Travel Discount Coupon

This coupon entitles
when you book

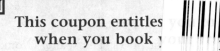

RESERVATION SERVICE

Hotels ♦ Airlines ♦ Car Rentals ♦ Cruises
All Your Travel Needs

Here's what you get: *

♦ A discount of $50 USD on a booking of $1,000** or more for two or more people!

♦ A discount of $25 USD on a booking of $500** or more for one person!

♦ Free membership for three years, and 1,000 free miles on enrollment in the unique Travel Network Miles-to-Go® frequent-traveler program. Earn one mile for every dollar spent through the program. Redeem miles for free hotel stays starting at 5,000 miles. Earn free roundtrip airline tickets starting at 25,000 miles.

♦ Personal help in planning your own, customized trip.

♦ Fast, confirmed reservations at any property recommended in this guide, subject to availability.***

♦ Special discounts on bookings in the U.S. and around the world.

♦ Low-cost visa and passport service.

♦ Reduced-rate cruise packages and special car rental programs worldwide.

Visit our website at http://www.travelnetwork.com/Frommer or call us globally at 201-567-8500, ext. 55. In the U.S., call toll-free at 1-888-940-5000, or fax 201-567-1838. In Canada, call at 1-905-707-7222, or fax 905-707-8108. In Asia, call 60-3-7191044, or fax 60-3-7185415.

---

* To qualify for these travel discounts, at least a portion of your trip must include destinations covered in this guide. No more than one coupon discount may be used in any 12-month period, for destinations covered in this guide. Cannot be combined with any other discount or promotion.

**These are U.S. dollars spent on commissionable bookings.

***A $10 USD fee, plus fax and/or phone charges, will be added to the cost of bookings at each hotel not linked to the reservation service. Customers must approve these fees in advance. If only hotels of this kind are booked, the traveler(s) must also purchase roundtrip air tickets from Travel Network for the trip.

Valid until December 31, 1998. Terms and conditions of the Miles-to-Go® program are available on request by calling 201-567-8500, ext 55.

ITY234

"Amazingly easy to use. Very portable, very complete."

—Booklist

◆

"The only mainstream guide to list specific prices. The Walter Cronkite of guidebooks—with all that implies."

—Travel & Leisure

◆

"Complete, concise, and filled with useful information."

—New York Daily News

◆

"Hotel information is close to encyclopedic."

—Des Moines Sunday Register

Frommer's® 98

Italy

by Darwin Porter and Danforth Prince

Macmillan • USA

ABOUT THE AUTHORS

A native of North Carolina, **Darwin Porter** was bureau chief for the *Miami Herald* when he was 21 and later worked in television advertising. A veteran travel writer, he wrote Frommer's first-ever guide to Italy, and he has been a frequent traveler in Italy every since. He is joined by **Danforth Prince,** formerly of the Paris bureau of the *New York Times,* who has lived and traveled in Italy extensively. This team writes a number of best-selling Frommer's guides, notably to England, France, Germany, and the Caribbean.

MACMILLAN TRAVEL

A Simon & Schuster Macmillan Company
1633 Broadway
New York, NY 10019

Find us online at **http://www.frommers.com** or on America Online at Keyword: **Frommers**.

ISBN 0-02-861653-7
ISSN 1044-2170

Editor: Suzanne Roe Jannetta
Special thanks to Vanessa Rosen and Reid Bramblett
Production Editor: John Carroll
Design by Michele Laseau
Digital Cartography by John Decamillis and Ortelius Design

SPECIAL SALES

Bulk purchases (10+ copies) of Frommer's and selected Macmillan travel guides are available to corporations, organizations, mail order catalogs, institutions, and charities at special discounts, and can be customized to suit individual needs. For more information write to Special Sales, Simon & Schuster, 1633 Broadway, New York, NY 10019.

Manufactured in the United States of America

Contents

1   The Best of Italy   1

1   The Best Travel Experiences   1

2   The Most Romantic Getaways   3

3   The Best Museums   3

4   The Best Cathedrals   5

5   The Best Ruins   5

6   The Best Wineries   7

7   The Best Luxury Hotels   9

8   The Best Moderately Priced Hotels   10

9   The Best Restaurants   11

10   The Best Buys   12

2   Getting to Know Italy   14

1   The Regions in Brief   14

2   Italy Today   20

3   A Look at the Past   22

★   *Dateline*   22

4   Italian Architecture & Art 101: A Guide to What You'll See   31

5   Italian Cuisine   42

3   Planning a Trip to Italy   48

1   Visitor Information & Entry Requirements   48

2   Money   48

★   *The Italian Lira, the U.S. Dollar & the U.K. Pound*   49

★   *What Things Cost in Rome*   50

★   *What Things Cost in Florence*   51

3   When to Go—Climate, Holidays & Events   51

★   *Italy Calendar of Events*   53

4   Health & Insurance   55

5   Tips for Travelers with Special Needs   56

6   Getting to Italy from North America   59

7   Getting to Italy from the United Kingdom   62

8   Getting to Italy from Within Europe   64

9 Getting Around Italy 66

10 Tips on Accommodations 70

11 Tips on Dining 71

★ *Fast Facts: Italy* 71

4 Settling into Rome 77

1 Orientation 78

2 Getting Around 85

★ *Fast Facts: Rome* 88

3 Accommodations 91

★ *Family-Friendly Hotels* 98

4 Dining 114

★ *Family-Friendly Restaurants* 119

5 Exploring Rome 133

★ *Millennium Milestones: Roma 2000* 134

1 The Vatican & St. Peter's 135

2 The Forum, the Colosseum & Highlights of
   Ancient Rome 143

3 The Pantheon & Attractions Near Piazza Navona &
   Campo de' Fiori 149

4 More Attractions 153

★ *Beneath It All: Touring Roma Sotteranea* 160

★ *Walking Tour—Rome of the Caesars* 163

5 Especially for Kids 173

6 Organized Tours 173

7 Soccer Matches & Other Outdoor Activities 174

8 Shopping 175

9 Rome After Dark 185

10 Side Trips from Rome 194

6 Florence (Firenze) 204

1 Orientation 205

2 Getting Around 209

★ *Fast Facts: Florence* 211

3 Accommodations 213

★ *Family-Friendly Hotels* 222

4 Dining 229

★ *Family-Friendly Restaurants* 237

5 Seeing the Sights   242

6 Soccer Matches & Other Outdoor Activities   258

7 Shopping   259

★ *The Art of Marbleizing*   266

8 Florence After Dark   267

9 A Side Trip to Fiesole   271

7 Tuscany & Umbria   274

1 Montecatini Terme   275

★ *Tuscan Tours*   279

2 Lucca   280

3 Pisa   286

4 San Gimignano   291

5 Siena   296

★ *The Palio: Spectacle of Violence*   299

6 La Chiantigiana: The Aroma of the Grape   306

7 Arezzo   315

8 Gubbio   317

9 Perugia   320

10 Assisi   327

11 Spoleto   334

12 Orvieto   339

8 Bologna & Emilia-Romagna   344

1 Bologna   344

★ *The World's Greatest China Shop*   351

2 Ferrara   358

3 Ravenna   364

4 Modena   368

5 Parma   372

9 Settling into Venice   378

1 Orientation   379

2 Getting Around   385

★ *Fast Facts: Venice*   386

3 Accommodations   388

★ *Family-Friendly Hotels*   398

4 Dining   402

★ *Family-Friendly Restaurants*   408

10 Exploring Venice 414

1 Piazza San Marco (St. Mark's Square) 414

2 The Lido & the Grand Canal 420

3 Museums & Galleries 421

★ *Plan of the Accademia* 422

4 More Attractions 425

★ *Walking Tour—From Piazza San Marco to the Grand Canal* 429

5 Especially for Kids 433

6 Organized Tours 433

7 Shopping 434

★ *Venetian Carnival Masks* 436

8 Venice After Dark 440

9 Side Trips from Venice 445

11 The Veneto 449

1 Riviera del Brenta 449

2 Padova (Padua) 453

★ *Cappuccino in the Elegance of 19th-Century Padua* 458

3 Treviso 459

4 Asolo 463

5 Bassano del Grappo 465

6 Vicenza 468

★ *La Città del Palladio* 470

7 Verona 473

12 Trieste, the Dolomites & South Tyrol 482

1 Trieste 482

2 Cortina d'Ampezzo 489

★ *Exploring the Peaks of the Dolomiti* 492

3 Bolzano 496

4 Merano 499

5 Trento (Trent) 502

13 Milan, Lombardy & the Lake District 506

1 Milan 506

★ *Italian Design: From Retro to the Restless* 530

2 Bergamo 537

3 Cremona 540

4 Mantova (Mantua) 542

5 Lake Garda 546

6 Lake Como 555

7 Lake Maggiore 563

14 Piedmont & Valle d'Aosta 567

1 Torino (Turin) 567

2 Aosta 575

3 Courmayeur & Entrèves 578

15 Genova & the Italian Riviera 584

1 San Remo 584

2 Genova (Genoa) 590

3 Rapallo 599

4 Santa Margherita Ligure 602

5 Portofino 605

6 Cinque Terre 608

16 Naples, Pompeii & Ischia 613

1 Naples 614

★ *A Sweet Shop & a Grand Cafe* 632

2 The Environs of Naples 632

★ *Treading Lightly on Mount Vesuvius* 634

3 Pompeii 636

4 Ischia 639

17 The Amalfi Coast & Capri 646

1 Sorrento 646

2 Positano 651

3 Amalfi 655

4 Ravello 660

5 Paestum 665

6 Capri 666

18 Apulia (Puglia) 678

1 Foggia 678

2 The Gargano Peninsula 682

3 Bari 688

4 The Trulli District 693

★ *The Mystery of the Trulli* 694
5 Brindisi 696
★ *Gateway to Greece* 697
6 Lecce 698
7 Taranto 702

19   Sicily   706

1 Taormina 709
2 Siracusa (Syracuse) 719
3 Agrigento 724
4 Selinunte 727
5 Segesta 728
6 Palermo 729
★ *Exploring La Kalsa* 732
7 Journeys off the Beaten Path 742
8 Isole Eolie o Lipari (Aeolian Islands) 744

Index   751

List of Maps

Italy

Regions of Italy   17

Rome

Rome Orientation   82

Rome Metro   87

Rome Accommodations   92

Accommodations & Dining
  Near Campo de' Fiori &
  Piazza Navona   96

Accommodations & Dining
  Near Piazza di Spagna   99

Accommodations & Dining
  Near Termini & Via
  Veneto   105

Accommodations & Dining in
  the Vatican Area   111

Dining in Trastevere   129

Rome Attractions   136

Vatican City   139

Ancient Rome & Attractions
  Nearby   145

The Pantheon & Attractions
  Near Piazza Navona &
  Campo de' Fiori   151

Walking Tour—Rome of
  the Caesars   165

Side Trips from Rome   195

Florence

Florence Accom-
  modations   214

Florence Dining   230

Florence Attractions   244

Venice

Venice Orientation   381

Venice Accommodations &
  Dining   390

Venice Attractions   416

Piazza San Marco   419

Walking Tour—From Piazza
  San Marco to the Grand
  Canal   431

Regional Maps

Tuscany & Umbria   276

Chianti Region   309

Emilia-Romagna   345

The Veneto   451

Trieste, the Dolomites &
  South Tyrol   485

Lombardy & the
  LakeDistrict   507

Piedmont & Valle
  d'Aosta   569

Italian Riviera   587

Bay of Naples & the
  Amalfi Coast   649

Capri   667

Southern Italy   679

Sicily   707

City Maps

Lucca   281

Pisa   287

Siena   297

Perugia   321

Assissi   329

Spoleto   337

Orvieto   341

Bologna   347

Milan   509

Genova   593

Naples   619

Herculaneum   635

Pompeii   637

AN INVITATION TO THE READER

In researching this book, we discovered many wonderful places—hotels, restaurants, shops, and more. We're sure you'll find others. Please tell us about them, so we can share the information with your fellow travelers in upcoming editions. If you were disappointed with a recommendation, we'd love to know that, too. Please write to:

Darwin Porter/Danforth Prince
Frommer's Italy '98
Macmillan Travel
1633 Broadway
New York, NY 10019

AN ADDITIONAL NOTE

Please be advised that travel information is subject to change at any time—and this is especially true of prices. We therefore suggest that you write or call ahead for confirmation when making your travel plans. The authors, editors, and publisher cannot be held responsible for the experiences of readers while traveling. Your safety is important to us, however, so we encourage you to stay alert and be aware of your surroundings. Keep a close eye on cameras, purses, and wallets, all favorite targets of thieves and pickpockets.

WHAT THE SYMBOLS MEAN

✪ Frommer's Favorites

Our favorite places and experiences—outstanding for quality, value, or both.

The following abbreviations are used for credit cards:

AE	American Express	DISC	Discover
CB	Carte Blanche	MC	MasterCard
DC	Diners Club	V	Visa

FIND FROMMER'S ONLINE

Arthur Frommer's Outspoken Encyclopedia of Travel (www.frommers.com) offers more than 6,000 pages of up-to-the-minute travel information—including the latest bargains and candid, personal articles updated daily by Arthur Frommer himself. No other Web site offers such comprehensive and timely coverage of the world of travel.

The Best of Italy

Our aim is to save you time and money since you've come to Italy to relax—not to exhaust yourself searching for the best deals and the most evocative experiences. Spend your vacation in peace, and let us do the work. Italy is one of the most beautiful, diverse, and culturally rich countries in the world, with some of the world's best offerings in everything from monuments to cuisine. Although the selections below represent the best of Italy, they by no means exhaust the list of wonderful things to see and do, as you'll soon find out for yourself. For Italy is a land of enchanting discoveries, and whether this is your first trip to the peninsula or your 50th, you're bound to come away with your own favorites to add to your personal "best of" list.

1 The Best Travel Experiences

Italy is a feast for the senses and the intellect, and some of the country's most thrilling experiences involve the simple act of living in the Italian style. Although the country is literally stuffed with the potential for memorable experiences, here's an abbreviated list of some that are, by anyone's estimate, spectacular:

- **Visiting the Art Cities of Italy:** When Italy consisted of dozens of principalities, its art treasures were concentrated in many small capitals. Each of these cities, blessed with the patronage of a papal representative or ducal family, amassed vast quantities of art. Exquisite paintings, statues, and frescoes are displayed in churches, monasteries, and palaces whose architects are world acclaimed. Although the best known of these troves reside in Florence, Rome, and Venice, stunning art collections are also found in the cities of Assisi, Cremona, Genoa, Mantua, Padua, Parma, Palermo, Pisa, Siena, Taormina, Tivoli, Turin, Verona, and Vicenza.
- **Eating Out:** One of the most cherished pastimes of the Italians is eating out. Regardless of how much lasagne you've had in your life, it's never better than the real thing in Italy. Each region has its own specialties, some handed down for centuries. If the weather is fine and you're dining outdoors with a view of, perhaps, a medieval church or piazza, it's the closest thing to heaven in Italy. *Buon appetito!*

- **Celebrating Mass in St. Peter's** (The Vatican, Rome): With the possible exception of some sites in Jerusalem, St. Peter's is the most visible and important building in Christendom. The huge size of the church is daunting. For many visitors, celebrating mass here is a spiritual highlight of their lives. Your co-celebrants are likely to come from every corner of the world. See chapter 5.

- **Taking a Boat Ride on the Grand Canal of Venice:** The S-shaped Grand Canal, curving for 2 miles along historic buildings and under ornate bridges, is the most romantic and evocative waterway in the world. Most first-timers are stunned by the variety of Gothic and Renaissance buildings, the elaborate styles of which could fill a book on architecture. A ride on the canal will give you ever-changing glimpses of the city's poignant beauty. Your ride doesn't have to be on a gondola; any public *vaporetto* (ferry) sailing between Venice's railway station and the Piazza San Marco will provide a heart-stopping view. See chapter 10.

- **Walking in Venice:** The most obvious means of transport in Venice is by boat; an even more appealing method is on foot, traversing hundreds of canals, large and small, and crossing over the arches of medieval bridges. Getting from one point to another can be like walking through a maze; but you won't be hassled by traffic, and the sense of the city's beauty, timelessness, and slow decay is almost mystical. See chapter 10.

- **Attending an Opera:** It's estimated that more than 2,000 new operas were staged in Italy during the 18th century, and since then Italian opera fans have earned a reputation as the toughest and most demanding in the world. For a firsthand view of their devotion to this art form, consider attending an opera. Likely choices include Venice's Teatro di San Cassiano (opened in 1637 as the first opera house in Italy); Milan's La Scala (the most prestigious opera house in the world, especially for *bel canto*); and a wide assortment of outdoor settings, such as the Arena in Verona, one of the largest surviving amphitheaters in the ancient world. Suitable for up to 20,000 spectators, and known for its fine acoustics, the Arena presents operas throughout July and August, when moonlight and the perfumed air of the Veneto add to the charm. See chapters 10, 11, and 13.

- **Shopping Milan:** Milan is one of the most enchanting fashion capitals of Europe. You'll find a range of shoes, clothing, and accessories unequaled anywhere else in the world. Even if you weren't born to shop, stroll along the streets bordering Via Montenapoleone and check out the elegant offerings from Europe's most famous designers. See chapter 13.

- **Experiencing the Glory of the Romans:** Even after centuries of looting, much remains of the glory of the Roman Empire—from architectural monuments to art. Of course, Rome itself has the greatest share (the popes didn't tear down everything to recycle into churches). Here you'll find everything from the Roman Forum to the Colosseum, symbol of Imperial Rome. On the outskirts, the long-buried city of Ostia Antica, the port of Ancient Rome, has been unearthed. But Rome doesn't have a monopoly on such ancient treasures; they're scattered throughout Italy, especially in Sicily. The tourist hordes also descend on Pompeii, once buried by lava. Our favorite Roman ruins are at Paestum, along the coast of Campania. Its ruins, especially the Temple of Neptune, are worth the trip to Italy. See chapters 5, 16, 17, and 18.

- **Rejuvenating at a Spa:** Although the spas of Germany are infinitely busier, the *terme* (spas) of Italy enjoy a relaxed charm and thousands of devoted aficionados. Head to Montecatini Terme, or the island of Ischia to learn why Italians are so passionate about "the cure." If you're affluent and exhausted, you can opt for a regime of mud baths and immersion in the sulfurous waters bubbling out of geothermal springs. Regardless of how extensively you participate in the spa rituals, you're likely to emerge refreshed and relaxed. See chapters 7 and 16.

- **Reliving the Grand Tour:** During the 18th and 19th centuries, enlightened schoolmasters believed that a tour through Italy was the proper conclusion to a well-rounded education. The sons of prosperous families from France, Britain, and Germany swept southward on grand loops through the Alps; the great art cities of the Veneto, Umbria, and Tuscany; the monuments and churches of Rome; and the ancient ruins of Naples and Sicily. Part of the enchantment of a grand tour of Italy is stumbling upon unexpected charms in the smaller towns as well, as you travel the length of the country.

2 The Most Romantic Getaways

These destinations are known throughout the world as enchanting, secluded places to recuperate from stress and/or rejuvenate a romance.

- **Spoleto:** It's as ancient as the Roman Empire and as timeless as the music presented here every summer during its world-renowned arts festival. The architecture of this quintessential Umbrian hill town is centered around a core of religious buildings dating from the 13th century. It's less chic but more romantic during the off-season, when the crowds are less dense. See chapter 7.
- **Portofino:** It's the most famous small port in the world, largely because of the well-preserved buildings surrounding its small, circular harbor. Located 22 miles southeast of Genoa, in the heart of the Italian Riviera, it's charming, chic, and cosmopolitan. A cluster of top-notch hotels cater to the very rich and famous. See chapter 15.
- **Capri:** Floating amid azure seas south of Naples, Capri is called the "Island of Dreams." Roman emperors Augustus and Tiberius both came here for R&R, and since the late 1800s celebrities have flocked here for an escape. A boat ride around the island's rugged coastline is one of our favorite things to do on Capri. See chapter 17.
- **Ravello:** It's small, sunny, and loaded with notable buildings (such as its cathedral, founded in 1086). Despite its choice position on the Amalfi coast, it manages to retain the aura of an old-fashioned village. Famous residents have included writer Gore Vidal. See chapter 17.
- **Taormina:** The most charming place in Sicily, this resort is loaded with regional charm, chiseled stonework, and a sense of the ages. Favored by wealthy Europeans and dedicated artists, especially in midwinter when the climate is delightful, it's a fertile oasis of olive groves, grapevines, and orchards. Visitors will relish the delights of the sun, the sea, and the medieval setting. See chapter 19.

3 The Best Museums

Although some fans argue that the entire Italian peninsula is a display of human civilization, the country's museums are incomparable. You're likely to stumble upon many of them in out-of-the-way places, but here's a short list of the country's best:

- **Musei Vaticani** (The Vatican, Rome): Rambling, disjointed, and unbelievably well stocked with the artistic treasures accumulated over the centuries by the popes, this complex contains some of the most famous attractions of Italy. Among them are the Sistine Chapel, such sculptures as *Laocooün and His Sons* and the *Belvedere Apollo,* buildings whose walls were almost completely executed by Raphael, and endless collections of art ranging from (very pagan) Greco-Roman antiquities to Christian art by famous European masters. See chapter 5.

- **Museo Nazionale di Villa Giulia** (Rome): Mysterious and for the most part undocumented, the Etruscans were the ancestors of the ancient Romans, who later conquered most of the known world. They left a legacy of bronze and marble sculpture, sarcophagi, jewelry, and representations of mythical heroes, some of which were excavated at Cerveteri, an Etruscan stronghold north of Rome. Most startling about the artifacts is their sophisticated, almost mystical sense of design. The building that houses this Etruscan collection was a papal villa in the 1500s. See chapter 5.

- **Galleria degli Uffizi** (Florence): This 16th-century Renaissance palace functioned as the administrative headquarters, or *uffizi* (offices), for the Medici's administration of Florence. It's estimated that up to 90% of Italy's artistic patrimony is stored in this building, the crown jewel of Italy's museums. (The Galleria degli Uffizi was the target of a very destructive car bomb that caused considerable damage in 1993.) See chapter 6.

- **Museo Nazionale del Bargello** (Florence): The severely angular 12th-century exterior of the Bargello, located in the heart of Florence, is permeated with the raw power of the governing magistrate who built it. Today its collection of sculpture and decorative accessories is without equal in Italy. See chapter 6.

- **Palazzo Pitti** (Florence): The spheres of influence that dominated Florence during its most creative years revolved around the Medicis and the Pittis, two families who ruled the city from their respective banks of the Arno. The Pittis moved into this palazzo in 1560, after it was enlarged with two new wings. Today it houses a museum containing everything from paintings by old masters (such as Raphael and Titian) to works by modern artists and a collection of antique silver. See chapter 6.

- **Galleria Nazionale dell'Umbria** (Perugia): Italian Renaissance art has roots in Tuscan and Umbrian painting of the 1200s. This collection, set on the uppermost floor of the Palazzo dei Priori (parts of which date from the 1400s), contains a world-class collection of paintings, most executed in Tuscany or Umbria between the 13th and the 18th centuries. The museum contains works by Perugino, Piero della Francesco, Duccio, Fra Angelico, and Benozzo Gozzoli, among others. See chapter 7.

- **Gallerie dell'Accademia** (Venice): It's one of the most richly stocked art museums in Italy, boasting hundreds of paintings, many of them Venetian, executed between 1300 and 1790. Among the highlights are works by Bellini, Giorgione, Carpaccio, and Titian. See chapter 10.

- **Pinacoteca di Brera** (Milan): Although Milan is usually associated with wealth and corporate power, it contains a worthy assortment of cultural icons as well. Foremost among these is the Brera Picture Gallery, whose collection—shown in a 17th-century palace—is especially rich in paintings from the schools of Lombardy and Venice. See chapter 13.

- **Museo Poldi-Pezzoli** (Milan): In 1881 this museum's namesake donated his extensive art collection to his hometown, thereby creating the base for one of Italy's most influential museums. The collection includes Persian carpets, portraits by Cranach of Martin Luther and his wife, works by Botticelli and Bellini, and massive amounts of decorative art, including furniture. See chapter 13.

- **Museo Archeologico Nazionale** (Naples): Naples and the region around it have yielded more sculptural treasures from the ancient Roman Empire than anywhere else in Italy. Many of these riches have been accumulated in a rambling building originally designed as a barracks for the Neapolitan cavalry in the 1500s. Today much of the loot excavated from Pompeii and Herculaneum, as well as the Renaissance collections of the Farnese family, are in this museum, which boasts one of the richest troves of Greco-Roman antiquities in the world. See chapter 16.

4 The Best Cathedrals

As the home of many of Christianity's most important monuments, Italy has always combined a reverence for churches with a vivid sense of architectural showmanship. The result has been some of the most spectacular cathedrals in the world.

- **Basilica di San Pietro** (The Vatican, Rome): Its roots began with the first Christian emperor, Constantine, in A.D. 324. By 1400 the Roman basilica was in danger of collapsing, prompting the Renaissance popes to commission plans for the largest, most impressive cathedral that the world had ever seen. Amid the rich decor of gilt, marble, and mosaics are countless artworks, including Michelangelo's *Pietà*. Other sights here are a small museum of Vatican treasures and the eerie, underground grottoes containing the tombs of former popes. An elevator ride (or rigorous climb) up the tower to Michelangelo's dome provides panoramic views of Rome. See chapter 5.

- **Il Duomo** (Santa Maria del Fiore, Florence): Begun in the final years of the 1200s, and consecrated 140 years later, the Duomo was a symbol of the prestige and wealth of Florence. With an exterior of pink, green, and white marble, and loaded with world-class art, it's one of the largest and most distinctive religious buildings in Italy. A view of its dome, erected over a 14-year period in what was at the time a radical new design by Brunelleschi, is worth the trip to Florence. Other elements of the Duomo include the Campanile (one of the most charming bell towers in Italy) and the Baptistery (a Romanesque outbuilding with renowned bronze doors and a sheath of green-and-white marble). See chapter 6.

- **Basilica di San Francesco** (Assisi): St. Francis, protector of small animals and birds, was long dead when construction began on this double-tiered showcase of the Franciscan brotherhood. Interior decoration, in many cases by Cimabue and Giotto, reached a new kind of figurative realism in Italian art around 1300, long before later masters of the Renaissance carried the technique even further. Consecrated in 1253, the cathedral is one of the highlights of Umbria and the site of many religious pilgrimages. See chapter 7.

- **Il Duomo** (Orvieto): A well-designed transition between the Romanesque and Gothic styles, this cathedral was begun in 1290 and completed in 1600. It sheltered an Italian pope (Clement VII) when Rome was sacked by French soldiers in 1527. Part of the building's mystery derives from Orvieto's role as an Etruscan stronghold long before Italy's recorded history. See chapter 7.

- **Il Duomo** (Milan): Begun in 1386, and finally completed in 1809 on orders of Napoléon, Il Duomo of Milan is an ornate and unusual building. Gathered around a triangular gable bristling with 135 pointed and chiseled spires, it's both massive and airy. The interior is as severe as its exterior is ornate. It's one of the most remarkable buildings in Italy, although it's often overlooked. See chapter 13.

5 The Best Ruins

During the 18th century, no self-respecting aristocrat from England or Germany would have dreamed of entering middle age without having first taken a tour through the ruins of the ancient world, perhaps picking up a load of ancient Greek or Roman mementos en route. Here's a list of the ruins they were bound to have visited:

- **Ostia Antica:** During the height of the Roman Empire, Ostia ("mouth" in Latin) was the harbor town set at the point where the Tiber flowed into the sea. As Rome declined, so did Ostia. By the early Middle Ages, the town had almost disappeared, its population decimated by malaria. In the early 1900s archeologists excavated the ruins of hundreds of ancient buildings, many of which can be viewed. See chapter 5.

- **Il Foro Romano** (Rome): Two thousand years ago most of the known world was directly affected by decisions made in the Roman Forum. Today classicists and archeologists wander among its ruins, conjuring up the glory that was Rome. What you'll see today is a pale, rubble-strewn version of the site's original majesty— it's now surrounded by modern boulevards packed with whizzing cars. See chapter 5.

- **Il Palatino** (Rome): According to legend, the Palatine Hill was the site where Romulus and Remus (the orphaned infant twins who survived in the wild by suckling a she-wolf) eventually founded the city. Although Il Palatino is one of the seven hills of Ancient Rome, it's hard to distinguish it as such because of the urban congestion that rises all around it. Despite that, scholars come to pay frequent homage. The site is enhanced by the presence of the Farnese Gardens (Orti Farnesiani), laid out in the 1500s on the site of Tiberius's palace. See chapter 5.

- **Il Coliseo** (Rome): Rome boasts only a handful of other ancient monuments that survive in such well-preserved condition. A massive amphitheater set incongruously amid a maze of modern traffic, the Colosseum was once the setting for gladiator combat, lion-feeding frenzies, and public entertainment whose cruelty was a noted characteristic of the Roman Empire. All three of the ancient world's classical styles (Doric, Ionic, and Corinthian) are represented here, superimposed in tiers one above the other. See chapter 5.

- **Villa Adriana** (near Tivoli): Hadrian's Villa slumbered in rural obscurity until the 1500s, when Renaissance popes ordered its excavation. Only then was the scale of this massive and very beautiful villa from A.D. 134 appreciated. Its builder, Hadrian, who had visited almost every part of his empire, wanted to incorporate the widespread wonders of the world into one fantastic building site. See chapter 5.

- **Ercolano** (Herculaneum, near Naples): Legend says that it was founded by Hercules. The historical facts tell us that it was buried under rivers of volcanic mud one fateful day in A.D. 79 after the eruption of Vesuvius. Seeping into the cracks of virtually every building in town, the scalding mud preserved the timbers of hundreds of structures that would otherwise have rotted in the normal course of time. Devote at least 2 hours to seeing some of the best-preserved houses to survive from the ancient world. See chapter 16.

- **Pompeii** (Campania): Once it was an opulent resort filled with 25,000 wealthy Romans. In A.D. 79 the same eruption that devastated Herculaneum (see above) buried Pompeii under at least 20 feet of scalding volcanic ash. Beginning around 1750, Charles of Bourbon ordered the systematic excavation of the ruins—the treasures hauled out of Pompeii sparked a wave of interest throughout northern Europe in the classical era. See chapter 16.

- **Paestum** (Campania): Paestum was discovered by accident around 1750, when local bureaucrats tried to build a road across the heart of what had been a thriving ancient city. Paestum originated as a Greek colony around 600 B.C., fell to the Romans in 273 B.C., and declined into obscurity in the final days of the empire.

Today amateur archeologists can follow a well-marked walking tour through the excavations. See chapter 17.

- **La Valle dei Templi** (Sicily): Although most of it lies in ruins, the Valley of the Temples in Agrigento is one of the most beautiful classical sites in Europe, especially in February and March when the almond trees surrounding it burst into pink blossoms. One of the site's five temples dates from as early as 520 B.C.; another— although never completed—ranks as one of the largest temples in the ancient world. See chapter 19.

- **Segesta** (Sicily): Even its site is impressive: a rocky outcropping surrounded on most sides by a jagged ravine. Built around 430 B.C. by the Greeks, Segesta's Doric colonnade is one of the most graceful in the ancient world. Believed to have been destroyed by the Saracens (Muslim raiders) in the 11th century, Segesta is stark, mysterious, and highly evocative of the ancient world. See chapter 19.

- **Selinunte** (Sicily): Although its massive columns lie scattered on the ground, as if an earthquake had punished its builders, this is one of our favorite ancient ruins in Italy. Around 600 B.C., immigrants from Syracuse built Selinunte into an important trading port. The city was a bitter rival of the neighboring city of Segesta (see above) and was destroyed around 400 B.C., and again in 250 B.C. by the Carthaginians. See chapter 19.

6   The Best Wineries

Italy has thousands of vineyards, many of which have been run by families for generations, in some cases with grape stock whose genetic forebears were first developed by predecessors of the ancient Romans. Here's a guide to the major wine-growing regions of Italy (listed geographically, from the alpine northwest to Sicily), with a short list of the most hospitable and interesting vineyards within each region:

- **The Piedmont:** Reds with rich and complex flavors make up most of the wine output of this rugged, high-altitude region near Italy's border with France. One of the most interesting vineyards is headquartered in a 15th-century abbey near the hamlet of Alba. For information, contact the **Antiche Cantine dell'Annunziata,** Abbazia dell'Annunziata, La Morra, 12064 Cuneo (☎ **0173/50-185**).

- **Lombardy:** The Po Valley has always been known for its flat vistas, its midsummer humidity, its fertile soil, and its excellent wines. The region produces everything from dry flat reds to sparkling whites with a champagne-like zest. **Guido Berlucchi,** Piazza Duranti 4, Borgonato di Cortefranca, 25040 Brescia (☎ **030/ 984-381**), one of Italy's largest wineries, is especially willing to receive visitors.

- **The Veneto:** The humid flatlands of the eastern Po Valley have produced memorable red and white wines in great abundance since the days of the Venetian doges. Output includes massive quantities of everything from soft white Soaves and Pinot Grigios to Valpolicellas and red Merlots. Important vineyards in the region include **Nino Franco** (known for its sparkling prosecco), in the hamlet of Valdobbiadene, Via Garibaldi 177, 31049 Treviso (☎ **0423/972-051**); **Azienda Vinicola Fratelli Fabiano,** Via Verona 6, 37060 Sona, near Verona (☎ **045/ 608-1111**); and **Fratelli Bolla,** Piazza Cittadella 3, 37122 Verona (☎ **045/ 809-0911**). For information on these and any of the dozens of other producers within the Veneto, contact the region's **Azienda di Promozione Turistica,** Via Leoncino 61, 37121 Verona (☎ **045/592-828**).

- **Trentino and the Alto Adige:** The northwest region of Italy is divided into two provinces: Alto Adige and Trento. The loftier of the two districts, the Alto Adige, was once part of the Austro-Hungarian province of the South Tyrol and occupies the region around Bolzano in Italy's extreme alpine north. More Germanic than Italian, it clings to its Austrian traditions and folklore and grows an Italian version of the *gewuürtztraminers* (a fruity white wine) that would more often be found in Germany, Austria, and Alsace. Venerable wine growers include Alois Lageder (founded in 1855) and Schloss Turmhof, in Entiklar, both near Bolzano. The latter boasts a castle that exudes Teutonic history and some of the highest-altitude vineyards in the South Tyrol. For information, contact **Alois Lageder,** Tenuta Loüwengang, Vicolo dei Conti, Magré, Strada del Vino (☎ **0471/817-256**); or **Schloss Turmhof,** Entiklar, Kurtatsch, 39040 (☎ **0471/880-122**).

The Trentino area, a short distance to the south of the Alto Adige, is one of the leading producers of Chardonnay and sparkling wines that are fermented using methods originally developed centuries ago. A winery worth a visit is **Cavit Cantina Viticoltori,** Via del Ponte 31, 38100 Trento (☎ **0461/922-055**).

- **Friuli–Venezia Giulia:** This region within the cool alpine foothills of northeastern Italy produces a light, fruity vintage that is especially appealing when young. One of the most important vineyards is **Livio Felluga,** near Gorizia. For information, contact **Livio Felluga,** Via Risorgimento 1, Brazzano di Cormons, 34071 Gorizia (☎ **0481/60-052**). Another worthy producer known for its high-quality wines is **E. Collavini Vini & Spumante,** Via della Ribolla Galla 2, Corno di Rosazzo, Udine (☎ **0432/753-222**).

- **Emilia-Romagna:** Comprised of two distinct areas (Emilia, to the west of Bologna, and Romagna, to the east) the region is known to some gastronomes as the producer of some of Italy's best food, with wines worthy of its legendary cuisine. Emilia's most famous wine is Lambrusco, 50 million bottles of which are produced every year near the towns of Modena and Reggio. Less well known but also highly rated wines from Emilia include the Colli Piacentini wines, the most famous producer of which is **Cantine Romagnoli,** Via Provinciale, Villo di Vigolzone 29020 (☎ **0523/870-129**). Wines from Romagna crop up on wine lists throughout the country and include the rigidly defined wine-producing regions of Sangiovese, Trebbiano, and Albana.

- **Tuscany and Umbria:** Some of Italy's most scenic vineyards lie nestled among the verdant and rolling hills of these two stately regions. Virtually any winery in either of the two districts is likely to be permeated with history and architectural character, but one of the most appealing in Umbria is **Azienda Vallesant di Luigi Barberani,** Azienda Agricola Vallesant, Loc. Cerreto, Baschi, 05023 Terni (☎ **0763/41-820**). One of Tuscany's largest vintners is **Villa Banfi,** Castello Banfi, Sant'Angelo Scalo, Montalcino, 53020 Siena (☎ **0577/840-111**). Equally worthwhile, and also near Siena, are **Biondi-Santi,** Loc. Greppo, 53024 Montalcino (☎ **0577/847-121**); and **Casa Vinicola L. Cecchi,** Loc. Casina dei Ponti, 53011 Castellina in Chianti (☎ **0577/743-057**).

- **Latium:** The region around Rome is known for predominantly white wines that include Marino, Est! Est!! Est!!!, Colli Albani, and the widely visible Frascati—"the wine of the popes and the people." All of these are derived almost exclusively from Malvasia and Trebbiano grapes and, in some cases, from combinations of the two. Two of the region's most famous producers of Frascati are **Fontana Candida,** whose winery, 14 miles southwest of Rome, was built around 1900; and **Gotto D'Oro-Cantina Sociale di Marino,** Via del Divino Amore, 115, 00040 Frattocchie, Roma (☎ **06/9354-6931**). To arrange visits, contact the **Gruppo Italiano Vini,** Villa Belvedere, 37010 Calmasino, Verona (☎ **045/626-0600**).

- **Campania:** The wines produced in the harsh, hot landscapes of Campania, around Naples in southern Italy, seem stronger, rougher, and in many cases more powerful than those grown in gentler climes. Among the most famous are the Lacryma Christi (Tears of Christ), a white that grows in the volcanic soil near Naples, Herculaneum, and Pompeii; Taurasi, a potent red; and Greco di Turo, a pungent white laden with the odors of apricots and apples that are particularly aromatic when consumed with local anchovies and salted cheese. One of the most frequently visited vineyards is **Mastroberardino,** 75 Via Manfredi, Atripalda, 83042 Avellino (**☎ 0825/626-123**).

- **Sicily:** Its hot climate and volcanic soil foster the growth of more vineyards than any other region of Italy. Most of these are devoted to the production of simple table wines. Of the better vintages, the best-known wines are Marsala and, to a lesser extent, muscat dessert wines. One producer of the heady Marsala wine is **Corvo Duca di Salaparuta,** a 19th-century winery set in the hills above Palermo. For information, contact **Casa Vinicola Duca di Salaparuta,** Via Nazionale, SS113, Casteldaccia, 90014 Palermo (**☎ 091/945-223**). A leading competitor, also near Palermo, is **Regaleali,** Contrada Regaleali, 93010 Vallclunga, Pratameno Caltanisseha (**☎ 0921/542-522**), a historic enterprise maintained by the Tasca d'Almerita family. Known mainly for its still and sparkling whites (Nozze d'Oro) and to a lesser extent its reds (Rosso del Conte) and rosés, it welcomes visitors. A name that evokes years of wine-making traditions, thanks to its skill at producing Cerasuolo di Vittoria and Moscato di Pantelleria, is **Cantine Torrevecchia di Favuzza Giuseppe,** Via Ariosto 10A, 90144 Palermo (**☎ 0932/989-400**).

7 The Best Luxury Hotels

- **Hassler** (Rome; **☎ 800/223-6800** in the U.S.): Hollywood mingles easily with old European wealth at the Hassler. The setting (near an obelisk and a baroque Renaissance church) at the top of the Spanish Steps is among the most evocative in Rome. The bar attracts an invigorating mixture of clients. The restaurant offers panoramic views over the city. See chapter 4.
- **Villa San Michele** (Fiesole, near Florence; **☎ 055/59-451**): This former 15th-century monastery is set behind a facade reputedly designed by Michelangelo. Brigitte Bardot once selected it for one of her honeymoons (no one remembers which husband it was). It lies in a scented garden, in one of the hill towns near Florence. Many visitors consider this charming hotel a worthy escape from the often oppressive midsummer congestion of Florence. With fewer than 45 rooms, and a decor that no set designer could ever duplicate, it evokes the charm of an aristocratic private villa. See chapter 6.
- **Hotel Cipriani** (Venice; **☎ 800/992-5055** in the U.S.): This exclusive and elegant hotel is in a 3-acre garden on Isola della Giudecca, one of the calmer islands that comprise the ancient city of Venice. The grand hotel was originally built as a cloister in the 15th century and is centered around a very large, modern, and well-maintained swimming pool. See chapter 9.
- **Gritti Palace** (Venice; **☎ 800/325-3535** in the U.S.): Andrea Gritti, a doge who ruled Venice with an iron hand until his death in 1538, is the namesake for this property, gem of one of the most elegant hotel chains (CIGA) in the world. The exquisite interiors offer a taste of Venice's historic opulence. See chapter 9.
- **Miramonti Majestic Grand Hotel** (Cortina d'Ampezzo; **☎ 0436/4201**): Designed like a massive mountain fortress, this hotel is located in the heart of Italy's most glamorous alpine resort. The clientele seems to relish the hotel's Italian panache amid the bracing air of the Dolomites. Despite the modern amenities, there's a 19th-century quality about this place. See chapter 12.

- **Grand Hotel Villa d'Este** (Cernobbio; ☎ 031/3481): Originally built in 1568, this splendid palace in the Lake District is one of the most famous Renaissance-era hotels in the world. Step inside and you're surrounded by frescoed ceilings, impeccable antiques, and many other exquisite details. Ten magnificently land-scaped acres, parts of which have been nurtured since the 1500s, surround the hotel. Cool breezes are provided by nearby Lake Como and the proximity to the Swiss and Italian Alps. See chapter 13.

- **Albergo Splendido** (Portofino; ☎ 800/237-1236 in the U.S.): Originally built as a monastery in the 14th century, and later abandoned because of attacks by North African pirates, this monument was rescued during the 19th century by an Italian baron and converted into a summer home for his family. The posh hillside retreat on the Italian Riviera now accommodates a sophisticated clientele, including many film stars. The scent of mimosas fills the air, and the sea views are blissful. See chapter 15.

- **Grand Hotel Quisisana Capri** (Capri; ☎ 081/837-0788): This hotel, situated on a part of the island sheltered from the sometimes annoying winds of Capri, was originally established as a health spa by an English doctor around 1850. It is large (165 rooms), supremely comfortable, and intricately linked to the allure that made Capri popular with the ancient Roman emperors. See chapter 17.

- **San Pietro** (Positano; ☎ 089/875-455): The only marker that identifies this cliffside hotel, located in the Campania region, is a 15th-century chapel set beside the winding road. The hotel doesn't advertise, protects the privacy of its guests, and offers frequent transportation into that hub of midsummer Italian glamor, Positano, less than a mile away. The bedrooms resemble suites and offer views of the sea. Strands of bougainvillea twine around the dramatically terraced, glisten-ing white exterior walls. See chapter 17.

- **Palazzo San Domenico** (Taormina, Sicily; ☎ 0942/23-701): This is one of the great, stylish old hotels of Europe, a 500-year-old Dominican monastery whose severe lines and dignified bulk are softened with antique tapestries, fragrant gar-dens, and a sense of the eternal that only Sicily can give. Since its transformation into a hotel in 1896, its clients have included movie legends Dietrich, Garbo, and Loren. See chapter 19.

8   The Best Moderately Priced Hotels

Italy has hundreds of charming inns, *pensiones,* and hotels with reasonable rates. Here's a short list of some of our top choices:

- **Hotel Venezia** (Rome; ☎ 800/526-5497 in the U.S.): Set near Rome's main rail-way terminal, this hotel features Murano glass chandeliers in the bedrooms and public areas, which were recently renovated. Some units have balconies overlooking the street, and everything is clean. See chapter 4.

- **Romantik Hotel J and J** (Florence; ☎ 055/234-5005): This charming hotel was built in the 1500s as a monastery and is set on a rarely visited street near the historic Church of Santa Croce. It's named after the initials of its owners' children (James and Jacqueline). The property was renovated in 1990, but still retains much of its Renaissance charm. See chapter 6.

- **Hotel Palazzo Bocci** (in Spello, near Assisi; ☎ 0742/301-021): Built in the late 18th century, and renovated and transformed into a hotel in 1992, this palace is posh, tasteful, and reasonably priced. Many of the public and private rooms have sweeping views of the valley below. See chapter 7.

- **Hotel Roma** (Modena; ☎ **059/222-218**): In the 1700s this building was among the real-estate holdings of the duca d'Este. Today it's likely to be the temporary home of whatever opera star happens to be singing in Pavarotti's hometown. Flourishing as a hotel since the 1950s, the Roma, located in the historic heart of town, is comfortable and uncomplicated. See chapter 8.
- **La Residenza** (Venice; ☎ **041/528-5315**): Many of this hotel's clients are art lovers who return to Venice year after year. Originally built in the 14th century, its interior walls have some of the most charming stucco work in Venice. On the medieval piazza outside, older citizens feed pigeons while younger ones play soccer. See chapter 9.
- **Menardi** (Cortina d'Ampezzo; ☎ **0436/2400**): Built a century ago, this alpine inn exudes Austrian *gemütlichkeit* (coziness), with blazing fireplaces and windows that overlook a view of alpine meadows and rugged crags. Best of all, it's a short uphill walk from one of Italy's most glamorous resorts. See chapter 12.
- **Hotel Asnigo** (Cernobbio; ☎ **031/510-062**): The Asnigo embodies the Edwardian style of the age in which it was built (1914) and has the atmosphere of a genteel retreat. Set in a garden, it's clean and run in a friendly, low-key style. Some visitors return year after year. See chapter 13.
- **Hotel Florence** (Bellagio; ☎ **031/950-342**): A private villa in the 19th century, this hotel has a dignified facade, an arbor with tumbling wisteria, and stone-sided terraces overlooking a lake. A series of renovations in 1990 brought it tastefully up-to-date, and Saturday-night jazz concerts and an American-style bar have made it better than ever. See chapter 13.
- **Albergo Nazionale** (Portofino; ☎ **0185/269-575**): This excellent moderately priced choice is situated right in the heart of the most photographed harbor of Italy, in the most expensive pocket of posh on the Italian Riviera. Antique furnishings, coved ceilings, and hand-painted Venetian furniture add to the charm and luxury, but nothing equals the view of the harbor from some bedroom windows. See chapter 15.

9 The Best Restaurants

- **Relais le Jardin** (Rome; ☎ **06/361-3041**): Located in the dignified Lord Byron Hotel, in an upscale residential neighborhood a short drive from the center of Rome, the Relais is always on the short list of the country's best. The menu varies according to what's in season. See chapter 4.
- **Harry's Bar** (Venice; ☎ **041/528-5777**): It's legendary, it's lighthearted, and it's fun. First made famous by writer Ernest Hemingway, Harry's Bar still serves sublime food in the formal dining room upstairs. The Bellini, peach juice with prosecco (Italian sparkling wine), was born here. See chapter 9.
- **Antico Martini** (Venice; ☎ **041/522-4121**): Founded in 1720 as a spot to savor the newly developed rage of coffee drinking, this restaurant is one of the very best in Venice. Replete with paneled walls and glittering chandeliers, the Antico Martini specializes in Venetian cuisine. See chapter 9.
- **Ristorante il Desco** (Verona; ☎ **045/595-358**): Set in a former palazzo, this restaurant is the best in the Veneto region of northeastern Italy. Its culinary repertoire emphasizes a *nuova cucina* (nouvelle cuisine) that makes use of the freshest ingredients. The wine selections are excellent. See chapter 11.
- **Ristorante Tivoli** (Cortina d'Ampezzo; ☎ **0436/866-400**): At this charming and friendly restaurant, a cozy chalet on a hillside above the town, enjoy such

flavorful dishes as stuffed rabbit in an onion sauce, filet of veal with pine nuts and basil, and a delectable saffron-flavored salmon. See chapter 12.

- **Ristorante Emiliano** (Stresa; ☎ **0323/31-396**): Overlooking the soothing waters of Lake Garda, Emiliano attracts many conservative clients from throughout northern Europe who come to the Italian Lake District for R&R. Recipes adhere to the traditions of the Emilia-Romagna region, which is known for its pastas, sausages, and cheeses. See chapter 13.
- **Peck's Restaurant** (Milan; ☎ **02/876-774**): In the 19th century an entrepreneur from Prague moved to Lombardy and founded the most upscale delicatessen (Peck's) in Milan. The same management also runs this sumptuously elegant restaurant. You're likely to dine surrounded by the business moguls who run Italy. See chapter 13.
- **Ristorante da Vittorio** (Bergamo; ☎ **035/218-060**): Set on a busy commercial boulevard in a town known for its feudal fortifications, this restaurant stresses regional cuisine with an array of risottos, pastas, and game dishes. See chapter 13.
- **L'Aquila Nigra** (Mantua; ☎ **0376/327-180**): To reach this restaurant, which used to be a Renaissance palace, you'll have to meander through a labyrinth of narrow alleyways in the historic heart of Mantua. Inside, the high-ceilinged rooms offer elegant food, served with dignified panache by a well-trained staff. See chapter 13.
- **Vecchia Lanterna** (Turin; ☎ **011/537-047**): Ornate 19th-century furniture, *belle époque* lighting fixtures, and art nouveau accessories add to the charm and elegance you'll enjoy here. The food is rich and savory, too. See chapter 14.
- **Gran Gotto** (Genoa; ☎ **010/564-344**): Despite its excellent cuisine, this place manages to remain lighthearted, irreverent, and richly connected to the seafaring life of this ancient Italian port. The *zuppa di pesce* (a Riviera version of a Marseillaise bouillabaisse) is worth the trip to Genoa. See chapter 15.

10 The Best Buys

- **Ceramics:** The town of Faenza, in the Emilia-Romagna region, has been the center of pottery making, especially *majolica,* ever since the Renaissance. Majolica, also known as *faïence,* is a type of hand-painted, glazed, and heavily ornamented earthenware. Of course, you don't have to go to Faenza to purchase it, as shops throughout the country carry it. Tuscany and Umbria are also known for their earthenware pottery, carried by many shops in Rome and Florence.
- **Fashion:** Italian fashion is world renowned. Pucci and Valentino lead the parade to be followed in time by Armani, Versace, Missoni, and, of course, Gucci. Following World War II, Italian design began to compete seriously against the French fashion monopoly. Today Italian designers such as Krizia are among the fashion arbiters of the world. Milan dominates the fashion scene with the largest selection of boutiques, followed by Rome and Florence. Ironically, a lot of "French" fashion is now designed and manufactured in Italy, in spite of what the label says.
- **Glass:** Venetian glass, ranging from the delicate to the grotesque, is famous the world over. In Venice you'll find literally hundreds of stores peddling Venetian glass in a wide range of prices. Here's the surprise: A great deal of Venetian glass today isn't manufactured on Murano (an island in the Venetian lagoon) but in the Czech Republic. That doesn't mean that the glass is unworthy. Many factories outside Italy turn out high-quality glass products that are then shipped to Murano, where many so-called glass factories aren't factories at all but storefronts selling this imported "Venetian" glass.

- **Gold:** The tradition of shaping jewelry out of gold dates from the time of the Etruscans, and this ancient tradition is going strong in Italy today, with artisans still working in tiny studios and workshops. Many of the designs they follow are based on ancient Roman originals. Of course, many gold jewelers don't follow tradition at all, but design original and often daring pieces. Many shops throughout Italy will even melt down your old gold jewelry and refashion it into something more modern.

- **Lace:** For centuries Italy has been known for its exquisite and delicate lace— fashioned into everything from women's undergarments to heirloom-type tablecloths. Florence long ago distinguished itself for the *punto Firenze* or "Florentine stitch" made by cloistered nuns, although this tradition isn't as plentiful as it used to be. Venetian lace is even more famous, including some of the finest lace products in the world, especially *tombolo* (pillow lace), macramé, and an expensive form of lace known as *chiacchierino*. Of course, the market today is also flooded with cheap machine-made stuff, which a trained eye can quickly spot. Although some pieces of lace, such as a bridal veil, might cost millions of lire, you'll often find reasonably priced collars, handkerchiefs, and doilies in boutiques in Venice and Florence.

- **Leather:** The Italians—not just Gucci designers—are the finest leather craftspeople in the world. From boots to luggage, from leather clothing to purses (or wallets), Italian cities, especially Rome, Florence, Venice, and Milan, abound in leather shops selling quality goods. Leather is one of the best values in Italy, in spite of the substandard work that's now appearing. If you shop carefully, you can still find lots of handcrafted Italian leather products.

- **Prints & Engravings:** Ever since the Renaissance, Italy has been a shopping mecca for engravings and prints, especially Rome and Florence. Wood engravings, woodcuts, mezzotints, copper engravings—you name it and you'll find it in Italy. Of course, you have to be a careful shopper when purchasing. Some prints are genuine antiques and works of rare art, whereas others are rushed off the assembly line and into the shops. Since you can no longer go to Italy and take home Roman antiques or a crate of Raphaels, visitors today content themselves with these relatively inexpensive prints and engravings—admittedly reproductions but collectors' items nonetheless.

- **Religious Objects & Vestments:** The religious objects industry in Italy is big and bustling, centered mostly in the Greater Vatican area in Rome. The greatest concentration of shops in Rome is near the ancient Church of Santa Maria Sopra Minerva. They've got it all, from cardinals' birettas and rosary beads to religious art and vestments.

2 Getting to Know Italy

Conquerors, scholars, artists, and saints as well as curious travelers have been drawn to Italy for centuries. Across turbulent seas and stormy mountains they came, even risking their lives to see Italy. Getting here by plane, sea, rail, or car is considerably easier today, but the age-old attraction remains.

Some have been fascinated by its people, including the novelist E. M. Forster, who wrote that the Italians were "more marvellous than the land." Others have been drawn to its artistic treasures, left by geniuses such as Leonardo da Vinci and Michelangelo.

Although ancient, Italy is still a relatively modern country in terms of political unity. Unlike the rest of Europe, Italy was late in developing a national identity. It wasn't until 1870 that the country's 20 regions were united under one central government. Although Italy may be a late bloomer among European nations, its culture has flourished since antiquity, and no country in the world has as many reminders of its cultural heritage as does Italy. They range from Rome's Colosseum to Sicily's Greek ruins.

Other visitors come to Italy for the scenery—cypress-studded landscapes, coastal coves, jagged Dolomite peaks, fishing ports, sandy beaches, and charming little hill towns whose historic cores haven't changed much in hundreds of years.

Many travelers visit Italy just to have fun, and given the country's sense of *la dolce vita*, that goal is almost guaranteed. Other, more serious visitors come here to immerse themselves in Italy's history and culture, and most of them leave thinking that this country is one of the world's most rewarding travel destinations.

1 The Regions in Brief

Italy is about the size of the state of Arizona. The peninsula's shape, however, gives visitors the impression of a much larger area; the ever-changing seacoast contributes to this feeling, as do the large islands of Sicily and Sardinia. Bordered on the northwest by France, on the north by Switzerland and Austria, and on the east by Slovenia (formerly part of Yugoslavia), Italy is still a land largely surrounded by the sea.

Two areas within the boundaries of Italy not under the control of the Italian government are the State of Vatican City and the Republic of San Marino. The 109 acres of Vatican City in Rome were established in 1929 by a concordat, or formal agreement, between Pope Pius XI and Benito Mussolini, acting as head of the Italian government; the agreement also gave the Roman Catholic religion special status in the country. The pope is the sovereign of the State of Vatican City, which has its own legal system and its own post office.

Here is a brief rundown of the cities and regions covered in this book:

ROME   The region of **Latium** is dominated by Rome, capital of the ancient empire and the modern nation of Italy, and Vatican City, the independent papal state. Containing vast lodes of the world's artistic treasures, Latium is a land of myth, legend, grandeur, and ironies. Much of the civilized world was once ruled from here, going back to the days when Romulus and Remus are said to have founded Rome on April 21, 753 B.C. For generations Rome was justifiably referred to as *caput mundi* (capital of the world). It no longer enjoys such a lofty position, of course, but remains a timeless city, ranking with Paris and London as one of the most visited of Europe. There's no place else in all the world with more artistic monuments than Rome, not even Venice or Florence. Rome is the country's storehouse of treasures, from the Sistine Chapel to the Roman Forum. It remains the city of *la dolce vita*. How much time should you budget? The Italian writer Silvio Negro said, "A lifetime is not enough."

FLORENCE, TUSCANY & UMBRIA   **Tuscany** is one of the most culturally and politically influential provinces in Italy—the development of Italy without Tuscany is simply unthinkable. It was the vistas of Tuscany, with its sun-warmed vineyards and towering cypresses fluttering in gentle breezes, that inspired the artists of the Renaissance. Nowhere in the world does the Renaissance live on more than it does in its birthplace, **Florence,** with its artistic works left by da Vinci and Michelangelo, among others. Since the 19th century, travelers have been flocking to Florence to see the Donatello bronzes, the Botticelli smiles, and all the other preeminent treasures. Unfortunately, it's now an invasion, and Florence is overrun like Venice. All the world knows of Florence's astounding artistic wealth, including the most reproduced statue on earth (Michelangelo's *David*), so you run the risk of being trampled underfoot as you explore the historic heart of the city. To escape, head for nearby attractions in the Tuscan hill towns, former stamping ground of the Guelphs and Ghibellines. The main cities to visit include Lucca, Pisa, and especially Siena, Florence's great historical rival with an inner core that appears to be caught in a time warp. As a final treat, visit San Gimignano, northwest of Siena, which is celebrated for its medieval "skyscrapers."

Pastoral, hilly, and fertile, **Umbria** is similar to Tuscany, but with fewer tourists. Its once-fortified network of hill towns is among the most charming in Italy. Crafted from millions of tons of gray-brown rocks, each town is a testament to the masonry and architectural skills of many generations of Italian craftsmen. Cities worth a visit include Perugia, Gubbio, Assisi, Spoleto (site of the world-renowned annual arts festival), and Orvieto, a mysterious citadel once used as a stronghold by the Etruscans. Called the land of shadows, Umbria is often covered in a bluish haze that evokes an ethereal painted look. Many local artists have tried to capture the province's special glow, with its sun-dappled hills, terraced vineyards, and miles upon miles of olive trees. If you're short on time, visit Assisi to check out Giotto's frescoes at the Basilica di San Francesco, and Perugia, the largest and richest of the provence's cities.

EMILIA-ROMAGNA   Italians seem to agree on only one thing: The food in Emilia-Romagna is the best in Italy. The region's capital, Bologna, boasts a stunning Renaissance core with plenty of majestic churches and arcades, a fine university with roots in the early Middle Ages, and a populace with a reputation for leftist leanings.

The region also has one of the highest standards of living in Italy. Should you budget time for a visit? Definitely yes, although the pluckings are richer in Tuscany and Umbria. But Emilia-Romagna has a lot going for it, including tortellini, lasagne, and fettuccine, its greatest contributions to world gastronomy. When not dining in Bologna, you can take time to explore its artistic heritage. Other art cities also abound in the region—none more noble than the Byzantine city of Ravenna, still living off its past glory as the one-time capital of the declining Roman Empire.

If you can visit only one more city in the region, make it Parma, to see its city center with its Duomo and Battistero and to view its National Gallery. Parma is also the home of Parmesan cheese and prosciutto. Another noteworthy city is Modena, hometown of opera star Pavarotti—known for its cuisine, its cathedral, and its Este Gallery. The crowded Adriatic resort of Rimini and the medieval stronghold of San Marino are both at the periphery of Emilia-Romagna.

VENICE & THE VENETO This region, dotted with richly stocked museums and some of the best architecture in Italy, sprawls across the verdant hills and flat and fertile plains of northeastern Italy, between the Adriatic, the Dolomites, Verona, and the edges of Lake Garda. The fortunes of the Veneto revolved, for many generations, around Venice. Few travelers need to be sold on the glories of Venice, with its sumptuous palaces, romantic waterways, Palazzo Ducale, and Basilica di San Marco. Aging, decaying, and sinking into the sea, Venice is so alluring that we almost want to say visit it if you have to skip Rome and Florence. However, we don't dare because each of the top three tourist cities of Italy is so special and unique that we hope you can accommodate all of them in your itinerary. As special as Venice and its islands in the lagoon are, we also recommended that you tear yourself away and visit at least three fabled art cities in the "Venetian Arc"—Verona of *Romeo and Juliet* fame, Vicenza to see the villas of Andrea Palladio where 16th-century aristocrats lived, and Padua (Padova), ennobled by its Giotto frescoes.

TRIESTE, THE DOLOMITES & SOUTH TYROL Before the South Tyrol region **(Trentino–Alto Adige)** was annexed by Italy after World War I, it was an integral part of Austria. Despite the changes made almost 80 years ago, passions continue to run deep here as family loyalties cling tenaciously to Austrian ways. The region's split personality is enhanced by the mixture of Italian and German spoken on an everyday basis. Also, the architecture dotting the rocky sides of the Dolomites seems mostly influenced by either the chalet or the Austrian Jugendstil style. This region is far richer in culture, artistic treasures, and activities than the Valle d'Aosta (see below), and its ski resort, Cortina d'Ampezzo, is far more fashionable than Courmayer or Breuil-Cervina in the northwestern corridor. Its most interesting bases—especially if you want to see the Austrian version of Italy—are Bolzano (Bozen) and Meran (Merano). Trent (Trento), the capital of Trentino, is more historic than either Merano or Bolzano, but lacks their scenic beauty.

Set in the extreme northeastern corner of Italy, adjacent to the border of modern-day Slovenia, the region of **Friuli–Venezia Giulia** is, in its own way, one of the most cosmopolitan and culturally sophisticated regions of Italy. Set at the crossroads of the Balkans and the Teutonic world, it was highly influenced by the Austro-Hungarian Empire. Its capital is the seaport of Trieste, although worthy sites of interest include Udine, Gorizia, and Pordenone. The area is filled with artistic treasures from the Roman, Byzantine, and Romanesque-Gothic eras, and many of the public buildings (especially those of Trieste) might remind you more of Vienna. This area is not a mainstream tourist destination, and that forms its particular appeal. For those on the whirlwind tour, Trieste could be skipped. But those who come to Trieste will be

Regions of Italy

VAL D'AOSTA
Courmayeur
Aosta
Novara
Lake Maggiore
Como
Milan
Turin
Asti
Vercelli
PIEDMONT
Cuneo
Savona
Genoa
LIGURIA
San Remo
Rapallo
Gulf of Genoa
La Spezia

Alps
Lake Como
Lake Garda
Bergamo
Brescia
Cremona
LOMBARDY

Merano
Bolzano
Trent
Belluno
TRENTINO-ALTO ADIGE
Cortina d'Ampezzo
Vicenza
VENETO
Verona
Padua
Treviso
Venice
FRIULI-VENEZIA GIULIA
Udine
Trieste
Gulf of Venice

Northern Apennine
Parma
Mantua
Modena
Ferrara
EMILIA-ROMAGNA
Bologna
Ravenna
Rimini

Ligurian Sea
Livorno
Pisa
Florence
Siena
TUSCANY
Elba
SAN MARINO
Pesaro
Perugia
Macerata
Ancona
Assisi
Viterbo
Orvieto
UMBRIA
Spoleto
THE MARCHES
Terano
Terni
Civitavecchia

Adriatic Sea

ROME
VATICAN CITY
LATIUM
L'Aquila
Pescara
Chieti
ABRUZZI
Campobasso
MOLIZE
Caserta
Gulf of Gaeta
Benevento
Foggia

SARDINIA
Sassari
Ólbia
Nuoro
Cagliari

Tyrrhenian Sea

Ischia
Naples
Pompeii
Mt. Vesuvius
Capri
Amalfi
Sorrento
Salerno
Avellino
Paestum
CAMPANIA
Potenza
APULIA
Bari
BASILICATA
Brindisi
Taranto
Lecce
Gulf of Taranto

Southern Apennine

CALABRIA
Cosenza
Catanzaro

Trapani
Marsala
Selinunte
Palermo
Lipari Islands
Mediterranean Sea
SICILY
Enna
Agrigento
Taormina
Mt. Etna
Messina
Reggio di Calabria
Catania
Ragusa
Syracuse
Ionian Sea

0   100 m
        160 km
N

3-0651

17

richly rewarded by the unique atmosphere of the largest seaport on the Adriatic. Trieste has enough attractions to fill one busy day and is an easy drive from Venice.

MILAN, LOMBARDY & THE LAKES   Flat, fertile, prosperous, and politically conservative, Lombardy is dominated by Milan in the same way that Latium is dominated by Rome. Lombardy is one of the world's leading commercial and cultural centers—it has been immersed in the mercantile ethic ever since Milan developed into Italy's gateway to northern, German-speaking Europe during the early Middle Ages. Although it's fashionable to belittle Milan for its industrial power and its contempt of the poorer regions of Italy's south, its fans compare it to New York. Milan's cathedral is the third largest in Europe, its opera house (La Scala) is the site of some of the finest performances anywhere, and its museums and churches are world class. Nevertheless, in spite of its formidable attractions—everything from da Vinci's *Last Supper* to one of Europe's greatest cathedrals—Milan is still not in the tourist league of Rome, Florence, and Venice. Work in Milan if you have the time, although you'll find more charm in the neighboring art cities of Bergamo, Brescia, Pavia, Cremona, and Mantua. Also competing for your time will be the lakes of Garda and Maggiore, which lie near Lombardy's eastern edge and are the preferred vacation destinations of the Milanese themselves.

PIEDMONT & VALLE D'AOSTA   Set at the extreme northwestern edge of Italy, sharing a set of alpine peaks with France (which in some ways it resembles), the **Piedmont** was the district from which Italy's dreams of unification spread in 1861. Long under the domination of the Austro-Hungarian Empire, the Piedmont enjoys a cuisine laced with alpine cheeses and dairy products. It's proud of its largest city, Turin (Torino in Italian). Called the "Detroit of Italy," Turin is the home of the Fiat empire, as well as vermouth, Asti Spumante, and the Borsalino hat. Although a great cosmopolitan center, it doesn't have the antique charm of its seafront sibling, Genoa, or the sophistication, world-class dining, and chic shopping of its Lombard cousin, Milan. Turin's most controversial sight is the *Sacra Sindone*, or the Holy Shroud, which many Catholics believe is the exact cloth in which Christ's body was wrapped when removed from the cross.

Italy's window on Switzerland and France, the **Valle d'Aosta**—the smallest region of Italy—often serves as an introduction to the country itself, especially for those journeying from France through the Mont Blanc tunnel into Italy. The introduction is misleading, as the Valle d'Aosta stands apart from the rest of Italy, a semiautonomous, high-altitude region of towering peaks and valleys in the northwestern corridor of the country. Known for its alpine sunshine and the ancient French-derived dialect of its citizens, it's more closely linked to France (especially the French alpine region of Savoy) than to Italy. An area rich in scenery, dairy products, and wine, its most important city is the ancient Roman city of Aosta, which except for some ruins is rather dull. More intriguing are two of Italy's major ski resorts, Courmayeur and Breuil-Cervinia, which are rivaled—and topped—only by Cortina d'Ampezzo in the Dolomites. Many of the region's villages are crafted from gray rocks culled from the mountains that rise on all sides. The best time to visit is either in the summer or the deep of winter. Late spring and fall get rather sleepy in this part of the world.

LIGURIA & THE ITALIAN RIVIERA   Comprising most of the Italian Riviera, the unexpected capital of which is the steeply sloping city of Genoa (Genova), the region of Liguria incorporates medieval ports known for their charm (Portofino, Ventimiglia, and San Remo), a massive naval base (La Spezia), and a quintet of coastal communities (Cinque Terra) that cling tenaciously to traditional values. There's also a series of *belle époque* seaside resorts (Rapallo and Santa Margherita Ligure) whose style and nonchalance are reminiscent of resorts along the nearby French Riviera. As chic as the Italian Riviera is, it's still rivaled and surpassed by the French. But the Italian Riviera has its unique appeal. Although it's overbuilt and overrun with tourists, just as its French counterpart is, it's still a land of great beauty. It's actually two Rivieras—the *Riviera di Ponente,* or western Riviera, which runs from the French border to Genoa, and the *Riviera di Levante* to the east. Faced with a choice, make it the Riviera di Levante, as it's more glamorous and cosmopolitan. Italy's largest port, Genoa, also merits a visit to learn of its rich culture and history. The historic harbor was given a face-lift for the celebrations honoring Columbus in 1992.

NAPLES, THE AMALFI COAST & CAPRI   More than any other region of Italy, **Campania** reverberates with the memories of the ancient Romans, who favored its strong sunlight, fertile soil, and bubbling sulfurous springs. It manages to incorporate the anarchy of Naples with the elegant beauty of Capri and the Amalfi coast. The district also contains many sites specifically identified in ancient mythology (lakes defined as the entrance to the Kingdom of the Dead, for example) and some of the most prolific ancient ruins (including Pompeii and Herculaneum) in the world. No longer the treat of artists, kings, and emperors, Campania is overrun, overcrowded, and over everything, but it still lures visitors. Allow at least a day for Naples, which has amazing museums and the world's worst traffic outside of Cairo. Pompeii and Herculaneum are for the ruin collectors, whereas those seeking Italian sun head for Capri, rivaled only by Portofino in the north for chicdom. The best towns along the Amalfi Drive, even though they're no longer unspoiled, are Ravello (not on the sea) and Positano (which is on the sea). Amalfi and Sorrento are much tackier and more overrun.

APULIA   Sun-drenched and poor, Apulia forms the heel of the Italian boot. It is the most frequently visited province of Italy's Deep South; part of its allure lies in its string of resorts, which line the elongated seacoast. Depending on the dialect you're hearing, the region is referred to as Puglia, Le Puglie, or Apulia. The *trulli* houses of Alberobello are known for their unique cylindrical shapes and conical, flagstone-sheathed roofs. Among the region's largest cities are Bari (the capital), Foggia, and Brindisi (gateway to nearby Greece, with which the town shares many characteristics). Each of these cities is a modern disaster, filled with tawdry buildings, heavy traffic, and rising crime rates (tourists are often the victims). Visitors mostly pass through Bari at night—it's a favorite with backpackers—and the only reason to spend a night in Brindisi is the wait to catch the ferry to Greece the next morning.

SICILY   The largest island of the Mediterranean, Sicily is a land of beauty, mystery, and world-class monuments. Cynical yet passionate, it's endlessly fascinating, a bizarre mixture of bloodlines and architecture from medieval Normandy, Aragonese Spain, Moorish North Africa, ancient Greece, Phoenicia, and Rome. Since the advent of modern times, part of the island's primitiveness has faded, as thousands of newly arrived cars clog the narrow lanes of its biggest city, Palermo. Although poverty remains widespread, the age-old stranglehold of the Mafia seems less certain because of the increasingly vocal protests of an outraged Italian public. On the eastern edge of the island is Mount Etna, the tallest active volcano in Europe. Many of Sicily's larger cities (Trapani, Catania, and Messina) are relatively unattractive, but areas of ravishing beauty and eerie historic interest include Siracusa, Taormina, Agrigento, and Selinunte. Sicily's ancient ruins are rivaled only by those of Rome itself. The Valley of the Temples, for example, is worth the trip here.

2 Italy Today

TOURIST OVERLOAD　As the end of the second millennium approaches, Italy is scrambling to prepare itself for the onslaught of tourists who will make pilgrimages to the country for **Jubilee 2000,** the Holy Year declared by the pope to celebrate the transition into a new era. This upcoming onslaught will dwarf the invasions of the Etruscans, Langobards, or Normans in previous centuries. The mayor of Venice, Massimo Cacciari, using metaphors appropriate to his city, said of the oncoming Holy Year invasion, "If the floods are not channeled, we all risk capsizing." His fear was echoed by city authorities in Rome and Florence.

Even the present hordes pouring into the country—the numbers are swollen by millions of Roman Catholics from lands like Poland and Croatia—are flooding Italy's ancient meccas. One Italian politician facetiously suggested placing a NO VACANCY sign at the border.

In 1996, Florence, out of desperation, refused to allow more than 150 tour buses within the city center at any time. Cacciari, the Venetian mayor, has threatened to go even farther. He has suggested that tourists to Venice may have to "register" in advance of their arrival or else risk not being allowed to enter the city gates.

Of course, these Draconian measures and suggestions have met with violent opposition in some quarters. Pierluigi Bolla, the regional commisioner for tourism in the Veneto area, angrily denounced the Venetian registration plan, calling the mayor's proposal "boisterous" and claiming it masked "an implicit admission of the absence of any tourism strategy." He also claimed that visitors to Rome's millennial Jubilee were being treated as an "invasion of wild horses."

THE NORTHERN LEAGUE　Outsiders, however, are not the only problem Italians face today. The Northern League's Umberto Bossi is making a strong stand for Italian regions north of the Po River to secede from Italy and create a new nation: the Federal Republic of Padania. The area, from Turin in the west to below Venice in the east, is the home of the industries that have revived and/or maintained the Italian economy in recent decades. In fact, measured seperately from the rest of the nation, it is the area of highest per capita income in all of Europe, and taxes paid by northerners are used to subsidize poorer regions in the south. Critics nationwide agree that a great deal of tax money has been squandered, and Bossi insists that the Mafia is the true beneficiary of public works projects in the southern regions of the country.

Bossi has set himself up in the political backwater of Mantua, a small Renaissance city of 53,000. Besides naming the city as his new capital, after declaring a symbolic split from Italy on September 15, 1996, he has also set up a provisional government consisting of a cabinet and an unarmed—for the time being—security force known as the "Green-shirts"—a moniker chillingly reminiscent of Mussolini's Black-shirts.

Few people seem to consider the issue of secession very seriously, however, and a September 1996 poll showed only 7.6% of Italians in favor of a split. Even within the ghost state of Padania, Bossi faces challenges, as Mantua's salami and cheese companies, among Italy's best, say they've seen sales fall in protest to their location within the proposed separatist capital. Emilia-Romagna, among the most prosperous of the northern regions, has maintained its leftist leanings, thereby aligning itself with Prime Minister Romano Prodi's central government.

Still, Bossi has set up camp and doesn't appear to be going away. The national media has dubbed the separatist phenomenon "Bossismo." Prodi dismisses the issue, preferring to concentrate on national budget battles. Regardless of how they're handled, though, the issues underlying Bossi's movement—taxation and spending—cannot be ignored. The Government Accounting Office projects that a majority of Italians will be of southern origin within 30 years. This will increase not only the cost of public works projects in the south but the existing tensions between the north and the south as well.

A LAND OF CONTRADICTIONS Modern Italy is a land of contradictions: a Roman Catholic state ruled by the mores and values of a staunchly religious consciousness that nevertheless is the most corrupt country in Western Europe. Italy is a land whose sons and daughters emigrated to form large populations throughout the world, especially in America, but its citizens today in large numbers remain viciously opposed to and prejudiced against immigrants arriving on their own shore. In 1997, the most recent flood washed in from embattled Albania to the east.

"In the course of a century, we've gone from being a land of emigrants to one that takes in immigrants," said Luigi Manconi, a Milan sociologist. "We're just not equipped."

Widespread unemployment has enhanced racism and prejudice in Italy, primarily directed toward the North African contingent that has descended upon Italy in search of jobs. Despite attempts to turn them back, they continued to arrive in 1997. Most work in the agricultural community as migrant workers. Some are prostitutes in the bustling resorts on the Italian Riviera. These workers are not accepted into the tight-knit Italian communities.

POLITICS ARE DIRTY Although the government might try to limit immigration, any attempt to clean up its own image seems hopeless. *La politica e una cosa sporca* (politics are dirty) is an expression often heard in Italy. The charge is certainly justified. Corruption, scandal, and political chaos are parts of everyday life on the Italian landscape. The word *politician* is almost always preceded by the word *corrupt*. It's virtually assumed that anyone entering politics is doing so for personal gain.

Italy's precarious modern political system, with 55 governments since World War II, has been compared by many political analysts to the ill-fated First Republic.

THE ECONOMY, THE MAFIA & IL SORPASSO Although Italy ranks sixth among world economic powers, the instability of the lira in global markets has forced Italy to remain a second-class participant in global commerce. Its true economy cannot be measured because of the vast underground economy *(economia sommersa)* controlled by the Mafia. Almost every Italian has some unreported income or expenditure. Other global competitors refrain from investing in Italian ventures because of lack of confidence in the government.

Besides soccer *(calcio),* the family, and affairs of the heart, the national obsession of Italy as it faces the millennium is *il sorpasso,* a term that describes Italy's surpassing of its archrivals France and Britain in economic indicators. Economists disagree about whether or not *il sorpasso* has happened, and statistics (complicated by the presence of Italy's vast underground economy) vary widely from source to source. All levels of Italian society are actively engaged to some degree in withholding funds from the government. Today Italy's underground economy competes on a monumental scale with the official economy, with participation by all sorts of otherwise respectable businesses and individuals. Complicating Italy's problems for economists, the police, and politicians is the constant interference of the Mafia, whose methods—despite numerous more or less heartfelt crackdowns—continue today even more ruthlessly than ever.

Another complicating factor is the surfeit of laws in Italy and their effect on the citizens. Before they get thrown out of office, Italian politicians pass laws and more laws, adding to the horde already on the books. Italy has more laws on the books than any other nation of Western Europe and also suffers from a bloated bureaucracy. Something as simple as cashing a check or paying a bill can devour half a day. To escape the brambles of red tape, Italians have become marvelous improvisers and corner-cutters. Whenever possible they bypass the sclerotic public sector and negotiate private deals *fra amici*—among friends.

WHAT THE FUTURE HOLDS   Italy can no longer bask in its glorious past. The country today is a land in transition, struggling to become a stable, viable contender in the global community. It's probably safe to say, though, that Italy will continue to be a land of contradictions: Although some view with dread the upcoming invasion of visitors during Jubilee 2000, zillions of trinket peddlers are eagerly awaiting the hordes. Even as we speak, factories are busy turning out the souvenirs to be hawked.

3 A Look at the Past

Dateline

- **Bronze Age** Celts, Teutonic tribes, and others from the Mediterranean and Asia Minor inhabit the peninsula.
- **1000 B.C.** Large colonies of Etruscans settle in Tuscany and Campania, quickly subjugating many of the Latin inhabitants of the Italian peninsula.
- **800 B.C.** Rome begins to take shape, evolving from a strategically located shepherd village into a magnet for Latin tribes fleeing the Etruscans.
- **600 B.C.** Etruscans occupy Rome, designating it the capital of their empire; the city grows rapidly and a major seaport opens at Ostia.
- **510 B.C.** The Latin tribes, still centered in Rome, revolt against the Etruscans; alpine Gauls attack from the north; Greeks living in Sicily destroy the Etruscan navy.
- **250 B.C.** The Romans, allied with the Greeks, Phoenicians, and native Sicilians, defeat the Etruscans; Rome flourishes and begins the accumulation of a vast empire.

continues

THE ETRUSCANS   Among the early inhabitants of Italy, the most significant were the Etruscans— but who were they, actually? No one knows, and the many inscriptions they left behind—mostly on graves—are of no help, since the Etruscan language has never been deciphered by modern scholars. It's thought that they arrived on the eastern coast of Umbria several centuries before Rome was built, which was around **800 B.C.** Their religious rites and architecture show an obvious contact with **Mesopotamia;** the Etruscans may have been refugees from Asia Minor who traveled westward about 1200 to 1000 B.C. Within two centuries they had subjugated Tuscany and Campania and the Villanova tribes who lived there.

While the Etruscans built temples at Tarquinia and Caere (present-day Cerveteri), the few nervous Latin tribes who remained outside their sway gravitated to **Rome,** then little more than a sheepherding village. As its power grew, however, Rome increasingly profited from the strategically important Tiber crossing where the ancient **Salt Way (Via Salaria)** turned northeastward toward the central Apennines.

From their base at Rome, the Latins remained free of the Etruscans until about **600 B.C.** But the Etruscan advance was inexorable, and although the tribes concentrated their forces at Rome for a last stand, they were swept away by the sophisticated Mesopotamian conquerors. The new overlords introduced gold tableware and jewelry, bronze urns and terra-cotta statuary, and the best of Greek and Asia Minor art and culture; they also made Rome the governmental seat of all Latium. Roma is an Etruscan name, and the kings of Rome had Etruscan names: Numa, Ancus, Tarquinius, even Romulus.

The Estruscans ruled until the Roman revolt around **510 B.C.,** and by **250 B.C.** the Romans and their Campania allies had vanquished the Etruscans, wiping out their language and religion. However, many of the former rulers' manners and beliefs remained, assimilated into the culture. Even today certain Etruscan customs and bloodlines are believed to exist in Italy, especially in Tuscany.

The best places to see the legacy left by these mysterious people are in **Cerveteri** and **Tarquinia** outside Rome. Especially interesting is the Etruscan **necropolis,** just 4 miles southeast of Tarquinia, where thousands of tombs have been discovered. To learn more about the Etruscans, visit the **Museo Nazionale di Villa Giulla** in Rome, housed in a 16th-century papal palace in the Villa Borghese.

THE ROMAN REPUBLIC After the Roman Republic was established in **510 B.C.,** the Romans continued to increase their power by conquering neighboring communities in the highlands and forming alliances with other Latins of the lowlands. They gave to their Latin allies, and then to conquered peoples, partial or complete Roman citizenship, with the obligation of military service. Citizen colonies were set up as settlements of Roman farmers, and many of the famous cities of Italy today originated as colonies. The colonies were for the most part fortified, and they were linked to Rome by military roads.

The stern Roman republic was characterized by belief in the gods, the necessity of learning from the past, strength of the family, education through books and public service, and—most important—obedience. The **all-powerful Senate** presided as Rome defeated rival powers one after the other and grew to rule the Mediterranean. The **Punic Wars** with Carthage in the **3rd century B.C.** cleared away a major obstacle to Rome's growth, although people said later that Rome's breaking of its treaty with Carthage (which led to the total destruction of that city) put a curse on the Italian city. No figure was more towering during the republic than **Julius Caesar,** the charismatic conqueror of Gaul. He was called "the wife of every husband and the husband of every wife," among other honors. After defeating the last resistance of the Pompeians in Spain in 45 B.C., he came to Rome and was made dictator and consul for 10 years. He was at that point almost a king. Conspirators led by Marcus Junius Brutus stabbed him to death in the Senate on March 15, 44 B.C.

- **49 B.C.** Italy (through Rome) controls the entire Mediterranean world.
- **44 B.C.** Julius Caesar assassinated; his successor, Augustus, transforms Rome from a city of brick to a city of marble.
- **3rd century A.D.** Rome declines under a series of incompetent and corrupt emperors.
- **4th century A.D.** Rome is fragmented politically as administrative capitals are established in such cities as Milan and Trier, Germany.
- **A.D. 395** The empire splits; Constantine establishes a "New Rome" at Constantinople (Byzantium); Goths successfully invade Rome's northern provinces.
- **410–455** Rome is sacked by barbarians.
- **475** Rome falls, leaving only the primate of the Catholic Church in control; the pope slowly adopts many of the powers once reserved for the Roman emperor.
- **800** Charlemagne is crowned Holy Roman Emperor by Pope Leo III; Italy dissolves into a series of small warring kingdoms.
- **Late 11th century** The popes function like secular princes with private armies.
- **1065** The Holy Land falls to the Muslim Turks; the Crusades are launched.
- **1303–77** Papal schism; the pope and his entourage move from Rome to Avignon.
- **1377** The papacy returns to Rome.
- **1443** Brunelleschi's dome caps the Duomo in Florence as the Renaissance ("rebirth") bursts into full bloom.
- **1469–92** Lorenzo il Magnifico rules in Florence

continues

as the Medici patron of Renaissance artists.

- **1499** The *Last Supper* is completed by Leonardo da Vinci in Milan.
- **1508** Michelangelo begins work on the Vatican's Sistine Chapel.
- **1527** Rome is sacked by Charles V of Spain, who is crowned Holy Roman Emperor the following year.
- **1796–97** Napoléon's series of invasions arouses Italian nationalism.
- **1861** The Kingdom of Italy is established.
- **1915–18** Italy enters World War I on the side of the Allies.
- **1922** Fascists march on Rome; Benito Mussolini becomes premier.
- **1929** A concordat between the Vatican and the Italian government is signed delineating the rights and responsibilities of each party.
- **1935** Italy invades Abyssinia (Ethiopia).
- **1936** Italy signs "Axis" pact with Germany.
- **1940** Italy invades Greece.
- **1943** U.S. Gen. George Patton lands in Sicily and soon controls the island.
- **1945** Mussolini is killed by a mob in Milan.
- **1946** The Republic of Italy is established.
- **1957** The Treaty of Rome, founding the European Community (EC), is signed by six nations.
- **1960s** The country's economy grows under the EC, but the impoverished south lags behind.
- **1970s** Italy is plagued by left-wing terrorism; former premier Aldo Moro is kidnapped and killed.
- **1980s** Political changes in Eastern Europe induce Italy's strong Communist Party to

continues

Mark Antony then assumed control by seizing Caesar's papers and wealth. Intent on expanding the Republic, Mark Antony met with **Cleopatra** at Tarsus in 41 B.C. She seduced him, and he stayed in Egypt for a year. When Mark Antony eventually returned to Rome, still smitten with Cleopatra, he made peace with Caesar's willed successor, **Octavius,** and, through the pacts of Brundisium, soon found himself married to Octavius's sister, Octavia. This marriage, however, did not prevent Antony from openly marrying Cleopatra in 36 B.C. The furious Octavius gathered western legions and defeated Antony at the **Battle of Actium** on September 2, 31 B.C. Cleopatra fled to Egypt, followed by Antony, who committed suicide in disgrace 1 year later. Cleopatra, unable to seduce his successor and thus retain her rule of Egypt, followed suit the same year with a snake bite.

THE ROMAN EMPIRE By **49 B.C.,** Italy ruled all of the Mediterranean world either directly or indirectly, with all political, commercial, and cultural pathways leading directly to Rome. The possible wealth and glory to be found in Rome lured many, draining other Italian communities of human resources. Foreign imports, especially agricultural imports, hurt local farmers and landowners. Municipal governments faltered, and civil wars ensued. Public order was restored by the Caesars (planned by Julius but brought to fruition under Augustus). On the eve of the **birth of Christ,** Rome was a mighty empire whose generals had brought the Western world under the sway of Roman law and civilization.

Born Gaius Octavius in 63 B.C., **Augustus,** the first Roman emperor, reigned from 27 B.C. to A.D. 14. His reign, called **"the golden age of Rome,"** led to the Pax Romana, or two centuries of peace. He had been adopted by, and eventually became the heir of, his great-uncle Julius Caesar. In Rome today you can still visit the remains of the **Forum** of Augustus, built before the birth of Christ, and the **Domus Augustana,** where the imperial family lived on Palatine Hill.

The emperors, whose succession started with Augustus's principate after the death of Julius Caesar, brought Rome to new, almost giddy, heights. Augustus transformed the city from brick to marble—much the way that Napoléon III transformed Paris many centuries later. But success led to **corruption.** The emperors wielded autocratic power, and the centuries witnessed a steady decay in the ideals and traditions upon which the empire had been founded.

The army became a fifth column of barbarian mercenaries, the tax collector became the scourge of the countryside, and for every good emperor (Augustus, Trajan, Vespasian, and Hadrian, to name a few) there were three or four debased heads of state (Caligula, Nero, Domitian, Caracalla, and more).

After Augustus died, his widow, **Livia**—a crafty social climber who had divorced her first husband to marry Augustus—set up her son **Tiberius** as ruler through a series of intrigues and poisonings. A long series of murders ensued, and Tiberius, who ruled during Pontius Pilot's trial and crucifixion of Christ, was eventually murdered in an uprising of landowners. Murder was, in fact, so common, that a short time later the emperor Domitian (A.D. 81–96) became so obsessed with the possibility of assassination that he had the walls of his palace covered in mica so he could see behind him at all times. (He was killed anyway.)

Excesses and scandal ruled the day, from **Caligula** appointing his horse a lifetime member of the Senate, to his successor, **Claudius,** being poisoned by his wife, **Agrippina,** to secure the succession of **Nero,** her son by a previous marriage. Nero's thanks was to later murder not only his mother but his wife as well. The disgraceful Nero was removed as emperor while visiting Greece; he committed suicide with the cry "What an artist I destroy."

- modify its program and even to change its name; the Socialists head their first post-1945 coalition government.
- **1994** A conservative coalition, led by Silvio Berlusconi, wins general elections.
- **1995** Following the resignation of Berlusconi, Lamberto Dini, Treasury minister, is named prime minister to head transitional government.
- **1996** Dini steps down as prime minister, as president dissolves both houses of parliament; in general elections, the center-left coalition known as the Olive Tree sweeps both the Senate and the Chamber of Deputies.
- **1997** Prime Minister Prodi makes deep slashes in budget in hopes to enter European monetary union; threats of secession from north make world headlines.

By the 3rd century A.D., corruption was so prevalent that there were 23 emperors in 73 years. How bad had things gotten? So bad that **Caracalla,** to secure control of the empire, had his brother Geta slashed to pieces while lying in his mother's arms. Rule of the empire changed hands so frequently that news of the election of a new emperor commonly reached the provinces together with a report of his assassination.

The 4th-century reforms of **Diocletian** held the empire together, but at the expense of its inhabitants, who were reduced to tax units. He reinforced imperial power while paradoxically weakening Roman dominance and prestige by **dividing the empire** into two halves, east and west, and establishing administrative capitals at such outposts as Milan, Trier in Germany, and elsewhere. Diocletian not only instituted heavy taxes but also a socioeconomic system that made profession hereditary. This edict was so strictly enforced that the son of a silversmith could be tried as a criminal if he attempted to become a sculptor instead.

Constantine became emperor in 306 B.C., and in 330 B.C. he made Constantinople (also known as **Byzantium**) the **new capital** of the Roman Empire, moving the administrative functions away from Rome altogether, partly because the menace of possible barbarian attack in the West had increased greatly. Constantine took the best Roman artisans, politicians, and public figures with him to the new capital, creating a city renowned for its splendor, intrigue, jealousies, and passion. Constantine was the **first Christian emperor,** allegedly converting after he saw the True Cross in the heavens, accompanied by the legend, "In This Sign Shall You Conquer," after which he defeated the pagan Maxentius and his followers in battle.

THE EMPIRE FALLS The eastern and western sections of the Roman Empire split in A.D. 395, leaving Italy without the support it once received from east of the Adriatic. When the **Goths** moved toward Rome in the early **5th century,** citizens in the provinces, who had grown to hate and fear the cruel bureaucracy set up by Diocletian and followed by succeeding emperors, welcomed the invaders. And then the pillage began.

Rome was first sacked by **Alaric** in **August of 410.** The populace made no attempt to defend the city (other than trying vainly to buy off the Goth, a tactic that admittedly had worked 3 years before); most people simply fled into the hills or headed to their country estates if they were rich. The feeble Western emperor, Honorius, hid out in Ravenna the entire time.

More than 40 troubled years passed until the siege of Rome by **Attila the Hun.** Strangely enough, it was the daughter of Honorius's stepsister, Placidia, who sent her seal ring to the barbarian and precipitated his march on the city. Attila was, however, dissuaded from attacking thanks largely to a peace mission headed by **Pope Leo I.** That was in 452, but relief was short-lived, for in 455 **Gaiseric the Vandal** carried out a 2-week sack that was unparalleled in its pure savagery. The empire of the West lasted for only another 20 years; finally the sacks and chaos ended it in A.D. 476, and Rome was left to the popes, under the nominal auspices of an exarch from Byzantium (Constantinople.)

The last would-be Caesars to walk the streets of Rome were both **barbarians:** The first was **Theodoric,** who established an Ostrogoth kingdom at Ravenna from 493 to 526; and the second was **Totilla,** who held the last chariot races in the Circus Maximus in 549. Totilla was engaged in a running battle with Belisarius, the general of the Eastern emperor Justinian, who sought to regain Rome for the Eastern Empire. The city changed hands several times, recovering some of its ancient pride by bravely resisting Totilla's forces, but eventually being entirely depopulated by the continuing battles.

Christianity, a new religion that created a new society, was probably founded in Rome about a decade after Jesus' crucifixion. Gradually gaining strength despite early persecution, it was finally accepted as the official religion of the empire. The best way today to relive the early Christian era is to visit Rome's **Appian Way** and its **Catacombs,** along Via Appia Antica, built in 312 B.C. According to Christian tradition, it was here that an escaping Peter encountered the vision of Christ. The Catacombs of St. Callixtus form the first cemetery of the Christian community of Rome.

THE MIDDLE AGES So a ravaged Rome entered the Middle Ages, her once-proud population scattered and unrecognizable in rustic exile. A modest population started life again in the swamps of the Campus Martius, while the seven hills, now without water since the aqueducts were cut, stood abandoned and crumbling.

After the **fall of the Western Empire,** the pope took on more and more imperial powers, although there was no political unity in the country. Decades of rule by barbarians and then Goths were followed by takeovers in different parts of the country by various strong warriors, such as the **Lombards.** Italy was thus divided into several spheres of control. In 731 **Pope Gregory II** renounced Rome's dependence on Constantinople and thus ended the twilight era of the Greek exarch who had nominally ruled Rome.

Papal Rome turned toward Europe, where the papacy found a powerful ally in **Charlemagne,** a king of the barbarian Franks. In 800 he was crowned emperor by **Pope Leo III.** The capital that he established at Aachen (in French, Aix-la-Chapelle) lay deep within territory known to the Romans a half millennium ago as the heart of the barbarian world. Although Charlemagne pledged allegiance to the church and looked to Rome and its pope as the final arbiter in most religious and cultural affairs, he launched northwestern Europe on a course toward bitter political opposition to the meddling of the papacy in temporal affairs.

The successor to the empire of Charlemagne was a political entity known as the **Holy Roman Empire,** which lasted from **962 to 1806.** The new empire defined the **end of the Dark Ages,** but it ushered in a period of long and bloody warfare as well. The Lombard leaders battled **Franks.** Magyars from Hungary invaded northeastern Lombardy and were in turn defeated by the increasingly powerful **Venetians.** Eventually **Normans** gained military control of **Sicily** in the 11th century, divided it completely from the rest of Italy, and altered forever both the island's racial and ethnic makeup and its architecture.

As Italy dissolved into an increasingly fragmented collection of **city-states,** the papacy fell under the power of the feudal landowners of Rome. Eventually even the process for choosing popes came into the hands of the increasingly Germanic Holy Roman Emperors, although this power balance would very soon shift.

Rome during the Middle Ages was a quaint, rural town. Narrow lanes with overhanging buildings filled many areas that were originally planned as showcases of ancient imperial power, including the Campus Martius. Great **basilicas** were built and embellished with golden-hued mosaics. The forums, mercantile exchanges, temples, and great theaters of the Imperial Era slowly disintegrated and collapsed. The decay of Ancient Rome was assisted by periodic **earthquakes,** centuries of neglect, and, in particular, the growing need for building materials. Rome receded into a dusty provincialism. As the seat of the **Roman Catholic Church,** the state was almost completely controlled by priests, who had an insatiable need for new churches and convents.

By the end of the 11th century the **popes** shook off control of the Roman aristocracy, rid themselves of what they considered the excessive influence of the emperors at Aachen, and began an aggressive expansion of church influence and acquisitions. The deliberate organization of the church into a format modeled on the hierarchies of the ancient Roman Empire put the church on a collision course with the empire and the other temporal leaders of Europe, resulting in an endless series of not-very-flattering power struggles.

THE RENAISSANCE   The story of Italy from the dawn of the Renaissance in the **15th century** to the Age of Enlightenment in the 17th and 18th centuries is as varied and fascinating as that of the rise and fall of the empire. The papacy soon became essentially a feudal state, and the pope was a medieval (later Renaissance) prince engaged in many of the worldly activities that brought criticism upon the church in later centuries. The **fall of the Holy Land** to the Turks in **1065** catapulted the papacy into the forefront of world politics, primarily because of the **Crusades,** many of which the popes directly caused or encouraged (but most of which were judged military and economic disasters). During the 12th and 13th centuries the bitter rivalries that rocked the secular and spiritual bastions of Europe took their toll on the stability of the Holy Roman Empire, which grew weaker as city-states buttressed by mercantile and trade-related prosperity grew stronger and as France emerged as a potent nation in its own right. Each investiture of a new bishop to any influential post resulted in endless jockeying for power among many factions.

These conflicts reached their most visible impasse in **1303,** when the papacy was moved to the French city of **Avignon.** For more than 70 years, until 1377, viciously competing popes (one in Rome, another under the protection of the French kings in Avignon) made simultaneous claims to the legacy of St. Peter, underscoring as never before the degree to which the church was both a victim and a victimizer in the temporal world of European politics.

The seat of the papacy was eventually returned to Rome, where a series of popes were every bit as interesting as the Roman emperors they replaced. The great families—**Barberini, Medici, Borgia**—enhanced their status and fortunes impressively when one of their sons was elected pope. For a look at life in Rome during this tumultuous period, you can visit **Castel Sant'Angelo** in Rome, which became a papal residence in the 14th century.

Despite the centuries that had passed since the collapse of the Roman Empire, the age of siege was not yet over. In **1527, Charles V,** king of Spain, carried out the worst **sack of Rome** ever. To the horror of **Pope Clement VII** (a Medici), the entire city was brutally pillaged by the man who was to be crowned Holy Roman Emperor the next year.

During the years of the Renaissance, the **Reformation,** and the **Counter-Reformation,** Rome underwent major physical changes. The old centers of culture reverted to pastures and fields, whereas great churches and palaces were built with the stones of Ancient Rome. This building boom, in fact, did far more damage to the temples of the Caesars than any barbarian sack had done. Rare marbles were stripped from the imperial baths and used as altarpieces or sent to lime kilns. So enthusiastic was the papal destruction of Imperial Rome that it's a miracle anything is left.

Politics aside, this era is best remembered because of its art. The great ruling families of Italy, especially the **Medici** in Florence, but also the **Gonzaga** in Mantua and the **d'Este** in Ferrara, not only reformed law and commerce, they also sparked a **renaissance in art.** Out of this period arose such towering figures as **Leonardo da Vinci** and **Michelangelo.** Many visitors come to Italy today to view what's left of the art and glory of that era—everything from Michelangelo's **Sistine Chapel** at the Vatican to his statue of **David** in Florence, from Leonardo da Vinci's **Last Supper** in Milan to the **Duomo** in Florence graced by **Brunelleschi's** dome.

UNITED ITALY   The **19th century** witnessed the final **collapse of the Renaissance city-states,** which had existed since the end of the 13th century. These units, eventually coming under the control of a **signore** (lord), were, in effect, regional states, with mercenary soldiers, civil rights, and assistance for their friendly neighbors. Some had attained formidable power under such *signori* as the d'Este family in Ferrara, the Medici in Florence, and the Visconti and the Sforza families in Milan.

During the 17th, 18th, and 19th centuries, decades of turmoil in Italy had lasted through the many years of succession of different European dynasties; **Napoléon** made a bid for power in Italy beginning in **1796,** fueling his war machines with what was considered a relatively easy victory. During the **Congress of Vienna** (1814–15), which followed Napoléon's defeat, Italy was once again divided among many different factions: Austria was given Lombardy and Venetia, and the Papal States were returned to the pope. Some duchies were put back into the hands of their hereditary rulers, and southern Italy and Sicily went to a Bourbon dynasty. One historic move, which eventually contributed to the unification of Italy, was the assignment of the former republic of Genoa to Sardinia (which at the time was governed by the House of Savoy).

Political unrest became a fact of Italian life, at least some of it encouraged by the rapid industrialization of the north and the almost total lack of industrialization in the Italian south. Despite those barriers, in **1861,** thanks to the brilliant efforts of the patriots **Camillo Cavour** (1810–61) and **Giuseppe Garibaldi** (1807–82), the

Kingdom of Italy was proclaimed and **Victor Emmanuel (Vittorio Emanuele) II** of the House of Savoy, king of Sardinia, became head of the new monarchy.

Garibaldi, the most respected of all Italian heroes, must be singled out for his efforts, which included taking Sicily, then returning to the mainland and marching north to meet Victor Emmanuel II at Teano, and finally declaring a unified Italy (with the important exception of Rome itself.) It must have seemed especially sweet to a man whose efforts at unity had caused him to flee the country fearing for his life on four separate occasions. It is a tribute to the tenacity of this red-bearded hero that he never gave up, even in the early 1850s when he was forced to wait out one of his exiles as a candlemaker on Staten Island in New York.

Although the hope, pushed by Europe's theocrats and some of its devout Catholics, of attaining one empire ruled by the pope and the church had long ago faded, there was still a fight, followed by generations of hard feelings, when the **Papal States**—a strategically and historically important principality under the temporal jurisdiction of the pope—were **confiscated** by the new Kingdom of Italy.

The establishment of the kingdom, however, did not signal a complete unification of Italy because the city of **Rome** was still under papal control and **Venetia** was still held by Austria. This was partially resolved in 1866, when Venetia joined the rest of Italy after the **Seven Weeks' War** between Austria and Prussia; and in 1871 Rome became the **capital** of the newly formed country. The **Vatican,** however, did not yield its territory to the new order, despite guarantees of nonintervention proffered by the Italian government, and relations between the pope and the country of Italy remained rocky.

THE RISE OF IL DUCE On October 28, 1922, **Benito Mussolini,** who had started his Fascist Party in 1919, knew the time was ripe to demand change in Italy. He gathered together 50,000 supporters for a **march on Rome.** Inflation was soaring and workers had just called a general strike in protest, so king Victor Emmanuel II, rather than recognizing a state under siege, recognized Mussolini as the new government leader.

In **1929,** Mussolini defined the divisions between the Italian government and the **Vatican** by signing a **concordat** that granted political and fiscal autonomy to Vatican City. It also made Roman Catholicism the official state religion of Italy; that designation was removed in 1978 through a revision of the concordat.

WORLD WAR II & THE AXIS During the Spanish Civil War (1936–39), Mussolini's support of the Falangists, under **Francisco Franco,** helped encourage the formation of the "Axis" alliance between Italy and **Nazi Germany.** Despite its outdated military equipment, Italy added to the general horror of the era by invading Abyssinia (Ethiopia) in 1935, supposedly to protect Italian colonial interests there. In 1940 Italy invaded Greece through Albania, and in 1942 sent thousands of Italian troops to assist Hitler in his disastrous campaign along the Russian front. In **1943** Allied forces, under the command of U.S. Gen. George Patton and British Gen. Bernard Montgomery, landed in Sicily and quickly secured the island as they prepared to move north, toward Rome.

In the face of likely defeat and humiliation, Mussolini was overthrown by his own cabinet (Grand Council). The Allies made a separate deal with Italy's king, Victor Emmanuel III, who had more or less gracefully collaborated with the Fascists during the previous two decades, and who now shifted allegiances without too much visible fuss. A politically divided Italy watched as battalions of fanatical German Nazis released Mussolini from his Italian jail cell to establish the short-lived Republic of Salò, headquartered on the edge of Lake Garda. Mussolini had hoped for a groundswell of popular opinion in favor of Italian Fascism, but events quickly proved this nothing more than a futile dream.

In **April 1945,** with almost half a million Italians rising in a **mass demonstration** against him and the German war machine, Mussolini was captured by Italian partisans as he fled to Switzerland. Along with his mistress, Claretta Petacci, and several others of his intimates, he was shot and strung upside-down from the roof of a gasoline station in Milan.

POSTWAR ITALY   Disaffected with the monarchy and its identification with the fallen Fascist dictatorship, Italian voters in 1946 voted for the establishment of a republic. The major political party that emerged in the aftermath of World War II was the **Christian Democratic Party,** a right-of-center group whose leader, Alcide De Gasperi (1881–1954), served as premier until 1953. The second-largest party was the **Communist Party,** which, however, by the mid-1970s had abandoned its revolutionary program in favor of a democratic form of "Eurocommunism" (in 1991 the Communists even changed their name, to Democratic Party of the Left).

Although after the war Italy was stripped of all its overseas colonies, it quickly succeeded, in part because of U.S. aid under the **Marshall Plan** (1948–52), in rebuilding its economy, both agriculturally and industrially. By the **1960s,** as a member of the **European Community** (founded in Rome in 1957), Italy had become one of the leading industrialized nations of the world, prominent in the manufacture of automobiles and office equipment.

But the country continued to be plagued by **economic inequities** between the prosperous, industrialized north and the economically depressed south. It suffered an unprecedented flight of capital (frequently aided by Swiss banks only too willing to accept discreet deposits from wealthy Italians) and an increase in bankruptcies, inflation (almost 20% during much of the 1970s), and unemployment.

During the **late 1970s and early 1980s,** Italy was rocked by the rise of **terrorism,** instigated both by neo-Fascists and by left-wing intellectuals from the Socialist-controlled universities of the north.

THE 1990s   In the early 1990s, Italians were stunned as many leading politicians were accused of wholesale corruption. As a result, a newly formed right-wing grouping, led by media magnate **Silvio Berlusconi,** swept to victory in general elections in 1994. Berlusconi became prime minister at the head of a coalition government.

In December 1994, Berlusconi resigned as prime minister after the federalist **Northern League Party** defected from his coalition and he lost his parliamentary majority. Treasury Minister **Lamberto Dini,** a nonpolitical banker with international financial credentials, was named to replace Berlusconi.

Dini signed on merely as a transitional player in Italy's topsy-turvy political game. His austere measures enacted to balance Italy's budget, including cuts in pensions and health care, were not popular among the mostly blue-collar Italian workers or the highly influential labor unions. Pending a predicted defeat in a no-confidence vote, Dini stepped down as prime minister. His resignation in January 1996 left beleaguered Italians shouting "*Basta!*" (Enough!). This latest shuffling in Italy's political deck prompted **President Oscar Scalfaro** to dissolve both Italian houses of parliament.

Impressions

It is not impossible to govern Italians. It is merely useless.

—Benito Mussolini

Once again the Italians were faced with forming a new government. The elections in **April 1996** proved a shocker, not only for the defeated politicians, but for the victors as well. The center-left coalition known as the **Olive Tree,** led by **Romano Prodi,** swept both the Senate and the Chamber of Deputies. The Olive Tree, whose roots stem from the old Communist Party, achieved victory by shifting toward the center and focusing their campaign on a strong platform protecting social benefits and supporting Italy's bid to become a solid member of the European Community.

Prodi carried through on his commitment when he announced a stringent budget for 1997 in a bid to be among the first countries to enter the monetary union. The latest budget contained $40 billion in spending cuts and tax increases. All this is done in the hope that a single currency, called the Euro, will be launched on schedule on January 1, 1999.

4 Italian Architecture & Art 101: A Guide to What You'll See

ARCHITECTURE

THE ETRUSCANS & ROMANS   The mysterious Etruscans, whose earliest origins lay probably somewhere in **Mesopotamia,** brought the first truly impressive architecture to mainland Italy. Little remains of their architecture, but historical writings by the Romans record powerful Etruscan **walls, bridges,** and **aqueducts.** As Rome asserted its own identity and overpowered its Etruscan masters, it borrowed heavily from themes already established by Etruscan architects.

Architecture flourished magnificently in **Rome,** advancing in size and majesty far beyond the examples set by the Etruscans and the **Greeks.** Part of this was because of the development of a primitive form of concrete, but even more important was the fine-tuning of the **arch,** which was used with a logic, rhythm, and ease never before seen. **Monumental buildings** were erected, each an embodiment of the strength, power, and careful organization of the Roman Empire itself. Examples include forums and baths scattered across the Mediterranean world (the greatest of which were **Trajan's Forum** and **Caracalla's Baths,** both in Rome). Equally magnificent were the **Colosseum** and a building that later greatly influenced the Palladians during the Renaissance, **Hadrian's Pantheon,** both erected in Rome.

Of course, these immense achievements were made possible by two major resources: almost limitless funds pouring in from all regions of the empire and an unending supply of slaves captured during military campaigns abroad.

Although it doesn't sound very romantic, it was the use of **concrete,** as mentioned, that had a major influence on Roman architecture—as well as on buildings to come. Concrete, which seemingly lasts forever—as evidenced by the giant concrete dome of Rome's Pantheon and the Baths of Caracalla—made vast buildings possible. **Insulae** (apartment blocks) climbed to seven floors or more, something almost unheard of before. Even though Romans didn't invent the arch or the aqueduct, or even concrete, they perfected these building forms, and their methods and styles were to be used throughout Western culture.

THE ROMANESQUE PERIOD   The art and architecture in the centuries that followed the **collapse of Rome** became known as **early medieval** or Romanesque. In its many variations, it flourished between A.D. **1000 and 1250,** although in isolated pockets away from Europe's commercial mainstream it continued for several centuries later.

During the Romanesque period, Italian architects were influenced by the innumerable **Roman ruins**—classical columns, entablatures, vaults, ornamentation, and whole facades were left intact to inspire future generations. While inspired by the Romans, however, designs during this time were decidedly Italian, as the architecture put emphasis on width and on the horizontal lines of a building. Italian buildings of this period, especially churches, were **larger and lower to the ground** than parallel examples of Romanesque designs from northern European countries. **Churches** were designed in **three parts,** with a separate baptistry and campanile, and earlier Romanesque examples took early Christian basilicas as their example, retaining colonnaded atriums and narthex entrances. After about 1100, the influence of the atrium on overall design declined, and the traditional Italian **portico** became more common. **Arcading** (a series of decorative arches—either open or closed with masonry—supported on columns) was commonly used as facade, and **timber roofs** became the norm instead of stone vaults.

Climate also affected the way in which Italian Romanesque designs differed from Romanesque designs found in the rest of Europe during this time. Because snow and heavy rain were not factors in Italy, architects could design roofs of a lower pitch than was common through much of Europe. Intensive sunlight and heat also led to the incorporation of **smaller windows** to exclude rather than trap some of the light. Because of the sunny climate, facades were brightly decorated with **glass mosaic** and **variegated marble,** which would reflect the sunlight in a dramatic and beautiful way. Northern European designs still depended on the more traditional stone sculptural and statuary facades. In addition, stone was not as plentiful in Italy as in other parts of Europe. Because of the almost unlimited availability of clay, **brick** became a popular material for structural elements of the building, with marble, also readily available in a variety of rich colors, becoming a primary material for facades.

Italy, being a series of city-states as opposed to a unified country like many other European nations, also had regional variations of Romanesque design. In the north, with Milan as its center, were found Lombard Romanesque designs, which most closely resembled the designs of France and Germany during this time. In central Italy, the Tuscan or Pisan school, strongly influenced by the Catholic Church, was most closely based on ancient Roman designs. In the south, including Sicily, Norman Romanesque was similar to Norman-influenced architecture found in other European nations, but with additional Saracenic, Byzantine, and Greek elements.

Existing examples of **Lombard Romanesque** date mostly from the 11th and 12th centuries and are most evident in **Milan,** Pavia, Verona, and near the lakes and Alps at Como, Aosta, and Ivrea. Structures are mainly of brick in shades of red, pink, and brown, some decorated with stone or marble. With a cooler climate than the rest of Italy, buildings in this region tended to share elements of design, such as more steeply pitched roofs and larger windows, with the rest of Europe. **Stone groin and rib vaults** were also used extensively, as opposed to the timber roofs favored in the rest of Italy. Arcading was the common external decoration, and **wheel-pattern windows** dominated all other designs. Column designs were in line with the rest of Italy, with columns usually resting on the backs of animals, but the decorations were less classical than in other regions and introduced a wide range of animals, devils, monsters, flowers, and plants into facade designs. The most distinctive feature of Lombard Romanesque is the design of tall slender squared **bell towers,** separate from the main body of the church. An excellent example is the bell tower of the **Abbey Church at Pomposa,** circa 1063. Other fine examples of Lombard Romanesque design include the Church of Saint Ambrogio in Milan; the cathedral groups (campanile, cathedral, and baptistery) at Cremona, Ferrara, and Parma; the Modena Cathedral; the Church of Saint Abbondio at Como; the Church of Saint Zeno at Verona; the Church of Saint Michele at Pavia, and the cathedrals at Aosta, Ivrea, and Piacenza.

Tuscan Romanesque extended from northern Tuscany to Naples, with its center being around Florence, Pisa, and Lucca. It is known for its brilliant colored **marble facades in intricate patterns,** churches built by **basilican plan** (rectangular, with a semicircular apse at one of the short ends and a narthex at the other) with timber roofs and exterior arcading. Columns, capitals, and decoration reflect classical influences. The single most outstanding example of Tuscan Romanesque is the **cathedral group at Pisa** (including the famous leaning bell tower). Other examples in the region are the Cathedral of Saint Martino (exterior only) and the churches of Saint Michele and Saint Frediano at Lucca, the Church of Saint Miniato al Monte in Florence, cathedrals at Assisi and Spoleto, the Church of Saint Maria in Cosmedin at Rome, and the Amalfi and Salerno cathedrals.

The **Norman Romanesque** architecture of southern Italy, particularly Apulia and Sicily, is unique. It **blends different cultures** and illustrates the turbulent history of the area—colonized by the Greeks, absorbed into the Byzantine Empire, held under Mohammedan domination, and conquered by the Normans in the 11th century. The Normans built the cathedrals of Apulia and Sicily using local craftsmen who incorporated brilliant, intricate **Byzantine mosaics,** richly carved **Greek sculpture,** and **Saracenic** (rounded) **arches and vaults.** Romanesque designs here also share characteristics with cathedrals built by the Normans in England, including massive stonework, brick walls, little or no abutment, solid square towers, and rounded doorways and windows. Of course, the differences were the above-mentioned flatter roofs and smaller windows. Examples of Norman Romanesque include the Cathedral at Cefalu, the Monreale Abbey Church and the Cappella Palatina in Palermo, the Palazzo Farsetti and Palazzo Loredan in Venice, and the town of San Gimignano near Siena.

THE GOTHIC PERIOD What followed was the Gothic period **(1250–1450),** with the popes in exile in France, and Sicilo-Norman rule giving way to Angevin culture and shifting from Palermo to Naples. During this time, architecture in Lombardy remained essentially Romanesque—indeed, it has been argued that Italy did not have a Gothic period of architecture. But it did, with Italian designs differing from the rest of Europe, again, in their **continued acknowledgment of Roman culture.** What Italy did not have were the soaring towers and spires, complex ribbed vaults, slender paneled towers, and quadrangles of similar English designs. What it did have were **timber roofs, brick faced with marble, pointed arches,** and **carved white marble** tracery and sculpture (mainly in relief). Ornament and detail remained mainly **classical.** Towers became less common, but when incorporated, were still constructed separately instead of moving into the main body of the church as in other parts of Europe.

The **best examples** of the Gothic in Italy are in **Tuscany,** south toward **Rome,** and in **Venice.** Fine examples of the style include the cathedrals of Florence, Siena, and Orvieto. Many of the churches are less interesting and have largely been altered, but there are numerous exceptions, including the Church of Saint Maria della Spina at Pisa, the Church of Saints Giovanni and Paolo and the Church of Saint Maria Gloriosa dei Frari in Venice, the Church of Saint Croce in Florence, and the Church of Saint Francesco in Assisi. Palaces include the Ca'd'Oro, fronting the Grand Canal, and the Doge's Palace in Venice. Town halls include the Palazzo Pubblico in Siena; the Palazzo Vecchio in Florence; the Palazzo dei Priori in Perugia; the Palazzo dei Priori in Volterra; the Palazzo Pubblico in Montepulciano; the Palazzo dei Consoli at Gubbio; the Palazzo Contarini-Fasan, the Palazzo Foscari, the Palazzo Franchetti, and the Palazzo Pisani, all in Venice; and the Palazzo Stefano in Taormina, Sicily.

THE EARLY RENAISSANCE   The Renaissance began in Italian art in the 14th century, but came relatively late to architecture, first being incorporated in **1420.** Designs from this period represent the **pinnacle of Italian architecture.** During the Renaissance, scholars and artists, the men of learning in that time, began not so much to question the importance of God, but the alleged unimportance of man. They turned their gaze to the accomplishments, advancements, and innovations of antiquity, with numerous Roman examples all around them. These examples, which had likewise influenced previous eras of architectural design, came to the forefront (appreciation of all things Greek came much later) as outstanding examples of man's ingenuity. All of man's experiences—along with nature in human, animal, and landscape forms—were explored in sculpture, relief, mosaic, and stained glass, without a definitive hierarchy topped by God and religion.

Renaissance architectural style included a return to the incorporation of the **barrel vaults and domes** favored by the ancient Romans. In about 1425, Renaissance painters discovered the laws of perspective, and **Brunelleschi** was the first to incorporate this in architectural form. As a result, building designs showed control and **unity of space** and achieved breadth and a feeling of **light** not to be found in Gothic churches. Architects became fascinated with **Roman and Greek designs** of the centrally planned church, which came to be seen as the ultimate classical metaphor. The effect was that design became increasingly concerned with **proportion and detail.**

During this time, artists became the most important members of the community and, owing to their education and creativity, became more versatile. They embraced multiple forms of expression. Thus, the first Renaissance architect of the Florence Duomo was **Giotto,** the painter. Church-builder **Alberti** was first a scholar, writer, and mathematician.

Brunelleschi's masterpiece of the era is the **dome** of the **Florence Cathedral,** which overcame mathematical complications about how to cover an existing 138-foot octagonal span—too great for timber centering—without exterior abutment. Besides being a sculptor, Brunelleschi had studied mathematics and spent time drawing ancient Roman buildings in and around Rome, which had aroused his interest in using large vaults and domed construction in the manner of the Roman baths. His solution for the cathedral was to build a dome on Gothic principles with medieval-style ribs and one that—because of the limitations he was facing—was taller than a true hemisphere (which, being a classicist, he would have preferred). To retain the shape of the dome, and reduce the strain of its weight, it was built as two domes, one within the other.

Other examples of Brunelleschi's early Renaissance designs around Florence include the churches of **Saint Spirito** and **Saint Lorenzo,** and the unfinished **Church of Saint Maria degli Angeli,** which, when started in 1437, became the first centrally planned work of the Renaissance. Still other examples of Renaissance architecture include the Church of Saint Maria Novella in Florence, the Church of Saint Andrea in Mantua, and the Ducal Palace in Urbino. Florentine palaces include Alberti's Palazzo Rucellai, Medici-Riccardi, and the Palazzo Pitti. Lombardy has few examples because, like Germany and England, its Renassaince was more in decoration than construction.

Perhaps the **greatest example** of the Renaissance and its **marriage of Christian and pagan ideals** is the small temple in the courtyard of the **Church of Saint Pietro** in Montorio, which exhibits superb form and simplicity in its undecorated architectural elements, while commemorating a Christian event (the spot where Saint Peter was allegedly crucified).

The **Veneto,** under the domination of the Venetian republic, always had different influences because of its close ties with Constantinople, Dalmatia, and the East, and its cultural isolation within Italy itself. Here Renaissance designs continued with semi-Gothic facades, and in Venice itself there was no need or room for arcaded courtyards. Examples of the early Venetian Renaissance include the **Scuola di San Rocco** and the **Church of Saint Zaccaria.** After the collapse of Rome in 1527, some artists moved north, and the architecture began to reflect southern Renaissance styles. In Venice this can be seen in the Biblioteca Sansoviniana (Library of Saint Mark), the Zecca (Mint), and the Palazzo Cornaro. Other examples include the Bevilacqua in Verona.

PALLADIO & THE HIGH RENAISSANCE   The High Renaissance was dominated by **Bramante, Raphael,** and **Michelangelo,** and its inception is symbolized by Milan falling to the French and Bramante moving to Rome at the beginning of the **16th century.** After the French exile of the popes, Pope Sixtus IV began restoring Rome to prominence, with the construction of **St. Peter's Basilica** (see below) being the crowning achievement. Other examples of High Renaissance include the cloisters at the Monastery of Saint Ambrogio, an exercise in pure classicism, and Michelangelo's New Sacristy in Saint Lorenzo and the Medici Family Mausoleum, both in Florence.

Andrea di Pietro (or **"Palladio"** as he is known to the world) became the towering architect of the High Renaissance and left many buildings in his native **Vicenza.** The city outside Venice is still called *Città del Palladio.* Although his designs were adopted around the world, especially in England and America, Vicenza remains the best place to view his **villas.** Palladio arrived in Vicenza in 1523 and worked there until his death in 1580. Palladio was not a daring innovator but an academician following the rules of **classical Roman architecture.** His roofs are tiled and hipped; on each of the four external sides is a pillared, rectangular portico. The effect is like a Roman temple. The so-called "attic" in his design was usually surmounted by **statues.** His most acclaimed building remains the **Villa Rotonda** in Vicenza, a cube with a center circular hall topped by a dome.

THE LATE RENAISSANCE & THE BAROQUE   In 1573, **Giacomo da Vignola** undertook a challenge that was to pave the way for the transition to the **baroque** period **(1590–1780).** He was called upon to design **Il Gesu,** the mother church of the Society of Jesus, in Rome, so that every person in a large congregation could hear the church service. He responded with a design that included a wide, short barrel-vaulted nave and shallow transepts for good acoustics and to give the illusion of space. There were no aisles or colonnades, only side chapels, which gave the building a sense of spaciousness and dignity. It was then topped with a large dome with fenestrated drums, flooding the church with dramatic light and unity unknown in Gothic or Renaissance churches.

The church inspired late Renaissance architects, already eager to incorporate more of themselves into their designs, to adapt their classical influences into a **functional unity** that more readily suited the needs of contemporary society. The transition was not without criticism, and the term *baroque* actually means "mis-shapen pearl" from the Spanish or Portuguese—a derogatory name stemming from the accentuated curves that evolved in this style.

Still entirely classical in concept, baroque architecture became freer than Renaissance structures with the use of **curves**—not only in ceiling design but in whole walls, which might be alternately concave and convex. The **oval** became the favored building plan, as curves symbolized vitality and movement, and were further accented by the use of **dramatic lighting** from only one or two sources.

These changes, as exemplified by the requests made of Vignola in designing Il Gesu, stemmed from a movement away from humanism and back toward the **Catholic Church,** whose Jesuit visionaries were attempting to reintroduce spiritual values more suited to the modern world. Thus the curve, a more sensual form than the Renaissance rectangle, was used with great exuberance, as the church adopted gaiety and pageantry to try to retain followers who had been seduced by the secular nature of the Renaissance.

One of the great baroque designs is **Bernini's piazza at St. Peter's Basilica** in Rome. The use of vast elliptical colonnade symbolized St. Peter's—the mother church of Christendom—embracing the world. The western ends are joined to the basilica facade by two long corridors, successfully creating space to accommodate vast crowds wanting to witness the pope's blessing of the city. The columns stand four deep, 60 feet high, and are surmounted by an excessive procession of saints starting along the facade and proceeding outward along the piazza.

In addition to St. Peter' Basilica (see below), **other examples of early baroque works** include the New Cathedral of Brescia, the Cathedral of Saint Pietro in Bologna, and the Church of Saint Susanna in Rome. The period reached its zenith in such Rome designs as the Church of Saint Andrea al Quirinale, the Church of Saint Carlo alle Quattro Fontane, the fountain of the rivers at the Piazza Navona, and the Triton Fountain of the Piazza Barberini. Other good examples include the Church of Saint Maria della Salute in Venice; the Sindone Chapel (home of the shroud), the Church of Saint Lorenzo, and the Basilica di Superga, all in Turin; the Church of Saint Maria Egiziaca in Naples; the Church of Saint Croce in Lecce; and Sicily's Cathedral of Palermo.

ST. PETER'S BASILICA   Behind Bernini's piazza rises St. Peter's itself, the stellar achievement of the late High Renaissance and the early baroque period. Bramante was only the first in a series of architects to tackle this awesome edifice. Directed by the popes, St. Peter's was built over a span of 120 years. Because of the decades upon decades necessary for its construction, it is not a towering piece of organized architecture. Therefore, it's almost impossible to discuss it as a harmonious unit. Each piece stands alone, it seems, as exemplified by **Michelangelo's dome.** Even so, the design of the cathedral is truly a feat, being so beautifully proportioned from one part to another as to disguise its huge size. In the classical tradition, it makes use of **coffered and paneled barreled vaults,** plus vast **crossing dome and drum designs.**

Michelangelo designed and began the construction of the massive **dome** from 1547 to 1564. Upon his death, the work was continued from models, but other architects added their own ideas. The distance you see today, from the top of the lantern over the dome, is **450 feet,** a staggering achievement considering building techniques in those days. The sheer mass of the structure—about five times the area of a football field—is the impression one gets today. The **nave** is an enormous barreled vault, coffered and frescoed. No central plan was followed, and little remains of Bramante's original concept, which was that of a dome-topped Greek cross based on Rome's Pantheon. The baroque ornamentation Bernini sumptuously supplied from 1629 onward was certainly not in adherence to Bramante's simpler plan.

THE 18th & 19th CENTURIES—A PERIOD OF DECLINE   Around 1780, Italy began to lose the place that it had held for several centuries as the leader of architectural innovation. Other nations were not so directly influenced by the Catholic Church as Italy, so the eyes and designs of the world turned to the French **rococo style,** which was freer, more lighthearted, and showed an abandonment of order symbolized by its senseless elegant decoration. The rococo style took over as the dominant tradition throughout Europe, and at the same time the Germans, French, and English began to credit the Greeks as originators of the classical style, thus denying the influence of Italy and its Roman heritage.

Perhaps as a result of these snubs of church and history, Italy did not respond to the rococo movement with the same enthusiasm as the rest of Europe. The Italian designs that came **between 1780 and 1920** were for the most part rather lackluster. Rather than responding to a challenge of Italy's role as an architectural innovator, designers began simply to knock off classical models with just a hint of Byzantine decoration or treatment, as evidenced by the facade of the Florence Duomo.

In the rest of the world, the Belgian-initiated **art nouveau** movement attempted to challenge the dominance of the rococo, but came and died quickly, springing up in the 1890s and disappearing almost without a trace by 1910. Neither was Italy much inspired by this outside movement, although Milan's **Galleria Vittorio Emanuele II,** with its glass-and-metal roof and iron sculpture, as well as its **Casa Castiglione,** located at 47 Corso Venezia, are good examples of the fleeting art nouveau trend.

THE 20th CENTURY   Since the beginning of the 20th century, with a few notable exceptions, architecture worldwide has developed a sameness of design and materials that pays little regard to location and culture. In Italy, the marriage of classicism and innovation has given way to large functional squared concrete structures such as the apartment block for the **Societa Novocomum** in Como, the **Saint Maria Novella Railway Station** in Florence, and the **University of Rome's** Instituto Fisico (Department of Physics).

For a short while, **Mussolini** attempted to resurrect national pride through the design of **neoclassical** structures, but the result was the construction of pompous buildings like Milan's **Central Railway Station.** Rather than gaining unity through design, the architecture is simply made busy by repeating rectangular arches and windows. Facade decorations were seemingly tacked onto the building just to acknowledge that it is indeed classically inspired. In Rome the **Foro Italico** stands as one of Mussolini's monumental architectural achievements. It is a large complex of sports arenas, with the name DUCE as a design repeated thousands of times in black-and-white tiles. If Italy produced any great modern architect in the 20th century, it was **Pier Luigi Nervi,** born in 1891 in Milan. He was innovative, creating new buildings in daring styles and shapes best represented by Rome's **Palazzo della Sport** designed for the 1960 Olympics.

More recently, **steel and concrete designs** have attempted the marriage of sharp angles and curves with mixed results, but some examples that work fairly well include the Palace of Labor in Turin, the Church of Saint Ildefonso in Milan, and Rome's Palazzetto dello Sport, Flaminio Stadium, and Termini Station. But where giants of architecture once trod, men and women with visions less grand rule modern building in Italy today. Instead of creating great architecture today, many Italian architects are trying to preserve that which already exists. The best example is Venice. Although there are those who claim that the city of palaces and gondolas may already be dead, few want to give up so easily. There is much talk but little effort to build colossal dikes to protect Venice from the relentless sea. The reason is money—or the lack of it. When money is available, work proceeds to save buildings from imminent collapse, but it's like a bottomless pit. We view it as trying to rebuild Ancient Rome in a single day.

ART

There's an amazing richness of Italian art—there's so much, in fact, that it's often stuck away in dark corners of unlighted churches. In fact, it's a good idea to carry a pocketful of **small coins** to drop in boxes to turn on the lights in some churches. Italy has so much art that some paintings—world masterpieces—that would be the focal point of major museums in other parts of the world are often tucked away in obscure rooms—small salons, really—of rarely visited museums. There's too much of a good thing and not enough room to display the bounty, much less maintain the art and protect it from thieves.

How did it all begin?

ETRUSCAN & ROMAN ART   Although not much Etruscan architecture remains, Etruscan art survives in the form of a handful of **murals** discovered in tombs and more numerous examples of finely sculptured **sacrophagi,** many of which rest today in Italian museums. The Etruscans were surpassed in the area of sepulchral painting only by the Egyptians. These paintings, most often done as true frescoes right into wet plaster, took as their subject the people and items the deceased would need to live comfortably in the spirit world—thus servants, horses, chariots, drinking vessels. In coloration, however, Etruscan art moved away from everyday reality—horses might perhaps have bright blue or green legs or the coats of animals might be brightened with vivid spots or stripes—all in an effort to create a celebratory setting for postlife, as opposed to a grim memorial for grieving survivors. Features of human figures in these works are strongly **Oriental,** perhaps giving a clue to the origins of the mysterious Estruscans themselves, and the use of line and presentation of figures are strongly influenced by **Greek art** of the same time period, owing largely to the popularity Greek artists enjoyed among wealthy Etruscan patrons. Several of the most frequently seen of these tombs can be visited on day trips from Rome. The best collection of sarcophagi is at the **Museo Nazionale di Villa Giulia** in Rome.

As **Rome** asserted its own identity and overpowered its Etruscan masters, it borrowed heavily from themes already established by Etruscan artists and architects. In time, however, the Romans discovered **Greek art,** fell in love with that country's statuary, and looted much of it.

Eventually, as Rome continued to develop its empire, its artisans began to turn out an exact, **realistic portrait sculpture,** which differed distinctly from the more idealized forms of Greek sculpture. Rome was preoccupied with sculpted images—in fact, sculptors made "bodies" en masse and later fitted a particular head on the sculpture upon the demand of a Roman citizen. Most Roman painting that survives is in the form of **murals** in the fresco technique, and most of these were uncovered when **Pompeii** and **Herculaneum** were dug up. Basically, Roman art continued the Hellenistic tradition. Rome's greatest artistic expression was in architecture, not in art such as painting.

EARLY CHRISTIAN & BYZANTINE ART   The aesthetic and engineering concepts of the Roman Empire eventually evolved into early Christian and Byzantine art. More concerned with **moral and spiritual values** than with the physical beauty of the human form or the celebration of political grandeur, early Christian artists turned to the supernatural and spiritual world for their inspiration. Basilicas and churches were lavishly decorated with **mosaics** and **colored marble,** whereas painting depicted the earthly suffering (and heavenly rewards) of **martyrs and saints,** with symbols used in the compositions strictly dictated to the artist by the church. **Three-dimensional representation was disallowed,** following the Eastern tradition that all illusions of action or reality were taboo. In fact, the only freedom the painter enjoyed was in choosing colors and composing shapes.

ROMANESQUE ART   Supported by monasteries or churches, Romanesque art, which flourished between **A.D. 1000 and 1200,** was almost wholly concerned with **ecclesiastical subjects,** often with the intention of educating the worshippers who studied it. Biblical parables were carved in stone or painted into frescoes and became useful teaching aids for a church eager to spread its message. For the most part, **sculpture** from this period, created only as architectural decoration, remained largely **Byzantine,** with a flatness that disallowed detail. An exception was the sculpture of the **Lombard region,** which was under the influence of Germanic tribes. Here sculpture regained a **bulkiness** that had been lost since antiquity. One school of Lombard sculpture took the name of its master, **Benedetto Antelami,** and is characterized by stiff posturing that, combined with the dominance of raised features, gives the sculpture its characteristic rigid vigor.

Painting at this time was still limited to church frescoes and illustrations of Christian documents.

GOTHIC ART & THE FORERUNNERS OF THE RENAISSANCE   As the appeal of the Romanesque faded, the Gothic, or **late medieval,** style greatly altered preconceptions of Italian art and encouraged a vast increase in the number of art works produced. The Italians were inspired by 14th-century **French art,** because a weakened papacy had fallen under the influence of the French monarchy. French art at the time had an affected sentiment—the pose was everything—and this gradually made itself known in Italian works.

Prior to the Renaissance, Italy's greatest **sculptor** was **Nicola Pisano,** who lived from 1206 to 1278 and whose major work was the pulpit in the **baptistery in Pisa,** a piece classical in form. The Roman inspiration is evident in the relief figures—relaxed in gesture and lacking individuality—around a high hexagonal box supported on seven Corinthian columns, three of which are propped on the backs of marble lions.

Late in the 13th century, painting finally began to break away from its role as architectural adornment, and with the arrival of **Cimabue,** the great age of Italian art was about to dawn. Facts about the life of this towering artist aren't well documented, but he worked, mainly in Tuscany, from 1270 to 1300. He painted a number of **frescoes** for the upper and lower churches of the **Sacred Convent of San Francesco** at Assisi, but they're in bad condition, his colors obscured over the ages. Cimabue, breaking with the rigidity of Byzantine art, revealed the spirit of his subject, expressing emotion in realistic detail as opposed to the church's symbolic terms. This trail-blazing artist was the harbinger of the greatest art movement in the history of the world: the Italian Renaissance.

He would be followed by **Giotto** (1266–1336), a painter from Florence, a city where commerce was valued more than an obscure God shrouded in the Catholic Church's increasingly abstract codes and rituals. Giotto was undoubtedly influenced by the rise of **St. Francis,** who arrived in the city preaching that all things were of God and should be loved and treated as God, with no priestly intercession needed in matters of religion. Another person who influenced Giotto was his friend **Dante,** who had just published his *Divine Comedy* "in the volgare," the language of the people. By writing in the language of the people rather than in Latin, the language of the intellectuals, he was the first great poet to embrace the working man rather than alienate him.

Although Giotto's paintings continued to explore Christian themes and stories, they did so figured with people who walked and talked equally with Christ, allowing viewers to equate themselves with the painted subjects. This was obviously a big step toward the Renaissance, when artists and intellectuals began to strongly question the insignificance of man in the face of God, exploring human feats and accomplishments down through the ages.

THE ITALIAN RENAISSANCE   The Italian Renaissance was born in **Florence** during the **15th century,** when members of the powerful **Medici** family emerged as some of the greatest art patrons in history. The Renaissance began with great artistic events, such as **Ghiberti defeating Brunelleschi** in a contest to design bronze doors for the baptistery of the Cathedral of Florence. (The original doors have been removed to the Duomo Museum for safekeeping and replaced by copies.)

Until the Renaissance, most painters had been viewed as nothing more than stone masons, for example. But in the Renaissance, the artist became an inventor, an architect, an intellectual, a discoverer, and mainly an interpreter of life. Renaissance painting developed mainly in Florence, where it was formal and intellectual, and in Venice, where art was designed to create pleasure. **Portraits** began to appear in art—the delight and triumph of the individual personality. **Perspective, space composition,** and **anatomy** came into vogue. The plastic and human values in painting were emphasized as never before. An example of that is **Maccio's** *Adam and Eve* in Florence.

The Renaissance gave birth to artists who excelled in both painting and sculpture. Emerging on the scene was **Jacopo della Quercia** (1375–1438), who brought vitality and a robust quality to sculpture, as exemplified by his major work, *Fonte Gaia,* in the Duomo Museum at Siena. His sculpture brought in the new quality of emotion, which would be seen to greater effect later in the works of Michelangelo.

Donatello (1386–1466) emerged as the first great name in Renaissance sculpture, and his *David* became the first important freestanding nude done in Europe since the days of the Romans. His most famous equestrian statue, *Gattamelata,* done in 1444, stands in the piazza of the Church of Sant'Antonio in Padua.

Michelangelo continued to think of himself as a sculptor, although his greatness also lies in his skills as an architect and painter. His early triumph came with a *Pietà,* begun at the age of only 23 and now in St. Peter's in Rome.

Working virtually day and night for 2 years, from 1501 to 1503, Michelangelo created the idealized man, his magnificent *David* (now on display in Florence at the Accademia), a statue of titanic power and grace. His other legacies include the **Medici tombs,** executed between 1521 and 1534 (next door to the Church of San Lorenzo in Florence). The figures of *Night and Day* are the best known.

The towering Renaissance painter, of course, was **Leonardo da Vinci** (1452–1519), who was the very epitome of a Renaissance man. Naturalist, anatomist, and engineer, he even conceived of the practicability of mechanical flight. His *Mona Lisa* (now in the Louvre in Paris) is the most famous painting in the world, and his wall painting the *Last Supper* (now in the process of being restored at the Monastery of Santa Maria delle Grazie in Milan) is his most impressive.

Italy had so many great artists during this period that it's mind-boggling, considering that entire centuries have gone by without the emergence of even one great artist. Chief among the lesser lights was **Raphael** (1483–1520). He died early, but not before creating lasting works of art, including his masterpiece, *Madonna del Granduca,* in the Pitti Palace in Florence. He painted **frescoes** in the apartments of Pope Julius II in the Vatican while Michelangelo was painting (very reluctantly) his immortal Sistine Chapel nearby.

The **Venetian school** was different from the Florentine. In Venice color was crucial, whereas in Florence it was only a decorative note, as most Renaissance artists here were concerned with formal relationships and space through the laws of perspective.

Jacopo Bellini (ca. 1400–70) was the founder of the most celebrated family of artists from the Venetian school. **Giovanni Bellini** (ca. 1430–1516) was the greatest master of Venetian painting in the 1400s. He created rich, serene landscapes to depict mankind's spiritual harmony with nature.

Giorgione (1477–1510) created works of mystical charm and surpassed the Bellini family in his achievements. He is credited with one of the great steps forward in the history of painting as a fine art, the popularization of **easel painting**—a picture existing for its own sake, the purpose of which was simply to give pleasure to the viewer. His *La Tempesta,* for example, was, like many of his paintings, both brooding and tranquil—a painting of haunting, hypnotic beauty, defying interpretation.

The period known as the **High Renaissance** was said to last for only about 25 years, beginning in the **early 16th century.** This period in art saw more and more emphasis on rich color and subtle variations within forms. Works of great technical mastery emerged. Despite the subtle differences between the stages of the Renaissance, Italy remained Europe's artistic leader for nearly 200 years.

MANNERISM   The **transitional period** between the Renaissance and the baroque came to be called Mannerism. This transition was the result of great turmoil in Europe at the time, with Francis I of France and Charles V of Spain battling for domination of the continent. Much of the fighting took place in northern Italy, and in 1527 Spain's hired German warriors stormed Rome, the beginning of 3 years of rape and pillage that ended only when the pope crowned Charles an emperor of the Holy Roman Empire. Not surprisingly, artists reacted to the strife that had become everyday life by overturning many of the principles that defined the Renaissance. Painting and sculpture were stripped of balance, stability, and naturalism, which were replaced with **distortion, restlessness,** and **false rigidity.** Out of this period emerged such great artists as **Tintoretto,** whose major work was the cycle of frescoes for the Scuola di San Rocco in Venice (it took 23 years to finish); Verona-born **Paolo Veronese;** and the most sensitive, and some critics say the finest, of the Mannerists, **Parmigianino.**

THE BAROQUE   On the trail of Mannerism, the baroque movement swept Italy in the **early 1600s** and lasted until well into the 1700s. It was a period that attempted to find balance between the spirituality of the Gothic and the secular nature of the Renaissance—a result of the Catholic Counter-Reformation (in response to the Protestant Reformation) and the absolutism that dominated the politics of Europe. Rather than glorifying the universal man, as in the Renaissance, there was exploration of human ceremony, a result of a rigid code of courtly behavior. Still the pessimism of the Mannerists was slowly lifting as tight control of kingdoms and the certainty of Jesuit principles allowed a feeling of stability to return to the European nations. Religion continued to play a key role in society, but its expression in the arts was tempered by the worldly scars of the very human conflicts that had occurred. Art responded with an exploration of depth and the suggested illusion of distance, incorporating a strong sense of **light, color,** and **motion.** It was an age of intensity, drama, and power, which not surprisingly led to a flowering of the dramatic arts as well.

Great artists to emerge during this period included **Giovanni Bernini,** who became renowned both as a sculptor and as a painter, but the two painters who best represented the movement were **Carracci,** who decorated the Roman palace of Cardinal Farnese, and **Michelangelo da Caravaggio,** one of the pioneers of baroque painting. The even more flamboyant **rococo**—with its increasingly dramatic posturing and use of light—grew out of the baroque style. Much of the work from the baroque period, in fact, is a bit heavy-handed, resulting in an art of unbalanced sentimentality.

THE 19TH CENTURY TO THE PRESENT   By the 19th century the great light had gone out of art in Italy. (The beacon was picked up instead by France.) **Neoclassicism**—a return to the aesthetic ideals of ancient Greece and Rome, whose ideals of patriotism were resonant with the growing sense of Pan-Italian patriotism—swept through almost every aspect of the Italian arts. The neoclassicist movement was largely the product of the excitement that resulted from the discovery of Pompeii and Herculaneum. **Antonio Canova** (1757–1822) became the most famous of the neo-classical sculptors. But neoclassicism never attained the grandeur in Italy that it did in France.

The **20th century** witnessed the birth of several major Italian artists whose works once again captured the imagination of the world. **Giorgio De 'Chirico** and **Amedeo Modigliani** (the latter's greatest contribution lay in a new concept of portraiture) were only two among many. **Giorgio Morandi,** the Bolognese painter of bottles and jugs, also became known around the world. The greatest Italian sculptor of the 20th century was **Mcdardo Rosso,** who died in 1928.

Since then Italy has been a European leader in sophisticated and witty interpre-tations of buildings, paintings, fashion, industrial design, and decor. Many modern Italian artists have infused Italian flair into workaday and utilitarian objects, whose quality, humor, and usefulness have become legendary.

5 Italian Cuisine

Italians are among the world's greatest cooks. Just ask any one of them. Despite the unification of Italy, regional tradition still dominates the various kitchens, ranging from Rome to Lombardy, from the Valle d'Aosta to Sicily. "Italian food" perhaps has little meaning unless it's more clearly defined as Neapolitan, Roman, Sardinian, Sicilian, Venetian, Piedmontese, Tuscan, or whatever. Each region has a flavor and a taste of its own, as well as a detailed repertoire of local dishes.

Whereas in some countries to the north food was consumed as a means of stay-ing alive, the cuisine in Italy has always been a paramount reason to live. This was true from the earliest days. Even the Etruscans—to judge from the lifelike scenes of banquets in their tombs—loved food and took delight in enjoying it. The Romans became famous for their never-ending banquets and for their love of exotic treats such as flamingo tongues.

Although culinary styles vary, Italy abounds in trattorie specializing in local dishes—some of which are a delight for carnivores, such as the renowned *bistecca alla fiorentina,* which is cut from flavorful Chianina beef, then charcoal-grilled and served with a fruity olive oil. Other dishes, especially those found at the antipasti buffet, would appeal to every vegetarian's heart: peppers, greens, onions, pastas, beans, to-matoes, and fennel.

Many North American visitors erroneously think of Italian cuisine as limited. Of course, everybody has heard of minestrone, spaghetti, chicken cacciatore, and spumoni. But Italian chefs hardly confine themselves to such a restricted repertoire. Incidentally, except in the south, Italians don't use as much garlic in their food as many foreigners seem to believe. Most Italian dishes, especially those in the north, are butter based. Spaghetti and meatballs, by the way, is not an Italian dish, although certain restaurants throughout the country have taken to serving it "for homesick Americans."

CUISINE AROUND THE COUNTRY

Rome is the best place to introduce yourself to Italian cuisine, as it has specialty restaurants that represent all the culinary centers of the country. Throughout your Roman holiday, you'll encounter such savory viands as *zuppa di pesce* (a soup or stew of various fish, cooked in white wine and flavored with herbs), *cannelloni* (tube-shaped pasta baked with any number of stuffings), *riso col gamberi* (rice with shrimp, peas, and mushrooms, flavored with white wine and garlic), *scampi alla griglia* (grilled prawns, one of the best-tasting, albeit expensive, dishes in the city), *quaglie col risotto e tartufi* (quail with rice and truffles), *lepre alla cacciatore* (hare flavored with tomato sauce and herbs), *zabaglione* (a cream made with sugar, egg yolks, and marsala), *gnocchi alla romana* (potato-flour dumplings with a sauce made with meat and covered with grated cheese), *abbacchio* (baby spring lamb, often roasted over an open fire), *saltimbocca alla romana* (literally "jump-in-your-mouth"—thin slices of veal with sage, ham, and cheese), *fritto alla romana* (a mixed fry that's likely to include everything from brains to artichokes), *carciofi alla romana* (tender artichokes cooked with such herbs as mint and garlic, and flavored with white wine), *fettuccine all'uovo* (egg noodles served with butter and cheese), *zuppa di cozze* (a hearty bowl of mussels cooked in broth), *fritto di scampi e calamaretti* (baby squid and prawns, fast-fried), *fragoline* (wild strawberries, in this case from the Alban Hills), and *finocchio* (fennel, a celery-like raw vegetable with the flavor of anisette, often eaten as a dessert or in a salad).

From Rome, it's on to **Florence** and **Siena,** where you'll encounter the hearty, rich cuisine of the Tuscan hills.

The next major city to visit is **Venice,** where the cookery is typical of the Venetia district. It has been called "tasty, straightforward, and homely" by one long-ago food critic, and we concur. One of the most typical dishes is *fegato alla veneziana* (liver and onions), as well as *risi e bisi* (rice and fresh peas). Seafood figures heavily in the Venetian diet, and grilled fish is often served with the bitter red radicchio, a lettuce that comes from Treviso.

In **Lombardy,** of which Milan is the center, the cookery is more refined and flavorful, in our opinion. No dish here is more famous than *cotoletta alla milanese* (cutlets of tender veal, dipped in egg and bread crumbs, and fried in olive oil until they're a golden brown)—the Viennese called it Wiener schnitzel. *Ossobuco* is the other great dish of Lombardy; this is cooked with the shin bone of veal in a ragoût sauce and served on a bed of rice and peas. *Risotto alla milanese* is also a classic Lombard dish. This is rice that can be dressed in almost any way, depending on the chef's imagination. It's often flavored with saffron and butter, to which chicken giblets have been added. It's always served, seemingly, with heaps of Parmesan cheese. *Polenta,* a cornmeal mush that's "more than mush," is the staff of life in some parts of northeastern Italy and is eaten in lieu of pasta.

The cooking in the **Piedmont,** of which Turin is the capital, and the Aosta Valley is different from that in the rest of Italy. Its victuals are said to appeal to strong-hearted men returning from a hard day's work in the mountains. You get such dishes as *bagna cauda,* a sauce made with olive oil, garlic, butter, and anchovies in which you dip uncooked fresh vegetables. *Fonduta* is also celebrated: It's made with melted Fontina cheese, butter, milk, egg yolks, and, for an elegant touch, white truffles.

In the **Trentino–Alto Adige area,** whose chief towns are Bolzano, Merano, and Trent, the cooking is naturally influenced by the traditions of the Austrian and Germanic kitchens. South Tyrol, of course, used to belong to Austria, and here you get such tasty pastries as strudel.

Liguria, whose chief town is Genoa, turns to the sea for a great deal of its cuisine, as reflected by its version of bouillabaisse, a *burrida* flavored with spices. But its most famous food item is *pesto,* a sauce made with fresh basil, garlic, cheese, and walnuts, which is used to dress pasta, fish, and many other dishes.

Emilia-Romagna, with such towns as Modena, Parma, Bologna, Ravenna, and Ferrara, is one of the great gastronomic centers of Italy. Rich in produce, its school of cooking produces many notable pastas that are now common around Italy. They include *tagliatelle, tortellini,* and *cappelletti* (larger than tortellini and made in the form of "little hats"). Tagliatelle, of course, are long strips of macaroni, and tortellini are little squares of dough that have been stuffed with chopped pork, veal, or whatever. Equally popular is *lasagne,* which by now everybody has heard of. In Bologna it's often made by adding finely shredded spinach to the dough. The best-known sausage of the area is *mortadella,* and equally famous is a *cotoletta alla bolognese* (veal cutlet fried with a slice of ham or bacon). The distinctive and famous cheese, *parmigiana,* is a product of Parma and also Reggio Emilia. *Zampone* (stuffed pig's foot) is a specialty of Modena.

Much of the cookery of **Naples**—spaghetti with clam sauce, pizzas, and so forth— is already familiar to North Americans because so many Neapolitans moved to the New World and opened restaurants. *Mozzarella,* or buffalo cheese, is the classic cheese of this area. Mixed fish fries, done a golden brown, are a staple of nearly every table.

Sicily has a distinctive cuisine, with good strong flavors and aromatic sauces. A staple of the diet is *maccheroni con le sarde* (spaghetti with pine seeds, fennel, spices, chopped sardines, and olive oil). Fish is good and fresh in Sicily (try swordfish). Among meat dishes, you'll see *involtini siciliani* on the menu (rolled meat with a stuffing of egg, ham, and cheese cooked in bread crumbs). A *caponata* is a special way of cooking eggplant in a flavorful tomato sauce. The desserts and homemade pastries are excellent, including *cannoli,* cylindrical pastry cases stuffed with ricotta and candied fruit (or chocolate). Their ice creams, called *gelati,* are among the best in Italy.

AND SOME VINO TO WASH IT ALL DOWN

Italy is the largest wine-producing country in the world; as far back as 800 B.C. the Etruscans were vintners. It's said that more soil is used in Italy for the cultivation of grapes than for food. Many Italian farmers produce wine just for their own consumption or for their relatives in "the big city." However, it wasn't until 1965 that laws were enacted to guarantee regular consistency in wine-making. Wines regulated by the government are labeled DOC *(Denominazione di Origine Controllata).* If you see DOCG on a label (the "g" means *garantita*), that means even better quality control.

THE VINEYARDS OF ITALY Based on traditions and priorities established by the ancient Greeks, Italy produces more wine than any other nation on earth. More than four million acres of Italian soil are cultivated as vineyards, and in recent years there has been an increased emphasis on recognizing vintages from lesser-known growers who may or may not be designated as working within a zone of controlled origin and name. (It's considered an honor, and usually a source of profit, to own vines within a DOC. Vintners who are presently limited to marketing their products as unpretentious table wines—*vino di tavola*—often expend great efforts lobbying for an elevated status as a DOC.)

Italy's wine producers range from among the most automated and technologically sophisticated in Europe to low-tech, labor-intensive family plots turning out just a few hundred bottles of wine a year. You can sometimes save costs by buying direct from a producer (the signs beside the highway of any wine-producing district will advertise VENDITTA DRETTA). Not only will you avoid paying the retailer's markup, but you also might get a glimpse of the vines that produced the vintage you carry home with you.

Useful vocabulary words for such endeavors include *bottiglieria* (a simple wine shop) and *enoteca* (a more upscale shop where many different vintages, from several different growers, are displayed and sold like magazines in a bookstore). In some cases you can buy a glass of the product before you buy the bottle, and in some cases platters of cold cuts and/or cheeses are available to offset the tang (and alcoholic effects) of the wine.

REGIONAL WINES Coming from the volcanic soil of Vesuvius, the wines of **Campania** (Naples) have been extolled for 2,000 years. Homer praised the glory of **Falerno,** which is straw yellow in color. Neapolitans are fond of ordering a wine known as **Lacrima Christi,** or "tears of Christ," to accompany many seafood dishes. It comes in amber, red, and pink. With meat dishes, try the dark mulberry-colored **Gragnano,** which has a faint bouquet of faded violets. Also, the red and white wines of Ischia and Capri are justly renowned.

The heel of the Italian boot, **Apulia,** produces more wine than any other part of Italy. Try **Castel del Monte,** which comes in shades of pink, white, and red.

Latium (Rome) is a major wine-producing region of Italy. Many of the local wines come from the Castelli Romani, the hill towns around Rome. Horace and Juvenal sang the praises of Latium wines even in imperial times. These wines, experts agree, are best drunk when young, and they're most often white, mellow, and dry (or else "demi-sec"). There are seven different types, including **Falerno** (straw yellow in color) and **Cecubo** (often served with roast meat). Try also **Colli Albani** (straw yellow with amber tints and served with both fish and meat). The golden-yellow wines of **Frascati** are famous, produced both in a demi-sec and sweet variety, the latter served with dessert.

The wines of **Tuscany** (Florence and Siena) are also famous, and they rank with some of the finest reds in France. **Chianti** is the best known, and it comes in several varieties. The most highly regarded is **Chianti Classico,** a lively ruby-red wine mellow in flavor with a bouquet of violets. A good label is Antinori. A less known but remarkably fine Tuscan wine is **Brunello di Montalcino,** a brilliant garnet red that's served with roasts and game. The ruby-red, almost-purple **Vino Nobile di Montepulciano** has a rich, rugged body; it's a noble wine that's aged for 4 years.

The sparkling **Lambrusco** of **Emilia-Romagna** is by now best known by Americans, but this wine can be of widely varying quality. Most of it is a brilliant ruby red. Be more experimental and try such wines as the dark ruby-red **Sanglovese** (with a delicate bouquet) and the golden-yellow **Albana,** which is somewhat sweet. **Trebbiano,** generally dry, is best served with fish.

From the **Marches** (capital: Ancona) comes one major wine, **Verdicchio dei Castelli di Jesi,** which is amber-straw in color, clear, and brilliant. Some have said that it's the best wine in Europe "to marry with fish."

From **Venetia** (Venice and Verona) in northeastern Italy, a rich breadbasket of the country, come such world-famous wines as **Bardolino** (a light ruby-red wine often served with poultry), **Valpolicella** (produced in "ordinary quality" and "superior dry," and best served with meats), and **Soave,** so beloved by W. Somerset Maugham, which has a pale amber-yellow color with a light aroma and a velvety flavor. Also try one of the Cabernets, either the ruby-red **Cabernet di Treviso** (ideal with roasts and game) or the even deeper ruby-red **Cabernet Franc,** which has a marked herbal bouquet and is also served with roasts.

The **Friuli–Venezia Giulia** area, whose chief towns are Trieste and Udine, attract those who enjoy a "brut" wine with a trace of flint. From classic grapes comes **Merlot,**

Impressions

In Italy, the pleasure of eating is central to the pleasure of living. When you sit down to dinner with Italians, when you share their food, you are sharing their lives.

—Fred Plotkin, *Italy for the Gourmet Traveler,* 1996

deep ruby in color, and several varieties of Pinot, including **Pinot Grigio,** whose color ranges from straw yellow to gray-pink (good with fish). Also served with fish, the **Sauvignon** has a straw-yellow color and a delicate bouquet.

The **Trentino–Alto Adige** area, whose chief towns are Bolzano and Trent, produces wine influenced by Austria. Known for its vineyards, the region has some 20 varieties of wine. The straw-yellow, slightly pale-green **Riesling** is served with fish, as is the pale green-yellow **Terlano. Santa Maddalena,** a cross between a garnet and a ruby in color, is served with wild fowl and red meats, and **Traminer,** straw yellow in color, has a distinctive aroma and is served with fish. A **Pinot Bianco,** straw yellow with greenish glints, has a light bouquet and a noble history, and is also served with fish.

The wines of **Lombardy** (Milan) are justly renowned, and if you don't believe us, would you then take the advice of Leonardo da Vinci, Pliny, and Virgil? These great men have sung the praise of this wine-rich region bordered by the Alps to the north and the Po River to the south. To go with the tasty, refined cuisine of the Lombard kitchen are such wines as **Frecciarossa** (a pale straw yellow in color with a delicate bouquet; order with fish), **Sassella** (bright ruby red in color; order with game, red meat, and roasts), and the amusingly named **Inferno** (a deep ruby red in color with a penetrating bouquet; order with meats).

The finest wines in Italy, mostly red, are said to be produced on the vine-clad slopes of the **Piedmont** district (Turin). Of course, **Asti Spumante,** the color of straw with an abundant champagne-like foam, is the prototype of Italian sparkling wines. While traveling through this area of northwestern Italy, you'll want to sample **Barbaresco** (brilliant ruby red with a delicate flavor; order with red meats), **Barolo** (also brilliant ruby red, best when it mellows into a velvety old age), **Cortese** (pale straw yellow with green glints; order with fish), and **Gattinara** (an intense ruby-red beauty in youth that changes with age). Piedmont is also the home of **vermouth,** a white wine to which aromatic herbs and spices, among other ingredients, have been added; it's served as an aperitif.

Liguria, which includes Genoa and the Italian Riviera, doesn't have as many wine-producing regions as other parts of Italy, yet grows dozens of different grapes. These are made into such wines as **Dolceacqua** (lightish ruby red, served with hearty food) and **Vermentino Ligure** (a pale yellow in color with a good bouquet; often served with fish).

The wines of **Sicily,** called a "paradise of the grape," were extolled by the ancient poets, including Martial. Caesar himself lavished praise on **Mamertine** when it was served at a banquet honoring his third consulship. **Marsala,** of course, an amber-yellow wine served with desserts, is the most famous wine of Sicily; it's velvety and fruity and is sometimes used in cooking, as in veal marsala. The wines made from grapes grown in the volcanic soil of Etna come in both red and white varieties. Also try the **Corvo Bianco di Casteldaccia** (straw yellow in color, with a distinctive bouquet) and the **Corvo Rosso di Casteldaccia** (ruby red in color, almost garnet in tone, full-bodied and fruity).

We've only cited a few popular wines. Rest assured that there are hundreds more you may want to discover for yourself.

OTHER DRINKS Italians drink other libations as well. Their most famous drink is **Campari,** bright red in color and flavored with herbs; it has a quinine bitterness to it. It's customary to serve it with ice cubes and soda.

Limoncello, a bright yellow drink made by infusing pure alcohol with lemon zest, has become Italy's second most popular drink. Long a staple in Italy's lemon-producing region along the Amalfi Coast in Capri and Sorrento, recipes for the sweetly potent concoction have been passed down by families there for generations. About a decade ago restaurants in Sorrento, Naples, and Rome started making their own versions. Tourists visiting those restaurants as well as the Sorrento peninsula began singing limoncello's praises—and requesting bottles to go. Enterprising businesses started manufacturing the drink, and its popularity has reached global proportions, recently becoming the best-selling liqueur in the world.

Beer, once treated as a libation of little interest, is still far inferior to wines produced domestically, but foreign beers, especially those of Ireland and England, are gaining great popularity with Italian youths, especially in Rome. This popularity is mainly because of atmospheric pubs, which now number more than 300 in Rome alone, where young people will linger over a pint and a conversation. Most pubs are in the Roman center, and many are licensed by Guinness and its Guinness Italia operations. In a city with 5,000 watering holes, 300 pubs may seem like a drop, but since the clientele is young, the wine industry is trying to devise a plan to keep that drop from becoming a steady stream of Italians who prefer grain to grapes.

High-proof **grappa** is made from the "leftovers" after the grapes have been pressed. Many Italians drink this before or after dinner (some put it into their coffee). It's an acquired taste—to an untrained foreign palate, it often seems rough and harsh.

Italy has many **brandies** (according to an agreement with France, Italians are not supposed to use the word "cognac" in labeling them). A popular one is **Vecchia Romagna.**

Besides limoncello, there are several other popular **liqueurs** to which the Italians are addicted. Try herb-flavored **Strega,** or perhaps an amaretto tasting of almonds. One of the best known is **Maraschino,** taking its name from a type of cherry used in its preparation. **Galliano** is also herb flavored, and **Sambucca** (anisette) is made of aniseed and is often served with a "fly" (coffee bean) in it. On a hot day, an Italian orders a vermouth, Cinzano, with a twist of lemon, ice cubes, and a squirt of soda water.

3 Planning a Trip to Italy

This chapter is devoted to the where, when, and how of your trip—the advance planning required to get it together and take it on the road.

1 Visitor Information & Entry Requirements

VISITOR INFORMATION   For information before you go, contact the **Italian National Tourist Office,** although Frommer's readers have noted that the office is not as helpful as it could be. In the United States branches are located at 630 Fifth Ave., Suite 1565, **New York,** NY 10111 (☎ **212/245-4822;** fax 212/586-9249); 401 N. Michigan Ave., **Chicago,** IL 60611 (☎ **312/644-0990;** fax 312/644-3109); and 12400 Wilshire Blvd., Suite 550, **Los Angeles,** CA 90025 (☎ **310/820-0098;** fax 310/820-6357). In Canada, contact the Italian National Tourist Office at 1 Place Ville Marie, Suite 1914, **Montreal,** PQ H3B 2C3 (☎ **514/866-7667;** fax 514/392-1429); and in England at 1 Princes St., **London** W1R 8AY (☎ **0171/408-1254;** fax 0171/493-6695).

You can also write directly (in English or Italian) to the provincial or local tourist boards of areas you plan to visit. Provincial tourist boards (known as **Ente Provinciale per il Turismo**) operate in the principal towns of the provinces. Local tourist boards (known as **Azienda Autonoma di Soggiorno e Turismo**) operate in all places of tourist interest; a list can be obtained from the Italian National Tourist Office.

ENTRY REQUIREMENTS   U.S., Canadian, British, Australian, New Zealand, and Irish citizens with a valid passport do not need a visa to enter Italy if they do not expect to stay more than 90 days and do not expect to work there. Those who, after entering Italy, find that they would like to stay more than 90 days can apply for a permit for an additional stay of 90 days, which as a rule is granted immediately. Travelers can apply for the permit at the nearest *questura* (police headquarters).

2 Money

CURRENCY   There are no restrictions as to how much foreign currency you can bring into Italy, although visitors should declare

The Italian Lira, the U.S. Dollar & the U.K. Pound

At this writing, $1 U.S. = approximately 1,666 lire (or 100 lire = 6¢), and this was the rate of exchange used to calculate the dollar values given throughout this book. The rate fluctuates from day to day, depending on a complicated series of economic and political factors, and might not be the same when you travel to Italy.

Likewise, the ratio of the British pound to the lira fluctuates constantly. At press time, £1 = approximately 2,778 lire (or 100 lire = 3.6p), an exchange rate reflected in the table below.

Lire	U.S. $	U.K. £	Lire	U.S. $	U.K. £
50	0.03	0.02	20,000	12.00	7.20
100	0.06	0.04	25,000	15.00	9.00
300	0.18	0.11	30,000	18.00	10.80
500	0.30	0.18	35,000	21.00	12.60
700	0.42	0.25	40,000	24.00	14.40
1,000	0.60	0.36	45,000	27.00	16.20
1,500	0.90	0.54	50,000	30.00	18.00
2,000	1.20	0.72	100,000	60.00	36.00
3,000	1.80	1.08	125,000	75.00	45.00
4,000	2.40	1.44	150,000	90.00	54.00
5,000	3.00	1.80	200,000	120.00	72.00
7,500	4.50	2.70	250,000	150.00	90.00
10,000	6.00	3.60	500,000	300.00	180.00
15,000	9.00	5.40	1,000,000	600.00	360.00

the amount brought in. This proves to the Italian Customs office that the currency came from outside the country and therefore the same amount or less can be taken out. Italian currency taken into or out of Italy may not exceed 200,000 lire in denominations of 50,000 lire or lower.

The basic unit of Italian currency is the **lira** (plural: **lire**). Coins are issued in denominations of 10, 20, 50, 100, 200, and 500 lire, and bills come in denominations of 1,000, 2,000, 5,000, 10,000, 50,000, 100,000, and 500,000 lire. Coins for 50 and 100 lire come in two sizes each, the newer ones both around the size of a dime. The most common coins are the 200- and 500-lire ones, and the most common bills are the 1,000, 5,000, and 10,000 lire.

For the best **exchange rate,** go to a bank, *not* to hotels or shops. Currency and traveler's checks (for which you'll receive a better rate than cash) can be changed at the airport and some travel agencies, such as American Express and Thomas Cook. Note the exchange rates offered—it can sometimes pay to shop around.

If you need a check drawn upon an Italian bank, for example, to pay a deposit on a hotel room, this can be arranged by a large commercial bank or by a currency specialist such as **Ruesch International,** 700 11th St. NW, Washington, DC 20001 (☎ **800/424-2923** or 202/408-1200), which can perform a wide variety of conversion-related financial transactions for individual travelers.

CREDIT CARDS   **Visa** and **MasterCard** are now almost universally accepted (and in many places preferred) at most hotels, restaurants, and shops in Italy. The majority also accept **American Express,** and **Diner's Club** is gaining some ground, especially

What Things Cost in Rome	U.S. $
Taxi (from central rail station to Piazza di Spagna)	6.00
Subway or public bus (to any destination)	0.90
Local telephone call	0.12
Double room at the Hassler (very expensive)	390.00
Double room at Hotel Columbus (moderate)	192.00
Double room at Hotel Corot (inexpensive)	96.00
Continental breakfast (cappuccino and croissant standing at most cafes and bars)	3.75
Lunch for one at Ristorante da Pancrazio (moderate)	27.00
Dinner for one, without wine, at Relais Le Jardin (expensive)	60.00
Dinner for one, without wine, at Girarrosto Toscano (moderate)	35.00
Dinner for one, without wine, at Otello alla Concordi (inexpensive)	21.60
Pint of beer	3.00
Glass of wine	2.00
Coca-Cola	1.50–2.40
Cup of coffee	1.30
Roll of color film, 36 exposures	6.50
Admission to the Vatican museums and Sistine Chapel	9.00
Movie ticket	7.50

in more expensive establishments. The only places that don't accept credit cards are the small mom-and-pop joints, be they one-star hotels, cheap dining spots, or neighborhood shops.

ATM NETWORKS   ATM machines are becoming more and more common in Italy. If your bank card has been programmed with a PIN, it's likely that you can use your card at ATMs abroad to withdraw money from your account or as a cash advance on your credit card—just look for ATM machines that display your network's (Plus, Cirrus, etc.) symbol. You might want to check with your home bank to see if your PIN code must be reprogrammed for usage in Italy. It's also a good idea to determine the frequency limits for withdrawals and cash advances on your credit card. American Express cardholders have access to the ATM machines of Banco Popolare di Milano; the transaction fee is 2% with a minimum charge of $2.50 and a maximum of $20. ATMs give a better exchange rate than banks, but some ATMs exact a service charge on every transaction. For Cirrus locations abroad call ☎ 800/424-7787, or check out MasterCard's World Wide Web site (www.mastercard.com). For PLUS usage abroad, contact your local bank or visit Visa's Web site (www.visa.com).

TRAVELER'S CHECKS   Traveler's checks are still a very safe way to carry money. In the event of theft, the value of your checks will be refunded if properly documented. Most large banks sell traveler's checks, charging fees that average between 1% and 2% of the value of the checks you buy, although some out-of-the-way banks, in rare instances, have charged as much as 7%. If your bank wants more than a 2% commission, it sometimes pays to call the traveler's check issuers directly for the address of outlets where this commission will be less.

What Things Cost in Florence	U.S.$
Taxi (from the train station to Piazza Signoria)	9.00
Public bus (to any destination)	.90
Local telephone call	.13
Double room at the Excelsior (deluxe)	432.00
Double room at the Villa Azalee (moderate)	153.00
Double room at the Hotel Elite (budget)	84.00
Continental breakfast (cappuccino and croissant standing at a cafe)	3.75
Lunch for one at Le Fonticine (budget)	12.00
Lunch for one, standing at an average bar/cafe	5.00
Dinner for one, without wine, at Sabatini (expensive)	47.00
Dinner for one, without wine, at Trattoria Antellesi (moderate)	20.00
Dinner for one, without wine, at Vecchia Firenze (inexpensive)	12.00
Pint of beer	4.60
Glass of wine	3.60
Coca-Cola	1.30
Cup of coffee	1.05
Roll of color film, 36 exposures	6.25
Admission to the Uffizi Galleries	7.90
Movie ticket	7.90

American Express (☎ 800/221-7282 in the U.S. and Canada) is one of the largest and most immediately recognized issuers of traveler's checks. No commission is charged to holders of certain types of American Express cards or members of the Automobile Association of America (AAA). For questions or problems that arise outside the United States and Canada, contact any of the company's many regional representatives.

Other issuers include **Citicorp** (☎ 800/645-6556 in the U.S. and Canada, or 813/623-1709, collect, from other parts of the world); **Thomas Cook** (☎ 800/223-7373 in the U.S. and Canada), which issues MasterCard traveler's checks; and **Interpayment Services** (☎ 800/221-2426 in the U.S. and Canada, or 212/858-8500, collect, from other parts of the world), which sells Visa checks that are issued by a consortium of member banks and the Thomas Cook organization.

Most Italian banks and *cambi* prefer traveler's checks denominated in either U.S. dollars or Swiss francs.

MONEYGRAM If you find yourself out of money, a wire service provided by **American Express** can help you tap willing friends and family for emergency funds. Call ☎ 800/926-9400.

3 When to Go—Climate, Holidays & Events

April to June and September and October are the best months for touring Italy—temperatures are usually mild and the tourist hordes are not quite so intense. Starting in mid-June, the summer tourist rush really picks up, and from July through mid-September the country is teeming with visitors. August is the worst month to visit. Not only does it get uncomfortably hot, muggy, and filled with tourists, but the entire country goes on vacation at least from August 15 until the end of the month, and a goodly percentage of Italians take off the entire month. Many hotels, restaurants, and shops are closed—except at the spas, beaches, and islands, which are where 70% of the Italians are headed. In winter (late October to Easter), most sights go on shorter winter hours or are closed for restoration/rearrangement, many hotels and restaurants take a month or two off between November and February, spa and beach destinations become padlocked ghost towns, and it can get much colder than most people expect—it may even snow on occasion.

High season on most airlines' routes to Rome usually stretches from June until the beginning of September. This is the most expensive and most crowded time to travel. **Shoulder season** is from April to May, early September to October, and December 15 to 24. **Low season** is November 1 to December 14 and December 25 to March 31.

CLIMATE

It's warm all over Italy in summer; it can be *very* hot in the south, especially inland. The high temperatures (measured in Italy in degrees Celsius) begin in Rome in May, often lasting until sometime in October. Winters in the north of Italy are cold with rain and snow, but in the south the weather is warm all year, averaging 50°F in winter.

For the most part, it's drier in Italy than in North America. High temperatures, therefore, don't seem as bad since the humidity is lower. In Rome, Naples, and the south, temperatures can stay in the 90s for days, but nights are most often comfortably cooler.

The average high temperatures in Rome during the summer are 82°F in June, 87°F in July, and 86°F in August; the average lows are 63°F in June, and 67°F in July and August. In Venice, the average high temperatures are 76°F in June, 81°F in July, and 80°F in August; the average lows are 63°F in June, 66°F in July, and 65°F in August.

Italy's Average Daily Temperature & Monthly Rainfall

		Jan	Feb	Mar	Apr	May	June	July	Aug	Sept	Oct	Nov	Dec
Florence	Temp. (°F)	45	47	50	60	67	75	77	70	64	63	55	46
	Rainfall (in.)	3	3.3	3.7	2.7	2.2	1.4	1.4	2.7	3.2	4.9	3.8	2.9
Rome	Temp. (°F)	49	52	57	62	70	77	82	78	73	65	56	47
	Rainfall (in.)	2.3	1.5	2.9	3.0	2.8	2.9	1.5	1.9	2.8	2.6	3.0	2.1
Venice	Temp. (°F)	43	48	53	60	67	72	77	74	68	60	54	44
	Rainfall (in.)	2.3	1.5	2.9	3.0	2.8	2.9	1.5	1.9	2.8	2.6	3.0	2.1

HOLIDAYS

Offices and shops in Italy are closed on the following dates: January 1 (New Year's Day), Easter Monday, April 25 (Liberation Day), May 1 (Labor Day), August 15 (Assumption of the Virgin), November 1 (All Saints' Day), December 8 (Feast of the Immaculate Conception), December 25 (Christmas Day), and December 26 (Santo Stefano).

Closings are also observed in the following cities on feast days honoring their patron saints: Venice, April 25 (St. Mark); Florence, Genoa, and Turin, June 24 (St. John the Baptist); Rome, June 29 (Sts. Peter and Paul); Palermo, July 15 (Santa Rosalia); Naples, September 19 (St. Gennaro); Bologna, October 4 (St. Petronio); Cagliari, October 30 (St. Saturnino); Trieste, November 3 (San Giusto); Bari, December 6 (St. Nicola); and Milan, December 7 (St. Ambrose).

ITALY CALENDAR OF EVENTS

For more information about these and other events, contact the various tourist offices throughout Italy. Dates often vary from year to year.

January

- **Carnival,** in Piazza Navona, Rome. Marks the last day of the children's market and lasts until dawn of the following day. Usually January 5.
- **Epiphany Celebrations,** nationwide. All cities, towns, and villages in Italy stage Roman Catholic Epiphany observances. One of the most festive celebrations is the Epiphany Fair at Rome's Piazza Navona. Usually January 5–6.
- **Festa di Sant'Agnese,** at Sant'Agnese Fuori le Mura in Rome. An ancient ceremony in which two lambs are blessed and shorn. Their wool is then used later for palliums. Usually January 17.
- **Festival of Italian Popular Song,** San Remo (the Italian Riviera). A 3-day festival with major artists performing the latest Italian song releases. Late January.
- **Foire de Saint Ours,** Aosta, Valle d'Aosta. Observing a tradition that has existed for 10 centuries, artisans from the mountain valleys come together to display their wares—often made of wood, lace, wool, or wrought iron—created during the long winter months. Late January.

February

- ✪ **Carnevale in Venice.** Carnevale is a riotous time in Venice. Theatrical presentations and masked balls take place throughout Venice and on the islands in the lagoon. The balls are by invitation, but the street events and fireworks are open to everyone. For more information contact the **Venice Tourist Office,** San Marco, Giardinetti Reali, Pal. Selva (☎ **041/522-6356**). The week before Ash Wednesday, the beginning of Lent.

March

- **Festa di Santa Francesca Romana,** at Piazzale del Colosseo near the Church of Santa Francesco Romana in the Roman Forum. A blessing of cars. Usually March 9.
- **Festa di San Giuseppe,** in the Trionfale Quarter, north of the Vatican. The heavily decorated statue of the saint is brought out at a fair with food stalls, concerts, and sporting events. Usually March 19.

April

- **Holy Week** observances, held nationwide. Processions and age-old ceremonies—some from pagan days, some from the Middle Ages—are staged. The most notable procession is led by the pope, passing the Colosseum in Rome and the Roman Forum up to Palatine Hill; a torchlit parade caps the observance. Sicily's observances are also noteworthy. Beginning 4 days before Easter Sunday; sometimes at the end of March, but often in April.
- **Scoppio del Carro** (Explosion of the Cart), in Florence. An ancient observance in which a cart laden with flowers and fireworks is drawn by three white oxen to the Duomo, where at noon mass a mechanical dove detonates it from the altar. Easter Sunday.
- **Festa della Primavera.** The Spanish Steps in Rome are decked out with banks of flowers, and later orchestral and choral concerts are presented in Trinità dei Monti. Dates vary.
- **Easter Sunday,** Piazza di San Pietro in Rome. In an event broadcast around the world, the pope gives his blessing from the balcony of St. Peter's.

May

○ **Maggio Musicale Fiorentino ("Musical May Florentine").** Italy's oldest and most prestigious festival takes place in Florence, with opera, ballet performances, and concerts at Teatro Comunale, Via Solferino 16; Teatro della Pergola, Via della Pergola 18; and various other venues, including Piazza della Signoria and the courtyard of the Pitti Palace. Schedule and ticket information is available from **Maggio Musicale Fiorentino/Teatro Comunale,** Via Solferino 16, 50123 Firenze (☎ **055/27-791**). Tickets cost 20,000L to 200,000L ($12 to $120). Late April into July.

• **International Horse Show,** at Piazza di Siena in the Villa Borghese, Rome. Usually May 1 to 10, but the dates can vary.

June

• **Son et Lumière.** The Roman Forum and Tivoli, Rome, areas are dramatically lit at night. Early June until the end of September.

• **San Ranieri,** Pisa. Pisa honors its patron saint with candlelit parades, followed the next day by eight rower teams competing in 16th-century costumes. June 16.

• **Gioco del Ponte,** Pisa. Teams in Renaissance costume take part in a much-contested tug-of-war contest on the Ponte di Mezzo, which spans the Arno River. Last Sunday in June.

○ **Festival dei Due Mondi/Festival di Spoleto.** Dating from 1958, this festival was the artistic creation of Maestro and world-class composer Gian Carlo Menotti, who continues to preside over the event today. International performers convene for 3 weeks of dance, drama, opera, concerts, and art exhibits in Spoleto, an Umbrian hill town north of Rome. Tickets and information are available from the **Festival dei Due Mondi,** Piazza Duomo 7, 06049 Spoleto (☎ **0743/44-325** or 0743/222-367; fax 0743/40-696). Information is also available from the box office, c/o **Teatro Nuovo,** Piazza Belli, 06049 Spoleto (☎ **0743/40-265** or 0743/223-419). June 25 to July 13.

• **Festa di San Pietro,** St. Peter's Basilica, Rome. The most significant Roman religious festival, observed with solemn rites in St. Peter's. Usually around June 29.

• **International Exposition of Modern Art,** Venice. Better known as the *Biennale d'Arte,* this is one of the most famous art events in Europe, taking place during alternate (odd-numbered) years. June to October.

July

○ **Il Palio,** Siena. Palio fever grips the Tuscan hill town of Siena for a wild and exciting horse race from the Middle Ages. Pageantry, costumes, and the celebrations of the victorious contrada mark the well-attended spectacle. It's a "no rules" event: Even a horse without a rider can win the race, which takes place on Siena's Piazza del Campo. For details contact the Azienda di Promozione Turistica, Piazza del Campo 56, 53100 Siena (% 0577/280-551). July 2 and August 16.

• **Arena Outdoor Opera Season,** Verona. Culture buffs flock to the 20,000-seat Roman amphitheater. Early July to mid-August.

• **La Festa di Nolantri,** Rome. Trastevere, the most colorful quarter of Old Rome, becomes a gigantic outdoor restaurant, with tables lining the streets and merry-makers and musicians providing the entertainment. Here's how to take part in the fun: After reaching the quarter, find the first empty table and try to get a waiter; but keep a close eye on your valuables. For more information contact **Ente Provinciale per il Turismo,** Via Parigi 11, 00185 Roma (☎ **06/4889-9200**). Mid-July.

- **La Festa del Redentore (Feast of the Redeemer),** Venice. This event marks the lifting of the plague in July 1578, with fireworks, pilgrimages, and boating on the lagoon. Third Saturday and Sunday in July.
- **Festival Internazionale di Musica Antica,** Urbino. A cultural extravaganza, as international performers converge on Raphael's birthplace. It's the most important Renaissance and baroque music festival in Italy. Details are available from **Azienda di Promozione Turistica,** Piazza del Rinascinento 1, I-61092 Urbino (☎ **0722/ 722-2613** or 0722/722-2788). Ten days in late July.

August
- **Festa delle Catene,** in the Church of San Pietro in Vincoli, Rome. The relics of St. Peter's captivity go on display. August 1.
- ✪ **Venice International Film Festival.** Ranking after Cannes, this film festival at Venice brings together stars, directors, producers, and filmmakers from all over the world. Films are shown at the Palazzo del Cinema, on the Lido, both day and night, to an international jury and to the public. Contact the **Biennale Office,** Ca'Giustinian–San Marco, 30124 Venice (☎ **041/521-8838**) for exact dates. Late August to early September.

September
- **Regata Storica,** on the Grand Canal in Venice. A maritime spectacular; many gondolas participate in the canal procession, although gondolas don't race in the regatta itself. First Sunday in September.
- **Sagra dell'Uva,** in the Basilica of Maxentius in the Roman Forum, Rome. At this harvest festival musicians in ancient costumes entertain, and grapes are sold at reduced prices. Dates vary, usually early September.

October
- **Sagra del Tartufo,** Alba, Piedmont. Honors the expensive truffle in Alba, the truffle capital of Italy, with contests, truffle-hound competitions, and tastings of this ugly but very expensive and delectable fungus. For details, contact the **Azienda di Promozione Turistica,** Piazza Medford, 12051 Alba (☎ **0173/35-833**). October 12–26.

December
- **Christmas Blessing of the Pope,** Piazza di San Pietro, Rome. Delivered at noon from the balcony of St. Peter's Basilica. It's broadcast around the world. December 25.

4 Health & Insurance

STAYING HEALTHY   You'll encounter few health problems traveling in Italy. The tap water is generally safe to drink, the milk pasteurized, and health services good.

If you take prescription medicine, it's a good idea to bring along copies of your prescriptions (written in the generic—not brand-name—form). If you need a doctor, your hotel can recommend one, or you can contact your embassy or consulate. You can also obtain a list of English-speaking doctors before you leave from the **International Association for Medical Assistance to Travelers (IAMAT),** in the United States at 417 Center St., Lewiston, NY 14092 (☎ **716/754-4883**); in Canada at 40 Regal Rd., Guelph, ON N1K 1B5 (☎ **519/836-0102**).

If you suffer from a chronic illness or special medical condition, consider purchasing a Medic Alert identification bracelet or necklace, which will immediately alert any doctor to your condition and will provide Medic Alert's 24-hour hotline phone number so that foreign doctors can obtain your vital medical facts at no charge. The initial membership is $35, and there's a $15 yearly fee. Contact the **Medic Alert Foundation,** 2323 Colorado Ave., Turlock, CA 95381-1009 (☎ **800/825-3785**).

INSURANCE   Insurance needs for the traveler fall into three categories: (1) health and accident, (2) trip cancellation, and (3) lost luggage. Before purchasing any additional insurance, check your homeowner's, automobile, and medical insurance policies, as well as the insurance provided by your credit- and charge-card companies and auto and travel clubs. You may already have adequate off-premises theft coverage. Note that to submit any insurance claim you must always have thorough documentation, including all receipts, police reports, medical records, and such. Remember, **Medicare** only covers U.S. citizens traveling in Mexico and Canada.

If you're prepaying for your vacation or are taking a charter or any other flight that has cancellation penalties, look into cancellation insurance. Some credit/charge-card companies, however, provide trip-cancellation coverage if you purchase your tickets with your credit/charge card.

Some companies offering **travel insurance**—ranging from trip cancellation, trip interruption, lost luggage, and accident and medical coverage—include **Travel Guard International,** 1145 Clark St., Stevens Point, WI 54481 (☎ **800/826-1300**); **Travel Insured International, Inc.,** P.O. Box 280568, East Hartford, CT 06128-0568 (☎ **800/243-3174** in the U.S., 203/528-7663 outside the U.S. between 7:45am and 7pm EST); **Healthcare Abroad (MEDEX),** c/o Wallach & Co., 107 W. Federal St. (P.O. Box 480), Middleburg, VA 20118-0480 (☎ **800/237-6615** or 703/687-3166); and **Access America,** 6600 W. Broad St., Richmond, VA 23230 (☎ **800/284-8300**).

British companies offering traveler's insurance include **Columbus Travel Insurance Ltd.** (☎ **0171/375-0011** in London) or, for students, **Campus Travel** (☎ **0171/730-3402** in London). Columbus Travel will sell travel insurance only to people who have been official residents of Britain for at least a year. Britain's Consumers' Association recommends that you insist on seeing the policy and reading the fine print before buying travel insurance.

5 Tips for Travelers with Special Needs

FOR TRAVELERS WITH DISABILITIES

If you're flying around Europe, the airlines and ground staff will help you on and off planes and reserve seats for you with sufficient legroom, but it's essential to arrange for this assistance in advance by contacting your airline.

Recent laws in Italy have compelled railway stations, airports, hotels, and most restaurants to follow a stricter set of regulations about **wheelchair accessibility** to rest rooms, ticket counters, and the like. Even museums and other sightseeing attractions have conformed to the regulations, which mimic many of the regulations presently in effect in the United States. **Alitalia,** as the most visible airline in Italy, has made special efforts to make its planes, public areas, rest rooms, and access ramps as wheelchair-friendly as possible.

Before you go, there are several agencies that can provide advance-planning information. One is the **Travel Information Service** of Philadelphia's Moss Rehab Hospital, (☎ **215-456-9600,** or 215/456-9602 for TTY), which provides information to telephone callers only.

You may also want to consider joining a tour for visitors with disabilities. For the names and addresses of operators offering such tours—as well as other miscellaneous travel information—contact the **Society for the Advancement of Travel for the Handicapped,** 347 Fifth Ave., Suite 610, New York, NY 10016 (☎ **212/ 447-7284**). Annual membership dues are $45, or $30 for senior citizens and students.

FEDCAP Rehabilitation Services (formerly known as the Federation of the Handicapped), 211 W. 14th St., New York, NY 10011 (☎ **212/727-4200;** fax 212/ 721-4374), offers expert information on travel problems that persons with disabilities often face and how to solve them. Membership is $4 per year.

You can also obtain a copy of **"Air Transportation of Handicapped Persons"** from the Distribution Unit, U.S. Department of Transportation, Publications Division, M-4332, Washington, DC 20590. Write for Free Advisory Circular No. AC12032.

For the blind or visually impaired, the best source of travel advice is the **American Foundation for the Blind,** 11 Penn Plaza, Suite 300, New York, NY 10001 (☎ **800/232-5463** for ordering information kits and supplies, or 212/502-7600). It offers information on travel and the various requirements for transporting seeing-eye dogs, including border formalities. It also issues identification cards to those who are legally blind.

Another good organization is **Flying Wheels Travel,** 143 W. Bridge (P.O. Box 382), Owatonna, MN 55060 (☎ **800/525-6790**), which offers various escorted tours, cruises, and private tours all over the world for persons with disabilities.

For a $25 annual fee, **Mobility International USA,** P.O. Box 10767, Eugene, OR 97440 (☎ **541/343-1284** voice and TDD; fax 541/343-6182), provides members with information on various destinations and also offers discounts on videos, publications, and programs it sponsors.

For British travelers, the **Royal Association for Disability and Rehabilitation (RADAR),** Unit 12, City Forum, 250 City Rd., London EC1V 8AF (☎ **0171/ 250-3222**), publishes three holiday "fact packs" that sell for £2 each or £5 for a set of all three. The first one provides general information, including planning and booking a holiday, insurance, and finances. The second outlines transportation available when going abroad, and equipment for rent. The third deals with specialized accommodations. Another good resource is the **Holiday Care Service,** Imperial Building, 2nd Floor, Victoria Road, Horley, Surrey RH6 7PZ (☎ **01293/774-535;** fax 01293/ 784-647), a national charity that advises on accessible accommodations for the elderly and persons with disabilities. Annual membership costs £30.

FOR GAY & LESBIAN TRAVELERS

Since 1861 Italy has had liberal legislation regarding homosexuality, but that doesn't mean that it has always been looked upon favorably in a Catholic country. Homosexuality is much more accepted in the north than in the south, especially in Sicily, although Taormina has long been a gay mecca. However, all major towns and cities have an active gay life, especially Florence, Rome, and Milan, which considers itself the "gay capital" of Italy, and is the headquarters of **ARCI Gay,** the country's leading gay organization with branches throughout Italy. Capri is the gay resort of Italy, rivaled only by the gay beaches of Venice.

PUBLICATIONS   Men can order *Spartacus,* the international gay guide ($32.95), or *Odysseus 1997, The International Gay Travel Planner,* a guide to international gay accommodations ($27). Both lesbians and gay men might want to pick up a copy of *Gay Travel A to Z* ($16), which specializes in general information, as well as listings of bars, hotels, restaurants, and places of interest for gay travelers throughout the world. These books and others are available from **Giovanni's Room,** 1145 Pine St., Philadelphia, PA 19107 (☎ **215/923-2960;** fax 215/923-0813).

Our World, 1104 N. Nova Rd., Suite 251, Daytona Beach, FL 32117 (☎ 904/ 441-5367; fax 904/441-5604), is a magazine devoted to options and bargains for gay and lesbian travel worldwide. It costs $35 for 10 issues. The upscale *Out and About,* 8 W. 19th St., Suite 401, New York, NY 10011 (☎ 800/929-2268; fax 800/ 929-2215), has been hailed for its "straight" reporting about gay travel. It profiles the best gay or gay-friendly hotels, gyms, clubs, and other places throughout the world. Its cost is $49 a year for 10 information-packed issues. Both publications are also available at most gay and lesbian bookstores.

ORGANIZATIONS   The **International Gay Travel Association (IGTA),** P.O. Box 4974, Key West, FL 33041 (☎ 800/448-8550 for voice mailbox, or 305/ 292-0217), encourages gay and lesbian travel worldwide. With around 1,200 member travel agencies, it specializes in networking travelers with the appropriate gay-friendly service organization or tour specialist. It offers a quarterly newsletter, marketing mailings, and a membership directory that's updated four times a year.

FOR SENIOR TRAVELERS

Many senior discounts are available, but note that some may require membership in a particular association.

PUBLICATIONS   For information before you go, obtain the free booklet **"101 Tips for the Mature Traveler,"** from **Grand Circle Travel,** 347 Congress St., Suite 3A, Boston, MA 02210 (☎ 800/221-2610 or 617/350-7500; fax 617/350-6206).

ORGANIZATIONS   The **American Association of Retired Persons (AARP),** 601 E St. NW, Washington, DC 20049 (☎ 202/434-AARP), is the nation's leading organization for people 50 and older. It serves their needs and interests through advocacy, research, informative programs, and community services provided by a network of local chapters and experienced volunteers throughout the country. The organization also offers members a wide range of special membership benefits, including *Modern Maturity* magazine and the monthly *Bulletin.*

Information is also available from the **National Council of Senior Citizens,** 8403 Colesville Road, Suite 1200, Silver Spring, MD 20910 (☎ 301/578-8800), which charges $13 per person or per couple, for which you receive a bimonthly magazine, part of which is devoted to travel tips. Reduced discounts on hotel and auto rentals are also offered.

Mature Outlook, P.O. Box 9390, Des Moines, IA 50306-9519 (☎ 800/ 336-6330; fax 847/286-5024), is a travel organization for people over 50. Members are offered discounts at ITC-member hotels and a bimonthly magazine. The $14.95 to $19.95 annual membership fee entitles members to coupons for discounts at Sears, Roebuck & Co. Savings are also offered on selected auto rentals and restaurants.

TRAVEL SERVICES   If you're 45 or older and need a companion with whom to share your travel and leisure, consider contacting **Golden Companions,** P.O. Box 5249, Reno, NV 89513 (☎ 702/324-2227; fax 702/324-2236). Founded in 1987, this helpful service has found companions for hundreds of mature travelers from all over the United States and Canada. Members meet through a confidential mail network.

SAGA International Holidays, 222 Berkeley St., Boston, MA 02116 (☎ 800/ 343-0273; fax 617/375-5951), runs inclusive tours and cruises for travelers 50 years of age or older.

DISCOUNT RAIL CARD   See "Getting to Italy from the United Kingdom," "Getting to Italy from Within Europe" and "Getting Around Italy" later in this chapter for information on the various special rail discounts available for senior travelers.

FOR STUDENT TRAVELERS

Council Travel Service (CTS) (a subsidiary of the Council on International Educational Exchange) is America's largest student, youth, and budget travel group, with more than 60 offices worldwide. The main office is at 205 E. 42nd St., New York, NY 10017 (☎ **800/226-8624** in the U.S. to find your local branch, or 212/822-2700). Council Travel can issue **International Student Identity Cards (ISIC)**, available to all bona fide students for $19, which entitle holders to generous travel and other discounts. ISIC cards also provide holders with a basic health and life insurance plan and a 24-hour help line. If you're no longer a student but are still under 25, you can get a **GO 25,** which will get you the insurance and some of the discounts as well (but not student admission prices in museums). CTS also sells Eurail and YHA (Youth Hostel Association) passes and can book hostel or hotel accommodations. The CTS in the United Kingdom is at 28A Poland Street (Oxford Circus), London WIV 3DB (☎ **0171/437-7767**). CTS's Italy office is in Rome, near the train station, at Via Genova 16, 00184 Roma (☎ **06/467-9271;** fax 06/467-9207). In Canada, **Travel CUTS,** 187 College St., Toronto, Ont. M5T 1P7 (☎ **416/798-2887**), offers similar services.

Campus Travel, 52 Grosvenor Gardens, London SW1W OAG (☎ **0171/730-3402**), opposite Victoria Station, open 7 days a week, is Britain's leading specialist in student and youth travel worldwide. Founded to meet the needs of students and young people, it provides a comprehensive travel service specializing in low rail, sea, and airfares, holiday breaks, and travel insurance, plus student discount cards.

YOUTH HOSTELS   Students on a budget can also join **Hostelling International,** or IYHF as it's known abroad. For $25 annually ($10 for those under 18, $15 for those over 54), you get a card that entitles you to a discount at official IYH/AIG hostels (of which there are more than 50 in Italy), but not at most private hostels (of which there are a few). In the United States the address is 733 15th St. NW, Suite 840, Washington, DC 20005 (☎ **800/444-6111**). In the United Kingdom, you can get a card at Covent Garden, 14 Southampton St., London WC23 7HY (☎ **0171/836-8541**). For more information in Britain contact the **Youth Hostels Association of England and Wales,** 8 St. Stephen's Hill, St. Alban, Hertfordshire AL1 2DY (☎ **01727/855-215**).

Youth hostels are likely to be overcrowded in summer, particularly at popular tourist meccas, so be sure to book ahead of time.

DISCOUNT RAIL CARD   See "Getting to Italy from the United Kingdom," "Getting to Italy from Within Europe," and "Getting Around Italy" later in this chapter for information on special student/youth rail discounts.

6 Getting to Italy from North America

BY PLANE

High season on most airlines' routes to Rome usually stretches from June until the beginning of September. This is the most expensive and most crowded time to travel. **Shoulder season** is from April to May, early September to October, and December 15 to 24. **Low season** is November 1 to December 14 and December 25 to March 31.

Fares to Italy are constantly changing, but you can expect to pay somewhere in the range of $400 to $800 for a direct round-trip ticket from New York to Rome in coach class.

Flying time to Rome from New York, Newark, and Boston is 8 hours; from Chicago, 10 hours; and from Los Angeles, 12¹/₂ hours. Flying time to Milan from New York, Newark, and Boston is 8 hours; from Chicago, 9 hours and 15 minutes; and from Los Angeles, 11¹/₂ hours.

THE MAJOR NORTH AMERICAN CARRIERS

American Airlines (☎ 800/624-6262) was among the first North American–based newcomers to fly into Italy. From Chicago's O'Hare Airport, American flies nonstop every evening to Milan. Flights from all parts of American's vast network fly regularly into Chicago. **TWA** (☎ 800/221-2000) offers daily nonstop flights from New York's JFK to both Rome and Milan. **Delta** (☎ 800/241-4141) flies from New York's JFK to both Milan and Rome. Separate flights depart every evening for both destinations. For a few months in midwinter, service to one or both of these destinations might be reduced to six flights a week. **United Airlines** (☎ 800/538-2929) has service to Milan only from Dulles Airport in Washington, D.C. **US Airways** (☎ 800/428-4322) offers one flight daily to Rome out of Philadelphia (you can connect through Philly from most major U.S. cities).

British Airways (☎ 800/AIRWAYS), **Air France** (☎ 800/237-2747), **KLM** (☎ 800/374-7747), and **Lufthansa** (☎ 800/645-3880) offer some attractive deals for anyone interested in combining a trip to Italy with a stopover in, say, Britain, Paris, Amsterdam, or Germany along the way.

Canada's second-largest airline, Calgary-based **Canadian Airlines International** (☎ 800/426-7000), flies every day of the week from Toronto to Rome. Two of the flights are nonstop, whereas the others touch down en route in Montréal, depending on the schedule.

THE MAJOR ITALIAN CARRIER

Alitalia (☎ 800/223-5730) flies nonstop to Rome from different North American cities, including New York (JFK), Newark, Boston, Chicago, and Miami. Nonstop flights into Milan are from New York (JFK), Newark, and Los Angeles. Schedules are carefully designed to facilitate easy transfers to all the major cities. Alitalia participates in the frequent-flyer programs of other airlines, including Continental and US Airways.

OTHER GOOD-VALUE CHOICES

BUCKET SHOPS In its purest sense, a bucket shop, also known as a consolidator, acts as a clearinghouse for blocks of tickets that airlines discount and consign during normally slow periods of air travel.

Tickets are sometimes—but not always—priced at up to 35% less than the full fare. Perhaps your reduced fare will be no more than 20% off the regular fare. Terms of payment can vary—say, anywhere from 45 days prior to departure to last-minute sales offered in a final attempt by an airline to fill an empty aircraft.

One of the biggest U.S. consolidators is **Travac,** 989 Ave. of the Americas, New York, NY 10018 (☎ 800/TRAV-800 or 212/563-3303), which offers discounted seats throughout the United States to most cities in Europe on airlines that include TWA, United, and Delta. Another branch office is at 2601 E. Jefferson St., Orlando, FL 32803 (☎ 407/896-0014).

Since dealing with unknown bucket shops might be a little risky, it's wise to call the Better Business Bureau in your area to see if complaints have been filed against the company from which you plan to purchase a ticket.

CHARTER FLIGHTS Strictly for reasons of economy (never for convenience), some travelers are willing to accept the possible uncertainties of a charter flight to Italy.

In a strict sense, a charter flight occurs on an aircraft reserved months in advance for a one-time-only transit to some predetermined point. Before paying for a charter, check the restrictions on your ticket or contract. You may be asked to purchase a tour package and pay far in advance. You'll pay a stiff penalty (or forfeit the ticket entirely) if you cancel. Charters are sometimes canceled when the plane doesn't fill up. In some cases, the charter-ticket seller will offer you an insurance policy for your own legitimate cancellation (hospitalization, death in the family, whatever).

There's no way to predict whether a proposed flight to Rome will cost less on a charter or less through a bucket shop. You'll have to investigate at the time of your trip. Some charter companies have proved unreliable in the past.

One reliable charter-flight operator is **Council Charter,** run by the Council on International Educational Exchange, 205 E. 42nd St., New York, NY 10017 (☎ **800/2-COUNCIL** or 212/822-2900), which arranges charter seats on regularly scheduled aircraft.

One of the biggest New York charter operators is **Travac,** 989 Sixth Ave., New York, NY 10018 (☎ **800/TRAV-800** or 212/563-3303.).

BY PACKAGE TOUR

With a good tour group, you can know ahead of time just what your trip will cost. Perhaps best of all, you won't be bothered with having to arrange your own transportation in places where language might be a problem, look after your own luggage, cope with reservations and payment at individual hotels, or deal with other "nuts and bolts" requirements of travel. Although several of the best-rated tour companies are described below, you should consult a good travel agent for the latest offerings and advice.

TOUR OPERATORS

There are many different operators eager for a share of your business, but one that meets with consistent approval from participants is **Perillo Tours,** 577 Chestnut Ridge Rd., Woodcliff Lake, NJ 07675-9888 (☎ **800/431-1515** in the U.S. or 201/307-1234), family operated for three generations. Since it was established in 1945, it has sent more than a million travelers to Italy. Perillo tours cost much less than you would spend if you arranged a comparable trip yourself. Accommodations are in first-class hotels, and guides tend to be well qualified, well informed, and sensitive to the needs of tour participants.

Perillo operates hundreds of departures year-round. Between April and October, nine different itineraries are offered, ranging from 8 to 15 days each, covering broadly different regions of the peninsula. Between November and April, the "Off-Season Italy" tour covers three of Italy's premier cities during a season when they're likely to be less crowded with tourists.

Another contender for the package-tour business in Italy is **Italiatour,** a company of the Alitalia Group (☎ **800/845-3365** or 212/765-2183), which offers a wide variety of tours through all parts of the peninsula. It specializes in tours for independent travelers who ride from one destination to another by train or rental car. In most cases the company sells pre-reserved hotel accommodations, which are usually less expensive than if you had reserved the accommodations yourself. Because of the company's close link with Alitalia, the prices quoted for air passage are sometimes among the most reasonable on the retail market.

Trafalgar Tours, 11 E. 26th St., New York, NY 10010 (☎ **800/854-0103**), is one of Europe's largest tour operators. It offers cost-conscious packages with lodgings in unpretentious hotels. The 14-day "Best of Italy" tour begins and ends in Rome, with five stops including Sorrento, Venice, and Florence. Some meals and twin-bed accommodations in first-class hotels are part of the package. The 12-day "Bellissimo" tour also begins and ends in Rome and includes the Isle of Capri, Assisi, Venice, and Montecatini. Check with your travel agent for more information on these tours. Trafalgar only takes calls from agents.

One of Trafalgar's leading competitors, known for offering roughly equivalent, cost-conscious tours, is **Globus/Cosmos Tours,** 5301 S. Federal Circle, Littleton, CO 80123-2980 (☎ **800/338-7092**). Globus offers first-class escorted coach tours of various regions of Italy lasting from 8 to 16 days. Cosmos, a budget branch of Globus, sells escorted tours of about the same length. Tours must be booked through a travel agent, but you can call the 800 number for brochures. Other competitors are **Insight International Tours,** 745 Atlantic Ave., #720, Boston, MA 02111 (☎ **800/582-8380**), who books superior first-class, fully escorted motor-coach tours lasting from 1 week to a 36-day grand tour of Italy, and **Tauck Tours,** P.O. Box 5027, Westport, CT 01661 (☎ **800/468-2855**).

Finally, **Abercrombie & Kent,** 1520 Kensington Rd., Oak Brook, IL 60521 (☎ **800/323-7308**) and Sloane Square House, Holbein Place, London SW1W 8NS (☎ **0171/730-9376**), offers a medley of luxurious premium packages. Your overnight stays will be in meticulously restored castles and exquisite Italian villas, most of which are four- and five-star accommodations. Several trips are offered, including tours of the Lake Garda region and the southern territory of Calabria.

7 Getting to Italy from the United Kingdom

Because getting to Italy from the U.K. is often expensive, savy Brits usually call a travel agent for a "deal." That could be in the form of a charter flight or some other special promotion. These so-called deals—by land or air—are always available because of the great popularity of Italy as a tourist destination.

BY PLANE

If a special air-travel promotion is not available or feasible at the time of your anticipated visit, then an APEX ticket might be the way to keep costs trimmed. These tickets must be reserved in advance. However, an APEX ticket offers a discount without the usual booking restrictions. You might also ask the airlines about a "Eurobudget ticket," which imposes restrictions or length-of-stay requirements.

British newspapers are always full of classified advertisements touting "slashed" fares to Italy. One good source is *Time Out,* a magazine published in London. London's *Evening Standard* has a daily travel section, and the Sunday editions of almost any newspaper will run many ads. Although competition is fierce, one well-recommended company that consolidates bulk ticket purchases and then passes the savings on to its consumers, is **Trailfinders** (☎ **0171/937-5400** in London). It offers access to tickets on such carriers as SAS, British Airways, and KLM.

CEEFAX, a British television information service included on many home and hotel TVs, runs details of package holidays and flights to Italy and beyond. Just switch to your CEEFAX channel, and you'll find a menu of listings that includes travel information.

Both **British Airways** (☎ **0345/222-111** in the U.K.) and **Alitalia** (☎ **0171/602-7111**) have frequent flights from London's Heathrow Airport to Rome, Milan,

Venice, Pisa (the gateway to Florence), and Naples. Flying time from London to these cities is anywhere from 2 to 3 hours. BA also has one direct flight a day from Manchester to Rome.

BY TRAIN

Many different rail passes are available in the U.K. for travel in Europe. For details, stop in at the **International Rail Centre,** Victoria Station, London SW1V 1JZ (☎ **0171/834-7066**). The staff there can help you find the best option for the trip you're planning. Some of the most popular are the **Inter-Rail** and **EuroYouth** passes, which entitle pass holders to unlimited second-class travel in 26 European countries.

"**Route 26**" **tickets** are another worthwhile option for travelers under age 26. They allow passengers to move in a leisurely fashion from London to Rome, with as many stopovers en route as their holders want, using a different route southbound (through Belgium, Luxembourg, and Switzerland) from the return route northbound (exclusively through France). All travel must be completed within 2 months of the date of departure. Route 26 tickets from London to Rome cost £173 for the most direct routing, or £198 for a roundabout route that takes passengers through the south of France.

Wasteels, adjacent to Platform 2 in Victoria Station, London SW1V 1JZ (☎ **071/ 834-6744**), will sell a **Rail Europe Senior Pass** to U.K. residents for £5. With it, a British resident more than 60 years of age can buy discounted rail tickets on many of the rail lines of Europe. To qualify, British residents must present a valid British Senior Citizen rail card, which is available for £16 at any BritRail office upon presentation of proof of age and British residency.

BY BUS

Eurolines, 52 Grosvenor Gardens (opposite Victoria Rail Station), Victoria, London SW1 (☎ **0171/730-8235,** or 01582/404511 for information and reservations by credit or charge card), is the leading operator of scheduled coach service across Europe. Its comprehensive network of services includes regular departures to destinations throughout Italy, including Turin, Milan, Bologna, Florence, and Rome; plus summer services to Verona, Vicenza, Padua, and Venice.

Eurolines' services to Italy depart from London's Victoria Coach Station and are operated by modern coach, with reclining seats and a choice of smoking or nonsmoking areas. Return tickets are valid for up to 6 months, and for added flexibility passengers may leave their return date open.

A round-trip ticket from London to Rome using as direct a route as possible costs £127, and from £89 one-way, depending on the season. Travelers under 26 pay around £10 less each way. Departures in either direction are daily, and the trip takes around 37 hours each way. Tickets are for direct travel to Rome only.

BY PACKAGE TOUR

The oldest travel agency in Britain, **Cox & Kings** (☎ **0171/873-5006**) was established in 1758 as the paymasters and transport directors for the British armed forces in India. The company continues to send large numbers of travelers from Britain throughout the rest of the world, specializing in unusual, if pricey, holidays. Their offerings in Italy include organized tours through the country's gardens and sites of historic or aesthetic interest, opera tours, pilgrimage-style visits to sites of religious interest, and food- and wine-tasting tours. The company's staff is noted for their focus on tours of ecological and environmental interest.

If your interests are more varied than those items mentioned in this brief list, call the London headquarters of the **International Association of Travel Agencies (IATA)** (☎ **0181/607-9080**) for the names and addresses of tour operators that specialize in travel relating to your particular interest.

8 Getting to Italy from Within Europe

BY TRAIN

If you plan to travel heavily on the European and/or British railroads, you'll do well to secure the latest copy of the *Thomas Cook European Timetable of Railroads.* This comprehensive, 500-plus-page timetable accurately documents all of Europe's mainline passenger rail services. It's available exclusively in North America from **Forsyth Travel Library,** P.O. Box 480800, Kansas City, MO 64146 (☎ **800/ 367-7984**), for $27.95 (plus $4.50 shipping in U.S. and $5.50 in Canada), or at travel specialty stores.

New electric trains running between France and Italy have made travel between the two countries faster and more comfortable than ever before. France's TGVs travel at speeds of up to 185 miles per hour, and have cut travel time between Paris and Turin from 7 to 5$^1/_2$ hours, and between Paris and Milan from 7$^1/_2$ hours to 6 hours and 40 minutes.

Italy's ETRs travel at speeds of up to 145 miles per hour and currently run between Milan and Lyon (5 hours), with a stop in Turin.

EUROPEAN-WIDE RAILPASSES

EURAILPASS Many travelers to Europe take advantage of one of the greatest travel bargains, the Eurailpass, which permits unlimited first-class rail travel in any country in Western Europe (except the British Isles) and Hungary in Eastern Europe. Oddly, it does *not* include travel on the rail lines of Sardinia, which are organized independently of the rail lines of the rest of Italy.

The advantages are tempting: No tickets; simply show the pass to the ticket collector, then settle back to enjoy the scenery. Seat reservations are required on some trains. Many of the trains have *couchettes* (sleeping cars), for which an additional fee is charged.

Obviously, the 2- or 3-month traveler gets the greatest economic advantages. To obtain full advantage of a 15-day or 1-month pass, you'd have to spend a great deal of time on the train.

Eurailpass holders are entitled to considerable reductions on certain buses and ferries, as well. You'll get a 20% reduction on second-class accommodations from certain companies operating ferries between Naples and Palermo, or for crossings to Sardinia and Malta.

Types of Eurailpasses A **consecutive-day Eurailpass** lets you travel first-class only on unlimited trains for a set period of time ranging from 15 days to 3 months. The cost is $522 for 15 days, $678 for 21 days, $838 for 1 month, $1,188 for 2 months, and $1,468 for 3 months. Children 3 and under travel free providing they don't occupy a seat (otherwise, they're charged half fare); children under 12 pay half fare.

The **Eurail Saverpass** is a money-saving ticket that offers discounted 15-day travel for groups of three or more people traveling together between April and September, or two people traveling together between October and March. The price of a Saverpass, valid all over Europe for first class only, is $444 for 15 days, $576 for 21 days, and $712 for 1 month.

The **Eurail Flexipass** allows passengers to visit Europe with more flexibility. It's valid in first class and offers the same privileges as the Eurailpass. The Flexipass, however, provides a number of individual travel days that can be used over a much longer period of consecutive days—making it possible to stay over in a city or town without losing a day of travel. There are two passes: 10 days of travel within 2 months for $616, and 15 days of travel within 2 months for $812.

If you're under 26, you can purchase a **Eurail Youthpass,** which entitles you to unlimited second-class travel wherever the Eurailpass is honored. The pass costs $418 for 15 consecutive days, $598 for 1 month, or $798 for 2 months. There's also a **Eurail Youth Flexipass** for travelers under 26. Two passes are available: 10 days of travel within 2 months for $438 and 15 days of travel within 2 months for $588.

EUROPASS   The Europass is more limited than the Eurailpass, but may offer better value for visitors traveling over a smaller area. The Europass is good for 2 months and allows unlimited rail travel within three to five European countries with shared (contiguous) borders. The countries included are Italy, France, Germany, Switzerland, and Spain.

For travel in three of the above-mentioned countries (Italy plus two other contiguous countries) the fare for adults in first class is $316 for 5 days of travel, $358 for 6 days of travel, and $400 for 7 days of travel.

For travel in four contiguous countries, the adult fare is $442 for 8 days of travel, $484 for 9 days of travel, and $526 for 10 days of travel. For travel in all five of the above-mentioned countries, the adult fare is $568 for 11 days of travel, $610 for 12 days of travel, and $736 for 15 days of travel.

If two adults travel together, the second adult receives a 50% discount on the above-quoted fares. You can add an "associate country" (Austria, Benelux, Greece, or Portugal) to your Europass by paying a surcharge of between $60 and $120 per country.

For travelers under 26, a **Europass Youth** is available. The fares are 35% off those quoted above, and the pass is only good for second-class travel. Unlike the adult Europass, there is no companion discount.

WHERE TO BUY A EURAILPASS OR EUROPASS   You can buy these passes from travel agents or from railway agents in major cities such as New York, Montréal, and Los Angeles. Eurailpasses are also available from the North American offices of CIT Travel Service, the French National Railroads, the German Federal Railroads, and the Swiss Federal Railways, or through **Rail Europe** (☎ **800/438-7245**). No matter what everyone tells you, Eurailpasses *can* be bought in Europe as well (at the major train stations), but are more expensive. Rail Europe can also give you information on the rail-and-drive versions of the passes.

HOW TO USE A EURAILPASS OR EUROPASS   In addition to saving you money, these easy-to-use passes can save you time. In most cases, you won't have to wait in line at the ticket window at the train station—you just need to scribble the date on the pass as you hop on the train. You will, however, need to go to the ticket window if the train you want to take requires you to reserve a seat (such as the Pendolino) or if you want a spot in a sleeping couchette. The Eurailpass only gets you a 33% discount on the TGV train through the Chunnel from London to Paris. To allow you to take night trains without using 2 days on your pass, a Eurail day begins at 7pm in the evening and runs until midnight of the following night.

BY CAR

If you're already on the Continent, particularly in a neighboring country such as France or Austria, you may want to drive to Italy. However, arrangements should be made in advance with your car-rental company.

It's also possible to drive from London to Rome, a distance of 1,124 miles, via Calais/Boulogne/Dunkirk, or 1,085 miles via Oostende/Zeebrugge, not counting channel crossings either by Hovercraft ferry or the Chunnel. Milan is some 400 miles closer to Britain than is Rome. If you cross over from England and arrive at one of the continental ports, you still face a 24-hour drive. Most drivers play it safe and budget 3 days for the journey.

Most of the roads from Western Europe leading into Italy are toll-free, with some notable exceptions. If you use the Swiss superhighway network, you'll have to purchase a special tax sticker at the frontier. You'll also pay to go through the St. Gotthard Tunnel into Italy. Crossings from France can be through the Mont Blanc Tunnel, for which you'll pay, or you can leave the French Riviera at Menton (France) and drive directly into Italy along the Italian Riviera toward San Remo.

If you don't want to drive such distances, ask a travel agent to book you on a Motorail arrangement where the train carries your car. This service, however, is good only to Milan, as there are no car and sleeper expresses running the approximately 400 miles south to Rome.

9   Getting Around Italy

BY PLANE

Italy's domestic air network on **Alitalia** (☎ 800/223-5730) is one of the largest and most complete in Europe. There are some 40 airports serviced regularly from Rome, and most flights are under an hour. Fares vary, but some discounts are available. Tickets are discounted 50% for passengers 2 to 11 years old; for passengers 12 to 22 years old, there's a youth fare. And anyone can get a 30% reduction by taking domestic flights that depart at night.

BY TRAIN

Trains provide a medium-priced means of transportation, even if you don't buy the Eurailpass or one of the special Italian Railway tickets (see below). As a rule of thumb, second-class travel regardless of the destination usually costs about two-thirds the price of an equivalent trip in first class. A *couchette* (a private fold-down bed in a communal cabin) requires a supplement above the price of first-class travel. In a land where *mamma* and *bambini* are highly valued, children ages 4 to 11 receive a discount of 50% off the adult fare, and children 3 and under travel free with their parents.

Senior citizens get a break, too. Anyone 60 and over can purchase a **Senior Citizen's Silver Card (Carta d'Argento)** by presenting proof of age at any railway station. The card, which can only be purchased in Italy, allows a 20% discount off the price of any ticket between points on the Italian rail network. It's good for 1 year and costs 40,000L ($24). It's not valid on Friday, Saturday, or Sunday between late June and late August or during Christmas week. The Italian railway system also offers a **Cartaverde,** good for anyone under 26. Valid for 1 year, the card costs 40,000L ($24) and entitles a passenger to a 20% reduction off any state train fare. This pass can only be purchased in Italy.

An **Italian Railpass** (known within Italy as a BTLC Pass) allows non-Italian citizens to ride as much as they like on the entire rail network of Italy. Buy the pass in the United States or at main train stations in Italy, have it validated the first time you use it at any railway station in Italy, and ride as frequently as you like within the time validity of your pass. An 8-day pass costs $254 in first class and $172 in second class, a 15-day pass is $320 in first class and $213 in second class, a 21-day pass runs $371 in first class and $248 in second class, and a 30-day pass costs $447 in first class and $297 in second class. All passes have a $15 issuing fee per class.

With the Italian Railpass and each of the other special passes, a supplement must be paid to ride on certain very rapid trains. These are designated ETR-450 trains (also known as "Pendolino" trains). The rail systems of Sardinia are administered by a separate entity and are not included in the Railpass or any of the other passes mentioned.

Another option is the **Italian Flexirail Card,** which entitles holders to a predetermined number of days of travel on any rail line of Italy within a certain period of time. It's ideal for passengers who plan in advance to spend several days sightseeing before boarding a train for another city. A pass giving 4 possible travel days out of a block of 1 month costs $199 in first class and $137 in second class, a pass for 8 travel days stretched over a 1-month period costs $291 in first class and $189 in second class, and a pass for 12 travel days within 1 month costs $365 in first class and $244 in second class.

In addition, the **Kilometric Ticket** is valid for 2 months' worth of travel on regular trains. (It can also be used on special train rides if you pay a supplement.) The ticket is valid for 20 trips, providing that the total distance covered does not exceed 1,875 miles (3,000km). The price is $264 in first class, $156 in second class.

You can purchase any of these passes from a travel agent or at **CIT Tours,** the official representative of Italian State Railway, with offices at 342 Madison Ave., New York, NY 10173 (☎ **800/223-7987** or 212/697-2100; fax 212/697-1394), and at 6033 W. Century Blvd., Suite 980, Los Angeles, CA 90045 (☎ **800/248-7245** or 310/338-8616; fax 310/670-4269). For price information call ☎ **800/248-7245.**

Warning: Many irate readers have complained about train service in Italy—they've found the railroads dirty, overcrowded, unreliable, and with little regard for schedules. As you may have heard, strikes plague the country, and you never know as you board a train when it will reach your hoped-for destination. A sense of humor (and a flexible itinerary) might be your best defense against aggravation and irritating delays.

BY BUS

Italy has an extensive and intricate bus network, covering all regions of the country. However, because rail travel is inexpensive, the bus is not the preferred method of travel. Besides, drivers seem to go on strike every 2 weeks.

One of the leading bus operators in Italy is **SITA,** Viale Cadorna 105, Florence (☎ **055/278-611**). SITA buses serve most parts of the country, especially the central belt, such as Tuscany—not the far frontiers.

Other companies operating buses are **Autostradale,** Piazzale Castello, Milan (☎ **02/801-161**), which serves a large chunk of northern Italy; and **Lazzi,** Via Mercadante 2, Florence (☎ **055/363-041**), which goes through Tuscany, including Siena, and much of central Italy.

Where these nationwide services leave off, local bus companies operate in most regions, particularly in the hill sections and in the alpine regions where travel by rail is not possible. For more information about these services, refer to the "By Bus" sections under "Getting There" in the various city, town, and village sections.

BY CAR

U.S. and Canadian drivers must carry an **International Driver's License** when touring Italy or else obtain a declaration from the **Automobile Club d'Italia (ACI)** that entitles them to drive on Italian roads. The declaration is available from any ACI frontier or provincial office; to obtain the declaration, U.S. or Canadian drivers must present a valid driver's license from their home country with an Italian translation. (Several organizations, including AAA, can provide translations.) The possession of such a translation is intended to facilitate procedures with Italian police personnel, who don't necessarily understand English text. In practice, however, the translation is often not even looked at. But if you're respecting the letter of the Italian law, it's necessary to have it.

Apply for an International Driver's License at any **American Automobile Association (AAA)** branch. You must be at least 18 years old and have two 2- by 2-inch photographs, a $10 fee, and a photcopy of your U.S. driver's license with a AAA application form. To find the AAA office nearest you, check the local telephone directory or contact AAA's national headquarters at 1000 AAA Dr., Heathrow, FL 32746-5063 (☎ 407/444-7000). Remember that an International Driver's License is valid only if physically accompanied by your original driver's license and if it is signed on the back. In Canada, you can get the address of the Canadian Automobile Association closest to you by calling ☎ 613/247-0117.

The **Automobile Club d'Italia (ACI)** is the equivalent of the American Automobile Association. It has offices throughout Italy, including the head office, Via Marsala 8, 00185 Rome (☎ 06/4998-2389), open Monday to Saturday from 8am to 2pm. The 24-hour **Information and Assistance Center (CAT)** of the ACI is at Via Magenta 5, 00185 Roma (☎ 06/4477). Both offices are located near the main railway station (Stazione Termini) in Rome.

RENTALS   Many of the most charming landscapes in Italy lie away from the main cities, far away from the train stations. For that, and for sheer convenience, renting a car is usually the best way to explore the country.

However, the legalities and contractual obligations of renting a car in Italy (where accident and theft rates are very high) are more complicated than in almost any other country in Europe. To rent a car in Italy, a driver must have nerves of steel, a sense of humor, a valid driver's license, a valid passport, and in most cases, be over age 25. In all cases, payment and paperwork are simpler if you present a valid credit or charge card with your completed rental contract. If that isn't possible, you'll almost certainly be required to pay a substantial deposit, sometimes in cash. Insurance on all vehicles is compulsory in Italy, although any reputable car-rental firm will arrange it in advance before you're even given the keys.

The three major car-rental companies in Italy are **Avis** (☎ 800/331-2112), **Budget Rent a Car** (☎ 800/472-3325), and **Hertz** (☎ 800/654-3001). Another option is **Kemwel** (☎ 800/678-0678).

In some, but not all, cases, slight discounts are offered to members of the American Automobile Association (AAA) or the American Association of Retired Persons (AARP).

Each company offers a **collision-damage waiver (CDW)** that costs between $14 and $21 a day (depending on the value of the car). Some companies include CDWs in the prices they quote; others don't. This extra protection will cover all or part of the repair-related costs if there is an accident. (In some cases, even if you purchase the CDW, you'll still pay between $200 and $300 per accident. It pays to ask some questions before you sign the contract.) If you don't have CDW and have an accident, you'll usually pay for all damages, up to the replacement cost of the vehicle. Because most newcomers are not familiar with local driving customs and conditions, we highly recommend that you buy the CDW, though certain credit/charge-card issuers will compensate you for any accident-related liability to a rented car if the imprint of their card appears on the original rental contract. In addition, because of the rising theft rate in Italy, all three of the major U.S.–based companies offer theft and break-in protection policies (Avis and Budget require it). For pickups at most airports in Italy, all three companies must impose a 10% government tax. To avoid that charge, consider picking your car up at an inner-city location. There's also an unavoidable 19% government tax, although more and more companies are including this in the rates they quote.

GASOLINE   Gasoline (known as *benzina*) is expensive in Italy, as are *autostrade* tolls. Carry enough cash if you're going to do extensive motoring, and be prepared for "sticker shock" every time you fill up even a medium-sized car with "super benzina," which has the octane rating that's appropriate for most of the cars you'll be able to rent. It's priced throughout the country at around 1,900L ($1.15) per liter, which is equivalent to approximately 7,200L ($4.30) a gallon. Filling up the tank of a medium-sized car can easily set you back around 75,000L ($45).

Gas stations on autostrade are open 24 hours a day, but on regular roads gas stations are rarely open on Sunday, many close between noon and 3pm for lunch, and most of them shut down after 7pm. Make sure the pump registers zero before an attendant starts refilling your tank. A popular scam, particularly in the south, is to fill your tank before resetting the meter so that you pay not only your bill but the charges run up by the previous motorist.

DRIVING RULES   The Italian Highway Code follows the Geneva Convention and Italy uses international road signs. Driving is on the right, passing on the left. Violators of the highway code are fined; serious violations may also be punished by imprisonment. In cities and towns, the speed limit is 50 kilometers per hour (kmph), or 31 miles per hour (m.p.h.). For all cars and motor vehicles on main roads and local roads, the limit is 90kmph or 56 m.p.h. For the autostrade (national express highways), the limit is 130kmph or 81 m.p.h. Use of seat belts is compulsory.

ROAD MAPS   The best touring maps are published by the **Automobile Club d'Italia (ACI)** and the **Italian Touring Club,** or you can purchase the maps of the **Carta Automobilistica d'Italia,** covering Italy in two maps on the scale of 1:800,000 (1cm = 8km). These two maps should fulfill the needs of most motorists. If you plan to explore one region of Italy in depth, then consider one of 15 regional maps (1:200,000; 1cm = 2km), published by **Grande Carta Stradale d'Italia.**

All maps mentioned above are sold at certain newsstands and at all major bookstores in Italy, especially those with travel departments. Many travel bookstores in the United States also carry them. If U.S. outlets don't have these maps, they often offer Michelin's red map (no. 988) of Italy, which is on a scale of 1:1,000,000 (1cm = 10km). This map covers all of Italy in some detail.

BREAKDOWNS/ASSISTANCE   In case of car breakdown or for any tourist information, foreign motorists can call ☎ **116** (nationwide telephone service). For road information, itineraries, and all sorts of travel assistance, call ☎ **06/499-8389** (ACI's information center). Both services operate 24 hours a day.

BY FERRY

Ferries are used primarily in the south. Driving time from Naples to Sicily is cut considerably by taking one of the vessels operated by **Tirrenia Lines,** Molo Angioino, Stazione Marittima, in Naples (☎ **081/720-1111**). Departures are daily at 8pm for the 11-hour trip to Palermo. Frequent ferry services and hydrofoils also depart from Naples for the offshore islands of Capri and Ischia.

10 Tips on Accommodations

Note that all accommodations listed in this guide have **private bath** unless specified otherwise. Most hotels in Italy do not have **parking garages;** for those that do, we have indicated any charges.

Italy controls the prices of its hotels, designating a minimum and a maximum rate. The difference between the two may depend on the season, the location of the room, or even its size. Hotels are classified by **stars** in Italy, indicating their category of comfort: five stars for deluxe, four stars for first class, three stars for second class, two stars for third class, and one star for fourth class. Government ratings do not depend on the decoration or on frescoed ceilings, but rather on facilities, such as elevators and the like. Many of the finest hostelries in Italy are rated second class because they serve only breakfast (a blessing really, for those seeking to escape the board requirements).

Reservations are advised, even in the so-called slow months from November to March. Tourist travel to Italy peaks from May to October, when moderate and budget hotels are full.

VILLAS & APARTMENTS For information on renting villas or apartments, you may write directly to the local tourist board or the provincial tourist office in the city or town where you expect to stay. For addresses, refer to "Essentials" in the individual city or town listings. Information on villas and apartments is also available in daily newspapers or through local real-estate agents in Italy. The following organizations deal in the rental of villas or apartments in Italy: **Hideaways International,** 767 Islington St. (P.O. Box 4433), Portsmouth, NH 03801 (☎ **800/843-4433** or 603/430-4433); **At Home Abroad, Inc.,** 405 E. 56th St., Suite 6H, New York, NY 10022-2466 (☎ **212/421-9165;** fax 212/752-1591); **Rent a Vacation Everywhere, Inc. (RAVE),** 135 Meigs St., Rochester, NY 14607 (☎ **716/256-0760;** fax 716/256-2676); **Hometours International, Inc.,** P.O. Box 11503, Knoxville, TN 37939 (☎ **800/367-4668**); **Grand Luxe International, Inc.,** 165 Chestnut St., Allendale, NJ 07401 (☎ **201/327-2333**); and **Rentals in Italy,** 1742 Calle Corva, Camarillo, CA 93010 (☎ **800/726-6702** or 805/987-5278; fax 805/482-7976).

FARMHOUSE ACCOMMODATIONS Another option is to stay in a house, an apartment, or a bedroom on an Italian farm as part of a program known as *agriturismo.* Most of the farms lie in rural areas outside the main tourist centers.

Italy Farm Holidays, 547 Martling Ave., Tarrytown, NY 10591 (☎ **914/631-7880;** fax 914/631-8831), represents about 50 working farms scattered for the most part in the Piedmont, Tuscany, Umbria, Veneto, and Puglia, any of which would be suitable as a base for touring the art cities of the regions.

Each farm or cooperative has passed inspection, and some of the most desirable ones lie just a few miles from the heart of Florence and Siena. Most properties require minimum stays of 3 to 7 days, and require payment in full in advance. Many offer meals (usually breakfast) as part of the arrangement; others provide such amenities as free use of bicycles or optional horseback-riding packages. Only a few of the establishments contain more than seven rentable accommodations, most have private bathrooms, and many contain kitchens of their own.

Weekly rates for two people begin at around $450 per week in low season in a modest apartment or B&B, rising to around $3,500 per week in high season for an elegant villa or a historic castle suitable for up to 10 occupants.

House cleaning or maid service is not provided during your occupancy unless it's specifically arranged as a supplement or when a client stays for more than 1 week in an apartment or house.

RELIGIOUS INSTITUTIONS   Convents, monasteries, and other religious institutions in Italy offer accommodations, generally of the fourth-class hotel or *pensioni* category. Some are just for men; others are for women only. Many, however, accept married couples. Italian tourist offices generally have abbreviated listings of these accommodations, or you can write directly to the archdiocese (Archidiocesi di Roma, for example) in cities in which you desire such an accommodation.

Accommodations can range from rather luxurious convents to bone-bare monastic cells. It all depends. One of the main reasons to stay in a religious institution is economy, as the accommodations are invariably cheaper than hotels or pensioni.

ALPINE LIVING   The **Club Alpino Italia,** Via Fomseca Pimentel 7, 20127 Milan (☎ 02/2614-1378), owns and operates hundreds of huts in mountain districts and annually publishes a miniguide with a map and information on access, equipment, and tariffs. A 1-year membership in the club costs 95,000L ($57) and includes a copy of this miniguide plus advice and information about skiing and climbing throughout northern Italy. Write or call for more information.

11 Tips on Dining

Some restaurants in Italy still offer a tourist menu, a *menu turistico,* at an all-inclusive price. This menu is sometimes called *menu del giorno,* or menu of the day. The tourist menu includes soup (nearly always minestrone) or pasta, followed by a meat dish with vegetables, topped off by dessert (fresh fruit or cheese), as well as a quarter liter of wine or mineral water, along with the bread, cover charge, and service (you'll still be expected to tip something extra). Some restaurants also offer a fixed-price menu, called *menu a presso fisso.* The fixed-price menu includes taxes and service (although it's considered proper to leave a tip) but rarely includes the cost of the wine.

Some restaurants virtually insist that diners order at least a first and second course. Owners highly disapprove of foreign visitors who come in and order pasta as a main course, perhaps a salad, and then leave. If you want only a plate of spaghetti or something light, you need not reserve a table in a proper restaurant, but can patronize a less formal *trattoria* or any number of fast-food cafeterias, *rosticcerias,* or *tavola caldas.* You don't pay a cover charge, and you can order as much or as little as you wish without the waiter showing obvious disapproval. Pizzerias are another good option for light meals or snacks. Many bars or cafe-bars also offer both hot and cold food throughout the day. For a light lunch, try *panini,* rolls stuffed with meat. *Tramezzini* are white-bread sandwiches with the crust trimmed. It's also possible to go into one of hundreds of general food stores throughout the country (called *alimentari*) and have sandwiches prepared on the spot, or purchase the makings for a picnic lunch to be enjoyed in a park.

A final caveat: Phone numbers of restaurants often aren't valid for more than a year or two. For reasons known only to the restaurateurs themselves, opening hours, even days of closing, are changed frequently. So, if possible, always check the specific details with the restaurant before heading here. If the staff doesn't speak English and you need a confirmed reservation (always a good idea), ask someone at your hotel reception desk to make a reservation for you.

FAST FACTS: Italy

American Express   Offices are found in Rome at Piazza di Spagna 38 (☎ 06/67-641), in Florence on Via Dante Alighieri (☎ 055/50-981), in Venice at San Marco 1471 (☎ 041/520-0844), and in Milan at Via Brera 3 (☎ 02/728-5571).

All offices are now open Monday through Friday from 9am to 5:30pm and Saturday from 9am to 12:30pm. The money transactions section of the Venice office is open Monday through Saturday from 8am to 8pm.

Business Hours   Regular business hours are generally Monday to Friday from 9am (sometimes 9:30am) to 1pm and 3:30 (sometimes 4) to 7 or 7:30pm. In July or August, offices may not open in the afternoon until 4:30 or 5pm. **Banks** in Italy are open Monday to Friday from 8:30am to 1 or 1:30pm, and 2 or 2:30 to 4pm, and are closed all day Saturday, Sunday, and national holidays. The midafternoon closing (called *riposo*) is often observed in Rome, Naples, and most cities of southern Italy; however, in Milan and other northern and central cities the custom has been completely abolished by some merchants. Most **shops** are closed on Sunday, except for certain barbershops that are open on Sunday morning and tourist-oriented stores in touristy areas that are now permitted to remain open on Sunday during the high season. If you're traveling in Italy in summer and the heat is intense, we suggest that you learn the custom of the riposo, too.

Camera/Film   U.S.–brand film is available in Italy, but it's expensive. Take in as much as Customs will allow if you plan to take a lot of pictures.

Currency   See "Money," earlier in this chapter.

Customs   Overseas visitors to Italy can bring along most items for personal use duty-free, including fishing tackle, a sporting gun and 200 cartridges, a pair of skis, two tennis racquets, a baby carriage, two ordinary hand cameras with 10 rolls of film, and 400 cigarettes (two cartons) or a quantity of cigars or pipe tobacco not exceeding 500 grams (1.1 lb). There are strict limits on importing alcoholic beverages. However, limits are much more liberal for alcohol bought tax-paid in other countries of the European Union.

For U.S. citizens: Upon leaving Italy, U.S. citizens who have been outside the country for 48 hours or more are allowed to take back to their home country $400 worth of merchandise duty-free—that is, if they have claimed no similar exemption within the past 30 days. If you make purchases in Italy, it's important to keep your receipts.

For EU citizens: On January 1, 1993, the borders between European countries were relaxed as the European markets united. When you're traveling within the EU, this will have a big impact on what you can buy and take home with you for personal use.

If you buy your goods in a duty-free shop, then the old rules still apply—you're allowed to take home 200 cigarettes and 2 liters of table wine, plus 1 liter of spirits or 2 liters of fortified wine. But if you buy your wine, spirits, or cigarettes in an ordinary shop in Italy, for example, you can take home *almost* as much as you like. (U.K. Customs and Excise does not set theoretical limits.) If you're returning home from a non-EU country, the allowances are the standard ones from duty-free shops. You must declare any goods in excess of these allowances. British Customs tends to be strict and complicated in its requirements. For details, get in touch with **Her Majesty's Customs and Excise Office,** New King's Beam House, 22 Upper Ground, London, SE1 9PJ (☎ **0171/620-1313**).

Driving Rules   See "Getting Around Italy," earlier in this chapter.

Drug Laws   Penalties are severe and could lead to either imprisonment or deportation. Selling drugs to minors is dealt with particularly harshly.

Drugstores   At every drugstore (*farmacia*) there's a list of those that are open at night and on Sunday, which rotates.

Electricity The electricity in Italy varies considerably. It's usually alternating current (AC), varying from 42 to 50 cycles. The voltage can be anywhere from 115 to 220. It's recommended that any visitor carrying electrical appliances obtain a transformer. Check the exact local current with the hotel where you're staying. Plugs have prongs that are round, not flat; therefore, an adapter plug is also needed.

Embassies/Consulates In case of an emergency, embassies have a 24-hour referral service.

The Embassy of the **United States** is in Rome at Via Vittorio Veneto 119A (☎ 06/46-741; fax 06/488-2672). Other U.S. consulates are in Florence at Lungarno Amerigo Vespucci 46 (☎ 055/239-8276; fax 055/284-088), and in Milan at Via Principe Amedeo 2/10 (☎ 02/290-351). These offices are open Monday to Friday from 8:30am to noon and 2 to 5:30pm. There's also a consulate in Naples on Piazza della Repubblica (☎ 081/583-8111), which is open Monday to Friday from 8am to 1pm and from 2 to 5pm. The consulate in Genoa is closed; however, there is an office of the U.S. Foreign Commercial Service in Genoa at Piazza Portello 6 (☎ 010/543-877), which is open Monday to Friday from 8:30am to 12:30pm and from 2 to 5:30pm.

Consulate and passport services for **Canada** are in Rome at Via Zara 30 (☎ 06/445-981), which is open Monday to Friday from 8:30am to 12:30pm. The Canadian Embassy in Rome is at Via G. B. Rossi 27 (☎ 06/445-981; fax 06/445-98754).

The **United Kingdom** Embassy is in Rome at Via XX Settembre 80A (☎ 06/482-5441; fax 06/487-3324), open Monday to Friday from 9:15am to 1:30pm. The U.K. consulate in Florence is at Lungarno Corsini 2 (☎ 055/284-133). The Consulate General's office in Naples is located at Via Francesco Crispi 122 (☎ 081/663-511), open Monday to Friday from 9am to 12:30pm and 2 to 4:30pm. In Milan, contact the office at Via San Paolo 7 (☎ 02/723-001), open Monday to Friday from 9:15am to 12:15pm and 2:30 to 4:30pm.

The Embassy of **Australia** is in Rome at Via Alessandria 215 (☎ 06/852-721; fax 06/852-723-00), which is open Monday to Thursday from 8:30am to 12:30pm and 1:30 to 5:30pm, and on Friday from 8:30am to 1:15pm. The consular services for Australia are in Rome at Corso Trieste 25 (☎ 06/852-2721), open Monday to Thursday from 9am to noon and 1:30 to 5pm, and on Friday from 9am to 1pm.

The **New Zealand** Embassy is in Rome at Via Zara 28 (☎ 06/440-2928; fax 06/440-2984), open Monday to Friday from 8:30am to 12:45pm and 1:45 to 5pm.

Emergencies Dial ☎ 113 for an ambulance, police, or fire. In case of a breakdown on an Italian road, dial ☎ 116 at the nearest telephone box; the nearest Automobile Club of Italy (ACI) will be notified to come to your aid.

Holidays See "When to Go—Climate, Holidays & Events," earlier in this chapter.

Information See "Visitor Information & Entry Requirements," earlier in this chapter and specific cities for local information offices.

Legal Aid The consulate of your country is the place to turn, although offices cannot interfere in the Italian legal process. They can, however, inform you of your rights and provide a list of attorneys. You'll have to pay for the attorney out of your pocket—there is no free legal assistance. If you're arrested for a drug offense, about all the consulate will do is notify a lawyer about your case and perhaps inform your family.

Liquor Laws Wine with meals has been a normal part of family life for hundreds of years in Italy. Children are exposed to wine at an early age, and consumption of alcohol is not anything out of the ordinary. There's no legal drinking age for buying or ordering alcohol. Alcohol is sold day and night throughout the year, as there is almost no restriction on the sale of wine or liquor in Italy.

Mail　Mail delivery in Italy is notoriously bad. One letter from a soldier, postmarked in 1945, arrived in his home village in 1982. Letters sent from New York, say, in November, are often delivered (if at all) the following year. If you're writing for hotel reservations, it can cause much confusion on both sides. Many visitors arrive in Italy long before their hotel deposits. A fax machine, if you have one, is the way to go. Likewise, your family and friends back home may not receive your postcards or aerograms for anywhere from 1 to 8 weeks (sometimes longer). Postcards, aerogrammes, and letters weighing up to 20 grams to the U.S. and Canada cost 1,300L (85¢), to the U.K. and Ireland 800L (35p), and to Australia and New Zealand 1,400L (AUS$1). You can purchase stamps at all post offices and at *tabacchi* (tobacco) stores.

Maps　See "Getting Around Italy," earlier in this chapter. Also see certain map recommendations in the city listings for Rome, Florence, and Venice.

Newspapers/Magazines　In major cities, it's possible to find the *International Herald Tribune* or *USA Today* as well as other English-language newspapers and magazines, including *Time* and *Newsweek,* at hotels and news kiosks.

Pets　A veterinarian's certificate of good health is required for dogs and cats and should be obtained by owners before entering Italy. Dogs must be on a leash or muzzled at all times. Other animals must undergo examination at the border or port of entry. Certificates for parrots or other birds subject to psittacosis must state that the country of origin is free of disease. All documents must be certified first by a notary public, then by the nearest Italian consulate.

Police　Dial ☎ 113, the all-purpose number for police emergency assistance in Italy.

Radio/TV　Major radio and television broadcasts are on RAI, the Italian state radio and television network. Occasionally, especially during the tourist season, the network will broadcast special programs in English. Announcements are made in the radio and TV guide sections of local newspapers. Vatican Radio also carries foreign-language religious news programs, often in English. Shortwave transistor radios pick up broadcasts from the BBC (British), Voice of America (United States), and CBC (Canadian). RAI television and private channels broadcast only in Italian. More expensive hotels often have TV sets in the bedrooms with cable subscriptions to the CNN news network. Also, see "Television," below.

Rest Rooms　All airport and railway stations, of course, have rest rooms, often with attendants, who expect to be tipped. Bars, nightclubs, restaurants, cafes, and all hotels have facilities as well. Public toilets are also found near many of the major sights.

Usually they are designated as WC (water closet) or *donne* (women) or *uomini* (men). The most confusing designation is *signori* (gentlemen) and *signore* (ladies), so watch those final *is* and *es*!

Safety　The most common menace, especially in large cities, particularly Rome, is the plague of pickpockets and roving gangs of gypsy children who virtually surround you, distract you in all the confusion, and steal your purse or wallet. Never leave valuables in a car, and never travel with your car unlocked. A U.S. State Department travel advisory warns that every car—whether parked, stopped at a traffic light, or even moving—can be a potential target for armed robbery.

Taxes   As a member of the European Union, Italy imposes a value-added tax (called IVA in Italy) on most goods and services. The tax most affecting visitors is the one imposed on hotel rates, which ranges from 9% in first- and second-class hotels to 19% in deluxe hotels.

Non-EU (European Union) citizens are entitled to a refund of the IVA if they spend more than 300,000L ($180) at any one store, before tax. To claim your refund, request an invoice from the cashier at the store and take it to the Customs office *(dogana)* at the airport to have it stamped before you leave. *Note:* If you are going to another EU country before flying home, have it stamped at the airport Customs office of the last EU country you will be in (for example, if you're flying home via Britain, have your Italian invoices stamped in London). Once back home, mail the stamped invoice (keeping a photocopy for your records) back to the original vendor within 90 days of the purchase. The vendor will, sooner or later, send you a refund of the tax you paid at the time of your original purchase. Reputable stores view this as a matter of ordinary paperwork and are very businesslike about it. Less honorable stores might lose your dossier. It pays to deal with established vendors on large purchases. You can also request that the refund be credited to the credit/charge card with which you made the purchase; this is usually a faster procedure.

Many shops are now part of the "Tax Free for Tourists" network (look for the sticker in the window). Stores participating in this network issue a check along with your invoice at the time of purchase. After you have the invoice stamped at Customs, you can redeem the check for cash directly at the Tax Free booth in the airport—in Rome, it's past Customs; in Milan's airports the booth is inside the Duty Free shop—or mail it back in the envelope provided within 60 days.

Telephone/Fax/Telegrams   To **call Italy from the United States,** dial ☎ 011 (international dialing prefix), then 39 (Italy's country code), then the city code (for example, 55 for Florence), then the actual number. Note that numbers in Italy do indeed range from four to eight digits in length. Also note that, when calling from outside Italy, you must drop the initial zero from the city codes that are cited throughout this book.

A **local phone call** in Italy costs 200L (13¢). **Public phones** either accept coins, precharged phone cards (*scheda* or *carta telefonica*), or both. You can buy a *carta telefonica* at any *tabacchi* (tobacconists; most display a sign with a white "T" on a brown background) in increments of 5,000L ($3.35), 10,000L ($6.65), and 15,000L ($10). To make a call, pick up the receiver and insert 200L or your card (break off the corner first). Most phones have a digital display that will tell you how much money you've inserted (or how much is left on the card). Dial the number, and don't forget to take the card with you after you hang up.

To call **from one city code to another** within Italy, dial the city code, complete with initial zero, then the number. To **dial direct internationally,** dial ☎ 00, then the country code, the area code, and number. Country codes are as follows: The United States and Canada are 1; the United Kingdom is 44; Ireland is 353; Australia is 61; New Zealand is 64. Make international calls from a public phone if possible, because hotels almost invariably charge ridiculously inflated rates for direct dial, but bring plenty of *schede* to feed the phone. Calls dialed directly are billed on the basis of the call's duration only. A reduced rate is applied from 11pm to 8am on Monday to Saturday and all day Sunday. Direct-dial calls from the United States to Italy are much cheaper, so arrange for whomever to call you at your hotel.

To ring free, national **telephone information** (in Italian) in Italy, dial ☎ 12. International information is available at 176, but costs 1,200L (80¢) a shot.

To make **collect or calling card calls,** drop in 200L or insert your card (don't worry—the call's free and you get the money back when you're done), dial one of the numbers below, and an American operator will be on shortly to assist you (as Italy has yet to discover the joys of the touch-tone phone, you'll always have to wait for the operator to come on). The following calling-card numbers work all over Italy: **AT&T,** ☎ 172-1011; **MCI,** ☎ 172-1022; and **Sprint,** ☎ 172-1877. To make collect calls to a country besides the United States, dial ☎ 170 (free) and practice your Italian counting in order to relay the number to the Italian operator. Tell them you want it *al carico del destinatario.*

Your hotel will most likely be able to send or receive **faxes** for you, sometimes at inflated prices, sometimes at cost. Otherwise, most *cartolerie* (stationery stores), *copisti* or *fotocopie* (photocopy shops), and some *tabacchi* (tobacconists) offer fax services. For **telegrams,** ITALCABLE operates services abroad, transmitting messages by cable or satellite. Both internal and foreign telegrams may be dictated over the phone (☎ 186).

Television   The RAI is the chief television network broadcasting in Italy, although its format is not as politically oriented as in the past. Every TV in the country receives RAI-1, RAI-2, and RAI-3. In addition, most Italians receive Canale 5, Rete 4, and Italia 1, which are controlled by media magnate Silvio Berlusconi, as well as several other private stations.

Time   In terms of standard time zones, Italy is 6 hours ahead of eastern standard time in the United States. Daylight saving time goes into effect in Italy each year from the end of March to the end of September.

Tipping   This custom is practiced with flair in Italy—many people depend on tips for their livelihoods. In **hotels,** the service charge of 15% to 19% is already added to a bill. In addition, it's customary to tip the chambermaid 1,000L (60¢) per day; the doorman (for calling a cab), 1,000L (60¢); and the bellhop or porter 3,000L to 5,000L ($1.80 to $3) for carrying your bags to your room. A concierge expects about 15% of his or her bill, as well as tips for extra services performed, which could include help with long-distance calls. In expensive hotels these lire amounts are often doubled.

In **restaurants,** 15% is added to your bill to cover most charges. An additional tip for good service is almost always expected. It's customary in certain fashionable restaurants in Rome, Florence, Venice, and Milan to leave an additional 10%, which, combined with the assessed service charge, is a very high tip indeed. The sommelier expects 10% of the cost of the wine. Checkroom attendants now expect 1,500L (90¢), although in simple places Italians still hand washroom attendants 200L to 300L (10¢ to 20¢), more in deluxe and first-class establishments. Restaurants are required by law to give customers official receipts.

In **cafes and bars,** tip 15% of the bill, and give a theater usher 1,500L (90¢). **Taxi drivers** expect at least 15% of the fare.

Tourist Offices   See "Visitor Information & Entry Requirements," earlier in this chapter, and also specific city chapters.

Visas   See "Visitor Information & Entry Requirements," earlier in this chapter.

Water   Although most Italians take mineral water with their meals, tap water is safe everywhere, as are any public drinking fountains you run across. Unsafe sources will be marked *"acqua non potabile."* If tap water comes out cloudy, it is only the calcium or other minerals inherent in a water supply that often comes untreated from fresh springs.

Settling into Rome 4

Even as Rome looks toward the millennium, remnants of its ancient past endure. Break ground for a new building foundation anywhere in Rome, and you might discover a valuable historical site. At least that's what happened when the Rome government forged ahead with plans for a new Philharmonic Hall. As excavation got underway, workers discovered an ancient villa, which has halted construction plans at least temporarily.

It hasn't always been that way. Mussolini didn't let a little history delay his Via del Impero, the wide boulevard that linked his office on the Piazza Venezia with the Colosseum. But now, with Fascism in the near past, ancient times are treated with more care, and Mussolini's street, renamed Via dei Fori Imperiali, is the site of the largest urban excavation of the city in more than 60 years.

As archaeologists from the University of Rome attempt to probe the foundation of the communities and cultures that built Rome, you'll recognize their work in the form of a huge hole between the Piazza Venezia and the Colosseum. They're exploring the ancient Forum of Nerva, built by the emperor Domitian to honor his son in the first century A.D. It's part of an intricate complex of ancient squares known as the Imperial Forums, and the dig is an ambitious effort to expand the area of the Roman Forum in time for the Roman Jubilee in the year 2000. Though faced with that deadline, archaeologists are carefully peeling back layers of time, revealing an entire cross-section of ancient to contemporary civilizations.

These efforts will allow tourists to explore ancient treasures such as rough stone walls from the Carolingian era (A.D. 774 to 961), a deep ditch that functioned as an early Roman sewer (probably the first or second century B.C.), and the trail of a street used by the popes, up through the Middle Ages, to travel from the papal palace to St. Peter's. Tourists will also be able to wander over the heavy cement blocks and dark stones that served as footings for giant columns that bordered Dommitian's extensive piazza.

Whether underground or above, Rome remains a city of images, vivid and unforgettable. One of the most striking may be seen at dawn—ideally from Janiculum Hill—when the city's silhouette, with its bell towers and cupolas, gradually comes into focus. Rome is also a city of sounds, beginning early in the morning with the peal of church bells calling the faithful to mass. As the city awakens and comes to life, the streets fill with cars, taxis, and motor scooters, blaring their horns as they weave in and out of traffic. The sidewalks become over-run with bleary-eyed office workers rushing off to their desks, but not before steal-ing into crowded cafes for their first cappuccino of the day. The shops lining the streets open for business by raising their protective metal grilles as loudly as possible, seeming to delight in their contribution to the general din. Even the many fruit-and-vegetable stands buzz with activity, as an eclectic group of Romans arrive to purchase their day's supply of fresh produce, haggling over price and caviling over quality.

By 10am the tourists take to the streets, battling the crowds and traffic as they wend their way from Renaissance palaces and baroque buildings to the famous ruins of antiquity—the Colosseum and the Forum, symbols of a once-great empire whose heart was Rome, the Eternal City. Indeed, Rome often appears to have two populations: one of Romans and one of visitors. During the summer months espe-cially, countless sightseers converge upon the city, guidebooks and cameras in hand. Of course, if you visit in August, you may not see many true Romans—the locals flee at that time. Or as one Roman woman once told us, "Even if we're too poor to go on vacation, we close the shutters and pretend we're away so neighbors won't find out we couldn't afford to leave the city."

The traffic, unfortunately, is worse than ever, restoration programs seem to drag on forever, and, as the capital, Rome remains at the center of the major political scan-dals and corruption known as *Tangentopoli* ("bribe city") that sends hundreds of gov-ernment bureaucrats to jail each year.

But in spite of all this metropolitan and political chaos, Romans still live the good life. After you've wandered through the Colosseum, marveled at the Pan-theon, traipsed through St. Peter's Basilica, and thrown a coin in Trevi Fountain, you can pause in the early evening to experience the charm of Rome at dusk. Find a cafe at summer twilight and watch the shades of pink turn to gold and copper before the night finally falls. That's when a new Rome awakens. The restaurants and cafes grow more animated and more fun, especially if you've found one on an antique piazza or along a narrow alley deep in Trastevere. After dinner you can stroll by the fountains, or through Piazza Navona, have a *gelato* (or *espresso* in win-ter), and the night is yours.

As the city prepares for Roma 2000 and the millennium, it will be upgrading its urban landscape with better traffic signals, trees along the roads, flower beds in traf-fic islands, small public gardens in various parts of the city, and the restoration of ancient monuments, among many other improvements.

That's on the horizon. But if you go now, you'll still experience a vast array of activities to delight you, in spite of the traffic, overcrowding, and little gypsy chil-dren out to snatch your purse or wallet.

In chapter 5 we'll take you on fascinating walks through the major historical and architectural sites of Rome. And although the sites are an important ingredient in the appreciation of this centuries-old city, they represent only one aspect of Rome—the past. Rome is also a vibrant, exciting *modern* metropolis, pulsing with all kinds of daytime and nighttime activities. As you take part in them, you'll find yourself em-bracing the city's life with intensity, like a Roman. As the saying goes, "When in Rome . . ."

1 Orientation

ARRIVING

BY PLANE Chances are that you'll arrive in Italy at Rome's **Leonardo da Vinci International Airport** (☎ **06/65-951** or 06/6595-3640 for information), popularly known as **Fiumicino**, 18¹/₂ miles from the center of the capital. (If you're flying by charter, you might wing into Ciampino Airport; see below.)

After leaving Passport Control, two information desks—one for Rome, one for Italy—come into view. At the Rome desk you can pick up a general (not a detailed) map and some pamphlets Monday to Saturday from 8:30am to 7pm. A *cambio* (money exchange) operates daily from 7:30am to 11pm. Luggage storage is available in the main arrivals building and is open daily, 5,000L ($3) per bag.

To get into the city, follow the signs marked TRENI for the shuttle service directly to the main rail station, **Stazione Termini** (arriving on Track 22). It runs between 7am and 10pm for 13,000L ($7.80) one-way. A local train, costing 7,000L ($4.20), runs between the airport and the Tiburtina Station, from which you can go the rest of the way to the Termini by subway Line B, costing another 1,000L (60¢). The shuttle train takes about 30 minutes, and the local train, because of the transfer, will add another hour to the trip. Should you arrive on a charter flight at **Ciampino** (☎ 06/794-941), take a COTRAL bus, departing every 30 minutes or so, which will deliver you to the Anagnina stop of Metropolitana Line A. Take Linea A to Stazione Termini where you can make your final connections. Trip time is about 45 minutes, and the cost is 2,000L ($1.20).

Taxis from Fiumicino **(Da Vinci)** to the city are expensive—70,000L ($42) and up. From **Ciampino,** the rate is the same (70,000L/$42), but the trip is shorter.

BY TRAIN OR BUS Trains and buses arrive in the center of old Rome at the **Stazione Termini,** Piazza dei Cinquecento (☎ 1478/880-881), the train, bus, and subway transportation hub for all of Rome, which is surrounded by many hotels (especially cheaper ones).

If you're taking the **Metropolitana** (Rome's subway network), follow the illuminated red M signs. To catch a bus, go straight through the outer hall of the Termini and enter the sprawling bus lot of Piazza dei Cinquecento. You'll also find taxis here (see "Getting Around," later in this chapter, for details on public transportation). Beware of the taxi drivers soliciting passengers right outside the terminal; they can charge unaware travelers as much as triple the normal amount. Instead, line up in the taxi queue in the Piazza dei Cinquecento.

The Termini is filled with services. At a branch of the Banca Nazionale delle Communicazioni (between Tracks 8–11 and Tracks 12–15) you can exchange money. *Informazioni Ferroviarie* (in the outer hall) dispenses information on rail travel to other parts of Italy. There's also a tourist information booth here, along with baggage services, barbershops, gift shops, restaurants, and bars. But beware of pickpockets, perhaps quick-fingered young children. The station is also home to the **Albergo Diurno** (☎ 06/323-5457), a hotel without beds but with baths, showers, and well-kept toilet facilities open daily from 7am to 8pm.

BY CAR From the north the main access route is the **Autostrada del Sole (A1),** cutting through Milan and Florence, or you can take the coastal route, SS1 Aurelia, from Genoa. If you're driving north from Naples, you take the southern lap of the **Autostrada del Sole (A2).** All these autostrade join with the **Grande Raccordo Anulare,** a ring road that encircles Rome, channeling traffic into the congested city. Long before you reach this ring road, you should study a map carefully to see what part of Rome you plan to enter and mark your route accordingly. Route markings along the ring road tend to be confusing.

VISITOR INFORMATION

Some tourist information is available at the **Ente Provinciale per il Turismo,** Via Parigi 5, 00185 Roma (☎ 06/4889-9253), open Monday to Friday from 8:15am to 7:15pm, Saturday 8:15am to 2:15pm—but the information dispensed here is meager. There's another information bureau at the Stazione Termini (☎ 06/ 487-1270), open daily from 8:15am to 7:15pm.

Rome also operates three **Info-Tourism "Boxes,"** kiosks set up in trailers in the historic center. The kiosks offer some brochures and maps, but their main asset is a database with information on attractions, hotels, restaurants, and more. The booths are located on Largo Carlo Goldoni (☎ 06/687-5027), off Via del Corso, across from Via dei Condotti; on Via Nazionale (☎ 06/474-6262) near the Palazzo delle Esposizioni; and on Largo Corrado Ricci (☎ 06/678-0992), near the Colosseum. All three are open Tuesday to Saturday from 10am to 6pm and Sunday from 10am to 1pm.

CITY LAYOUT

Inside the still remarkably intact **Great Aurelian Wall** (started in A.D. 271 to calm Rome's barbarian jitters), you'll find a city designed for a population that walked to get where it was going. Parts of Rome actually feel more like an oversized village than the former imperial capital of the Western world.

The Stazione Termini faces a huge plaza, **Piazza dei Cinquecento,** named after 500 Italians who died heroically in a 19th-century battle in Africa.

The bulk of ancient, Renaissance, and baroque Rome (as well as the train station) lies on the east side of the **Tiber River (Fiume Tevere),** which meanders through town flowing through 19th-century stone embankments. However, several important monuments lie on the other side of the river: **St. Peter's Basilica** and the **Vatican,** the **Castel Sant'Angelo** (formerly the tomb of the Emperor Hadrian), and the colorful **Trastevere** neighborhood.

The various quarters of the city are linked by large boulevards (large at least in some places) that have mostly been laid out since the late 19th century. Starting from the **Vittorio Emanuele monument,** a highly controversial pile of snow-white Brescian marble, there's a street running practically due north to **Piazza del Popolo** and the city wall. This is **Via del Corso,** one of the main streets of Rome—noisy, congested, always crowded with buses and shoppers, called simply "Il Corso." To its left (west) lie the Pantheon, Piazza Navona, Campo de' Fiori, and the Tiber River. To its right (east) you'll find the Spanish Steps, Trevi Fountain, Borghese Gardens, and Via Veneto. Back at the Vittorio Emanuele monument, the major artery going west (and ultimately across the Tiber to St. Peter's) is **Corso Vittorio Emanuele.** Behind you to your right, heading toward the Colosseum, is **Via del Fori Imperiali,** laid out in the 1930s by Mussolini to show off the ruins of the imperial forums he had excavated, which line it on either side. Yet another central conduit is **Via Nazionale,** running from **Piazza Venezia** (just in front of the Vittorio Emanuele monument) east to **Piazza della Repubblica** (near the Termini). The final lap of Via Nazionale is called **Via Quattro Novembre.**

FINDING AN ADDRESS   Finding an address in Rome can be a problem because of the narrow streets of old Rome and the little, sometimes hidden *piazze* (squares). Numbers usually run consecutively, with odd numbers on one side of the street and evens on the other. However, in the old districts the numbers will sometimes run up one side to the end, then back in the opposite direction on the other side. Therefore, no. 50 could be opposite no. 308.

STREET MAPS   Arm yourself with a detailed street map, not the general overview handed out free at tourist offices. You'll need a detailed map even to find such attractions as the Trevi Fountain. The best ones are published by **Falk,** available at most newsstands. The best selections of maps are sold in bookstores (see "Shopping," in chapter 5).

TRAFFIC For the $2^1/_2$ millennia before the wide boulevards mentioned above were built, the citizens had to make their way through narrow byways and curves that defeated all but the best senses of direction. These streets—among the most charming aspects of the city—still exist in large quantities, mostly unspoiled by the advances of modern construction. However, this tangled street plan has one troublesome element: automobiles. The traffic in Rome is awful! When the claustrophobic street plans of the Dark Ages open unexpectedly onto a vast piazza, every driver accelerates full throttle for the distant horizon, while pedestrians flatten themselves against marble fountains for protection or stride with firm jaws right into the thick of the howling traffic.

The traffic problem in Rome is nothing new. Julius Caesar was so exasperated by it that he banned all vehicular traffic during daylight hours. Sometimes it's actually faster to walk than to take a bus, especially during any of Rome's four daily rush hours (that's right, *four:* to work, home for lunch/*riposo,* back to work, home in the evening). The hectic crush of urban Rome is considerably less during August, when many Romans are out of town on vacation. If you visit at any other time of year, however, be prepared for the general frenzy that characterizes the average Roman street.

NEIGHBORHOODS IN BRIEF

Here are the main districts of interest, spiraling roughly out from the ancient center, through the heart of old Rome, and on to some of the more interesting outlying residential areas. This section will give you some idea of where you may want to stay and where the major attractions are.

Ancient Rome   Most visitors to Rome explore this district first, taking in the Colosseum, Palatine Hill, the Roman Forum, the Fori Imperiali (Imperial Forums), and Circus Maximus. It forms part of the *centro storico* or historic district (along with Campo de' Fiori and Piazza Navona and the Pantheon described below). With its narrow streets, airy piazzas, antique atmosphere, and great location, vistors enjoy staying in this area instead of the uglier, duller, and more dangerous districts such as the section around the Termini. If you base yourself here—as many do—you can walk to the monuments and avoid the hassle of Rome's inadequate public transportation. But here's the bad news: Because hotel owners know that tourists want to stay here, room prices are often 30% to 50% higher than in other less desirable areas. So if you want atmosphere, you must pay for it.

Campo de' Fiori & the Jewish Ghetto   South of Corso Vittorio Emanuele, centered around Piazza Farnese and the market square of Campo de' Fiori, many buildings in this district were constructed in Renaissance times as private homes. Walk on **Via Giulia**—the most fashionable street in Rome in the 16th century—with its antique stores, interesting hotels, and modern art galleries.

West of Via Arenula lies one of the city's most intriguing districts, the old **Jewish Ghetto,** where the dining options far outnumber the hotel options. In 1556, Pope Paul IV ordered the Jews, about 8,000 at the time, to move into this area. The walls were not torn down until 1849. Although we think Ancient and medieval Rome have a lot more atmosphere, this area is close to many attractions and makes a great place to stay. Nevertheless, hoteliers still sock it to you on prices.

Piazza Navona & the Pantheon   One of the most alluring areas of Rome, this district is a maze of narrow streets and alleys dating back to the Middle Ages and is filled

Rome Orientation

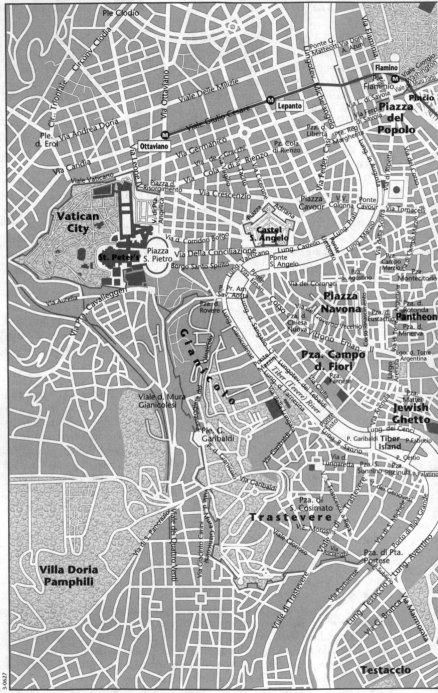

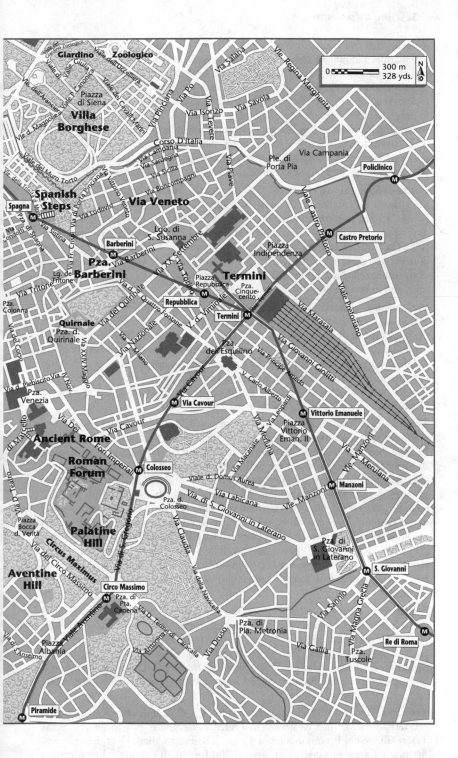

with churches and palaces built during the Renaissance and baroque eras, often with rare marbles and other materials stripped from Ancient Rome. The only way to explore it is on foot. Its heart is **Piazza Navona,** built over Emperor Domitian's stadium and bustling with sidewalk cafes, *palazzi* (palaces), street artists, musicians, and pickpockets. There are several hotels in the area and plenty of trattorie. Rivaling it— in general activity, the cafe scene, and nightlife—is the area around the **Pantheon,** which remains from ancient Roman times surrounded by a district built much later (this "pagan" temple was turned into a church and rescued, whereas the buildings that once surrounded it are long gone). If you'd like to stay in medieval Rome, you face the same 30% to 50% increase in hotel prices as you do for Ancient Rome.

Piazza di Spagna   Ever since the 17th century the **Spanish Steps**—former site of the Spanish ambassador's residence—have been the center of tourist Rome. Keats lived in a house opening onto the steps, and some of Rome's most prestigious shopping streets fan out from it, including Via Condotti. The most elegant address here is **the Hassler,** one of Rome's grandest hotels. If you want to sleep in the hippest part of town, you must be willing to part with a lot of extra lire. This area charges some of the capital's highest prices, not only for hotels, but for restaurants, designer silk suits, and leather loafers.

Via Veneto   In the 1950s and early 1960s this was the haunt of the *dolce vita* set, as the likes of King Farouk and Swedish actress Anita Ekberg paraded up and down the boulevard to the delight of the *paparazzi.* The street is still here, still the site of luxury hotels and elegant cafes and restaurants, although it no longer has the allure it did in its heyday. Rome city authorities would like to restore this legendary street to some of its former glory. Frank Sinatra and Elizabeth Taylor may never pass through it again, but Rome is trying to spruce up Via Vittorio Veneto by banning vehicular traffic on the top half of the street.

Termini   The main train station adjoins Piazza della Repubblica, and for many, this is your introduction to Rome. Much of the area is seedy and filled with gas fumes from all the buses and cars, but there's still a lot to see here, including the **Basilica di Santa Maria Maggiore** and the **Baths of Diocletian.** Although this is one of the least desirable places to stay in Rome—and also one of the most dangerous because of muggings—it's also the cheapest. There are some high-class hotels in the area, including the Grand, but many are long past their heyday. The area directly south of the Termini is more chaotic and seedier than the district to the north. Even though the hotel prices are lower, you'll still be overcharged—if innkeepers think they can get away with it. The best *pensioni* and hotels lie north of the Termini, within a 15-minute walk. Many of these hotels are run-down and in dire need of major renovation, although some have recently been improved. There's talk of a "renaissance" for the area.

Appian Way   Via Appia Antica is a 2,300-year-old road that has witnessed much of the history of the ancient world. By 190 B.C. it extended from Rome to Brindisi on the southeast coast, and its most famous sights today are the **catacombs,** the graveyards of patrician families (despite what it says in *Quo Vadis?,* they were not used as a place for Christians to hide out while fleeing persecution). This is one of the most historically rich areas of Rome to explore—but don't go there seeking a hotel. There are several restaurants, however.

Testaccio   In A.D. 55, Nero ordered that Rome's thousands of broken amphoras and terra-cotta roof tiles be stacked in a carefully designated pile to the east of the Tiber, just west of Pyramide and today's Ostia Railway Station. Over the centuries, the mound grew to a height of around 200 feet, then compacted to form the centerpiece for one of the city's most unusual neighborhoods. Eventually, houses were built on the terra-cotta mound, and caves were dug into its mass for the storage of wine and foodstuffs (a constant temperature of 50°F was maintained year-round, thanks to the porosity of the terra-cotta). Bordered by the Protestant cemetery, today Testaccio is home to restaurants with *very* Roman cuisine (see "Dining," later in this chapter).

Trastevere   This is the most authentic district of Rome, lying "across the Tiber," and its people are of mixed ancestry, including Jewish, Roman, and Greek, and speak their own dialect. The area centers around the ancient churches of **Santa Cecilia** and **Santa Maria in Trastevere.** Home to many young expatriates, the district became a gathering place for hedonists and bohemians after World War II. It has been called the last of the capital's old *rioni* (neighborhoods). There are those who speak of it as a "city within a city"—or at least a village within a city. It's said that the language is rougher and the cuisine spicier, and although Trastevere doesn't have the glamorous hotels of central Rome, it does have some of the last remaining authentic Roman dining. Trastevere used to be a bastion of the budget traveler, but foreigners from virtually everywhere have been buying real estate en masse here, so change is in the air.

Around Vatican City   Also across the river, Vatican City is a small city-state, but its influence extends around the world. The Vatican museums and St. Peter's take up most of the land area, and the popes have lived here for six centuries. Although the neighborhhood contains some good hotels (and several bad ones), it's somewhat removed from the more happening scene of Ancient and Renaissance Rome, and getting to and from it can be time-consuming. Also, the area is rather dull at night and contains few if any of Rome's finest restaurants. Vatican City and its surrounding area is best for exploring during the day.

Prati   This little-known district is really a 19th-century middle-class suburb north of the Vatican. It's been discovered by budget travelers because of its low-cost *pensioni* (boardinghouses). The **Trionfale flower-and-food market** itself is worth the trip. The area also abounds in shopping streets less expensive than those found in central Rome. If safety is a main concern for you, Prati is a more tranquil district, usually devoid of the pickpockets and thieves who prey on tourists in Ancient Rome and around the Termini.

Parioli   The most elegant residential section of Rome is framed by the green spaces of the Villa Borghese to the south and the Villa Glori and Villa Ada to the north. It's a setting for some of the city's finest restaurants, hotels, and nightclubs. It's not the most central, however, and can be a hassle if you're dependent on public transportation. Parioli lies adjacent to Prati, but across the Tiber to the east, and, like Prati, is one of the safer districts of Rome.

Monte Mario   On the northwestern precincts of Rome, Monte Mario is the site of the deluxe Cavalieri Hilton, an excellent stop to take in a drink and the panorama of Rome. If you plan to spend a lot of time shopping and sightseeing in the heart of Rome, it's a difficult and often expensive commute. The area lies north of Prati, away from the hustle and bustle of central Rome. Bus 913 runs from Piazza Augusto Imperator near the Piazza del Popolo to Monte Mario.

2 Getting Around

BY PUBLIC TRANSPORTATION

BY SUBWAY   The **Metropolitana,** or **Metro** for short, is the fastest means of transportation in Rome. It has two underground lines: Line A goes between **Via**

Ottaviano, near St. Peter's, and **Anagnina,** stopping at **Piazzale Flaminio** (near Piazza del Popolo), **Piazza di Spagna, Piazza Vittorio Emanuele,** and **Piazza San Giovanni** in Laterano. Line B connects the Rebibbia District with Via Laurentina, stopping at **Via Cavour, Stazione Termini,** the **Colosseum, Circus Maximus,** the **Pyramid, St. Paul's Outside the Walls,** and **E.U.R.** A big red letter "M" indicates the entrance to the subway.

Tickets are 1,500L (90¢) and are available from vending machines at all stations. These machines accept 50L, 100L, and 200L coins, and some of them will take 1,000L notes. Some stations have managers, but they won't make change. Booklets of tickets *(carnet)* are available at *tabacchi* (tobacco shops) and in some terminals. You can also purchase a tourist pass on either a daily or weekly basis (see "By Bus & Tram").

Building a subway system for Rome has not been easy, since every time workers start digging they discover an old temple or other archeological treasure and heavy earth-moving has to cease for a while.

BY BUS & TRAM Roman buses and trams are operated by an organization known as **ATAC (Azienda Tramvie e Autobus del Commune di Roma),** Via Volturno 65 (☎ **06/46-951** for information).

For only 1,500L (90¢) you can ride to most parts of Rome on quite good bus service. The ticket is valid for 1 hour and 15 minutes, and you can get on many buses and trams during that time period using the same ticket. At the Stazione Termini, you can purchase a special tourist bus pass, costing 6,000L ($3.60) for 1 day or 24,000L ($14.40) for a week. This allows you to ride on the ATAC network without bothering to purchase individual tickets. The tourist pass is also valid on the subway—but never ride the trains when the Romans are going to or from work or you'll be mashed flatter than fettuccine. On the first bus you board, you place your ticket in a small machine that prints the day and hour you boarded. And you do the same on the last bus you take during the validity period of the ticket.

Buses and trams stop at areas marked FERMATA. At most of these, a yellow sign will display the numbers of the buses that stop there, and then a list of all the stops along each bus's route in order, so you can easily search out your destination. In general they're in service from 6am to midnight daily. After that and until dawn, you can ride on special night buses (they have an "N" in front of their bus number), which only run on main routes. It's best to take a taxi in the wee hours—if you can find one.

At the bus information booth at Piazza dei Cinquecento, in front of the Stazione Termini, you can purchase a directory complete with maps summarizing the particular routes. *Warning:* Any maps of the Rome bus system will likely be outdated before they are printed. Many buses listed on the "latest" map no longer exist; others are enjoying a much-needed rest, and new buses suddenly appear without warning. A few old reliable routes remain valid, however, such as the **27** from the Termini to the Colosseum, the **75** and **170** from the Termini to Trastevere, and the **492** from the Termini to the Vatican. But if you're going somewhere and dependent on the bus, be sure to carefully research where the bus stop is, and exactly what bus goes there—don't assume it'll be the same bus the next day. Ask about where to purchase bus tickets, or buy them in *tabacchi* or at bus terminals. You must have your ticket before boarding the bus, as there are no ticket-issuing machines on the vehicles.

Take extreme caution riding the overcrowded buses of Rome—pickpockets abound! This is particularly true on **bus no. 64,** a favorite of tourists because of its route through Rome's historic districts, and thus also a favorite of Rome's vast pickpocketing community. Bus no. 64 has earned various nicknames: "The Pickpocket Express" or "The Wallet Eater."

Rome Metro

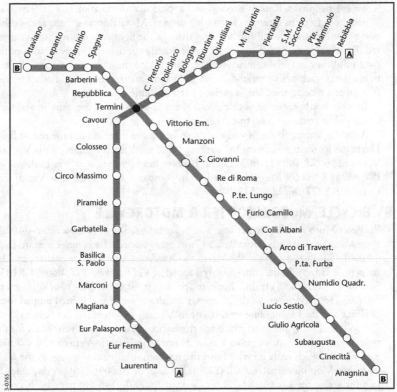

BY TAXI

If you're accustomed to hopping a cab in New York or London, then do so in Rome. If not, take less expensive means of transport. Avoid paying your fare with large bills—invariably, taxi drivers claim they don't have change, hoping for a bigger tip (stick to your guns and only give about 10%). Don't count on hailing a taxi on the street or even getting one at a stand. If you're going out, have your hotel call one. At a restaurant, ask the waiter or cashier to dial for you. If you want to phone for yourself, try one of these numbers: ☎ **06/6645, 06/3570,** or **06/4994.**

The meter begins at 4,500L ($2.70) for the first 3 kilometers, then increases 200L (10¢) per 150 meters. Every suitcase is 2000L ($1.20), and on Sunday a 5,000L ($3) supplement is assessed, plus another 2,000L ($1.20) supplement from 10pm to 7am.

BY CAR

For general information, see "Getting Around" in chapter 3.

All roads may lead to Rome if you're driving, but don't count on doing much driving once you get here. Since the reception desks of most Roman hotels have at least one English-speaking person, it's wise to call ahead to find out the best route into Rome from wherever you're starting out.

Find out if the hotel has a garage. If not, you're usually allowed to park your car in front of the hotel long enough to unload your luggage. Someone at the hotel—a doorman, if there is one—will direct you to the nearest garage or place to park. Garage prices range from 6,000L to 60,000L ($3.60 to $36) depending on proximity to the center of the city and amenities such as enclosed and guarded areas.

To the neophyte, Roman driving will appear like the chariot race in *Ben-Hur*. When the light turns green, go forth with caution. Many Roman drivers at the other part of the intersection will still be going through the light even though it has turned red. Roman drivers in traffic gridlock move bravely on, fighting for every inch of the road until they can free themselves from the tangled mess. To complicate matters, many zones, such as that around Piazza di Spagna, are traffic-free, and other traffic-free zones are being tried out in various parts of Rome.

In other words, try to get your car into Rome as safely as possible, park it, and walk or use public transportation from then on.

As you're leaving Rome, if you want to rent a car to drive around the rest of Italy, **Hertz** has its main office near the parking lot of the Villa Borghese, at Via Vittorio Veneto 156 (☎ 06/321-6831). The **Budget** headquarters is at Via Ludovisi 60 (☎ 06/482-0966). **Maggiore,** an Italian company, has an office at Via di Tor Cervara 225 (☎ 06/229-351).

BY BICYCLE, MOTORSCOOTER & MOTORCYCLE

St. Peter Moto Renting & Selling, Via di Porta Castello 43 (☎ 06/6880-04608), open Monday to Saturday from 9am to 7pm, rents mopeds. Rates range upward from 40,000L ($24) per day. Take the Metro to Ottaviano. Another agency that provides mopeds is **Happy Rent,** conveniently located at Via Farimi 3 (☎ 06/481-8185), 300 yards from the Termini. Most mopeds cost 40,000L ($24) for 4 hours or 60,000L ($36) for the entire day. Happy Rent also offers several guided moped tours of Rome and the surrounding area. It's open Monday to Saturday from 9am to 7pm.

You'll find many places to rent bikes throughout Rome. Ask at your hotel for the nearest rental location, or go to **I Bike Rome,** Via Vittorio Veneto 156 (☎ 06/322-5240), which rents bicycles from the underground parking garage at the Villa Borghese. Most bikes cost 4,000L ($2.40) per hour or 10,000L ($6) per day. Mountain bikes rent for 7,000L ($4.20) per hour or 18,000L ($10.80) per day. It's open daily from 9am to 7pm.

Bike riders are permitted anywhere in the city, including pedestrian-only zones and traffic-free areas such as St. Peter's Square, where you can ride within the arcaded confines of what's been called the world's most magnificent oval. Also appealing is a 30km (18.5-mile) bike lane beside the Tiber that extends from central Rome north, to the industrial suburb of Castel Jubileo.

BY FOOT

Although it's a large city, Rome is an excellent walking city—you'll find sites of interests often clustered together rather than spread out among large distances. Much of the inner core of Rome is traffic-free—so you'll need to walk whether you like it or not. Walking is the perfect way to see the ancient narrow cobbled streets of Old Rome. However, in many parts of the city it's hazardous and uncomfortable because of the crowds, heavy traffic, and very narrow sidewalks. Sometimes sidewalks don't exist at all, and it becomes a sort of free-for-all with pedestrians competing for space against vehicular traffic (the traffic always seems to win). *Caution:* When walking, always be on your guard for speeding traffic.

FAST FACTS: Rome

American Express   The Rome offices of American Express are at Piazza di Spagna 38 (☎ 06/67-641). The travel service is open Monday to Friday from 9am to 5:30pm and Saturday from 9am to 12:30pm. Hours for the financial and mail services are Monday to Friday from 9am to 5pm and Saturday from 9am to noon. The tour desk is open during the same hours as those for travel services and also Saturday afternoon from 2 to 2:30pm from May to October.

Bookstores See "Shopping," in chapter 5.

Business Hours In general, **banks** are open Monday to Friday from 8:30am to 1:30pm and 3 to 4pm. Some banks keep afternoon hours ranging from 2:45 to 3:45pm. Two U.S. banks in Rome are Chase Manhattan Bank, Via Michele Mercati 39 (☎ 06/808-5655), and Citibank, Via Abruzzi 2 (☎ 06/478-171). **Shopping** hours are governed by the *riposo* (siesta). Most stores are open year-round Monday to Saturday from 9am to 1pm and then from 3:30 or 4pm to 7:30 or 8pm. Most shops are closed Sunday.

Car Rentals See "Getting Around," earlier in this chapter.

Climate In the summer months, the temperature reaches into the high 80s. The coldest months are December and January when the temperature can dip into the 40s. The most rainfall occurs in October and November.

Crime See "Safety," below.

Currency Exchange This is possible at all major rail and airline terminals in Rome, including the **Stazione Termini,** where the *cambio* (exchange booth) beside the rail information booth is open daily from 8am to 8pm. At some cambi you'll have to pay commissions, often $1^1/2$%. Banks, likewise, often charge commissions. Many so-called moneychangers will approach you on the street, but often they're pushing counterfeit lire. However, they offer very good rates for their fake money! To be on the safe side, we recommend that money be exchanged only at banks, hotels, or currency exchange booths.

Dentist To secure a dentist who speaks English, call the U.S. Embassy in Rome (☎ 06/46-741). You may have to call around in order to get an appointment. There's also the 24-hour G. Eastman Dental Hospital, Viale Regina Elena 287 (☎ **06/844-831**).

Doctor Call the U.S. Embassy (see "Dentist," above), which will provide a list of doctors who speak English. All big hospitals in Rome have a 24-hour first-aid service (go to the emergency room). You'll find English-speaking doctors at the privately run **Salvator Mundi International Hospital,** Viale delle Mura Gianicolensi 67 (☎ **06/588961**). For medical assistance, the **International Medical Center** is on 24-hour duty at Via Giovanni Amendola 7 (☎ **488-2371**). You could also contact the **Rome American Hospital,** Via Emilio Longoni 69 (☎ **06/22-551**), with English-speaking doctors on duty 24 hours a day. Another medical service is **MEDI-CALL Sr 1,** Studio Medico, Via Salaria, 300 Palazzina C interno 5 (☎ **06/844-0113**), which is a new Medical Society that provides private assistance to foreigners in Rome. It offers quick, efficient, and organized medical services with a team of experienced and capable doctors who can fulfill every medical need.

Drugstores A reliable pharmacy is **Farmacia Internazionale,** Piazza Barberini 49 (☎ **06/679-4680**). Most pharmacies are open from 8:30am to 1pm and 4 to 7:30pm. In general, pharmacies follow a rotation system so that several are always open on Sunday (the rotation schedule is posted outside each one).

Embassies/Consulates See "Fast Facts: Italy" in chapter 3.

Emergencies The police "hotline" number is ☎ **21-21-21.** Usually, however, dial ☎ **112** for the police, to report a fire, or summon an ambulance.

Eyeglasses   Try **Vasari,** Piazza della Repubblica 61 (☎ **06/488-2240**), adjacent to the Grand Hotel, a very large shop with lots of choices.

Hospitals   See "Doctor," above.

Hotlines   Dial ☎ **113,** which is a general SOS, to report any kind of danger, such as rape. You can also dial ☎ **112,** the police emergency number. For an ambulance call ☎ **5100;** for personal crises, call Samaritans, Via San Giovanni in Laterano 250 (☎ **06/7045-4444**), daily from to 1 to 10pm.

Lost Property   Usually lost property is gone forever. But you might try checking at **Oggetti Rinvenuti,** Via Nicolò Bettoni 1 (☎ **06/581-6040**), open Monday to Friday from 9am to 1pm and Tuesday to Thursday from 2:30 to 6pm. At the **Stazione Termini** off Track 1 (☎ **06/4730-6682**), open daily from 7am to 11pm, you may reclaim objects that have been found in the station.

Luggage Storage/Lockers   These are available at the Stazione Termini along Tracks 1 and 22 daily from 5am to 1am. The charge is 5,000L ($3) per piece per 12-hour period.

Mail   Post office boxes in Italy are red and are attached to walls. The left slot is only for letters intended for the city; the right is for all other destinations. Vatican post office boxes are blue, and you can buy special stamps at the Vatican City Post Office. Letters mailed at Vatican City reach North America far more quickly than does mail sent from within Rome for the same cost. The **Vatican City Post Office** is adjacent to the information office in St. Peter's Square. It's open Monday to Friday from 8:30am to 7pm and Saturday from 8:30am to 6pm.

The main post office of Rome is at **Piazza San Silvestro 19,** 00186 Roma (☎ **06/6771**), between Via del Corso and Piazza di Spagna, open Monday to Friday from 9am to 6pm and Saturday from 9am to noon. Mail addressed to you at this central office, with *fermo posta* written after the name and address of the post office, will be given to you upon identification by passport. Stamps *(francobolli)* can be purchased at *tabacchi* (tobacconists).

Newspapers/Magazines   You can get the *International Herald Tribune, New York Times,* and *Time* and *Newsweek* magazines at most newsstands. The expat magazine (in English) *Wanted in Rome* comes out monthly and lists current events and shows. If you want to try your hand at reading Italian, the Thursday edition of the newspaper *La Repubblica* contains *Trova Roma,* a magazine supplement full of cultural and entertainment listings.

Police   See "Emergencies," above.

Rest Rooms   Facilities are found near many of the major sights, often with attendants, as are those at bars, nightclubs, restaurants, cafes, and hotels, plus the airports and the railway station. You're expected to leave 200L to 500L (10¢ to 30¢) for the attendant.

Safety   Pickpocketing is the most common problem. Men—keep your wallets in your front pocket or inside jacket pocket. Women—purse-snatching is also commonplace, with young men on Vespas who will ride past you and grab your purse. To avoid trouble, stay away from the curb, and keep your purse on the wall side of your body and the strap over both shoulders across your chest. Don't lay anything valuable on tables or chairs where it can be grabbed up easily. Gypsy children are a particular menace. You'll often virtually have to fight them off, if they completely surround you. They'll often approach you with pieces of cardboard hiding their stealing hands.

Taxes A **value-added tax** (called **IVA** in Italy) is added to all consumer products and most services, including restaurants and hotels. The tax is not the same for all goods and services. The tax is 12% on clothing and 19% on most luxury goods.

Taxis See "Getting Around," earlier in this chapter.

Telegrams/Fax If your hotel doesn't have a fax, try a tobacconist or photocopy shop. You can send telegrams from all post offices during the day and from the telegraph office at the central post office in San Silvestro, off Via della Mercede, at night. See also "Fast Facts: Italy," in chapter 3.

Transit Information Leonardo da Vinci International Airport (☎ **06/65-951**); Ciampino Airport (☎ 06/794-941); bus information (☎ **06/46-951**); rail information (☎ **1478/880-881**).

Water Rome is famous for its drinking water, which is generally safe, even from the outdoor fountains. If it isn't, there's a sign reading *acqua non potabile*. Nevertheless, Romans traditionally order bottled mineral water in restaurants to accompany the wine with their meals.

3 Accommodations

The good news is that Roman hoteliers are sprucing up for the Holy Year visitors who are expected to flood the city at the millennium. The bad news is that some of that ripping out and repairing of old plumbing and seedy hotel rooms may be going on when you visit in 1998.

Among the luxury leaders, there has been no earth-shaking news since the opening of the **Hotel Eden,** which is now a market leader. After all, it's almost impossible to open a five-star palace hotel in Rome today because real estate isn't available. One of Rome's newest four-star hotels, the **Mecenate Palace,** has made a splash and is becoming better known.

A number of small hotels have either opened or undergone renovations. That makes them worthy contenders for your visit today. The best example is the **Hotel Nerva** (see below). We've previewed the best of these newly discovered or rediscovered candidates, some of which were not highly recommended only a short time ago.

You'll find the cheapest hotels (and probably the most run-down) around the Stazione Termini—one of the city's seedier neighboorhoods. The most central are in the **Centro Storico** near all the sights and monuments—but you pay for the location. Some elegant ones—such as the **Cavalieri Hilton**—can be found in residential suburb areas. See "Neighborhoods in Brief" under "Orientation," earlier in this chapter, to get an idea of where you may want to base yourself.

Rome is a year-round tourist destination, so you'll need to make reservations no matter what the season. Because of Rome's importance as a religious center, some groups book hundreds of rooms in the winter "low season" because they get better discounts. Many hotels will grant winter discounts—usually no more than 10%—and you may have to negotiate this at the reception desk.

Rome has more than 500 hotels. Recommendations are based on value—regardless of the price range—and special considerations, such as charm, comfort, and location.

All the hotels recommended serve breakfast, and many of them also have good restaurants. The deluxe hotels house some of the finest restaurants in Rome. Breakfast is not always included in the room rate, so always determine this when checking in. Breakfast will be of the continental variety—cappuccino and croissants, along with jam and butter.

Rome Accommodations

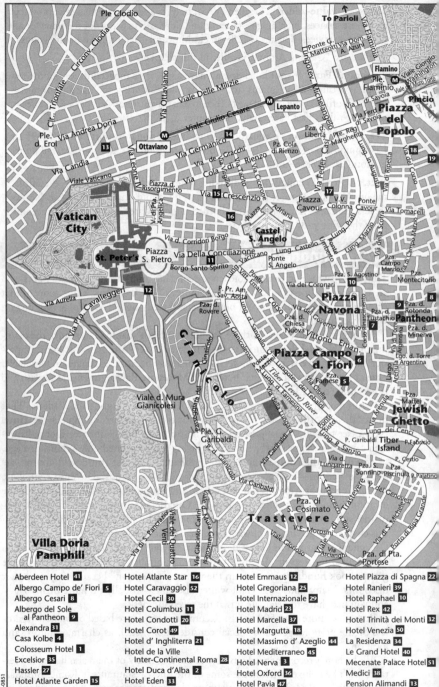

Aberdeen Hotel **41**
Albergo Campo de' Fiori **5**
Albergo Cesari **8**
Albergo del Sole
  al Pantheon **9**
Alexandra **31**
Casa Kolbe **4**
Colosseum Hotel **1**
Excelsior **35**
Hassler **27**
Hotel Atlante Garden **15**

Hotel Atlante Star **16**
Hotel Caravaggio **52**
Hotel Cecil **30**
Hotel Columbus **11**
Hotel Condotti **20**
Hotel Corot **49**
Hotel d' Inghliterra **21**
Hotel de la Ville
  Inter-Continental Roma **28**
Hotel Duca d'Alba **2**
Hotel Eden **33**

Hotel Emmaus **12**
Hotel Gregoriana **25**
Hotel Internazionale **29**
Hotel Madrid **23**
Hotel Marcella **37**
Hotel Margutta **18**
Hotel Massimo d' Azeglio **44**
Hotel Mediterraneo **45**
Hotel Nerva **3**
Hotel Oxford **36**
Hotel Pavia **47**

Hotel Piazza di Spagna **22**
Hotel Ranieri **39**
Hotel Raphael **10**
Hotel Rex **42**
Hotel Trinità dei Monti **32**
Hotel Venezia **50**
La Residenza **34**
Le Grand Hotel **40**
Mecenate Palace Hotel **51**
Medici **38**
Pension Alimandi **13**

3-0851

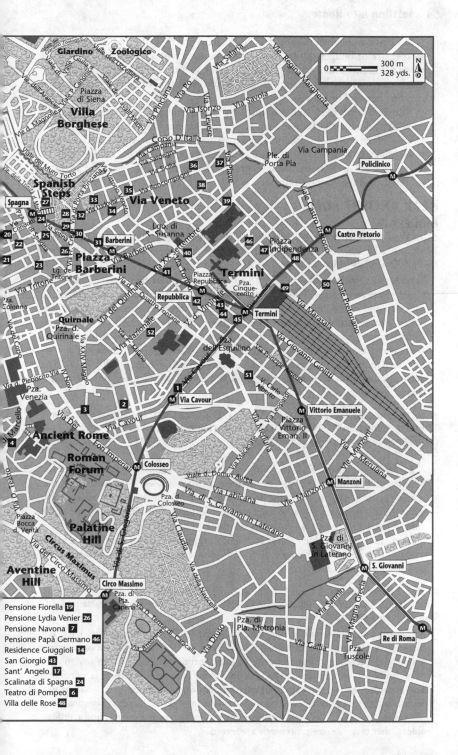

Pensione Fiorella **19**
Pensione Lydia Venier **26**
Pensione Navona **7**
Pensione Papà Germano **46**
Residence Giuggioli **14**
San Giorgio **43**
Sant' Angelo **17**
Scalinata di Spagna **24**
Teatro di Pompeo **6**
Villa delle Rose **48**

Most well-recommended hotels in Rome have private baths, but in some of the inexpensive or budget choices you'll have to share with other guests. Nearly all hotels are heated in the cooler months, but not all are air-conditioned in summer, which can be vitally important during July and August. The deluxe and first-class ones are, but after that it's a toss-up.

Nearly all hotels today quote an inclusive rate, including service and value-added taxes—but double-check upon arrival. It's rare for Roman hotels to have private garages. Hotel reception desks will advise about nearby garages, where fees usually range from 6,000L to 60,000L ($3.60 to $36). Of course, the higher price would be for garage space in the heart of Rome, whereas the lower price would be for an open-air, unguarded space on the outskirts.

NEAR ANCIENT ROME
MODERATE

Colosseum Hotel. Via Sforza 10, 00184 Roma. ☎ **06/482-7228.** Fax 06/482-7285. 50 rms. TV TEL. 170,000L–220,000L ($102–$132) double. Rates include breakfast. AE, DC, MC, V. Parking 30,000L ($19.20). Metro: Cavour.

Set two short blocks southwest of the Santa Maria Maggiore Basilica, the Colosseum Hotel offers comfortable (albeit small) but affordable accommodations. Someone with flair and lots of lira notes designed the public areas and upper hallways, which have a hint of baronial grandeur. The bedrooms are furnished with well-conceived antique reproductions (beds of heavy carved wood, dark-paneled wardrobes, leatherwood chairs)—and all with monklike white walls and sometimes rather old-fashioned plumbing. Air-conditioning is available on request for 20,000L ($12). The drawing room, with its long refectory table, white walls, red tiles, and provincial armchairs, invites lingering.

Hotel Duca d'Alba. Via Leonina 14, 00184 Roma. ☎ **06/484-471.** Fax 06/488-4840. 27 rms, 11 with shower only. A/C MINIBAR TV TEL. 190,000L ($114) double with shower only, 270,000L ($162) double with bath. Rates include breakfast. AE, DC, MC, V. Parking 35,000L ($21). Metro: Cavour.

A bargain close to the Roman Forum and the Colosseum, this hotel lies in the Suburra *quartier* where the "plebes" of ancient Rome resided. This sector of Rome is being gentrified—it had become pretty seedy—and this hotel is part of that renaissance. Although completely renovated and air-conditioned, it still retains some of the aura of the 19th century, when it was first built. The bedrooms are tasteful, even a bit decorated, with soothing colors and light wood pieces and restored private baths. The most desirable rooms are the four with private balconies. The rooms also have personal safes and hair dryers.

✪ **Hotel Nerva.** Via Tor di Conti 3-5. 00184 Roma. ☎ **06/678-1835.** Fax 06/699-22204. 19 rms. AC MINIBAR TV TEL. 200,000L–325,000L ($128–$208). Rates include breakfast. AE, DC, MC, V. Metro: Colosseo.

Some of its walls and foundations date from the 1400s, others a century later, but fortunately, the modern amenities only date back to 1997. The site, set on a terrace above, and a few steps away from the Roman Forum, would appeal to any student of archaeology and literature. The welcome from the Cirulli brothers is warm and accommodating. You can expect an environment that's accented with wood panels, terra-cotta tiles, and, in the case of some of the bedrooms, the building's original, very old ceiling beams. Otherwise, furniture is serviceable, contemporary, and comfortable. Other than breakfast, no meals are served.

INEXPENSIVE

Casa Kolbe. Via San Teodoro 44. ☎ **06/679-4974.** 65 rms. TEL. 115,000L ($69) double.
AE, DC, MC, V. Metro: Circo Massimo.

More than many of its competitors, this three-story hotel receives groups of travelers from North America and Germany, who arrive *en masse* by bus. (Many are students form Colorado and Louisiana, and members of senior citizens groups from virtually everywhere.) Bedrooms, painted in old-fashioned tones of deep red and brown, evoke the decorative styles of around 1900, and are deliberately very simple, well scrubbed, and in some cases, a bit battered from frequent use. Many overlook a small garden, and the hotel's location, underneath the Palatine, is convenient to the archaeological treasures of Old Rome. Although you'll have to look hard to find evidence of it, the hotel was built on ancient Roman foundations and functioned during separate periods of the Middle Ages as both a convent and monastery. The in-house dining room, which is open only to residents, serves set menus priced at 25,000L ($15) each. The hotel, incidentally, was named in honor of Maximilian Kolbe, a Polish-born resistance fighter killed by the Nazis during World War II.

NEAR CAMPO DE' FIORI
MODERATE

✪ **Teatro di Pompeo.** Largo del Pallaro 8, 00186 Roma. ☎ **06/6830-0170.** Fax 06/6880-5531. 13 rms. A/C TV TEL. 280,000L ($168) double. Rates include breakfast. AE, DC, MC, V. Bus: 46, 62, or 64

Built on top of the ruins of the Theater of Pompey, which dates from about 55 B.C., this small charmer lies near the spot where Julius Caesar met his end. Intimate and refined, it's on a quiet piazzetta near the Palazzo Farnese and Campo de' Fiori. The bedrooms, all doubles, are decorated in an old-fashioned Italian style with hand-painted tiles. The beamed ceilings date from the days of Michelangelo. There's no restaurant, but breakfast is served. Since this is such a historic gem with so few rooms, reserve as early as possible.

INEXPENSIVE

✪ **Albergo Campo de' Fiori.** Via del Biscione 6, 00186 Roma. ☎ **06/6880-6865.** Fax 06/687-6003. 27 rms, 9 with bath (shower); 1 honeymoon suite. 140,000L ($84) double without bath; 160,000L ($96) double with shower only; 200,000L ($120) double with bath; 175,000L ($105) triple without bath; 200,000L ($120) triple with shower only; 250,000L ($150) triple with bath. Rates include breakfast. MC, V. Bus: 46, 62, or 64 from the Termini to Museo di Roma; then arm yourself with a good map for the walk.

This seems to be everybody's favorite budget hideaway. Right in the historic center of Rome in a market area that has existed since the 1500s, this cozy, narrow six-story hotel offers rustic rooms, many quite tiny and sparsely adorned, others with a lot of character. The best, on the first floor, have been renovated. Yours might have a ceiling of clouds and blue skies along with mirrored walls. The best accommodation is the honeymoon suite on the sixth floor, with a canopied king-size bed. (Honeymooners beware: There's no elevator.) Guests can enjoy the panorama from the terrace overlooking the vegetable-and-flower market below, and, in the distance, St. Peter's.

NEAR PIAZZA NAVONA & THE PANTHEON
VERY EXPENSIVE

✪ **Albergo del Sole al Pantheon.** Piazza della Rotonda 63, 00186 Roma. ☎ **06/678-0441.** Fax 06/6994-0689. 26 rms, 4 suites. A/C MINIBAR TV TEL. 500,000L ($300) double; 650,000L ($390) suite. Rates include breakfast. AE, DC, MC, V. Parking 35,000L ($21). Bus: 119.

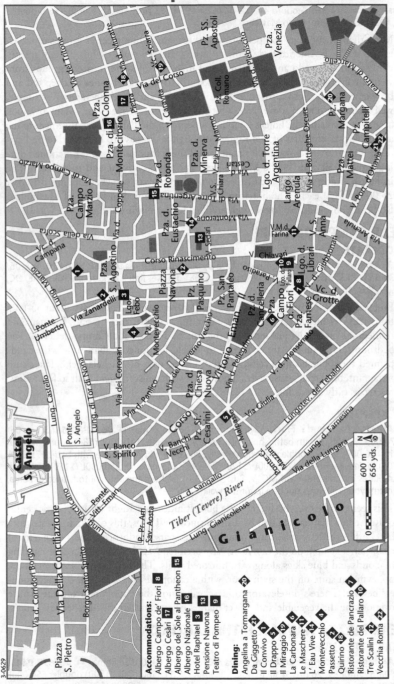

Accommodations:

Albergo Campo de' Fiori **8**
Albergo Cesàri **17**
Albergo del Sole al Pantheon **16**
Albergo Nazionale **13**
Hotel Raphael **3**
Pensione Navona **9**
Teatro di Pompeo **15**

Dining:

Angelina a Tormargana **20**
Da Giggetto **21**
Il Convivo **1**
Il Drappo **5**
Il Miraggio **19**
La Carbonara **6**
Le Maschere **11**
L' Eau Vive **14**
Montevecchio **4**
Passetto **2**
Quirino **18**
Ristorante de Pancrazio **7**
Ristorante del Pallaro **10**
Tre Scalini **12**
Vecchia Roma **22**

3-0629

The Albergo del Sole al Pantheon, overlooking the Pantheon, is an absolute gem. The present-day *albergo* is one of the oldest hotels in the world; the first records of it as a hostelry appear in 1467. Long known as a retreat for emperors and sorcerers, the hotel has hosted such guests as Frederick III of the Habsburg family. Later it drew such distinguished company as Jean-Paul Sartre and his companion, Simone de Beauvoir. Today the rooms are exquisitely furnished and decorated with period pieces and stylized reproductions.

Hotel Raphael. Largo Febo 2, 00186 Roma. ☎ **06/682-831.** Fax 06/687-8993. 53 rms, 20 suites. A/C MINIBAR TV TEL. 475,000L–655,000L ($285–$393) double; 615,000L–710,000L ($369–$426) suite. AE, DC, MC, V. Bus: 70, 81, 87, or 115.

In the heart of ancient Rome, adjacent to Piazza Navona, this hotel is within easy walking distance of many of Rome's attractions. Its rooftop garden terrace boasts a panorama of the ancient city. The charming ivy-covered facade invites you to enter the lobby, which is decorated with antiques that might rival local museums. Some of the suites have private terraces, and all the well-appointed bedrooms have direct-dial phones and satellite TV. Some of the rooms are quite small, however.

Dining/Entertainment: The elegant restaurant and bar, Café Picasso, serves a French/Italian hybrid cuisine.

Services: Room service, baby-sitting, laundry, and currency exchange.

Facilities: Fitness room.

MODERATE

Albergo Cesàri. Via di Pietra 89A, 00186 Roma. ☎ **06/679-2386.** Fax 06/679-0882. 50 rms, 40 with bath. A/C TV TEL. 170,000L–180,000L ($102–$108) double without bath, 200,000L–230,000L ($120–$138) double with bath; 245,000L–280,000L ($147–$168) triple with bath; 285,000L–315,000L ($171–$189) quad with bath. AE, DC, MC, V. Parking 45,000L ($27). Bus: 492 from Termini.

The Albergo Cesàri, on an ancient street in the old quarter of Rome, has occupied its desirable location between the Trevi Fountain and the Pantheon since 1787. Its guests have included Garibaldi and Stendhal, and its well-preserved exterior harmonizes with the Temple of Neptune and many little antique shops nearby. The bedrooms have mostly functional modern pieces, but there are a few traditional trappings as well to maintain character. In 1996, 16 bedrooms and the breakfast room were completely renovated.

INEXPENSIVE

Pensione Navona. Via dei Sediari 8, 00186 Roma. ☎ **06/686-4203.** Fax 06/6880-3802. 26 rms, 22 with bath (shower). 125,000L ($75) double without bath; 140,000L ($84) double with bath. Rates include breakfast. No credit cards. Bus: 70, 81, 87, or 115.

Although the rooms are not as glamorous as the exterior of this palace, the Pensione Navona offers clean and decent accommodations, many of which have been renovated and some of which open to views of the building's central (and quiet) courtyard. Run by an Australian-born family of Italian descent, the place has tiled bathrooms, ceilings high enough to relieve the midsummer heat, and an array of architectural oddities (the legacy of the continual construction this palace has undergone since 1360). The *pensione* lies on a small street that radiates out from the southeastern tip of Piazza Navona.

NEAR PIAZZA DI SPAGNA & PIAZZA DEL POPOLO

VERY EXPENSIVE

Hassler. Piazza Trinità dei Monti 6, 00187 Roma. ☎ **800/223-6800** in the U.S., or 06/699-340. Fax 06/678-9991. 85 rms, 15 suites. A/C MINIBAR TV TEL. 650,000L–980,000L

🙂 Family-Friendly Hotels

Cavalieri Hilton *(see p. 113)*   This hotel is like a resort at Monte Mario, with a swimming pool, gardens, and plenty of grounds for children to run and play, yet it's only 15 minutes from the center of Rome, reached by the hotel shuttle bus.

Hotel Massimo d'Azeglio *(see p. 106)*   Near the Stazione Termini, this place has long been a family favorite. The rooms are large, well kept, and comfortable, and the well-trained staff is solicitous of children.

Hotel Ranieri *(see p. 108)*   This hotel offers a family-style atmosphere in rooms that are air-conditioned with private bath. Many are large enough to house families of three or four, and baby cots are on hand as well.

Hotel Venezia *(see p. 108)*   At this good, moderately priced family hotel near the Stazione Termini, the rooms have been renovated and most are large enough for extra beds for children.

($390–$588) double; from 1,600,000L ($960) suite. AE, DC, MC, V. Parking 40,000L ($24). Metro: Piazza di Spagna.

The Hassler, the only deluxe hotel in this old part of Rome, uses the Spanish Steps as its grand entrance. The original 1885 Hassler was rebuilt in 1944, and while the crown worn by the Hassler is a bit tarnished these days (as is the tiara of the Grand), both hostelries have such a mystique that they continue to prosper and endure in spite of their overpriced rooms. The brightly colored rooms, the lounges with a mixture of modern and traditional furnishings, and the bedrooms with their "Italian Park Avenue" trappings all strike a faded 1930s note.

The bedrooms, some of which are small, have a personalized look—Oriental rugs, tasteful draperies at the French windows, brocade furnishings, comfortable beds, and (the nicest touch of all) bowls of fresh flowers. Some rooms have balconies with views of the city. Each accommodation contains a private bath, usually with two sinks and a bidet. In spite of all this, the Excelsior, for the most part, has better rooms.

Dining/Entertainment: The Hassler Roof Restaurant, on the top floor, is a favorite with visitors and Romans alike for its fine cuisine and view. Its Sunday brunch is a popular rendezvous time in Rome. The Hassler Bar is ideal for an aperitif or a drink; in the evening it has piano music.

Services: Room service, telex and fax, limousine, in-room massages, in-house laundry.

Facilities: Fitness center, tennis court (in summer), free bicycles available; nearby garage.

Hotel de la Ville Inter-Continental Roma. Via Sistina 67–69, 00187 Roma. ☎ **800/ 327-0200** in the U.S. and Canada, or 06/67-331. Fax 06/678-4213. 192 rms, 23 suites. A/C MINIBAR TV TEL. 532,000L–640,000L ($319.20–$384) double; from 900,000L ($540) suite. Rates include breakfast. AE, DC, MC, V. Parking 35,000L ($21). Metro: Piazza di Spagna or Barberini.

The Hotel de la Ville Inter-Continental Roma looks deluxe (it's officially rated first class) from the minute you walk through the revolving door, where a smartly uniformed doorman immediately greets you. Once inside this palace, built in the 19th century on the site of the ancient Gardens of Lucullus, you'll find Oriental rugs, marble tables, brocade-covered furniture, and a staff who speak English. There are endless corridors leading to what at first seems a maze of ornamental lounges, all elegantly upholstered and hung with their quota of crystal lighting fixtures. Some of

Accommodations & Dining Near Piazza di Spagna

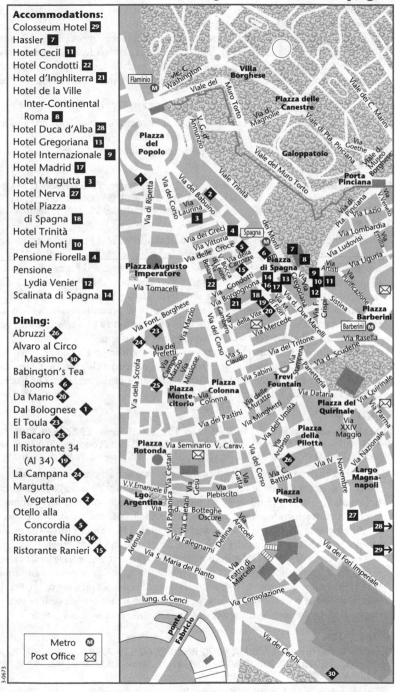

Accommodations:
Colosseum Hotel 29
Hassler 7
Hotel Cecil 11
Hotel Condotti 22
Hotel d'Inghliterra 21
Hotel de la Ville
   Inter-Continental
   Roma 8
Hotel Duca d'Alba 28
Hotel Gregoriana 13
Hotel Internazionale 9
Hotel Madrid 17
Hotel Margutta 3
Hotel Nerva 27
Hotel Piazza
   di Spagna 18
Hotel Trinità
   dei Monti 10
Pensione Fiorella 4
Pensione
   Lydia Venier 12
Scalinata di Spagna 14

Dining:
Abruzzi 26
Alvaro al Circo
   Massimo 30
Babington's Tea
   Rooms 6
Da Mario 20
Dal Bolognese 1
El Toula 23
Il Bacaro 25
Il Ristorante 34
   (Al 34) 19
La Campana 24
Margutta
   Vegetariano 2
Otello alla
   Concordia 5
Ristorante Nino 16
Ristorante Ranieri 15

Metro M
Post Office ✉

3-0673

99

the public rooms have a sort of 1930s elegance, others are strictly baroque, and in the middle of it all is an open courtyard.

The bedrooms and the public areas have been completely renovated in a beautifully classic and yet up-to-date way. The higher rooms with balconies have the most panoramic views of Rome to be found anywhere, and all guests are free to use the roof terrace with the same view. Many savvy guests prefer this hotel to the overpriced glory of the Hassler next door.

Dining/Entertainment: La Piazzetta de la Ville Restaurant, on the second floor overlooking the garden, serves an Italian and international cuisine. The hotel also has an American bar with a pianist during cocktail hours.

Services: Room service (24 hours), baby-sitting, laundry and valet service.

Facilities: Roof terrace.

✪ **Hotel d'Inghliterra.** Via Bocca di Leone 14, 00187 Roma. ☎ **06/69-981.** Fax 06/6992-2243. 86 rms, 12 suites. A/C MINIBAR TV TEL. 574,000L ($344.40) double; 650,000L ($390) triple; 994,000L ($596.40) suite. Rates include breakfast. AE, DC, MC, V. Metro: Piazza di Spagna.

Hotel d'Inghliterra nostalgically holds onto its traditions and heritage, even though it has been completely renovated. The most fashionable small hotel in Rome, it has hosted big names from Anatole France, Ernest Hemingway, and Franz Liszt to Alec Guinness. (In the 19th century the king of Portugal met here with the pope.) The bedrooms have mostly old pieces—gilt and lots of marble, mahogany chests, and glittery mirrors complemented with modern conveniences. Some, however, are just too small. The preferred bedrooms are higher up, opening onto a tile terrace, with a balustrade and a railing covered with flowering vines and plants.

Dining/Entertainment: The hotel's restaurant, the **Roman Garden,** serves excellent Roman dishes. The English-style bar with its paneled walls, tip-top tables, and old lamps casting soft light is a favorite gathering spot in the evening. The Roman Garden Lounge offers light lunches and snacks.

EXPENSIVE

✪ **Scalinata di Spagna.** Piazza Trinità dei Monti 17, 00187 Roma. ☎ **06/679-3006.** Fax 06/6994-0598. 15 rms, 1 suite. A/C MINIBAR TV TEL. 420,000L ($252) double; 500,000L ($300) triple; 700,000L ($420) suite. AE, MC, V. Parking 45,000L ($27). Metro: Piazza di Spagna.

This hotel near the Spanish Steps has always been one of the most sought-after in Rome. It's right at the top of the steps, directly across from the Hassler, in a delightful little building—only two floors are visible from the outside—nestled between much larger structures, with four relief columns across the facade and window boxes with bright blossoms. The recently redecorated interior is like an old inn—the public rooms are small with bright print slipcovers, old clocks, and low ceilings.

The decorations vary radically from one room to the next. Some have low, beamed ceilings and ancient-looking wood furniture; others have loftier ceilings and more run-of-the-mill appointments. Everything is spotless and most pleasing to the eye. In season, breakfast is served on the patio or on the roof-garden terrace with its sweeping view of the dome of St. Peter's across the Tiber. Reserve well in advance.

MODERATE

Hotel Cecil. Via Francesco Crispi 55A, 00187 Roma. ☎ **06/679-7998.** Fax 06/679-7996. 41 rms. TV TEL. 300,000L–350,000L ($180–$210) double. Rates include breakfast. AE, MC, V. Parking 25,000L–30,000L ($15–$18). Metro: Piazza Barberini.

This hotel, in a 17th-century building, lies in the heart of Rome, near Piazza di Spagna and the Fontana di Trevi. It has entertained everybody from Casanova to

Henrik Ibsen, who wrote *Brandt* and conceived *Peer Gynt* here. Today it's attractively streamlined, with comfortable bedrooms, each with a private newly renovated bath, satellite TV, and radio. Since this is an extremely noisy part of Rome, double windows have been installed in accommodations facing the busy street. There's a panoramic terrace for viewing "monumental Rome."

Hotel Condotti. Via Mario de' Fiori 37, 00187 Roma. ☎ **06/679-4661.** Fax 06/679-0484. 14 rms, 2 minisuites. A/C MINIBAR TV TEL. 230,000L–320,000L ($147.20–$204.80) double; 290,000L–350,000L ($185.60–$224) minisuite. Rates include breakfast. AE, DC, MC, V. Metro: Piazza di Spagna.

Small, choice, and terrific for shoppers intent on being near the city's toniest boutiques, this hotel is chic, intimate, and comfortable. Other than a cooperative and hardworking staff, it offers few amenities (no bar, no restaurant). However, there is a breakfast room. The roster of comfortably modern, mostly blue-and-white bedrooms may be devoid of any sense of historic nostalgia, but they're comfortable and soothing. Most of the staff speaks English.

Hotel Gregoriana. Via Gregoriana 18, 00187 Roma. ☎ **06/679-4269.** Fax 06/678-4258. 19 rms. A/C TV TEL. 320,000L ($192) double. Rates include breakfast. No credit cards. Parking 25,000L ($15). Metro: Piazza di Spagna.

Although surrounded by much more expensive neighbors like the pricey Hassler, the small Gregoriana has some fans of its own—mainly members of the Italian fashion industry. The ruling matriarch of an aristocratic family left the building to an order of nuns in the 19th century, but they eventually retreated to other quarters. Today there might be a slightly more elevated spirituality in Room C than in the rest of the hotel, as it used to be a chapel. Throughout the hotel, the smallish rooms provide comfort and Italian design. The elevator cage is a black-and-gold art deco fantasy, and the door to each room has a reproduction of an Erté print whose fanciful characters indicate the letter designating that room. You'll pay the bill in the tiny, rattan-covered lobby.

Hotel Internazionale. Via Sistina 79, 00187 Roma. ☎ **06/6994-1823.** Fax 06/678-4764. 42 rms, 2 suites. A/C MINIBAR TV TEL. 315,000L ($189) double; from 700,000L ($420) suite. Rates include breakfast. AE, MC, V. Parking 35,000L ($21). Metro: Piazza di Spagna or Barberini.

Although this *albergo* sits on the ruins of a series of buildings known as Horti Lucullani from the 1st century B.C., the present structure is rooted in a series of buildings dating from the 1500s. Since 1870 the present hotel has operated, just half a block from the top of the Spanish Steps, on one of the most fashionable shopping streets of Rome. It has antique charm of its own, in spite of the modern intrusions. Accommodations facing the narrow Via Sistina have double windows to cut down the noise. Some antique wingback chairs and coffered ceilings charm the bedrooms, contrasting with contemporary built-in pieces.

Hotel Madrid. Via Mario de' Fiori 93–95, 00187 Roma. ☎ **06/699-1511.** Fax 06/679-1653. 26 rms, 7 suites. A/C MINIBAR TV TEL. 290,000L ($174) double; 400,000L ($240) suite for four. Rates include breakfast. AE, DC, MC, V. Parking 34,000L–39,000L ($20.40–$23.40). Metro: Piazza di Spagna.

The Hotel Madrid evokes *fin-de-siècle* Roma in its interior in spite of the modern character of its well-maintained and comfortable, if rather minimalist, bedrooms. The hotel appeals to the individual traveler who wants a good standard of service. Guests often take their breakfast amid ivy and blossoming plants on the roof terrace with a panoramic view of rooftops and the distant dome of St. Peter's. Some of the doubles are large, equipped with small scatter rugs, veneer armoires, and shuttered windows.

Others are quite small—so make sure you know what you're getting before you check in. The hotel is an ocher building with a shuttered facade on a narrow street practically in the heart of the boutique area centering around Via Frattina, near the Spanish Steps.

Hotel Piazza di Spagna. Via Mario de' Fiori 61, 00187 Roma. ☎ **06/679-6412.** Fax 06/679-0654. 16 rms. A/C MINIBAR TV TEL. 280,000L–310,000L ($168–$186) double. Rates include breakfast. AE, MC, V. Metro: Piazza di Spagna. Bus: 590.

Set about a block from the downhill side of the Spanish Steps, this hotel was once just an unknown, run-down *pensione* until new owners in the 1990s took it over and substantially upgraded it. Originally built in the early 1800s, it has always occupied prime real estate. It's small but classic, with a warm, inviting atmosphere. Some rooms even have a Jacuzzi. The decor of the rooms is functional and streamlined.

Hotel Trinitàdei Monti. Via Sistina 91, 00187 Roma. ☎ **06/679-7206.** Fax 06/699-0111. 23 rms. MINIBAR TV TEL. 200,000L–250,000L ($128–$160) double. Rates include breakfast. AE, MC, V. Metro: Barberini or Piazza di Spagna.

Set between two of the most oft-visited piazzas in Rome (Barberini and di Spagna), this is a well-maintained and friendly hotel. Bedrooms come in subdued colors and are comfortable if not flashy. They're outfitted with elaborate, herringbone-patterned parquet floors and big windows flooding the interior with sunlight. The hotel's social center is a simple coffee bar near the reception desk. Don't expect anything terribly fancy, but the welcome is warm and the location is ultra-convenient.

INEXPENSIVE

Hotel Margutta. Via Laurina 34, 00187 Roma. ☎ **06/322-3674.** Fax 06/320-0395. 21 rms. 156,000L ($93.60) double; 210,000L ($126) triple. Rates include breakfast. AE, DC, MC, V. Metro: Flaminio.

The Hotel Margutta, on a cobblestone street near Piazza del Popolo, offers attractively decorated rooms and a helpful staff. The hotel is housed in a 200-year-old building that was transformed into a small hotel in 1961. Located off the paneled, black stone–floored lobby is a simple breakfast room with framed lithographs. The best rooms are on the top floor, each with a view. Two of these three rooms (nos. 50 and 51) share a terrace, and the larger bedroom has a private terrace. Management always reserves the right to charge a 20% to 35% supplement for these accommodations. Be alert to the fact that the hotel is not air-conditioned, nor does it have room phones.

Pensione Fiorella. Via del Babuino 196, 00187 Roma. ☎ **06/361-0597.** 7 rms, none with bath. 95,000L ($57) double. Rates include breakfast. No credit cards. Metro: Flaminio.

A few steps from Piazza del Popolo is this utterly basic but comfortable *pensione*. Antonio Albano and his family are one of the best reasons to stay here—they speak little English, but their humor and warm welcome make renting one of their well-scrubbed bedrooms a lot like visiting a lighthearted Italian relative. The bedrooms open onto a high-ceilinged hallway. The doors of the Fiorella shut at 1am. Reservations can only be made a day before you check in.

Pensione Lydia Venier. Via Sistina 42, 00187 Roma. ☎ **06/679-1744.** Fax 06/679-7263. 30 rms, 10 with shower only, 10 with bath. TV TEL. 150,000L ($90) double without bath; 180,000L ($108) double with shower only; 200,000L ($120) double with bath. Rates include breakfast. AE, DC, MC, V. Metro: Piazza Barberini or Piazza di Spagna.

This respectable *pensione* is set on one of the upper floors of a gracefully proportioned apartment building on a street that juts out from the top of the Spanish Steps. The bedrooms are utterly simple with understated furnishings—a dignified combination of slightly battered modern and antique and an occasional reminder of an earlier era (such as a ceiling fresco). The rooms include both a TV and a telephone. The service here is wonderful, and the staff is more than accommodating. They go out of their way to be helpful, especially to those who don't speak Italian. The location is ideal, with its proximity to the Spanish Steps, an American Express office, a subway stop, three different piazzas, and the Villa Borghese.

NEAR VIA VENETO
VERY EXPENSIVE

✪ **Excelsior.** Via Vittorio Veneto 125, 00187 Roma. ☎ **800/325-3589** in the U.S. and Canada, or 06/47-081. Fax 06/482-6205. 321 rms, 44 suites. A/C MINIBAR TV TEL. 580,000L–640,000L ($348–$384) double; from 1,100,000L ($660) suite. AE, MC, V. Metro: Piazza Barberini.

This hotel is far livelier and better than its sibling, the Grand. It's also got a lot more *joie de vivre*, even though Elizabeth Taylor checked out a long time ago. She has been replaced by Arab princesses and international financiers. The Excelsior (pronounced Ess-*shell*-see-or) is a limestone palace whose baroque corner tower, which looks right over the U.S. Embassy, is a landmark in Rome. Guests enter a string of cavernous reception rooms with thick rugs, marble floors, gilded garlands and pilasters decorating the walls, and Empire furniture (supported by winged lions and the like). Everything looks just a little bit tarnished today, and the celebrities have gone elsewhere, but the Excelsior endures, seemingly as eternal as Rome itself. In no small part that's because of the exceedingly hospitable staff.

The rooms come in two basic varieties: new (the result of a major renovation) and traditional. The old ones are a bit shopworn while the newer rooms have more imaginative color schemes and very plush carpeting. The doubles are spacious and elegantly furnished, often with antiques and silk curtains. The furnishings in the singles are also of high quality. Most of the bedrooms are different, many with a sumptuous Hollywood-style bath—marble-walled with separate bath and shower, sinks, bidet, and a mountain of fresh towels.

Dining/Entertainment: The Excelsior Bar, open daily from 10:30am to 1am, is the most famous on Via Vittorio Veneto, and La Cupola is known for its national and regional cuisine, with dietetic and kosher food prepared on request.

Services: Room service, baby-sitting, laundry and valet service.

Facilities: Beauty salon, barbershop.

✪ **Hotel Eden.** Via Ludovisi 49, 00187 Roma. ☎ **800/225-5843** in the U.S., or 06/478-121. Fax 06/482-1584. 101 rms, 11 suites. A/C MINIBAR TV TEL. 720,000L–850,000L ($432–$510) double; from 1,600,000L ($960) suite. AE, DC, MC, V. Parking 50,000L ($30). Bus: 119.

For several generations after its inauguration in 1889, this richly ornate five-story hotel reigned over one of the most stylish shopping neighborhoods in the world. Hemingway, Maria Callas, Ingrid Bergman, Fellini—all the big names checked in here during its heyday. In 1994, after its purchase in 1989 by Trusthouse Forte, it reopened after 2 years (and $20 million) of radical renovations that enhanced its original *fin-de-siècle* grandeur and added the modern amenities its five-star status calls for. Set near the top of the Spanish Steps, its hilltop position guarantees a panoramic view over the city from most bedrooms that guests consider worth the rather high expense. The rooms contain marble-sheathed bathrooms, draperies worthy of *Architectural Digest*, and decor that harks back to the late 19th century. Understated elegance is the rule.

Dining/Entertainment: A piano bar, and a glamorous restaurant, La Terrazza, that's recommended separately (see "Dining," later in this chapter).

Services: Concierge, 24-hour room service, dry cleaning/laundry, newspaper delivery on request, secretarial service (proir notification necessary), valet parking.
Facilities: Gym and health club on the premises.

MODERATE

Alexandra. Via Vittorio Veneto 18, 00187 Roma. ☎ **06/488-1943.** Fax 06/487-1804. 39 rms, 6 suites. A/C MINIBAR TV TEL. 280,000L ($168) double; 320,000L ($192) triple; 360,000L ($216) suite. Rates include buffet breakfast. AE, DC, MC, V. Parking 35,000L ($21). Metro: Piazza Barberini.

Although lots of guidebooks ignore it, this is one of your few chances to stay on Via Veneto without going broke. Set behind the dignified stone facade of what was originally a 19th-century private mansion, this hotel offers immaculately maintained, comfortable rooms filled with antique furniture and modern conveniences. Rooms facing the front are exposed to the roaring traffic and animated street life of Via Veneto; those in back are quieter but with less of a view. No meals are served other than breakfast, although the hall porter or a member of the staff can carry drinks to clients in the reception area. The breakfast room is especially appealing: Inspired by an Italian garden, it was designed by the noted architect Paolo Portoghesi.

Hotel Marcella. Via Flavia 106, 00187 Roma. ☎ **06/47-46-451.** Fax 06/481-5832. 75 rms. A/C MINIBAR TV TEL. 300,000L ($192) double. Rates include breakfast. AE, DC, MC, V. Bus: 37, 60, 61, or 62.

Originally built in the 1920s, this six-story hotel was renovated into its present three-star status in the early 1990s. Bedrooms are contemporary yet individual, each slightly different from its neighbor in motif and color scheme. They're comfortable enough to take up residence in for several days without feeling cramped or anonymous. The architectural highlight of the hotel is the glass-enclosed conservatory on the uppermost floor, site of panoramic breakfasts that extend out over the Via Veneto neighborhood where the place is located. Other than breakfast, no meals are served, although there's an American-style bar on the premises.

Hotel Oxford. Via Boncompagni 89, 00187 Roma. ☎ **06/4282-8952.** Fax 06/4281-5349. 57 rms, 2 suites. A/C MINIBAR TV TEL. 240,000L ($144) double; 290,000L ($174) triple; 350,000L ($210) suite. Rates include buffet breakfast. 20% reductions Jan–Mar 15, Aug, and Nov–Dec. AE, DC, MC, V. Parking 30,000L–50,000L ($18–$30). Bus: 56 or 58.

The centrally located Hotel Oxford is a decent, although not spectacular, choice adjacent to the Borghese Gardens. Recently renovated, the Oxford is now centrally heated and fully carpeted throughout. There's a pleasant lounge and Tony's bar (which serves snacks), plus a dining room offering a good Italian cuisine. The bedrooms, which were recently renovated, are now air-conditioned in summer and centrally heated in winter, with simple modern furnishings and full carpeting. The rooms are a bit sterile and functional in decor, but well maintained.

La Residenza. Via Emilia 22–24, 00187 Roma. ☎ **06/488-0789.** Fax 06/485721. 27 rms, 6 suites. A/C MINIBAR TV TEL. 287,000L–295,000L ($172.20–$177) double; 325,000L–340,000L ($195–$204) suite. Rates include buffet breakfast. AE, MC, V. Parking (limited) 5,000L ($3). Metro: Piazza Barberini.

La Residenza successfully combines the intimacy of a generously sized town house with the elegant appointments of a well-decorated four-star hotel. It's a bit old-fashioned and homelike, but is still a favorite among international travelers. The location is superb but noisy. The converted villa has an ivy-covered courtyard and a labyrinthine series of upholstered public rooms with Oriental rugs, Empire divans, oil portraits, and warmly accommodating cushioned rattan chairs. A series of terraces is scattered strategically throughout the hotel.

Accommodations & Dining Near Termini & Via Veneto

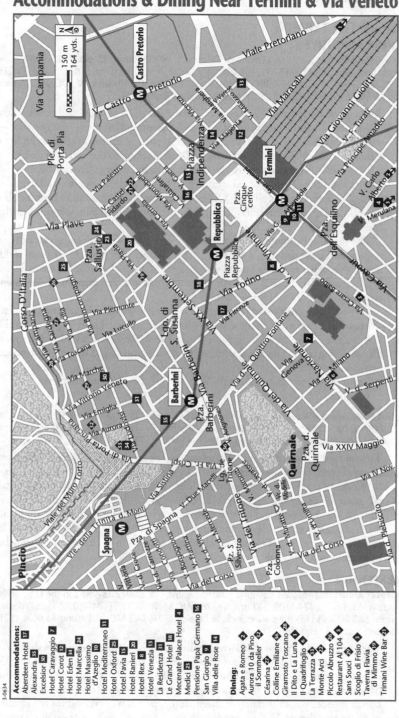

Accommodations:
Aberdeen Hotel 17
Alexandra 35
Excelsior 30
Hotel Caravaggio 7
Hotel Corot 12
Hotel Eden 34
Hotel Marcella 24
Hotel Massimo d'Azeglio 10
Hotel Mediterraneo 11
Hotel Oxford 25
Hotel Pavia 15
Hotel Ranieri 20
Hotel Rex 8
Hotel Venezia 13
La Residenza 31
Le Grand Hotel 18
Mecenate Palace Hotel 4
Medici 23
Pensione Papa Germano 16
San Giorgio 9
Villa delle Rose 14

Dining:
Agata e Romeo 4
Aurora 10 da Pino il Sommelier 27
Césarina 27
Colline Emiliane 45
Girarrosto Toscano 28
Il Dito e La Luna 5
Il Quadrifoglio 1
La Terrazza 22
Monte Arci 22
Piccolo Abruzzo 29
Restaurant Al 104 5
Sans Souci 29
Scoglio di Frisio 3
Taverna Flavia di Mimmo 26
Trimani Wine Bar 21

105

NEAR THE TERMINI
VERY EXPENSIVE

Le Grand Hotel. Via Vittorio Emanuele Orlando 3, 00185 Roma. ☎ **800/325-3589** in the U.S. and Canada, or 06/47-091. Fax 06/474-7307. 134 rms, 36 suites. A/C MINIBAR TV TEL. 580,000L–640,000L ($348–$384) double; from 900,000L ($540) suite. AE, DC, MC, V. Parking 50,000L–60,000L ($30–$36). Metro: Piazza della Repubblica.

When it was inaugurated by its creator, Cesar Ritz, in 1894, Le Grand struck a note of grandeur it has tried to maintain ever since. Its location near the railway station—once highly desirable—has lost its charm. The Hassler at the top of the Spanish Steps is more dramatically located, and many VIPs are flocking to the restored Eden. Only a few minutes from Via Veneto, the Grand looks like a large late-Renaissance palace, its five-floor facade covered with carved loggias, lintels, quoins, and cornices. Inside, the floors are marble with Oriental rugs, the walls are a riot of baroque plasterwork, and crystal chandeliers, Louis XVI furniture, potted palms, antique clocks, and wall sconces complete the picture.

The spacious bedrooms are conservatively decorated with matching curtains and carpets, and equipped with a dressing room and fully tiled bath. Every room is different, although some are less grand than you might expect from the impressive lobby. While most are traditional, with antique headboards and Venetian chandeliers, some are modern. Every room is soundproof.

Dining/Entertainment: The hotel's Le Grand Bar is an elegant meeting place where tea is served every afternoon—in winter, accompanied by a harpist or pianist. You can enjoy quick meals at the Salad Bar, or else try Le Restaurant, the hotel's more formal dining room. Dietetic and kosher foods can be arranged with advance notice. Service is first-rate.

Services: Room service (24 hours), baby-sitting, laundry and valet service.

Facilities: Beauty salon.

Hotel Massimo d'Azeglio. Via Cavour 18, 00184 Roma. ☎ **800/223-9832** in the U.S., or 06/487-0270. Fax 06/482-7386. 210 rms. A/C MINIBAR TV TEL. 440,000L ($264) double. Rates include breakfast. DC, MC, V. Parking 35,000L–45,000L ($21–$27). Metro: Termini.

This up-to-date hotel near the train station and opera was established as a small restaurant by one of the founders of an Italian hotel dynasty more than a century ago. In World War II it was a refuge for the king of Serbia and also a favorite with Italian generals. Today this centrally located hotel is the flagship of the Bettoja chain. Run by Angelo Bettoja and his charming wife, who hails from America's southland, it offers clean, comfortable accommodations, plus a bar and a well-trained staff. Its facade is one of the most elegant neoclassical structures in the area, and its lobby has been renovated, with light paneling.

EXPENSIVE

Hotel Mediterraneo. Via Cavour 15, 00184 Roma. ☎ **800/223-9832** in the U.S., or 06/488-4051. Fax 06/474-4105. 262 rms, 9 suites. A/C MINIBAR TV TEL. 480,000L ($288) double; from 580,000L ($348) suite. Rates include breakfast. AE, DC, MC, V. Parking 35,000L ($21). Metro: Stazione Termini.

The Hotel Mediterraneo sports vivid Italian art deco styling. Because of the war, it wasn't completed until 1944, but its blueprints were executed from 1936 to 1938 in anticipation of the 1942 World's Fair. Because of its position beside what Mussolini planned as his triumphant passageway through Rome, each of the local building codes was deliberately violated, and approval was granted for the creation of an unprecedented 10-floor hotel. Its height, coupled with its position on one of

Rome's hills, provides panoramic views from its roof garden and bar, which is especially charming at night.

Mario Loreti, one of Mussolini's favorite architects, was the genius who planned for an interior sheathing of gray marble, the richly allegorical murals of inlaid wood, and the art deco friezes ringing the ceilings of the enormous public rooms. Don't overlook the gracefully curved bar, crafted from illuminated cut crystal, or the ships' figureheads that adorn the ceiling of the wood-sheathed breakfast room. The lobby is also decorated with antique busts of Roman emperors, part of the Berttoja family's collection.

Our only quibble with this otherwise award-winning hotel involves the furniture in the bedrooms. Even the hotel's most ardent fans have to admit it's what you'd find in a 1940s summer camp in the Adirondacks. Rustic, slightly battered, solid, and dependable, it's a slight imperfection in an otherwise marvelous and historically evocative setting.

Hotel Rex. Via Torino 149, 00184 Roma. ☎ **06/482-4828.** Fax 06/488-2743. 48 rms, 2 suites. A/C MINIBAR TV TEL. 370,000L ($236.80) double; 500,000L ($320) suite. Rates include breakfast. AE, DC, MC, V. Metro: Piazza della Repubblica.

Its four-story facade is simpler than you might expect, considering this four-star hotel's illustrious origins. In the early 1700s, it functioned as the residence of the Spanish ambassador to the papal court, and served as the setting for a sometimes disconcerting blend of politics and religion. Around 1900, it was transformed into a prestigious hotel, and today retains some of the marble and paneled touches from that renovation. Accommodations are conservatively modern, frequently renovated, and contain soundproofing, marble bathrooms, and all the amenities you'd expect from a hotel of this price range. There's a bar on the premises, but the only meal served is breakfast.

Mecenate Palace Hotel. Via Carlo Alberto 3. 00185 Roma. ☎ **06/4470-2024.** Fax 06/446-1354. 59 rms, 3 suites. A/C MINIBAR TV TEL. 300,000L–470,000L ($192–$300.80) double; 500,000L ($320) suite. AE, DC, MC, V. Metro: Termini.

One of Rome's newest four-star hotels opened on the premises of what was once a private villa originally built in the Liberty (art nouveau) style around 1900. It rises five floors above a neighborhood near the city's main railway station. The pastel-colored bedrooms, with traces of the original turn-of-the-century detailing and contemporary furnishings, overlook such monuments as Santa Maria Maggiore, in the city's monumental core. Each contains a safe deposit box and multilanguage satellite TV. The hotel offers a bar and a dignified restaurant that serves lunch and dinner every day except Sunday, and a roof garden with sweeping views over Roman rooftops and the above-mentioned church.

San Giorgio. Via Giovanni Amendola 61, 00185 Roma. ☎ **800/223-9832** in the U.S., or 06/482-7341. Fax 06/488-3191. 186 rms, 5 suites. A/C MINIBAR TV TEL. 380,000L ($228) double; from 495,000L ($297) suite. Rates include breakfast. AE, DC, MC, V. Parking 35,000L–45,000L ($21–$27). Metro: Termini.

A four-star hotel built in 1940, the San Giorgio is constantly being improved by its founders, the Bettoja family (it was the first air-conditioned hotel in Rome, and is now also soundproof). It's connected to the Massimo d'Azeglio so guests can patronize its fine restaurant. The hotel is ideal for families, as many of its corner rooms can be converted into larger quarters. Each bedroom has a radio, along with other amenities that often lie behind wood-veneer doors. Breakfast is served in a light and airy room, and the staff is most helpful.

MODERATE

Aberdeen Hotel. Via Firenze 48, 00184 Roma. ☎ **06/482-3920.** Fax 06/482-1092. 26 rms. A/C MINIBAR TV TEL. 245,000L ($147) double. Rates include buffet breakfast. AE, DC, MC, V. Metro: Termini.

This is a completely renovated hotel near the Rome Opera House, central to both landmarks and the train station. It's in a quiet and fairly safe area of Rome—in front of the Ministry of Defense. The rooms are furnished with an uninspired modern styling and include modern amenities such as hair dryers. Only a breakfast buffet is served, but many inexpensive trattorie lie nearby.

Hotel Caravaggio. Via Palermo 73. 00184 Roma. ☎ **06/485-915.** Fax 06/474-363. 25 rms. MINIBAR TV TEL. 180,000L–250,000 ($115.20–$160) double. AE, DC, MC, V. Metro: Termini.

Originally built a century ago, in a location near the railway station that is not as stylish today as it used to be, this building was transformed into a hotel in the early 1970s. This hotel rises only two floors above a busy commercial neighborhood. Clients tend to return here year after year, partly because of its reasonable prices, no-nonsense dignity, and the unpretentious comfort of its soundproofed bedrooms. Most (but not all) contain air-conditioning. Breakfast is the only meal served. On the premises is a sauna and Jacuzzi with hydrotherapy as well as laundry facilities.

Hotel Ranieri. Via XX Settembre 43, 00187 Roma. ☎ **06/481-4467.** Fax 06/481-8834. 40 rms. A/C MINIBAR TV TEL. 180,000L–270,000L ($108–$162) double. Rates include breakfast. Weekend discounts granted in Jan, Feb, and Dec and daily discount rates in Aug. AE, MC, V. Parking 20,000L–30,000L ($12–$18). Metro: Piazza della Repubblica.

The Ranieri is a winning three-star hotel in a very old but freshly restored building. The guest rooms received a substantial renovation in 1995, complete with new furniture, carpets, wall coverings, and even new bathrooms. The location is good; from the hotel you can stroll to the Rome Opera, Piazza della Repubblica, and Via Vittorio Veneto. The public rooms, the lounge, and the dining room are attractively decorated, in part with contemporary art. You can arrange for a home-cooked meal in the dining room.

Hotel Venezia. Via Varese 18 (near Via Marghera), 00185 Roma. ☎ **06/445-7101.** Fax 800/526-5497 or 06/495-7687. 61 rms. A/C MINIBAR TV TEL. 235,000L ($141) double; 320,000L ($192) triple. Rates include breakfast. AE, DC, MC, V. Parking 30,000L ($18). Metro: Termini.

The Hotel Venezia is the type of place that restores your faith in affordably priced hotels. The location is good—three blocks from the railroad station, in a part-business, part-residential area dotted with a few old villas and palm trees. The Venezia had a total renovation in 1991, transforming it into a good-looking and cheerful hostelry with a charming collection of public rooms with brown marble floors. In some cases, the bedrooms are furnished with a 17th-century style, although some are beginning to look shopworn. All units have Murano chandeliers, and some have a balcony for surveying the action on the street below. The housekeeping is superb—the management really cares.

Medici. Via Flavia 96, 00187 Roma. ☎ **06/482-7319.** Fax 06/474-0767. 68 rms. MINIBAR TV TEL. 160,000L–250,000L ($96–$150) double. Rates include breakfast. AE, DC, MC, V. Parking 28,000L–35,000L ($16.80–$21). Metro: Piazza della Repubblica.

The Medici, built in 1906, is still a substantial hotel with easy access to the shops along Via XX Settembre and the train station. Many of its better rooms overlook an inner patio garden, with Roman columns holding up greenery and climbing ivy. The lounge, with its white coved ceiling, has many nooks connected by wide white arches. The furnishings in the public areas and the generous-sized rooms are traditional, with lots of antiques. The few rooms that are air-conditioned are 20,000L ($12) extra.

Villa delle Rose. Via Vicenza 5, 00185 Roma. ☎ **06/445-1788.** Fax 06/445-1639. 38 rms. A/C TV TEL. 240,000L–260,000L ($144–$156) double. Rates include breakfast. AE, DC, MC, V. Metro: Termini or Castro Pretorio.

Set less than two blocks north of the railway station, behind a dignified cut-stone facade inspired by the Renaissance, this hotel was originally built in the late 1800s as a private home. Despite many renovations, the ornate trappings of the wealthy family who constructed the place are still visible, including a set of Corinthian-capped marble columns in the lobby and a flagstone-covered terrace that fills part of a verdant garden in back. Much of the interior has been redecorated with traditional wall coverings and new carpets. Morning breakfasts in the garden, where rows of pink and red roses bloom, do a lot to add country flavor to an otherwise very urban and noisy location. The English-speaking staff is helpful and tactful.

INEXPENSIVE

Hotel Corot. Via Marghera 15–17, 00185 Roma. ☎ **06/4470-0900.** Fax 06/4470-0905. 20 rms. A/C MINIBAR TV TEL. 160,000L–190,000L ($96–$114) double; 180,000L–220,000L ($108–$132) triple; 200,000L–250,000L ($120–$150) quad. Rates include breakfast. 15% weekend discounts for multiple-night stays. AE, DC, MC, V. Parking 25,000L–28,000L ($15–$16.80). Metro: Termini.

Modernized and comfortable, this hotel occupies the second and third floors of a turn-of-the-century building that contains a handful of private apartments and another, somewhat inferior hotel. The Corot is a safe but lackluster bet north of the Termini, and far better than some of the horrors south of the station. Guests register in a small, paneled area on the building's street level, and then take an elevator to their respective floors. The bedrooms are airy, with high ceilings, and are filled with simple but traditional furniture and soothing colors. The bathrooms are modern and contain hair dryers. There's a residents' bar near a sun-flooded window in one of the public rooms.

Hotel Pavia. Via Gaeta 83, 00185 Roma. ☎ **06/483-801.** Fax 06/481-9090. 25 rms. A/C MINIBAR TV TEL. 160,000L–215,000L ($96–$129) double. Rates include breakfast. AE, DC, MC, V. Parking 15,000L–20,000L ($9–$12). Metro: Termini.

The Hotel Pavia is a popular choice on this quiet street near the gardens of the Baths of Diocletian. Established in the 1980s, it occupies a much-renovated century-old private villa. You'll pass through a wisteria-covered passageway that leads to the recently modernized reception area and the public rooms, tastefully covered in light-grained paneling with white lacquer accents and carpeting, where the staff is attentive and friendly.

The front rooms tend to be noisy, but that's the curse of all Termini hotels. Nevertheless, the rooms are comfortable and fairly attractive, with simple, modern wood furnishings and soothing colors. All in all, it's a safe haven in an unsafe area.

Pensione Papà Germano. Via Calatafimi 14A, 00185 Roma. ☎ **06/486-919.** 16 rms, 6 with bath. TEL. 68,000L ($40.80) double without bath, 80,000L ($48) double with bath; 80,000L ($48) triple without bath, 100,000L ($60) triple with bath. 10% discount Nov–Mar. AE, MC, V. Metro: Termini.

This is about as basic and simple as anything in this book. This 1892 *belle époque* building has undergone some recent renovations, yet retains its modest ambience. Chances are that your fellow travelers will arrive, backpack in tow, directly from the train station four blocks to the south. Located on a block-long street immediately east of the Baths of Diocletian, this *pensione* has simple, clean accommodations with plain furniture, hair dryers, well-maintained showers, and a high-turnover clientele of European and North American students. The energetic, English-speaking owner,

Gino Germano, offers advice on sightseeing to anyone who asks. The *pensione* doesn't serve breakfast, but there are dozens of cafes nearby that open early.

NEAR VATICAN CITY
VERY EXPENSIVE

✪ **Hotel Atlante Star.** Via Vitelleschi 34, 00193 Roma. ☎ **06/687-3233.** Fax 06/687-2300. 55 rms, 10 suites. A/C MINIBAR TV TEL. 525,000L ($315) double; from 600,000L ($360) suite. Rates include breakfast. AE, DC, MC, V. Parking 40,000L ($24). Metro: Ottaviano. Tram: 19 or 30.

The Atlante Star is a first-class hotel a short distance from the Vatican, with the most striking views of St. Peter's of any hotel in Rome. The tastefully renovated lobby is covered with dark marble, chrome trim, and lots of exposed wood, whereas the upper floors give the impression of being inside a luxuriously appointed ocean liner. This stems partly from the lavish use of curved and lacquered surfaces, walls uphol-stered in freshly colored printed fabrics, modern bathrooms, and wall-to-wall carpet-ing. Even the door handles are art deco–inspired. The rooms are small but posh, outfitted with all the modern comforts. There's also a royal suite with a Jacuzzi. If there's no room at this inn, the owner will try to get you a room at his less expen-sive Atlante Garden nearby.

Dining/Entertainment: The restaurant, Les Etoiles, is an elegant roof-garden choice at night, with a 360° panoramic view of Rome and an illuminated St. Peter's in the background. The flavorful cuisine is inspired in part by Venice.

Services: Room service (24 hours), laundry/valet, baby-sitting, express checkout.

Facilities: Roof garden, foreign-currency exchange, secretarial services in English, translation services.

EXPENSIVE

Hotel Atlante Garden. Via Crescenzio 78, 00193 Roma. ☎ **06/687-2361.** Fax 06/687-2315. 60 rms. A/C MINIBAR TV TEL. 420,000L ($252) double. Rates include breakfast. AE, DC, MC, V. Parking 40,000L ($24). Metro: Ottaviano. Tram: 19 or 30.

Atlante Garden stands on a tree-lined street near the Vatican. It's much cheaper than its nearby sibling, the Atlante Star. The entrance takes you through a garden tunnel lined with potted palms, which eventually leads into a series of handsomely decorated public rooms. More classical in its decor than the Atlante Star, the Garden offers 19th-century-style bedrooms that have been freshly papered and painted and contain tastefully conservative furniture and all the modern accessories. The renovated baths are tiled, and each is equipped with a Jacuzzi.

Hotel Columbus. Via della Conciliazione 33, 00193 Roma. ☎ **06/686-5435.** Fax 06/686-4874. 92 rms. MINIBAR TV TEL. 320,000L ($192) double. Rates include buffet breakfast. AE, DC, MC, V. Free parking. Bus: 62.

In an impressive 15th-century palace, built some 12 years before its namesake set off for America, the Hotel Columbus was once the private home of the wealthy cardi-nal who later became Pope Julius II and tormented Michelangelo into painting the Sistine Chapel. The building looks much as it must have centuries ago—a severe, time-stained facade, small windows, and heavy wooden doors leading from the street to the colonnades and arches of the inner courtyard. The cobbled entranceway leads to a reception hall with castlelike furniture, then on to a series of baronial public rooms. Note especially the main salon with its walk-in fireplace, oil portraits, battle scenes, and Oriental rugs.

The bedrooms are considerably simpler than the tiled and tapestried salons, done in soft beiges and furnished with comfortable and serviceable modern pieces. All the

Accommodations and Dining in the Vatican Area

Accommodations:
Hotel Atlante Star **3**
Hotel Atlante Garden **2**
Hotel Columbus **5**
Hotel Emmaus **7**
Pension Alimandi **8**
Residence Giuggioli **9**
Sant'Angelo **4**

Dining:
Les Etoiles **3**
Ristorante Giardinaccio **6**
Ristorante Il Matriciano **1**
Ristorante Pierdonati **5**

accommodations are spacious, but a few are enormous and still have such original details as decorated wood ceilings and frescoed walls. However, only some of them are air-conditioned. The hotel restaurant serves lunch and dinner.

MODERATE

Hotel Emmaus. Via delle Fornaci 23, 00165 Roma. ☎ **06/638-0370.** Fax 06/635-658. 26 rms. MINIBAR TV. 150,000L–170,000L ($96–$108.80) double. AE, DC, MC, V. Metro: Ottaviano.

Because of its relatively low prices, and a location a short walk west of the Vatican, you'll probably share this hotel with at least one, and in some cases, entire busloads of fervent Catholic pilgrims from all parts of the world. Set within a short walk west of the Vatican, within an older, four-story building that was radically renovated and upgraded in 1992, it offers unpretentious and basic but comfortable accommodations. There's an elevator on the premises, a breakfast area, and a different color scheme for rooms on each floor of this two-star, four-story hotel.

INEXPENSIVE

Pension Alimandi. Via Tunisi 8, 00192 Roma. ☎ **06/3972-6300.** Fax 06/3972-3943. 35 rms. TV TEL. 160,000L ($96) double. AE, DC, MC, V. Parking 25,000L ($15). Metro: Ottaviano.

Named after the three brothers who run it (Luigi, Enrico, and Paolo), this is an amicable, well-managed, and recently (in 1995) renovated guesthouse that was originally conceived as an apartment house in 1908. It's set within a bland residential neighborhood very close to the Vatican. Bedrooms are comfortable, albeit a bit small, and clean, with modern, generically international furniture and cramped but modern-looking bathrooms. Each of the three upper floors is serviced by two elevators leading down to a simple lobby. The social center and most appealing spot in the hotel is the roof garden. Here, potted plants and a bar contribute to an ambience that includes views toward the dome of the Basilica of St. Peter's, a short walk from the hotel. No meals are served other than breakfast.

Residence Giuggioli. Via Germanico 198, 00192 Roma. ☎ **06/324-2113.** 5 rms (1 with bath). 110,000L ($66) double without bath; 130,000L ($78) double with bath. No credit cards. Parking 20,000L ($12) in a nearby garage. Metro: Ottaviano.

The force behind virtually everything that happens here is Sra. Gasparina Giuggioli, whose ancestors founded this family-style guesthouse in the 1940s. It occupies most of the second floor of a five-story apartment house from the 1870s, with accommodations in high-ceilinged rooms that were originally much grander than they are today, but whose noble proportions are still obvious. Three of the five rooms have balconies overlooking the street outside; the one with the private bath is no. 6. Sra. Giuggioli has abandoned any pretense of providing morning breakfast (there are cafes nearby that serve whatever you want) or any other kind of meal service. But the site is nonetheless popular and crowded, partly because of her conviviality, partly because of the rooms' larger-than-expected sizes and scattering of antique and semiantique furniture. If this place should happen to be full, walk a few flights up for an almost-equivalent lodging, the *Pensione Lady* (☎ 06/324-2112), where up to seven rooms might be available at approximately the same rates.

Sant'Angelo. Via Mariana Dionigi 16, 00193 Roma. ☎ **06/322-0758.** Fax 06/320-4451. 25 rms. AC TV TEL. 130,000L–180,000L ($78–$108) double; 190,000L–220,000L ($114–$132) triple. Rates include continental breakfast. AE, DC, MC, V. Parking 25,000L ($15). Metro: Cavour.

Right off Piazza Cavour (northeast of the Castel Sant'Angelo) and just a 10-minute walk from St. Peter's Basilica, this hotel stands in a relatively untouristy area. Maintained and operated by several members of the Torre family, the hotel occupies the second and third floors of an imposing 200-year-old building whose other floors are devoted to offices and private apartments. The bedrooms are simple, modern, clean, and uncomplicated, with wooden furniture and views of either the street or of a rather bleak but quiet courtyard in back. The rooms have a bath, shower, telephone, satellite TV, and air-conditioning. Although the hotel serves only breakfast, the neighborhood offers many acceptable dining choices.

IN PARIOLI
VERY EXPENSIVE

✪ **Hotel Lord Byron.** Via G. de Notaris 5, 00197 Roma. ☎ **06/322-0404.** Fax 06/322-0405. 28 rms, 9 suites. A/C MINIBAR TV TEL. Apr–July and Sept–Oct, 440,000L–620,000L ($264–$372) double; 800,000L–1,300,000L ($480–$780) suite. July–Aug and Nov–Mar, 400,000L–560,000L ($228–$348) double; 700,000L–1,300,000L ($420–$780) suite. Rates include buffet breakfast. AE, DC, MC, V. Metro: Flaminio. Bus: 26 or 52.

Savvy travelers (with hefty wallets), fleeing those landmarks of yesterday (the Grand and the Excelsior), are likely to check in here. Lord Byron exemplifies modern Rome—an art deco villa set on a residential hilltop in Parioli, an area of embassies and exclusive town houses at the edge of the Villa Borghese. From the curving entrance steps off the staffed parking lot in front, you'll notice design accessories that attract the most sophisticated clientele in Italy. An oval Renaissance urn in chiseled marble occupies a niche in the reception area. Flowers are everywhere, the lighting is discreet, and everything is on a cultivated small scale that makes it seem more like a well-staffed private home than a hotel. Each of the guest rooms is different, but most have lots of mirrors, upholstered walls, a spacious bathroom with gray marble accessories, a big dressing room/closet, and all the amenities. Check into room 503, 602, or 603 for the most panoramic views of Rome.

Dining/Entertainment: On the premises is one of Rome's best restaurants, Relais Le Jardin, recommended separately (see "Dining," later in this chapter).

Services: Concierge, room service (24 hours), laundry and valet service.

MODERATE

Hotel degli Aranci. Via Barnaba Oriani 9–11, 00197 Roma. ☎ **06/808-5250.** Fax 06/808-5250. 54 rms, 3 suites. A/C MINIBAR TV TEL. 280,000L ($168) double; 350,000L ($210) suite. Rates include breakfast. AE, DC, MC, V. Free parking. Bus: 3 or 53.

Hotel degli Aranci is a former private villa on a tree-lined residential street in Parioli, surrounded by similar villas now used, in part, as consulates and ambassadorial town houses. Most of the accommodations have tall windows opening onto city views and are filled with provincial furnishings or English-style reproductions. The public rooms have memorabilia of Ancient Rome scattered about, including bisque-colored medallions of soldiers in profile, old engravings of ruins, and classical vases highlighted against the light-grained paneling. A marble-topped bar in an alcove off the sitting room adds a relaxed touch. From the glass-walled breakfast room, at the rear of the house, you can see the tops of orange trees.

INEXPENSIVE

Hotel delle Muse. Via Tommaso Salvini 18, 00197 Roma. ☎ **06/808-8333.** Fax 06/808-5749. 61 rms. TV TEL. 160,000L–190,000L ($96–$114) double; 220,000L–240,000L ($132–$144) triple. Rates include buffet breakfast. AE, CB, DC, DISC, MC, V. Bus: 4. Tram: 19.

The three-star Hotel delle Muse, half a mile north of the Villa Borghese, is a winning but undiscovered choice. It's run by the efficient, English-speaking Giorgio Lazar. Most rooms have been renovated but remain rather spartan and minimalist. In the summer Lazar operates a restaurant in the garden. A bar is open 24 hours a day in case you get thirsty at 5am. There's also a TV room, plus a writing room and a dining room.

IN MONTE MARIO

Cavalieri Hilton. Via Cadiolo 101, 00136 Roma. ☎ **800/445-8667** in the U.S. and Canada, or 06/35091. Fax 06/3509-2241. 376 rms, 17 suites. A/C MINIBAR TV TEL. 520,000L ($312) double; from 1,150,000L ($690) suite. AE, CB, DC, DISC, MC, V. Parking 5,000L–30,000L ($3–$18). Free shuttle bus to/from the city center.

Cavalieri Hilton combines all the advantages of a resort hotel with the convenience of being a 15-minute drive from the center of Rome. Overlooking Rome and the Alban Hills from its perch on top of Monte Mario, it's set in 15 acres of trees, flowering shrubs, and stonework. Its facilities are so complete that many visitors (at least those who have seen the city before) never leave the hotel grounds. The entrance leads into a lavish red-and-gold lobby, whose sculpture and winding staircases are usually flooded with sunlight from the massive windows.

The guest rooms and suites, many with panoramic views, are designed to fit contemporary standards of comfort, quality, and style. Soft furnishings in pastel colors are paired with Italian furniture in warm-toned woods. Each unit has a keyless electronic lock, independent heating and air-conditioning, color TV with in-house movies, radio, and bedside control for all electric apparatus in the room, as well as a spacious balcony. The bathrooms, sheathed in Italian marble, are equipped with large mirrors, a hair dryer, international electric sockets, vanity mirror, piped-in music, and phone.

Dining/Entertainment: The hotel's stellar restaurant, La Pergola, has one of the best dining views in Rome. In summer, a garden restaurant, Il Giardino dell'Uliveto, with a pool veranda, is an ideal choice.

Services: Concierge (24 hours), room service, laundry/valet, bus to/from the city center.

Facilities: Tennis courts, jogging paths, fitness center, spa, indoor arcade of shops, indoor and outdoor swimming pools, facilities for persons with disabilities.

4 Dining

Rome remains one of the world's great capitals for dining, even though you can no longer order those flamingo tongues that the Romans were once so fond of. If anything, you'll find more diversity in Roman cuisine today than ever before. Of course, Rome's dining scene is hardly the equal of London and Paris, but what you get isn't bad and is, in fact, often sublime.

From elegant, deluxe palaces with lavish trappings to little trattorie opening onto hidden piazzas deep in the heart of Old Rome, the city abounds in good restaurants in all price ranges.

It's difficult to compile a list of the best restaurants in such a city. Everybody—locals, expatriates, even those who have chalked up only one visit—has favorites ("What . . . you don't know about that little trattoria three doors down from Piazza Navona?"). What follows is not a list of all the best restaurants of Rome, but simply a running commentary on a number of our personal favorites. For the most part, we've chosen not to review every deluxe spot known to all big spenders. Rather, we've tried to seek out equally fine (or better) restaurants often patronized by some of the finest palates in Rome—but not necessarily by the fattest wallets.

Rome's cooking is not subtle, but its kitchen rivals anything the chefs of Florence or Venice can turn out. A feature of Roman restaurants is skill at borrowing—and sometimes improving upon—the cuisine of other regions. Throughout the capital you'll come across Neapolitan *(alla neapolitana),* Bolognese *(alla bolognese),* Florentine *(alla fiorentina),* and even Sicilian *(alla siciliana)* specialties. One of the oldest sections of the city, Trastevere, is a gold mine of colorful streets and restaurants with inspired cuisine.

In general, lunch is served from 1 to 3pm and dinner from 8 to around 10:30pm. August is a popular month for Romans to leave on vacation and many restaurants will be closed.

NEAR ANCIENT ROME
EXPENSIVE

Alvaro al Circo Massimo. Via dei Cerchi 53. ☎ **06/678-6112.** Reservations required. Main courses 40,000L–60,000L ($24–$36). AE, CB, DC, DISC, MC, V. Tues–Sat 11am–3pm and 7–11pm, Sun 11am–3pm. Closed Aug. Metro: Circo Massimo. ITALIAN.

Alvaro al Circo Massimo, at the edge of the Circus Maximus, is the closest thing in Rome to a genuine provincial inn right down to the corncobs hanging from the ceiling and rolls of fat sausages. Their antipasti and pasta dishes are fine, the meat courses well prepared, and there's an array of fresh fish—never overcooked. Other specialties include tagliolini with mushrooms and truffles, and roasted turbot with potatoes. They're especially well stocked with exotic seasonal mushrooms, including black truffles that rival the ones you'd find in Spoleto. A basket of fresh fruit rounds out the repast. With a comfortable, mellow atmosphere, Alvaro al Circo Massimo

And just in case.

We're here with American Express® Travelers Cheques and Cheques *for Two*.® They're the safest way to carry money on your vacation and the surest way to get a refund, practically anywhere, anytime.

Another way we help you...

do more

AMERICAN
EXPRESS

**Travelers
Cheques**

provides a welcome setting for relaxing and turning your meal into a tranquil evening affair.

Restaurant Al 104. 104 Via Urbana. ☎ **06/484-556.** Reservations recommended. Main courses 30,000L–48,000L ($19.20–$30.70); fixed-price menu 70,000L ($44.80). DC, MC, V. Tues–Sun 8:30pm–midnight. Metro: Cavour. SHELLFISH/SARDINIAN.

The setting is small, intimate, even cramped, and the ambience befits the family heritage of the owners, firmly rooted in the seafaring traditions of faraway Sardinia. A few types of grilled fish are available, as well as one or two meat dishes. But the heart and soul of the place is kept alive and healthy in bubbling aquariums containing clams, mussels, crayfish, squid, and a variety of Mediterranean (again, Sardinian) shellfish whose dialectical nicknames (*farro, fasolari, telline*) simply don't translate into "conventional" English or Italian.

The best way to experience all this is with the *menu dégustazione* whose price is noted above; otherwise, à la carte selections include platters of snails, crab-stuffed ravioli, spaghetti with lumpfish caviar and parsley, and another version of spaghetti that's enhanced with *bottarga*, a Sardinian delicacy that's concocted from the dried roe of mullet, fresh parsley, and olive oil. Locals swear by it, and all but the most adventurous of newcomers usually steer clear. Main courses include *seppie* (cuttlefish) with black olives, and *totani* (a Sardinian version of squid) served with potatoes. Looking for a light-textured dessert to end your meal with a crescendo? Opt for a *spuma di limone* (lemon mousse) with berries.

MODERATE

Il Quadrifoglio. 19 Via del Boschetto. ☎ **06/482-6096.** Reservations recommended. Main courses 20,000L–24,500L ($12.80–$15.70). AE, DC, MC, V. Mon–Sat 7pm–midnight. Metro: Cavour. NEAPOLITAN.

The grandiose palace housing this likable and well-managed restaurant was built as part of the spree that transformed the face of the Via Nazionale around the time of the unification of Italy. The cuisine is redolent with the flavors and herbs of Naples and southern Italy. You'll find a tempting selection of antipasti, featuring anchovies, peppers, capers, onions, and breaded and fried eggplant, many of these garnished with herbs and olive oil. Pastas are made daily, usually with sauces that are tomato or oil based, always with herbs and usually aged crumbling cheeses, and at their best garnished with squid or octopus. Try a rice dish (one of the best is sartù di riso) that's studded with vegetables, herbs, and meats), followed by fish dishes such as octopus (*polipetto alla posillipo*) in sauce, or a simple but savory version of *granatine* (meatballs, usually of veal, bound together with mozzarella). Dessert anyone? An enduring favorite here is torta caprese, fashioned with hazelnuts and chocolate.

INEXPENSIVE

Abruzzi. Via del Vaccaro 1. ☎ **06/679-3897.** Reservations recommended. Main courses 9,000L–20,000L ($5.40–$12). DC, MC, V. Sun–Fri 12:30–3pm and 7:30–10:30pm. Closed 2 weeks in Aug (dates vary). ABRUZZESE.

Abruzzi takes its name from a little-explored region east of Rome known for its haunting beauty and curious superstitions. The restaurant is located at one side of Piazza S. S. Apostoli, just a short walk from Piazza Venezia. Good food and reasonable prices make it a big draw for students. The chef is justly praised for his satisfying assortment of cold antipasti. With your starter, we suggest a liter of garnet-red wine; we once had one whose bouquet was suggestive of the wildflowers of Abruzzi. If you'd like a soup as well, you'll find a good stracciatella (an egg-and-Parmesan soup). A typical main dish is vitella tonnata con capperi, a veal in tuna-fish sauce with capers.

Ristorante al Cardello. Via del Cardello 1 (corner of Via Cavour). ☎ **06/474-5259.** Reservations recommended. Main courses 9,000L–14,000L ($5.40–$8.40). AE, DC, MC, V. Mon–Sat 12:30–3:30pm and 7:30–10:45pm. Closed Aug. Metro: Cavour. ROMAN/ABRUZZI.

It's charming and it's conveniently close to the Colosseum. This restuarant has thrived here since the 1920s, when it was established in the semicellar of an 18th-century building. Our favorite culinary experience here involves access to an antipasti buffet, where an all-vegetarian medley of marinated vegetables (including eggplant, zucchini, and various squash and corn choices) reveal the bounty of the Italian harvest. The price of 9,000L ($5.40) per person for reasonable quantities represents flavorful good value. Any of these might be followed with such dishes as *bucatini* (thick spaghetti) *alla matriciana*; roasted lamb with potatoes, garlic, and mountain herbs; thick stews; and desserts that include fresh fruit with sorbet, or tiramisù.

NEAR CAMPO DE' FIORI & THE JEWISH GHETTO
EXPENSIVE

Angelino a Tormargana. Piazza Margana 37. ☎ **06/678-3328.** Reservations not necessary. Main courses 52,000L–78,000L ($31.20–$46.80). MC, V. Mon–Sat noon–3:30pm and 7:30–11pm. ROMAN.

Goethe once frequented this tavern three blocks from Piazza Venezia, as did Anna Magnani, Jean-Paul Sartre, and even Richard Nixon. Back in fashion after a number of years, the tavern has responded by jacking up its prices. Everything else—from the atmosphere to the food—has remained unchanged, and that's why Romans like it so. You can dine alfresco in a setting of old palazzi and cobblestone squares. The food is very much in the typical Roman trattoria style—not exceptionally imaginative, but good. We'd recommend the cold seafood risotto or the peppery penne all'arrabbiata (with a tomato and hot pepper sauce). For a main course, you might select kidneys with mushrooms or veal scaloppine flavored with lemon juice. Other main-dish selections are pollo alla diavola and that staple of Roman cuisine, tripe.

Il Drappo. Vicolo del Malpasso 9. ☎ **06/687-7365.** Reservations required. Main courses 22,000L–28,000L ($13.20–$16.80); fixed-price menu (including Sardinian wine) 62,000L ($37.20). AE, CB, DC, V. Mon–Sat 8pm–midnight. Closed 2 weeks in Aug. SARDINIAN.

Il Drappo, on a narrow street near the Tiber, is operated by a woman known to her habitués only as "Valentina." This is a favorite of the art and film worlds. You'll have your choice of two tastefully decorated dining rooms festooned with yards of patterned cotton draped from supports on the ceiling. Flowers and candles are everywhere. Fixed-price dinners may include a wafer-thin appetizer called carte di musica (sheet-music paper), which is topped with tomatoes, green peppers, parsley, and olive oil, followed by fresh spring lamb in season, a fish stew made with tuna caviar, or a changing selection of strongly flavored regional specialties that are otherwise difficult to find in Rome. Another favorite menu item is pasta with fish eggs and chicory tips. For dessert, try the *seadas* (cheese-stuffed fried cake in a special dark honey). Service is first-rate.

MODERATE

Da Giggetto. Via del Portico d'Ottavia 21–22. ☎ **06/686-1105.** Reservations recommended. Main courses 20,000L–26,000L ($12–$15.60). AE, DC, MC, V. Tues–Sun 12:30–3pm and 7:30–11pm. Closed Aug 1–15. ROMAN.

Da Giggetto, in the old ghetto, is right next to the Theater of Marcellus and old Roman columns extend practically to its doorway. Romans flock to this bustling trattoria for its special traditional dishes. None is more typical than carciofi alla giudia, baby-tender fried artichokes—thistles to make you whistle with delight—a true delicacy. The cheese concoction, mozzarella in carrozza, is another delight, as are the zucchini flowers stuffed with mozzarella and anchovies. You could also sample fettuccine al'Amatriciana, shrimp sautéed in garlic and olive oil, a bold tripe dish, or saltimbocca (the eternal favorite of veal and ham).

La Carbonara. Piazza Campo de' Fiori 23. ☎ **06/686-4783.** Reservations recommended. Main courses 16,000L–24,000L ($9.60–$14.40). AE, MC, V. Wed–Mon noon–2:30pm and 6:30–10:30pm. Closed 3 weeks in Aug. ROMAN.

In an antique *palazzetto* at the edge of the market square, this amiable trattoria claims to be the home of the original spaghetti carbonara. According to a much-disputed legend, the forebears of the present owners devised the recipe in the final days of World War II, when American GIs donated their K-rations of powdered eggs and salted bacon to the chef. The result was the egg yolk, cheese, and bacon-enriched pasta dish that's famous throughout the world. The dining room features succulent antipasti, grilled meats, fresh and intelligently prepared seasonal vegetables, and—in addition to the carbonara—several other kinds of pasta, including tagliolini with porcini mushrooms. Another specialty is bucatini al'Amatriciana, with a sauce of tomato, bacon, and hot peppers.

Ristorante da Pancrazio. Piazza del Biscione 92. ☎ **06/686-1246.** Reservations recommended. Main courses 18,000L–32,000L ($10.80–$19.20); fixed-price menu 45,000L ($27). AE, DC, MC, V. Thurs–Tues noon–3pm and 7:30–11:15pm. Closed 2 weeks in Aug (dates vary). ROMAN.

Ristorante da Pancrazio is popular as much for its archaeological interest as for its culinary allure. One of its two dining rooms is gracefully decorated in the style of an 18th-century tavern; the other occupies the premises of Pompey's ancient theater, and as such is lined with marble columns, carved capitals, and bas-reliefs that would be the envy of many museums. Classified as a national monument, it's probably the only such site that feeds your body as well as your sense of history. They serve the full range of traditional Roman dishes, such as risotto alla pescatora (with seafood), several kinds of scampi, saltimbocca (veal with ham), and abbacchio al forno (roast lamb with potatoes). You might also order ravioli stuffed with artichoke hearts. No one gets innovative around here—these dishes are prepared according to time-tested recipes. If it was good enough for Caesar, it's good enough for the patrons of da Pancrazio.

✪ **Ristorante del Pallaro.** Largo del Pallaro 15. ☎ **06/6880-1488.** Reservations recommended for dinner on weekends. Fixed-price menu 31,000L ($18.60). No credit cards. Tues–Sun 1–3pm and 7:30pm–12:30am. ROMAN.

The cheerful and kindhearted woman in white who emerges with clouds of steam from the bustling kitchen is the owner, Paola Fazi. She maintains a simple duet of very clean dining rooms where price-conscious Romans go for good food at bargain prices. She also claims—although others dispute it—that Julius Caesar was assassinated on this very site. No à la carte meals are served, but the fixed-price menu has made the place famous. As you sit down, your antipasto, the first of eight courses, will appear. Then comes the pasta of the day, followed by roast veal, white meatballs or (only on Friday) dried cod, along with potatoes and eggplant. For your final courses, you're served mozzarella, cake with custard, and fruit in season. The meal also includes bread, mineral water, and half a liter of the house wine. This is the type of food you might be served if you were invited to the home of a prosperous Roman family.

Vecchia Roma. Via della Tribuna di Campitelli 18. ☎ **06/686-4604.** Reservations recommended. Main courses 24,000L–30,000L ($14.40–$18). AE, DC. Thurs–Tues 1–3:30pm and 8–11:30pm. Closed 10 days in Aug. Bus: 64, 90, 90b, 97, or 774. ROMAN/ITALIAN.

Vecchia Roma is a charming, moderately priced trattoria in the heart of the ghetto. Movie stars have frequented the place, sitting at the crowded tables in one of the four small dining rooms (the back room is the most popular). The owners are known for their "fruits of the sea," a selection of fresh seafood. The minestrone of the day is made with fresh vegetables, and an interesting selection of antipasti, including salmon or vegetables, is always available. The pastas and risottos are savory, including linguine alla marinara with scampi. A "green" risotto with porcini mushrooms is invariably good. The chef prepares excellent cuts of meat, including his specialty, lamb and la spigola (a type of white fish).

INEXPENSIVE

Le Maschere. Via Monte della Farina 29. ☎ **06/687-9444.** Reservations recommended. Main courses 12,000L–30,000L ($7.20–$18). AE, DC, MC, V. Tues–Sun 7:30pm–midnight. Closed Aug. CALABRESE.

Le Maschere, near Largo Argentina, specializes in the fragrant, often-fiery cookery of Calabria's Costa Viola—lots of fresh garlic and wake-up-your-mouth red peppers. In a cellar from the 1600s that's decorated with regional artifacts of Calabria, it has recently enlarged its kitchen and added three more dining rooms festooned with fantastic medieval- and Renaissance-inspired murals. Begin with a selection of antipasti calabresi. For *primo* (first course), you can try one of their many different preparations of eggplant or a pasta—perhaps with broccoli or with devilish red peppers, garlic, bread crumbs, and more than a touch of anchovy. The chef also grills meats and fresh swordfish caught off the Calabrian coast. For dessert, finish with a Calabrian sheep cheese or a fresh fruit salad. If you don't want a full meal, you can just visit for pizza and beer and listen to the music at the piano bar. In summer you can dine at a small table outside overlooking a tiny piazza.

NEAR PIAZZA NAVONA & THE PANTHEON

EXPENSIVE

Il Convivio. Via dell'Orso 44. ☎ **06/686-9432.** Reservations recommended. Main courses 39,000L–45,000L ($24.95–$28.80). AE, DC, MC, V. Tues–Sat 1–2:30pm; Tues–Sun 8–10:30pm. ITALIAN/ROMAN.

A meal at Il Convivio is a logical (and restful) way to revive yourself after a tour around the nearby Piazza Navona. It's housed within a Renaissance (circa 1550) building, and contains space for only 30 diners who are always made to feel like part of all the activity bubbling within the kitchens. The setting (pink marble floors, pink accessories scattered over a trio of small rooms) is an appropriate foil for the creative cuisine that emerges from the kitchens, at least some of which varies according to the inspiration of the chefs and owners. Even the ravioli is stuffed creatively, with ingredients that change with the seasons, and might include blends of, among others, scamorza cheese with pulverized Swiss chard, or crayfish and fresh tarragon. Saddle of rabbit might be stuffed with porcini mushrooms and served with an onion marmalade; or a boned rack of lamb cooked in an herb and vegetable crust are worthy main courses. Dessert? Consider a slice of almond and bitter chocolate cake accented with fresh currants.

MODERATE

Montevecchio. Piazza Montevecchio 22. ☎ **06/686-1319.** Reservations required. Main courses 26,000L–32,000L ($15.60–$19.20). AE, MC, V. Tues–Sun 1–3pm and 8–11:30pm. Closed Aug 10–25 and Dec 26–Jan 9. ROMAN/ITALIAN.

To visit, you must negotiate the winding streets of one of Rome's most confusing neighborhoods, near Piazza Navona. The heavily curtained restaurant on this

☺ Family-Friendly Restaurants

Césarina *(see p. 124)* A longtime family favorite, this restaurant serving the cuisine from the Emilia-Romagna region offers the most kid-pleasing pastas in town, each handmade and presented with a different sauce. You can request a selection of three kinds of pasta on one plate for a little taste of each.

Otello alla Concordia *(see p. 123)* This place is as good as any to introduce your child to the hearty Roman cuisine. If your child doesn't like the spaghetti with clams, then maybe the eggplant parmigiana will do. Families can dine in an arbor-covered courtyard.

Tre Scalini *(see p. 119)* All families visit Piazza Navona at some point, and this is the best choice if you'd like a dining table overlooking the square. The cookery is Roman and the menu is wide enough to accommodate most palates—including children's. Even if your child doesn't like the main course, the tartufo (ice cream with a coating of bittersweet chocolate, cherries, and whipped cream) at the end of the meal is a classic bound to please.

Renaissance piazza is where both Raphael and Bramante had studios and where Lucrezia Borgia spun many of her intrigues. The entrance opens onto a high-ceilinged room filled with rural mementos and bottles of wine. Your meal might begin with a strudel of porcini mushrooms followed by the invariably good pasta of the day, perhaps a bombolotti stuffed with prosciutto and spinach. Then select roebuck with polenta, roast Sardinian goat, or one of several veal dishes (on one occasion, served with salmon mousse). Many of these recipes, such as the mushroom strudel and the Sardinian goat, are virtually impossible to find on Roman menus anymore.

Passetto. Via Zanardelli 14. ☎ **06/6880-6569.** Reservations recommended. Main courses 24,000L–60,000L ($14.40–$36). AE, DC, MC, V. Daily noon–3pm and 7pm–midnight. ROMAN/ITALIAN/INTERNATIONAL.

Passetto, dramatically positioned at the north end of Piazza Navona, has drawn patrons with its reputation for excellent Italian food for 145 years. Regrettably, its success has spoiled it somewhat and service is now no longer among the most polished. The interior is stylish—three rooms, one containing frosted-glass-cylinder chandeliers. In summer, however, sit outside looking out on Piazza Sant'Apollinare. The pastas are exceptional, including penne alla Norma. One recommended main dish is orata (sea bass) al cartoccio (baked in a paper bag with tomatoes, mushrooms, capers, and white wine). Another house specialty is rombo passetto (a fish similar to sole) cooked in cognac and pine nuts. Fresh fish is often priced by its weight, so tabs can soar quickly. Fresh vegetables are abundant in summer, and a favorite dessert is seasonal berries with fresh thick cream.

Tre Scalini. Piazza Navona 30. ☎ **06/687-9148.** Reservations recommended. Main courses 22,000L–32,000L ($13.20–$19.20). AE, DC, MC, V. Daily 12:15–3pm and 7–11pm. Closed Dec–Feb. ROMAN.

Established in 1882, this is the most famous and respected restaurant on Piazza Navona—a landmark for ice cream as well as more substantial meals. Yes, it's literally crawling with tourists, but its waiters are a lot friendlier and more helpful than those at the nearby Passetto. Although there's a cozy bar on the upper floor, outfitted with simple furniture and a view over the piazza, most visitors opt for a seat either in the ground-floor cafe or restaurant, or, during warm weather, at tables on the piazza.

House specialties include risotto con porcini, spaghetti with clams, roast duck with prosciutto, a carpaccio of sea bass, saltimbocca, and roast lamb in the Roman style. No one will object if you order just a pasta and salad, unlike at other restaurants nearby. Their famous tartufo (ice cream disguised with a coating of bittersweet chocolate, cherries, and whipped cream) and other ice creams cost 10,000L ($6) each.

INEXPENSIVE

Il Miraggio. Vicolo Sciarra 59. ☎ **06/678-0226.** Reservations recommended. Main courses 12,000L–18,000L ($7.20–$10.80). AE, V. Thurs–Tues 12:30–3:30pm and 7:30–10:30pm. Closed Feb 5–20. ROMAN/SARDINIAN/SEAFOOD.

While shopping near Piazza Colonna, you may want to escape the roar of traffic along the corso by dining at this informal, hidden-away "mirage" in a charming location on a crooked street. It's a cozy, neighborhood setting with good food. A specialty of the house is tortellini alla papalina, spaghetti alla bottarga (spaghetti with soft roe sauce), and spigola alla vernaccia (sea bass sautéed in butter and vernaccia wine). Meat courses are well prepared, and there is an array of fresh fish. For dessert try seadas, a typical Sardinian dessert made of thin-rolled pastry filled with fresh cheese, fried, and served with honey.

✪ **L'Eau Vive.** Via Monterone 85. ☎ **06/6880-1095.** Reservations recommended. Main courses 10,000L–28,000L ($6–$16.80); fixed-price menus 15,000, 22,000, and 30,000L ($9, $13.20, and $18). AE, MC, V. Mon–Sat 12:30–2:30pm and 8–10:30pm. Closed Aug 1–20. FRENCH/INTERNATIONAL.

This offbeat spot is run by lay missionaries who wear the dress or costumes of their native countries. The restaurant occupies the cellar and the ground floor of the 17th-century Palazzo Lantante della Rovere, and is filled with monumental paintings under vaulted ceilings. In this formal atmosphere, at 10 o'clock each evening, the waitresses sing religious hymns and *Ave Marias.* Pope John Paul II used to dine here when he was still archbishop of Krakow, and today some flamboyant jet-setters have adopted L'Eau Vive as their favorite spot. Specialties include hors d'oeuvres and frogs' legs, and the cellar is well stocked with French wines. Main dishes range from guinea hen with onions and grapes in a wine sauce to couscous. Other selections include several kinds of homemade pâté, salad niçoise, and beefsteak in wine sauce. A smooth finish is the chocolate mousse. The tasteful place settings include fresh flowers and good glassware. Your tip will be turned over for religious purposes.

Quirino. Via delle Muratte 84. ☎ **06/679-4108.** Main courses 15,000L–20,000L ($9–$12) and fish courses 30,000L ($18). AE, MC, V. Mon–Sat 12:30–3:30pm and 7–10pm. Closed 3 weeks in Aug. Metro: Piazza Barberini. ROMAN/ITALIAN/SICILIAN.

Quirino is a good place to dine right after you've tossed your coin into the Trevi Fountain. The atmosphere inside is typical Italian, with hanging chianti bottles, a beamed ceiling, and muraled walls. The food is strictly in the "home-cooking" style of Roman trattorie. We're fond of a mixed fry of tiny shrimp and squid rings that resemble onion rings. Specialties include vegetarian antipasti, homemade pasta with clams and porcini mushrooms, pasta alla Norma (a typical Sicilian plate), and a variety of fresh tasty fish. For dessert there is chestnut ice cream with hot chocolate sauce or homemade cannoli Siciliani among others.

NEAR PIAZZA DI SPAGNA & PIAZZA DEL POPOLO
EXPENSIVE

✪ **El Toulà.** Via della Lupa 29B. ☎ **06/687-3498.** Reservations required for dinner. Main courses 38,000L–55,000L ($22.80–$33); fixed-price menus 90,000L–100,000L ($54–$60). AE, DC, MC, V. Mon 8–11pm, Tues–Sat 1–3pm and 8–11pm. Closed Aug. ROMAN/VENETIAN.

El Toulà ("The Hayloft" in the alpine dialect of Cortina d'Ampezzo) offers the quin-tessence of Roman haute cuisine with a creative flair, and is the glamorous flagship of an upscale, now international chain. The elegant setting of vaulted ceilings and large archways attracts the international set. Guests stop in the charming bar to order a drink while perusing the impressive, always-changing menu (one section devoted to Venetian specialties, in honor of the restaurant's origins). Items include fegato (liver) alla veneziana, calamari stuffed with vegetables, baccala (codfish mousse served with polenta), and another Venetian classic, broetto, a fish soup made with monkfish and clams. The selection of sherbets changes seasonally—the cantaloupe and fresh strawberry are celestial concoctions—and you can request a mixed plate if you'd like to sample several of them. El Toulà usually isn't crowded at lunchtime.

MODERATE

Babington's Tea Rooms. Piazza di Spagna 23. ☎ **06/678-6027.** Main courses 19,000L–37,000L ($11.40–$22.20); brunch 45,000L ($27). AE, MC, DC, V. Wed–Mon 9am–11:30pm. Metro: Piazza di Spagna. ENGLISH/MEDITERRANEAN.

When Victoria was on the English throne in 1893, an Englishwoman named Anne Mary Babington arrived in Rome and couldn't find a place for "a good cuppa." With stubborn determination, she opened her own tearooms near the foot of the Spanish Steps, and the rooms are still going strong, although prices are terribly inflated because of its fabulous location. You can order everything from Scottish scones and Ceylon tea to a club sandwich and American coffee. Brunch is served at all hours. Pastries cost 4,000 to 13,000L ($2.40 to $7.80); a pot of tea (dozens of varieties available) goes for 12,000L ($7.20).

Dal Bolognese. Piazza del Popolo 1–2. ☎ **06/361-1426.** Reservations required. Main courses 22,000L–28,000L ($13.20–$16.80); fixed-price menu 60,000L ($36). AE, MC, V. Tues–Sun 12:30–3pm and 8:15pm–1am. Closed 20 days in Aug. Metro: Flaminio. BOLOGNESE.

If *La Dolce Vita* were being filmed now, this restaurant would be used as a back-drop—it's one of those rare dining spots that's not only chic, with patrons in the lat-est Fendi drag, but noted for its food as well. Young actors, shapely models, artists from nearby Via Margutta, even industrialists on expense accounts show up here, quickly booking the limited sidewalk tables. To begin your feast, we suggest a misto de pasta—four pastas, each with a different sauce, arranged on the same plate. A worthy substitute would be thin, savory slices of Parma ham or perhaps the prosciutto and melon (try a little freshly ground pepper on the latter). For your main course, specialties include lasagne verde, tagliatelle alla bolognese, and a most recommend-able cotolette alla bolognese (veal cutlet topped with cheese).

You may want to cap your evening by calling on the Rosati cafe next door (or its competitor, the Canova, across the street), to enjoy one of the tempting pastries.

Il Bacaro. Via degli Spagnoli 27, near Piazza delle Coppelle. ☎ **06/686-4110.** Reservations recommended. Main courses 18,000L–28,000L ($11.50–$17.90). MC, V. Mon–Sat 8pm–midnight. ITALIAN.

Unpretentious and accommodating to the tastes and customs of the many foreign visitors who dine here, this restaurant contains only about a half-dozen tables and operates from an ivy-edged hideaway alleyway near the Piazza di Spagna. Long ago, the site was a palazzo from the 1600s, and some vestiges of the building's former gran-deur remain intact, despite an impossibly cramped kitchen where the efforts of the staff to keep the show moving are nothing short of heroic. Menu items are time-tested, flavorful, and enduring, and include homemade ravioli stuffed with mush-rooms and Parmesan cheese; grilled filet of beef with roasted potatoes; a succulent radicchio stuffed with Gorgonzola; and an unusual version of warm carpaccio of beef that isn't very often seen within other restaurants.

Ristorante Nino. Via Borgognona 11 (off Via Condotti). ☎ **06/679-5676.** Reservations recommended. Main courses 22,000L–32,000L ($13.20–$19.20). AE, DC, MC, V. Mon–Sat 12:30–3pm and 7:30–11pm. Closed Aug. Metro: Piazza di Spagna. TUSCAN.

Ristorante Nino, a short walk from the Spanish Steps, is a tavern mecca for writers, artists, and an occasional model from one of the nearby high-fashion houses. Nino's enjoys deserved acclaim for its Tuscan cooking—hearty and completely unpretentious. The restaurant is particularly known for its steaks shipped in from Florence and charcoal broiled, priced according to weight. A plate of cannelloni Nino is one of the chef's specialties. Other good dishes include grilled veal liver, fagioli cotti al fiasco, codfish alla livornese, and zucchini pie.

Ristorante Ranieri. Via Mario de' Fiori 26 (off Via Condotti). ☎ **06/678-6505.** Reservations required. Main courses 22,000L–32,000L ($13.20–$19.20). AE, DC, MC, V. Mon–Sat 12:30–3pm and 7:30–11pm. Metro: Piazza di Spagna. INTERNATIONAL/ITALIAN.

Ristorante Ranieri is well into its second century (it was founded in 1843). Neapolitan-born Giuseppe Ranieri was the chef to Queen Victoria, and his namesake restaurant still maintains its Victorian trappings. Nothing ever seems to change here. Start with prosciutto or melon, or else that classic Roman soup stracciatella made with eggs and cheese. Another starter might be the crêpes alla Ranieri, which we've ordered here for years. Beefsteak from Florence is meltingly tender, as is the veal liver. You might also try the ossobuco in the style of Lombardy. For dessert, the tiramisû is a winner. Most of the dishes are French and Italian, although overall the cookery is international.

INEXPENSIVE

Da Mario. Via della Vite 55–56. ☎ **06/678-3818.** Reservations recommended. Main courses 16,000L–22,000L ($9.60–$13.20); fixed-price menu 38,000L–43,000L ($22.80–$25.80). AE, DC, MC, V. Mon–Sat 12:30–3pm and 7:30–11pm. Closed Aug. Metro: Piazza di Spagna. ROMAN/FLORENTINE.

Da Mario is noted for its moderately priced game specialties. Mario also does excellent Florentine dishes, although the typical steak is too costly these days for most budgets. You can dine in air-conditioned comfort on the street level or descend to the cellars. A good beginning is the wide-noodle pappardelle, best when served with a game sauce (caccia) or with chunks of rabbit (lepre), available only in winter. Capretto (kid) and beefsteaks are served in the Florentine fashion, although you may prefer roast quail with polenta. We heartily recommend the gelato misto, a selection of mixed ice cream.

Il Ristorante 34 (also Al 34). Via Mario de' Fiori 34. ☎ **06/679-5091.** Reservations required. Main courses 18,000L–30,000L ($10.80–$18); fixed-price menu 55,000L ($33). AE, DC, MC, V. Tues–Sat 12:30–3pm and 7:30–10:30pm, Sun 12:30–3pm. Closed 1 week at Easter and 3 weeks in Aug. Metro: Piazza di Spagna. ROMAN.

Il Ristorante 34 is a very good and increasingly popular restaurant close to the most famous shopping district of Rome. Its long and narrow interior is sheathed in scarlet wallpaper, ringed with modern paintings, and capped with a vaulted ceiling. In the rear, stop to admire a display of antipasti proudly exhibited near the entrance to the bustling kitchen. The cookery is highly reliable and the chef might whip caviar and salmon into the noodles to enliven the dish, or else cook chunks of lobster into the risotto. He also believes in rib-sticking fare such as pasta lentil soup, or meatballs in a sauce with "fat" mushrooms. One of his most interesting pastas comes with a pumpkin-flavored cream sauce, and his spaghetti with clams is among the best in Rome.

La Campana. Vicolo della Campana 18. ☎ **06/686-7820.** Reservations recommended. Main courses 18,000L–21,000L ($11.50–$13.45). AE, DC, MC, V. Tues–Sun 12:30–2:30pm and 7:30–10:45pm. Metro: Piazza di Spagna. ROMAN.

If you opt for a meal in this comfortable, not-particularly-innovative restaurant, you won't be alone. The place has been dishing up traditional Roman specialties since it first began welcoming locals and religious pilgrims in 1518, a year when the food probably wasn't nearly as well crafted as it is today. Added benefits not afforded to pilgrims of yesteryear include air-conditioning. Look for a well-stocked antipasti buffet; rich pastas with names like l'arrabiatta and alla matriciana; juicy, herb-laden versions of roasted lamb with potatoes; roast hen with roasted vegetables; and grilled fish or squid. The welcome has managed to remain warm, despite the passage of literally thousands of diners.

Margutta Vegetariano. Via Margutta 119. ☎ **06/3600-1805.** Reservations recommended. Main courses 12,000L–18,000L ($7.20–$10.80). AE, DC, MC, V. Mon–Sat 1–3pm and 7:30–10:30pm. Closed 2 weeks in Aug. Metro: Piazza di Spagna. VEGETARIAN.

Established in 1980 by Claudio Vannini, an enthusiast of new-wave thinking and Indian philosophy, this place functioned for many years as one of Rome's only vegetarian restaurants. Partly because of the patronage of Signor Vannini's friend and neighbor, the late Federico Fellini, and partly because of its excellent cuisine, the restaurant quickly became a stylish favorite of Italian film stars and TV personalities. You can order from a sophisticated list of risotto and pasta, herb-enriched soups, mixed salads, a mélange of fried vegetables, meatless goulash, soyburgers, and a selection of soufflés made with potatoes, spinach, or wild mushrooms. Eggplant parmigiana is a perennial favorite. There's also a large selection of wines and ciders.

Otello alla Concordia. Via della Croce 81. ☎ **06/679-1178.** Main courses 16,000L–36,000L ($9.60–$21.60); fixed-price menu 36,000L ($21.60). AE, DC, MC, V. Mon–Sat 12:30–3pm and 7:30–11pm. Closed 2 weeks in Feb. Metro: Piazza di Spagna. ROMAN.

Set on a side street amid the glamorous boutiques near the northern edge of the Spanish Steps, this is one of the most popular and consistently reliable restaurants of Rome. A stone corridor from the street leads into a dignified building, the Palazzo Povero. Choose a table (space permitting) in either the arbor-covered courtyard or in the cramped but convivial series of inner dining rooms. Displays of Italian bounty decorate an interior well known to many of the shopkeepers from the surrounding fashion district. The spaghetti alle vongole veraci (spaghetti with clams) is excellent, as are Roman-style saltimbocca (veal with ham), abbacchio arrosto (roasted baby lamb), eggplant parmigiana, a selection of grilled or sautéed fish dishes (including swordfish), and several different preparations of veal.

NEAR VIA VENETO
VERY EXPENSIVE

✪ **La Terrazza.** In the Hotel Eden, Via Ludovisi 49. ☎ **06/478-121.** Reservations recommended. Main courses 42,000L–68,000L ($25.20–$40.80); fixed-price menu 120,000L ($72). AE, DC, MC, V. Daily 12:30–2:30pm and 7:30–10:30pm. Metro: Piazza Barberini. ITALIAN/INTERNATIONAL.

This restaurant serves the finest cuisine in the city (a title shared with Relais Le Jardin) along with a sweeping view over St. Peter's from the fifth floor of the Eden Hotel. Service manages to be formal and flawless, yet not at all intimidating. Chef Enrico Derfligher, the commercial and culinary catalyst behind about a dozen top-notch

Italian restaurants throughout Europe, prepares a menu that varies with the season and is among the most urbane and polished in Rome. Examples include a warm salad of grilled vegetables lightly toasted with greens in balsamic vinegar, red tortelli (whose pink coloring comes from a tomato mousse) stuffed with mascarpone cheese and drizzled with lemon, grilled tagliata of beef with eggplant and tomatoes, and a superb "symphony" of seafood. Artfully arranged on a platter, and prepared only for two or more diners, it includes perfectly seasoned Mediterranean sea bass, turbot, gilthead, and prawns.

✪ **Sans Souci.** Via Sicilia 20. ☎ **06/482-1814.** Reservations required. Main courses 36,000L–58,000L ($21.60–$34.80). AE, DC, MC, V. Tues–Sun 8pm–1am. Closed Aug 10–30. Metro: Piazza Barberini. FRENCH/ITALIAN.

Sans Souci, which was getting a little tired, has now bounced back, and Michelin has restored its coveted star. It is now the market leader for glitz, glamor, and nostalgia for *la dolce vita.* Nothing quite matches the overly decorated Sans Souci, which serves sublime food to those on the see-and-be-seen circuit, and might be your best bet for spotting a movie star, albeit a faded one. You enter a small dimly lit lounge to the right at the bottom of the steps. Here, amid tapestries and glittering mirrors, the maître d' will present you with the menu, which you can peruse while sipping a drink. The menu is ever changing, as "new creations" are devised. You might begin with a terrine of goose liver with truffles, a special creation of the chef. The fish soup is, according to one Rome restaurant critic, "a legend to experience." The soufflés are also popular, including artichoke, asparagus, and spinach. Risottos are prepared for two. One of the most popular pasta dishes is ravioli filled with truffle. Other specialties are homemade fois gras and lamb from Normandy. Dessert soufflés, also prepared for two, are a specialty, including chocolate and Grand Marnier.

MODERATE

Aurora 10 da Pino il Sommelier. Via Aurora 10. ☎ **06/474-2779.** Reservations recommended. Main courses 22,000L–32,000L ($13.20–$19.20). AE, DC, MC, V. Tues–Sun noon–3pm and 7–11:15pm. Metro: Piazza Barberini. ITALIAN.

Just a few paces from the top of Via Veneto, this restaurant lies in the vaulted interior of what was originally a Maronite convent. The high-energy direction of its Sicilian manager, Pino Salvatore, and his staff have attracted some of the capital's most influential diplomats and a sprinkling of film stars. The place is noted for its awesome array of more than 250 wines, representing every province of Italy. Unusual for Rome, the restaurant features a large soup menu, along with a tempting array of fresh antipasti. Dishes include linguine with lobster, a Sicilian-style fish fry, swordfish in herb sauce, filet of beef with porcini mushrooms, risotto with asparagus, and beef stew flambé. The cookery is savory and first-rate, using top-quality ingredients.

Césarina. Via Piemonte 109. ☎ **06/488-0828.** Reservations recommended. Main courses 18,000L–26,000L ($10.80–$15.60). AE, DC, MC, V. Mon–Sat 12:30–3pm and 7:30–11pm. EMILIANA-ROMAGNOLA/ROMAN.

Specializing in the cuisines of Rome and the region around Bologna, this former hole-in-the-wall has grown since matriarch Césarina Masi established it around 1960 (many Rome veterans fondly remember Ms. Masi's strict supervision of her kitchens, and how she would lecture regulars who didn't finish their tagliatelle). Although Césarina died in the mid-1980s, the restaurant perpetuates her culinary traditions. The tactful and polite staff roll an excellent bollito misto (an array of well-seasoned boiled meats) from table to table on a trolley, and often follow with a misto Césarina—three kinds of handmade pasta, each served with a different sauce. Equally appealing is the saltimbocca and the cotoletta alla bolognese, a veal cutlet baked with ham and cheese. A dessert specialty is semifreddo Césarina with hot chocolate. The food is excellent, and the selection of fresh antipasti is very appealing.

Colline Emiliane. Via Avignonesi 22 (right off Piazza Barberini). ☎ **06/481-7538.** Reservations required. Main courses 18,000L–26,000L ($10.80–$15.60). MC, V. Sat–Thurs 12:45–2:45pm and 7:45–10:45pm. Closed Aug. Metro: Piazza Barberini. EMILIANA-ROMAGNOLA.

Colline Emiliane, established in 1936, is a small restaurant serving the *classica cucina bolognese*. It's a family-run place—the owner is the cook and his wife makes the pasta (which, incidentally, is about the best you'll encounter in Rome). The house specialty is an inspired tortellini alla panna (cream sauce) with truffles, but the less expensive pastas are all excellent as well—maccheroni al funghetto and tagliatelle alla bolognese. As an opener for your meal, we suggest culatello di Zibello, a delicacy from a small town near Parma known for having the finest prosciutto in the world. Main courses include braciola di maiale, boneless rolled pork cutlets that have been stuffed with ham and cheese, breaded, and sautéed. Giambonnetto (roast veal Emilian style with roast potatoes) is another specialty. To finish your meal, we'd recommend budino al cioccolato, a chocolate pudding that's baked like flan.

Girarrosto Toscano. Via Campania 29. ☎ **06/482-3835.** Reservations required. Main courses 22,000L–50,000L ($13.20–$30). AE, DC, MC, V. Thurs–Tues 12:30–3pm and 7:30–11:30pm. TUSCAN.

Girarrosto Toscano, facing the walls of the Borghese Gardens, draws large crowds, so you may have to wait. Under the vaulted ceilings of a cellar it serves some of the finest Tuscan specialties in Rome. Begin by enjoying an enormous selection of antipasti, from succulent little meatballs and melon with prosciutto, to frittate (omelets) and an especially delicious Tuscan salami. You're then given a choice of pasta, such as fettuccine in a cream sauce. Although expensive, bistecca alla fiorentina—grilled steak seasoned with oil, salt, and pepper—is the best item to order. The oysters and fresh fish from the Adriatic are served every day. Order with care if you're on a budget—both meat and fish are all priced according to weight and can run considerably higher than the prices quoted above. For dessert, we'd recommend the assortment of ice cream called gelato misto.

INEXPENSIVE

Piccolo Abruzzo. Via Sicilia 237. ☎ **06/482-0176.** Reservations recommended. Main courses 16,000L–22,000L ($9.60–$13.20). AE, DC, MC, V. Mon–Sat 12:30–3pm and 7pm–midnight. Closed 1 week in August. ABRUZZESE.

An imaginative array of antipasti and copious portions make Piccolo Abruzzo one of the most popular restaurants in its neighborhood. In a brick- and stucco-sheathed room, perfumed with hanging cloves of garlic, salt-cured hams, and beribboned bunches of Mediterranean herbs, the regulars plan a meal either early or late to avoid the jam, as the place is small and popular. Full meals are priced according to what you take from the antipasti buffet groaning with at least 20 offerings. You can follow with a pasta course, which might be samples of three different versions, followed by a meat course, then cheese and dessert. A meat specialty is agnello d'Abruzzi, roast lamb full of flavor and herbally scented.

NEAR THE TERMINI
EXPENSIVE

Agata e Romeo. 45 Via Carlo Alberto. ☎ **06/446-6115.** Reservations recommended. Main courses 40,000L–50,000L ($25.60–$32). AE, DC, MC, V. Mon–Sat 1–3pm and 8–10:30pm. Metro: Piazza Vittorio. ROMAN.

Named after the husband-wife team who direct the place (Romeo), and cook (Agate), this is a small-scale and warmly charming enclave of culinary creativity in the shadow of the Church of Santa Maria Maggiore. Menus, while based on mainline culinary traditions, are changed with the seasons to reflect the bounty of the Italian harvest, as well as the whims and inspiration of both kitchen and wine cellar. Examples include a purée of eggplant capped with slices of rabbit fillet, or a deceptively simple version of white beans topped with fried cuttlefish. Spaghetti is often prepared with shellfish, especially clams or any of a roster of Mediterranean bivalves you might not have seen in North American waters. Breast of duck with porcini and herb sauce, or rack of lamb with rosemary sauce, are perennial favorites. One of the restaurant's classic dessert specialties is their own version of *millefiori*—chantilly cream laced with liqueur and served in puff pastry.

MODERATE

Scoglio di Frisio. Via Merulana 256. ☎ **06/487-2765.** Reservations recommended. Main courses 18,000L–32,000L ($10.80–$19.20). AE, DC, MC, V. Mon–Fri 12:30–3pm and 7:30–11pm, Sat–Sun 7:30–11pm. Bus: 714 from the Termini. NEAPOLITAN/PIZZA.

Scoglio di Frisio is the choice *suprême* to introduce yourself to the Neapolitan kitchen. While here, you should get reacquainted with a genuine, plate-sized Neapolitan pizza (crunchy, oozy, and excellent) with clams and mussels. After a medley of stuffed vegetables and antipasti, you may then settle for chicken cacciatore or veal scaloppine. Scoglio di Frisio also makes for an inexpensive night of enchanting entertainment, as cornball "O Sole Mio" and Neapolitan *bel canto* elements spring forth from a guitar, mandolin, and strolling tenor (who is like Mario Lanza reincarnate). The nautical decor—in honor of the top-notch fish dishes—is complete with a high-ceilinged grotto with craggy walls, fisher's nets, crustaceans, and a miniature three-masted schooner hanging overhead.

Taverna Flavia di Mimmo. Via Flavia 9. ☎ **06/474-5214.** Reservations recommended. Main courses 18,000L–32,000L ($10.80–$19.20). AE, DC, MC, V. Mon–Fri 12:30–3pm and 7:30–11pm, Sat 7:30–11pm. Metro: Piazza della Repubblica. ROMAN/INTERNATIONAL.

The Taverna Flavia di Mimmo, just a block from Via XX Settembre, is a robustly Roman restaurant. It still serves the same food that used to delight Frank Sinatra and the "Hollywood on the Tiber" crowd in the 1950s. It may not be chic anymore, but we still recommend it as a dining experience. Specialties include a risotto with scampi and spaghetti al whisky. A different regional dish is featured daily, which might be Roman-style tripe prepared in such a savory manner that it tastes far better than it sounds. Exceptional dishes include ossobuco with peas, a seafood salad, and fondue with truffles.

INEXPENSIVE

Il Dito e La Luna. 47–51 Via dei Sabelli, San Lorenzo. ☎ **06/494-0726.** Reservations recommended. Main courses 16,000L–22,000L ($10.25–$14.10). No credit cards. Daily 8pm–midnight. Metro: Termini. SICILIAN/ITALIAN.

This charming, small-scale restaurant has a rather schizophrenic menu that's equally divided between traditional Sicilian and more creative and up-to-date recipes that are prepared with gusto and flair. Consequently, it's the kind of place where both your Sicilian grandmother and your trendy, young nephews can simultaneously experience culinary happiness. Il Dito e La Luna is an unpretentious bistro, with countertops and service areas accented with the fruits of a bountiful harvest. The menu includes fresh orange-infused anchovies served on orange segments, a creamy flan of mild onions and mountain cheese, and a seafood couscous loaded with shellfish in a style traditionally served in both North Africa and coastal Sicily. Pastas such as a square-cut spaghetti (tonnarelli) prepared with mussels, bacon, and tomatoes, and exotic mushrooms are succulent. Even those not particularly enamored with fish should try the *baccalà mantecato* (baked and pulverized salt cod) served with lentils. Traditional and soothing, it's a nutrient-rich comfort food beloved by many Sicilians since the days of their youth.

Monte Arci. Via Castelfidardo 33. ☎ **06/494-1220.** Reservations recommended. Main courses 14,000L–22,000L ($8.40–$13.20). V. Mon–Fri 12:30–3pm and 7–11:30pm, Sat 7–11:30pm. ROMAN/SARDINIAN.

Monte Arci, on a cobblestone street near Piazza Indipendènza not far from the Termini, is set behind a sienna-colored facade. The restaurant features low-cost Roman and Sardinian specialties (you'll spend even less for pizza). Typical dishes include malloreddus (a regional form of gnocchetti); pasta with clams or lobster or those delectable porcini mushrooms; green and white spaghetti with bacon, spinach, cream, and cheese; saltimbocca (veal with ham); and lamb sausage flavored with herbs and pecorino cheese. Much of this food is just like mamma used to make.

Trimani Wine Bar. Via Cernaia 37b. ☎ **06/446-9630.** Fixed-price lunch 26,000L ($15.60); salads and platters of light food 12,000L–20,000L ($7.20–$12); glass of wine (depending on the vintage) 4,000L–12,000L ($2.40–$7.20). AE, DC, MC, V. Mon–Sat 11:30am–3pm and 5:30pm–midnight. Closed several weeks in Aug. Metro: Piazza della Repubblica or Castro Pretorio. CONTINENTAL.

Conceived as a tasting center for French and Italian wines, spumantis, and liqueurs, this elegant wine bar lies at the edge of a historic district. Amid a postmodern, award-winning interior decor inspired by classical Rome, you'll find comfortable seating, occasional live music, and a staff devoted to pressurizing half-full bottles of wine between pours. Menu items are inspired by the stylish bistros of Paris, and might include vegetarian pastas (in summertime only), salades niçoises, herb-laden bean soups (fagiole), slices of quiche, Hungarian goulash, and platters of French and Italian cheeses and pâtés. Trimani, a family of wine brokers whose company was established in 1821, maintains a well-stocked shop about 40 yards from its wine bar, at Via Goito 20 (☎ **06/446-9661**), where an astonishing array of the enological bounty of Italy is for sale.

ON THE APPIAN WAY

Hostaria l'Archeologia. Via Appia Antica 139. ☎ **06/788-0494.** Reservations recommended, especially on weekends. Main courses 14,000L–26,000L ($8.40–$15.60); fixed-price menu 26,000L ($15.60). AE, DC, MC, V. Fri–Wed 12:30–3:30pm and 8–10:30pm. Bus: 660 from San Giovanni. ROMAN/ITALIAN.

Hostaria l'Archeologia is only a short walk from the catacombs of St. Sebastian. The family-run restaurant is like an 18th-century village tavern with lots of atmosphere, strings of garlic and corn, oddments of copper hanging from the ceiling, earth-brown beams, and sienna-washed walls. In summer, guests dine in the garden out back under the wisteria. The Roman victuals are first-rate; you can glimpse the kitchen from behind a partition in the exterior garden parking lot. Many Roman families visit on the weekend, sometimes as many as 30 diners in a group. Of special interest is the wine cellar, excavated in an ancient Roman tomb, with bottles dating back to 1800. You go through an iron gate, down some stairs, and into the underground cavern. Along the way, you can still see the holes once occupied by funeral urns.

IN TESTACCIO

Checchino dal 1887. Via di Monte Testaccio 30. ☎ **06/574-3816.** Reservations recommended. Main courses 13,000L–32,500L ($7.80–$19.50). AE, DC, MC, V. Tues–Sat 12:30–3pm

and 8–11pm, Sun 12:30–3pm. Closed Aug, 1 week around Christmas, and Sun in June–Sept.
ROMAN.

During the 1800s, a local wine shop flourished by selling drinks to the butchers working in the neighborhood's many slaughterhouses. In 1887 the ancestors of the present owners obtained a license to sell food, thus giving birth to the restaurant you'll find here today. Slaughterhouse workers in those days were paid part of their meager salaries with the *quinto quarto* (fifth quarter) of each day's slaughter (the tail, the feet, the intestines, and the offal), which otherwise had no commercial value. Following many centuries of Roman traditions, Ferminia, the wine shop's cook, somehow transformed these products into the tripe and oxtail dishes that form an integral part of the menu.

Many Italian diners come here to relish these dishes, which might not appeal to every foreign visitor's taste. They include rigatone con pajata (pasta with small intestines), coda alla vaccinara (oxtail stew), fagiole e cotiche (beans with intestinal fat), and other examples of *la cocina povera* (food of the poor). Less adventurous, and possibly more appetizing, are the restaurant's array of well-prepared salads, soups, pastas, steaks, cutlets, grills, and ice creams, which the kitchens produce in abundance. The English-speaking staff is helpful and kind, tactfully proposing well-flavored alternatives if you're not ready for Roman soul food.

IN TRASTEVERE
EXPENSIVE
Alberto Ciarla. Piazza San Cosimato 40. ☎ **06/581-8668.** Reservations required, especially on weekends. Main courses 26,000L–46,000L ($15.60–$27.60); fixed-price menus 80,000L–90,000L ($48–$54). AE, DC, MC, V. Mon–Sat 8:30pm–12:30am. Closed 1 week in Jan and 1 week in Aug. SEAFOOD.

Alberto Ciarla is the best and most expensive restaurant in Trastevere. Some critics still consider it one of the finest restaurants in all of Rome, although it's not as chic as it was when discovered by fickle fashion in the late 1980s. In an 1890 building, set into an obscure corner of an enormous square, it serves some of the most elegant fish dishes in the city. You'll be greeted at the door with a cordial reception and a lavish display of seafood on ice. A dramatically modern decor plays shades of brilliant light against patches of shadow for a Renaissance chiaroscuro effect. Specialties include a handful of ancient recipes subtly improved by Signor Ciarla (an example is the soup of pasta and beans with seafood). Original dishes include a delectable salmon Marcel Trompier with lobster sauce, a well-flavored sushi, spaghetti with clams, and a full array of shellfish. The fillet of sea bass is prepared in at least three different ways, including an award-winning version with almonds.

MODERATE
La Cisterna. Via della Cisterna 13. ☎ **06/581-2543.** Reservations recommended. Main courses 16,000L–32,000L ($9.60–$19.20). AE, DC, MC, V. Mon–Sat 7pm–midnight. ROMAN.

La Cisterna, named for an ancient well from imperial times discovered in the cellar, lies deep in the heart of Trastevere. For more than half a century it has been run by the Simmi family, who are genuinely interested in serving only the best as well as providing a good time for all guests. In good weather you can dine outside at sidewalk tables. If it's rainy or cold you'll be in rooms decorated with murals, including the *Rape of the Sabine Women*. Food critics have never awarded any stars to this place—and probably never will—but if you like traditional cookery based on the best of regional produce, then come here. In summer you can inspect the antipasti right

Dining in Trastevere

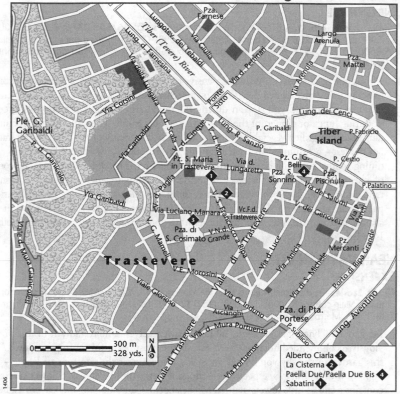

Alberto Ciarla ❸
La Cisterna ❷
Paella Due/Paella Due Bis ❹
Sabatini ❶

out on the street before going in. Specialties of the house include Roman-style suckling lamb (abbacchio), rigatoni a l'amatriciana, pappallini romana (wide noodles flavored with prosciutto, cheese, and eggs), shrimp, and fresh fish—especially sea bass baked with herbs.

Sabatini. Piazza Santa Maria in Trastevere 13. ☎ **06/581-2026.** Reservations recommended. Main courses 20,000L–42,000L ($12–$25.20). AE, DC, MC, V. Daily noon–3pm and 8pm–midnight. Closed 2 weeks in Aug (dates vary). ROMAN/SEAFOOD.

This is one of the most popular dining spots in Rome, although the glitz and glitter crowd have moved on to other places. At night, Piazza Santa Maria—one of the settings used in Fellini's *Roma*—is the center of the liveliest action in the neighborhood. The place is very tied to the hustle-bustle of the Trastevere landscape. In summer, tables are placed out on this charming piazza and you can look across at the floodlit golden frescoes of the church. If you can't get a table outside, you may be assigned to a room under beamed ceilings, with stenciled walls, lots of paneling, and framed oil paintings. So popular is this place that you may have to wait for a table even if you have a reservation. The spaghetti with seafood is excellent, and fresh fish and shellfish, especially grilled scampi, may tempt you as well (although these aren't as good as at Alberto Ciarla). For a savory treat, try pollo con pepperoni, chicken cooked with red and green peppers. The meal price will rise exorbitantly if you order grilled fish or the Florentine steaks. For wine, try a white Frascati or an Antinori chianti in a hand-painted pitcher.

INEXPENSIVE

Paella Due/Paella Due Bis. Via della Lungarette 173. ☎ **06/588-2876.** Pizzas 8,000L–12,000L ($4.80–$7.20); main courses 15,000L–30,000L ($9–$18); fixed-price meals (paella) 35,000L–70,000L ($21–$42) for two diners. No credit cards. Tues–Sun noon–midnight. SPANISH.

This is one of the best relatively inexpensive restaurants in Trastevere, with references to Spain that derive from a decade the owner/chef spent cooking in a restaurant there. No one will mind if you stop in during the midafternoon for just a cup of coffee, or during lunch or dinner for the array of pizzas and pastas. The antipasti buffet contains focaccia, grilled vegetables, sliced mozzarella, and many of the fruits of the Italian harvest—a minimeal in itself beginning at 10,000L ($6). You'll find a trio of dining rooms, paintings of the nearby Tiber, and a sense of Old Trastevere. The cost of a heaping paella platter for two varies widely according to what you want it to contain. Least expensive is the vegetarian version; the most expensive is the authentic paella valenciana with seafood and meat. Most diners are served in Paella Due, although if it's full, the overflow heads next door to additional seating in Paella Due Bis.

NEAR VATICAN CITY
EXPENSIVE

✪ **Les Etoiles.** In the Hotel Atlante Star, Via Vitelleschi 34. ☎ **06/689-3434.** Reservations required. Main courses 85,000L–125,000L ($51–$75). AE, DC, MC, V. Daily 12:30–2:30pm and 7:30–11pm. Metro: Ottaviano. MEDITERRANEAN.

Les Etoiles, "The Stars," deserves all the stars it receives. The restaurant in this previously recommended hotel has been called "the most beautiful rooftop in Italy." At this garden in the sky you'll have an open window over the rooftops of Rome—a 360° view of landmarks, especially the floodlit dome of St. Peter's. A flower terrace contains a trio of little towers, named Michelangelo, Campidoglio, and Ottavo Colle. In summer everyone wants a table outside, but in winter almost the same view is available from tables near the picture windows. The color and fragrance of a refined Mediterranean cuisine, with perfectly balanced flavors, includes quail cooked either with radicchio or in a casserole with mushrooms and herbs, artichokes stuffed with ricotta and pecorino cheese, Venetian-style risotto with squid ink, and roast suckling lamb with mint. The creative chef is rightly proud of his many regional dishes, and the service is refined with an exciting wine list.

MODERATE

Ristorante Il Matriciano. Via dei Gracchi 55. ☎ **06/321-2327.** Reservations required, especially for dinner. Main courses 14,000L–26,000L ($8.40–$15.60). AE, DC, MC, V. Daily 12:30–3pm and 8–11:30pm. Closed Aug 5–25, Wed in Nov–Apr, and Sat in May–Oct. Metro: Lepanto or Ottaviano. ROMAN.

Il Matriciano is a family restaurant with a devoted following. Its location near St. Peter's makes it all the more distinguished. The food is good, but it's mostly country fare—nothing fancy. The decor, likewise, is kept to a minimum. In summer try to get one of the sidewalk tables behind a green hedge and under a shady canopy. For openers you might enjoy a zuppa di verdura or ravioli di ricotta. From many dishes, we recommend scaloppa alla valdostana, abbacchio (suckling lamb) al forno, and trippa (tripe) alla romana. The most obvious specialty of the house, bucatini matriciana, is derived from the favorite sauce in the Roman repertoire: Amatriciana. Here, it's prepared with bucatini pasta, and richly flavored with bacon, tomatoes, and basil. Dining at the homelike convivial tables, you're likely to see an array of Romans, from prelates and cardinals escaping from the confines of the nearby Vatican for a while, to stars of the Italian cinema.

Ristorante Pierdonati. Via della Conciliazione 39. ☎ **06/6880-3557.** Reservations not necessary. Main courses 14,000L–30,000L ($8.40–$18); fixed-price menu 25,000L ($15). AE, MC, V. Fri–Wed noon–3:30pm and 7–10:30pm. Closed Aug. ROMAN.

Ristorante Pierdonati has been serving wayfarers to the Vatican since 1868. In the same building as the previously recommended Hotel Columbus, this restaurant was the former home of Cardinal della Rovere. Today it's the headquarters of the Knights of the Holy Sepulchre of Jerusalem, and the best restaurant in the gastronomic wasteland of the Vatican area. Its severely classical facade is relieved inside by a gargoyle fountain spewing water into a basin. You'll dine beneath a vaulted ceiling. Try the calves' liver Venetian style, the stewed veal with tomato sauce, or ravioli bolognese. To get really Roman, order the tripe. The cuisine isn't refined or pretentious, but robust and heavy. It can get rather crowded here on days that see thousands upon thousands flocking to St. Peter's. Tuesday and Friday are fresh fish days.

INEXPENSIVE

Ristorante Giardinaccio. Via Aurelia 53. ☎ **06/631-367.** Reservations recommended, especially on weekends. Main courses 10,000L–15,000L ($6–$9). AE, DC, MC, V. Wed–Mon 12:15–3:30pm and 7:15–11pm. ITALIAN/MOLISIAN/INTERNATIONAL.

This popular restaurant, operated by Nicolino Mancini, is only 200 yards from St. Peter's. Unusual for Rome, it offers Molisian specialties from southeastern Italy. It's rustically decorated in the country-tavern style with dark wood and exposed stone. Flaming grills provide succulent versions of perfectly done quail, goat, and other dishes, but perhaps the mutton goulash would be more adventurous. You can order many versions of pasta, including taconelle, a homemade pasta with lamb sauce, which is often served. Vegetarians and others will like the large self-service selection of antipasti. Snooty diners might dismiss this food as too regional—or "too peasant"— but it's a perfect introduction to the hearty cuisine of an area rarely visited by Americans.

IN PARIOLI
VERY EXPENSIVE

✪ **Relais Le Jardin.** In the Hotel Lord Byron, Via G. de Notaris 5. ☎ **06/361-3041.** Reservations required. Main courses 45,000L–55,000L ($27–$33). AE, DC, MC, V. Mon–Sat 1–3pm and 8–10:30pm. Closed Aug. ITALIAN/TRADITIONAL.

Relais Le Jardin is one of the best places to go in Rome for both traditional and creative cuisine, and a chichi crowd with demanding palates patronizes it nightly. There are places in Rome with greater views, but not with such an elegant setting. Inside one of the most exclusive small hotels of the capital, the aggressively lighthearted decor combines white lattice with bold colors and flowers. Many of the cooks and service personnel were trained at embassies or diplomatic residences abroad. A *relais gourmands*, the establishment serves a seasonally changing array of dishes. The pasta and soups are among the finest in town, as exemplified by the tonnarelli pasta with asparagus and smoked ham served with concassé tomatoes. The chef can take a dish once served only to the plebes in Roman days, bean soup with clams, and make it elegantly refined. For your main course you can choose from roast loin of lamb with artichoke romana or grilled beef sirloin with hot chicory and sautéed potatoes. The single best risotto served in Rome in our view is the chef's risotto with pheasant sauce, asparagus, and black truffle flakes with a hint of fresh thyme.

MODERATE

Al Ceppo. Via Panama 2. ☎ **06/841-9696.** Reservations recommended. Main courses 18,000L–26,000L ($10.80–$15.60). AE, DC, MC, V. Tues–Sun 12:30–3pm and 8–11pm. Closed the last 3 weeks of Aug. ROMAN.

Because of its somewhat hidden location (although it's only two blocks from the Villa Borghese, near Piazza Ungheria), the clientele is likely to be Roman rather than foreign. This is a longtime favorite, and the cuisine is as good as it ever was. "The Log" (its name in English) features an open wood-stoked fireplace on which the chef does lamb chops, liver, and bacon to charcoal perfection. The beefsteak, which hails from Tuscany, is also succulent. Other dishes on the menu include linguine monteconero (made with clams and fresh tomatoes); a savory spaghetti with peppers, fresh basil, and pecorino cheese; a fillet of swordfish filled with grapefruit, Parmesan cheese, pine nuts, and dry grapes; and a fish carpaccio (raw sea bass) with a green salad, onions, and green pepper. Save room for dessert, especially the apple cobbler, the pear and almond tart, or the chocolate meringue hazelnut cake.

Exploring Rome 5

With the imminent approach of its millennium-ending Jubilee 2000, Rome has been working hard to spruce up its appearance. You'll be amazed by the new sense of cleanliness and vitality especially among the historic buildings and monuments. The greenish-black grime of automobile and other pollution has disappeared, revealing the original glory of the structures of the Eternal City, and every nuance of their intricate decorations.

Many of the tourist-trodden squares such as the Piazza di Trevi (of *Three Coins in the Fountain* fame) and the Piazza Navona are bright, sparkling, and alluring again. The Frommer prize for cleanup goes to the "artists" who transformed the dingy Piazza di Sant'Ignazio into the rococo gem it was always meant to be. Even the churches along Via del Corso, including that jewel of the baroque era, San Marcello, shine again along the streets of this magnificently historic city.

Whether under grime or grime-free, the ancient monuments silently evoke the enchanted historic aura of one of the greatest centers of Western civilization. In the millennium of the Eternal City's influence, all roads led to Rome with good reason. It was one of the first cosmopolitan cities in the world, importing slaves, gladiators, great art—even citizens—from the far corners of the empire. Along with all its carnage and mismanagement, it left a legacy of law and an uncanny lesson in how to conquer enemies by absorbing their cultures.

But ancient Rome is only part of the spectacle. The Vatican has had a tremendous influence on making the city a center of world tourism. Although Vatican architects stripped down much of the glory of the past, they created great Renaissance treasures, occasionally incorporating the old—as Michelangelo did in turning the Baths of Diocletian into a church.

In the years that followed, Bernini adorned the city with the wonders of the baroque, especially the fountains. The modern sightseer even owes a debt (as reluctant as one may be to acknowledge it) to Mussolini, who did much to dig out the past, particularly at the Imperial Forum. Today, besides being the Italian capital, Rome, in a larger sense, belongs to the world.

Millennium Milestones: Roma 2000

In A.D. 1,000, at the dawn of Christendom's second millennium, thousands of devoutly religious Romans gathered on the city's hilltops, anxiously awaiting the return of Christ the Majesty to judge the living and the dead. Despite the fanatical predictions of many mystics and visionaries that the world would end a thousand years after the arrival of Christ, nothing particularly eventful happened. The dejected masses of the Roman faithful returned to their homes, churches, and work-day rituals to continue their lives in the Eternal City.

This time around, they may simply be waiting for the government to finish—or even start—the many proposed work projects that were supposed to make the end of the second millennium more event-filled than its dawn. Since 1997 locals and visitors alike have had a sense of the fuss being raised. Restoration efforts have blocked access to the Colosseum and the Spanish Steps. A lengthy green construction fence surrounding excavations at the Forum of Nerva has hindered views along the Via dei Fori Imperiali. Renovation of neighborhood squares has created hectic street detours and reduced the amount of available parking.

Consequently, this urban chaos has left a question in many minds as to whether the benefits of these restoration projects will outweigh the inconvenience. Progress is being made very slowly through a path of governmental red tape, a lack of definitive central planning, and archaeological projects that almost daily uncover new difficulties or setbacks in meeting projected completion deadlines.

Indeed, broad-based powers and funds have been allocated for these improve-ments. Yet, the initiation—let alone progress—of many projects has proved to be as frustrating as driving the city's streets. Unfortunately, civic-mindedness gives way to businesses vying for their slice of the pie, and groundbreaking just about any-where exposes multiple layers of history that require new plans of exploration and protection.

Inconveniences are also evident in more contemporary structures, as many mu-seums and restaurants have limited their hours of operation, decreased the space accessible to customers, or even closed their doors to enlarge gallery and dining space or renovate toilet facilities. There's a rush to transform churches, schools, homes, and abandoned buildings into lodging as well, causing pedestrian detours and increased levels of noise pollution.

The plans sound good: banning vehicular traffic in whole neighborhoods, trans-forming inner-city parking lots into open squares for socialization, opening new parking areas closer to the autostrada and rail lines at the outskirts of the city, sched-uling high-speed trains and bus connections to depart every five minutes toward the core historical district, and planting scores of trees and flowerbeds to beautify the face of the city. But the details remain out of focus even at this late date. Anxi-ety and speculation rise as individual links in the master plan fall apart or simply remain ignored.

Perhaps the city's cultural program series, begun in 1997 to focus attention on the role of Rome as a crucible of civilization, will provide the impetus needed to get its politicos and engineers in gear in 1998 and 1999. But then again, the suc-cess of that program has been largely tied to the enthusiasm of outsiders, as musi-cians and artists from around the world have responded to the city's call to honor the spirit of Western Civilization—a decidedly easier feat than altering the con-crete structure from which it sprang.

1 The Vatican & St. Peter's

On the left side of Piazza San Pietro, near the Arco delle Campane, is the **Vatican Tourist Office** (☎ **06/6988-4466**), open Monday to Saturday from 8:30am to 7pm. Here you can buy a map of the Vatican and have your questions answered about St. Peter's or the Vatican museums.

✪ **St. Peter's Basilica (Basilica di San Pietro).** Piazza San Pietro. ☎ **06/6988-4466.** Basilica (including the sacristy, treasury, and grottoes), free; guided tour of the excavations around St. Peter's tomb, 10,000L ($6); dome, 5,000L ($3) adults, 1,000L (60¢) students, or 6,000L ($3.60) to take the elevator. Basilica (including the sacristy and treasury), Mar–Sept, daily 7am–7pm; Oct–Feb, daily 7am–6pm. Grottoes daily 7am–5pm. Dome, Mar–Sept, daily 8am–6pm; Oct–Feb, daily 8am–4:30pm. Bus: 46. *Note:* To be admitted to St. Peter's, women must wear longer skirts or pants—anything that covers the knees. Men cannot wear shorts. Sleeveless tops are not allowed for either gender. You *will* be turned away.

As you stand in Bernini's **St. Peter's Square** (Piazza San Pietro), you'll be in the arms of an ellipse dominated by St. Peter's Basilica. Like a loving parent, the Doric-pillared colonnade reaches out to embrace the faithful. Holding 300,000 is no problem for this square.

In the center of the square is an Egyptian obelisk, brought from the ancient city of Heliopolis on the Nile Delta and used to adorn the nearby Nero's Circus. Flanking the obelisk are two 17th-century fountains—the one on the right (facing the basilica) by Carlo Maderno, who designed the facade of St. Peter's, was placed here by Bernini himself; the other is by Carlo Fontana.

Inside, the size of this famous church is awe-inspiring—although its dimensions (about two football fields) are not immediately apparent. St. Peter's is said to have been built over the tomb of the crucified saint. Originally it was erected on the order of Constantine, but the present structure is essentially High Renaissance and baroque; it showcases the talents of some of Italy's greatest artists: Bramante, Raphael, Michelangelo, and Maderno.

In a church of such grandeur—overwhelming in its detail of gilt, marble, and mosaic—although you can't expect much subtlety, you will encounter an extraordinary display of art. In the nave on the right (the first chapel) stands the best-known piece of sculpture, the *Pietà* that Michelangelo sculpted while still in his early 20s. In the 1970s, in one of the worst acts of vandalism on record, a madman screaming "I am Jesus Christ" attacked the *Pietà*, battering the Madonna's stone arm, the folded veil, her left eyelid, and nose. Now restored, the *Pietà* is protected by a wall of reinforced glass. Much farther on, in the right wing of the transept near the Chapel of St. Michael, rests Canova's neoclassic sculptural tribute to **Pope Clement XIII.** The truly devout are prone to kiss the feet of the 13th-century bronze of **St. Peter,** attributed to Arnolfo di Cambio (at the far reaches of the nave, against a corner pillar on the right). Under Michelangelo's dome is the celebrated *baldacchino* by Bernini, resting over the papal altar. The canopy was created in the 17th century—in part, so it's said, from bronze stripped from the Pantheon. However, analysis of the bronze seems to prove otherwise.

In addition, you can visit the **sacristy and treasury,** filled with jewel-studded chalices, reliquaries, and copes. One robe worn by Pius XII strikes a simple note in these halls of elegance. Later you can make an underground visit to the **Vatican grottoes,** with their tombs, both ancient and modern (Pope John XXIII gets the most adulation).

To go even farther down, to the area around St. Peter's tomb, you must apply several days beforehand to the **excavations** office. You can make your applications

Rome Attractions

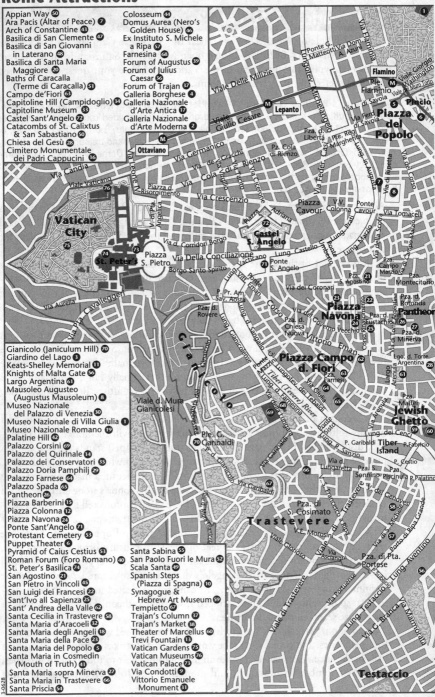

Appian Way 50
Ara Pacis (Altar of Peace) 7
Arch of Constantine 43
Basilica di San Clemente 47
Basilica di San Giovanni
  in Laterano 48
Basilica di Santa Maria
  Maggiore 20
Baths of Caracalla
  (Terme di Caracalla) 51
Campo de'Fiori 63
Capitoline Hill (Campidoglio) 34
Capitoline Museum 33
Castel Sant'Angelo 72
Catacombs of St. Calixtus
  & San Sabastiano 50
Chiesa del Gesù 28
Cimitero Monumentale
  dei Padri Cappucini 16

Colosseum 44
Domus Aurea (Nero's
  Golden House) 46
Ex Instituto S. Michele
  a Ripa 57
Farnesina 68
Forum of Augustus 39
Forum of Julius
  Caesar 36
Forum of Trajan 37
Galleria Borghese 4
Galleria Nazionale
  d'Arte Antica 17
Galleria Nazionale
  d'Arte Moderna 2

Gianicolo (Janiculum Hill) 70
Giardino del Lago 3
Keats-Shelley Memorial 11
Knights of Malta Gate 56
Largo Argentina 61
Mausoleo Augusteo
  (Augustus Mausoleum) 8
Museo Nazionale
  del Palazzo di Venezia 30
Museo Nazionale di Villa Giulia 1
Museo Nazionale Romano 19
Palatine Hill 42
Palazzo Corsini 69
Palazzo del Quirinale 14
Palazzo dei Conservatori 35
Palazzo Doria Pamphilj 29
Palazzo Farnese 64
Palazzo Spada 65
Pantheon 26
Piazza Barberini 15
Piazza Colonna 12
Piazza Navona 24
Ponte Sant'Angelo 71
Protestant Cemetery 53
Puppet Theater 6
Pyramid of Caius Cestius 53
Roman Forum (Foro Romano) 40
St. Peter's Basilica 74
San Agostino 21
San Pietro in Vincoli 45
San Luigi dei Francesi 22
Sant'Ivo all Sapienza 62
Sant' Andrea della Valle 25
Santa Cecilia in Trastevere 58
Santa Maria d'Aracoeli 32
Santa Maria degli Angeli 18
Santa Maria della Pace 23
Santa Maria del Popolo 5
Santa Maria in Cosmedin
  (Mouth of Truth) 41
Santa Maria sopra Minerva 27
Santa Maria in Trastevere 66
Santa Priscia 54

Santa Sabina 55
San Paolo Fuori le Mura 52
Scala Santa 49
Spanish Steps
  (Piazza di Spagna) 10
Synagogue &
  Hebrew Art Museum 59
Tempietto 67
Trajan's Column 37
Trajan's Market 38
Theater of Marcellus 60
Trevi Fountain 13
Vatican Gardens 75
Vatican Museums 76
Vatican Palace 73
Via Condotti 9
Vittorio Emanuele
  Monument 31

3-0628

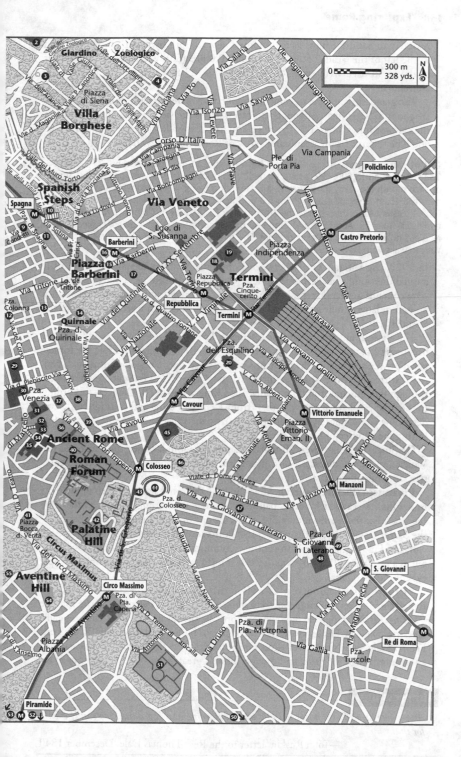

137

Monday to Saturday from 9am to noon and 2 to 5pm by passing under the arch to the left of the facade of St. Peter's. For 10,000L ($6), you'll take a guided tour of the tombs that were excavated in the 1940s, 23 feet beneath the floor of the church.

The grandest sight is yet to come: the climb to **Michelangelo's dome,** which towers about 375 feet high. Although you can walk up the steps, we recommend taking the elevator for as far as it'll carry you. You can also walk along the roof, for which you'll be rewarded with a panoramic view of Rome and the Vatican.

✪ **Vatican Museums & the Sistine Chapel.** Vatican City, Viale Vaticano. ☎ **06/6988-3333.** Admission 15,000L ($9) adults, 10,000L ($6) children, free for everyone the last Sunday of each month (be ready for a crowd). July–Sept and Easter week, Mon–Sat and final Sun of month 8:45am–4pm; off-season, Mon–Sat and final Sun of month 9am–2pm. Closed Jan 6, Feb 11, Easter Mon., Thurs before the 7th Sun after Easter, May 1, Corpus Christi (9th Sun after Easter), June 29, Aug 15, Nov 1, and Dec 8. Last admission 1 hour before closing. Closed religious holidays. Metro: Ottaviano. *Note:* The museum entrance is a long walk around the Vatican walls from St. Peter's Square.

In 1929, the Lateran Treaty between Pope Pius XI and the Italian government created the world's smallest independent state, located in Rome. Though small, this state contains a gigantic repository of treasures from antiquity and the Renaissance housed in labyrinthine galleries. The Vatican's art collection reaches its apex in the Sistine Chapel.

The Vatican museums comprise a series of lavishly adorned palaces and galleries occupying a part of the papal palaces built from the 1200s onward. From the former papal private apartments, the museums were created over a period of time to display the vast treasure trove of art acquired by the Vatican. You can choose your route through the museum from four color-coded itineraries—A, B, C, or D—according to the time you have at your disposal (from 1 1/2 to 5 hours) and your interests. You determine your choice by consulting large-size panels placed at the entrance and following the letter/color of your choice.

Obviously, 1, 2, or even 20 trips will not be enough to see the wealth of the Vatican, much less digest it. With that in mind, we've previewed only a representative sampling of the masterpieces on display here.

Pinacoteca (Picture Gallery): After climbing the spiral stairway, keep to the right to the Pinacoteca, which houses paintings and tapestries from the 11th to the 19th centuries. For the break with the Byzantine, see one of the Vatican's finest artworks— the *Stefaneschi Triptych* (six panels) by Giotto and his assistants. You'll also see the works of Fra Angelico, the 15th-century Dominican monk who distinguished himself as a miniaturist (his *Virgin with Child* is justly praised—look for the microscopic eyes of the Madonna).

In the Raphael salon you can view three paintings by that giant of the Renaissance—the *Coronation of the Virgin,* the *Virgin of Foligno,* and the massive *Transfiguration* (completed by Raphael shortly before his death). There are also eight tapestries made by Flemish weavers from cartoons by Raphael. In Room IX, seek out Leonardo da Vinci's masterful—but uncompleted—*St. Jerome with the Lion,* as well as Giovanni Bellini's *Pietà,* and one of Titian's greatest works, the *Virgin of Frari.*

Impressions

As a whole St. Peter's is fit for nothing but a ballroom, and it is a little too gaudy even for that.

—John Ruskin, letter to the Rev. Thomas Dale, December 1840

Vatican City

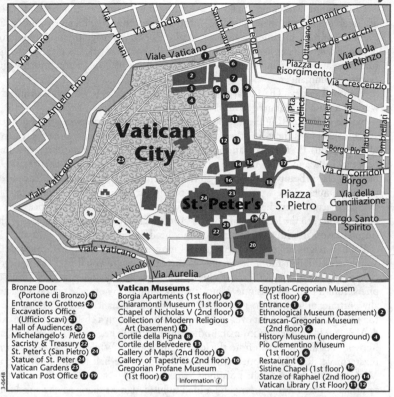

Bronze Door
  (Portone di Bronzo) 18
Entrance to Grottoes 24
Excavations Office
  (Ufficio Scavi) 21
Hall of Audiences 20
Michelangelo's *Pietà* 23
Sacristy & Treasury 22
St. Peter's (San Pietro) 24
Statue of St. Peter 24
Vatican Gardens 25
Vatican Post Office 17 19

Vatican Museums
Borgia Apartments (1st floor) 14
Chiaramonti Museum (1st floor) 9
Chapel of Nicholas V (2nd floor) 15
Collection of Modern Religious
  Art (basement) 14
Cortile della Pigna 8
Cortile del Belvedere 13
Gallery of Maps (2nd floor) 12
Gallery of Tapestries (2nd floor) 10
Gregorian Profane Museum
  (1st floor) 2   Information ⓘ

Egyptian-Gregorian Musem
  (1st floor) 7
Entrance 1
Ethnological Museum (basement) 2
Etruscan-Gregorian Museum
  (2nd floor) 6
History Museum (underground) 4
Pio Clementino Museum
  (1st floor) 6
Restaurant 5
Sistine Chapel (1st floor) 16
Stanze of Raphael (2nd floor) 14
Vatican Library (1st Floor) 11 12

Finally, in Room X feast your eyes on one of the masterpieces of the baroque period, Caravaggio's *Deposition from the Cross.*

Egyptian-Gregorian Museum: Review the grandeur of the Pharaohs by studying sarcophagi, mummies, statues of goddesses, vases, jewelry, sculptured pink-granite statues, and hieroglyphics.

Estruscan-Gregorian Museum: With sarcophagi, a chariot, bronzes, urns, jewelry, and terra-cotta vases, this gallery affords remarkable insights into an ancient civilization. One of the most acclaimed exhibits is the Regolini-Galassi tomb, unearthed at Cerveteri (see "Side Trips from Rome," later in this chapter) in the 19th century. It shares top honors with the *Mars of Todi,* a bronze sculpture that probably dates from the 5th century B.C.

Pio Clementino Museum: Here you'll find Greek and Roman sculptures, many of which are immediately recognizable masterpieces. The rippling muscles of the *Belvedere Torso,* a partially preserved Greek statue (1st century B.C.) that was much admired by the artists of the Renaissance, especially Michelangelo, reveal an intricate knowledge of the human body. In the rotunda is a large gilded bronze of Hercules that dates from the late 2nd century A.D. Other major works of sculpture are under porticoes that open onto the Belvedere courtyard. Dating from the 1st century B.C., one sculpture shows Laocoön and his two sons locked in an eternal struggle with the serpents. The incomparable *Apollo of Belvedere* (a late Roman reproduction of an authentic Greek work from the 4th century B.C.) has become the symbol of classic male beauty.

Chiaramonti Museum: You'll find a dazzling array of Roman sculpture and copies of Greek originals in these galleries. In the Braccio Nuovo, which was built as an extension of the Chiaramonti, you can admire *The Nile,* a magnificent reproduction of a long-lost Hellenistic original, and one of the most remarkable pieces of sculpture from antiquity. The imposing statue of Augustus of Prima Porta presents him as a regal commander.

Vatican Library: The Library is richly decorated and frescoed, representing the work of a team of Mannerist painters commissioned by Sixtus V.

Stanze of Raphael: While still a young man, Raphael was given one of the greatest assignments of his short life: the decoration of a series of rooms in the apartments of Pope Julius II. The decoration was carried out by Raphael and his workshop between 1508 and 1524. In these works, Raphael achieves the Renaissance aim of blending classic beauty with realism. In the first chamber, the **Stanza dell'Incendio,** you'll see much of the work of Raphael's pupils but little of the master—except in the fresco across from the window. The figure of the partially draped Aeneas rescuing his father (to the left of the fresco) is sometimes attributed to Raphael, as is the surprised woman with a jug balanced on her head to the right.

Raphael reigns supreme in the next and most important salon, the **Stanza della Segnatura,** the first room decorated by the artist, where you'll find the majestic *School of Athens,* one of the artist's best-known works, which depicts such philosophers from the ages as Aristotle, Plato, and Socrates. Many of these figures are actually portraits of some of the greatest artists of the Renaissance, including Bramante (on the right as Euclid, bent over and balding as he draws on a chalkboard), Leonardo da Vinci (as Plato, the bearded man in the center pointing heavenward), even Raphael himself (looking out at you from the lower right corner). While he was painting this masterpiece, Raphael stopped work to walk down the hall for the unveiling of Michelangelo's newly finished Sistine Chapel ceiling. He was so impressed that he returned to his *School of Athens* and added to his design a sulking Michelangelo sitting on the steps. Another well-known masterpiece in this room is the *Disputà del Sacramento.*

The Stanza d'Eliodoro, also by the master, manages to flatter Raphael's papal patrons (Julius II and Leo X) without compromising his art (although one rather fanciful fresco depicts the pope driving Attila from Rome). Finally, there's the Sala di Constantino, which was completed by his students after Raphael's death. And the loggia, frescoed with more than 50 scenes from the Bible, was designed by Raphael, although the actual work was done by his loyal students.

Collection of Modern Religious Art: This museum, opened in 1973, represents the American artists' first invasion of the Vatican (the church had previously limited itself to European art created before the 18th century). But Pope Paul VI's hobby changed all that. Of the 55 rooms in the new museum, at least 12 are devoted to American artists. All the works chosen for the museum were judged on the basis of their "spiritual and religious values." Among the American works is Leonard Baskin's 5-foot bronze sculpture of *Isaac.* Modern Italian artists such as de Chirico and Manzù are also displayed, and there's a special room for the paintings of the French artist Georges Rouault.

Borgia Apartments: These apartments, frescoed with biblical scenes by Pinturicchio of Umbria and his assistants, were designed for Pope Alexander VI (the infamous Borgia pope). The rooms, although badly lit, have great splendor and style. At the end of the Stanze of Raphael is the Chapel of Nicholas V, an intimate room frescoed by the Dominican monk Fra Angelico, the most saintly of all Italian painters.

Sistine Chapel: Michelangelo considered himself a sculptor, not a painter. While in his 30s, he was commanded by Julius II to stop work on the pope's own tomb and to devote his considerable talents to painting ceiling frescoes—an art form of which the Florentine master was contemptuous.

Michelangelo labored for 4 years (1508–12) over this epic project, which was so physically taxing that it permanently damaged his eyesight. All during the task he had to contend with the pope's incessant urgings to hurry up; at one point Julius threatened to topple Michelangelo from the scaffolding—or so Vasari relates.

It's ironic that a project undertaken against the artist's wishes would form his most enduring legend. Glorifying the human body as only a sculptor could, Michelangelo painted nine panels, taken from the pages of Genesis, and surrounded them with prophets and sibyls. The most notable panels detail the expulsion of Adam and Eve from the Garden of Eden, and the creation of man—where God's outstretched hand imbues Adam with spirit.

The Florentine master was in his 60s when he began to paint the masterly *Last Judgment* on the altar wall. Again working against his wishes, Michelangelo presents a more jaundiced view of people and their fate; God sits in judgment, and sinners are plunged into the mouth of hell.

A master of ceremonies under Paul III, Monsignor Biagio da Cesena, protested to the pope against the "shameless nudes" painted by Michelangelo. Michelangelo showed he wasn't above petty revenge by painting the prude with the ears of a jackass in hell. When Biagio complained to the pope, Paul III maintained that he had no jurisdiction in hell. However, Daniele de Volterra was summoned to drape clothing over some of the bare figures—thus earning for himself a dubious distinction as a haberdasher.

On the side walls are frescoes by other Renaissance masters such as Botticelli, Perugino, Luca Signorelli, Pinturicchio, Cosimo Roselli, and Ghirlandaio. We'd guess that if these paintings had been displayed by themselves in other chapels, they would be the object of special pilgrimages. But since they have to compete unfairly with the artistry of Michelangelo, they're virtually ignored by the average visitor.

The restoration of the Sistine Chapel in the 1990s touched off a worldwide debate among art historians. The Sistine Chapel was on the verge of collapse, both from its age and the weather, and restoration has taken years, as restorers used advanced computer analyses in their painstaking and controversial work. They reattached the fresco and repaired the ceiling. No longer dark and shadowy, Michelangelo's frescoes are now bright and pastel. Critics claim that in addition to removing centuries of dirt and grime—and several of the added "modesty" drapes— a vital second layer of paint was removed as well. Purists argue that many of the restored figures seem flat compared to the original, which had more shadow and detail. Others in the media have hailed the project for having saved Michelangelo's masterpiece for future generations to appreciate.

History Museum: This museum, founded by Pope Paul VI, was established to tell the history of the Vatican. It exhibits arms, uniforms, and armor, some of which dates back to the early days of the Renaissance. The carriages on display are those used by the popes and cardinals in religious processions. Among the showcases of dress uniforms are the colorful outfits worn by the Pontifical Army Corps, which was discontinued by Pope Paul VI.

Ethnological Museum: The Ethnological Museum is an assemblage of works of art and objects of cultural significance from all over the world. The principal route is a half-mile walk through 25 geographical sections, which display thousands of objects covering 3,000 years of world history. The section devoted to China is especially interesting and worthwhile.

VATICAN GARDENS

Separating the Vatican from the secular world on the north and west are 58 acres of lush, carefully tended gardens filled with winding paths, brilliantly colored flowers, groves of massive oaks, and ancient fountains and pools. In the midst of this pastoral setting is a small summer house, the Villa Pia, built for Pope Pius IV in 1560 by Pirro Ligorio. You can visit the gardens only on a guided tour, which must be arranged in advance and is limited to 33 people; so reserve as far in advance as possible during the busy summer period. (*Note:* You cannot get tickets by phone.) Tours run Monday and Tuesday and Thursday through Saturday at 10am. Tickets are 18,000L ($10.80) per person and are available at the Vatican Tourist Office.

PAPAL AUDIENCES

When in Rome, the pope gives public audiences every Wednesday morning. The audience begins at 10:30am, but sometimes at 10am in the hot summer. It takes place in the Paul VI Hall of Audiences, although sometimes the Basilica of St. Peter and St. Peter's Square are used to accommodate a large attendance. Anyone is welcome, but you must obtain a free ticket first from the office of the Prefecture of the Papal Household, accessible from St. Peter's Square by the Bronze Door, where the right-hand colonnade (as you face the basilica) begins. The office is open Monday to Saturday from 9am to 1pm. Tickets are readily available on Monday and Tuesday, but sometimes you won't be able to get into the office on Wednesday morning. Occasionally, if there's enough room, you can attend without a ticket.

You can also write ahead of time to the **Prefecture of the Papal Household,** 00120 Città del Vaticano (☎ **06/6988-3017**), indicating your language, the dates of your visit, the number of people in your party, and, if possible, the hotel in Rome to which the cards should be sent the afternoon before the audience. American Catholics, armed with a letter of introduction from their parish priest, should apply to the **North American College,** Via dell'Umiltà 30, 00187 Rome (☎ **06/690-011**).

At noon on Sunday the pope speaks briefly from his study window and gives his blessing to the visitors and pilgrims gathered in St. Peter's Square. From about mid-July to mid-September the Angelus and blessing take place at the summer residence at Castelgandolfo, some 16 miles out of Rome and accessible by Metro and bus.

ANOTHER ATTRACTION AROUND VATICAN CITY

Castel Sant'Angelo. Lungotevere Castello 50. ☎ **06/687-5036.** Admission 8,000L ($4.80) adults, free for children 17 and under and seniors 60 and over. Daily 9am–2pm, Sun 9am–noon. Closed second and last Tues of each month. Metro: Ottaviano.

This overpowering structure, in a landmark position on the Tiber, was originally built in the 2nd century A.D. as a tomb for the emperor Hadrian; it continued as an imperial mausoleum until the time of Caracalla. If it looks like a fortress, it should—that was its function in the Middle Ages, built over the Roman walls and linked to the Vatican by an underground passageway that was much used by the fleeing papacy, who escaped from unwanted visitors like Charles V during his sack of the city in 1527.

In the 14th century it became a papal residence, enjoying various connections with Boniface IX, Nicholas V, even Julius II, patron of Michelangelo and Raphael. But its legend rests largely on its link with Pope Alexander VI, whose mistress bore him two children—Cesare and Lucrezia Borgia.

Today the highlight of the castle is a trip through the Renaissance apartments with their coffered ceilings and lush decoration. Their walls have witnessed plots and intrigues that make up some of the archtreachery of the High Renaissance. Later, you can go through the dank cells that once rang with the screams of Cesare's victims of torture. The most famous figure imprisoned here was Benvenuto Cellini, the eminent sculptor and goldsmith, remembered chiefly for his classic, candid *Autobiography*. Now an art museum, the castle halls display the history of the Roman mausoleum, along with a wide-ranging selection of ancient arms and armor. You can climb to the top terrace for another one of those dazzling views of the Eternal City.

2   The Forum, the Colosseum & Highlights of Ancient Rome

✪ **Roman Forum (Foro Romano).** Via dei Fori Imperiali. ☎ **06/699-0110.** Admission 12,000L ($7.20) adults, free for children 17 and under and seniors 60 and over. Apr–Sept, Mon–Sat 9am–6pm, Sun 9am–1pm; Oct, Mon 9am–3pm, Sun 9am–1pm. Last admission 1 hour before closing. Closed Jan 16–Feb 15. Metro: Colosseo.

When it came to cremating Caesar, raping Sabine women, purchasing a harlot for the night, or sacrificing a naked victim, the Roman Forum was the place to be. Traversed by Via Sacra (the Sacred Way), it was built in the marshy land between the Palatine and the Capitoline hills. It flourished as the center of Roman life in the days of the Republic, before it gradually lost prestige to the Imperial Forums.

Be warned: Expect only fragmented monuments, an arch or two, and lots of overturned boulders. That any semblance of the Forum remains today is miraculous, as it was used for years, like the Colosseum, as a quarry. Eventually it reverted to what the Italians call *campo vaccino* (cow pasture). But excavations in the 19th century began to bring to light one of the world's most historic spots.

By day, the columns of now-vanished temples and the stones from which long-forgotten orators spoke are mere shells. Bits of grass and weed grow where a triumphant Caesar was once lionized. But at night, when the Forum is silent in the moonlight, it isn't difficult to imagine that vestal virgins still guard the sacred temple fire. (*Historical footnote:* The function of the maidens served to keep the temple's sacred fire burning—but their own flame under control. Failure to do the latter sent them to an early grave . . . alive!)

You can spend at least a morning wandering alone through the ruins of the Forum. If you're content with just looking at the ruins, you can do so at your leisure. But if you want the stones to have some meaning, you'll have to purchase a detailed plan at the gate, as the temples are hard to locate otherwise. The first half of our walking tour "Rome of the Caesars," later in this chapter, will take you around what remains of the ancient buildings and temples, as well as up the Palatine Hill.

A long walk up from the Roman Forum leads to the **Palatine Hill** (which you can visit on the same ticket and at the same hours as the Forum), one of the seven hills of Rome. The Palatine, tradition tells us, was the spot on which the first settlers built their huts, under the direction of Romulus. In later years the hill became a patrician residential district that attracted such citizens as Cicero. In time, however, the area was gobbled up by imperial palaces, and it drew a famous and infamous roster of tenants, such as Caligula (who was murdered here), Nero, Tiberius, and Domitian.

Only the ruins of its former grandeur remain today, and you really need to be an archaeologist to make sense of them, as they're more difficult to understand than those in the Forum. But even if you're not interested in the past, it's worth the climb for the panoramic, sweeping view of both the Roman and Imperial forums, as well as the Capitoline Hill and the Colosseum. To explore, again, see our "Rome of the Caesars" walking tour, later in this chapter.

✪ **Colosseum (Colosseo).** Piazzale del Colosseo, Via dei Fori Imperiali. ☎ 06/700-4261. Street level, free; upper levels, 8,000L ($4.80). Apr–Sept, Mon–Tues and Thurs–Sat 9am–6pm (until 7pm June–Aug), Wed and Sun 9am–1pm; Oct–Mar, Mon–Tues and Thurs–Sat 9am–3pm, Wed and Sun 9am–1pm. Metro: Colosseo.

In spite of the fact that it's a mere shell, the Colosseum remains the greatest architectural inheritance from ancient Rome. Vespasian ordered the construction of the elliptically shaped bowl, called the Amphitheatrum Flavium, in A.D. 72; it was inaugurated by Titus in A.D. 80 with a many-weeks-long bloody combat between gladiators and wild beasts. At its peak, under the cruel Domitian, the Colosseum could seat 50,000 spectators. The vestal virgins from the temple screamed for blood, as more and more exotic animals were shipped in from the far corners of the empire to satisfy jaded tastes (lion vs. bear, two humans vs. hippopotamus, or whatever). Not-so-mock naval battles were staged (the canopied Colosseum could be flooded) in which the defeated combatants might have their lives spared if they put up a good fight. Many historians now believe that one of the most enduring legends linked to the Colosseum—that Christians were fed to the lions here—is unfounded.

Long after it ceased to be an arena to amuse sadistic Romans, the Colosseum was struck by an earthquake. Centuries later it was used as a quarry, its rich marble facing stripped away to build palaces and churches.

On one side, part of the original four tiers remains; the first three levels were constructed in Doric, Ionic, and Corinthian styles to lend variety.

A highly photogenic memorial (next to the Colosseum), the **Arch of Constantine** was erected in honor of Constantine's defeat of the pagan Maxentius (A.D. 306). It's a landmark in every way. Physically, it's beautiful, perhaps marred by the aggravating traffic that zooms around it at all hours, but so intricately carved and well preserved that you almost forget the racket of the cars and buses. Many of the reliefs have nothing whatsoever to do with Constantine or his works, but tell of the victories of earlier Antonine rulers—they were apparently lifted from other, long-forgotten memorials.

Historically, the arch marks a period of great change in the history of Rome and therefore the history of the world. Converted to Christianity by a vision on the battlefield, Constantine officially ended the centuries-long persecution of the Christians during which many devout followers of the new religion had often been put to death, in a most gruesome manner. While Constantine did not ban paganism (which survived officially until the closing of the temples more than half a century later), he espoused Christianity himself and began the inevitable development that culminated in the conquest of Rome by the Christian religion. The arch, a tribute to the emperor, was erected by the Senate in A.D. 315.

After visiting the Colosseum, it's also convenient to look at the site of the **Domus Aurea,** or the Golden House of Nero, on Via Labicana on the Esquiline Hill; it faces the Colosseum and is adjacent to the Forum. The Domus Aurea was one of the most sumptuous palaces of all time, constructed by Nero after disastrous fire swept over Rome in A.D. 64. Not much remains of its former glory, but once the floors were made of mother-of-pearl and the furniture of gold. The area that is the Colosseum today was an ornamental lake, which reflected the grandeur and glitter of the Golden House. The hollow ruins—long stripped of their lavish decorations—lie near the entrance to the Oppius Park.

During the Renaissance, painters such as Raphael chopped holes in the long-buried ceilings of the Domus Aurea to gain admittance. Once here, they were inspired by

Ancient Rome & Attractions Nearby

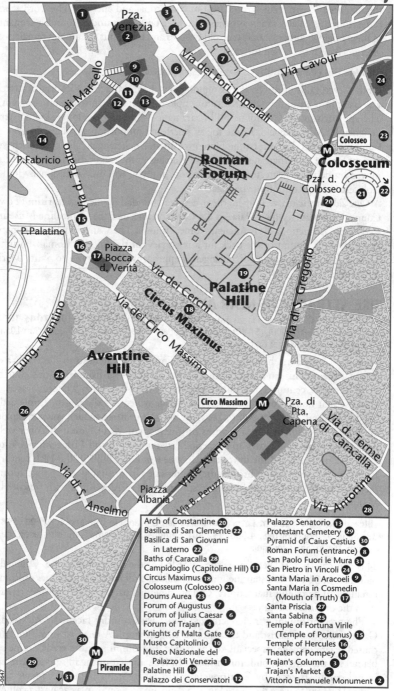

Pza. Venezia

Via dei Fori Imperiali

Via Cavour

di Marcello

P.Fabricio

Via d. Teatro

Colosseo

Colosseum

Roman Forum

Pza. d. Colosseo

P.Palatino

Piazza Bocca d. Verità

Via dei Cerchi

Palatine Hill

Via di S. Gregorio

Circus Maximus

Via dei Circo Massimo

Lung. Aventino

Aventine Hill

Circo Massimo

Pza. di Pta. Capena

Via d. Terme di Caracalla

Viale Aventino

Via di S. Anselmo

Piazza Albania

Via B. Peruzzi

Via Antonina

Piramide

Arch of Constantine 20
Basilica di San Clemente 22
Basilica di San Giovanni in Laterno 22
Baths of Caracalla 28
Campidoglio (Capitoline Hill) 11
Circus Maximus 18
Colosseum (Colosseo) 21
Doums Aurea 23
Forum of Augustus 7
Forum of Julius Caesar 6
Forum of Trajan 4
Knights of Malta Gate 26
Museo Capitolinio 10
Museo Nazionale del Palazzo di Venezia 1
Palatine Hill 19
Palazzo dei Conservatori 12

Palazzo Senatorio 13
Protestant Cemetery 29
Pyramid of Caius Cestius 30
Roman Forum (entrance) 8
San Paolo Fuori le Mura 31
San Pietro in Vincoli 24
Santa Maria in Aracoeli 9
Santa Maria in Cosmedin (Mouth of Truth) 17
Santa Priscia 27
Santa Sabina 25
Temple of Fortuna Virile (Temple of Portunus) 15
Temple of Hercules 16
Theater of Pompey 14
Trajan's Column 3
Trajan's Market 5
Vittorio Emanuele Monument 2

3-0647

145

the frescoes and the small "grotesques" of cornucopia and cherubs. The word *grotto* came from this palace, as it was believed to have been built underground. Remnants of these original, almost-2,000-year-old frescoes and fragments of mosaics remain. All interiors have been closed for years.

Capitoline Hill (Campidoglio). Piazza del Campidoglio.

Of the Seven Hills of Rome, the Campidoglio is the most sacred—its origins stretch way back into antiquity (an Etruscan temple to Jupiter once stood on this spot). The approach to the Capitoline Hill is dramatic—climbing the long, sloping steps designed by Michelangelo. At the top is a perfectly proportioned square, Piazza del Campidoglio, also laid out by the Florentine artist. Michelangelo also positioned the ancient bronze equestrian statue of Marcus Aurelius in the center, but it has now been moved inside to be protected from pollution, and you will only occasionally find a replacement copy out on the pedestal.

One side of the piazza is open; the others are bounded by the **Senatorium** (Town Council), the statuary-filled **Palazzo dei Conservatori,** and the **Capitoline Museum** (see "More Attractions Near Ancient Rome," below). The Campidoglio is dramatic at night (walk around to the back for a regal view of the floodlit Roman Forum). The other steps adjoining Michelangelo's approach will take you to Santa Maria d'Aracoeli.

MORE ATTRACTIONS NEAR ANCIENT ROME

Basilica di San Clemente. Piazza San Clemente, Via Labicana 95. ☎ **06/7045-1018.** Basilica, free; grottoes, 3,000L ($1.80). Mon–Sat 9:30am–12:30pm and 3:30–6pm, Sun 10am–noon and 3:30–6pm. Metro: Colosseo.

From the Colosseum, head up Via di San Giovanni in Laterano to the Basilica of Saint Clement. This isn't just another Roman church—far from it! In this church-upon-a-church, centuries of history peel away. In the 4th century a church was built over a secular house from the 1st century, beside which stood a pagan temple dedicated to Mithras (god of the sun). Down in the eerie grottoes (which you can explore on your own—unlike the catacombs on the Appian Way), you'll discover well-preserved frescoes dating back to the period between the 9th and 11th centuries. After the Normans destroyed the lower church, a new one was built in the 12th century. Its chief attraction is the bronze-orange mosaic (from that period) that adorns the apse, as well as a chapel honoring St. Catherine of Alexandria with frescoes by Masolino.

Basilica di San Giovanni in Laterano. Piazza San Giovanni in Laterano 4. ☎ **06/6988-6433.** Basilica, free; cloisters, 4,000L ($2.40). Summer, daily 7am–7pm; off-season, daily 7am–6pm. Metro: San Giovanni.

This church—not St. Peter's—is the cathedral of the diocese of Rome. Originally built in A.D. 314 by Constantine, the cathedral has suffered the vicissitudes of Rome, forcing it to be rebuilt many times. Only fragmented parts of the baptistery remain from the original structure.

The present building is characterized by its 18th-century facade by Alessandro Galilei (statues of Christ and the Apostles ring the top). A terrorist bomb in 1993 caused severe damage, especially to the facade. Borromini gets the credit (some say blame) for the interior, built for Innocent X. It's said that in the misguided attempt to redecorate, frescoes by Giotto were destroyed (remains believed to have been painted by Giotto were discovered in 1952 and are now on display against a column near the church entrance on the right inner pier). In addition, look for the unusual ceiling and the sumptuous transept, and explore the 13th-century cloisters with their twisted double columns.

The popes used to live next door at the **Lateran Palace** before the move to Avignon in the 14th century. But the most unusual sight is across the street at the "Palace of the Holy Steps," called the **Santuario della Scala Sancta,** Piazza San Giovanni in Laterano (☎ **06/7049-4619**). It's alleged that these were the actual steps that Christ climbed when he was brought before Pilate. These steps are supposed to be climbed only on your knees, which you're likely to see the faithful doing throughout the day.

Baths of Caracalla (Terme di Caracalla). Via delle Terme di Caracalla 52. ☎ **06/ 575-8302.** Admission 8,000L ($4.80) adults, free for children 11 and under. Apr–Sept, Tues–Sat 9am–6pm, Sun–Mon 9am–1pm; Oct–Mar, Tues–Sat 9am–3pm, Sun–Mon 9am–1pm. Bus: 628.

Named for the emperor Caracalla, the Terme di Caracalla were completed in the early part of the 3rd century. The richness of decoration has faded and the lushness can only be judged from the shell of brick ruins that remain.

✪ Museo Capitolino and Palazzo dei Conservatori. Piazza del Campidoglio. ☎ **06/ 6710-2071.** Admission (to both) 10,000L ($6). 5,000L ($3) for children under 18 and adults over 60. Tues–Sat 9am–7pm; Sun and holidays 9am–2pm. Bus: 57, 75, 81, 94, or 95.

These museums house some of the greatest pieces of classical sculpture in the world. The **Capitoline Museum** was built in the 17th century, based on an architectural sketch by Michelangelo. In the first room is *The Dying Gaul,* a work of majestic skill. It's a copy of a Greek original that dates from the 3rd century B.C. In a special gallery all her own is the *Capitoline Venus,* who demurely covers herself. This statue was the symbol of feminine beauty and charm down through the centuries (also a Roman copy of a 3rd century B.C. Greek original). *Amore* (Cupid) and *Psyche* are up to their old tricks near the window.

The famous equestrian statue of Marcus Aurelius, whose years in the middle of the piazza made it a victim of pollution, has recently been restored and is now kept in the museum for protection. This is the only bronze equestrian statue to have survived from Ancient Rome, mainly because for centuries it was thought to be a statue of Constantine the Great and papal Rome respected the memory of the first Christian emperor. It's a beautiful statue even though the perspective is rather odd. The statue is housed in a glassed-in room on the street level called Cortile di Marforio; it's a kind of Renaissance greenhouse, surrounded by windows.

The **Palace of the Conservatori,** across the way, was also based on an architectural plan by Michelangelo and is rich in classical sculpture and paintings. One of the most notable bronzes—a work of incomparable beauty—is *Lo Spinario* (a little boy picking a thorn from his foot), a Greek classic that dates from the 1st century B.C. In addition, you'll find *Lupa Capitolina* (the *Capitoline Wolf*), a rare Etruscan bronze that may go back to the 5th century B.C. (Romulus and Remus, the legendary twins that the wolf suckled, were added at a later date). The palace also contains a "Pinacoteca"—mostly paintings from the 16th and 17th centuries. Notable canvases include Caravaggio's *Fortune-Teller* and his curious *John the Baptist,* the *Holy Family* by Dosso Dossi, *Romulus and Remus* by Rubens, and Titian's *Baptism of Christ.* The entrance courtyard is lined with the remains—head, hands, foot, and a kneecap—of an ancient colossal statue of Constantine the Great.

Saint Peter in Chains (Chiesa di San Pietro in Vincoli). Piazza San Pietro in Vincoli 4A (off Via degli Annibaldi). ☎ **06/488-2865.** Free admission. Spring/summer, daily 7am–12:30pm and 3:30–7pm; Autumn/winter, 7am–12:30pm and 3:30–6pm. Metro: Via Cavour.

From the Colosseum, head up the "spoke" street Via degli Annibaldi to this church, founded in the 5th century to house the chains that bound St. Peter in Palestine. The chains are preserved under glass. But the drawing card is the tomb of Julius II, with one of the world's most famous pieces of sculpture, *Moses* by Michelangelo. As readers of Irving Stone's *The Agony and the Ecstasy* know, Michelangelo was to have carved 44 magnificent figures for Julius's tomb. That didn't happen, of course, but the pope was given one of the greatest consolation prizes—a figure intended to be "minor" that is now numbered among Michelangelo's masterpieces. In the *Lives of the Artists*, Vasari wrote about the stern father symbol of Michelangelo's *Moses*: "No modern work will ever equal it in beauty, no, nor ancient either."

Museo Nazionale del Palazzo di Venezia. Via del Plebiscito 118. ☎ **06/6999-4216.** Admission 8,000L ($4.80) adults, free for children under 18 and adults over 60. Tues–Sat 9am–2pm, Sun 9am–1pm. Bus: 57, 64, 65, 70, or 75.

The Museum of the Palazzo Venezia, in the geographic heart of Rome, served as the seat of the Embassy of Austria until the end of World War I. During the Fascist regime (1928–43), it was the seat of the Italian government. The balcony from which Mussolini used to speak to the Italian people was built in the 15th century. You can now visit the rooms and halls containing oil paintings, porcelain, tapestries, ivories, and ceramics. No one particular exhibit stands out—it's the sum total that adds up to a major attraction. The State Rooms occasionally open to host temporary exhibitions.

Standing outside the museum, you can't help but notice the 20th-century **monument of Victor Emmanuel II,** king of Italy, built on part of the Capitoline Hill and overlooking the piazza, a lush work that has often been compared to a wedding cake. Here you'll find the Tomb of the Unknown Soldier that was created in World War I.

Chiesa di Santa Maria in Cosmedin. Piazza della Bocca della Verità 18. ☎ **06/678-1419.** Free admission. Daily 9am–1pm and 2:30–6pm.

This little church was founded in the 6th century, but was subsequently rebuilt—and a campanile was added in the 12th century in the Romanesque style. The church is ever popular with pilgrims drawn not by the great art treasures but by the "Mouth of Truth," a large disk under the portico. As Gregory Peck demonstrated to Audrey Hepburn in *Roman Holiday,* the mouth is supposed to chomp down on the hand of liars who insert their paws. According to local legend, a former priest used to keep a scorpion in back to bite the fingers of anyone he felt was lying. On one of our visits to the church, a little woman, her head draped in black, sat begging a few feet from the medallion. A scene typical enough—except that this woman's right hand was covered with bandages.

Chiesa di Santa Maria d'Aracoeli. Piazza d'Aracoeli. ☎ **06/679-8155.** Free admission. Daily 7am–noon and 4–7pm.

Sharing a spot on Capitoline Hill, this landmark church was built for the Franciscans in the 13th century. According to legend, Augustus once ordered a temple erected on this spot, where a sibyl, with her gift of prophecy, forecast the coming of Christ. In the interior of the present building you'll find a coffered Renaissance ceiling and a mosaic of the Virgin over the altar in the Byzantine style. If you're sleuth enough, you'll also find a tombstone carved by the great Renaissance sculptor Donatello. The church is known for its Bufalini Chapel, a masterpiece of Pinturicchio, who frescoed it with scenes illustrating the life and death of St. Bernardino of Siena. He also depicted St. Francis receiving the stigmata. These frescoes are a highpoint in early Renaissance Roman painting. You have to climb a long flight of steep steps to reach the church, unless you're already on the neighboring Piazza del Campidoglio, in which case you can cross the piazza and climb the steps on the far side of the Museo Capitolino.

3 The Pantheon & Attractions Near Piazza Navona & Campo de' Fiori

✪ **Pantheon.** Piazza della Rotonda. ☎ **06/6830-0230.** Free admission. July–Sept, daily 9am–6pm; Oct–June, Mon–Sat 9am–4:30pm, Sun 9am–1pm. Bus: 119.

Of all the great buildings of Ancient Rome, only the Pantheon ("All the Gods") remains intact today. It was built in 27 B.C. by Marcus Agrippa and later reconstructed by the emperor Hadrian in the first part of the 2nd century A.D. This remarkable building is among the architectural wonders of the world because of its dome and its concept of space.

The Pantheon was once ringed with white marble statues of Roman gods in its niches. Animals were sacrificed and burned in the center, and the smoke escaped through the only means of light, an opening at the top 27 feet in diameter. The Pantheon is 142 feet wide and 142 feet high. Michelangelo came here to study the dome before designing the cupola of St. Peter's (whose dome is 2 feet smaller than the Pantheon's).

Other statistics are equally impressive. The walls are 25 feet thick and the bronze doors leading into the building weigh 20 tons each. The temple was converted into a church in the early 7th century, which helped save it from destruction.

About 125 years ago the tomb of Raphael was discovered in the Pantheon (fans still bring him flowers). Victor Emmanuel II, king of Italy, and his successor, Umberto I, are interred here.

ATTRACTIONS AROUND PIAZZA NAVONA & THE PANTHEON

Piazza Navona, surely one of the most beautifully baroque sites in all of Rome, is like an ocher-colored gem, unspoiled by new buildings or even by traffic. The shape results from the ruins of the Stadium of Domitian, which lie underneath. Great chariot races were once held here, some rather unusual, such as the one in which the head of the winning horse was lopped off as it crossed the finish line and was carried by runners to be offered as a sacrifice by the vestal virgins on top of the Capitoline Hill. In medieval times the popes used to flood the piazza to stage mock navel encounters. Today the most strenuous activities are performed by occasional fire-eaters, who go through their evening paces before an interested crowd of Romans and visitors.

Beside the twin-towered facade of the Church of Saint Agnes (17th century), the piazza boasts several other baroque masterpieces. The best known, in the center, is Bernini's **Fountain of the Four Rivers,** whose four stone personifications symbolize the world's greatest rivers—the Ganges, Danube, della Plata, and Nile. It's fun to try to figure out which is which. (*Hint:* The figure with the shroud on its head is the Nile, so represented because the river's source was unknown at the time.) The fountain at the south end, the **Fountain of the Moor,** is also by Bernini and dates from the same period as the church and the Fountain of the Four Rivers. The **Fountain of Neptune,** which balances that of the Moor, is a 19th-century addition. During the summer there are outdoor art shows in the evening, but visit during the day—it's best time to inspect the fragments of the original stadium under a building on the north side of the piazza. If you're interested, walk out at the northern exit and turn left for a block. It's astonishing how much the level of the ground has risen since ancient times.

Chiesa del Gesù. Piazza del Gesù, Via degli Astalli 16. ☎ **06/678-6341.** Free admission. Apr–Sept, daily 6am—12:30pm and 4–7pm; Oct–Mar, daily 6am–12:30pm and 4:30–7:15pm.

Built between 1568 and 1584 by donations from a Farnese cardinal, this structure functioned for several centuries as the most potent and powerful church in the Jesuit order. Conceived as a bulwark against the perceived menace of the Protestant Reformation, it's an important symbol and legacy from the Catholic Counter-Reformation. The sheathing of yellow marble that covers part of the interior was added during the 1800s.

Galleria Doria Pamphilj. Piazza del Collegio Romano 2. ☎ **06/679-4365.** Gallery, 12,000L ($7.20) per person adults, 9,000L ($5.40) students and senior citizens; apartments, 5,000L ($3). Fri–Wed 10am–5pm. Private visits may be arranged.

Located off Via del Corso, this museum offers visitors a look at what it's really like to live in an 18th-century palace. Like many Roman palaces of the period, the mansion is partly leased to tenants (on the upper levels), and there are even shops on the street level, but all this is easily overlooked after you enter the grand apartments of the historic princely Doria Pamphilj family, which traces its lines to before the great 15th-century Genoese admiral Andrea Doria. The regal apartments surround the central court and gallery of the palace. The 18th-century decor pervades the magnificent ballroom, drawing rooms, dining rooms, and even the family chapel. Gilded furniture, crystal chandeliers, Renaissance tapestries, and portraits of family members are everywhere. The Green Room is especially rich in treasures, with a 15th-century Tournay tapestry, paintings by Memling and Filippo Lippi, and a seminude portrait of Andrea Doria by Sebastiano del Piombo. The Andrea Doria Room is dedicated to the admiral and to the ship of the same name. It contains a glass case with mementos of the great maritime disaster of the 1950s.

Skirting the central court is a picture gallery with a memorable collection of frescoes, paintings, and sculpture. Most important among a number of great works are the portrait of Innocent X by Velázquez, called one of the four best portraits ever painted; *Salome* by Titian; and works by Rubens and Caravaggio. Notable also are the *Bay of Naples* by Pieter Brueghel the Elder and a copy of Raphael's portrait of Principessa Giovanna d' Aragona de Colonna (who looks remarkably like Leonardo's *Mona Lisa*). Most of the sculpture came from the Doria country estates. It includes marble busts of Roman emperors, bucolic nymphs, and satyrs. Even without the paintings and sculptures, that gallery would be worth a visit just for its fresco-covered walls and ceilings.

Chiesa di San Agostino. Piazza Sant'Agostino/Via della Scrofa 80. ☎ **06/6880-1962.** Free admission. Daily 7:45am–noon and 4:30–7:30pm.

Built between 1479 and 1483, this was one of the first churches erected during the Roman Renaissance. Originally commissioned by the archbishop of Rouen, France, its interior was altered and redecorated in the 1700s and 1800s. A painting by Caravaggio, *Madonna of the Pilgrims* (1605), hangs in the first altar on the left, as you enter.

Chiesa di San Luigi dei Francesi. Via Santa Giovanna d'Arco. ☎ **06/688-271.** Fri–Wed 8am–12:30pm and 3:30–7pm, Thurs 8am–12:30pm.

This has been the national church of France in Rome since 1589. There's a stone salamander—the symbol of the Renaissance French monarch François I—subtly carved into its facade. Inside, in the last chapel on the left, is a noteworthy series of frescoes by Caravaggio—the celebrated *Calling of St. Matthew* on the left, *St. Matthew and the Angel* in the center, and the *Martyrdom of St. Matthew* on the right.

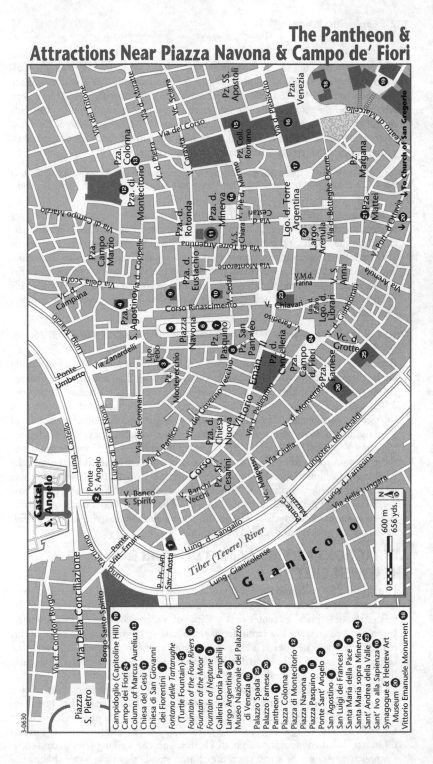

Campidoglio (Capitoline Hill) **19**
Campo dei Fiori **24**
Column of Marcus Aurelius **17**
Chiesa del Gesù **13**
Chiesa di San Giovanni
  dei Fiorentini **1**
Fontana delle Tartarughe
  (Turtle Fountain) **21**
Fountain of the Four Rivers **6**
Fountain of the Moor **7**
Fountain of Neptune **5**
Galleria Doria Pamphilj **15**
Largo Argentina **22**
Museo Nazionale del Palazzo
  di Venezia **16**
Palazzo Spada **25**
Palazzo Farnese **26**
Pantheon **11**
Piazza Colonna **13**
Piazza di Montecitorio **12**
Piazza Navona **6**
Piazza Pasquino **8**
Ponte Sant' Angelo **2**
San Agostino **4**
San Luigi dei Francesi **9**
Santa Maria della Pace **3**
Santa Maria sopra Minerva **14**
Sant' Andrea della Valle **23**
Sant' Ivo alla Sapienza **10**
Synagogue & Hebrew Art
  Museum **20**
Vittorio Emanuele Monument **18**

151

Piazza Colonna. Off Via del Corso. Bus: 119.

The centerpiece of this square is one of the most dramatic obelisks in town, the **Column of Marcus Aurelius,** a hollow bronze column rising 83 feet above the piazza. Built between A.D. 180 and 196, and restored (some say "defaced") in 1589 by a pope who replaced the statue of the Roman warrior on top with a statue of St. Paul, it's one of the ancient world's best examples of heroic bas-relief and one of the most memorable sights of Rome. The Palazzo Chigi, the official residence of the Italian prime minister, hovers above the piazza's northern edge.

Chiesa di Santa Maria della Pace. Vicolo del Arco della Pace 5 (off Piazza Navona). ☎ **06/6880-1962.** Free admission. Tues–Sat 10am–noon and 4–6pm, Sun 9–11am. Currently under renovation.

According to legend, blood flowed from a statue of the Virgin above the altar after someone threw a pebble at it. This legend motivated Pope Sixtus to rebuild the church in the 1500s on the foundations of an even older sanctuary. For generations after that, its curved porticos, cupola atop an octagonal base, cloisters by Bramante, and frescoes by Raphael helped make it one of the most fashionable churches for aristocrats residing in the surrounding palazzos. Before you go, check to make sure it's open because it's currently undergoing renovations and there's no definite completion date.

Chiesa di Santa Maria Sopra Minerva. Piazza della Minerva 42. ☎ **06/679-3926.** Free admission. Daily 7am–noon and 4–7pm.

Beginning in 1280, early Christian leaders ordained that the foundation of an already ancient temple dedicated to Minerva (goddess of wisdom) be reused as the base for Rome's only Gothic church. Architectural changes and redecorations during the 1500s and the 1900s stripped this building of some of its original allure. Despite that, the roster of ornaments inside—including an awe-inspiring collection of medieval and Renaissance tombs—creates an atmosphere that's something akin to a religious museum. You'll find a beautiful chapel frescoed by Fillipino Lippi and, to the left of the apse, a muscular *Risen Christ* carrying a rather small cross carved from marble by Michelangelo himself (the bronze drapery covering Christ's shocking nudity was added later). Under the altar lies the body of St. Catherine of Siena, and in the passage to the left of the choir, surrounded by a small fence, is the floor tomb of the great monastic painter Fra Angelico. The amusing baby elephant carrying a small obelisk in the piazza outside was designed by Bernini.

ATTRACTIONS AROUND CAMPO DE' FIORI & THE JEWISH GHETTO

During the 1500s **Campo de' Fiori** was the geographic and cultural center of secular Rome, site of dozens of inns that would almost certainly have been reviewed by this guidebook. From its center rises a statue of a severe-looking monk (Giordano Bruno) whose presence is a reminder of the occasional burning at the stake in this piazza of religious heretics. Today, ringed with venerable and antique houses, the campo is the site of an open-air food market held Monday to Saturday from early in the morning until around noon, or whenever the food runs out.

The best way to see the **Jewish Ghetto** is to go on a free walking tour offered by **Service International de Documentation Judeo-Chrétienne,** Via Plebiscito 112 (☎ **06/679-5307**). An interesting remnant from the era of the ghetto is the **Church of San Gregorio,** Ponte Quattro Capi at the end of Via del Portico d'Ottavia. It has an inscription in both Hebrew and Latin asking Jews to convert to Catholicism. Across the street from the church stands the **Sinagoga Ashkenazita**

(☎ **06/6875-051**), which is open only for services. Trying to avoid all resemblance to a Christian church, the building, constructed from 1874 to 1904, evokes Babylonian and Persian architectural details. The synagogue was attacked by terrorists in 1982 and since then has been heavily guarded by *carabinieri* armed with machine guns. It houses the **Jewish Museum** (☎ **06/6840-061**), which is open daily in July and September from 9am to 4:30pm. Off-season hours are Monday through Thursday from 9:30am to 1pm and 2 to 4:30pm, Friday from 9:30am to 1:30pm, and Saturday 9:30am to noon. Admission is 8,000L. Many rare and even priceless treasures are exhibited here, including a Moroccan prayer book from the early 14th century and ceremonial objects from the 17th-century Jewish Ghetto.

Palazzo Farnese. Piazza Farnese. Closed to the public.

Built between 1514 and 1589, this palace designed by Sangallo, Michelangelo, and others was astronomically expensive at the time. Its famous residents have included a 16th-century member of the Farnese family, Pope Paul III, Cardinal Richelieu, and the former Queen Christina of Sweden, who moved to Rome after abdicating her throne. During the 1630s, when the building's heirs could not afford to maintain it, the palace became the site of the French Embassy, a function it has served ever since. It's closed to the public. For the best view of the palazzo, cut west from Via Giulia along any of the narrow streets—we recommend Via Mascherone or Via dei Farnesi.

Palazzo Spada. Capo di Ferro 3. ☎ **06/686-1158.** Admission 8,000L ($4.80) adults, free for children 17 and under and seniors 60 and over. Tues–Sat 9am–7pm, Sun 9am–12:30pm.

Built around 1550 for Cardinal Gerolamo Capo di Ferro, and later inhabited by the descendants of several other cardinals, this palace was sold to the Italian government in the 1920s. Its richly ornate facade, covered in high-relief stucco decorations in the Mannerist style, is the finest of any building from 16th-century Rome. Although the State Rooms are closed to the public, the richly decorated courtyard and a handful of galleries of paintings are open.

4 More Attractions

THE SPANISH STEPS, THE TREVI FOUNTAIN & ATTRACTIONS NEARBY

✪ **Spanish Steps (Piazza di Spagna).** Metro: Piazza di Spagna.

The Spanish Steps were the last part of the outside world that Keats saw before he died in a house at the foot of the stairs (see the Keats–Shelley Memorial, later in this section). The steps—filled in the spring with flower vendors, jewelry dealers, and photographers snapping pictures of tourists—and the square take their names from the Spanish Embassy, which used to have its headquarters here. Designed by Italian architect Francesco de Sanctis between 1723 and 1725, they were funded almost entirely by the French as a preface to the French national church, Trinità dei Monti, at the top. Unfortunately, in recent years, even during tourist season, the steps have been vacant because of massive restorations. Work is underway to complete the project by the year 2000.

At the foot of the steps is a boat-shaped fountain designed by Pietro Bernini (not to be confused with his son, Giovanni Lorenzo Bernini, who proved to be a far greater sculptor). About two centuries ago, when the foreign art colony was in its ascendancy, the 136 steps were covered with young men and women who wanted to pose for the painter—men with their shirts unbuttoned to show off what they hoped was a Davidesque physique, and women consistently draped like Madonnas.

Trevi Fountain (Fontana dei Trevi). Piazza di Trevi. Metro: Piazza Barberini.

As you elbow your way through the summertime crowds around the Trevi Fountain, you'll find it hard to believe that this little piazza was nearly always deserted before *Three Coins in the Fountain* brought the tour buses. Today it's a must on everybody's itinerary. To do it properly, hold your lira coin in the right hand, turn your back to the fountain, and toss the coin over your shoulder (being careful not to bean anyone behind you). Then the spirit of the fountain will see to it that you return to Rome one day—or that's the tradition, at least. Actually, this is an evolution of an even older tradition of drinking from the fountain. Nathaniel Hawthorne (1804–64), in the novel *The Marble Faun,* wrote that anyone drinking from this fountain's water "has not looked upon Rome for the last time." Because of pollution, no one drank from it for years. Since the fountain has been restored in 1994 and is running again, the water is supposedly pure, owing to an electronic device that keeps the pigeons at bay. We'd still suggest that you skip a "Trevi cocktail" and have a mineral water at a cafe instead.

Supplied by water from the Acqua Vergine aqueduct, and a triumph of the baroque style, it was based on the design of Nicolo Salvi (who is said to have died of illness contracted during his supervision of the project) and was completed in 1762. The design centers around the triumphant figure of Neptunus Rex, standing on a shell chariot drawn by winged steeds and led by a pair of tritons. Two allegorical figures in the side niches represent good health and fertility.

On the southwestern corner of the piazza that contains the fountain, you'll see a somber, not particularly spectacular-looking church (Chiesa S. S. Vincenzo e Anastasio) with a strange claim to fame. Within this church survive the hearts and intestines of several centuries of popes. According to legend, the church was built on the site of a spring that burst from the earth after the beheading of St. Paul, at one of three sites where his head is said to have bounced off the ground.

Altar of Peace (Ara Pacis). Via di Ripetta. ☎ **06/719-0071.** Admission 4,000L ($2.40). Apr–Sept, Tues–Wed and Fri–Sun 9am–1:30pm, Thurs and Sat 4–7pm; Oct–Mar, Tues–Wed and Fri–Sun 9am–1:30pm. Bus: 81.

In an airy glass-and-concrete building beside the eastern banks of the Tiber at Ponte Cavour rests a reconstructed treasure from the reign of Augustus. It was built by the Senate as a tribute to that emperor and the peace he had brought to the Roman world. You can see portraits of the imperial family—Augustus, Livia (his wife), Tiberius (Livia's son and the successor to the empire), even Julia (the unfortunate daughter of Augustus, exiled by her father for her sexual excesses)—on the marble walls. The altar was reconstructed from literally hundreds of fragments scattered in museums for centuries. A major portion came from the foundations of a Renaissance palace on the Corso. The reconstruction—quite an archaeological adventure story in itself—was executed (and sometimes enhanced) by the Fascists during the 1930s.

✪ **Galleria Borghese.** Piazza Scipione Borghese, off Via Pinciano, in the Villa Borghese. ☎ **06/8424-1607** for reservations, 06/841-7645 for information. Admission 12,000L ($7.20). Tues–Sun 9am–7pm; July 10–Sept 14, also Tues–Sun 8:30–11:30pm.

This legendary art gallery shut its doors early in 1984 and appeared virtually to have closed forever. However, in the spring of 1997, after a complete restoration, it is back in all its fabulous glory. The bad news is that it may be hard to get in because of limited access (see below). The Italian state purchased the museum in 1902, but, as it turned out, it was resting on an unstable honeycomb of subterranean grottos and watercourses.

A whole new generation has come into adulthood in Rome without sampling this treasure trove of art, ranging from such masterpieces as Bernini's *Apollo and Daphne,* Titian's *Sacred and Profane Love,* and Raphael's *Deposition,* even Caravaggio's *Jerome.*

The collection began with the gallery's founder, Scipione Borghese, who by the time of his death in 1633 had accumulated some of the greatest art of all time, even managing to acquire Bernini's early sculptures. Some paintings were spirited out of Vatican museums and even confiscated when their rightful owners were hauled off to prison until they became "reasonable" about turning over their art. The great collection suffered at the hands of Napoléon's sister, Pauline, who married Camillo Borghese in 1807 and sold most of the ancient collection (many works now in the Louvre in Paris). One of the most viewed pieces of sculpture in today's gallery, ironically, is Canova's life-size sculpture of Pauline in the pose of *Venus Victorious.* When Pauline was asked if she felt uncomfortable posing in the nude, she replied, "Why should I? The studio was heated."

No more than 300 visitors are allowed on the ground floor at one time, no more than 90 on the upper floor. Therefore, prebooking is essential if you want to visit. Regrettably, you can call for a reservation, but the number invariably seems busy. For those who do get through and who are able to make a reservation, the chance to see such works as Bernini's *David* and his *The Rape of Persephone* are worth the effort.

After visiting the gallery, you may want to join the Romans in their strolls through the **Villa Borghese** (see below), replete with zoological gardens and small bodies of water. Horse shows are occasionally staged at **Piazza Siena.**

Galleria Nazionale d'Arte Moderna. Viale delle Belle Arti 131. ☎ **06/322-981.** Admission 8,000L ($4.80) adults, free for children 17 and under and seniors 60 and over. Tues–Sat 9am–7pm, Sun 9am–1pm.

The National Gallery of Modern Art is in the Villa Borghese Gardens, a short walk from the Etruscan Museum. With its neoclassic and romantic paintings and sculpture, it's a dramatic change from the glories of the Renaissance and the Romans. Its 75 rooms also house the largest collection in Italy of 19th- and 20th-century artists. Included are important works of Balla, Boccioni, de Chirico, Morandi, Manzù, Marini, Burri, Capogrossi, and Fontana, and a large collection of Italian optical and pop art.

Look for Modigliani's *La Signora dal Collaretto* and the large *Nudo.* Several important sculptures, including one by Canova, are on display in the museum's gardens. The gallery also houses a large collection of foreign artists, including French impressionists Degas, Cézanne, and Monet, and the postimpressionist van Gogh. Surrealism and expressionism are well represented in works by Klee, Ernst, Braque, Miró, Kandinsky, Mondrian, and Pollock. You'll also find sculpture by Rodin. The collection of graphics, the storage rooms, and the Department of Restoration can be visited by appointment from Tuesday to Friday.

Keats-Shelley Memorial. Piazza di Spagna 26. ☎ **06/678-4235.** Admission 5,000L ($3). May–Sept, Mon–Fri 9am–1pm and 3–6pm; Oct–Apr, Mon–Fri 9am–1pm and 2:30–5:30pm. Metro: Piazza di Spagna.

At the foot of the Spanish Steps is this 18th-century house where Keats died of consumption on February 23, 1821, at the age of 25. "It is like living in a violin," wrote Italian author Alberto Savinio. Since 1909, when it was bought by well-intentioned English and American aficionados of English literature, the building has been a working library established in honor of Keats, and the poet Shelley, who drowned off the coast of Viareggio with a copy of Keats in his pocket. Mementos inside range from the kitsch to the immortal and are almost relentlessly laden with literary nostalgia. The apartment where Keats spent his last months, carefully tended by his close friend, Joseph Severn, shelters a strange death mask of Keats as well as the "deadly sweat" drawing by Severn.

Augustus Mausoleum (Mausoleo Augusteo). Via di Ripetta and Piazza Augusteo Imperatore.

This seemingly indestructible pile of bricks along Via di Ripetta has been here for 2,000 years and will probably remain for another 2,000. Like the larger tomb of Hadrian across the river, this was once a circular, marble-covered affair with tall cypress trees, symmetrical groupings of Egyptian obelisks, and some of the most spectacular ornamentation in Europe. Many of the emperors of the 1st century had their ashes deposited in golden urns inside this building, and it was probably because of the resultant crowding that Hadrian later decided to construct an entirely new tomb (today, the Castel Sant'Angelo) for himself in another part of Rome. The imperial remains stayed intact in this building until the 5th century, when invading bar-barians smashed the bronze gates and stole the golden urns, emptying the ashes on the ground outside. After periods when it functioned as a Renaissance fortress, a bullfighting ring, and a private garden, the tomb was restored in the 1930s by Mussolini, who might have envisioned it as a burial place for himself. You cannot enter the mausoleum, but you should walk along the four streets that encircle it.

✪ **Museo Nazionale di Villa Giulia (Etruscan).** Piazzale di Villa Giulia 9. ☎ **06/322-6571.** Admission 8,000L ($4.80) adults, free for children 18 and under and seniors 60 and over. Tues–Sat 9am–7pm, Sun 9am–2pm. Metro: Flaminio.

A 16th-century papal palace in the Villa Borghese Gardens shelters this priceless collection of art and artifacts of the mysterious Etruscans, who predated the Romans. Known for their sophisticated art and design, the Etruscans left a legacy of sarcophagi, bronze sculptures, terra-cotta vases, and jewelry, among other items.

If you have time only for the masterpieces, head for Sala 7, which has a remarkable 6th-century B.C. *Apollo* from Veio (clothed, for a change). The other two widely acclaimed pieces of statuary in this gallery are *Dea con Bambino (Goddess with a Baby)* and a greatly mutilated, but still powerful, *Hercules* with a stag. In the adjoining room, Sala 8, you'll see the lions' sarcophagus from the mid-6th century B.C., which was excavated at Cerveteri, north of Rome.

Finally, one of the world's most important Etruscan art treasures is the bride and bridegroom coffin from the 6th century B.C., also dug out of the tombs of Cerveteri (in Sala 9). Near the end of your tour, another masterpiece of Etruscan art awaits you in Sala 33: the *Cista Ficoroni,* a bronze urn with paw feet, mounted by three figures, which dates from the 4th century B.C.

Palazzo del Quirinale. Piazza del Quirinale. Free admission (but a passport or similar ID is required for entrance). Sun 9am–1pm. Metro: Barberini.

Until the end of World War II this palace was the home of the king of Italy, and before that it was the residence of the pope. Despite its origins during the Renaissance, when virtually every important architect in Italy worked on some aspect of its sprawling premises, it's rich in associations with ancient emperors and deities. The colossal statues of the *dioscuri* Castor and Pollux, which now form part of the fountain in the piazza, were found in the nearby great baths of Constantine, and in 1793 Pius VI had the ancient Egyptian obelisk moved here from the Mausoleum of Augustus. The sweeping view of Rome from the piazza, which crowns the highest of the seven ancient hills of Rome, is itself worth the trip.

VILLA BORGHESE

This park in the heart of Rome is 3¹/₂ miles in circumference. One of the most elegant parks in Europe, it was created by Cardinal Scipione Borghese in the 1600s. Umberto I, king of Italy, acquired it in 1902 and presented it to the city of Rome, renaming it Villa Umberto I. However, Romans preferred their old name, which has stuck. A park of landscaped vistas and wide-open "green lungs," the greenbelt is crisscrossed by roads, but you can escape from the traffic and seek a shaded area—usually pine or oak—to enjoy a picnic or simply relax. In the northeast of the park is a small zoo, and the park is also home to the Galleria Borghese (see above), one of the finest museums of Rome, with many masterpieces by Renaissance and baroque artists.

AROUND VIA VENETO

Cimitero Monumentale dei Padri Cappucini. Under the Church of the Immaculate Conception, Via Vittorio Veneto 27. ☎ **06/487-1185.** Admission 2,000L ($1.20). Daily 9am–noon and 3–6pm. Metro: Barberini.

Qualifying as one of the most horrifying sights in all Christendom, this is a cemetery of skulls and crossbones woven into mosaic "works of art" just a short walk from Piazza Barberini. To make this allegorical dance of death, the bones of more than 4,000 Capuchin brothers were used. Some of the skeletons are intact, draped with Franciscan habits. The creator of this chamber of horrors? The tradition of the friars is that it was the work of a French Capuchin. Their literature suggests that the cemetery should be visited keeping in mind the historical moment of its origins, when Christians had a rich and creative cult for their dead, when great spiritual masters meditated and preached with a skull in hand. Those who have lived through the days of crematoriums and other such massacres may view the graveyard differently, but to many who pause to think, this macabre sight of death has a message. It's not for the squeamish. The entrance is halfway up the first staircase on the right of the church.

Piazza Barberini. Metro: Piazza Barberini.

This piazza lies at the foot of several Roman streets, among them Via Barberini, Via Sistina, and Via Vittorio Veneto. It would be a far more pleasant spot were it not for the heavy traffic swarming around its principal feature, Bernini's **Fountain of the Triton.** For more than three centuries the strange figure sitting in a vast open clam has been blowing water from his triton. Off to one side of the piazza is the clean, aristocratic side facade of the Palazzo Barberini, named for one of Rome's powerful families. The Renaissance Barberini reached their peak when a son was elected pope (Urban VIII). This Barberini pope encouraged Bernini and gave him great patronage.

As you go up Via Vittorio Veneto, look for the small fountain on the right-hand corner of Piazza Barberini, which is another of Bernini's works, the small **Fountain of the Bees.** At first they look more like flies, but they are the bees of the Barberini, the crest of that powerful family complete with the crossed keys of St. Peter above them (the keys were always added to a family crest when a son was elected pope).

Galleria Nazionale d'Arte Antica. Via delle Quattro Fontane 13. ☎ **06/481-4430.** Admission 8,000L ($4.80) adults, free for children 17 and under and seniors 60 and over. Tues–Sat 9am–7pm, Sun 9am–12:30pm. Metro: Barberini.

The Palazzo Barberini, right off Piazza Barberini, is one of the most magnificent baroque palaces in Rome. It was begun by Carlo Maderno in 1627 and completed in 1633 by Bernini, whose lavishly decorated rococo apartments, called the Gallery of Decorative Art, are on view.

The bedroom of Princess Cornelia Costanza Barberini and Prince Giulio Cesare Colonna di Sciarra still stands just as it was on their wedding night, and many household objects are displayed in the decorative art gallery. In the chambers, which have frescoes and hand-painted silk linings, you can see porcelain from Japan and Bavaria, canopied beds, and a wooden baby carriage.

On the first floor of the palace, a splendid array of paintings includes works from the 13th to the 16th centuries, most notably the *Mother and Child* by Simone Martini, and works by Filippo Lippi, Andrea Solario, and Francesco Francia. Il Sodoma has some brilliant pictures here, including *The Rape of the Sabines* and *The Marriage of St. Catherine.* One of the best-known paintings is Raphael's beloved *La Fornarina,* the baker's daughter who was his mistress and who posed for his Madonna portraits. Titian is represented by his *Venus and Adonis.* Other artists exhibited include Tintoretto, El Greco, and Holbein the Younger. Many visitors come here just to see the magnificent Caravaggios, including *Narcissus.*

AROUND THE TERMINI

Basilica di Santa Maria Maggiore. Piazza di Santa Maria Maggiore. ☎ **06/483-195.** Free admission. Daily 7am–7pm (until 8pm in summer). Metro: Termini.

This great church, one of the four major basilicas of Rome, was originally founded by Pope Liberius in A.D. 358, but was rebuilt by Pope Sixtus III in 432–40. Its campanile, erected in the 14th century, is the loftiest in the city. Much doctored in the 18th century, the church's facade is not an accurate reflection of the treasures inside. The basilica is especially noted for the 5th-century Roman mosaics in its nave, as well as for its coffered ceiling, said to have been gilded with gold brought from the New World. In the 16th century Domenico Fontana built a now-restored "Sistine Chapel." In the following century Flaminio Ponzo designed the Pauline (Borghese) Chapel in the baroque style. The church contains the tomb of Bernini, Italy's most important sculptor and architect during the baroque era in the 17th century. Ironically, the man who changed the face of Rome with his elaborate fountains is buried in a tomb so simple it takes a sleuth to track it down (to the right near the altar). Restoration of the 1,600-year-old church has begun and is scheduled for completion in the year 2000.

✪ **National Roman Museum (Museo Nazionale Romano).** Via Enrico de Nicola 79. ☎ **06/488-2298.** Admission 12,000L ($7.20). Tues–Sat 9am–2pm, Sun and holidays 9am–1pm. Metro: Piazza della Repubblica.

Located near Piazza dei Cinquecento, which fronts the railway station, this museum occupies part of the 3rd-century A.D. Baths of Diocletian and a section of a convent that may have been designed by Michelangelo. It houses one of Europe's finest collections of Greek and Roman sculpture and early Christian sarcophagi.

The Ludovisi Collection is the highlight of the museum, particularly the statue of the Gaul slaying himself after he has done in his wife (a brilliant copy of a Greek original from the 3rd century B.C.). Another prize is a one-armed Greek *Apollo.* A galaxy of other sculptured treasures includes *The Discus Thrower of Castel Porziano* (an exquisite copy), *Aphrodite of Cirene* (a Greek original), and the so-called *Hellenistic Ruler,* a Greek original of an athlete with a lance. A masterpiece of Greek sculpture, *The Birth of Venus,* is in the Ludovisi Throne room. *The Sleeping Hermaphrodite* (Ermafrodito Dormiente) is an original Hellenistic statue. You can stroll through the cloister, filled with statuary and fragments of antiquity, including a fantastic mosaic.

Chiesa di Santa Maria degli Angeli. Piazza della Repubblica 12. ☎ **06/488-0812.** Free admission. Daily 7:30am–12:30pm and 4–6:30pm. Metro: Piazza della Repubblica.

On this site, which adjoins the National Roman Museum near the railway station, once stood the "tepidarium" of the 3rd-century Baths of Diocletian. But in the 16th century Michelangelo—nearing the end of his life—converted the grand hall into one of the most splendid churches in Rome. Surely the artist wasn't responsible for "gilding the lily"—that is, putting trompe-l'oeil columns in the midst of the genuine pillars. The church is filled with tombs and paintings, but its crowning treasure is the genuine statue of St. Bruno by the great French sculptor Jean-Antoine Houdon. His sculpture is larger than life and about as real.

THE APPIAN WAY & THE CATACOMBS

Of all the roads that led to Rome, **Via Appia Antica**—built in 312 B.C.—was the reigning leader. It eventually stretched all the way from Rome to the seaport of Brindisi, through which trade with the colonies in Greece and the East was funneled. According to Christian tradition, it was along the Appian Way that an escaping Peter encountered the vision of Christ, which caused him to go back into the city to face subsequent martyrdom.

Of the Roman monuments on Via Appia Antica, the most impressive is the **Tomb of Cecilia Metella,** within walking distance of the catacombs. The cylindrical tomb honors the wife of one of Julius Caesar's military commanders from the Republican era. Why such an elaborate tomb for such an unimportant person in history? Cecilia Metella happened to be singled out for enduring fame because her tomb remained and the others decayed.

Along the Appian Way the patrician Romans built great monuments above the ground, and Christians met in the catacombs beneath the earth. The remains of both can be visited today. In some dank, dark grottoes (never stray too far from either your party or one of the exposed lightbulbs), you can still discover the remains of early Christian art. Only someone wanting to write a sequel to *Quo Vadis?* would visit all the catacombs, but of those open to the public, the catacombs of St. Callixtus and St. Sebastian are the most important.

Tomb of St. Sebastian (Catacombe di San Sebastiano). Via Appia Antica 136. ☎ 06/785-0350. Admission 8,000L ($4.80) adults, 4,000L ($2.40) children 6–15, free for children 5 and under. Fri–Wed 8:30am–noon and 2:30–5:30pm. Bus: 118 near the Colosseo metro station.

Today the tomb of the martyr is in the basilica (church), but his original tomb was in the catacombs under the basilica. From the reign of the emperor Valerian to the reign of the emperor Constantine, the bodies of Saint Peter and Saint Paul were hidden in the catacombs. The big church was built here in the 4th century. None of the catacombs, incidentally, is a grotto; all are dug from *tufo,* a soft volcanic rock. This is the only Christian catacomb in Rome that's always open. The tunnels here, if stretched out, would reach a length of 7 miles. In the tunnels and mausoleums are mosaics and graffiti, along with many other pagan and Christian objects from centuries even before the time of Constantine.

Catacombe di San Callisto (Callixtus). Via Appia Antica 110. ☎ 06/513-6725. Admission 8,000L ($4.80) adults, 4,000L ($2.40) children 6–15, free for children 5 and under. Thurs–Tues 8:30am–noon and 2:30–5pm (until 5:30pm in summer). Bus: 218 from Piazza San Giovanni in Laterano to Fosse Ardeatine; ask driver to let you off at Catacombe di San Callisto.

"The most venerable and most renowned of Rome," said Pope John XXIII of these funerary tunnels. The founder of Christian archaeology, Giovanni Battista de Rossi (1822–94), called them "catacombs par excellence." They are the first cemetery of the Christian community of Rome, burial place of 16 popes in the 3rd century. They

Beneath It All: Touring Roma Sotteranea

Talk about the "underground" and a growing legion of Romans will excitedly take up the story, offering tidbits about where to go, who to talk to, what's been seen, and what's allegedly awaiting discovery, just around the next bend in the sewer. The sewer? That's right. This underground is neither subway nor trendy arts movement but the vast historical ruins of a city that has seen occupation for nearly 3,000 years, the first two millenniums of which are now largely buried by natural sediment and manmade landfills. In fact, archaeologists estimate that these processes over time have left the streets of Ancient Rome as much as 20 yards beneath the surface.

A little to deep for you? Consider this: Each year, an inch of dust in the form of pollen, leaves, pollution, sand, and silt from disintegrating ruins settles over Rome. That silt has really taken a toll in its own right. Archeologists estimate that the ruins of a one-story Roman house will produce debris six feet deep over its entire floor plan. When you multiply that by more than 40,000 apartment buildings, 1,800 palaces, and numerous giant public buildings, a very real picture of the burial of the ancient city presents itself. You should also take note of the centuries-old Roman tradition of burying old buildings in landfills, which can raise the level of the earth up to several yards all at once. In fact, past builders have often filled up massive stone ruins with dirt or dug down through previous landfills to the columns and vaults of underlying structures, then laid a foundation for a new layer of Roman architecture.

As a result, many of the buildings on the streets today actually provide direct access to Rome's inner world. Secret doorways lead down to hidden crypts and shrines—the existence of which are closely guarded secrets. Nondescript locked doors in churches and other public buildings often open upon whole blocks of the ancient city—streets still intact. Take for instance San Clemente, the 12th-century basilica east of the Colosseum, where a staircase in the sacristy leads down to the original 4th-century church. Not only that, but a staircase near the apse of the church goes down to an earlier Roman apartment building and temple, which in turn leads down to a giant public building dating back to the Great Fire (A.D. 64). Another

---

bear the name of St. Callixtus, the deacon who Pope St. Zephyrinus put in charge of them and who was later elected pope (217–22) in his own right. The cemeterial complex is made up of a network of galleries stretching for nearly 12 miles, structured in five different levels, and reaching a depth of about 65 feet. There are many sepulchral chambers and almost half a million tombs. Paintings, sculptures, and epigraphs (with such symbols as the fish, the anchor, and the dove) provide invaluable material for the study of the life and customs of the ancient Christians and the story of their persecutions.

Entering the catacombs, you see at once the most important crypt, that of the nine popes. Some of the original marble tablets of their tombs are still preserved. The next crypt is that of St. Cecilia, the patron of sacred music. This early Christian martyr received three ax strokes on her neck, the maximum allowed by Roman law, which failed to kill her outright. Farther on, you'll find the famous Cubicula of the Sacraments with its 3rd-century frescoes. The catacombs were dug in the middle of the 2nd century up until the middle of the 5th century as cemeteries and places of prayers—never private dwellings.

interesting doorway to the past is the one in the south exterior wall of St. Peter's, which leads down to an intact necropolis. That crumbling brick entry, located in the gardens on the east side of Esquiline Hill, carries you into the vast Golden House, Nero's residence, built upon the ruins left by the Great Fire.

Several tour companies now offer selected views of what's beneath the feet of Rome. Two tours, the **Itinera** (☎ **06/275-7323**) and **LU.PA.** (☎ **06/519-3570**), are run by trained archeologists with vast amounts of experience studying the structures and layout of the underlying city. **Genti e Paesi** (☎ **06/8530-1755**) and **Città Nascosta** (☎ **06/321-6059**) take more of an artsy historical approach. Romans seemingly can't get enough of the underground, and a complete listing of scheduled visits appears weekly in the publication *Romac'e,* available at newsstands.

For those who want still more access to the world that lies beneath Rome, the Italian monthly magazine *Forma Urbis* features the photographs of Carlo Pavia, who, armed with lights, camera, hip boots, and oxygen mask, slogs through ancient sewage and hordes of jumping spiders, giant rats, and albino insect populations to record part of the ancient city that has never been seen before. Pavia's most bizarre discovery was a series of plants from North Africa and the Arab world growing in rooms beneath the Colosseum. The theory is they grew from seeds that fell from the coats of exotic animals sent into the arena to battle gladiators.

It's probably true that much of the underground will remain inaccessible to the general public. However, influential citizens such as Emanuele Gattis, a retired government archaeologist who oversaw more than 30 years worth of construction projects in Rome, are urging government leaders to seize their opportunity and direct part of the billions of lire being spent to beautify Rome for Jubilee 2000 into opening up more of the city's buried past.

Citizens speculate about what such activity might uncover, and a new branch of urban folklore has blossomed, with Romans retelling old legends about vast palaces still adorned in decorative finery, and whole blocks so intact that the spirits of an older Rome go about their daily business unhindered by the turmoil of their contemporary cousins, just yards above their heads.

THE TESTACCIO AREA & SOUTH

Protestant Cemetery. Via Caio Cestio 6. ☎ **06/574-1900.** Free admission (but a 1,000L/ 60¢ offering is customary). Apr–Sept, Tues–Sun 9am–6pm; Oct–Mar, Tues–Sun 9am–5pm. Metro: Piramide.

Near Porta San Paola, in the midst of a setting of cypress trees, lies the old cemetery where John Keats is buried. In a grave nearby, Joseph Severn, his "deathbed" companion, was interred beside him six decades later. Dejected, and feeling his reputation as a poet diminished by the rising vehemence of his critics, Keats asked that the following epitaph be written on his tombstone: "Here lies one whose name was writ in water." A great romantic poet Keats certainly was, but a prophet, thankfully not.

Percy Bysshe Shelley, author of *Prometheus Unbound,* drowned off the Italian Riviera in 1822, before his 30th birthday. His ashes rest alongside those of Edward John Trelawny, fellow romantic and man of the sea. Trelawny maintained—but this was not proved—that Shelley may have been murdered, perhaps by petty pirates bent on robbery.

Pyramid of Caius Cestius. Piazzale Ostiense. Metro: Piramide.

Dating from the 1st century B.C., the Pyramid of Caius Cestius, about 120 feet high, looks as if it belongs to the Egyptian landscape. It was constructed during the "Cleopatra craze" in architecture that swept across Rome. The pyramid can't be entered, but it's fun to circle and photograph. Who was Caius Cestius? A rich magistrate in imperial Rome whose tomb is more impressive than his achievements. You can visit at any time.

St. Paul Outside the Walls (Basilica di San Paolo Fuori le Mura). Via Ostiense. ☎ 06/ 541-0341. Free admission. Basilica, daily 7am–6:30pm; cloisters, daily 9am–12:45pm and 3–6pm. Metro: San Paolo Basilica.

The Basilica of St. Paul, whose origins go back to the time of Constantine, is the fourth great patriarchal church of Rome. It burned in 1823 and was subsequently rebuilt. This basilica is believed to have been erected over the tomb of St. Paul. From the inside, its windows may appear at first to be stained glass, but they're actually translucent alabaster. With its forest of single-file columns and its mosaic medallions (portraits of the various popes), this is one of the most streamlined and elegantly decorated churches in Rome. Its single most important treasure is a 12th-century candelabra designed by Vassalletto, who is also responsible for the remarkable cloisters— in themselves worth the trip "outside the walls." They contain twisted pairs of columns enclosing a rose garden. The Benedictine monks and students sell a fine collection of souvenirs, rosaries, and bottles of Benedictine every day except Sunday and religious holidays.

IN TRASTEVERE

From many vantage points in the Eternal City the views are panoramic. Scenic gulpers, however, have traditionally preferred the outlook from the **Gianicolo (Janiculum Hill),** across the Tiber, not one of the "Seven Hills" but certainly one of the most visited (and a stopover on many bus tours). The view is at its best at sundown, or at dawn, when the skies are often fringed with mauve. The Janiculum was the site of a battle between Guiseppe Garibaldi and the forces of Pope Pius IX in 1870—an event commemorated today with statuary. To reach the Gianicolo, take bus no. 41 from Ponte Sant'Angelo.

Chiesa di Santa Cecilia in Trastevere. Piazza Santa Cecilia. ☎ 06/589-9289. Church, free; Cavallini frescoes, free (but a donation is requested); excavations, 12,000L ($7.20). Main church, daily 10am–noon and 4–6pm; frescoes, Tues and Fri 10–11am.

A cloistered and still-functioning convent with a fine garden, Santa Cecilia contains a difficult-to-visit fresco by Cavallini in its inner sanctums and a late 13th-century baldacchino by Arnalfo di Cambio over the altar. The church is built on the reputed site of Cecilia's long-ago palace, and for a small fee you can descend under the church to inspect the ruins of some Roman houses as well as peer through a gate at the highly stuccoed grotto underneath the altar.

Chiesa di Santa Maria in Trastevere. Piazza Santa Maria in Trastevere. ☎ 06/581-4802. Free admission. Daily 7:30am–12:30pm and 4–7pm.

This Romanesque church at the colorful center of Trastevere was originally built around A.D. 350 and is one of the oldest churches in Rome. The body was added around 1100, and the portico in the early 1700s. The restored mosaics on the apse date from around 1140, and below them are the 1293 mosaic scenes depicting the life of Mary done by Pietro Cavallini. The faded mosaics on the facade are 12th or 13th century, and the octagonal fountain in the piazza is an ancient Roman original restored and added to in the 17th century by Carlo Fontana.

PONTE SANT'ANGELO

The trio of arches in the river's center has been basically unchanged since the bridge was built around A.D. 135; the arches that abut the river's embankments were added late in the 19th century as part of a flood-control program. On December 19, 1450, so many pilgrims gathered on this bridge (which at the time was lined with wooden buildings) that about 200 of them were crushed to death. Since the 1960s the bridge has been reserved exclusively for pedestrians who can stroll across and admire the statues designed by Bernini. On the southern end is the site of one of the most famous executions of the Renaissance, **Piazza San Angelo.** Here, in 1599, Beatrice Cenci and several members of her family were beheaded on orders of Pope Clement VIII. Their crime? Plotting the successful death of their very rich and very brutal father. Their tale later inspired a tragedy by Shelley and a novel by a 19th-century Italian politician named Francesco Guerrazzi.

WALKING TOUR
Rome of the Caesars

Start: Via Sacra in the Roman Forum.
Finish: Circus Maximus.
Time: 5½ hours.
Best Time: Any sunny day.
Worst Times: After dark, or when the place is overrun with tour groups.

This tour tries to incorporate the most centrally positioned of the monuments that attest to the military and architectural grandeur of Rome. As a whole, they comprise the most famous and evocative ruins in the world, despite such drawbacks as roaring traffic that's the bane of the city's civic planners, and a general dustiness and heat that might test the strength of even the hardiest of amateur archaeologists.

After the collapse of Rome and during the Dark Ages, the Forum and many of the other sites on this tour were lost to history, buried beneath layers of debris, until Mussolini set out to restore the grandeur of Rome by reminding his compatriots of their glorious past.

THE ROMAN FORUM   The more westerly of the two entrances to the Roman Forum is at the corner of Via dei Fori Imperiali and Via Cavour, adjacent to Piazza Santa Maria Nova. The nearest Metro is Colosseo.

As you walk down into the Forum along a masonry ramp you'll be heading for the **Via Sacra,** the ancient Roman road that ran through the Forum connecting the Capitoline Hill, to your right, with the Arch of Titus (1st century A.D.), situated off to your left. The Roman Forum is the more dignified and more austere of the two forums you'll visit on this walking tour. Although it consists mostly of artfully evocative ruins scattered confusingly around a sun-baked terrain, it represents almost 1,000 years of Roman power during the severely disciplined period before the legendary decadence of the later Roman emperors.

During the Middle Ages, when this was the *campo vaccino* (cow pasture) and all these stones were underground, there was a dual column of elm trees connecting the Arch of Titus, off to your left, with the Arch of Septimius Severus (A.D. 200), to your right.

Arriving at the Via Sacra, turn right. The random columns on the right as you head toward the Arch of Septimius Severus belong to the:

1. Basilica Aemilia, formerly the site of great meeting halls and shops all maintained for centuries by the noble Roman family who gave it its name. At the corner nearest the Forum entrance are some traces of melted bronze decoration that fused to the marble floor during a great fire set by invading Goths in A.D. 410.

The next important building is the:

2. Curia, or Senate house—it's the large brick building on the right that still has its roof. Romans had been meeting on this site for centuries before the first structure was erected, and that was still centuries before Christ. The present building is the fifth (if one counts all the reconstructions and substantial rehabilitations) to stand on the site. Legend has it that the original building was constructed by an ancient king with the curious name of Tullus Hostilius. The tradition he began was a noble one indeed, and modern legislative systems owe much to the Romans who met in this hall. Unfortunately, the high ideals and inviolate morals that characterized the early Republican senators gave way to the bootlicking of imperial times, when the Senate became little more than a rubber stamp. Caligula, who was only the third emperor, had his horse appointed to the Senate (it was a life appointment), and that pretty much sums up where the Senate was by the middle of the 1st century A.D.

The building was a church until 1937, when the Fascist government tore out the baroque interior and revealed what we see today. The original floor of Egyptian marble and the tiers that held the seats of the senators have miraculously survived. In addition, at the far end of the great chamber we can see the stone on which rested the fabled golden statue of *Victory*. Originally installed by Augustus, it was disposed of in the 4th century by a fiercely divided Senate, whose Christian members convinced the emperor that it was improper to have a pagan statue in such a revered place.

Outside, head down the Curia stairs to the:

3. Lapis Niger, the remains of black marble that reputedly mark the tomb of Romulus. They bask today under a corrugated roof. Go downstairs for a look at the excavated tomb. There's a stone here with the oldest Latin inscription in existence, which unfortunately is nearly unintelligible. All that can be safely assumed is that it genuinely dates from the Rome of the kings, an era that ended in a revolution in 510 B.C.

Across from the Curia, the:

4. Arch of Septimius Severus was dedicated at the dawn of the troubled 3rd century to the last decent emperor who was to govern Rome for some time. The friezes on the arch depict victories over the Arabs and the Parthians by the cold but upright Severus and his two dissolute sons, Geta and Caracalla. Severus died on a campaign to subdue the unruly natives of Scotland, and at the end of the first decade of the 3rd century Rome unhappily fell into the hands of young Caracalla, chiefly remembered today for the baths he built.

Walk around to the back of the Severus arch, face it, and look to your right. There amid the rubble you'll find a semicircular stair that led to the famous:

5. Rostra, the podium from which dictators and caesars addressed "friends, Romans, countrymen," in the Forum below. One can just imagine the emperor, shining in his white toga surrounded by imperial guards and distinguished senators, gesticulating grandly like one of the statues on a Roman roofline. The motley crowd falls silent, the elegant senators pause and listen, the merchants put down their measures, and even the harlots and unruly soldiers lower their voices in such an august presence. Later emperors didn't have much cause to use the Rostra, making their policies known through edict and assassination instead.

Walking Tour—Rome of the Caesars

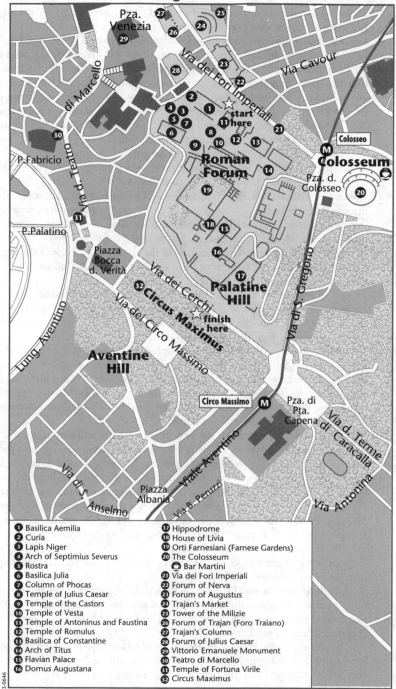

1 Basilica Aemilia
2 Curia
3 Lapis Niger
4 Arch of Septimius Severus
5 Rostra
6 Basilica Julia
7 Column of Phocas
8 Temple of Julius Caesar
9 Temple of the Castors
10 Temple of Vesta
11 Temple of Antoninus and Faustina
12 Temple of Romulus
13 Basilica of Constantine
14 Arch of Titus
15 Flavian Palace
16 Domus Augustana
17 Hippodrome
18 House of Livia
19 Orti Farnesiani (Farnese Gardens)
20 The Colosseum
   Bar Martini
21 Via dei Fori Imperiali
22 Forum of Nerva
23 Forum of Augustus
24 Trajan's Market
25 Tower of the Milizie
26 Forum of Trajan (Foro Traiano)
27 Trajan's Column
28 Forum of Julius Caesar
29 Vittorio Emanuele Monument
30 Teatro di Marcello
31 Temple of Fortuna Virile
32 Circus Maximus

3-0646

Now, facing the colonnade of the Temple of Saturn, once the public treasury, and going to the left, you'll come to the ruins of the:

6. **Basilica Julia,** again little more than a foundation. The basilica gets its name from Julius Caesar, who dedicated the first structure in 46 B.C. Like many buildings in the Forum, the basilica was burned and rebuilt several times, and the last structure dated from those shaky days after the Gothic invasion of A.D. 410. Throughout its history it was used for hearing civil court cases, which were conducted in the pandemonium of the crowded Forum, open to anyone who happened to pass by. The building was also reputed to be particularly hot in the summer, and it was under these sweaty and unpromising circumstances that Roman justice, the standard of the world for a millennium, was meted out.

Walking back down the ruined stairs of the Basilica Julia and into the broad area whose far side is bounded by the Curia, you'll see the:

7. **Column of Phocas.** Probably lifted from an early structure in the near vicinity, this was the last monument to be erected in the Roman Forum, and it commemorates the Byzantine emperor Phoca's generous donation of the Pantheon to the pope of Rome, who almost immediately transformed it into a church.

Now make your way down the middle of the Forum nearly back to the ramp from which you entered. The pile of brick with the semicircular indentation that stands in the middle of things was the:

8. **Temple of Julius Caesar,** erected some time after the dictator was deified. Judging from the reconstruction, it was quite an elegant building. As you stand facing the ruins, with the entrance to the Forum on your left, you'll see on your right three columns that originally belonged to the:

9. **Temple of the Castors.** This temple perpetuated the legend of Castor and Pollux, who appeared out of thin air in the Roman Forum and were observed watering their horses at the fountain of Juturna (still visible today), just as a major battle against the Etruscans turned in favor of Rome. Castor and Pollux, the heavenly twins—and the symbol of the astrological sign Gemini—seem a favorite of Rome.

The next major monument is the circular:

10. **Temple of Vesta,** wherein dwelt the sacred flame of Rome and the Atrium of the Vestal Virgins. A vestal virgin was usually a girl of good family who signed a contract for 30 years. During that time she lived in the ruin you're standing in right now. Of course, back then it was an unimaginably rich marble building with two floors. There were only six vestal virgins at a time during the Imperial Era, and even though they had the option of going back out into the world at the end of their 30 years, few did. The cult of Vesta came to an end in 394, when a Christian Rome secularized all its pagan temples. A man standing on this site before then would have been put to death immediately.

Stand in the atrium with your back to the Palatine and look beyond those fragmented statues of former vestals to the:

11. **Temple of Antoninus and Faustina.** It's the building with the freestanding colonnade just to the right of the ramp where you first entered the Forum. Actually, just the colonnade dates from imperial times; the building behind is a much later church dedicated to San Lorenzo.

After you inspect the beautifully proportioned Antoninus and Faustina temple, head up Via Sacra away from the entrance ramp toward the Arch of Titus. Pretty soon, on your left you'll see the twin bronze doors of the:

12. **Temple of Romulus.** It's the doors themselves that are really of note here—they're the original Roman doors and swing on the same massive hinges they were originally mounted on in A.D. 306. In this case, the temple is not dedicated to the

legendary cofounder of Rome, but to the son of its builder, the emperor Maxentius. Unfortunately for both father and son, they competed with a general who deprived them of both their empire and their lives. That man was Constantine, who, while camped outside Rome during preparations for one of his battles against Maxentius, saw the sign of the cross in the heavens with the insignia *in hoc signo vinces* (in this sign shall you conquer). Raising the standard of Christianity above his legions, he defeated the emperor Maxentius and became the first Christian emperor.

At the time of Constantine's victory (A.D. 306) the great:

13. **Basilica of Constantine** (marked by those three gaping arches up ahead on your left) was only half finished, having been started by the unfortunate Maxentius. However, Constantine finished the job and affixed his name to this, the largest and most impressive building in the Forum. To our taste, the more delicate, Greek-influenced temples are more attractive, but you have to admire the scale and the engineering skill that erected this monument. The fact that portions of the original coffered ceiling are still intact is amazing. The basilica once held a statue of Constantine so large that his little toe was as wide as an average man's waist. You can see a few fragments from this colossus—the remnants were found in 1490—in the courtyard of the Conservatory Museum on the Capitoline Hill. As far as Roman emperors went, Christian or otherwise, ego knew no bounds.

From Constantine's basilica, follow the Roman paving stones of Via Sacra to the:

14. **Arch of Titus,** clearly visible on a low hill just ahead. Titus was the emperor who sacked the great Jewish temple in Jerusalem, and the bas-relief sculpture inside the arch shows the booty of the Jews being carried in triumph through the streets of Rome, while Titus is crowned by Victory, who comes down from heaven for the occasion. You'll notice in particular the candelabra, for centuries one of the most famous pieces of the treasure of Rome. In all probability it lies at the bottom of the Busento River in the secret tomb of Alaric the Goth.

THE PALATINE HILL   When you've gathered your strength in the shimmering hot sun, head up the Clivus Palatinus, the road to the palaces of the Palatine Hill. With your back to the Arch of Titus, it's the road going up the hill to the left.

It was on the Palatine Hill that Rome first became a city. Legend tells us that the date was 753 B.C. At that time the city originally consisted of nothing more than the Palatine, which was soon enclosed by a surprisingly sophisticated wall, remains of which can still be seen on the Circus Maximus side of the hill. As time went on and Rome grew in power and wealth, the boundaries were extended and later enclosed by the Servian Wall. When the last of the ancient kings was overthrown (510 B.C.), Rome had already extended onto several of the adjoining hills and valleys. As Republican times progressed, the Palatine became a fashionable residential district. So it remained until Tiberius—who, like his predecessor, Augustus, was a bit too modest to really call himself "emperor" out loud—began the first of the monumental palaces that were to cover the entire hill.

It's difficult today to make sense out of the Palatine. The first-time viewer might be forgiven for suspecting it to be an entirely artificial structure built on brick arches. Those arches, which are visible on practically every flank of the hill, are actually supports that once held imperial structures. Having run out of building sites, the emperors, in their fever, simply enlarged the hill by building new sides on it.

The Clivius Palatinus, goes on only a short way, through a small sort of valley filled with lush, untrimmed greenery. After about 5 minutes (for walkers going at a leisurely pace), you'll see the ruins of a monumental stairway just to the right of the road. The Clivus Palatinus turns sharply to the left here, skirting the monastery of San Bonaventura, but we'll detour to the right and take a look at the remains of the:

15. **Flavian Palace.** As you walk off the road and into the ruins, you'll be able to discern that there were once three rooms here. But it's impossible for anyone but an archaeologist to comprehend quite how splendid these rooms were. The entire Flavian Palace was decorated in the most lavish of colored marbles and gold. Much of the decoration survived as late as the 18th century, when the greedy duke of Parma removed most of what was left. The room closest to the Clivus Palatinus was called the Lararium and held statues of the divinities that protected the imperial family. The middle room was the grandest of the three. It was the imperial throne room, where the ruler of the world, the emperor of Rome, would sit. The far room was a basilica and as such was used for miscellaneous court functions, among them audiences with the emperor. This part of the palace was used entirely for ceremonial functions. Adjoining these three rooms are the remains of a spectacularly luxurious peristyle. You'll recognize it by the hexagonal remains of a fountain in the middle. Try, if you can, to imagine this fountain surrounded by marble arcades, planted with mazes, and equipped with mica-covered walls. On the opposite side of the peristyle from the throne room are several other great reception and entertainment rooms. The banquet hall was here, and beyond it, looking over the Circus Maximus, are a few ruins of former libraries. Although practically nothing remains except the foundations, every now and again you'll catch sight of a fragment of colored marble floor, in a subtle, sophisticated pattern.

The imperial family lived in the:

16. **Domus Augustana,** the remains of which lie toward the Circus Maximus and slightly to the left of the Flavian Palace. The new building that stands here—it looks old to us—is a museum (usually closed). It stands in the absolute center of the Domus Augustana. In the field adjacent to the Hippodrome stadium (see below) stood the Villa Mills, a gingerbread Gothic villa of the 19th century. It was quite a famous place, owned by a rich Englishman who came to Rome from the West Indies. Villa Mills was the scene of many fashionable entertainments in Victorian times, and it's interesting to note that the last dinner parties that took place on the Palatine Hill were given by an Englishman. At any of several points along this south-facing belvedere of the Palatine Hill, you'll be able to see the faraway oval-shaped walls of the Circus Maximus. Continue with your exploration of the Palatine Hill by heading across the field parallel to the Clivus Palatinus and you'll come to the north end of the:

17. **Hippodrome,** or Stadium of Domitian. The field was apparently occupied by parts of the Domus Augustana, which in turn adjoined the enormous stadium. The stadium itself is worth examination, although sometimes it's difficult to get down inside it. The perfectly proportioned area was usually used for private games, staged for the amusement of the imperial family. As you look down the stadium from the north end, you can see, on the left side, the semicircular remains of a structure identified as Domitian's private box. Some archaeologists claim that the "stadium" was actually an elaborate sunken garden.

The aqueduct that comes up the wooded hill used to supply water for the Baths of Septimius Severus, whose difficult-to-understand ruins lie in monumental poles of arched brick at the far end of the stadium.

Returning to the Flavian Palace, leave the peristyle on the opposite side from the Domus Augustana and follow the signs to the:

18. House of Livia. They take you down a dusty path to your left. Although legend says that this was the house of Augustus's consorts, it actually was Augustus's all along. The place is notable for some rather well-preserved murals showing mythological scenes. But more interesting is the aspect of the house itself—it's not very big, and there never were any great baths or impressive marble arcades. Augustus, even though he was the first emperor, lived simply compared to his successors. His wife, Livia, was a fiercely ambitious aristocrat who divorced her own husband to marry the emperor (the ex-husband was forced to attend the wedding, incidentally) and, according to some historians, was the true power behind Roman policy between the death of Julius Caesar and the ascension of Tiberius. She even controlled Tiberius, her son, since she had engineered his rise to power through a long string of intrigues and poisonings.

After you've examined the frescoes in Livia's parlor, head up the steps that lead to the top of the embankment to the north. Once on top, you'll be in the:

19. Farnese Gardens (Orti Farnesiani), the 16th-century horticultural fantasies of a Farnese cardinal. They're constructed on top of the Palace of Tiberius, which, you'll remember, was the first of the great imperial palaces to be built on this hill. It's impossible to see any of it, but the gardens are cool and nicely laid out. You might stroll up to the promontory above the Forum and admire the view of the ancient temples and the Capitoline heights off to the left.

You've now seen the best of the Forum and the Palatine. To leave the archaeological area, you should continue walking eastward along the winding road that meanders steeply down from the Palatine Hill to Via di San Gregorio. When you reach the roaring traffic of that busy thoroughfare, walk north toward the bulk of what some Romans consider the most potent symbol of their city, the:

20. Colosseum. Its crumbling, oval-shaped bulk is the greatest monument of Ancient Rome, and visitors are impressed with its size, its majesty, and its ability to conjure up the often cruel entertainments that were devised inside for the pleasure of the Roman masses. Either visit it now or return later.

☕ **TAKE A BREAK** After all this exposure to the glory that was Rome, you'll want to retreat to a cozy modern cafe for a caffeine or food fix. The best-sited choice is **Bar Sael (Lazio),** Piazza del Colosseo 21–23 (☎ **06/488-0677**), adjacent to the piazza's subway stop leading underground. (Don't worry if you can't pronouce this establishment's unusual name, as the only indication you'll see outside is BAR.) Come here for frothy cappuccino, and—if you're in the mood—beer and wine. Food is limited to a wide selection of *panini* (sandwiches) priced between 4,000L and 6,000L ($2.40 and $3.60) each and pastas that average 12,000L ($7.20) per heaping platter. Because it's the only cafe on the busy piazza, it's often quite crowded and popular. Hours are 6am to 9pm daily.

THE IMPERIAL FORUMS With your back to the Colosseum, walk westward along the:

21. Via dei Fori Imperiali, keeping to the right side of the street. It was Mussolini who issued the controversial orders to cut through centuries of debris and junky buildings to carve out this boulevard, thereby linking the Colosseum to the grand 19th-century monuments of Piazza Venezia. Excavations under his Fascist regime began at once, and many archaeological treasures were revealed. Today the vistas over the ruins of Rome's Imperial Forum, visible from the northern side of the boulevard, make for one of the most fascinating walks in Rome.

Begun by Julius Caesar as an answer to the overcrowding of Rome's older forums during the days of the empire, the Imperial Forums were at the time of their construction flashier, bolder, and more impressive than the buildings in the Roman Forum we've just visited, and as such represented the unquestioned authority of the Roman emperors at the height of their absolute power. After the collapse of Rome and during the Dark Ages, they, like many other ancient monuments, were lost to history, buried beneath layers of debris until Mussolini, in an egomaniacal attempt to draw comparisons between his Fascist regime and the glory of ancient Rome, helped to restore the grandeur of Rome by reminding his compatriots of their glorious imperial past.

Some of the rather confusing ruins you'll see from the boulevard include the shattered remnants of the colonnade that once surrounded the Temple of Venus and Roma. Next to it, you'll see the back wall of the Basilica of Constantine. Shortly, on the street's north side, you'll come to a large outdoor restaurant, where Via Cavour joins the boulevard. Just beyond the small park across Via Cavour are the remains of the:

22. **Forum of Nerva,** built by the emperor whose 2-year reign (A.D. 96–98) followed that of the paranoid Domitian. The Forum of Nerva is best observed from the railing that skirts it on Via dei Fori Imperiali. You'll be struck by just how much the ground level has risen in 19 centuries. The only really recognizable remnant is a wall of the Temple of Minerva with two fine Corinthian columns. This forum was once flanked by that of Vespasian, which is now, however, completely gone. It's possible to enter the Forum of Nerva from the other side, but you can see it just as well from the railing.

The next forum you approach is the:

23. **Forum of Augustus,** built before the birth of Christ to commemorate the emperor's victory over the assassins Cassius and Brutus in the Battle of Philippi (42 B.C.). Fittingly, the temple that once dominated this forum—and whose remains can still be seen—was that of Mars Ultor, or Mars the Avenger. In the temple once stood a mammoth statue of Augustus, which has unfortunately completely vanished. Like the Forum of Nerva, you can enter the Forum of Augustus from the other side (cut across the wee footbridge).

Continuing along the railing, you'll see next the vast semicircle of:

24. **Trajan's Market,** Via Quattro Novembre 95 (☎ 06/679-0048), whose teeming arcades stocked with merchandise from the far corners of the Roman world long ago collapsed, leaving only a few ubiquitous cats to watch after things. The shops once covered a multitude of levels, and you can still wander around many of them. In front of the perfectly proportioned semicircular facade—designed by Apollodorus of Damascus at the beginning of the 2nd century—are the remains of a great library, and fragments of delicately colored marble floors still shine in the sunlight between stretches of rubble and tall grass.

While the view from the railing is of interest, Trajan's Market is worth the descent below street level. To get here, follow the service road you're on until you reach the monumental Trajan's Column on your left, where you turn right and go up the steep flight of stairs that leads to Via Nazionale. At the top of the stairs, about half a block farther on the right, you'll see the entrance to the market. It's open Tuesday to Saturday from 9am to 7pm and Sunday from 9am to 1pm. Admission is 3,750L ($2.25) for adults, 2,500L ($1.50) for students, and free for children 17 and under and seniors 60 and over.

Before you head down through the labyrinthine passageways, you might like to climb the:

25. Tower of the Milizie, a 12th-century structure that was part of the medieval head-quarters of the Knights of Rhodes. The view from the top (if it's open) is well worth the climb. From the tower, you can wander where you will through the ruins of the market, admiring the sophistication of the layout and the sad beauty of the bits of decoration that still remain. When you've examined the brick and travertine corridors, head out in front of the semicircle to the site of the former library; from here, scan the retaining wall that supports the modern road and look for the entrance to the tunnel that leads to the:

26. Forum of Trajan (Foro Traiano), entered on Via Quattro Novembre near the steps of Via Magnanapoli. Once through the tunnel, you'll emerge in the newest and most beautiful of the Imperial Forums, designed by the same man who laid out the adjoining market. There are many statue fragments and pedestals that bear still-legible inscriptions, but more interesting is the great Basilica Ulpia, whose gray marble columns rise roofless into the sky. You wouldn't know it to judge from what's left, but the Forum of Trajan was once regarded as one of the architectural wonders of the world. Constructed between A.D. 107 and 113, it was designed by the Greek architect Apollodorus of Damascus.

Beyond the Basilica Ulpia is:

27. Trajan's Column, which is in magnificent condition, with intricate bas-relief sculpture depicting Trajan's victorious campaign (although from your vantage point you'll only be able to see the earliest stages). The emperor's ashes were kept in a golden urn at the base of the column. If you're fortunate, someone on duty at the stairs next to the column will let you out there. Otherwise, you'll have to walk back the way you came.

The next stop is the:

28. Forum of Julius Caesar, the first of the Imperial Forums. It lies on the opposite side of Via dei Fori Imperial, the last set of sunken ruins before the Victor Emmanuel Monument. While it's possible to go right down into the ruins, you can see everything just as well from the railing. This was the site of the Roman stock exchange, as well as of the Temple of Venus, a few of whose restored columns stand cinematically in the middle of the excavations.

ON TO THE CIRCUS MAXIMUS   From here, retrace your last steps until you're in front of the white Brescian marble monument around the corner on Piazza Venezia, where the:

29. Vittorio Emanuele Monument dominates the piazza. The most flamboyant landmark in Italy, it was constructed in the late 1800s to honor the first king of Italy. It has been compared to everything from a frosty wedding cake to a Victorian typewriter. An eternal flame burns at the Tomb of the Unknown Soldier. The interior of the monument has been closed to the public for many years.

Keep close to the monument and walk to your left, in the opposite direction from Via dei Fori Imperiali. You might like to pause at the fountain that flanks one of the monument's great white walls and splash some icy water on your face. Stay on the same side of the street and just keep walking around the monument. You'll be on Via del Teatro Marcello, which takes you past the twin lions that guard the sloping stairs and along the base of the Capitoline Hill.

Keep walking along this boulevard until you come to the:

30. Teatro di Marcello, on your right. You'll recognize the two rows of gaping arches, which are said to be the models for the Colosseum. Julius Caesar is credited with starting the construction of this theater, but it was finished many years after his death (in 11 B.C.) by Augustus, who dedicated it to his favorite nephew, Marcellus.

A small corner of the 2,000-year-old arcade has been restored to what presumably was the original condition. Here, as everywhere, there are numerous cats stalking around the broken marble.

The bowl of the theater and the stage were adapted many centuries ago as the foundation for the Renaissance palace of the Orsini family. The other ruins belong to old temples. To the right is the Porticus of Octavia, dating from the 2nd century B.C. Note how later cultures used part of the Roman structure without destroying its original character. There's another good example of this on the other side of the theater. There you'll see a church with a wall that completely incorporates part of an ancient colonnade.

Keep walking along Via del Teatro Marcello away from Piazza Venezia for two more long blocks, until you come to Piazza della Bocca della Verità. The first item to notice in the attractive piazza is the rectangular:

31. Temple of Fortuna Virile. You'll see it on the right, a little off the road. Built a century before the birth of Christ, it's still in magnificent condition. Behind it is another temple, dedicated to Vesta. Like the one in the Forum, it's round, symbolic of the prehistoric huts where continuity of the hearthfire was a matter of survival.

About a block to the south you'll pass the facade of the Church of Santa Maria in Cosmedin, set on Piazza della Bocca della Verità. Even more noteworthy, a short walk to the east, is the:

32. Circus Maximus, whose elongated oval proportions and ruined tiers of benches might remind visitors of the setting for *Ben-Hur*. Today a formless ruin, the victim of countless raids upon its stonework by medieval and Renaissance builders, the remains of the once-great arena lie directly behind the church. At one time 250,000 Romans could assemble on the marble seats, while the emperor observed the games from his box high on the Palatine Hill.

The circus lies in a valley formed by the Palatine Hill on the left and the Aventine Hill on the right. Next to the Colosseum, it was the most impressive structure in Ancient Rome, located certainly in one of the most exclusive neighborhoods. Emperors lived on the Palatine, while the great palaces of patricians sprawled across the Aventine, which is still a rather nice neighborhood. For centuries the pomp and ceremony of imperial chariot races filled this valley with the cheers of thousands.

When the dark days of the 5th and 6th centuries fell on the city, the Circus Maximus seemed a symbol of the complete ruination of Rome. The last games were held in 549 on the orders of Totilla the Goth, who had seized Rome in 547 and established himself as emperor. He lived in the still-glittering ruins on the Palatine and apparently thought that the chariot races in the Circus Maximus would lend credence to his charade of empire. It must have been a pretty miserable show, since the decimated population numbered something like 500 when Totilla recaptured the city. The Romans of these times were caught between Belisarius, the imperial general from Constantinople, and Totilla the Goth, both of whom fought bloodily for control of Rome. After the travesty of 549, the Circus Maximus was never used again, and the demand for building materials reduced it, like so much of Rome, to a great dusty field.

To return to other parts of town, head for the bus stop adjacent to the Santa Maria in Cosmedin Church, or walk the length of the Circus Maximus to its far end where you can pick up the Metro.

5 Especially for Kids

Beyond the ancient monuments, Rome offers other attractions that will be equally appealing, educational, and fun for kids. For example, many children also enjoy the climb to the top of **St. Peter's Basilica.**

The **Fun Fair (Luna Park),** along Via delle Tre Fontane (☎ **06/592-5933**), at E.U.R. (a suburban area south of the city; take the Metro Line B to the Magliana stop, or less desirably to the San Paolo stop), is one of the largest in Europe. It's known for its "big wheel" at the entrance, and there are merry-go-rounds, miniature railways, and shooting galleries, among other attractions. Admission is free, but you pay for each ride. Open Monday to Saturday from 5pm to midnight. Metro: Magliana.

The **Teatro delle Marionette degli Accettella,** performing at the Teatro Mongiovino, Via Giovanni Genocchi 15 (☎ **06/513-9405**), has marionette performances for children on Saturday and Sunday (except in July and August) at 4:30pm. Tickets are 12,000L ($7.20) per person, adult or child.

The **Puppet Theater** on Pincio Square in the **Villa Borghese gardens** above Piazza del Popolo has "Punch and Judy" performances nearly every day. While here, you might also like to take your children through the park to enjoy the fountain displays and the lake and the many wide spaces in which they can play. You can **rent boats** at the Giardino del Lago, or stop by the **zoo** at Viale del Giardino Zoologico 20 (☎ **06/321-6564**). The zoo is open in summer, Monday to Friday from 8:30am to 5pm, and Saturday and Sunday from 8:30am to 6pm; in winter, Monday to Friday from 8:30am to 4pm and Saturday and Sunday from 8:30am to 5pm. Admission is 10,000L ($6) for adults, free for small children.

At 4pm every day there's a military band and a parade as the guard changes at the **Quirinale Palace,** Piazza del Quirinale, the residence of the president of Italy.

6 Organized Tours

Because of the sheer volume of artistic riches, some visitors prefer to begin their stay in Rome with an organized tour. While few things can really be covered in any depth on these "overview tours," they're sometimes useful for getting the feel and geography of a complicated city. One of the leading tour operators (among the zillions of possibilities) is **American Express,** Piazza di Spagna 38 (☎ **06/67-641**), open Monday to Friday from 9am to 5:30pm and Saturday from 9am to 12:30pm. Its tours are the most closely geared to American visitors, and all tours are conducted strictly in English.

One of the most popular tours is a 4-hour orientation tour of Rome and the Vatican, which departs most mornings at 9:30am and costs 60,000L ($36) per person. Another 4-hour tour, which focuses on the Rome of antiquity (including visits to the Colosseum, the Roman Forum, the ruins of the Imperial Palace, and the Church of San Pietro in Vincoli), costs 50,000L ($30). Of the many excursions offered to sites outside the city limits of Rome, the most popular is a 5-hour bus tour to **Tivoli,** where visits are conducted to the **Villa d'Este** and its spectacular gardens and the ruins of the **Villa Adriana,** all for the price of 63,000L ($37.80) per person.

If your time in Italy is rigidly limited, you might opt for 1-day excursions to points farther afield on tours that are marketed (but not conducted) by American Express. Although rushed and far too short to expose the many-layered majesty of these destinations, a series of 1-day tours is offered to Pompeii, Naples, and Sorrento for a price of 140,000L ($84) per person; to Florence for 170,000L ($102); and to Capri for 193,000L ($115.80). Lunch is included on each of these full-day trips, but to participate you'll need a lot of stamina, as each tour departs from Rome around 7am and returns sometime after 9 or 10pm to your hotel.

Another option is **Scala Reale,** Via Varese 46 (☎ **800/732-2863,** ext. 4052, in the U.S., or 06/4470-0898). Scala Reale is a cultural association founded by the American architect Tom Rankin. He offers small-group tours and excursions focusing on the architectural and artistic significance of Rome. Tours include visits to monuments, museums, and piazzas as well as to neighborhood trattorie. In addition, custom-designed tours are available. Tours begin at 30,000L ($18). Children 11 and under are admitted free to walking tours.

7 Soccer Matches & Other Outdoor Activities

SOCCER   Soccer is one of the four all-consuming passions of thousands of Italians, richly intertwined with their image of the country. Rome boasts two intensely competitive teams, Lazio and Roma, which tend to play either against each other or against visiting teams from other parts of the country every Sunday afternoon. Matches are held at the **Stadio Olimpico,** Foro Italico dei Gladiatori (☎ **06/ 36-851**), originally built by Mussolini as a nationalistic (Fascist) statement. Thousands of tickets are sold during the 2 or 3 hours before each game. (Tickets are also sold at the stadium Monday to Friday from 9am to 5pm.) The players usually take a break during June, July, and August, beginning the season with something approaching pandemonium in September.

BIKING   The traffic is murderous and the pollution might make your head spin, but there are quiet times (early mornings and Sunday) when a spin beside the Tiber or through the Borghese Gardens might prove very appealing. It's highly advisable to wear a helmet when bicycling, even if the local Vespa riders don't.

Bike riders are permitted anywhere in the city, including pedestrian-only zones, and traffic-free areas such as St. Peter's Square, where you can ride within the arcaded confines of what's been called the world's most magnificent oval. Also appealing is a 30km (18.5-mile) bike lane beside the Tiber that extends from central Rome north, to the industrial suburb of Castel Jubileo.

Bike-rental concession stands are found in the following areas: Piazza del Popolo, Largo San Silvestro, Largo Argentina, Piazza di Spagna, and Viale della Pineto in the Villa Borghese.

BOWLING   One of the city's largest bowling complexes, whose hordes of participants provide a spectacle almost more interesting than the game itself, **Bowling Roma** is at Viale Regina Margherita 181 (☎ **06/855-1184**), off Via Nomentana.

GOLF   Rome boasts several golf courses that will usually welcome members of other golf clubs. Each, of course, will be under the greatest pressure on Saturday and Sunday, so as a nonmember try to schedule arrival for a weekday.

One of the capital's best courses, with a clubhouse in a villa built during the 1600s and fairways designed by Robert Trent Jones, is the **Country Club Castelgandolfo,** Via Santo Spirito 13, Castelgandolfo (☎ **06/931-2301**). An older, more entrenched, and more prestigious course is the **Circolo del Golf Roma,** Via Appia Nuova 716/ A (☎ **06/780-3407**). About 8½ miles from the center of town lies the **Olgiata Golf Club,** Largo Olgiata 15, off Via Cassia (☎ **06/3088-9141**).

HORSEBACK RIDING   The most convenient of Rome's several riding clubs is the **Associazione Sportiva Villa Borghese,** Via del Galoppatoio 23 (☎ **06/ 320-0487**). Other stables are in the **Circolo Ippico Olgiata,** Largo Olgiata 15

(☎ 06/3088-8792), near Cassia and the **Società Ippica Romana,** Via del Monti della Farnesina 18 (☎ 06/324-0591). Tack and equipment are English style.

JOGGING Jogging provides a moving view of the city's monuments—but beware of the city's heat and be alert to speeding traffic. Several possible itineraries include the park of the **Villa Borghese,** where the series of roads and pathways, some of them beside statuary, provide a verdant oasis in the city's congestion. The best places to enter the park are at Piazza del Popolo or at the top of Via Vittorio Veneto. The **Cavalieri Hilton,** Via Cadlolo 101, Monte Mario (☎ 06/35-091), offers a jogging path (measuring a third of a mile) through the trees and flowering shrubs of its landscaping. The grounds that surround the **Villa Pamphilj** contain three running tracks, although they might either be locked or in use by local sports teams. A final possibility, not recommended for jogging after dark, is the rounded premises of the Circus Maximus (about half a mile).

SWIMMING There are more than 90 swimming pools in Rome besides those found at hotels. Be warned that many require an annual membership fee even if you only plan to be in the city a short time. For more information on pools and their requirements or fees, contact the **Comitato Regionale Lazio Federazione Italiana Nuoto,** 8 Via Virgilio, 00193 Rome, Italy (☎ 06/687-4367). One of the busiest all-year pools is at the **Roman Sport Center,** Via del Galoppatoio 33 (☎ 06/320-1667), which lies adjacent to the parking lot on the grounds of the Villa Borghese. Open to the public, it contains two large swimming pools, squash courts, a gym, and saunas. In another part of town, the **Piscina della Rose,** Viale America (☎ 06/592-6717), is an Olympic-size pool open to the public (and crowded with teenagers and *bambini*) between June and September. More sedate, set in lushly landscaped gardens, and open to nonresidents, is the pool on the resort-inspired premises of the **Cavalieri Hilton,** Via Cadlolo 101 (☎ 06/35-091). Lap swimmers can exercise year-round at the **Villa Pamphili Sporting Club,** Via della Nocetta (☎ 06/6615-8555), adjacent to the Hotel Villa Pamphili.

TENNIS The best tennis courts are at private clubs, many of which are in a handful of suburbs. Players are highly conscious of proper tennis attire, so be prepared to don your most sparkling whites and your best manners. One of the city's best-known clubs is the **Tennis Club Parioli,** Via Salaria (☎ 06/8620-0882), open daily from 8am to noon only.

8 Shopping

Rome offers temptations of every kind, but this section will try to focus on the urge to shop that sometimes overcomes even the most stalwart of visitors. You might find hidden oases of charm and value in unpublicized streets and districts, but what follows is a listing and description of certain streets known throughout Italy for their shops. The monthly rent on these famous streets is very high, and those costs are passed on to the consumer. Nonetheless, a stroll down some of these streets presents a cross section of the most desirable wares in Italy.

Cramped urban spaces and a well-defined sense of taste have encouraged most Italian stores to elevate the boutique philosophy to its highest levels. The theory is that if you like what you see in a shop window, you'll find it duplicated, in spirit and style, inside. Lack of space, and definition of a merchandising program, usually restrict an establishment's merchandise to one particular style, degree of formality, or mood.

Caveat: We won't pretend that Rome is Italy's finest shopping center (Florence and Venice are) or that its shops are unusually inexpensive—many of them aren't. But even on the most elegant of Rome's thoroughfares, there are values mixed in with the costly boutiques.

Shopping hours are generally Monday from 3:30 to 7:30pm, and Tuesday to Saturday from 9:30 or 10am to 1pm and from 3:30 to 7 or 7:30pm. Some shops are open on Monday mornings, however, and some shops don't close for the afternoon break.

THE SHOPPING SCENE

Via Borgognona   Beginning near Piazza di Spagna, both the rents and the merchandise are chic and very, very expensive. Like its neighbor, Via Condotti, it's a mecca for wealthy, well-dressed women from around the world. Its storefronts have retained their baroque or neoclassical facades.

Via Condotti   Easy to find because it begins at the base of the Spanish Steps, this is the poshest and the most visible upper-bracket shopping street in Rome, and the best example in Europe of avidly elegant consumerism. Even the recent incursion of some less elegant stores hasn't diminished the allure of this street as a consumer's playground for the rich and the very, very rich.

Via del Corso   Not attempting the stratospheric image (or prices) of Via Condotti or Via Borgognona, the styles here are aimed at younger consumers. There are, however, some gems scattered amid the shops selling jeans and sporting equipment. The most interesting shops are in the section nearest the fashionable cafes of Piazza del Popolo.

Via Francesco Crispi   Most shoppers reach this street by following Via Sistina (see below) one long block from the top of the Spanish Steps. Near the intersection of these streets are several shops well suited for unusual and less expensive gifts.

Via Frattina   Running parallel to Via Condotti, it begins, like its more famous sibling, at Piazza di Spagna. Part of its length is closed to traffic. Here, the concentration of shops is denser, although some aficionados claim that its image—and its prices—are slightly less chic and slightly lower than its counterparts on Via Condotti. It's usually thronged with shoppers who appreciate the lack of motor traffic.

Via Nazionale   The layout here recalls 19th-century grandeur and ostentatious beauty, but the traffic is horrendous; crossing Via Nazionale requires a good sense of timing and a strong understanding of Italian driving patterns. It begins at Piazza della Repubblica and runs down almost to the 19th-century monuments of Piazza Venezia. There's an abundance of leather stores—more reasonable in price than those in many other parts of Rome—and a welcome handful of stylish boutiques.

Via Sistina   Beginning at the top of the Spanish Steps, Via Sistina runs to Piazza Barberini. The shops are small, stylish, and based on the personalities of their owners. The pedestrian traffic is less dense than on other major streets.

Via Vittorio Veneto & Via Barberini   Evocative of *La Dolce Vita* fame, Via Veneto is filled these days with expensive hotels and cafes and an array of relatively expensive stores selling shoes, gloves, and leather goods.

SHOPPING A TO Z
ANTIQUES

Some visitors to Italy consider the trove of antiques for sale the country's greatest treasure. The value of almost any antique has risen to alarming levels as increasingly wealthy Europeans outbid each other in frenzies of acquisitive lust. You might remember that any antique dealer who risks the high rents of central Rome is acutely aware of the value of almost everything ever made and will probably recognize anything of value long before his or her clients. Beware of fakes, remember to insure anything you have shipped home, and for larger purchases—anything more than 300,000L ($180) at any one store—keep your paperwork in order to obtain your tax refund.

Via dei Coronari is buried in a colorful section of the Campus Martius and is an antiquer's dream, literally lined with magnificent vases, urns, chandeliers, breakfronts, chaises, refectory tables, and candelabra. To find the entrance to the street, turn left out of the north end of Piazza Navona, pass the excavated ruins of Domitian's Stadium, and the street will be just ahead of you. There are more than 40 antique stores in the next four blocks. Bring your pocket calculator with you, and keep in mind that stores are frequently closed between 1 and 4pm.

Ad Antiqua Domus. Via Paola 25–27. ☎ **06/686-1530.**

Italian furniture from the days of Caesar through the 19th century is for sale here. It's as much a museum of Italian furniture design through the ages as it is a shop. There's a second location at Via dei Coronari 227 (☎ **06/687-5384**).

Artimport. Via del Babuino 150. ☎ **06/679-6585.**

A bargain and antique shopper's mecca, this bazaar always has something for sale that's intriguing and tasteful. Merchandise is duly certified as to its authenticity. Although there is a wide assortment of merchandise, the owners specialize in silver.

Galleria Coronari. Via dei Coronari 59. ☎ **06/686-9917.**

The Galleria Coronari is a desirable shop that might be used as a starting point. Many of its antiques are nostalgia-laden bric-a-brac small enough to fit into a suitcase, including jewelry, dolls, paintings, and elaborately ornate picture frames from the 19th century. Also represented is furniture from the 18th, 19th, and early 20th centuries, and such oddities as a completely furnished dollhouse, accurate down to the miniature champagne bottles in the miniature pantry.

ARTS & PRINTS

Alberto di Castro. Via del Babuino 71. ☎ **06/361-3752.**

Alberto di Castro is one of the largest dealers of antique prints and engravings in Rome. You'll find rack after rack of depictions of everything from the Colosseum to the Pantheon, each evocative of the best architecture in the Mediterranean world, priced between $25 and $1,000 depending on the age and rarity of the engraving.

Alinari. Via d'Albert 16A. ☎ **06/679-2923.**

This print shop takes its name from the famed Florentine photographer of the 19th century. Original prints of Alinari are almost as prized as paintings in national galleries, and you can pick up your own here.

Galleria d'Arte Schneider. Rampa Mignanelli 10. ☎ **06/678-4019.**

Near the top of the Spanish Steps, this is one of the most enduring art galleries in Rome. Established in 1953 by an American-born professor of languages and art connoisseur, it specializes in lesser-known sculpture and paintings by Italians or foreign residents of Rome. Among the artists promoted early in their careers by this gallery are Dimitre Hadzi, George d'Almeida, Paolo Buggiani, and Mirko Balsedella. The frequently changing inventories are relatively affordable. The building that contains the gallery, incidentally, was designed in the 19th century by a Danish sculptor with the intention that it serve as a refuge for artists ever after. The day-to-day operations of the gallery are conducted by Mr. Schneider's charming wife, Dolores.

The gallery keeps no set hours, and some days it doesn't open at all—so call first. When the gallery is open, it's only in the late afternoon. Always closed in August.

Galleria 2 RC. Via dei Delfini 16. ☎ **06/6992-2141.**

This gallery has the best print studio in Rome where you'll find a collection of beautifully reproduced works from famous artists. It's almost as good as owning the real thing.

Giovanni B. Panatta Fine Art Shop. Via Francesco Crispi 117. ☎ **06/679-5948.**

You'll find excellent color and black-and-white prints covering a variety of subjects from 18th-century Roman street scenes to astrological charts in this fine art shop up the hill toward the Borghese Gardens. There's also a good selection of reproductions of medieval and Renaissance art that are attractive and reasonably priced.

Fava. Via del Babuino 180. ☎ **06/361-0807.**

Fava recaptures the era when Neapolitans sold 17th- and 18th-century pictures of the eruptions of Vesuvius, once highly sought by collectors. Many of these "volcanic paintings" of yesteryear—so eagerly sought by British collectors in particular—can still cause a conflagration today. This is really unusual art from the attics of the days of yore.

Olivi. Via del Babuino 126. ☎ **06/3600-0064.**

This is called "The Old Curiosity Shop of Rome." Professor Olivi is a whiz when it comes to knowing Roman history and collecting a treasure trove of old prints.

BOOKSTORES

Economy Book and Video Center. Via Torino 136. ☎ **06/474-6877.**

Catering to the English-speaking communities of Rome, this bookstore sells only English-language books (both new and used, paperback and hardcover), greeting cards, and videos. Staffed by British, Australian, and American workers, it lies about a block from the Piazza della Repubblica Metro station, and bus lines no. 64 and 70.

Lion Bookshop. Via del Babuino 181. ☎ **06/322-5837.**

The Lion Bookshop is the oldest English-language bookshop in town, specializing in literature, both American and English. It also sells children's books and photographic volumes on both Rome and Italy. A vast choice of English-language videos is for sale or rent. The store is closed in August.

Rizzoli. Largo Chigi 15. ☎ **06/679-6641.**

Rizzoli's collection of Italian-language books is one of the largest in Rome, but if your native language is French, English, German, or Spanish, the interminable shelves of this very large bookstore have a section to amuse, enlighten, and entertain you.

CHINA & GLASSWARE

Barduagni. Via del Tritone 99–100. ☎ **06/488-4324.**

Established in Rome in 1912, this shop and gallery features all that is fine in European china and glassware. Specializing in Rosenthal tableware and objet d'art, the list of items and manufacturers represented here spans the continent, including Wedgwood.

DEPARTMENT STORES

La Rinascente. In Piazza Colonna, at Via del Corso 189. ☎ **06/679-7691.**

This upscale department store offers clothing, hosiery, perfume, cosmetics, house-wares, and furniture. It also has its own line of clothing (Ellerre) for men, women, and children. This is the largest of the Italian department-store chains.

Standa. Corso Francia 124. ☎ **06/333-8719.**

Rome's six Standa branches could not be considered stylish by any stretch of the imagination, but some visitors find it enlightening to wander—just once—through the racks of department-store staples to see what an average Italian household might accumulate. Other branches are at Corso Trieste 200, Via Trionfale, Via Cola di Rienzo 173, Viale Regina Margherita, and Viale Trastevere 60.

DISCOUNT SHOPPING

Certain stores that can't move their merchandise at any price often consign these goods to discounters. In Italy, the original labels are usually still inside the garment, and you'll find some very chic ones strewn in with mounds of other garments. Why wouldn't they sell at higher prices in more glamorous shops? Some garments are the wrong size, some have gone out of fashion, and some are a stylistic mistake that the original designer wishes had never been produced.

Discount System. Via del Viminale 35. ☎ **06/482-3917.**

Discount System sells men's and women's wear by many of the big names (Armani, Valentino, Nino Cerruti, Fendi, and Krizia). Even if an item isn't from a famous designer, it often came from a factory that produces some of the best quality of Italian fashion. However, don't give up hope: If you find something you like, know that it will be priced at around 50% of its original price tag, and it just might be a cut-rate gem well worth your effort. To get here, take the Metro to Repubblica and walk.

FASHION

For Men

Angelo. Via Bissolati 34. ☎ **06/474-1796.**

This exclusive store is a custom tailor for discerning men. It has been featured in such publications as *Esquire* and *Gentleman's Quarterly.* Angelo employs the best cutters and craftspeople, and his taste in style and design is impeccable. Custom shirts, dinner jackets, even casual wear, can be made on short notice. If you don't have time to wait, Angelo will ship anywhere in the world. The outlet also sells ready-made items such as cardigans, cashmere pullovers, evening shirts, suits, and overcoats.

Battistoni. Via Condotti 61A. ☎ **06/678-6241.**

This fashion store is known for the finest men's shirts in the world. As Marlene Dietrich once noted, "With that said, you don't need to sell the shop anymore." In addition, it also hawks a men's cologne, called Marte (Mars), for the "man who likes to conquer."

Emporio Armani. Via del Babuino 119. ☎ **06/322-151.**

This store stocks relatively affordable men's wear crafted by the couturier who has dressed perhaps more stage and screen stars than any other designer in Italy. If these prices aren't high enough for you, try the designer's more expensive line—a short walk away, at Giorgio Armani, Via Condotti 77 (☎ **06/699-1460**). The merchandise here is sold at sometimes staggering prices that are still often 30% less than what you'd pay in the United States.

Schostal. Via del Corso. ☎ **06/679-1240.**

Dating to 1870, this is the clothing store for men who like their garments conservative and well crafted. Featuring everything from underwear to cashmere overcoats, the prices are more reasonable than you might think, and a devoted staff is both courteous and attentive.

Valentino. Via Condotti 13. ☎ **06/678-3656.**

Behind all the chrome mirrors at Via Condotti is this swank emporium where you can become the most fashionable man in town—if you can afford the high prices. Valentino's women's haute couture is sold around the corner, in an even bigger showroom at Via Bocca di Leone 15 (☎ **06/679-5862**).

For Women
Benetton. Via Condotti 18. ☎ **06/679-7982.**

Prices at this branch of the worldwide sportswear distributor are about the same as those at less glamorous addresses. Famous for woolen sweaters, tennis wear, blazers, and the kind of outfits you'd want to wear on a private yacht, this company has suffered (like every other clothier) from inexpensive Asian copies of its designs. The original, however, is still the greatest.

Gianfranco Ferre. Via Borgognona 42B. ☎ **06/679-0050.**

Here you can find the women's line of this famous designer whose clothes have been called "adventurous."

Givenchy. Via Borgognona 21. ☎ **06/678-4058.**

This is the Roman headquarters of one of the great designer names of France, Givenchy, a company known since World War I for its couture. Here the company emphasizes ready-to-wear garments for stylish women with warm Italian weather in mind.

Max Mara. Via Frattina 28, at Largo Goldoni. ☎ **06/679-3638.**

Max Mara is one of the best outlets in Rome for women's clothing if you like to look chic. The fabrics are appealing and the alterations are free.

Renato Balestra. Via Sistina 67. ☎ **06/679-5424.**

Rapidly approaching the stratospheric upper levels of Italian fashion is Renato Balestra, whose women's clothing attains standards of lighthearted elegance at its best when designed and worn in Italy. This branch carries a complete line of the latest Balestra ready-to-wear designs for women. The company's administrative headquarters and the center of its couture department are nearby at Via Ludovisi 35 (☎ **06/482-1723**), although advance appointments are recommended there. It's advisable to stop into the Via Sistina branch for an idea of the designer's style before launching yourself into a dialogue with Balestra's couture department, if only to save costs.

For Children
Baby House. Via Cola di Rienzo 117. ☎ **06/321-4291.**

Baby House offers what might be the most label-conscious collection of children's and young people's clothing in Italy. With an inventory of clothes suitable for children and adolescents to age 15, it sells clothing by Valentino, Bussardi, and Laura Biagiotti, whose threads are usually reserved for adult, rather than juvenile, playtime.

Benetton. Via Condotti 19. ☎ **06/679-7982.**

Despite its elegant address (see above), Benetton isn't as expensive as you might expect. This store is an outlet for children's clothes (from infants to age 12) of the famous sportswear manufacturer. You can find rugby shirts, corduroys and jeans, and accessories in a wide selection of colors and styles.

The College. Via Vittoria 52. ☎ **06/678-4073.**

The College has everything you'll need to make adorable children more adorable—and less-adorable children at least presentable. Part of the inventory of this place is reserved for adult men and women, but the majority is intended for the infant and early adolescent offspring of the store's older clients. This establishment maintains another branch at Via Condotti 47 (☎ **06/678-4036**), which sells only clothes for women.

FOOD

Castroni. Via Cola di Rienzo 196. ☎ **06/687-4383.**

Castroni carries an amazing array of unusual foodstuffs from throughout the Mediterranean. If you want herbs from Apulia, pepperoncino oil, cheese from the Valle d'Aosta, or that strange brand of balsamic vinegar whose name you can never remember, Castroni will have it. Large, old-fashioned, and filled to the rafters with the abundance of agrarian Italy, it also carries certain foods that are exotic in Italy but commonplace in North America, such as taco shells, corn curls, and peanut butter.

GIFTS

A. Grispigni. Via Francesco Crispi 59 (at Via Sistina). ☎ **06/679-0290.**

A. Grispigni has a large assortment of leather-covered boxes, women's purses, compacts, desk sets, and cigarette cases. Many items, like Venetian wallets and Florentine boxes, are inlaid with gold.

Anatriello del Regalo. Via Frattina 123. ☎ **06/678-9601.**

This store is known for stocking an inventory of new and antique silver, some of it among the most unusual in Italy. All the new items are made by Italian silversmiths, in designs ranging from the whimsical to the severely formal and dignified. Also on display are antique pieces of silver from England, Germany, and Switzerland.

HOME ACCESSORIES

Avignonese. Via Margutta 16. ☎ **06/361-4004.**

This specialty shop can be counted on to come up with unusual and tasteful objects for the home. Each object, from lamps to terra-cotta boxes, is unique.

JEWELRY

Bulgari. Via Condotti 10. ☎ **06/679-3876.**

Bulgari has been Rome's most prestigious jeweler for more than a century. The shop window, on a conspicuously affluent stretch of Via Condotti, is a visual attraction in its own right. Bulgari designs combine classical Greek aesthetics with Italian taste, changing in style with the years, yet clinging to tradition as well. Prices range from "affordable" to "the sky's the limit."

E. Fiore. Via Ludovisi 31 (near Via Veneto). ☎ **06/481-9296.**

At E. Fiore you can choose a jewel and have it set to your specifications. Or you can make your selection from a rich assortment of charms, bracelets, necklaces, rings, brooches, corals, pearls, and cameos. Also featured are elegant watches, silverware, and goldware. Fiore does expert repair work on jewelry and watches.

Siragusa. Via delle Carrozze 64. ☎ **06/679-7085.**

This is more like a museum than a shop, specializing in unusual jewelry based on ancient carved stones or archaeological pieces. Handmade chains, for example, often hold coins and beads discovered in Asia Minor that date from the 3rd and 4th centuries B.C.

LEATHER

Italian leather is among the very best in the world; it can attain butter-soft textures more pliable than cloth. You'll find hundreds of leather stores in Rome, many of them excellent.

Alfieri. Via del Corso 2. ☎ **06/361-1976.**

With the exception of blatant erotica, you'll find virtually any garment you can think of, fashioned from leather, inside this richly stocked store. Established in the 1960s, with a somewhat more funky and counterculture slant than Casagrande or Campanile, it prides itself on leather jackets, boots, bags, belts, shirts, hats, and pants for men and women, short shorts in leather that might remind you of the *lederhosen* of the Austrian alps, and skirts that come in at least ten different—sometimes neon-inspired—colors. Although everything sold is made in Italy, be alert that the virtue of this place involves reasonable prices rather than ultra-high quality in every case. So although you'll definitely find whimsy, an amazingly wide selection, and affordable prices, check the stitching and operability of zippers, or whatever, before you invest.

Campanile. Via Condotti 58. ☎ **06/678-3041.**

Despite the postmodern sleekness of its premises, this outfit bears a pedigree going back to the 1870s and an impressive inventory of well-crafted leather jackets, belts, shoes, bags, and suitcases for both men and women. Quality is relentlessly high, and as such, the store might function as the focal point for your window-shopping energies along either side of Rome's most glamorous shopping street.

Casagrande. Via Cola di Rienzo 206. ☎ **06/687-4610.**

If famous names in leatherware appeal to you, you'll find most of the biggies here, including Fendi and its youth-conscious offspring, Fendissime, Cerruti, Mosquino, and Valentino. This is a well-managed store that has developed an impressive reputation for quality and authenticity since the 1930s. Although they don't give the stuff away (who does?), prices are more reasonable than equivalent merchandise sold in some other parts of town.

Fendi. Via Borgognona 36A–39. ☎ **06/679-7641.**

Fendi is mainly known for its avant-garde leather goods, but it also has furs, stylish purses, ready-to-wear clothing, and a new men's line of clothing and accessories. Fendi's also carries gift items, home furnishings, and sports accessories. Closed Saturday afternoon from July to September.

Gucci. Via Condotti 8. ☎ **06/679-0405.**

Gucci, of course, is a legend, an established firm since 1900. Its merchandise consists of high-class leather goods, such as suitcases, handbags, wallets, shoes, and desk accessories. It also has departments of elegant men's and women's wear, including beautiful shirts, blouses, and dresses, as well as ties and neck scarves of numerous designs. *La bella figura* is alive and well at Gucci, and prices have never been higher.

Saddlers Union. Via Condotti 26. ☎ **06/679-8050.**

This is a great place to look for well-crafted leather accessories. The wide selection of bags might lure you here, but there is plenty more—belts, wallets, shoes, briefcases, and other finely crafted items.

LINGERIE

Brighenti. Via Frattina 7–8. ☎ **06/679-1484.**

At Brighenti, amid several famous neighbors on Via Frattina, you might run across a "seductive fantasy." It's strictly *lingerie di lusso,* or perhaps better phrased, *haute corseterie.* Closed in August.

Tomassini di Luisa Romagnoli. Via Sistina 119. ☎ **06/488-1909.**

Tomassini di Luisa Romagnoli offers delicately beautiful lingerie and negligees, all original designs of Luisa Romagnoli. Most of the merchandise sold here is of shimmery Italian silk; other items, to a lesser degree, are of fluffy cotton or frothy nylon. Highly revealing garments are sold either ready-to-wear or are custom-made.

Vanità. Via Frattina 70. ☎ **06/679-1743.**

Featuring underthings from across the color spectrum, no rainbow can match the lingerie selection here. Yes, you can get black or white, but take the time to browse and you'll discover hues you've never dreamed of as well.

LIQUORS

Ai Monasteri. Piazza delle Cinque Lune 76. ☎ **06/6880-2783.**

Ai Monasteri is a treasure trove of liquors (including liqueurs and wines), honey, and herbal teas made in monasteries and convents all over Italy. You can buy excellent chocolates and other candies here as well. You make your selections in a quiet atmosphere reminiscent of a monastery, just two blocks from Bernini's Fountain of the Four Rivers in Piazza Navona. The shop will ship some items home for you.

MARKETS

At the sprawling **Porta Portese** open-air flea market of Rome held every Sunday morning, every peddler from Trastevere and the surrounding Castelli Romani sets up a temporary shop. The vendors are likely to sell merchandise ranging from second-hand paintings of Madonnas and termite-eaten Il Duce wooden medallions, to pseudo-Etruscan hairpins, bushels of rosaries, 1947 TV sets, and books printed in 1835. Serious shoppers can often ferret out a good buy. If you've ever been impressed with the bargaining power of the Spaniard, you haven't seen anything till you've viewed an Italian.

Go to this Trastevere flea market, near the end of Viale Trastevere (bus no. 75 to Porta Portese, then a short walk to Via Portuense), to catch the workday Roman in an unguarded moment. By 10:30am the market is full of people. Some of the vendors arrive here as early as midnight to get their choice space. As at any street market, beware of pickpockets. Open on Sunday from 7am to 1pm.

MOSAICS

Savelli. Via Paolo VI 27. ☎ **06/6830-7017.**

Mosaics are an art form as old as the Roman Empire itself. Many of the objects displayed in this company's gallery were inspired by ancient originals discovered in thousands of excavations throughout the Italian peninsula, including those at Pompeii and Ostia. Others, especially the floral designs, depend on the whim and creativity of the artist. Objects include tabletops, boxes, and vases. The cheapest mosaic objects begin at around $125 and are unsigned products crafted by students at an art school partially funded by the Vatican. Objects made in the Savelli workshops that are signed by the individual artists (and that tend to be larger and more elaborate) range from $500 to as much as $25,000. The outlet also contains a collection of small souvenir items such as keychains and carved statues.

RELIGIOUS OBJECTS

Anna Maria Gaudenzi. Piazza delle Minerva 69A. ☎ **06/679-0431.**

Set in a neighborhood loaded with purveyors of religious art and icons, this shop claims to be the oldest of its type in Rome. If you collect depictions of the Madonna, paintings of the saints, exotic rosaries, chalices, small statues, or medals, you can feel secure in knowing that thousands of pilgrims have spent their money here before you. Whether you view its merchandise as a devotional aid or as bizarre kitsch, this shop has it all. Closed August 10–20.

SHOES

Dominici. Via del Corso 14. ☎ **06/361-0591.**

Dominici, located behind an understated facade a few steps from Piazza del Popolo, shelters an amusing and lighthearted collection of men's and women's shoes in a pleasing variety of vivid colors. The style is aggressively young at heart and the quality is good.

Ferragamo. Via Condotti 73–74. ☎ **06/679-8402.**

Ferragamo sells elegant and fabled footwear, plus women's clothing and accessories, and ties, in an atmosphere full of Italian style. The name became famous in America when such silent screen vamps as Pola Negri and Greta Garbo began appearing in Ferragamo shoes. There are always many customers waiting to enter the shop. Management allows them to enter in small groups. Figure on a 30-minute wait outside.

Fragiacomo. Via Condotti 35. ☎ **06/679-8780.**

Fragiacomo sells shoes for men and women in a champagne-colored showroom with gilt-painted chairs and big display cases.

Lily of Florence. Via Lombardia 38 (off Via Vittorio Veneto). ☎ **06/474-0262.**

This famous Florentine shoemaker has a shop in Rome, with the same merchandise that made the outlet so well known in the Tuscan capital. The colors come in a wide range, the designs are stylish, and the leather texture is of good quality. Lily sells shoes for both men and women, and features American sizes with prices 30% to 40% less than in the U.S.

SUITCASES

Livio di Simone. Via San Giacomo 23. ☎ **06/3600-1732.**

Unusual suitcases (in many shapes and sizes) in which hand-painted canvas has been sewn into the bags are sold here. This outlet has one of the most tasteful yet durable collections in Rome.

WINE

Buccone. Via Ripetta (near Piazza del Popolo). ☎ **06/361-2154.**

At this historic wine shop the selection of wines and gastronomic specialties is among the finest in Rome.

Trimani. Via Goito 20. ☎ **06/446-9661.**

Trimani, established in 1821, sells wines and spirits from Italy, among other offerings. Purchases can be shipped to your home. Trimani collaborates with the Italian wine magazine *Gambero Rosso,* organizing some lectures about wine where devotees can improve their knowledge and educate their tastebuds.

9   Rome After Dark

When the sun goes down across the city, palaces, ruins, fountains, and monuments are bathed in a theatrical white light. There are actually few evening occupations quite as pleasurable as a stroll past the solemn pillars of old temples or the cascading torrents of Renaissance fountains glowing under the blue-black sky. Of the **fountains,** the Naiads (Piazza della Repubblica), the Tortoises (Piazza Mattei), and, of course, the Trevi are particularly beautiful at night. The **Capitoline Hill** is magnificently lit after dark, with its measured Renaissance facades glowing like jewel boxes. Behind the Senatorial Palace is a fine view of the illuminated **Roman Forum.** If you're staying across the Tiber, **Piazza San Pietro** (in front of St. Peter's Basilica) is impressive at night without tour buses and crowds. And a combination of illuminated architecture, Renaissance fountains, and, frequently, sidewalk shows and art expositions enliven **Piazza Navona.** If you're ambitious and have a good sense of direction, try exploring the streets to the west of Piazza Navona, which look like a stage set when they're lit at night.

There are no inexpensive nightclubs in Rome. *Another important warning:* During the peak of the summer visiting days, usually in August, all nightclub proprietors seem to lock their doors and head for the seashore, where they operate alternate clubs. Some of them close at different times each year, so it's hard to keep up-to-date. Always have your hotel check to see if a club is operating before you make a trek to it. Many of the legitimate nightclubs, besides being expensive, are highlighted by hookers plying their trade. Younger people fare better than some more sedate folk, as the discos open and close with freewheeling abandon.

But remember that for many Romans, a night on the town means dining late at a trattoria. The locals like to drink wine and talk after their meal, even when the waiters are putting chairs on top of empty tables.

Even if you don't speak Italian, you can generally follow the listings of special events and evening entertainment featured in *La Repubblica,* one of the leading Italian newspapers. *TrovaRoma,* a special weekly entertainment supplement—good for the coming week—is published in this paper on Thursday.

THE PERFORMING ARTS
CLASSICAL MUSIC
Academy of St. Cecilia. Via della Conciliazione 4. ☎ **06/688-01044.** Tickets 25,000L–80,000L ($15–$48).

Concerts given by the orchestra of the Academy of St. Cecilia usually take place at Piazza Villa Giulia, site of the Etruscan Museum, from the end of June to the end of July; in winter they're held in the academy's concert hall on Via della Conciliazione. Depending on the circumstances, the organization sometimes selects other addresses in Rome for its concerts, including a handful of historic churches, when available. Performance nights are either Saturday, Sunday, Monday, or Tuesday.

Teatro Olimpico. Piazza Gentile da Fabriano. ☎ **06/323-4890.** Tickets 20,000L–80,000L ($12–$48).

Large and well publicized, this echoing stage hosts a widely divergent collection of singers, both classical and pop, who perform according to a schedule that sometimes changes at the last minute. Occasionally the space is devoted to chamber orchestras or visiting foreign orchestras.

OPERA

Teatro dell'Opera. Piazza Beniamino Gigli 1. ☎ **06/481-601.** Tickets 20,000L–260,000L ($12–$156).

If you're in the capital for the opera season, usually from the end of December until June, you may want to attend the historic Rome Opera House, located off Via Nazionale. Nothing is presented here in August. In the summer, the venue switches to Piazza Siena.

BALLET & DANCE

Performances of the **Rome Opera Ballet** are given at the Teatro dell'Opera (see above). The regular repertoire of classical ballet is supplemented by performances of internationally acclaimed guest artists, and Rome is on the major agenda for troupes from around the world. Watch for announcements in the weekly entertainment guides to Rome about venues outside the Teatro dell'Opera, including Teatro Olimpico or even open-air ballet performances. Both modern (such as the Alvin Ailey dancers) and classical dance troupes appear frequently in Rome.

A MEAL & A SONG

Da Ciceruacchio. On Piazza dei Mercanti, at Via del Porto 1, in Trastevere. ☎ **06/580-6046.**

This restaurant was once a sunken jail—the ancient vine-covered walls date from the days of the Roman Empire. Folkloric groups appear throughout the evening, especially singers of Neapolitan songs, accompanied by guitars and harmonicas—a rich repertoire of old-time favorites, some with bawdy lyrics. There are charcoal-broiled steaks and chops along with lots of local wine, and bean soup is a specialty. The grilled mushrooms are another good opening, as is the spaghetti with clams. You can dine here Tuesday to Sunday from 8pm to midnight for 35,000L to 60,000L ($21 to $36).

Da Meo Patacca. Piazza dei Mercanti 30, in Trastevere. ☎ **06/5833-1086.**

Da Meo Patacca would have pleased Barnum and Bailey. On a gaslit piazza from the Middle Ages, it serves bountiful self-styled "Roman country" meals to flocks of tourists. The atmosphere is one of extravaganza—primitive, colorful, theatrical in a carnival sense—good fun if you're in the mood. Downstairs is a vast cellar with strolling musicians and singers. Utilizing a tavern theme, the restaurant is decked out with wagon wheels, along with garlands of pepper and garlic. And many offerings are as adventurous as the decor—wild boar, wild hare, and quail. But fear not. They also serve corn on the cob, pork and beans, thick-cut sirloins, and chicken on a spit. Come here for general fun and entertainment—not refined cuisine. Expect to spend 60,000L ($36) and up for a meal here. In summer, you can dine at outdoor tables. It's open daily from 8 to 11:30pm.

Fantasie di Trastevere. Via di Santa Dorotea 6, in Trastevere. ☎ **06/588-1671.**

Roman rusticity is combined with theatrical flair at Fantasie di Trastevere, the people's theater where the famous actor Petrolini made his debut. In the 16th century, this restaurant was an old theater built for Queen Cristina of Sweden and her court. The cuisine isn't subtle, but it's bountiful. Such dishes as the classic saltimbocca (ham with veal) are preceded by tasty pasta, and everything is aided by Castelli Romani wines. Accompanying the main dishes is a big basket of warm, country-coarse herb bread (you'll tear off hunks). Expect to pay 80,000L to 120,000L ($48 to $72) for a full meal. If you visit for a drink, the first one will cost 35,000L ($21). Some two dozen folk singers and musicians in regional costumes perform, making it a festive affair. Meals begin daily at 8pm, with piano bar music from 8:30 to 9:30pm, followed by the show, lasting until 10:30pm.

THE CLUB & MUSIC SCENE
NIGHTCLUBS

Alien. Via Velletri 13–17. ☎ **06/841-2212.** Cover 30,000L–35,000L ($18–$21) including the first drink.

In a setting devoted to celebrating hi-tech, futuristic rows of exposed pipes and ventilation ducts, you'll find a deliberately bizarre space-age view of future shock, bathed in strobe lights and electronic music. Dull moments in any evening are punctuated with a cabaret-esque master or mistress of ceremonies whose brief interludes of cabaret or comedy accent a diet of very new-wave music. Open Tuesday through Saturday from 11pm to 4am.

Alpheus. Via del Commercio 36. ☎ **06/574-7826.** Cover 10,000L ($6), 15,000L ($9) on Sat.

One of Rome's largest and most energetic nightclubs contains three sprawling rooms, each with a different musical sound and an ample number of bars. You'll find areas devoted to Latin music packed with Spanish-speaking Catholics eager for a break from too constant an exposure to Rome's churches, other areas playing rock, and an area devoted to jazz. Live bands come and go, and there's enough cultural variety in the crowd to keep virtually anyone amused throughout the course of the evening. Open Wednesday to Sunday from 10:30pm to 4am.

Arciliuto. Piazza Monte Vecchio 5. ☎ **06/687-9419.** Cover 35,000L ($22.40) including the first drink. Closed July 20–Sept 3.

Arciliuto is one of the most romantic candlelit spots in Rome. It was reputedly the former studio of Raphael. From 10pm to 2am on Monday to Saturday guests enjoy a musical salon ambience, listening to a guitarist, a pianist, and a violinist. The evening's presentation also includes live Neapolitan songs and new Italian madrigals, even current hits from Broadway or London's West End. The setting and atmosphere are intimate. Drinks run 10,000L ($6). This highly recommended establishment is hard to find, but it's within walking distance of Piazza Navona.

Black Out. Via Saturnia 18. ☎ **06/7049-6791.** Cover 10,000L ($6) including the first drink.

Counterculture, blasé, and clinging to musical models of the punk-rock and the UK–Indie music culture of faraway London, Black Out occupies an industrial-looking site that opens between 1am and 4am only on Friday and Saturday. Whenever it can manage, a live band is presented Thursday—very late. It's one of the best sites in town for a view of counterculture alienation and rage as interpreted by modern Italian youth. Recorded music (Friday and Saturday) includes punk, retro, rhythm and blues, grunge, and whatever else happens to be in fashion at the moment of your arrival. The Thursday-night live acts, when presented at all, can be just about anything. Regardless of the musical venue in effect on Friday or Saturday, there's always one room (with an independent sound system) devoted exclusively to black music of one genre or another, be it Los Angeles rap or South African jazz or South American calypso.

La Cabala/The Blue Bar/Hostaria dell'Orso. Via dei Soldati 25. ☎ **06/686-4221.** No cover, but a one-drink minimum of 15,000L–35,000L ($9–$21) in the Blue Bar and La Cabala.

During the heyday of *la dolce vita*, these premises were the most talked-about evening venue of Rome, and although the spotlight has since shifted, many Romans continue to view the place with affection and nostalgia. The setting is a 14th-century palazzo, near Piazza Navona, which began its life as a simple inn. Clients who used its dining and/or overnight facilities through the ages have included St. Francis of Assisi, Dante, Rabelais, Montaigne, and Goethe.

Today the establishment contains three separate areas. In the cellar, the **Blue Bar** is a moody but mellow enclave featuring cocktails and the music from two pianists and guitarists. On the street level, the formal **Hostaria dell'Orso** restaurant serves international cuisine. Main courses include spigolo in cartoccio con frutti di mar (sea bass cooked in a paper bag, garnished with shellfish) and spaghetti in cartoccio with lobster and risotto served with scampi and radicchio. One floor above street level is **La Cabala,** a disco that attracts a well-dressed, over-25 crowd who tend to know their way around. Some clients combine a trip to all three areas during a night on the town. You can visit only the disco or only the bar if you wish. The restaurant serves dinner only, Monday to Saturday from 7:30pm to midnight. The Blue Bar and La Cabala are open Monday to Saturday from 10:30pm to 3 or 4am, depending on business. All three floors are closed on Sunday. If you plan to dine here, reservations are recommended.

Club Picasso. Via Monte di Testaccio 63. ☎ **06/574-2975.** No cover Tues–Thurs, 15,000L ($9) Fri–Sat including the first drink.

Everything about this place was inspired by the large, gregarious L.A.–style nightclubs, where rhythm and blues, rock 'n' roll, and funk blare out across a crowd that loves to dance, dance, dance. Don't expect only a crowd full of teeny-boppers, as clients here include 20-year-olds, 50-year-olds (who remember some of the music as original to their college years), and lots of high-energy people-watchers in between. A bouncer at the door maintains strict provisions against anyone who looks like troublemaking is part of his or her entertainment. Open Tuesday to Saturday from 10pm to 4am.

Folkstudio. Via Frangipane 42. ☎ **06/487-1063.** Tickets 10,000L–20,000L ($6–$12), plus a one-time membership fee of 5,000L ($3).

Very little about this place has changed since it was founded in 1962. It prides itself on a battered and well-used venue that resembles "an old underground cantina" from the earliest days of the hippie era. The sound system and lighting aren't very sophisticated, but the ambience is refreshing and can be fun, and the musical acts manage to draw out some likable performances of old-fashioned soul music, gospel, funk, and folk, as well as traditional music from such countries as Ireland. From time to time a musician might even break into a recital of poetry. Some kind of act is presented Tuesday to Sunday from 9:30 to 11pm. No drinks are served inside, as the place considers itself a concert hall rather than a nightclub, but several bars and cafes in the neighborhood sell bottles of beer and whisky in plastic cups to go, and no one at Folkstudio will object if you carry them in with you. The place is closed from early July until late September.

Magic Fly. Via Bassanello 15, Cassia-Grottarossa. ☎ **06/3326-8956.** Cover 25,000L–30,000L ($15–$18) including the first drink.

Small-scale, and somewhat cramped when it really begins to rock, this disco and piano bar is more elegant than the norm and lies outside the ring road that encircles the center of Rome, about 3 miles northeast of the city's center. It changes its sound depending on the night of the week and might include Latin salsa and merengue, American-style rock, or British new wave, according to a schedule that most of underground, late-night Rome seems to understand instinctively. Throughout the place, there's often a sense of poshness that encourages many of the men to wear neckties. Transportation to the place is invariably a taxi. Open Tuesday to Sunday from 10:30pm to dawn.

Radio Londra. Via Monte Testaccio. No phone. Cover 15,000L ($9).

More than any other club on this list of recommendations, this one revels in the counterculture ambience of punk rock, inspired, as its name would imply, by the chartreuse-haired, nose-pierced devotees so common in London. There's no phone and very few rules inside, except for an emphasis on allowing clients to look and act as weird and freaky as possible. Since the location is near the popular gay club, L'Alibi, the club downstairs attracts a large number of the brethren, although the crowd is sexually mixed. Upstairs is a pub and pizzeria where bands often appear. You can even order a veggie burger here with a Bud. The club is open Wednesday through Monday from 11:30am to 4am, and the pub/pizzeria serves Wednesday through Friday and Sunday and Monday from 9pm to 3am (until 4am on Saturday).

Yes, Brazil. Via San Francesco a Ripa 103. ☎ **06/581-6267.** No cover.

This is one of Rome's most animated and popular Latin American nightspots. Set in the dimly lit recesses of a 16th-century Trastevere building, it manages to incorporate the mobs of Italians and South Americans who dip and sway to dance steps that are usually some derivation of the samba. There's live music every night of the week, a point of honor at the club. It's open every night from 9:30pm to 2am.

JAZZ, SOUL & FUNK

Alexanderplatz. Via Ostia 9. ☎ **06/3974-2171.** No cover, but a 3-month membership costs 12,000L ($7.70).

At this leading club you can hear jazz (not rock) every night except Sunday from 9pm to 2am, with live music beginning at 10:15pm. There's also a restaurant, with a good kitchen, that serves everything from gnocchi alla romana to Japanese.

Big Mama. Vicolo San Francesco a Ripa 18. ☎ **06/581-2551.** Cover 20,000L–30,000L ($12–$18) for big acts (free for minor shows), plus 20,000L ($12) for a one-time membership fee.

Big Mama is a hangout for jazz and blues musicians where you're likely to meet the up-and-coming jazz stars of tomorrow, and sometimes even the big names. The club is open Monday to Saturday from 9pm to 1:30am. Closed July to September.

Fonclea. Via Crescenzio 82A. ☎ **06/689-6302.** Cover: none Sun–Thurs, 10,000L ($6.40) on Sat.

Fonclea offers live music every night—Dixieland, rock, rhythm and blues. This is basically a cellar jazz establishment and crowded pub that attracts patrons from all walks of Roman life. The music starts at 9:15pm and usually lasts until 12:30am. The club is open nightly from 7pm to 2am (on Friday and Saturday it stays open until 3:30am). There's also a restaurant that features grilled meats, salads, and crêpes. A meal starts at 35,000L ($21), but if you want dinner it's best to reserve a table.

Gilda. Via Mario dei Fiori 97. ☎ **06/678-4838.** Cover 40,000L ($24) including the first drink.

Gilda is an adventurous combination of nightclub, disco, and restaurant known for its glamorous acts. In the past it has hosted Diana Ross and splashy, Paris-type revues. The artistic direction assures first-class shows, a well-run restaurant, and disco music played between the live musical acts. The restaurant and pizzeria open at 9:30pm and occasionally present shows. An international cuisine is featured, with meals costing from 35,000L ($21). The nightclub, opening at midnight, presents music of the 1960s as well as modern recordings. The club stays open until 4am.

There's also an attractive piano bar on the premises called Swing, featuring Italian and Latin music.

Music Inn. Largo dei Fiorentini 3. ☎ **06/6880-2220.** Cover 15,000L ($9).

The Music Inn is among the leading jazz clubs of Rome. Some of the biggest names in jazz, both European and American, have performed here. Open Thursday to Sunday from 8pm to 2am. Closed July and August.

Notorious. Via San Nicola de Tolentino 22. ☎ **06/474-6888.** Cover 40,000L ($24).

Notorious really isn't. It's one of the most popular discos of Rome, open Tuesday to Saturday from 11pm to 4am. The music is always recorded. Some of the most beautiful people of Rome show up in these crowded confines, often in their best disco finery. Show up late—it's more fashionable.

Saint Louis Music City. Via del Cardello 13A. ☎ **06/474-5076.** Cover 7,000L ($4.20) including club membership.

Saint Louis Music City is another leading jazz venue with large, contemporary surroundings, but it doesn't necessarily attract the big names in jazz. What you get instead are young and sometimes very talented groups beginning their careers. Many celebrities patronize the place. Soul and funk are also performed on occasion. You can dine at a restaurant on the premises, where meals cost 35,000L ($21) and up. Open Tuesday to Sunday from 9pm to 2am.

GAY CLUBS

Angelo Azzuro. Via Cardinal Merry del Val 13. ☎ **06/580-0472.** Cover 10,000L ($6) including the first drink on Fri and Sun, 12,000L ($7.20) on Sat.

Angelo Azzuro is a gay "hot spot" deep in the heart of Trastevere, open on Friday, Saturday, and Sunday from 11pm to 4am. There's no food or live music—men dance with men to recorded music, and women are also invited to patronize the club. Friday is for women only.

The Hangar. Via in Selci 69. ☎ **06/488-1397.** No cover.

Established in 1984 by a Louisiana-born expatriate, John, and his Italian partner, Gianni, this is the premier gay bar in Rome. It's set on one of Rome's oldest streets, adjacent to the Roman Forum, in the house on the site of the palace inhabited by Emperor Claudius's deranged wife, Messalina. (Her ghost is rumored to inhabit the premises.) Each of the establishment's two bars has its own independent sound system. Women are welcome any night except Monday, when the club features videos and entertainment for gay men. The busiest nights are Saturday, Sunday, and Monday, when as many as 500 people cram inside. It's open Wednesday to Monday from 10:30pm to 2:30am. The Hangar is closed for 3 weeks in August.

Joli Coeur. Via Sirte 5. ☎ **06/8621-5827.** Cover 15,000L ($9) including the first drink.

A fixture upon the city's lesbian nighttime scene, Joli Coeur attracts women from around Europe during its very limited hours—it's open only on Saturday and Sunday nights from 10:30pm to 2am. Saturday night is reserved for women only, although Sunday the crowd can be mixed. Information about Joli Coeur is available at The Hangar (see above) because of the difficulties in reaching Joli Coeur directly.

L'Alibi. Via Monte Testaccio 44. ☎ **06/574-3448.** Cover 20,000L ($12).

L'Alibi, in the Testaccio sector, away from the heart of Rome, is a year-round venue on many a gay man's agenda. The crowd, however, tends to be mixed, both Roman and international, straight and gay, male and female. One room is devoted to dancing. It's open Wednesday to Sunday from 11pm to 5am.

THE BAR & CAFE SCENE

Unless you're dead set on making the Roman nightclub circuit, try what might be a far livelier and less expensive scene—sitting late at night on Via Veneto or Piazza del Popolo, all for the cost of an espresso.

ON VIA VENETO

Back in the 1950s—a decade that *Time* magazine gave to Rome, in the way it conceded the 1960s to London—Via Vittorio Veneto rose in fame and influence as the choicest street in Rome, crowded with aspiring and actual movie stars, their directors, and a fast-rising group composed of card-carrying members of the so-called jet set. Today the *bella gente* (beautiful people), movie stars, and directors wouldn't be caught dead on Via Veneto—even with night-owl sunglasses, and the street has moved into the mainstream of world tourism. It's about as "in" and undiscovered today as pretzels, but you may want to spend some time there.

Caffè de Paris. Via Vittorio Veneto 90. ☎ **06/488-5284.**

Caffè de Paris rises and falls in popularity depending on the decade. In the 1950s it was a haven for the fashionable, and now it's a popular restaurant in summer when the tables spill right out onto the sidewalk and the passing crowd walks through the maze.

Harry's Bar. Via Vittorio Veneto 150. ☎ **06/484643.**

Harry's Bar is a perennial favorite. Every major Italian city (Florence and Venice, for example) seems to have one, and Rome is no exception, although the one here has no connection with the others. The haunt of the IBF—International Bar Flies—at the top of Via Veneto is elegant, chic, and sophisticated. In summer, sidewalk tables are placed outside. For those who wish to dine outdoors, but want to avoid the scorching Roman sun, a new air-conditioned sidewalk cafe is open from May to November. Meals inside cost about double what you'd pay outside. In back is a small dining room, which serves some of the finest food in central Rome; meals go for 90,000L to 100,000L ($54 to $60). The restaurant inside is open Monday to Saturday from 12:30 to 3pm and 7:30pm to 1am, while outside you can eat from noon to midnight. The bar is open from 11am to 2am; closed Sunday and August 1–10. The Piano Bar is open nightly from 11pm.

PIAZZA DEL POPOLO

This piazza is haunted with memories. According to legend, the ashes of Nero were enshrined here, until 11th-century residents began complaining to the pope about his imperial ghost. The Egyptian obelisk seen here today dates from the 13th century B.C., removed from Heliopolis to Rome during the reign of Augustus (it originally stood at the Circus Maximus). The present piazza was designed in the early 19th century by Valadier, Napoléon's architect. Two almost-twin baroque churches stand on the square, overseeing the never-ending traffic.

Café Rosati. Piazza del Popolo 5A. ☎ **06/322-5859.**

Café Rosati, which has been around since 1923, attracts guys and dolls of all persuasions who drive up in Maseratis and Porsches. It's really a sidewalk cafe/ice-cream parlor/candy store/confectionery/ristorante that has been swept up in the fickle world of fashion. The later you go, the more interesting the action. The restaurant serves lunch only, daily from noon to 4pm.

Canova Café. Piazza del Popolo. ☎ **06/361-2231.**

Although management has filled the interior with boutiques that sell expensive gift items, including luggage and cigarette lighters, many Romans still consider this as "the place" on Piazza del Popolo. The Canova has a sidewalk terrace for pedestrian-watching, plus a snack bar, a restaurant, and a wine shop inside. In summer you'll have access to a courtyard whose walls are covered with ivy and where flowers grow in terra-cotta planters. A meal costs 20,000L ($12) and up. Food is served daily from noon to 3:30pm and 7 to 11pm, but the bar is open from 7am to midnight or 1am.

Near the Pantheon

Many visitors to the Eternal City now view Piazza della Rotonda, located across from the Pantheon and reconstructed by the emperor Hadrian in the first part of the 2nd century A.D., as the "living room" of Rome. This is especially true on a summer night.

Caffè Sant'Eustachio. Piazza Sant'Eustachio 82. ☎ **06/686-1309.**

Strongly brewed coffee is one of the elixirs of Italy, and many Romans will walk many blocks for what they consider a superior brew. The Caffè Sant'Eustachio is one of Rome's most celebrated espresso shops, where the water supply is funneled into the city by an aqueduct built in 19 B.C. Rome's most experienced espresso judges claim that the water plays an important part in the coffee's flavor, although steam forced through ground Brazilian coffee roasted on the premises has a significant effect as well. Purchase a ticket from the cashier for as many cups as you want, and leave a small tip—about 200L (10¢)—for the counterperson when you present your receipt. Open Tuesday to Friday and Sunday from 8:30am to 1am, and Saturday from 8:30am to 1:30am.

Di Rienzo. Piazza della Rotonda 8–9. ☎ **06/686-9097.**

Di Rienzo, the most desirable cafe here, is open daily from 7am to either 1 or 2am. In fair weather you can sit at one of the sidewalk tables (if you can find one free). In cooler weather you can retreat inside, where the walls are inlaid with the type of marble found on the Pantheon's floor. Many types of pastas appear on the menu, as does risotto alla pescatora (fisherman's rice) and several meat courses. You can also order pizzas.

In Trastevere

Piazza del Popolo lured the chic and sophisticated from Via Veneto, and now several cafes in the district of Trastevere, across the Tiber, threaten to attract the same from Popolo. Fans who saw Fellini's *Roma* know what **Piazza Santa Maria in Trastevere** looks like at night. The square—filled with milling throngs in summer—is graced with an octagonal fountain and a church that dates from the 12th century. Children run and play on the piazza, and occasional spontaneous guitar fests break out when the weather's good.

Café-Bar di Marzio. Piazza Santa Maria in Trastevere 18B. ☎ **06/581-6095.**

This warmly inviting place, which is strictly a cafe (not a restaurant), has both indoor and outdoor tables at the edge of the square with the best view of its famous fountain. Open Tuesday to Saturday from 7am to 2am.

On the Corso

Café Alemagna. Via del Corso 181. ☎ **06/678-9135.**

The monumental Café Alemagna is usually filled with busy shoppers. You'll find just about every kind of dining facility a hurried resident of Rome could want, including a stand-up sandwich bar with dozens of selections from behind a glass case, a cafeteria, and a sit-down area with waiter service. The decor includes high coffered ceilings, baroque wall stencils, crystal chandeliers, and black stone floors.

NEAR THE SPANISH STEPS

Antico Caffè Greco. Via Condotti 84. ☎ **06/679-1700.**

Since 1760 the Antico Caffè Greco has been the poshest and most fashionable coffee bar in Rome—the gathering place of the literati. Previous sippers have included Stendhal, Goethe, even D'Annunzio. Keats would also sit here and write. Today, however, you're more likely to see dowagers on a shopping binge and American tourists, but there's plenty of atmosphere here. In the front is a wooden bar, and beyond that a series of small salons. You sit at marble-topped tables of Napoleonic design, against a backdrop of gold or red damask, romantic paintings, and antique mirrors. Waiters are attired in black tailcoats. The house specialty is paradisi, made with lemon and orange. The cafe is open Monday to Saturday from 8am to 9pm, but closed for 10 days in August.

Enoteca Fratelli Roffi Isabelli. Via della Croce 76B. ☎ **06/679-0896.**

The fermented fruits of the vine have played a prominent role in Roman life since the word *bacchanalian* was first invented (and that was very early indeed), and one of the best places to taste the wines of Italy is at the Enoteca Fratelli Roffi Isabelli. A stand-up drink in its darkly antique confines is the perfect ending to a visit to the nearby Spanish Steps. Set behind an unflashy facade in a chic shopping district, this is the city's best repository for Italian wines, brandies, and grappa. You can opt for a postage-stamp table in back, if you desire, or stay at the bar with its impressive display of wines that lie stacked on shelves in every available corner.

NEAR PIAZZA COLONNA

Giolitti. Via Uffici del Vicario 40. ☎ **06/699-1243.**

For devotees of gelato (addictively tasty ice cream), Giolitti is one of the city's most popular nighttime gathering spots and the oldest ice-cream shop in the city; in the evening it's thronged with strollers with a sweet tooth. To satisfy that craving, try a whipped cream–topped cup of Giolitti gelato. Some of the sundaes look like Vesuvius about to erupt. Many people take gelato out to eat on the streets; others enjoy it in the postempire splendor of the salon inside. You can have your "cuppa" daily from 7am to 2am. There are many excellent, smaller *gelaterie* throughout Rome, wherever you see the cool concoction advertised as *produzione propria* (homemade).

NEAR PIAZZA NAVONA

Bar della Pace. Via della Pace 3-5. ☎ **06/686-1216.**

Bar della Pace, located near Piazza Navona, has elegant neighbors, such as Santa Maria della Pace. The bar dates from the beginning of this century, with wood, marble, and mirrors forming its decor.

Hemingway. Piazza delle Coppelle 10. ☎ **06/686-4490.**

Hemingway's discreet door is located off one of the most obscure piazzas in Rome. Inside, the owners have re-created a 19th-century decor beneath soaring vaulted ceilings that shimmer from the reflection of glass chandeliers. Evocations of a Liberty-style salon are strengthened by the sylvan murals and voluptuous portraits of reclining odalisques. Assorted painters, writers, and creative dilettantes occupy the clusters of overstuffed armchairs, listening to conversation or classical music. On Saturday and Sunday after 5pm there are small musical concerts and shows. It's open during the winter, Monday and Wednesday to Saturday from 9pm to 2am; in summer, daily from 9pm to 2am.

IRISH PUBS

It's an indication of the diversity of their tastes that young Italians are drawn in large numbers to Irish-style pubs. The two most popular ones are:

Druid's Den. Via San Martino ai Monti 28. ☎ **06/488-0258.**

The popular Druid's Den is open daily from 5pm to 12:30am. Here, while enjoying a pint of beer at 7,500L ($4.50), you can listen to recorded Irish music and dream of Eire. A group of young Irishmen one night even did an Irish jig in front of delighted Roman spectators. Live music, Irish style, is usually presented on Wednesday. The "den" is near Piazza Santa Maria Maggiore and the train station.

Fiddler's Elbow. Via dell'Olmata 43. ☎ **06/487-2110.**

Fiddler's Elbow, near Piazza Santa Maria Maggiore and the railway station, is reputedly the oldest pub in the capital. It's open daily from 4:30pm to 12:30am. Sometimes, however, the place is so packed you can't find room to drink.

CINEMA

Pasquino Cinema. Vicolo del Piede 19 (just off Piazza Santa Maria in Trastevere). ☎ **06/683-3551.**

In the Trastevere neighborhood, across the Tiber, just off the corner of Piazza Santa Maria in Trastevere, the little Pasquino draws a faithful coterie of English-speaking fans, including Italians and expatriates. The average film—usually of recent vintage or a classic—costs 10,000L ($6). There are three theaters with screenings daily. There is also a bookshop, a cafe, and a video-bar. The cinema was getting overhauled in 1997 but should open its doors again in 1998 under new management. Call to be sure it's reopened.

10 Side Trips from Rome

Most European capitals are ringed with a number of scenic attractions, and as far as sheer variety, Rome tops all of them. Just a few miles away you can go back to the dawn of Italian history and explore the dank tombs the Etruscans left as their legacy or drink the golden wine of the Alban hill towns (Castelli Romani).

You can wander around the ruins of Hadrian's Villa, the "queen of villas of the ancient world," or be lulled by the music of baroque fountains in the Villa d'Este. You can turn yourself bronze on the beaches of Ostia di Lido—or explore the ruins of Ostia Antica, the ancient seaport of Rome.

Unless you're rushed beyond reason, allow at least 3 days to take a look at the attractions in the environs. We've highlighted the best of the lot below:

TIVOLI

The town of Tivoli is 20 miles east of Rome on Via Tiburtina—about an hour's drive with traffic. If you don't have a car, take Metro Line B to the end of the line, the Rebibbia station. After exiting the station, take an Acotral bus the rest of the way to Tivoli. Generally, buses depart about every 20 minutes during the day.

EXPLORING THE VILLAS

Tivoli, known as Tibur to the ancient Romans, was the playground of emperors. Today its reputation continues unabated: It's the most popular half-day jaunt from Rome.

Side Trips from Rome

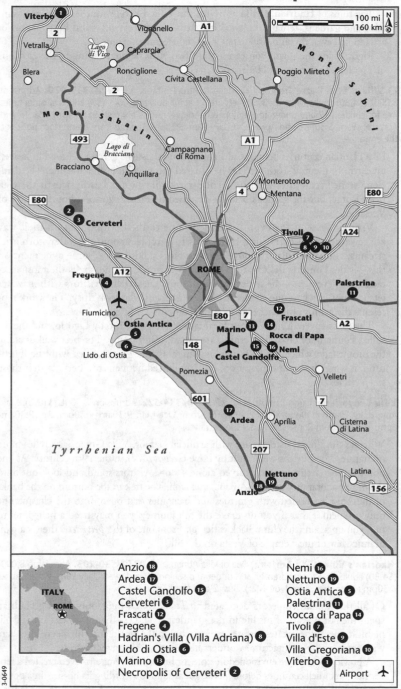

0 ____ 100 mi
0 ____ 160 km

Viterbo ①
2
Vetralla
Blera
Viganello
Caprarola
Lago di Vico
Ronciglione
Cívita Castellana
A1
Poggio Mirteto
M o n t i   S a b i n i

M o n t i   S a b a t i n i
2
493
Lago di Bracciano
Bracciano
Anguillara
Campagnano di Roma
A1
Monterotondo
Mentana
4
E80

E80
②
③ Cerveteri
Fregene
④
A12
Fiumicino
Ostia Antica
⑤
ROME
Tivoli **⑦**
⑧ **⑨** **⑩**
A24
Palestrina
⑪
⑫
E80
7
Frascati
A2

Marino
⑬
⑭
Rocca di Papa
Castel Gandolfo
⑮ **⑯ Nemi**
6
Lido di Ostia
148
Pomezia
Velletri
601
⑰
Ardea
Aprília
7
Cisterna di Latina

T y r r h e n i a n   S e a
207
Latina
Nettuno
⑱ **⑲**
Anzio
156

Anzio ⑱	Nemi ⑯
Ardea ⑰	Nettuno ⑲
Castel Gandolfo ⑮	Ostia Antica ⑤
Cerveteri ③	Palestrina ⑪
Frascati ⑫	Rocca di Papa ⑭
Fregene ④	Tivoli ⑦
Hadrian's Villa (Villa Adriana) ⑧	Villa d'Este ⑨
Lido di Ostia ⑥	Villa Gregoriana ⑩
Marino ⑬	Viterbo ①
Necropolis of Cerveteri ②	Airport ✈

ITALY
ROME

3-0649

The ruins of **Hadrian's Villa** as well as the **Villa d'Este,** with their fabulous fountains and gardens, remain the two chief attractions of Tivoli—and both *are* major attractions, even if you must curtail your sightseeing in Rome.

Right inside the town, you can look at two villas before heading to the environs of Tivoli and the ruins of Hadrian's Villa.

✪ **Villa d'Este.** Piazza Trento, Viale delle Centro Fontane. ☎ **0774/312-070.** Admission 8,000L ($4.80) adults when the water jets are set at full power, 5,000L ($3) adults at other times; free for children 17 and under and seniors 60 and over. Nov–Feb, daily 9am–4pm; Mar to mid-Apr, daily 9am–5:30pm; mid-Apr to Oct daily 9am–6:30pm. The bus from Rome stops right near the entrance.

Like Hadrian centuries before, Cardinal Ippolito d'Este of Ferrara believed in heaven on earth. In the mid-16th century he ordered this villa built on a hillside. The dank Renaissance structure, with its second-rate paintings, is hardly worth the trek from Rome, but the gardens below—designed by Pirro Ligorio—dim the luster of Versailles.

Visitors descend the cypress-studded slope to the bottom, and on their way are rewarded with everything from lilies to gargoyles spouting water, torrential streams, and waterfalls. The loveliest fountain—and there is some agreement on this—is the **Fontana del'Ovato,** designed by Ligorio. But nearby is the most spectacular achievement—the hydraulic organ fountain, dazzling visitors with its water jets in front of a baroque chapel, with four maidens who look tipsy. The work represents the genius of Frenchman Claude Veanard.

The moss-covered, slime-green Fountain of Dragons, also by Ligorio, and the so-called Fountain of Glass by Bernini, are the most intriguing. The best walk is along the promenade, which has 100 spraying fountains. The garden, filled with rhododendron, is worth hours of exploration, but you'll need frequent rest periods after those steep climbs.

Villa Gregoriana. Largo Sant'Angelo. ☎ **0774/334-522.** Admission 2,500L ($1.50). May–Aug, daily 10am–7:30pm; Sept, 9:30am–6:30pm; Oct–Mar, 9:30am–4:30pm; Apr 9:30am–6pm. The bus from Rome stops near the entrance.

Whereas the Villa d'Este dazzles with artificial glamor, Villa Gregoriana relies more on nature. The gardens were built by Pope Gregory XVI in the 19th century. At one point on the circuitous walk carved along a slope, visitors stand and look out onto the most panoramic waterfall (Aniene) at Tivoli. The trek to the bottom on the banks of the Anio is studded with grottoes and balconies that open onto the chasm. The only problem is that if you do make the full journey, you may need a helicopter to pull you up again (the climb back is fierce). From one of the *belvederes* there's a panoramic view of the Temple of Vesta on the hill.

Hadrian's Villa (Villa Adriana). Via di Villa Adriana. ☎ **0774/530-203.** Admission 8,000L ($4.80) adults, free for children 17 and under and seniors 60 and over. Daily 9am–sunset (about 6:30pm in summer, 4pm Nov–Mar). Bus: 2 or 4 from Tivoli.

Of all the Roman emperors dedicated to *la dolce vita,* the globe-trotting Hadrian spent the last 3 years of his life in the grandest style. Less than 4 miles from Tivoli, he built one of the greatest estates ever erected in the world and filled acre after acre with some of the architectural wonders he'd seen on his many travels.

A preview of what he envisioned in store for himself, the emperor even created a representation of hell centuries before Dante got around to recording its horrors in a poem. A patron of the arts, a lover of beauty, and even something of an architect, Hadrian directed the staggering feat of constructing much more than a villa—a self-contained world for a vast royal entourage and the hundreds of servants and guards they required to protect them, feed them, bathe them, and satisfy their libidos.

Hadrian erected theaters, baths, temples, fountains, gardens, and canals bordered with statuary throughout his estate. He filled the palaces and temples with sculpture, some of which now rests in the museums of Rome. In later centuries, barbarians, popes, and cardinals, as well as anyone who needed a slab of marble, carted off much that made the villa so spectacular. But enough of the fragmented ruins remain for us to piece together the story.

For a glimpse of what the villa used to be, see the plastic reconstruction at the entrance. Then, following the arrows around, look in particular for the Marine Theater (ruins of the round structure with Ionic pillars); the Great Baths, with some intact mosaics; and the Canopus, with a group of caryatids whose images are reflected in the pond, as well as a statue of Mars. For a closer look at some of the items excavated, you can visit the museum on the premises and a museum and visitor center near the villa parking area.

STAYING FOR A MEAL

Albergo Ristorante Adriano. Via di Villa Adriana 194. ☎ **0774/535-028.** Main courses 22,000L–40,000L ($13.20–$24); fixed-price menu 75,000L ($45). AE, DC, MC, V. Mon–Sat 12:30–2:30pm and 8–10pm, Sun 12:30–2:30pm. Bus: 2 or 4 from Tivoli. ITALIAN.

At the bottom of the villa's hill, in a stucco-sided villa a few steps from the ticket office, sits an idyllic stopover point either before or after you visit Hadrian's Villa. It offers terrace dining under plane trees or indoor dining in a high-ceilinged room with terra-cotta walls, neoclassical moldings, and white Corinthian pilasters. The food is home-style cooking—nothing fancy. The menu includes roast lamb, saltimbocca (veal cooked with ham), a variety of veal dishes, deviled chicken, a selection of salads and cheeses, and simple desserts—everything homemade. They're especially proud of their homemade pasta dishes.

Le Cinque Statue. Via Quintillio Varo 8. ☎ **0774/335-366.** Reservations recommended. Main courses 12,000L–25,000L ($7.20–$15). AE, DC, MC, V. Sat–Thurs 12:30–3pm and 7:30–10pm. Closed Aug 15–Sept 7. The ACOTRAL bus from Rome stops nearby. ROMAN.

Established in the 1950s, this restaurant takes its name from the quintet of old carved statues, including Apollo Belvedere and gladiators, that decorate the place. Today this comfortable restaurant is maintained by a hardworking Italian family, who prepare an honest and unpretentious cuisine. Everything is accompanied by the wines of the hill towns of Rome. Begin with a pastiche of mushrooms or brains, or make a selection from the excellent antipasti. Try the rigatoni with fresh herbs, tripe fried Roman style, or a mixed fry of brains and vegetables. All the pasta is freshly made on the premises. They also have a wide array of ice creams and fruits.

OSTIA

Ostia Antica is one of the area's major attractions, particularly interesting to those who can't make it to Pompeii. If you want to see both ancient and modern Rome, get your bikini and take the Metropolitana (subway) Line B from the Stazione Termini to the Magliana stop. Change here for the Lido train to Ostia Antica, about 16 miles from Rome. Departures are about every half hour, and the trip takes only 20 minutes. The Metro lets you off across the highway that connects Rome with the coast. It's just a short walk to the excavations.

Later, board the Metro again to visit the **Lido di Ostia,** the beach. Italy may be a strongly Catholic country, but the Romans don't allow religious conservatism to affect their bathing attire. This is the beach where the denizens of the capital frolic on the seashore and at times create a merry carnival atmosphere, with dance halls, cinemas, and pizzerias. The Lido is set off best at Castelfusano, against a backdrop of pinewoods. This stretch of shoreline is referred to as the Roman Riviera.

Ostia Antica: Rome's Ancient Seaport. Viale dei Romagnoli 717. ☎ **06/5635-8099.** Admission 8,000L ($4.80) adults, free for children 17 and under. Apr–Sept, daily 9am–6pm; Oct–Mar, daily 9am–5pm. Metro: Ostia Antica Line Roma-Ostia-Lido.

Ostia, located at the mouth of the Tiber, was the port of ancient Rome. It served as the gateway for all the riches from the far corners of the empire. It was founded in the 4th century B.C., and became a major port and naval base primarily under two later emperors, Claudius and Trajan.

A thriving, prosperous city developed, full of temples, baths, theaters, and patrician homes. Ostia Antica flourished for about eight centuries before it began to wither away. Gradually it became little more than a malaria bed, a buried ghost city that faded into history. Although a papal-sponsored commission launched a series of digs in the 19th century, the major work of unearthing was carried out under Mussolini's orders from 1938 to 1942 (the work had to stop because of the war). The city is only partially dug out today, but it's believed that all the chief monuments have been uncovered.

The principal monuments are clearly labeled. The most important spot in all the ruins is **Piazzale delle Corporazioni,** an early version of Wall Street. Near the theater, this square contained nearly 75 corporations, the nature of their businesses identified by the patterns of preserved mosaics.

Greek dramas were performed at the ancient **theater,** built sometime in the early days of the empire. The classics are still aired here in summer (check with the tourist office for specific listings), but the theater as it looks today is the result of much rebuilding. Every town the size of Ostia had a forum, and during the excavations a number of pillars of the ancient **Ostia Forum** were uncovered. At one end is a 2nd-century B.C. temple honoring a trio of gods—Minerva, Jupiter, and Juno (little more than the basic foundation remains). In addition, there's a well-lit museum in the enclave that displays Roman statuary along with some Pompeii-like frescoes. There are perfect picnic spots beside fallen columns or near old temple walls.

CASTELLI ROMANI

For the Roman emperor and the wealthy cardinal in the heyday of the Renaissance, the Castelli Romani (Roman Castles) exerted a powerful lure, and they still do. Of course, the Castelli are not castles, but hill towns—many of them with an ancient history. The wines from the Alban Hills will add a little *feu de joie* to your life. The ideal way to explore the hill towns is by car. But you can get a limited review by taking one of the buses that leaves every 20 minutes from Rome from the Subaugusta stop of the Metro system (A).

CASTELGANDOLFO

Since the early 17th century this resort on Lake Albano, 16 miles from Rome, has been the summer retreat of the popes. As such, it attracts thousands of pilgrims yearly, although the papal residence, Villa Barberini, and its surrounding gardens are private and open only on special occasions. Interestingly, the pope's summer place incorporates part of the notoriously despotic emperor Domitian's palace (but the pastimes have changed).

On days that the pope grants a mass audience, thousands of visitors—many of whom arrive on foot—stream into the audience hall. Pope Pius XII, worried about the thousands of people who waited out in the rain to see him, built this air-conditioned structure to protect the faithful from the elements. On a summer Sunday the pope usually appears on a small balcony in the palace courtyard, reciting with the crowd the noon Angelus prayers.

The seat of the papacy opens onto a little square in the center of the town, where holiday-makers sip their wine—nothing pontifical here. A chairlift transports visitors from the hillside town to the lake, where some of the aquatic competitions were held in the 1960 Olympics. The Church of St. Thomas of Villanova, on the principal square, as well as the fountain, reveal Bernini's hand. If you need to be sold more on visiting Castelgandolfo, remember that it was praised by the eminent guidebook writer Goethe.

NEMI

The Romans flock to Nemi in droves, particularly from April to June for the succulent strawberry of the district—acclaimed by some gourmets as the finest in Europe. In May, there's a strawberry festival. Nemi was also known to the ancients. A temple to the huntress Diana was erected on Lake Nemi, which was said to be her "looking glass." In A.D. 37 Caligula built luxurious barges to float on the lake. Mussolini, much later, drained Nemi to find the barges, but it was a dangerous time to excavate them from the lake's bottom. They were senselessly destroyed by the Nazis during the infamous retreat.

EXPLORING THE TOWN

At the Roman Ship Museum, or **Museo delle Navi,** Via di Diana (☎ **06/939-8040**), you can see two scale models of the ships destroyed by the Nazis. The major artifacts on display are mainly copies, as the originals now rest in world-class museums. The museum is open April to September, Monday to Saturday from 9am to sunset, Sunday from 9am to 1pm; October to March, daily from 9am to 1pm. Admission is 8,000L ($4.80) for adults, free for children 18 and under and seniors 60 and over. To reach the museum, head from the center of Nemi toward the lake.

The 15th-century **Palazzo Ruspoli,** a baronial estate, is the focal point of Nemi, but the hill town itself invites exploration—particularly the alleyways the local denizens call streets and the houses with balconies jutting out over the slopes. While darting like Diana through the Castelli Romani, try to time your schedule to have lunch here in Nemi.

AN EXCELLENT RESTAURANT

La Taverna. Via Nemorense 13. ☎ **06/936-8135.** Reservations required. Main courses 14,000L–18,000L ($8.40–$10.80). AE, DC, MC, V. Thurs–Tues 12:30–2pm and 8–10pm. INTERNATIONAL.

Offering a large array of regional dishes and a rustic atmosphere, La Taverna is worth the trouble it takes to get here. In April the fragole (wild strawberries) signs go out. Try fettuccine with mushrooms. For a main dish we suggest the chef's specialty, arrosto di abbacchio e maiale (it consists of both a pork chop and grilled lamb) or a fresh fish dish. If you want to have a Roman feast, accompany your main dish with large roasted mushrooms, priced according to size, and a small fennel salad. To top off the galaxy of goodies, it's traditional to order Sambucca, a clear white drink like anisette, "with a fly in it." The "fly" is a coffee bean, which you suck on for added flavor.

FRASCATI

Located about 13 miles from Rome on Via Tuscolana, and some 1,073 feet above sea level, Frascati is one of the most beautiful of the hill towns—known for the wine to which it lends its name and its villas—which luckily bounced back from the severe destruction caused by bombers in World War II.

To get here, take one of the Cotral buses leaving from the Subaugusta stop of the Metro system (A). You can also board a small train that leaves from the Ferrovie Laziali section of the central Stazione Termini in Rome. This train runs only to Frascati.

WINE TASTING, RENAISSANCE GARDENS & ANCIENT RUINS

Although bottles of Frascati wine are exported—and served in many of the restaurants and trattorie of Rome—tradition holds that the wine is best near the golden vineyards from which it came. Romans drive up on Sunday just to drink the *vino*. To sample some of the golden white wine yourself, head for **Cantina Comandini,** Via E. Filiberto 1 (☎ **06/942-0915**), right off Piazza Roma. The Comandini family welcomes you to the wine cellar, a regional tavern in which they sell Frascati wine from their own vineyards. You can stop and drink the wine on the spot for 6,000L ($3.60) for a liter or 1,500L (90¢) for a glass. This is not a restaurant, but they sell sandwiches to go with your wine. The tavern is open Monday to Saturday from 4 to 8pm.

For your other sightseeing, stand in the heart of Frascati, at Piazza Marconi, to see the most important of the estates: **Villa Aldobrandini,** Via Massala. The finishing touches to this 16th-century villa were applied by Maderno, who designed the facade of St. Peter's in Rome, but you can only visit the gardens. Still, with its grottoes, yew hedges, statuary, and splashing fountains, it makes for an exciting outing. The gardens are open only in the morning, but you must go to the Azienda di Soggiorno e Turismo, Piazza Marconi 1 (☎ **06/942-0331**) and ask for a free pass. The office is open Monday to Friday from 8am to 2pm and 3:30 to 6:40pm and Saturday from 8am to 2pm.

If you have a car, you can continue past the Villa Aldobrandini to **Tuscolo,** about 3 miles beyond the villa. An ancient spot with the ruins of an amphitheater dating from about the 1st century B.C., Tuscolo offers what may be one of Italy's most panoramic views.

You may also want to visit the bombed-out **Villa Torlonia.** Its grounds have been converted into a public park whose chief treasure is the "Theater of the Fountains," also designed by Maderno.

A MEAL TO GO WITH YOUR WINE

Cacciani Restaurant. Via Armando Diaz 13. ☎ **06/942-0378.** Reservations required on weekends. Main courses 16,000L–28,000L ($9.60–$16.80). AE, DC, MC, V. Tues–Sun 12:30–3pm and 7:30–10:30pm. Closed Jan 7–19 and Aug 18–27. ROMAN.

Cacciani is the choicest restaurant in Frascati, where the competition has always been tough (Frascati foodstuffs once attracted the epicurean Lucullus). A large, modern restaurant in the center of town, with a terrace commanding a view of the valley, the long-enduring Cacciani has drawn such long-ago celebrities as Clark Gable. The kitchen is exposed to the public, and it's fun just to watch the women wash the sand off the spinach. To get you started, we recommend the pasta specialties, such as fettuccine or rigatoni alla vaccinara (oxtail in tomato sauce). For a main course, the baby lamb with a special sauce of white wine and vinegar is always reliable. There is, of course, a large choice of wines, which are kept in a cave under the restaurant. The owners, the Cacciani family, will arrange a combined visit to several of the wine-producing villas of Frascati along with a memorable meal at their elegant restaurant, if you call ahead.

PALESTRINA

If you go out of Rome through the Porta Maggiore and travel on Via Prenestina for about 24 miles, you'll eventually come to Palestrina, a medieval hillside town that overlooks a wide valley.

When U.S. airmen flew over in World War II and bombed part of the town, they scarcely realized their actions would launch Palestrina as an important tourist attraction. After the debris was cleared, a pagan temple—once one of the greatest in the world—emerged: the **Fortuna Primigenia,** rebuilt in the days of the empire but dating from centuries before.

Palestrina predates the founding of Rome by several hundred years. It resisted conquest by the early Romans, and later took the wrong side in the civil war between Marius and Sulla. When Sulla won, he razed every stone in the city except the Temple of Fortune and then built a military barracks on the site. Later, as a favorite vacation spot for the emperors and their entourages, it sheltered some of the most luxurious villas of the Roman Empire.

In medieval feuds, the city was repeatedly destroyed. Its most famous child was Pier Luigi da Palestrina, who is recognized as the father of polyphonic harmony.

The **Colonna–Barberini Palace** (☎ 06/955-8100), high on a hill overlooking the valley, today houses Roman statuary found in the ruins, plus Etruscan artifacts, such as urns the equal of those in the Villa Giulia Museum in Rome. But the most famous work—worth the trip itself—is the *Nile Mosaic,* a well-preserved ancient Roman work, the most remarkable one ever uncovered. The mosaic details the flooding of the Nile, a shepherd's hunt, mummies, ibises, and Roman warriors, among other things. The museum is open daily from 9am to an hour before sunset. Admission is 4,000L ($2.40) for adults and free for children 17 and under and seniors 60 and over.

You'll also find a cathedral here that dates from 1100, with a mostly intact bell tower. It rests on the foundation of a much earlier pagan temple.

SPENDING THE NIGHT

Albergo Ristorante Stella (Restaurant Coccia). Piazza della Liberazione 3, Palestrina, 00036 Roma. ☎ **06/953-8172.** Fax 06/957-3360. 27 rms, 2 suites. AC TV TEL. 90,000L ($54) double; 150,000L ($90) suite. AE, DC, V.

Albergo Ristorante Stella, a buff-colored hotel set in the commercial center of town, is located on a cobblestone square filled with parked cars, trees, and a small fountain. It was renovated in 1995, although the bedrooms remain rather basic, but comfortable. The simple lobby is filled with warm colors, curved leather couches, and autographed photos of local sports heroes. The restaurant is sunny. There's a small bar where you might have an aperitif before lunch. Meals cost from 40,000L ($24), and the restaurant is open daily from noon to 3pm and 7 to 9pm.

FREGENE

The fame of this coastal city north of the Tiber—24 miles from Rome—dates back to the 1600s when the land belonged to the Rospigliosi, a powerful Roman family. Pope Clement IX, a member of that wealthy family, planted a forest of pine that extends along the shoreline for 2 1/2 miles and stands half a mile deep to protect the land from the strong winds of the Mediterranean. Today the wall of pines makes a dramatic backdrop for the golden sands and luxurious villas of the resort. You can take a Civitavecchia-bound train from the Stazione Termini in Rome to Fregene, the first stop. Or you can take the bus, which leaves from the Lepanto Metro stop and takes passengers to the center of Fregene.

WHERE TO STAY & DINE

La Conchiglia. Lungomare di Ponente 4, Fregene, 00050 Roma. ☎ **06/668-5385.** Fax 06/668-5385. 36 rms. A/C MINIBAR TV TEL. 160,000L ($96) double. Rates include breakfast. AE, DC, MC, V.

La Conchiglia means "The Shellfish" in Italian—an appropriate name for this hotel and restaurant right on the beach with views of the water and the pines. Built in 1934, the hotel features a white, circular lounge with built-in curving wall banquettes that face a cylindrical fireplace with a raised hearth—seemingly a setting for a modern Italian film. A resort aura, however, is created by the large green plants. The bar in the cocktail lounge, which faces the terrace, is also circular. The rooms are comfortable and well furnished.

It's also possible to stop by just for a meal, and the food is good. Try, for example, spaghetti with lobster and grilled fish or one of many excellent meat dishes. Meals start at 50,000L ($30). The restaurant is in the garden, shaded by bamboo. Oleander flutters in the sea breezes. The restaurant is open daily from 1 to 3pm and 8 to 10pm.

ETRUSCAN HISTORICAL SIGHTS

CERVETERI (CAERE)

As you walk through the Etruscan Museum in Rome (Villa Giulia), you'll often see the word *Caere* written under a figure vase or a sarcophagus. This is a reference to the nearby town known today as Cerveteri, one of the great Etruscan cities of Italy, whose origins may go as far back as the 9th century B.C. Of course, the Etruscan town has long since faded, but not the **Necropolis of Cerveteri** (☎ 06/995-0003). The effect is eerie; Cerveteri is often called a "city of the dead."

When you go beneath some of the mounds, you'll discover the most striking feature of the necropolis—the tombs are like rooms in Etruscan homes. The main burial ground is called the Necropolis of Banditacca. Of the graves thus far uncovered, none is finer than the Tomba Bella (sometimes called the Reliefs' Tomb), the burial ground of the Matuna family. Articles such as utensils and even house pets were painted in stucco relief. Presumably these paintings were representations of items the dead family would need in the world beyond. The necropolis is open May to September, Tuesday to Sunday from 9am to 7pm; October to April, Tuesday to Sunday from 9am to 3:30pm. Admission is 8,000L ($4.80).

Relics from the necropolis are displayed at the **Museo Nazionale Cerite,** Piazza Santa Maria Maggiore (☎ 06/994-1354). The museum is housed within the ancient walls and crenellations of Ruspoldi Castle. It's open May to September, Tuesday to Sunday from 9am to 7pm; October to April, Tuesday to Sunday from 9am to 2pm. Admission is free.

You can reach Cerveteri by bus or car. If you're driving, head out Via Aurelia, northwest of Rome, for a distance of 28 miles. By public transportation, take Metro Line A in Rome to the Lepanto stop; from Via Lepanto you can take a Cotral bus (☎ 06/324-4724) to Cerveteri; the trip takes about an hour and costs 4,900L ($2.95). Once at Cerveteri, it's a 1 1/4-mile walk to the necropolis. Just follow the signs that point the way.

TARQUINIA

If you wish to see tombs even more striking and more recently excavated than those at Cerveteri, go to Tarquinia. The medieval turrets and fortifications atop the rocky cliffs overlooking the sea seem to contradict the Etruscan name of Tarquinia. Actually, Tarquinia is the adopted name of the old medieval community of Corneto, in honor of the major Etruscan city that once stood nearby. The main attraction in the town is the **Tarquinia National Museum,** Piazza Cavour (☎ **0766/856-036**), devoted to Etruscan exhibits and sarcophagi excavated from the necropolis a few miles away. The museum is housed in the Palazzo Vitelleschi, a Gothic palace that dates from the mid-15th century. Among the exhibits are gold jewelry, black vases with carved and painted bucolic scenes, and sarcophagi decorated with carvings of animals and relief figures of priests and military leaders. But the biggest attraction is in itself worth the ride from Rome—the almost life-size pair of winged horses from the pediment of a Tarquinian temple. The finish is worn here and there, and the terra-cotta color shows through, but the relief stands as one of the greatest Etruscan masterpieces ever discovered. The museum is open Tuesday to Sunday from 9am to 7pm, and charges 8,000L ($4.80) for adults, free admission for children 17 and under and seniors 60 and over.

The same ticket also admits you to the **Etruscan Necropolis** (☎ **0766/856-308**), which covers more than 2½ miles of rough terrain near where the ancient Etruscan city once stood. Thousands of tombs have been discovered here, some of which have not been explored even today. Others, of course, were discovered by looters, but many treasures remain even though countless pieces were removed to museums and private collections. The paintings on the walls of the tombs have helped historians reconstruct the life of the Etruscans—a heretofore impossible feat without a written history. They depict feasting couples in vivid colors mixed from iron oxide, lapis lazuli dust, and charcoal. One of the oldest tombs (from the 6th century B.C.) depicts young men fishing while dolphins play and colorful birds fly high above. Many of the paintings convey an earthy, vigorous, sex-oriented life among the wealthy Etruscans. The tombs are generally open Tuesday to Sunday from 9am to an hour before sunset (until 2pm November to March). You can reach the grave sites by taking a bus from the Barriera San Giusto to the Cimitero stop. Or try the 20-minute walk from the museum. Inquire at the museum for directions.

To reach Tarquinia by car, take Via Aurelia outside Rome and continue on the autostrada toward Civitavecchia. Bypass Civitavecchia and continue another 13 miles north until you see the exit signs for Tarquinia. As for public transportation, going by train is the preferred choice: A *diretto* train from Roma Ostiense station takes 50 minutes. Also, eight buses a day leave from the Via Lepanto stop in Rome for the 2-hour trip to the neighboring town, Barriera San Giusto, which is 1½ miles from Tarquinia. Bus schedules are available at the tourist office in Barriera San Giusto (☎ 0766/856-384), which is open Monday to Saturday from 8am to 2pm.

6 Florence (Firenze)

No other city today in Europe, with the exception of Venice, lives off its past the way Florence does. The city was the birthplace of the Renaissance, an amazing outburst of activity between the 14th and the 16th centuries that completely changed the face of the Tuscan town, and the world has been beating a path here ever since. During the heyday of the Renaissance, under the benevolent eye (and purse) of the Medicis, the city became the world's greatest repository of art treasures. The list of geniuses who lived or worked here reads like a "who's who" in the world of art and literature: Dante, Boccaccio, Fra Angelico, Brunelleschi, Donatello, da Vinci, Raphael, Cellini, Michelangelo, Ghiberti, and Giotto.

At first glance, Florence is a bit foreboding and architecturally not the Gothic fantasy of lace that Venice is, for example. Many of its *palazzi* look like severe fortresses, as was the Medici style. They were built, after all, to keep foreign enemies at bay. These facades, though, however uninviting, contain treasures within, as the thousands upon thousands of visitors who overrun the too-narrow streets of the city today know and appreciate.

Ever since the 19th century Florence has been visited by seemingly half the world—wanting to see Michelangelo's *David*, Botticelli's *Venus on the Half Shell*, or Brunelleschi's dome. The city has impressed some hard-to-impress people, including Mark Twain, who found that it overwhelms with "tides of color that make all the sharp lines dim and faint and turn the old city to a city of dreams."

Although to some extent Florence appears to be caught in a time warp, the city virtually pulsates with present-day life while jealously guarding its Renaissance treasures. Students racing to and from the university quarter add renewed vibrance and culture to the city, and it's amusing to watch how many local businesspeople avoid the city's impossible traffic today: They whiz by on Vespas while cars are stalled in traffic.

The locals both bemoan the fact that their city is overrun with visitors and at the same time welcome them, because they know that it puts tripe on the table (tripe is a Florentine's favorite dish). The 400,000 people of Florence are almost guaranteed a good living off the tourists, whereas Milan, which gets far fewer visitors, is subjected to various economic depressions that come and go. "It's the price we pay for fame," laments one local merchant. "The visitors have crowded our city and strained our facilities, but they make it possible for me to own a villa in Fiesole and take my children on vacation to San Remo every year."

City fathers or mothers have been wise to keep the inner Renaissance core relatively free of modern architecture and polluting industry. Florence has industry, but it's sent packing to the suburbs. It's a relatively clean city and safe as Italian cities go, with far less crime than Rome, and certainly far less than Naples. You can generally walk the narrow cobblestone streets at night unmolested, although caution is always advised.

Florentines say that they like to present *una bella figura,* or "a good appearance," to the rest of the world, and are incredibly upset when that appearance is attacked, as in the case of the May 1993 bombing of the Uffizi that cost them many treasures. The entire city rallied to reopen this treasure trove of Renaissance and other works of art.

By all means, Florence should be on the itinerary of even the most rushed tours of Europe. There's nothing like it anywhere else in the world. Venice and Rome are too different from Florence to invite sane comparisons. The one myth you must not believe—and it's heard more and more frequently—is that Florence is becoming "the Los Angeles of Italy." How did the rumor get started? Perhaps because Florentines have the highest per capita number of cellular phones in Europe. That's because they're trying to be modern and keep up with the changing world, but they also know that you're coming to pay homage to their glorious past and not to their achievements of today. Even though still a great cultural center of art and fashion, nobody seriously suggests that anything magnificent has been created in Florence in a few centuries at least.

May and September are the ideal times to visit Florence. The worst times are the week before and including Easter and from June until the first week of September—Florence is literally overrun with tourists during these times, and the city streets, or anything else, weren't designed for mass tourism. Temperatures in July and August hover in the 70s, dropping to a low of 45° or 46°F in December and January, the coldest months.

1 Orientation

ARRIVING

BY PLANE If you're flying from North America the best air connection is Rome, where you can board a domestic flight to the **Galileo Galilei Airport** at Pisa (☎ 050/500-707), 58 miles west of Florence. There's a shuttle train (trip time: a little over 1 hour) every hour or two between the airport and Florence's train station from 6 or 7am to 7 or 8pm.

Florence's small airport, **Amerigo Vespucci** (☎ 055/30-615), lies 3¹/₂ miles northwest of the city on Via del Termine, near the A11 autostrada. This airport receives domestic flights from such cities as Rome and Milan, as well as international flights from such cities as Brussels, Frankfurt, London, Munich, Nice, and Paris. ATAF bus no. 62 runs between the airport and the main Santa Maria Novella rail terminal every 20 minutes. The 15-minute taxi ride from the airport to the city should cost about $20. Domestic air service is provided by **Alitalia,** Lungarno degli Acciaiuoli 10–12 in Florence (☎ 055/27-881).

BY TRAIN Florence lies in the heart of Italy and is a major stopover in Europe for Eurailpass holders. If you're coming north from Rome, count on a 2- to 3-hour trip, depending on your connection. Bologna is just an hour away by train, and Venice, 4 hours. The **Santa Maria Novella rail station,** in Piazza della Stazione

(☎ **055/288-785** for railway information), adjoins Piazza Santa Maria Novella, which has one of the great churches of Florence. From here, most of the major hotels are within easy reach, either on foot or by taxi or bus.

Facilities in the train station include a currency exchange open Monday to Saturday from 8:20am to 6:30pm; a day hotel, **Albergo Diurno,** where you can take a shower after a long train ride and rest up; and luggage storage at the top of Track 16.

Some trains into Florence stop at the **Stazione Campo di Marte,** on the eastern side of Florence. A 24-hour bus service (no. 91) runs between the two rail terminals.

BY BUS   Two long-distance bus lines service Florence: **SITA,** Viale Cadorna 103-105 (☎ **055/483-651**), and **Lazzi Eurolines,** Piazza della Stazione 4-6 (☎ **055/ 215-154**). SITA connects Florence with such Tuscan hill towns as Siena, Arezzo, Pisa, and San Gimignano, and Lazzi Eurolines provides service from such cities as Rome and Naples.

BY CAR   Florence, because of its central location, enjoys good autostrada connections with the rest of Italy, especially Rome and Bologna.

Autostrada A1 connects Florence with both the north and south of Italy. Florence lies 172 miles north of Rome, 65 miles west of Bologna, and 185 miles south of Milan. Bologna is about an hour away by car, and Rome is 3 hours away. The Tyrrhenian coast is only an hour from Florence on the A11 heading west.

Use a car only to get to Florence. Don't even contemplate using it once here, as most of central Florence is closed to all vehicles except those of local residents.

VISITOR INFORMATION

Contact the **Azienda Promozione Turistica,** Via A. Manzoni 16 (☎ **055/ 234-6284;** fax 055/234-6286), open Monday to Saturday from 8:30am to 1:30pm. Another helpful office handling data about Florence and Tuscany is at Via Cavour 1R (☎ **055/290-832;** fax 055/276-0383), open Monday to Saturday from 8:15am to 7:15pm and Sunday from 8:15am to 1:45pm. Yet another helpful information office is near Piazza della Signoria, at Chiasso dei Baroncelli 17R (☎ **055/230-2124**), open Monday to Saturday from 8:15am to 1:45pm. There's also a small visitor information office inside the main train terminal.

CITY LAYOUT

Florence is a city seemingly designed for walking. It's amazing how nearly all the major sights can be discovered on foot. The only problem is that the sidewalks in summer are so crowded that we only hope you don't suffer from claustrophobia.

MAIN ARTERIES & STREETS   The city is split by the **Arno River,** which usually looks serene and peaceful, but can turn ferocious with floodwaters on rare occasions. The major part of Florence, certainly its historic core with most of the monuments, lies on the north or "right" side of the river. But the "left" side is not devoid of attractions. Many longtime visitors frequent the Oltrarno ("across the Arno") for its tantalizing trattorie; they also maintain that the shopping here is less expensive. Even the most hurried visitor will want to cross over the Arno to see the Pitti Palace with its many art treasures and walk through the Giardini di Boboli, a series of formal gardens, the most impressive in Florence. In addition, you'll also want to cross over to check out the panoramic views of the city from Piazzale Michelangelo. To reach it, follow Viale Michelangelo up the flank of the hill (one easy way to go is to take bus no. 13 from the train station).

The Arno is spanned by eight bridges, of which the **Ponte Vecchio,** which is lined with jewelry stores, is the most celebrated and most central. Many of these bridges were ancient structures until the Nazis, in a hopeless and last-ditch effort, senselessly destroyed them in their "defense" of Florence in 1944. With tenacity, Florence rebuilt its bridges, using pieces from the destroyed structures whenever possible. The **Ponte Santa Trínita** is the second-most important bridge. It leads to the **Via dei Tornabuoni,** which is the most important shopping street on the right bank (don't look for bargains, however). At the Ponte Vecchio you can walk, again on the right bank of the Arno, along Via por Santa Maria, which will become Via Calimala. This will lead you into **Piazza della Repubblica,** a commercial district known for its cafes.

From here, you can take Via Roma, which leads directly into **Piazza di San Giovanni,** where you'll find the baptistery and its neighboring sibling, the larger **Piazza del Duomo,** with the world-famous cathedral and bell tower by Giotto. From the far western edge of Piazza del Duomo you can take Via del Proconsolo south to **Piazza della Signoria,** to see the landmark **Palazzo Vecchio** and its sculpture-filled **Loggia della Signoria.**

High in the hills overlooking Florence is the ancient town of **Fiesole,** with Etruscan and Roman ruins and a splendid cathedral.

FINDING AN ADDRESS   Florence has two different systems for street numbering—red (*rosso*) numbers or blue or black (*blu or nero*) numbers. Red numbers identify commercial enterprises, such as shops and restaurants. Blue or black numbers identify office buildings, private homes, apartment houses, or hotels.

Since street numbers are chaotic in Florence, it's better to get a cross street or some landmark if you're looking for an address along a long boulevard.

STREET MAPS   At the very least, arm yourself with a map from the tourist office (see "Visitor Information," above, for the location of the tourist offices). But if you'd like to see Florence in any depth—particularly those little side streets—buy a **Falk** map (indexes are included), which gives all the streets. Falk maps are available at all bookstores and at most newsstands.

NEIGHBORHOODS IN BRIEF

Florence isn't divided into neighborhoods the way many cities are. Most locals refer to either the left bank or the right bank of the Arno and that's about it, unless they head out of town for the immediate environs, such as Fiesole. The following selection of "neighborhoods"—most of them grouped around a palace, church, or square—is therefore rather arbitrary.

Centro   Called simply that by the Florentines, Centro could, in effect, be all the historic heart of Florence, but mostly the term is used to describe the area southwest of the Duomo. This district is not as important as it used to be, as Piazza della Signoria (see below) now attracts more visitors. The heyday of Centro was in the 1800s when it was filled with narrow medieval streets that were torn down to make a grander city center. Lost forever were great homes of the Medici and the Sacchetti families, among others. **Piazza della Repubblica,** although faded, is still lively day and night with its celebrated cafes, such as **Giubbe Rosse,** founded in 1888, and **Caffè Gilli,** which opened in 1733. The most fashionable artery of Centro is Via dei Tournabuoni, the most elegant shopping street in Florence. Pause on this street at no. 83 (**La Giacosa**) for a pâtisserie before continuing to survey the *palazzi* and the high-quality but lethally priced merchandise.

Piazza del Duomo   Situated in the heart of Florence, this square and its surrounding area are dominated by the **Duomo,** Santa Maria del Fiore, site of the former local grain and hay markets. One of the largest buildings in the Christian world, this cathedral is exceeded only by St. Peter's in Rome. You come upon it unexpectedly because the surrounding buildings were not torn down to give it breathing room. Capped by Brunelleschi's dome—an amazing architectural feat—the structure now dominates the skyline of Florence. Every visitor flocks to the area, to see not only the Duomo but the neighboring *campanile* (bell tower), one of the most beautiful in all of Italy, and the **baptistery** across the way. Now consecrated to St. John the Baptist, the baptistery was originally a pagan temple honoring Mars. Its doors are among the jewels of Italian Renaissance sculpture. Here, too, in this same neighborhood is the **Museo dell'Opera del Duomo,** a sculpture haven that includes some of the most important works of Donatello. A few touristy hotels and trattorie are also found around the Duomo.

Piazza della Signoria   This section of Florence—and the piazza in particular—has been the site of many dramatic moments in the city's history, including Savonarola's "bonfire of the vanities," in which Florentines burned precious items such as jewelry and paintings to purify themselves. Today the most visited square in Florence is home to the **Loggia dei Lanzi,** with Cellini's *Perseus* holding a beheaded Medusa. This is the most photographed original statue in Florence still standing outside. Michelangelo's *David* on the square is a copy, the original having been moved inside to protect it from the elements. To the south are the **Galleria degli Uffizi** and the **Palazzo Vecchio.**

Piazza Santa Maria Novella/Termini   On the northwestern edge of central Florence is the large Piazza Santa Maria Novella with its church of the same name. Founded in the 13th century by the Dominicans, the church is one of the most important and most visited in Florence. Completed in 1360, it is filled with admirable frescoes by Domenico Ghirlandaio and a *Crucifix* by Brunelleschi. Donatello allegedly was so taken with the crucifix that upon seeing it he dropped a basket of eggs he was carrying. This area is not all art and culture, however. Northwest of Santa Maria Novella lies the busiest section of Florence, centered at Piazza della Stazione, the **main railway terminal** of the city. Like all railway stations in Italy, it's surrounded by budget hotels, some of dubious quality. Leading off of Piazza dell'Unita Italiana, Via del Melarancio goes a short distance east to **San Lorenzo,** the first cathedral of Florence. Beyond San Lorenzo is Piazza Madonna degli Aldobrandini, one of the more forgettable squares of Florence were it not the entrance to the **Medici Chapels.** Because it is, half the world can be seen flocking here to see the famous Medici tombs, the work of Michelangelo whose allegorical figures of *Day* and *Night* are among the most famous sculptures of all time. Southwest of Piazza Santa Maria Novella, toward the Arno, is **Piazza Ognissanti,** a fashionable—albeit car-clogged—Renaissance square opening onto the river. On this square are two of the most legendary hotels in the city: the **Grand** and the **Excelsior.**

Piazza San Marco   Although it has none of the grandeur of the square of the same name in Venice, this district is nevertheless one of the most important in Florence—centered around its church, now the **Museo di San Marco.** Located in a former Dominican monastery, the museum houses a collection of the greatest works of Fra Angelico, who decorated the walls of the monks' cells with edifying scenes. Like the other areas previously previewed, this *quartier* of Florence is also overrun by visitors, most of them rushing to the **Galleria dell'Accademia** on Via Ricasoli to see the monumental figure of *David* (1501–04) sculpted by Michelangelo. A perfect example of the sculptor's humanism, it's the most reproduced statue in the world. Other highlights of the area include **Piazza della Santissima Annunziata,** one of the most beautiful in Florence and dominated by an equestrian statue of Ferdinand I de'Medici by Bologna.

Piazza Santa Croce   This section is in the southeastern part of the old town of Florence, near the Arno, and is dominated by the Gothic Santa Croce (or Holy Cross) Church, completed in 1442. Once the scene of jousts and festivals, even *calcio* (a local game of football), the **Piazza San Croce** in time became the headquarters of the Franciscans, who established a firm base here in 1218. Although the piazza and the area have little of their former prestige, the section remains a much-visited part of Florence, although not as tourist trodden as the areas mentioned above. Today the church is the virtual Pantheon of Florence, containing the tombs, among others, of Michelangelo and Machiavelli. A little distance to the north of Santa Croce is **Casa Buonarroti,** on Via Ghibellina, which Michelangelo acquired for his nephew. Today it's a museum with a collection of works by Michelangelo, mainly drawings, gathered by his nephew. From here you can follow Via Buonarroti to the **Piazza dei Ciompi,** a lively square unknown to many visitors. It's filled with stalls peddling secondhand goods. Look for old coins, books, and even antique Italian uniforms.

Ponte Vecchio   Southwest of Piazza della Signoria is the Ponte Vecchio (Old Bridge) area. The oldest of the bridges of Florence, it's flanked by jewelry stores and will carry you to the Oltrarno. This has always been a strategic crossing place in Florence, even when it was an old stone bridge. In the Middle Ages it was the center for leather craftspeople, fishmongers, and butchers, but over the years jewelers' shops have replaced these less-glamorous industries. Corridoio Vasariano runs the length of the Ponte Vecchio above the shops—built by Vasari in just 5 months. Actually, the Ponte Vecchio was almost destroyed on the night of August 4, 1944, when the Nazi heirarchy gave orders to blow up all the bridges along the Arno. Even though mined, the Ponte Vecchio was miraculously spared. This area is one of the most congested parts of Florence, but on every visitor's itinerary nonetheless.

Across the Arno   The "left bank" of the Arno River, known as the **Oltrarno,** is home to the **Palazzo Pitti,** with its picture gallery and **Giardini di Boboli,** Massacio's frescoes in the church of **Santa Maria del Carmine,** artisans' workshops, some good restaurants, and the postcard panorama of Florence and its dome from **Piazzale Michelangiolo.** Even those visitors who stay glued to the right bank cross the Arno to visit the Pitti Palace. It's outranked only by the Uffizi in its treasure troves of art. When the crowds at the Pitti get you down, you can always escape to the lush greenery of the Boboli Gardens. At the top of the gardens is an elegant fortress known as **Forte Belvedere,** built between 1590 and 1595. It affords one of the most panoramic views of Florence and is well worth the climb.

Fiesole   Although a town in its own right, Fiesole is treated by some as a neighborhood or suburb of Florence. An ancient town on a hill overlooking Florence, it has panoramic views of the city of the Renaissance and of the Arno Valley. It was founded by the Etruscans, perhaps as early as the 7th century B.C. Its center is the large **Piazza Mino da Fiesole.** The fresh, clean air of Fiesole makes it an ideal retreat when the heart of Florence is sultry and overrun with visitors. There are hotels here, as well as trattorie, or you can visit to see the sights, including the **Convent of San Fancesco** and the **Duomo,** or to just take in the view.

2 Getting Around

ON FOOT   Because Florence is so compact, walking is the ideal way—and at times the only way, because of numerous pedestrian zones—to get around. In theory at least, pedestrians have the right of way at uncontrolled zebra crossings, but don't count on that should you encounter a speeding Vespa.

BY PUBLIC TRANSPORTATION The major sights in the small city of Florence are within walking distance of most hotels, but you might prefer to use the public **buses.** You must purchase your ticket before boarding, but for 2,000L ($1.20) you can ride on any public bus in the city for a total of 70 minutes. A 24-hour pass costs 5,000L ($3). Bus tickets can be purchased from tobacconists and news vendors. The local **bus station** (which serves as the terminal for ATAF city buses) is at Piazza del Duomo 57F (☎ 055/56-501). Bus routes are posted at bus stops, but the numbers of routes can change overnight, because of sudden repair work going on at one of the ancient streets—perhaps a water main broke overnight and caused flooding. We recently found that a bus route map printed only 1 week prior was already out of date. Therefore, if you're dependent on bus transport in Florence, you'll need to inquire that day for the exact number of the vehicle you wish to board. If you're caught riding a bus without a ticket, you'll be fined 80,000L ($48).

BY TAXI Taxis can be found at stands at nearly all the major squares in Florence. If you need a radio taxi, call ☎ 055/4390 or 055/4798.

BY CAR As mentioned, driving a car in Florence is a hopeless undertaking—not only because of the snarled traffic and the maze of one-way streets, but because much of the district you've come to see is a pedestrian zone. In addition, **parking** seems to become more difficult every summer. Unless you are particularly gifted at squeezing your rental car into impossibly tight spaces, don't even think of parking aboveground. Instead, look for prominently posted blue signs emblazoned with the letter "P" that will lead you to the nearest garages. If your hotel doesn't have its own garage, someone on the staff will direct you to the nearest garage after you've unloaded your luggage or else will arrange valet parking. Garage fees for the night average 35,000L to 40,000L ($21 to $24), although vans or large luxury cars may cost as much as 50,000L ($30) per night.

Although there are dozens of garages throughout the city, some of the most visible and centrally located include the **International Garage,** Via Palazzuolo 29 (☎ 055/282-386); **Garage La Stazione,** Via Alamanni (☎ 055/284-768); the **Autoparking SLL,** Via Fiesolana 19 (☎ 055/247-7871); and the **Garage Anglo-Americano,** Via dei Barbadori 5 (☎ 055/214-418). If these garages are full, you can almost always find a space at the **Garage Porte Nuova,** Via Portenuove (☎ 055/333-355).

You will, however, need a car to explore the surrounding countryside of Tuscany in any depth. Car-rental agencies in Florence include **Avis,** Borgo Ognissanti 128R (☎ 055/213-629); **Budget,** Borgo Ognissanti 134R (☎ 055/287-161); and **Hertz,** Via del Termine 1 (☎ 055/307-370).

BY BICYCLE OR MOTOR SCOOTER Bicycles and motor scooters, if you avoid the whizzing traffic, are two other practical ways of getting around. **Alinari,** located near the railway station at Via Guelfa 85R (☎ 055/280-500), rents bikes for 4,000L to 5,000L ($2.40 to $3) per hour, or 20,000L to 30,000L ($12 to $18) per day, depending on the model. Also available are small-engined, rather loud motor scooters that rent for 9,000L ($5.40) per hour, or 45,000L ($27) per day. Renters must be 18 or over, and must leave either a cash deposit of 200,000L ($120) or a passport, driver's license, and the number of a valid credit or charge card. Alinari is open Monday to Saturday from 9am to 1pm and 3 to 7:30pm and Sunday from 10am to 1pm and 3 to 7:30pm.

BY GUIDED TOUR If you have a limited amount of time in Florence, or want to get an overall view before exploring on your own, many companies run guided bus tours of the city's main sights. The two virtually indistinguishable big names are

American Express (☎ **055/50-981**) and **SitaSightseeing** (☎ **055/214-721**). Both run morning tours of the major sights and separate afternoon tours of the top secondary sights. They cost 50,000L ($33.35) per person for each half-day tour, museum admissions included. Both companies also run afternoon tours to Pisa (50,000L/$33.35) and the Chianti (54,000L/$36), and an all-day trip that combines Siena and San Gimignano (73,000L/$48.65). To arrange any other kind of guided tour, visit the **Ufficio Guide Turistiche** (☎ **055/247-8188**) at Viale Gramsci 9a.

FAST FACTS: Florence

American Express   Amex is at Via Dante Alighieri 20–22r (☎ **055/50-981**) and at Via Guicciardini 49r (☎ **055/288-751**). Both offices are open Monday to Friday from 9am to 5:30pm and Saturday from 9am to 12:30pm.

Business Hours   From mid-June to mid-September most shops and businesses are open Monday to Friday from 9am to 1pm and 4 to 8pm. Off-season hours, in general, are Monday from 3:30 to 7:30pm and Tuesday to Saturday from 9am to 1pm and 3:30 to 7:30pm.

Consulates   The consulate of the **United States** is at Lungarno Amerigo Vespucci 46 (☎ **055/239-8276**); it's open Monday to Friday from 9am to 2pm. The consulate of the **United Kingdom** is at Lungarno Corsini 2 (☎ **055/284-133**), near Piazza Santa Trínita; it's open Monday to Friday from 9:30am to 12:30pm and 2:30 to 4:30pm.

Citizens of other English-speaking countries, including Canada, Australia, and New Zealand, should contact their diplomatic representatives in Rome.

Currency Exchange   Local banks in Florence grant the best rates. Most banks are open Monday to Friday from 8:30am to 1:30pm and 2:45 to 3:45pm. The tourist office (see "Orientation," earlier in this chapter) exchanges money at official rates when banks are closed and on holidays, but a commission is often charged. You can also go to the Ufficio Informazione booth at the rail station, which is open daily from 7:30am to 7:40pm. American Express (see locations above) also exchanges money.

One of the best places to exchange currency is the post office (see below).

Dentist   For a list of English-speaking dentists, consult your consulate, if possible, or contact **Tourist Medical Service,** Via Lorenzo il Magnifico 59 (☎ **055/ 475-411**). Visits without an appointment are only possible Monday to Friday from 11am to noon and 5 to 6pm and Saturday from 11am to noon. After hours, an answering service gives names and phone numbers of dentists and doctors who are on duty.

Doctor   Contact your national consulate for a list of English-speaking physicians. You can also contact **Tourist Medical Service,** Via Lorenzo il Magnifico 59 (☎ **055/475-411**). See also "Dentist," above.

Drugstores   See "Pharmacies," below.

Emergencies   For fire, call ☎ **115;** for an ambulance, call ☎ **118;** for the police, ☎ **113;** and for road service, ☎ **116.**

Eyeglass Repair   Two well-accessorized and centrally located possibilities are **Salmoiraghi,** Via dei Calzaioli 77R (☎ **055/290-869**), and the **Centro Ottico Optometrico,** Via Cavour 94R (☎ **055/287-210**).

Hairdressers/Barbers   Both women and men are fond of **Big Art,** Piazza della Repubblica 3 (☎ **055/212-016**), located right in the center of Florence. Call for an appointment. It's on the floor above street level.

Hospitals   Call the **General Hospital of Santa Maria Nuova,** Piazza Santa Maria Nuova 1 (☎ 055/27-581).

Information   See "Visitor Information," earlier in this chapter.

Laundry/Dry Cleaning   The self-service **Lavanderia Superlava Splendid,** Via del Sole 29R (☎ 055/218-836), is a good choice because of its central location off Piazza Santa Maria Novella. It's open Monday to Friday from 8:30am to 7:30pm. Most hotels can arrange for dry cleaning, although you'll pay extra for the convenience. You can also ask at your hotel reception desk for the nearest dry cleaner in your neighborhood.

Lost Property   The lost-and-found office, **Oggetti Smarriti,** is at Via Circondaria 19 (☎ 055/32-831), near the rail terminal.

Luggage Storage   This is available at **Santa Maria Novella Stazione,** in the center of the city on Piazza della Stazione (☎ 055/278-785). It's open daily from 4:15am to 1:45am.

Pharmacies   **Farmacia Molteni,** Via Calzaiuoli 7R (☎ 055/215-472), is open 24 hours a day, including Sunday.

Photographic Needs   One of the best places is **Bottega della Foto,** Piazza del Duomo 17 (☎ 055/283-006), across from the cathedral in the center of Florence.

Police   Dial ☎ 113 in an emergency. English-speaking foreigners who want to see and talk to the police should go to the **Ufficio Stranieri station** at Via Zara 2 (☎ 055/49-771), where English-speaking personnel are available daily from 9am to 2pm.

Post Office   The **Central Post Office** is at Via Pellicceria 3, off Piazza della Repubblica (☎ 055/277-4322 for English-speaking operators, or 055/277-4539 or 055/211-038), open Monday to Saturday from 8:15am to 7pm. You can purchase stamps and telephone cards at Windows 21–22. If you want your mail sent to Italy general delivery (*fermo posta*), have it sent in care of this post office (use the 50100 Firenze postal code). Mail can be picked up at Windows 23–24. A telegram, telex, and fax office on the second floor is open Monday through Saturday from 8:15am to 6pm (you can also send telegrams by phoning ☎ 186 24 hours a day). A **foreign exchange** office is open Monday to Friday from 8:15am to 6pm; you can also exchange money (notes only) at automatic tellers on the ground floor daily from 8:15am to 7pm. If you want to send packages of up to 20kg, go to the rear of the building and enter at Piazza Davantzi 4; hours are the same as the main post office.

Radio   Although there are some private stations, the air waves are dominated by RAI, the national radio network. In the summer months RAI broadcasts some news in English. Vatican Radio's foreign news broadcasts (in English) also reach Florence. Shortwave radio reception is also possible, and you can pick up American (VOA), British (BBC), and Canadian (CBC) radio broadcasts. The American Southern European Broadcast Network (SEB) from Vicenza can also be heard on regular AM radio (middle or medium wave).

Rest Rooms   Public toilets are found in most galleries, museums, bars and cafes, and restaurants, as well as bus, train, and air terminals. Usually they are designated as WC (water closet) or *donne* (women) or *uomini* (men). The most confusing designation is *signori* (gentlemen) and *signore* (ladies), so watch those final *i*s and *e*s!

Safety Violent crimes are rare in Florence; most crime consists mainly of pick-pockets who frequent crowded tourist centers, such as corridors of the Uffizi Galleries. Members of group tours who cluster together are often singled out as victims. Car thefts are relatively common: Don't leave your luggage in an unguarded car, even if it's locked in the trunk. Women should be especially careful in avoiding purse snatchers, some of whom grab a woman's purse while whizzing by on a Vespa, often knocking the woman down. Documents such as passports and extra money are better stored in safes at your hotel if available.

Taxes A value-added tax (IVA) is added to all consumer products and most services, including those at hotels and restaurants. The tax is refundable if you spend more than 300,000L ($180) at any one store.

Taxis See "Getting Around," earlier in this chapter.

Transit Information For international flights from **Galileo Galilei Airport,** call ☎ **050/500-707;** for domestic flights at **Peretola,** call ☎ **055/30-615;** for railway information, dial ☎ **055/278-785;** for long-distance bus information, call ☎ **055/483-651;** and for city buses, dial ☎ **055/56-501.**

3 Accommodations

For sheer charm and luxury, the hotels of Florence are among the finest in Europe. Many of the city's grand old villas and palaces have been converted into hotels. There are not too many tourist cities where you can find a 15th- or 16th-century palace—tastefully decorated and most comfortable—rated as a second-class *pensione.* Florence is equipped with hotels in virtually all price ranges and with widely varying standards, comfort, service, and efficiency.

However, during the summer months there simply aren't enough rooms to meet the demand, and if you arrive without a reservation you may not find a place for the night and will have to drive to nearby Montecatini, where you'll always stand a good chance of securing accommodations.

In Florence, the most desirable—and often most expensive—place to stay in terms of shopping, nightlife, sightseeing attractions, and restaurants is in the historic heart of the city on the right bank of the Arno, especially in the Centro and around the Duomo and Piazza della Signoria. Yes, this area is much too touristy, and in summer the streets are like an international camp, but it's still a lot better than staying on the outskirts, where commuting into the historic center is difficult because of inadequate public transportation. Driving into the center is almost impossible, because of the heavy traffic and because major districts of Florence are pedestrian-only zones.

The cheapest lodgings in the historic center are found around the Termini (rail station); these are also the least desirable, of course. The area directly around the Termini and Santa Maria Novella, although generally safe during the day, is the center of major drug dealing late at night and should be avoided then for safety reasons. The Santa Maria Novella area isn't all budget lodgings, however; also in this general area is Piazza Ognissanti—south of Piazza Santa Maria Novella toward the Arno—one of the most fashionable squares in Florence and the home of two of the city's most famous hotels.

Also in the historic center, but less tourist trodden and a bit more tranquil, is the area around Piazza San Marco and the University quarter.

Once you cross the Arno, lodgings are much scarcer, although there are places to stay, including some *pensioni.* In general, prices are lower across the Arno, and you'll be located next to one of the major attractions of Florence: the Pitti Palace.

Florence Accommodations

Albani Firenze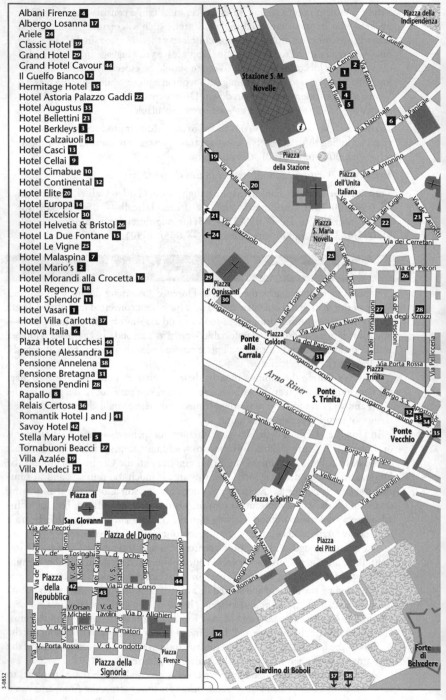
Albergo Losanna
Ariele
Classic Hotel
Grand Hotel
Grand Hotel Cavour
Il Guelfo Bianco
Hermitage Hotel
Hotel Astoria Palazzo Gaddi
Hotel Augustus
Hotel Bellettini
Hotel Berkleys
Hotel Calzaiuoli
Hotel Casci
Hotel Cellai
Hotel Cimabue
Hotel Continental
Hotel Elite
Hotel Europa
Hotel Excelsior
Hotel Helvetia & Bristol
Hotel La Due Fontane
Hotel Le Vigne
Hotel Malaspina
Hotel Mario's
Hotel Morandi alla Crocetta
Hotel Regency
Hotel Splendor
Hotel Vasari
Nuova Italia
Plaza Hotel Lucchesi
Pensione Alessandra
Pensione Annelena
Pensione Bretagna
Pensione Pendini
Rapallo
Relais Certosa
Romantik Hotel J and J
Savoy Hotel
Stella Mary Hotel
Tornabuoni Beacci
Villa Azalée
Villa Medeci

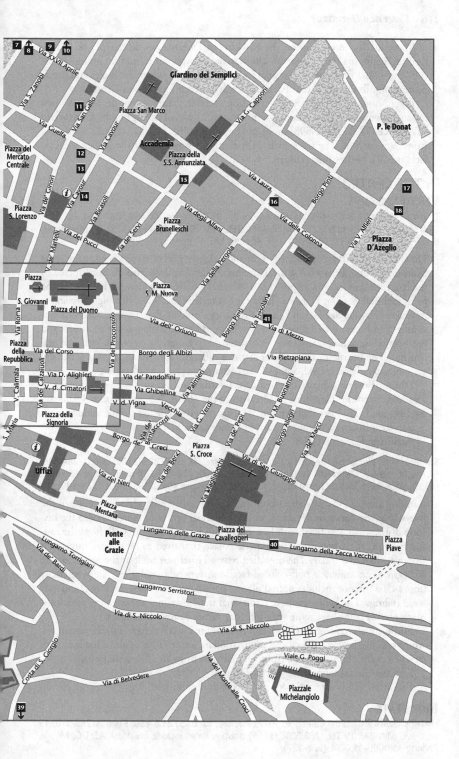

Many luxury hotels exist on the outskirts of Florence, as do cheaper boarding-houses. Again, these are acceptable alternatives if you don't mind the commute into the center. As a final option, consider lodging in Fiesole, where it's cooler and much more tranquil. Bus no. 7 runs back and forth between Fiesole and Centro.

If you should arrive without a reservation and don't want to wander around town on your own looking for a room, go in person (instead of calling) to the **Consorizio ITA office** (☎ **055/282-893**) in the rail terminal at Piazza della Stazione, open daily from 9am to 9pm. The Consorizio ITA charges a small fee for the service and collects the first night's room charge.

IN THE CENTRO
VERY EXPENSIVE

✪ **Hotel Helvetia & Bristol.** Via dei Pescioni 2, 50123 Firenze. ☎ **055/287-814.** Fax 055/ 288-353. 50 rms, 15 suites. A/C MINIBAR TV TEL. 420,000L–540,000L ($252–$324) double; 660,000L–1,400,000L ($396–$840) suite. AE, DC, MC, V. Parking 40,000L ($24).

Hotel Helvetia & Bristol is located in the most elegant part of Florence, just a few steps from the Duomo between Via dei Tornabuoni and Via degli Strozzi. Constructed in the late 19th century, and reopened in 1989 after a massive restoration, it was once the most exclusive hotel in Florence. Today it has reclaimed a lot of that old glory and is rivaled only by the Regency. It lacks the Regency's modern flair, however, and is rather somber and heavy, with draped windows, tasseled chairs, 15th-century paintings, and regal period furnishings. Strict attention was paid to preserving its original architectural features. The bedrooms come in about three different sizes, ranging from extremely generous to rather cramped. Some of the better rooms have whirlpool tubs.

Dining/Entertainment: The first-class Giardino d'Inverno (Winter Garden) was a gathering spot for Florentine intellectuals in the 1920s. It's now a cocktail bar serving light food. The main dining room, the Bristol, serves a deluxe cuisine (dinner only).

Services: Room service, baby-sitting, laundry, valet.

Facilities: Car-rental desk.

Savoy Hotel. Piazza della Repubblica 7, 50123 Firenze. ☎ **055/283-313.** Fax 055/284-840. 97 rms, 4 suites. A/C MINIBAR TV TEL. 410,000L–450,000L ($246–$270) double; from 550,000L ($330) suite. Rates include breakfast. AE, DC, MC, V. Parking 40,000L–50,000L ($24–$30).

Ranking after (a long way after) both the Grand and the Excelsior (see below), the five-star Savoy stands in the clamorous commercial center of Florence (also the historic district), an area filled with fine stores and just a 5-minute walk from the railway station. It's a five-story *fin-de-siècle* palace that used to be a more important stopover than it is today. The dignified Savoy Hotel was built at the height of the *belle époque* era and has a buff-colored facade with neoclassical trim. The predictably upper-class interior includes potted plants, period art, patterned carpeting, and coffered ceilings. The bedrooms have traditional Italian styling, although the pink-and-black marble baths have more style than the rather somber bedrooms.

Dining/Entertainment: Guests can dine in the hotel's elegant Tuscan restaurant, which features both a regional and international cuisine. There's also a bar area with frescoed walls reminiscent of a trompe l'oeil view from an 18th-century balcony.

Services: Room service, baby-sitting, laundry, valet.

Facilities: Limited facilities for persons with disabilities.

MODERATE

Hotel Calzaiuoli. Via dei Calzaiuoli, 50122 Firenze. ☎ **055/212-456.** Fax 055/268-310. 45 rms. A/C MINIBAR TV TEL. 260,000L ($156) double. Rates include breakfast. AE, DC, MC, V. Parking 35,000L–45,000L ($21–$27).

Hotel Calzaiuoli has one of the city's most desirable locations in terms of sightseeing, as the major attractions lie virtually on its doorstep. Although the building is old (it was a private home in the 1800s) and the location historic, the interior has been completely modernized in a rather severe contemporary style. The rooms are simple but comfortable, each furnished with functional and efficient pieces.

Pensione Pendini. Via degli Strozzi 2, 50123. ☎ **055/211-170.** Fax 055/281-807. 42 rms. TEL. 230,000L ($138) double. AE, DC, MC, V. Rates include breakfast. Parking 35,000L–40,000L ($21–$24).

Founded in 1879, the family-owned and -run Pensione Pendini offers an old-fashioned environment in a distinguished but faded setting. Your room may overlook the active piazza or front an inner courtyard (more peaceful). One of the oldest *pensioni* in Florence, it's located on the fourth floor of an arcaded building. The all-purpose lounge is furnished family style with a piano and card tables. The breakfast room, a redecorated large room inside one of the arcades, offers a view of the whole of Via degli Strozzi. All the bedrooms are soundproof, and some have quite a lot of character, with reproduction antiques. The bar/lounge is open 24 hours. The Pendini is not for everyone, but it's one of the long-enduring favorites among *pensione* fans visiting Florence. Only breakfast is served.

Tornabuoni Beacci. Via dei Tornabuoni 3, 50123 Firenze. ☎ **055/212-645.** Fax 055/283-594. 34 rms. A/C MINIBAR TV TEL. 250,000L–280,000L ($150–$168) double. Rates include breakfast. AE, DC, MC, V. Parking 30,000L ($18).

Tornabuoni Beacci is located near the Arno and Piazza Santa Trínita, on the city's principal shopping street. The *pensione* occupies the three top floors of a 14th-century *palazzo*. All its living rooms have been furnished in a tatty provincial style, with bowls of flowers, parquet floors, a formal fireplace, old paintings, murals, and rugs. Although it still has an aura of old-fashioned gentility, the hotel was recently renovated, with more air-conditioning added to some rooms. The roof terrace, surrounded by potted plants and flowers, is for late-afternoon drinks or breakfast. Dinner, typically Florentine and Italian dishes, is served here in summer. The view of the nearby churches, towers, and rooftops is worth experiencing. The bedrooms are moderately well furnished.

INEXPENSIVE

Pensione Bretagna. Lungarno Corsini 6, 50123 Firenze. ☎ **055/289-618.** Fax 055/289-619. 18 rms, 9 with bath. TV TEL 145,000L ($87) double without bath, 155,000L ($93) double with bath; 210,000L ($126) triple with bath. Rates include breakfast. AE, MC, V. Parking 30,000L ($18).

The centrally located Pensione Bretagna is in an early Renaissance palace that was the residence of Louis Napoléon in the 1820s, although it's a rather basic and simply furnished place today. It's a good cost-conscious choice though, and is run by a helpful staff, most of whom speak English. The rates depend on the plumbing, as some rooms don't have private bath. The bedrooms are rather plain, but the public rooms are impressive, with gilded stucco work, painted ceilings, fireplaces, and a balcony overlooking the Arno.

NEAR PIAZZA DEL DUOMO
MODERATE

Grand Hotel Cavour. Via del Proconsolo 3, 50122 Firenze. ☎ **055/282-461.** Fax 055/218-955. 92 rms. A/C MINIBAR TV TEL. 255,000L ($153) double. Rates include breakfast. AE, DC, MC, V. Parking 30,000L–55,000L ($18–$33).

Located opposite the Bargello Museum, between Via del Proconsolo and Via Dante Alighieri, the Grand Hotel Cavour, originally an elaborate 13th-century palace, stands on one of the busiest and noisiest streets in Florence. The hotel is located on an important corner of the city, near the Badia Church, between the houses of the Cerchi and Pazzi families. It once belonged to the Cerchis, and in the lounge you can see where the old courtyard was laid out. The Cavour maintains its architectural splendor. The coved main lounge, with its frescoed ceiling and crystal chandelier, is of special interest, as is the old chapel, now used as a dining room. The altar and confessional are still there. The ornate ceiling and stained-glass windows reflect superb crafting. The bedrooms are traditionally styled and comfortably furnished.

NEAR PIAZZA SANTA MARIA NOVELLA & TERMINI
VERY EXPENSIVE

Grand Hotel. Piazza Ognissanti 1, 50123 Firenze. ☎ **800/325-3589** in the U.S. and Canada, or 055/288-781. Fax 055/217-400. 90 rms, 17 suites. A/C MINIBAR TV TEL. 620,000L–750,000L ($372–$450) double; from 1,900,000L ($1,140) suite. AE, DC, MC, V. Parking from 50,000L ($30).

The Grand Hotel is a bastion of luxury. It fronts the Piazza Ognissanti and is across from the Hotel Excelsior, which is more luxurious with more facilities. Neither the Grand nor the Excelsior, although among the top three or four hotels of Florence, is as exclusive as the more refined Hotel Regency (see below). A hotel of history and tradition, the Grand is known for its halls and salons. Its rooms and suites have a refined elegance, and the most desirable overlook the Arno. Each bedroom contains silks, brocades, and real or reproduction antiques.

Dining/Entertainment: A highlight of the hotel is the restored Winter Garden, an enclosed court lined with arches where regional and seasonal specialties are served along with an array of international dishes. Guests gather at night in the Fiorino Bar to listen to piano music.

Services: Room service, baby-sitting, laundry, valet.

Facilities: Foreign currency exchange.

✪ Hotel Excelsior. Piazza Ognissanti 3, 50123 Firenze. ☎ **800/325-3535** in the U.S. and Canada, or 055/264-201. Fax 055/210-278. 172 rms, 23 suites. A/C MINIBAR TV TEL. 550,000L–640,000L ($330–$384) double; from 720,000L ($432) suite. AE, DC, MC, V. Parking 50,000L ($30).

Hotel Excelsior is the ultimate in well-ordered luxury in Florence. Grander than the Grand (see above), the Excelsior for years has reigned as the most famous luxury hotel in Florence. Cosmpolitan and sophisticated, it has the best trained staff in town, but in recent years more tranquil and less commercial establishments, including the Regency and Helvetia & Bristol, have been attracting some of its customers. But if you like glamor and glitz, check into the Excelsior (but be sure to make reservations well in advance). Part of the hotel was once owned by Carolina Bonaparte, sister of Napoléon. The present hotel was formed in 1937. The opulent bedrooms have 19th-century Florentine antiques and sumptuous fabrics. The spacious rooms offer lots of comfortable chairs, and baths with heated racks, thick terrycloth towels, and high ceilings. All the rooms reflect a heavy-handed style of decorating, and some are much more luxurious than others. In these old palaces, expect accommodations to come in a variety of configurations. Naturally, the rooms on the top floor with balconies overlooking the Arno and the Ponte Vecchio are the best and most sought after.

Dining/Entertainment: Il Cestello is the hotel's deluxe restaurant, serving an elegantly prepared international cuisine. The Donatello Bar is reviewed in "Florence After Dark," later in this chapter.

Services: Room service, baby-sitting, laundry, valet, express checkout, translation services.

Facilities: Foreign currency exchange.

Grand Hotel Villa Medici. Via il Prato 42, 50123 Firenze. ☎ **055/238-1331.** Fax 055/238-1336. 89 rms, 14 suites. A/C MINIBAR TV TEL. 450,000L–620,000L ($270–$372) double; 950,000L ($570) suite. AE, CB, DC, MC, V. Parking 45,000L–60,000L ($27–$36).

This old-time favorite—former stomping grounds of kings and princesses—is an 18th-century Medici palace lying two blocks southwest of the train station. Turned into a luxury hotel in 1962, it's an enduring favorite. In general this hotel appeals more to tradition-oriented Europeans than to Americans who may want more up-to-date facilities. Out back is a private garden (not Florence's finest), with a motel sized swimming pool. The most peaceful rooms front the garden. However, during the day there's noise from the convent school next door. The rooms are traditionally and often handsomely furnished, although rather cramped. Thick towels, hair dryers, and minibars are some of the amenities. We prefer the accommodations on the sixth floor, as they open onto terraces. The staff is one of the best trained in Florence.

Dining/Entertainment: The Lorenzo de' Medici Restaurant serves both international and Florentine cuisine. The restaurant is graced with marble pilasters and illuminated by Murano chandeliers, but the cuisine is only standard fare.

Services: Room service, baby-sitting, laundry, valet.

Facilities: Cleaning and pressing facilities, swimming pool.

EXPENSIVE

Albani Firenze. Via Fiume 12. 50123 Firenze. ☎ **055/26-030.** Fax 055/211-045. 77 rms, 3 suites. A/C MINIBAR TV TEL. 350,000L–440,000L ($210–$264) double; from 800,000L ($480) suite. AE, DC, MC, V.

In 1993, a respected nationwide chain transformed a run-down pensione, within a 10-minute walk from the Duomo, into one of the most appealing four-star luxury hotels in Florence. The setting is the august and dignified premises of what was originally built around 1900 as a private villa. Today, you'll find a grand setting with up-to-date comforts and *House & Garden*-style draperies, artwork, and architectural embellishments. The formal, high-ceilinged interiors sometimes verge on the theatrical, but are never forbidding. There's a restaurant on the premises, where lunch and dinners are served every day except Sunday.

Dining/Entertainment: A restaurant on the premises serves traditional Italian and international food. There's also a bar.

Services: Concierge, 24-hour room service, dry cleaning/laundry, newspaper delivery, valet parking.

Facilities: None.

Hotel Astoria Palazzo Gaddi. Via del Giglio 9, 50123 Firenze. ☎ **055/239-8095.** Fax 055/214-632. 90 rms, 5 suites. A/C MINIBAR TV TEL. 430,000L ($258) double; 800,000L ($480) suite. Rates include buffet breakfast. AE, DC, MC, V. Parking 40,000L ($24) nearby.

In spite of its location in a setting of cheap Termini hotels, this is an impressive and classic Renaissance palace, the finest in the area. The Hotel Astoria at one time housed the office of a now-defunct newspaper. In the 17th century John Milton wrote parts of *Paradise Lost* in one of the bedrooms. This 16th-century palace has been renovated and turned into a serviceable and enduring choice, with a helpful staff and experienced management. From the bedrooms on the upper floors you'll have a view over the terra-cotta rooftops of Florence. The bedrooms have stylish and traditional furnishings for the most part, although some are decorated in a more sterile modern manner. The bathrooms are first-rate, with fluffy towels and hair dryers. The front rooms are the noisiest as they overlook a traffic-clogged avenue.

Dining/Entertainment: The garden-style Palazzo Gaddi restaurant serves an international cuisine.

Services: Room service, laundry, baby-sitting.

Facilities: Car-rental desk, shopping boutique, foreign currency exchange.

MODERATE

Hotel Malaspina. Piazza della Indipendenza 24. 50129 Firenze. ☎ **055/489-869.** Fax 055/474-809. 32 rms. MINIBAR TV TEL. 260,000L ($156) double. Rates include buffet breakfast. AE, DC, MC, V.

Set within a 10-minute walk north of the Duomo, this hotel opened in 1993 within the 19th-century premises of what was originally a dormitory for students at a nearby school of dentistry. The inviting interior has been carefully renovated and outfitted with dignified, traditional furniture that fits gracefully into the airy, high-ceilinged public rooms and bedrooms. Windows are big, and floors tend to be covered in either glazed or terra-cotta tiles. Each room contains a safe for locking up valuables. Breakfast is the only meal served.

Villa Azalée. Viale Fratelli Rosselli 44, 50123 Firenze. ☎ **055/214-242.** Fax 055/268-264. 24 rms. A/C MINIBAR TV TEL. 255,000L ($153) double; 315,000L ($189) triple. Rates include buffet breakfast. AE, DC, MC, V. Parking from 30,000L ($18).

The Villa Azalée, a handsome structure set on a street corner with a big garden, is a remake of a private home originally built in the 1860s and transformed into a hotel in 1964. The personal touch of the owners is reflected in both the atmosphere and the tasteful decor, which features tall, white-paneled doors with ornate brass fittings, parquet floors, crystal chandeliers, and antiques intermixed with credible reproductions. The lounge is like a private home, and the bedrooms are distinctive (one, in particular, boasts a flouncy canopy bed). The hotel is a 5-minute walk from the rail station. Guests can rent bicycles at the hotel for 5,000L ($3) per day.

INEXPENSIVE

Ariele. Via Magenta 11, 50123 Firenze. ☎ **055/211-509.** Fax 055/268-521. 40 rms. AC TV TEL. 210,000L ($126) double; 240,000L ($144) triple. Rates include breakfast. AE, DC, MC, V. Parking 15,000L ($9).

Located just a block from the Arno, the Ariele, an old corner villa that has been converted into a roomy *pensione*, bills itself as "Your Home in Florence." The building is architecturally impressive, with large salons and lofty ceilings. The furnishings, however, combine antique with functional. The bedrooms are a grab bag of comfort.

✪ **Hotel Bellettini.** Via dei Cerretani, 50123 Firenze. ☎ **055/213-561.** Fax 055/283-551. 27 rms, 22 with bath. A/C TEL. 140,000L ($84) double without bath; 170,000L ($102) double with bath. Rates include buffet breakfast. AE, DC, MC, V.

For the kind of historic ambience this Renaissance palazzo offers, plus its good location in the heart of town, midway between the Duomo and the railway station, this hotel charges refreshingly reasonable rates. It was built in the 1300s, with a history of innkeeping that goes back at least 300 years, and is maintained by a pair of Tuscany-born sisters (Marzia and Gina), who, along with their helpful staff, are well versed in explaining the labyrinth of Florence's streets to confused newcomers. This place is so traditional—with terra-cotta floors, beamed ceilings, and touches of stained glass—that you expect Henry James, Elizabeth Barrett Browning, or Nathanial

Hawthorne to check in at any minute. Bedrooms are plain, although occasionally somewhat ascetic, but comfortable. About half the rooms have TV, and many have sweeping views of Florence that turn even a postcard-jotter into E. M. Forster.

Hotel Berkleys. Via Fiume 11, 50123 Firenze. ☎ and fax **055/212-302**. 9 rms. TV TEL. 140,000L ($84) double; 180,000L ($108) triple; 215,000L ($129) quad. Rates include breakfast. MC, V.

This pleasant but modest hotel occupies the top floor of a 19th-century apartment building whose lower floors contain two less desirable two-star hotels. It lies about a block east of the railway station. The owners, the Andreoli family, are polite and friendly, and there's an employee on duty throughout the day and night. The simple lobby leads into a breakfast nook and a bar area, where drinks are served on request. The bedrooms are simple but clean. Of course, you stay here for the prices, not for any grandeur.

Hotel Elite. Via della Scala 12, 50123 Firenze. ☎ **055/215-395**. 8 rms, 3 with shower only, 5 with bath (shower). TV TEL. 100,000L ($60) double with shower only, 160,000L ($96) double with bath. Rates include breakfast. No credit cards. Parking from 30,000L ($18).

The Elite is an attractive little *pensione* worthy of being better known. It lies two floors above street level in a 19th-century apartment building about a two-block walk from the railway station. It's also convenient for exploring most of the major monuments. The owner, Maurizio Maccarini, speaks English and is a helpful, welcoming host. The small hotel rents light and airy bedrooms, divided equally between singles and doubles. Some singles have only a shower (no toilet).

Hotel Le Vigne. Piazza S. Maria Novella 24, 50123 Firenze. ☎ **055/294-449**. Fax 055/230-2263. 19 rms, 16 with bath; 2 suites. A/C TEL. 150,000L ($90) double with bath; 200,000L ($120) triple with bath; 250,000L ($150) suite for four. Rates include buffet breakfast. AE, DC, MC, V. Parking 25,000L ($15).

Hotel Le Vigne offers comfortably furnished bedrooms and enjoys a prime location on one of the most central squares of Florence. Its sitting room overlooks the square. An Italian family took over this 15th-century building and restored it in the early 1990s, preserving the old features, including frescoes, whenever possible. The small hotel is on the first floor (second to Americans) of this old-fashioned building. Five of the units are air-conditioned, and a few singles don't have baths. Breakfast, a generous self-service buffet, is the only meal served.

Hotel Mario's. Via Faenza 89, 50123 Firenze. ☎ **055/216-801**. Fax 055/212-039. 16 rms. A/C TV TEL. 130,000L–220,000L ($78–$132) double; 210,000L–270,000L ($126–$162) triple. Rates include breakfast. AE, DC, MC, V.

Two blocks from the train station and close to San Lorenzo Market, this winning choice on the first floor of an old Florentine building has been a hotel since 1872 when the "Room with a View" crowd started arriving in Florence in search of the glory of the Renaissance. The spotless little hotel has been completely restored and furnished in a typical Florentine style. Mario Noce is a gracious host, and he and his staff speak English. Although you'll find cheaper inns in Florence, the service and hospitality make Mario's worth your lire. Some of the rooms open onto a small garden, and furnishings are often antique reproductions, including armoires and wrought-iron headboards. Fresh flowers and fresh fruit are put out daily. Some of the beams in the public areas are 300 years old.

Hotel Vasari. Via B. Cennini 9–11, 50123 Firenze. ☎ **055/212-753**. Fax 055/294-246. 30 rms. A/C MINIBAR TV TEL. 150,000L–210,000L ($90–$126) double. Rates include breakfast. AE, DC, MC, V. Parking 15,000L ($9).

👪 Family-Friendly Hotels

Hotel Casci *(see p. 223)*   This inexpensive gem has a great location in the historic district, and many of its bedrooms are rented as triples and quads, ideal for families.

Nuova Italia *(see p. 222)*   Families get special discounts at this 17th-century building near the rail station, and the hotel offers some very spacious rooms suitable for large broods.

Relais Certosa *(see p. 229)*   Families wanting to escape the congestion of over-crowded Florence can head to this *relais* hotel—a former monastery 10 minutes southwest of the city. Set on 5 acres of land, it offers wide-open spaces and an inviting, family-type atmosphere.

Vasari has ties to some of Florence's most prestigious literary associations, thanks to the fact that for several years it was the home of 19th-century French poet Alphonse de la Martine. Originally built in the 1840s as a private home, it was a run-down two-star hotel until 1993, when its owners poured money into its renovation and upgraded it to one of the most reasonably priced three-star hotels in town. Its three stories are connected by elevator, and the bedrooms are comfortable, albeit somewhat Spartan, and clean. Some of the public areas retain their original elaborate vaulting.

Nuova Italia. Via Faenza 26, 50123 Firenze. ☎ **055/287-508.** Fax 055/210-941. 20 rms. A/C TEL. 130,000L–180,000L ($78–$108) double; 180,000L–230,000L ($108–$138) triple; 220,000L–260,000L ($132–$156) quad. Rates include breakfast. AE, MC, V. Parking 35,000L–40,000L ($21–$24) nearby.

This little hotel, situated in a renovated 17th-century building in the center of Florence, has been welcoming Frommer's readers since 1958. All the bedrooms have private bath, soundproof windows, and air-conditioning, and are pleasantly furnished and decorated with paintings and posters. Some large rooms are suitable for families, to whom the management—the Viti family—grants special discounts. The Vitis, who happen to serve a fantastic cappuccino, also help guests figure out how to get around Florence and offer tips on where to shop and what to do. The hotel is located only a block from the railway station, near the San Lorenzo Market and the Medici Chapels. Despite the soundproofed windows, some readers have complained about the noise here.

Stella Mary Hotel. Via Fiume 17, 50123 Firenze. ☎ **055/215-694.** Fax 055/264-206. 7 rms. TV TEL. 65,000L–135,000L ($39–$81) double; 95,000L–165,000L ($57–$99) triple. AE, MC, V. Parking 27,000L ($16.20).

Stella Mary Hotel is a small *pensione* lying 12 blocks from the train station and around the corner from a busy bus station. The English-speaking owners, Mrs. Vittoria and her son, personally operate a clean and comfortable "home in Firenze." The rooms are cozy and full of light, and a sitting room with a TV set is reserved for guests. Although the hotel only serves breakfast, the staff can recommend several good restaurants nearby. The hotel, in a classic Florentine-style building with an elevator, is only a short walk from the San Lorenzo Church and the San Lorenzo Market.

NEAR PIAZZA SAN MARCO
MODERATE

Hotel Cellai. Via 27 Aprile, 14. 50129 Firenze. ☎ **055/489-291.** Fax 055/470-387. 45 rms. A/C MINIBAR TV TEL. 250,000L ($150) double. AE, DC, MC, V.

The origins of this hotel date to the 1930s, when members of the Cellai family first started renting a handful of rooms. Eventually the enterprise grew to incorporate the large-scale structure you see today. Set two blocks east of the landmark Piazza della Indipendenza, a 10-minute walk north of the Duomo, it has a dignified, much-used series of public rooms with terra-cotta floors and architectural details. All rooms are individually decorated, some with appealing contemporary paintings. No two are alike, but it sometimes pays to ask for a room, if one is available, with a varnished wooden ceiling supported by very old beams—these rooms seem more appealing and a bit warmer than their neighbors.

Hotel Le Due Fontane. Piazza della SS. Annunziata 14, 50122 Firenze. ☎ **055/210-185.** Fax 055/294-461. 53 rms, 3 suites. A/C MINIBAR TV TEL. 260,000L ($156) double; 400,000L ($240) suite. Rates include breakfast. AE, CB, DC, DISC, MC, V. Parking 20,000L ($12).

Hotel Le Due Fontane is a small palace on the best-known Renaissance square in Florence, right in the heart of the artistic center of the city, within an easy walk of the Duomo. Although the building dates back to the 14th century, the hotel has been completely renovated and modernized, and today it offers simply but tastefully furnished bedrooms that are well kept if a bit uninspired. The upper-floor rooms offer the most tranquil night's sleep. Services and facilities include laundry, personal hotel bus service, car-rental facilities, shopping boutiques, a concierge, a business center, baby-sitting, and a bar.

Il Guelfo Bianco. Via Cavour 29. 50129 Firenze. ☎ **055/288-330.** Fax 055/295-203. 39 rms, 1 suite. A/C MINIBAR TV TEL. 220,000L–260,000L ($132–$156) double; 300,000L–400,000L ($180–$240) suite. AE, DC, MC, V. Parking 12,000L ($7.20).

This comfortable, well-positioned hotel consists of a pair of side-by-side 15th-century buildings, which would have been interconnected with a hallway long ago except for the necessary permission from the city's unyielding construction committees. Renovations occurred most recently in 1989 and 1994. Most rooms have timbered ceilings and views over the historic neighborhood. The white-walled bedrooms contain simple, conservatively contemporary furniture.

Rapallo. Via Santa Caterina d'Alessandria 7, 50129 Firenze. ☎ **055/472-412.** Fax 055/470-385. 30 rms. MINIBAR TV TEL. 190,000L–273,000L ($114–$163.80) double; 256,000L–381,000L ($153.60–$228.60) triple. Rates include breakfast. AE, DC, MC, V. Parking 35,000L ($21).

Although the Rapallo is not typical of Florence, it is, nevertheless, completely revamped and inviting. The small lounge is brightened by planters, Oriental rugs, and barrel stools set in the corners for drinking and conversation. The bedrooms are furnished mostly with blond-wood suites, quite pleasant, and all have a private safe and, upon request, a TV. The hotel is within walking distance of the railway station.

INEXPENSIVE

Hotel Casci. Via Cavour 13, 50129 Firenze. ☎ **055/211-686.** Fax 055/239-6461. 25 rms. TV TEL. 100,000L–160,000L ($60–$96) double; 135,000L–215,000L ($81–$129) triple; 170,000L–270,000L ($102–$162) quad. Rates include breakfast. AE, DC, MC, V. Parking 35,000L–40,000L ($21–$24).

The Casci is a well-run little hotel in the historic district, 200 yards from the main railway station and 100 yards from Piazza del Duomo. As one reader wrote, "For *location, location, location,* there's nothing better in Florence." The building dates from the 14th century, and some of the public rooms feature the original frescoes. Gioacchio Rossini, the famous composer of *The Barber of Seville* and *William Tell,* lived in the building between 1851 and 1855. The hotel is both traditional and modern, and the English-speaking reception staff looks after guests very well. The bedrooms are comfortably furnished, and each contains a hair dryer. Each year four or five bedrooms are upgraded and renovated. The few rooms that overlook the busy street are soundproof.

Hotel Cimabue. Via B. Lupi 7, 50129 Firenze. ☎ **055/471-989.** Fax 055/475-601. 16 rms. TV TEL. 160,000L–180,000L ($96–$108) double. Rates include buffet breakfast. AE, DC, MC, V. Parking 22,000L ($13.20).

This building was constructed in 1904 as a private, Tuscan-style *palazzo*. The most charming bedrooms are the five that contain original frescoed ceilings. Four of these lie one floor above street level, the fifth on the ground floor. The hotel was last renovated in 1991, but contains Liberty-style, turn-of-the-century antiques that correspond to the building's age. Its Belgian-Italian management team extends a warm, multicultural welcome.

Hotel Europa. Via Cavour 14, 50129 Firenze. ☎ **055/210-361.** Fax 055/210-361. 13 rms. TV TEL. 160,000L ($96) double. Rates include breakfast. AE, MC, V.

Located two long blocks north of the Duomo, this 16th-century building has functioned as a family-run hotel since 1925. Despite the antique appearance of the simple exterior, much of the interior has been modernized, although the hotel contains plenty of homey touches. All but four of the bedrooms overlook the back, usually opening onto a view of the campanile of the Duomo. Those that face the street are noisier, but benefit from double glazing that keeps out at least some of the traffic noise. Breakfast is the only meal served.

Hotel Morandi alla Crocetta. Via Laura 50, 50121 Firenze. ☎ **055/234-4747.** Fax 055/248-0954. 10 rms. A/C MINIBAR TV TEL. 210,000L ($126) double; 280,000L ($168) triple. AE, DC, MC, V. Parking 14,000L–18,000L ($8.40–$10.80).

This small, charming hotel is administered by one of the most experienced hoteliers in Florence, a sprightly matriarch named Katherine Doyle who came to Florence from her native Ireland when she was 12. It contains all the elements needed for a Florence *pensione* and is situated on a little-visited backstreet near a university building. The structure was built in the 1500s as a convent. The bedrooms have been tastefully restored, filled with framed examples of 19th-century needlework, beamed ceilings, and antiques. In the best Tuscan tradition, the tall windows are sheltered from the summer sunlight with heavy draperies. You register in a high-ceilinged and austere salon filled with Persian carpets. The hotel lies right behind the Archeological Museum and two blocks from the Accademia.

Hotel Splendor. Via S. Gallo 30, 50129 Firenze. ☎ **055/483-427.** Fax 055/461-276. 31 rms, 25 with bath (tub or shower). TV TEL. 140,000L ($84) double without bath, 200,000L ($120) double with bath; 270,000L ($162) triple with bath. Rates include buffet breakfast. AE, MC, V. Parking 30,000L ($18).

Although Hotel Splendor is within a 10-minute walk of the Duomo, the residential neighborhood it occupies is a world away from the milling hordes of the tourist district. The hotel occupies three high-ceilinged floors of a 19th-century apartment building. Its elegantly faded public rooms evoke the kind of family-run *pensione* that early in the century attracted the genteel, "Room with a View"–type crowd who descended on Florence from northern Europe for prolonged art-related visits. This is the domain of the Masoero family, whose homelike rooms contain an eclectic array of semiantique furniture. All the singles have baths. There is no restaurant, but room service is available.

NEAR PIAZZA SANTA CROCE
VERY EXPENSIVE

✪ Romantic Hotel J and J. Via di Mezzo 20, 50121 Firenze. ☎ **055/234-5005.** Fax 055/ 240-282. 15 rms, 5 suites. A/C MINIBAR TV TEL. 350,000L–500,000L ($210–$300) double; 550,000L–650,000L ($330–$390) suite. Rates include breakfast. AE, DC, MC, V. Parking 35,000L ($21).

This charming hotel, located within a 5-minute walk of the Church of Santa Croce, was originally built in the 16th century as a monastery. It underwent massive restoration in 1990 and was soon after transformed into the hotel you'll see today. Although acquired by the Romantic Hotel chain in 1994, the hotel has managed to preserve its familial atmosphere. You'll find many sitting areas throughout the property, including a flagstone-covered courtyard with stone columns, and a salon with vaulted ceilings and several preserved frescoes. The bedrooms combine modern furniture, some of it built in, with the monastery's original beamed ceilings. The suites usually contain sleeping lofts, and in some cases rooftop balconies overlooking Florence's historic center. There's a bar on the premises, but breakfast is the only meal served.

Dining/Entertainment: There's a very small bar in the lobby. Other than breakfast, no meals are served.

Services: Very limited room service (drinks and small snacks); it's usually—but not always, depending on the staff—available 24 hours. Dry cleaning/laundry, valet parking.

Facilities: None.

EXPENSIVE

Plaza Hotel Lucchesi. Lungarno della Zecca Vecchia 38, 50122 Firenze. ☎ **800/223-9832** in the U.S., or 055/26-236. Fax 055/248-0921. 97 rms, 10 suites. A/C MINIBAR TV TEL. 350,000L–500,000L ($210–$300) double; 630,000L ($378) suite. Rates include breakfast. AE, DC, MC, V. Parking 25,000L–40,000L ($15–$24).

Plaza Hotel Lucchesi—often a favorite with tour groups—was originally built in 1860 but has been renovated many times since then. It lies along the banks of the Arno, a 10-minute walk from the Duomo and a few paces from the imposing Church of Santa Maria della Croce. It also lies six blocks east of the Uffizi. Its interior decor includes lots of glossy mahogany, acres of marble, and masses of fresh flowers. Even though the bedrooms feature up-to-date equipment, they seem dated. Nevertheless, they're comfortable and well maintained, with many conveniences, including trouser presses and well-stocked bathrooms. About 20 accommodations open onto private terraces or balconies, some with enviable views over the heart of historic Florence.

Dining/Entertainment: A large breakfast buffet and dinner are served in the sunny lobby-level restaurant, La Serra. The food is only average, however; you'll fare better at one of the independently run restaurants nearby. There's also a bar.

Services: Room service (24 hours), baby-sitting, laundry, valet.

Facilities: Car-rental desk.

NEAR THE PONTE VECCHIO
EXPENSIVE

Hotel Augustus. Vicolo del'Oro 5, 50123 Firenze. ☎ **055/283-054.** Fax 055/268-557. 62 rms, 8 suites. A/C MINIBAR TV TEL. 420,000L ($252) double; 550,000L ($330) suite. Rates include buffet breakfast. AE, DC, MC, V. Parking 30,000L–40,000L ($18–$24).

Hotel Augustus is for those who require modern comforts in a historic setting. The Ponte Vecchio is just a short stroll away, as is the Uffizi Gallery. The exterior is rather pillbox modern, but the interior seems light, bright, and comfortable. The expansive lounge and drinking area is like an illuminated cave, with a curving ceiling and built-in conversation areas. Some of the bedrooms open onto little private balconies with garden furniture. The decor in the bedrooms consists of relatively simple provincial pieces, and the overall effect is rather lackluster but well maintained. Views of the Arno are often blocked by neighboring buildings. Laundry, baby-sitting, and 24-hour room service are provided.

Hotel Continental. Lungarno Acciaiuoli 2, 50123 Firenze. ☎ **055/282-392.** Fax 055/283-139. 48 rms, 1 suite. A/C MINIBAR TV TEL. 350,000L–450,000L ($210–$270) double; 530,000L–750,000 ($318–$450) suite. Rates include continental breakfast. AE, DC, MC, V. Parking 35,000L–40,000L ($21–$24).

Located at the entrance of the Ponte Vecchio, Hotel Continental occupies some select real estate and is a better choice than its sibling, the Hotel Augustus. Through the lounge windows and from some of the bedrooms you can see the little jewelry and leather shops that flank the much-painted bridge. Despite its perch in the center of historic Florence, the hotel was created in the 1960s, so its style of accommodation is utilitarian, with functional furniture that's softened by decorative accessories. The hotel was overhauled in 1992. You reach your bedroom by the elevator or by climbing a wrought-iron staircase (note that parts of the old stone structure have been retained). The management likes to put up North Americans, knowing they'll be attracted to the roof terrace, a vantage point for viewing Piazzale Michelangiolo, the Pitti Palace, the Duomo, the campanile, and Fiesole. Artists fight to get the penthouse suite up in the tower (Torre Guelfa dei Consorti).

Dining/Entertainment: There's a small bar, but no restaurant.

Services: Concierge (7am to midnight), room service, dry cleaning/laundry, baby-sitting, and valet parking.

Facilities: None.

MODERATE

Hermitage Hotel. Vicolo Marzio 1, Piazza del Pesce I, 50122 Firenze. ☎ **055/287-216.** Fax 055/212-208. 29 rms. AC TV TEL. 240,000L–310,000L ($144–$186) double; 370,000L ($222) triple; 450,000L ($270) family room. Rates include breakfast. MC, V. Parking 30,000L–40,000L ($18–$24).

The offbeat, intimate Hermitage Hotel is a charming place to stay right on the Arno. It has a rooftop sun terrace providing a view of much of Florence, including the nearby Uffizi. You can take your breakfast under a leafy arbor surrounded by potted roses and geraniums. The success of this small hotel has much to do with its English-speaking owner, Vincenzo Scarcelli, who has made the Hermitage an extension of his home, furnishing it in part with antiques and well-chosen reproductions. Best of all is his warmth toward guests, many of whom keep coming back.

The extremely small bedrooms are pleasantly furnished, many with Tuscan antiques, rich brocades, and good beds. The tiled baths are superb and contain lots of gadgets. Breakfast is served in a dignified, beam-ceilinged dining room. The rooms overlooking the Arno have the most scenic view, and they've been fitted with double-glass windows that reduce the traffic noise by 40%.

INEXPENSIVE

Pensione Alessandra. Borgo SS Apostoli 17, 50123 Firenze. ☎ **055/283-438.** Fax 055/210-619. 25 rms, 15 with bath. TEL. 130,000L ($78) double without bath, 175,000L ($105) double with bath. Rates include breakfast. AE, MC, V.

Within a block of the quays of the Arno, near the Ponte Vecchio, this is a three-story, two-star, completely unpretentious *pensione*. Although the facade has retained some of its 15th-century severity, the bedrooms inside have been modernized into efficient, if not particularly luxurious, accommodations that many visitors find well suited to their needs. Only those rooms on the uppermost floor are air-conditioned. Some of the rooms contain TV. Breakfast is the only meal served.

NEAR PIAZZA MASSIMO D'AZEGLIO

Piazza Massimo d'Azeglio is a 12-minute walk northeast of the historic core of Florence.

EXPENSIVE

✪ **Hotel Regency.** Piazza Massimo d'Azeglio 3, 50121 Firenze. ☎ **055/245-247.** Fax 055/234-6735. 29 rms, 5 suites. A/C MINIBAR TV TEL. 450,000L–580,000L ($270–$348) double; from 600,000L ($360) suite. Rates include breakfast. AE, DC, MC, V. Parking 45,000L ($27).

Much less overtly commercial than either the Grand or the Excelsior, the Regency is an intimate villa of taste and exclusivity. It's like lodging in a grand private residence, and to many savvy (and well-heeled) travelers it's *the* place to stay in Florence today. It lies a bit apart from the shopping and sightseeing center of Florence, but it's only a 15-minute stroll to the cathedral. And although its location isn't central (a blessing for tranquility seekers), it's conveniently and quickly reached by taxi or bus. This well-built, old-style villa, a member of Relais & Châteaux, has its own garden across from a park in a residential area of the city. This luxurious hideaway, filled with stained glass, paneled walls, and reproduction antiques, offers exquisitely furnished rooms, including some special rooms on the top floor with walk-out terraces.

Dining/Entertainment: The attractive dining room, Relais le Jardin, is renowned for its *alta cucina.* You can also take your meals in the well-lit winter garden.

Services: Room service (24 hours), baby-sitting, laundry, valet.

Facilities: Garden.

INEXPENSIVE

Albergo Losanna. Via Vittorio Alfieri 9, 50121 Firenze. ☎ and fax **055/245-840.** 10 rms, 4 with bath; 1 suite. TEL. 100,000L ($60) double without bath, 120,000L ($72) double with bath; 210,000L ($126) suite. Rates include breakfast. AE, MC, V. Parking 30,000L–35,000L ($18–$21).

A good, inexpensive choice, the Albergo Losanna is a tiny, family-run place off Viale Antonio Gramsci, between Piazzale Donatello and Piazza Massimo d'Azeglio. This affordable place offers utter simplicity and cleanliness as well as insight into a typical Florentine atmosphere. Buses stop a block and a half away. The bedrooms, all doubles, are homey and well kept, but the furnishings are simple and a bit tired.

ACROSS THE ARNO
EXPENSIVE

Hotel Villa Carlotta. Via Michele di Lando 3, 50125 Firenze. ☎ **055/220-530.** Fax 055/233-6147. 32 rms. A/C MINIBAR TV TEL. 360,000L–390,000L ($216–$234) double. Rates include breakfast. AE, DC, MC, V. Free parking.

The lavish renovations that the owner poured into her distinguished establishment transformed it into one of the most charming smaller hotels in Florence. It was built during the Edwardian age as a private villa and acquired in the 1950s by Carlotta Buchholz, who named it after herself. The aura here is still very much like that of a private villa, and it's located in a residential section of the city. In 1985 all bedrooms were upgraded with the addition of pink or blue silk wallpaper, reproduction antiques, silk bedspreads, private safety-deposit boxes, and crystal chandeliers; each also has a view of the surrounding garden. The hotel is only a 10-minute walk from the Ponte Vecchio; by taxi, it's a 5-minute ride.

Dining/Entertainment: The dining room, Il Bobolino, serves meals ranging from fresh salads to full culinary regalias.

Services: Room service, baby-sitting, laundry, valet.

Facilities: Garden, car-rental desk.

MODERATE

Pensione Annalena. Via Romana 34, 50125 Firenze. ☎ **055/222-402.** Fax 055/222-403. 20 rms. TV TEL. 250,000L ($150) double. Rates include breakfast. AE, DC, MC, V. Parking 20,000L ($12).

In existence since the 15th century, Pensione Annalena has had many owners, including the Medici family. Once a convent, in the past three-quarters of a century it has been a haven for artists, poets, sculptors, and writers (Mary McCarthy once wrote of its importance as a cultural center). During a great deal of that period it was the domain of the late sculptor Olinto Calastri. Now it's owned by Claudio Salvestrini, who attracts paying guests sympathetic to the *pensione*'s special qualities. Most of the simply furnished and rather severe accommodations overlook a garden. Don't be put off by this hotel's lack of air-conditioning, as the high ceilings and thick masonry walls almost guarantee a relatively constant and comfortable interior temperature throughout the summer. During the war the Annalena was the center of much of the underground, as many Jews and rebel Italians found safety hidden away in an underground room behind a secret door. The *pensione* is about a 5-minute walk from the Pitti Palace, 10 minutes from the Ponte Vecchio.

INEXPENSIVE

Classic Hotel. Viale Machiavelli 25, 50125 Firenze. ☎ **055/229-3512.** Fax 055/229-353. 19 rms, 3 suites. 190,000L ($114) double; 310,000L ($186) suite. AE, DC, MC, V.

Located within a 20-minute walk south of Il Duomo, this hotel occupies the stately pink-walled premises of what was originally built during the 19th century as a private villa. Set near the Porto Romano, it has its own garden where vines climb over a network of arbors and trellises. Inside you'll find cool interiors with high ceilings and either glazed tile or terra-cotta floors and comfortable bedrooms painted in pale colors with a medley of conservatively modern or traditional furniture. Don't expect opulence—this isn't that kind of hotel. Instead, you'll find an appealing, low-key, and completely unpretentious place geared to the tastes of an international body of sightseers.

ON THE OUTSKIRTS
AT COLLI

Torre di Bellosguardo. 2 Via Roti Michelozzi, 50124 Firenze. ☎ **055/229-8145.** Fax 055/229-008. 10 rms, 6 suites. MINIBAR TV TEL. 390,000L ($234) double; from 490,000L ($294) suite. MC, V.

Set on a hilltop near the south bank of the Arno, less than 2 miles southwest of the Duomo, this hotel occupies the palatial premises of what originated in the 1300s as a private villa. Until the 1950s, it functioned as a private home. A swimming pool is set within a sprawling park and garden that by standards so close to the city center is very, very large. You'll register under the frescoed ceiling of what used to be a ballroom, and the high-ceilinged bedrooms evoke the grandeur, albeit in a simplified manner, of another age. Plumbing fixtures are up-to-date and stylish, however, in vivid contrast to the otherwise antique setting. Rooms are not air-conditioned, but because of the building's site atop of a breezy hilltop, it isn't really missed.

Dining/Entertainment: There's a small bar, but no restaurant.

Services: Concierge, 24-hour room service (drinks, not food), valet parking.
Facilities: None.

AT GALLUZZO

Relais Certosa. Via di Colle Ramole 2, 50124 Firenze. ☎ **800/223-9832** in the U.S., or 055/204-7171. Fax 055/268-575. 63 rms, 6 suites. A/C MINIBAR TV TEL. 380,000L ($228) double; 550,000L ($330) suite. Rates include breakfast. DC, MC, V. Take the Rome–Milan expressway to exit A1, "Firenze/Certosa"; go 300 yards and turn left on a signposted road leading to the hotel.

The four-story Relais Certosa is set on 5 acres of land with tennis courts. It was originally a guesthouse for the nearby monastery, but during the Renaissance it became the villa that stands today. After centuries of use in private hands, it was converted into a hotel in the 1970s, and today could easily become your home in Florence. Convenient for motorists who want to avoid the hysterical city center, it's only 10 minutes from the monumental district and 5 minutes from the Rome–Milan expressway. Its rooms are well furnished, and each has individual climate control. Somehow the owners, the Bettoja family, have managed to blend Renaissance charm and style with modern comfort. All rooms face a park with views of the Tuscan hills and the Certosa monastery. There's parking space for 200 cars.

Dining/Entertainment: The Greenhouse Restaurant offers guests and nonguests alike some of the best Tuscan dining in the area, featuring regional specialties as well as continental dishes. Guests also enjoy a garden and terrace for drinks and snacks and a bar.

Services: Room service, laundry, valet.
Facilities: Tennis courts, parking.

4 Dining

The Florentine table has always been set with the abundance provided by the Tuscan countryside. That means the region's best olive oil and wine, such as chianti; succulent fruits and vegetables; fresh fish from the coast; and game in season. Meat-lovers all over Italy sing the praise of *bistecca alla fiorentina,* a thick and juicy steak on the bone often served with white Tuscan beans.

The Tuscan cuisine (except for some of its hair-raising specialties) should please most North Americans, as it's simply flavored, without rich spices, and based on the hearty, bountiful produce brought in from the hills. Florentine restaurants are not generally as acclaimed by gourmets as those of Rome, although good, moderately priced establishments abound. Florentines often assert that the cooking in the other regions of Italy "offends the palate."

IN THE CENTRO
MODERATE

Al Lume di Candela. Via delle Terme 23R. ☎ **055/294-566.** Reservations required. Main courses 20,000L–30,000L ($12–$18). AE, MC, V. Mon–Sat 7:30–11pm. Closed 1 week in Aug. TUSCAN/INTERNATIONAL.

Established in 1948, Al Lume di Candela is uniquely located in a 13th-century tower that was partially leveled when its patrician family fell from grace (the prestige of Tuscan families was once reflected in how high their family towers soared). The restaurant offers a typically Florentine cuisine in a tavern decor, although candlelight makes for a romantic atmosphere. In the past, celebrities were known to patronize the place. The food is precise and often inventive, combining rich tastes and unusual flavors. Dishes include taglierini with sage and porcini mushrooms; a very light

Florence Dining

Al Lume di Candela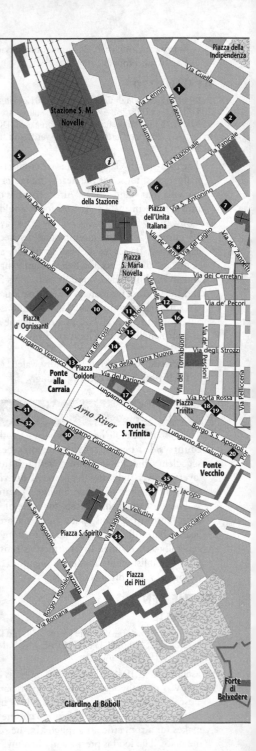
Buca dell' Orafo 21
Buca Lapi 12
Buca Mario 11
Cafaggi 4
Cantinetta Antinori 16
Cibreo 28
Da Ganino 39
Da Pennello 38
Del Fagioli 22
Don Chisciotte 1
Gelateria Vivoli 24
Harry's Bar 13
Il Cavallino 40
I Quattro Amici 5
I' Toscano 3
La Baraonda 27
La Carabaccia 10
La Nandina 20
Le Capannina di Sante 29
Le Fonticine 2
Le Mossacce 36
Le Quattro Stagioni 33
Mamma Gina 35
Oliviero 19
Osteria Numero Uno 15
Paoli 37
Pierot 32
Ristorante Dino 26
Ristorante Otello 6
Sabatini 8
Sostanza 9
Trattoria Angiolino 30
Trattoria Antellesi 7
Trattoria Cammillo 34
Trattoria Coco Lezzone 17
Trattoria Garga 14
Trattoria Pallottino 23
Trattoria Vittoria 31
Vecchia Firenze 25

3-0853

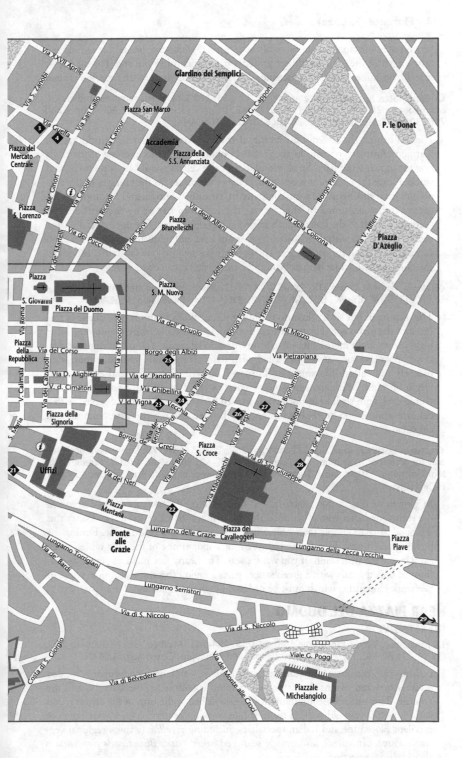

version of house-smoked salmon; veal chops stuffed with white beans *(cannellini)* and arugula; entrecôte (sirloin) of beef grilled with pepper, olive oil, and Tuscan herbs; maccheroncini served with thyme; and calamari seared in sherry with pecorino cheese.

✪ Cantinetta Antinori. Piazza Antinori 3. ☎ **055/292-234.** Reservations recommended. Main courses 25,000L–30,000L ($15–$18). AE, DC, MC, V. Mon–Fri 12:30–2:30pm and 7–10:30pm. Closed Aug and Dec 24–Jan 6. ITALIAN/TUSCAN.

Hidden behind the severe stone facade of the 15th-century Palazzo Antinori is the Catinetta Antinori, one of Florence's most popular restaurants and one of the city's few top-notch wine bars. Small wonder that the cellars should be supremely well stocked since the restaurant is one of the city's showplaces for the vintages of the oldest and most distinguished wine company in Tuscany, Umbria, and Piedmont. Vintages can be consumed by the glass at the stand-up bar or by the bottle as an accompaniment to the Italian meals served at wooden tables. The not especially large room is decorated with floor-to-ceiling racks of aged and undusted wine bottles. You can eat a full meal or just snacks. The cookery is standard but satisfying, especially the sausages with white haricot beans and the fresh Tuscan ewe's cheese.

Oliviero. Via delle Terme 51R. ☎ **055/287-643.** Reservations required. All main courses 30,000L ($18). AE, CB, DC, DISC, MC, V. Mon–Sat 7–11pm. Closed Aug. TUSCAN.

This is a small but smart, luxurious dining room. From 8pm on, live music is featured in the piano bar. The finest traditions of Tuscan cookery are maintained here; highly select, fresh ingredients are used in the seasonal menu. You might, for example, savor appetizers such as octopus salad with basil, string beans, and tomatoes; fried mussels and squash blossoms; or Tuscan ham with figs and bread coated with virgin olive oil. Main courses usually include fresh fish; grilled, boned rabbit and young cock with shell beans; or ravioli stuffed with chopped liver and served with a delicate white onion sauce. For dessert, try the green fig mousse with almonds and chocolate.

Trattoria Coco Lezzone. Via del Parioncino 26R. ☎ **055/287-178.** Reservations accepted only for groups of 10 or more. Main courses 16,000L–50,000L ($9.60–$30). No credit cards. Mon–Sat noon–2:30pm and 7–10pm. Closed the last week of July to Aug and Dec 25–Jan 6. FLORENTINE.

In Florentine dialect this establishment's name refers to the sauce-stained apron of the extroverted chef who established this place more than a century ago. Today this is a good place to sample the wholesome fare of the Tuscan countryside. During the bustling lunch hour Florentines crowd in for a spot at one of the long tables, so go early before the rush begins if you want a seat. The hearty fare includes generous portions of boiled meats with a green sauce, pasta e fagioli (beans), osso buco, tripe, or beefsteak Florentine, which must be ordered by phone in advance.

NEAR PIAZZA DEL DUOMO
INEXPENSIVE

Le Mossacce. Via del Proconsolo 55R. ☎ **055/294-361.** Main courses 12,000L–15,000L ($7.20–$9). AE, MC, V. Mon–Fri noon–2:30pm and 7–9:30pm. Closed Aug. TUSCAN.

Le Mossacce, patronized by a long list of faithful Tuscan fans, is conveniently located midway between two of the city's most famous monuments, the Bargello and the Duomo. This small 35-seat restaurant was established at the turn of the century, and within its 300-year-old walls, a team of hardworking waiters serves a wide range of excellent Florentine and Italian specialties, including *ribollita* (a thick regional vegetable soup), cannelloni, and heavily seasoned baked pork. *Bistecca alla fiorentina* is also a favorite selection.

Vecchia Firenze. Borgo degli Albizi 18. ☎ **055/234-0361.** Main courses 12,000L–22,000L ($7.20–$13.20). AE, DC, MC, V. Daily noon–2pm and 7–10pm. FLORENTINE.

Established in the 1950s, Vecchia Firenze combines atmosphere and budget meals. It's housed in an old palace with an elegant entrance through high doors. Some of the tables are in the courtyard; others are inside the vaulted dining rooms. The restaurant is lit by a wrought-iron chandelier, although the place is not elaborately voguish—in fact, it caters to students and the working people of Florence, who eat here regularly and never seem to tire of its simple but good-tasting offerings. You might begin with a tagliatelle Vecchia Firenze (the chef prepares a different version everyday), then follow with a quarter of a roast chicken or sole in butter.

NEAR PIAZZA DELLA SIGNORIA
MODERATE

Da Ganino. Piazza dei Cimatori 4R. ☎ **055/214-125.** Reservations recommended. Main courses 15,000L–30,000L ($9–$18). AE, DC, MC, V. Mon–Sat 1–3pm and 8–11pm. FLORENTINE/TUSCAN.

The small and intimate Da Ganino is staffed with the kind of waiters who take the quality of your meal as their personal responsibility. Someone will recite to you the frequently changing specialties of the day, which might include well-seasoned versions of Tuscan beans, spinach risotto, grilled veal liver, grilled veal chops, and Florentine beefsteak on the bone. The *tagliatelle con tartufi* (pasta with truffles) makes an excellent, if expensive, appetizer. Also worthwhile is filet of chicken with a lemon-cream sauce and a *fritto misto* of meats, including brains, kidneys, beef filets, lamb chops, and a selection of grilled vegetables.

Paoli. Via dei Tavolini 12R. ☎ **055/216-215.** Reservations required. Main courses 15,000L–30,000L ($9–$18); fixed-price menu 40,000L ($24). AE, DC, MC, V. Wed–Mon noon–2:30pm and 7–10:30pm. Closed 3 weeks in Aug. TUSCAN/ITALIAN.

Paoli, located between the Duomo and Piazza della Signoria, and one of the finest restaurants in Florence, was established in 1824 by the Paoli brothers in a building that dated in part from the 13th century. It turns out a host of specialties, but it could be recommended almost solely for its medieval-tavern atmosphere, with arches and ceramics stuck into the frescoe-adorned walls like medallions. The pastas are homemade, and the chef also does a superb *rognoncino* (kidney) trifolato and a sole meunière. A recommendable side dish is *piselli* (garden peas) alla fiorentina.

INEXPENSIVE

Da Pennello. Via Dante Alighieri 4R. ☎ **055/294-848.** Main courses 15,000L–22,000L ($9–$13.20); fixed-price menu 30,000L ($18). AE, MC, V. Tues–Sat noon–3pm and 7–10pm, Sun noon–3pm. Closed Aug 1–30 and Dec 25–Jan 3. FLORENTINE/ITALIAN.

This informally operated trattoria offers many Florentine specialties on its à la carte menu and is known for its wide selection of antipasti; you can make a meal out of these delectable hors d'oeuvres. The ravioli is homemade and one pasta specialty—loved by locals—is spaghetti carrettiera, made with tomatoes and pepperoni. To follow, you can have deviled roast chicken. The chef posts daily specials, and sometimes it's best to order one of these, as the food offered was bought fresh that day at the market. A Florentine cake, *zuccotto*, rounds out the meal. The restaurant is on a narrow street, near Dante's house, about a 5-minute walk from the Duomo toward the Uffizi.

Il Cavallino. Via della Farine 6R. ☎ **055/215-818.** Reservations recommended. Main courses 13,000L–26,000L ($7.80–$15.60); fixed-price menu 30,000L ($18). AE, DC, MC, V. Thurs–Tues noon–2:30pm and 7–10pm. TUSCAN/ITALIAN.

Il Cavallino has been a local favorite since the 1930s. It's on a tiny street (which probably won't even be on your map) that leads off Piazza della Signoria at its northern end, not far from the equestrian statue. There's usually a gracious reception at the door, especially if you called ahead for a reservation. Two of the three dining rooms have vaulted ceilings and peach-colored marble floors. The main room looks out over the piazza. Menu items are typical hearty Tuscan fare, including an assortment of boiled meats in green herb sauce, grilled filet of steak, breast of chicken Medici style, and the inevitable Florentine spinach.

NEAR PIAZZA SANTA MARIA NOVELLA & TERMINI
EXPENSIVE

Harry's Bar. Lungarno Vespucci 22R. ☎ **055/239-6700.** Reservations required. Main courses 18,000L–34,000L ($10.80–$20.40). AE, MC, V. Mon–Sat noon–3pm and 7–11pm. Closed Dec 18–Jan 8 and 1 week in Aug. ITALIAN/AMERICAN.

Harry's Bar, located in an 18th-century building in a prime position on the Arno, has been an enclave of expatriate and well-heeled visiting Yankees since 1953. Harry's is the easiest place in Florence to meet fellow Americans. The international menu is small but select, and beautifully prepared, including risotto or tagliatelle with ham, onions, and cheese, and a very tempting *gamberetti* (crayfish) cocktail. Harry has created his own tortellini, but his hamburger and his club sandwich are the most popular items. The chef also prepares about a dozen specialties every day: breast of chicken "our way," grilled giant-sized scampi, and a lean broiled sirloin steak. An apple tart with cream nicely finishes off a meal.

I Quattro Amici. Via degli Orti Oricellari 29. ☎ **055/215-413.** Reservations recommended. Main courses 43,000L–70,000L ($25.80–$42). AE, DC, MC, V. Daily noon–3pm and 7–10:30pm. SEAFOOD.

Established in 1990 by four Tuscan entrepreneurs who had known each other since childhood, this restaurant occupies the street level of a modern building near the railway station. Inside, amid a vaguely neoclassical decor, the place serves endless quantities of fish to a landlocked clientele eager for memories of the sea. Specialties include pasta with fish sauce and fragments of sausage, fish soup, fried shrimp, and squid in the style of Livorno, and grilled, stewed, or baked versions of all the bounty of the Mediterranean. The roast sea bass and roast snapper, flavored with Mediterranean herbs, are among the finest dishes. The vegetables are fresh and flavorful. Every Thursday, Friday, and Saturday evening, guests are treated to live music while they dine.

MODERATE

Buca Lapi. Via del Trebbio 1R. ☎ **055/213-768.** Reservations required for dinner. Main courses 22,000L–35,000L ($13.20–$21). AE, DC, MC, V. Tues–Sat 12:30–2:30pm and 7:30–10:30pm. Closed 2 weeks in Aug. TUSCAN.

This cellar restaurant was founded in 1880 and is big on glamor, good food, and the enthusiasm of fellow diners. Its decor alone—under the Palazzo Antinori—makes it fun: The vaulted ceilings are covered with travel posters from all over the world. The cooks know how to turn out the most classic dishes of the Tuscan kitchen with superb finesse, and there's a long table of interesting fruits, desserts, and vegetables. Specialties include *scampi giganti alla griglia,* a super-sized shrimp, and *bistecca alla fiorentina* (local beefsteak). In season, the *fagioli toscani all'olio* (Tuscan beans in the native olive oil) are a delicacy to many palates. For dessert, try the international favorite, crêpes Suzette, or the local choice, zuccotto, a Florentine cake that's *delicato.*

✪ Don Chisciotte. Via Ridolfi 4R. ☎ **055/475-430.** Reservations recommended. Main courses 26,000L–32,000L ($15.60–$19.20). AE, DC, MC, V. Mon 8–10:30pm, Tues–Sat 1–2:30pm and 8–10:30pm. ITALIAN/SEAFOOD.

Set one floor above street level in a venerable Florentine *palazzo* near the railway station, this restaurant is known for its creative cuisine and its changing array of very fresh fish. We feel we discovered this place, as we were touting its glory long before Michelin got around to giving it a star. The dining room, outfitted in soft pink, green, and ivory, reflects the colors of the menu items, which are produced with a flourish from the kitchens. The cuisine is creative, based on flavors that are often enhanced by an unusual assortment of fresh herbs, vegetables, and fish stocks. Choose from risotto of broccoli and baby squid; red taglierini with clams, pesto, and cheese; black ravioli colored with squid ink and stuffed with a purée of shrimp and crayfish; and filet of turbot with a radicchio sauce.

✪ Sabatini. Via de' Panzani 9A. ☎ **055/211-559.** Reservations recommended. Main courses 26,000L–38,000L ($15.60–$22.80). AE, DC, MC, V. Tues–Sun 12:30–2:30pm and 7:30–10:30pm. FLORENTINE.

Despite its less-than-chic location near the railway station, Florentines and visitors alike have long extolled Sabatini as the finest of the restaurants characteristic of the city. You'll get better food here than at the highly touted Enoteca Pinchiorri, Via Ghibellina 87, which Michelin gives two stars but which has consistently drawn more reader disapproval (and we concur) than any other restaurant in Florence. To celebrate our annual return visit to Sabatini, we order the same main course we had when we first visited—boiled Valdarno chicken with a savory green sauce. Back then we complained to the waiter that the chicken was tough. He replied, "But, of course!" The Florentines like chicken with muscle, not the hot-house variety so favored by Americans. Having eaten a lot of Valdarno chicken since then, we're now more appreciative of Sabatini's dish. But on subsequent visits we've found some of the other main courses more delectable, especially the veal scaloppine with artichokes. Of course, you can always order a good sole meunière or the classic beefsteak Florentine. Another specialty is spaghetti Sabatini, a cousin of spaghetti carbonara but enhanced with fresh tomatoes. American-style coffee is also served, following the Florentine cake, called zuccotto.

✪ Trattoria Garga. Via del Moro 48R. ☎ **055/239-8898.** Reservations required. Main courses 24,000L–60,000L ($14.40–$36). AE, DC, MC, V. Tues–Sat 12:30–3pm and 7:30pm–midnight, Sun 7:30pm–midnight. TUSCAN.

Some of the most creative cuisine in Florence is served here. The building's thick Renaissance walls contain paintings by both Florentine and American artists, including those painted by the owners themselves, Giuliano Gargani and his Canadian wife, Sharon. Both operatic arias and heavenly odors emerge from a postage-stamp-sized kitchen. Many of the Tuscan menu items are so unusual that Sharon's bilingual skills are put to good use. Dishes include octopus with peppers and garlic, boar with juniper berries, grilled marinated quail, and "whatever strikes the mood" of Giuliano. One dish, created in 1992, has earned a lot of publicity—*tagliarini magnifico*, made with angel-hair pasta, orange and lemon rind, mint-flavored cream, and Parmesan cheese. The location is between the Ponte Vecchio and Santa Maria Novella.

INEXPENSIVE

Buca Mario. Piazza Ottaviani 16R. ☎ **055/214-179.** Reservations required. Main courses 15,000L–25,000L ($9–$15). AE, DC, MC, V. Fri–Tues 12:15–2:30pm and 7:15–10:30pm. Closed Aug. FLORENTINE.

Buca Mario, in business for a century, is one of the most famous cellar restaurants of Florence. It's located right in the historic center in the 1886 Palazzo Niccolini. While diners sit at tables placed beneath the vaulted ceilings, the waiters—some of whom have worked in the States—will suggest an array of Florentine pastas, beef-steak, Dover sole, or beef carpaccio, followed by a tempting selection of desserts. The cookery bursts with flavor in the robust *buca* style. There's a wonderful exuberance about the place, but in the enigmatic words of one longtime patron: "It's not for the fainthearted."

La Carabaccia. Via Palazzuolo 190R. ☎ **055/214-782.** Main courses 18,000L–30,000L ($10.80–$18). AE, MC, V. Tues–Sat 12:30–2:30pm; daily 7:30–10:30pm. Closed 15 days in Aug. FLORENTINE.

Two hundred years ago a *carabaccia* was a workaday boat, shaped like a hollowed-out half onion and used on the Arno to dredge silt and sand from the river bottom. The favorite onion soup of the Medici was *zuppa carabaccia*, which this restaurant still features today. It's a creamy white onion soup served with croûtons (not in the French style, the chef rushes to tell you). You can, of course, eat more than onions here. The menu changes every day and is based on whatever fresh local ingredients are available. There's always one soup, followed by four or five pastas, including crespelle (crêpe) of such fresh vegetables as asparagus or artichokes. The restaurant was established in the 1970s in a building two centuries old.

Le Fonticine. Via Nazionale 79R. ☎ **055/282-106.** Reservations recommended for dinner. Main courses 16,500L–28,000L ($9.90–$16.80). AE, DC, MC, V. Tues–Sat noon–3pm and 7:30–10:30pm. Closed Jan 1–15 and Aug. TUSCAN/BOLOGNESE.

Le Fonticine used to be part of a convent until the owner, Silvano Bruci, converted both it and its adjoining garden into one of the most hospitable restaurants in Florence, lying close to the San Lorenzo food market. Today the richly decorated interior contains all the abundance of an Italian harvest, as well as the second passion of Signor Bruci's life, his collection of original modern paintings. The first passion, as a meal here reveals, is the cuisine that he and his wife produce from recipes she collected from her childhood in Bologna.

Proceed to the larger of the establishment's two dining areas; along the way you can admire dozens of portions of freshly made pasta decorating the table of an exposed grill. At the far end of the room a wrought-iron gate shelters the wine collection that Mr. Bruci has amassed, like his paintings, over many years. The food, served in copious portions, is both traditional and delectable. Begin with a platter of fresh antipasti, or with samplings of three of the most excellent pasta dishes of the day. This might be followed by *fegatina di pollo* (chicken), veal scaloppine, or one of the other main dishes.

Osteria Numero Uno. Via del Moro 22. ☎ **055/284-897.** Reservations recommended. Main courses 18,000L–25,000L ($10.80–$15). AE, DC, MC, V. Mon 7–11pm, Tues–Sat 12:30–2:30pm and 7:30–11:30pm. Closed Aug. INTERNATIONAL/FLORENTINE.

This restaurant derives its name from its original location, since 1959, at number one *(numero uno)* on a street near its present location on Via del Moro. In 1985 the restaurant moved to its new premises in a 15th-century *palazzo* within a 3-minute walk from the railway station. Its cuisine is a well-prepared, well-presented blend of international foods and Italian dishes.

Many patrons prefer a seat in the main dining room, with its vaulted ceiling and oversized fireplace, although two adjacent dining rooms contain part of the spillover. Menu choices include taglierini with mushrooms (with or without truffles); ravioli stuffed with either ricotta and basil or fresh artichokes; risotto with asparagus or sweet

🛈 Family-Friendly Restaurants

Da Pennello *(see p. 233)*   This family-style trattoria near Dante's house offers filling, tasty, and inexpensive dishes.

Gelateria Vivoli *(see p. 242)*   After tasting the ice cream here—in virtually every known flavor—your child might agree that this place was worth the trip to Florence.

La Nandina *(see p. 240)*   Florentine families frequent this place off the Arno, a 4-mile walk from the Uffizi.

peppers; carpaccio of beef or salmon; the classic Florentine tripe; chicken with marsala or Parmesan; turbot baked with artichokes, herbs, and potatoes; and Florentine-style beefsteak, which is usually prepared for two diners. Dessert might be succulent *torta della nonna.*

Ristorante Otello. Via degli Orti Oricellari 36R. ☎ **055/216-517.** Reservations recommended. Main courses 14,000L–30,000L ($8.40–$18). AE, DC, MC, V. Daily noon–3pm and 7:30–11pm. FLORENTINE/TUSCAN.

Located next to the train station, Ristorante Otello is a long-established Florentine dining room that serves an animated clientele in comfortably renovated surroundings. Its antipasto Toscano is one of the best in town, an array of appetizing hors d'oeuvres that practically becomes a meal in itself. The waiter urges you to *"Mangi, mangi, mangi!"* ("Eat, eat, eat!") and that's what diners do here, as the victuals at Otello have been known to stir the most lethargic of appetites. The true trencher-person goes on to order one of the succulent pasta dishes, such as spaghetti with small baby clams or pappardelle with garlic sauce. The meat and poultry dishes are equally delectable, including sole meunière or veal pizzaiola with lots of garlic.

Sostanza. Via del Porcellana 25R. ☎ **055/212-691.** Reservations recommended. Main courses 14,000L–28,000L ($8.40–$16.80). No credit cards. Mon–Fri noon–2:10pm and 7:30–9:30pm. Closed Aug and 2 weeks at Christmas. FLORENTINE.

Sostanza is the city's oldest and most revered trattoria. It has long been where working people have gone for excellent, moderately priced food. In recent years, however, it has begun attracting a more sophisticated set as well. Florentines call the place Troia, which means "hog," but also suggests a woman of easy virtue. The small dining room has crowded family tables, but when you taste what comes out of that kitchen, you'll know that fancy decor would be superfluous. Specialties include breaded chicken breast and a succulent T-bone steak. You might also want to try tripe in the Florentine way—that is, cut into strips, then baked in a casserole with tomatoes, onions, and Parmesan cheese.

Trattoria Antellesi. Via Faenza 9R. ☎ **055/216-990.** Reservations recommended. Main courses 16,000L–24,000L ($9.60–$14.40). AE, DC, MC, V. Daily noon–3pm and 7–10:30pm. TUSCAN.

Set on the ground floor of a 15th-century historic monument, a few steps from the Medici Chapels, this restaurant is devoted almost exclusively to well-prepared versions of time-tested Tuscan recipes. Owned by Enrico Verrecchia and his Arizona-born wife, Janice, the restaurant prepares at least seven *piatti del giorno* (daily specials) that change according to the availability and seasonality of the ingredients. Dishes might include tagliatelle with porcini mushrooms or braised arugula, *crespelle alla fiorentina* (cheesy spinach crêpe introduced to France by Catherine de Medici's kitchen staff), pappardelle with wild boar, market-fresh fish (generally on Friday), flavorful Valdostana chicken, and properly grilled bistecca alla fiorentina. The array of quality Italian wines (with an emphasis on Tuscany) has for the most part been selected by Janice herself.

NEAR PIAZZA SAN MARCO
INEXPENSIVE

Cafaggi. Via Guelfa 35R. ☎ **055/294-989.** Reservations recommended. Main courses 12,000L–30,000L ($7.20–$18); fixed-price menu 22,000L ($13.20). AE, MC, V. TUSCAN.

Atmospheric and charming best describe this small-scale (50-seat) trattoria that has flourished on this site since 1922, when it was established within a modestly proportioned *palazzo* that predates the Renaissance. Tables are scattered throughout two old-fashioned dining rooms. The menu features Tuscan dishes, including Florentine beefsteak, steaming bowls of vegetarian soup, and grilled fish accompanied with rice, potatoes, or a medley of very fresh salads and vegetables. Forget counting calories and try the succulent *millefoglie alle creme* for dessert; it positively overflows with cream.

I'Toscano. Via Guelfa 70R. ☎ **055/215-475.** Reservations recommended at dinner. Main courses 12,000L–25,000L ($7.20–$15); fixed-price menu 27,000L ($16.20). AE, DC, MC, V. Wed–Mon noon–2:30pm and 7:30–10:30pm. Closed Aug 1–15. TUSCAN.

Bouquets of flowers liven up this restaurant's monochromatic, mostly beige interior, but despite the understated setting, the place is a magnet for gastronomes who appreciate the succulent, all-Tuscan specialties that emerge from its pungently scented kitchens. Menu items change with the seasons, but are often at their best during late autumn and winter, when mixed platters containing slices of wild boar, venison, partridge, and, when available, pheasant are a worthy substitute for the roster of antipasti that tempts visitors the rest of the year. Ravioli, made on the premises and stuffed with spinach, are always popular, as well as any of several forms of gnocchi or tagliatelle. Fish (usually sea bass or monkfish, pan-fried or grilled) is most prominent on the menu on Friday, but veal, turkey, and pork dishes, as well as Florentine beefsteaks, are also offered.

NEAR PIAZZA SANTA CROCE
MODERATE

La Baraonda. Via Ghibellina 67R. ☎ **055/234-1171.** Reservations recommended. Main courses 23,000L ($13.80). AE, DC. Tues–Fri 1–2:30pm; Mon–Sat 7:30pm. Bus: 14. TUSCAN.

Locals make up about 80% of the clientele of this bustling trattoria, many of them merchants and hotel employees. This small, gregarious establishment—with a name that translates as "hubbub" or "disorder"—serves a Tuscan cuisine flavored with seasonally available local ingredients. Some members of the staff speak fluent English, and in many cases will propose carefully assembled fixed-price meals. Examples from the ever-changing menu include an array of *sformato di verdure* (vegetable soufflé made with, among other ingredients, artichokes, or whatever else is in season at the moment), risotto with fresh greens, and a savory meat loaf *(polpettone in umido)* made with veal and fresh tomatoes. At the end of the meal, complimentary sweets and grappa are served.

Cibreo. Via dei Macci 118R. ☎ **055/234-1100.** Reservations recommended in the restaurant, not accepted in the trattoria. Main courses 45,000L ($27) in the restaurant, 20,000L ($12) in the trattoria. AE, DC, MC, V (restaurant only). Tues–Sat 12:30pm and 8–11pm. Closed late July to early Sept. MEDITERRANEAN.

The unpretentious Cibreo consists of a restaurant, a less formal tavern-style trattoria, and a cafe-bar across the street. The small and impossibly old-fashioned kitchen is noteworthy for not containing a grill and for not serving pastas. Instead, Cibreo specializes in food cooked in a wood-burning oven and cold marinated dishes (especially vegetables). Menu items include a sformato (a soufflé made from potatoes and ricotta, served with Parmesan cheese and tomato sauce), *inzimmino* (Tuscan-style squid stewed with spinach), and a flan of Parmesan cheese, veal tongue, and artichokes.

Some of the staff are expatriate New Yorkers who excel at explaining the restaurant's culinary themes. The restaurant takes its name from (and serves) an old Tuscan dish *(cibreo)* that was allegedly so delectable it nearly killed Catherine de' Medici. (She consumed so much that she was overcome with near-fatal indigestion.) The dish is prepared about eight times a year at the restaurant, but only on special request, and usually for specially catered meals ordered in advance. It combines the organs, the meat, and the crest (or comb) of a chicken with tons of garlic, rosemary, sage, and wine, with lots of fussing over intermediary steps before the final presentation.

Del Fagioli. Corso dei Tintori 47R. ☎ **055/244-285.** Reservations recommended. Main courses 18,000L–26,000L ($10.80–$15.60). No credit cards. Mon–Fri noon–2:30pm and 7:30–10:30pm. Closed Aug. FLORENTINE/TUSCAN.

Devoted to the pleasures of country-style Tuscan cuisine, this restaurant (whose name translates as "beans") was established in 1966 in a pair of dining rooms lined with old engravings of the monuments of Florence. It serves a choice of locally made *affettati toscani* (sausages, pâtés, and dried or salted meats), a hearty *ribollita* (cabbage and bread soup), several types of spaghetti and tagliatelle, sliced breast of turkey, Florentine beefsteak, and game dishes in season. Fish might include oven-roasted sea bass or monkfish, its flavor enhanced with herbs. Fagioli, incidentally, was also a traditional name for the buffoons (clowns and humorists) who performed throughout the Renaissance for the political rulers of Florence.

INEXPENSIVE

Ristorante Dino. Via Ghibellina 51R. ☎ **055/241-452.** Reservations recommended. Main courses 15,000L–30,000L ($9–$18). AE, DC, MC, V. Tues–Sat noon–3pm and 7:30–10:30pm, Sun noon–2:30pm. TUSCAN.

In a 14th-century building near the Casa Buonarroti, this restaurant has vaulted ceilings and a cuisine inspired by members of the Casini family. Specialties include spaghetti alla Dino, flavored with carrots, celery, chile peppers, and aromatic herbs; risotto della Renza, rich with aromatic herbs and fresh tomatoes; and ribollita, the cabbage, bean, and bread soup of Tuscany. Tuscan purists are often jolted with memories of their childhood at the mention of one of the restaurant's ever-present dishes, *garetto Ghibellino,* a historic recipe made from pork shanks with celery and sage. The excellent wine list features vintages from throughout Italy, especially Tuscany.

Trattoria Pallottino. Via Isola della Stinche 1R. ☎ **055/289-573.** Reservations recommended at dinner. Main courses 12,000L–32,000L ($7.20–$19.20). AE, DC, MC, V. Tues–Sun 12:30–2:30pm and 7:30–10:30pm. TUSCAN.

Set within a narrow street less than a block from the Piazza Santa Croce, this distinctive Tuscan-style restaurant contains only two small and sometimes cramped dining rooms. Flickering candles illuminate a timeless, all-Italian scene where the staff works hard, usually with humor and style. Menu specialties include everything you ever associated with Tuscan cuisine (succulent antipasti, tagliolini with cream and herbs, ravioli with spinach or pine nuts and cream sauce) as well as dishes that are distinctive and specific to this restaurant, such as *peposa,* a slab of beef marinated for at least

4 hours in a rich broth of ground black pepper, olive oil, and tomatoes; and *spaghetti fiecchiraia* (spaghetti laden with red chili peppers, olive oil, and tomatoes)—it derives its name from the sharp exhalation of breath a 19th-century fiacre driver would make to his horses when prompting them to gallop. In your case, it will be because of the spiciness of the dish, and have nothing to do with horse-drawn carriages. Dessert might be a vanilla custard drizzled with a compôte of fresh fruit.

NEAR THE PONTE VECCHIO
MODERATE

La Nandina. Borgo SS. Apostoli 64R. ☎ **055/213-024.** Reservations recommended. Main courses 20,000L–32,000L ($12–$19.20). AE, DC, MC, V. Mon 7–10:30pm, Tues–Sat noon–3pm and 7–10:30pm. Closed 2 weeks in Aug. TUSCAN/INTERNATIONAL.

This family-run restaurant is located just off the Arno, about a 4-minute walk from the Uffizi (in fact, it's an excellent choice for lunch if you're visiting the galleries). Established in 1924, this elegant restaurant is an old favorite with both Florentines and visitors alike. You can have an aperitif in the intimate and plushly upholstered cocktail lounge and dine in the 14th-century cellar. The cuisine consists of dishes from the provinces as well as from Rome and Venice, and might include ravioli with flap mushrooms, spinach crêpes, curried breast of capon, veal piccatina, several kinds of beefsteak, and a changing array of daily specials. All the food is high quality but not fussy.

INEXPENSIVE

Buca dell'Orafo. Via Volta dei Girolami 28R. ☎ **055/213-619.** Main courses 10,000L–30,000L ($6–$18). No credit cards. Tues–Sat 12:30–2:30pm and 7:30–10:30pm. Closed Aug and 2 weeks in Dec. FLORENTINE.

Established in the 1940s, Buca dell'Orafo is a little dive (one of the many cellars or *buca*-type establishments beloved by Florentines). An *orafo* is a goldsmith, and it was in this part of Florence that the goldsmith trade grew. The buca, once part of an old goldsmith shop, is reached via a street under a vaulted arcade right off Piazza del Pesce. The trattoria is usually stuffed with regulars, so if you want a seat, go early. Over the years the chef has made little concession to the foreign palate, turning out instead genuine Florentine specialties, including tripe and mixed boiled meats with a green sauce and *stracotto e fagioli* (beef braised in a sauce of chopped vegetables and red wine), served with beans in a tomato sauce. There's a feeling of camaraderie among the diners here.

ACROSS THE ARNO
EXPENSIVE

La Capannina di Sante. Piazza Ravenna, adjacent to the ponte Giovanni da Verrazzano. ☎ **055/68-8345.** Reservations recommended. Main courses 20,000L–40,000L ($12–$24); fixed-price menu 90,000L ($54). AE, DC, MC, V. Mon–Sat 7:30pm–1am. Closed 1 week in Aug. SEAFOOD.

This simple and unpretentious restaurant, featuring a river-view terrace for outdoor dining, has functioned in more or less the same way on and off since 1935. The restaurant serves only the best and freshest seafood, prepared in a simple and healthy manner, usually with olive oil or butter and Mediterranean seasonings. Examples include filets of sea bass or turbot, mixed seafood grills, and an occasional portion of veal or steak for anyone who doesn't care for fish. For an appetizer, we recommend the sampling of hot seafood—there's none finer in Florence. The wines are simple and straightforward, and the greeting is warm and friendly.

Trattoria Vittoria. Via della Fonderia 52R. ☎ **055/225-657.** Reservations recommended. Main courses 25,000L–60,000L ($15–$36). AE, DC, MC, V. Thurs–Tues noon–3:30pm and 7:30–10:30pm. SEAFOOD.

This unheralded and untouristy establishment serves some of the finest fish dishes in Florence. It's a big and bustling trattoria, and service is frenetic. Most of the fresh fish dishes of the day are priced according to weight, making a main dish considerably higher than the prices quoted above. Sole is the most expensive, although you can also order equally tempting lower-priced dishes. Two savory choices to begin your meal include risotto alla marinara and spaghetti alla vongole (clams). The mixed fish fry gives you a little bit of everything. Desserts are homemade and extremely rich.

MODERATE

Mamma Gina. Borgo Sant' Jacopo 37R. ☎ **055/239-6009.** Reservations required for dinner. Main courses 20,000L–30,000L ($12–$18). AE, DC, MC, V. Mon–Sat noon–2:30pm and 7–10pm. Closed Aug 7–21. TUSCAN.

Mamma Gina is a rustic left-bank restaurant that prepares fine foods in the traditional bustling manner. Although it's run by a corporation that operates other restaurants scattered throughout Tuscany, this restaurant is named after its founding matriarch (Mamma Gina), whose legend has continued despite her death in the 1980s. This exceptional trattoria, well worth the trek across the Ponte Vecchio, is a center for hearty Tuscan fare. Some of the rich and savory menu items include cannelloni Mamma Gina (stuffed with a purée of minced meats, spices, and vegetables); tagliolini with artichoke hearts or mushrooms, and whatever else is in season at the time; and chicken breast Mamma Gina, baked in the northern Italian style with prosciutto and Emmenthaler cheese. This is an ideal spot for lunch after visiting the Pitti Palace.

Trattoria Cammillo. Borgo Sant' Jacopo 57. ☎ **055/212-427.** Reservations required. Main courses 15,000L–45,000L ($9–$27). AE, DC, MC, V. Fri–Tues noon–2:30pm and 7:30–10:30pm. Closed mid-Dec to Jan and Aug 1–21. TUSCAN.

Housed on the ground floor of a former Medici palace, the Trattoria Cammillo is one of the most popular—and perhaps the finest—of the Oltrarno dining spots. Its most serious rival is Mamma Gina, which is also good, but not quite as good as this savvy choice. Snobbish boutique owners cross the Arno regularly to feast here; they know they'll get such specialties as tagliatelle flavored with fresh peas and truffles. This sounds like such a simple dish, but when it's prepared right, as it most often is here, it's a real treat. You'll also find excellent assortments of fried or grilled vegetables; superfresh scampi and sole; fried, deboned pigeon served with artichokes; and breast of chicken with truffles and Parmesan. The trattoria is between the Ponte Vecchio and the Ponte Santa Trínita. Because of increased business, you're likely to be rushed through a meal.

INEXPENSIVE

Le Quattro Stagioni. Via Maggio 61R. ☎ **055/218-906.** Reservations recommended. Main courses 8,000L–16,000L ($4.80–$9.60). AE, DC, MC, V. Mon–Sat 12:15–2:30pm and 7:30–10:30pm. Closed Aug and Dec 25. TUSCAN/SEAFOOD.

Set in a historic building near the Pitti Palace, this charming and old-fashioned restaurant specializes in both seafood and classic Tuscan recipes, and does so exceedingly well. An efficient and professional staff serves such dishes as gnocchi, crostini, pasta with squid in its own ink, roast lamb with artichokes, sea bass roasted with fennel, a succulent array of fresh vegetables, beefsteak, several different preparations of veal, and homemade desserts. As the establishment's name (The Four Seasons) implies, the menu changes according to the seasonal availability of the ingredients.

Pierot. Piazza Tadeo Gaddi 25R. ☎ **055/702-100.** Reservations recommended. Main courses 15,000L–25,000L ($9–$15). AE, DC, MC, V. Mon–Sat noon–3pm and 7–11:30pm. Closed July 15–31. SEAFOOD/TUSCAN.

Pierot, which has been a fixture of Florence since 1955, is housed in a 19th-century building constructed during the reign of Vittorio Emanuel. Although a few other places—already previewed—also specialize in seafood, this place is a bit of an oddity in landlocked Florence. The seasonal menu varies with the availability of ingredients, but might include linguine with *frutti di mare* (fruits of the sea), pasta with lobster sauce, and a choice of traditional Tuscan steaks, soups, and vegetables. Seafood risotto is deservedly a perennial favorite.

Trattoria Angiolino. Via San Spirito 36R. ☎ **055/239-8976.** Reservations recommended. Main courses 16,000L–18,000L ($9.60–$10.80). AE, DC, MC, V. Daily 12:30–1:30pm and 7–10:30pm. ITALIAN/TUSCAN.

This restaurant has thrived within this 14th-century building since the 1920s, and as such has fed a friend or relative of virtually everyone in Florence. The decor is old-timey and warm, with a potbellied stove and brick floors, and the menu includes Tuscan and Italian dishes that many visitors remember from their childhood. Choose from an array of antipasti, steaming bowls full of pasta e fagioli, a roster of home-made pastas that include ravioli and taglioni, veal and chicken cutlets prepared either Milanese or parmigiana style, and rich, homemade cakes and pastries.

GELATO

✪ **Gelateria Vivoli.** Via Isola delle Stinche 7R. ☎ **055/292-334.** Gelati 2,500L–16,000L ($1.50–$9.60). No credit cards. Tues–Sun 8am–1am. Closed 3 weeks in Aug (dates vary). ICE CREAM.

Established in the 1930s, and today run by the third generation of the Vivoli family, this establishment produces some of the finest ice cream in Italy. Of course, to hear it here, it's *the* finest. They provide the gelati for many of the restaurants of Florence. Buy your ticket first and then select your flavor. Choose from blueberry, fig, melon, and other fruits in season, as well as chocolate mousse, or even coffee ice cream flavored with espresso. A special ice cream is made from rice. The establishment offers a number of semifreddi concoctions—an Italian ice cream using cream as a base instead of milk. The most popular flavors are almond, marengo (a type of meringue), and zabaglione (eggnog). Other flavors include *limoncini alla crema* (candied lemon peels with vanilla-flavored ice cream) and *aranciotti al cioccolate* (candied orange peels with chocolate ice cream). The shop is located on a backstreet near the church and cloisters of Santa Croce.

5 Seeing the Sights

Florence was the fountainhead of the Renaissance, the city of Dante and Boccaccio. Characteristically, it was the city of Machiavelli, and uncharacteristically, of Savonarola. For three centuries it was dominated by the Medici family, patrons of the arts, masters of assassination. But it is chiefly through its artists that we know of the apogee of the Renaissance: Ghiberti, Fra Angelico, Donatello, Brunelleschi, Botticelli, and the incomparable Leonardo da Vinci and Michelangelo.

In Florence we can trace the transition from medievalism to an age of "rebirth." For example, all modern painters owe a debt to an ugly, awkward, unkempt man named Masaccio (Vasari's "Slipshod Tom") who died at age 27. Modern painting began with his frescoes in the Brancacci Chapel in the Church of Santa Maria del Carmine, which you can go see today. Years later Michelangelo painted a more celebrated Adam and Eve in the Sistine Chapel, but even this great artist never realized the raw humanity of Masaccio's Adam and Eve fleeing from the Garden of Eden.

Group tourism has so overwhelmed the city of the Renaissance that officials in 1996 demanded that organized tour groups book visits to the city in advance and pay an admission fee. No more than 150 tour buses will be allowed into the city center at one time—and, considering the smallness of the place, that is still a large amount. Today, there are more than seven tourists for each native Florentine. And that doesn't even count the day-trippers, who rush off to Venice in the late afternoon.

If you get trampled underfoot at the Uffizi or elsewhere seeking the treasures of the Renaissance, know that many famous visitors have lodged their complaints as well. In 1817, Stendhal called the city, "Nothing better than a vast museum of foreign tourists." Henry James complained about the crush of winter traffic along the Cascine, John Ruskin attacked the hackney coaches filling the squares, and Mary McCarthy, much later in the 1950s, denounced Florence as "A terrible city, in many ways, uncomfortable and dangerous to live in, a city of drama, argument, and struggle."

Despite all its traffic and inconveniences, Florence is still one the world's greatest art cities. Those tour buses are here for a reason.

For information on specialized sightseeing tours in Florence and the surrounding countryside, see the "Tuscan Tours" box in chapter 7, "Tuscany & Umbria."

THE TOP MUSEUMS

✪ **Galleria degli Uffizi.** Piazzale degli Uffizi 6. ☎ **055/2388-6512.** Admission 12,000L ($7.20). Tues–Sat 8:30am–6:50pm, Sun and holidays 8:30am–1:30pm (last entrance 45 minutes before closing).

You can now avoid hours waiting in line at the Uffizi by booking a reservation and purchasing tickets in advance. Call ☎ **055/471-960** or visit the **ITA** (Informazioni Turistiche Alberghiere) office at 9A Viale Gramsci. Tickets must be paid for at least 5 days before entrance and must be picked up at the tourist information office on Via Chiasso Baroncelli only on the morning of the reserved date.

When the last grand duchess of the Medici family died, she bequeathed to the people of Tuscany a wealth of Renaissance, even classical, art. The paintings and sculpture had been accumulated by the powerful grand dukes in three centuries of rule that witnessed the height of the Renaissance. Vasari designed the palace in the 16th century for Cosimo I.

To see and have time to absorb all the Uffizi paintings would take at least 2 weeks. We'll present only the sketchy highlights. The Uffizi is nicely grouped into periods or schools to show the development and progress of Italian and European art.

The first room begins with classical sculpture. You'll then meet up with those rebels from Byzantium, Cimabue and his pupil Giotto, with their madonnas and bambini. Since the Virgin and Child seem to be the overriding theme of the earlier Uffizi artists, it's enlightening just to follow the different styles over the centuries, from the ugly, almost midget-faced babies of the post-Byzantine works to the chubby, red-cheeked cherubs that glorified the baroque.

Look for Simone Martini's *Annunciation,* a collaborative venture. The halo around the head of the Virgin doesn't conceal her pouty mouth. Fra Angelico of Fiesole, a 15th-century painter, lost in a world peopled with saints and angels, makes his Uffizi debut with (naturally) a *Madonna and Bambino.* A special treasure is a work by Masaccio, who died at an early age, but is credited as being the father of modern painting. In his madonnas and bambini we see the beginnings of the use of perspective in painting. Fra Angelico's *Coronation of the Virgin* is also in this salon.

Florence Attractions

Archaeological Museum 10
Badia 32
Baptistry 19
Bargello 33
Boboli Gardens 50
Campanile di Giotto 17
Casa Buonarotti 41
Casa Guidi 47
Cascine park 25
Cenacolo di Foligno 2
Cenacolo di
    Sant 'Appollonia 3
Cenacolo di Santo
    Spirito Museum 45
Chiostro dello Scalzo 4
Duomo 16
Forte di Belvedere 51
Fortezza del Basso 1
Galleria Corsini 27
Galleria dell 'Accademia 7
Giardino dei Semplici 6
Instituto e Museo di Storia
    della Scienza 37
Loggia dei Lanzi 35
Loggia del Bigallo 18
Medici Chapels 22
Museo Bardini 52
Museo dell'Opera
    dell Duomo 15
Museo dell'Opera
    di Santa Croce 39
Museo di Santa Maria
    Novella 24
Museo Horne 38
Museo Zoologico
    La Specola 48
Ognissanti 26
Orsanmichele 30
Palazzo Medici-Riccardi 20
Pallazo Pitti 49
Palazzo Strozzi 29
Palazzo Vecchio 34
Piazzale Michelangelo 53
Ponte Vecchio 42
Protestant Cemetery 11
Raccolta della Ragione 31
San Lorenzo 21
San Marco 5
San Miniato al Monte 54
Sant 'Ambrogio 14
Santa Croce 40
Santa Felicità 43
Santa Maria della Carmine 46
Santa Maria Maddalena
    dei Pazzi 12
Santa Maria Novella 23
Santa Trinita 28
Santissima Annunziata 8
Santo Spirito 44
Spedale degli Innocenti 9
Synagogue 13
Uffizi Galleries 36

3-0838

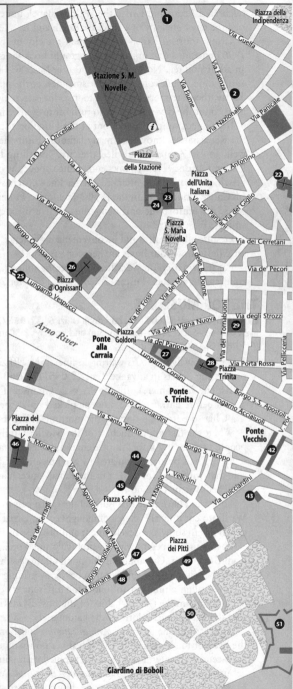

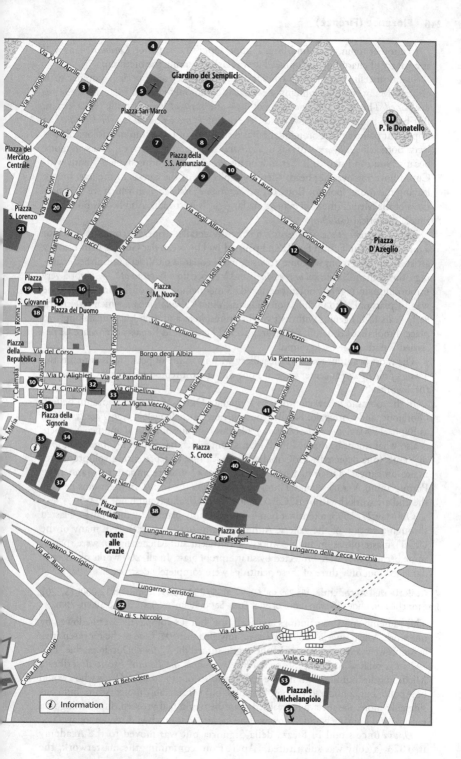

In another room you'll find Friar Filippo Lippi's far-superior *Coronation*, as well as a galaxy of charming madonnas. He was a rebel among the brethren.

The Botticelli rooms, which contain his finest works, are especially popular with visitors. Many come to contemplate what is commonly referred to as *Venus on the Half Shell*. This supreme conception of life—the *Birth of Venus*—really packs 'em in. But before being captured by Venus, check out *Minerva Subduing the Centaur*, an important painting that brought about a resurgence of interest in mythological subjects. Botticelli's *Allegory of Spring* or *Primavera* is a gem; it's often called a symphony because you can listen to it. Set in a citrus grove, the painting depicts Venus with Cupid hovering over her head. Mercury looks out of the canvas to the left. Before leaving the room, look for Botticelli's *Adoration of the Magi*, in which we find portraits of the Medici (the vain man at the far right is Botticelli). Also here is Botticelli's small, allegorical *Calumny*.

The *Adoration of the Shepherds* is a superbly detailed triptych, commissioned for a once-important Tuscan family and painted by Hugo van der Goes, a 15th-century artist. In another room we come across one of Leonardo da Vinci's unfinished paintings, the brilliant *Adoration of the Magi*, and Verrocchio's *Baptism of Christ*, not a very important painting, but noted because da Vinci painted one of the angels when he was 14 years old. Also in this salon hangs da Vinci's *Annunciation*, which reflects the early years of his genius with its twilight atmosphere and each leaf painstakingly in place. Proof that Leonardo was an architect? The splendid Renaissance palace he designed is part of the background.

The most beautiful room in the gallery with its dome of pearl shells contains the *Venus of the Medici* at center stage; it's one of the most reproduced of all Greek sculptural works.

In the rooms to follow are works by Perugino, Dürer, Mantegna, Giovanni Bellini, Giorgione, and Correggio. Finally, you can view Michelangelo's *Holy Family*, as well as Raphael's *Madonna of the Goldfinch*, plus his portraits of Julius II and Leo X. There is also what might be dubbed the Titian salon, which has two of his interpretations of Venus (one depicted with Cupid). When it came to representing voluptuous females on canvas, Titian had no rival. In other rooms are important Mannerists: Parmigianino, Veronese, and Tintoretto *(Leda and the Swan)*. In the rooms nearing the end are works by Rubens, Caravaggio *(Bacchus)*, and Rembrandt.

On May 27, 1993, a terrorist bomb—presumably planted by the Mafia—blasted through a section of the gallery. Although paintings were destroyed, many of the Uffizi's masterpieces, including works by Botticelli and Michelangelo, were spared, some because they were protected by shatterproof glass. In all, 200 works of art were damaged, but only three of these paintings were completely destroyed.

✪ Galleria dell'Accademia. Via Ricasoll 60. ☎ **055/238-8609.** Admission 12,000L ($7.20); free for children under 18 with proof of age. Tues–Sat 8:30am–6:50pm, Sun 8:30am–2pm.

This museum contains paintings and sculpture, but it's completely overshadowed by one work, Michelangelo's colossal *David*, unveiled in 1504. One of the most sensitive accounts we've ever read of how Michelangelo turned the 17-foot "Duccio marble" into *David* is related in Irving Stone's *The Agony and the Ecstasy*. Stone describes a Michelangelo "burning with marble fever" who set out to create a *David* who "would be Apollo, but considerably more; Hercules, but considerably more; Adam, but considerably more; the most fully realized man the world had yet seen, functioning in a rational and humane world." How well he succeeded is much in evidence today.

David once stood in Piazza della Signoria but was moved to the Academy in 1873 (a copy was substituted). Apart from containing the masterwork, the sculpture gallery is also graced with Michelangelo's unfinished quartet of slaves, carved around 1520 and intended for the ill-fated tomb of Julius II, and his *St. Matthew,* which he worked on (shortly after completing *David*) for the Duomo. His unfinished *Palestrina Pietà* displayed here is a much later work, dating f rom 1550.

In the connecting picture gallery is a collection of Tuscan masters, such as Botticelli, and Umbrian works by Perugino (teacher of Raphael).

✪ **Palazzo Pitti.** Piazza dei Pitti. ☎ **055/213-440.** Admission: Palatina, 12,000L ($7.20); Modern Art Gallery, 8,000L ($4.80); Argenti, 8,000L ($4.80). Tues–Sat 9am–7pm.

The Pitti Palace, built in the mid-15th century (Brunelleschi was the original architect), was once the residence of the powerful Medici family. It's located across the Arno (a 5-minute walk from the Ponte Vecchio).

There are actually several museums in this complex, the most important of which is the **Galleria Palatine,** which houses one of Europe's great art collections, with masterpieces hung one on top of the other, as in the days of the Enlightenment. If for no other reason, it should be visited for its Raphaels alone. Other museums include the **Appartamenti Reali,** which the Medici family once called home, and the **Museo degli Argenti,** 16 rooms devoted to displays of the "loot" acquired by the Medici dukes. Others are the **Coach and Carriage Museum** and the **Galleria d'Arte Moderna,** as well as the **Museo della Porcellane** (porcelain) and the **Galleria del Costume.**

After passing through the main door, proceed to the Sala di Venere (Room of Venus). In it are Titian's *La Bella,* of rich and illuminating color (entrance wall), and his portrait of Pietro Aretino, one of his most distinguished works. On the opposite wall are Titian's *Concert of Music,* often attributed to Giorgione, and his portrait of Julius II.

In the Sala di Apollo (on the opposite side of the entrance door) are Titian's *Man with Gray Eyes*—an aristocratic, handsome romanticist—and his *Mary Magdalene,* covered only with her long hair. On the opposite wall are Van Dyck portraits of Charles I of England and Henrietta of France.

In the Sala di Marte (entrance wall) is an important *Madonna and Child* by Murillo of Spain, as well as the Pitti's best-known work by Rubens: *The Four Philosophers.* On the left wall is one of Ruben's most tragic and moving paintings, depicting the *Consequences of War*—an early *Guernica.*

In the Sala di Giove (entrance wall) are Andrea del Sarto's idealized John the Baptist in his youth, Fra Bartolomeo's *Descent from the Cross,* and one of Rubens's most exciting paintings (even for those who don't like art), which depicts a romp of nymphs and satyrs. On the third wall (opposite the entrance wall) is the Pitti's second famous Raphael, the woman under the veil, known as *La Fornarina,* his bakery-girl mistress.

In the following gallery, the Sala di Saturno, look to the left on the entrance wall to see Raphael's *Madonna of the Canopy.* On the third wall near the doorway is the greatest Pitti prize, Raphael's *Madonna of the Chair,* his best-known interpretation of the Virgin, and what is in fact probably one of the six most celebrated paintings in all of Europe.

In the Sala dell'Iliade (to your left on the entrance wall) is a work of delicate beauty, Raphael's rendition of a pregnant woman. On the left wall is Titian's *Portrait of a Gentleman,* which he was indeed. (Titian is the second big star in the Palatine Gallery.) Finally, as you're leaving, look to the right of the doorway to see one of Velázquez's representations of the many faces of Philip IV of Spain.

❂ Museo Nazionale del Bargello. Via del Proconsolo 4. ☎ **055/238-8606.** Admission 8,000L ($4.80). Tues–Sat 8:30am–1:50pm; 2nd and 4th Sun of the month 9am–2pm, 1st and 3rd Mon of the month 9am–2pm.

The National Museum, a short walk from Piazza della Signoria, is a 13th-century fortress palace whose dark underground chambers once resounded with the echoing cries of the tortured. Today it's a vast repository of some of the most important sculpture of the Renaissance, including works by Michelangelo and Donatello.

Here you'll see another Michelangelo *David* (referred to in the past as *Apollo*), chiseled perhaps 25 to 30 years after the statuesque figure in the Academy Gallery. The Bargello *David* is totally different—even effete when compared to its stronger brother. The gallery also displays Michelangelo's grape-capped *Bacchus* (one of his earlier works), who is tempted by a satyr. Among the more significant sculptures is Giambologna's *Winged Mercury.*

The Bargello displays two versions of Donatello's *John the Baptist*—one emaciated, the other a younger and much kinder edition. Donatello, of course, was one of the outstanding and original talents of the early Renaissance. In this gallery you'll learn why. His *St. George* is a work of heroic magnitude. According to an oft-repeated story, Michelangelo, upon seeing it for the first time, commanded it to "March!" Donatello's bronze *David* in this salon is one of the most remarkable figures of all Renaissance sculpture—it was the first freestanding nude since the Romans stopped chiseling. As depicted, *David* is narcissistic (a stunning contrast to Michelangelo's latter-day virile interpretation). For the last word, however, we'll have to call back our lady of the barbs, Mary McCarthy, who wrote: "His David . . . wearing nothing but a pair of fancy polished boots and a girlish bonnet, is a transvestite's and fetishist's dream of alluring ambiguity."

Look for at least one more notable work, another *David*—this one by Andrea del Verrocchio, one of the finest of the 15th-century sculptors. The Bargello contains a large number of terra-cottas by the della Robbia clan.

Museo di San Marco. Piazza San Marco 3. ☎ **055/210-741.** Admission 8,000L ($4.80). Tues–Sun 8:30am–1:50pm. Closed 1st, 3rd, and 5th Sun of the month, and 2nd and 4th Mon of the month. Closed Jan 1, May 1, and Dec 25.

Museo di San Marco, a state museum, is a handsome Renaissance palace whose cell walls are decorated with frescoes by the mystical Fra Angelico, one of Europe's greatest 15th-century painters. In the days of Cosimo dei Medici, San Marco was built by Michelozzo as a Dominican convent. It originally contained bleak, bare cells, which Angelico and his students then brightened considerably with some of the most important works of this pious artist of Fiesole, who portrayed recognizable landscapes in strong, vivid colors.

One of his better-known paintings found here is *The Last Judgment,* which depicts people with angels on the left dancing in a circle, and lordly saints towering overhead. Hell, as it's depicted on the right, is naive—Dante-esque—infested with demons, reptiles, and sinners boiling in a stew. Much of hell was created by his students; Angelico's brush was inspired only by the Crucifixion, madonnas, and bambini—or landscapes, of course. Henry James claimed that Angelico "never received an intelligible impression of evil; and his conception of human life was a perpetual sense of sacredly loving and being loved." Here, also, are his *Descent from the Cross* and a panel of scenes from the life of Christ, including the *Flight into Egypt.*

In one room are frescoes and panels by Fra Bartolomeo, who lived from 1475 to 1517 and was highly influenced by Raphael. Note his *Madonna and Child with Saints.* In the Capitolo is a powerful *Crucifixion* by Angelico.

Turn right at the next door and you'll enter a refectory devoted to the artistic triumph of Domenico Ghirlandaio, who taught Michelangelo how to fresco. Ghirlandaio's own *Last Supper* in this room is rather realistic; his saints have tragic faces and silently evoke a feeling of impending doom.

Upstairs on the second floor—at the top of the hallway—is Angelico's masterpiece, *The Annunciation.* From here, you can walk down the left corridor to explore the cells of the Dominicans. Most of the frescoes depict scenes from the Crucifixion.

After turning to the right, you may want to skip the remaining frescoes, which appear to be uninspired student exercises. But at the end of the corridor is the cell of Savonarola, which was the scene of his arrest. The cell contains portraits of the reformer by Bartolomeo, who was plunged into acute melancholy by the jailing and torturing of his beloved teacher. Pictures of the reformer on the pyre at Piazza della Signoria are on display.

If you retrace your steps to the entrance, then head down still another corridor, you'll see more frescoes, past a library with Ionic columns designed by Michelozzo. Finally, you'll come to the cell of Cosimo dei Medici, with a fresco by Gozzoli, who worked with Angelico.

THE DUOMO, THE BELL TOWER & THE BAPTISTERY

In the heart of Florence, at Piazza del Duomo and Piazza San Giovanni (named after John the Baptist), is a complex of ecclesiastical buildings that form a triumvirate of top sightseeing attractions.

✪ **Cathedral of Santa Maria del Fiore (Duomo).** Piazza del Duomo. ☎ **055/213-229.** Cathedral, free; excavations, 3,000L ($1.80); cupola, 8,000L ($4.80). Apr–Oct, Mon–Fri 9am–6pm, Sat 8:30am–5pm, Sun 1–5pm; Nov–Mar, Mon–Fri 10am–7pm, Sat 9:30am–5pm, Sun 1–5pm.

The Duomo, graced by Brunelleschi's dome, is the crowning glory of Florence. But don't rush inside too quickly, as the view of the exterior, with its bands of white, pink, and green marble—geometrically patterned—is, along with the dome, the best feature. One of the world's largest churches, the Duomo represents the flowering of the "Florentine Gothic" style. Typical of the history of cathedrals, construction stretched over centuries. Begun in 1296, it was finally consecrated in 1436, although finishing touches on the facade were applied as late as the 19th century. The cathedral was designed by Arnolfo di Cambio in the closing years of the 13th century, and the funds were raised in part by a poll tax.

Brunelleschi's efforts to build the dome (1420–36) would make the subject of a film, as did Michelangelo's vexations over the Sistine Chapel. At one time before his plans were eventually accepted, the architect was tossed out on his derrière and denounced as an idiot. He eventually won the commission by a clever "egg trick," as related in Giorgio Vasari's *Lives of the Painters,* written in the 16th century, a book to which we are here indebted (as are all authors of books dealing with Italian Renaissance art). The architect challenged his competitors to make an egg stand on a flat piece of marble. Each artist tried to make the egg stand, but failed. When it was Brunelleschi's turn, he took the egg and cracked its bottom on the marble and thus made it stand upright on the marble. Each of the other artists said that he could have done the same thing, if he had known he could crack the egg. Brunelleschi retorted that they would also have known how to vault the cupola if they had seen his model or plans.

His dome—a "monument for posterity"—was erected without supports. When Michelangelo began to construct a dome over St. Peter's, he paid tribute to

Brunelleschi's earlier cupola in Florence: "I am going to make its sister larger, yes, but not lovelier."

Inside, the overall effect of the cathedral is bleak, except when you stand under the cupola, frescoed in part by Vasari. Some of the stained-glass windows in the dome were based on designs by Donatello (Brunelleschi's friend) and Ghiberti (Brunelleschi's rival). If you resisted scaling Giotto's bell tower, you may want to climb Brunelleschi's ribbed dome. The view is well worth the trek.

Also in the cathedral are some terra-cottas by Luca della Robbia. In 1432 Ghiberti, taking time out from his "Gateway to Paradise," designed the tomb of St. Zenobius. Excavations in the depths of the cathedral have brought to light the remains of the ancient Cathedral of Santa Reparata (tombs, columns, and floors), which was probably founded in the 5th century and transformed in the following centuries until it was demolished to make way for the present cathedral.

Incidentally, during some 1972 excavations the tomb of Brunelleschi was discovered, and new discoveries indicate the existence of a second tomb nearby. Giotto's tomb, which has never been found, may be in the right nave of the cathedral, beneath the campanile that bears his name.

✪ **Giotto's Bell Tower (Campanile).** Piazza del Duomo. ☎ **055/230-2885.** Admission 8,000L ($4.80). Mar–Oct, daily 9am–6:50pm; Nov–Feb, daily 9am–4:20pm.

If we can believe the accounts of his contemporaries, Giotto was the ugliest man ever to walk the streets of Florence. Ironically, then, he left to posterity the most beautiful bell tower, or campanile, in Europe, rhythmic in line and form. That Giotto was given the position of *capomastro* and grand architect (and pensioned for 100 gold florins for his service) is remarkable in itself, for he is famous for freeing painting from the confinements of Byzantium. He designed the campanile in the last 2 or 3 years of his life, and he died before its completion.

The final work was admirably carried out by Andrea Pisano, one of the greatest Gothic sculptors in Italy (see his bronze doors on the nearby baptistery). The 274-foot tower, a "Tuscanized" Gothic, with bands of colored marble, can be scaled for a panorama of the sienna-colored city. The view will surely rank among your most memorable—it encompasses the enveloping hills and Medici villas. If a medieval pageant happens to be passing underneath (a likely possibility in spring), so much the better. After Giotto's death, Pisano and Luca della Robbia did some fine bas-relief and sculptural work, now in the Duomo Museum behind the cathedral.

✪ **Battistero San Giovanni (Baptistery).** Piazza S. Giovanni. ☎ **055/230-2885.** Admission 5,000L ($3). Mon–Sat 1–5pm, Sun 9am–12:30pm.

Named after the city's patron saint, Giovanni (John the Baptist), the present octagonal Battistero dates from the 11th and 12th centuries. The oldest structure in Florence, the baptistery is a highly original interpretation of the Romanesque style, with its bands of pink, white, and green marble. Visitors from all over the world come to gape at its three sets of bronze doors. In his work on two sets of doors, Lorenzo Ghiberti reached the pinnacle of his artistry in *quattrocento* Florence. To win his first commission on the north door, the then-23-year-old sculptor had to compete against such formidable opposition as Donatello, Brunelleschi (architect of the dome crowning the cathedral), and Siena-born Jacopo della Quercia. Upon seeing Ghiberti's work, Donatello and Brunelleschi conceded defeat. By the time he completed the work, Ghiberti was around 44 years old. The gilt-covered panels—representing scenes from the New Testament, including the Annunciation, the Adoration, and Christ debating the elders in the temple—make up a flowing rhythmic narration in bronze.

To protect them from the elements, the originals were removed to the Museo dell'Opera del Duomo; but the copies are works of art unto themselves.

After his long labor, the Florentines gratefully gave Ghiberti the task of sculpting the east door (directly opposite the entrance to the Duomo). Upon seeing the doors, Michelangelo is said to have exclaimed, "The Gateway to Paradise!" Given carte blanche, Ghiberti designed his masterpiece, choosing as his subject familiar scenes from the Old Testament, including Adam and Eve at the creation. This time Ghiberti labored over the rectangular panels from 1425 to 1452 (he died in 1455). Ghiberti wasn't exactly modest: He claimed he personally planned and designed the Renaissance—all on his own.

Shuttled off to adorn the south entrance and to make way for Ghiberti's "gate" to paradise were the oldest doors of the baptistery, by Andrea Pisano, mentioned earlier for his work on Giotto's bell tower. For his subject, the Gothic sculptor represented the "Virtues" as well as scenes from the life of John the Baptist, whom the baptistery honors. The door was completed in 1336. On the interior (just walk through Pisano's door—no charge) the dome is adorned with 13th-century mosaics, dominated by a figure of Christ. Mornings are reserved for worship.

Museo dell'Opera del Duomo. Piazza del Duomo 9. ☎ **055/230-2885.** Admission 8,000L ($4.80). Apr–Oct, Mon–Sat 9am–6:50pm; Nov–Mar, Mon–Sat 9am–5:20pm.

Museo dell'Opera del Duomo, across the street but facing the apse of Santa Maria del Fiore, is beloved by connoisseurs of Renaissance sculpture. It houses the sculpture removed from the campanile and the Duomo—not only to protect the pieces from the weather, but from visitors who want samples. A major attraction here is an unfinished *Pietà* by Michelangelo, which is in the middle of the stairs. It was carved between 1548 and 1555 when the artist was in his 70s. In this vintage work, a figure representing Nicodemus (but said to have Michelangelo's face) is holding Christ. The great Florentine intended it for his own tomb, but he is believed to have grown disenchanted with it and to have attempted to destroy it. The museum has a Brunelleschi bust, as well as della Robbia terra-cottas. The museum's premier attraction is the restored panels of Ghiberti's "Doors to Paradise" removed from the baptistery.

You'll see bits and pieces from what was the old Gothic-Romanesque fronting of the cathedral, with ornamental statues, as conceived by the original architect, Arnolfo di Cambio. One of Donatello's early works, *St. John the Evangelist,* is here—not his finest hour certainly, but anything by Donatello is worth looking at, including one of his most celebrated works, the *Magdalene,* which is in the room with the *cantorie* (see below). This wooden statue once stood in the baptistery, and had to be restored after the flood of 1966. Dating from 1454–55, it's stark and penitent.

A good reason for visiting the museum is to see the marble choirs—*cantorie*—of Donatello and Luca della Robbia (the works face each other and are in the first room you enter after climbing the stairs). The Luca della Robbia choir is more restrained, but it still "Praises the Lord" in marble—with clashing cymbals and sounding brass that constitute a reaffirmation of life. In contrast, all restraint breaks loose in the *cantoria* of dancing cherubs in Donatello's choir. It's a romp of chubby bambini. Of all of Donatello's works, this one is the most lighthearted. But, in total contrast, lavish your attention on Donatello's *Zuccone,* one of his greatest masterpieces; it was created for Giotto's bell tower.

PIAZZA DELLA SIGNORIA

This square, although never completed, is one of the most beautiful in Italy; it was the center of secular life in the days of the Medici. Through it pranced church robbers, connoisseurs of entrails, hired assassins seeking employment, chicken farmers from Valdarno, book burners, and many great men—including Machiavelli, on a secret mission to the Palazzo Vecchio, and Leonardo da Vinci, trailed by his inevitable entourage.

On the square is the **Fountain of Neptune,** the sea god surrounded by creatures from the deep, as well as frisky satyrs and nymphs. It was designed by Ammannati, who later repented for chiseling Neptune in the nude. But Michelangelo, to whom Ammannati owes a great debt, judged the fountain inferior.

Near the fountain is a spot where Savonarola walked his last mile. This zealous monk was a fire-and-brimstone reformer who rivaled Dante in conjuring up the punishment hell would inflict on sinners. Two of his chief targets were Lorenzo the Magnificent and the Borgia pope, Alexander VI, who excommunicated him. Savonarola whipped the Florentine faithful into an orgy of religious fanaticism, but eventually fell from favor. Along with two other friars, he was hanged in the square in 1498. Afterward, as the crowds threw stones, the pyre underneath the men consumed their bodies. It's said that the reformer's heart was found whole and grabbed up by souvenir collectors. His ashes were tossed into the Arno.

For centuries Michelangelo's *David* stood in Piazza della Signoria, but it was moved to the Academy Gallery in the 19th century. The work you see on the square today is an inferior copy, commonly assumed by many first-time visitors to be Michelangelo's original.

The 14th-century **Loggia della Signoria** (sometimes called the Loggia dei Lanzi) houses a gallery of sculpture often depicting fierce, violent scenes. The most famous and the best piece is a rare work by Benvenuto Cellini, the goldsmith and tell-all autobiographer. Critics have said that his exquisite but ungentlemanly *Perseus,* who holds the severed head of Medusa, is the most significant Florentine sculpture since Michelangelo's *Night* and *Day.* Two other well-known, although less skillfully created, pieces are Giambologna's *Rape of the Sabines,* an essay in three-dimensional Mannerism, and his *Hercules with Nessus the Centaur,* a chorus line of a half-dozen Roman vestal wallflowers. For those on the mad rush, we suggest saving the interior of the Palazzo Vecchio for another day.

Palazzo Vecchio. Piazza della Signoria. ☎ **055/276-8325.** Admission 10,000L ($6). Mon–Wed and Fri–Sat 9am–7pm, Sun 8am–1pm. Last admission 1 hour before closing.

The secular "Old Palace" is without doubt the most famous and imposing palace in Florence. It dates from the closing years of the 13th century. Its remarkable architectural feature is its 308-foot tower, an engineering feat that required supreme skill. Once home to the Medici, the Palazzo Vecchio (also called the Palazzo della Signoria) is occupied today by city employees, but much of it is open to the public.

The 16th-century "Hall of the 500" (Dei Cinquecento), the most outstanding part of the palace, is filled with Vasari & Co. frescoes as well as sculpture. As you enter the hall, look for Michelangelo's *Victory.* It depicts an insipid-looking young man treading on a bearded older man (it has been suggested that Michelangelo put his own face on that of the trampled man).

Later you can stroll through the rest of the palace, through its apartments and main halls. You can also visit the private apartments of Eleanor of Toledo, wife of Cosimo I, and a chapel that was begun in 1540 and frescoed by Bronzino. The palace displays the original of Verrocchio's bronze *putto* (from 1476) from the courtyard fountain. This work is called both *Winged Cherub Clutching a Fish* and *Boy with a Dolphin.* The palace also shelters a 16th-century portrait of Machiavelli that's attributed to Santi di Tito. Donatello's famous bronze group, *Judith Slaying Holofernes,* once stood on Piazza della Signoria, but it was brought inside.

The salons, such as a fleur-de-lis apartment, have their own richness and beauty. Following his arrest, Savonarola was taken to the Palazzo Vecchio for more than a dozen torture sessions, including "twists" on the rack. The torturer pronounced him his "best" customer.

MORE ATTRACTIONS
PONTE VECCHIO

Spared by the Nazis in their bitter retreat from the Allied advance in 1944, "The Old Bridge" is the last remaining medieval *ponte* spanning the Arno (the Germans blew up the rest). The bridge was again threatened in the flood of 1966 when the waters of the Arno swept over it and washed away a fortune in jewelry from the goldsmiths' shops that flank the bridge.

Today the restored Ponte Vecchio is closed to vehicular traffic. The little shops continue to sell everything from the most expensive of Florentine gold to something simple—say, a Lucrezia Borgia poison ring. Florentine hog butchers once peddled their wares on this bridge.

NEAR PIAZZA SAN LORENZO

✪ **Cappelle Medici.** Piazza Madonna degli Aldobrandini 6. ☎ **055/23 885.** Admission 12,000L ($7.20). Tues–Sat 8:30am–6:30pm, Sun 8:30am–1:50pm.

A mecca for all pilgrims, the Medici tombs are sheltered adjacent to the Basilica of San Lorenzo (see below). The tombs, housing the "blue-blooded" Medici, are actually entered in back of the church by going around to Piazza Madonna degli Aldobrandini. First you'll pass through the baroque Chapel of the Princes, that octagon of death often denounced for its "trashy opulence." In back of the altar is a collection of Italian reliquaries.

The real reason the chapels are visited en masse, however, is the **New Sacristy,** designed by Michelangelo as a gloomy mausoleum. "Do not wake me; speak softly here," Michelangelo wrote in a bitter verse. Working from 1521 to 1534, he created the Medici tomb in a style that foreshadowed the coming of the baroque. Lorenzo the Magnificent—a ruler who seemed to embody the qualities of the Renaissance itself, and one of the greatest names in the history of the Medici family—was buried near Michelangelo's uncompleted *Madonna and Child* group, a simple monument that evokes a promise unfulfilled.

Ironically, the finest, world-renowned groups of sculpture were reserved for two Medici "clan" members, who (in the words of Mary McCarthy) "would better have been forgotten." Both are represented by Michelangelo as armored, regal, idealized princes of the Renaissance. In fact, Lorenzo II, duke of Urbino, depicted as "the thinker," was a deranged young man (just out of his teens before he died). Clearly, Michelangelo was not working to glorify these two Medici dukes. Rather, he was chiseling for posterity. The other two figures on Lorenzo's tomb are most often called *Dawn* and *Dusk,* with morning represented as woman and evening as man.

The two best-known figures—Michelangelo at his most powerful—are *Night* and *Day* at the feet of Giuliano, the duke of Nemours. *Night* is chiseled as a woman in troubled sleep; *Day* is a man of strength awakening to a foreboding world. These two figures were not the sculptural works of Michelangelo's innocence.

Discovered in a sepulchral chamber beneath the Medici Chapel was Michelangelo's only group of mural sketches. Access is through a trap door and a winding staircase. The walls apparently had been used by the great artist as a giant doodling sheet. Drawings include a sketch of the legs of Duke Giuliano, Christ risen, and a depiction of the Laocoön, the Hellenistic figure group. Fifty drawings, done in charcoal on plaster walls, were found. The public can sometimes view these sketches in the choir.

Basilica di San Lorenzo. Piazza San Lorenzo. ☎ **055/216-634.** Free admission. Library, Mon–Sat 9am–1pm; study room, Mon–Sat 8am–2pm.

This is Brunelleschi's 15th-century Renaissance church, where the Medici used to attend services from their nearby palace on Via Larga, now Via Camillo Cavour. Critic Walter Pater found it "great rather by what it designed or aspired to do, than by what it actually achieved." Most visitors flock to see Michelangelo's New Sacristy with his *Night* and *Day* (see the Medici Chapels, above), but Brunelleschi's handiwork deserves some time, too.

Built in the style of a Latin cross, the church is distinguished by harmonious grays and rows of Corinthian columns. The Old Sacristy (walk up the nave, then turn left) was designed by Brunelleschi and decorated in part by Donatello (see his terra-cotta bust of St. Lawrence). This is often cited as the first and finest work of the early Renaissance. Even more intriguing are the pulpits of Donatello, among his last works, a project carried out by students following his death in 1466. Scenes depict Christ's passion and resurrection.

After exploring the Old Sacristy, go through the first door (unmarked) on your right, then turn right again and climb the steps.

The **Biblioteca Medicea Laurenziana** (☎ **055/210-760**) is entered separately at Piazza San Lorenzo 9 and was designed by Michelangelo to shelter the expanding library of the Medici. The library is filled with some of Italy's greatest manuscripts—many of which are handsomely illustrated. Visitors are kept at a distance by protective glass, but it's well worth the visit. Open Monday through Saturday from 8am to 2pm.

Palazzo Medici–Riccardi. Via Camillo Cavour 1. ☎ **055/276-0340.** Admission 6,000L ($3.60). Mon–Tues and Thurs–Sat 9am–12:30pm and 3–6pm, Sun 9am–noon.

This palace, a short walk from the Duomo, was the home of Cosimo dei Medici before he took his household to the Palazzo della Signoria. In the apogee of the Medici power, it was once adorned with some of the world's greatest masterpieces, such as Donatello's *David.* Built by palace architect Michelozzo in the mid-15th century, the brown stone building was also the scene, at times, of the court of Lorenzo the Magnificent. Art lovers visit today chiefly to see the mid-15th-century frescoes by Benozzo Gozzoli in the Medici Chapel. Gozzoli's frescoes, which depict the *Journey of the Magi,* form his masterpiece—in fact, they're a hallmark in Renaissance painting. Although taking a religious theme as his subject, the artist turned it into a gay romp, a pageant of royals, knights, and pages, with such fun mascots as greyhounds and even a giraffe. It's a fairytale world come alive, with faces of the Medici along with local celebrities who were as famous as Madonna and Michael Jackson in their day but are known only to scholars today.

Another gallery, which has to be entered by a separate stairway, was frescoed by Luca Giordano in the 18th century, but his work seems merely decorative. The apartments, where the prefect lodges, are not open to the public. The gallery, incidentally, may also be viewed free.

NEAR PIAZZA DELLA SANTISSIMA ANNUNZIATA

Ospedale degli Innocenti. Piazza della Santissima Annunziata 12. ☎ **055/249-1723.** Admission 4,000L ($2.40). Mon–Sat 9am–1pm, Sun 8am–noon.

The Hospital of the Innocents was the first hospital for foundlings in the world, although the Medici and Florentine bankers were not known for Reagan trickle-down economics. The building, and the loggia with its Corinthian columns, was conceived by Brunelleschi and marked the first architectural bloom of the Renaissance in Florence. On the facade are terra-cotta medallions done in blues and opaque whites by Andrea della Robbia that depict babes in swaddling clothes.

Still used as an orphanage, the building also contains an art gallery. Notable among its treasures is a terra-cotta *Madonna and Child* by Luca della Robbia, plus works by Sandro Botticelli. One of the gallery's most important paintings is an *Adoration of the Magi* by Domenico Ghirlandaio (the chubby bambino looks a bit pompously at the Wise Man kissing his foot).

Museo Archeologico. Via della Colonna 38. ☎ **055/23-575.** Admission 8,000L ($4.80). Tues–Sat 9am–2pm, Sun 9am–1pm.

The Archeological Museum, a short walk from Piazza della Santissima Annunziata, houses one of the most outstanding Egyptian and Etruscan collections in Europe in a palace originally built for Grand Duchess Maria Maddalena of Austria. The Etruscan-loving Medici began that collection, although the Egyptian loot was first acquired by Leopold II in the 1830s. Its Egyptian mummies and sarcophagi are on the first floor, along with some of the better-known Etruscan works. Pause to look at the lid to the coffin of a fat Etruscan (unlike the blank faces staring back from many of these tombs, this overeater's countenance is quite expressive).

One room is graced with three bronze Etruscan masterpieces, among the rarest objets d'art of these relatively unknown people. They include the *Chimera,* a lion with a goat sticking out of its back. This was an Etruscan work of the 5th century B.C., found near Arezzo in 1555. The lion's tail—in the form of a venomous reptile—lunges at the trapped beast. The others are a statue of *Minerva* and one of an *Orator.* These pieces of sculpture range from the 5th to the 1st century B.C. Another rare find is a Roman bronze of a young man, the so-called *Idolino from Pesaro.* The François vase on the ground floor, from the year 570 B.C., is celebrated. A prize in the Egyptian department is a wood-and-bone chariot, beautifully preserved, that astonishingly dates back to a tomb in Thebes from the 14th century B.C.

NEAR PIAZZA SANTA MARIA NOVELLA

Basilica di Santa Maria Novella. Piazza Santa Maria Novella. ☎ **055/210-113.** Church, free; Spanish Chapel and cloisters, 5,000L ($3). Church, Mon–Fri 7–11:30am and 3:30–6pm, Sat 10–11:30am and 3:30–5pm, Sun 3:30–5pm; Spanish Chapel and cloisters, Mon–Thurs and Sat 9am–2pm, Sun 8am–1pm.

Near the railway station is one of Florence's most distinguished churches, begun in 1278 for the Dominicans. Its geometric facade, with bands of white and green marble, was designed in the late 15th century by Leon Battista Alberti, an aristocrat and true Renaissance man (philosopher, painter, architect, poet). The church borrows from and harmonizes the Romanesque, Gothic, and Renaissance styles.

In the left nave as you enter, the third large painting is the great Masaccio's *Trinity,* a curious work that has the architectural form of a Renaissance stage setting, but whose figures—in perfect perspective—are like actors in a Greek tragedy. If you view the church at dusk you'll see the stained-glass windows in the fading light cast kaleidoscope fantasies on the opposite wall.

Head straight up the left nave to the Gondi Chapel for a look at Brunelleschi's wooden *Christ on the Cross,* which is said to have been carved to compete with Donatello's same subject in Santa Croce (see below). According to Vasari, when Donatello saw Brunelleschi's completed Crucifix, he dropped his apron full of eggs intended for their lunch. "You have symbolized the Christ," Donatello is alleged to have said. "Mine is an ordinary man." (Some art historians reject this story.)

In the late 15th century Ghirlandaio contracted with a Tornabuoni banker to adorn the choir with frescoes illustrating scenes from the lives of Mary and John the Baptist. Michelangelo, only a teenager at the time, is known to have studied under Ghirlandaio (perhaps he even worked on this cycle).

If time remains, you may want to visit the cloisters, going first to the "Green Cloister," and then the splendid Spanish Chapel frescoed by Andrea di Bonaiuto in the 14th century (one panel depicts the Dominicans in triumph over heretical wolves).

NEAR PIAZZA SANTA CROCE

Basilica di Santa Croce. Piazza Santa Croce 16. ☎ **055/244-619.** Church, free; cloisters and church museum, 4,000L ($2.40). Church, daily 8am–12:30pm and 3–6:30pm. Museum and cloisters, Mar–Sept, Thurs–Tues 10am–12:30pm and 2:30–6:30pm; Oct–Feb, daily 10am–12:30pm and 3–5pm.

The **Pantheon of Florence,** or Tuscany's "Westminster Abbey," this church shelters the tombs of everyone from Michelangelo to Machiavelli, from Dante (he was actually buried at Ravenna) to an astronomer (Galileo) who—at the hands of the Inquisition—"recanted" his concept that the earth revolves around the sun. Just as Santa Maria Novella was the church of the Dominicans, Santa Croce, said to have been designed by Arnolfo di Cambio, was the church of the Franciscans. Believe us, you can brave a visit here better than Stendhal who, after seeing Santa Croce, gushed: "I had attained to that supreme degree of sensibility where the divine intimations of art merge with the impassioned sensuality of emotion. As I emerged, I was seized with a fierce palpitation of the heart; I walked in constant fear of falling to the ground."

In the right nave (first tomb) is the Vasari-executed monument to Michelangelo, whose body was smuggled back to his native Florence from its original burial place in Rome. Along with a bust of the artist are three allegorical figures who represent the arts. In the next memorial a prune-faced Dante, a poet honored belatedly in the city that exiled him, looks down. Farther on, still on the right, is the tomb of Machiavelli, whose *The Prince* became a virtual textbook in the art of wielding power. Nearby is a lyrical bas-relief, *The Annunciation* by Donatello.

The *Trecento* frescoes are reason enough for visiting Santa Croce—especially those by Giotto to the right of the main chapel. Once whitewashed, the Bardi and Peruzzi chapels were "uncovered" in the mid-19th century in such a clumsy fashion that they had to be drastically restored. Although badly preserved, the frescoes in the Bardi Chapel are most memorable, especially the deathbed scene of St. Francis. The cycles in the Peruzzi Chapel are of John the Baptist and St. John. In the left transept is Donatello's once-controversial wooden *Crucifix*—too gruesome for some Renaissance tastes, including that of Brunelleschi, who is claimed to have said: "You [Donatello] have put a rustic upon the cross." (For Brunelleschi's "answer," go to Santa Maria Novella.) Incidentally, the Pazzi Chapel, entered through the cloisters, was designed by Brunelleschi, with terra-cottas by Luca della Robbia.

Inside the monastery of this church the Franciscan fathers established the **Leather School** at the end of World War II. The purpose of the school was to prepare young boys technically to specialize in Florentine leather work. The school has flourished and produced many fine artisans who continue their careers here. Stop in and see the work when you visit the church.

Casa Buonarroti. Via Ghibellina 70. ☎ **055/241-752.** Admission 10,000L ($6) adults, 7,000L ($4.20) students, seniors 60 and over, and children. Wed–Mon 9:30am–1:30pm.

Only a short walk from Santa Croce stands the house that Michelangelo managed to buy for his nephew. Turned into a museum by his descendants, the house was restored in 1964. It contains some fledgling work by the great artist, as well as some models by him. Here you can see his *Madonna of the Stairs,* which he did when he was 16 years old, as well as a bas-relief he did later, depicting the *Battle of the Centaurs.* The casa is enriched by many of Michelangelo's drawings, shown to the public in periodic exhibitions.

ACROSS THE ARNO

For a view of the wonders of Florence below and Fiesole above, climb aboard bus no. 13 from the central station and head for **Piazzale Michelangiolo,** a 19th-century belvedere overlooking a view seen in many a Renaissance painting. It's best at dusk, when the purple-fringed Tuscan hills form a frame for Giotto's bell tower, Brunelleschi's dome, and the towering hunk of stones that stick up from the Palazzo Vecchio. Another copy of Michelangelo's *David* dominates the square.

Warning: At certain times during the day the square is overcrowded with tour buses and peddlers selling trinkets and cheap souvenirs. If you go at these times, often midday in summer, you'll find that the view of Florence is still intact—but you may be run down by a Vespa if you try to enjoy it.

Giardini di Boboli (Boboli Gardens). Piazza de' Pitti 1. ☎ **055/213-370.** Admission 5,000L ($3). Apr–May and Oct, daily 8:30am–6:30pm; June–Sept, daily 8:30am–7:30pm; Nov–Mar, daily 9am–5:30pm. Last admission 1 hour before closing.

Behind the Pitti Palace are the Giardini di Boboli, through which the Medici romped. The gardens were originally laid out by Triboli, a great landscape artist, in the 16th century. The Boboli is ever-popular for a promenade or an idyllic interlude in a pleasant setting. The gardens are filled with fountains and statuary, such as a *Venus* by Giambologna in the "Grotto" of Buontalenti. Our favorite? An absurd Mannerist piece depicting Cosimo I's dwarf or court jester posing as a chubby Bacchus riding a turtle (found next to Vasari's corridor). You can climb to the top of the Fortezza di Belvedere for a dazzling view of the city.

Santa Maria del Carmine. Piazza Santa Maria del Carmine. ☎ **055/238-2195.** Admission 5,000L ($3). Mon and Wed–Sat 10am–4:30pm, Sun 1–4:30pm.

This baroque church, a result of rebuilding after a fire in the 18th century, is located a long walk from the Pitti Palace. Miraculously, the renowned Brancacci Chapel was spared—miraculous because it contains frescoes by Masaccio, who ushered in the great century of *Quattrocento* Renaissance painting. Forsaking the ideal, Masaccio depicted man and woman in their weakness and their glory.

His technique is seen at its most powerful in the expulsion of Adam and Eve from the Garden of Eden. The artist peopled his chapel, a masterpiece of early perspective, with scenes from the life of St. Peter (the work was originally begun by his master, Masolino). Note especially the fresco *Tribute Money,* and the baptism scene with the nude youth freezing in the cold waters.

Masaccio did the upper frescoes, but because of his early death, the lower ones were completed by Filippino Lippi (not to be confused with his father, Filippo Lippi, a greater artist).

FOR THE LITERARY ENTHUSIAST

Casa di Dante. Via Santa Margherita 1. ☎ **055/219-416.** Admission 5,000L ($3) adults, free for children 9 and under. Wed–Mon 10am–6pm, Sun 10am–2pm. Closed approximately 3 weeks during July–Aug (dates vary).

For those of us who were spoon-fed hell but spared purgatory, a pilgrimage to this rebuilt medieval house may be of passing interest, although it contains few specific exhibits of note. Dante was exiled from his native Florence in 1302 for his political involvements. He never returned, and thus wrote his *Divine Comedy* in exile, conjuring up fit punishment in the *Inferno* for his Florentine enemies. Dante certainly had the last word. The house is reached by walking down Via Dante Alighieri.

Casa Guidi. Piazza S. Felice Felice 8. ☎ **055/219-416.** Admission free. Mon–Fri 3–6pm (but call first to verify).

Just across from the Pitti Palace, not far from the Arno, is the former residence of Elizabeth Barrett and Robert Browning. They chose this location less than a year after their clandestine marriage in London, and it became their home for the remaining 14 years of their life together. Casa Guidi is where their son was born and where they wrote some of their best-known works. Elizabeth died here in 1861. Her tomb can be visited at the English cemetery in Florence. After her death, a heart-broken Browning left Florence, never to return (he died in Venice in 1889 and is buried in Westminster Abbey in London). The poets' son, Pen, acquired the residence in 1893, intending to make a memorial to his parents; however, he died before completing his plans. The rooms were first opened to the public in 1971 when the Browning Institute, an international charitable organization, acquired the apartment. "White doves in the ceiling" and frescoes of "angels looking down from a cloud," both of which Elizabeth wrote about, will interest Browning aficionados.

In a more cynical age, there is the possibility of rejecting the Brownings' life in Florence as "sentimental." Regardless, it's admirable what the institute has done to pay homage to the two 19th-century poets who were the center of the Anglo-Florentine community, much as Keats and Shelley were the stars in "English Rome." Elizabeth Barrett Browning wrote regarding Casa Guidi that "the charm of a home is a home to come back to."

FOR VISITING AMERICANS

Florence American Cemetery and Memorial. Via Cassia, 50023 Impruneta. ☎ **055/202-0020.** Free admission. May 15–Sept 15, daily 8am–6pm; Sept 16–May 14, daily 8am–5pm. The SITA city bus stops at the cemetery entrance every 2 hours, except on holidays, when there's usually no bus service; the bus follows Via Cassia.

The Florence American Cemetery and Memorial is on a 70-acre site about 7¹/₂ miles south of the city on the west side of Via Cassia, the main highway connecting Florence with Siena and Rome. One of 14 permanent American World War II military cemetery memorials built on foreign soil by the American Battle Monuments Commission, the memorial is on a site that was liberated on August 3, 1944, and later became part of the zone of the U.S. Fifth Army. It's adjacent to the Greve River and framed by wooded hills. Most of the 4,402 servicemen and women interred here died in the fighting that occurred after the capture of Rome in June 1944.

A SYNAGOGUE

La Sinagoga di Firenze. Via Farini 4. ☎ **055/245-252.** Admission 6,000L ($3.60) adults, 5,000L ($3) children 15–18, free for children 13 and under. Apr–Sept, Sun–Thurs 10am–1pm and 2–5pm, Fri 10am–1pm; Oct–Mar, Mon–Thurs 11am–1pm and 2–5pm, Fri and Sun 10am–1pm. Closed Jewish holidays.

The synagogue is in the Moorish style, inspired by Constantine's Byzantine church of Hagia Sophia. Completed in 1882, it was badly damaged by the Nazis in 1944 but has been restored to its original splendor. A museum is upstairs.

6 Soccer Matches & Other Outdoor Activities

GOLF   You'll find an 18-hole golf course, **Golf Club Ugolino,** in the nearby suburb of Impruneta, at Via Chiantigiana 3 (☎ **055/230-1009**). Impruneta lies about 9 miles south of the center.

JOGGING   One of the city's finest stretches of uninterrupted pedestrian foot-paths is in **La Cascine Park,** west of the center on the north bank of the Arno. Its eastern end begins beside the Ponte della Vittoria. (You can jog there by follow-ing the river to Piazza Vittorio Veneto, although bus no. 17 will carry you there from the cathedral.) The park also has tennis courts, a racetrack, and a public swim-ming pool. Another possibility is to jog amid the ornamental walkways of the **Boboli Gardens,** behind the Pitti Palace, although there you might find greater crowds of art lovers. If none of this appeals to you, you might jog along any of the city's **riverside quays** (the best time is early morning, if you're up to it), although you'll have to pay close attention to breakneck traffic feeding onto the Arno bridges.

SOCCER   Florence's hometown team is Fiorentina, and the city's residents take their games very seriously indeed. To watch them, head for the **Stadio Comunale,** Viale Manfredi Fanti 4-6 (☎ **055/26-241**), near Campo di Marte, about 1¹/₂ miles northeast of the town's historic center. Games are usually held on Sunday afternoon between September and May, and tickets go on sale at the stadium 2 or 3 hours be-fore the scheduled beginning. Any hotel receptionist in Florence can give you details for the upcoming week.

If you're interested in practicing your dribble and playing with local enthusiasts, head for the previously mentioned La Cascine Park, beside the river west of town, or to Campo di Marte, the soccer headquarters of Florence, where a handful of youths will likely be practicing.

SWIMMING   There's a public pool at the eastern edge of La Cascine, open June to September, the **Piscine Le Pavoniere,** Viale degli Olmi (☎ **055/367-506**). An-other possibility is the **Piscina Bellariva,** Lungarno Aldo Moro 6 (☎ **055/333-979**). These pools are crowded, however, with lots of *bambini.*

TENNIS   Although technically classified as semiprivate clubs, you'll often find an available court at the **Tennis Club Rifredi,** Via Facibeni (☎ **055/432-552**); **Il Poggetto,** Via Michele Mercati 24B (☎ **055/481-285**); or the **Circolo Tennis alle Cascine,** Viale Visarno 1 (☎ **055/332-651**). Be aware of dress codes; tennis whites with appropriate shoes are often strongly encouraged.

7 Shopping

THE SHOPPING SCENE

Skilled craftsmanship and traditional design unchanged since the days of the Medici have made Florence a serious shopping destination. Florence is noted for its hand-tooled **leather goods** and its various **straw merchandise,** as well as superbly crafted **gold jewelry.** Its reputation for fashionable custom-made clothes is no longer what it was, having lost its position to Milan.

The whole city of Florence strikes many visitors as a gigantic department store. Entire neighborhoods on both sides of the Arno offer good shops, although those along the medieval Ponte Vecchio (with some exceptions) strike most people as too touristy.

Florence is not a city for bargain shopping. In general the merchandise is rather high priced. Most visitors interested in gold or silver jewelry head for the **Ponte Vecchio** and its tiny shops. It's difficult to tell one from the other, but you really don't need to since the merchandise is similar. If you're looking for a charm or sou-venir, these shops are fine. But the heyday of finding gold jewelry bargains on the Ponte Vecchio is long gone.

The street for antiques in Florence is **Via Maggio;** some of the furnishings and objets d'art here are from the 16th century. Another major area for antique shopping is **Borgo Ognissanti.**

Florence's Fifth Avenue is **Via dei Tornabuoni.** This is the place to head for the best-quality leather goods, for the best clothing boutiques, and for stylish but costly shoes. Here you'll find everyone from Giorgio Armani to Salvatore Ferragamo.

The better shops are for the most part along Tornabuoni, but there are many on **Via Vigna Nuova, Via Porta Rossa,** and **Via degli Strozzi.** You might also stroll on the lungarno along the Arno.

For some of the best buys in leather, check out **Via del Parione,** a short narrow street off of Tornabuoni.

Shopping hours are generally Monday from 4 to 7:30pm and Tuesday to Saturday from 9 or 10am to 1pm and 3:30 or 4pm to 7:30pm. During the summer some shops are open Monday morning. However, don't be surprised if some shops are closed for several weeks in August or for the entire month.

SHOPPING A TO Z
ANTIQUES

There are many outlets for antiques in Florence (but those high prices!). If you're in the market for such expensive purchases, or if you just like to browse, try the following:

Adriana Chelini. Via Maggio 28. ☎ **055/213-471.**

This chic shop specializes in 16th- and 17th-century furniture, from small to large pieces. It also carries some paintings and porcelain and glass items from later periods. The staff will assist in shipping.

Bottega San Felice. Via Maggio 39R. ☎ **055/215-479.**

Bottega San Felice offers many intriguing items from the 19th century, sometimes in the style known as "Charles X." The shop also sells more modern pieces. Many art deco items are for sale, as are many Biedermeier pieces.

Gallori Turchi. Via Maggio 10-12-14R. ☎ **055/282-279.**

Gallori Turchi is one of the best antique stores in Florence for the serious collector— that is, the serious well-heeled collector. Some of its rare items date to the 15th century. Each item seems well chosen, ranging from polychrome figures to gilded Tuscan pieces. The shop is closed from July 20 to August 20.

Guido Bartolozzi. Via Maggio 18R. ☎ **055/215-602.**

The Bartolozzis have been doing business in this same shop for 120 years. Their specialty is European antiques from the 16th to the 19th centuries. Furniture, tapestries, china, glassware, and many other items are on display.

Paolo Romano. Borgo Ognissanti 20. ☎ **055/293-294**.

This eclectic shop carries furniture, accessories, and objets d'art from the 16th to the 19th centuries. Many pieces are small and demure; others are more suitable to the place you'll move to when you become the next Bill Gates.

ART
Galleria Masini. Piazza Goldoni 6R. ☎ **055/294-000.**

Established in 1870, the oldest art gallery in Florence, Galleria Masini lies a few minutes' walk from the Hotel Excelsior and other leading hotels. The selection of modern and contemporary paintings by top artists is extensive, representing the work of more than 500 Italian painters. Even if you're not a collector, this is a good place to select a picture that will be a lasting reminder of your visit to Italy—you can take it home duty-free.

BOOKS

Bm Bookshop. Borgo Ognissanti 4R. ☎ **055/294-575.**

This is the oldest English bookstore in Florence devoted to American and British books and one of the finest bookstores in Europe. It carries a large and excellent selection of paperbacks, travel guides, art and architecture books, history, Italian interest, fashion, design, and children's books, plus the largest collection of Italian cookbooks in English to be found in the city. Books are chosen by an expert staff and can be shipped anywhere in the world at nominal rates. The bookshop is near the Excelsior Hotel.

Libreria il Viaggio. Borgo degli Albizi 41R. ☎ **055/240-489.**

This specialty bookstore in the center of Florence sells maps and guidebooks from all over the world, in a wide variety of languages, including English. It's one of the finest bookstores of its type in Italy, with a tempting variety of titles and merchandise.

FABRIC

Casa di Tessuti. Via de' Pecori 20R. ☎ **055/215-961.**

In business for more than half a century, Casa di Tessuti is a shop for fabric connoisseurs. It has some of the nation's largest and highest-quality selections of linen, silk, wool, and cotton. The Romoli family, longtime proprietors, are proud of their assortment of fabrics, and rightly so, and are known for their selections of design and colors.

Cirri. Via por Santa Maria. ☎ **055/239-6593.**

Although once considered a dying art, Cirri keeps the art of Florentine embroidery alive, with literally hundreds of beautiful designs in linen, cotton, and silk.

FASHION (MEN & WOMEN)

Glamour. Borgo San Jacopo 49. ☎ **055/210-334.**

Italian clothing from lesser-known designers such as Caractere is available here. Although style is first rate, prices are more affordable than most fashion houses in Florence. You'll find good-quality sweaters as well as blouses and skirts in various materials. This is for the savvy shopper interested in good buys—minus the famous names.

Loretta Caponi. Piazza Antinori 4. ☎ **055/213-668.**

This shop's arched ceiling and decorative gold-and-turquoise trim create a perfect atmosphere in which to browse through a beautiful selection of slipdresses, robes, linens, and children's wear in luxurious silks, velvets, and cottons.

Mariposa. Lungarno Corsini 2. ☎ **055/284-259.**

Mariposa offers women's fashions from such famous designers as Krizia, Fendi, Rocco Barocco, Missoni, and Mimmina. Foreign customers are often granted a 10% discount.

Max Mara. Via del Pecori 14. ☎ **055/239-6590.**

Featured here are high-quality women's clothes designed and produced by Max Mara, a name synonymous with classic elegance—even a touch of flamboyance. The selection covers everything from hats and coats to suits and slacks. You don't find the big names in design here, but many of the "unknowns" are getting better known every day.

Romano. Piazza della Repubblica. ☎ **055/239-6890.**

In the commercial center of town near the Duomo is Romano, a glamorous clothing store for both women and men. The owners commissioned a curving stairwell to be constructed under the high ornate ceiling. But even more exciting are leather and suede goods found here, along with an assortment of stylish dresses, shoes, and handbags—prices are high, but so is the quality.

GIFTS

Balatresi Gift Shop. Lungarno Acciaiuoli 22R. ☎ **055/287-851.**

Among the many treasures found here are Florentine mosaics created for the shop by Maestro Metello Montelatici, who is arguably one of the greatest mosaicists alive today. The store also sells original ceramic figurines by the sculptor Giannitrapani, and a fine selection of hand-carved alabaster, enamel ware, and Tuscan glass. Many Americans come here every year to do their Christmas shopping.

Menegatti. Piazza del Pesce, Ponte Vecchio 2R. ☎ **055/215-202.**

The wide inventory here includes pottery from Florence, Faenza, and Deruta. There are also della Robbia reproductions made in red clay like the originals. Items can be sent home if you arrange it at the time of your purchase.

GLASS

Cose Del '900. Borgo San Jacopo 45. ☎ **055/283-491.**

This small shop is full of glass items of every description from 1900 to 1950. There are shot glasses, drinking glasses, centerpieces, and many art deco pieces.

HERBALISTS

Alessandro Bizzarri. Via della Condotta 32R. ☎ **055/211-580.**

Alessandro Bizzarri is one of those musty old stores found only in Europe. It's been dispensing spices and minerals since 1842. Some of its extracts and essences are based on formulas in use in the Middle Ages or Renaissance era.

Antica Farmacia del Cinghiale. Piazza del Mercato Muovo 4R. ☎ **055/282-128.**

Antica Farmacia del Cinghiale, in business for some three centuries, is an *erboristeria,* dispensing herbal teas and fragrances, along with herbal potpourris. A pharmacy is also situated here.

Officina Profumo Farmaceutica di Santa Maria Novella. Via della Scala 16N. ☎ **055/216-276.**

This is the most fascinating pharmacy in Italy. Located northwest of the Church of Santa Maria Novella, it opened its doors to the public in 1612, offering a selection of herbal remedies that were created by friars of the Dominican order. Those closely guarded secrets have been retained, and many of the same elixirs are still sold today. You've heard of papaya as an aid to digestion, but what about elixir of rhubarb? A wide selection of perfumes, scented soaps, shampoos, and of course potpourris, along with creams and lotions, is also sold. The shop is closed on Saturday afternoon in July and August.

JEWELRY

Buying jewelry is almost an art in itself, so proceed with caution. Florence, of course, is known for its jewelry. You'll find some stunning antique pieces, and, if you know how to buy, some good values.

Befani e Tai. Via Vacchereccia 13R. ☎ **055/287-825.**

Befani e Tai is one of the most unusual jewelry stores in Florence—some of its pieces date back to the 19th century. The store was established right after World War II by expert goldsmiths who were childhood friends. Some of their clients even design their own jewelry for special orders. Artisans are skilled at working in gold and platinum.

Faraone-Settepassi. Via dei Tornabuoni 25R. ☎ **055/215-506.**

Faraone-Settepassi, one of the most distinguished jewelers of the Renaissance city, draws a well-heeled patronage.

Fratelli Favilli. Piazza del Duomo 16R. ☎ **055/211-846.**

Fratelli Favilli is the finest engraver in the city, with a specialty in signet rings. Virtually any design you bring to them can be crafted here.

Mario Buccellati. Via dei Tornabuoni 69-71R. ☎ **055/239-6579.**

Located away from the Ponte Vecchio, Mario Buccellati specializes in exquisite handcrafted jewelry and silver. A large selection of intriguing pieces at high prices is offered.

Rudolfo Fallaci. Ponte Vecchio 10 and 22. ☎ **055/294-981.**

Modern 18-carat gold jewelry is the specialty here, all made in Florence. Look also for the beautiful enameled silver boxes from the 1800s. Also to be found are cameos and pieces set with diamonds.

LEATHER

Universally acclaimed, Florentine leather is still the fine product it always was—smooth, well shaped, and often in vivid colors.

Beltrami. Via del Tornabuoni 48. ☎ **055/287-779.**

The well-known Beltrami leather goods are sold here as well as expensive evening clothes, heavyweight silk scarves, and fashions of the best quality. This is one of several Beltrami shops in the area. High fashion, high prices, and high quality are what you'll find here, but prices are significantly lower than what you'll pay for Beltrami in the States.

Beltrami Spa. Via del Panzani 1. ☎ **055/212-661.**

This Beltrami shop offers last season's fashions at discounts of 20% to 50%. There are further discounts for multiple purchases, and since the original prices are still on the items, you can tell how much you are saving.

Bojola. Via dei Rondinelli 25R. ☎ **055/211-155.**

Sergio Bojola, a leading name in leather, has distinguished himself in Florence by the variety of his selections, in both synthetic materials and beautiful leathers. Here you'll find first-class quality and craftsmanship.

Gucci. Via del Tornabuoni 73. ☎ **055/264-011.**

You've heard of the mother of all battles: This is the mother of all Gucci shops. Although much imitated around the world, this Gucci product is real. In general, prices are a bit cheaper here than in Milan and a lot less expensive than in the United States. If you want to shop for Gucci in Italy, head here. There's every Gucci item imaginable—belts to shoes to shawls, and, of course, the chic Gucci scarf.

John F. Lungarno Corsini 2. ☎ **055/239-8985.**

John F., located near the Santa Trínita Bridge, is a high-fashion house of leather located in a Florentine palace. The leather clothing is of exclusive design, and the salon shows models from the *crème de la crème* of its collection. Although many foreigners shop here, John F. also dresses some of the most chic Florentine women. Beautifully styled and crafted accessories, including handbags and leather articles, are also offered. There's also a vast selection of Missoni sports sweaters.

Leonardo Leather Works. Borgo dei Greci 16A. ☎ **055/292-202.**

Leonardo Leather Works concentrates on two of the oldest major crafts of Florence: leather and jewelry. Leather goods include wallets, bags, shoes, boots, briefcases, clothing, travel bags, belts, and gift items, with products by famous designers. No imitations are permitted here. The jewelry department has a large assortment of gold chains, bracelets, rings, earrings, and charms.

Pollini. Via Calimala 12R. ☎ **055/214-738.**

Pollini, one of the leading leather-goods stores of Florence, offers a wide array of stylized merchandise, including shoes, suitcases, clothing, belts, and virtually anything made of leather. It's located in the historic heart of Florence, near the Ponte Vecchio.

Taddei. Via Santa Margherita 11R. ☎ **055/239-8960.**

Taddei is the place for exquisitely made leather boxes and desk accessories. This family-owned and -run business has been turning out quality items for three generations.

LINGERIE

Garbo. Borgo Ognissanti 2. ☎ **055/295-338.**

The meticulously crafted lingerie offered here—including ready-made and custom linens, silks, and cottons with handstitched embroidery—is inspired by bygone days.

MARKETS

After checking into their hotels, the most intrepid shoppers head for **Piazza del Mercato Nuovo (the Straw Market),** called "Il Porcellino" by the Italians because of the bronze statue of a reclining wild boar here. (It's a copy of the one in the Uffizi.) Tourists pet its snout (which is well worn) for good luck. The market stands in the monumental heart of Florence, an easy stroll from the Palazzo Vecchio. It sells not only straw items but leather goods as well, along with an array of typically Florentine merchandise—frames, trays, hand-embroidery, table linens, and hand-sprayed and -painted boxes in traditional designs. Open Monday to Saturday from 9am to 7pm.

However, even better bargains await those who make their way through pushcarts to the stalls of the open-air **Mercato Centrale** (also called the Mercato San Lorenzo), in and around Borgo San Lorenzo, near the railway station. If you don't mind bargaining, which is imperative here, you'll find an array of merchandise, including raffia bags, Florentine leather purses, salt-and-pepper shakers, straw handbags, and art reproductions.

MASKS

I Mascherari. Via dei Tavolini 13R. ☎ **055/231-823.**

I Mascherari is the best shop for masks, which after a long sleep have become a fad again. Some of the masks are based on Florentine Renaissance patterns; others are in the Venetian *commedia dell'arte* style.

MOSAICS

Arte Musiva. Largo Bargellini 2-4. ☎ 055/241-647.

Florentine mosaics are universally recognized. Bruno Lastrucci, the director of Arte Musiva, located in the old quarter of Santa Croce, is one of the most renowned living exponents of this art form. In the workshop you can see artisans—including some of the major mosaicists of Italy—plying their craft, creating both traditional Florentine and modern designs. A selection of the most significant works is permanently displayed in the gallery, including decorative panels and tiles.

PAPER & STATIONERY

Giulio Giannini & Figlio. Piazza Pitti 37R. ☎ 055/212-621.

Giulio Giannini & Figlio has been a family business for more than 140 years and is the leading stationery store in Florence. Foreigners often snap up the exquisite merchandise for gift-giving later in the year.

Il Papiro. Via Cavour 55R. ☎ 055/215-262.

Its specialty is party-colored marbleized paper that's skillfully incorporated into objects ranging from bookmarks to photo albums. (Have a favorite relative who's getting married soon? These make great wedding albums.) More unusual are the marbleized wood (such as music boxes) and leather (couture-style purses and bags) items, as well as the marbleized fabric. The staff is charming, and the prices are reasonable, considering the high quality of virtually everything sold in the store. The flagship store is on Via Cavour, but there are branches at Piazza del Duomo 24R (☎ 055/215-262) and Lugarno Acciaiuoli 42R (☎ 055/215-262).

Pineider. Piazza della Signoria 13R. ☎ 055/284-4655.

Established on this site in 1774, and maintained today by descendants of the original founders, this is the oldest store in Florence specializing in the art of printing and engraving. The most aristocratic-looking greeting cards, business cards, stationery, and formal invitations come from this outfit, which employs a battalion of artisans who custom-make the steel plates for each engraving job. This is the flagship of a discreet, small-scale chain. Because most orders take between 2 and 3 weeks to fill, many clients place their orders at this store, then arrange to have the final product shipped home. The store also stocks a wide range of gift items, including beautifully crafted diaries, stationery, the kinds of desk sets you'd offer your favorite CEO, portfolios, address books, photo albums, and etchings of vistas unique to Florence. A less extensive branch of this store, that doesn't take custom engraving orders, is at Via dei Tornbuoni 76 (☎ 055/211-605).

PRINTS & ENGRAVINGS

Ducci. Lungarno Corsini 24. ☎ 055/214-550.

This shop hawks the best selection of historical prints and engravings covering the history of Florence from the 13th century. Also available are Florentine boxes covered with gold leaf, marble fruit, and wooden items.

Giovanni Baccani. Via della Vigna Nuova 75R. ☎ 055/214-467.

Giovanni Baccani has long been a specialist in this field. Everything it sells is old—there's nothing new here. "The Blue Shop," as it's called, offers a huge array of prints

---

The Art of Marbleizing

The city that prides itself as the literary cradle of Italy has always known how best to present its folios and manuscripts.

The brilliantly colored marbleized end pages that decorate the inside covers of books and photo albums use techniques that were originally developed in Persia and Turkey, and were imported to Italy during the 1400s by Florentine and Venetian merchants. The technique was improved and kept alive in Florence throughout the 19th and 20th centuries.

How do they do it? The "marbleizing" technique takes advantage of the relative densities of water and oil-based pigments to "float" layers of ink above the basins of water. By jiggling sheets of paper through multicolored brew, teams of trained artisans create the peacock-feathered effect that has been so popular throughout the ages. Part of the expense of marbleized paper involves the need to discard large amounts of ink, as the basin of pigment is usually thrown away after the treatment of each piece of paper.

---

and engravings, often of Florentine scenes. These are found in bins, and you're free to look as long as you want. Tuscan paper goods are also sold.

SHOES

Casadei. Via del Tornabuoni. ☎ **055/287-240.**

An interesting shop painted white with pillars, making the room look like a small colonnade, this is one of four Casadei shops in Italy (others are in in Rome, Ferrara, and near Bologna). Locally produced women's shoes, boots, and handbags are sold here, all with the Casadei label. Prices run from 300,000L ($180).

Ferragamo. Via dei Tornabuoni 16R. ☎ **055/292-123.**

Salvatore Ferragamo has long been one of the most famous names in shoes. Although he started in Hollywood just before the outbreak of World War I, the headquarters of this famed manufacturer were installed here in the Palazzo Ferroni, on the most fashionable shopping street of Florence, before World War II broke out. Ferragamo sells shoes for both men and women, along with some of the most elegant boutique items in the city, including men's and women's clothing, scarves, handbags, ties, luggage, and other merchandise. But chances are you'll want to visit it for its stunning shoes, known for their durability and style.

If you're really interested, check out the **Ferragamo Museum** at Via dei Tornabuoni 2 (☎ **055/336-0456**), open on Monday, Wednesday, and Friday from 9am to 1pm and 2 to 6pm. This free museum, set on the second floor of a block devoted completely to the Ferragamo aesthetic, chronicles the family-run empire from its beginnings, and documents everything from the design to the manufacturing process. There's also a display of exquisite shoes from other eras.

Lily of Florence. Via Guicciardini 2R. ☎ **055/294-748.**

Lily of Florence offers both men's and women's shoes in American sizes. For women, Lily distributes both her own creations and those of other well-known designers. The stylish shoes come in a wide range of colors and are made of high-quality leather.

SILVER

Pampaloni. Borgo Santi Apostoli, 47R. ☎ **055/289-094.**

This shop is headed by Gianfranco Pampaloni, the third-generation silversmith in his family. An inspired artist, he often bases designs on past achievements, for example, a 1604 drinking goblet by the Roman artist Giovanni Maggi. The business was launched in 1902, and some of the classic designs turned out back then are still being made. Gianfranco doesn't live in the past, however, as his own adventurous designs are carried in such prestigious outlets as the Rome-based jeweler Bulgari and Tiffany & Co.

WINES

Il Cantinone. Via Santo Spirito 6. ☎ **055/218-898.**

Although this restaurant is self-described as presenting a typical Florentine menu, the emphasis here is on wine—principally the wines of Tuscany, such as Black Label, Santo Cristo, and Villa Antinori. Purchase your choice by the glass or by the bottle to take with you. And don't forget to try the Vin Santo, a Tuscan dessert wine, with almond cookies.

8 Florence After Dark

Evening entertainment in Florence is not an exciting prospect, unless you simply like to walk through the narrow streets or head up toward Fiesole for a view of the city at night (truly spectacular). The typical Florentine begins an evening early at one of the cafes listed below.

For theatrical and concert listings pick up a free copy of *Welcome to Florence,* available at the tourist office. This handy publication contains information on recitals, concerts, theatrical productions, and other cultural offerings.

Many cultural presentations are performed in churches. These might include open-air concerts in the cloisters of the Badia Fiesolana in Fiesole, or at the Ospedale degli Innocenti, the foundling "hospital of the innocents," on summer evenings only.

Orchestral offerings—performed by the **Regional Tuscan Orchestra**—are often presented at the church of Santo Stefano al Ponte Vecchio.

From late April until July, the city welcomes classical musicians for its festival of cantatas, madrigals, concertos, operas **Maggio Musicale,** and ballets, many of which are presented in Renaissance buildings. Schedule and ticket information is available from Maggio Musicale Fiorentino/Teatro Comunale, Via Solferino 16, 50123 Firenze (☎ **055/27-791**). Tickets cost 20,000L to 200,000L ($12 to $120).

THE PERFORMING ARTS

Teatro Comunale di Firenze/Maggio Musicale Fiorentino. Corso Italia 16. ☎ **055/211-158.** Tickets 36,000L–200,000L ($21.60–$120) for the opera; 35,000L–100,000L ($21–$60) for concerts; 16,000L–50,000L ($9.60–$30) for the ballet.

This is the main theater in Florence, with opera and ballet seasons presented from September to December, and concert season from January to April. This theater is also the venue for the **Maggio Musicale Fiorentino,** Italy's oldest and most prestigious festival that takes place in Florence from May to July and offers opera, ballet, concerts, recitals, cinema, and meetings. The box office is open Tuesday to Friday from 11am to 5:30pm, Saturday from 9am to 1pm, and 1 hour before the curtain.

Teatro della Pergola. Via della Pergola 18. ☎ **055/247-9651.** Tickets 12,000L–70,000L ($7.20–$42).

This is the major legitimate theater of Florence, but you'll have to understand Italian to appreciate most of its plays, except for opera, which is universal, of course. Plays are performed year-round except during the Maggio Musicale, when the theater becomes the setting for many of the musical presentations of the festival. Performances are Tuesday to Saturday at 8:45pm. The box office is open Tuesday to Saturday from 9:30am to 1pm and 3:45 to 6:45pm and Sunday from 9:45am to noon.

THE CLUB & MUSIC SCENE

Full-Up. Via della Vigna Vecchia 23-25R. ☎ **055/293-006.** Cover 15,000L–25,000L ($9–$15) includes the first drink.

Contained in the cellar of an antique building in the historic heart of town, this well-known establishment attracts college students from the city's many universities, who appreciate the club's two-in-one format. One section contains a smallish dance floor and recorded dance music; another is devoted to the somewhat more restrained ambience of a piano bar. The place can be fun, and even older clients usually feel at ease here. Open Wednesday to Monday from 9pm to 3am.

Meccanò. Viale degli Olmi 1. ☎ **055/331-371.** Cover 22,000L–30,000L ($13.20–$18) includes the first drink.

This is Florence's best and most internationally sophisticated disco. Set within a 20-minute bus ride from Piazza Duomo, near the Parco della Cascine, it's one of the few discos in Italy to offer an indoor-outdoor setting that includes century-old trees, a terrace, and three dance floors on two different levels. The musical venue includes everything from punk to rock to funk to garage. Gays mix with the mostly hetero crowd with ease, and the average age of the clientele is from 18 to around 32. There's no real dress code, but if you opt to dine at the club's restaurant, you'll find that the clientele there is better dressed and more prosperous than that of the average dance-till-you-drop clubber. Set menus cost 35,000L ($21) and are served beginning at 9pm. Don't be surprised if someone decides to dance on your table after you've finished eating. Dancing reigns supreme every night except Sunday, Monday, and Wednesday, from 11:30pm to 4am. Fortunately, the place is air-conditioned.

Red Garter. Via de' Benci 33R. ☎ **055/234-4904.** No cover.

Perhaps nothing could be more unexpected in this city of Donatello and Michelangelo than a club called the Red Garter, right off Piazza Santa Croce. The club, which has an American Prohibition–era theme, attracts young people from all over the world and features everything from rock to bluegrass. A mug of Heineken lager on tap goes for 7,000L ($4.20), and most tall drinks, made from "hijacked hootch," as it's known here, begin at 10,000L ($6). The club is open Monday to Thursday from 8:30pm to 1am and Friday to Sunday from 9pm to 1:30am. "Happy Hour" is every evening until 9:30pm.

Space Electronic. Via Palazzuolo 37. ☎ **055/293-082.** Cover 25,000L ($15) includes the first drink.

This is the only club in Florence with karaoke. The decor consists of gigantic carnival heads, wall-to-wall mirrors, and an imitation space capsule that goes back and forth across the dance floor. If karaoke doesn't thrill you, however, head to the new ground-floor pub, which stocks an ample supply of imported beers. On the upper level is a large dance floor with a wide choice of music and the best sound-and-light show in town. This place attracts a lot of foreign women who want to hook up with Florentine men on the prowl. The disco opens nightly at 9:30pm and usually goes until 2:30am or later, depending on business.

Tenax. Via Pratese 46. ☎ **055/308-160.** Cover 20,000L–50,000L ($12–$30).

Set within a 10-minute bus ride from the Piazza Duomo (take bus no. 29 or 30 to a point near Florence's airport), this is Florence's premier venue for live rock. The bands come from throughout Italy and the rest of Europe. This place used to be a garage and is appropriately battered and grungy. Shows begin nightly except Monday at 10pm and continue until around 4am. Dress as you would for a punk-rock recital in London.

Yab Yum. Via Sassetti 5R. ☎ **055/215-161.** Cover 22,000L–30,000L ($13.20–$18) includes the first drink.

Much of this joint's popularity derives from its location in the heart of Florence's historic core—a boon for art-weary visitors who want to dance, dance, dance. Owned and operated by the same entrepreneurs who maintain the larger, more fun, and less inhibited Meccanò, it offers much the same kind of music, albeit in a smaller and more cramped setting. Partly because its interior is less well air-conditioned, it closes between May and October. Otherwise, hours are Wednesday through Saturday from 11pm to 4am.

THE BAR & CAFE SCENE
BARS & PUBS
Donatello Bar. In the Hotel Excelsior, Piazza Ognissanti 3. ☎ **055/264-201.**

Donatello Bar, on the ground floor of this previously recommended deluxe hotel, is the city's most elegant watering hole. Named in honor of the great Renaissance artist, this bar and its adjoining restaurant, Il Cestello, attracts well-heeled international visitors along with the Florentine cultural and business elite. The ambience is enlivened by a marble fountain and works of art. Piano music is featured daily from 7pm to 1am.

Dublin Pub. Via Faenza 27R. ☎ **055/293-049.**

If you ask whether this is an Italian pub, the all-Italian staff will respond rather grandly that such a concept doesn't exist, and that pubs are by definition Irish. And once you get beyond the fact that virtually no one on the staff here has ever been outside of Tuscany, and that there's very little to do here except drink and perhaps practice your Italian, you might settle down and have a rollicking old (very Latin) time. Beers, at least, are appropriately Celtic, and include Harp, Guinness, Kilkenny, and Strong's on tap. You'll find it near the Santa Maria Novella railway station.

Fiddler's Elbow. Piazza Santa Maria Novella 7R. ☎ **055/215-056.**

After an initial success in Rome, this Irish pub has now invaded the city of Donatello and Michelangelo. It quickly became one of the most popular watering holes in Florence. An authentic pint of Guinness is the most popular item to order. The location is in the vicinity of the rail station.

CAFES
Café Rivoire. Piazza della Signoria 4R. ☎ **055/214-412.**

Café Rivoire offers a classy and amusing old-world ambience with a direct view of the statues of one of our favorite squares in the world. You can sit at one of the metal tables set up on the flagstones outside, or at one of the tables in a choice of inner rooms filled with marble detailing and unusual oil renderings of the piazza outside. If you don't want to sit at all, try the mahogany and green-marble bar, where many of the more colorful characters making the Grand Tour of Europe talk, flirt, or gossip. There's also a selection of small sandwiches, omelets, and ice creams. The cafe is noted for its hot chocolate.

Giacosa. Via dei Tornabuoni 83R. ☎ **055/239-6226.**

Giacosa is a deceptively simple-looking cafe whose stand-up bar occupies more space than its limited number of sit-down tables. Set behind three Tuscan arches on a fashionable shopping street in the center of the old city, it has a warmly paneled interior, a lavish display of pastries and sandwiches, and a reputation as the birthplace of the Negroni. That drink, as you probably know, is a combination of gin, Campari, and red vermouth. You can also wet your whistle with Singapore slings, Italian and American coffee, and a range of aperitifs. Light meals are also served, and the cafe is famous for its ice cream.

Gilli. Piazza della Repubblica 39R, via Roma 1. ☎ **055/213-896.**

Gilli, the oldest and most beautiful cafe in Florence, occupies a desirable position in the center of the city, a few minutes' walk from the Duomo. It was founded in 1733, when Piazza della Repubblica had a different name. You can sit at a small, brightly lit table near the bar, or retreat to an intricately paneled pair of rooms to the side and enjoy the flattering light from the Venetian-glass chandeliers. Daily specials, sandwiches, toasts, and hard drinks are sold, along with an array of "tropical" libations.

Giubbe Rosse. Piazza della Repubblica 13-14R. ☎ **055/212-280.**

The waiters of this place still wear the red coats as they did when the establishment was founded in 1888. Originally a beer hall, today it's an elegantly paneled cafe, bar, and restaurant filled with turn-of-the-century chandeliers and polished granite floors. You can enjoy a drink or cup of coffee at one of the small tables near the zinc-top bar. An inner dining room has a soaring vaulted ceiling of reddish brick. Light lunches are a specialty, as are full American breakfasts.

GAY NIGHTLIFE

Crisco. Via S. Egidio 43R. ☎ **055/248-0580.** Cover 12,000L–20,000L ($7.20–$12), depending on the night of the week.

This, Florence's leading gay bar, caters only to men and is located in an 18th-century building that contains both a bar and a dance floor. Classified as a *club privato*, it's open on Wednesday, Thursday, Sunday, and Monday from 10:30pm to 3:30am, and Friday and Saturday from 10:30pm to 5 or 6am.

Santanassa Bar. Via del Pandolfini 29R. ☎ **055/243-356.** Cover 12,000L ($7.20) Sun–Thurs, 15,000L–20,000L ($9–$12) Fri–Sat, includes the first drink.

Many of Tuscany's gay community consider this club a Saturday-night staple. In summertime the crowd gets very international, looking like a cross section of all the nations of Europe. There's a crowded bar on the street level, sometimes with a live piano player, where many of the clients seem to have known one another for years. On Friday and Saturday the cellar is transformed into a disco. It's open Sunday to Thursday from 10pm to 4am and Friday and Saturday from 10pm to 6am. The bar is open year-round; the disco is open September through June.

Tabasco. Piazza Santa Cecelia 3. ☎ **055/213-000.** Cover 15,000L–20,000L ($9–$12) includes the first drink.

One of the leading gay bars of Florence, Tabasco stands near Piazza della Signoria in the heart of the city. The club offers a bar, along with video games and X-rated male-action movies. Sometimes cabaret shows and karaoke are offered. You must be 18 to be admitted. It's open Tuesday to Sunday from 10pm to at least 3am or later on weekends.

9   A Side Trip to Fiesole

For more extensive day trips, you can refer to the next chapter. But Fiesole is a virtual suburb of Florence.

When the sun shines too hot on Piazza della Signoria and tourists try to prance bare-backed into the Uffizi, Florentines are likely to head for the hills—usually to Fiesole. But they'll encounter more tourists, as this town—once an Etruscan settlement—is the most popular outing from the city. Bus no. 7, which leaves from Piazza San Marco, will take you here in 25 minutes and give you a panoramic view along the way. You'll pass fountains, statuary, and gardens strung out over the hills like a scrambled jigsaw puzzle.

EXPLORING THE TOWN

When you arrive at Fiesole, by all means don't sit with the throngs all afternoon in the central square sipping Campari (although that isn't a bad pastime). Explore some of Fiesole's attractions. You won't find anything as dazzling as the Renaissance treasures of Florence, however—the charms of Fiesole are more subtle. Fortunately, all major sights branch out within walking distance of the main piazza, beginning with the **Cattedrale di San Romolo**. At first this cathedral may seem austere, with its concrete-gray Corinthian columns and Romanesque arches. But it has its own beauty. Dating from A.D. 1000, it was much altered during the Renaissance. In the Salutati Chapel are important sculptural works by Mino da Fiesole. It's open daily from 7:30am to noon and 4 to 7pm.

Bandini Museum. Via Dupre. ☎ **055/59-477.** Admission 6,000L ($3.60) adults, 3,000L ($1.80) children 17 and under, students, and seniors 60 and over. Daily 9am–6pm.

This ecclesiastical museum, around to the side of the Duomo, belongs to the Fiesole Cathedral Chapter, established in 1913. On the ground floor are della Robbia terracotta works, as well as art by Michelangelo and Nino Pisano. On the top floors are paintings by the best Giotto students, which reflect ecclesiastical and worldly themes, most of them the work of Tuscan artists of the 14th century.

Museo Missionario Francescano Fiesole. Via San Francesco 13. ☎ **055/59-175.** Free admission (but a donation is expected). Mon–Fri 9am–noon and 3–6pm, Sat 3–6pm.

The hardest task you'll have in Fiesole is to take the steep goat-climb up to the Convent of San Francesco. You can visit the Gothic-style Franciscan church, which was built in the first years of the 1400s. The church was consecrated in 1516. Inside are many paintings by well-known Florentine artists. In the basement of the church is the ethnological museum. Begun in 1906, the collection has a large section of Chinese artifacts, including ancient bronzes. An Etruscan-Roman section contains some 330 archaeological pieces, and an Egyptian section also has numerous objects.

Teatro Romano e Museo Civico. Via Portigiani 1. ☎ **055/59-477.** Admission 6,000L ($3.60) adults; 3,000L ($1.80) children 6–16, students, and seniors 60 and over; free for children 5 and under. Daily 9:30am–6:30pm. Closed first Tues every month.

On this site is the major surviving evidence that Fiesole was an Etruscan city six centuries before Christ, and later a Roman town. In the 1st century B.C. a theater was built, the restored remains of which you can see today. Near the theater are the skeleton-like ruins of the baths, which may have been built at the same time. Try to visit the Etruscan-Roman museum, with its many interesting finds that date from the days when Fiesole—not Florence—was supreme (a guide is on hand to show you through).

WHERE TO STAY

Hotel Aurora. Piazza Mino da Fiesole 39, Fiesole, 50014 Firenze. ☎ **055/59-100.** Fax 055/ 59-587. 27 rms. A/C MINIBAR TV TEL. 227,000L–335,000L ($136.20–$201) double. Rates include breakfast. AE, DC, MC, V.

Set on Fiesole's main square, behind a facade of green shutters and ocher-colored stucco, the Aurora occupies a structure built in the 18th century as a private house. In 1890 it became a hotel that catered almost exclusively to arts-conscious English people making their grand tour through the historic cities of Italy. The hotel continues to rent rooms, which have been modernized and simplified to meet today's needs and even include Jacuzzis. Views over faraway Florence are visible from the hotel's back bedrooms, which cost more than those overlooking the piazza in front. On the premises are a back terrace with hanging vines, a pergola, and views of the city. Connecting doors can be opened between some rooms to create suites, which cost around 550,000L ($330) each.

Pensione Bencista. Via Benedetto de Maiano 4, Fiesole, 50014 Firenze. ☎ **055/59-163.** Fax 055/59-163. 44 rms, 32 with bath. TEL. 115,000L ($69) per person without bath, 135,000L ($81) per person with bath. Rates include half board. No credit cards.

Pensione Bencista has been the family villa of the Simoni family for years. One guest found that it was like E. M. Forster's "*A Room with a View* gone to the country." It was built around 1300, with additions made to the existing building about every 100 years after that. In 1925 Paolo Simoni opened the villa to paying guests. Today it's run by his son, Simone Simoni. Its position, high up on the road to Fiesole, is commanding, with an unmarred view of the city and the hillside villas. The driveway to the formal entrance, with its circular fountain, winds through olive trees. The spread-out villa has many lofty old rooms furnished with family antiques. The bedrooms vary in size and interest; many are without bath and have hot and cold running water only. In chilly weather guests meet each other in the evening in front of a huge fireplace. The Bencista is suitable for parents who might want to leave their children in the country while they take jaunts into the city. It's a 10-minute bus ride from the heart of Florence.

✪ **Villa San Michele.** Via Doccia 4, Fiesole, 50014 Firenze. ☎ **055/59-451.** Fax 055/598-734. 26 rms, 10 suites. A/C MINIBAR TV TEL. 1,240,000L ($744) double; 2,380,000L ($1,428) suite. Rates include half board. AE, DC, MC, V. Closed mid-Nov to mid-Mar.

Villa San Michele is an ancient monastery of unsurpassed beauty—the setting is memorable. On a hill just below Fiesole, a 15-minute walk south of the center, and complete with gardens, the monastery was built in the 15th century on a wide ledge. After being damaged in World War II, the villa was carefully restored. It is said that the facade and the loggia were designed by Michelangelo. A curving driveway, lined with blossoming trees and flowers, leads to the entrance. A 10-arch covered loggia continues around the view side of the building to the Italian gardens at the rear. On the loggia, chairs are set out for drinks and moonlight dinners. Most of the bedrooms open onto the view, or the inner courtyard. Each room is unique, all with private baths, some with iron or wooden canopy beds, antique chests, Savonarola chairs, formal draperies, old ecclesiastical paintings, candelabra, and statues—in other words, a stunning tour de force of rich but restrained design. Poets and artists have stayed at the San Michele and sung its praise.

WHERE TO DINE

Trattoria le Cave di Maiano. Via delle Cave 16. ☎ **055/59-133.** Reservations required. Main courses 28,000L–32,000L ($16.80–$19.20). AE, DC, MC, V. Tues–Sun noon–3pm; daily 7–11:30pm. Closed Aug 10–20. TUSCAN.

This restaurant, at Maiano, is a 15-minute ride east from the heart of Florence and just a short distance south of Fiesole. It's a family-run establishment that since the 17th century has been an esoteric address to discerning Florentines. The rustically decorated trattoria is a garden restaurant, with stone tables and large sheltering trees. Inside, the restaurant is in the tavern style, with a beamed ceiling. We recommend highly the antipasto and the homemade green tortellini. For a main course, there's a golden grilled chicken or perhaps a savory herb-flavored roast lamb. For side dishes, we suggest fried polenta, Tuscan beans, and fried potatoes. As a final treat, the waiter will bring you homemade ice cream with fresh raspberries.

7

Tuscany & Umbria

Rome may rule Italy but Tuscany presides over its heart. Its landscapes, some little changed since the days of the Medici, are like Renaissance paintings, even today, with their cypress trees and olive groves, along with those fabled Chianti vineyards.

That ancient race, the Etruscans, first appeared in Italy in the region of Tuscany—those "long nosed, sensitive footed, subtly smiling Etruscans," to quote D. H. Lawrence. The Romans followed and absorbed and conquered them, and by the 11th century the region had evolved into a collection of independent city-states, such as Florence and Siena, each trying to dominate the other.

Many of these cities that we'll soon visit, including Siena, knew the apogee of their economic and political power in the 13th century. So popular in Florence, the Renaissance was slow to come to Siena, which remains a gem of Gothic glory.

But in time the Renaissance did arrive with its titans of art, including those hometown sons, Giotto, Michelangelo, and Leonardo da Vinci, who passed through these landscapes centuries ago. Ever since these grand artists "invented" the Renaissance (although it wasn't called that at the time), the world has flocked to Tuscany to see not just the land but some of the world's greatest art. Critics claim, without too much exaggeration, that Western civilization was "rediscovered" in Tuscany. To call Lawrence back for judgment, Tuscany became "the perfect center of man's universe."

Under the tutelage of the powerful Medici family, art flourished, and the legacy remains of Masaccio, Piero della Francesca, Luca Signorelli, Raphael, Donatello, Botticelli, and countless others, including the unprecedented engineering feats of such architects as Brunelleschi. This first Renaissance is well known. Lesser known is the virtual second Renaissance that came to Tuscany, long after the Medici dynasty expired in 1737. Drawn to Tuscany to write about its art, history, and landscapes was a stellar literary brigade that included Gorky, Twain, Shelley, Stedhal, Dostoyevsky, the Brownings, and even Dylan Thomas.

Such Tuscan men of letters as Dante, Petrarch, and Boccaccio, who put the seal of approval on the Tuscan dialect by writing in the vernacular rather than Latin, might look down their pointed noses at their neighbor, Umbria. But that would be Tuscan snobbism. A small, landlocked region that lies at the heart of the Italian peninsula, Umbria is more associated with saints than great artists like

Tuscany. Christendom's most beloved saints were born here, foremost of which was St. Francis of Assisi, founder of the Franciscans. St. Valentine, a 3rd-century bishop of Terni, was also born here, as was St. Clare, founder of the Order of Poor Clares.

Umbria painters also contributed to the glory of the Renaissance, including Il Perugino, whose lyrical works can be seen today in the Galleria Nazionale dell'Umbria in Perugia. Umbria's landscapes, also the subject of countless paintings, are as alluring as ever, as you pass through a hilly, chestnut-wooded terrain interspersed with fertile plains of olive groves and vineyards (Pliny the Elder was among the first to rhapsodize over the vino of Umbria).

How much time to spend in each province? A countess at a Tuscan villa told us: "Give each a year. Who knows? Perhaps you'll write two bestsellers—*A Year in Tuscany,* followed by *A Year in Umbria.*"

1 Montecatini Terme

19 miles NE of Florence, 26 miles NE of Pisa

The best known of all Italian spas, Montecatini Terme has long been frequented for its cures and scenic location. It's a peaceful Tuscan town set among green hills of the valley called Valdinievole.

The spa's fame began in the latter part of the 18th century when the grand duke of Tuscany, one Pietro Leopoldo, opened a thermal spa here. But centuries before that it had been discovered by the Romans. The fame of Montecatini spread rapidly, and by 1890 it was a regular stopover for some of the titled aristocrats of Europe. In the 20th century it drew such luminaries as Gary Cooper, Rose Kennedy, and Gabriel D'Annunzio, and was further immortalized in Fellini's *8½.*

Many visitors are just regular tourists who enjoy a restful stopover in a spa town; others come to lose weight, to take the mud baths, and to visit the sauna-cum-grotto. The mineral waters are said to be the finest in Europe, and the most serious visitors go to the 19th-century **Tettuccio** spa, with its beautiful gardens, to fill their cups from the curative waters.

The spa is filled with dozens of hotels and *pensiones,* mostly art nouveau buildings from the beginning of this century, and many would-be visitors to Florence—unable to find a room in that overcrowded city—journey east to Montecatini instead. The spa has a season lasting from April to October, and the town really shuts down in the off-season.

When you tire of all that rest, you can take a funicular cable car from Viale Diaz up to **Montecatini Alto,** enjoying its panoramic view. Montecatini Alto was important in the Middle Ages, containing about two dozen towers that were demolished in 1554 on orders of Cosimo Medici I. You can walk along narrow streets to the ruins of a fortress here, paying a short visit to St. Peter's Church. You'll invariably come across the main square, named for the poet Giuseppe Giusti. From the hillside town, you can see Florence on a clear day. Today Montecatini, the Vichy of France or the Baden-Baden of Germany, no longer draws La Loren, Arturo Toscanini, or even Verdi (who wrote the last act of *Otello* here), but it attracts some of the world's most fashionable people on the see-and-be-seen circuit, especially during the horse-racing season from April through October. It's filled with some of the most expensive boutiques in Europe—but don't come here for shopping bargains.

ESSENTIALS

GETTING THERE   From Florence a train leaves every hour during the day for Montecatini. Trip time is 45 minutes, and a one-way passage costs 7,300L ($4.40). The railroad station at Montecatini is at Piazza Italia (☎ **0572/78-551**) in the center.

Tuscany & Umbria

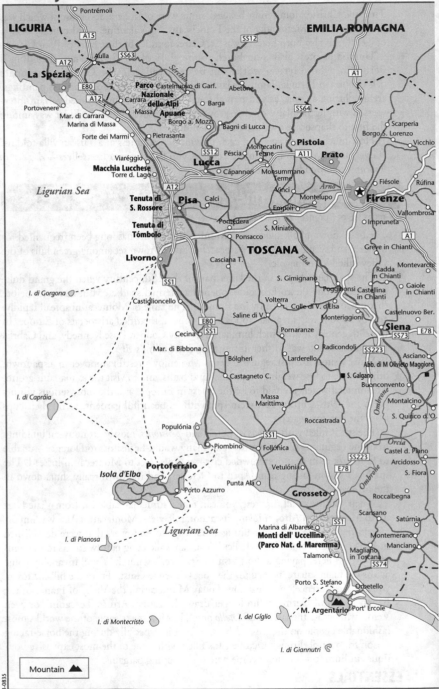

Mountain ▲

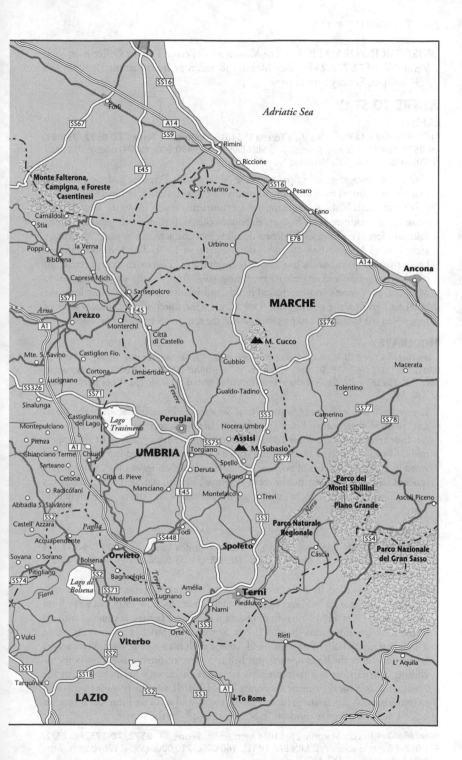

VISITOR INFORMATION   The **Montecatini Terme Tourist Office** is on Viale Verdi (☎ **0572/772-244**), open Monday to Saturday from 9am to 12:30pm and 3:30 to 7pm, Sunday 9am to noon.

WHERE TO STAY
EXPENSIVE

✪ **Gran Hotel e la Pace.** Via della Toretta 1, 51016 Montecatini Terme. ☎ **0572/75-801.** Fax 0572/78-451. 142 rms, 8 suites. A/C MINIBAR TV TEL. 490,000L ($294) double; 700,000L ($420) suite. AE, DC, MC, V. Closed Nov–Apr 4.

This is the dowager grand empress hotel of Montecatini Terme, a gilded-age bastion that has maintained its white-glove formality since its establishment in 1869. Rivaled only by the Bella Vista, a competing five-star hotel that doesn't have the Gran Hotel's panache, it's outfitted with frescoes, elaborate ceilings, flowered sun terraces, soaring columns, lots of gilt, and all the ornate detailing that characterizes formal 19th-century architecture. A renovation upgraded the premises in 1994. The bedrooms are less lavish than the public areas, but discreetly comfortable. There's an elegant restaurant (the Michelangelo) and an outdoor swimming pool. Anyone who wants full access to Montecatini Terme's most technical health and beauty treatments must leave the hotel and go into the nearby park. Despite that, the hotel offers a limited array of supervised spa facilities on its premises, one of the few hotels in town that does.

MODERATE

Gran Hotel Croce di Malta. Viale IV Novembre 18, 51016 Montecatini Terme. ☎ **0572/ 9201.** Fax 0572/767-516. 92 rms, 12 suites. A/C MINIBAR TV TEL. 270,000L ($162) double; 360,000L ($216) suite. Rates include breakfast. Half board 40,000L ($24) per person extra. AE, DC, MC, V.

Located in a residential neighborhood near the spa, the imposing facade of this pleasant, turn-of-the-century hotel rises from behind a screen of shrubbery and an outdoor terrace. It's the most accommodating, and most attractive, of the upper-middle-bracket hotels of Montecatini, with a vaguely modernized interior last renovated in 1995 and touches of polished marble scattered throughout the conservatively modern bedrooms and the public areas. A genteel, helpful staff and affordable prices make this a perennial favorite, with a list of habitués who return "same time next year."

INEXPENSIVE

Grand Hotel Vittoria. Viale della Libertà, 51016 Montecatini Terme. ☎ **0572/79-271.** Fax 0572/910-520. 84 rms. A/C MINIBAR TV TEL. 180,000L ($108) double. Rates include breakfast. AE, DC, MC, V.

Despite a renovation in 1993, this cost-conscious hotel retains a pleasantly old-fashioned aura that's a holdover from its initial construction in 1905. Set away from the center of town amid a dignified collection of private homes, it's one of the best of the town's many middle-bracket hotels. Semiantique touches abound, including a double stairway built of travertine and flanked with masses of flowers. Verdi stayed here shortly after the hotel opened, just before it went through other transitions, including a brief stint as a monastery. It served as the town's headquarters for the Nazis, and later, for the Americans during World War II. On the premises are a small swimming pool, a pleasant garden, a tennis court, and a covered terrace. It receives a good number of conventioneers, especially throughout the winter.

Hotel Manzoni. Viale Manzoni 28, 51016 Montecatini Terme. ☎ **0572/70-175.** Fax 0572/ 911-012. 58 rms, 3 suites. A/C MINIBAR TV TEL. 160,000L–210,000L ($96–$126) double. Rates include half board. AE, DC, MC, V.

Tuscan Tours

I Bike Italy offers leisurely, professionally guided and supported, single-day rides in the Tuscan countryside around Florence. You'll see olive groves, vineyards, Florentine castles, and hillside villa estates. You can also taste wine at local Chianti vineyards. They provide a shuttle to take you in and out of the city center, 21-speed bicycles, helmets, water bottles, lunch (on full-day tours), and a bilingual bike guide to show you the way and fix any flats. Tours begin in Florence at 9am with a shuttle pickup on the north end (Duomo end) of Ponte alle Grazie (one bridge upriver from Ponte Vecchio). All tours are back in Florence by 4pm. Full-day tours cover up to 20 scenic miles (average 3.2 mph—a leisurely pace!). The cost is 75,000L ($45). For more information, call **I Bike Italy** in Florence (☎ **055/234-2371** or 0368/459-123).

Custom Tours in Tuscany offers historical and epicurean adventures in Florence and throughout Tuscany. Whether your interests lie with artisans, wine makers, and chefs, or with art, architecture, and history, Custom Tours is an invaluable resource. Let them know what it is that you wish to see or do, and they will do their best to arrange your day for you. They can help you buy antiques, leather, extra-virgin olive oil, or the most superb bed linens and table linens at a fraction of Madison Avenue prices. Some possible day tours include Florence/Art, Artisans, and Markets; Wineries and Tastings; Outlet Shopping; Lucca; Siena/San Gimignano/Monteriggioni; Pietrasanta's Marble Carvers and Quarries; Pienza/ Montepulciano/Monte Oliveto Maggiore; Medici Villas and Gardens; or a custom-designed tour to suit your needs and interests. These tours begin and end in Florence, but they may be customized to fit into longer countryside itineraries. In Florence, plan to do a lot of walking; outside of Florence, the guides will accompany you in your own rented car or will arrange for a car and driver. Fees are $275 per day for Florence tours or $375 for tours in the Tuscan countryside (6 to 7 hours) for up to six people. Additional persons are $25 each. Transportation, meals, highway tolls, museum admissions, and gratuities are not included. For further information or to make reservations, contact Vivian Kramer at **Custom Tours in Tuscany,** 206 Ivy Lane, Highland Park, IL 60035 (☎ **847/432-1814** or fax 847/ 432-1889).

Mountain Travel/Sobek—a company known for adventure trips—also offers 8-day walking tours through the Tuscan countryside. Such medieval towns as Siena and Gaiole are explored. This is not for roughing it—it's a walking tour where you're pampered. Guests stay in everything from a Relais & Châteaux to a town house from the 1400s. Departures are only in June, September, and October. Land prices start at a high $3,150, with most meals included. This is the most luxurious walking tour outfit in Italy. For more information, phone **Mountain Travel/Sobek** (☎ **800/227-2384**).

Located in a building that's more than 600 years old, the Simoncini-Greco family has run this comfortable hotel since 1921. They offer the best of both worlds, with 17th- through 19th-century furnishings spread throughout an inn that features modern amenities. There's also a landscaped garden, swimming pool, lounge, recreation room, bar, formal dining room, and two elevators. You can leave your car in their private lot, and make use of free 18-speed touring bicycles to better enjoy the green parks and olive-covered hillsides. The restaurant's fine Mediterranean cuisine is rich in locally gathered or produced seafood, meats, poultry, and homemade pastas, along with a delectable selection of fresh vegetables and recently prepared desserts—all from the kitchen supervised by both Canadian and Italian chefs.

Hotel Villa Ida. Viale G. Marconi 55, 51016 Montecatini Terme. ☎ **0572/78-201.** Fax 0572/772-008. 21 rms. A/C MINIBAR TV TEL. 110,000L ($66) double with breakfast, 170,000L ($102) double with half board. AE, DC, MC, V.

Spa devotees who are bargain hunters gravitate to this 19th-century building that was radically upgraded in the late 1980s to enter today's world. Fancy prices and even the fancy *la dolce vita* are far removed here. This place offers simple comforts but everything is cozy and refined in a genteel sort of way. You could check in with Proust's aunt. A modern decor now graces the place and the bedrooms are immaculately maintained. The hotel also offers such extras as a library, TV lounge, and a tavern for wine tasting. Two outside terraces are ideal for an alfresco breakfast or dinner. The food is very generous of portion and well prepared, though not necessarily aimed at the diet conscious.

WHERE TO DINE

Gourmet. Via Amendola 6. ☎ **0572/771-012.** Reservations recommended. Main courses 25,000L–42,000L ($15–$25.20). AE, DC, MC, V. Wed–Mon noon–2pm and 8–11pm. Closed Jan 7–20 and Aug 1–20. ITALIAN.

In a 19th-century building with a Liberty-style interior, this is the best independent restaurant in Montecatini. Established in 1984, it prides itself on formal, elegant service and dishes that are more unusual than the run-of-the-mill pastas and veal dishes of lesser competitors. Menu items change with the seasons and the availability of the ingredients. You'll find a spectacular array of antipasti (the restaurant refers to it as "antipasti fantasia") concocted from seafood and fresh vegetables, ravioli stuffed with pulverized sea bass and herbs, risotto with scampi, and a medley of fruit garnishes (melon slices with lobster and a honey-vinegar sauce, for example). Most items are delicious, impeccably fresh, and beautifully presented by a gracious team of servers. The desserts are made fresh daily and might include a soufflé flavored with Grand Marnier.

2 Lucca

45 miles W of Florence, 13 miles E of Pisa, 209 miles N of Rome

At the time of the collapse of the Roman Empire, Lucca was virtually the capital of Tuscany. Long before that, Caesar, Crassus, and Pompey met here and agreed to rule Rome as a triumvirate in 56 B.C. Periodically in its valiant, ever-bloody history, it functioned as an independent principality, similar to Genoa. This autonomy attests to the fame and prestige Lucca enjoyed. Now, however, it's largely bypassed by time and travelers, rewarding the discriminating few.

By the end of the 1600s Lucca had gained its third and final set of city walls. This girdle of ramparts is largely intact today, and is one of the major reasons to visit the town, with its medley of architecture that ranges from the Roman to Liberty (the Italian term for art nouveau). Lucca was the birthplace of Giacomo Puccini, whose favorite watering hole, the Antico Caffè di Simo (see below), still stands.

Today, it is best known for its *olio d'oliva lucchese,* the quality olive oil produced in the region outside the town's walls, and shoppers will be delighted to find a number of upscale boutiques located within the city, testimony to an affluence not dependent on the tourist trade. Thriving, cosmopolitan, and perfectly preserved, Lucca is a sort of Switzerland of the south. Banks have latticed Gothic windows; shops look like well-stocked linen cupboards. Plump children play in landscaped gardens, and geraniums bloom from the roofs of medieval tower houses.

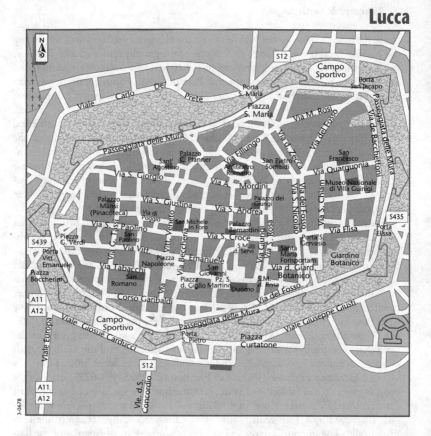

ESSENTIALS

GETTING THERE   By Train   There are about eight trains per day between Florence and Lucca. The trip takes 1¼ hours and costs 7,000L ($4.20) each way. The railway station lies south of Lucca's historic core, a short walk from the city's ramparts. For railway information in Lucca, call ☎ **0583/47-013.** If you don't have a lot of luggage, you can walk into the center; otherwise buses and taxis stand ready to take you there.

By Bus   The **Lazzi** bus company (☎ **0583/587-897**) operates half a dozen buses per day between Florence and Lucca. They take less time than the train (about 50 minutes to an hour) and cost the same. Buses pick up passengers in front of the railway station in Florence and drop them off in Lucca at both the railway station and in the historic core of town at Piazzale Verdi, near the tourist office.

VISITOR INFORMATION   The **Lucca Tourist Office** is on Piazzale Verdi (☎ **0583/419-689**), open from April to October daily from 9am to 7pm, off-season daily from 9am to 1:30pm.

EXPLORING THE TOWN

✪ **Le Mura,** Lucca's city walls, built largely in the days of the Renaissance, enclose the old town, the zone of the most interest to visitors. The Lucchesi are fiercely proud of these walls, the best preserved Renaissance defense ramparts in Europe, although old enemies, such as Napoléon, are long gone. The present walls, which measure 115 feet at the base and soar 40 feet high, replaced crumbling ramparts constructed during the Middle Ages. If you'd like to join in one of the grand promenades of Tuscany, you can gain access to the ramparts from one of 10 bastions, the most frequently used of which is in back of the tourist office at Piazzale Verdi. For orientation, you may want to walk completely around the city on the tree-shaded ramparts, a distance of 2¹/₂ miles.

Afterward, we suggest that you head to Piazza San Martino to visit the **Cathedral of San Martino (Duomo)** (☎ 0583/494-726), dating back to 1060, although the present structure was mainly rebuilt. The facade is exceptional, evoking the "Pisan-Romanesque" style, but with enough originality to distinguish it from the Duomo at Pisa. Designed mostly by Guidetto da Como in the early years of the 13th century, the west front contains three wide ground-level arches, surmounted by three scalloped galleries with taffy-like twisting columns tapering in size.

The main relic inside St. Martin is the *Volto Santo*, a crucifix carved by Nicodemus (so tradition has it) from the Cedar of Lebanon. The face of Christ was supposedly chiseled onto the statuary. The main art treasure in the Duomo is Jacopo della Quercia's tomb of Ilaria del Carretto, who died in 1405 (while still young), the wife of Paolo Guinigi. The marble effigy of the young lady, in regal robes, rests atop the sarcophagus—the cathedral's diffused mauve light in the afternoon casts a ghostly glow on her countenance. The tomb in the sacristy is fringed with chubby bambini. It's open daily from 9am to 5:30pm; admission to the church is free, but the tomb costs 3,000L ($1.80) for adults, 2,000L ($1.20) for children under 14. You can also get a cumulative ticket good for the tomb, the adjacent Duomo Museum, and the nearby church of San Giovanni for 7,000L ($4.20) adults, 4,000L ($2.40) children under 14.

The **Chiesa San Frediano,** Piazza San Frediano (☎ 0583/493-627), is one of the most important and famous in Lucca. Romanesque in style, it was erected when Lucca enjoyed its greatest glory, in the 12th and 13th centuries. Its severe white facade is relieved by a 13th-century mosaic of Christ ascending. Its campanile rises majestically. The interior is dark, and visitors often speak in whispers. But the bas-reliefs on the Romanesque font add a note of comic relief. Supposedly depicting the story of Moses, among other themes, it shows Egyptians in medieval armor chasing after the Israelites. Two tombs in the basilica were the work of Jacopo della Quercia, the celebrated Sienese sculptor. They're in the fourth chapel on the left. The church is open Monday to Saturday from 7:30am to noon and 3 to 6pm and Sunday from 9am to 1pm and 3 to 6pm.

At Piazza San Michele, a short walk away, **San Michele in Foro** (☎ 0583/48-459) often surprises first-timers to Lucca, who mistake it for the Duomo. Begun in 1143, it's the most memorable example of the style and flair the denizens of Lucca brought to the Pisan-Romanesque school of architecture. Its exquisite west front, again employing the scalloped effect, is spanned by seven arches on the ground level, then surmounted by four tiers of galleries, utilizing imaginatively designed columns. Dragon-slaying St. Michael, wings outstretched, rests on the friezelike peak of the final tier. Inside, seek out a Filippo Lippi painting of four saints. It's open daily from 7:30am to 12:30pm and 3 to 6pm. If you're here in September, the piazza outside, which was the old Roman forum, holds a daily colorful open market selling everything from olive oil to souvenirs of Tuscany.

The Lucchesi horde their art treasures in the **Pinacoteca Nazionale e Museo di Palazzo Mansi,** Via Galli Tassi 43 (☎ 0593/55-570), which is open Tuesday through Saturday from 9am to 7pm and Sunday from 9am to 2pm, charging 8,000L ($4.80) for admission. This palace was constructed for the powerful Mansi family, whose descendants are still some of the movers and shakers in the town today. Although Tuscany has far greater preserves of art, there are some treasures here, notably a portrait of Princess Elisa by Marie Benoist. Elisa Bonaparte (1777–1820) was "given" the town by her brother Napoléon in 1805. She became princess of Lucca and Piombino. Unlike her profligate sister, Pauline Borghese in Rome, Elisa was a strong woman, showing a remarkable aptitude for public affairs. A patron of the arts and letters, she laid out the Piazza Napoleone and achieved other accomplishments, earning her the nickname semiramis of Lucca. The collection is enriched by works from Lanfranco, Luca Giordano, and Tintoretto, among others, although not their greatest works. A Veronese is damaged, but Tintoretto's *Miracle of St. Mark Freeing the Slave* is amusing. The patron saint of Venice literally dive-bombs from heaven to save the day.

Worth seeking out, and overlooked by most visitors to Lucca, **Anfiteatro Romano** or Roman Amphitheater is found at Piazza Anfiteatro, reached along Via Fillungo. The outlines of its arches can still be seen in its outer walls, and within the inner ring only the rough form remains to evoke what must have been. Once the theater was adorned with rich Tuscan marble in many hues, but greedy builders hauled off its materials to create some of the many churches of Lucca, including San Michele and the cathedral. The foundations of the former grandstands, which once rang with the sound of Tuscans screaming for gladiator blood, now support an ellipse of houses from the Middle Ages. The theater was from the 2nd century A.D.

Napoléon's widow, Marie Louise, ordered the clearing of the medieval buildings, for which Lucca's boys playing soccer on the asphalt today can be thankful. Lucca was given later to Marie Louise following its rule by Elisa, the French dictator's sister. Marie Louise became Lucca's favorite ruler and they erected a statue to her, still seen today in Piazza Napoleone (her son sold Lucca to Leopold II of Tuscany in 1847). If you want to catch a glimpse at Lucca life, find a chair at one of the sleepy cafes and pass the day away. In July and August, you can come here (actually the Piazza Guidiccioni nearby) and see a screening of the latest Italian and U.S. hits in the open air.

SHOPPING   The rolling and sometimes sunblasted hills around Lucca have been famous since the days of the Romans for their gnarled olive trees and scenic beauty. They produce an amber-colored oil that's prized by gastronomes throughout the world as the finest available anywhere.

You won't have to look far for access to the product, as every supermarket, butcher shop, and delicatessen in Lucca sells a baffling variety of the oil, in glass or metal containers ranging from pocketbook-sized to mega-drums suitable for institutional kitchens. But if you want to travel into the hills that surround the town to check out the production of this heart-healthy product directly, two of the region's best-known producers of olive oil sell their products directly on premises that evoke Tuscan farmhouse life of the early 20th century. They include **Maionchi,** in the hamlet of Tofori (localitá Tofori; ☎ **0583/978-194**), 11 miles northeat of Lucca; and **Camigliano,** Via per Sant'Andrea 49 (☎ **0583/490-420**), 6 miles northeast of Lucca.

Looking for souvenirs of your stopover in Lucca? A fast promenade amid the town's richest inventories of consumer goods, the Via Fillungo and the Via del Battistero (Lucca's answer to Milan's Via Montenapoleone) can satisfy most materialistic cravings. The town's best gift and souvenir shops include **Insiene,** Via Vittorio Emanuele 9 (☎ **0583/419-649**). Its leading competitor, placing a special emphasis on Lucca's rustically appealing porcelain, pottery, tiles, and glittering crystal, is **Incontro,** Via Buia (☎ **0583/491-225**).

WHERE TO STAY

⭘ **Piccolo Hotel Puccini.** Via di Poggio 9, 55100 Lucca. ☎ **0583/55-421.** Fax 0583/53-487. 14 rms. TV TEL. 125,000L ($75) double. AE, MC, V.

Your best bet in the center is this palace constructed in the 1400s, across the street from the house where the city's favorite son, Giacomo Puccini, was born. The classical music played in the lobby area—often Puccini—commemorates the long-ago association. Lying right off Piazza San Michele, one of the most enchanting in Lucca, this little hotel is better than ever now that an energetic couple, Raffaella and Paolo, have taken it over, breathing new life into the property. Intimate, cozy, and comfortable, the bedrooms are beautifully maintained with freshly starched curtains, good beds, crisp linens, and tasteful furnishings. Some bedroom windows open onto the small square in front with its bronze statue of the great Puccini.

⭘ **Principessa Elisa.** Strada Statale 12, 55050 Massa Pisana (Lucca). ☎ **0583/379-737.** Fax 0583/379-019. 8 junior suites. A/C MINIBAR TV TEL. 410,000L–530,000L ($246–$318) suite for two. AE, DC, MC, V.

In 1992 this blue-fronted 18th-century villa was reunited with its neighbor (the Hotel Villa La Principessa, below), renewing a pattern established long ago when this villa housed the army officer who was the favorite escort of Napoléon's sister, owner of the larger villa across the road. When the Principessa Elisa was transformed into a posh country-house hotel, it replaced its better-established neighbor as the most elegant lodging of Lucca, and a Relais & Châteaux property. That didn't really matter to the Mugnani family, since both lodgings belong to them anyway. The neoclassical villa has verdant gardens, a worthy collection of antiques, discreet and charming service, and bedrooms larger and more plushly decorated than those in its elegant but simpler sibling. Each accommodation is a skillfully decorated junior suite, with views either of gardens or a park, and furnishings that the Bonapartes themselves might have lived with comfortably. The restaurant, Il Gazebo, is recommended separately below.

Villa La Principessa. Strada Statale 12 bis, 55050 Massa Pisana (Lucca). ☎ **0583/370-037.** Fax 0583/379-136. 35 rms, 5 suites. A/C MINIBAR TV TEL. 335,000L–385,000L ($201–$231) double; 425,000L ($255) suite. AE, DC, MC, V. Closed Nov–Mar.

Associated with the Principessa Elisa (above) set across the highway, this is a well-managed, four-star hotel. It's less luxurious than its sibling, but also less expensive. Like its five-star neighbor, it's less than 2 miles south of Lucca's center, beside a meandering highway with sharp turns and limited visibility. It's sheltered with hedges, flowering trees, and the best kinds of architectural detailings from other eras. It was built in 1320 as the private home of one of the dukes of Lucca, Castruccio Castracani, who was later depicted by Machiavelli as "The Ideal Prince." Later, when the hills around Lucca were dotted with the homes of members of the Napoleonic court, the house was rebuilt in a severely dignified 18th-century style. The bedrooms are comfortably renovated with everything you'll need. There's a swimming pool set in a garden. Breakfast is the only meal served.

WHERE TO DINE

⭘ **Buca di Sant'Antonio.** Via della Cervia 1. ☎ **0583/55-881.** Reservations recommended. Main courses 18,000L–26,000L ($10.80–$15.60). AE, DC, MC, V. Tues–Sat noon–3pm and 7:30–10:30pm, Sun noon–3pm. Closed 2 weeks in Jan. TUSCAN.

Set in the historic core of Lucca, on a difficult-to-find alleyway near Piazza San Michele, this is the finest restaurant in Lucca, serving far better food than it did in the first decades of its operation in the 1950s. Today's cuisine is refined and inspired, respecting the old traditional ways but also daring to be modern and innovative as well. It's outfitted with country-rustic implements (such as copper pots and an open fireplace) and has a hearty and hospitable staff. Menu items include grilled dishes; a savory compendium of stews designed to ward off midwinter chills; and such regional specialties as red-bean minestrone, a succulent version of codfish, and such pastas as tortellini in meat sauce.

Da Giulio in Pelleria. Via della Conce 45. ☎ **0583/55-948.** Reservations recommended. Main courses 13,000L–18,000L ($7.80–$10.80). AE, DC, MC, V. Tues–Sat and third Sun of every month, noon–2:30pm and 7:15–10:15pm. Closed Aug. LUCCHESE.

Less expensive than many of its competitors, this restaurant occupies a 200-year-old building near the Porta San Donato, and attracts lots of habitués with uncompromising allegiance to local traditions and time-honored recipes. Under its present management since 1991, it presents dishes such as succulent minestrones, pastas, veal, hearty soups, and chicken dishes served in generous, robust portions. There are also some regional dishes that might just be a little too ethnic for most North American tastebuds, such as *cioncia*, which is concocted with veal snout and herbs.

Giglio. Piazza del Giglio 2. ☎ **0583/494 058.** Reservations recommended. Main courses 20,000L–50,000L ($12–$30). AE, DC, MC, V. Thurs–Mon noon–3pm and 7–10pm. REGIONAL/ TUSCAN.

In earthy regional appeal and popularity this place is rivaled only by the previously recommended Buca di Sant'Antonio. It has flourished in this location in the heart of town since 1957. The secret to its appeal might be its rustic decor (including 15th-century architectural detailing), its attentive and helpful staff, and its succulent interpretations of time-honored Tuscan and regional recipes. You'll find nothing experimental here, a fact that doesn't seem to bother any of its local clients one bit. Chow down on red-bean soup with local greens; all kinds of pasta, including a local version of macaroni with rabbit meat; well-prepared antipasti; and a wide choice of Tuscan wines.

Il Gazebo della Principessa Elisa. In the Hotel Principessa Elisa, Strada Statale 12. ☎ **0583/ 379-737.** Reservations recommended. Fixed-price menu 75,000L–85,000L ($45–$51). AE, DC, MC, V. Mon–Sat 12:30–2:30pm and 8–10pm. ITALIAN/TUSCAN.

Some patrons from the surrounding region chose to dine here as a means of visiting one of Tuscany's most elegant hotels. Set in a previously recommended country house less than 2 miles south of Lucca's center, the restaurant is in a re-creation of an English conservatory. Wraparound windows in an almost circular room offer views over a garden that was replanted at great expense in the early 1990s. Service, as you'd expect from a five-star hotel with Relais & Châteaux status, is impeccable. Menu items include upscale versions of local Luccan recipes, including, among others, a *farro Lucchese*, red-bean soup with locally grown greens. Other, less ethnic dishes include steamed scampi with fresh tomato sauce, smoked swordfish with grilled eggplant, and ravioli stuffed with herbed eggplant and served with prawn sauce. Each is prepared with refinement and skill.

LUCCA AFTER DARK

Sleepy Lucca comes to life during July and August at the time of the classical music festival, **Estate Musicale Lucchese.** Venues spring up everywhere. The tourist office keeps a list. The town also comes alive on **July 12** when residents don medieval costumes and parade through the city, the revelry continuing late into the night.

In the hometown of Puccini, there is a devotion to opera, which is showcased at **Teatro Comunale del Giglio,** Piazza di Giglio (☎ **0583/442-103**), in September and October. At least one opera by Lucca's world-renowned composer is presented annually. More classical musical venues fill the town in September during the **Settembre Lucchese Festival,** highlighted by Volto Santo feast day on September 13. The Tempietto's crucifix bearing the "face" of Christ is hauled through the town to commemorate its miraculous journey to Lucca. Cafes that night fill up with wine-drinking revelers.

If you're not in Lucca during one of these special events, follow in the footsteps of Puccini and head to **Antico Caffè di Simo,** Via Fillungo 58 (☎ **0583/46-234**), where the composer used to come to eat and drink, perhaps to dream about his next opera. At this historical cafe you can order the best gelato (ice cream) in town while taking in the old-timey aura of faded mirrors, brass, and marble. In off-season (usually December through February) the place becomes a piano bar with frequent jazz nights. It's open Tuesday through Sunday from 8am to 8pm.

3 Pisa

47 miles W of Florence, 207 miles NW of Rome

One of Katherine Anne Porter's best short stories is called "The Leaning Tower." A memorable scene deals with a German landlady's sentimental attachment to a 5-inch plaster replica of the Leaning Tower of Pisa, a souvenir whose ribs caved in at the touch of a prospective tenant. "'It cannot be replaced,' said the landlady, with a severe, stricken dignity. 'It was a souvenir of the Italian journey.'" Ironically the year (1944) Miss Porter published her "Leaning Tower," a bomb fell near the real campanile. Fortunately, the original wasn't damaged.

Few buildings in the world have captured imaginations as much as the Leaning Tower of Pisa. It's the single most instantly recognizable building in all the Western world. Perhaps visitors are drawn to it as a symbol of the fragility of people, or at least the fragility of their work. The Leaning Tower is a landmark powerful enough to entice visitors to call, and once there, they usually find other sights to explore as well.

There's more to Pisa than meets the typical tourist's eye. There's the present. Go into the busy streets surrounding the university and the market and you'll find a town that resounds with the exuberance of its student population and residents making the purchases necessitated by everyday life.

ESSENTIALS

GETTING THERE By Plane Both domestic and international flights arrive at Pisa's Galileo Galilei Airport (☎ **050/500-707** for information). Trains make the 5-minute trip into the center of Pisa for 1,500L (90¢) per person; buses, for 1,200L (70¢).

By Train Trains link Pisa and Florence every 30 minutes. Trip time is 1 hour, and a one-way fare is 7,200L ($4.30). Coastal trains also link Pisa and Rome. Arrivals are at the **Pisa Centrale,** Piazza Stazione (☎ **050/41-385**), a major stop for trains on the Genoa/Rome line. The station is about a 10- to 15-minute walk from the Leaning Tower and the other major attractions. Otherwise you can take a bus (no. 1) from the station to the heart of the city.

By Bus There is frequent bus service to Florence operated by **APT** (call ☎ **050/505-511** in Pisa for information and schedules).

By Car From Florence, take the autostrada west (A11) to the intersection (A12) going south to Pisa.

Pisa

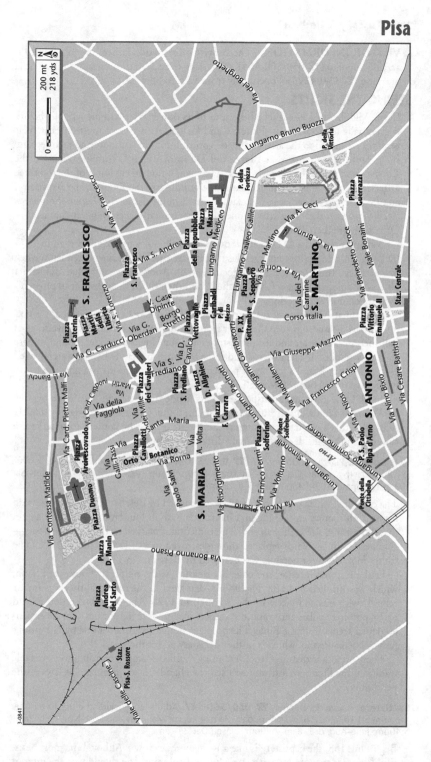

VISITOR INFORMATION   The **tourist information offices** are located at Piazza del Duomo (☎ **050/560-464**), open daily from 9am to sunset; and Piazza della Stazione (☎ **050/42291**), open daily from 9am to 7pm.

SEEING THE SIGHTS

In the Middle Ages, Pisa reached the apex of its power as a maritime republic before it eventually fell to its rivals, Florence and Genoa. As is true of most cities at their zenith, Pisa turned to the arts, and made contributions in sculpture and architecture. Its greatest legacy remains at **Piazza del Duomo,** which D'Annunzio labeled the *Campo dei Miracoli* (Field of Miracles). Here you'll find an ensemble of the top three attractions, all original Pisan-Romanesque buildings—the Duomo, the Baptistery, and the Leaning Tower itself. Nikolaus Pevsner, in his classic *An Outline of European Architecture,* wrote: "Pisa strikes one altogether as of rather an alien character—Oriental more than Tuscan."

Construction of the ✪ **Leaning Tower,** an eight-story campanile, began in 1174 by Bonanno, and a persistent legend is that the architect deliberately intended the bell tower to lean (but that claim is undocumented). Another legend is that Galileo let objects of different weights fall from the tower, then timed their descent to prove his theories on bodies in motion.

Unfortunately, the tower is in serious danger of collapse. The government is taking various measures to keep the tower from falling, including clamping five rings of half-inch steel cable around its lower stones and stacking tons of lead around its base to keep it stabilized. The tower is said to be floating on a sandy base of water-soaked clay; it leans at least 14 feet from perpendicular. If it stood up straight, the tower would measure about 180 feet tall.

In 1990 the government suspended visits inside the tower. In years gone by, one of the major attractions in Europe was to climb the Tower of Pisa—taking all 294 steps. But that's too dangerous today, and visitors must be content to observe the tower from the outside—but at a safe distance, of course.

✪ **Il Duomo.** Piazza del Duomo 17. ☎ **050/560-547.** Free admission. Dec–Feb, 2,000L ($1.20); Mar–Nov. May–Oct, Mon–Sat 10am–7:40pm, Sun 1–7:40pm; Nov–Apr, Mon–Sat 10am–12:45pm and 3–4:45pm, Sun 3–4:45pm.

The cathedral, which dates from 1063, was designed by Buschetto, although Rainaldo in the 13th century erected the unusual facade with its four layers of open-air arches that diminish in size as they ascend. The cathedral is marked by three bronze doors—rhythmic in line—which replaced those destroyed in a disastrous fire in 1596. The south door, the most notable, was designed by Bonanno in 1180.

In the restored interior, the chief art treasure is the pulpit by Giovanni Pisano, which was finished in 1310. The pulpit, damaged in the cathedral fire, was finally rebuilt (with bits and pieces of the original) in 1926. The polygonal pulpit is held up by porphyry pillars and column statues that symbolize the Virtues. The relief panels depict scenes from the Bible. The pulpit is similar to an earlier one by Giovanni's father, Nicola Pisano, which is in the baptistery across the way.

There are other treasures, too, including Galileo's lamp (according to unreliable tradition, the Pisa-born astronomer used the chandelier to formulate his laws of the pendulum).

Battistero. Piazza del Duomo. ☎ **050/560-547.** Admission (including entry to another monument) 10,000L ($6). Dec–Feb, daily 9am–4:40pm; Mar–May and Sept–Nov, daily 9am–5:40pm; June–Aug, daily 8am–7:40pm. Closed Dec 31–Jan 1.

Begun in 1153, the baptistery is like a Romanesque crown. Although its most beautiful feature is the exterior, with its arches and columns, you should visit the interior to see the hexagonal pulpit made by Nicola Pisano in 1260. Supported by pillars that rest on the backs of three marble lions, the pulpit contains bas-reliefs of the Crucifixion, the Adoration of the Magi, the presentation of the Christ child at the temple, and the Last Judgment (many angels have lost their heads over the years). Column statues represent the Virtues. At the baptismal font is a contemporary John the Baptist by a local sculptor. The echo inside the baptistery shell has enthralled visitors for years.

Museo dell'Opera. Piazza Arcivescovado. ☎ **050/560-547.** Admission (including entry to another monument) 10,000L ($6). Dec–Feb, daily 9am–4:20pm; Mar–May and Sept–Nov, daily 9am–5:20pm; June–Aug, daily 8am–7:20pm.

Opened in 1986, this museum exhibits works of art removed from the monumental buildings on the piazza. The heart of the collection, on the ground floor, consists of sculptures spanning the 11th to the 13th centuries. The most famous exhibit is an ivory *Madonna* and the *Crucifix* by Giovanni Pisano. Also exhibited is the work of French goldsmiths, which was presented by Maria de' Medici to Archbishop Bonciani in 1616. Upstairs are paintings from the 16th to the 18th centuries. Some of the textiles and embroideries date from the 15th century. Another section of the museum is devoted to Egyptian, Etruscan, and Roman works of art.

Camposanto. Campo dei Miracoli. ☎ **050/560-547.** Admission 10,000L ($6). Dec–Feb, daily 9am–4:40pm; Mar–May and Sept–Nov, daily 9am–5:40pm; June–Aug, daily 8am–7:40pm.

This cemetery was designed by Giovanni di Simone in 1278, but a bomb hit it in 1944 and destroyed most of the famous frescoes that once covered the inside. Recently it has been partially restored. It's said that earth from Calvary was shipped here by the Crusaders on Pisan ships (the city was a great port before the water receded). The cemetery is of interest because of its sarcophagi, statuary, and frescoes. One room contains three of the frescoes from the 14th century that were salvaged from the bombing: *The Triumph of Death, The Last Judgment,* and *The Inferno,* with the usual assortment of monsters, reptiles, and boiling caldrons. *The Triumph of Death* is the most interesting, with its flying angels and devils. In addition, you'll find lots of white-marble bas-reliefs, including Roman funerary sculpture.

Museo Nazionale di San Matteo. Piazzetta San Matteo 1 (near Piazza Mazzini). ☎ **050/541-865.** Admission 8,000L ($4.80) adults, free for children 17 and under and seniors 60 and over. Tues–Sat 9am–7pm, Sun 9am–1pm.

The well-planned Museo Nazionale di San Matteo contains a good assortment of paintings and sculptures, many of which date from the 13th to the 16th centuries. In the museum are statues by Giovanni Pisano; Simone Martini's *Madonna and Child with Saints,* a polyptych, as well as Nino Pisano's *Madonna del Latte (Madonna of the Milk),* a marble sculpture; Masaccio's *St. Paul,* painted in 1426; Domenico Ghirlandaio's two *Madonna and Saints* depictions; works by Strozzi and Alessandro Magnasco; and very old copies of works by Jan and Pieter Brueghel.

SHOPPING

On the second weekend of every month, an antique fair fills the Ponte di Mezzo. Virtually everything from the Tuscans hills is for sale, from virgin fresh olive oil to what one dealer told us was the "original" *Mona Lisa* (not the one hanging in the Louvre). If you're not in town for this market, head for the Piazza Vettovaglie, just off Via Borgo Stretto, which has a market every morning from 7am to 1:30pm. Everything is for sale here, from old clothing to fresh Tuscan food products. The market sprawls outside its boundaries, spilling onto the Via Domenio Cavalca as well. You can skip the Pisan restaurants for lunch and eat here, as there is an array of little trattorie that will fill you up—all at an affordable price. You can also pick up the makings for a picnic here to enjoy later in the Tuscan hillsides. A horde of intriguing stores also line the Via Borgo Stretto, which is an arcaded street evocative of the ones in Bologna. Mimes and street performers often entertain the shoppers.

WHERE TO STAY

Grand Hotel Duomo. Via Santa Maria 94, 56126 Pisa. ☎ 050/561-894. Fax 050/560-418. 94 rms, 2 suites. A/C MINIBAR TV TEL. 290,000L ($174) double; 340,000L ($204) suite. Rates include breakfast. AE, DC, MC, V. Parking 30,000L ($18).

The five-story Grand Hotel Duomo, dating from the 1940s (and showing it), lies in the heart of Pisa, a short walk from the Leaning Tower, which is the most compelling reason to stay here. A buff-colored stucco building, it has a covered roof garden for uninterrupted views. Inside there's a liberal use of marble, crystal chandeliers, even tall murals in the dining room. The restaurant, serving very standard fare, is often filled with tour groups. The bedrooms are furnished haphazardly, with parquet floors, big windows, built-in headrests, and individual lights. They provide laundry service and 24-hour room service, and baby-sitting can be arranged.

Hotel D'Azeglio. Piazza Vittorio Emanuele II 18B, 56125 Pisa. ☎ 050/500-310. Fax 050/ 28-017. 29 rms. A/C MINIBAR TV TEL. 216,000L ($129.60) double. Rates include breakfast. AE, DC, MC, V. Parking 15,000L ($9).

This is an unremarkable hotel in the vicinity of the railway station and the air terminal, in the commercial center of Pisa. It's viewed as the third-best hotel in town, after the Duomo and Cavalieri, but don't expect too much, as competition in innkeeping isn't too keen in Pisa. On the premises is an American bar and roof garden with a view of the city. The standard rooms are well maintained and reasonably comfortable.

Jolly Hotel Cavalieri. Piazza della Stazione 2, 56125 Pisa. ☎ 050/43-290. Fax 050/502-242. 100 rms. A/C MINIBAR TV TEL. 310,000L ($186) double. Rates include breakfast. AE, DC, MC, V. Parking 30,000L ($18).

This is supposedly the best hotel in Pisa, which doesn't say a lot for Pisan innkeeping standards. A bland commercial chain-run property, it opens onto a view of the monumental train station and the piazza in front of it. The seven-story hotel was constructed in 1948, but since then has been practically rebuilt from the inside out. The rooms are filled with time-worn furniture, paneling, and large expanses of glass. The hotel hosts dozens of business travelers, who appreciate the quiet bar and restaurant for their meetings. The Restaurant Cavalieri, with an adjacent piano bar, serves lunch and dinner daily. Parking is often possible in the square in front of the station or in a nearby garage.

Royal Victoria. Lungarno Pacinotti 12, 56126 Pisa. ☎ 050/940-111. Fax 050/940-180. 48 rms, 42 with bath (tub or shower). TEL. 94,000L ($56.40) double without bath, 155,000L ($93) double with bath; 169,000L ($101.40) triple with bath; 180,000L ($108) quad with bath. Rates include breakfast. AE, DC, MC, V. Parking 30,000L ($18).

Royal Victoria is conveniently located on the Arno, within walking distance of most of the jewels in Pisa's crown. The oldest hotel in Pisa, it was launched in 1839 and is still under the same family management today. Although hardly a perfect hotel, its location is second only to the Grand Hotel. Also, it's less sterile in atmosphere than the choices previously recommended. Its tastefully decorated lounge sets the hospitable scene. Most rooms are devoted to the past only through painted ceilings, spaciousness, and the warmth of antiques suitable to contemporary comfort. The decor can also be a functional modern.

WHERE TO DINE

✪ **Al Ristoro dei Vecchi Macelli.** Via Volturno 49. ☎ **050/20-424.** Reservations required. Main courses 15,000L–26,000L ($9–$15.60); fixed-price menu 40,000L–90,000L ($24–$54). AE, DC. Mon–Tues and Thurs–Sat noon–3pm and 8–10:30pm. Closed 2 weeks in Aug. INTERNATIONAL/TUSCAN.

This is the best restaurant in Pisa, set in a comfortably rustic 1930s building near Piazzetta di Vecchi Macelli. Residents of Pisa claim that the cuisine is prepared with something akin to love, and they prove their devotion by returning frequently. After selecting from a choice of two dozen varieties of seafood antipasti, you can enjoy a homemade pasta with scallops and zucchini or fish-stuffed ravioli in a shrimp sauce. Other dishes include gnocchi with pesto and shrimp and roast veal with a velvety truffle-flavored cream sauce.

Da Bruno. Via Luigi Bianchi 12. ☎ **050/560-818.** Reservations recommended for dinner. Main courses 25,000L–45,000L ($15–$27); fixed-price menu 30,000L ($18). AE, DC, MC, V. Mon noon–2:30pm, Wed–Sun noon–2:30pm and 7:30–10pm. PISAN.

For around half a century Da Bruno has survived in its location some 400 yards from the Leaning Tower. One of Pisa's finest restaurants, although charging moderate tabs, Da Bruno is decorated like a Tuscan inn under beamed ceilings. Locals are particularly fond of this place, which lies outside Pisa's old walls but still within walking distance of the Duomo. Many in-the-know diners prefer the old-fashioned dishes of the Tuscan kitchen, including hare with pappardelle (a wide noodle), a thick regional vegetable soup *(zuppa alla paesana)*, and codfish with leeks *(baccalà con porri)*.

Emilio. Via del Cammeo 44. ☎ **050/562-141.** Fax 050/562-096. Reservations recommended. Main courses 15,000L–30,000L ($9–$18); fixed-price menu 26,000L ($15.60). AE, DC, MC, V. Sat–Thurs noon–3:30pm and 7–10:30pm. PISAN/ITALIAN.

Partly because of its well-prepared food, and partly because of its proximity to the Piazza dei Miracoli (site of the Leaning Tower), this restaurant attracts more foreign tourists than almost any other restaurant in Pisa. Built in the 1960s, and renovated in 1991 in a style some visitors compare to a South American hacienda, it contains a large, high window similar to what you might expect in a church, which filters light down on the brick-walled interior. The menu features a very fresh assortment of antipasti, spaghetti with clams, risotto with mushrooms, such fish dishes as *branzini à l'Isolana* oven-baked with tomatoes and vegetables, and Florentine-style beefsteaks.

PISA AFTER DARK

After dinner, Pisans seem to go to bed. But on summer evenings there are free classical music concerts presented on the steps of the Duomo or cathedral. Music aficionados from all over the world can be seen sprawled out on the lawn. Concerts are also presented within the Duomo, which is known for its phenomenal acoustics. The tourist office has details. The best time to be in Pisa is the last Sunday in June, when Pisans stage their annual tug-of-war, the *Gioco del Ponte,* which revives some of their pomp and ceremony from the Middle Ages. Each quadrant of the city presents richly costumed parades.

4 San Gimignano

26 miles NW of Siena, 34 miles SW of Florence

A golden lily of the Middle Ages! Called the Manhattan of Tuscany, the town preserves 13 of its noble towers, which give it a skyscraper skyline. The approach to the walled town today is dramatic, but once it must have been fantastic, as San

Gimignano in the heyday of the Guelph and Ghibelline conflict had as many as 72 towers. Today its fortress-like severity is softened by the subtlety of its quiet, harmonious squares, and many of its palaces and churches are enhanced by Renaissance frescoes, as San Gimignano could afford to patronize major painters.

But despite its beauty and authenticity, the town can seem like a made-to-order tourist mecca during the day, with large groups shuffling through the sites and in and out of the numerous restaurants and gift shops that have popped up to capitalize on the trade. Wait until late afternoon or early evening, and you can get a sense of the town without so many distractions. Go to one of the tasting rooms for a sample of the famous *Vernaccia,* the light white wine bottled in the region, or see if you can identify set locations from the movie adaptation of E. M. Forster's *Where Angels Fear to Tread.*

ESSENTIALS

GETTING THERE   By Bus   TRA-IN buses service San Gimignano (☎ 0577/ **204-111**) from Florence with a change at Poggibonsi (trip time: 75 minutes); the one-way fare is 9,500L ($5.70). The same company also operates service from Siena, with a change at Poggibonsi (trip time: 50 minutes); the one-way fare is 7,900L ($4.75). In San Gimignano, buses stop at Piazzale Montemaggio, outside Porta San Giovanni, the city's southern gate. You'll have to walk into the center, as vehicles aren't allowed.

By Car   From Florence or Siena, take the Firenze-Siena autostrada to Poggibonsi, where you'll need to cut west along a secondary route (S324) to San Gimignano.

VISITOR INFORMATION   Information is available from the **Associazione Pro Loco,** Piazza del Duomo 1 (☎ 0577/940-008), open daily November through February from 9am to 1pm and 2 to 6pm, and daily March through October from 9am to 1pm and 3 to 7pm.

EXPLORING THE MANHATTAN OF TUSCANY

In the center of town is the palazzo-flanked **Piazza della Cisterna**—so named because of the 13th-century cistern in its heart. Connected with the irregularly shaped square is its satellite, **Piazza del Duomo.** The square's medieval architecture—towers and palaces—is almost unchanged, and it's the most beautiful spot in town. One ticket, available at any of the sites listed below, allows admission to all of them. The ticket costs 16,000L ($9.60) for adults and 12,000L ($7.20) for students and children.

The **Palazzo del Popolo** was designed in the 13th century. Its tower, the Torre Grossa, built a few years later, is believed to have been the tallest "skyscraper" (about 178 feet high) in town. Passing through the Museo Civico (see below), you can scale this tower and be rewarded with a bird's-eye view of this most remarkable town. The tower, the only one in town you can climb, is open March through October daily from 9:30am to 7:30pm; off-season, Tuesday through Saturday from 9:30am to 1:30pm and 2:30 to 4:30pm. Admission is 8,000L ($4.80).

Duomo Collegiata o Basilica di Santa Maria Assunta. Piazza del Duomo. ☎ 0577/ **940-316.** Church, free; chapel, 3,000L ($1.80) adults, 2,000L ($1.20) students ages 6–18. Daily 9:30am–12:30pm and 3–5:30pm.

Residents of San Gimignano still call this a Duomo or cathedral, even though it was demoted to a "Collegiata" once the town lost its bishop. Do not judge this book—or rather facade—by its cover. Plain and austere on the outside, dating from the 12th century, it is richly decorated inside. Actually, the facade for some reason was never finished.

Escaping from the burning Tuscan sun, retreat inside to a world of tiger-striped arches and a galaxy of gold stars. Head for the north aisle where Bartolo di Fredi depicted scenes in the 1360s from the Old Testament. Two memorable ones include *The Trials of Job* and *Noah with the Animals*. Other outstanding works by this artist are in the lunettes off the north aisle, including a medieval view of the cosmography of the Creation. In the right aisle panels trace scenes from the life of Christ—the kiss of Judas, the Last Supper, the Flagellation, and the Crucifixion. As a bizarre curiosity, seek out Bartolo's horrendous *Last Judgment*, one of the most perverse in Italy. Abandoning briefly his rosy-cheeked Sienese madonnas, he depicted distorted and suffering nudes, which were shocking for its day.

The chief attraction of the basilica is the Chapel of Santa Fina, designed by Giuliano and Benedetto da Maiano. The fresco teacher of Michelangelo, Domenico Ghirlandaio, frescoed the chapel with scenes from the life of a local girl, Fina, who became the town's patron saint. Her deathbed scene is memorable. According to accounts of the day, the little girl went to the well for water and, once there, accepted an orange from a young swain. When her mother scolded her for her wicked ways, she was so mortified that she prayed for the next five years until St. Anthony called her to heaven.

Museo Civico. In the Palazzo del Popolo, Piazza del Duomo 1. ☎ **0577/940-340.** Admission 7,000L ($4.20) adults, 5,000L ($3) students, 3,500L ($2.10) children. Apr–Oct, daily 9:30am–7:30pm; Nov–Mar, Tues–Sun 9:30am–1:30pm and 2:30–4:30pm.

Installed upstairs in the Palazzo del Popolo (*Comune*, or town hall) is the Museo Civico. Most notable here is the Sala di Dante, where the White Guelph–supporting poet spoke out for his cause in 1300. Look for one of the masterpieces of San Gimignano—the *Maestà*, or Madonna enthroned, by Lippo Memmi (later "touched up" by Gozzoli).

The first large room you enter upstairs contains the other masterpieces of the museum—a *Madonna in Glory*, with Saints Gregory and Benedict, painted by Pinturicchio. On the other side of it are two different depictions of the *Annunciation* by Filippino Lippi. On the opposite wall, note the magnificent Byzantine *Crucifix* by Coppo di Marcovaldo.

Around to the left of the cathedral on a little square (Piazza Luigi Pecori) is the Museum of Sacred Art, an unheralded museum of at least passing interest for its medieval tombstones and wooden sculpture. It also has an illustrated-manuscript section and an Etruscan section.

Museo di Criminologia Medioevale. Via di Castello 1. ☎ **0577/942-243.** Admission 8,000L ($4.80). Apr–Oct, daily 10am–1pm and 2–6:30pm; off-season, Sat–Sun 11am–1pm and 2–6pm.

The Marquis de Sade would take delight here. In this Tuscan chamber of horrors some of the most horrendous antique instruments of torture are on display. For torture in the style of the Middle Ages, this chamber has the cutting edge. In case you don't know just how the devices of torture worked on the victims, descriptions are provided in English. All are ghoulish. As the curator explained, the museum has a political agenda even today. The exhibitions such as cast-iron chastity belts inherently reveal some of the sexism involved in torture devices with the revelation that many have been updated for use around in the world today, ranging from Africa to South America. These include the garrote, that horror of the Inquisition trials of the 1400s. Fittingly enough, this bizarre sight is housed in what locals call the Torre del Diavolo or devil's tower.

WHERE TO STAY

Bel Soggiorno. Via San Giovanni 91, 53037 San Gimignano. ☎ **0577/940-375.** Fax 0577/943-149. 18 rms, 4 suites. A/C TV TEL. 150,000L ($90) double; from 200,000L ($120) suite. AE, CB, DC, MC, V. Parking 15,000L ($9).

Although no longer the town's best, having bowed to increasing competition from the Relais Santa Chiara and La Cisterna, this hotel is still the best value. The rear bedrooms and dining room open on the lower pastureland and the bottom of the village. Although rated only three stars by the government, the lodgings are far superior to what you might expect. The rooms are small and pleasantly revamped, and some have antiques and terraces. About half open onto views of the Val d'Elsa. All of them were designed in the High Tuscan style by an architect from Milan; eight contain air-conditioning and four offer minibars. In summer you'll be asked to have your meals here—which is no great hardship as the cuisine is excellent. Done in the medieval style, the dining room contains murals depicting a wild boar hunt. Nonresidents are welcome to dine here Tuesday to Sunday.

Hotel Leon Bianco. Piazza della Cisterna, 63037 San Gimignano. ☎ **0577/941-294.** Fax 0577/942-123. 20 rms. A/C TV TEL. 260,000L–310,000L ($156–$186) double. AE, DC, MC, V. Parking 19,000L ($11.40).

This restored 11th-century villa, a Tuscan classic, offers San Gimignano at its best—front rooms look out over the stark medieval Piazza della Cisterna, whereas rear rooms have a sweeping view of the Elsa Valley. Features include vaulted ceilings, terra-cotta floors, and bedrooms individualized by the quirks and construction of an ancient dwelling—one room is rustically romantic with vaulted ceilings and alcoves composed entirely of rough brick. A sunny roof terrace is a good place to order breakfast, a drink, or just to lounge and relax. There is no restaurant on the premises, but several are a short stroll away.

La Cisterna. Piazza della Cisterna 24, 53037 San Gimignano. ☎ **0577/940-328.** Fax 0577/942-080. 50 rms, 2 suites. TV TEL. 141,000L–181,000L ($84.60–$108.60) double; 206,000L ($123.60) suite. Rates include breakfast. AE, DC, MC, V. Closed Jan and Feb. Parking 20,000L ($12).

Opened in 1919, ivy-covered La Cisterna is modernized but still retains its medieval lines (it was built at the base of some 14th-century patrician towers). For years, it was the only hotel in town, and it's still one of the town's leading inns. Many tourists visit it just for the day and to patronize Le Terrazze restaurant (see "Where to Dine," below). The hotel was renovated in 1996. The bedrooms are generally large; some of the best rooms open onto terraces with views of the Val d'Elsa (the hotel rests on a hilltop). Because of the narrow, cobble-covered streets that surround this historic inn, guests may drop off their luggage at the hotel's entrance, then drive a short distance to a point outside the city's medieval walls to park their cars. It's located just a few dozen feet from all the major sightseeing attractions.

Pescille. Località Pescille, 53037 San Gimignano. ☎ and fax **0577/940-186.** 31 rms, 9 suites. TEL. 145,000L–150,000L ($87–$90) double; 200,000L–220,000L ($120–$132) suite. AE, DC, MC, V. Closed Nov 6–Mar 10.

This is the most tranquil hotel in the San Gimignano area, set in olive groves and vineyards 2$^{1}/_{2}$ miles outside town. A castle stood on this site as early as A.D. 1000, and later the property was a monastery. Napóléon came this way in 1812 and chased out the monks. Later the building became a winery, and, finally, in 1971 was turned into a hotel. The most desirable of the traditional accommodations is the two-level Tower Room, opening onto a picture-perfect view of San Gimignano. Since it costs the same as the other accommodations, this room with a view is naturally every guest's first choice. The Pescille lies north of the center of town heading toward Volterra, and therefore is best suited to motorists.

Relais Santa Chiara. Via Matteotti 15, 53037 San Gimignano. ☎ **0577/940-701.** Fax 0577/942-096. 39 rms, 2 suites. A/C MINIBAR TV TEL. 200,000L–310,000L ($120–$186) double; 240,000L–370,000L ($144–$222) suite. Rates include buffet breakfast. AE, DC, MC, V.

Originally built in the 1960s as a lingerie factory, this solid and comfortable hotel lies in a residential neighborhood about a 10-minute walk south of the medieval ramparts of San Gimignano. It's the prestige place to stay in town, far superior to either La Cisterna or the Bel Soggiorno. It's surrounded with elegant gardens and a swimming pool, and its spacious public rooms contain Florentine terra-cotta floors and mosaics. The comfortable bedrooms are furnished in precious brierwood and walnut and include a Jacuzzi, radio, and hair dryer. Although the hotel is relatively new, the furnishings and ambience blend in harmoniously with the Tuscan countryside. The hotel does not have a restaurant, but serves a buffet breakfast, along with snacks at lunch in summer.

WHERE TO DINE

Ristorante Le Terrazze. In La Cisterna hotel, Piazza della Cisterna 24. ☎ **0577/940-328.** Reservations required. Main courses 20,000L–40,000L ($12–$24). AE, DC, MC, V. Wed 7:30–10pm, Thurs–Mon 12:30–2:30pm and 7:30–10pm. Closed Nov–Mar 9. TUSCAN.

Set in the center of San Gimignano, one of this restaurant's two dining rooms boasts stones originally laid in the 1300s. The newer dining room, which was added in 1969, has lots of rustic accessories and large windows overlooking the old town and the Val d'Elsa beyond. The setting is one of a country inn, and the food features an assortment of produce from the surrounding Tuscan farms. The soups and pastas make fine beginnings, and specialties of the house include such delectable and unusual items as sliced filet of wild boar prepared with polenta and Chianti; breast of goose with walnut sauce and roasted potatoes; vitello (veal) alla Cisterna, served with buttered beans; and breaded lamb cutlets with fried artichokes.

WINE TASTING

San Gimignano produces its own white wine (Vernaccia), which is one of Italy's relatively esoteric (at least to foreigners) vintages. One of the widest selections in town, as well as samplings of Chianti from throughout Tuscany, is displayed and sold at **Da Gustavo,** Via San Matteo 29 (☎ 0577/940-057). Small but select, and set within the tourist and historic core of the town, it's run by the Beccuci family. Don't think you'll have to select a vintage based solely on the recommendation of the salespeople here: There's an informal stand-up bar set up on the premises where glasses cost from 2,000 to 6,000L ($1.20 to $3.60). If you don't see what you're looking for on the shelves, ask—someone will probably haul it out from a storeroom the moment you mention its name. A worthy and even larger competitor, with a similar format, is **Bar Enoteca il Castello,** Via di Castello 20 (☎ 0577/940-878), run since 1988 by members of the Rainieri family. A bar at one end of the premises dispenses generous doses of bread, cheese, salami, and simple platters designed as flavorful foils to glasses of wine priced from 3,000L ($1.80) each. There are views over the nearby hills, tables to sit at (a fact you'll appreciate after a glass or two), and take-away bottles of every conceivable Italian (especially Tuscan and the local Vernaccia) vintage.

EN ROUTE TO SIENA

Traveling from San Gimignano to Siena, you can take Route S324 east from San Gimignano to Poggibonsi, then turn south on Route S2, following the path of the ancient Roman highway Via Cassia, now a little traveled byway into Siena. Not only will you avoid the heavily trafficked autostrada, but you'll also absorb more of the history, architecture, and geography of the region, taking in the sight of its hillside vineyards, ancient walled villages, and historic tales of struggle. On the SS323, 9 miles north of Siena, is the town of **Monteriggioni,** built as a Sienese lookout fortress to guard against attack by the Florentines in 1213. The original walls are still intact and contain the 14 towers that once gave it an imposing skyline, looming up out of the wild, a symbol of Sienese might. A stop here will take you back in time, wandering the streets of a village little changed after more than 700 years of civilization.

5 Siena

21 miles S of Florence, 143 miles NW of Rome

After visiting Florence, it's altogether fitting, certainly bipartisan, to call on what has been labeled in the past its natural enemy. In Rome we saw classicism and the baroque; in Florence, the Renaissance; but in the walled city of Siena we stand solidly planted back in the Middle Ages. On three sienna-colored hills in the center of Tuscany, Sena Vetus lies in Chianti country. Perhaps preserving its original character more markedly than any other city in Italy, it is even today a showplace of the Italian Gothic.

William Dean Howells, the American novelist *(The Rise of Silas Lapham),* called Siena "not a monument but a light." Although it's regrettably too often visited on a quick day's excursion, Siena is a city of contemplation and profound exploration. It's characterized by Gothic palaces, almond-eyed Madonnas, aristocratic mansions, letter-writing St. Catherine (patron saint of Italy), narrow streets, and medieval gates, walls, and towers.

Although such a point of view may be heretical, one can almost be grateful that Siena lost its battle with Florence. Had it continued to expand and change after reaching the zenith of its power in the 14th century, chances are it would be markedly different today, influenced by the rising tides of the Renaissance and the baroque (represented here only in a small degree). But Siena retained its uniqueness—certain Sienese painters were still showing the influence of Byzantium in the late 15th century.

The university, founded in 1240, is still a leading industry, and the conversation you'll overhear between locals in the streets is the purest Italian dialect in the country. But you may have to wait until evening, since most residents retreat within the seclusion of their homes during the days full of tourist buses. They emerge to reclaim the cafes and squares in the evenings, when most of the visitors have gone away. In a nod to its reputation as a commercial leader during the Middle Ages, you can also convert your dollars to lire at the Monte dei Paschi, the oldest bank in the world.

SPECIAL EVENTS The best time to visit is usually on July 2 or August 16, the occasions of the ✪ **Palio delle Contrade,** a historical pageant and tournament known throughout Europe, which draws thousands annually. In the horse race, each bareback-riding jockey represents a *contrada* (one of the wards into which the city is divided). The race, which requires tremendous skill, takes place on Piazza del Campo, the historic heart of Siena. Before the race, much pageantry evoking the 15th century parades by, with colorfully costumed men and banners. The flag-throwing ceremony, depicted in so many travelog films, takes place at this time. And just as enticing is the victory celebration.

Don't buy expensive tickets for the day of the Palio. It's free to stand in the middle—and a lot more fun. Just get here very early, and bring a book and a

Siena

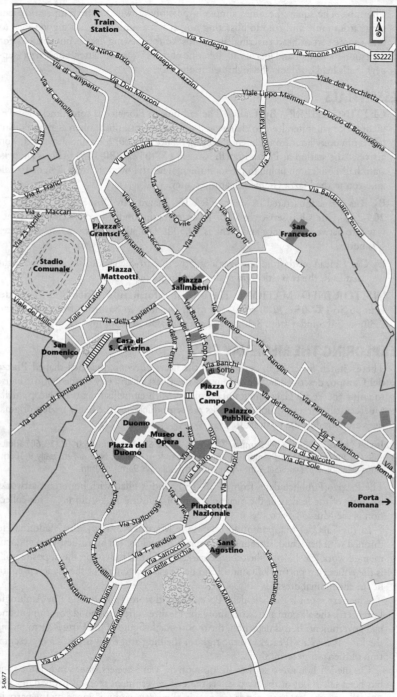

Thermos. The square becomes almost impossibly crowded. The temperature can range from rainy and cold to blistering hot. If it's a sunny day, it's a good idea to bring some sort of head covering, since most of the viewing area is not shaded. For a memorable dinner and lots of fun, join one of the 17 *contrade* attending a *cena* (supper) that's held outdoors the night before the race.

ESSENTIALS

GETTING THERE   By Train   The rail link to Florence is sometimes inconvenient, since you often have to change and wait at other stations, often at Empoli. But trains run every hour from Florence, costing 8,000L ($4.80) for a one-way ticket. You arrive at the station at Piazza Fratelli Rosselli (☎ 0577/280-115). This is an awkward half-hour climb uphill to the monumental heart; however, buses 2, 4, or 10 will take you to the Piazza Gramsci near the center.

By Bus   Headquartered in Siena, **TRA-IN,** Piazza San Domenico 1 (☎ 0577/204-245), offers bus service to all of Tuscany in air-conditioned coaches. The one-way fare between Florence and Siena is 10,500L ($6.30) per person. The trip takes 1¹/₄ hours.

By Car   Head south from Florence along the Firenze-Siena autostrada, a superhighway that links the two cities, going through Poggibonsi.

VISITOR INFORMATION   The **tourist information office** is at Piazza del Campo 56 (☎ 0577/280-551). It's open Monday to Saturday from 8:30am to 7:30pm and Sunday from 8:30am to 1pm and 3:30 to 6:30pm.

EXPLORING THE MEDIEVAL CITY

There's much to see here. Let's start in the heart of Siena, the shell-shaped **Piazza del Campo,** described by Montaigne as "the finest of any city in the world." Pause to enjoy the Fonte Gaia, the fountain of joy, with embellishments by Jacopo della Quercia (the present sculptured works are reproductions; the badly beaten original ones are found in the town hall).

Palazzo Pubblico. Piazza del Campo. ☎ **0577/292-263.** Admission 6,000L ($3.60) adults, 3,000L ($1.80) students and seniors 65 and over, free for children. Nov 6–Feb, daily 9:30am– 1:30pm; Mar–Nov 5, Mon–Sat 9am–7pm, Sun and holidays 9am–1:30pm.

The Palazzo Pubblico dates from 1288–1309 and is filled with important artworks by some of the leaders in the Sienese school of painting and sculpture. This collection is the Museo Civico.

In the Sala del Mappomondo is Simone Martini's *Majesty,* the Madonna enthroned with her Child, surrounded by angels and saints. It's his earliest-known documented work (ca. 1315). The other remarkable Martini fresco (on the opposite wall) is the equestrian portrait of Guidoriccio da Fogliano, general of the Sienese Republic, in ceremonial dress.

The next room is the Sala della Pace, frescoed from 1337 to 1339 by Ambrogio Lorenzetti; the allegorical frescoes show the idealized effects of good government and bad government. In this depiction, the most notable figure of the Virtues surrounding the king is *La Pace* (Peace). To the right of the king and the Virtues is a representation of Siena in peaceful times.

On the left Lorenzetti showed his opinion of "ward heelers," but some of the sting has been taken out of the frescoes, as the evil-government scene is badly damaged. Actually, these were propaganda frescoes in their day, commissioned by the party in power, but they are now viewed as among the most important of all secular frescoes to come down from the Middle Ages.

The Palio: Spectacle of Violence

Like the Spanish bullfight, Siena's major event of the year, its Palio della Contrade (see "Italy Calendar of Events," in chapter 3) is coming under increasing fire for its brutality. For the event, the temperature in town rises higher than the blistering Tuscan sun. All the pomp and ritual of the Middle Ages live again, as heralds, child drummers, flag-bearers, and Renaissance costumes evoke the pomp of the festival.

Three days before the big race, trial races are held, the final trial on the morning of the event. Siena is divided into 17 *contrade,* or wards, and each district—identified by its characteristic colors—competes. However, because the site of the event, Il Campo, will hold only 10 *contrade,* wards are chosen by lot. Young partisans, flaunting the colors of their *contrada,* race through the medieval streets of Siena in packs. Food and wine are bountiful on the streets of each *contrada* on the eve of the race.

The event could easily be considered all in good fun, except that some partisans take it too seriously. There have been kidnappings of the most skilled jockeys before the race. Bribery has been reported as commonplace. So fiercely competitive is the race that all that seems to remain taboo is the sabotaging of the horse's reins.

During the race jockeys have been known to unseat the competition, although a horse without a rider is allowed to win. The event has been cited for its cruelty to animals, as horses are sometimes impaled by guardrails along the track. TV cameras move in on the gore, capturing live the spurting blood as a horse collides with the rail. Jockeys have been caught on camera kicking the horses. In theory, riders are supposed to alternate whip strokes between their mounts and their competitors.

The crowd screams with an excitement unheard in Italy since gladiators battled lions in the Roman Colosseum. One local Sienese who has attended 30 different Palios said, "Winning, not sportsmanship, is the only thing that's important. There are rules, but we Italians never bother to worry about rules. Instead of a horse race, you might call the event a rat race."

Accessible from the courtyard of the Palazzo Pubblico is the **Torre del Mangia,** which is the most characteristic architectural landmark on the skyline of Siena. Dating from the 14th century, it soars to a height of 335 feet. The tower takes its name from a former bell-ringer, a fat, sleepy fellow called *mangiagaudagni,* or "eat the profits." Surprisingly, the tower has no subterranean foundations. If you climb this needle-like tower, which Henry James called "Siena's declaration of independence," you'll be rewarded with a drop-dead view of the city skyline and the enveloping Tuscan landscape. In the Middle Ages, this was the second-tallest tower in Italy; Cremona has Siena beat. The tower is open daily from 10am to dusk, charging 5,000L ($3) for you to risk cardiac arrest by climbing it.

✪ **Il Duomo.** Piazza del Duomo. ☎ **0577/283-048.** Free admission. Nov–Mar 16, daily 7:30am–1:30pm and 2:30pm–sunset; Mar 17–Oct, daily 7:30am–7:30pm.

At Piazza del Duomo, directly southwest of Piazza del Campo, stands an architectural fantasy. With its colored bands of marble, the Sienese cathedral is an original and exciting building, erected in the Romanesque and Italian Gothic styles and dating from the 12th century. The dramatic facade—designed in part by Giovanni Pisano—dates from the 13th century, as does the Romanesque bell tower.

The zebra-like interior, with its black-and-white stripes, is equally stunning. The floor consists of various embedded works of art, many of which are roped off to preserve the richness in design, which depict both biblical and mythological subjects. Numerous artists worked on the floor, notably Domenico Beccafumi. For most of the year a large part of the cathedral floor is covered to protect it.

The octagonal 13th-century pulpit is by Nicola Pisano (Giovanni's father), who was one of the most significant Italian sculptors before the dawn of the Renaissance (see his pulpit in the baptistery at Pisa). The Siena pulpit is his masterpiece; it reveals in relief such scenes as the slaughter of the innocents and the Crucifixion. The elder Pisano finished the pulpit in 1268, aided by his son and other artists. Its pillars are supported by four marble lions, again reminiscent of the Pisano pulpit at Pisa.

In the chapel of the left transept (near the library) is a glass-enclosed box with an arm that tradition maintains is the one John the Baptist used to baptize Christ, and Donatello's bronze of John the Baptist. To see another Donatello work in bronze— a bishop's gravemarker—look at the floor in the chapel to the left of the pulpit's stairway. Some of the designs for the inlaid wooden stalls in the apse were by Riccio. A representational blue starry sky twinkles overhead.

Libreria Piccolomini. Inside Il Duomo, Piazza del Duomo. ☎ **0577/283-048.** Admission 3,000L ($1.80). Mar 16–Oct, daily 9am–7:30pm; Nov–Mar 15, daily 10am–1pm and 2:30–5pm. Closed Jan 1 and Dec 25.

Founded by Cardinal Francesco Piccolomini (later Pius III) to honor his uncle (Pius II), the library inside Il Duomo is renowned for its cycle of frescoes by the Umbrian master Pinturicchio. His frescoes are well preserved, even though they date from the early 16th century. In Vasari's words, the panels illustrate "the history of Pope Pius II from birth to the minute of his death." Raphael's alleged connection with the frescoes, if any, is undocumented. In the center is an exquisite *Three Graces*, a Roman copy of a 3rd-century B.C. Greek work from the school of Praxiteles.

Museo dell'Opera Metropolitana. Piazza del Duomo 8. ☎ **0577/283-048.** Admission 5,000L ($3). Mar 16–Sept, daily 9am–7:30pm; Oct, daily 9am–6pm; Nov–Mar 15, daily 9am–1:30pm. Closed Dec 25–Jan 1.

This museum houses paintings and sculptures originally created for the cathedral. On the ground floor you'll find much interesting sculpture, including works by Giovanni Pisano and his assistants. But the real draw hangs on the next floor in the Sala di Duccio: his fragmented *La Maestà*, a Madonna enthroned, painted from 1308 to 1311. The panel was originally an altarpiece by Duccio di Buoninsegna for the cathedral, filled with dramatic moments that illustrate the story of Christ and the Madonna. A student of Cimabue's, Duccio was the first great name in the school of Sienese painting. In the rooms upstairs are the collections of the treasury, and on the very top floor is a display of paintings from the early Sienese school.

Battistero. Piazza San Giovanni (behind the Duomo). ☎ **0577/283-048.** Admission 3,000L ($1.80). Mar 16–Sept, daily 9am–7:30pm; Oct, daily 9am–6pm; Nov–Mar 15, daily 10am–1pm and 2:30–5pm. Closed Jan 1 and Dec 25.

The facade of the baptistery dates from the 14th century. In the center of the interior is the baptismal font by Jacopo della Quercia, which contains some bas-reliefs by Donatello and Ghiberti.

Pinacoteca Nazionale (Picture Gallery). In the Palazzo Buonsignori, Via San Pietro 29. ☎ **0577/281-161.** Admission 8,000L ($4.80) adults, free for children 17 and under and seniors 60 and over. Apr–Oct, Tues–Sat 9am–7pm, Sun 8am–1pm; Nov–Mar, Tues–Sun 8:30am–1:30pm.

Housed in a 14th-century palazzo near Piazza del Campo is the national gallery's collection of the Sienese school of painting, which once rivaled that of Florence.

Displayed here are some of the giants of the pre-Renaissance. Most of the paintings cover the period from the late 12th century to the mid-16th century.

The principal treasures are on the second floor, where you'll contemplate the artistry of Duccio in the early salons. The gallery is rich in the art of the two Lorenzetti brothers, Ambrogio and Pietro, who painted in the 14th century. Ambrogio is represented by an *Annunciation* and a *Crucifix*, but one of his most celebrated works, carried out with consummate skill, is an almond-eyed *Madonna and Bambino* surrounded by saints and angels. Pietro's most important entry here is an altarpiece—*The Madonna of the Carmine*—made for a church in Siena in 1329. Simone Martini's *Madonna and Child* is damaged but one of the best-known paintings here.

In the salons to follow are works by Giovanni di Paolo *(Presentation at the Temple)*, Sano di Pietro, and Giovanni Antonio Bazzi (called "Il Sodoma," allegedly because of his sexual interests).

Santuario e Casa di Santa Caterina (St. Catherine's Sanctuary). Costa di S. Antonio. ☎ **0577/280-330.** Free admission (but an offering is expected). Mon–Sat and holidays 9am–12:30pm and 3:30–6:30pm.

Of all the personalities associated with Siena, the most enduring legend surrounds that of St. Catherine, acknowledged by Pius XII in 1939 as the patron saint of Italy. The mystic, who was the daughter of a dyer, was born in 1347 in Siena. She was instrumental in persuading the papacy to return to Rome from Avignon. The house where she lived, between Piazza del Campo and San Domenico, has now been turned into a sanctuary—it's really a church and oratory, with many works of art, located where her father had his dyeworks. On the hill above is the 13th-century **Basilica of St. Domenico,** where a chapel dedicated to St. Catherine was frescoed by Il Sodoma.

Enoteca Italica Permanente. Fortezza Medicea, Viale Maccari. ☎ **0577/288-497.** Free admission. Tues–Sat noon–1am, Mon noon–8pm.

Owned and operated by the Italian government, the Enoteca Italica Permanente, which serves as a showcase for the finest wines of Italy, would whet the palate of even the most demanding wine lover. An unusual architectural setting is designed to show bottles to their best advantage. The establishment lies just outside the entrance to an old fortress, at the bottom of an inclined ramp, behind a massive arched doorway. Marble bas-reliefs and wrought-iron sconces, along with regional ceramics, are set into the high brick walls of the labyrinthine corridors, the vaults of which were built for Cosimo de'Medici in 1560. There are several sunny terraces for outdoor wine tasting, an indoor stand-up bar, and voluminous lists of available vintages, which are for sale either by the glass or by the bottle. Count yourself lucky if the bartender will agree to open an iron gate for access to the subterranean wine exposition. Here, in the lowest part of the fortress, carpenters have built illuminated display racks containing bottles of recent vintages.

SHOPPING

Despite the fact that Siena's role as a shopping emporium has always played second fiddle to its larger rival, Florence, there's nonetheless a cornucopia of exotic inventories within the city's stores and boutiques. You're likely to find boutiques and souvenir stands in even the smallest cubbyhole of the town's historic core, but the best of the lot includes **Arcaico,** Via di Citta 81 (☎ 0577/280-551). This is the centerpiece of three almost-adjacent shops, each with the same name, that stock the richest trove of ceramics and souvenir items in Siena. Examples of their merchandise include cachepots for dressing up a potted plant, religious figurines, decorative tiles, dinnerware painted in pleasing floral patterns, and wine and water jugs.

A worthy competitor is **Martini Marisa,** Via del Capitano 11 (☎ **0577/288-177**), purveyor of gift items, local stoneware, and porcelain, in patterns and modes that evoke your visit to Siena. Also try the nearby premises of **Zina Proveddi,** Via del Citta 96 (☎ **0577/286-078**), smaller than either of its competitors, but with a co-zier, homier feel and an emphasis on the rustic and affordable in pottery and painted tiles set into wood. Displaying a wide variety of handmade ceramics, **Ceramiche Santa Caterina,** Via di Città 51 (☎ **0577/283-098**), offers sculpture, dishes, and tile among the items for sale in its shop, but custom orders are available upon re-quest—and the owners say they can make anything you can describe.

Specializing in older jewelry, **Antichita Saena Vetus,** Via di Città 53 (☎ **0577/ 42-395**), handles furniture and paintings from the 1800s, and always has a few smaller pieces reasonably priced for the bargain hunter. **La Balzana,** Piazza del Campo (☎ **0577/285-380**), has a few older engravings as remnants of its antique-dealing days, but now features an assortment of local pottery and souvenirs.

Specializing in handmade paper products, **Il Papiro,** Via di Città 37 (☎ **0577/ 284-241**), has the town's best selection of stationery, notebooks, wrapping paper, boxes, and a variety of pens.

Utilizing the colors and designs of Renaissance Siena, **Siena Ricama,** Via di Città 61 (☎ **0577/288-339**), is the place to order custom-made hand-embroidered table and bed linens. The handwoven knits at **Il Telaio,** Chiasso del Bargello 2 (☎ **0577/ 47-065**), are turned into beautiful women's jackets, scarves, and jumpers.

Don't overlook Siena as an outlet for some of Tuscany's finest wines. There's an outlet for local Chianti—sold in individual bottles, and sometimes four-packs and six-packs—on virtually every street corner. Many of the finer bottles are wrapped in the distinctive straw sheathing that has prompted the fabrication of lamps in countless jazz bars and private homes throughout North America. For the largest selection pos-sible, head for the permanent wine exposition maintained by a consortium of world-class producers, the previously recommended **Enoteca Italiana Permanente,** Fortezza Medicei, Viale Maccari (☎ **0577/288-497**).

A Tuscan gourmet's delight, **Enoteca San Domenico,** Via del Paradiso 56 (☎ **0577/271-181**), sells regional wines and grappa by the bottle, and also hawks pasta, virgin olive oils, sauces, jams, and assorted sweets. With a focus on smaller leather goods, **Mercatissimo della Calzatura e Pelletteria,** Viale Curtatone 1 (☎ **0577/2813-05**), has a fashionable selection of Italian shoes and bags, as well as budget objects like king rings.

WHERE TO STAY

You'll *definitely* need hotel reservations if you're here in summer for the Palio. Make them far in advance, and secure your room with a deposit.

VERY EXPENSIVE

✪**Certosa di Maggiano.** Strada di Certosa 82, 53100 Siena. ☎ **0577/288-180.** Fax 0577/ 288-189. 5 rms, 12 suites. A/C MINIBAR TV TEL. 500,000L–600,000L ($300–$360) double; 900,000L–1,300,000L ($540–$780) suite. Rates include breakfast. AE, DC, MC, V. Parking 50,000L ($30).

This early 13th-century Certosinian monastery lay in dusty disrepair until 1975, when Anna Grossi Recordati renovated it and began attracting some of the world's social luminaries to its 700-year-old interior. It lacks the facilities and the formal ser-vice of the Park Hotel Siena, but many savvy guests prefer the intimacy of this cozy retreat. The stylish and plush public rooms fill the spaces between what used to be the ambulatory of the central courtyard, and the complex's medieval church still holds mass on Sunday. There are only 17 accommodations, one of which has a private walled garden. Most are spacious and filled with antiques mixed with art objects. The hotel is not easy to find, set away from the center of town on a narrow road. Although there are some signs, you may want to phone ahead for directions.

Dining/Entertainment: The small vaulted dining room contains a marble fireplace and entire walls of modern ceramics. It's open to nonresidents who make a reservation. The cuisine is excellent.

Services: Room service, guide service, massages, baby-sitting.

Facilities: Heliport, tennis courts, swimming pool.

EXPENSIVE

Jolly Hotel Excelsior. Piazza La Lizza, 53100 Siena. ☎ **0577/288-448.** Fax 0577/41-272. 123 rms, 3 suites. A/C MINIBAR TV TEL. 275,000L–400,000L ($165–$240) double; 350,000L–600,000L ($210–$360) suite. Rates include breakfast. AE, DC, MC, V. Parking 45,000L ($27).

Set in the commercial center of the newer section of Siena, near the sports stadium, this hotel is a distinguished member of a nationwide chain, although it lacks the ambience and beauty of either the Certosa di Maggiano or the Park Hotel Siena. It was originally built as the Excelsior Hotel in the 1880s and was completely renovated about a century later. The high-ceilinged lobby is stylishly Italian, with terra-cotta accents and white columns. The bedrooms have modern but uninspired furniture, a trim monochromatic color scheme, and many conveniences. The hotel's restaurant features both regional and international dishes. Room service, laundry, valet, and baby-sitting are available.

Park Hotel Siena. Via di Marciano 18, 53100 Siena. ☎ **0577/44-803.** Fax 0577/49-020. 63 rms, 6 suites. A/C MINIBAR TV TEL. 390,000L ($234) double; from 650,000L ($390) suite. AE, DC, MC, V. Closed Dec 3–Feb.

This building was originally commissioned in 1530 by one of Siena's most famous Renaissance architects. It was transformed into a luxurious hotel around the turn of the century and has remained the leading hotel in Siena ever since. It doesn't have the antique charm of the Certosa di Maggiano, but it's more professionally run. A difficult access road leads around a series of hairpin turns (watch the signs carefully) to a buff-colored villa set with a view over green trees and suburbanite houses about a 12-minute drive (1½ miles) southwest of the city center. The landscaped swimming pool, double-glazed windows, upholstered walls, and plush carpeting have set new standards around here. The hotel is well tended, with stylish modern decoration and comfortably furnished public salons.

Dining/Entertainment: Meals in the hotel restaurant might include wild mushroom salad with black truffles, tortellini with spinach and ricotta, and a regularly featured series of regional dishes from Tuscany, Umbria, or Emilia-Romagna.

Services: Room service, laundry, valet.

Facilities: Swimming pool, public salons, two tennis courts.

Villa Scacciapensieri. Via di Scacciapensieri 10, 53100 Siena. ☎ **0577/41-441.** Fax 0577/270-854. 30 rms, 2 suites. A/C MINIBAR TV TEL. 260,000L–350,000L ($156–$210) double; 420,000L ($252) suite. Rates include breakfast. AE, DC, MC, V. Closed Jan–Feb.

This is one of the lovely old villas of Tuscany, where you can stay in a personal, if timeworn, atmosphere. Standing on the crest of a hill about 2 miles from Siena, the villa is approached by a private driveway under shade trees. Although it's not as state-of-the-art as it once was, it's still preferred by many tradition-minded Europeans, who seem to appreciate its antiquated charms. The bedrooms vary widely in style and comfort, and your opinion of this hotel may depend on your room assignment. The hotel also features a handsomely landscaped swimming pool and a tennis court. Services include room service, laundry, valet, and baby-sitting. The informal restaurant serves Tuscan and Italian cuisine. You can dine here Thursday to Tuesday (reserve ahead).

MODERATE

Garden Hotel. Via Custoza 2, 53100 Siena. ☎ **0577/47-056.** Fax 0577/46-050. 136 rms. TV TEL. 183,000L–280,000L ($109.80–$168) double. Rates include breakfast. AE, DC, MC, V.

Garden Hotel is a well-styled country house, built by a Sienese aristocrat in the 16th century. Located on the edge of the city, high up on the ledge of a hill, it commands a view of Siena and the surrounding countryside that has been the subject of many a painting. The hotel stands formal and serene, with a long avenue of clipped hedges, a luxurious sense of space, and an aura of freshness. Its outstanding feature is obviously its garden, plus its price, and many prefer it because they can partially escape the noise of Siena here. Rooms are divided between the old villa and adjoining buildings. Some 100 rooms contain a minibar and 60 are air-conditioned. The breakfast room has a flagstone floor, decorated ceiling, and view of the hills. You can take your other meals in an open-air restaurant on the premises. There's also a swimming pool open June to September.

Hotel Santa Caterina. Via Enea Silvio Piccolomini 7, 53100 Siena. ☎ **0577/221-105.** Fax 0577/271-087. 19 rms. A/C MINIBAR TEL. 200,000L ($120) double. Rates include breakfast. AE, DC, MC, V. Parking 15,000L ($9).

This 18th-century villa is beautifully preserved, featuring original terra-cotta floors, sculpted marble fireplaces and stairs, arched entryways, beamed ceilings, and antique wooden furniture. Its grounds include a terraced rear garden overlooking the valley south of Siena. When booking, you may want to specify one of the 12 rooms that overlook the garden and valley beyond it. Each accommodation is well-furnished and tasteful, and the hotel features a bar and breakfast veranda. There is no restaurant, but several good eateries are a short walk away.

Villa Belvedere. Belvedere, 53034 Colle di Val d'Elsa Siena. ☎ **0577/920-966.** Fax 0577/924-128. 15 rms. TV TEL. 170,000L–225,000L ($102–$135) double. Rates include breakfast. AE, DC, MC, V. Exit the autostrada from Florence at Colle di Val d'Elsa Sud and follow the signs.

Villa Belvedere, about 7¹/₂ miles from Siena and halfway to San Gimignano, occupies a structure built in 1795. In 1820 it was the residence of Ferdinand III, archduke of Austria and grand duke of Tuscany, and in 1845 of Grand Duke Leopold II. Surrounded by a large park with a swimming pool, the hotel has bar service, a garden with a panorama, and elegant dining rooms where typical Tuscan and classic Italian dishes are served. The old-fashioned bedrooms, furnished in part with antiques, all have central heating and overlook the park. Each room is a double. There's also a tennis court.

INEXPENSIVE

Albergo Chiusarelli. Via Curtatone 15, 53100 Siena. ☎ **0577/280-562.** Fax 0577/271-177. 50 rms. TV TEL. 130,000L ($78) double; 175,000L ($105) triple. AE, MC, V.

Near Piazza San Domenico, Albergo Chiusarelli is housed in an ocher-colored building with Ionic columns and Roman caryatids supporting a second-floor loggia. It looks much older, but the building was constructed in 1870. The interior has been almost completely renovated, and each functional, albeit lackluster, room contains a modern bath and an electric hair dryer. Ask for a room in back to escape the street noise. The hotel is just at the edge of the old city, and is convenient to the parking areas at the sports stadium a 5-minute walk away. A bar and restaurant on the basement level serve standard full meals—often to tour groups.

Castagneto Hotel. Via del Cappuccini 39, 53100 Siena. ☎ **0577/45-103.** Fax 0577/283-266. 11 rms. TV TEL. 170,000L ($102) double. No credit cards. Closed Dec 15–Mar 15.

Set on a low hill commanding a view over Siena, about a mile northwest of the center, this modestly proportioned brick villa was built in the 1700s as a farmhouse. Today it's a hotel maintained by the Francioni brothers, and is set behind a gravel-covered parking lot near a garden with birds, vines, and trees. It was renovated into a hotel in 1973, and contains simple, unpretentious rooms in clean and functional working order. Only doubles are available, although single travelers are often accepted at the rate quoted above. It's way down the scale from the hostelries previously considered, but an acceptable choice because of its prices.

WHERE TO DINE

Even those on a brief excursion sometimes find themselves in Siena for lunch, and that's a happy prospect, as the Sienese are good cooks, in the best of the Tuscan tradition.

MODERATE

Al Mangia. Piazza del Campo 43. ☎ **0577/281-121.** Reservations recommended. Main courses 18,000L–30,000L ($10.80–$18); fixed-price menu 60,000L–80,000L ($36–$48). AE, DC, MC, V. Daily noon–3pm and 7–10pm. Closed Mon in Nov–Mar. TUSCAN.

Al Mangia, one of the finest restaurants in the heart of the city, dates from 1937 and has outside tables that overlook the town hall. The food is not only well cooked but appetizingly presented. The house pasta specialty is *cannoli alla Mangia*. Craving a savory Tuscan main dish? Try a *bollito di manzo con salsa verde* (boiled beef with an herby green sauce). Another excellent course is the ossobuco with artichokes, and roast boar hunter's style is featured in season. This is also a good place for *bisteca fiorentino*. For dessert, it's got to be *panforte*, made of spicy delights, including almonds and candied fruits. It's known all over Europe.

INEXPENSIVE

Al Marsili (Ristorante Enoteca Gallo Nero). Via del Castoro 3. ☎ **0577/47-154.** Reservations recommended. Main courses 15,000L–30,000L ($9–$18). AE, DC, MC, V. Tues–Sun 12:30–2:30pm and 7:30–10:30pm. SIENESE/ITALIAN.

This beautiful restaurant stands between the Duomo and Via di Città in a neighborhood packed with medieval and Renaissance buildings. You dine beneath crisscrossed ceiling vaults whose russet-colored brickwork was designed centuries ago. Specialties of the chef include roast boar with tomatoes and herbs, *ribollita* (a savory vegetable soup), spaghetti covered with a sauce of seasonal mushrooms, and veal scaloppine with tarragon and tomato sauce. There's also a *cantina* of wines (the *enoteca* part of its name), where glasses begin at 6,000L ($3.60) if you'd like to indulge in a little wine tasting.

Da Guido. Vicolo Pier Pettinaio 7. ☎ **0577/280-042.** Reservations required. Main courses 15,000L–25,000L ($9–$15). AE, DC, MC, V. Thurs–Tues 12:30–3:30pm and 7:30–10:30pm. SIENESE/INTERNATIONAL.

Da Guido is a medieval Tuscan restaurant about 100 feet off the promenade street near Piazza del Campo. It's decked out with crusty old beams, time-aged brick walls, arched ceilings, and iron chandeliers. Our approval is backed up by the public testimony of more than 300 prominent people who have left autographed photographs to adorn the walls of the three dining rooms—film stars, diplomats, opera singers, and car-racing champions, even popes and presidents. There's a grill for steaks, chickens, and roasts. The antipasti are most rewarding. For a main dish, you may want to stick to the roasts, or try a pasta, tagliata alla Guido. The signature appetizer is *fiocchi di neve alla tartufo,* a gnocchi-like object made with wheat flour, filled with ricotta, eggs, basil, and spices—everything topped with a black truffle. The desserts are good, too.

Grotta Santa Caterina—Da Bagoga. Via della Galluzza 26. ☎ **0577/282-208.** Reservations recommended. Main courses 11,000L–20,000L ($6.60–$12); fixed-price menu 23,000L ($13.80). AE, MC, V. Tues–Sat 12:30–3pm and 7–10pm, Sun 12:30–3pm. Closed July 21–30 and Nov–Mar. TUSCAN/INTERNATIONAL.

Located in the heart of historic Siena, this building dates from the 1400s, although the restaurant wasn't established until 1953. Midway up a narrow, steeply inclined cobblestone street, the restaurant is an unpretentious gathering place popular with local residents. Inside are brick arches, lots of rustic detailing, plants, and wooden chairs. Specialties include eight kinds of scaloppine, beef or gnocchi with truffles, and chicken cooked in beer. Rabbit in champagne is a favorite, and the kitchen will also prepare a wide variety of mixed roast meats, including veal, pork, and lamb. Many dishes are based on 16th-century recipes—which means no tomatoes and no potatoes, since these vegetables were not in use at the time.

Nello La Taverna. Via del Porrione 28–30. ☎ **0577/289-043.** Reservations required. Main courses 15,000L–26,000L ($9–$15.60). AE, DC, MC, V. Mar–Nov, daily noon–3pm and 7–10pm; Dec and Feb, Tues–Sat noon–3pm and 7–10pm. Closed Jan. TUSCAN/VEGETARIAN.

Established in the 1930s, Nello La Taverna offers an ambience that's about as typical of the Sienese region as anything you'll find. Situated on a narrow stone-covered street about half a block from Piazza del Campo, the restaurant, as its name implies, offers a tavern decor that includes brick walls, hanging lanterns, racks of wine bottles, and sheaves of corn hanging from the ceiling. Best of all, you can view the forgelike kitchen with its crew of uniformed cooks busily preparing your dinner from behind a row of hanging copper utensils. Specialties include a salad of fresh radicchio, green lasagne ragoût style, and lamb cacciatore with beans. Freshly made pasta is served every day. Your waiter will gladly suggest a local vintage for you.

SIENA AFTER DARK

Although Siena doesn't contain a cornucopia of nightclubs, you can mingle with your nocturnal counterparts at **Blue Eyes Pub,** Via Giovanni Duprè 64 (☎ **0577/42-650**), which offers an indulgently permissive setting that's neither completely English nor completely Italian. There are touches of marble, battered Formica tables, and five kinds of beer on tap. Mugs cost from 6,500L ($3.90) and can be consumed amid a widely diverse crowd that's either wildly experimental or rather conservative, depending on your luck and timing. It's open Wednesday through Monday from 7pm to 3am.

6 La Chiantigiana: The Aroma of the Grape

La Chiantigiana, as Route S222 is known, twists and turns narrowly through the hilly terrain that makes up Tuscany's famous wine region. **Chianti,** once associated with cheap, sweet Italian wines, has finally captured the attention of wine connoisseurs with well-crafted *classicos* and *riservas.* This is the result of improved attention to growing and vinification techniques over the last two decades. The year 1990 proved to be a landmark, producing a vintage that quickly disappeared from world markets, some labels of which are highly prized by dedicated collectors. The area is also home to **vin santo,** a dessert wine something like old sherry that's difficult to find elsewhere.

The entire area is only 30 miles from north to south and 20 miles at its widest point. You could conceivably rent a bike or scooter for your tour. But if you do you'll have to cope with hills, dust, and the driving habits of "road king" Italians who call this turf their own. The rental of a small and easily maneuverable car is preferable, but even with an auto you still must deal with road-hogging buses and flying Fiats. A car will let you stop at vineyards along the dirt lanes that stray from the main road, an option not provided by any bus tour of the region. Still, be prepared for hairpin turns, ups and downs, and narrow and unidentified lanes.

Signs touting DEGUSTAZIONE or VENDITÀ DIRETTA lead you to wineries open to the public and offering tastings.

GETTING AROUND BY PUBLIC TRANSPORTATION   If you don't have a car, you can reach the central town of Greve by a SITA bus leaving from the main station in Florence, at the rate of one every 1¹/₂ hours. The trip takes an hour and costs 4,700L ($2.80) for a one-way ticket. Once in Greve, you can go to **Marco Ramuzzi,** Via Italo Stecchi 23 (☎ 055/853-037), and rent a mountain bike for 15,000L ($9) per day or a scooter for 40,000L ($24). Armed with a map from the tourist office, you can set out, braving the winding roads of Chianti country.

VISITOR INFORMATION   The tourist information office in the town of Greve in Chianti, at Via Luca Cino 1 (☎ 055/854-5243), is a useful source of data for the entire area, offering maps of the region and up-to-date listings about wineries that admit visitors.

TOURING THE WINERIES

In Florence, get on S222 off autostrada E35 and head south. At Petigliolo, 2¹/₂ miles south of the city, turn left and follow the signs to the first attraction along the road— not a winery but the vine-clad **Santo Stefano à Tizzano,** a church from the Romanesque era. Nearby stands a castle fortress dating from the 11th century. Today, this **Castello di Tizzano** (☎ 055/482-737) is part of a consortium of farms producing Chianti Classico under the Gallo Nero label. You can visit the cellars here and sample and perhaps buy bottles of Chianti or vin santo, and most definitely their award-winning olive oil, among the finest we've ever tasted. Here you'll feel you're in the very heart of Tuscany, enjoying two of its most famous products of the earth: wine and olive oil.

About 1¹/₄ miles farther along, following the same road, you arrive at **San Polo,** which is the heart of the iris industry of Italy. So many flowers grow in this region that in May (dates vary) an Iris Festival is held honoring the flower and source of livelihood for many of the area's growers. Far removed from the bustle and hordes of Florence, San Polo seems like a lonely time capsule, with a structure that once belonged to the powerful Knights Templar. A church of ancient origins stands here, **San Miniato in Robbiana,** which, if we are to believe the inscription, was consecrated in 1077 by the then-reigning bishop of Fiesole.

At San Polo, turn left and follow the signs back to S222 and the village of **Strada,** which is only 9 miles from Florence. "Street" seems a stange name for a town. Locals claim that the name came from an old Roman road or strada that ran through here. A still-standing castle, Castello di Mugano, one of the best preserved in Tuscany, stands guard over the region.

Continue along the Chiantigiana until you reach Vicchiomaggio where a castle here once hosted the illustrious Leonardo da Vinci. You'll be following in his footsteps by visiting **Fattorio Casatello di Vicchiomaggio** (☎ 055/854-078), which is open daily from 9am to 1pm and 2 to 7pm. Here you can sample and buy wines and grappa. You can also taste vin santo. The winery, too, offers olive oil for sale, so you can do a bit of shopping. It once sold the greatest honey of Tuscany—but no more. Perhaps the owners save the precious nectar for their own enjoyment.

Nearby lies the village of **Verrazzano,** a name more familiar to New Yorkers today than Tuscans. Giovanni da Verrazzano left the land of the grape and set to sea in the service of François I of France. In 1524 he discovered the harbor of New York and the island of Manhattan before disappearing without a trace on his second voyage to Brazil. The Verrazzano bridge to Staten Island honors this brave explorer today.

His birthplace is still standing. Called **Castello di Verrazzano** (☎ 0577/ 854-243), it is open Monday to Friday from 8am to 5pm to those who have called ahead and made a reservation to visit. You can sample and buy wine here. Unless the staff is rushed, you might even get instruction about how to become a wine snob. If you didn't make reservations, there's a *punto vendita,* or shop, open during daylight hours on Saturday and Sunday, lying on S222 heading south toward Greve.

About a mile north of Greve you come to **Castello di Uzzano,** Via Uzzano 5 (☎ 0577/854-032), which you can visit in summer by dropping in, although in winter you need a reservation. This winery charges an admission of 20,000L ($12), which allows you to tour the cellars and enjoy a tasting of the wine. Later, if you wish, you can purchase wine, olive oil, and honey, each product seemingly more delectable than the next. Long before it became one of the great wineries of Tuscany, Castello di Uzzano was constructed for the bishop of Florence some time in the 1200s.

At one time this castle was the residence of Niccolò da Uzzano, the philanthropist and humanist who was a great Tuscan patron of the arts as well. The garden around this estate is one of the loveliest in Tuscany. For the highlight of your tour of the Chianti country, ask the owner, Marion de Jacobert, to prepare a picnic lunch for you, costing 30,000L ($18), which includes admission to the garden. Here you can enjoy scenery that would have inspired da Vinci while feasting on prosciutto, the finest Tuscan salami you are likely to ever taste, vine-ripened tomatoes, country fresh bread, and that fruity Chianti, of course. Visitors are welcome here Monday through Saturday from 8am to noon and from 1 to 6pm. You can even stroll over here in about an hour from the Greve bus station (see below). If your schedule allows only one Tuscan winery in your itinerary, make it this one, especially if you're dependent on public transportation from Florence.

The road continues to **Greve,** which is the capital of Chianti. The grandest wine fair in Tuscany takes place here every September in this medieval town with its population of 11,000, most of whom make their living from the grape. One of the more colorful towns of Tuscany, it lies on the banks of the Greve River. Its heartbeat square is the funnel-shaped Piazza del Mercatale, which has a statue honoring that fabled native son, Verrazzano. Greve's castle long ago burned to the ground, but you can visit the parish church, Santa Croce, with a triptych by Lorenzo di Bicci. Greve is filled with wine shops or *enoteche,* although we find it far more adventurous to buy from the wineries themselves.

If you get hungry, there's a delectable little place to eat. Head for **La Mia Cucina,** Piazza Matteotti 80 (☎ 055/854-4718), which serves every day but Monday. The aroma of their roasting meats—tender and succulent—drifts across the square. They also make a creamy lasagne and delectably stuffed cannelloni. Their penne, in the words of one member of the staff, is "the best in Tuscany," an exaggeration perhaps, but is it ever good. The place is cheap, too, with most dishes costing 5,000 to 6,000L ($3 to $3.60).

Chianti Region

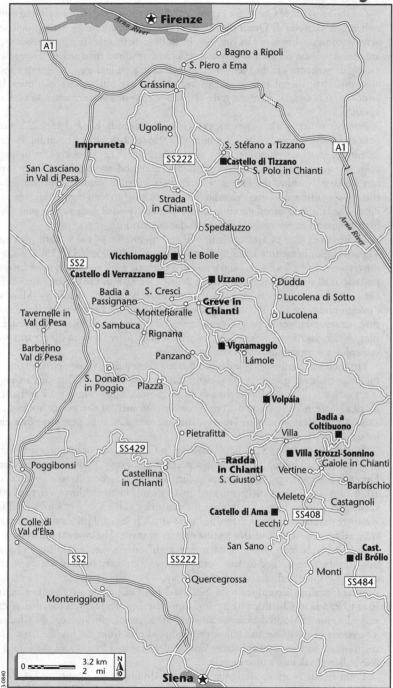

★ **Firenze**

A1

○ Bagno a Ripoli
○ S. Piero a Ema

Grássina

Ugolino ○

Impruneta ○

SS222

S. Stéfano a Tizzano

■ **Castello di Tizzano**
○ S. Polo in Chianti

A1

San Casciano
in Val di Pesa ○

Strada
in Chianti

○ Spedaluzzo

SS2

Vicchiomaggio ■ ○ le Bolle

Castello di Verrazzano ■

■ **Uzzano**

○ Dudda
○ Lucolena di Sotto

Badia a ○
Passignano

S. Cresci

**Greve in
Chianti**

Tavernelle in
Val di Pesa ○

Montefióralle

○ Sambuca

Rignana

○ Lucolena

Barberino
Val di Pesa ○

Vignamaggio ■

Panzano ○

○ Lámole

S. Donato ○
in Poggio

Piazza

Volpáia ■

○ Pietrafitta

Villa

**Badia a
Coltibuono** ■

Poggibonsi ○

SS429

■ **Villa Strozzi-Sonnino**
Gaiole in Chianti

Castellina
in Chianti

**Radda
in Chianti**

Vertine ○

○ Barbíschio

S. Giusto ○

Meleto ○

○ Castagnoli

Colle di
Val d'Elsa ○

Castello di Ama ■

Lecchi ○

SS408

San Sano ○

**Cast.
di Brólio** ■

SS2

SS222

○ Quercegrossa

○ Monti

SS484

Monteriggioni ○

0 ▬▬ 3.2 km
2 mi

N

3-0840

★ **Siena**

309

On the outskirts of Greve, the Figline Val d'Arno road leads to a lovely and tranquil estate, **Castello di Querceto** (☎ **055/854-9064**). Although these people are very welcoming, they won't let you visit the castle (strictly private quarters), but they are proud to show off their winery and will allow you into their cellars. They sell a variety of wines they make themselves, as well as grappa and a golden-green virgin olive oil. Their special vino is Sangiovese, which is aged in wooden barriques. Its aroma, so it is said, is "from the gods." Parties of four or more are advised to call in advance.

Another winery within easy reach of Greve is **Fontodi,** lying along S222, near Sant'Eufrosino. Fontodi, Via S. Leonino (☎ **055/852-005**), is a beautiful Tuscan farmstead. It, too, ages its wines in wooden barriques. The wines here are of good color (by now you're a wine snob), fine solidity, and moderate tannins. "Thirty years ago we lagged behind the French wine makers," a staff member confided. "But come—taste our wine—don't you think we're catching up with them?" They are indeed. The farm sells wines, vin santo, and Tuscan olive oil of such virginal purity it's been compared to one of those saintly Madonna paintings.

Immediately east of Greve lies one of the highlights of the Chianti district: **Vignamaggio,** home to a beautiful Renaissance villa (☎ **055/853-559**). This was the residence of La Gioconda, who with her enigmatic smile sat for the most famous portrait of all time, Leonardo da Vinci's *Mona Lisa,* now in the Louvre Museum in Paris. You can tour the gardens—some of the most beautiful in Tuscany—Monday through Friday for 15,000L ($9) if you call in advance for a reservation. If the classical statues and towering hedges seem familiar, it means you saw Kenneth Branagh's film, *Much Ado About Nothing,* which was shot here. After a tour of the gardens you can enjoy a wine tasting in the front estate office.

From Greve, continue 3¹/₂ miles south along the winding Chiantigiana to one of the most enchanting spots in the Chianti, the little agricultural village of **Panzano.** It's worth a walk around, and parts of its medieval castle—which once witnessed battles between Florence and Siena—remain. Women of the village are said to make the finest embroidery in Tuscany, and you may want to acquire some from the locals.

Further south on the S222 lies **Castellina in Chianti,** one of the most delightful of all the Tuscan hilltop villages, with a population of only 3,000. Once a fortified Florentine outpost against the armies in Siena, it fell to Sienese-Aragonese forces in 1478. But when Siena itself collapsed in 1555 to Florentine forces, sleepy little Castellina was left alone to slumber for centuries. That's why it's preserved its *quattrocento* look, with its once fortified walls virtually intact. Little houses were constructed into the walls and also nesting on top of them. The covered walkway, Via della Volte, is the most historic in town. Although bottegas here sell Chianti and olive oils, you are better advised to delay your purchases until later, because you are on the doorstep of some of the finest wineries in Italy.

After Castellina, detour from the S222 and head east along a tortuous, winding road to **Radda in Chianti,** with a population of 1,700. Radda is surrounded by the rugged region of Monti del Chianti and was the ancient capital of Lega del Chianti. The streets of the village still follow their original plan from the Middle Ages. The main square with its somber Palazzo Comunale, bearing a fresco from the 1400s, is like walking back into a time capsule.

From Radda continue along the tortuous, winding road, signposted Gaiole in Chianti. Along the way you'll come upon ✪ **Tenuta Badia a Coltibuono** (☎ **0577/749-124**), a wine estate and a restaurant (see "Where to Dine," below). Try to time your arrival for lunch, as the Tuscan food is excellent and most typical of the region.

Called "the abbey of the good harvest," this place was founded by Vallombrosian monks about a thousand years ago. They were the first vine growers of Chianti. For around a century and a half, the Stucchi Prinetti family has been linked to the property.

You should call for a reservation to visit the winery. In summer only, there are guided tours from 10:30am to 1pm, including a wine tasting for 5,000L ($3). A shop on site sells the wines of the region along with Coltibuono olive oil. The olives are picked by hand, crushed in old stone mills, and cold-pressed to obtain a high-quality oil with a strong, slightly spicy flavor. The shop also sells wine vinegars aged in casks, strongly scented balsamic vinegar, and exquisite varieties of acacia, chestnut, heather, and manna honey.

After a meal here, you can continue to the market town of **Gaiole in Chianti,** with a population of 5,000. This is a distance of 6 miles east of Radda. At a local cooperative here, **Agricoltori Chianti Geografico,** Via Mulinaccio 10 (☎ 0577/749-489), you can enjoy wine tasting on Monday through Saturday from 9am to 12:30pm and from 2 to 5pm and also purchase some of the famous wines of the region—not only Chianti but also the delectable white, Vernaccia di San Gimignano. The local vin santo is made of trebbiano and malvasia grapes left to dry before pressing. They are then fermented in small oak barrels for about 4 years. The cooperative also sells the extra-virgin olive oil produced in the region.

Use Gaiole as a starting point for interesting wine tours in the area, notably to the towering **Castello di Brolio** (☎ 0577/749-066), lying 6 miles south of Gaiole along S484. This is home of the Barone Ricasoli Wine House, famous since the 19th century for Baron Ricasoli's experiments aimed at improving the quality of Chianti wines. The history of this property goes back to the closing years of the 11th century when monks from Florence came here to live. Caught up many times in the bombardments between the warring forces of Florence and Siena, the castle was later torn down until authorities in Florence ordered that it be reconstructed.

If you're a true devotee, you'll find many other wineries in the area—all easily reached by car from Gaiole. The best include **Fattoria dei Pagliaresi** (☎ 0577/359-070), lying south of Gaiole on S484 in Castelnuovo. You should call the day before a visit. There are no cellars, but you can tour the farm and taste or buy wine, along with grappa and virgin pure olive oil. The winery is known for some excellent old vintages.

Yet another possibility lies 3 miles to the east in little Monti. Here, **Fattoria San Giusto** (☎ 0577/747-121) requires advance warnings of visits. It not only sells wines, vin santo, and olive oil, but offers horseback riding as well.

If you backtrack, taking S408 to Siena, you can follow the signposts about 6 miles north to **Fattoria della Aiola** (☎ 0577/322-615), where you can visit the gardens and cellars, sampling wines and grappa Monday through Friday throughout the year but also on Saturday and Sunday in summer. The farm sells Chianti, sangiovese, champagne, grappa, brandy, olive oil, and honey. It even produces its own vinegar. Reservations are required for parties of four or more.

WHERE TO STAY ALONG LA CHIANTIGIANA

The atmospheric Tuscan inns along the Chianti road are fabled, and many motorists like to break up a visit between Florence and its old enemy, Siena, with a night at one of these hotels. The best centers for overnighting are Greve in Chianti, Radda, Gaiole, and, our personal favorite, Castellina in Chianti. In addition to the restaurants recommended above, many of these inns are also noted for their good food and wine. Even if you're not a guest, you might visit for a meal.

Albergo del Chianti. Piazza Matteotti 86, 50022 Greve in Chianti. ☎ **0577/853-763.** Fax 0577/853-763. 16 rms. A/C MINIBAR TV TEL. 140,000L ($84) double. Rates include breakfast. MC, V.

Wine lovers head to this hotel in the center of Greve in Chianti. It offers antique rooms on one floor and modern on another—a total of 16 well-furnished accommodations. A fine Tuscan restaurant on site serves regional specialties, accompanied by the wines of the region.

Castello di Spaltenna. Pieve di Spaltenna, 53013 Gaiole in Chianti. ☎ **0577/749-483.** Fax 0577/749-269. 21 rms, 4 suites. A/C MINIBAR TV TEL. 300,000L–380,000L ($180–$228) double; 425,000L ($255) suite. Rates include breakfast. AE, DC, MC, V. Closed mid-Jan to Feb.

This inn is located in an ancient former monastery that stands on a hill above the village of Gaiole. It is a choice property, with some of the theatrical flair of the Middle Ages still evident. An ancient castle refectory, for example, remains. The panoramic views around here are among the finest in the area. Some of the traditionally furnished rooms include such modern amenities as a hydromassage or a Jacuzzi. Suites also have fireplaces. Room decor varies but might include wrought-iron bed frames and 1,000-year-old terra-cotta floors. The Tuscan cuisine here is solidly grounded in the classics, but, depending on the shopping for the day, the chef also has creative flair.

Il Girarrosta. Via Roma 41, 53107 Radda in Chianti. ☎ **0577/738-010.** 9 rms. 50,000L ($30) double. No credit cards.

Smaller and more informal than Villa Miranda, this hotel is the bargain of the Chianti country. It has been a family-run inn since 1927 at the center of Radda village. The rooms are simple and informal, but neat and comfortable, spread across two floors. The family is extremely welcoming and will serve you a hearty Tuscan cuisine any day except Wednesday. The building is very old (no one is quite sure how old), but it's been renovated.

Salivolpi. Via Fiorentina 89, 53011 Castellina in Chianti. ☎ and fax **0577/740-484.** 19 rms. TEL. 130,000L–140,000L ($78–$84) double. Rates include breakfast. AE, DC, MC, V.

The good living continues at this farm setting against a backdrop that looks like a Renaissance painting in the Uffizi. After it was turned from farm to hotel in 1984, Salivolpi has been visited by some of the world's most discriminating travelers, drawn to its setting and ambience. The rooms are spread across three buildings, each decorated with Tuscan antiques and beautifully maintained. Although there is a swimming pool and garden, there is no restaurant, but several good ones are a short drive away.

✪ Tenuta di Ricavo. Ricavo, 53011 Castellina in Chianti (2 miles north of town). ☎ **0577/740-221.** Fax 0577/741-016. 12 rms, 11 suites. MINIBAR TV TEL. 300,000L ($180) double; 440,000L ($264) suite. Rates include breakfast. MC, V. Closed early Nov to Apr 30.

This place is a fantasy of what a Tuscan inn should look like. In fact, the hotel of several buildings is like a medieval hamlet of stone-built houses, complete with a swimming pool. Rooms are furnished with antiques, and on nippy nights guests gather in the public lounge filled with a blazing fireplace. It's our favorite inn in all the Chianti country. The innkeepers rent beautifully furnished and maintained bedrooms, furnished with a regional decor. The Tuscan restaurant serves an elegant, refined cuisine.

Villa Casalecchi. Casalecchi 18, 53001 Castellina in Chianti. ☎ **0577/740-240.** Fax 0577/741-111. 16 rms, 3 suites. TV TEL. 300,000L–360,000L ($180–$216) double; up to 400,000L ($240) suite. Rates include breakfast. AE, DC, MC, V. Closed Nov to 1 week before Easter.

Almost as elegant as the Tenuta di Ricavo, this four-star property is built against a hill. You arrive on the hilltop and enter into what is actually the top floor. You then have to go down to the other floors. Although the building is quite old, it was remodeled extensively in 1984 and further rebuilding was necessary because of World War II damage. Since 1962, it has been receiving guests and housing them in a refined Tuscan ambience with beautifully furnished bedrooms. The hotel restaurant is used for catering to some of the finest palates in the world, and it serves a perfect Tuscan cuisine, with extremely fresh ingredients.

Villa Miranda. Loc. Villa, 53107 Radda in Chianti. ☎ **0577/738-021.** Fax 0577/738-668. 60 rms. 120,000L–170,000L ($72–$102) double. MC, V.

Villa Miranda was built on the site of an old posthouse that became a small Tuscan inn in 1842. Nowadays, most of the antique-filled rooms in the outbuildings have such amenities as a minibar, air-conditioning, TV, and phone, while those in the main structure are simpler. There are also two swimming pools on the grounds along with a tennis court. The restaurant here is one of the finest in the area, specializing in regional fare such as wild boar cooked in white wine.

WHERE TO DINE ALONG LA CHIANTIGIANA

Some of the best food in Italy is served in the Chianti district—all dishes, of course, accompanied by the wine of the region. Many visitors to the region view a stopover at one of these restaurants almost as important as touring the wineries. We've selected the places that serve the finest food in the area—all at affordable prices.

GREVE & ENVIRONS

Borgo Antico. Via Case Sparse 15, Lucolena (east of Greve). ☎ **0577/851-024.** Reservations required. Main courses 14,000L–28,000L ($8.40–$16.80). Fixed-price menus 60,000L–80,000L ($36–$48). AE, MC, V. Wed–Mon noon–3pm and 7–9:30 or 10pm. Closed Jan 7–Feb 12. TUSCAN.

This small place may be more upscale than you first thought. Renovated from a former stable, it is an alluring restaurant where the owners cook all the meals themselves. We've had better Florentine beefsteak here—tender and delicately flavored—than in Florence itself (but at far less the price). Very large cultivated strawberries of the region are cooked into a risotto. Their best pasta, in our view, is served with a spicy cream sauce flaked with red peppers.

Bottega del Moro. Piazza Trieste 14R, Greve in Chianti. ☎ **0577/853-753.** Reservations recommended. Main courses 17,000L–26,000L ($10.20–$15.60). AE, DC, MC, V. Thurs–Tues 12:15–2:15pm and 7:15–9:30pm. Closed Nov and first week of June. TUSCAN.

Modern paintings are in sharp contrast to the antique Tuscan atmosphere of rough brick walls and old tile floors. This is really a simple trattoria, right in the heart of town, but the cuisine is robust and hearty, made with fresh seasonable ingredients. They serve succulent homemade pastas, from crespelle to ravioli. The Florentine favorite, tripe, is always served, as well as rabbit from the hillside. Worth the trek across the village is the herb-flavored pieces of skewered meat grilled to perfection.

La Cantinetta. Via Mugnano 93, Spedaluzzo (north of Greve). ☎ **0577/857-2000.** Reservations required. Main courses 13,000L–23,000L ($7.80–$13.80). AE, DC, MC, V. Wed–Mon noon–2:30pm and 7:30–10:30pm. TUSCAN.

Armed with a good map from the tourist office, you can strike out from Greve along S93, heading nearby for Spedaluzzo. La Cantinetta's large garden for outdoor dining in summer is such a magnet that reservations are necessary. The restaurant offers some of the best pastas in Tuscany, none better than tagliata with truffles. Spaghetti made with porcini mushrooms would have pleased (surely) the demanding palate of da Vinci himself. Chicken cooked with fresh fried vegetables is another winning dish, as are stuffed rabbit and pigeon.

Montagliari. Via di Montagliari 27, Panzano (between Montagliari and Greve). ☎ **055/852-184.** Reservations recommended. Main courses 23,000L–25,000L ($13.80–$15). MC, V. Nov–Feb, daily 12:30–3pm; Thurs–Sun 7:30–10:30pm. March–Oct, daily 12:30–3pm and 7:30–10:30 or 11pm. TUSCAN.

This rustic restaurant is noted for its robust Tuscan cookery. Tables are set out in a garden, and the place is decorated like an old Tuscan farmhouse. The specialty here is wild boar cacciatora, which deserves a star. You can also order wide noodles with rabbit, herb-flavored veal cutlets, and ravioli filled with walnuts. A plate of penne with raw chopped tomatoes and home-grown basil disappears quickly.

CASTELLINA & ENVIRONS

Albergaccio di Castellina. Via Fiorentina 35, Castellina (on road to San Donato). ☎ **0557/741-042.** Reservations appreciated. Main courses 22,000L–27,000L ($13.20–$16.20). Fixed-price menu 65,000L ($39). No credit cards. Mon, Fri, and Sat 12:30–2pm; Tues–Thurs 7:30–9:30pm. Closed Nov 1–20. TUSCAN.

With is rough stone walls and beamed ceilings, this restaurant is a Tuscan cliche of charm. It's noted for its Tuscan fare prepared with very fresh ingredients deftly handled by a local staff. A winning combination is the platter of gnocchi and ricotta with white truffles of the region, or else you can order a dish of wide noodles cooked with wild boar. Ravioli stuffed with shredded pork and chestnuts is a dish to savor before getting *Gourmet* magazine on the phone. The tender, tasty, and herb-flavored Tuscan lamb is definitely a dish to order.

Antica Trattoria La Torre. Piazza del Comune 1, Castellina. ☎ **0577/740-236.** Reservations required in summer. Main courses 12,000L–20,000L ($7.20–$12). AE, DC, MC, V. Sat–Thurs noon–2:30pm and 7:30–9:30pm. Closed Oct 1–15. TUSCAN.

This old family-run dining room depends on the harvest from the field, stream, and air to keep its good cooks busy. The Tuscan game, the birds such as pigeons and guinea fowl, and the local beef are the finest in the area. The Florentine beefsteak alone is worth the trip. The surroundings may be simple, but the food is sublime and reasonably priced.

Il Vignale. Via XX Settembre 2, Radda in Chianti. ☎ **0577/738-094.** Reservations recommended. Main courses 25,000L–35,000L ($15–$21). AE, MC, V. Daily 1–2:30pm and 7:30–9:30pm. Closed Nov 20 to mid-March. TUSCAN.

This rustic yet elegant establishment is the best family-run dining room in the area, turning out a finely honed Tuscan version of a cuisine that is both flavorful and prepared with the freshest of ingredients. A habitué told us, "This is as close as you can get to being served food that you might be offered in a local home in the area." It is popular with both residents and visitors alike. The menu highlights the best on the market that day. Every day something new appears, and the cuisine is quite creative. You can go for the whole wild boar and order the gargantuan *menu degustazione* at 80,000L ($48).

Pietraffita Bar-Ristorante. Località Pietrafitta 41 (north of Castellina). ☎ **0577/741-123.** Reservations recommended. Main courses 17,000L–25,000L ($10.20–$15). AE, DC, MC, V. Summer, Thurs–Tues 12:30–2:30pm and 7:30–10pm; winter, Fri–Sun 12:30–2:30pm and 7:30–10pm. Closed Jan–March 6. ITALIAN/INTERNATIONAL.

Summer meals here are consumed outside under umbrellas in fair weather. On cool or rainy days, patrons retreat inside to the small dining room. Run by a team of Austrian and British expatriates deeply immersed in the traditions of Tuscan cuisine, this remote spot surprisingly offers zesty regional and international dishes, some of the finest in the area. Try their flat noodles with boiled beef. The catch of the field, rabbit and wild boar, gets great attention here. Menus change based on market availability, but the fare is fresh and always generous of portion.

Tenuta Badia a Coltibuono. ☎ 0577/749-031. Reservations required. Main courses 20,000L–26,000L ($12–$15.60); fixed-price menus 55,000L–60,000L ($33–$36). MC, V. Apr–Oct, daily 12:30–3pm and 7–9pm. Closed Nov–Mar. MC, V. TUSCAN/INVENTIVE.

This restaurant occupies a medieval building adjacent to the winery recommended above. It's very much a family affair here, with owner Paolo Stucchi Prinetti the host in the dining room, and the chef preparing food from recipes given a touch of originality by the mistress of the domain, Lorenza de' Medici. Dishes are based on simple, seasonal ingredients whose flavors are accented by fresh herbs and greens. Fresh pasta is made daily, and regional meat specialties include rabbit, lamb, and the extraordinary Chianina beef of Tuscany. Local goat and sheep's milk cheese are served, and homemade desserts conclude the banquets here. The wine list highlights the vintages of Coltibuono.

7　Arezzo

50 miles SE of Florence

The most landlocked of all towns or cities of Tuscany, Arezzo was originally an Etruscan settlement and later a Roman center. The city flourished in the Middle Ages before its capitulation to Florence.

The walled town grew up on a hill, but large parts of the ancient city, including native son Petrarch's house, were bombed during World War II before the area fell to the Allied advance in the summer of 1944. Apart from Petrarch, famous sons of Arezzo have included Vasari, the painter-architect remembered chiefly for his history of the Renaissance artists, and Guido of Arezzo (sometimes known as Guido Monaco), who gave the world the modern musical scale before his death in the mid-11th century.

Today, Arezzo looks a little rustic, as if the glory of the Renaissance has long past it by. But this isn't surprising when you consider that it lost its prosperity when Florence annexed it in 1348. Arezzo might look a bit down at the heel, but it really isn't. The city today has one of the biggest jewelry industries in Western Europe. Little firms on the outskirts turn out an array of rings and chains, and bank vaults are overflowing with gold ingots. But all that's on the outskirts. The inner core, which most visitors want to explore, didn't share in this gold and looks as if it needs a rehab.

ESSENTIALS

GETTING THERE　By Train　There's a train that comes from Florence every 50 minutes throughout the day. The trip takes between 40 and 60 minutes, and a one-way ticket costs 7,500L ($4.50). Trains depart and arrive at the **Stazione Centrale,** Piazza della Repubblica (☎ **0575/22-663**), in the center of town. Because there are no direct train routes from Siena to Arezzo, railway passengers from Siena are required to make hot, prolonged, and tiresome rail transfers in Florence. Therefore, unless it happens to be Sunday (see below), it's better to opt for bus transfers if your point of origin is Siena.

By Bus　Travel by bus from Florence to Arezzo is not a good idea. Bus routes from Siena to Arezzo, however, are preferable to the bothersome train transfers. Monday to Saturday, five buses per day travel from Siena directly to Arezzo. On Sunday, however, you'll have to take the train. For information on bus routes, call the bus station in Siena (☎ **0577/280-551**).

VISITOR INFORMATION   The **Arezzo Tourist Information Office,** at Piazza della Repubblica 28 (☎ 0575/377-678), is open Monday to Saturday from 9am to 1pm and 3 to 7pm and Sunday from 9am to 1pm.

EXPLORING THE TOWN

The biggest event on the Arezzo calendar is the **Giostra** (joust) **del Saraceno,** staged the third Sunday of June and the first Sunday of September on **Piazza Grande.** Horsemen in medieval costumes reenact the lance-charging ritual—with balled whips cracking in the air—as they have since the 13th century. But Piazza Grande should be visited at any time of the year for the medieval and Renaissance palaces and towers that flank it, including the 16th-century **Loggia** by Vasari.

The **Church of Santa Maria della Pieve,** Corso Italia (☎ 0575/22-629), is a Romanesque structure, with a front of three open-air loggias (each pillar designed differently). The 14th-century bell tower is known as "the hundred holes," as it's riddled with windows. Inside, the church is bleak and austere, but there's a notable polyptych of the *Virgin with Saints* by one of the Sienese Lorenzetti brothers (Pietro), painted in 1320. The church is open daily from 8am to 1pm and 3 to 6:30pm.

A short walk away is **Petrarch's House,** Via dell'Orto 28A (☎ 0575/24-700), which has been rebuilt after war damage. Born at Arezzo in 1304, Petrarch was, of course, the great Italian lyrical poet and humanist, who immortalized his love, Laura, in his sonnets. His house is open Monday to Saturday from 10am to noon and 3 to 5pm. Ring the bell for admission.

If you have only an hour for Arezzo, run to the ✪ **Basilica di San Francesco,** Piazza San Francesco (☎ 0575/20-630), a Gothic church finished in the 14th century for the Franciscans. In the church is a fresco cycle—*Legend of the True Cross*—by Piero della Francesca, his masterpiece.

Piero's frescoes are remarkable for their grace, clearness, dramatic light effects, well-chosen colors, and ascetic severity. Vasari credited della Francesca as a master of the laws of geometry and perspective, and Sir Kenneth Clark called Piero's frescoes "the most perfect morning light in all Renaissance painting." The frescoes depict the burial of Adam, Solomon receiving the queen of Sheba at the court (the most memorable scene in the cycle), the dream of Constantine with the descent of an angel, as well as the triumph of the Holy Cross with Heraclius, among other subjects. The church can be visited daily from 8am to noon and 2 to 6:30pm. Admission is free.

You might also want to check out **Il Duomo,** Piazza del Duomo (☎ 0575/23-991), which was built in the so-called pure Gothic style—rare for Tuscany. The cathedral was begun in the 13th century, but the final touches (the facade) weren't applied until the outbreak of World War I. Its art treasures include stained-glass windows by Marcillat and a main altar in the Gothic style. Its main treasure, though, is the *Mary Magdalene,* a della Francesca masterpiece. It's open daily from 8am to noon and 2 to 6:30pm.

SHOPPING   Arezzo hosts one of Europe's biggest gold jewelry industries. In the very center of town, around Piazza Grande, are dozens of antique shops that have earned for Arezzo the title of "ye olde curiosity shop of Tuscany." These spill out onto the piazza during the Antiques Fair, held the first weekend of every month.

WHERE TO STAY

There are no outstanding hotels here that will induce you to linger, the way you might in San Gimignano or Siena. They're comfortable and affordable, but usually attract people in Arezzo on "gold business."

Hotel Continentale. Piazza Guido Monaco 7, 52100 Arezzo. ☎ **0575/20-251.** Fax 0575/350-485. 74 rms. MINIBAR TV TEL. 150,000L ($96) double. AE, DC, MC, V. Parking 18,000L ($10.80).

This modern, geometric hotel is certainly different from the more antique architecture that characterizes most of the town's historic core. However, located less than 200 yards from the town's railway station, in the town's commercial core, the Continentale offers cost-conscious accommodations in an early 1950s setting. Renovations have kept the place up-to-date. About 70% of the bedrooms—which are scattered over five efficiently decorated floors—have air-conditioning, and since the price is the same for all rooms in the hotel, it pays to request one specifically in advance. The hotel restaurant is open for three meals a day every day except Sunday evening and Monday.

WHERE TO DINE

Buca di San Francesco. Via San Francesco 1. ☎ **0575/23-271.** Reservations recommended. Main courses 16,000L–36,000L ($9.60–$21.60). AE, DC, MC, V. Wed–Sun 12:30–3pm and 7–11pm. ITALIAN.

Located in the historic core of the old city, this admirable restaurant—the city's finest—is set in the cellar of a building from the 1300s, and decorated with medieval references and strong Tuscan colors of sienna and blue. Menu items include pollo del Valdarno arrosto (roast chicken from the valley of the Arno) flavored with anise, homemade tagliolini with tomatoes and ricotta, and calves' liver with onions according to a regional recipe. A popular first course is green noodles with a rich meat sauce, oozing with creamy cheese and topped with a hunk of fresh butter. All ingredients are fresh, many of the staples are produced in-house, and even the establishment's olive oil is from special, private sources not shared by other restaurants.

8 Gubbio

25 miles NE of Perugia, 135 miles N of Rome, 57 miles SE of Arezzo, 34 miles N of Assisi

Gubbio is one of the best-preserved medieval towns in Italy. It has modern apartments and stores on its outskirts, but once you press through that, you're firmly back in the Middle Ages. The best-known streets of its medieval core are Via XX Settembre, Via dei Consoli, Via Galeotti, and Via Baldassini. All these streets are found in the old town, or Città Vecchia, set against the steep slopes of Monte Ingino.

Since Gubbio is off-the-beaten track, it remains a fairly sleepy backwater today except for intrepid shoppers who drive here to shop for ceramics (see below). Gubbio is almost as well known for ceramics as is Deruta. The last time Gubbio entered the history books was in 1944 when 40 hostages were murdered by the Nazis. Today, the central Piazza dei Quaranta Martiri is named for and honors those victims.

ESSENTIALS

GETTING THERE   By Bus   Because Gubbio doesn't have a rail station, visitors arrive by car or bus. There are eight buses a day from Perugia. Trip time is 1 hour 10 minutes, and a one-way ticket costs 7,400L ($4.45). Buses arrive and depart from Piazza 40 Martiri (☎ **075/922-0066**), in the heart of town.

By Car   From Rome, follow the autostrada A1 to Orte, then take SS3 north 88 miles to its intersection with SS298 at Schéggia. Go southwest on SS298 for 8 miles to Gubbio. From Perugia, this turnoff is 25 miles northeast on the SS298.

VISITOR INFORMATION   The **Gubbio Tourist Office,** at Piazza Oderisi 6 (☎ 075/922-0693), is open Monday to Saturday from 8am to 2pm and 3 to 6pm, and Sunday from 9am to 1pm.

EXPLORING THE OLD TOWN

If the weather is right you can take a cable car up to **Monte Ingino,** at a height of 2,690 feet, for a panoramic view of the area. In July and August service is Monday to Saturday from 8:30am to 7:30pm and Sunday from 8:30am to 8pm; in June and September, from 9:30am to 1:15pm and 2:30 to 7:30pm; off-season, daily from 10am to 1:15pm and 2:30 to 5pm. A round-trip ticket costs 6,000L ($3.60).

Back in Gubbio, you can set about exploring a town that knew its golden age in the 1300s. Begin at Piazza Grande, the most important square. Nearby you can visit the **Palazzo dei Consoli,** Piazza Grande (☎ 075/927-4298), a Gothic edifice housing the famed bronze *tavole eugubine,* a series of tablets as old as Christianity, which were discovered in the 15th century. The tablets contain writing in the mysterious Umbrian language. The museum has a display of antiques from the Middle Ages and a collection of not very worthwhile paintings. It's open Tuesday to Saturday from 9am to 12:30pm and 3:30 to 6pm and Sunday from 9am to 1pm. Admission is 4,000L ($2.40) for adults and 3,000L ($1.80) for children.

The other major sight is the **Palazzo Ducale,** or ducal palace, Via Ducale (☎ 075/927-5872). This palace is associated with the memories (not always good ones) of the ruling dukes of Urbino. It was built for Federico of Montefeltro. It's open Monday through Saturday from 9am to 1pm and 2:30 to 6:30pm, Sunday from 9am to 1pm; admission is 4,000L ($2.40).

After visiting the ducal palace, you can go inside **Il Duomo,** Via Ducale (☎ 075/927-3980), across the way. The cathedral of Gubbio is a relatively unadorned pink Gothic building with some stained-glass windows from the 12th century. It has a single nave. It's open daily from 9am to 12:30pm and 3:30 to 8:30pm.

Gubbio has some minor attractions as well, including the **Chiesa di San Francesco,** Piazza Quaranta Martiri (☎ 075/927-3460), built in the Gothic style. The interior walls of the north apse are covered with a set of stunning frescoes executed in the early 1400s. The name of the local painter, Ottaviano Nelli, is relatively unknown, but reproductions of his work often appear in Italian art books.

You can also visit the **Teatro Romano,** Via del Teatro Romano—at least from the outside. Dating from the time of Augustus, this former theater is now a ruin and is closed to the public. Special permission is needed to enter (usually granted only for academic research).

SHOPPING   This is the major reason many visitors flock to Gubbio. Gubbio's fame as a ceramics center can trace its beginnings to the 14th century. In the 1500s the industry rose to the height of its fame. Sometime during this period a Mastro Giorgio pioneered a particularly intense, irridescent ruby red that awed the competitors of his day. Today, pottery workshops are found all over town, the beautiful flowery plates lining walls of shop doorways. You can't miss them.

Two of the best outlets in Gubbio for the product lie within the town's historic center, and between them offer a staggering array of ceramics. Head for **Ceramica Rampini,** Via Leonardo da Vinci 94 (☎ 075/927-2963), or its largest competitor, **La Mastro Giorgio,** 3 Piazza Grande (☎ 075/927-1574). La Mastro Giorgio opens its factory, at Via Tifernate 10 (☎ 075/927-3616), about a half-mile from the center of Gubbio, to well-intentioned visitors who phone in advance for a convenient hour.

Gubbio is known for more than pots and vases: Its replicas of medieval crossbows *(balestre)* are prized as children's toys and macho decorative ornaments by aficionados of such things. If you want to add a touch of medieval authenticity to your den or office, head for the showrooms of either of two outfits that manufacture these—priced from 20,000L ($12) for a cheap version to as much as 150,000L ($90) for something much more substantial. They include **Negocio Medioevo,** Ponte d'Assi (☎ 075/927-2596), and **Rafael & Giuliani Morelli,** Ponte d'Assi (☎ 075/927-2934).

WHERE TO STAY

Hotel Gattapone. Via Beni 6, 06024 Gubbio. ☎ **075/927-2489.** Fax 075/927-1269. 15 rms. TV TEL. 90,000L ($54) double. AE, DC, MC, V. Closed Jan.

This is a pleasant but not particularly plush hotel. What the hotel lacks in luxuries it makes up for in low prices. It's set at the bottom of a narrow alleyway whose flagstone pavement is spanned with soaring medieval buttresses. Guests enter a modernized lobby, in place since the site became a hotel in the 1970s, and head for a sun-flooded breakfast room where large windows offer glimpses of a tiny garden. Although the furniture throughout is modern and relatively uninspired, there are a few handcrafted details, such as timbered ceilings and arches of chiseled stone, here and there. Breakfast is the only meal served. For other meals, the hotel staff usually refers its clients to the Taverna del Lupo (see below).

Palace Hotel Bosone. Via XX Settembre 22, 06024 Gubbio. ☎ **075/922-0698.** Fax 075/922-0552. 25 rms, 5 suites. A/C MINIBAR TV TEL. 125,000L ($75) double; 220,000L–295,000L ($132–$177) suite. Closed 3 weeks in Feb.

This is the most scenically located hotel in town, and also one of the most lavishly historic. Set at the meeting point of an almost endless flight of stone steps and a narrow street in the upper regions of town, it was built in the 1300s and enlarged during the Renaissance. The three-story stone building was converted from a private home into a hotel in 1974, welcoming guests ever since into cozy bedrooms trimmed with stone. No meals are served other than breakfast, although the hotel usually directs its clients to the Taverna del Lupo, a short walk from the hotel.

San Marco. Via Perugino 5, 06024 Gubbio. ☎ **075/922-0234.** Fax 075/927-3716. 63 rms. TV TEL. 132,000L ($79.20) double. AE, DC, MC, V. Parking 15,000L ($9) in nearby garage.

Its unpromising location on the busiest street corner in town is the San Marco's only real drawback. Other than that, this is a worthwhile, not particularly expensive, hotel set near the town's municipal parking lot. Built in solid, stone-sided stages between 1300 and the 1700s, it contains an arbor-covered terrace in back and cozy and traditionally furnished bedrooms that are comfortable and well maintained. The Restaurant San Marco serves Italian food beneath russet-colored brick vaulting.

WHERE TO DINE

Ristorante Federico de Montefeltro. Via della Repubblica 35. ☎ **075/927-3949.** Reservations recommended. Main courses 16,000L–24,000L ($9.60–$14.40). AE, DC, MC, V. Fri–Wed 12:30–2:30pm and 7:20–10:30pm. Closed Feb. ITALIAN/REGIONAL.

Named after the feudal lord who built the ducal palace of Gubbio, this restaurant stands beside steeply inclined flagstones in the oldest part of the city. Inside is a pair of tavern-style dining rooms ringed with exposed stone and pinewood planking. Many of the specialties are based on ancient regional recipes, although the selection of tasty, fresh antipasti covers the traditions of most of the Italian peninsula. Dishes are executed here with a polished technique. Menu items include chicken cooked with garlic, rosemary, and wine; roast suckling pig; several preparations of polenta; and broad noodles (pappardelle) with wild hare. You'll also be served a local version of unleavened bread fried in oil as part of the meal.

Taverna del Lupo. Via Giovanni Ansidei 21. ☎ **075/927-4368.** Reservations recommended. Main courses 20,000L–25,000L ($12–$15). AE, DC, MC, V. Tues–Sun 12:30–11pm. Closed Jan. ITALIAN/TUSCAN.

This is the most authentically medieval of the many competing restaurants in Gubbio. Originally built in the 1200s, with unusual rows of tiles, it contains ceilings supported by barrel vaults and ribbing of solid stone, from which are suspended iron chandeliers. For such a relatively modest place, the menu is surprisingly sophisticated and filled with the rich bounty from this part of Italy, each dish deftly prepared by a talented kitchen staff. Menu items include a terrine of duck studded with truffles, suprême of pheasant, rich and steaming minestrones, and many of the pork, veal, and beef dishes that are distinctly Tuscan.

9 Perugia

50 miles SE of Arezzo, 117 miles N of Rome, 96 miles SE of Florence

Perugia was one of a dozen major cities in the mysterious Etruscan galaxy. In Perugia we can peel away the epochs. For example, one of the town gates is called the **Arco di Augusto,** or Arch of Augustus. The loggia spanning the arch dates from the Renaissance, but the central part is Roman. Builders from both periods used the reliable Etruscan foundation, which was the work of architects who laid stones to last.

Today the city—home to Perugina chocolate—is the capital of Umbria; it has retained much of its Gothic and Renaissance charm, although it has been plagued with wars and swept up in disastrous events. The city is one of universities and art academies, attracting a young, vibrant crowd—some of whom can be seen in one of the zillions of local bars, pizzerias, music shops, and cafes enjoying the famous chocolate *baci* (kisses). To capture the essence of the Umbrian city, you must head for Piazza IV Novembre in the heart of Perugia. During the day the square is overrun, so try to go late at night when the old town is sleeping. That's when the ghosts come out to play.

ESSENTIALS

GETTING THERE   By Train   Perugia has rail links with Rome and Florence, but connections can be awkward. Trains from Rome often connect in Foligno, where, if you miss a train, there can be a wait up to an hour or more. If possible, try to get one of the infrequent direct trains that take only 3 hours, or even an IC train that cuts the trip down to 2¹/₂ hours. A one-way ticket from Rome costs 25,400L ($15.25), but direct trains may impose a 10,000L ($6) supplement. Most trains from Florence connect in Terontola, although there are occasional direct trains as well. A one-way fare costs 20,900L ($12.55), although direct trains impose a supplement, usually about 9,000L ($5.40). For information and schedules, call ☎ 075/500-7467. Arrivals are at the train station lying away from the town's monumental core at Piazza Vittorio Veneto. Buses 20, 26, 27, 28, and 29 run to Piazza Italia, as close as you get to the center.

By Bus   A daily bus motors here from the heart of Rome every day, costing 19,000L ($11.40) for a one-way ticket and taking 2¹/₂ hours. The same price will get you a bus trip from Florence in 2 hours. For information and schedules, call ☎ 075/500-9641.

By Car   From either Rome or Florence, Autostrada del Sole (A1) takes you to the cutoff east to Perugia. Just follow the signs. From Siena, S73 winds its way to Perugia. A73 connects with the autostrada. If you arrive by car, you can drive to your hotel to unload your baggage; after that, you'll be directed to a parking lot on the outskirts.

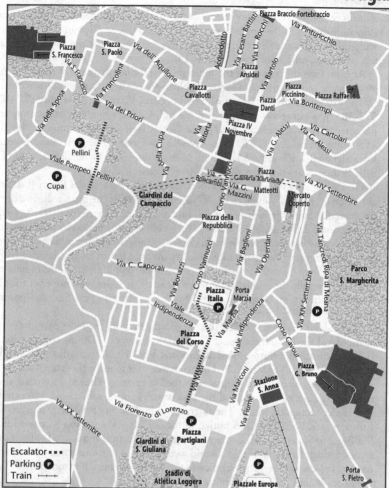

VISITOR INFORMATION The **tourist information office** is at Piazza IV Novembre 3 (☎ 075/573-6458). It's open Monday to Saturday from 8:30am to 1:30pm and 3:30 to 6:30pm, Sunday and holidays 9am to 1pm. It is closed January 1 and December 25 and 26.

EXPLORING THE CITY

As the villages of England compete for the title of most picturesque, so the cities of Italy vie for the honor of having the most beautiful square. As you stand on the central ✪ **Piazza IV Novembre,** you'll know that Perugia is among the top contenders for that honor.

In the heart of the Piazza is the **Fontana Maggiore** (Grand Fountain), built some time in the late 1270s by a local architect, a monk named Bevignate. A major restoration is in the process of returning it to some of its former glory. The fountain's artistic triumph stems from the sculptural work by Nicola Pisano and his son, Giovanni. Along the lower basin of the fountain—which is the last major work of the elder Pisano—is statuary that symbolizes the arts and sciences, Aesop's fables, the months of the year, the signs of the zodiac, and scenes from the Old Testament and Roman history. On the upper basin (mostly the work of Giovanni) is allegorical sculpture, such as one figure representing Perugia, as well as saints, biblical characters, even local officials of the city in the 13th century.

After viewing the marvels of the fountain, you'll find that most of the other major attractions either open onto Piazza IV Novembre or lie only a short distance away.

The exterior of the **Cathedral of San Lorenzo,** Piazza IV Novembre (☎ 075/ 572-3832), is rather raw-looking, as if the builders were suddenly called away and never returned. The basilica is built in the Gothic style and dates from the 14th and 15th centuries. Inside, you'll find the *Deposition* of Frederico Barocci. In the museum, Luca Signorelli's *Virgin Enthroned* with saints is displayed. Signorelli was a pupil of della Francesca. It's open daily from 8:30am to noon and 4 to 6:45pm.

On the opposite side of Piazza IV Novembre is the **Palazzo dei Priori** (Palace of the Priors), at Corso Vannucci 19 (☎ 075/572-0316). The town hall, one of the finest secular buildings in Italy, dates from the 13th century and shelters the Galleria Nazionale dell'Umbria (see below). Its facade is characterized by a striking row of mullioned windows. Over the main door is a Guelph (member of the papal party) lion and a griffin of Perugia, which hold chains once looted from a defeated Siena. You can walk up the stairway—the Vaccara—to the pulpit. By all means explore the interior, especially the vaulted Hall of the Notaries, frescoed with stories of the Old Testament and from Aesop. It's open Monday to Saturday from 9am to 7pm and Sunday from 9am to 1pm.

An escalator has been installed to take passengers from the older part of Perugia at the top of the hill and the upper slopes to the lower city. During construction of the escalator the old fortress, **Rocca Paolina,** Via Marzia, was rediscovered, along with buried streets. The fortress had been covered over to make the gardens and viewing area at the end of Corso Vannucci in the last century. The old streets and street names have been cleaned up, and the area is well lighted, with an old wall exposed and modern sculpture added. The fortress was built in the 1500s by Sangallo. The Etruscan gate, Porta Marzia, is buried in the old city walls and can be viewed from Via Baglioni Sotterranea. This street lies within the fortress and is lined with houses, some of which date from the 1400s and were buried at one time when gardens were constructed above them. The escalator to the Rocca operates daily from 6am to 1am; the Rocca is open daily from 8am to 7pm.

✪ **Galleria Nazionale dell'Umbria.** Upstairs in the Palazzo dei Priori (see above), Corso Vannucci 19. ☎ **075/574-1247.** Admission 8,000L ($4.80) adults, free for children 17 and under and seniors. Mon–Sat 9am–7pm, Sun 9am–1pm. Closed the first Mon of every month.

Upstairs in the Palace of the Priors is the National Gallery of Umbria, which houses the most comprehensive collection of Umbrian art from the 13th to the 19th centuries. It is one of the art treasure troves of Italy, and viewing here is better than ever now that it's undergone a restoration and reorganization. Among the earliest paintings of interest is a *Virgin and Child* by Duccio di Buoninsegna, the first important master of the Sienese school. You'll see statuary by the Pisano family, who designed the Grand Fountain out front, and by Arnolfo di Cambio, the architect of the Palazzo Vecchio in Florence.

Tuscan artists are well represented—the pious Fra Angelico's *Virgin and Child* with saints and angels is there, as well as the same subject treated differently by Piero della Francesca and Benozzo Gozzoli.

You'll also see works of native-son Perugino, among them his *Adoration of the Magi.* Perugino was the master of Raphael. Often accused of sentimentality, Perugino does not enjoy the popularity today that he did at the peak of his career, but he remains a key painter of the Renaissance, who is noted especially for his landscapes.

The gallery also displays art by Pinturicchio, who studied under Perugino, and whose most notable work was the library of the Duomo of Siena.

Collegio del Cambio. Corso Vannucci 25. ☎ **075/572-8599.** Admission 5,000L ($3) adults, free for children under 12. Mar–Oct and Dec 20–Jan 6, Mon–Sat 9am–12:30pm and 2:30–5:30pm, Sun and holidays 9am–12:30pm; Jan 7–Feb and Nov 1–Dec 19, Tues–Sat 8am–2pm, Sun and holidays 9am–12:30pm. Closed New Year's Day, May Day, and Christmas Day.

Right off Piazza IV Novembre, this medieval exchange building—part of the Palazzo dei Priori—opens onto the main street of Perugia, Corso Vannucci (Vannucci was the real name of Perugino). The collegio is visited chiefly by those seeking to view the Hall of the Audience, frescoed by Perugino and his assistants, including a teenage Raphael. On the ceiling Perugino represented the planets allegorically. The Renaissance master peopled his frescoes with the Virtues, sybils, and such biblical figures as Solomon. But his masterpiece is his own countenance. It seems rather ironic that—at least for once—Perugino could be realistic. Another room of interest is the Chapel of S. J. Battista, which contains many frescoes painted by a pupil of Perugino, G. Nicola di Paolo.

SHOPPING

By far the most famous foodstuff in town derives from one of Italy's best-loved manufacturers of chocolates and bon-bons, Perugina. Don't expect a hi-glam, high-profile outlet for this product, as the company has traditionally opted to flood Italy and the world with as broad an access to their product as possible. Consequently, displays of the foil-wrapped chocolates crop up at tobacco shops, supermarkets, newspaper kiosks, and sometimes gas stations throughout the city. Confused about the product? The selection includes milk chocolate *(cioccolato al latte)*, and its darker counterpart, *cioccolato fondente*, both sold in everything from mouth-sized morels *(baci)* to romance-sized, appropriately impressive decorative boxes. One always-reliable outlet for the product within the town center is the **Bar Ferrari,** Corso Vannucci 43 (☎ 075/575-6197), which stockpiles Perugina products prominently amid the workaday bustle of one of the most popular bars and cafes in town. Chocoholics who want even stronger doses of the stuff sometimes opt to visit the factory itself, which offers tours to clients who phone in advance. The **Fabrica Perugina,** 3 miles west of Perugia's historic core, forms the centerpiece of the hamlet of San Sisto. Telephone ☎ 075/52-761 to make an appointment.

Looking for ceramics and the kind of souvenirs that are more enduring than your hunger pangs? Head for either of Perugia's most interesting shops, **La Bottega dei Bassai,** Via Baglioni (☎ 075/572-3108), or **Ceccucci,** Corso Vannucci 38 (☎ 075/573-5143). If you're searching for fashion, particularly the cashmere garments that are tailored and often designed in Perugia, consider a jaunt 4 miles south of town to the village of Ponta San Giovanni. Here, one of the largest inventories of cashmere garments (coats, suits, dresses, and sweaters) for men and women is stockpiled at **Big Bertha,** Ponta San Giovanni (☎ 075/599-7572), the well-signposted direct factory outlet for one of Italy's most visible mail-order clothiers.

A SHOPPING SIDE TRIP: THE CERAMICS OF DERUTA

One of the artisanal highlights of a trip to this part of Italy involves shopping for a product that's been associated with Umbria since the days of the Renaissance painters. The manufacturing town of Deruta, 12½ miles south of Perugia off the Via Flaminia, has the densest concentration of shops and factories that sell the distinctive product anywhere in Italy. Don't even think of mentioning the word "porcelain" within earshot of virtually anyone in town. ("Stoneware," or even better, "glazed terra-cotta," is preferred.) The process involves forming the region's terra-cotta clay into sturdy-looking bowls, umbrella stands, plates, cups, and art objects, firing them, glazing them with distinctive arabesques and bright colors, and firing them again. Especially popular is a design associated with the region since the Renaissance, when Raphael commissioned some of this ceramic-ware here, a motif of dragons cavorting amid flowers and vines.

The largest, most deeply entrenched manufacturer in town, with some of the most reliable shipping services and the biggest sampling of wares, is **Ubaldo Grazie,** Via Tiberina 181 (☎ 075/971-0201). Although its roots go back to the 15th century, the sprawling factory that produces the stuff, built in the 1920s, predates Mussolini. Look for sophisticated marketing programs, authentic copies of antique pieces, as well as more contemporary interpretations based on style-conscious Italian modernism. Anything you buy on site can be shipped via UPS to any destination in the world. The factory outlet can be visited daily except Saturday afternoon and Sunday from 8am to noon and 2 to 6pm. Tours of the factory, lasting about an hour each, are sometimes offered, free, to clients who phone and reserve in advance.

A less comprehensive nearby competitor, whose namesake began his career within the above-mentioned Ubaldo Grazie factories, is **Antonio Margaritelli,** Via Tiberina 214 (☎ 075/971-1572). Founded in 1975, this factory outlet stocks material that's roughly equivalent to that at the Ubaldo Grazie factories, but in a less diverse selection.

What should you look for in your Deruta ceramics? You can get a fast education in the town's ceramic traditions from a quick visit to the **Museo della Ceramica Umbra,** Palazzo del Comune (City Hall), Piazza dei Consoli (☎ 075/971-1143). It's open Tuesday to Saturday from 9am to noon and 1:30 to 5pm, and charges 3,500L ($2.10) per person for a view of ceramics produced within the region between the 1500s and today. Look for a radical enlargement of this museum during the lifetime of this edition.

WHERE TO STAY

Hotel Brufani. Piazza Italia 12, 06100 Perugia. ☎ **075/573-2541.** Fax 075/572-0210. 20 rms, 4 suites. A/C MINIBAR TV TEL. 330,000L–450,000L ($198–$270) double; 650,000L ($390) suite. AE, CB, DC, MC, V. Parking 25,000L ($15).

Located at the top of the city, this five-star hotel, the best in town, was built by Giacomo Brufani in 1884 on the ruins of the ancient Rocca Paolina, a site known to the ancient Romans that later served as the home of one of the Renaissance popes. It's placed on a cliff edge, only a few yards from the main street of Perugia, Corso Vannucci. Most of the accommodations offer a view of the Umbrian landscape so beloved by painters. Recent renovations have upgraded most of the rooms and bathrooms. The hotel has a good cafe-restaurant, Collins, named for the great-grandfather of Mr. Bottelli, who succeeded the original owner, Mr. Brufani, nearly a century ago.

Hotel Fortuna Perugia. Via Bonazzi 19, 06123 Perugia. ☎ **075/572-2845.** Fax 075/573-5040. 33 rms. MINIBAR TV TEL. 90,000L–158,000L ($54–$94.80) double. AE, DC, MC, V.

Here is a chance to stay at a formerly four-star hotel that deliberately "downgraded" itself in 1996 to three-star status, and consequently lowered its prices. In the historic heart of Perugia, the building itself dates from the 14th century, but has been extensively rebuilt and remodeled over the years. Today, arched leaded glass doors lead to an interior of hardwood floors, sleek modern styling, tasteful art, and a welcoming atmosphere. Bedrooms are designed with sleek, contemporary styling—often blond woods and flamboyant fabrics—and are filled with modern amenities, including up-to-date plumbing. Even better than the rooms are the views, some of which might have inspired Perugino himself. The hotel has a reading room, a cozy bar, and a roof-top terrace opening onto the tile roofs of the town and the Umbrian landscape in the distance. When the weather's right, guests take their cappuccino and croissants here. There's no restaurant, but many trattorie are available almost literally outside the door.

Hotel La Rosetta. Piazza Italia 19, 06121 Perugia. ☎ and fax **075/572-0841.** 95 rms, 1 suite. MINIBAR TV TEL. 210,000L–260,000L ($126–$156) double; 295,000L ($177) suite. Rates include breakfast. AE, DC. Parking 25,000L–35,000L ($15–$21).

Since 1927 when this Perugian landmark was established, it has expanded from a seven-room pensione to a labyrinthine complex. It's one of the leading inns in town, although not quite as desirable as its nearest competitor, the Locanda della Posta. With its frescoed ceiling, Room 55 has been declared a national treasure. (The bullet holes that papal mercenaries shot into the ceiling in 1848 have been artfully preserved.) The other, less grandiose accommodations include decors ranging from slickly contemporary to Victorian to 1960s style. Each unit is peaceful, clean, and comfortable. The in-house restaurant is recommended separately (see "Where to Dine," below).

Locanda della Posta. Corso Vannucci 97, 06121 Perugia. ☎ **075/572-8925.** Fax 075/572-2413. 40 rms, 1 suite. A/C MINIBAR TV TEL. 200,000L–295,000L ($120–$177) double; 300,000L–350,000L ($180–$210) suite. Rates include breakfast. AE, DC, MC, V. Parking 20,000L ($12) in nearby garage.

Goethe slept here. So did Hans Christian Andersen—in fact, this used to be the only hotel in Perugia. The hotel sits on the main street of the oldest part of Perugia, behind an impressive ornate facade that was sculpted in the 1700s. We prefer this luxuriously decorated small hotel to the Brufani Hotel, which is five stars only in the eyes of the local government raters. The Della Posta's views may not be as grand, but it's better run and has more comfortable and better-kept rooms. The hotel lies in the center of town, 15 yards from Piazza Italia, at the beginning of a pedestrian zone on Perugia's main street.

WHERE TO DINE

✪ **Il Falchetto.** Via Bartolo 20. ☎ **075/573-1775.** Main courses 25,000L–60,000L ($15–$36). AE, DC, MC, V. Tues–Sun 12:30–2:30pm and 7:30–10:30pm. UMBRIAN/ITALIAN.

The restaurant has flourished in this 19th-century building since it was established in 1941. Many of the dishes here adhere to traditional themes and have a certain zest that has won critical approval for this medieval-style restaurant. Menu items include tagliatelle with truffles, grilled trout from the Nera River, prosciutto several different ways, pasta with chickpeas, grilled filet of goat, and filet steak with truffles. One special dish, of which the chef is justly proud, is falchetti (gnocchi with ricotta and spinach). Some of the best Umbrian wines are served here. The restaurant is a short walk from Piazza Piccinino (where you'll be able to park).

La Rosetta. In the Hotel La Rosetta, Piazza Italia 19. ☎ **075/572-0841.** Reservations recommended, especially in summer. Main courses 18,000L–28,000L ($10.80–$16.80). AE, DC, MC, V. Tues–Sun 12:30–3pm and 7:30–10pm. UMBRIAN.

La Rosetta has gained more fame than the hotel in which it's lodged. Every politician from the region uses the restaurant, and during the Perugia jazz festival (10 days in midsummer), virtually every jazz star always stays and dines here. Food-smart

Italian travelers manage to arrive here at mealtime—it's that good and reasonable. You'll find three areas in which to dine: an intimate wood-paneled salon, a main dining area divided by Roman arches and lit by brass chandeliers, and a courtyard enclosed by the walls of the villa-style hotel. Under shady palm trees you can have a leisurely meal that's both simple and reliable. The menu choice is vast, but a few specialties stand out over the rest. To begin, the finest dishes are either *spaghetti alla Norcina* (with a truffle sauce) or *vol-au-vent di tortellini Rosetta*. Among the main dishes, the outstanding entry is *scaloppine alla Perugina*.

La Taverna. Via delle Streghe 8. ☎ **075/572-4128.** Reservations recommended. Main courses 16,000L–30,000L ($9.60–$18). AE, DC, MC, V. Tues–Sun 12:30–2:30pm and 7:30–10:30pm. UMBRIAN.

One of the finest and most innovative restaurants in Umbria, La Taverna is in a medieval house built around 700 years ago. Its entrance is at the bottom of one of the narrowest alleyways in town, in the heart of Perugia's historic center. (Prominent signs indicate its position off Corso Vannucci at the bottom of a flight of stairs.) Three dining rooms, each filled with exposed masonry, oil paintings, and a polite staff, radiate out from the high-ceilinged vestibule. The cuisine is inspired by Claudio Brugalossi, an Umbrian chef who spent part of his career in Tampa, Florida, working for the Hyatt chain. Your meal might include ravioli filled with rapini and ricotta, a soup of lima beans and artichokes, half-moon-shaped ravioli filled with salmon and saffron, or a creative array (depending on what's in season) of fish, polentas, risottos, and fresh meats.

✪ **Osteria del Bartolo.** Via Bartolo 30. ☎ **075/573-1561.** Reservations recommended. Main courses 26,000L–36,000L ($15.60–$21.60); fixed-price all-Umbrian menu 40,000L ($24); *menu degustazione* 75,000L ($45). AE, DC, MC, V. Mon–Sat 1–2:45pm and 8–10:30pm. Closed Jan 7–25 and July 26–Aug 5. UMBRIAN.

Set in the historic center of town in a palazzo whose foundations date from the 14th century, this family-run restaurant is known for its fresh ingredients, culinary flair, and elegant presentations. It's the pacesetter in Perugia. Many dishes are quite traditional. Straight from the cookbooks of the 1600s, *botaccio* is made with farmer's bread stuffed with sausage, vegetables, and a sharp pecorino cheese that's baked in the oven. Also tempting are fresh tortelli with porcini (flap mushrooms), ricotta di pecora, steamed tomatoes, and olive oil. The restaurant makes its own butter twice a day, its own bread once a day, and its own pasta fresh with every order. The chef also makes his own desserts. There's enough distance between tables to allow discreet conversations.

Trattoria Ricciotto. Piazza Danti 19. ☎ or fax **075/572-1956.** Reservations recommended. Main courses 18,000L–25,000L ($10.80–$15); fixed-price menu 35,000L ($21). AE, DC, MC, V. Mon–Sat 12:30–3pm and 7:30–10pm. UMBRIAN.

Since 1888 this rustically elegant restaurant has been owned and operated by members of the Betti family, who cook, serve the food, uncork the wine, and welcome visitors to Perugia. In a building that dates in part from the 14th century, the restaurant offers a variety of well-prepared specialties, including fettuccine with truffles, *maccheroni arrabbiata* (pasta with tomatoes and red and green peppers), spring lamb chasseur, and *fagotti Monte Bianco* (turkey with parmigiano, ham, and a cream sauce). One of the most satisfying meals in town is prepared here as a time-tested specialty of the house. Composed of a platter containing two different cuts of veal, served with a spinach soufflé and roasted potatoes, it's a bargain at 20,000L ($12), and sought after by hardworking locals year-round. What's a good preface for this? Consider tagliatelle with green olives, or maccheroni with mushrooms and cream sauce.

PERUGIA AFTER DARK

Begin your evening by joining in Italy's liveliest *passeggiata* (a promenade at dusk) along the main street of Perugia, Corso Vannucci. This is a traffic-free pedestrian strip running north to south. As a main street of a town, it's been called "noble," and it's named for Perugia's most famous resident, Pietro Vannucci, known to most of the world as Perugino. Everyone, especially the students of Perugia, seem to stroll here. Many drop into one of the little cafes or *enoteche* for an aperitivo. If you cafe hop or wine bar crawl, you can sample as many as 150 wines from some 60 vineyards in Umbria at these cafes—providing you can keep on your feet.

There are two cafes better than the rest, foremost of which is **Sandri Pasticceria,** Corso Vannucci 32 (☎ 075/572-4112), offering drinks, cakes, pastries, and sandwiches to clients who cluster around the shiny marble-top bar area. You can also order full meals here, including Parmesan eggplant or a veal cutlet Milanese. Here's another outlet for purchasing some of the city's famous chocolates. The bar is lit by crystal chandeliers. Its main competitor, and also worthy, is **Caffé del Cambio,** Corso Vannucci 29 (☎ 075/575-4165), which is a favorite of university students. The first room is most impressive. Capped with a vaulted ceiling, it contains racks of pastries, cones of ice cream, a long stand-up bar, and a handful of tiny tables. The low-ceilinged room in back is smoky, more crowded, and much livelier.

The hottest time to visit Perugia is for Italy's foremost jazz festival, **Umbria Jazz,** which sprawls over a 10-day period in early or mid-July (dates vary). Such jazz heavies as Sonny Rollins or Keith Jarrett have shown up here to perform. For ticket sales, information, and schedules, call ☎ 075/573-2432. Tickets range from 20,000L to 70,000L ($12 to $42).

Perugia has a goodly number of pubs where you can sit around and chew on more than just the town's famous chocolates. Foremost among them is the **Australian Pub,** Via del Verzaro 39 (☎ 075/572-0206), where four kinds of beer (including Australia's most famous, Fosters) are served on tap from 7,000L ($4.20) a mug. There's no music, no dancing—only an ambience that's more southern hemisphere than southern Mediterranean. It's open Tuesday to Sunday from 7pm to 2am. One of its most visible competitors is **Hostaria del Lupo Mannaro,** Via Guardabassi 4, near the Piazza Morlacchi (☎ 075/573-6827), which functions as a cost-conscious Umbrian restaurant until 10pm, then transforms itself into a wine bar from around 10:15pm to 1am. Pizza and beer are served until closing, and there's usually live music presented every Tuesday beginning at 9:30pm. Closed Monday.

10   Assisi

110 miles N of Rome, 15 miles SE of Perugia

Ideally placed on the rise to Mount Subasio, watched over by the medieval Rocco Maggiore, this purple-fringed Umbrian hill town retains a mystical air. The site of many a pilgrimage, Assisi is forever linked in legend with its native son, St. Francis. The gentle saint founded the Franciscan order and shares honors with St. Catherine of Siena as the patron saint of Italy. But he is remembered by many, even non-Christians, as a lover of nature (his preaching to an audience of birds is one of the legends of his life). Dante compared him to John the Baptist.

St. Francis put this town on the map, and making a pilgrimage here is one of the highlights of a visit to Umbria, as exemplified by the friars in brown habits and belts of knotted rope wandering about. Today, Italy's Catholic youth flock here for religious conferences, festivals, and reflection. But even without St. Francis, the hill town merits a visit for its interesting sights and architecture. Sightseers and pilgrims mingling together get a little thick in summer, and at Easter or Christmas you are likely to be trampled underfoot. We've found it best and less crowded in spring or fall.

ESSENTIALS

GETTING THERE   By Train   Assisi lies on the Foligno-Teròntola train line, a 30-minute ride from the terminal at Foligno. The one-way fare from Perugia is 3,500L ($2.10). At Teròntola you can connect from Florence and at Foligno from Rome. A one-way fare from Rome costs 18,000L ($10.80), but 20,000L ($12) from Florence. The small station is in Santa Maria degli Angeli, down in the valley. From here, buses run every half hour to the central Piazza Matteotti in Assisi itself.

By Bus   Frequent buses connect Perugia (see above) with Assisi, the trip taking 1 hour and costing 5,000L ($3) for a one-way ticket. One bus a day arrives from Rome in 3 hours, costing 30,000L ($18) for a one-way ticket, and two buses pull in from Florence, taking 2 1/2 hours and costing 25,000L ($15) for a one-way ticket.

By Car   In 30 minutes from Perugia you can be in Assisi by taking S3 southwest from that city. At the junction of Route 147, just follow the signs toward Assisi. But, once here, you'll have to park on the outside, as the monumental core is closed to traffic (you can drop off luggage at a hotel before returning to a parking lot on the outskirts).

VISITOR INFORMATION   The **tourist information office** is at Piazza del Comune 12 (☎ 075/812-534). It's open Monday to Friday from 8am to 2pm and 3:30 to 6:30pm, Saturday from 9am to 1pm and 3:30 to 6:30pm, and Sunday from 9am to 1pm.

WHAT TO SEE & DO

In addition to the sights listed below, you might also visit the **Cattedrale di San Rufino** (☎ 075/812-285). Built in the mid-12th century at Piazza San Rufino, the Duomo of Assisi is graced with a Romanesque facade, greatly enhanced by rose windows. It's one of the finest churches in the hill towns, as important as the one at Spoleto. Adjoining the cathedral is a bell tower, or campanile. Inside, the church has been baroqued, an unfortunate decision that lost the purity that the front suggests. St. Francis and St. Clare were both baptized here. It is open March 1 to November 4 daily from 10am to noon and from 2:30 to 6pm (closes at 5pm off-season). It costs 2,500L ($1.50) to visit the crypt.

The **Basilica of Santa Chiara** (Clare), on Piazza Santa Chiara (☎ 075/812-282), is dedicated to "the little plant of Blessed Francis," as St. Clare liked to describe herself. Born in 1193 into one of the richest and noblest families of Assisi, Clare was to give all her wealth to the poor and to found, together with St. Francis, the Order of the Poor Clares. She was canonized by Pope Alexander IV in 1255. Pope Pius XII declared her Patroness of Television in 1958. It was decided to entrust to her this new means of social communication on the basis of a vision that she related she had on Christmas Eve in 1252 in which she saw the manger and heard the friars sing in the Basilica of St. Francis while she was bedridden in the Monastery of San Damiano.

Although many of the frescoes that once adorned the basilica have been either completely or partially destroyed, much remains that's worthy of note. On entering, your attention is caught by the striking *Crucifix* behind the main altar, a painting on wood dating from the time of the church itself (ca. 1260). The work is by "the Master of St. Clare," who is also responsible for the beautiful icons on either side of the transept. An oft-reproduced fresco of the Nativity from the 14th century can be admired in the left transept. The basilica houses the remains of St. Clare as well as the crucifix under which St. Francis received his command from above.

Assisi

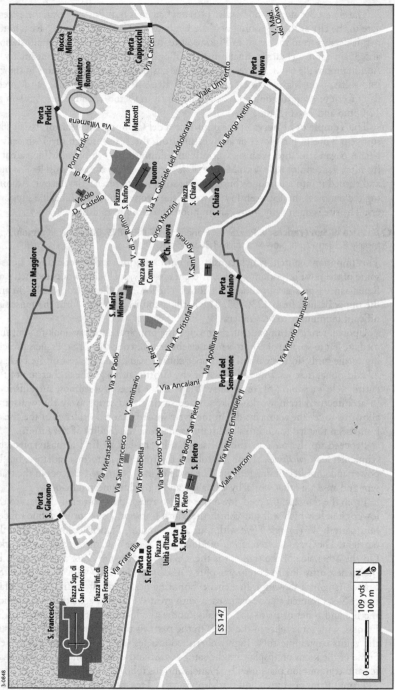

3-0848

The closest bus stop to the Basilica of Santa Chiara is near Porta Nuova, the eastern gate to the city at the beginning of Viale Umberto I. The bus does not have a number; it departs from the depot in Piazza Matteotti for its first run to the train station at 5:35am and concludes its final run at 11:59pm. Buses arrive at half-hour intervals. Admittance to the basilica is free; however, the custodian turns away visitors in shorts, miniskirts, plunging necklines, and backless attire. It's open November to March, daily from 6:30am to noon and 2 to 6pm; April to October, daily from 6:30am to 12:05pm and 2 to 6:55pm.

The **Temple of Minerva** opens onto Piazza del Comune, the heart of Assisi. The square is a dream for a lover of architecture from the 12th through the 14th centuries. A pagan structure, with six Corinthian columns, the Temple of Minerva dates from the 1st century B.C. With Minerva-like wisdom, the people of Assisi let it stand, and turned it into a baroque church inside so as not to offend the devout. Adjoining the temple is the 13th-century Tower of the People, built by Ghibelline supporters. The site is open daily from 7am to noon and 2:30pm to dusk.

✪ **Basilica di San Francesco.** Piazza San Francesco. ☎ **075/819-001.** Free admission. Apr–Oct, daily 8:30am–7pm; Nov–Mar, daily 8:30am–6pm.

This important church, which consists of both an upper and lower church, houses some of the most important cycles of frescoes in Italy, including works by such pre-Renaissance giants as Cimabue and Giotto. The lower basilica is from 1228–30 and the upper basilica from 1230–53. The basilica and its paintings form the most significant monument to St. Francis.

Upon entering the upper church through the principal doorway, look to your immediate left to see one of Giotto's most celebrated frescoes, that of St. Francis preaching to the birds. In the nave of the upper church you'll find the rest of the cycle of 27 additional frescoes, some of which are by Giotto, although the authorship of the entire cycle is a subject of controversy. Many of the frescoes are almost surrealistic—in architectural frameworks—like a stage setting that strips away the walls and allows us to see the actors inside. In the cycle we see pictorial evidence of the rise of humanism that led to Giotto's and Italy's split from the rigidity of Byzantium.

Proceed up the nave to the transept and turn left to find a masterpiece by Cimabue, his *Crucifixion.* Time has robbed the fresco of its former radiance, but its power and ghostlike drama remain. The cycle of badly damaged frescoes in the transept and apse are other works by Cimabue and his paint-smeared helpers.

From the transept, proceed down the stairs through the two-tiered cloisters to the lower church, which will put you in the south transept. Look for Cimabue's faded but masterly *Virgin and Child* with four angels and St. Francis looking on from the far right. The fresco is often reproduced in detail as one of Cimabue's greatest works. On the other side of the transept is the *Deposition from the Cross,* a masterpiece by the Sienese artist Pietro Lorenzetti, plus a *Madonna and Child* with St. John and St. Francis (stigmata showing). In a chapel honoring St. Martin of Tours, Simone Martini of Siena painted a cycle of frescoes, with great skill and imagination, that depicts the life and times of that saint. Finally, under the lower church is the crypt of St. Francis, with some relics of the saint. In the past, visitors were not allowed access to the vaults containing these highly cherished articles, only scholars and clergymen. Some of the items on display are the saint's tunic and cowl, his shoes, and the chalice and communion plate used by Francis and his followers.

From the lower church you can also visit the **Treasury** and **Perkins Collection.** The treasury shelters precious church relics, often in gold and silver, and even the original gray sackcloth worn by St. Francis before the order adopted the brown tunic. Here also is the Perkins Collection, a limited but rich exhibition of art donated by a philanthropist from the United States who had assembled a masterful collection of Tuscan/Renaissance works, including paintings by Luca Signorelli and Fra Angelico. To view the treasury and the collection costs 3,000L ($1.80), and hours are daily from 9:30am to noon and 2 to 6pm (closed Sunday and from November to March).

Eremo delle Carceri. Via Eremo delle Carceri. ☎ **075/812-301.** Free admission (donations accepted). Daily 8am–6pm.

Eremo delle Carceri (Prisons' Hermitage), in a setting 2¹/₂ miles east of Assisi (out Via Eremo delle Carceri), dates from the 14th and 15th centuries. The "prison" is not a penal institution but rather a spiritual retreat. It's believed that St. Francis retired to this spot for meditation and prayer. Out back is a gnarled, moss-covered ilex (or live oak) tree, more than 1,000 years old, where St. Francis is believed to have blessed the birds, after which they are said to have flown in the four major directions of the compass to symbolize that Franciscans, in coming centuries, would spread out from Assisi all over the world. The friary contains some faded frescoes. One of the handful of friars who still inhabit the retreat will show you through. Donations are accepted to defray the cost of maintenance. In keeping with the Franciscan tradition, the friars at Le Carceri are completely dependent on alms for their support.

Rocca Maggiore. ☎ **075/815-292.** Reached by an unmarked stepped street opposite the basilica. Admission 5,000L ($3). Daily 10am–dusk.

The Rocca Maggiore (Great Fortress) sits astride a hill overlooking Assisi. It should be visited if for no other reason than for the panoramic view of the Umbrian countryside from its ramparts. The present building—now in ruins—dates from the 14th century, and the origins of the structure go back beyond time.

WHERE TO STAY

Space in Assisi tends to be tight—so reservations are vital. Still, for such a small town, Assisi has a good number of accommodations.

MODERATE

Hotel Giotto. Via Fontebella 41, 06082 Assisi. ☎ **075/812-209.** Fax 075/816-479. 70 rms, 2 suites. MINIBAR TV TEL. 195,000L ($117) double; 325,000L ($195) suite. Rates include breakfast. AE, DC, MC, V. Parking 15,000L ($9).

The five-story Hotel Giotto is an up-to-date and well-run hotel, built at the edge of town on several levels. Although targeted by tour groups, the Giotto is the second-best hotel in Assisi (we find the Subasio, discussed below, more tranquil and better appointed). Located near the Basilica of St. Francis, and opening onto panoramic views, the Giotto offers small formal gardens and terraces for meals or sunbathing. It has spacious modern public rooms, which lead to the well-furnished and comfortable rooms. Bright colors predominate, although many accommodations look tatty. The hotel is open all year.

Hotel Subasio. Via Frate Elia 2, 06082 Assisi. ☎ **075/812-206.** Fax 075/816-691. 66 rms, 5 suites. MINIBAR TV TEL. 290,000L ($174) double; 345,000L ($207) triple; from 370,000L ($222) suite. Rates include breakfast. AE, DC, MC, V.

This is a first-class four-story hotel with a decidedly old-fashioned aura. The Subasio has been the unquestioned choice of many a famous visitor—from movie stars to royalty. But such a chic clientele from yesterday has often given way today to milling groups. Despite that, however, the Subasio still reigns as the finest choice in Assisi in which to lay your head for the night. The hotel is linked to the Church of St. Francis by a covered stone arched colonnade, and its dining terrace (with extremely good food) is the most dramatic in Assisi. Dining is also an event on the vaulted medieval loggia. The bedrooms at the front open onto balconies with a good view.

INEXPENSIVE

Albergo Ristorante del Viaggiatore. Via San Antonio 14, 06081 Assisi. ☎ **075/816-297** or 075/812-424. Fax 075/813-051. 16 rms. TEL. 110,000L ($66) double. Rates include breakfast. MC, V.

In Michelin's lineup of the hotel properties of Assisi, this one is at the bottom of the totem pole, yet it is among the very tops for value. This ancient town house has been totally renovated, although the stone walls and arched entryways of the lobby hint at its age. Bedrooms are spacious with high ceilings but are very contemporary, as are the bar and dining room, which offers an excellent Umbrian cuisine. The restaurant has been operated by the same family for years, and offers local and regional fare and wines. Half board is available upon request, costing 80,000L ($48) per person.

Hotel dei Priori. Corso Mazzini 15, 06081 Assisi. ☎ **075/812-237.** Fax 075/816-804. 34 rms. TEL. 139,000L–179,000L ($83.40–$107.40) double. Rates include breakfast. AE, DC, MC, V.

Founded in 1923, this hotel has been continuously renovated to keep up to date with the times and continue welcoming clients from all over the world. The hotel lies in one of the town's most historic buildings, dating back to the 17th century when it was known as the Nepis Palace designed by Galeazzo Alessi. A homelike, somewhat old-fashioned Umbrian atmosphere prevails. Marble staircases and floors, terra-cotta, and vaulted ceilings along with stone-arched doorways remain from its seigniorial palazzo heyday. Antiques and tasteful prints in both the rooms and the public areas add further grace notes, along with a collection of Oriental rugs. Rooms, many of which are a bit small, have style and tradition. The hotel also has an on-site bar and serves Umbrian specialties only to hotel guests and only from April through October.

Hotel Sole. Corso Mazzini 35, 06081 Assisi. ☎ **075/812-373** or 075/812-922. Fax 075/813-706. 35 rms. TV TEL. 100,000L ($60) double; 130,000L ($78) triple. AE, DC, MC, V.

For Umbrian hospitality and a general down-home feeling, the Sole is a winning combination in the heart of medieval Assisi—comfortable but traditional, thoroughly renovated, and affordable. No dank, musty cells of St. Francis here. The severe beauty of rough stone walls and ceilings, terra-cotta floors, and marble staircases pay homage to the past, balanced by big-cushioned chairs in the TV lounge and contemporary wrought-iron bed frames and furnishings in the guest rooms. Rooms, some of which are across the street in an annex, are spacious for the most part and feature up-to-date baths. The family owners also offer one of the town's best cuisines under the 15th-century vaults of their restaurant. The food is so savory you might want to take half board, costing from 85,000L ($51) per person. This would be a good choice for dining even if you aren't a guest of the hotel.

St. Anthony's Guest House. Via Galeazzo Alessi 10, 06081 Assisi. ☎ and fax **075/812-542.** 20 rms. 72,000L–76,000L ($43.20–$45.60) double. Rates include breakfast. No credit cards. Closed Nov–Mar 15.

This special hotel provides economical and comfortable accommodations in a medieval villa turned guesthouse. Operated by the Franciscan Sisters of the Atonement (an order that originated in Graymoor, New York), the guesthouse offers the pilgrim/ traveler hospitality and a peaceful atmosphere. Located on the upper ledges of Assisi, St. Anthony's Guest House contains its own terraced garden and panoramic view. In all, 35 people can be accommodated. For an additional 20,000L ($12.80), a midday meal is served at 1pm. Meals and companionship are enjoyed in a restored 12th-century dining room. The sisters and their co-workers welcome you, showing you their library with English-language books.

Umbra. Via degli Archi 6, 06081 Assisi. ☎ **075/812-240.** Fax 075/813-653. 25 rms, 5 suites. TEL. 140,000L–170,000L ($84–$102) double; from 170,000L ($102) suite. AE, DC, MC, V. Closed mid-Jan to Feb. Parking 15,000L ($9).

With origins that go back to the 1400s, the Umbra is the most centrally located accommodation in Assisi, in a position right off Piazza del Comune with its Temple of Minerva. The hotel is built on Roman foundations. The outdoor terraced dining room, a local favorite (see "Where to Dine" below), forms an important part of the hotel's entryway. You enter through old stone walls covered with vines and walk under a leafy pergola. The lobby is compact and functional. The rooms are arranged as small apartments. The bedrooms offer comfortable beds; some have a tiny balcony overlooking the crusty old rooftops and the Umbrian countryside. By the time of your arrival more rooms are supposed to be air-conditioned, but all of them are graced with at least one or two antiques from the 18th or 19th century.

A NEARBY PLACE TO STAY

Hotel Palazzo Bocci. Via Cavour 17, 06038 Spello. ☎ **0742/301-021.** Fax 0742/301-464. 17 rms, 6 suites. A/C MINIBAR TV TEL. 180,000L–220,000L ($108–$132) double; 260,000L–320,000L ($156–$192) suite. Rates include breakfast. AE, DC, MC, V. Head 6^1/2 miles southeast of Assisi along S147.

Located in the historic center of Spello, this palace dates from the second half of the 18th century. The owner purchased the palace in 1989, renovated it, and opened it as a hotel in 1992. Inside is a courtyard with a view of the valley, a beautiful fountain, and two age-old palms. Taste and restraint went into designing both public and private rooms, some of which open onto panoramic views. The bedrooms have such equipment as hydromassage, a safe, a writing desk with two chairs, a hair dryer, and soundproofing. There's a nice bar and a large, lush garden with a panoramic view where drinks are served. A buffet breakfast is offered, and a well-known restaurant, Il Molino, is just in front of the hotel. The village has a pool (7,500L/$4.50 per hour) and tennis courts (15,000L/$9 per hour, but you can continue playing if no one is waiting) within a 5-minute walk.

WHERE TO DINE

Il Medio Evo. Via dell'Arco dei Priori 4B. ☎ **075/813-068.** Reservations recommended. Main courses 22,000L–32,000L ($13.20–$19.20). AE, DC, MC, V. Thurs–Tues noon–2:30pm and 7:30–9:45pm. Closed Jan 7–Feb 7 and July 1–20. UMBRIAN/INTERNATIONAL.

Assisi's best restaurant is one of the architectural oddities of the town's historic center. The foundations on which the restaurant rests are at least 1,000 years old. During the Middle Ages and again in Renaissance times the structure was successively enlarged and modified until today it's an authentic medieval gem of heavy stonework. Fresh ingredients and skill go into the genuine Umbrian cooking served here. Alberto Falsinotti and his family prepare superb versions of Umbrian recipes whose origins are as old as Assisi itself. Specialties include tortelloni stuffed with minced turkey, veal, and beef, served simply but flavorfully with butter and Parmesan; gnocchi stuffed with ricotta and spinach, and sprinkled with Parmesan; roasted rabbit with red-wine sauce and truffles; and roast lamb with rosemary, potatoes, and herbs.

Ristorante Buca di San Francesco. Via Brizi 1. ☎ **075/812-204.** Reservations recommended. Main courses 25,000L–40,000L ($15–$24). AE, DC, MC, V. Tues–Sun noon–2:30pm and 7:30–9:30pm. Closed July 1–15. UMBRIAN/ITALIAN.

This characteristic *ristorante* is set in a medieval palace, with masonry believed to be as old as St. Francis himself. The menu changes frequently, according to the availability of ingredients. You can savor such specialties as *spaghetti alla buca*, as well as onion soup. Grilled meats are always featured, and sometimes they are served with the *tartufo nero* (black truffle)—so popular in the Umbrian countryside. In summer, guests can dine outside on a terrace.

Umbra. Via degli Archi 6. ☎ **075/812-240.** Reservations recommended. Main courses 14,000L–25,000L ($8.40–$15). AE, DC, MC, V. Tues–Sat noon–2pm; Mon–Sat 7:30–9pm. Closed Jan 10–Mar 15. UMBRIAN.

Although most of the building that contains this venerable restaurant dates from the Middle Ages, the walls of the laundry and the kitchens (which occupy the basement) are from the final days of the Roman Empire. The restaurant was originally established as an inn in either 1926 or 1928 (the owners can't remember exactly which), and its shaded garden is charming enough to have pleased even St. Francis—on a warm day you'll hear birds chirping. Situated in the heart of the old city, not far from the basilica, the establishment is the personal statement of the owner and his staff of capable helpers. The Umbrian menu items range from the fanciful to the classically popular. In any event, ample use is made of truffles. The best cuts of meat are generally used, along with very fresh vegetables. A specialty is roast lamb infused with Umbrian herbs.

11 Spoleto

80 miles N of Rome, 30 miles SE of Assisi, 130 miles S of Florence, 40 miles SE of Perugia

Hannibal couldn't conquer it, but Gian-Carlo Menotti did—and how! Before Maestro Menotti put Spoleto on the tourist map in 1958, it was known mostly to art lovers, teachers, and students. Today the chic and fashionable, artistic and arty flood the Umbrian hill town to attend performances of the world-famous **Festival dei Due Mondi** (Festival of Two Worlds), most often held in June and July. Menotti searched and traveled through many hill towns of Tuscany and Umbria before making a final choice. When he saw Spoleto, he fell in love with it. And quite understandably.

Long before Tennessee Williams first arrived to premiere a new play, Thomas Schippers to conduct the opera *Macbeth,* or Shelley Winters to do three one-act plays by Saul Bellow, Spoleto was known to St. Francis and to Lucrezia Borgia (she occupied the 14th-century castle that towers over the town, the **Rocca dell'Albornoz**). The town is filled with palaces of Spoletan aristocracy, medieval streets, and towers built for protection during the time when visitors weren't as friendly as they are today. There are churches, churches, and more churches—some of which, such as **San Gregorio Maggiore,** were built in the Romanesque style in the 11th century.

But the tourist center is **Piazza del Duomo,** with its cathedral and **Teatro Caio Melisso** (Chamber Theater). The cathedral is a hodgepodge of Romanesque and medieval architecture, with a 12th-century campanile. Its facade is of exceptional beauty, renowned especially for its mosaic by Salsterno in 1207. The interior should be visited if for no other reason than to see the cycle of frescoes in the chancel by Filippo Lippi from 1467 to 1469. His son, Filippino, also an artist, designed the tomb for his father, but a mysterious grave robber hauled off the body one night about two centuries later. The keeper of the apse will be happy to unlock it for you. These frescoes, believed to have been carried out largely by students, were the elder Lippi's last work; he died in Spoleto in 1469. As friars went in those days, Lippi was a bit of a swinger; he ran off with a nun, Lucrezia Buti, who later posed as the

Madonna in several of his paintings. The Duomo is open daily from 8am to 1pm and 3 to 6:30pm (closes at 5:30pm off-season).

Spoleto should be visited even when the festival isn't taking place, as it's a most interesting town. It has a number of worthwhile sights, including the remains of a **Roman theater** off Piazza della Libertà (entrance on Via S. Agata). Motorists wanting a view can continue up the hill from Spoleto around a winding road (about 5 miles) to **Monteluco,** an ancient spot 2,500 feet above sea level. Monteluco is peppered with summer villas. The monastery here was once frequented by St. Francis of Assisi.

✪ **THE FESTIVAL**   Since the late 1950s, the artistic world has shown up here for the **Festival dei Due Mondi** or Festival of the Two Worlds, an internationally acclaimed event. It's held every year here from late June to mid-July and attracts the elite of the operatic, ballet, and theatrical worlds, both from Europe and America. Tickets for most events cost from 10,000L to 50,000L ($6 to $30), plus a 15% handling charge. For tickets in advance, write to the Associazione Festival dei Due Mondo, Biglietteria Festival dei Due Mondi, **Teatro Nuovo,** Piazza Belli 06049 Spoleto. Once in Spoleto, you can also go to the Teatro Nuovo for tickets (☎ **0743/ 40-265**). Another contact is the **Associazione Festival dei Due Mondi,** Via Cesare Beccaria 18, Rome 00196 (☎ **06/321-0288**).

ESSENTIALS

GETTING THERE   By Train   Daily trains arrive from Rome, most of which are IC (Inter-City trains), which are more expensive than ordinary trains. The one-way IC fare from Rome to Spoleto costs 21,400L ($12.85), but only 15,600L ($9.35) on a regular train. IC trains also run frequently between Perugia and Spoleto, costing 10,800L ($6.50), although the ordinary train fare is just 5,900L ($3.55). Trip time from Rome is 1 hour, 40 minutes; from Perugia, 1 hour. The train station at Spoleto (☎ **0743/48-720**) is at Piazza Polvani outside of town. Note the huge Alexander Calder sculpture outside the station. Circolare and Navetta buses A, B, C, and E will take you into the center, letting you off at Piazza della Libertà.

By Bus   Two buses daily arrive from Perugia, taking 1 1/2 hours and costing 5,600L ($3.35) for a one-way ticket. There is also one daily bus from Rome (trip time: 1 hour, 50 minutes), with a one-way ticket going for 6,500L ($3.90). The tourist information office posts schedules.

By Car   From either Assisi or Perugia (see above), continue along the S3 south to Spoleto. Driving time from Assisi is only half an hour or so. Once here, park your car in the Upper Town.

VISITOR INFORMATION   The **tourist information office** is at Piazza della Libertà 7 (☎ **0743/220-311**). It's open April to September, daily from 4:30 to 7:30pm; October to March, Monday to Friday from 9am to 1pm and 3:30 to 6:30pm, Saturday from 10am to 1pm and 3:30 to 6:30pm, and Sunday from 10am to 1pm.

WHERE TO STAY

Spoleto offers an attractive range of hotels, but when the "two worlds" crowd in at festival time, the going's rough (one year a group of students bedded down on Piazza del Duomo). In an emergency, the **tourist information office,** at Piazza della Libertà 7 (☎ **0743/220-311**), can arrange for you to stay in a private home at a moderate price—it's imperative to telephone in advance for a reservation. Many of the private rooms are often rented well in advance to artists appearing at the festival. Innkeepers are likely to raise all the prices listed below to whatever the market will bear.

MODERATE

Albornoz Palace Hotel. Viale Matteotti, 06049 Spoleto. ☎ **0743/221-221.** Fax 0743/221-600. 92 rms, 4 suites. A/C MINIBAR TV TEL. 160,000L–370,000L ($96–$222) double; from 590,000L ($354) suite. Rates include breakfast. AE, DC, MC, V.

Starkly modern, and perched in a residential neighborhood half a mile south of the town center, this five-story building is the largest and best equipped in Spoleto. Although this is the most prestigious address in town, with the best facilities, the tiny Gattapone (below) is more luxurious and much more tranquil. A small garden in back contains a swimming pool. On the premises are two restaurants, a bar, and a marble-trimmed lobby decorated with large modern paintings by American-born artist Sol Lewitt. The bedrooms are painted in cool tones of blue-gray, and contain modern bathrooms and views over either Spoleto, Monteluco, or the surrounding hills. The hotel, incidentally, is named after the 14th-century cardinal-soldier (Albornoz) who built parts of Spoleto.

Dei Duchi. Viale Giacomo Matteotti 4, 06049 Spoleto. ☎ **0743/44-541.** Fax 0743/44-543. 51 rms, 2 suites. MINIBAR TV TEL. 180,000L ($108) double; 350,000L ($210) suite. Rates include breakfast. AE, DC, MC, V.

This bare-brick, modern hotel is within walking distance of the major sights—yet it perches on a hillside with views and terraces. It lacks the style of the Gattapone and Albornoz Palace and seems more geared to commercial travelers. Near the Roman theater, Dei Duchi is graced with brick walls, open-to-the-view glass, and lounges with modern furnishings and original paintings. Some bedrooms have their own balconies, plus bland bed coverings, wood-grained furniture, and built-in cupboards—in all, a bit drab. In high season half board is required. In summer you have a choice of two dining rooms, each airy, light, and roomy.

✪ Gattapone. Via del Ponte 6, 06049 Spoleto. ☎ **0743/223-447.** Fax 0743/223-448. 7 rms, 9 junior suites. MINIBAR TV TEL. 230,000L ($138) double; from 330,000L ($198) suite. Rates include continental breakfast. AE, DC, MC, V.

The Gattapone is more a spectacle than a hotel, and we'd rank it as the finest choice for the discriminating traveler visiting Spoleto, with a lot more personality and style than the Albornoz Palace. Probably the only 16-room hotel in Italy to be rated first class, it's among the clouds, high on a twisting road leading to the ancient castle and the 13th-century Ponte delle Torri, a bridge 250 feet high. The hotel occupies two side-by-side stone cottages. The buildings cling closely to the road, and each descends the precipice overlooking the gorge. The hotel's view side is equipped with a two-story picture window and an open spiral stairway that leads from the intimate lounge to the bedrooms. Each of the rooms is individually furnished, with comfortable beds, antiques, and plenty of space. Only breakfast is served.

✪ San Luca. Via Interna della Mura 21, 06049 Spoleto. ☎ **0743/223-399.** Fax 0743/223-800. 33 rms, 2 suites. A/C TV TEL. 200,000L ($120) double; from 250,000L ($150) suite. AE, DC, MC, V.

In a restored and impressive building from the 19th century, this hotel is now the most up-to-date in town, filled with ambience, style, and grace. It has the best of modern, but wherever you turn there is a grace note of the past, including a roof garden and a spacious courtyard with a fountain dating back to 1602. All the elegant bedrooms are spacious and are furnished in a sober yet comforting style, with all the modern amenities. The bathrooms are particularly welcoming with such extras as a

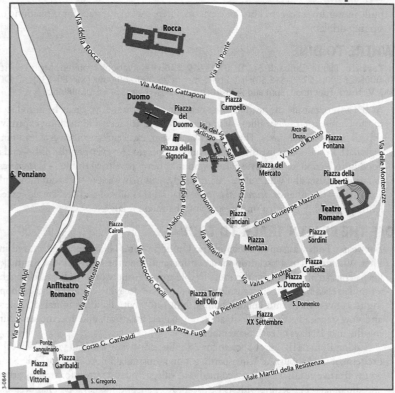

hair dryer, phone, and towel-warmer. Many rooms are also fitted with a massage bath. The public rooms respect the style of the building, with period furniture. Elevators, a garden solarium, and a good restaurant serving Umbrian specialties make this hotel even more alluring.

INEXPENSIVE

Hotel Charleston. Piazza Collicola 10, 06049 Spoleto. ☎ **0743/220-052.** Fax 0743/222-010. 18 rms. MINIBAR TV TEL. 155,000L ($93) double; 190,000L ($114) triple. Rates include breakfast. AE, DC, MC, V. Parking 15,000L ($9).

This tile-roofed, sienna-fronted building was built in the 17th century. Today it serves as a pleasantly accessorized hotel, conveniently located in the historic center. It's a solid and reliable choice, with wood-beamed ceilings, terra-cotta floors, and open fireplaces. Each of the bedrooms has a ceiling accented with beams of honey-colored planking and comfortable mattresses. Many of the guest rooms have been updated with new furnishings and bathrooms. On the premises is a sauna, as well as a bar, library, and a sitting room with sofas and a writing table.

Hotel Clarici. Piazza della Vittoria 32, 06049 Spoleto. ☎ **0743/223-311.** Fax 0743/222-010. 24 rms. A/C MINIBAR TV TEL. 150,000L ($90) double. Rates include breakfast. AE, DC, MC, V. Parking 10,000L ($6).

Clarici is rated only third class, but it's airy and modern, the best of the budget bets in Spoleto. Each accommodation has a private balcony that opens onto a view. The hotel doesn't emphasize style, but rather the creature comforts: soft low beds, built-in wardrobes, steam heat, an elevator. There's a large terrace for sunbathing or sipping drinks.

WHERE TO DINE

Il Tartufo. Piazza Garibaldi 24. ☎ **0743/40-236.** Reservations required. Main courses 16,000L–26,000L ($9.60–$15.60); fixed-price menus 28,000L–60,000L ($16.80–$36). AE, DC, MC, V. Thurs–Tues noon–3pm and 7:30–10:30pm. Closed July 15–31. UMBRIAN.

At Il Tartufo, outside the heart of town near the amphitheater, you may be introduced to the Umbrian *tartufo* (truffle)—if you can afford it. It's served in the most expensive appetizers and main courses. This immaculately kept, excellent tavern serves at least nine regional specialties that use the black tartufo of Spoleto. An ever-popular dish—and a good introduction for neophyte palates who may never have tried truffles—is *strengozzi al tartufo*, a pasta dish with truffles. Alternatively, you may want to start your meal with an omelet—for instance, *frittata al tartufo*. Main dishes of veal and beef are also excellently prepared. For such a small restaurant, the menu is large.

OFF THE BEATEN TRACK TO TODI

For years, Todi was sound asleep in the Umbrian sun. Then the world moved in. First, Visa used it as a backdrop for a commercial, then the University of Kentucky keeps consistently voting it "the most livable town in the world." This has brought a monied class from America rushing in to purchase decaying castles and villas, hoping to convert them into holiday homes. Not only that: Todi has imitated Spoleto and now stages a Festival di Todi, attracting ballet, theatrical, and operatic stars during the first 10 days of each September.

Taking Route 418 out of Spoleto for 28 miles northwest will lead you to what the excitement is all about. At Acquasparta, get on autostrada 3 northwest to Todi. Soon you will arrive at this well-preserved medieval village, today a retreat for wealthy artists and diplomats. The setting with its Etruscan, Roman, and medieval past has been likened to a fairytale of long ago.

Upon arriving, you'll enter the triangularly walled town through one of its three gates, named for the destinations of the roads leading away: Rome in the southwest wall, Perugia to the north, and Orvieto to the southeast. Remains of **original Roman and Etruscan walls** are also evident just inside the Rome gate. The town's central square, **Piazza del Popolo,** was built over a Roman forum and is as harmonious as any in Italy, containing the 12th-century Romanesque-Gothic cathedral and three beautiful palaces—the **Palazzo del Popolo,** built in 1213, the **Palazzo del Capitano,** dating from 1292, and the 14th-century **Palazzo dei Priori** with its trapezoidal tower, all of which are filled with the wares of the **National Exhibit of Crafts** *(Mostra Nazionale dell'Artigianato)* each summer.

Also on view in the town are the **Church of Santa Maria della Consolazione,** standing guard over Todi with its domes and exquisite stained glass, and the 13th-century **Church of San Fortunato,** in the Piazza della Repubblica, burial site of the town's most famous citizen, the monk and medieval poet Jacopone. To the right of the church, a path leads uphill to the ruins of a 14th-century castle known as **La Rocca.** From here, a walk up the twisting **Viale della Serpentina** will reward you with a bird's-eye view of the surrounding valley—fitting in a town allegedly founded on the spot where an eagle used a stolen Umbrian tablecloth to line its aerie. If the climb seems a bit much, check the view from **Piazza Garibaldi.**

Today, the artisans of Todi are particularly renowned for their woodwork. Examples of historical as well as contemporary craft are available for perusal or purchase in the town, especially surrounding the summer craft exhibition along the Piazza del Popolo.

12 Orvieto

75 miles N of Rome, 47 miles SW of Perugia, 70 miles SW of Assisi

Built on a pedestal of volcanic rock above vineyards in a green valley, Orvieto is the closest hill town to Rome and, as such, is often visited by those who don't have the time to explore other spots in Umbria.

Lying on the Paglia, a tributary of the Tiber, Orvieto sits on an isolated rock some 1,035 feet above sea level. Crowning the town is its world-famed cathedral. A road runs from below up to Piazza del Duomo.

The most spectacularly sited hill town in Umbria (but not the most spectacular town), Orvieto was founded by the Etruscans, who were apparently drawn to it because of its good defensive possibilities. Likewise, long after its days as a Roman colony, Orvieto became a papal stronghold. It was a natural fortress, as its cliffs rise starkly from the valley below, even though Orvieto, when you finally reach it, is relatively flat. Although the tall, sheer cliffs on which the town stands saved it from the incursion of railroads and superhighways, which are down in the valley, time and traffic vibrations have caused the soft volcanic rock to disintegrate so that work is imminently necessary to shore up the town.

Orvieto is known for its white wine, which is best enjoyed at a wine cellar at Piazza del Duomo 2 as you contemplate the facade of the cathedral.

ESSENTIALS

GETTING THERE   Three trains a day arrive from Perugia. Because of frequent stops, the trip takes 1¹/₂ hours. A one-way ticket costs 9,800L ($5.90). From Florence, the trip time is 2 hours, and a one-way ticket costs 16,200L ($9.70). From Rome, the train takes 1¹/₂ hours and costs 12,500L ($7.50) one-way. The trains arrive in the valley; shuttle buses run back and forth between the train station and Piazza del Duomo. For information, call ☎ **0763/300-434.**

By Bus   From Perugia, you can take an ATC bus to Orvieto for 10,700L ($6.40) one-way, but the only departure is at 5:55am Monday to Saturday. You can purchase tickets on the bus. For more information, call ☎ **0763/41-921.**

By Car   From Rome, drive 75 miles north on autostrada A1 to Orvieto. From Perugia, head 26 miles south on route SS3bis to Todi, then take SS448 for 15¹/₂ miles southwest to the intersection of autostrada E35, and drive 5¹/₂ miles to Orvieto.

VISITOR INFORMATION   The **Orvieto Tourist Office,** at Piazza del Duomo 24 (☎ **0763/341-772**), is open Monday to Friday from 8am to 2pm and 4 to 7pm, Saturday from 10am to 1pm and 4 to 7pm, and Sunday from 9am to 7pm.

EXPLORING THE TOWN

Erected on the site of two older churches, the ✪ **Duomo,** Piazza del Duomo (☎ **0763/341-147**), dedicated to the Virgin, was begun in 1288 (maybe even earlier). The cathedral was built to commemorate the Miracle of Bolsena. This alleged miracle came out of the doubts of a priest who questioned the transubstantiation (that is, the incarnation of Jesus Christ in the Host). However, so the story goes, at the moment of consecration, the Host started to drip blood. The priest doubted no more and the Feast of Corpus Christi was launched.

The cathedral is known for its elaborately adorned facade, rich statuary, marble bas-reliefs, and mosaics. Pope John XXIII once proclaimed that on Judgment Day, God would send his angels down to earth to pick up the facade of this cathedral and transport it back to heaven.

There's a rose window over the main door, but the most controversial parts of the cathedral are the modern bronze portals that many art historians journey from around the world to see. The doors, installed in 1970, were the work of Emilio Greco, an eminent sculptor. He took as his theme the Misericordia, the seven acts of corporal charity. One panel depicts Pope John XXIII's famous visit to the prisoners of Rome's Queen of Heaven jail in 1960. Some critics have called the doors "outrageous"; others have praised them as "one of the most original works of modern sculpture." You decide for yourself.

On the west facade the richly sculptured marble was based on designs of Lorenzo Maitani of Siena. It's divided into three gables. Four wall surfaces around the three doors were adorned with sculpture in relief, also based on designs of Maitani. He worked on the cathedral facade until his death in 1330. The bas-reliefs depict scenes from the Bible, including the Last Judgment. After Maitani's death, Andrea Pisano took over, but the actual work carried on until the dawn of the 17th century.

For decades every guidebook writer has suggested that the cathedral facade is best viewed at sunset. However, there's nothing wrong with dawn's early light.

Inside, the nave and aisles were constructed in alternating panels of black and white stone. You'll want to seek out the Cappella del Corporale with its mammoth silver shrine based on the design of the facade of the cathedral. This 1338 masterpiece, richly embellished with precious stones, was the work of Ugolino Vieri of Siena. It was designed to shelter the Holy Corporal from Bolsena (the cloth in which the bleeding Host was wrapped). The most celebrated chapel inside is the Chapel of San Brizio, which contains newly restored frescoes of the Last Judgment and the Apocalypse by Luca Signorelli. Michelangelo was said to have been inspired by the frescoes at the time he was contemplating the Sistine Chapel. The masterpiece was produced between 1499 and 1503 and cost $4.4 million to renovate. Signorelli was called to Orvieto to complete the frescoes, which were begun in 1447 by Fra Angelico. The church is open April to September, daily from 7am to 1pm and 2:30 to 7:30pm; November to February, daily from 7am to 1pm and 2:30 to 5:30pm; and in March and October, daily from 7am to 1pm and 2:30 to 6:30pm.

The famous **Pozzo di San Patrizio** (St. Patrick's Well), Viale Sangallo, off Piazza Cahen (☎ 0763/343-768), is an architectural curiosity. In its day it was an engineering feat. Pope Clement VII ordered the well built when he feared that Orvieto might come under siege and its water supply be cut off. The well was entrusted to the design of Antonio da Sangallo the Younger in 1527. It's some 200 feet deep and about 42 feet in diameter, cut into volcanic rock. Two spiral staircases, with about 250 steps, lead into the wells. These spiral ramps never meet. Admission is 6,000L ($3.60). It's open April to September, daily from 10am to 7pm; October to March, daily from 10am to 6pm.

Across from the cathedral stands the **Palazzo Faina,** Piazza Duomo 29 (☎ 0763/341-511), a 19th-century palace. Originally a private collection, the museum here contains many Etruscan artifacts found in and around Orvieto. In addition to the stone sarcophagi, terra-cotta portraits, and vials of colored glass left by the Etruscans, the museum also contains many beautiful Greek vases. Three of the most important objects in the collection are a trio of amphorae attributed to one of the finest of the Attic vase painters, Exekias (550–540 B.C.). They were found in a necropolis near Orvieto and are a gauge as to the richness reached by the city-state of Velzna, as

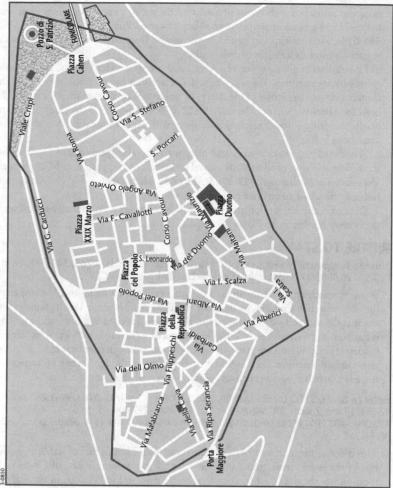

Orvieto used to be known. It's open Tuesday to Sunday from 10am to 1pm and 3 to 7pm. Admission is 7,000L ($4.20).

The **Emilio Greco Museum,** Piazza Duomo (☎ **0763/344-605**), opened in 1991 to house an important collection of art donated to the city of Orvieto by the emminent sculptor, Emilio Greco. In the collection are 32 Greco sculptures, plus 60 graphic works (including lithographs, etchings, and drawings). Greco's artistic ties to Orvieto date from the 1960s when he sculpted the bronze doors of the Duomo. The modern museum was designed by architect Giulio Savio on the ground floor of the 14th-century Palazzo Soliano facing Piazza Duomo. The museum is open daily from April through September from 10:30am to 1pm and 3 to 7pm (closes at 6pm off-season).

SHOPPING   Since the days of the Etruscans, Orvieto has been known for its lim-pid white wine, **Orvieto Classico,** made from grapes that thrive in the local chalky soil and are sometimes fermented in caves that riddle the surrounding topography. You'll be able to buy glasses of the fruity wine—called "liquid gold"—at any bar or tavern in town, but if you want to haul a bottle or two back to your own digs, head for the town's most appealing wine shop, **Foresi,** Piazza Duomo 2 (☎ 0763/ 341-611), where stockpiling esoteric local vintages from virtually every vintner in the region is viewed as a matter of civic pride.

Fabrications of gift items, especially lace and carved wooden objects, are also noteworthy local enterprises. For access to styles of lace that have embroidered everything from courtesan's petticoats to the sleeves of priests during mass at the local cathedral, head for **Duranti,** Via del Duomo 10 (☎ 0763/344-606). Tablecloths, handkerchiefs, and frilly curtains are available, along with an occasional baptismal robe for a newborn infant.

Woodworking, woodcarving, and inlay work are also specialties of Orvieto. For the widest selection of laboriously carved or inlaid objects, patronize **Michelangeli,** Via Gualverio Michelangeli (☎ 0763/342-660), where you can find everything from full-scale furniture to an ornate cup and bowl.

Orvieto is also known for its pottery, which is best seen on Saturday mornings at the pottery market at the Piazza del Popolo.

WHERE TO STAY

Albergo Filippeschi. Via Filippeschi 19, 05019 Orvieto. ☎ and fax **0763/343-275.** 16 rms. TV TEL. 120,000L ($72) double. Rates include breakfast. AE, DC, MC, V.

If you're searching for a bargain, and the high prices of La Badia and Maitani aren't for you, head like a pilgrim to the door of Filippeschi. Managed by its family owners, it is the most affordable property in the center. Housed in a historical mansion, it has been restored with a certain style and grace by gutting a decaying structure and modernizing it. Rooms are generally spacious, and although they lack style, they contain modern amenities such as a small refrigerator. Although there's no restaurant, there is a cozy bar, and a generous breakfast is served in a tasteful room.

Hotel La Badia. S.N.C. Località La Badia 8, 05019 Orvieto Terni. ☎ **0763/90-359.** Fax 0763/ 92-796. 19 rms, 7 suites. A/C MINIBAR TV TEL. 261,000L–291,000L ($156.60–$174.60) double; 406,000L–482,000L ($243.60–$289.20) suite. Half board 67,000L ($40.20) per person extra. AE, MC, V.

This is one of the most memorable of the country inns in this part of Italy. Set 3 miles east of the town center atop a hill that faces the rocky foundations of Orvieto, the location was the site of a Benedictine abbey (*Badia,* in local dialect) in the 8th century A.D. It was upgraded to a monastery in the 12th century, when a church was erected nearby with funds donated by a local noblewoman. In the 19th century the buildings were renovated by an aristocratic family called Fiumi, who did what they could to preserve the irreplaceable stonework. Today the hotel is the finest, most historic, and most charming hotel in Orvieto, with tennis courts, a swimming pool, a well-chosen collection of antiques, and luxurious bedrooms with an appealing sense of history. Views extend over the surrounding countryside, and a restaurant provides elegant meals with discreet service.

Hotel Maitani. Via Maitani 5, 05018 Orvieto. ☎ and fax **0763/342-011.** 20 rms, 8 suites. A/C TV TEL. 195,000L ($117) double; 230,000L–270,000L ($138–$162) suite. AE, DC, MC, V. Parking 15,000L ($9).

The stone-sided building that houses this family-run hotel was originally built as a palazzo around 600 years ago. It was transformed into a hotel in 1966. The bedrooms, scattered over four floors of the structure, are mostly modernized but do retain some reminders of their medieval origins. The rooms are small but cozy and comfortable. Other than breakfast, no meals are served on the premises, though several restaurants are nearby. Both the hotel and the street it sits on were named after the architect who designed Orvieto's famous cathedral, a short walk away. If you have a car, it's best to try to check in early, as the hotel has parking space for only eight vehicles.

✪ **Villa Ciconia.** Via dei Tigli 69, 05019 Orvieto. ☎ **0763/92-982.** Fax 0763/90-677. 10 rms. A/C MINIBAR TV TEL. 200,000L–210,000L ($120–$126) double. Rates include breakfast. AE, DC, MC, V.

This beautiful 16th-century villa—the best hotel in the environs—sits in an 8-acre park at the confluence of the Chiani and Paglia rivers. It has the thick walls, terra-cotta floors, and beamed ceilings typical of its era. Huge chestnut beams run more than 13 yards along the ceiling of the lobby, and the main dining room features a great stone fireplace and a lacunar ceiling with ornate molding and allegorical and natural frescoes around the walls. All of the spacious rooms have views into the park, private bath facilities, and period furnishings. Guests can use a public sports center nearby that features an indoor Olympic swimming pool, indoor and outdoor red-clay tennis courts, and horseback riding. The hotel restaurant features a wide variety of well-prepared Tuscan dishes and a large selection of local and national wines. Truffles figure prominently on the menu.

WHERE TO DINE

La Grotte del Funaro. Via Rip Serancia 41. ☎ **0763/343-276.** Main courses 15,000L–30,000L ($9–$18). AE, DC, MC, V. Tues–Sun noon–2:30pm and 7pm–1am. UMBRIAN.

The cuisine here is the type of solid, traditional fare that Umbrian grandmothers have served their families for generations—fresh, flavorful, and nutritious, with absolutely no attempt to be creative or newfangled in any way. The setting, however, a surprisingly dry cave below the city center, includes many eerie references to other days and other times. No one seems to have any idea how long the cave has been in everyday use—the staff believes that it was part of the storerooms used by the ancient Etruscans. Menu items include an array of grilled meats, including grilled lamb, grilled pork with potatoes and vegetables, pastas flavored with local mushrooms and truffles, and well-prepared, very fresh vegetables. The steps that lead down to this restaurant are only about a hundred yards from Piazza della Repubblica, in the historic town, a bit to the west of the center.

8 Bologna & Emilia-Romagna

Lying in the northern reaches of central Italy, Emilia-Romagna is known for gastronomy and for its art cities, Modena and Parma. Once-great families, including the Renaissance dukes of Ferrara, rose in power and influence, creating courts that attracted painters and poets, notably Tasso and Ariosto.

Bologna, the capital, stands at the crossroads between Venice and Florence, and is linked by express highways to Milan and Tuscany. By basing yourself in this ancient university city, you can branch out in all directions: north for 32 miles to Ferrara, southeast for 31 miles to the ceramics-making town of Faenza, northwest for 25 miles to Modena with its Romanesque cathedral, or 34 miles farther northwest to Parma, the legendary capital of the Farnese family duchy in the 16th century. Ravenna, famed for its mosaics, lies 46 miles east of Bologna on the Adriatic Sea.

Most of our sightseeing destinations lie on the ancient Roman road, **Via Emilia,** that began in Rimini and stretched all the way to Piacenza, a Roman colony that often attracted invading barbarians.

This ancient land (known to the Romans as Æmilia, and to the Etruscans before them) is rich in attractions—the cathedral and baptistery of Parma, for instance—and in scenic beauty (the green plains and the slopes of the Apennines). Emilia is one of the most bountiful farming districts in Italy and sets a table highly praised in Europe—both for its wines and for its imaginatively prepared pasta dishes.

1 Bologna

32 miles S of Ferrara, 94 miles SW of Venice, 235 miles N of Rome

The manager of a hotel in Bologna laments: "The Americans! They spend a week in Florence, a week in Venice. Why not 6 days in Florence, 6 days in Venice, and 2 days in Bologna?" That's a good question. Bologna is one of the most sadly overlooked Italian cities—we've found cavernous accommodation space here in July and August, when the hotels in Venice and Florence were packed as tightly as a can of Progresso clam sauce.

"But what is there to see in Bologna?" is also a common question. True, it boasts no Uffizi or Doge's Palace. However, it does offer a beautiful city that's one of the most architecturally unified in Europe—a panorama of marbled sidewalks and porticos that, if spread out, would surely stretch all the way to the border.

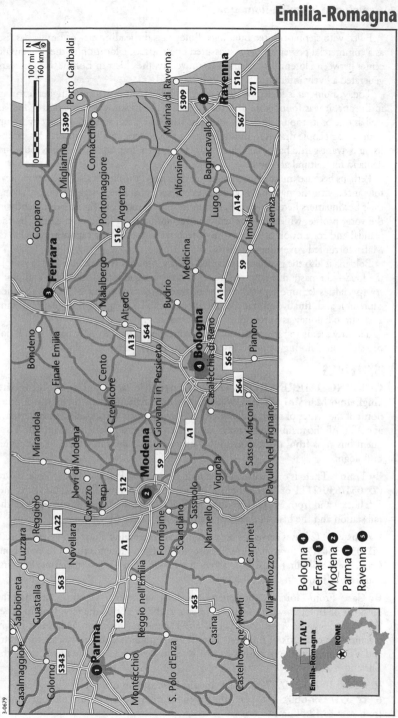

Filled with sienna-colored buildings, Bologna is the leading city of Emilia. Its rise as a commercial power was almost assured by its strategic location as the geographic center between Florence and Venice. Its university, the oldest in Europe, has for years generated a lively interest in art and culture.

Today, Bologna is fueled by its university. The oldest institute of higher learning in Europe, it was founded in 1088 and features the nation's best medical school as well as one of its top business schools. The bars, cafes, and squares of the city fill up with young people drawn to its academy, and an eclectic mix of concerts, art exhibits, and avant-garde ballet and theater are booked to keep up with a corresponding demand for cultural activity.

Perhaps because the student population is so large, the city is also a center of great tolerance, with the national gay alliance and several student organizations making their headquarters here. Politically, communism and socialism figure prominently in the voter profile, which may be why the region has been largely unscathed by the scandal and corruption of neighboring precincts where blatant capitalism has led to Mafia-corrupted government activity.

Bologna is also the gastronomic capital of Italy. Gourmets flock here just to sample the food—the pasta dishes (tortellini, tagliatelle, lasagne verde), the meat and poultry specialties (zampone, veal cutlet bolognese, tender breasts of turkey in sauce supreme), and, finally, mortadella, the incomparable sausage of Bologna, as distant a cousin to baloney as porterhouse is to the hot dog.

The city seems to take a vacation in August, becoming virtually dead. You'll notice signs proclaiming *chiuso* ("closed") almost everywhere you look.

ESSENTIALS

GETTING THERE **By Plane** The international airport, the **Aeroporto Guglielmo Marconi** (☎ **051/389-469** for information about flights), is 4 miles north of the center of town and serviced by such domestic carriers as Aermediterranea and ATI. All the main European airlines have connections through this airport. A frequent bus runs from the airport to the air terminal at the rail station in the center of Bologna.

By Train There is one **railroad station** in Bologna, at Piazza delle Medaglie d'Oro (☎ **051/630-2111** or 1478/88-088). Trains arrive every hour from Rome (trip time: 3¹/₂ hours) and from Milan (trip time: 1³/₄ hours). Buses 25 and 30 run between the rail station and the historical core of Bologna, the Piazza Maggiore.

By Bus ATC buses serve the area from their terminal at Piazza XX Settembre 6 (☎ **051/350-172** for information). Buses to and from Florence run once every hour (trip time: 1¹/₂ hours). Buses also arrive every hour from Venice (trip time: 2 hours) and from Milan (trip time: 3 hours).

By Car From Florence, continue north along autostrada A1 until you reach the outskirts of Bologna where signs direct you to the center of the city. Coming over the Apennines, the Autostrada del Sole (A1) runs northwest to Milan just before reaching the outskirts of Bologna. The A13 superhighway cuts northeast to Ferrara and Venice and the A14 dashes east to Rimini, Ravenna, and the towns along the Adriatic.

VISITOR INFORMATION The **tourist information office** is at Piazza Maggiore 6 (☎ **051/239-660**). It's open Monday to Saturday from 9am to 7pm and Sunday from 9am to 12:30pm.

GETTING AROUND Bologna is easy to cover on foot; most of the major sights are in and around Piazza Maggiore, the heart of the city. However, if you don't want

To Piazza D. Medaglie d' Oro
Via Riva di Reno
Piazza dell'Otto Agosta
Via A. Righi Via delle Moline
Via delle Belle Arti
Via della Lame
Via G. Marconi
Via S. Felice
Via N. Sauro
Via San Giorgio
Via Galliera
Via dell'Indipendenza
Via Marsala
Via del Pratello
Via Ugo Bassi
Via Goito
Via Oberdan
Via Zamboni
S. Giacomo Maggiore ①
Pza. di Porta Ravegnana
S. Francesco
Via Rizzoli ②
Via S. Vitale
Piazza Malpighi
⑤ Pze. Maggiore e del Nettuno ④
Strada Maggiore
To Madonna di S. Luca
Via Val d'Aposa
⑥
Piazza Galiléo
Via Barberia
Via M. d'Azeglio
Via Castiglione
⑧ S. Stefano
Via S. Stefano
Via Nosadella
Via Tagliapietre
⑦
Via Farini
Pza. Cavour
Via Saragozza
Via Urbana
Via Garibaldi
⑨ S. Domenico
3-0656

Basilica di San Petronius ⑥
Basilica di St. Domenico ⑨
Chiesa di San
    Giacomo Maggiore ②
Fontana del Nettuno ⑤
Museo Civico Archeologico ⑦

Palazzo Comunale ④
Pinacoteca Nazionale
    di Bologna ①
Santo Stefano ⑧
Torre degli Asinelli ③

Church ✝

to walk, **city buses** leave for most points from either Piazza Nettuno or Piazza Maggiore. Free maps are available at the storefront office of the AT (Azienda Trasporti) at Piazza Galvani 4, behind the Church of San Petronio. Tickets can be purchased at one of many booths and tobacconists throughout Bologna. Once on board, however, you must have your ticket validated.

   Taxis are on radio call (☎ 051/372-727 or 051/534-141).

SEEING THE SIGHTS

Basilica di San Petronio. Piazza Maggiore. ☎ 051/225-442. Free admission. Daily 7am–noon and 3:30–7:30pm.

Sadly, the facade of this enormous Gothic basilica honoring the patron saint of Bologna was never completed. Legend has it that the entire construction was greatly curtailed by papal decree when the Vatican learned that Bologna city fathers planned to erect a Duomo larger than St. Peter's. Although the builders went to work in 1390, after three centuries the church was still not finished (even though Charles V was crowned emperor here in 1530). However, Jacopo della Quercia of Siena did grace the central door with a masterpiece Renaissance sculpture. Inside, the church could accommodate the traffic of New York's Grand Central Terminal. The central nave is separated from the aisles by pilasters shooting upward to the flying arches of the ceiling. Of the 22 art-filled chapels, the most interesting is the Bolognini Chapel, the fourth chapel on the left as you enter. It's embellished with frescoes representing heaven and hell. The purity and simplicity of line represent some of the best of the Gothic in Italy.

✪ **Fontana del Nettuno.** Piazza del Nettuno.

Characteristic of the pride and independence of Bologna, this fountain has gradually become a symbol of the city, but it was in fact designed in 1566 by a Frenchman named Giambologna by the Italians (his fame rests largely on the work he did in Florence). Viewed as irreverent by some, "indecent" by the Catholic Church, and magnificent by those with more liberal tastes, this 16th-century fountain depicts Neptune with rippling muscles, a trident in one arm, and a heavy foot on the head of a dolphin. The church forced Giambologna to manipulate Neptune's left arm to cover a monumental endowment. Giambologna's defenders of the time denounced this as "artistic castration." Around his feet are four highly erotic cherubs, also with dolphins. At the base of the fountain, four very sensual sirens spout streams of water from their breasts.

Palazzo Comunale. Piazza Maggiore 6. ☎ **051/203-526.** Each museum separately, 5,000L ($3) adults, 2,500L ($1.50) children 14–18 and seniors 60 and over, free for children 13 and under; combined ticket to both museums, 8,000L ($4.80) adults, 4,000L ($2.40) children 14–18 and seniors 60 and over, free for children 13 and under. Tues–Sat 10am–6pm, Sun guided tour at 4pm. Closed holidays.

Built in the 14th century, this town hall has seen major restorations, but happily retains its splendor. Enter through the courtyard, then proceed up the steps on the right to the **Comunal Collection of Fine Arts,** which includes many paintings from the 14th- and 19th-century Emilian school. Another section comprises the **Museum of Giorgio Morandi,** an entire section devoted to the works of this famed painter of Bologna (1890–1964). His subject matter such as a vase of flowers or a box might have been mundane, but he transformed these objects into works of art of startling intensity and perception. Some of his finest works here are landscapes of Grizzana, a village where he spent many a lazy summer working and drawing. There is also a reconstruction of his studio.

Basilica di St. Domenico. Piazza San Domenico 13. ☎ **051/640-0411.** Free admission. Daily 7am–1pm and 2:15–7pm.

The basilica dates from the 13th century, but it has seen many alterations and restorations. The church houses the beautifully crafted tomb of St. Domenico, in front of the Capella della Madonna. The sculptured tomb—known as an *area*—is a Renaissance masterpiece, a joint enterprise of Niccolò Pisano, Guglielmo (a friar), Niccolò dell'Arca, Alfonso Lombardi, and the young Michelangelo. Observe the gaze and stance of Michelangelo's San Procolo, which appears to be the "rehearsal" for his later David. The choir stalls, the second major artistic work in the basilica, were carved by Damiano da Bergamo, another friar, in the 16th century.

Torre degli Asinelli. Piazza di Porta Ravegnanna. Admission 3,000L ($1.80). May–Sept, daily 9am–6pm; Oct–Apr, daily 9am–5pm.

These leaning towers keep defying gravity year after year. They are also the virtual symbol of Bologna. Stendhal observed that a Bolognese far from home is likely to burst into tears at the thought of his beloved two towers. In Canto 31 of the Inferno, Dante wrote that when the giant Antaeus picked him up, along with Virgil, and lowered him into a well, he likened the experience to the dizzy sensation of looking up at the **Garisenda Tower** as a cloud drifts "over against the slant of it, swimming low." The *Due Torri* were built by patricians in the 12th century. In the Middle Ages Bologna had dozens of these skyscraper towers, ahead of Manhattan by several centuries. They were status symbols: The more powerful the family, the taller the tower. The smaller one, the **Garisenda,** is only 162 feet tall and leans approximately 10½ feet from the perpendicular. The family who built this tower did not prepare a solid foundation, and the tower sways tipsily to the south today. When the Garisenda clan saw what they had done, they gave up. In 1360 part of the tower was lopped off, because it was viewed as a threat to public safety. The taller one, the **Asinelli** (334 feet tall, a walk up of nearly 500 steps), inclines almost $7\frac{1}{2}$ feet. Those who scale the Asinelli should be awarded a medal, but instead they're presented with a panoramic view of the red tile roofs of Bologna and the green hills beyond.

After visiting the towers, take a walk up what must be the most architecturally elegant street in Bologna, **Strada Maggiore,** with its colonnades and mansions.

Santo Stefano. Via Santo Stefano 24. ☎ **051/223-256.** Free admission to church and museum. Daily 9am–12:20pm and 3:30–6:30pm.

From the leaning towers, head up Via Santo Stefano to see a quartet of churches linked together like Siamese twins. A church has stood on this site since the 5th century, which even then was a converted temple of Isis. Charlemagne stopped here to worship on his way to France in the 8th century. The first church you enter is the Church of the Crucifix, relatively simple with only one nave and a crypt. It dates from the 11th century. To the left is the entrance to the Church of Santo Sepolcro, a polygonal temple dating principally from the 12th century. Under the altar is the tomb of San Petronio or Saint Petronius, modeled after the Holy Sepulchre in Jerusalem and adorned with bas-reliefs. Continuing left, you enter another rebuilt church, this one honoring Saints Vitale and Agricola. The present building, graced with three apses, also dates from the 11th century. To reenter Sepolcro, take the back entrance this time into the Courtyard of Pilate, onto which several more chapels open. Legend has it that the basin in the courtyard was the one in which Pontius Pilate washed his hands after condemning Christ to death. Actually, it's a Lombard bathtub from the 8th century. Through the courtyard entrance to the right, proceed into the Romanesque cloisters, dating from the 11th and 12th centuries. The names on the wall of the lapidary honor Bolognese war dead.

Chiesa di San Giacomo Maggiore. Piazza Rossini or Via Zamboni 15. ☎ **051/225-970.** Free admission. Daily 8am–noon and 3:30–6pm.

The Church of St. James was originally a Gothic structure in the 13th century. But, like so many others, it has been altered and restored at the expense of its original design. Still, it's one of Bologna's most interesting churches, filled with art treasures. The **Bentivoglio Chapel** is the most sacred haunt, even though time has dimmed the luster of its frescoes. Near the altar, seek out a *Madonna and Child* enthroned, one of the most outstanding works of the artist Francesco Erancia. The holy pair are surrounded by angels and saints, as well as by a half-naked Sebastian to the right. Nearby is a sepulchre of Antonio Bentivoglio, designed by Jacopo della Quercia, who labored so long over the doors to the Basilica of San Petronio. In the Chapel of Santa Cecilia you'll discover important frescoes by Francia and Lorenzo Costa.

Museo Civico Archeologico. Via dell'Archiginnasio 2. ☎ **051/233-849.** Admission 8,000L ($4.80) adults, 4,000L ($2.40) students and seniors over 60, free for children under 14. Tues–Fri 9am–2pm, Sat–Sun 9am–1pm and 3:30–7pm.

This museum houses one of the major Egyptian collections in Italy, as well as important discoveries dug up in Emilia. As you enter, look to the right in the atrium to see a decapitated marble torso, said to be that of Nero. Opened in 1994, on the lower floor, a modern new Egyptian section presents a notable array of mummies and sarcophagi. The chief attraction in this collection is a cycle of bas-reliefs from Horemheb's tomb. On the ground floor a new wing contains a gallery of casts, displaying copies of famous Greek and Roman sculptures. On the first floor, reached through a gallery of casts, two exceptional burial items from Verucchio (Rimini) are exhibited. Note the wood furnishings, footrests, and the throne of tomb 89, which is decorated with scenes from everyday life and ceremonial parades.

Upstairs are cases of prehistoric objects, tools, and artifacts. The relics of the Etruscans comprise the best part of the museum, especially the highly stylized Askos Benacci, depicting a man on a horse that is perched on yet another animal. Also displayed are terra-cotta urns, a vase depicting fighting Greeks and Amazons, and a bronze Certosa jar dating from the 6th century B.C. The museum's greatest single treasure is Phidias's head of Athena Lemnia, a copy of the 5th-century B.C. Greek work.

Pinacoteca Nazionale di Bologna. Via delle Belle Arti 56. ☎ **051/243-222.** Admission 8,000L ($4.80), free for children 17 and under and seniors 60 and over. Tues, Wed, and Fri 9am–2pm, Thurs and Sat 9am–7:30pm, Sun 9am–1pm. Closed holidays.

The most significant works of the school of painting that flourished in Bologna from the 14th century to the heyday of the baroque have been assembled under one roof in this second-floor *pinacoteca.* The gallery also houses works by other major Italian artists, such as Raphael's *St. Cecilia in Estasi.* Guido Reni (1575–1642) of Bologna steals the scene with his *St. Sebastian* and his *Pietà,* along with his equally penetrating *St. Andrea Corsini, The Slaying of the Innocents,* and his idealized *Samson the Victorious.* Other Reni works at the National include *The Flagellation of Christ, The Crucifixion,* and his masterpiece—*Ritratto della Madre*—a revealing portrait of his mother that must surely have inspired Whistler. Then seek out Vitale de Bologna's (1330–61) rendition of St. George slaying the dragon—a theme in European art that parallels Moby Dick in America. Also displayed are works by Francesco Francia, and especially noteworthy is a polyptych attributed to Giotto.

SHOPPING

Serious collectors of art deco and art nouveau designs will find a variety of objets d'art at **Art Decorativi,** Via Santo Stefano 12/A (☎ **051/222-758**), which features functional wares and curios from the turn of the century through the 1930s. Obviously the stock changes, but expect to find items such as Murano glass, dish sets, furniture, and lamps. If you call the puppeteer **Demitrio Presini** (☎ **051/649-1837**), you might catch him and set up an appointment to see his creations, but your chances are better if you just show up at his workshop, Via Rizzoli 17 (no telephone), afternoons between 1:30 and 6:30pm. Here you can tour the facilities and see how his puppets, including *burratini,* wooden puppets in handmade costumes, are made. Nothing can be purchased on the premises, but you can order a puppet that will be made and shipped to you within 1 to 3 months. Presini specializes in local and regional characters, but is capable of any custom work you may want.

Galleria Marescalchi, Via Marescalchi 116/B (☎ **051/240-368**), features more traditional art, offering paintings and prints for view or sale by native son Morandi, Italian modern master De Chirico, and such foreigners as Chagall and Magritte.

Fans of musical mastery should head over to **Bongiovanni,** 28/E Via Rizzoli (☎ **051/225-722**), which stocks rare and popular recordings of operatic and classical scores on cassette, CD, and vinyl.

There are a number of shops that more than adequately illustrate the city's nickname *Bologna la Grassa* (Bologna the Fat), which alludes to its strong gastronomical heritage. An array of breads, pasta, and pastries make **Atti,** with locations at Via Caprarie 7 (☎ **051/220-425**) and Via Drapperie 6 (☎ **051/233-369**), a tempting stop whether you're hungry or not. Among the pastries is the Bolognese specialty *certosino,* a heavy loaf resembling fruitcake. Also available at the Via Caprarie location are an assortment of *gastronomie*—delectable heat-and-serve starters and main

The World's Greatest China Shop

Faenza lent its name to a form of ceramics known as faïence, which had originated on the Balearic island of Majorca, off the east coast of Spain. The town of Faenza, only 36 miles southeast of Bologna, became the Italian center of this industry. Faenza potters found inspiration in the work coming out of Majorca and in the 12th century began to produce their own designs—characterized by brilliant, rich colors and floral decorations. The art reached its pinnacle in the 16th century when the "hot-fire" process was perfected, during which ceramics were baked at a temperature of 1,742°F.

The legacy of this fabled industry is preserved today at the **Museo Internazionale delle Ceramiche** (International Museum of Ceramics), Via Campidoro 2 (☎ **0546/ 21-240**), called "the world's greatest china shop." Housed here are works not only from the artisans of Faenza but from throughout the world, including pre-Colombian pottery from Peru. Of exceptional interest are Etruscan and Egyptian ceramics, as well as a wide-ranging collection from the Orient, even from the days of the Roman Empire.

Deserving special attention is the section devoted to modern ceramic art, including works by Matisse and Picasso. On display are Picasso vases and a platter with his dove of peace, a platter in rich colors by Chagall, a "surprise" from Matisse, and a framed ceramic plaque of the Crucifixion by Georges Rouault. Another excellent work, the inspiration of a lesser-known artist, is a ceramic woman by Dante Morozzi. Even the great Léger tried his hand at ceramics.

The museum, which attracts not only ceramic makers but interested visitors worldwide, is open June to September, Tuesday to Saturday from 9am to 7pm and Sunday from 9:30am to 1pm; October to May, Tuesday to Friday from 9am to 1:30pm, Saturday from 3 to 6pm, and Sunday from 9:30am to 1pm. Admission is 8,000L ($4.80) for adults, 4,000L ($2.40) for children 17 and under and seniors 65 and over.

courses made fresh at the shop. If you want chocolate, **Majani,** Via Carbonesi 5 (☎ **051/234-302**), claims to be Italy's oldest sweets shop, having made and sold confections since 1796. A wide assortment of chocolates awaits you, accompanied by several types of biscuits, and at Easter they also make eggs, "rabbits," and "lamb." A stop at **Tamburini,** Via Caprarie 1 (☎ **051/234-726**), lends credence to claims that it is Italy's most lavish food shop. Shoppers choose from an incredible array of *gastronomie,* including meats and fish, soups and salads, vegetables, and sweets, as well as fresh pasta to prepare at home. If you don't have anything to cook or serve your pasta in, **Schiavina,** Via Clavature 18 (☎ **051/223-438**), sells every kitchen utensil you might ever need, including cookware, silverware, glasses, dinnerware, and knives.

If you have hard-to-fit feet, head to **Piero,** Via delle Lame 56 (☎ **051/558-680**), which carries attractive, well-made footwear for men and women in large sizes, ranging up to European size 53 for men (the equivalent of an American size 20) and size 46 for women. **Bruno Magli** quickly made a name for himself after he opened his first shoe factory in 1934. Today, Bruno Magli shops that sell leather bags, jackets, and coats for men and women—in addition to shoes—are located at Galeria Cavour 9 (☎ **051/266-915**) and Piazza della Mercanzia 2 (☎ **051/231-126**). **Draganczuk** offers women's tailoring at Galleria Cavour 2/E (☎ **051/239-576**), but also sells a range of designer outfits at Via Farini 14 (☎ **051/221-815**). With styles ranging from elegant to casual, **Marisell,** Via Farini 4 (☎ **051/234-670**), offers women's wear by some of today's best-known Italian designers. A range of men's and women's clothes are available at **Paris, Texas,** Via Altabella 11 (☎ **051/225-751**), including, but not limited to designer evening wear, whereas the location at Via dell'Indipendenza 67/2 (☎ **051/241-994**) focuses more on casual clothing like jeans and T-shirts.

The Veronesi family has been closely tied to the jewelry trade for centuries. Now split up and competing among themselves, the various family factions are represented by **Arrigo Veronesi,** Via dell'Archiginnasio 4/F (☎ **051/235-790**), which sells modern jewelry and watches; **F. Veronesi & Figli,** Piazza Maggiore 4 (☎ **051/224-835**), which offers contemporary jewelry, watches, and silver using ancient designs; and **Giulio Veronesi,** with locations at Piazza di Re Enzo 1 (☎ **051/234-237**) and **Galleria Cavour** (☎ **051/234-196**), which also sells modern jewelry and Rolex watches.

WHERE TO STAY

Bologna has four to six trade fairs a year, during which hotel room rates rise dramatically. Some hotels announce their prices in advance; others prefer to wait until bookings are actually being accepted, perhaps to see what the market will bear. Be duly warned: At trade fair times (dates vary yearly; check with the tourist office) business clients from throughout Europe book the best rooms, and you—as a tourist—will be paying a lot of money to visit Bologna.

VERY EXPENSIVE

Grand Hotel Baglioni. Via dell'Indipendenza 8, 40121 Bologna. ☎ **051/225-445.** Fax 051/234-840. 117 rms, 8 suites. A/C MINIBAR TV TEL. 540,000L–660,000L ($324–$396) double; from 1,000,000L ($600) suite. Rates include breakfast. AE, DC, MC, V. Parking 45,000L ($27).

Far better and more atmospheric than its chief rival, the Royal Hotel Carlton, the Grand Hotel Baglioni boasts a desirable location in the center of Bologna, near the main square and Neptune's fountain. Its four-story facade is crafted of the same reddish brick that distinguishes many of the city's older buildings. The interior is noted for its wall and ceiling frescoes. Each soundproof room contains reproductions of antique furniture as well as all the modern conveniences that one would expect in a grand hotel. The rooms are generally spacious, the fourth-floor units being the largest of all.

Dining/Entertainment: Good-tasting Bolognese cooking is served in the elegant à la carte restaurant, I Carracci (see "Where to Dine," below).

Services: Room service, baby-sitting, laundry, valet.

Facilities: Hairdresser.

EXPENSIVE

Grand Hotel Elite. Via Aurelio Saffi 36, 40131 Bologna. ☎ **051/649-1432.** Fax 051/649-2426. 153 rms, 20 suites. A/C MINIBAR TV TEL. 350,000L ($210) double; 410,000L ($246) suite. Rates include breakfast. AE, DC, MC, V. Parking 18,000L–35,000L ($10.80–$21).

Located on the city's northwestern edge, a 12-minute walk to the center, this eight-story establishment was originally built in the 1970s as a combination of private apartments and hotel rooms. In 1993, the entire structure was transformed into a hotel. The bedrooms are comfortable but lackluster. Even if you're not staying at the hotel, you may want to patronize its restaurant, the Cordon Bleu, which features international food and the classic cuisine of Emilia-Romagna. Also popular is a bar with comfortable banquettes and a good selection of whisky and regional wines. The restaurant is closed on Sunday.

Royal Hotel Carlton. Via Montebello 8, 40121 Bologna. ☎ 051/249-361. Fax 051/249-724. 251 rms, 22 suites. A/C MINIBAR TV TEL. 420,000L ($252) double; 600,000L–700,000L ($360–$420) suite. Rates include breakfast. AE, DC, MC, V. Parking 25,000L–35,000L ($15–$21).

Royal Hotel Carlton, only a few minutes' walk from the railway station and many of the national monuments, is L-shaped, rises six stories high, and has a triangular garden. Some claim it's the best hotel in Bologna, but we happen to think that that honor goes to the Baglioni. The Hilton-style Carlton, two blocks south of the station, is a rather austere commercial establishment, catering mainly to business travelers. It's in the modern style, with a balcony and picture window for each bedroom, although the views aren't particularly inspiring.

Dining/Entertainment: One of the most dramatic staircases in Bologna sweeps from the second floor in an elegant crescent to a point near the comfortable American Bar, a grill restaurant that serves decent regional and international food.

Services: Room service, baby-sitting, laundry, valet.

Facilities: Limited facilities for travelers with disabilities.

MODERATE

Dei Commercianti. Via de'Pignattari 11, 40124 Bologna. ☎ 051/233-052. Fax 051/224-733. 35 rms. A/C MINIBAR TV TEL. 290,000L–450,000L ($174–$270) double. Rates include breakfast. AE, DC, MC, V. Parking 30,000L ($18).

This hotel was once the site of the "Domus" (the first seat of the town hall) for the *comune* of Bologna in the 12th century. Recent restoration work uncovered original wooden features that are seen in the hall and the rooms built in the old tower. In spite of the centuries-old history, the atmosphere is bright and the hotel offers all the modern amenities. The rooms decorated with antique furniture feature air-conditioning, minibar, satellite TV, and a safe. The hotel, which is located beside the Church of San Petronio in the pedestrian area of Piazza Maggiore, offers panoramic views of the cathedral.

Hotel Corona D'Oro 1890. Via Oberdan 12, 40126 Bologna. ☎ 051/236-456. Fax 051/262-679. 35 rms. A/C MINIBAR TV TEL. 290,000L–450,000L ($174–$270) double. Rates include breakfast. AE, DC, MC, V. Parking 30,000L ($18).

This fine palazzo, formerly the home of the noble Azzoguidi family in the 15th century, still preserves the architectural features of various periods, from the art nouveau in the hall to the medieval severity of the coffered ceiling in the meeting room, and the frescoes, depicting coats-of-arms and landscapes, in the rooms. Although the rooms are decorated according to various periods, they have air-conditioning, minibar, satellite TV, fax and computer hookups, and a safe. The hotel is just a short distance from the Two Towers and Piazza Maggiore.

Hotel Milano Excelsior. Viale Pietramellara 51 (near Piazza Medaglie d'Oro), 40121 Bologna. ☎ 051/246-178. Fax 051/249-448. 70 rms, 6 suites. A/C MINIBAR TV TEL. 285,000L ($171) double; 360,000L ($216) suite. During trade fairs, 410,000L ($246) double; 480,000L ($288) suite. Rates include breakfast. AE, DC, MC, V. Parking 10,000L ($6).

Hotel Milano Excelsior, built in the 1950s, is a first-class hotel, and it has all the trappings and fringe benefits associated with its class: an American bar as well as a restaurant decorated with crystal chandeliers. The location is particularly convenient for motorists because of its proximity to the approach roads to many other Italian citizens. However, the nearby rail station is equally attractive to travelers without cars. It has a completely modern decor, although a number of its bedrooms contain more traditional furnishings. The hotel offers excellent service and an attentive staff and the dining room, the Ristorante Felsineo, serves tasty Emilian food. The restaurant is closed on Sunday.

Hotel Orologio. Via IV Novembre, 10, 40123 Bologna. ☎ **051/231-253.** Fax 051/260-552. 35 rms. A/C MINIBAR TV TEL. 290,000L–450,000L ($174–$270) double. Rates include breakfast. AE, DC, MC, V. Parking 30,000L ($18).

This charming, small hotel, so called because it faces the clock *(orologio)* on the civic center, is situated in the historical center of medieval Bologna with a view of Piazza Maggiore and of the Podestà Palace. The rooms are decorated with modern furnishings and have air-conditioning, minibar, satellite TV, and a safe. This is the ideal hotel for those who wish to steep themselves in the past without forfeiting modern comforts.

Tre Vecchi. Via dell'Indipendenza 47, 40121 Bologna. ☎ **051/231-991.** Fax 051/224-143. 96 rms. A/C MINIBAR TV TEL. 250,000L ($150) double. During trade fairs, 320,000L ($192) double. Rates include breakfast. AE, DC, MC, V. Parking 30,000L ($18); free on street.

This hotel was established in the 1970s in a century-old building on a much-traveled street in the center of town, a 5-minute walk from the train station. Despite the traffic, the bedrooms are clean, bright, and relatively quiet, thanks to the insulated windows and soundproofing. The gentle humor in the establishment's name ("Three Geriatrics") was conceived by the trio of aging entrepreneurs who originally founded it. The four-story hotel contains two elevators and several lounges where guests can relax and watch TV. No meals are served except breakfast.

INEXPENSIVE

Albergo Al Cappello Rosso. Via de Fusari 9, 40123 Bologna. ☎ **051/261-891.** Fax 051/227-179. 33 rms. A/C MINIBAR TV TEL. 180,000L–280,000L ($108–$168) double. During trade fairs and congresses, 450,000L ($270) double. Rates include breakfast. AE, DC, MC, V.

In the 14th century "The Red Hat," as the name translates, referred to the preferred head gear of the privileged tradesmen who stayed at this inn. More than 600 years later, the hotel still claims the name, but has been revamped into an ultramodern facility that offers no hint of its past. It's conveniently located in the heart of Bologna, in a busy shopping district cloaked in the long history of the city. If modern comfort is what you want or if you need a break from the more rustic charms of many Italian lodges, this is the place. Although individual rooms tend to be rather modular, the staff is gracious and willing to help you meet your individual needs. A sleek brass-topped bar is located within the hotel, and excellent meals are available only steps away in any of the plethora of nearby restaurants that help Bologna retain its culinary status.

Alexander. Viale Pietramellara 47, 40121 Bologna. ☎ **051/247-118.** Fax 051/247-248. 108 rms. A/C MINIBAR TV TEL. 245,000L ($147) double. During trade fairs, 275,000L ($165) double. Rates include breakfast. AE, DC, MC, V. Parking 10,000L ($6) outside. Closed Aug.

Built in the early 1960s, the Alexander is the best hotel buy near the Piazza Medaglie d'Oro, the main hub of car and trail traffic in the city. Perched near the more expensive Hotel Milano Excelsior, the Alexander features desirable bedrooms, with brightly painted foyers, compact furnishings, and neat tidy baths. The double glass windows help to blot out street noise. The main lounge is crisp and warm, with wood paneling and lounge chairs placed on Turkish rugs.

WHERE TO DINE
EXPENSIVE

Diana. Via dell'Indipendenza 24. ☎ **051/231-302.** Reservations recommended. Main courses 18,000L–35,000L ($10.80–$21); fixed-price menu 75,000L ($45). AE, DC, MC, V. Tues–Sun noon–2:30pm and 7–10:30pm. Closed Jan 1–10 and Aug. REGIONAL/INTERNATIONAL.

Set in a late medieval building in the heart of town, this well-recommended restaurant has been a popular fixture in Bologna since 1920. It offers three gracefully decorated dining rooms and a verdant terrace for outdoor dining. This restaurant was named in honor of the goddess of the hunt because of the many game and seasonal dishes it served when it was first established. In recent years, although game is still featured in season, it opts for a staple of regional and international cuisine, all of it competently prepared. Begin your meal with one of the city's most delicious appetizers—spuma di mortadella, a pâté made of mortadella sausage and served with dainty white toast. You'll never eat baloney again.

I Carracci. In the Grand Hotel Baglioni, Via dell'Indipendenza 8. ☎ **051/225-445.** Reservations required. Main courses 25,000L–30,000L ($15–$18). AE, DC, MC, V. Mon–Sat 12:30–2:30pm and 7:30–10:30pm. Closed Aug 1–25. ITALIAN/INTERNATIONAL.

The most fashionable and *bellissimo* dining spot in Bologna—and arguably the best—this restaurant is named after the family of artists who decorated the premises with frescoes. Its cuisine equals that of the Notai (see below), and the service is impeccable. The elegant dining room, the most harmonious in the city, dates from the 16th century. The frescoes on the ceiling were painted in the 1700s by the Carracci brothers, and their interpretation of the four seasons is richly allegorical and mythical. The seasonally adjusted menu features the freshest produce and the highest-quality meat, poultry, and fish. Some dishes we've enjoyed here include tortellini in brodo, tagliatelle in ragoût, veal scallop alla bolognese, wild boar, cacciatore, and grilled fillet of salmon. The wine list is among the finest of any restaurant in the province.

Nuovi Notai. Via de'Pignattari 1. ☎ **051/228-694.** Reservations required. Main courses 18,000L–26,000L ($10.80–$15.60); fixed-price menus 48,000L–65,000L ($28.80–$39). AE, DC, MC, V. Mon–Sat 12:30–2:30pm and 8–10:30pm. ITALIAN/TUSCAN/UMBRIAN.

Hidden behind a lattice- and ivy-covered facade next to the cathedral, within view of one of the most beautiful squares in Italy, this sublime restaurant, often cited as the city's best, draws from a loyal clientele. In summer, sidewalk tables are placed outside. Music lovers and relaxing businesspeople appreciate the piano bar. The decor combines the *belle époque* with Italian flair and includes artwork, hanging Victorian lamps, and clutches of beautifully arranged flowers on each table.

The fine cooking is based on the best local products Emilia-Romagna has to offer. An attachment to culinary traditions doesn't preclude a modern approach to the cuisine. Menu items include a flan of cheese fondue, gratin of gnocchi with truffles, a filet of beef cooked in *cartoccio* (a paper bag) and garnished with porcini mushrooms, and deboned breast of wild goose. Dessert might be a suprême of almonds served with ricotta cheese and coffee sauce.

Ristorante al Pappagallo. Piazza della Mercanzia 3C. ☎ **051/232-807.** Reservations required. Main courses 34,000L–35,000L ($20.40–$21). AE, DC, MC, V. Mon–Sat 12:30–2:30pm and 8–10:20pm. BOLOGNESE.

This restaurant has a faithful following. Diners have included Einstein, Hitchcock, and Toscanini. It's still going strong, with memories of a glorious past, but it's no longer the finest restaurant in Italy. "The Parrot" is housed on the ground floor of a Gothic mansion, across the street from the landmark 14th-century Merchants' Loggia (a short walk from the leaning towers).

For the best possible introduction, begin your meal with lasagne verde al forno (baked lasagne that gets its green color from minced spinach). And then, for the main course, the specialty of the house: *filetti di tacchino*, superb turkey breasts baked with white wine, parmigiano cheese, and truffles. Modern low-calorie offerings also appear on today's menu. With your meal, the restaurant serves the amber-colored Albana wine and the sparkling red Lambrusco, two of the best-known wines of Emilia.

MODERATE

Montegrappa da Nello. Via Montegrappa 2. ☎ **051/236-331.** Reservations recommended for dinner. Main courses 12,000L–40,000L ($7.20–$24). AE, DC, MC, V. Tues–Sun noon–3pm and 7–11:30pm. Closed Aug. BOLOGNESE/INTERNATIONAL.

Montegrappa da Nello has a faithful following that swears by its pasta dishes. It's one of the few restaurants that still does the old-fashioned and classic Bolognese cuisine. It's said that if you can't get an invitation to visit a local's house, this is the place to go for tasty Bolognesi specialties. Franco and Ezio Bolini are your hosts, and they insist that all produce be fresh. The restaurant, just a short walk from Piazza Maggiore, offers *tortellina Montegrappa,* a pasta favorite served in a cream-and-meat sauce. Another savory pasta is *graminia,* a very fine white spaghetti presented with mushrooms, cream, and pepper. The restaurant is also known for its fresh white truffles and mushrooms. Another sublime salad is made with truffles, mushrooms, Parmesan cheese, and artichokes. For a main course, *misto del cuoco* is a mixed platter from the chef, featuring a selection of his specialties, including zampone, cotoletta alla bolognese, and scaloppine with fresh mushrooms.

INEXPENSIVE

Antica Osteria Romagnola. Via Rialto 13. ☎ **051/263-699.** Reservations recommended for dinner. Main courses 18,000L–25,000L ($10.80–$15). AE, DC, MC, V. Tues 7:30–11pm; Wed–Sat 12:30–2:30pm and 7:30–11pm; Sun 12:30–2:30pm. Closed Jan 7–16 and Aug. ITALIAN.

Unlike many of its competitors in Bologna, this establishment offers cuisine from throughout Italy, including the distant south. You might begin your meal with one of the unusual and well-flavored risottos, or choose from a savory selection of antipasti. The variety of pastas is also impressive, including ravioli with essence of truffles, garganelli pasta with zucchini, or pasta whipped with asparagus tips. You might also select a terrine of ricotta and arugula; the latter was considered an aphrodisiac by the ancient Romans. For your main course you might try a springtime specialty of *capretto* (roast goat) with artichokes and potatoes, or filet mignon prepared with aromatic basil.

Grassilli. Via del Luzzo 3. ☎ **051/237-938.** Reservations required. Main courses 20,000L–26,000L ($12–$15.60). AE, DC, MC, V. Thurs–Tues 12:30–2:30pm; Thurs–Sat and Mon–Tues 8–10:15pm. Closed July 20–Aug 15, Dec 24–Jan 6, and for dinner on holidays. BOLOGNESE/INTERNATIONAL.

Grassilli is a good bet for conservative regional cooking with few deviations from the time-tested formulas that have made Bolognese cuisine famous. It's located in a 1750s building across from an antique store, on a narrow cobblestone alleyway a short block from the two leaning towers. The restaurant also has a summertime street-side canopy for outdoor dining. At night it can be festive, and your good time will be enhanced if you order such specialties as tortellini in a mushroom-cream sauce, the chef's special tournedos, maccheroni with fresh peas and prosciutto, or a range of succulent grilled and roasted meats.

Rosteria da Luciano. Via Nazario Sauro 19. ☎ **051/231-249.** Reservations recommended. Main courses 15,000L–28,000L ($9–$16.80); fixed-price lunch 20,000L–35,000L ($12–$21). AE, DC, MC, V. Thurs–Tues noon–2pm and 7:30–10:30pm. Closed Aug. BOLOGNESE.

Rosteria da Luciano is seriously challenging the competition. It serves some of the best food in Bologna. Located on a side street, within walking distance of the city center, it has an art deco style and contains three large rooms with a real Bolognese atmosphere. The front room, opening onto the kitchen, is preferred. As a novelty, there's a see-through window on the street that looks directly into the kitchen.

The chefs not only can't keep any secrets from you, but you get an appetizing preview of what awaits you before you step inside. To begin your gargantuan repast, request the tortellini in a rich cream sauce. Well-recommended main dishes include the *fritto misto all'Italiana* (mixed fry) and the *scaloppe con porcini* (veal with mushrooms). One savory offering is *cotoletta alla bolognese,* veal layered with ham and Parmesan, then baked. A dramatic dessert is crêpes flambés.

INEXPENSIVE

Osteria dell'Orso. 1/F Via Mentana. ☎ **051/231-576.** Reservations recommended. Main courses 10,000L–16,000L ($6–$9.60). AE, MC, V. Daily noon–2am. ITALIAN.

In the 1970s, a restaurant that was already well established moved from another part of town into this 15th-century building near the university, and—thanks to some of the best *ragú bolognese* in town—has continued to thrive ever since. Most clients opt for a seat within the high-ceilinged, medieval-looking main floor, although an informal cantina-like room in the cellar is open for additional seating whenever it's needed. You won't go wrong if you preface a meal here with any kind of pasta labeled "bolognese." Members of the staff even admit that they're reluctant to stop eating it themselves, despite regular access to the stuff that's been on the menu in some cases for many years. Other options include homemade tagliolini (with the above-mentioned ragú) or tortelloni with a cheese, ham, and mushroom sauce. Veal cutlet fiorentina (with spinach) is always worthwhile, and if you feel adventurous, you can always opt for grilled donkeymeat *(samarino)* that for the regulars is a culinary staple.

Osteria del Moretto. 5 Via di San Mamolo. ☎ **051/580-284.** Main courses 10,000L–12,500L ($6–$7.50). No credit cards. Mon–Sat 8pm–2:30am. BOLOGNESE.

This simple trattoria and bar has operated with very few obvious changes from the same duet of rooms, with basically the same simple menu, since it was founded around 1900. Built as a convent in the 13th century, you'll find it near the Porto San Mamolo, in the historic core of Bologna. Most of the stand-up clients drink wine and, in some cases, segue from drinks into a working-class meal. This might include selections from a platter of local cheese as an antipasto, steaming bowls full of pasta e fagiole (with beans), spaghetti bolognese, a cold salad of meat and vegetables known as *salata Trentino,* eggplant parmigiana, chicken, and a limited selection of fish.

A NEARBY PLACE TO DINE

✪ **San Domenico.** Via Gaspara Sacchi 1, Imola. ☎ **0542/29-000.** Reservations recommended. Main courses 35,000L–50,000L ($21–$30); fixed-price lunch (Tues–Sat) 55,000L ($33); fixed-price Sun lunch or fixed-price dinner (including wine) 80,000L ($48); menu degustazione 125,000L ($75). AE, DC, MC, V. Tues–Sat 12:30–2:30pm; Tues–Sun 8–10:30pm. Closed Jan 1–10 and July 27–Aug 25. ITALIAN.

To an increasing degree, gastronomes from all over Europe and America are traveling to the unlikely village of Imola, which lies 21 miles southeast of Bologna, to savor the offerings of what some food critics consider the best restaurant in Italy. The restaurant can also be easily reached from Ravenna.

The cuisine here is sometimes compared to modern cuisine creations in France. However, owner Gian Luigi Morini claims that his delectable offerings are nothing more than adaptations of festive regional dishes, except they are lighter, more subtle, and are served in manageable portions. He was born in this rambling stone building whose simple facade faces the courtyard of a neighboring church. For 25 years Signor Morini worked at a local bank, returning home every night to administer his restaurant. Now his establishment is among the primary attractions of Emilia-Romagna.

A tuxedo-clad member of his talented young staff will escort you to a table near the tufted leather banquettes. Meals include heavenly concoctions made with the freshest ingredients. You might select goose-liver pâté studded with white truffles, fresh shrimp in a creamy sweet bell-pepper sauce, roast rack of lamb with fresh rosemary, stuffed suprême of chicken wrapped in lettuce leaves, or fresh handmade spaghetti with shellfish. Signor Morini has collected some of the best vintages in Europe for the past 30 years.

BOLOGNA AFTER DARK

Since the Middle Ages, in both politics and art, Bologna has always been noted for a wild, sometimes self-indulgent side that has both intrigued and terrorized more sedate regions of Italy. This, coupled with a large population of students and persons under 35, contributes to a burgeoning night scene and some of the most diverse nightclubs of any city its size in Italy.

During July and August, the city authorities transform the parks along the town's northern tier into an Italian version of a German *biergarten* complete with disco music under colored lights. Vendors sell beer and wine from indoor/outdoor bars set up on the lawns, merchants hawk food and souvenirs from raffish-looking stands, while the milling midsummer crowd seems well aquainted with each other. Events range from live jazz to classical concerts. Ask any hotelier, or the city tourist office, for the schedule of midsummer events, or try your luck by taking either a taxi or—much less convenient—bus no. 25 from the main station to **Arena Parco Nord** (☎ 051/533-880).

The **Teatro Communale,** Via Largo Respighi (☎ 051/529-999), is the venue for major cultural presentations in Bologna, including opera, ballet, and orchestral presentations. **Circolo della Musica di Bologna,** Via Galleria 11 (☎ 051/227-032), presents free classical music concerts throughout the summer.

For the rest of the year, there's always a cafe, bar, or pub nearby. Fans of Irish ales, Teutonic dipthongs, and Celtic music can head for the **Irish Times Pub,** Via Paradiso (☎ 051/251-648), where Harp, Guinness, and Kilkenny flow along with a Latinized version of Olde Eire. Counterculture wannabes head to the **Piccolo Bar,** Piazza Guiseppe Verdi 4 (☎ 051/227-147), where you'll get a whiff of Generation X's hopes and dreams as interpreted by Italy. The nautical-looking, and somewhat dressier, **Porto di Mare,** Vicolo Sampieri 3 (☎ 051/222-650), offers a somewhat disorganized restaurant in addition to sprawling separate areas devoted to flirting, gossiping, and listening to music that ranges from jazz to funk.

Bologna's most popular gay bar is **Cassero,** Piazza Porta Saragozza 2 (☎ 051/644-6902), located in a venerable medieval building that opens onto a third-floor terrace with a view of the stars. Open nightly as a mostly gay male bar from 9:30pm to at least 2:30am, it's transformed into a disco Thursday through Sunday. Thursday night is for lesbians only; Friday through Sunday is mostly for *uomini* (men).

As a university city, Bologna has many student cafes. One of the most central and most popular is **Mocambo,** Via d'Azaglio 1E (☎ 051/229-516), which is near the Duomo. Its major competitor, also facing the Duomo, is **Bar Giuseppe,** Piazza Maggiore I (☎ 051/264-444), serving some of the best espresso in town.

2 Ferrara

259 miles N of Rome, 32 miles N of Bologna, 62 miles SW of Venice

When Papa Borgia, also known as Pope Alexander VI, was shopping around for a third husband for the apple of his eye, darling Lucrezia, his gaze fell on the influential house of Este. From the 13th century, this great Italian family had domi-nated Ferrara, building up a powerful duchy and a reputation as builders of palaces and patrons of the arts. Alfonse d'Este, son of the shrewd but villainous Ercole I, who was the ruling duke of Ferrara, was an attractive, virile candidate for Lucrezia's much-used hand (her second husband had already been murdered, perhaps by her brother, Cesare, who was the apple of nobody's eye—with the possible exception of Machiavelli).

Although the Este family may have had private reservations (after all, it was common gossip that the pope "knew" his daughter in the biblical sense), they finally consented to the marriage. As the duchess of Ferrara, a position she held until her death, Lucrezia was to have seven children. But one of her grandchildren, Alfonso II, wasn't as prolific as his forebear, although he had a reputation as a roué. He left the family without a male heir. The greedy eye of Pope Clement VIII took quick action on this, gobbling up the city as his fief in the waning months of the 16th century. The great house of Este went down in history, and Ferrara sadly declined under the papacy.

Incidentally, Alfonso II was a dubious patron of Torquato Tasso (1544–95), au-thor of the epic *Jerusalem Delivered,* a work that was to make him the most celebrated poet of the late Renaissance. The legend of Tasso—who is thought to have been in-sane, paranoid, or at least tormented—has steadily grown over the centuries. It didn't need any more boosting, but Goethe fanned the legend through the Teutonic lands with his late 18th-century drama *Torquato Tasso.* It's said that Alfonso II at one time made Tasso his prisoner.

Ferrara today is still relatively undiscovered, especially by globe-trotting North Americans. The city is richly blessed, with much of its legacy intact. Among the his-toric treasures remaining are a great cathedral and the Este Castle, along with enough ducal palaces to make for a fast-paced day of sightseeing. Its palaces, for the most part, have long been robbed of their lavish furnishings, but the faded frescoes, the paint-ings not carted off, and the palatial rooms are reminders of the vicissitudes of power.

Modern Ferrara is one of the most health-conscious places in all of Italy. Bicycles outnumber the automobiles on the road and more than half the citizens get exercise by jogging. In fact, it's almost surreal: Enclosed in medieval walls under a bright sky, everywhere you look, you'll find the people of Ferrara engaged in all sorts of self-powered locomotion.

ESSENTIALS

GETTING THERE   By Train   Getting here by train is fast and efficient, as Ferrara lies on the main train line between Bologna and Venice. A total of 33 trains a day originating in Bologna pass through here. Trip time is 40 minutes, and the fare is 4,200L ($2.50) one-way. Some 24 trains arrive from Venice (trip time: 1 1/2 hours); the one-way fare is 9,800L ($5.90). For information and schedules call ☎ **0532/ 770-340.**

By Bus   From most destinations the train is best, but if you're in Modena (see be-low), you'll find 11 bus departures a day for Ferrara. Trip time is between 1 1/2 and 2 hours, and a one-way ticket costs 8,400L ($5.05). In Ferrara, bus information for the surrounding area is available by calling ☎ **0532/771-302.**

By Car   From Bologna, take A13 north. From Venice, take A4 southwest to Padua and continue on A13 south to Ferrara.

VISITOR INFORMATION   The **tourist information office** is at Corso Gio-vecca 21 (☎ **0532/209-370**). It's open Monday to Saturday from 8:30am to 7pm and Sunday from 9am to 1pm and 2:30 to 5:30pm.

EXPLORING THE TOWN

Castello Estense. Piazza della Repubblica. ☎ **0532/299-111.** Admission 10,000L ($6) adults, 4,000L ($2.40) seniors 65 and over, free for children 9 and under. Tues–Sat 9:30am–5:30pm, Sun 9:30am–4pm.

A moated, four-towered castle (lit at night), this proud fortress began as a bricklayer's dream near the end of the 14th century, although its face has been lifted and wrenched around for centuries. It was home to the powerful Este family. Here the dukes went about their daily chores: murdering their wives' lovers, beheading or imprisoning potential enemies, whatever. Today it's used for the provincial and prefectural administration offices, and many of its once-lavish rooms may be inspected— notably the Salon of Games, the Room of Games, and the Room of Dawn, as well as a Lombardesque chapel that once belonged to Renata di Francia, daughter of Louis XII. Parisina, the wife of Duke Nicolò d'Este III, was murdered with her lover, Ugolino, the duke's natural son, in the dank prison below the castle, creating the inspiration for Browning's "My Last Duchess."

Il Duomo. Piazza Cattedrale. ☎ **0532/207-449.** Free admission. Church, Mon–Sat 7:30am– noon and 3–6:30pm, Sun 7:30am–1pm and 4–7:30pm; museum, Mon–Sat 10am–noon and 3–5pm. Closed Dec–Feb.

Located only a short stroll from the Este castle, the 12th-century Duomo weds the delicate Gothic with the more virile Romanesque. The offspring: an exciting pink marble facade. Behind the cathedral is a typically Renaissance campanile (bell tower). Inside, the massive structure is heavily baroqued, as the artisans of still another era festooned it with trompe l'oeil. The entrance to the **Museo del Duomo** lies to the left of the atrium as you enter. It's worth a visit just to see works by Ferrara's most outstanding painter of the 15th century, **Cosmé Tura.** Aesthetically controversial, the big attraction here is Tura's St. George slaying the dragon to save a red-stockinged damsel in distress. Opposite is a work by **Jacopo della Quercia** depicting a sweet, regal Madonna with a pomegranate in one hand and the Child in the other. This is one of della Quercia's first masterpieces. Also from the Renaissance heyday of Ferrara are some bas-reliefs, notably a *Giano bifronte,* a mythological figure looking at the past and the future, along with some 16th-century *arazzi,* or tapestries, woven by hand.

Palazzo Schifanoia. Via Scandiana 23. ☎ **0532/64-178.** Admission 6,000L ($3.60) adults, 3,000L ($1.80) students and seniors 60 and over, free for children 17 and under. Daily 9am– 7pm. Closed major holidays.

Home to the **Museo Civico d'Arte Antica,** the first part of the Schifanoia Palace was built in 1385 for Albert V d'Este, and later enlarged by Borso d'Este (1450–71). The museum was founded in 1758 and was transferred to its present site in 1898. The first part of the collection then exhibited, which consisted of coins and medals, was enhanced by donations of archaeological finds, antique bronzes, small Renaissance plates and pottery, and other collections.

Art lovers are lured to the Salon of the Months to see the astrological cycle. The humanist Pellegrino Prisciani at court conceived the subjects of the cycle, though Cosmé Tura, the official court painter for the Estes, was probably the organizer of the works. Tura was the founder of the Ferrarese School, to which belonged, among others, Ercole de' Roberti and Francesco del Cossa, who painted the March, April, and May scenes. In the wall cycle, which represents the 12 months of the year, each month is subdivided into three horizontal bands: The lower band shows scenes from the daily life of courtiers and people, the middle one displays the relative sign of the zodiac, and the upper one presents the triumph of the classical divinity for that

particular myth. The frescoes form a complex presentation, leading to varying interpretations as to their meaning.

Palazzo dei Diamanti. Corso Ercole d'Este 21. ☎ **0532/205-844.** Admission 10,000L
($6.00), free for children under 18 and seniors over 60. Tues–Sat 9am–2pm, Sun 9am–1pm.

The Palazzo dei Diamanti, another jewel of d'Este splendor, is so named because of
the 9,000 diamond-shaped stones on its facade. Of the handful of museums sheltered
here, the **Pinacoteca Nazionale** (National Picture Gallery) is the most important. It
houses the works of the Ferrarese artists—notably the trio of old masters, **Tura, del
Cossa,** and **Roberti.** The collection covers the chief period of artistic expression in
Ferrara from the 14th to the 18th centuries. The palace also houses the **Municipal
Gallery of Modern Art,** which sponsors the most important modern art exhibitions
in town.

Casa Romei. Via Savonarola 30. ☎ **0532/240-341.** Admission 4,000L ($2.40), free for chil-
dren under 18 and seniors over 60. Tues–Sun 8:30am–2pm.

This 15th-century palace was the property of John Romei, a friend and confidant of
the fleshy Duke Borso d'Este, who made the Este realm a duchy. John (or Giovanni)
was later to marry one of the Este princesses, although we don't know if it was for
love or power or both. In later years, Lucrezia and her gossipy coterie—riding in the
ducal carriage drawn by handsome white horses—used to descend on the Romei
house, perhaps to receive Borgia messengers from Rome. The house is near the Este
tomb. Its once-elegant furnishings have been carted off, but the chambers—many
with terra-cotta fireplaces—remain, and the casa has been filled with frescoes and
sculpture.

SHOPPING

Ferrara has a rich tradition of artisanship dating back to the Renaissance days of the
Este family. Some of the best, albeit expensive, products can be seen in the dozen or
so antique stores that dot the town's historic center. Two particularly appealing dealers include **Antichita San Michele,** Via del Turco 22 (☎ **0532/211-055**), and
Antica Ferrara, Corso Giovecca 112 (☎ **0532/206-845**). Newer goods, often fashioned in a style derivative of what was originally developed during the Renaissance,
include ceramics whose designs are etched directly into the clay in a style older than
virtually anyone can remember. Examples of the craft are displayed, sold, and shipped
from **Ceramica Artistica Ferrarese,** Via Baluardi 125 (☎ **0532/66-093**), and **La
Marchesana,** Via Cortevecchia 38A (☎ **0532/240-535**).

And if you want to dress up the private rooms of your house with the fruits of
Ferrara's looms, consider a visit to **Merletto,** Via Saraceno 29 (☎ **0532/202-088**),
located within a hundred yards of the cathedral. Here you'll find a roster of bed and
table linens as well as fabric sold by the meter that's suitable for either draperies or
upholstery. More unusual is an outfit specializing in wrought iron, **Chierici,** Via
Bartoli 17 (☎ **0532/67-057**), near the Ponte San Giorgio. Some of the smaller
pieces, such as decorative brackets or fireplace tools, make good souvenirs.

Food products? **Antica Salumeria Polesinati,** Via Mazzini 78 (☎ **0532/
206-833**), and **Enoteca Al Brindisi,** Via Adelardi 11 (☎ **0532/209-142**), stockpile
the fruits of the Ferrarese harvest in historically evocative settings. Outdoor markets?
Every month except August, on the first Saturday and first Sunday of every month,
the open-air antique and handcraft markets feature lots of junk scattered amidst the
increasingly rare treasures. They're conducted from 8am to 7pm in both the Piazza
Municipale (mostly antiques and bric-a-brac) and the Piazza Savonarola (mainly
handcrafts and bric-a-brac).

WHERE TO STAY

✪ **Duchessa Isabella.** Via Palestro 70, 44100 Ferrara. ☎ **0532/202-121.** Fax 0532/202-638. 22 rms, 6 suites. A/C MINIBAR TV TEL. 480,000L ($288) double; from 650,000L ($390) suite. Rates include breakfast. AE, DC, MC, V.

This hotel was the private home of the head of one of the region's most respected Jewish organizations until the late 1980s. In 1990 it reopened as a five-star hotel with a spectacular decor. Today it's a member of the illustrious Relais & Châteaux hotel chain. Named in honor of the d'Este family's most famous ancestor, Isabella, the hotel maintains a lavish garden. The bedrooms are each decorated in a different color scheme and are identified by the names of the flowers whose colors they most closely resemble. Each imbues a sense of history, is outfitted with all the electronic amenities a visitor might want, and is very, very comfortable.

Dining/Entertainment: The hotel operates an elegant restaurant that's set beneath lavishly gilded and painted ceilings. (In summer the venue moves outside into the garden.) The cuisine is based on the traditional recipes of Emilia-Romagna, although a wide choice of less esoteric dishes is also available.

Services: A horse-drawn landau will take guests on excursions around Ferrara's historic center. There's also room service, conference facilities, laundry and valet service, and free use of bicycles.

Hotel Europa. Corso della Giovecca 49. ☎ **0532/205-456.** Fax 0532/212120. 37 rms, 2 suites. A/C MINIBAR TV TEL. 175,000L ($105) double; 220,000L ($132) suite. Rates include breakfast. Parking 12,000L ($7.20). AE, DC, MC, V.

This hotel were originally built near the Castello d'Estense in the 1600s as a rich and ornate private palace. In 1880, it was transformed into one of the most prestigious hotels in town, but during World War II, portions of the rear were bombed, mutilated, and subsequently repaired in a less grandiose but conservatively comfortable style. Today, the three-story, three-star establishment continues in a worthy but less spectacular version of its original, offering a tactful and well-trained staff, relatively reasonable prices, and a handful of bedrooms overlooking the *corso* that retain ceiling frescoes from the building's original construction. The others are clean and comfortable, with antique furnishings and modern comforts. There's a bar on the premises, but no restaurant, as only breakfast is served.

✪ **Locanda Borgonuovo.** Via Cairoi 29. 44100 Ferrara. ☎ **0532/248-000.** Fax 0532/248-000. 4 rms. A/C MINIBAR TV TEL. 140,000L–150,000L ($84–$90) double. AE, MC, V.

This is the kind of pensione that contains so many aspects of a private home that loyal clients sometimes reserve their accommodations a full year in advance. It occupies the two lower floors of a four-story medieval palazzo that belonged to the owner's father, when it functioned as his law office. Bedrooms are outfitted with family antiques and mementos, containing new bathrooms that were upgraded in 1994—the year the site began accepting paying guests. Breakfasts are appealingly personable, directed by either Signora Adele Orlandini or her charming son Filippo. Although it lies within a traffic-free pedestrian zone about a hundred yards from the Castello d'Estense, rented cars can still park for free on the street outside.

Ripagrande Hotel. Via Ripagrande 21, 44100 Ferrara. ☎ **0532/765-250.** Fax 0532/764-377. 20 rms, 20 junior suites. A/C MINIBAR TV TEL. 290,000L ($174) double; from 330,000L ($198) junior suite. Rates include breakfast. AE, DC, MC, V. Parking 20,000L ($12). Bus: 1, 2, 3, or 9.

The Ripagrande, one of the most unusual hotels in town, occupies one of the city's Renaissance palaces. Rich coffered ceilings, walls in Ferrarese brickwork,

16th-century columns, and a wide stairway with a floral cast-iron handrail characterize the broad entrance hall. Inside the hotel are two Renaissance courtyards decorated with columns and capitals. Half of the hotel's 40 rooms are junior suites with sleeping areas connected to an internal stairway. The rooms are spacious with modern and tasteful furnishings, often antique reproductions. Some of the accommodations are on three levels, with a garret-like bedroom above. The most desirable rooms are on the top floor, opening onto terraces overlooking the red tile roofs of Ferrara. Laundry and room service are provided.

WHERE TO DINE

Grotta Azzurra. Piazza Sacrati 43. ☎ **0532/209-152.** Reservations recommended. Main courses 13,000L–25,000L ($7.80–$15); fixed-price menus 18,000L–50,000L ($10.80–$30). AE, DC, MC, V. Mon–Tues and Thurs–Sat 12:30–2:30pm and 7:30–9:30pm, Sun 12:30–2:30pm. Closed July 5–31. FERRARESE/SEAFOOD.

Behind a classic brick facade on a busy square, the Grotta Azzurra seems like a restaurant you might encounter on the sunny isle of Capri, not in Ferrara. It was established back in the *la dolce vita* days of the 1950s. However, the cuisine is firmly entrenched in the northern Italian kitchen. It's best to visit in the autumn when favorite dishes include wild boar and pheasant, usually served with polenta. Many sausages, served as antipasti, are made with game as well. More esoteric dishes include a boiled calf's head and tongue, while a local favorite is boiled stuffed pork leg. The chef is also an expert at grilled meats, especially pork, veal, and beef.

La Provvidenza. Corso Ercole I d'Este 92. ☎ **0532/205-187.** Reservations required. Main courses 15,000L–35,000L ($9–$21). AE, DC, MC, V. Tues–Sun noon–2:30pm and 8–10pm. Closed Aug 11–17. FERRARESE/ITALIAN.

La Provvidenza stands on the same street as the Palazzo dei Diamanti. The building itself is from around 1750, and there has been a restaurant here for at least a century, although the present management dates only from the 1970s. It has a farm-style interior, with a little garden where the regulars request tables in fair weather. The antipasti table is the finest we've seen—or sampled—in Ferrara. Really hearty eaters should order a pasta, such as fettuccine with smoked salmon, before tackling the main course, perhaps perfectly grilled and seasoned veal chops. Other specialties include *pasticchio alla Ferrarese* (macaroni mixed with a mushroom-and-meat sauce laced with a creamy white sauce) and *fritto misto di carne* (mixed grill). The dessert choice is wide and luscious. Take a large appetite to this local favorite.

FERRARA AFTER DARK

During July and August, concerts and temporary art exhibitions are offered as part of the **Estate a Ferrara** program. The tourist office will provide you with a schedule of events and dates, which vary from year to year. During the rest of the year, you can rub elbows with fellow drinkers, and usually lots of students, at a refreshingly diverse collection of bars, pubs, and discos. **Osteria Al Brindisi,** Via Adelardi 9B (☎ **0532/209-142**) claims, with some justification, to be the oldest wine bar in the world, with a tradition of uncorking bottles that goes back to the early 1400s. Wine begins at around 2,500L ($1.50) a glass and seems to taste best when accompanied by a dozen kinds of *panini* (sandwiches).

For something unusual head for **Birreria Sebastien,** Via Darsena 53A (☎ **0532/ 768-233**), an animated beer hall that occupies an old barge and now floats next to an embankment on the town's river. Pizzas, priced at 11,000L ($6.60), are big enough for two and go well with the foaming mugs of brew.

3 Ravenna

46 miles E of Bologna, 90 miles S of Venice, 81 miles NE of Florence, 227 miles N of Rome

Ravenna is one of the most unusual towns in Emilia-Romagna. Today, you'll find a sleepy town, but one with memories of a great past, luring hordes of tourists to explore what remains. As the capital of the Western Roman Empire (from A.D. 402), the Visigoth Empire (from A.D. 473), and the Byzantine Empire under the emperor Justinian and the empress Theodora (A.D. 540–752), Ravenna became one of the greatest cities on the Mediterranean.

Having achieved its cultural peak as part of the Byzantine Empire between the 6th and 8th centuries, Ravenna is known today for the many well-preserved mosaics created during that time—the finest in all of Western art and the most splendid outside Istanbul. Although it now looks much like any other Italian city, the low Byzantine domes of its churches still evoke its Eastern past.

ESSENTIALS

GETTING THERE   By Train   With frequent service and only 1¼ hours by train from Bologna, Ravenna can be easily visited on a day trip; a one-way fare is 7,200L ($4.30). There's also frequent service to Ferrara; a one-way fare is 6,500L ($3.90). At Ferrara, you can make connections to Venice, for 17,800L ($10.70) each way. The train station is a 10-minute walk from the center.

By Bus   Trains are better. Once at Ravenna, however, you'll find both a regional (ATR) system and a municipal (ATM) bus network serving the area. Buses depart from outside the train station at Piazza Farini. The tourist office (see below) will have bus schedules and more details, depending on where you want to go, or call ☎ 0544/35-288 for information.

By Car   From Bologna, head east along autostrada A14 or southeast of Ferrara on S309.

VISITOR INFORMATION   The **tourist information center** is at Piazza Mameli 4 (☎ 0544/35-404). Here you can purchase a ticket to visit six monuments for a single cost of 10,000L ($6). These sights are the **Battistero Neoniano,** the **Archepiscopal Museum and Church of St. Andrea,** the **Church of San Vitale,** the **Mausoleum of Galla Placidia,** the **Adrian Baptistery,** and the **Basilica of St. Apollinare Nuovo.** The office is open Monday to Saturday from 8:30am to 6pm; in summer it's also open Sunday from 9am to noon and 3 to 6pm.

EXPLORING THE TOWN

You can actually see all the sights within 1 busy day. The center of Ravenna is **Piazza del Popolo,** which has a Venetian aura to it. To the south, off the colonnaded Piazza San Francesco, you can visit the **Tomba di Dante** on Via Dante Alighieri. After crossing Piazza dei Caduti and heading northward along Via Guerrini, you can reach the **Battistero Neoniano** at the Piazza del Duomo. Directly southeast of here and opening onto Piazza Arcivescovado is the **Museo Arcivescovile** and the **Church of St. Andrea.** After seeing these attractions, you can head back to the tourist information office, cutting west along Via San Vitale. This will take you to the **Basilica di San Vitale.** After a visit here, you can explore the **Mausoleum of Gallo Placidia** in back of the basilica. Also nearby is the **Museo Nazionale di Ravenna** along Via Fiandrini (adjacent to Via San Vitale). Finally to cap off your day, you can take bus 4 or 44 from the railroad station or Piazza Caduti to visit **Basilica of St. Appollinare** in Classe, reached along Via Romeo Sud.

Leaning Towers of Ravenna   Lying north of the Piazza del Popolo, is the 12th-century leaning tower of Ravenna, the **Torre Pubblica.** This tower (which can't be visited) leans even more than the Tower of Pisa. Nearby along Viale Farini is another leaning tower, the 12th-century **Campanile of San Giovanni Evangelista,** which is even tipsier than Torre Pubblica. When Allied bombs struck the church in World War II, its apse was destroyed, but the mighty tower couldn't be toppled.

Battistero Neoniano. Piazza del Duomo. ☎ **0544/33-696.** Admission (including admission to Museo Arcivescovile) 5,000L ($3). Daily 9am–7pm; off-season, daily 9:30am–4:30pm. Closed Christmas and New Year's Day.

The octagonal baptistery was built in the 5th century. In the center of the cupola is a tablet showing John the Baptist baptizing Christ. The circle around the tablet depicts in dramatic mosaics of deep violet-blues and sparkling golds the 12 crown-carrying Apostles. The baptistery originally serviced a cathedral that no longer stands. (The present-day Duomo of Ravenna was built around the mid-18th century and is of little interest except for some unusual pews.) Beside it is a campanile from the 11th century, perhaps earlier.

Museo Arcivescovile and Church of St. Andrea. Piazza Arcivescovado. ☎ **0544/33-696.** Admission 5,000L ($3). Tues–Sat 9am–7pm (until 4:30pm in winter), Sun 9am–1pm.

This twofold attraction is housed in the Archbishop's Palace, which dates from the 6th century. In the museum, the major exhibit is a throne carved out of ivory for Archbishop Maximian, which dates from around the mid-6th century.

In the chapel or oratory dedicated to St. Andrea are brilliant mosaics. Pause a while in the antechamber to look at an intriguing mosaic above the entrance. It's an unusual representation of Christ as a warrior, stepping on the head of a lion and a snake. Although haloed, he wears partial armor, evoking "Onward, Christian Soldiers." The chapel—built in the shape of a cross—contains other mosaics that are "angelic," both figuratively and literally. Busts of saints and apostles stare down at you with the ox-eyed look of Byzantine art.

Basilica di San Vitale. Via San Vitale 17. ☎ **0544/33-696.** Admission 6,000L ($3.60). Apr–Sept, daily 9am–7pm; off-season, daily 9am–4:30pm.

This octagonal domed church dates from the mid-6th century. The mosaics inside—in brilliant greens and golds, lit by light from translucent panels—are among the most celebrated in the Western world. Covering the apse is a mosaic rendition of a clean-shaven Christ astride the world, flanked by saints and angels. To the right is a mosaic of Empress Theodora and her court, and to the left, the man who married the courtesan-actress, Emperor Justinian, and his entourage. If you can tear yourself away from the mosaics long enough, you might admire the church's marble decoration. Seven large arches span the temple, but the frescoes of the cupola are unimaginative.

✪ **Mausoleum of Galla Placidia.** Via San Vitale. ☎ **0544/34-266.** Entrance included with admission to Basilica di San Vitale (see above). Apr–Sept, daily 9am–7pm; Oct–Mar, daily 9am–4:30.

This 5th-century chapel is so unpretentious that you'll think you're at the wrong place. But inside it contains some exceptional mosaics that date back to antiquity, although they may not look it. Translucent panels bring the mosaics alive in all their grace and harmony—rich and vivid with peacock-blue, moss-green, Roman gold, eggplant, and burnt orange. The mosaics in the cupola literally glitter with stars. Popular tradition claims that the cross-shaped structure houses the tomb of Galla Placidia, sister of Honorius, Rome's last emperor. Galla Placidia, who died in Rome in A.D. 450, is one of history's most powerful women. She became virtual ruler of the Western world after her husband, Ataulf, king of the Visigoths, died—only a virtual ruler because in reality she became a regent for Valentinian III, who was only 6 at the time of his father's death.

Museo Nazionale di Ravenna. Via Fiandrini (adjacent to Via San Vitale). ☎ **0544/34-424.** Admission 8,000L ($4.80) adults, free for children 17 and under and seniors 60 and over. Tues–Sun 8:30am–7:30pm.

This museum contains archaeological objects from the early Christian and Byzantine periods—icons, fragments of tapestries, medieval armaments and armory, sarcophagi, ivories, ceramics, and bits of broken pieces from the stained-glass windows of St. Vitale.

Basilica of St. Apollinare in Classe. Via Romeo sud. ☎ **0544/527-004.** Free admission. Daily 8:30am–noon and 2–5:30pm (until 6:30pm in summer). Bus: 4 or 44 from the railroad station (every 20 minutes) or Piazza Caduti.

Located about 3¹/₂ miles south of the city (it can be visited on the way to Ravenna if you're heading north from Rimini), this church dates from the 6th century, having been consecrated by Archbishop Maximian. Before the waters receded, Classe was a seaport of Rome's Adriatic fleet. Dedicated to St. Apollinare, the bishop of Ravenna, the early basilica stands side-by-side with a campanile—symbols of faded glory now resting in a lonely low-lying area. Inside the basilica is a central nave flanked by two aisles, the latter containing tombs of ecclesiastical figures in the Ravenna hierarchy. The floor—once carpeted with mosaics—has been rebuilt. Along the central nave are frescoed tablets. Two dozen marble columns line the approach to the apse, where you'll find the major reason for visiting the basilica. The mosaics are exceptional, rich in gold and turquoise, set against a background of top-heavy birds nesting in shrubbery. St. Apollinare stands in the center, with a row of lambs on either side lined up as in a processional, the 12 lambs symbolizing the Apostles, of course.

Tomba di Dante. Via Dante Alighieri. Free admission. Daily 8am–7pm.

Right off Piazza Garibaldi, the final monument to Dante Alighieri, "the divine poet," isn't much to look at—graced as it is with a bas-relief in marble. But it's a far better place than he assigned to some of his fellow Florentines. The author of the *Divine Comedy*, in exile from his hometown of Florence, died in Ravenna on September 14, 1321. To the right of the small temple is a mound of earth in which Dante's urn went "underground" from March 1944 to December 1945 because it was feared that his tomb might suffer from the bombings. Near the tomb is the Church of San Francesco, dating from the 5th century, the site of the poet's funeral.

OTHER DIVERSIONS

A DAY AT THE BEACH   Reached by bus (no. 70) in just 20 minutes from Ravenna, you can enjoy white-sand beaches set against a backdrop of pine forests. Lined with beach clubs, snack shops, and ice-cream stands, these beaches are extremely overcrowded during the sultry months of summer. The most beautiful beaches are found along a stretch called Punta Marina di Ravenna. Marina di Ravenna is also a lively venue at night with pubs and discos open until the early hours.

SHOPPING   No one can enter or leave Ravenna without being influenced by the severely dignified mosaics that adorn the interior of the town's most important churches. One of the best places to admire (and buy) examples of the art form is **Studio Acomena,** Via di Roma 60 (☎ **0544/37-119**). Here, replicas of Christ figures, Madonnas, the saints, and penitent sinners appear in all their majesty amid more secular forms whose designs were inspired by Roman gladiators or floral and geometric motifs. Virtually anything can be shipped. **Scianna,** Via di Roma 30 (☎ 0544/37-556), and **Luciana Notturni,** Via Arno 13 (☎ 0544/63-002), are two worthy competitors with similar merchandise.

WHERE TO STAY

Bisanzio. Via Salara 30, 48100 Ravenna. ☎ **0544/217-111.** Fax 0544/32-539. 38 rms. A/C MINIBAR TV TEL. 163,000–205,000L ($98–$123) double. Rates include breakfast. AE, DC, MC, V. Parking 25,000L ($15).

Bisanzio stands in the heart of town, just a few minutes' walk from many of Ravenna's treasures. It's cheaper and has more personality than the Jolly (see below). This is a pleasantly coordinated and completely renovated modern hotel. The guest rooms have attractive Italian styling, some with mottled batik wall coverings. It's ideal for those who want the comfort of a well-organized hotel, with good bedrooms, offering simplicity and all the other modern conveniences that travelers have come to expect. There's an uncluttered breakfast room with softly draped windows, and guests also have use of a garden.

Hotel Centrale Byron. Via IV Novembre 14, 48100 Ravenna. ☎ **0544/212-225.** Fax 0544/34-114. 54 rms. A/C TV TEL. 116,000L–124,000L ($69.60–$74.40) double. Rates include breakfast. AE, DC, MC, V. Parking 20,000L ($12).

Hotel Central E. Byron is an art deco–inspired hotel located a few steps from Piazza del Popolo. The lobby is an elegantly simple combination of white marble and brass detailing. The long, narrow public rooms, arranged "railroad style," include an alcove sitting room, a long hallway, and a combination TV room, bar, and snack and breakfast-room area. The rooms are simply but comfortably furnished. Why Lord Byron and not the literary legend of the city—Dante? Dante may have died here, but Lord Byron and his mistress of the moment (who both happened to be married) once shared a nearby palace.

Jolly Hotel. Piazza Mameli 1, 48100 Ravenna. ☎ **0544/35-762.** Fax 0544/216-055. 75 rms, 3 suites. A/C MINIBAR TV TEL. 170,000L–210,000L ($102–$126) double; from 300,000l ($180) suite. Rates include breakfast. AE, DC, MC, V. Parking 20,000L–30,000L ($12–$18).

This four-story hotel, 50 yards from the train station, built in 1950 in the postwar crackerbox style with a bunkerlike facade, contains two elevators and a conservative decor of stone floors and lots of paneling. As Ravenna suffers from a dearth of first-class accommodations, the Jolly has become a favorite of business travelers. However, it's too sterile for our tastes. Its La Matta restaurant serves a standard local and international cuisine. Services include baby-sitting, laundry, and room service from 7am to 11pm.

WHERE TO DINE

Bella Venezia. Via IV Novembre 16. ☎ **0544/212-746.** Reservations required. Main courses 14,000L–22,000L ($8.40–$13.20); fixed-price menu 28,000L ($16.80). AE, DC, MC, V. Mon–Sat noon–2:30pm and 7–10pm. Closed Dec 23–Jan 15. ROMAGNOLA/ITALIAN.

Bella Venezia, located a few steps from Piazza del Popolo and next door to the Hotel Centrale Byron, is the kind of well-known restaurant hotel managers recommend to their clients. Despite this restaurant's name, the only Venetian dish prepared here is *fegato alla veneziana* (liver fried with onions), which is, admittedly, delicious. Other than that, the repertoire is almost exclusively regional, with such dishes as risotto, *cappelletti alla romagnola* (round, cap-shaped pasta stuffed with a mixture of ricotta, roasted pork loin, chicken breast, and nutmeg, served with a meat sauce), and garganelli pasta served with whatever happens to be in season (baby asparagus, mushrooms, or peas). All pastas are made by hand, and the place is very family run, very warm, very old Italy.

Ristorante La Gardèla. Via Ponte Marino 3. ☎ **0544/217-147.** Reservations recommended. Main courses 8,000L–18,000L ($4.80–$10.80). AE, DC, MC, V. Fri–Wed noon–1:45pm and 7–10pm. Closed Feb 23–Mar 2 and Aug 10–25. EMILIA-ROMAGNA/SEAFOOD.

Ristorante La Gardèla, located a few steps from one of Ravenna's most startling leaning towers, is spread out over two levels with paneled walls lined with racks of wine bottles. The waiters bring out an array of typical but savory dishes. Specialties include *tortelloni della casa* (made with ricotta, cream, spinach, tomatoes, and herbs) and *spezzatino alla contadina* (roast veal served with potatoes, tomatoes, and herbs). Ravioli is stuffed with truffles and one of their past best pasta dishes, tagliatelle, is offered with porcini mushrooms. The chefs prepare more fresh fish than ever before, most often from the Adriatic. Considering the quality of the food and the first-rate ingredients, this is Ravenna's best restaurant buy.

Ristorante Tre Spade. Via Faentina 136. ☎ **0544/500-522.** Reservations recommended. Main courses 18,000L–30,000L ($10.80–$18); fixed-price menu 65,000L ($39). AE, DC, MC, V. Tues–Sat 12:30–2:30pm and 7:30–10:30pm, Sun 12:30–2:30pm. Closed the first 3 weeks of Aug. INTERNATIONAL/EMILIAN.

This is an appealing spot that has been serving good cuisine since 1980. The town's finest dining choice, Ristorante Tre Spade keeps prices under control while magically combining solid technique and inventiveness. Specialties include an asparagus parfait accompanied by a zesty sauce of bits of green peppers and black olives. This might be followed by taglioni with smoked-salmon sauce, veal cooked with sage, spaghetti with fruits of the sea (including clams in their shells), green gnocchi in Gorgonzola sauce, or roast game in season, plus a good collection of wines. The menu changes frequently, and daily specials are offered according to the market.

RAVENNA AFTER DARK

Some of the most spontaneous good times in Ravenna tend to unfold beside the city's waterside Marina di Ravenna, where a roster of pubs and dance bars combine big-city glitter with the charm and idiosyncracies of this very ancient city. Although lots of holes-in-the-wall within the neighborhood might appeal to you, two of the most appealing bars are **Santa Fe,** Viale delle Nazioni 180 (☎ **0544/530-249**), and **Hemingway,** Via T. de Revel (☎ **0544/590-159**), nearly adjacent to the city's railway station. Both of these offer drinks and dialogue every night and are positioned in places that might encourage you to drop in on nearby competitors.

4 Modena

25 miles NW of Bologna, 250 miles NW of Rome, 81 miles N of Florence

After Ferrara fell to Pope Clement VIII, the duchy of the Este family was established at Modena in the closing years of the 16th century. Lying in the Po Valley, the provincial and commercial city possesses many great art treasures that evoke its more glorious past. On the food front, the chefs of Modena enjoy an outstanding reputation in hard-to-please gastronomic circles. Traversed by the ancient Roman road, Via Emilia, although unknown to overseas travelers, Modena is a hot spot for European art connoisseurs.

An industrial zone blessed with Italy's highest per-capita income, Modena can seem as sleek as the sports cars it produces. This is partially because of its 20th-century face-lift, the result of the city being largely rebuilt in contemporary styles following the destructive bombing of the Second World War. These factors create a stark contrast to both the antiquity and poverty so noticeable in other regions of Italy. It is best known abroad as home to automobile and racing giants Ferrari, Maserati, and De Tomaso, as well as for its production of Lambrusco wine and balsamic vinegar. Locals also proudly claim opera star Luciano Pavarotti as one of their greatest exports.

Many visitors who care little about antiquities come to Modena just to visit the Ferrari and Maserati car plants. However, you can't visit the Ferrari factory. Instead, you can go to the showroom, **Galleria Ferrari**, in Maranello, Via Dino Ferrari 43 (☎ **0536/943-204**), a suburb of Modena. The showroom displays engines, trophies, and both antique and the latest Ferrari cars. It is open Tuesday through Sunday from 9:30am to 12:30pm and 3 to 6pm, charging an admission of 12,000L ($7.20). From the bus station on Via Bacchini in Modena, a bus marked Maranello departs hourly during the day. Ask at the tourist office (see below) for details and a map.

ESSENTIALS

GETTING THERE   By Train   There are good connections to and from Bologna (one train every 30 minutes); trip time is 20 minutes, and a one-way fare is 3,400L ($2.05). Trains arrive from Parma once per hour (trip time: 40 minutes); the one-way fare is 5,000L ($3). For information and schedules call ☎ **059/218-226.**

By Bus   The train is better. However, if you're in Ferrara (see above), one local ATCM bus (no. 7) leaves Ferrara for Modena every hour; trip time is 1 1/2 hours and a one-way fare is 8,400L ($5.05). In Modena, call ☎ **059/308-801** for information.

By Car   From Bologna, take autostrada A1 northeast until you see the turnoff for Modena.

VISITOR INFORMATION   The **tourist information office** is on Via Canalgrande (☎ **059/206-660**), open Monday, Tuesday, and Thursday to Saturday from 8:30am to 1pm and 3 to 7pm.

SEEING THE SIGHTS

✪ **Il Duomo.** Piazza del Duomo. ☎ **059/216-078.** Free admission. Apr–Oct, daily 7am–noon and 3:30–7pm; Nov–Mar, daily 7am–12:30pm and 3:30–7pm.

One of the glories of the Romanesque in northern Italy, the Duomo of Modena was built in a style that will be familiar to those who've been to Lombardy. It was founded in the summer of the closing year of the 11th century and designed by an architect named Lanfranco, with Viligelmo serving as decorator.

The work was carried out by Campionesi masons from Lake Lugano. The cathedral, consecrated in 1184, was dedicated to St. Geminiano, the patron saint of Modena, a 4th-century Christian and defender of the faith. Towering from the rear is the Ghirlandina, a 12th- to 14th-century campanile, 285 feet tall. Leaning slightly, the bell tower guards the replica of the Secchia Rapita (stolen bucket), which was garnered as booty from a defeated Bolognese.

The facade of the Duomo features a 13th-century rose window by Anselmo da Campione. It also boasts Viligelmo's main entryway, with pillars supported by lions, as well as Viligelmo bas-reliefs depicting scenes from Genesis. But don't confine your look to the front. The south door, the so-called Princes' Door, was designed by Viligelmo in the 12th century and is framed by bas-reliefs that illustrate scenes in the saga of the patron saint. You'll find an outside pulpit from the 15th century, with emblems of Matthew, Mark, Luke, and John.

Inside, there's a vaulted ceiling, and the overall effect is gravely impressive. The Modenese wisely and prudently restored the cathedral during the first part of the 20th century, so that its present look resembles the original design. The gallery above the crypt is an outstanding piece of sculpture, supported by four lions. The pulpit, also intriguing, is held up by two hunchbacks. The crypt, where the body of the patron saint was finally taken, is a forest of columns. In it, you'll find Guido Mazzoni's *Holy Family* group in terra-cotta, which was completed in 1480.

After visiting the crypt, head up the stairs on the left, where the custodian (tip expected) will lead you to the Museum of the Cathedral. In many ways the most intriguing of the Duomo's art displayed here are the metopes, which used to adorn the architecture. Like gargoyles, these profane bas-reliefs are a marvelous change of pace from solemn ecclesiastical art. One, for example, is part bird and part man—with one hoof. But that's not all: He's eating a fish whole.

✪ **Galleria Estense.** Palazzo del Musei, Largo Sant'Agostino 48 (off Via Emilia). ☎ 059/222-145. Gallery, 8,000L ($4.80) adults, free for children 17 and under and seniors 60 and over; library, free. Gallery, Tues and Fri–Sat 9am–7pm, Wed–Thurs 9am–2pm, Sun 9am–1pm; library, Mon–Thurs 9am–7pm, Fri–Sat 9am–1pm.

The Estense Gallery is noted for its paintings from the Emilian or Bolognese school from the 14th to the 18th centuries. The nucleus of the collection was created by the Este family in the heyday of their duchies in Ferrara, and afterward, Modena. Some of the finest work is by Spanish artists, including a miniature triptych by El Greco of Toledo and a portrait of Francesco I d'Este by Velázquez. Other works of art include Bernini's bust of Francesco I, plus paintings by Cosmé Tura, Correggio, Veronese, Tintoretto, Carracci, Reni, and Guercino.

One of the greatest libraries in southern Europe, the **Biblioteca Estense** (☎ 059/222-248), contains around 500,000 printed works and 13,000 manuscripts. An assortment of the most interesting volumes is kept under glass for visitors to inspect. Of these, the most celebrated is the 1,200-page *Bible of Borso d'Este*, bordered with stunning miniatures.

SHOPPING   If you want to go shopping, you can always cruise the car lots of the city (which has more Fiat factories than anywhere else in the world), looking for the best deal and hinting for invitations to one of the Agnelli family's cocktail parties. But if a car is not in your budget, consider a bottle or two of the vinegar that changed the face of salad making forever—balsamic vinegar.

Until the advent of nouvelle cuisine, which fundamentally changed many of the tenets of how North Americans ate, few people outside Italy had ever heard of balsamic vinegar. Today, gastronomes tend to panic in a kitchen without a goodly supply of the stuff, and Modena produces Italy's largest and most aromatic offerings. A worthwhile shop in the town center that sells esoteric food products, as well as bottles of the aromatic vinegar from virtually every producer in the region, is **Fini**, Piazza San Francesco (☎ 059/223-314). **Justi**, Via Capitani 47 (☎ 059/441-203) exports crates of the vinegar throughout Europe, as well as bottles on the premises.

WHERE TO STAY

Canalgrande Hotel. Corso Canalgrande 6, 41100 Modena. ☎ 059/217-160. Fax 059/221-674. 68 rms, 4 suites. A/C MINIBAR TV TEL. 275,000L ($165) double; from 432,000L ($259.20) suite. Rates include breakfast. AE, DC, MC, V. Parking 15,000L ($9). Bus: 7, 12, or 14.

Located in the old town, the Canalgrande Hotel is housed in a 300-year-old stucco palace. It has more atmosphere and charm than the much bigger and more highly rated Hotel Real Fini on Via Emilia. The Canalgrande has elaborate mosaic floors, Victorian-era furniture, carved and frescoed ceilings, and chandeliers. There's a garden behind the hotel whose central flowering tree seems filled with every kind of bird in Modena. Some visitors find the monumental oil paintings of the salons like a museum. Under the basement's vaulted ceiling is a tavern, La Secchia Rapita (the Stolen Bucket).

Hotel Daunia. Via del Pozzo 159, 41100 Modena. ☎ **059/371-182.** Fax 059/374-807. 46 rms. A/C MINIBAR TV TEL. 155,000L ($93) double. Rates include breakfast. AE, DC, MC, V. Parking 25,000L ($15).

Located away from the city center, recently built, this hotel's exterior is a modified 18th-century design. Inside, however, it's modern Italian all the way with gleaming brass, polished woods, eclectic contemporary furniture designs, and marble and tiled floors. The bar is comfortable enough, with a curved wood surface and sleek black wood and leather seating. But the breakfast room has a rather claustrophobic cafeteria feel owing to its long narrow parameters, low ceiling, black-and-white checkerboard floor, and lack of decoration, windows, or adequate lighting. Guest rooms all have private baths and are comfortable, but they also seem rather bare, being composed of light-colored walls and neutral fabrics contrasted by dark wood furnishings with a lack of colorful or patterned accessories to help brighten their interiors. In an unusual arrangement, the hotel restaurant, L'Aragosta, is located on the far side of the city center, and a free taxi service shuttles hungry lodgers back and forth. The restaurant serves numerous variations of pizzas, antipasti, and Italian wines along with traditional regional dishes. A private guarded parking lot ensures the safety of your vehicle.

Hotel Libertà. Via Blasia 10, 41100 Modena. ☎ **059/222-365** or 059/222-305. Fax 059/ 222-502. 50 rms, 1 suite. A/C MINIBAR TV TEL. 190,000L ($114) double; 280,000L ($168) suite. Rates include breakfast. AE, DC, MC, V. Parking 25,000L ($15).

A modern hotel wrapped in an aged exterior, this lodge is mere steps away from the cathedral and the Palazzo Ducale in the heart of the city. Marble and terra-cotta floors run throughout the hotel, and a large sleek bar features plush comfortable leather chairs and couches. Guest rooms favor floral wallpapers and blond wood furniture highlighted by plaid and other geometrically designed fabrics. Some top-floor rooms are made cozy by sloping ceilings that feature skylight windows. All accommodations include a private bathroom. The hotel has an elevator, breakfast room, television lounge, meeting room, and second garage. Several restaurants are close by, and the hotel staff particularly recommends the traditional Da Enzo restaurant located only 25 yards from the front door.

Hotel Roma. Via Farini 44, 41100 Modena. ☎ **059/222-218.** Fax 059/223-747. 53 rms, 2 suites. MINIBAR TV TEL. 135,000L ($81) double; 135,000L–155,000L ($81–$93) suite. Rates include breakfast. AE, DC, MC, V. Parking 15,000L ($9).

Hotel Roma, which became a hotel around 1950, is a buff-and-white neoclassical building about two blocks from the cathedral. The building dates from the 17th century, when it belonged to the duke of Este. It's one of our favorite hotels in its category in Modena. It's also the preferred hotel of many of the opera stars who gravitate to Pavarotti's hometown for concerts and auditions. The windows and doors are soundproof, presumably so anyone can privately imitate his or her favorite diva while practicing an aria. The guest rooms have high ceilings, tasteful colors, and comfortable and attractive furnishings. The lobby is a long skylit room with an arched ceiling, a bar, and a snack bar at the far end.

WHERE TO DINE

✪ **Fini.** Rue Frati Minori 54. ☎ **059/223-314.** Reservations recommended. Main courses 30,000L–50,000L ($18–$30). AE, DC, MC, V. Wed–Sun 12:30–2:30pm and 8–10:30pm. Closed July 25–Aug 25 and Dec 22–Jan 3. MODENESE/INTERNATIONAL.

A visit to this restaurant alone is well worth making the trip to Modena. Proudly maintaining the high reputation of the city's kitchens, Fini is one of the best restaurants you're likely to encounter in Emilia-Romagna. It's Pavarotti's favorite restaurant when he's in town. In spite of its modernized art nouveau decor, including Picasso-esque murals and banquettes, the restaurant was founded in 1912.

For an appetizer, try the creamy green lasagne or the tortellini (prepared in six different ways here—for example, with truffles). For a main dish, the gran bollito misto reigns supreme. A king's feast of boiled meats, accompanied by a selection of four different sauces, is wheeled to your table. The meat board includes zampone, a specialty of Modena, here prepared with stuffed pigs' trotters boiled with beef, a calf's head, ox tongue, chicken, and ham. After all this rich fare, you may settle for the fruit salad for dessert. For wines, Lambrusco is the local choice, and it's superb.

Ristorante Da Enzo. Via Coltellini 17 (off Piazza Mazzini). ☎ **059/225-177.** Reservations recommended. Main courses 13,000L–30,000L ($7.80–$18); fixed-price menus 30,000L–45,000L ($18–$27). AE, DC, MC, V. Tues–Sun noon–3pm and 7–10:30pm. Closed Aug. MODENESE.

Clean, conservative, and well known in Modena, this restaurant lies one floor above street level in an old building in the historic center's pedestrian zone. Specialties of the house include all the classic dishes of Modena, such as pappardelle (wide noodles) with rabbit meat, lasagne verde, several kinds of tortellini, and an array of grilled meats liberally seasoned with herbs and balsamic vinegar. Zampone (stuffed pigs' trotters) is another specialty.

MODENA AFTER DARK

This bustling powerhouse of Italy's industrial machine offers enough evening diversion to amuse an entire assembly line of factory workers and enough culture to absorb an entire theater of Pavarotti fans. Opera arrives in winter at the **Teatro Comunale,** Corso Canal Grande 85 (☎ **059/225-663**). However, culture doesn't sleep all summer. In July and August, Modena presents a series of theater, ballet, opera, and musical performances called **Sipario in Piazza.** You might even get to see Pavarotti perform. For more information contact Ufficio Sipario in Palazzo Comunale, Piazza Grande (☎ **059/206-460**). Tickets range from 15,000 to 30,000L ($9 to $18).

You can always stroll through the neighborhood where everyone seems to gravitate on long hot evenings, the Parco Amendola, to the south of Modena's historic core, filled with ice-cream stands, cafes, and bars.

5 Parma

284 miles NW of Rome, 60 miles NW of Bologna, 75 SE of Milan

Parma, which straddles Via Emilia, was the home of Correggio, Il Parmigianino, Bodoni (of type fame), Toscanini, and Parmesan cheese. It rose in influence and power in the 16th century as the seat of the Farnese duchy.

Upon the extinction of the male Farnese line, Parma came under the control of the French Bourbons. Its most loved ruler, Marie-Louise, widow of Napoléon and niece of Marie-Antoinette, arrived in 1815 after the Congress of Vienna awarded her this duchy. Marie-Louise became a great patron of the arts, and much of the collection she acquired is on display at the Galleria Nazionale (see below). Rising unrest forced her abdication in 1859, and in 1860, following a plebiscite, Parma was incorporated into the kingdom of Italy.

It has also been a mecca for opera lovers such as Verdi, the great Italian composer whose works include Il Trovatore and Aïda. He was born in the small village of Roncole, north of Parma, in 1813. In time, his operas echoed through the Teatro Regio, the opera house that was constructed under the orders of Queen Marie Louise.

Because of Verdi, Parma became a center of music, and even today the opera house is jam-packed in season. It's said that the Teatro Regio is the most "critical Verdi house" in Italy.

Today, Parma, one of Italy's most prosperous cities, is known for its production of Parmesan cheese and prosciutto, as well as the graciousness of its citizens, considered the most polite in all of Italy.

ESSENTIALS

GETTING THERE   By Train   Parma is conveniently served by the Milan-Bologna rail line, with 20 trains a day arriving from Milan (trip time: 80 minutes); the one-way fare is 11,700L ($7). From Bologna, 34 trains per day arrive in Parma (trip time: 1 hour); the one-way fare is 7,200L ($4.30). There are also seven connections a day from Florence; a one-way fare is 15,500L ($9.30); the trip takes 3 hours. For information and schedules call ☎ 05219/771-118.

By Bus   From major towns or cities in Italy, trains are usually more efficent than the buses because of faster connections. However, the bus comes into play if you're planning on visiting provincial towns in the Parma area. Information and schedules are available at the bus terminal at Piazzale Carlo Alberto della Chiesa 7 near the train station (☎ 0521/273-251).

By Car   From Bologna, head northwest along autostrada A1.

VISITOR INFORMATION   The tourist information center is at Piazza del Duomo 5 (☎ 0521/234-735), open Monday to Saturday from 9am to 7pm and Sunday from 9am to 12:30pm.

WHAT TO SEE & DO
THE TOP ATTRACTIONS

✪ **Il Duomo.** Piazza del Duomo. ☎ 0521/235-886. Free admission. Daily 7am–12:30pm and 3–7pm.

Built in the Romanesque style in the 11th century, with 13th-century Lombard lions guarding its main porch, the dusty pink Duomo stands side-by-side with a *campanile* (bell tower) constructed in the Gothic-Romanesque style and completed in 1294. The facade of the cathedral is highlighted by three open-air loggias. Inside, two darkly elegant aisles flank the central nave. The octagonal cupola was frescoed by the "divine" Correggio. Master of light and color, Correggio (1494–1534) was one of Italy's greatest painters of the High Renaissance. His fresco here, *Assumption of the Virgin,* foreshadows the baroque. The frescoes were painted from 1522 to 1534. In the transept to the right of the main altar is a Romanesque bas-relief, *The Deposition from the Cross* by Benedetto Antelami, which is somber, with each face bathed in tragedy. Made in 1178, the bas-relief is the best-known work of the 12th-century artist, who was the most important sculptor of the Romanesque in northern Italy.

✪ **Battistero.** Piazza del Duomo 7. ☎ 0521/235-886. Admission 4,000L ($2.40). Daily 9am–12:30pm and 3–7pm.

Among the greatest Romanesque buildings in northern Italy, the baptistery was the work of Antelami. The project was begun in 1196, although the date it was actually completed is unclear. Made of salmon-colored marble, it's spanned by four open tiers (the fifth one is closed off). Inside, the baptistery is richly frescoed with biblical scenes: a *Madonna Enthroned* and a *Crucifixion.* But it's the sculpture by Antelami that forms the most worthy treasure and provides the basis for that artist's claim to enduring fame.

Abbey of St. John (San Giovanni Evangelista). Piazzale San Giovanni 1. ☎ **0521/ 235-592.** Free admission to church; 4,000L ($2.40) for the pharmacist's shop. Daily 8:30am–noon and 3–6pm.

Behind the Duomo is this church of unusual interest. After admiring the baroque front, pass into the interior to see yet another cupola by Correggio. Working from 1520 to 1524, the High Renaissance master depicted the *Vision of San Giovanni*. Vasari liked it so much that he became completely carried away in his praise, suggesting the "impossibility" of an artist conjuring up such a divine work and marveling that it could actually have been painted "with human hands." Correggio also painted a St. John with pen in hand, in the transept (over the doorway to the left of the main altar). Il Parmigianino, the second Parmesan master, also did some frescoes in the chapel at the left of the entrance. You can visit the abbey, the school, the cloister, and a pharmacist's shop where monks made potions for some six centuries, a practice that lasted until the closing years of the 19th century. Mortars and jars, some as old as the Middle Ages, line the shelves.

Casa Natale e Museo di Arturo Toscanini. Via Rodolfo Tanzi 13. ☎ **0521/285-499.** Admission 3,000L ($1.80). Tues–Sun 10am–1pm; Tues–Sat 3–6pm.

This is the house where the great musician and conductor was born in 1867. Toscanini was unquestionably the greatest orchestral conductor of the first half of the 20th century and one of the most astonishing musical interpreters of all time. He spent his childhood and youth in this house, which has been turned into a museum with interesting relics and a record library, containing all the recorded works that he conducted.

MORE ATTRACTIONS

After viewing Parma's ecclesiastical buildings, you'll find its second batch of attractions conveniently sheltered under one roof at the **Palazzo della Pilotta,** Via della Pilotta 5. This palazzo once housed the Farnese family in Parma's heyday as a duchy in the 16th century. Badly damaged by bombs in World War II, it has been restored and turned into a palace of museums.

✪ **Galleria Nazionale.** In the Palazzo della Pilotta, Piazza della Pace, Via della Pilotta 5. ☎ **0521/233-309.** Admission 12,000L ($7.20) adults, free for children 17 and under and seniors 60 and over. Daily 9am–1:45pm.

The most important component of the Palazzo della Pilotta is the National Gallery. Filled with the works of Parma artists from the late 15th century to the 19th century—notably paintings by Correggio and Parmigianino—the National Gallery offers a limited but well-chosen selection of art. In one room is an unfinished head of a young woman attributed to da Vinci. Correggio's *Madonna della Scala* (of the stairs), the remains of a fresco, is also displayed. But his masterpiece—one of the celebrated paintings of northern Italy—is *St. Jerome with the Madonna and Child*. Imbued with a delicate quality, it represents age, youth, love—a gentle ode to tenderness. In the next room is Correggio's *Madonna della Scodella* (with a bowl), with its agonized faces. You'll also see Correggio's *Coronation*, a golden fresco and a work of great beauty, and his less successful *Annunciation*. One of Parmigianino's best-known paintings, *St. Catherine's Marriage*, is here, with its rippling movement and subdued colors.

You can also view **St. Paul's Chamber,** which Correggio frescoed with mythological scenes, including one of Diana. The chamber faces onto Via Macedonio Melloni. On the same floor as the National Gallery is the **Farnese Theater,** a virtual jewel box, evocative of Palladio's theater at Vicenza. Originally built in 1618, the structure was bombed in 1944 and has been restored. Admission to the theater is included in the admission to the gallery; however, should you wish to visit it and not the gallery, there's a separate charge of 5,000L ($3).

Museo Archeologico Nazionale. In the Palazzo della Pilotta, Piazza della Pace, Via della Pilotta 5. ☎ **0521/233-718.** Admission 4,000L ($2.40) adults, free for children 17 and under and seniors 60 and over. Tues–Sun 9am–2pm.

This most interesting museum houses Egyptian sarcophagi, Etruscan vases, Roman- and Greek-inspired torsos, Bronze Age relics, and its best-known exhibit called *Tabula Alimentaria,* a bronze-engraved tablet dating from the reign of Trajan and excavated at Velleia in the province of Piacenza.

SHOPPING

Parma's most famous food product—Parmesan cheese—or one of its non-Italian clones, is savored all over the world. Virtually every corner market sells thick wedges of the stuff, but if you're looking to buy your cheese in a setting that's both historic and redolent with herbs, spices, and a sense of Old Italy, head for either the **Salumerí Garibaldi,** Via Garibaldi 42 (☎ **0521/234-735**), or its nearby competitor, **Specialitá di Parma,** Via Farini 9 (☎ **0521/233-591**).

If the idea of a spectacular inventory of wine, sold by folk who really know their product, appeals to you, head for the **Enoteca Fontana,** Via Farina 24a (☎ **0521/ 286-037**), which sells bottles from virtually every vineyard in the region.

Hoping to learn more about the region's famous hams and cheeses? There are well-funded bureaucracies in Parma whose sole functions are to encourage the world at large to use greater quantities of the city's tastiest products. They can arrange tours and visits to the region's most famous producers. For information about Parma cheeses, contact the **Consorzio del Parmigiano Reggiano,** Via Gramsci 266 (☎ **0521/292-700**). For insights into the dressing and curing of Parma hams, contact the **Consorzio del Prosciutto di Parma,** Via M. dell' Arpe 8B (☎ **0521/243-987**).

Looking for a souvenir of Parma that's more durable? Head to **Palma,** Via Bixio 17C (☎ **0521/284-939**), for a selection of locally made handcrafts, including ceramics, wood carvings, and textiles.

WHERE TO STAY

Farnese International. Via Reggio 51A, 43100 Parma. ☎ **0521/994-247.** Fax 0521/ 992-317. 76 rms. A/C MINIBAR TV TEL. 169,000L ($101.40) double. Rates include buffet breakfast. AE, DC, MC, V. Free parking outdoors, 12,000L ($7.20) indoors.

This hotel is not up to the standards of the Stendhal (see below) but makes for a good overnight stopover. It's located in a quiet area that's convenient to the town center, airport, and fairs. Parma specialties are served in the hotel restaurant, Il Farnese. The bedrooms are comfortably furnished in Italian marble. Laundry and room service are provided.

Hotel Button. Strada San Vitale 7 (off Piazza Garibaldi), 43100 Parma. ☎ **0521/208-039.** Fax 0521/238-783. 41 rms. TV TEL. 160,000L ($96) double. Rates include continental breakfast. AE, DC, MC, V. Closed July.

Off Piazza Garibaldi, Hotel Button is a local favorite, one of the best bargains in the town center. This is a family-owned and -run hotel, and you're made to feel welcome. Perhaps you'll even join the locals in the lounge gathered around the TV to watch the soccer games. The rooms are simple but comfortably furnished, and generally spacious, although the decor is dull. The hotel doesn't have a restaurant but will serve you a complimentary continental breakfast.

Hotel Verdi. Via Pasini 18, 43100 Parma. ☎ **0521/293-539** or 0521/293-549. Fax 0521/293-559. 17 rms, 3 suites. A/C MINIBAR TV TEL. 290,000L ($174) double; 330,000L ($198) suite. AE, DC, MC, V. Parking 20,000L ($12).

Facing the expansive beauty of the Ducal Gardens, this art nouveau construction has preserved the elegance of its era while meeting the needs of the present-day visitor to Parma. In public areas sheer draperies warm the sunlight to a golden glow reflected off the black-and-gold marble floors. Guest rooms feature wooden parquet floors, briarwood furnishings in period design, fine linen, and a safe. The private bathrooms are lined in marble and include luxurious soaps and body oils as well as the more commonplace hair dryer. The adjacent Santa Croce restaurant offers a refined yet cordial atmosphere resplendent with period art, furnishings, and lighting in which to savor traditional cuisine and fine Italian wines. In the summer, a brick courtyard alive with greenery allows you to dine outdoors. To ensure vehicle safety, a guarded parking garage is situated at the rear of the hotel.

Palace Hotel Maria Luigia. Viale Mentana 140, 43100 Parma. ☎ **0521/281-032.** Fax 0521/231-126. 102 rms, 5 junior suites. A/C MINIBAR TV TEL. 330,000L ($198) double; 500,000L ($300) suite. Rates include breakfast. AE, CB, DC, MC, V. Parking 20,000L ($12).

This hotel, built of brick in 1974 and located near the station, was and still is a welcome addition to the Parma hotel scene. It caters especially to business travelers and is still superior to the Stendhal (see below). Bold colors and molded-plastic built-ins set the up-to-date mood, and the comfortable modern bedrooms feature soundproof walls as well as other amenities such as tiled baths with toiletries. There's a very Italian-looking American bar on the premises. The hotel also has one of the best restaurants in Parma, Maxim's, which serves excellent Italian and international specialties daily. Room service is available around the clock.

Park Hotel Stendhal. Piazzetta Bodini 3, 43100 Parma. ☎ **0521/208-057.** Fax 0521/285-655. 60 rms. A/C MINIBAR TV TEL. 294,000L ($176.40) double. Rates include breakfast. AE, DC, MC, V. Parking 15,000L ($9).

Park Hotel Stendhal sits on a square near the opera house, a few minutes' walk from many of the city's important sights and six blocks south of the station. The bedrooms are well maintained and furnished with contemporary pieces that are reproductions of various styles, ranging from rococo to provincial. Try for one of the traditional-looking rooms where the furnishings are classic with matching fabrics and patterned carpets. Some of the rooms are more standard and modern. There's a traditional American bar and lounge, with comfortable armchairs for before- and after-dinner drinks. La Pilotta, the hotel restaurant, serves a cuisine typical of Parma, with a medley of international dishes. Laundry service and room service are also provided.

WHERE TO DINE

The chefs of Parma are known throughout Italy for the quality of their cuisine. Of course, Parmesan cheese has added just the right touch to millions of Italian meals, and the word *parmigiana* is quite familiar to American diners.

Croce di Malta. Borgo Palmia 8. ☎ **0521/235-643.** Reservations recommended. Main courses 16,000L–26,000L ($9.60–$15.60). AE, DC, MC, V. Mon–Sat 12:30–2:30pm and 7:30–10:30pm. PARMIGIANA.

Local legend has it that angry citizens plotted to assassinate the last duke of Parma while he was drowning in *vino* at this tavern. All the dishes for which Parma is famous are served here, even some esoteric ones, such as cappellotti, a pasta that turns magenta because it's made with beets, or tortelli, made a golden amber with the addition of pumpkin, although another version is made with potatoes. Tagliatelle is served here in almost any style. Other dishes include roast veal stuffed with cheese and chicken flavored with wine and Gorgonzola cheese.

✪ **La Greppia.** Strada Garibaldi 39A. ☎ **0521/233-686.** Reservations required. Main courses 20,000L–40,000L ($12–$24). AE, DC, MC, V. Wed–Sun 12:30–2:30pm and 7:30–10:30pm. Closed July. PARMIGIANA.

La Greppia has an unpretentious decor yet it's near the top of every gourmet's list of the finest dining rooms of Parma. The competition is keen in Parma, but its only serious rival is Parizzi, with which it's locked in a neck-to-neck race. Through a plate-glass window at one end of the dining room, you can see the all-woman staff at work in the kitchen. Leading the team is the co-owner, Paola Cavassini, and her good-natured husband, Maurizio Rossi, who presides over the dining room. The chefs adjust their menus depending on the season. Likely dishes include veal kidneys sautéed with fines herbes and a demi-glacé sauce, breast of chicken with orange sauce, *pappardella alla Greppia* (prepared with cream and dried flap mushrooms), and roast rack of rabbit flavored with thyme. Many dishes are flavored, in season, with fresh thyme or mushrooms, even cherries. All of this good food is served in a building dating from the 17th century. The tarts made with fresh fruit are succulent desserts. Even better, the kitchen is known for its compelling chocolate cake, which one reviewer claimed was much better than the famed Sachertorte served at the Hotel Sacher in Vienna.

✪ **Parizzi.** Strada della Repubblica 71. ☎ **0521/285-952.** Reservations required. Main courses 60,000L–80,000L ($36–$48); fixed-price menu 65,000L ($39). Tues–Sat noon–2:30pm and 7–9:30pm. Closed Dec 24–25. AE, DC, MC, V. PARMIGIANA.

Located in the historic core of Parma, the building that houses Parizzi dates to 1551, when it was first established as an inn. Seated under the restaurant's skylit patio, the people of Parma, known for their exacting tastes and demanding palates, here enjoy the rich cuisine for which their town is celebrated. This restaurant is among the two best in Parma, comparable in cuisine to La Greppia. Both richly deserve their Frommer stars. After you're shown to a table in one of the good-sized dining rooms, a trolley cart filled with antipasti is wheeled before you, containing shellfish and salmon among its many delectable offerings. The stuffed vegetables are especially good (try the zucchini). You might begin with the chef's specialty, crêpes alla parmigiana—that is, crêpes stuffed with Fontina, Parma ham, and ricotta, or with truffles in September. In May you'll want to try the asparagus fresh from the fields. A good main course is the veal scaloppine with Fontina and ham. Desserts include zabaglione laced with marsala.

PARMA AFTER DARK

Life in Parma extends beyond munching on strips of salty ham and cheese. The **Teatro di Reggio,** near Piazza della Pace (☎ **0521/218-910**), is the site of concerts throughout the year as well as the annual midsummer **Concerti Nei Chiostri.**

One of our favorite pubs is **La Corriera Stravagante,** Via C. Prati 4 (☎ **0521/ 52-263**), filled with stonework, wooden tables, and lots of animated clients. Also within the historic center is **Bacco Verde,** Via Cavalloti (no phone), where sandwiches, glasses of beer, and wine are all dispensed in a cramped but engaging setting that's enhanced by antique stonework. If you're looking for a glass or two of some alarmingly esoteric wines, head for the bar section of an establishment recommended in the shopping section, the **Enoteca Fontana,** Via Farina 24A (☎ **0521/286-037**).

In the mood for dancing? Students and the under-25 set gravitate to **Astrolabio,** Via Zarotta 86A (☎ **0521/460-538**), while older folk (i.e., persons 25 to 40) usually opt for the more stylish and nominally more restrained **Disco Nabila,** Via Emilio Lepido 28 (☎ **0521/45-763**).

9 Settling into Venice

One rainy morning as we were leaving our hotel—a converted *palazzo*—decorative stone fell from the lunette, narrowly missing us. For a second it looked as if we were candidates for a gondola funeral cortège to the island of marble tombs, San Michele. In dismay, we looked back at the owner, a woman straight from a Modigliani portrait. From the doorway, she leaned like the Tower of Pisa, mocking the buildings of her city. Throwing up her hands, she sighed: "Venezia, Venezia," then turned and went inside.

Stoically, she had long ago surrendered to the inevitable decay that embraces Venice like at the base of the pilings. Venice is a preposterous monument to both the folly and the obstinacy of humankind. It shouldn't exist . . . but it does, much to the delight of thousands upon thousands of tourists, gondoliers, lacemakers, hoteliers, restaurateurs, and glassblowers.

Centuries ago, in an effort to flee the barbarians, Venetians left drydock and drifted out to a flotilla of "uninhabitable" islands in the lagoon. Survival was difficult enough, but no Venetian has ever settled for mere survival. The remote ancestors of the present inhabitants created the world's most beautiful city.

To your children's children, however, Venice may be nothing more than a legend. It's sinking at a rate of about $2^{1}/_{2}$ inches per decade. It's estimated that if no action is taken soon, one-third of the city's art will deteriorate hopelessly within the next decade or so. Clearly, Venice is in peril. One headline proclaimed, "The Enemy's at the Gates."

But for however long it lasts, the Venice of today, decaying or not, will be one of the highlights of your trip through Italy. It lacks the speeding cars and roaring mopeds of Rome; instead, you make your way through Venice either by boat or on foot. The city would be ideal were it not for the hordes upon hordes—far more than any barbarian invasion—who descend upon Venice today, creating a virtual emergency for those who need space to walk and air to breathe. These masses overwhelm the squares, such as Piazza San Marco, and make thoroughfares almost impossible to navigate.

In the sultry heat of the Adriatic in summer, the canals of Venice become a smelly stew. The steamy and overcrowded months of July and August are the worse times to visit. May and June and September and October are much more ideal.

Although it's one of the most—if not *the* most—enchantingly lovely and evocative cities on earth, you do pay a price, literally and figuratively, for all this beauty. The city is virtually selling its past to the world, even more so than Florence, and anybody who's been here leaves complaining of the outrageous prices.

In addition, tourists have virtually eroded what local life and flavor are left in the city. Since the 19th century, Venice has thrived on its visitors, including the likes of Lord Byron and Thomas Mann, but high prices have forced out many locals who used to live here. They fled across the lagoon to tacky, dreary Mestre, an industrial complex that was launched to help boost the regional economy and make it far less dependent on tourism. Mestre, with its factories, helps keep Venice relatively industry-free, although it spews pollution across the city, which is hardly what the art of Venice needs.

Today the city is trying belatedly to undo the damage that its watery environs and tourist-based economy have wrought. In 1993, after a 30-year hiatus, the canals were once again dredged in an attempt to reduce water loss and reduce the stench brought in with the low tides. In an effort to curb the other 30-year-old problem of residential migration to nearby Mestre, state subsidies are now being offered to the citizens of Venice as an incentive to not only stay but renovate their crumbling properties as well.

The Guggenheim Museum in conjuction with the local government has been working to drain floods of a different sort—namely the crowds of tourists pouring into Piazza San Marco—and the surrounding cathedral, hotels, cafes, and popular vaporetto. The museum is working to open branches in other parts of Venice (the Peggy Guggenheim Collection is already in the Palazzo Venier dei Leoni on the Grand Canal). Two of those sites, the Italian and American pavilions in the Castello Gardens, home of the Venice Biennale, will hopefully draw a big chunk of the tourist flow a mile outside of the San Marco area into Castello Gardens. When the Biennale (June through mid-October, every other year) is not taking place, this area is a veritable ghost town. The other location, a 16th-century salt factory on the Giudecca Canal, is located close to the Peggy Guggenheim Collection, but funnels the crowds away from the San Marco area.

The project also allows for reparations to these properties, with the city kicking in $6.7 million toward renovating the Castello Gardens, and another $3 million investment in the salt factory. Once refurbished, the three sites would all house contemporary art—some of it from among the 6,500 works of the museum's permanent collection that go largely unseen because of a shortage of exhibition space.

In spite of all its problems and relatively modest plans (so far) for saving itself, Venice still endures.

For how long? That is the question.

1 Orientation

ARRIVING

All roads lead not necessarily to Rome but, in this case, to the docks on the mainland of Venice. The arrival scene at the unattractive Piazzale Roma is filled with nervous expectation; even the most veteran traveler can become confused. Whether you arrive by train, bus, car, or airport limo, everyone walks to the nearby docks to select a method of transport to his or her hotel. The cheapest way is by *vaporetto* (public motorboat), the more expensive by gondola or motor launch (see "Getting Around," later in this chapter).

If your hotel lies near one of the public vaporetto stops, you can sometimes struggle with your own luggage until you reach the hotel's reception area. In any event, the one time-tested piece of advice for Venice-bound travelers is that excess baggage is bad news, unless you're willing to pay dearly to have it carried for you. Porters cannot accompany you and your baggage on the vaporetto.

BY PLANE   You can now fly from North America to Venice via Rome on Alitalia. You'll land at the **Marco Polo Aeroporto** (☎ 041/260-6111) at Mestre. Boats or *motoscafo* (shuttle boat) operated by **Cooperative San Marco** (☎ 041/522-2303) depart directly from the airport, taking visitors to a terminal near Piazza San Marco. The fare is 15,000L ($9). The motoscafo runs between the airport and Piazza San Marco with a stop at the Lido and takes about a half hour.

It's less expensive, however, to take a bus from the airport to the public hookup for transportation into Venice. Run by **Azienda Trasporti Veneto Orientale** (☎ 041/520-5530), a shuttle bus links the airport with the Piazzale Roma, costing 5,000L ($3). The trip takes about half an hour, and departures are usually on the hour. Even cheaper is a local bus company, **ACTV** (☎ 041/780-111), whose bus no. 5 makes the run for 1,500L (90¢). The ACTV buses also depart hourly, but take about an hour to reach Piazzale Roma. From Piazzale Roma, you can hook up with a vaporetto to take you to your hotel (or near your hotel).

BY TRAIN   Trains pull into the **Stazione di Santa Lucia,** at Piazzale Roma (☎ 04178/88-088 for information about rail connections). Travel time from Rome is about 5¼ hours; from Milan, 3½ hours; from Florence, 4 hours; and from Bologna, 2 hours. The best—and least expensive—way to get from the station to the rest of town is to take a vaporetto, which departs near the main entrance to the station.

BY BUS   Buses from mainland Italy arrive at Piazzale Roma. For information about schedules, call the **ACTV office** at Piazzale Roma (☎ 041/528-7886). If you're coming from a distant city in Italy, it's better to take the train. But Venice has good bus connections with nearby cities such as Padua. A one-way fare from Padua to Venice (or vice versa) is 5,000L ($3). The cheapest way to reach the heart of Venice from the bus station is by vaporetto.

BY CAR   Venice has autostrada links with the rest of Italy, with direct routes from such cities as Trieste (driving time: 1½ hours), Milan (3 hours), and Bologna (2 hours). Bologna is 94 miles southwest of Venice; Milan, 165 miles west of Venice; and Trieste, 97 miles east. Rome is 327 miles to the southwest.

If you arrive by car, there are several multitiered **parking areas** at the terminus where the roads end and the canals begin. One of the most visible is the **Garage San Marco,** Piazzale Roma (☎ 041/523-5101 or 041/523-2213), near the vaporetto, gondola, and motor launch docks. You'll be charged 34,000L to 46,000L ($20.40 to $27.60) per day, maybe more, depending on the size of your car, and from 20,000L to 33,000L ($12 to $19.80) for 12 hours. From spring to fall this municipal car park is nearly always filled. You're more likely to find parking on **Isola del Tronchetto** (☎ 041/520-7555), which costs 25,000L ($15) per day. From Tronchetto, take vaporetto no. 82 to Piazza San Marco. If you have heavy luggage, you'll need a water taxi. Parking is also available at Mestre.

VISITOR INFORMATION

Visitor information is available at the **Azienda di Promozione Turistica,** Palazzetto Selva-Giardinetti Reali (Molo S. Marco) (☎ 041/522-6356). Summer hours are

daily from 9:30am to 6:30pm; off-season, Monday through Saturday from 9:30am to 3:30pm.

CITY LAYOUT

MAIN ARTERIES & STREETS   Venice lies 2¹/₂ miles from the Italian mainland and 1¹/₄ miles from the open seas of the Adriatic. It's an archipelago of some 117 islands. Most visitors, however, concern themselves only with Piazza San Marco and its vicinity. In fact, the entire city has only *one* piazza, which is San Marco. Venice is divided into six quarters that local residents call *sestieri*. These are **San Marco** (the most frequented), **Santa Croce, San Polo, Castello, Cannaregio,** and **Dorsoduro.**

Many of the so-called streets of Venice are actually **canals,** 150 in all, spanned by a total of 400 bridges. A canal is called a *rio*. Venice's version of a main street is the **Grand Canal,** which is spanned by three bridges: the Rialto, the Academy Bridge, and the stone Railway Bridge. The Grand Canal splits Venice into two unequal parts.

Be prepared for a lot of unfamiliar street designations. A street running alongside a canal is called a *fondamenta,* and a major thoroughfare is known as a *salizzada, ruga,* or *calle larga.* But what's a *sottoportego?* That's a passageway beneath buildings. You'll often encounter the word *campo* when you come to an open-air area. That's a reference to the fact that such a place was once grassy, and in days of yore cattle grazed there.

South of the section called Dorsoduro, which is south of the Grand Canal, is **Canele della Guidecca,** a major channel separating Dorsoduro from the large island of La Guidecca. At the point where Canale della Guidecca meets the Canale di San

Impressions

When I went to Venice—my dream became my address.
                    —Marcel Proust, letter to Madame Strauss, May 1906

Marco, you'll spot the little **Isola di San Giorgio Maggiore,** with a church by Palladio. The most visited islands in the lagoon, aside from the **Lido,** are **Murano, Burano,** and **Torcello.**

FINDING AN ADDRESS   A maniac must have numbered the buildings of Venice at least six centuries ago. The numbering system is completely illogical. Therefore, before you set out for a specific place, get detailed instructions and have someone mark the establishment on your map. Instead of depending on street numbers, try to locate the nearest cross street. Since old signs and numbers have decayed over time, it's best to look for signs posted outside rather than a number.

Even with all the directions and signposts in the world, getting lost in Venice is inevitable, expected, and a great way to explore the city. Still, a little background can't hurt—you can at least try to understand why you're lost. *A helpful hint:* Every building has a street address and a mailing address, which are never the same thing. For example, a business at Calle delle Botteghe 3150 (Botteghe Street) will have a mailing address of San Marco 3150, since it is in the San Marco *sestiere* (district) and all buildings in an individual district are numbered continuously from 1 to 6,000. Therefore, landmarks become important, and one of the biggest landmarks is the Grand Canal that splits the city into two. It does this in a reversed-S pattern rather than a straight line, so the canal can actually appear on more than one side of you at once. Even with that advice, the sun and other navigational devices are valuable resources that can help lead you in the right direction.

It's also helpful to know that the city is divided into six *sestieri:* To the east of the Grand Canal, from north to south, runs Cannaregio, San Marco, and Castello; to the west, from north to south runs Santa Croce, San Polo, and Dorsoduro. Confused yet? Go ahead and factor in that most districts are not clearly marked, either along their boundaries or within them. Also, streets are subdivided into types of streets: You may be on a *fondamenta* (street), *salizzada* (paved road), *calle* (street alongside a canal), or *rio terra* (a filled canal channel now used as a walkway).

Squares also take on their own Venetian character, with only San Marco actually having the *piazza* designation used in other Italian communities—all the other squares are known as *campos.* Now that everything is as clear as the sludgy water that fills a summertime canal at low tide, realize that asking directions and maintaining good humor while being thoroughly disoriented are the most important factors in getting around Venice. It's no wonder that so many tourists stick to the sights immediately surrounding the Piazza San Marco—but press on, get lost, and explore the charming nooks and crannies of Venice unspoiled by the crowds of that famous square.

STREET MAPS   If you really want to tour Venice and experience that hidden, romantic trattoria on a nearly forgotten street, don't even think about using a map that doesn't detail every street and have an index in the back. The best of the lot is the **Falk** map of Venice. It details everything (well, almost), and since it's pocket size, you can open it in the Adriatic winds without fear of it blowing away as many larger maps do. It's sold at many news kiosks and at all bookstores. Another good source is *Frommer's Walking Tours: Venice,* which includes 13 maps of the city and the environs.

NEIGHBORHOODS IN BRIEF

San Marco   Welcome to the center of Venice. Napoléon called it the drawing room of Europe, and it's one crowded drawing room today. The heart of Venetian life for more than a thousand years, it's here that you'll find the major attractions: **Piazza San Marco**, or St. Mark's Square, dominated by St. Mark's Basilica. Just outside the basilica is the campanile, or bell tower, a reconstruction of the one that collapsed in 1902. Around the corner is the **Palazzo Ducale**, or Doge's Palace, with its **Bridge of Sighs.** In spite of these stellar attractions, this is basically a gaudy tourist belt filled with some of the most overpriced coffee shops in the world, including Florian's, founded in 1720, and Quadri, which opened in 1775. The most celebrated watering hole, however, is away from the square—Harry's Bar, founded by Giuseppe Cipriani but made famous by Hemingway. In and around the square are some of the most convenient hotels in Venice (although not necessarily the best) and an array of expensive shops and trattorie catering to the Yankee dollar, the British pound, the German mark, or whatever.

Castello   The shape of Venice is often likened to a fish. If so, Castello is the tail of the fish. The largest and most varied of the six sestieri, Castello is home to many attractions, such as the **Arsensal,** and some of the city's plushest hotels, including the Danieli. One of the district's most notable attractions is the **Gothic Church of Santa Giovanni e Paolo,** or **Zanipolo.** This was the Pantheon of the doges of Venice. Cutting through the sestiere is **Campo Santa Maria Formosa,** one of the largest open squares of Venice. The district's most elegant and frequented street is **Riva degli Schiavoni,** running along the Grand Canal and the site of some of the finest hotels and restaurants in Venice. It's also one of the city's favorite promenades.

Cannaregio   This is the gateway to Venice. It lies away from the railroad station at the northwest side of Venice and is the first of the six sestieri. It shelters about a third of the population of Venice, some 20,000 residents. At its heart is Santa Lucia Station, dating from 1955. The area also embraces the old **Jewish Ghetto,** the first one on the continent. Jews began to move here at the beginning of the 16th century, when they were segregated from the rest of the city. From here, the word *ghetto* later became a generic term all over Europe. Attractions in this area include the **Ca' d'Oro,** the finest example of the Venetian Gothic style of palatial architecture; the **Chiese della Madonna dell'Orto,** a 15th-century church known for its Tintorettos; and **Church of Santa Maria dei Miracoli,** with a Madonna portrait supposedly able to raise the dead. Unless you're coming here to view some church or palace, or even the ghetto, this area of Venice doesn't offer much else, as its hotels and restaurants are not the best. Some of the cheapest lodging is found along Lista di Spagna, immediately to the left as you exit the train station.

San Polo   This is the heart of commerical Venice and the smallest of the six sestieri. It's reached by crossing the **Ponte di Rialto** (Rialto Bridge) spanning the Grand Canal. The shopping here is much cheaper than in the boutiques around Piazza San Marco. One of the major attractions is the **Erberia,** which Casanova wrote about in his 18th-century biography. Both wholesale and retail markets still pepper this ancient site. At its center is the **Church of San Giacomo di Rialto,** oldest in the city. The district also encloses the **Scuola Grande di San Rocco,** a repository of the works of Tintoretto, which is the reason most upmarket tourists visit San Polo. Campo San Polo is one of the oldest and widest squares in Venice and is one of the principal venues for Carnival. San Polo is also filled with moderately priced hotels and a large number of trattorie, many of which specialize in seafood. In general, the hotels and restaurants are cheaper here than along San Marco but not as cheap as those around the Termini in Cannaregio.

Santa Croce This district, which takes its name from an old church that was long ago destroyed, generally follows the snakelike curve of the Grand Canal from Piazzale Roma to a point just short of the Ponte di Rialto. It's split into two rather different neighborhoods. The eastern part is in the typically Venetian style and is one of the least crowded parts of Venice, although it has some of the Grand Canal's loveliest palazzi. The western side is more industrialized and isn't very interesting to explore.

Dorsoduro This district is compared variously to New York's Greenwich Village or London's Chelsea, although in truth it doesn't resemble either section very much. The least populated of the sestieri, it's filled with old homes and half-forgotten churches. It's the southernmost section of the historic district, and its major attraction is the **Gallerie dell'Accademia.** Its second-most-visited attraction is the **Guggenheim Foundation.** It's less trampled than the areas around the Rialto Bridge and Piazza San Marco. Its most famous church is **La Salute,** whose first stone was laid in 1631. The **Zattere,** a broad quay built after 1516, is one of the favorite promenades in Venice. Cafes and pensiones abound in the area, as do trattorie.

LAGOON ISLANDS

The Lido This slim, sandy island cradles the Venetian lagoon, offering protection against the Adriatic Sea. The Lido is Italy's most fashionable bathing resort and site of the fabled Venice Film Festival. It's $7^1/2$ miles long and about half a mile wide, although reaching $2^1/2$ miles at its broadest point. It was the setting for many famous books, including Thomas Mann's *Death in Venice* and Evelyn Waugh's *Brideshead Revisited.* Some of the most fashionable and expensive hotels in Venice are found along the Lido Promenade. The most famous places to stay include the **Grand Hotel Excelsior** and the **Grand Hotel des Bains,** but there are cheaper establishments as well. The best way to get around is by bike or tandem, which can be rented at Via Zara and Gran Viale.

Torcello Lying $5^1/2$ miles northeast of Venice, Torcello is called "the mother of Venice," having been settled in the 9th century. It was once the most populous of the islands in the lagoon, but since the 18th century it has been nearly deserted. If you ever hope to find solitude in Venice, you'll find it here, following in the footsteps of Hemingway. It's visited today chiefly by those wishing to see its **Cattedrale di Torcello,** with its stunning Byzantine mosaics, and to lunch at **Locanda Cipriani.**

Burano Perched $5^1/2$ miles northeast of Venice, Burano is the most populous of the lagoon islands. In the 16th century, it produced the finest lace in Europe. Lace is still made here today, but it's nothing like the product of centuries past. Inhabited since Roman times, Burano is different from either Torcello or Murano. Forget lavish palaces. The houses are often simple and small and painted in deep blues, strong reds, and striking yellows. The island is still peopled by fisherfolk, and one of the reasons to visit is to dine in one of its trattorie where, naturally, the specialty is fish.

Murano This island, located three-quarters of a mile northeast of Venice, has been famed for its glassmaking since 1291. Today Murano is the most visited island in the lagoon. Once a closely guarded secret, Murano glassmaking is now clearly visible to any tourist who wants to visit the island and observe the technique on a guided tour. You can also visit a glass museum, the **Museo Vetrario di Murano,** and see two of the island's notable churches, **San Pietro Martire** and **Santi Maria e Donato.** You will likely be on the island for lunch, and there are a number of moderately priced trattorie to be found here as well.

2 Getting Around

Since you can't hail a taxi, at least not on land, get ready to walk and walk and walk. Of course, you can break up your walks with vaporetto or boat rides.

Provided that you can overcome the problem of getting yourself and your luggage transported safely—and without fisticuffs—to your hotel, you'll be set to embark on one of life's grand experiences: the exploration of Venice.

BY PUBLIC TRANSPORTATION   Much to the chagrin of the once-ubiquitous gondolier, the motorboats, or *vaporetti,* of Venice provide inexpensive and frequent, if not always fast, transportation in this canal-riddled city. The service is operated by **ACTV (Azienda del Consorzio Trasporti Veneziano),** Calle Fisero 1810 (☎ 041/ 528-7886). An *accelerato* is a vessel that makes every stop and a *diretto* makes only express stops. The average fare is 4,000L ($2.40). Note that in the summer the vaporetti are often fiercely crowded. Pick up a map of the system at the tourist office. Rarely will you have to wait more than 15 minutes for the approach of a vaporetto. The vaporetti run daily, with frequent service from 7am to midnight, then hourly between midnight and 7am.

If you'd like to ride more than walk around Venice, several discount tickets—sold at the various stations—are available. The most popular is the Biglietto 24 Ore, costing 15,000L ($9) and offering 24 hours of unlimited travel on any ACTV vaporetto. For 3 full days of unlimited travel, opt for the Biglietto 3 Giorni, costing 30,000L ($18), and, if you plan to be in Venice for 1 week, the Biglietto 7 Giorni, costing 55,000L ($33) and allowing 7 days of unlimited travel. Another bargain is the Biglietto Isole, which is good for unlimited travel for 1 day in one direction on line 12, serving the more remote islands in the lagoon, including the most visited: Murano, Burano, and Torcello. Its cost is 5,000L ($3).

The Grand Canal is long and snakelike and can only be crossed via one of three bridges, including the one at Rialto. If there's no bridge in sight, the trick in getting across is to use one of the **traghetti gondolas** strategically placed at key points. Look for them at the end of any passageway called Calle del Traghetto. Under government control, the fare is ony 1,000L (60¢), allowing you to cross the Grand Canal without having to walk for miles searching for a bridge.

BY WATER TAXI/MOTOR LAUNCH   It costs more than the public vaporetto, but you won't be hassled as much when you arrive with your luggage if you hire one of the city's many private motor launches, called *taxi acquei.* You may or may not have the cabin of one of these sleek vessels to yourself, since the captains fill their boats with as many passengers as the law allows before taking off. Your porter's uncanny radar will guide you to one of the inconspicuous piers where a water taxi waits.

The price of a transit by water taxi from Piazzale Roma (the road and rail terminus) to Piazza San Marco costs 80,000L ($48) for up to four passengers and 100,000L ($60) for more than four. The sailors seem to follow in the footsteps of the most cunning of doges. To their credit, the captains adroitly deliver you, with your luggage, to the canalside entrance of your hotel or on one of the smaller waterways within a short walking distance of your destination. You can also call for a water taxi—try the **Cooperativa San Marco** (☎ 041/522-2303).

BY GONDOLA   When riding in a gondola, two major agreements have to be reached: the price of the ride and the length of the trip. If you even vaguely seem like one of Barnum's suckers, you're likely to be taken on both counts. It's a common sight in Venice to see a gondolier huffing and puffing to take his passengers on a "quickie," often reducing the hour to 15 minutes. The gondolier, with his eye on his

Wonderful city, streets full of water, please advise.

—Robert Benchley

watch, is anxious to dump his load and pick up the next batch of passengers. Consequently, his watch almost invariably runs fast.

There *is* an accepted official rate schedule for gondoliers, but we've never known anyone to honor it. The actual fare depends on how effective you are in standing up to the gondolier's attempt to get more money out of you. The official rate is 100,000L ($60), but virtually no one pays that amount. Prices begin at 150,000L ($90) for up to 50 minutes, maybe a lot more. One gondolier confided to us that he settled for that amount in 1972. Today most gondoliers will ask *at least* double the official rate and will reduce your time aboard to 30 to 40 minutes, or even less. Prices go up after 8pm. In fairness to the gondoliers, it must be said that they have an awful job, which is romanticized out of perspective by the world. They row boatloads of tourists across hot, smelly canals with such endearments screamed at them as "No sing! No pay!" And these fellows must make plenty of lire while the sun shines, as their work ends when the first cold winds blow in from the Adriatic.

Two major **gondola stations** at which you can rent gondolas include Piazza San Marco (☎ **041/520-0685**) and Ponte di Rialto (☎ **041/522-4904**).

ON FOOT　Everybody walks in Venice—there's no other way. The streets are too crowded for bicycles or much else. In summer the overcrowding is so severe that you'll often have a hard time finding room for your feet on the street.

FAST FACTS: Venice

American Express　AMEX is located at San Marco 1471 on Salizzada San Moisé (☎ **041/520-0844**), in the San Marco area. City tours and mail handling can be obtained here. The office is open May to October, Monday to Saturday from 8am to 8pm for currency exchange and from 9am to 5:30pm for all other transactions; November to April, Monday to Friday from 9am to 5:30pm and Saturday from 9am to 12:30pm.

Baby-sitters　In lieu of a central booking agency, arrangements have to be made individually at various hotels. Obviously, the more advanced your notice, the better your chances of getting an English-speaking sitter.

Bookstores　The most centrally located is **Libreria Sansovino** at Bacino Orseolo 84 (☎ **041/522-2623**), lying to the north of Piazza San Marco. It carries both hard- and softcover books in English. Also central, in the vicinity of the American Express office (see above), is **Libreria San Giorgio,** Calle Larga XXII Marzo 2087 (☎ **041/523-8451**). One of the latter store's specialties is books on Venetian art, including Tiepolo among others.

Car Rentals　Obviously you won't need a car in Venice. But you may need one upon departure. You can make arrangements at **Europcar,** Piazzale Roma 496H (☎ **041/523-8616**), or at **Avis,** Piazzale Roma 496G (☎ **041/522-5825**). Both offices are open Monday to Friday from 8:30am to 12:30pm and 2:30 to 6pm and Saturday from 8:30am to noon.

Consulates　There is no **U.S. Consulate** in Venice; the closest is in Milan, at Via Principe Amedeo 2 (☎ **02/290-351**). The **British Consulate** is at Dorsoduro 1051 (☎ **041/522-7207**), open Monday to Friday from 10am to noon and 2 to 3pm.

Currency Exchange   There are many banks in Venice where you can exchange money. You might try the **Deutsche Bank SPA,** San Marco 2216 (☎ 041/520-7024). Many travelers find that **Guetta Viaggi,** San Marco 1261 (☎ 041/528-5101), offers the best rates in Venice.

Dentist   Your best bet is to have your hotel call and set up an appointment with an English-speaking dentist. The American Express office and the British Consulate also have lists.

Doctors   See "Hospitals," below. The suggestion given for a dentist in Venice (see above) also pertains to English-speaking doctors.

Drugstores   If you need a drugstore in the middle of the night, call ☎ 192 for information about which one is open. Pharmacies take turns staying open late. A well-recommended centrally located pharmacy is **International Pharmacy,** Via XXII Marzo 2067 (☎ 041/522-2311).

Emergencies   Call ☎ 113 for police, ☎ 118 for an ambulance, and ☎ 115 to report a fire.

Eyeglasses   This service is available at Benvenuti, Piazza San Marco (☎ 041/523-0430).

Hairdressers/Barbers   A good choice for both women and men is Bruno, Cannaregio 3924 (☎ 041/528-5833). Call first for an appointment.

Holidays   See "When to Go," in chapter 3.

Hospitals   Get in touch with the Civili Riuniti di Venezia, Campo Santi Giovanni e Paolo (☎ 041/529-4111), which is staffed with English-speaking doctors 24 hours a day.

Laundry/Dry Cleaning   Go to Lavaget, Cannaregio 1269 (☎ 041/715-976), on Fondamenta Pescaria off rio Tera San Leonardo. It's open Monday to Friday from 8:15am to 12:30pm and 3 to 7pm. This is the most convenient self-service laundry to the rail station, only a 5-minute walk away. It also does dry cleaning.

Lost Property   The central office for recovering lost property is the Ufficio Oggetti Rinvenuti, an annex to the Municipio (town hall) at San Marco 4134 (☎ 041/274-8225), on Calle Piscopia o Loredan, lying off Rive del Carbon on the Grand Canal. It's open on Monday, Wednesday, and Friday from 9:30am to 12:30pm.

Luggage Storage/Lockers   These services are available at the main rail station, Stazione di Santa Lucia, at Piazzale Roma (☎ 041/715-555). The cost is 5,000L ($3) per package.

Newspapers/Magazines   The *International Herald Tribune* and *USA Today* are sold at most newsstands and in many first-class and deluxe hotels, as are the European editions (in English) of *Time* and *Newsweek.*

Police   See "Emergencies," above.

Post Office   The main post office is at Fondaco dei Tedeschi (☎ 041/271-7111), in the vicinity of the Rialto Bridge. It's open Monday to Saturday from 8:15am to 7pm.

Radio   The main station is run by RAI, the Italian state radio and TV network, and broadcasts in Italian only (you can listen to the music even if you don't speak the tongue). Vatican Radio is received in Venice and often carries English-language news broadcasts. Throughout the night and for part of the day, shortwave radio reception in Venice is excellent, including British (BBC), American (VOA), and Canadian (CBC). At night, the American Armed Forces Network (AFN) from Munich or Frankfurt can be heard on regular AM radio (middle or medium wave).

Rest Rooms These are available at Piazzale Roma and various other places in Venice, but are not as plentiful as they should be. Often you'll have to rely on the facilities of a cafe, although you should purchase something, perhaps a light coffee, as in theory commercial establishments reserve their toilets for customers only. Most museums and galleries have public toilets. You can also use the public toilets at the Albergo Diurno, on Via Ascensione, just behind Piazza San Marco. Remember, *signori* means men and *signore* is for women.

Safety The curse of Venice is the pickpocket artist. Violent crime is rare. But because of the overcrowding in vaporetti and even on the small narrow streets, it's easy to pick pockets. Purse snatchers are commonplace as well. A purse snatcher can dart out of nowhere, grab a purse, and disappear in seconds down some narrow dark alleyway. Keep valuables locked in a safe in your hotel, if one is provided.

Taxes A 19% value-added tax (called IVA) is added to the price of all consumer goods and products and most services, such as those in hotels and restaurants.

Taxis See "Getting Around," earlier in this chapter.

Telegrams/Telex/Fax The post office maintains a telegram and fax service 24 hours a day. You can also call Italcable at ☎ **170** if you wish to send an international telegram; otherwise, call ☎ **186.**

Television The RAI is the chief television network broadcasting in Italy. Every TV in Venice receives three government-sponsored channels—RAI-1, RAI-2, and RAI-3—as well as numerous independent channels including Rete 4, Canale 5, and Italia 1.

Transit Information For flight information, call ☎ **041/260-6111;** for rail information, ☎ **01478/88-088;** and for bus schedules, ☎ **041/528-7886.**

Useful Telephone Numbers To check on the time, call ☎ **161.**

3 Accommodations

Venice has some of the most expensive hotels in the world, including the Gritti Palace and the Cipriani. But there are also dozens of unheralded and moderately priced places to stay, often on narrow, hard-to-find streets. Venice has never been known, however, as an inexpensive destination.

Because of their age and lack of uniformity, hotels in Venice offer widely varying rooms. For example, it's entirely possible to stay in a hotel generally considered " expensive," while paying only a "moderate" rate—that is, if you'll settle for the less desirable accommodation. Many so-called inexpensive hotels and boardinghouses have two or three rooms considered in the "expensive" category. Usually these accommodations are more spacious and open to a view.

The cheapest way to visit Venice is to book in a *locanda,* or small inn, which are rated below the *pensioni* (boardinghouses). Standards are highly variable in these places, many of which are dank, dusty, and dark. Rooms even in many second- or first-class hotels are often cramped, as space has always been a problem in Venice. It's estimated that in this "City of Light," at least half the bedrooms in any category are dark, so be duly warned. Rooms with lots of light opening onto the Grand Canal carry a hefty price tag.

Often facilities normally associated with first-class and deluxe hotels don't exist in Venetian hotels, many of which have floor plans laid out centuries ago. If an elevator is essential for you, always inquire in advance when booking a room.

The most difficult times to find rooms are during the February Carnevale, Easter, and anytime from June to September. Because of the tight hotel situation, it's advisable to make reservations as far in advance as possible. After those peak times, you can virtually have your pick of rooms, as many travelers avoid the damp, cold, and windy months of winter.

Most hotels, if you ask at the reception desk, will grant you a 10% to 15% discount in winter (that is, from November until March 15). But getting this discount may require a little negotiation at the desk. A few hotels close in January if there's no prospect of business.

Should you arrive without a reservation, go to one of the **AVA (Hotel Association) reservations booths** located throughout the area at the train station, the municipal parking garage at Piazzale Roma, the airport, and the information point on the mainland where the highway comes to an end. The main office is at Piazzale Roma (☎ **041/921-638**). You're required to post a deposit to secure a room, which is then rebated on your final hotel bill. Depending on the classification of hotel, deposits range from 20,000L to 75,000L ($12 to $45) per person. All hotel booths are open daily from 9am to 8 or 9pm.

If you want to avoid the crowds, consider staying in San Polo or Dorsoduro, which aren't as touristy and where you stand a chance of experiencing the "real" Venice. Connoisseurs of Venice often prefer the Dorsoduro because as the university part of town, it attracts informal cafes and inexpensive trattorie.

Most visitors, however, prefer the hotels in and around Piazza San Marco, although these tend to be expensive and the district is virtually overrun with visitors. Hotels around the more commercial Ponte de Rialto are often far less expensive, but also less desirable. In the Castello district, hotel prices vary according to the proximity to Piazza San Marco. The farther you go into Castello away from Piazza San Marco, the lower the prices.

NEAR PIAZZA SAN MARCO
VERY EXPENSIVE

✪ **Gritti Palace.** Campo Santa Maria del Giglio, San Marco 2467, 30124 Venezia. ☎ **800/ 325-3535** in the U.S., 416/947-4864 in Canada, or 041/794-611. Fax 041/520-0942. 93 rms, 6 suites. A/C MINIBAR TV TEL. 710,000L–900,000L ($426–$540) double; from 1,700,000L ($1,020) suite. AE, DC, MC, V. Vaporetto: Santa Maria del Giglio.

Gritti Palace, in a stately setting on the Grand Canal, is the renovated four-story palazzo of the 15th-century doge Andrea Gritti. It's a bit starchy, but in terms of prestige, only the Cipriani tops it. The place has a bit of a museum aura to it (some of the original furnishings are roped off, for example). For Ernest Hemingway it was "our home in Venice," and for years it has drawn a select clientele of some of the world's greatest theatrical, literary, political, and royal figures—Queen Elizabeth and Prince Philip, Greta Garbo, Herbert von Karajan, Winston Churchill. The range and variety of guest rooms seem almost limitless, from elaborate suites to relatively small singles. But in every case, the glamor is evident. For a splurge, ask for Hemingway's old suite or the Doge Suite, once occupied by W. Somerset Maugham.

Dining/Entertainment: The hotel's Ristorante Club del Doge is among the best in Venice, but also egregiously priced.

Services: Room service (24 hours), baby-sitting, laundry, valet.

Facilities: Use of the Hotel Excelsior's facilities on the Lido.

Venice Accommodations & Dining

Accommodations

Alloggi ai do Mori **21**
American Hotel **57**
Boston Hotel **44**
Danieli Royal Excelsior **37**
Doni Pensione **34**
Giorgione **5**
Gritti Palace **56**
Hotel Bisanzio **31**
Hotel Campiello **33**
Hotel Carpaccio **65**
Hotel Casanova **43**
Hotel Cipriani **38**
Hotel Concordia **22**
Hotel Do Pozzi **55**
Hotel la Fenice
  et Des Artistes **51**
Hotel Geremia **63**
Hotel Montecarlo **19**
Hotel Rialto **12**
Hotel San Cassiano
  Ca'Favretto **1**
Hotel Scandinavia **17**
La Calcina **59**
La Residenza **30**
Locanda Montin **60**
Locanda Remedio **14**
Locanda Sturion **3**
Londra Palace **32**
Marconi **4**
Pensione Accademia **62**
Pensione Seguso **58**
Saturnia-International **53**
Savoia & Jolanda **36**

Dining

Alfredo, Alfredo **25**
Al Covo **29**
"Al graspo de ua" **11**
Antico Martini **50**
Arcimboldo **18**
Da Ivo **46**
Do Forni **20**
Do Leoni **35**
Favorita **27**
Fiachetteria Toscana **9**
Harry's Bar **40**
Il Milion **8**
La Caravella **52**
La Furatola **64**
Le Chat Qui Rit **23**
Locanda Montin **61**
Nuova Rivetta **24**
Osteria da Fiore **66**
Poste Vecchie **2**
Quadri **41**
Restaurant da Bruno **16**
Ristorante à la Vecia
  Cavana **6**
Ristorante al
  Mondo Novo **15**
Ristorante Belvedere **26**
Ristorante Cipriani **39**
Ristorante Corte
  Sconta **28**
Ristorante da Raffaele **54**
Ristorante Noemi **45**
Rôsticceria
  San Bartolomeo **10**
Sempione **13**
Taverna la Fenice **49**
Tiziano Bar **7**
Trattoria Antica Besseta **67**
Trattoria La Colomba **42**
Trattoria alla Madonna **48**
Vini da Arturo **47**

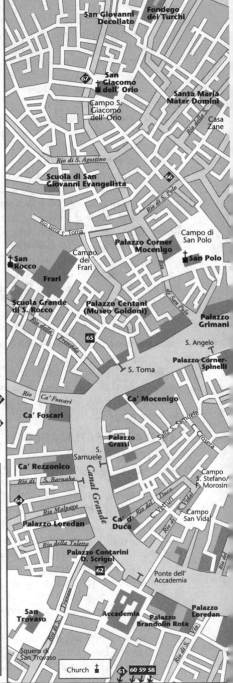

Near the Stazione FS. S. Lucia

3-0689

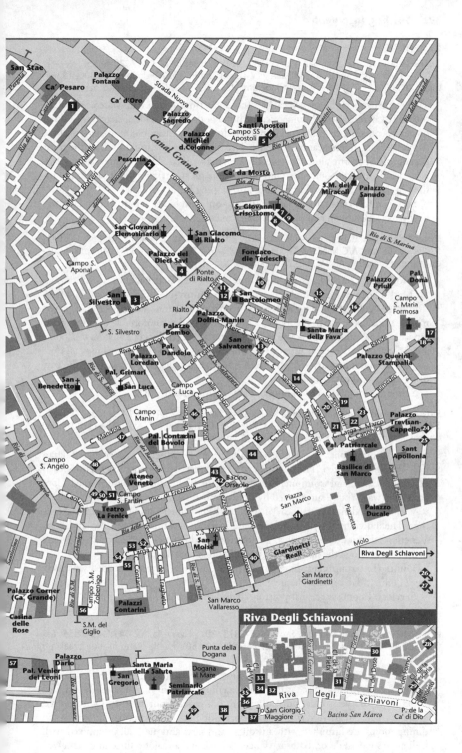

San Stae

Ca' Pesaro

1

Rio di Sant'

Palazzo
Fontana

Strada Nuova

Ca' d'Oro

Palazzo
Sagredo

Palazzo
Michiel
d.Colonne

Santi Apostoli
Campo SS
Apostoli **5** **6**

Rio D. Santi

Apostoli

Rio della Pietà

Canal Grande

Ca' da Mosto

Rio di
S.G. Crisostomo

S.M. dei
Miracoli

Palazzo
Sanudo

Pescaria

2

S. Giovanni
Crisostomo **7** **9**
8

Rio di S. Marina

Calle del Campanile

Calle D. Botteri

Rio della Racchetta

Fond. delle Prigioni

San Giovanni
Elemosinario

San Giacomo
di Rialto

Campo S.
Aponal

Palazzo del
Dieci Savi

4

Fondaco
die Tedeschi

Ponte
di Rialto

Palazzo
Priuli

Pal.
Dona

Campo
S. Maria
Formosa

San
Silvestro

3

Rio del Vin

11
12

San
Bartolomeo **10**

Rialto

Riva del Ferro

Stagneri

Rio della Fava

Salizzada S. Lio

15

16

17
18

S. Silvestro

Palazzo
Dolfin-Manin

Palazzo
Bembo

Merc. S. Salvador

Santa Maria
della Fava

C. Bande

Riva del Carbon

Pal.
Dandolo

San
Salvatore **13**

Merc.

C. Larga Mazzini

Palazzo Querini-
Stampalla

Palazzo
Loredan

Merc.

Rio di S. Salvador

Merc. Orologio

Rimedio

Pal. Grimani

San Luca

Campo
S. Luca

14

Salvatore

San
Benedetto

Campo
Manin

Calle Fuseri

Calle Cortoni

Fianchei

C. d. Teatro

C. Stechetti

19

23

Palazzo
Trevisan-
Cappello **24**

25

46

21
22

Larga S. Marco

Pal. Contarini
del Bovolo

47

45

Merc. Orologio

Pal. Patriarcale

Sant
Apollonia

Campo
S. Angelo

48

44

Basilica di
San Marco

Rio di Palazzo

Rio di S.M.

Rio di S. Angelo

Ateneo
Veneto

43
42

Bacino
Orseolo

Piazza
San Marco

41

Piazzetta

Palazzo
Ducale

49 50 51

Campo
S. Fantin

Pisc. di Frezzeria

Frezzeria

Ascension

Teatro
La Fenice

Caolina

C. della Veste

C. Larga XXII Marzo

53 52

54

55

S.S. Moise

San
Moise

Giardinetti
Reali

Molo

Riva Degli Schiavoni →

Palazzo Corner
(Ca' Grande)

Campo S.M.
Zobenigo

56

Calle Contarini

Calle del Traghetto

Calle Vallaresso

San Marco
Giardinetti

26

27

Casina
delle
Rose

S.M. del
Giglio

Palazzi
Contarini

San Marco
Vallaresso

Palazzo
Dario

Pal. Venier
dei Leoni

57

Rio D. Fornace

San
Gregorio

Santa Maria
della Salute

Seminario
Patriarcale

Punta della
Dogana

Dogana
al Mare

Rio di S. Moise

Riva Degli Schiavoni

30

28

C. del Forno

C. de la
Pescaria

C. della
Canonica

33

34 **32**

31

Ca' di Dio

C. del Dose

Riva degli Schiavoni

39

38

35

36

37

To San Giorgio
Maggiore

Bacino San Marco

P. de la
Ca' di Dio

Expensive

Hotel Casanova. Frezzeria, San Marco 1284, 30124 Venezia. ☎ **041/520-6855.** Fax 041/
520-6413. 45 rms, 5 suites. A/C MINIBAR TV TEL. 350,000L ($210) double; 440,000L ($264)
triple; 455,000L ($273) suite. Rates include breakfast. AE, DC, MC, V. Vaporetto: San Marco.

This former private home is located a few steps from Piazza San Marco. Although
the name Casanova sounds romantic, the hotel doesn't have a lot of character. It does,
however, contain a collection of church art and benches from old monasteries. These
sit on flagstone floors near oil portraits. The modernized bedrooms are for the most
part devoid of charm, although generally well maintained. The accommodations vary
considerably in size—some are quite small. The most intriguing units are found on
the top floor, with exposed brick walls and sloping beam ceilings.

Services: Concierge, room service (drinks only, no food) 7am to 10pm, laundry,
newspaper delivery on request, twice-daily maid service.

Hotel Concordia. Calle Larga, San Marco 367, 30124 Venezia. ☎ **041/520-6866.** Fax 041/
520-6775. 55 rms. A/C MINIBAR TV TEL. 290,000L–560,000L ($174–$336) double. Rates include buffet breakfast. AE, DC, MC, V. Vaporetto: San Marco.

The four-star Concordia is the only hotel in Venice that has rooms overlooking
St. Mark's Square. The completely renovated, century-old hotel is housed in a five-
story russet-colored building with stone-trimmed windows. A series of gold-plated
marble steps takes you to the lobby, where you'll find a comfortable bar area, good
service, and elevators to whisk you to the labyrinthine corridors upstairs. All bedrooms
are decorated in a Venetian antique style and contain, among other amenities, an electronic safe and a hair dryer. Light meals and Italian snacks are available in the bar;
otherwise only breakfast is served.

Services: Room service (24 hours), baby-sitting, laundry valet.

Saturnia-International. Calle Larga XXII Marzo, San Marco 2398, 30124 Venezia. ☎ **041/
520-8377.** Fax 041/520-7131. 95 rms. A/C MINIBAR TV TEL. 300,000L–520,000L ($180–$312)
double. Rates include breakfast. AE, DC, MC, V. Vaporetto: San Marco.

Saturnia-International was skillfully created from a 14th-century Venetian palazzo
near Piazza San Marco. The hotel is not as commercially oriented as the Moncaco
& Grand Canal, and is infinitely superior to the highly touted but cramped Flora
across the way. You're surrounded by richly embellished beauty here—a grand hallway with a wooden staircase, heavy iron chandeliers, fine paintings, and beamed ceilings. The individually styled bedrooms are spacious and furnished with chandeliers,
Venetian antiques, tapestry rugs, gilt mirrors, and ornately carved ceilings. Many
bedrooms overlook the hotel's quiet and dignified courtyard.

Dining/Entertainment: Its restaurant, La Caravella, is recommended separately
(see "Dining," later in this chapter).

Services: Room service, baby-sitting, laundry, valet.

Moderate

Hotel do Pozzi. Corte do Pozzi, San Marco 2373, 30124 Venezia. ☎ **041/520-7855.** Fax
041/522-9413. 35 rms. MINIBAR TV TEL. 250,000L ($150) double. Rates include breakfast.
AE, DC, MC, V. Vaporetto: Santa Maria del Giglio.

Small, modernized, and centrally located just a short stroll from the Grand Canal and
Piazza San Marco, this place is more like a country tavern than a hotel. Its original
structure is 200 years old, and it opens onto a paved front courtyard with potted
greenery. You can arrive via water taxi, boat, gondola, or vaporetto. The sitting and
dining rooms are furnished with antiques (and near antiques), all intermixed with
utilitarian modern decor. Baths have been added, and a major refurbishing has given
everything a fresh touch. Laundry and baby-sitting are available.

Hotel La Fenice et Des Artistes. Campiello de la Fenice, San Marco 1936, 30124 Venezia. ☎ **041/523-2333.** Fax 041/520-3721. 65 rms, 4 suites. TV TEL. 310,000L ($186) double; 420,000L ($252) suite. Rates include breakfast. AE, DC, MC, V. Vaporetto: San Marco.

This hotel offers widely varying accommodations in two connected buildings, each at least 100 years old. One building is rather romantic, although a bit timeworn, with an impressive staircase leading to the overly decorated bedrooms (one room was once described as "straight out of the last act of *La Traviata*, enhanced by small gardens and terraces"). Your satin-lined room may have an inlaid desk and a wardrobe painted in the Venetian manner to match a baroque bed frame. The carpets might be thin, however, and the fabrics aging. The bedrooms in the other building are far less glamorous, with modern, rather sterile furniture. All but about three of the rooms are air-conditioned.

Hotel Montecarlo. Calle dei Specchieri, San Marco 463, 30124 Venezia. ☎ **800/528-1234** or 041/520-7144. Fax 041/520-7789. 48 rms. A/C TV TEL. 180,000L–400,000L ($108–$240) double. Rates include breakfast. AE, DC, MC, V. Vaporetto: San Marco.

Located just a 2-minute walk from Piazza San Marco, this hotel was established some years ago in a 17th-century building, but was recently renovated to include modern baths. The upper hallways are lined with paintings by Venetian artists. The double rooms are comfortably proportioned and decorated with Venetian style furniture and Venetian-glass chandeliers. The hotel's restaurant, Antico Pignolo, serves lunch and dinner and features both Venetian and international dishes.

Hotel Scandinavia. Campo Santa Maria Formosa, Castello 5240, 30122 Venezia. ☎ **041/522-3507.** Fax 041/523-5232. 34 rms. A/C MINIBAR TV TEL. 300,000L–500,000L ($180–$300) double. Rates include breakfast. AE, MC, V. Vaporetto: San Zaccaria or Rialto.

This hotel is not in San Marco—it's in neighborhing Castello—but it has a convenient location not far from Piazza San Marco, so we've placed it in this section. A radical overhaul in 1992 added a third star to this hotel's rating. The entrance to the hotel, located in an old Venetian palace, is set behind a dark-pink facade just off one of the most colorful squares in Venice. The public rooms are filled with copies of 18th-century Italian chairs, Venetian-glass chandeliers, and a re-created rococo decor. The bedrooms are decorated in the Venetian style, but modern comforts have been added. A lobby lounge overlooks Campo Santa Maria Formosa.

INEXPENSIVE

Alloggi ai do Mori. Calle Larga San Marco, San Marco 658, 30124 Venezia. ☎ **041/520-4817.** Fax 041/520-5328. 11 rms, 7 with bath. TV TEL. 90,000L–105,000L ($54–$63) double without bath, 140,000L–160,000L ($84–$96) double with bath. MC, V. Vaporetto: San Marco.

Don't expect a tuckaway or obscure corner of Venice if you check into this small-scale hotel, as it's about 10 paces from the densest concentration of nonstop tourists in Europe. You'll have to balance your need for space with your love of panoramas here, as the lower-level rooms of this circa 1450 town house are larger, but don't have any particular views, whereas rooms on the 3rd and 4th floor are cramped but have sweeping panoramas over the Byzantine-inspired domes of San Marco's basilica. The site is frequently upgraded, re-wallpapered, and repainted by the conservation-minded owner, Antonella Bernardi, who's often stationed within the reception area on the building's second floor. The dozens of cafes within the neighborhood, some of them celebrated, compensate for the fact that no meals are served here. It derives its name from the metallic moors who exit from the Duomo's nearby campanile to strike chimes at hourly intervals. Most of the noise from the surrounding neighborhood is muffled within the bedrooms thanks to double-paned windows. Furniture within them is simple and modern, with few attempts to duplicate the styles of yesteryear.

Boston Hotel. Ponte dei Dai, San Marco 848, 30124 Venezia. ☎ **041/528-7665.** Fax 041/
522-6628. 42 rms. TEL. 170,000L–290,000L ($102–$174) double. Rates include buffet breakfast. AE, DC, MC, V. Closed Nov–Feb. Vaporetto: San Marco.

Built in 1962, the Boston Hotel is just a whisper away from St. Mark's. The hotel
was named after an uncle who left to seek his fortune in Boston . . . and never returned. The little living rooms combine the old and the new, containing many antiques and Venetian ceilings. For the skinny guest, there's a tiny, self-operated elevator
and a postage-stamp-sized street entrance. Most of the bedrooms, with parquet floors,
have built-in features, snugly designed beds, chests, and wardrobes. Several even have
tiny balconies that open onto canals. Some rooms are air-conditioned, and a TV is
available upon request.

Locanda Remedio. Calle del Remedio, Castello 4412, 30122 Venezia. ☎ **041/520-6232.**
Fax 041/521-0485. 12 rms. A/C MINIBAR TV TEL. 170,000L–230,000L ($102–$138) double.
Rates include breakfast. MC, V. Vaporetto: San Zaccharia.

This is another hotel that is not actually in San Marco, but in nearby Castello; it's
so close to Piazza San Marco, however, we've included it here. This hotel was constructed around 1500, in a gray fronted style that's not as intricate as the many nearby
buildings. From the street-level reception area, you climb a narrow flight of stairs up
to the public salons that have been turned into private bedrooms. Each has simple
but durable furniture, but none has a particularly memorable view. Breakfast is served
in a room graced with faded ceiling frescoes overlooking a neighborhood that despite
its proximity to San Marco is surprisingly calm and quiet.

ON OR NEAR RIVA DEGLI SCHIAVONI
VERY EXPENSIVE

✪ **Danieli Royal Excelsior.** Riva degli Schiavoni, Castello 4196, 30122 Venezia. ☎ **800/
325-3535** in the U.S. and Canada, or 041/522-6480. Fax 041/520-0208. 231 rms, 9 suites.
A/C MINIBAR TV TEL. 695,000L–845,000L ($417–$507) double; from 1,255,000L ($753) suite.
Rates include buffet breakfast. AE, DC, MC, V. Vaporetto: San Zaccaria.

Danieli Royal Excelsior was built as a grand showcase by the doge Dandolo in the
14th century. In 1822 it was transformed into a deluxe "hotel for kings." It's the most
ornate hotel in Venice, surpassed only by the Cipriani and the Gritti Palace. Placed
in a most spectacular position, right on the Grand Canal, it has sheltered not only
kings, but princes, cardinals, ambassadors, and such literary figures as George Sand
and Charles Dickens.

You enter into a four-story-high stairwell, with Venetian arches and balustrades.
The atmosphere is luxurious throughout—even the balconies opening off the main
lounge are illuminated by stained-glass skylights. The bedrooms range widely in price,
dimension, decor, and vistas, and those opening onto the lagoon cost a lot more. De
Musset and Ms. Sand made love in Room 10, the most requested accommodation
at the Danieli.

Dining/Entertainment: From the rooftop dining room, Terrazza Danieli, you
have an unblocked view of the canals and "crowns" of Venice. There's also an intimate cocktail lounge and a bar offering piano music.

Services: Room service, baby-sitting, laundry, valet.

Facilities: Hotel launch to the Lido in summer.

EXPENSIVE

✪ **Londra Palace.** Riva degli Schiavoni, Castello 4171, 30122 Venezia. ☎ **041/520-0533.**
Fax 041/522-5032. 53 rms, 33 junior suites. A/C MINIBAR TV TEL. 310,000L–620,000L ($186–
$372) double; 520,000L–720,000L ($312–$432) junior suite. Rates include breakfast. AE, DC,
MC, V. Vaporetto: San Zaccaria.

Londra Palace is a six-story gabled manor with 100 windows on the Venetian lagoon, a few yards from Piazza San Marco. The hotel's most famous patron was arguably Tchaikovsky, who wrote his *Fourth Symphony* in Room 108 in December 1877. He also composed several other works here. The cozy reading room off the main lobby is reminiscent of an English club, with leaded windows and paneled walls with framed blowups of some of Tchaikovsky's sheet music. The bedrooms are luxuriously furnished, often with lacquered Venetian furniture. Romantics ask for one of the two attic rooms decorated in the Regency style with beamed ceilings. The courtyard rooms are quieter and cheaper, opening onto rooftop views of Venice instead of the Grand Canal.

Dining/Entertainment: The hotel has a popular piano bar and an excellent restaurant, Do Leoni.

Services: Room service, baby-sitting, laundry, valet.

Facilities: Conference hall.

Savoia & Jolanda. Riva degli Schiavoni, Castello 4187, 30122 Venezia. ☎ **041/520-6644.** Fax 041/520-7494. 80 rms, 3 suites. TEL. 320,000L–350,000L ($192–$210) double; from 450,000L ($270) suite. Rates include breakfast. AE, DC, MC, V. Vaporetto: San Zaccaria.

Savoia & Jolanda occupies a prize position on Venice's main street, with a lagoon at its front yard. The hotel was established at the turn of the century as one of the most prominent along Riva degli Schiavoni, transformed from an old Venetian palazzo. Most of the bedrooms have a view of the boats and the Lido. Although its exterior reflects much of old Venice, the interior is somewhat spiritless. However, the staff makes life here comfortable and relaxed. The modern bedrooms have plenty of space for daytime living as they contain desks and armchairs. An addition to the hotel contains 20 rooms, each with air-conditioning, minibar, and TV.

MODERATE

Hotel Bisanzio. Calle della Pietà, Castello 3651, 30122 Venezia. ☎ **800/528-1234** in the U.S., or 041/520-3100. Fax 041/520-4114. 43 rms, 4 suites. A/C MINIBAR TV TEL. 330,000L ($198) double. Rates include buffet breakfast. AE, DC, MC, V. Vaporetto: San Zaccaria.

Lying a few steps from St. Mark's Square, in one of the oldest parts of Venice, this hotel offers hospitality and a good standard of service. Occupying the former home of sculptor Alessandro Vittoria, the hotel has an elevator and terraces, plus a private little bar and a mooring for gondolas and motorboats. The bedrooms are generally quiet, each decorated in a Venetian antique style. Amenities include 24-hour room service, baby-sitting, and laundry. The lounge opens onto a traditional old Venetian courtyard.

INEXPENSIVE

Doni Pensione. Calle de Vino, Castello 4656, 30122 Venezia. ☎ **041/522-4267.** Fax 041/522-4267. 12 rms, 2 with bath. 100,000L ($60) double without bath, 140,000L ($84) double with bath. Rates include breakfast. No credit cards. Vaporetto: San Zaccaria.

Doni Pensione sits in a private position, about a 3-minute walk from St. Mark's. Most of its very basic rooms either overlook a little canal, where four or five gondolas are usually tied up, or a garden with a tall fig tree. Simplicity (and cleanliness) prevails, especially in the pristine and down-to-earth bedrooms.

Hotel Campiello. Campiello del Vin, Castello 4647, 30122 Venezia. ☎ **041/520-5764.** Fax 041/520-5798. 16 rms. A/C TV TEL. 190,000L–240,000L ($114–$144) double. Rates include breakfast. AE, MC, V. Closed Jan. Vaporetto: San Zaccaria.

The pink-fronted Venetian town house that contains this hotel dates back to the 1400s. Today you'll find cost-conscious Venetian-style accommodations that were renovated in the mid-1990s. Although rated only two stars by the local tourist office, it's better than its status would imply, partly because of a spectacular location nearly adjacent to the more expensive hotels, and also because of such Renaissance touches as marble mosaic floors, lots of carefully polished hardwoods, and a helpful staff. Elderly or infirm guests sometimes opt for the only room with a separate entrance, a ground-floor hideaway that fortunately, has only been flooded by high tides once during the previous century. Only breakfast is served.

La Residenza. Campo Bandiera e Moro, Castello 3608, 30122 Venezia. ☎ **041/528-5315.** Fax 041/523-8859. 16 rms. A/C MINIBAR TV TEL. 220,000L ($132) double. Rates include breakfast. MC, V. Vaporetto: Arsenale.

La Residenza is in a pleasingly proportioned 14th-century building that looks a lot like a miniature version of the Doge's Palace. It's on a residential square where children play soccer and older people feed the pigeons. After gaining access (just press the button outside the entrance), you'll pass through a stone vestibule lined with ancient Roman columns before ringing another bell at the bottom of a flight of stairs. First an iron gate and then a door will open into an enormous salon filled with elegant antiques, 300-year-old paintings, and some of the most marvelously preserved walls in Venice.

The bedrooms are far less opulent than the public salons, however, and are furnished with contemporary pieces and functional accessories. The choice ones are usually booked far in advance, especially for Carnival season.

NEAR THE PONTE DI RIALTO
EXPENSIVE

Hotel Rialto. Riva del Ferro, San Marco 5149, 30124 Venezia. ☎ **041/520-9166.** Fax 041/523-8958. 77 rms. A/C MINIBAR TV TEL. 300,000L ($180) double. Rates include breakfast. AE, DC, MC, V. Vaporetto: Rialto.

Hotel Rialto opens right onto the Grand Canal at the foot of the Ponte di Rialto, the famous bridge flanked with shops. Its bedrooms are quite satisfactory, combining modern or Venetian furniture with ornate Venetian ceilings and wall decorations. The hotel has been considerably upgraded to second class, and private baths with tub or shower have been installed in each unit. The most desirable and expensive double rooms overlook the Grand Canal, and these go first.

Dining/Entertainment: The in-house dining room and its adjacent bar are open daily, but only between April and October.

Services: Concierge, room service (7am to midnight), newspaper delivery on request.

INEXPENSIVE

✪ **Locanda Sturion.** Calle des Sturion, San Polo 679, 30125 Venezia. ☎ **041/523-6243.** Fax 041/522-8378. 11 rms. A/C MINIBAR TV TEL. 200,000L–320,000L ($120–$192) double. Rates include continental breakfast. AE, DC, MC, V. Vaporetto: Rialto.

In the early 1200s, the Venetian doges commissioned a site where foreign merchants, who traded goods at the time near the Rialto Bridge, could be sheltered for the night after a hard day's bargaining. After long stints as a private residence, the site continues its tradition of catering to the overnight needs of foreign visitors. A private entrance leads up four steep flights of marble steps, past private apartments on the lower floors, to a labyrinth of cozy, clean, but not overly large bedrooms. Most have views over the terra-cotta rooftops of this congested neighborhood; two, however, open onto views of the Grand Canal. Bedrooms have wooden headboards and functional and somewhat old-fashioned but livable furniture. The intimate breakfast room is a honey: It's almost like a parlor with red brocaded walls, a Venetian chandelier, and a trio of big windows opening onto the Grand Canal.

Marconi. Riva del Vin, San Polo 729, 30125 Venezia. ☎ **041/522-2068.** Fax 041/522-9700. 26 rms. A/C MINIBAR TV TEL. 164,000L–327,000L ($98.40–$196.20) double. Rates include breakfast. AE, MC, V. Vaporetto: Rialto.

Marconi was built in 1500 when Venice was at the height of its naval supremacy. The drawing-room furnishings would be appropriate for visiting archbishops. The hotel lies less than 50 feet from the much portraited Rialto Bridge. The Maschietto family operates everything efficiently. Only four of the lovely old bedrooms open onto the Grand Canal, and these, of course, are the most eagerly sought after. Meals are usually taken in an L-shaped room with Gothic chairs. In fair weather, the sidewalk tables facing the Grand Canal are preferred by many.

IN CANNAREGIO
EXPENSIVE

Giorgione. SS. Apostoli, Cannaregio 4587, 30131 Venezia. ☎ **041/522-5810.** Fax 041/523-9092. 70 rms, 8 suites. A/C MINIBAR TV TEL. 310,000L–350,000L ($186–$210) double; 390,000L–420,000L ($234–$252) suite. Rates include buffet breakfast. AE, DC, MC, V. Vaporetto: Ca' d'Oro.

In spite of modernization, the decor here is traditionally Venetian. The lounges and public rooms are equipped with fine furnishings and decorative accessories. Likewise, the comfortable and stylish bedrooms are designed to coddle guests. The hotel also has a typical Venetian garden. It's rated second class by the government, but the Giorgione maintains higher standards than many of the first-class establishments. Only breakfast is served.

INEXPENSIVE

Hotel Geremia. Campo San Geremia, Cannaregio 290A, 30121 Venezia. ☎ **041/716-245.** Fax 041/524-2342. 20 rms, 14 with bath. TV TEL. 125,000L ($75) double without bath, 190,000L ($114) double with bath. Rates include breakfast. Discounts of 20% in winter. AE, MC, V. Vaporetto: Ferrovie.

For years, this small-scale hotel survived as a low-cost, one-star hotel that many guests considered worthy of two-star status. In 1997, the government finally raised its status to two stars, a long-awaited event that justified an almost immediate increase in the rates. In a modernized turn-of-the-century setting, this hotel is a 5-minute walk from the railway station. Inside, you'll find a well-maintained roster of pale-green bedrooms, none of which have water views, and some of whose bathrooms are shared by other guests on the same hallway. There's no elevator on the premises, but St. Mark's Square is within a brisk 25-minute walk, and no one can deny that the price, despite the recent increase, is still relatively appealing. Each room contains a safe for valuables.

IN SAN POLO
MODERATE

Hotel Carpaccio. San Tomà, San Polo 2765, 30125 Venezia. ☎ **041/523-5946.** Fax 041/524-2134. 20 rms. MINIBAR TV TEL. 310,000L ($186) double. Rates include breakfast. MC, V. Closed mid-Nov through Feb. Vaporetto: San Tomà.

Don't be put off by the narrow, winding alleyways that lead to the wrought-iron entrance of this second-class hotel—the building was meant to be approached by

---

🏠 Family-Friendly Hotels

American Hotel *(see p. 398)*   This secluded hotel is located across the Grand Canal away from the tourist hordes. It's a solid moderately priced choice where many rooms are rented as triples.

Pensione Accademia *(see p. 399)*   The best of the *pensioni* of Venice, this villa has a garden and large rooms. The former Russian Embassy was the fictional home of Katharine Hepburn in the film classic *Summertime*.

Pensione Seguso *(see p. 399)*   An antique-filled palace dating from the 15th century, this is a relatively secluded family-type place where the half-board rates are good value.

Quattro Fontane *(see p. 401)*   Long a Lido family favorite, this hotel guarantees summertime fun. It's somewhat like staying in the big chalet of a Venetian family. There's a private beach, too.

---

gondola. Once inside, you'll realize that your location in the heart of the oldest part of the city justifies your confusing arrival. This building used to be the Palazzo Barbarigo della Terrazza, and part of it is still reserved for private apartments. The tasteful and spacious bedrooms are filled with serviceable furniture. The salon is decorated with gracious pieces, marble floors, and a big arched window overlooking the Grand Canal. Breakfast is the only meal served.

IN SANTA CROCE
MODERATE
Hotel San Cassiano Ca' Favretto. Calle della Regina, Santa Croce 2232, 30135 Venezia. ☎ **041/524-1768.** Fax 041/721-033. 36 rms. A/C MINIBAR TV TEL. 190,000L–343,000L ($114–$205.80) double. Rates include breakfast. AE, DC, MC, V. Vaporetto: San Stae.

Hotel San Cassiano Ca' Favretto used to be the studio of the 19th-century painter Giacomo Favretto. The hotel's gondola pier and the dining room porch both afford views of the lacy facade of the Ca' d'Oro, sometimes considered the most beautiful building in Venice. The building is a former 14th-century palace, and the present owner has worked closely with Venetian authorities to preserve the original details, which include a 20-foot beamed ceiling in the entrance area. Patrons have included George McGovern and guests of the U.S. Embassy. Fifteen of the conservatively decorated rooms overlook one of two canals, and many of them are filled with antiques or high-quality reproductions.

IN DORSODURO
MODERATE
American Hotel. Campo San Vio, Dorsoduro 628, 30123 Venezia. ☎ **041/520-4733.** Fax 041/520-4048. 29 rms. A/C MINIBAR TV TEL. 320,000L ($192) double; 380,000L ($228) triple. Rates include buffet breakfast. AE, MC, V. Vaporetto: Accademia.

Set on a small waterway, the American Hotel (there's nothing American about it) lies in an ocher building across the Grand Canal from the most heavily touristed areas. It's one of your best budget bets in Venice. The modest lobby is filled with murals, warm colors, and antiques, and the location is perfect for anyone wanting to avoid the crowds that descend on Venice in summer. The bedrooms are comfortably furnished in a Venetian style, but they vary in size; some of the smaller ones are a bit cramped. Many rooms with their own private terrace face the canal. On the second floor is a beautiful terrace where guests can relax over drinks. The staff is attentive and helpful.

La Calcina. Zattere al Gesuati, Dorsoduro 780, 30123 Venezia. ☎ **041/520-6466.** Fax 041/ 522-7045. 30 rms. A/C TEL. 240,000L–280,000L ($144–$168) double. Rates include buffet breakfast. AE, MC, V. Closed Jan 9–Feb 4. Vaporetto: Zattere.

Recently renovated (and just in time!), La Calcina lies in a secluded, dignified, and less-trampled district of Venice. This used to be the English enclave before the area developed a broader base of tourism. John Ruskin, who wrote *The Stones of Venice*, stayed here in 1877, and he charted the ground for his latter-day compatriots. This pensione is absolutely spotless, and the furnishings are well chosen, but hardly elaborate. The rooms are cozy and comfortable.

✪ **Pensione Accademia.** Fondamenta Bollani, Dorsoduro 1058, 30123 Venezia. ☎ **041/ 523-7846.** Fax 041/523-9152. 29 rms. 270,000L ($162) double. Rates include breakfast. AE, DC, MC, V. Vaporetto: Accademia.

Pensione Accademia is the most patrician of the *pensioni*. It's in a villa whose garden extends into an angle created by the junction of two canals. The interior features Gothic-style paneling, Venetian chandeliers, and Victorian-era furniture. The building served as the Russian Embassy before World War II, and as a private house before that. There's an upstairs sitting room flanked by two large windows and a formal rose garden. The bedrooms are spacious and decorated with original furniture from the 19th century. Some of the rooms are air-conditioned, and most have been renovated. Pensione Accademia was the fictional residence of Katharine Hepburn's character in the film *Summertime*. Incidentally, it was when Hepburn was in Venice for the film that she fell into a canal and got a permanent eye infection.

Pensione Seguso. Zattere al Gesuati. Dorsoduro 779, 30123 Venezia. ☎ **041/528-6858.** Fax 041/522-2340. 40 rms, 30 with bath (tub or shower). TEL. 280,000L ($168) double without bath, 300,000L ($180) double with bath. Rates include breakfast. AE, DC, MC, V. Closed Dec–Feb. Vaporetto: Accademia.

Set at the junction of two canals, this hotel is located on a less-traveled side of Venice across the Grand Canal from Piazza San Marco. Its relative isolation made it attractive to such tenants as Ezra Pound and John Julius Norwich and his mother, Lady Diana Cooper. The interior is furnished with the family antiques of the Seguso family, who have maintained the hotel for more than 80 years. Small tables are set up near the hotel entrance, where breakfast is served on sunny days. Half board, obligatory, is served in the elegantly upper-crust dining room, where family heirlooms and family cats vie for the attention of the many satisfied guests.

INEXPENSIVE

✪ **Locanda Montin.** Fondamenta di Borgo, Dorsoduro 1147, 31000 Venezia. ☎ **041/ 522-7151.** Fax 041/520-0255. 9 rms, 3 with bath (shower). 80,000L ($48) double without bath, 90,000L ($54) double with bath. AE, DC, MC, V. Vaporetto: Accademia.

The well-recommended Locanda Montin is an old-fashioned Venetian inn whose adjoining restaurant is one of the most loved and frequented in the area. The hotel is located in the Dorsoduro section, an area across the Grand Canal from the most popular tourist zones. The establishment is officially listed as a fourth-class hotel, but its accommodations are considerably larger and better than that rating would suggest. Reservations are virtually mandatory because of the reputation of this locanda. The inn is a little difficult to locate—it's marked only by a small carriage lamp etched with the name of the establishment—but worth the search.

ON ISOLA DELLA GIUDECCA
VERY EXPENSIVE

✪ Hotel Cipriani. Isola della Giudecca 10, 30133 Venezia. ☎ **800/992-5055** in the U.S., or 041/520-7744. Fax 041/520-7745. 76 rms, 28 suites. A/C MINIBAR TV TEL. 900,000L–1,280,000L ($540–$768) double; from 1,950,000L ($1,170) suite. Rates include breakfast. AE, DC, MC, V. Closed Nov–Mar. Vaporetto: Zitelle.

With its isolated location, haute service, and exorbitant prices, the Cipriani outclasses every other posh contender in the city, including those traditional favorites, the Danieli and the Gritti Palace. Set in a 16th-century cloister on the residential island of Giudecca, this pleasure palace was established in 1958 by the late Giuseppe Cipriani, the founder of Harry's Bar and the one real-life character in Hemingway's Venetian novel. Clients in the past have included everyone from Margaret Thatcher to Barbra Streisand. The Cipriani, incidentally, is the only hotel on Giudecca, which otherwise is calm and quiet. Today the hotel is owned and operated by Orient Express Hotels. The guest rooms have different amenities—ranging from tasteful contemporary to an antique design—but all have splendid views.

Dining/Entertainment: Lunch is served in the bar, Il Gabbiano, either indoors or on terraces overlooking the water. More formal meals are served at night in the Restaurant.

Services: The best in Venice, with two employees for every room. A private launch service ferries guests, at any hour, to and from the hotel's own pier near Piazza San Marco. Room service, baby-sitting, laundry, and valet are available.

Facilities: Olympic-size swimming pool with filtered salt water, tennis courts, sauna, fitness center.

ON THE LIDO
VERY EXPENSIVE

✪ Excelsior Palace. Lungomare Marconi 41, 30126 Lido di Venezia. ☎ **800/325-3535** in the U.S. and Canada, or 041/526-0201. Fax 041/526-7276. 196 rms, 18 suites. A/C MINIBAR TV TEL. 572,000L ($343.20) double; from 1,650,000L ($990) suite. AE, DC, MC, V. Parking 30,000L ($18). Closed Nov–Mar 15. Vaporetto: Lido, then bus A, B, or C.

When the mammoth Excelsior Palace was built, it was the biggest resort hotel of its kind in the world. The Excelsior is a monument to *la dolce vita* and did much to make the Lido fashionable. Today it offers the most luxury along the Lido, although it doesn't have the antique character of the Hotel des Bains. Its rooms range in style and amenities from cozy singles to suites. Most of the social life here takes place around the angular swimming pool or on the flowered terraces leading up to the cabanas on the sandy beach. All guest rooms—some of them big enough for tennis games—have been modernized, often with vivid, summerlike colors.

Dining/Entertainment: On the premises is one of the most elegant dining rooms of the Adriatic, the Tropicana. The Blue Bar on the ground floor has piano music and views of the beach.

Services: Room service (24 hours), baby-sitting, laundry, valet.

Facilities: Six tennis courts, swimming pool, private pier with boat rental. A private launch makes hourly runs to the other CIGA hotels: the Gritti Palace and the Danieli Royal Excelsior on the Grand Canal.

EXPENSIVE

✪ Hotel des Bains. Lungomare Marconi 17, 30126 Lido di Venezia. ☎ **800/325-3535** in the U.S. and Canada, or 041/526-5921. Fax 041/526-0113. 191 rms, 19 suites. A/C MINIBAR TV TEL. 407,000L–605,000L ($244.20–$363) double; from 660,000L ($396) suite. AE, DC, MC, V. Closed Nov–Mar. Vaporetto: Lido, then bus A, B, or C.

Hotel des Bains was built in the grand era of European resort hotels, but its supremacy on the Lido was long ago lost to the Excelsior. It has its own wooded park and private beach with individual cabanas. Its confectionery-like facade dates from the turn of the century. Thomas Mann stayed here several times before making it the setting for his novella *Death in Venice,* and later it was used as a set for the film of the same name. The renovated interior exudes the flavor of the leisurely life of the *belle époque* era. The hotel, which overlooks the sea, has well-furnished, fairly large rooms.

Dining/Entertainment: Guests can dine in a large veranda room cooled by Adriatic sea breezes. The food is top-rate, and the service is superior.

Services: Room service, baby-sitting, laundry, valet. A motorboat shuttles back and forth between Venice and the Lido.

Facilities: Many resort-type amenities are available at the Golf Club Alberoni (tennis courts, a large swimming pool, a private pier, and a park).

✪ **Quattro Fontane.** Via Quattro Fontane 16, 30126 Lido di Venezia. ☎ **041/526-0227.** Fax 041/526-0726. 57 rms. A/C TV TEL. 360,000L–460,000L ($216–$276) double. Rates include breakfast. AE, DC, MC, V. Closed Easter and Nov–Apr 4. Free parking. Vaporetto: Lido, then bus A, B, or C.

In its price bracket, the Quattro Fontane is one of the most charming hotels on the Lido. The trouble is, a lot of people know that, so it's likely to be booked. This former summer home of a 19th-century Venetian family is most popular with British tourists. They seem to appreciate the homelike atmosphere, the garden, the helpful staff, and the rooms with superior amenities, not to mention the good food served at tables set under shade trees. Many of the rooms are furnished with antiques.

Dining/Entertainment: Hotel dining room open from April to October. There's a bar adjacent to the restaurant.

Services: Concierge, laundry/dry cleaning, newspaper delivery on request, twice-daily maid service, room service (7am to midnight).

Facilities: The hotel maintains changing booths and about a dozen private cabanas on the beach, a short walk from the hotel. There's also a tennis court on the premises.

MODERATE

Hotel Belvedere. Piazzale Santa Maria Elisabetta 4, 30126 Lido di Venezia. ☎ **041/526-0115.** Fax 041/526-1486. 30 rms. A/C TV TEL. 160,000L–240,000L ($96–$144) double. Rates include breakfast. AE, DC, MC, V. Vaporetto: Lido.

Built in 1857, Hotel Belvedere is still run by the same family. Restored and modernized, it also offers a popular restaurant (recommended in "Dining," later in this chapter). The hotel is open all year, which is unusual for the Lido. It offers simply furnished double rooms. All have air-conditioning or a view of the St. Mark lagoon. For the Lido, prices are reasonable. The hotel has parking in its garden, and it's located right across from the vaporetto stop. As an added courtesy, the Belvedere offers guests free entrance to the casino, and in summer guests can use the hotel's bathing huts that have been reserved on the Venetian Lido.

Hotel Helvetia. Gran Viale 4–6, 30126 Lido di Venezia. ☎ **041/526-0105.** Fax 041/526-8903. 56 rms. TEL. 180,000L–310,000L ($108–$186) double. Rates include breakfast. MC, V. Closed Nov–Mar. Parking 10,000L ($6). Vaporetto: Lido, then bus A, B, or C.

Hotel Helvetia is a four-story, russet-colored, 19th-century building with stone detailing on a side street near the lagoon side of the island, an easy walk from the vaporetto stop. The quieter rooms face away from the street, and rooms in the older wing have *belle époque* high ceilings and attractively comfortable furniture. The newer wing, dating from around 1950, is more streamlined and has been renovated in a more conservative and sterile style. Breakfast is served, weather permitting, in a flagstone-covered wall garden behind the hotel. Baby-sitting, laundry, and 24-hour room service are available.

4 Dining

Although Venice doesn't grow much foodstuff, and is hardly a victory garden, it's bounded by a rich agricultural district and plentiful vineyards in the hinterlands. The city gets the choicest items on its menu from the Adriatic, although the fish dishes, such as scampi, are very expensive. The many rich and varied specialties prepared in the Venetian kitchen will be surveyed in the restaurant recommendations to follow. For Italy, the restaurants of Venice are high priced, although there are many trattorie that cater to moderate budgets.

NEAR PIAZZA SAN MARCO
EXPENSIVE

✪ **Antico Martini.** Campo San Fantin, San Marco 1983. ☎ **041/522-4121.** Reservations required. Main courses 32,000L–50,000L ($19.20–$30); fixed-price menus 40,000L–55,000L ($24–$33) at lunch, 72,000L–98,000L ($43.20–$58.80) at dinner. AE, DC, MC, V. Wed 7–11:30pm, Thurs–Mon noon–2:30pm and 7–11:30pm. Vaporetto: San Marco or Santa Maria del Giglio. VENETIAN/INTERNATIONAL.

Antico Martini, the city's leading restaurant, elevates Venetian cuisine to its highest level. Inside, elaborate chandeliers glitter overhead and gilt-framed oil paintings adorn the paneled walls. The outside courtyard is splendid in the summer.

An excellent beginning is the risotto di frutti di mare ("fruits of the sea"), in a creamy Venetian style with plenty of fresh seafood. For a main dish, try the *fegato alla veneziana*, tender liver fried with onions and served with a helping of polenta, a yellow cornmeal mush. The chefs are better at regional dishes than they are at international ones. The restaurant has one of the city's best wine lists. The yellow Tocai is an interesting local wine and especially good with fish dishes.

La Caravella. Calle Larga XXII Marzo, San Marco 2398. ☎ **041/520-8901.** Reservations required. Main courses 45,000L–70,000L ($27–$42); fixed-price lunch 70,000L ($42). AE, DC, MC, V. Daily noon–3pm and 7pm–midnight. Vaporetto: San Marco. VENETIAN/INTERNATIONAL.

La Caravella, next door to the Hotel Saturnia International, offers an overblown nautical atmosphere and a leather-bound menu that makes you at first think this might be a tourist trap. Although it's expensive, it's not a trap but a citadel of good food and wine, with a cuisine that's almost as good as at the Antico Martini. The restaurant contains four different dining rooms, and outdoor dining is available in the courtyard during the summer months. The decor is rustically elegant, with frescoed ceilings, bouquets of flowers, and wrought-iron lighting fixtures. Many of the specialties are featured nowhere else in town. You might begin with an antipasti misto de pesce (fish) with olive oil and lemon juice, or perhaps prawns with avocado. Two specialties of the house are *granceola* (Adriatic sea crab on a bed of carpaccio) and chateaubriand for two. The best item to order, however, is one of the poached-fish dishes, such as bass—all priced according to weight and served with a tempting sauce. After all that, the ice cream in champagne is welcome.

Impressions

Venice is like eating an entire box of chocolate liqueurs at one go.

—Truman Capote

☻ Harry's Bar. Calle Vallaresso, San Marco 1323. ☎ **041/528-5777.** Reservations required. Main courses 75,000L–85,000L ($45–$51). AE, DC, MC, V. Daily 10:30am–11pm. Vaporetto: San Marco. VENETIAN.

Although Quadri and the Antico Martini have more elegant atmospheres, Harry's Bar serves the best food in Venice. A. E. Hotchner, in his *Papa Hemingway,* quoted the writer as saying, "We can't eat straight hamburger in a Renaissance palazzo on the Grand Canal." So he ordered a 5-pound "tin of beluga caviar" to "take the curse off it." Hemingway would probably skip the place today, and the prices would come as a shock even to him. Harry, by the way, is an Italian named Arrigo, son of the late Commendatore Cipriani. Like his father, Arrigo is an entrepreneur extraordinaire known for the standard of his cuisine. His bar is a watering spot for martini-thirsty Americans—the vodka martini is dry and well chilled, but Hemingway and Hotchner always ordered a Bloody Mary. Actually, the most famous drink of the house is one of the Bellinis (Prosecco and white peach juice). You can have your choice of dining in the bar downstairs or the room with a view upstairs. We recommend the Venetian fish soup, followed by the scampi Thermidor with rice pilaf or the seafood ravioli. The food is relatively simple, but absolutely fresh.

Quadri. Piazza San Marco, San Marco 120–124. ☎ **041/522-2105.** Reservations required. Main courses 41,000L–70,000L ($24.60–$42). AE, DC, MC, V. Wed–Sun noon–2:30pm and /–10:30pm. Vaporetto: San Marco. INTERNATIONAL.

One of the most famous restaurants of Europe, Quadri is even better known as a cafe (see "Venice After Dark," in chapter 10). This deluxe second-floor restaurant, with its elegant decor and clientele, overlooks the "living room" of Venice. Former patrons have included Marcel Proust and Stendhal. Many diners come here just for the view, and are often surprised by the memorable setting, high-quality cuisine, and impeccable service. Harry's Bar and the Antico Martini have better food, although the chef's skills here are considerable. The place is often packed with celebrities during art and film festivals, the world glitterati taking delight in this throwback to the days of *La Serenissima.* The chef is likely to tempt you with such dishes as octopus in fresh tomato sauce, salt codfish with polenta, scallops in a saffron sauce, or sea bass with crab sauce. Dessert specialties include "baked" ice cream and lemon mousse with fresh strawberry sauce.

MODERATE

☻ Al Covo. Campiello della Pescaria, Castello 3968. ☎ **041/522-3812.** Reservations recommended for dinner. Main courses 32,000L ($19.20); fixed-price lunch 45,000L ($27). AE, MC, V. Fri–Tues 12:45–2:15pm and 7:45–10:15pm. Vaporetto: Arsenale. VENETIAN/SEAFOOD.

This restaurant is near Piazza San Marco, in neighboring Castello. The antique setting and sophisticated management and cookery by Cesare Benelli and his Texas-born wife Diane create a special charm as well as very fresh and very appealing Venetian dishes. What is their preferred specialty? They respond, "That's like asking us, 'Which of your children do you prefer?' since we strongly attach ourselves to the development of each dish." Look for a succulent reinvention of a medieval version of a fish soup; potato gnocchi flavored with *go*—a local version of whitefish; seafood ravioli; linguine zestly blended with zucchini and fresh peas; and a delicious version of fritto misto that includes scampi, squid, a bewildering array of fish, and deep-fried vegetables that include zucchini flowers. The establishment prides itself on not having any freezers on the premises, a fact that guarantees that all food is imported fresh virtually every day. As you set out to find this place, be alert to the fact that it lies near Piazza San Marco, not near Rialto, as is frequently thought because of a square there with a similiar name.

Arcimboldo. Calle dei Furiani 3219, in Castello. ☎ **041/528-6569.** Reservations recommended for dinner. Main courses 27,000L–40,000L ($16.20–$24). DC, MC, V. Wed–Mon noon–2:30pm and 7:30–10:30pm. Vaporetto: Arsenale or San Zaccaria. VENETIAN/SEAFOOD.

At the corner where the Scuola di San Giorgio degli Schiavoni (containing Carpaccio's celebrated cycle of paintings) is located, turn into a little street and follow a narrow footpath leading deep into Venice's oldest quarter. At the end of the street, you'll stumble upon Arcimboldo, one of the city's most charming restaurants. It overlooks a canal and is named for Giuseppe Arcimboldo, a famous 16th-century painter who worked at the Hapsburg court, making fantastical portraits of fruits and vegetables. Reproductions of his work line the walls.

The intimate and romantic decor is a fitting backdrop for the traditional Venetian fare served here. Both old and modern dishes are prepared with the excellent fruit and vegetables grown on the neighboring islands. Diners can enjoy Venetian-style antipasti, excellent pasta dishes, fish, risotto, and the pick of poultry and meat. Everything is washed down with quality wines. In spring and summer tables are placed outside along the canal.

Da Ivo. Calle dei Fuseri, San Marco 1809. ☎ **041/528-5004.** Reservations required. Main courses 30,000L–45,000L ($18–$27). AE, DC, MC, V. Mon–Sat noon–2:40pm and 7pm–midnight. Closed Jan 6–31. Vaporetto: San Marco. TUSCAN/VENETIAN.

Da Ivo has such a faithful clientele you'll think at first that you're in a semiprivate club. The rustic atmosphere is both cozy and relaxing, and your well-set table flickers with the glow of candlelight. Homesick Florentines head here for some fine Tuscan cookery, but regional Venetian dishes are also served. In season, game, prepared according to ancient traditions, is cooked over an open charcoal grill. One cold December day our hearts and plates were warmed by an order of a homemade tagliatelli topped with slivers of tartufi bianchi, the unforgettable pungent white truffle from the Piedmont district. Dishes change according to the season and the daily availability of ingredients, but are likely to include anglerfish, a stewpot of fish, or cuttlefish in its own ink.

Do Forni. Calle dei Specchieri, San Marco 468. ☎ **041/523-2148.** Reservations required. Main courses 25,000L–40,000L ($15–$24). AE, DC, MC, V. Daily noon–3pm and 6–11pm. Vaporetto: San Marco. VENETIAN.

Centuries ago this was the site where bread was baked for some local monasteries, but today it's the busiest restaurant in Venice—even when the rest of the city slumbers under a wintertime Adriatic fog. It's divided into two sections, separated by a narrow alleyway. The Venetian cognoscenti prefer the front part, decorated in *Orient Express* style. The larger section at the back is like a country tavern, with ceiling beams and original paintings. The English menu is entitled "food for the gods" and lists such specialties as spider crab in its own shell, champagne-flavored risotto, calves' kidney in a bitter mustard, and sea bass in papillote (parchment). The food is international in scope, and dishes appear inspired not only by the cuisine of Venice but the kitchens of the United States, Morocco, England, and Germany as well.

Ristorante da Raffaele. Calle Larga XXII Marzo (Fondamenta delle Ostreghe), San Marco 2347. ☎ **041/523-2317.** Reservations recommended Sat–Sun. Main courses 22,000L–45,000L ($13.20–$27). AE, DC, MC, V. Fri–Wed noon–3pm and 7–10:30pm. Closed Dec 10 to mid-Feb. Vaporetto: San Marco or Santa Maria del Giglio. ITALIAN/VENETIAN.

Ristorante da Raffaele, a 5-minute walk from Piazza San Marco and a minute from the Grand Canal, has long been a favorite canalside restaurant. The place is often overrun with tourists, but the veteran kitchen staff handles the onslaught well. Dating from 1953, the restaurant offers the kind of charm and special atmosphere that are unique to Venice. However, the inner rooms are popular with Venetians and visitors alike. The huge inner sanctum has a high-beamed ceiling, 17th- to 19th-century pistols and sabers, exposed brick, wrought-iron chandeliers, a massive fireplace, and copper pots (hundreds of them). The food is excellent, beginning with a choice of tasty antipasti or well-prepared pastas. Seafood specialties include scampi, squid, and a platter of deep-fried fish from the Adriatic. The grilled meats are also succulent and can be followed by rich, tempting desserts. The crowded conviviality is part of the experience.

Ristorante Noemi. Calle dei Fabbri, San Marco 912. ☎ **041/522-5238.** Reservations recommended. Main courses 22,000L–35,000L ($13.20–$21). AE, DC, MC, V. Mon 7–10:30pm, Tues–Sat noon–2:30pm and 7–10:30pm. Closed Dec 15–Jan 15. Vaporetto: San Marco. INTERNATIONAL/VENETIAN.

This simple establishment is on a narrow street just a short walk from Piazza San Marco. Its decor features a multicolored marble floor in abstract patterns and swag curtains covering big glass windows. The foundations of the building date from the 14th century and the restaurant itself was established in 1927 and named after the matriarch of the family that continues to own it. House specialties, many of which border on *nuova cucina*, include thin black spaghetti with cuttlefish "in their own sauce" and fresh salmon crêpes with cheese, followed by the special lemon sorbet of the house, made with sparkling wine and fresh mint. More recent dishes include filet of salmon with white raisins, served with a sauce made from white wine and laurel leaves, and a filet of sole "Casanova," concocted with a velouté of white wine, shrimp, and mushrooms.

Taverna La Fenice. Campiello de la Fenice, San Marco 1938. ☎ **041/522-3856.** Reservations required. Main courses 18,000L–32,000L ($10.80–$19.20). AE, DC, MC, V. Aug–Apr, Mon 7–10:30pm, Tues–Sat noon–2:30pm and 7–10:30pm; May–July, daily noon–2:30pm and 7–10:30pm. Closed the second week in Jan. Vaporetto: San Marco. ITALIAN/VENETIAN.

Established in 1907, when Venetians were flocking in record numbers to hear the *bel canto* performances in the opera house nearby, this restaurant is one of the most romantic dining spots in Venice. The interior is suitably elegant, but the preferred spot during clement weather is outdoors beneath a canopy, a few steps from the burned Teatro La Fenice. The service is smooth and efficient. The most appetizing beginning is the selection of seafood antipasti. The fish is fresh from the Mediterranean. You might enjoy the risotto con scampi e arugula, the freshly made tagliatelle with cream and exotic mushrooms, John Dory filets with artichokes, turbot roasted with olive oil and broccoli, scampi with tomatoes and rice, or carpaccio alla Fenice.

Trattoria La Colomba. Piscina Frezzeria, San Marco 1665. ☎ **041/522-1175.** Reservations recommended. Main courses 32,000L–65,000L ($19.20–$39). AE, DC, MC, V. Daily noon–3pm and 7–11pm. Closed Wed from June 19–Aug, and Nov–Apr. Vaporetto: San Marco or Rialto. VENETIAN/INTERNATIONAL.

This is one of the most distinctive and popular trattorie in town, with a history going back at least a century and a by-now legendary association with some of the leading painters of Venice. In 1985 a $2-million restoration improved the infrastructure, making it a more attractive foil for the dozens of modern paintings that adorn its walls. These collections change seasonally and are discreetly available for sale. Menu items are likely to include at least five daily specials based exclusively on the time-honored cuisine of Venice. Otherwise, you can order such specialties as *risotto di funghi del Montello* (risotto with mushrooms from the local hills of Montello) or *baccalà alla vicentina* (milk-simmered dry cod seasoned with onions, anchovies, and cinnamon, and served with polenta). Fruits and vegetables used in the dishes are for the most part grown locally on the islands near Venice.

Vini da Arturo. Calle degli Assassini, San Marco 3656. ☎ **041/528-6974.** Reservations recommended. Main courses 25,000L–40,000L ($15–$24). No credit cards. Mon–Sat noon–2:30pm and 7–10:30pm. Closed Aug. Vaporetto: San Marco or Rialto. VENETIAN.

Vini da Arturo attracts many devoted regulars, including artists and writers. Here you get some of the most delectable of the local cooking—not just the standard Venetian cliches and not seafood, which may be unique for a Venetian restaurant. One local restaurant owner, who likes to dine here occasionally instead of at his own place, explained, "The subtle difference between good and bad food is often nothing more than the amount of butter and cream used." Instead of ordering plain pasta, try the tantalizing spaghetti alla Gorgonzola. The beef is also good, especially when prepared with a cream sauce flavored with mustard and freshly ground pepper. Salads are made with crisp, fresh ingredients, often in unusual combinations. The place is small and contains only seven tables; it's located between the Fenice Opera House and St. Mark's Square.

INEXPENSIVE

Alfredo, Alfredo. Campo San Filippo e Giacomo, Castello 4294. ☎ **041/522-5331.** Main courses 10,000L–35,000L ($6–$21). AE, DC, MC, V. Oct–Apr, Thurs–Tues 11am–2am. Vaporetto: San Zaccaria. VENETIAN/INTERNATIONAL.

Alfredo, Alfredo might be classified as a coffee shop. Here you can order any number of items, prepared in short order. These include pasta dishes such as spaghetti with a number of sauces, freshly made salads, crêpes, various grilled meats, and omelets. Its long hours make it a convenient spot for a light meal at almost any time of the day. The food is not always first-rate, and the atmosphere is a bit hysterical at times, but it still might come in handy.

Le Chat Qui Rit. Calle dei Fabbri 1138, San Marco 1131. ☎ **041/522-9086.** Main courses 10,000L–16,000L ($6–$9.60); pizzas 9,000L–14,000L ($5.40–$8.40). No credit cards. Nov–Aug, Sun–Fri 11am–9:30pm; Sept–Oct, daily 11am–9:30pm. Vaporetto: San Marco. VENETIAN/PIZZA.

This is a self-service cafeteria and pizzeria that offers Venetian dishes prepared "just like mama made." It's very popular because of its low prices. Dishes might include cuttlefish simmered in stock and served on a bed of yellow polenta or various fried fish. You can also order a steak grilled very simply, flavored with oil, salt, and pepper, perhaps a little garlic and herbs if you prefer. Main-dish platters are served rather quickly after you order them.

Nuova Rivetta. Campo San Filippo, Castello 4625. ☎ **041/528-7302.** Reservations required. Main courses 16,000L–30,000L ($9.60–$18). AE, MC, V. Tues–Sun 10am–10pm. Closed July 23–Aug 20. Vaporetto: San Zaccaria. VENETIAN/SEAFOOD.

Nuova Rivetta is an old-fashioned Venetian trattoria where you get good food at a good price. The restaurant stands in the monumental heart of the old city. Many find it best for lunch during a stroll around Venice. The most representative dish to order is frittura di pesce, a mixed fish fry from the Adriatic, which includes squid or various other "sea creatures" that turned up at the market on that day. Other specialties include gnocchi stuffed with Adriatic spider crab, pasticcio of fish (a main course), and spaghetti flavored with squid ink. The most typical wine of the house is Prosecco, whose bouquet is refreshing and fruity with a slightly sharp flavor. For centuries it has been one of the most celebrated wines of the Veneto region.

Restaurant da Bruno. Calle del Paradiso, Catello 5731. ☎ **041/522-1480.** Main courses 12,000L–20,000L ($7.20–$12); fixed-price menu 24,000L ($14.40). AE, DC, MC, V. Wed–Mon noon–3pm and 7–11pm. Closed 1 week in Jan. Vaporetto: San Marco or Rialto. VENETIAN.

Restaurant da Bruno is like a country taverna in the center of Venice. Located on a narrow street about halfway between the Rialto Bridge and Piazza San Marco, the restaurant attracts its crowds by grilling meats on an open-hearth fire. Get your antipasti at the counter and watch your prosciutto order being prepared—paper-thin slices of spicy flavored ham wrapped around breadsticks *(grissini)*. In the right season, da Bruno does some of the finest game specialty dishes in Venice. If featured, try in particular its capriolo (roebuck) and its fagiano (pheasant). A typical Venetian specialty prepared well here is the zuppa di pesce (fish soup). Other specialties include filet of beef with pepper sauce, veal scaloppine with wild mushrooms, scampi and calamari, and a local favorite, squid with polenta. After that rich fare, you may settle for a macedonia of mixed fruit for dessert.

Sempione. Ponte Beretteri 578. ☎ **041/522-6022.** Reservations recommended. Main courses 16,000L–28,000L ($9.60–$16.80). AE, DC, MC, V. Daily 11:30am–3pm and 6:30–10pm. Closed Tues and/or Thurs from Nov–Dec, depending on business. Vaporetto: Rialto. VENETIAN.

This restaurant has done an admirable job of feeding local residents and visitors for almost 90 years. Set adjacent to a canal, within a 15th-century building near St. Marks Square, it contains three dining rooms outfitted in a soothingly traditional style, a well-trained staff, and a kitchen that focuses on preparations of traditional Venetian cuisine. Examples include grilled fish, spaghetti with crabmeat, risotto with fish, fish soup, and a timeless and delectable version of Venetian calf's liver that hasn't been significantly changed since the restaurant was originally founded. Try for a table by the window so you can watch the gondolas glide by.

✪ Trattoria alla Madonna. Calle de la Madonna 594. ☎ **041/522-3824.** Reservations recommended but not always accepted. Main courses 17,000L–20,000L ($10.20–$12). AE, MC, V. Thurs–Tues noon–3pm and 7:15–10pm. Closed Jan 7–Feb 7 and Aug 1–15. Vaporetto: Rialto. VENETIAN/ITALIAN.

Despite the similarity of its name with that of a popular American singer (and many local jokes to that effect), this restaurant was established in 1954 in a 300-year-old building of historical distinction. Named after *another* famous Madonna, it's one of the most popular and characteristic trattorie of Venice, specializing in traditional Venetian recipes and an array of grilled fresh fish. A suitable beginning might be the antipasto frutti di mare (fruits of the sea). Pastas, polentas, risottos, meats (including *fegato alla veneziana,* liver with onions), and many kinds of irreproachably fresh fish are widely available. Many creatures of the sea are displayed in a refrigerated case near the entrance. The mixed fish fry of the Adriatic is a preferred dish, when available.

ON OR NEAR RIVA DEGLI SCHIAVONI
EXPENSIVE

Do Leoni. In the Londra Palace Hotel, Riva degli Schiavoni, Castello 4171. ☎ **041/520-0533.** Reservations recommended. Main courses 30,000L–60,000L ($18–$36); 3-course lunch (without drinks) 42,000L ($25.20). Residents of the Londra Palace Hotel receive a 20% discount (excludes fixed-price menu). AE, DC, MC, V. Restaurant, daily 11:30am–3pm and 7:30–11pm; bar, daily 10am–1am. Vaporetto: San Zaccaria. VENETIAN/INTERNATIONAL.

For years this restaurant was known by the French version of its name, Les Deux Lions. Set on the street level of an elegant and well-recommended hotel, it offers a panoramic view of a 19th-century equestrian statue ringed with heroic women

---

🍴 Family-Friendly Restaurants

Alfredo, Alfredo *(see p. 406)*   This is a great spot for the family on a sightseeing run. Short-order items are served quickly, including spaghetti with a number of sauces and freshly made salads.

Le Chat Qui Rit *(see p. 406)*   This is a self-service cafeteria where children are allowed to select what they want. Lots of pasta dishes.

Tiziano Bar *(see p. 410)*   You can order hot pasta dishes and sandwiches, consumed standing at the counter or seated on one of the high stools.

---

taming—you guessed it—lions. The restaurant is filled with scarlet and gold, a motif of lions patterned into the carpeting, and reproductions of English furniture.

Lunches are brief, buffet-style affairs, where clients serve themselves from a large choice of hot and cold Italian and international food. The appealing dinners by candlelight are more formal, with emphasis on Venetian cuisine. The chef's undeniable skill is reflected in such dishes as chilled fish terrine, baked salmon with truffles, and baby rooster with green-pepper sauce. At both lunch and dinner, the restaurant, depending on the weather, offers the option of dining outside on the piazza, overlooking the bronze lions and their masters.

NEAR THE ARSENALE
MODERATE
Ristorante Corte Sconta. Calle del Pestrin, Castello 3886. ☎ **041/522-7024.** Reservations required. Main courses 20,000L–30,000L ($12–$18); fixed-price menu 70,000L ($42). AE, DC, MC, V. Tues–Sat 12:30–2:30pm and 7:30–9:30pm. Closed Jan 7–Feb 7 and July 15–Aug 15. Vaporetto: Arsenale. SEAFOOD.

Ristorante Corte Sconta is located behind a narrow storefront that you'd probably ignore if you didn't know about this place. On a narrow alley whose name is shared by at least three other streets in Venice (this particular one is near Campo Bandiere e Moro and San Giovanni in Bragora), the modest restaurant whose name in Italian means "hidden courtyard" has a multicolored marble floor, plain wooden tables, and no serious attempt at decoration. It has become well known, however, as a sophisticated gathering place for artists, writers, and filmmakers. As the depiction of the satyr chasing the mermaid above the entrance implies, this is a fish restaurant, serving a variety of grilled creatures (much of the "catch" is largely unknown in North America). The fresh fish is flawlessly grilled. It's also flawlessly fresh—the gamberi, for example, is placed live on the grill. Begin with marinated salmon with arugula and pomegranate seeds in rich olive oil. If you don't like fish, a tender filet of beef is available. There's a big stand-up bar in an adjoining room that seems to be almost a private fraternity of the locals.

NEAR THE PONTE DI RIALTO
EXPENSIVE
Fiaschetteria Toscana. SS. San Giovanni Crisostomo 5719. ☎ **041/528-5281.** Reservations required. Main courses 28,000L–60,000L ($16.80–$36). AE, DC, MC, V. Wed–Mon 12:30–2:30pm and 7:30–10:30pm. Vaporetto: Rialto. VENETIAN/ TUSCAN.

The staff is hysterically busy, and despite the fact that this purports to be a rather stylish restaurant, there may be some rough points in the service and presentations. Nonetheless, this is the preferred choice of many food-savvy Venetians who often regard it as a venue for a celebration dinner. Despite the high prices and the fact that tables can be annoyingly close to the dialogue next to you, this place is a hot spot for trendoids who appreciate the see-and-be-seen ambience, and offers a vaguely permissive aura where filmmakers and photo-modèles can feel comfortable. Dining rooms are on two different levels, the upstairs of which is somewhat more claustrophobic than the downstairs. In the evening, the downstairs is especially appealing with its romantic candlelit ambience. Menu items include a *frittura della Serenissima* (a mixed platter of fried seafood with vegetables), veal scallops with lemon-marsala sauce and mushrooms, ravioli stuffed with whitefish and herbs, and several different kinds of Tuscan-style beefsteak.

MODERATE

✪ **"Al Graspo de Ua."** Calle Bombaseri, San Marco 5094. ☎ **041/520-0150.** Reservations required. Main courses 26,000L–35,000L ($15.60–$21). AE, DC, MC, V. Tues–Sun noon–3pm and 8–11pm. Closed Jan 2–17. Vaporetto: Rialto. SEAFOOD/VENETIAN.

"Al Graspo de Ua" is one bunch of grapes you'll want to pluck. For that special meal, it's a winner. Decorated in the old taverna style, it offers several air-conditioned dining rooms. One has a beamed ceiling, hung with garlic and copper bric-a-brac. Among the best fish restaurants in Venice, "Al Graspo de Ua" has been patronized by such celebs as Elizabeth Taylor, Jeanne Moreau, and even Giorgio de Chirico. You can help yourself to all the hors d'oeuvres you want—known on the menu as "self-service mammoth." Next try the *gran fritto dell'Adriatico,* a mixed treat of deep-fried fish from the Adriatic. The desserts are also good, especially the peach Melba.

Poste Vechie. Pescheria Rialto 1608. ☎ **041/721-822.** Reservations recommended. Main courses 22,000L–36,000L ($13.20–$21.60). AE, DC, MC, V. Wed–Mon noon–3:30pm and 7–10:30pm. Vaporetto: Rialto. SEAFOOD.

This is one of the most charming restaurants in Venice, set near the Rialto fish market and connected to the rest of the city by a small, privately owned bridge. It was established in the early 1500s as the local post office—when they used to serve food to fortify the mail carriers for their deliveries. Today it's one of the oldest restaurants in Venice, with a pair of intimate dining rooms (both graced with paneling, murals, and 16th-century mantelpieces) and an outdoor courtyard that evokes the countryside northwest of Venice.

Menu items include superfresh fish from the nearby markets; a salad of shellfish and exotic mushrooms; tagliolini flavored with squid ink, crabmeat, and fish sauce; and the restaurant's *pièce de résistance,* seppie (cuttlefish) à la veneziana with polenta. If you don't like fish, calves' liver or veal shank with ham and cheese are also well prepared. Desserts come rolling to your table on a trolley and are usually delicious.

Ristorante à la Vecia Cavana. Rio Terà SS. Apostoli 4624. ☎ **041/528-7106.** Main courses 35,000L–60,000L ($21–$36); fixed-price menu 35,000L ($21). AE, DC, MC, V. Fri–Wed noon–2:30pm and 7:30–10:30pm. Vaporetto: Ca' d'Oro. SEAFOOD.

Ristorante à la Vecia Cavana is off the tourist circuit and well worth the trek through the winding streets to find it. A *cavana* is a place where gondolas are parked, a sort of liquid garage, and the site of this restaurant used to be such a place in the Middle Ages. When you enter, you'll be greeted with brick arches, stone columns, terra-cotta floors, framed modern paintings, and a photograph of 19th-century fishermen relaxing after a day's work. It's an appropriate introduction to a menu that specializes in seafood, including a mixed grill from the Adriatic, fried scampi, fresh sole, squid, three different types of risotto (each prepared with seafood), and a spicy zuppa di pesce (fish soup). Another specialty of the house is *antipasti di pesce Cavana,* which includes an assortment of just about every sea creature. The food is authentic and seems prepared for the Venetian palate—not necessarily for the glitzy foreign tourist.

INEXPENSIVE

Ristorante al Mondo Novo. Salizzada di San Lio, Castello 5409. ☎ **041/520-0698.** Reservations recommended. Main courses 15,000L–35,000L ($9–$21); fixed-price lunch 23,000L–32,000L ($13.80–$19.20). AE, MC, V. Daily 11am–3pm and 7–11:30pm. Vaporetto: Rialto or San Marco. VENETIAN/SEAFOOD.

In a very old Venetian building originally built during the Renaissance, with a dining room outfitted in a regional style, this well-established restaurant offers professional service and a kindly staff. Plus, it stays open later than many of its nearby competitors. Menu items include a selection of seafood, prepared succulently as frittura misto dell'Adriatico, or charcoal grilled. Other items include macaroni alla verdura (with fresh vegetables and greens), an antipasti of fresh fish, and filets of beef with pepper sauce and rissole potatoes. Locals who frequent the place always order the fresh fish, knowing that the owner of the restaurant is a wholesaler in the Rialto fish market.

Rôsticceria San Bartolomeo. Calle della Bissa, San Marco 5424. ☎ **041/522-3569.** Main courses 15,000L–22,000L ($9–$13.20); fixed-price menus 26,000L–30,000L ($15.60–$18). AE, MC, V. Tues–Sun 9am–2:30pm and 4:30–9:30pm. Vaporetto: Rialto. VENETIAN/ITALIAN.

Rôsticceria San Bartolomeo is the most frequented fast-food eatery in Venice and has long been a haven for budget travelers. Downstairs is a *tavola calda* where you can eat standing up, but upstairs is a budget-level restaurant with waiter service. Typical dishes include *baccalà alla vicentina* (codfish simmered in herbs and milk), deep-fried mozzarella (which the Italians call *in carrozza*), and *seppie con polenta* (squid in its own ink sauce, served with a cornmeal mush). Everything is washed down with typical Veneto wine.

Once you leave the vaporetto, take an underpass on your left (that is, with your back facing the bridge). This passageway is labeled *sottoportego della Bissa*. The restaurant will be at the first corner, off Campo San Bartolomeo.

Tiziano Bar. SS. San Giovanni Cristostomo, midway between the Church of San Giovanne Cristostomo and the Teatro Mulibran. ☎ **041/523-5544.** Main dishes 8,000L–14,000L ($4.80–$8.40). Sun–Fri 8am–10:30pm. Vaporetto: Rialto. SANDWICHES/PASTA/PIZZA.

Tiziano Bar is a *tavola calda* (literally "hot table"). There's no waiter service—you eat standing at a counter or on one of the high stools. The place is known in Venice for selling pizza by the yard. From noon to 3pm it serves hot pastas such as rigatoni and cannelloni. But throughout the day you can order sandwiches or perhaps a plate of mozzarella.

IN CANNAREGIO
MODERATE

Il Milion. Corte Prima al Milion, Cannaregio 5841. ☎ **041/522-9302.** Reservations recommended. Main courses 19,000L–29,000L ($11.40–$17.40). No credit cards. Thurs–Tues noon–2pm and 6–10pm. Closed Aug. Vaporetto: Rialto. VENETIAN.

With a tradition of feeding wayfarers that extends back more than 300 years, and a location near the back side of the San Giovanni Crisostomo, this is one of the oldest restaurants in Venice. It's named after the book written by Marco Polo *(Il Milion)* describing his travels. In fact, the restaurant lies within a town house owned long ago by members of the explorer's family who, obviously, remained in Venice and did not share his sense of adventure. The bar, incidentally, is a favorite with some of the gondoliers of Venice. Menu items include what reads like a who's who of well-recognized Venetian platters, each fresh and well prepared. Examples include veal kidneys, calves' liver with fried onions, succulent platters of grilled sardines, spaghetti with clams, risotto flavored with squid ink, and a *fritto misto* of fried fish. The staff is charming and friendly, the setting not at all forbidding or off-putting.

IN SAN POLO
MODERATE

Osteria da Fiore. Calle del Scaleter, San Polo 2202. ☎ **041/721-308.** Reservations required. Main courses 34,000L–42,000L ($20.40–$25.20). AE, DC, MC, V. Tues–Sat 12:30–2:30pm and 8–9:30pm. Closed Aug and Dec 25–Jan 12. Vaporetto: San Tomà. SEAFOOD.

The breath of the Adriatic seems to blow through this place, although how the wind finds this little restaurant tucked away in a labyrinth is a mystery. The restaurant serves only fish, and has done so since 1910. An imaginative and changing fare is offered, depending on the availability of fresh fish and produce. If you have a love of maritime foods, you'll find them here—everything from scampi (a sweet Adriatic prawn, cooked in as many different ways as there are chefs) to granzeola, a type of spider crab. In days gone by we've sampled everything from fried calamari (cuttlefish) to bottarga (dried mullet roe eaten with olive oil and lemon). Try such dishes as *capelunghe alla griglio* (razor clams opened on the grill), *masenette* (tiny green crabs that you eat shell and all), and *canoce* (mantis shrimp). For your wine, we suggest Prosecco, which has a distinctive golden-yellow color and a bouquet that's refreshing and fruity. The proprietors extend a hearty welcome to match their fare.

IN SANTA CROCE
MODERATE

Trattoria Antica Besseta. SS. de Ca' Zusto, Santa Croce 1395. ☎ **041/721-687.** Reservations required. Main courses 25,000L–30,000L ($15–$18). AE, MC, V. Thurs–Mon noon–2:30pm and 7–10:30pm. Closed Aug 1–15. Vaporetto: Rive di Biasio. VENETIAN.

If you manage to find this place (go armed with a good map), you'll be rewarded with true Venetian cuisine at its most unpretentious. Head for Campo San Giacomo dell'Orio, then negotiate your way across infrequently visited piazzas and winding alleys. Push through saloon doors into a bar area filled with African masks and modern art. The dining room in back is ringed with paintings and illuminated with wagon-wheel chandeliers. Nereo Volpe, his wife, Mariuccia, and one of their sons are the guiding force, the chefs, the buyers, and even the "talking menus." The food depends on what looked good in the market that morning. The menu could include roast chicken, fried scampi, fritto misto, spaghetti in a sardine sauce, various roasts, and a selection from the day's catch. The Volpe family produces two kinds of their own wine, a pinot blanc and a cabernet.

IN DORSODURO
MODERATE

La Furatola. Calle Lunga San Barnaba, Dorsoduro 2870A. ☎ **041/520-8594.** Reservations recommended for dinner. Main courses 25,000L–45,000L ($15–$27). No credit cards. Fri–Tues noon–2:30pm and 7–9:30pm. Closed Aug. Vaporetto: Ca' Rezzonico. SEAFOOD.

La Furatola (an old Venetian word meaning "restaurant") is very much a Dorsoduro neighborhood hangout, but it has captured the imagination of local foodies. It's located in a 300-year-old building, along a narrow flagstone-paved street that you'll need a good map and a lot of patience to find. Perhaps you'll have lunch here after a visit to the Church of San Rocco, which is located only a short distance away. You'll push past double glass doors and enter a simple dining room. The specialty is fish brought to your table in a wicker basket so that you can judge its size and freshness by its bright eyes and red gills. A display of seafood antipasti is set out near the entrance. A culinary standout is the baby octopus boiled and eaten with a drop of red-wine vinegar. Eel comes with a medley of mixed fried fish, including baby cuttle-fish, prawns, and squid rings.

Locanda Montin. Fondamenta di Borgo, Dorsoduro 1147. ☎ **041/522-7151.** Reservations recommended. Main courses 15,000L–35,000L ($9–$21). AE, DC, MC, V. Tues 12:30–2:30pm, Thurs–Mon 12:30–2:30pm and 7:30–9:30pm. Vaporetto: Accademia. Closed 10 days mid-Aug and 20 days Jan. INTERNATIONAL/ITALIAN.

Locanda Montin is the kind of rapidly disappearing Venetian inn that virtually every literary and artistic figure in Venice has visited. Since it opened just after World War II, famous clients have included Ezra Pound, Jackson Pollock, Mark Rothko, and many of the assorted artist friends of the late Peggy Guggenheim. The inn is owned and run by the Carretins, who have covered the walls with paintings donated by or purchased from their many friends and clients.

Today the arbor-covered garden courtyard of this 17th-century building is filled with regular clients, many of whom allow their favorite waiter to select most of the items for their meal. The frequently changing menu includes a variety of salads, grilled meats, and fish caught in the Adriatic. Dessert might be a *semifreddo di fragoline,* a tempting chilled liqueur-soaked cake, capped with whipped cream and wild strawberries. The Locanda lies in one of the least-trampled sections of Venice, Dorsoduro, across the Grand Canal from Piazza San Marco.

ON ISOLA DELLA GIUDECCA
VERY EXPENSIVE

✪ **Ristorante Cipriani.** In the Hotel Cipriani, Isola della Giudecca 10. ☎ **041/520-7744.** Reservations required. Jacket and tie required for men. Main courses 55,000L–66,000L ($33–$39.60). AE, DC, MC, V. Daily 12:30–3pm and 8–10:30pm. Closed Nov–Mar. Vaporetto: Zitelle. ITALIAN.

The grandest and greatest of the hotel restaurants—better than the cuisine at the Gritti Palace—this restaurant offers dining terraces with extensive views over the lagoon. However, for lunch or dinner (more romantic) the view is not the only lure. The cuisine is sublime but relatively simple, depending on the freshest of ingredients perfectly prepared by one of the best-trained staffs along the Adriatic. This is not a family favorite, and children under 6 aren't allowed.

You can dine in the more formal room with Murano chandeliers and Fortuny curtains when the weather is nippy, or out on the terrace overlooking the lagoon. Freshly made pasta is a specialty, and it's among the finest we've ever sampled in Venice. Try the taglierini verdi with noodles and ham au gratin. Chef's specialties include mixed fried scampi and squid with tender vegetables and sautéed filets of veal with spring artichokes. Come here in October for the last Bellinis of the white peach season and the first white truffles of the season served in a champagne risotto.

EXPENSIVE

Harry's Dolci. Fondamenta San Biago 773, Isola della Giudecca 30133. ☎ **041/520-8337.** Reservations recommended, especially Sat–Sun. Main courses 30,000L–40,000L ($18–$24); fixed-price menu 75,000L ($45). AE, MC, V. Wed–Mon noon–3pm and 7–10:30pm. Closed Nov–March 30. Vaporetto: S. Eufemia. INTERNATIONAL/ITALIAN.

The people at the famed Harry's Bar have established their latest enclave far from the maddening crowds of St. Mark's Square on this little-visited island. From the quayside windows of this chic place, you can watch seagoing vessels, including everything from yachts to lagoon-based barges. White napery and uniformed waiters grace a modern room, where no one minds if you order only coffee and ice cream or perhaps a selection from the large pastry menu (the zabaglione cake is divine). Popular items include carpaccio Cipriani, chicken salad, club sandwiches, gnocchi, and house-style cannelloni. Dishes are deliberately kept simple, but each is well prepared.

ON THE LIDO
INEXPENSIVE

Favorita. Via Francesco Duodo 33, Lido di Venezia. ☎ **041/526-1626.** Main courses 23,000L–30,000L ($13.80–$18). AE, DC, MC, V. Tues–Sun 12:30–2:30pm and 7:30–10:30pm. Vaporetto: Lido di Venezia. SEAFOOD.

Occupying two dining rooms and a garden that has thrived here since the 1920s, this place was reputedly named after Gabriella, wife (and presumably, "the favorite") of Vittorio Emanuele, who occasionally stopped in for refreshment during her stopovers on the Lido. Since its debut, it's been operated by members of the Pradel family, now in their third generation of ownership. Their years of experience contribute to flavorful, impeccably prepared versions of seafood and shellfish, many of them grilled, that are served within the rustically beamed interior or at tables set up amid the flowering vines of the garden. What should you order? Try the trenette (spaghetti-like pasta) with baby squid and eggplant; potato-based gnocchi with crabs from the Venetian lagoon; and grilled versions of virtually every fish in the Adriatic, including eel, sea bass, turbot, and sole, some of which are combined into delectable platters.

Ristorante Belvedere. Piazzale Santa Maria Elisabetta 4, Lido di Venezia. ☎ **041/526-0115.** Reservations required. Main courses 12,000L–50,000L ($7.20–$30); fixed-price menu 28,000L ($16.80). AE, DC, MC, V. Tues–Sun noon–2:30pm and 7–9:30pm. Closed Nov 4 to mid-Feb. Vaporetto: Lido. VENETIAN.

Outside the big hotels, the best food on the Lido is served at the Ristorante Belvedere. Don't be put off by its location, across from where the vaporetto from Venice stops. In such a location, you might expect a touristy establishment. Actually, the Belvedere attracts some of the finest people of Venice. They often come here as an excursion, knowing that they can get some of the best fish dishes along the Adriatic. Sidewalk tables are placed outside, and there's a glass-enclosed portion for windy days. The main dining room is attractive, with cane-backed bentwood chairs and big windows. In back, reached through a separate entrance, is a busy cafe. Main dishes include the chef's special sea bass, along with grilled dorade (or sole), fried scampi, and other selections. You might begin with the special fish antipasti or spaghetti en papillote (cooked in parchment).

10 Exploring Venice

Venice appears to have been created specifically to entertain its legions of callers. Ever since the body of St. Mark was smuggled out of Alexandria and entombed in the basilica, Venice has been host to a never-ending stream of visitors—famous, infamous, and otherwise—from all over the world.

Venice has perpetually captured the imagination of poets, artists, and travelers. Wordsworth, Byron, and Shelley addressed poems to the city, and it has been written about or used as a setting by many contemporary writers.

In the pages ahead, we'll explore the city's great art and architecture. But, unlike Florence, Venice would reward its guests with treasures even if they never ducked inside a museum or church. In the city on the islands, the frame eternally competes with the picture it contains.

"For all its vanity and villainy," wrote Lewis Mumford, "life touched some of its highest moments in Venice."

1 Piazza San Marco (St. Mark's Square)

Piazza San Marco was the heartbeat of the Serenissima (the Serene Republic) in the heyday of Venice's glory as a seafaring republic, the crystallization of the city's dreams and aspirations. If you have only 1 day for Venice, you need not leave the square, as the city's major attractions, such as the Basilica of St. Mark and the Doge's Palace, are centered here or nearby.

The traffic-free square, frequented by tourists and pigeons, and sometimes by Venetians, is a constant source of bewilderment and interest. If you rise at dawn, you can almost have the piazza to yourself. As you watch the sun come up, the sheen of gold mosaics glistens into a mystic effect of incomparable beauty. At midmorning (9am) the overstuffed pigeons are fed by the city (if you're caught under the whir, you'll think you're witnessing a remake of Hitchcock's *The Birds*). At midafternoon the tourists reign supreme, and it's not surprising in July to witness a display of fisticuffs over a camera angle. At sunset, when the two Moors in the Clock Tower strike the end of another day, lonely sailors begin a usually frustrated search for those hot spots that characterized the Venice of yore. Deeper into the evening, the strollers parade by or stop for espresso at the fashionable Florian Caffè and sip while listening to a band concert.

Thanks to Napoléon, the square was unified architecturally. The emperor added the Fabbrica Nuova facing the basilica, thus bridging the Old and New Procuratie on either side. Flanked with medieval-looking palaces, Sansovinos Library, elegant shops, and colonnades, the square is now finished—unlike Piazza della Signoria in Florence.

✪ **Basilica di San Marco.** Piazza San Marco. ☎ **041/522-5205.** Basilica, free; treasury, 4,000L ($2.40); presbytery, 3,000L ($1.80); Marciano Museum, 3,000L ($1.80). Basilica (including the baptistery and presbytery), Apr–Sept, Mon–Sat 9:30am–5:30pm, Sun 2–5:30pm; Oct–Mar, Mon–Sat 9:30am–5pm, Sun 1:30–4:30pm. Treasury, Mon–Sat 9:30am–5pm, Sun 2–5pm. Marciano Museum, Apr–Sept, Mon–Sat 10am–5:30pm, Sun 2–4:30pm; Oct–Mar, Mon–Sat 10am–4:45pm. *Warning:* Visitors must wear appropriate clothing and remain silent during their visit. Photography is forbidden. Vaporetto: San Marco.

The so-called Church of Gold dominates Piazza San Marco. This is one of the world's greatest and most richly embellished churches. In fact, it looks as if it had been moved intact from Istanbul. The basilica is a conglomeration of styles, although it's particularly indebted to Byzantium. It incorporates other schools of design, such as Romanesque and Gothic, with freewheeling abandon. Like Venice, it's adorned with booty from every corner of the city's once far-flung mercantile empire—capitals from Sicily, columns from Alexandria, porphyry from Syria, and sculpture from old Constantinople.

The basilica is capped by a dome that—like a spider plant—sends off shoots, in this case a quartet of smaller-scale cupolas. Spanning the facade is a loggia, surmounted by replicas of the four famous St. Mark's horses—the *Triumphal Quadriga.*

On the facade, the rich marble slabs and mosaics depict scenes from the lives of Christ and St. Mark. One of the mosaics re-creates the entry of the evangelist's body into Venice. St. Mark's body, hidden in a pork barrel, was smuggled out of Alexandria in 828 and shipped to Venice. The evangelist dethroned Theodore, the Greek saint who up until then had been the patron of the city that had outgrown him.

In the **atrium,** there are six cupolas filled with mosaics illustrating scenes from the Old Testament, including the story of the Tower of Babel. The interior of the basilica, once the private chapel and pantheon of the doges, is a stunning wonderland of marbles, alabaster, porphyry, and pillars. Visitors walk in awe across the undulating multicolored ocean floor, which is patterned with mosaics.

To the right is the **baptistery,** dominated by the Sansovino-inspired baptismal font, upon which John the Baptist is ready to pour water. If you look back at the aperture over the entryway, you can see a mosaic of the dance of Salome in front of Herod and his court. Salome is wearing a star-studded russet-red dress and three white fox tails and is dancing under a platter that holds John's head. Her glassy face is that of a Madonna, not an enchantress.

After touring the baptistery, proceed up the right nave to the doorway to the oft-looted **treasury** *(tesoro).* Here, you'll find inevitable skulls and bones of some old ecclesiastical authorities under glass, plus goblets, chalices, and Gothic candelabra.

The entrance to the **presbytery** is nearby. In it, on the high altar, the alleged sarcophagus of St. Mark rests under a green marble blanket and is held up by four sculptured, Corinthian-style alabaster columns. The Byzantine-style **Pala d'Oro,** from Constantinople, is the rarest treasure at St. Mark's—made of gold and studded with precious stones.

On leaving the basilica, head up the stairs in the atrium to the **Marciano Museum** and the **Loggia dei Cavalli.** The star attraction of the museum is the world-famous *Triumphal Quadriga,* four horses looted from Constantinople by Venetian crusaders in the sack of that city in 1204. These horses once surmounted the basilica,

Venice Attractions

Accademia 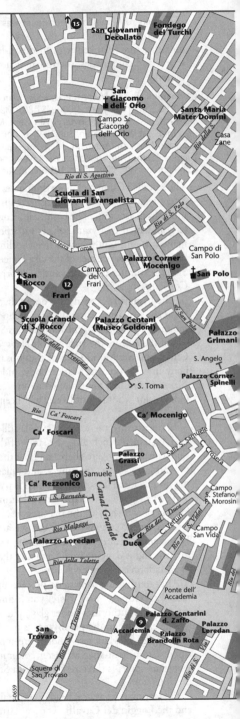 9
Arsenale 22
Basilica di San Giorgio Maggiore 23
Basilica di San Marco 1
Basilica di Santa Maria Gloriosa
 dei Frari 12
Bridge of Sighs 18
Campanile di San Marco 3
Ca' d'Oro 14
Ca' Rezzonico 10
Chiesa di San Zaccaria 20
Chiesa Madonna dell'Orto 16
Collezione Peggy Guggenheim 8
Museo Civico Correr 6
Museo Comunita Ebraica 15
Museo Storico Navale 21
Palazzo delle Prigioni 19
Palazzo Ducale 4
Piazza San Marco 5
Ponte di Rialto 13
Santa Maria della Salute 7
Santi Giovanni e Paolo Basilica 17
Scuola di San Rocco 11
Torre dell'Orologio 2

Church ✝

San Stae

Ca' Pesaro

Palazzo Fontana

Palazzo Sagredo

Ca' d'Oro
14

Strada Nuova

Palazzo Michiel d.Colonne

Santi Apostoli

Campo SS Apostoli

Canal Grande

Ca' da Mosto

Pescaria

C. del Campanile

Calle D. Botteri

Rio di

S.M. dei Miracoli

Palazzo Sanudo

Fonte delle pagioni

S. Giovanni Crisostomo

Rio di S. Marina

17

San Giovanni Elemosinario

Campo S. Aponal

San Giacomo di Rialto

Fondaco dei Tedeschi

Palazzo del Dieci Savi
13

Ponte di Rialto

Palazzo Priuli

Pal. Dona

Campo S. Maria Formosa

San Silvestro

Riva del Vin

Rialto

Riva del Ferro

San Bartolomeo

Stagneri

Santa Maria della Fava

S. Silvestro

Palazzo Dolfin-Manin

Palazzo Bembo

Merc S. Salvador

Pal. Dandolo

San Salvatore

Palazzo Querini-Stampalia

Riva del Carbon

Palazzo Loredan

Pal. Grimari

C. de Teatro

Palazzo Trevisan-Cappello

San Benedetto

San Luca

Campo S. Luca

Larga S. Marco

Canonica

Sant Apollonia

Campo Manin

C. dei Fuseri

C. Fabbri

Spadaria

Pal. Patriarcale
1

18

C. Mandola

Pal. Contarini del Bovolo

2

Basilica di San Marco

19

Campo S. Angelo

Ateneo Veneto

Bacino Orseolo

5   3

Piazza San Marco

4

Palazzo Ducale

Teatro La Fenice

Campo S. Fantin

Piz. di Frezzeria

6

Piazzetta

Ascension

S.S. Moise

San Moise

Molo

Area of Inset →

C. Larga XXII Marzo

Giardinetti Reali

Palazzo Corner (Ca' Grande)

Campo S.M. Zobenigo

San Marco Giardinetti

Casina delle Rose

S.M. del Giglio

Riva Degli Schiavoni

Pal. Venier dei Leoni

Palazzo Dario

8

Punta della Dogana

20

Cp. de l'Arsenal

22

Santa Maria della Salute

San Gregorio

Dogana al Mare

Riva   degli   Schiavoni

7

Seminario Patriarcale

To San Giorgio Maggiore

Bacino San Marco

21

23

417

but were removed because of damage by pollution. They were subsequently restored. This is the only quadriga (which means a quartet of horses yoked together) to have survived from the classical era. They are believed to have been cast in the 4th century. Napoléon once carted these much-traveled horses off to Paris for the Arc du Carousel, but they were returned to Venice in 1815. The museum, with its mosaics and tapestries, is especially interesting, but also be sure to walk out onto the loggia for a view of Piazza San Marco, called by Napoléon "the most beautiful salon in the world."

✪ **Palazzo Ducale.** Piazzetta San Marco. ☎ **041/522-4951.** Admission 14,000L ($8.40). Easter–Oct, daily 9am–6pm; Nov–Easter, daily 9am–4pm. Vaporetto: San Marco.

The Palace of the Doges is entered through the magnificent 15th-century Porta della Carta at the piazzetta. This palace is part of the legend and lore of Venice. It's somewhat like a frosty birthday cake in pinkish-red marble and white Istrian stone. The Venetian Gothic palazzo—with all the architectural intricacies of a paper doily—gleams in the tremulous Venetian light. The grandest civic structure in Italy, it dates back to 1309, although a fire in 1577 destroyed much of the original building.

The fire of 1577 made ashes of many of the palace's greatest masterpieces, and almost spelled doom for the building itself, as the new architectural fervor of the post-Renaissance was in the air. However, fortunately, sanity prevailed. Many of the greatest Venetian painters of the 16th century contributed to the restored palace, replacing the canvases or frescoes of the old masters.

If you enter from the piazzetta, past the four porphyry Moors, you'll be right in the middle of the splendid Renaissance courtyard, one of the most recent additions to a palace that has experienced the work of many different architects with widely varying tastes. You can take the "giants' stairway" to the upper loggia—so called because of the two Sansovino statues of mythological figures.

After climbing the Sansovino stairway of gold you'll enter some get-acquainted rooms. Proceed to the **Anti-Collegio Salon,** which houses the palace's greatest artworks—notably Veronese's *Rape of Europa,* to the far left on the right-hand wall. Tintoretto is well represented with his *Three Graces* and his *Bacchus and Ariadne.* Some critics consider the latter his supreme achievement. In the adjoining **Sala del Collegio,** you'll find allegorical paintings by Veronese on the ceiling. As you proceed to the right, you'll enter the Sala del Senato o Pregadi, with its allegorical painting by Tintoretto in the center of the ceiling.

It's in the **Sala del Consiglio dei Dieci,** with its gloomy paintings, that the dreaded Council of Ten (often called the Terrible Ten for good reason) used to assemble to decide who was in need of decapitation. In the antechamber, bills of accusation were dropped in the lion's mouth.

The excitement continues downstairs. Wander through the once-private apartments of the doges to the grand Maggior Consiglio, with an allegorical *Triumph of Venice* on the ceiling, painted by Veronese. The most outstanding feature, however, is Tintoretto's *Paradise,* over the Grand Council chamber—said to be the largest oil painting in the world. Paradise seems to have an overpopulation problem, perhaps a too-optimistic point of view on Tintoretto's part. Tintoretto was in his 70s when he began this monumental work (he died only 6 years later). The second grandiose hall, entered from the grand chamber, is the **Sala dello Scrutinio,** with paintings that tell of the past glories of Venice.

Reentering the Maggior Consiglio, follow the arrows on their trail across the **Bridge of Sighs,** linking the Doge's Palace with the Palazzo delle Prigioni. Here you'll see the cell blocks that once lodged the prisoners who felt the quick justice of the Terrible Ten. The "sighs" in the bridge's name stem from the sad laments of the

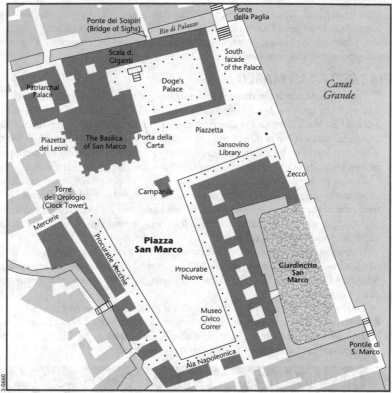

Map labels:
- Ponte dei Sospiri (Bridge of Sighs)
- Ponte della Paglia
- Rio di Palazzo
- Scala d. Giganti
- South facade of the Palace
- Doge's Palace
- Canal Grande
- Patriarchal Palace
- Piazzetta
- Piazzetta dei Leoni
- The Basilica of San Marco
- Porta della Carta
- Sansovino Library
- Zecco
- Torre dell'Orologio (Clock Tower)
- Campanile
- Mercerie
- Procuratie Vecchie
- Piazza San Marco
- Procuratie Nuove
- Giardinetto San Marco
- Museo Civico Correr
- Ala Napoleonica
- Pontile di S. Marco

numerous victims forced across it to face certain torture and possible death. The cells are somber remnants of the horror of medieval justice.

Campanile di San Marco. Piazza San Marco. ☎ **041/522-4064.** Admission 6,000L ($3.60). May–Oct, daily 9am–8pm; Nov–Apr, daily 9:30am–3:45pm. Vaporetto: San Marco.

One summer night back in 1902, the bell tower of St. Mark's Basilica, suffering from years of rheumatism in the damp Venetian climate, gave out a warning sound that sent the elegant and fashionable coffee drinkers in the piazza scurrying for their lives. But the campanile gracefully waited until the next morning—July 14—before it tumbled into the piazza. The Venetians rebuilt their belfry, and it's now safe to climb to the top. However, unlike other bell towers of Italy, where you have to brave narrow, steep, spiral staircases to reach the top, here, you can take an elevator. You can ride it and get a pigeon's view of the city. It's a particularly good vantage point for viewing the cupolas of the basilica.

Torre dell'Orologio. Piazza San Marco. ☎ **041/523-1879.** Vaporetto: San Marco.

Two Moors striking the bell atop the clock tower, Torre dell'Orologio, represent one of the most typical and characteristic Venetian scenes. This tower soars over the Old Procuratie. The clock under the winged lion not only tells the time, but is a boon to the astrologer: It matches the signs of the zodiac with the position of the sun. If the movement of the Moors striking the hour seems slow in today's fast, mechanized world, remember how many centuries the poor wretches have been at their task without time off. The "Moors" originally represented two European shepherds. However, after having been reproduced in bronze, they have grown darker with the passing of time. As a consequence, they came to be called Moors by the Venetians.

Unfortunately, because Venetian authorities have decided that interior visits are dangerous, you can only view the tower from the outside.

PIAZZETTA SAN MARCO

If Piazza San Marco is the drawing room of Europe, then its satellite, Piazzetta San Marco, is the antechamber. Hedged in by the Doge's Palace, Sansovinos Library, and a side of St. Mark's, the tiny square faces the Grand Canal. Two tall granite columns grace the square. One is surmounted by a winged lion, which represents St. Mark. The other is topped by a statue of a man taming a dragon, supposedly the dethroned patron saint Theodore. Both columns came from the East in the 12th century.

During the heyday of the Serene Republic, dozens of victims either lost their heads or were strung up here, many of them first being subjected to torture that would have made the Marquis de Sade flinch. One, for example, had his teeth hammered in, his eyes gouged out, and his hands cut off before being strung up. Venetian justice became notorious throughout Europe.

If you stand with your back to the canal, looking toward the south facade of St. Mark's Basilica, you'll see the so-called *Virgin and Child* of the poor baker, a mosaic honoring Pietro Fasiol (also Faziol), a young man unjustly sentenced to death on a charge of murder.

To the left of the entrance to the Doge's Palace are four porphyry figures, which, for want of a better description, the Venetians called "Moors." These puce-colored fellows are huddled close together, as if afraid. Considering the decapitations and torture that have occurred on the piazzetta, it's no wonder.

2 The Lido & the Grand Canal

THE LIDO

Along the white sands of the Lido strolled Eleonora Duse and Gabriele d'Annunzio *(Flame of Life)*, Goethe in Faustian gloom, a clubfooted Byron trying to decide with whom he was in love that day, de Musset pondering the fickle ways of George Sand, and Thomas Mann's Gustave von Aschenbach with his eye on Tadzio in *Death in Venice*. But gone is the relative isolation of yore. The de Mussets of today aren't mooning over lost loves—they're out chasing bikini-clad new ones.

Near the turn of the century, the Lido began to blossom into a fashionable beachfront resort, complete with deluxe hotels and its Casino Municipale (see "Venice After Dark," later in this chapter). However, like other beachfront resorts throughout the world, you'll find that Lido prices are usually stratospheric.

The Lido today is past its heyday. The fashionable and chic of the world still patronize the Excelsior Palace and the Hotel des Bains, but the beach strip is overrun with tourists and opens onto polluted waters. It's not just the beaches around Venice that are polluted, but reputedly the entire Adriatic. For swimming, guests use the pools of their hotels instead. They can, however, still enjoy the sands along the Lido.

Even if you aren't planning on staying in this area, you should still come over and explore for an afternoon. If you don't want to tread on the beachfront property of the rarefied hotel citadels—which have huts lining the beach like those of some tropical paradise—you can try the lungomare G. d'Annunzio Public Bathing Beach at the end of the Gran Viale (Piazzale Ettore Sorger), a long stroll from the vaporetto stop. You can book cabins—called *camerini*—and enjoy the sand. Rates change seasonally.

To reach the Lido, take vaporetto no. 1, 6, 52, or 82 (the ride takes about 15 minutes). The boat departs from a landing stage near the Doge's Palace.

✪ THE GRAND CANAL

Peoria may have its Main Street, Paris its Champs-Elysées—but Venice, for uniqueness, tops them all with its Canale Grande. Lined with palazzi—many in the elegant Venetian Gothic style—this great road of water is today filled with vaporetti, motorboats, and gondolas. Along the canal the boat moorings are like peppermint sticks. It begins at Piazzetta San Marco on one side and Longhena's Salute Church on the opposite bank. At midpoint it's spanned by the Rialto Bridge. Eventually, the canal winds its serpentine course to the railway station.

Some of the major and most impressive buildings along the Grand Canal have been converted into galleries and museums. Others have been turned into cooperative apartments, but often the lower floors are now deserted. Venetian housewives aren't as incurably romantic as foreign visitors. A practical lot, these women can be seen stringing up their laundry in front of thousands upon thousands of tourists.

On one foggy day, Madame Amandine Lucie Aurore Dudevant, née Dupin (otherwise known as George Sand), and her effete, poetic young lover, Alfred de Musset arrived via this canal. John Ruskin debunked and exposed it in his *The Stones of Venice*. Robert Browning, burnt out from the loss of his beloved Elizabeth and his later rejection at the hands of Lady Ashburton, settled down in a palazzo here, in which he eventually died. Eleonora Duse came this way with the young poet to whom she had given her heart, Gabriele d'Annunzio. Even Shakespeare came here in his fantasies. Intrepid guides will point out the "Palazzo de Desdemona."

The best way to see the Grand Canal is to board vaporetto no. 1 (push, shove, and gouge until you secure a seat at the front of the vessel). Settle yourself in, make sure you have your long-distance viewing glasses, and prepare yourself for a view that has thrilled even the hard-to-impress Ernest Hemingway, as well as millions of other visitors down through the ages.

3 Museums & Galleries

Venice is a city of art. Decorating its palazzi and adorning its canvases were artists such as Giovanni Bellini, Carpaccio, Giorgione, Titian, Lotto, Tintoretto, Veronese, Tiepolo, Guardi, Canaletto, and Longhi, to name just the more important ones. In the museums and galleries to follow, important works by all these artists are exhibited, as well as a number of modern surprises, such as those in the Guggenheim Collection.

Visiting hours are often subject to major variations, so keep this in mind as you go sightseeing. Many visitors who have budgeted only 2 or 3 days for Venice often express disappointment when, for some unknown reason, a major attraction closes abruptly.

✪ **Accademia.** Campo della Carità, Dorsoduro. ☎ **041/522-2247.** Admission 12,000L ($7.20) adults, free for children 17 and under and seniors 60 and over. Mon–Sat 9am–7pm, Sun 9am–2pm. Vaporetto: Accademia.

The pomp and circumstance, the glory that was Venice, lives on in this remarkable collection of paintings that span the period from the 14th to the 18th centuries. The hallmark of the Venetian school is color and more color. From Giorgione to Veronese, from Titian to Tintoretto, with a Carpaccio cycle thrown in, the Accademia has samples—often their best work—of its most famous sons. We'll highlight only some of the most-renowned masterpieces for the first-timer in a rush.

Plan of the Accademia

Room	What You'll Find There
1	Venetian painters; 14th century
2	Giovanni Bellini and Cima da Conegliano
3	Late 15th century to early 16th century
4	Italian painters; 15th century
5	Giovanni Bellini and Giorgione
6	16th century
7	Lorenzo Lotto and GG Savoldo
8	Palma the Elder
9	16th-century schools of painting
10	Titian, Veronese, and Tintoretto
11	Veronese, Tintoretto, and GB Tiepolo
12	18th-century landscape painters
13	Tintoretto and Bassano
14	Renovators of the 17th century
15	Minor painters of the 18th century
16	Giambattista Piazzetta
17	Longhi, Camaletto, Carriera, and Guardi
18	18th-century painters and engravers
19	15th-century painters
20	Gentile Bellini and Vittorio Carpaccio
21	Vittorio Carpaccio
22	Bookshop
23	Venetian painters; 15th century
24	Albergo Room and Titian

You'll first see works by such 14th-century artists as Paolo and Lorenzo Veneziano, who bridged the gap from Byzantine art to Gothic (see the latter's *Annunciation*). Next, you'll view Giovanni Bellini's *Madonna and Saint* (poor Sebastian, not another arrow), and Carpaccio's fascinating, although gruesome, work of mass crucifixion. As you move on, head for the painting on the easel by the window, attributed to the great Venetian artist Giorgione. On this canvas he depicted the *Madonna and Child*, along with the mystic St. Catherine of Siena and John the Baptist (a neat trick for Catherine, who seems to have perfected transmigration to join the cast of characters).

Two of the most important works with secular themes are Mantegna's armored *St. George*, with the slain dragon at his feet, and Hans Memling's 15th-century portrait of a young man. A most unusual *Madonna and Child* is by Cosmé Tura, the master of Ferrara, who could always be counted on to give a new twist to an old subject.

The Madonnas and bambini of Giovanni Bellini, an expert in the harmonious blending of colors, are the focus of another room. None but the major artists could stand the test of a salon filled with the same subjects, but under Bellini's brush each Virgin achieves her individual spirituality. Giorgione's *Tempest*, displayed here, is the single most famous painting at the Accademia. It depicts a baby suckling from the breast of its mother, while a man with a staff looks on. What might have emerged as a simple pastoral scene on the easel of a lesser artist comes forth as a picture of rare and exceptional beauty. Summer lightning pierces the sky, but the tempest seems to be in the background—far away from the figures in the foreground, who are menaced without knowing it.

The masterpiece of Lorenzo Lorto, a melancholy portrait of a young man, can be seen before you come to a room dominated by Paolo Veronese's *The Banquet in the House of Levi*. This is, in reality, a "Last Supper" that was considered a sacrilege in its day, so Veronese was forced to change its name to indicate a secular work. Impish Veronese caught the hot fire of the Inquisition by including dogs, a cat, midgets, Huns, and drunken revelers in the mammoth canvas. Four large paintings by Tintoretto—noted for their swirling action and powerful drama—depict scenes from the life of St. Mark. Finally, painted in his declining years (some have suggested in his 99th year, before he died from the plague) is Titian's majestic *Pietà*.

After a long and unimpressive walk, you can search out Canaletto's *Porticato*. Yet another room is heightened by Gentile Bellini's stunning portrait of St. Mark's Square, back in the days (1496) when the houses glistened with gold in the sunlight. All the works in this salon are intriguing, especially the re-creation of the *Ponte de Rialto,* and a covered wood bridge, by Carpaccio.

Also displayed is the cycle of narrative paintings that Vittore Carpaccio did of St. Ursula for the Scuola of Santa Orsola. The most famous is no. 578, which shows Ursula asleep on her elongated bed, with a dog nestled on the floor nearby, as the angels come for a visitation. Finally, on the way out, look for Titian's *Presentation of the Virgin,* a fit farewell to this galaxy of great Venetian art.

Museo Civico Correr. In the Procuratie Nuove, Piazza San Marco. ☎ **041/522-5625.** Admission 14,000L ($8.40) adults, 8,000L ($4.80) children 6–18, free for children 5 and under. June–Aug, Wed–Mon 10am–5pm; off-season, Wed–Mon 10am–4pm. Vaporetto: San Marco.

This museum traces the development of Venetian painting from the 14th to the 16th centuries. On the second floor are the red and maroon robes once worn by the doges, plus some fabulous street lanterns. There's also an illustrated copy of *Marco Polo in Tartaria.* You can see Cosmé Tura's *La Pietà,* a miniature of renown from the genius in the Ferrara School. This is one of his more gruesome works. It depicts a bony, gnarled Christ sprawled on the lap of the Madonna. Farther on, search out a Schiavone *Madonna and Child* (no. 545), our candidate for ugliest bambino ever depicted on canvas (no wonder the mother looks askance).

One of the most important rooms at the Correr is filled with three masterpieces: *La Pietà* by Antonello da Messina, a *Crucifixion* by the Flemish painter Hugo van der Goes, and a *Madonna and Child* by Dieric Bouts, who depicted the baby suckling his mother in a sensual manner. The star attraction of the Correr is the Bellini salon, which includes works by founding padre Jacopo and his son, Gentile. But the real master of the household was the other son, Giovanni, the major painter of the 15th-century Venetian school (look for his *Crucifixion* and compare it with his father's treatment of the same subject).

A small but celebrated portrait of St. Anthony of Padua by Alvise Vivarini is here, plus works by Bartolomeo Montagna. The most important work in the gallery, however, is Vittore Carpaccio's *Two Venetian Ladies,* although their true gender is a subject of much debate. In Venice they are popularly known as "The Courtesans." A lesser work, *St. Peter,* depicting the saint with the daggers in him, hangs in the same room.

The entrance is under the arcades of Ala Napoleonica at the western end of the square.

Ca'd'Oro. Cannaregio 3931–3932. ☎ **041/523-8790.** Admission 4,000L ($2.40). Daily 9am–1:30pm. Closed Jan 1, May 1, and Dec 25. Vaporetto: Ca'd'Oro.

This is one of the grandest and most handsomely embellished palaces along the Grand Canal. Although it contains the important **Galleria Giorgio Franchetti,** the House of Gold (so named because its facade was once gilded) competes with its own paintings. Today its facade is pink and white. Built in the first part of the 15th century in the ogival style, it has a lacy Gothic look. As a stellar example of Venetian Gothic, it is rivaled only by the doge's palace. Baron Franchetti, who restored the palace and filled it with his own collection of paintings, sculpture, and furniture, presented it to Italy during World War I.

You enter into a stunning courtyard, 50 yards from the vaporetto stop. The courtyard has a multicolored patterned marble floor and is filled with statuary. Proceed upstairs to the lavishly appointed palazzo. One of the gallery's major paintings is Titian's voluptuous *Venus.* She coyly covers one breast, but what about the other?

In a special niche reserved for the masterpiece of the Franchetti collection is Andrea Mantegna's icy-cold *St. Sebastian,* the central figure of which is riddled with what must be a record number of arrows. You'll also find works by Carpaccio. If you walk out onto the loggia, you'll have one of the grandest views of the Grand Canal, a panorama that even inspired Lord Byron when he could take his eyes off the ladies.

Ca'Rezzonico. Fondamenta Rezzonico, Dorsoduro 3136. ☎ **041/241-0100.** Admission 12,000L ($7.20) adults, 8,000L ($4.80) children 12–18, 4,000L ($2.40) children 11 and under. Oct–Apr, Sat–Thurs 10am–4pm; May–Sept, 10am–5pm. Vaporetto: Ca'Rezzonico.

This 17th- and 18th-century palace along the Grand Canal is where Robert Browning set up his bachelor headquarters. He was to die here in 1889. Pope Clement XIII also stayed here. It's a virtual treasure house, known for both its baroque paintings and furniture. First you enter the Grand Ballroom with its allegorical ceiling, then proceed through lavishly embellished rooms with Venetian chandeliers, brocaded walls, portraits of patricians, tapestries, gilded furnishings, and touches of chinoiserie. At the end of the first walk is the Throne Room, with its allegorical ceilings by Giovanni Battista Tiepolo.

On the first floor you can walk out onto a balcony for a view of the Grand Canal as the aristocratic tenants of the 18th century saw it. After this, another group of rooms follows, including the library. In these salons, look for a bizarre collection of paintings. One, for example, depicts half-clothed women beating up a defenseless naked man (one Amazon is about to stick a pitchfork into his neck, another to crown him with a violin). In the adjoining room, another woman is hammering a spike through a man's skull.

Upstairs you'll find a survey of 18th-century Venetian art. As you enter the main room from downstairs, head for the first salon on your right (facing the canal), which contains the best works of all, paintings from the brush of Pietro Longhi. His most famous work, *The Lady and the Hairdresser,* is the first canvas to the right on the entrance wall. Others depict the life of the idle Venetian rich. On the rest of the floor are bedchambers, a chapel, and salons—some with badly damaged frescoes, including a romp of satyrs.

✪ Collezione Peggy Guggenheim. Ca'Venier dei Leoni, Dorsoduro 701, Calle San Cristoforo. ☎ **041/520-6288.** Admission 12,000L ($7.20) adults, 8,000L ($4.80) students and children 16 and under. Wed–Mon 11am–6pm. Vaporetto: Accademia.

This is one of the most comprehensive and brilliant modern-art collections in the Western world, and it reveals both the foresight and critical judgment of its founder. The collection is housed in an unfinished palazzo, the former Venetian home of

Peggy Guggenheim, who died in 1979. In the tradition of her family, Peggy Guggenheim was a lifelong patron of contemporary painters and sculptors. Founder of the Art of This Century Gallery in New York in the 1940s, she created one of the most avant-garde galleries for the works of contemporary artists. Critics were impressed not only by the high quality of the artists she sponsored, but by her methods of displaying them.

As her private collection increased, she decided to find a larger showcase and selected Venice, steeped in a long tradition as a haven for artists. While the Solomon Guggenheim Museum was going up in New York according to Frank Lloyd Wright's specifications, she was creating her own gallery in Venice. Guests can wander through and enjoy art in an informal and relaxed way. Max Ernst was one of Peggy Guggenheim's early favorites, as was Jackson Pollock (she provided a farmhouse where he could develop his painting technique). Displayed here are works not only by Pollock and Ernst, but also by Picasso (see his cubist *The Poet* of 1911), Duchamp, Chagall, Mondrian, Brancusi, Delvaux, and Dalí, and a garden of modern sculpture that includes works by Giacometti, some of which he struggled to complete while resisting the amorous intentions of Marlene Dietrich. Temporary modern-art shows may be presented during the winter months. Since Peggy Guggenheim's death, the collection has been administered by the Solomon R. Guggenheim Foundation, which also operates the Solomon R. Guggenheim Museum in New York. Visitors can also enjoy a museum shop and cafe in the new wing of the museum, overlooking the sculpture garden.

Museo Storico Navale. Campo San Biasio, Castello 2148. ☎ **041/520-0276.** Admission 2,000L ($1.20): Mon–Sat 8:45am–1:30pm. Closed holidays. Vaporetto: Arsenale.

The Naval Museum of Campo San Biasio is filled with cannons, ships' models, and fragments of old vessels that date back to the days when Venice was supreme in the Adriatic. The prize exhibit is a gilded model of the *Bucintoro,* the great ship of the doge that surely would have made Cleopatra's barge look like an oil tanker in comparison. In addition, you'll find models of historic and modern fighting ships, local fishing and rowing craft, and a collection of 24 Chinese junks, as well as a number of maritime *ex voto* from churches of Naples.

If you walk along the canal as it branches off from the museum, you'll arrive at (about 270 yards from the museum and before the wooden bridge) the **Ships' Pavilion** where historic vessels are displayed. Proceeding along the canal, you'll soon reach the **Arsenale,** Campo del'Arsenale, guarded by stone lions, Neptune with a trident, and other assorted ferocities. You'll spot it readily enough because of its two towers that flank each side of the canal. In its day the Arsenale turned out galley after galley at speeds usually associated with wartime production.

4 More Attractions

CHURCHES & GUILD HOUSES

Much of the great art of Venice lies in its churches and *scuole* (guild houses or fraternities). Most of the guild members were drawn from the rising bourgeoisie of Venice. The guilds were said to fulfill both the material and spiritual needs of their (male) members, who often engaged in charitable works in honor of the saint for whom their scuola was named. Many of the greatest artists of Venice, including Tintoretto, were commissioned to decorate these guild houses. Some of the artists created masterpieces that can still be viewed today. Often the life of the patron saint of the scuola was commemorated. Narrative canvases that depicted the lives of the saints were called *teleri.*

✪ **Scuola di San Rocco.** Campo San Rocco, San Polo 3058. ☎ **041/523-4864.** Admission 8,000L ($4.80) adults, 6,000L ($3.60) students, 2,500L ($1.50) children. Mar 28–Nov 2, daily 9am–5:30pm; Nov 3–Mar 27, Mon–Fri 10am–1pm, Sat–Sun 10am–4pm. Closed Easter and Dec 25–Jan 1. Vaporetto: San Tomà; from the station, walk straight onto Ramo Mondoler, which becomes Larga Prima; then take Salizzada San Rocco, which opens into Campo San Rocco.

Of the scuole of Venice, none is as richly embellished as the Scuola di San Rocco, which is filled with epic canvases by Tintoretto. Born Jacopo Robusti in 1518, he became known for paintings of mystical spirituality and phantasmagoric light effects. By a clever trick he won the competition to decorate the darkly illuminated early 16th-century building. He began painting in 1564, and the work stretched on until his powers as an artist waned. He died in 1594. The paintings sweep across the upper and lower halls, mesmerizing the viewer with a kind of passion play. In the grand hallway they depict New Testament scenes, devoted largely to episodes in the life of Mary (the *Flight into Egypt* is among the best). In the top gallery are works that illustrate scenes from both the Old and New Testaments, the most renowned being those devoted to the life of Christ. In a separate room is Tintoretto's masterpiece—his mammoth *Crucifixion*, one of the world's most celebrated paintings. In it he showed his dramatic scope and sense of grandeur as an artist, creating a deeply felt scene that virtually comes alive—filling the viewer with the horror of systematic execution, thus transcending its original subject matter.

Basilica di Santa Maria Gloriosa dei Frari. Campo dei Frari, San Polo. ☎ **041/522-2637.** Admission 3,000L ($1.80), free Sun. Mon–Sat 9–11:45am and 3–6pm, Sun 3–6pm. Vaporetto: San Tomà.

Known simply as the Frari, this Venetian Gothic church is only a short walk from the Scuola di San Rocco. The church is filled with some great art. The best work is Titian's *Assumption* over the main altar—a masterpiece of soaring beauty that depicts the ascension of the Madonna on a cloud puffed up by floating cherubs. In her robe, but especially in the robe of one of the gaping saints below, "Titian red" dazzles as never before.

On the first altar to the right as you enter is Titian's second major work here—a *Madonna Enthroned,* painted for the Pesaro family in 1526. Although lacking the power and drama of the *Assumption,* it nevertheless is brilliant in its use of color and light effects. But Titian surely would turn redder than his Madonna's robes if he could see the latter-day neoclassical tomb built for him on the opposite wall. The kindest word for it: large.

Facing the tomb is a memorial to Canova, the Italian sculptor who led the revival of classicism. To return to more enduring art, head to the sacristy for a Giovanni Bellini triptych on wood, painted in 1488. The Madonna is cool and serene, one of Bellini's finest portraits of the Virgin. Also see the almost primitive-looking wood carving by Donatello of *St. John the Baptist.*

Scuola di San Giorgio degli Schiavoni. Calle Furiani, Castello. ☎ **041/522-8828.** Admission 5,000L ($3). Tues–Sat 10am–12:30pm and 3–6pm, Sun 10am–12:30pm. Vaporetto: San Zaccaria.

At the St. Antonino Bridge (Fondamenta dei Furlani) is the second important guild house to visit in Venice. Between 1502 and 1509 Vittore Carpaccio painted a pictorial cycle here of exceptional merit and interest. Of enduring fame are his works of St. George and the dragon—these are our favorite art in all of Venice and certainly the most delightful. For example, in one frame St. George charges the dragon on a field littered with half-eaten bodies and skulls. Gruesome? Not at all. Any moment you expect the director to call "Cut!" The pictures relating to St. Jerome are appealing but don't compete with St. George and his ferocious dragon.

Chiesa Madonna dell'Orto. Campo dell'Orto, Cannaregio 3512. ☎ **041/719-933.** Free admission. May–Oct, daily 9:30am–noon and 3:30–6pm; Nov–Apr, daily 9:30am–noon and 3–7pm. Vaporetto: Madonna dell'Orto.

This church provides a good reason to walk to this fairly remote northern district of Venice. At the church on the lagoon you'll be paying your final respects to Tintoretto. The brick structure with a Gothic front is famed not only because of its paintings by that artist, but because the great master is buried in the chapel to the right of the main altar. At the high altar are Tintoretto's *Last Judgment* (on the right) and *Sacrifice of the Golden Calf* (left)—two monumental paintings that curve at the top like a Gothic arch. Over the doorway to the right of the altar is Tintoretto's superb portrayal of the presentation of Mary as a little girl at the temple. The composition is unusual in that Mary is not the focal point—rather, a pointing woman bystander dominates the scene. The first chapel to the right of the main altar contains a masterly work by Cima de Conegliano, showing the presentation of a sacrificial lamb to the saints (the plasticity of St. John's body evokes Michelangelo). Finally, the first chapel on the left (as you enter) is graced with an exquisite Giovanni Bellini *Madonna and Child.* Note especially the eyes and mouth of both the mother and child. Two other pictures in the apse are *The Presentation of the Cross to St. Peter* and *The Beheading of St. Christopher.*

Chiesa di San Zaccaria. Campo San Zaccaria, Castello. ☎ **041/522-1257.** Admission 2,000L ($1.20). Daily 10am–noon and 4–6pm. Vaporetto: San Zaccaria.

Behind St. Mark's Basilica is this Gothic church with a Renaissance facade. The church is filled with works of art, notably Giovanni Bellini's restored *Madonna Enthroned,* painted with saints (second altar to the left). Many have found this to be one of Bellini's finest Madonnas, and it does have beautifully subdued coloring, although it appears rather static. Apply to the sacristan to see the Sisters' Choir, with works by Tintoretto, Titian, Il Vecchio, Anthony van Dyck, and Bassano. The paintings aren't labeled, but the sacristan will point out the names of the artists. In the Sisters' Choir are five armchairs in which the Venetian doges of yore sat. Also, if you save the best for last, you can see the faded frescoes of Andrea del Castagno in the shrine that honors San Tarasio.

Basilica di San Giorgio Maggiore. San Giorgio Maggiore, across from Piazzetta San Marco. ☎ **041/528-9900.** Free admission. Apr–Oct, daily 9:30am–12:30pm and 2:30–6pm; Nov–Mar, daily 10am–12:30pm and 2:30–4:30pm. Closed for Mass on Sunday and feast days 10:45am–noon. Vaporetto: Take the Giudecca-bound vaporetto (no. 82) on Riva degli Schiavoni and get off at the first stop, right in the courtyard of the church.

This church sits on the little island of San Giorgio Maggiore. The building was designed by Palladio, the great Renaissance architect of the 16th century—perhaps as a consolation prize since he was not chosen to rebuild the burnt-out Doge's Palace. The logical rhythm of the Vicenza architect is played here on a grand scale. But inside it's almost too stark since Palladio wasn't much on gilded adornment. The chief art hangs on the main altar—two epic paintings by Tintoretto, the *Fall of Manna* to the left and the far more successful *Last Supper* to the right. It's interesting to compare Tintoretto's *Cena* with that of Veronese at the Academy. Afterward you may want to take the elevator—for 3,000L ($1.80)—to the top of the belfry for a view of the greenery of the island itself, the lagoon, and the Doge's Palace across the way. In a word, it's unforgettable.

Santa Maria della Salute. Campo della Salute, Dorsoduro. ☎ **041/731-268.** Free admission (but an offering is expected); Sacristy 1,000L (60¢). Mar–Nov, daily 9am–noon and 3–6:30pm; Dec–Feb, daily 9am–noon and 3–5pm. Vaporetto: Salute.

Like the proud landmark that it is, La Salute—the pinnacle of the baroque movement in Venice—stands at the mouth of the Grand Canal overlooking Piazzetta San Marco. It opens onto Campo della Salute, in Dorsoduro. One of the most historic churches in Venice, it was built by Longhena in the 17th century—work began in 1631—as an offering to the Virgin for delivering the city from the grip of the plague. It was erected on enough pilings to support the Empire State Building (well, almost). Longhena, almost unknown when he got the commission for the church, was to dedicate a half a century to working on this church. Tragically, he would die 5 years before the long-lasting job was finally completed. Surmounted by a great cupola, the octagonal basilica makes for an interesting visit, as it houses a small art gallery in its sacristy (tip the custodian), which includes a marriage feast of Cana by Tintoretto, allegorical paintings on the ceiling by Titian, a mounted St. Mark, and poor St. Sebastian with his inevitable arrow.

Santi Giovanni e Paolo Basilica. Campo SS. Giovanni e Paolo, Castello 6363. ☎ **041/523-5913.** Free admission. Daily 7:30am–12:30pm and 3–7:30pm. Vaporetto: Rialto or Fondamenta Nuove.

This church, also known as Zanipolo, is called the unofficial pantheon of Venice since it houses the tombs of many doges. One of the great Gothic churches of Venice, the building was erected during the 13th and 14th centuries. Inside it contains artwork by many of the most noted Venetian painters. As you enter (right aisle), you'll find a retable by Giovanni Bellini (which includes a St. Sebastian filled with arrows). In the Rosary Chapel are ceilings by Veronese depicting New Testament scenes, including *The Assumption of the Madonna*. To the right of the church is one of the world's best-known equestrian statues—that of Bartolomeo Colleoni (paid for by the condottiere), sculpted in the 15th century by Andrea del Verrochio. The bronze has long been acclaimed as his masterpiece, although it was completed by another artist. The horse is far more beautiful than the armored military hero, who looks as if he had just stumbled upon a three-headed crocodile.

To the left of the pantheon is the Scuola di San Marco, with a stunning Renaissance facade (it's now run as a civic hospital).

THE GHETTO

The Ghetto of Venice, called the Ghetto Nuovo, was instituted in 1516 by the Venetian Republic in the Cannaregio district. It's considered to be the first ghetto in the world, and also the best kept. The word *geto* comes from the Venetian dialect and means "foundry." Originally there were two iron foundries here where metals were fused. The Ghetto stands in what is now the northwestern corner of Venice. Once Venetian Jews were confined to a walled area and obliged to wear distinctive red or yellow marks sewn onto their clothing and distinctive-looking hats. The walls that once enclosed and confined the Ghetto were torn down long ago, but much remains of the past.

There are five synagogues in Venice, each built during the 16th century. The oldest and most beautiful is the **Scola Tedesca** (German Synagogue), which was restored with funds from Germany. The others are the Spanish (the oldest continuously functioning synagogue in Europe), the Italian, **the Levantine-Oriental** (also known as the Turkish Synagogue), and the **Scola Canton.**

The best way to visit the synagogues is to take one of the guided tours that depart from the **Museo Comunità Ebraica,** Campo di Ghetto Nuovo 2902B (☎ **041/715-359;** Vaporetto: San Marcuola). The museum itself is open June to September, Sunday to Friday from 10am to 7pm; and October to May, Sunday to Friday from

10am to 4:30pm. Admission to the museum is 4,000L ($2.40) adults, 3,000L ($1.80) students. Guided tours cost 10,000L ($6) for adults and 8,000L ($4.80) for students. Tours last about an hour each, and depart Sunday to Friday at hourly intervals between 10:30am and 3:30pm from October to May, and at hourly intervals between 10:30am and 5:30pm from June to September. Tours include admission to the museum and visits to whatever three of the five synagogues happen to be open at the time of your visit.

WALKING TOUR
From Piazza San Marco to the Grand Canal

If this walking tour whets your appetite for more strolls through Venice, pick up a copy of *Frommer's Walking Tours: Venice,* which features 10 walking tours as well as detailed maps of the city.

Start: Piazza San Marco.
Finish: Grand Canal at the Ponte di Rialto.
Time: 2 hours, not including stops.
Best Times: Any sunny day.
Worst Times: Holidays and festivals (the streets are too crowded).

There are hundreds of byways, alleyways, and canals stretching across the faded splendor of Venice. This 2-hour walking tour will give you at least an exterior view plus a general orientation to the layout of parts of the city, often showing lesser-known sights, which can best be seen from the outside, on foot. Later, you can pick and choose at your leisure the sights you most want to revisit.

Our tour begins, appropriately enough, at the heart of the city:

1. **Piazza San Marco,** or St. Mark's Square, the most famous in Italy. Here and on its satellite square, Piazzetta San Marco, you can explore the major attractions of the city. These include the:

2. **Basilica di San Marco,** named for St. Mark, whose body was allegedly stolen from his tomb in Alexandria in 828 and brought to Venice. This basilica was built to enshrine the body of the man who became the city's patron saint. Next door is the:

3. **Palazzo Ducale,** a pink confection that was the home of the doges (dukes) who ruled Venice for years, with its adjoining Ponte dei Sospiri (Bridge of Sighs). In front of the palace is the:

4. **Campanile di San Marco,** the bell tower of Venice, which visitors climb for a view of the city and lagoon.

5. **Santa Maria della Salute.** The Renaissance mariners who supplied the lifelines that led to their Adriatic capital realized that the most impressive view of the city was, and perhaps still is, visible only from the water. To better see this unforgettable view, take a brief vaporetto ride across the Grand Canal to the baroque white walls of Santa Maria della Salute. Buy your ticket at either of two vaporetto stops: no. 16 (San Zaccaria), just east of St. Mark's Square, or no. 15 (San Marco), which lies just west of the square along the Grand Canal. Enjoy the short water ride and the view before getting off on the opposite side of the canal at the pier marked Salute. There you can look back across the Grand Canal at the rows of palazzi, many of which have been turned into glamorous hotels.

Walk to the right side of the church along Campo della Salute, past a pair of wooden bridges, and continue until you reach the third bridge, the only one of the three that's made of stone. Cross this bridge and head onto Rio Terradei

Catecumeni. After one block, turn left onto Calle Constantina. Now walk toward the water along a wide flagstone-covered walkway divided by a single row of trees that must struggle to survive in the salt air of Venice. The waterway you'll soon reach separates this section of Venice from the rarely visited:

6. **Island of Giudecca,** which lies across the broad Canale di Giudecca. Although you won't visit it as part of this walking tour, you might decide to return to explore its untrammeled streets later during your visit. From this vantage point, you can also gaze upon the cranes of the industrialized mainland town of Mestre, to the north.

   Turn right along the waterfront to a district known to Venetians as Dorsoduro. Much more of a residential neighborhood than the area around Piazza San Marco, it has often been compared to New York's Greenwich Village because artists and writers have traditionally been attracted to it. Many, of course, came to avoid the high prices charged on the opposite side of the Grand Canal. With water to your left and a changing panorama of brick and stone buildings to your right, you'll cross over the high arches of several bridges, always continuing along the canalside walkway which, in characteristically Venetian fashion, will change its name at least three times.

   At the third and last bridge, the Ponte della Calcina, at Campiello della Calcina, you'll notice two of the most famous pensiones of Venice—La Calcina, where John Ruskin stayed, and the Pensione Seguso. The name of the pavement that supports you here is Zattere ai Gesuati. You'll notice a pair of wooden platforms, managed by local cafes and separated from one another by dry-docked steel-hulled ships. After, perhaps, a coffee, you'll reach the acanthus-inspired pilasters of the baroque:

7. **Chiesa dei Gesuiti.** After visiting the church, take the street to its right, which is referred to variously as Rio Terrà Antonio Foscarini, Rio Terrà Marco Foscarini, or simply Rio Terrà Foscarini, and walk northwest. At the side of the church, admire Campo Santa Agnese, where tolling bells call the neighborhood to mass.

   Now continue north along Rio Foscarini until you reach the Grand Canal and the:

8. **Gallerie dell'Accademia.** You can either visit this great gallery of art or save it for another day. Cross the bridge, and you may notice the German consulate beside the elegant garden to the left. When you step off the bridge, you'll be on Campo San Vidal. At this point, the city of Venice has graciously mapped out one of the most logical walking tours in the city by posting prominent yellow signs with black lettering on dozens of appropriate street corners.

   Your walk, if you follow the signs, will take you back to St. Mark's Square through dozens of claustrophobic alleys, which are crumbling from exposure to the Adriatic winds, and into gloriously proportioned squares whose boundaries are often ornamented with exquisite detailing. From this point on, follow the signs that say PER S. MARCO. You can afford to ignore your map and lose yourself in the Renaissance splendor of this most unusual city.

   At Campo San Vidal, the pavement will funnel you in only one possible direction. After several twists and turns, you'll be in the huge expanse of:

9. **Campo San Stefano** (whose southern end is referred to on some maps as Campo Francesco Morosini). Keep walking across the square, past a wood-and-iron flagpole capped with the Lion of St. Mark. Midway along the right side of the square, follow the PER S. MARCO sign down a tiny alleyway called Calle del Spezier. The alley funnels across a bridge and then changes its name to Calle del Piovan. This will open to the wide expanses of:

10. **Campo San Maurizio.** Walk directly across the square, looking for yet another PER S. MARCO sign, which should direct you over another set of bridges.

Walking Tour—Piazza San Marco
To The Grand Canal

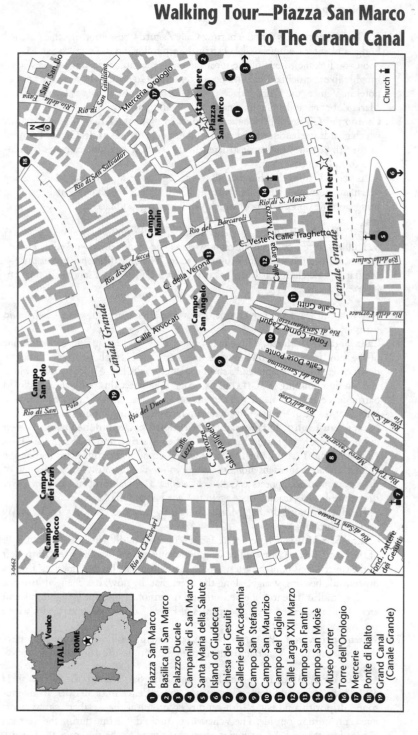

Church ✝

start here

Piazza San Marco

finish here

Merceria Orologio

Rio della Fava
Salz. San Lio
Rio di San Grilliano

Rio di San Salvador

Campo Manin

Rio di San Lucca

Campo San Angelo

C. della Verona

Calle Avvocati

Canăle Grande

Campo San Polo

Rio di San Polo

Campo del Frari

Campo San Rocco

Rio di Ca Foscari

Calle Lezzo

C. Carozzero

Salz. Malefatio

Rio del Duca

Rio del Sussinimo

Calle Dose Ponte

Rio di San Maurizio

Fond. Corner Zaguri

Calle Gritti

Rio del Barcaroli

C. Veste Calle Traghetto

Calle Larga 22 Marzo

Rio di S. Moisè

Canale Grande

Rio della Salute

Rio della Tornace

Salz. Marco Pascarini

Rio di S. Vio

Rio di San Trovaso

Fond. Zattere dei Gesuiti

Rio di San Tarià

3-0662

Venice
ITALY
ROME

1. Piazza San Marco
2. Basilica di San Marco
3. Palazzo Ducale
4. Campanile di San Marco
5. Santa Maria della Salute
6. Island of Giudecca
7. Chiesa dei Gesuiti
8. Gallerie dell'Accademia
9. Campo San Stefano
10. Campo San Maurizio
11. Campo del Giglio
12. Calle Larga XXII Marzo
13. Campo San Fantin
14. Campo San Moisè
15. Museo Correr
16. Torre dell'Orologio
17. Mercerie
18. Ponte di Rialto
19. Grand Canal (Canale Grande)

431

This square funnels into the narrow Calle Zaguri. Cross another canal's arched bridge and enter Campiello de la Feltrina. Keep following the signs to San Marco. Soon you'll come to one of the most famous Venetian squares, which is shaped roughly like a crucifix. One end opens onto the Grand Canal, near the famous hotel in Venice, the Gritti Palace. The full name of the square is Campo Santa Maria Zobenigo o del Giglio, a name usually shortened to:

11. **Campo del Giglio.** The square is dominated by a larger-than-life-sized statue, which guards the baroque facade of the Chiesa di Santa Maria del Giglio. Founded in the 9th century, but reconstructed in the 17th, it contains canvases by Tintoretto and Rubens.

As you exit from the church, follow once again the signs to San Marco, going down an alleyway, Calle delle Ostreghe. Cross the high arch of a canal-spanning bridge, on the opposite side of which you'll spot a good place to:

☕ **TAKE A BREAK**   The Bar Ducale, Calle delle Ostreghe (☎ 041/ 521-0002), offers cocktails and sandwiches. The owner once worked at Harry's Bar and learned the restaurant's culinary secrets. The only difference here is price— the Bar Ducale charges half the price of Harry's Bar. If not a sandwich, then enjoy a cappuccino.

When you leave the Bar Ducale, follow the street through several twists and turns onto:

12. **Calle larga XXII Marzo,** whose many shops, cafes, and restaurants make this one of the most frequented and crowded streets of Venice. In about a block, midway down its length, we recommend a short detour off to the left. Notice the gold, white, and red sign pointing to AL TEATRO LA FENICE. The street this points to is Calle del Sartor da Veste. Turn neither to the left nor right, but follow it over two bridges, into what is one of the most intimate summertime "living rooms" of Venice:

13. **Campo San Fantin.** In fair weather, the enclosed square is dotted with tables set out by the best restaurant in Venice, the **Antico Martini,** and its lesser rivals. Here you'll find the Teatro La Fenice and the Church of St. Fantin. After visiting the church, retrace your steps along the street you took previously. From the end of the square, its name appears as Calle del Cafetier. This walk will take you back over the pair of bridges leading once again to Calle Larga XXII Marzo.

Head left, toward the San Moisè Church. By now the PER S. MARCO signs will lead you through:

14. **Campo San Moisè,** whose ornate facade contrasts oddly with the modern bulk of the Hotel Bauer Grünwald & Grand on your right. Take the street to the left of the church, and note the PER S. MARCO sign as you pass by the American Express office while heading straight along the street that, by now, has changed its name once again, this time to Calle Seconda de l'Ascension. Continue straight under an arched tunnel to the sweeping expanses of Piazza San Marco, once again, where you may want to visit the:

15. **Museo Correr,** in the Procuratie Nuove, opposite the basilica. This museum traces the development of Venetian painting from the 14th to the 16th centuries.

☕ **TAKE A BREAK**   Since **Florian,** Piazza San Marco 56–59 (☎ 041/ 528-5338), was established, it has been the most Venetian of all cafes. Its interior rooms drip with a nostalgic 18th-century decor, but if the weather's sunny, most guests prefer to sit outside. The Venetians patronized this cafe during the Austrian occupation, whereas the occupying army's brass went to the rival cafe, the Quadri, across the square.

   Later, walk through the square and pass to the left of the Basilica of St. Mark, stopping perhaps to admire a pair of lions carved from red porphyry. As you gaze with the lions back across the wide expanse of the square, notice the arched tunnel that pierces the base of the:

16. **Torre dell'Orologio.** Pass beneath the Moorish bell ringers and the zodiac representations of the clock face. Here you'll be on the major shopping street of Venice, the:

17. **Mercerie.** Of course, this is the popular name of the street. It actually has many longer names, preceded by the word *merceria.* From now on, your guiding light will be the signs that say PER RIALTO. They will be either formally positioned at strategic corners in yellow or black or scrawled sometimes graffiti-style on the sides of buildings.

   Soon you'll reach the:

18. **Ponte Rialto,** from the Latin *rivo alto,* meaning high bank. The Istrian-stone bridge dates from 1588. The architect, Antonio da Ponte, actually beat out Michelangelo, Palladio, and Sansovino, among others, in a competition to design this bridge. Until 1854, the bridge was the only pedestrian crossing on the Grand Canal.

   Once at this point, you can board a vaporetto to take you back to Piazza San Marco. Along the way you can enjoy the:

19. **Grand Canal.** A ride along the palazzo-flanked banks of this highly touted waterway is not only one of the grandest experiences in all of Italy, but the entire world. It's the one experience visitors are likely to remember when memories of other monuments begin to fade away.

5 Especially for Kids

Unlike any other European city, Venice seems made for kids—providing you exercise caution around the edges of every canal you see (and you'll see plenty). Venice is like wandering around in a Disneyland fantasy for a child, complete with vaporetto rides to yet-unexplored islands.

   The most exciting activity for children is a **gondola ride.** Gondoliers are usually very patient with children, explaining (in Italian) the intricacies of their craft, although their actual demonstrations are more effective in getting the point across. Later in the day you can take your child to the **glass-manufacturing works** at **Murano** (see "Side Trips from Venice," later in this chapter), where the intricacies of the craft of blowing glass will be demonstrated.

   The one museum that seems to fascinate children the most is the **Naval Museum and Arsenale** (see "Museums & Galleries," earlier in this chapter), where the glorious remnants of Venice's maritime past are presented.

   To cap the day, you can always purchase a bag of corn from a street vendor so your child can feed the fat pigeons at **Piazza San Marco.**

6 Organized Tours

Tours through the streets and canals of Venice are distinctly different from tours through other cities of Italy because of the complete absence of traffic. You can always wander at will through the labyrinth of streets, but many visitors opt for a guided tour to at least familiarize themselves with the geography of the city.

   American Express, San Marco 1471 (☎ **041/520-0844**), which operates from a historic building a few steps from St. Mark's Square, offers an array of guided city tours. Some of the most popular offerings include the following:

Every morning at 9:10am, a 2-hour guided tour of the city departs from the front of the American Express building. The tour costs 36,000L ($21.60). Sights include St. Mark's Square, the basilica, the Doge's Palace, the prison, the bell tower, and in some cases a demonstration of the art of Venetian glassblowing.

Every afternoon, between 3 and 5pm, a 2-hour guided tour incorporates visits to the exteriors of several palaces along Campo San Benetto and other sights of the city. The tour eventually crosses the Grand Canal to visit the Church of Santa Maria dei Frari (which contains the *Assumption* by Titian). The tour continues by gondola down the canal to visit the Ca'd'Oro and eventually ends at the Rialto Bridge. The afternoon tour costs 38,000L ($22.80), and the combined price for both tours is just 60,000L ($36).

The **"Evening Serenade Tour,"** priced at 50,000L ($30) per person, allows a nocturnal view of Venice accompanied by the sound of singing musicians in gondolas. From May to October there are two daily departures, one at 7pm and another at 8pm, which leave from Campo Santa Maria del Giglio. Five to six occupants fit in each gondola. The experience lasts 50 minutes.

A **"Tour of the Islands of the Venetian Lagoon,"** priced at 25,000L ($15), departs twice daily, at 9:30am and again at 2:30pm, and lasts 3 hours. You'll pass— but not land at—the islands of San Giorgio and San Francesco del Deserto, and eventually land at Burano, Murano, and Torcello for brief tours of their churches and landmarks. This trip departs from and returns to the pier at Riva degli Schiavoni.

The American Express office is open for tours and travel arrangements Monday to Friday from 9am to 5:30pm and Saturday from 9am to 5pm.

If you'd like more personalized tours than those offered by American Express, contact the **Venice Travel Advisory Service,** 22 Riverside Dr., New York, NY 10023 (☎ and fax **212/873-1964,** or 041/523-2379 in Venice). Born in New York City, Samantha Durell is a professional photographer, and has lived and worked in Venice as a private tour guide for more than 10 years. Some locals claim that she knows Venice far better than they do.

She conducts orientation sessions and private walking tours by day or night. She also assists clients with advance planning services, and is an expert in making wedding arrangements for those who want to get married in Venice. Her expertise also includes advice on how to find out-of-the-way trattorie, where you can enjoy typical Venetian cuisine far away from the tourist hordes. In addition, she also has a wealth of information about shopping, sightseeing, art, history, dining, and entertainment. Private guided tours are individually tailored to your needs.

Morning and afternoon tours, for a maximum of six people, last at least 4 hours and cost $200 for two people, $50 for each additional adult, and $25 for each additional child.

For information on all-day boat tours of the **Villas** along the **Brenta Canal,** see "Riviera del Brenta" in chapter 11, "The Veneto."

7　Shopping

THE SHOPPING SCENE

Venetian **glass** and **lace** are known throughout the world. However, selecting quality products in either craft requires a shrewd eye, as there's much that is tawdry and shoddily crafted. Some of the glassware hawked isn't worth the cost of shipping it home. Yet other pieces represent some of the world's finest artistic and ornamental glass. Murano is the island famous for its handmade glass. However, you can find little glass animal souvenirs in shops all over Venice.

For lace, head out to Burano where the last of a long line of women put in painstaking hours to produce some of the finest lace in the world.

TIPS ON SHOPPING FOR GLASS   Venice is literally crammed with glass shops. It's estimated that there are at least 1,000 of them in the sestiere of San Marco alone. Unless you go to an absolutely top-quality and reliable dealer, such as those we recommend, most stores sell both shoddy and high-quality glassware. Only the most trained eye can sometimes tell the difference. The big secret (which is becoming less a secret all the time) is that a lot of so-called Venetian glass isn't Venetian at all, but comes from former Eastern Bloc countries, including the Czech Republic. Of course, the Czech Republic has some of the finest glassmakers in Europe, so that may not be bad either. It boils down to this: If you like an item, buy it. It may not be high quality, but then again, high-quality glassware can cost thousands of dollars. If you're looking for an heirloom, stick to such award-winning houses as Pauly & Co. or Venini. Even buyers of glassware for distribution outlets in other parts of the world have been fooled by the vast array of glass for sale in Venice. If even a buyer can be tricked, the layperson has only his or her own good instincts to follow.

TIPS ON SHOPPING FOR LACE   Most of the lace vendors are centered around Piazza San Marco. Although high, prices of Venetian lace are still reasonable considering the painstaking work that goes into it. Much of the lace is shoddy, and some of it—a lot of it, really—isn't Venetian lace but machine made in who knows what country. *The* name in Venetian lace is **Jesurum** (see below), which has stood for quality since the last century.

Jesurum has its own lacemakers and—to guarantee its future—even has a school to teach apprentices how to make lace. It offers the most expensive, but also the highest quality, lace in Venice. At other places you just have to take your chances. The lace shops are like the glassware outlets. They sell the whole gamut from the shoddy, to the machine-made, to the exquisite handmade pieces. Sometimes only the trained eye can tell the difference. However, even if a piece is handmade, you can never be sure exactly *where* it was handmade. Maybe China.

SHOPPING STROLLS   All the main shopping streets of Venice, even the side streets, are touristy and overrun. The greatest concentration of shops is around Piazza San Marco and around the Rialto. Prices are much higher at San Marco, but the quality of merchandise is also higher. There are two major shopping strolls in Venice. First, from Piazza San Marco you can stroll through Venice toward the spacious square of Campo Morosini. You just follow one shop-lined street all the way to its end (although the name will change several times along the way). You begin at Salizzada San Moisè, which becomes Via 22 Marzo, and then Calle delle Ostreghe, before it opens onto Campo Santa Maria Zobenigo. The street then narrows again and changes its name to Calle Zaguri before widening once more into Campo San Maurizio, finally becoming Calle Piovan before it reaches Campo Morosini. The only deviation from this tour is a detour down Calle Vallaressa, between San Moisè and the Grand Canal, which is one of the major shopping arteries with some of the biggest designer names in the business.

The other great shopping stroll in Venice wanders from Piazza San Marco to the Rialto in a succession of streets collectively known as **The Mercerie.** It's virtually impossible to get lost because each street name is preceded by the word *merceria,* such as Merceria dell'Orologio, which begins near the clock tower in Piazza San Marco. Many commercial establishments—mainly shops—line the Mercerie before it reaches the Rialto, which then explodes into one vast shopping emporium.

Venetian Carnival Masks

Venetian masks, considered collectors' items, originated during *carnevale,* which takes place the week before the beginning of Lent. In the old days there was a good reason to wear a mask during the riotous Carnival, as wives and husbands did their best to be unfaithful and priests tried to break their vows of chastity. Things got so out of hand that the Carnival was banned in the late 18th century. But it came back—and the masks went on again.

Shops selling masks can be found practically on every corner. As with glass and lace, however, quality varies. Many masks are great artistic expressions, whereas others are shoddy and cheap. The most sought-after mask is the *Portafortuna* (luck bringer), with its long nose and birdlike visage. *Orientale* masks evoke the heyday of the Serene Republic and its trade with the Far East. The *Bauta* was worn by men to assert their macho qualities, whereas the *Neutra* mask blends the facial characteristics of both sexes. The list of masks and their origins seem endless.

The best place to purchase Carnival masks is **Laboratorio Artigiano Maschere,** Castello 6657, Barbaria delle Tole (☎ 041/522-3110; Vaporetto: Rialto), which sells handcrafted masks in papier-mâché or leather. Masks are sold all over Venice, but this well-established store has a particularly good selection, including masks that depict characters of the Commedia dell'Arte. The shop also sells a variety of other handcrafted papier-mâché items, including picture and mirror frames, pots, consoles, and boxes in the shape of pets.

Another good outlet for masks is **Mondonovo,** Rio Terrà Canal (☎ 041/528-7344; Vaporetto: Ca'Rezzonico). Here, exceptionally talented artisans work perfecting these one-of-a-kind theatrical disguises.

MARKETS   If you're looking for some bargain-basement buys, head not for any basement but to one of the little shops that line the **Rialto Bridge.** The shops there branch out to encompass fruit and vegetable markets as well. The Rialto isn't the Ponte Vecchio in Florence, but, for what it offers, it isn't bad, particularly if your lire are running short. You'll find a wide assortment of merchandise here, from angora sweaters to leather gloves. Quality is likely to vary widely, so plunge in with the utmost discrimination. Vaporetto: Rialto.

SHOPPING A TO Z
ANTIQUES
Antichita Santomanco. Frezzeria, San Marco 1504. ☎ 041/523-6643. Vaporetto: San Marco.

This store is for the specialist only—especially the well-heeled specialist. It deals in antique furniture, jewels, silver, prints, and old Murano glasses. Of course, the merchandise is ever-changing, but you're likely to pick up some little heirloom item in the midst of the clutter. Many of the items date from the Venetian heyday of the 1600s.

BRASS OBJECTS
✪ **Valese Fonditore.** Calle Fiubera, San Marco 793. ☎ 041/522-7282. Vaporetto: San Marco.

Founded in 1913, Valese Fonditore serves as a showcase for one of the most famous of the several foundries that make their headquarters in Venice. Many of the brass copies of 18th-century chandeliers produced by this company grace fine homes in the United States, becoming valuable family heirlooms. If you're looking for a brass replica of the sea horses decorating the sides of gondolas, this shop stocks them in five or six different styles and sizes.

DOLLS

Bambole di Frilly. Foundamenta dell'Osmarin, Castello 4974. ☎ **041/521-2579.** Vaporetto: Mto. Vittorio Emanuele.

This studio-shop offers dolls with meticulously painted faces and hand-tailored costumes, including dressy pinafores. The smaller, reasonably priced, low-end dolls are made with the same painstaking care, offering a real souvenir value.

FASHION

Belvest Boutique. Calle Vallaresso, San Marco 1305 (near Harry's Bar). ☎ **041/528-7933.** Vaporetto: San Marco.

This is one of the finest boutiques of Venice, specializing in clothing for women and men, both handmade and ready to wear. Fabric from some of the world's leading clothmakers is used in the designs. Linked with Vogini, the famous purveyor of leatherwork, the boutique is a bastion of top-quality craftsmanship and high-fashion style.

La Bottega di Nino. Mercerie dell'Orologio, San Marco 223. ☎ **041/522-5608.** Vaporetto: San Marco.

In need of some new threads for the film festival? This is the place for elegant male attire. It features the work of many European designers, even some from England, but it shines brightest in its Italian names, such as Nino Cerruti, Valentino, and Zenia. The prices are also better for Italian wear.

La Fenice. Calle Larga XXII Marzo, San Marco 2255. ☎ **041/523-1273.** Vaporetto: San Marco.

Despite the similarity of its name with one of Venice's most visible theaters, this is a large and well-stocked outlet for some of the most visible clothing manufacturers of Italy. One of four outlets of a city-wide chain, La Fenice sells clothing for men and women from designers such as Ferré, Dior, Montana, and Mügler.

GIFTS

Il Papiro. Campo San Maurizio, San Marco 2764. ☎ **041/522-3055.** Vaporetto: Accademia.

Il Papiro is mainly noted for its stationery supplies, but it also carries and sells many different textures and colors of writing paper and cards. In addition to hand-printed paper, it sells any number of easy-to-pack gift items, such as wooden animals and copybooks. It's a good bet for those who want to take back small, inexpensive gifts.

GLASS

Anticlea. Campo San Provolo, Castello 4719. ☎ **041/528-6949.** Vaporetto: San Zaccaria.

Harking back to the days when they were used for trade in Venetian colonies, this shop offers scores of antique and reproduction glass beads, strung or unstrung, in many sizes, shapes, and colors.

The Domus. Fondamenta dei Vetrai 82, Murano. ☎ **041/739-215.** Vaporetto: 12 or 13 to Murano.

Located on the island of Murano, home of the actual glassworks, a good selection of designs by the island's top artisans can be found in this shop. Prevalent are smaller objects such as jewelry, vases, bowls, bottles, and drinking glasses. Here you'll find designs by Carlo Moretti.

L'Isola. Campo San Moisè, San Marco 1468. ☎ **041/523-1973.** Vaporetto: Vallaresso.

This is the shop of Carlo Moretti, one of the world's best-known contemporary artisans working in glass. You will find all his signature designs in decanters, drinking glasses, vases, bowls, and, of course, paperweights.

Marco Polo. Frezzeria, San Marco 1644. ☎ **041/522-9295.** Vaporetto: Vallaresso.

Quality Murano glass items fill this two-story shop. Among the items designed and handblown by the island's artisans you'll find one-of-a-kind sculptures, drinking glasses, boxes, and paperweights. The front display area on the ground floor features small pieces, which, although not cheap, make ideal souvenirs.

Marina Barovier. Calle delle Botteghe, San Marco 3172. ☎ **041/523-6748.** Vaporetto: San Samuele.

This gallery offers one of the most complete collections of 20th-century Murano glass available. In addition to the regular display, the shop mounts special exhibits every 3 months showcasing the work of various European and American designers.

✪ **Pauly & Co.** Ponte Consorzi, San Marco. ☎ **041/520-9899.** Vaporetto: San Zaccaria.

This award-winning house exports its products all over the world. You can wander through its 21 salons, enjoy an exhibition of artistic glassware, and later see a furnace in full action. Pauly's production, which is mainly made to order, consists of continually renewed patterns, subject to change and alteration based on the whims of its many customers.

Salviati. San Gregorio 195. ☎ **041/522-4257.** Vaporetto: San Zaccaria.

Like Pauly and Venin, this is one of the most prestigious stores in Venice offering glass, with designs that lean toward the old-fashioned and elaborate, the latter including a gigantic 12-branch chandelier. But, you can also find small and affordable objects here, such as an easy-to-pack ruby-red perfume bottle. Some of the pieces are spare and tastefully opaque; others in flamboyant hues. Prices are high, but you are paying for a reliable name. Salviati will insure and ship all purchases.

✪ **Venini.** Piazzetta Leoncini, San Marco 314. ☎ **041/522-4045.** Vaporetto: San Zaccaria.

Venini's Venetian art glass has caught the attention of collectors from all over the world. Many of their pieces, including anything-but-ordinary lamps, bottles, and vases, are works of art, and represent the best of Venetian craftsmanship in design and manufacture. Along with the previously recommended Pauly & Co. and Salviati, Venini represents the big triumvirate of Venetian glassmakers. Its best-known glass has a distinctive swirl pattern in several colors, which is called a venature. This shop is known for the refined quality of its glass, some of which appears almost transparent. Much of it is very fragile, but they learned long ago how to ship it anywhere safely. To visit the furnace, call ☎ **041/739-955.**

Vetri d'Arte. Piazza San Marco 140. ☎ **041/520-0205.** Vaporetto: Vallaresso.

Here you can find moderately priced glass jewelry for souvenirs and gifts, as well as a selection of pricier crystal jewelry and porcelain bowls.

GRAPHICS

Bac Art Studio. Campo San Maurizio, San Marco 2663. ☎ **041/522-8171.** Vaporetto: Santa Maria del Giglio.

This studio sells paper goods, but it's mainly a graphics gallery, noted for its selection of engravings, posters, and lithographs, which represent Venice at Carnival time. Items for the most part are reasonably priced, and it's clear that a great deal of care and selection have gone into the gallery's choice of merchandise.

Osvaldo Böhm. San Moisè, San Marco 1349–1350. ☎ **041/522-2255.** Vaporetto: San Marco.

Head here for that just right—and light—souvenir of Venice. Osvaldo Böhm has a rich collection of photographic archives specializing in Venetian art as well as original engravings and maps, lithographs, watercolors, and Venetian masks. You can also see modern serigraphs by local artists and some fine handcrafted bronzes.

HANDCRAFTS

Veneziartigiana. Calle Larga, San Marco 412. ☎ **041/523-5032.** Vaporetto: San Marco.

This is a market showcasing the work of many of the best artisans in the area. The volume and variety of goods surrounding you can be overwhelming, but search carefully and you can find many unusual, affordable handcrafted items, including works in glass, ceramics, dolls, posters, and masks.

JEWELRY

⭘ **Missiaglia.** Piazza San Marco 125. ☎ **041/522-4464.** Vaporetto: San Marco.

Since 1864, Missiaglia has been the private supplier to rich Venetians and savvy shoppers from around the world seeking the best in gold and jewelry. Go here for that special, classic piece. But, as the family keeps a sharp watch on the latest developments in the international jewelry design scene, something a little more cutting edge might catch your eye.

LACE

⭘ **Jesurum.** Mercerie del Capitello, San Marco 4857. ☎ **041/520-6177.** Vaporetto: San Zaccaria.

For serious purchases, Jesurum is the best place. This elegant shop, a center of noted lacemakers and fashion creators, has been located in a 12th-century church since 1868. You'll find Venetian handmade or machine-made lace and embroidery on table, bed, and bath linens; and hand-printed bathing suits. Quality and originality are guaranteed, and special orders are accepted. The exclusive linens created here are expensive, but the inventory is large enough to accommodate many budgets.

LEATHER

Bottega Veneta. Calle Vallaresso, San Marco 1337. ☎ **041/522-2816.** Vaporetto: San Marco.

Bottega Veneta is primarily known for its woven leather bags. These bags are sold elsewhere, but the prices are said to be less at the company's flagship outlet in Venice. The shop also sells shoes for women, suitcases, belts, and a wide array of high-fashion accessories. Men will enjoy the assortment of leather wallets.

Furla. Mercerie del Capitello, San Marco 4954. ☎ **041/523-0611.** Vaporetto: Rialto.

Furla is a specialist in women's leather bags, but sells belts and gloves for women as well. Many of the bags are stamped with molds, creating alligator- and lizard-like textures. These bags come in a varied choice of colors, including what the Austrians call "Maria Theresa ocher." You'll also find a varied selection of costume jewelry.

⭘ **Marforio.** Campo San Salvador, San Marco 5033. ☎ **041/522-5734.** Vaporetto: Rialto.

Marforio is located in the heart of the city. Founded in 1875, it's the oldest and largest leather-goods retail outlet in Italy. The company has been run by the same family for five generations. It's known for the quality of its leather products, and the outlet here has an enormous assortment, including all the famous European labels—Valentino, Giorgio Armani, Ferre, and Pierre Cardin, among others.

Vogini. Ascensione, San Marco 1291, 1292, and 1301 (near Harry's Bar). ☎ **041/522-2573.** Vaporetto: San Marco.

Every kind of leather work is offered at Vogini, especially women's handbags, which are exclusive models. There's also a large assortment of handbags in petit-point, plus men's and women's wear and shoes. The collection of artistic Venetian leather is of the highest quality. The travel-equipment department contains a large assortment of trunks and wardrobe suitcases as well as dressing cases—many of the latest models in luggage.

PAPER

Florence is still the major center in Italy for artistic paper—especially marbleized paper. However, craftspeople in Venice still make marble paper by hand—sheet by sheet. The technique of marbling paper originated in Japan as early as 1000, spreading through Persia and finally reaching Europe in the 1400s. Except for France, marbling had largely disappeared with the coming of the Industrial Revolution, but it was revived in Venice in the 1970s. The technique offers unlimited decorative possibilities and the widest range of possible colors (craftspeople are called "color alchemists"). Each sheet of handmade marbleized paper is one of a kind.

Antica Legatoria Piazzesi. Santa Maria del Giglio, San Marco 2511. ☎ **041/522-1202.** Vaporetto: San Marco.

You'll have fun just browsing among the displays of patterned, hand-painted paper here. Of course, buying is fun, too. The paper-covered objects in bright colors make great souvenirs of Venice. *Legatoria* means bookbindery, and some of this work is still done on special order, but the shop mainly offers such objects as scrapbooks, address books, diaries, Venetian Carnival statues, and paperweights. You can also find writing paper and decorative pieces.

Piazzesi. Campieilo della Feltrina, San Marco. ☎ **041/522-1202.** Vaporetto: Santa Maria del Giglio.

The oldest shop of its kind in the city, here you'll find hand-printed paper, memo pads, address books, and desk accessories. There are also prints available capturing scenes of bygone and contemporary Venice.

8 Venice After Dark

For such a fabled city, Venice's nightlife is pretty meager. Who wants to hit the nightclubs when strolling the city at night is more interesting than any spectacle staged inside? Ducking into a cafe or bar for a brief interlude, however, is a good way to break up your evening walk. Although it offers gambling and a few other diversions, Venice is pretty much an early-to-bed town. Most restaurants close at midnight.

The best guide to what's happening in Venice is **"Un Ospite di Venezia,"** a free pamphlet (part in English, part in Italian) distributed by the tourist office every 15 days. It lists any music and opera or theatrical presentations, along with art exhibitions and local special events.

In addition, classical concerts are often featured in various churches, such as the Chiesa di Vivaldi. To see if any **church concerts** are being presented at the time of your visit, call ☎ **041/520-8722** for information.

THE PERFORMING ARTS

In January 1996, a dramatic fire left the fabled La Fenice at Campo San Fantin, the city's main venue for performing arts, a blackened shell and a smoldering ruin. Opera lovers around the world, including Luciano Pavarotti, mourned its loss. The

Italian government has pledged $12.5 million for the reconstruction of the theater, the most beautiful in Italy. The theater's neoclassical facade survived the blaze, and is the subject of sightseeing interest today. Optimistic predictions suggest that the theater will reopen in 1998.

Fortunately, in the meantime, all has not been lost. Temporary venues will be found for performances of the Orchestra della Fenice and the Coro della Fenice. Information about La Fenice, Campo San Fantin, San Marco 1965, is available by calling ☎ 041/786-562. For a list of other cultural performances, contact the tourist office.

Teatro Goldoni. Calle Goldoni, near Campo San Luca, San Marco 4650B. ☎ **041/520-7583.** Tickets 20,000L–42,000L ($12–$25.20).

This theater, close to the Ponte di Rialto in the San Marco district, honors Carlo Goldoni (1707–93), the most prolific and one of the best Italian playwrights. The theater presents a changing repertoire of productions, often plays in Italian, but musical presentations as well. The box office is open Monday to Saturday from 10am to 1pm and 4:30 to 7pm.

THE BAR SCENE

Want more in the way of nightlife? All right, but be warned: The Venetian bar owners may sock it to you when they present the bill.

Bar ai Speci. In the Hotel Panada, Calle dei Specchieri, San Marco 646. ☎ **041/520-9088.** Vaporetto: San Marco.

Bar ai Speci is a charming corner bar located only a short walk from St. Mark's Basilica. Its richly grained paneling is offset by dozens of antique mirrors, each different, whose glittering surfaces reflect the rows of champagne and scotch bottles and the clustered groups of Biedermeier chairs.

Bar Ducale. Calle delle Ostreghe, San Marco 2354. ☎ **041/521-0002.** Vaporetto: San Marco.

Bar Ducale occupies a tiny corner of a building near a bridge over a narrow canal. Customers stand at the zinc bar facing the carved 19th-century Gothic-reproduction shelves. Mimosas are the specialty here, but tasty sandwiches are also offered. The ebullient owner learned his craft at Harry's Bar before going into business for himself. Today his small establishment is usually mobbed every day of the week. It's ideal for an early-evening aperitif as you stroll about.

Bar Salus. Campo Santa Margherita, Dorsoduro. ☎ **041/528-5279.** Vaporetto: Ca'Rezzonico.

Don't expect the aristocracies of Venice, or a group of monks and nuns, at this rough-and-ready bar near Ca'Rezzonica. A shot of whisky or a beer at the long stand-up bar offers insight into the sometimes raucous nuts and bolts that keep the city more or less intact. There's no music, and little emphasis on anything other than rendezvous between clients who seem to have known each another since the days of the Doges.

Devil's Forest. Calle Stagneri, San Marco 5185. ☎ **041/520-0623.** Vaporetto: Rialto.

Set within a stone's throw from the Rialto Bridge, this is an authentic British pub where long-term clients have reached a comfortable balance between the English- and Italian-speaking worlds. You'll find a comfortingly predictable roster of beers and ales on tap here (Guinness, Harp, Kilkenny, and Elephant Carlsberg), lots of references to European travel by the well-versed clients, and platters of food that average around 10,000L ($6). Don't expect bangers and mash, or steak and kidney pie, as things are more Mediterranean than that, with lots of emphasis on sandwiches, pastas, and simple grills. It's open daily from 10am to 1am.

Do Leoni. In the Londra Palace Hotel, Riva degli Schiavoni, Castello 4171. ☎ **041/520-0533.** Vaporetto: San Zaccaria.

The hotel's exclusive restaurant has already been recommended (see "Where to Dine," in chapter 9). Here the interior is a rich blend of scarlet-and-gold carpeting with a lion motif, English pub-style furniture, and Louis XVI–style chairs, along with plenty of exposed mahogany. While sipping your cocktail, you'll enjoy a view of a 19th-century bronze statue, the lagoon, and the foot traffic along the Grand Canal. A piano player entertains Monday through Saturday.

Fiddler's Elbow. Cannaregio 3847. ☎ **041/523-9930.** Vaporetto: Ca' d'Oro.

Five minutes from the Rialto Bridge, this pub called the "Irish pub" by the Venetians— is run by the same people who operate the equally popular Fiddler's Elbow in both Florence and Rome. Since its opening late in 1992 it has become one of Venice's most popular watering holes. They have the only satellite TV in Venice with all the channels—Sky, American, Sports, Music, whatever. In the summer, there is live outdoor music.

Guanotto. Ponte del Lovo 4819. ☎ **041/520-8439.** Vaporetto: Rialto.

This is a *gelateria/pasticceria/bar*. It's said to have virtually invented the spritzer, a combination of soda water, bitters, and white wine. Its drinks and cocktails are renowned, although enjoying a cappuccino here can take the chill off a rainy day in Venice as well.

✪ **Harry's Bar.** Calle Vallaresso 1323. ☎ **041/528-5777.** Vaporetto: San Marco.

The single most famous of all the watering holes of Ernest Hemingway, Harry's Bar is known for inventing its own drinks and exporting them around the world. It's also said that carpaccio, the delicate raw-beef dish, was invented here. Fans say that Harry's makes the best Bellini in the world, although many old-time visitors still prefer a vodka martini. Harry's Bar is now found around the world, from Munich to Los Angeles, from Paris to Rome, but this is the original. Except for a restaurant, Harry Cipriani, in New York City, the other bars are unauthorized knockoffs. In Venice, the bar is a Venetian tradition and landmark, not quite as famous as the Basilica di San Marco, but almost. Celebrities frequent the place during the various film and art festivals.

WINE BARS

Cantina do Spade. San Polo 860. ☎ **041/521-0574.** Vaporetto: Rialto.

This historic wine bar beneath an arcade near the main fish and fruit market of Venice dates from 1475. It was once frequented by Casanova. Venetians call it a *bacaro* instead of a wine bar. The place is completely rustic and bare-bones, but devotees come here to order chicchetti, the equivalent of Spanish tapas. Although there's no menu, the kitchen will occasionally turn out typical Venetian fare. Many diners prefer to order one of 250 different sandwiches the kitchen is usually willing to prepare. Often in season, game dishes, including boar, deer, and reindeer, are served, but don't count on this. Venetians delight in the 220 different types of wine. The place is a local favorite, and has been for centuries, but don't come here looking for glamor; head for Harry's Bar if that's what you're after.

Mascareta. Calle Lunga Santa Maria Formosa, Castello 5138. ☎ **041/523-0744.** Vaporetto: Rialto.

This wine bar was established in 1995. The focus is on dozens of bottles of Italian wines, many from the Veneto region. There's only room for 20 people seated at cramped tables in an old Venetian building, but if you're hungry you can order simple platters of snack-style food (prosciutto, cheese plates, and other dishes) priced from 8,000L ($4.80), depending on what's available that day. Closed from mid-December to mid-January.

Vino Vino. Calle del Caffettier 2007A. ☎ **041/523-7027.** Vaporetto: San Marco.

You can choose from more than 250 Italian and imported wines here. Vino Vino attracts a varied clientele: It wouldn't be unusual to see a Venetian countess sipping Prosecco near a gondolier eating a meal. This place is loved by everyone from snobs to young people to almost-broke tourists. It offers wines by the bottle or glass, including Italian grappas. Popular Venetian dishes are also served, including pastas, beans, baccalà (codfish), and polenta. The two rooms are always jammed like a vaporetto in rush hour, and there's take-away service if you can't find a place.

PIANO BARS

Linea d'Ombra. Fondamenta delle Zattere, Dorsoduro 19. ☎ **041/528-5259.** Vaporetto: Salute.

To the surprise of many of its visitors, Venice has few real nightclubs. However, if you're in the mood for a little night music, this place has a good piano bar with a restaurant. On Friday and Saturday, a pianist plays and sings international tunes, and if the night is right, it can make for one of the more romantic evenings in Venice. With a terrace that overlooks the Canale della Giudecca, drinkers and diners are treated to a view of the island of San Giorgio. You should reserve a table if you want to dine. The restaurant is open Monday, Tuesday, and Thursday to Saturday from 12:30 to 2:30pm and 8 to 10:30pm, and Sunday from 12:30 to 2:30pm; the bar is open Monday, Tuesday, and Thursday to Saturday from 8am to midnight.

Martini Scala Club. Campo San Fantin, San Marco 1980. ☎ **041/522-4121.** Vaporetto: San Marco or Santa Maria del Giglio.

Martini Scala Club is an elegant restaurant with a piano bar and has functioned as some kind of inn, in one manifestation or another, since 1724. You can enjoy its food and wine until 2am—it's the only kitchen in Venice that stays open late. Dishes include smoked goose breast with grapefruit and arugula, fresh salmon with black butter and olives, or gnocchi (dumplings) with butter and sage. The piano bar gets going after 10pm. It's possible to order drinks without having food. The restaurant is open Thursday to Monday from noon to 2:30pm and 7 to 11:30pm and Wednesday from 7 to 11:30pm. Main courses are from 36,000L ($21.60); a fixed-price dinner is 72,000L ($43.20) for four courses. The bar, which offers a piano bar and food, is open Wednesday to Monday from 10pm to 3:30am.

Paradiso Perduto. Fondamenta della Misericordia. ☎ **041/720-581.** Vaporetto: San Marcuola.

Early every evening except Wednesday, this authentic *hostaria* functions as a likable tavern, serving well-prepared platters of seafood to longtime residents who live close to Venice's train station, far from the touristic congestion around St. Mark's Square. If you're interested in dining (the *frittura mista* of fish, served with polenta, is wonderful), main courses range from 15,000L to 19,000L ($9 to $11.40), and are served Thursday to Tuesday from 7:30 to 10:30pm. But the real heart and soul of the place emerges after 11pm, when a mixture of soft recorded music and live piano music creates a backdrop for animated dialogues between the neighborhood crowd and visitors from abroad. The chitchat continues until at least 2am.

THE CAFE SCENE

✪ Florian. Piazza San Marco 56-59. ☎ **041/528-5338.** Vaporetto: San Marco.

This is the most famous cafe in Venice. The Florian was built in 1720, and it remains romantically and elegantly decorated—pure Venetian salons with red plush banquettes, intricate and elaborate murals under glass, and art nouveau lighting and lamps. It's the most fashionable and aristocratic rendezvous in Venice: The Florian roster of customers has included Casanova, Lord Byron, Goethe, Canova, de Musset, and Madame de Staël. Light lunch is served from noon to 3pm, costing 20,000L ($12) and up, and an English tea from 3 to 6pm, when you can select from a choice of pastries, ice creams, and cakes. Open Thursday to Tuesday from 9am to midnight. An espresso is 6,500L ($3.90); long drinks cost 19,000L ($11.40), plus 5,000L ($3) extra if you drink on the square when music is playing (April to October).

Gran Caffè Lavena. Piazza San Marco 133-134. ☎ **041/522-4070.**

The 18th-century Gran Caffè Lavena is a popular but intimate cafe located under the arcades of Piazza San Marco. During his stay in Venice, Richard Wagner was a frequent customer; he composed some of his greatest operas here. It has one of the most beautifully ornate glass chandeliers in town—the kind you'll love even if you hate Venetian glass. They hang from the ceiling between the iron rails of an upper-level balcony. The most interesting tables are near the plate-glass window in front, although there's plenty of room at the stand-up bar as well. Open daily from 9:30am to 7:30pm; closed for a few days in January and in November and on Thursday in winter. Coffee costs 1,500L (90¢) if you're standing, 5,500L ($3.30) if you're sitting at a table. And there's a music surcharge of 5,000L ($3).

✪ Quadri. Piazza San Marco 120-124. ☎ **041/522-2105.** Vaporetto: San Marco.

Quadri, previously recommended as a restaurant, stands on the opposite side of the square from the Florian. It, too, is elegantly decorated in antique style. It should be, as it was founded in 1638. Wagner used to drop in for a drink when he was working on *Tristan und Isolde.* Its prices are virtually the same as at the Florian, and it, too, imposes a surcharge on drinks ordered during concert periods. The bar was a favorite with the Austrians during their long-ago occupation. Open Wednesday to Sunday from noon to 2:30pm and 7 to 10:30pm. A whisky costs 17,000L ($10.20); coffee, 5,500L ($3.30). The music surcharge is 4,000L ($2.40).

ICE CREAM & PASTRIES

Gelateria Paolin. Campo San Stefano 2962A. ☎ **041/522-5576.** Vaporetto: S. Samuele.

For many, strolling to the Gelateria Paolin (set in a large colorful square) and ordering some of the tastiest ice cream (gelato) in Venice is nightlife enough. That's the way many a Venetian spends a summer evening. This gelateria has stood on the corner of this busy square since the 1930s, making it the oldest ice-cream parlor in Venice. You can order your ice cream to go or eat it at one of the sidewalk tables. Many interesting flavors are offered, including pistachio. The gelati cost more if consumed at a table. From June to September, the parlor is open daily from 7:30am to 11:30pm; October to May, Tuesday to Sunday from 7:30am to 9:30pm.

Pasticceria Marchini. San Maurizio 2769. ☎ **041/522-9109.** Vaparetto: Accademia.

If you'd like to escape the throngs of visitors that overrun Venice in the early evening, head here, have a pastry and a coffee, and contemplate your evening plans. This is where your Venetian friend (if you have one) would take you for the most delectable pastries served in the city. The small pastries are made according to old recipes—we recommend the **bigna.** Similar to zabaglione, this local pastry is divine, made with chocolate and cream.

CASINOS

Casino Municipale. Lungomare G. Marconi 4, Lido. ☎ **041/529-7111.** Admission 18,000L ($10.80).

If you want to risk your luck and your lire, take a vaporetto ride on the Casino Express, which leaves from stops at the railway station, Piazzale Roma, and Piazzetta San Marco, and delivers you to the landing dock of the Casino Municipale. The Italian government wisely forbids its nationals to cross the threshold unless they work here, so bring your passport. The building itself is foreboding, looking as if it had been inspired by Mussolini-era architects. Don't worry—the mood changes once you step inside. You can try your luck at blackjack, roulette, baccarat, or whatever. You can also dine, drink at the bar, or enjoy a floor show. Open May to October, daily from 3pm to 2:30am.

Vendramin-Calergi Palace. Cannaregio 2040, Strada Nuova. ☎ **041/529-7111.** Admission 18,000L ($10.80). Vaporetto: San Marcuola.

From November to April, the casino action moves to the 15th-century Vendramin-Calergi Palace. Incidentally, in 1883 Wagner died in this house, which opens onto the Grand Canal. Open daily from 3pm to 2:30am.

9 Side Trips from Venice

MURANO

This is the island where for centuries **glassblowers** have turned out those fantastic chandeliers that Victorian ladies used to prize so highly. They also produce heavily ornamented glasses so ruby-red or so indigo-blue you can't tell if you're drinking blackberry juice or pure grain alcohol. Happily, the glassblowers are still plying their trade, although increasing competition—notably from Sweden—has compelled a greater degree of sophistication in design.

Murano remains the chief expedition from Venice, but it's not the most beautiful nearby island. (Burano and Torcello are far more attractive.)

You can combine a tour of Murano with a trip along the lagoon. To reach it, take vaporetto no. 12 or 13 at Riva degli Schiavoni, a short walk from Piazzetta San Marco. The boat docks at the landing platform at Murano where—lo and behold—the first furnace awaits conveniently. It's best to go Monday to Friday from 10am to noon if you want to see some glassblowing action.

TOURING THE GLASS FACTORIES & OTHER SIGHTS

As you stroll through Murano, you'll find that the factory owners are only too glad to let you come in and see their age-old crafts. While browsing through the showrooms, you'll need stiff resistance to keep the salespeople at bay. Bargaining is expected. Don't—repeat *don't*—pay the marked price on any item. That's merely the figure at which to open negotiations.

However, the prices of made-on-the-spot souvenirs are not negotiable. For example, you might want to purchase a horse streaked with blue. The artisan takes a piece of incandescent glass, huffs, puffs, rolls it, shapes it, snips it, and behold—he has shaped a horse. The showrooms of Murano also contain a fine assortment of Venetian crystal beads, available in every hue of the rainbow. You may find some of the best work to be the experiments of apprentices.

An overcrowded little island where the women make splendid lace and the men make children.

—Ernest Hemingway, on Burano

While on the island, you can visit the Renaissance palazzo that houses the **Museo Vetrario di Murano,** Fondamenta Giustinian (☎ **041/739-586**), which contains a spectacular collection of Venetian glass. It's open April to October, Monday, Tuesday, and Thursday to Saturday from 10am to 5pm; November to March, Monday, Tuesday, and Thursday to Saturday from 10am to 4pm. Admission is 8,000L ($4.80) for adults and 5,000L ($3) for children.

If you're looking for a respite from the glass factories, head to the **Church of San Pietro Martire** (☎ **041/739-704**), which dates from the 1300s but was rebuilt in 1511 and is richly decorated with paintings by Tintoretto and Veronese. Its proud possession is a *Madonna and Child Enthroned* by Giovanni Bellini, plus two superb altarpieces by the same master. The church lies right before the junction with Murano's Grand Canal, about 250 yards from the vaporetto landing stage. It's open daily from 9am to noon and 2 to 6pm; closed for Mass on Sunday morning.

Even more notable is **Santi Maria e Donato,** Campo San Donato (☎ **041/739-056**), which is open daily from 9am to noon and 4 to 6pm with time variations for Sunday Mass. This building is a stellar example of the Venetian Byzantine style, in spite of its 19th-century restoration. It dates from the 7th century but was reconstructed in the 1100s. The interior is known for its mosaic floor—a parade of peacocks and eagles, as well as other creatures—and a 15th-century ship's-keel ceiling. Over the apse is an outstanding mosaic of the Virgin against a gold background, which dates from the early 1200s.

WHERE TO DINE

Ai Vetrai. Fondamenta Manin 29. ☎ **041/739-293.** Reservations recommended. Main courses 13,000–30,000L ($7.80–$18). DC, MC, V. Fri–Wed 10:30am–6pm. Closed 15 days from end of Dec to beginning of Jan. Vaporetto: 12 or 13 to Murano. VENETIAN.

Ai Vetrai entertains and nourishes its guests in a large room not far from the Canale dei Vetrai. If you're looking for fish prepared in the local style, with what might be called the widest selection on Murano, this is it. Most varieties of crustaceans and gilled creatures are available on the spot. However, if you phone ahead and order food for a large party, as the Venetians sometimes do, the owners will prepare what they call "a noble fish." You might begin with spaghetti in a green clam sauce.

Al Corallo. Fondamenta dei Vetrai 73. ☎ **041/739-080.** Main courses 10,000–25,000L ($6–$15); fixed-price menu 20,000L ($12). AE, DC, MC, V. Wed–Mon noon–3pm and 7–8:30pm. Closed mid-Dec to mid-Jan (dates vary). Vaporetto: 12 or 13 to Murano. VENETIAN.

Small and intimate, and somewhat isolated from the hustle and bustle of the larger islands of Venice, this family-run restaurant is one of the best established of the eateries on the island of Murano. Very little English is spoken, but the place is usually filled with a wide variety of clients from all walks of life. Specialties are typically Venetian, and the service is polite. Locals, many of them workers at the nearby glass factories, choose this place for a well-deserved meal after a morning of hard physical labor, and blend with the tourists. The menu changes daily, according to whatever's available in the local markets.

BURANO

Burano became world famous as a center of **lacemaking,** a craft that reached its pinnacle in the 18th century (recall Venetian point?). The visitor who can spare a morning to visit this island will be rewarded with a charming little fishing village far removed in spirit from the grandeur of Venice, but lying only half an hour away by ferry. Boats leave from Fondamente Nuove, which overlooks the Venetian graveyard (which is well worth the trip all on its own). To reach Fondamente Nuove, take vaporetto no. 12 or 52 from Riva degli Schiavoni.

EXPLORING THE ISLAND

Once at Burano, you'll discover that the houses of the islanders come in varied colors—sienna, robin's-egg or cobalt blue, barn red, butterscotch, grass green. If you need a focal point for your excursion, it should be the **Scoula di Merletti di Burano,** "Museo del Merletto," S. Martino Destra 184, Burano (☎ **041/730-034**), in the center of the fishing village at Piazza Baldassarc Galuppi. The museum is open Tuesday to Sunday from 10am to 4pm. Admission is 5,000L ($3). The Burano School of Lace was founded in 1872 as part of a movement aimed at restoring the age-old craft that had earlier declined, giving way to such other lacemaking centers as Chantilly and Bruges. Go up to the second floor where you can see the lacemakers, mostly young women, at their painstaking work and can purchase hand-embroidered or handmade-lace items.

After visiting the lace school, next walk across the square to the **Duomo** and its leaning campanile (inside, look for the *Crucifixion* by Tiepolo). However, do so at once, because the bell tower is leaning so precariously it looks as if it may topple at any moment.

WHERE TO DINE

Ostaria ai Pescatori. Piazza Baldassare Galuppi 371. ☎ **041/730-650.** Reservations recommended. Main courses 20,000L–30,000L ($12–$18). AE, MC, V. Thurs–Tues noon–3pm and 6–9:30pm. Closed Jan. Vaporetto: Line 12 or 52 from Murano. SEAFOOD.

The family that pools its efforts to run this well-known restaurant maintains strong friendships with the local fishers, who often reserve the best parts of their daily catch for preparation in the kitchen here. The cooking is performed by the matriarch of an extended family. The place has gained a reputation as the preserver of a type of simple and unpretentious restaurant unique to Burano. Locals in dialect call it a *buranello.* Clients often take the vaporetto from other sections of Venice (the restaurant lies close to the boat landing) to eat at the plain wooden tables set up either indoors or on the small square in front. Specialties feature all the staples of the Venetian seaside diet, including fish soup, risotto di pesce, pasta seafarer style, tagliolini in squid ink, and a wide range of crustaceans, plus grilled, fried, and baked fish. Dishes prepared with local game are also available, but you must request them well in advance. Your meal might also include a bottle of fruity wine from the region.

Trattoria de Romano. Via Baldassare Galuppi 223. ☎ **041/730-030.** Reservations recommended. Main courses 18,000L–25,000L ($10.80–$15). AE, MC, V. Wed–Mon noon–2:30pm and 7–8:30pm. Closed Dec 15 to beginning of Feb. Vaporetto: Line 12 or 52 from Murano. VENETIAN.

If you're on the island at mealtime, you may want to join a long line of people who enjoy this rather simple-looking *caratteristico* Trattoria de Romano, which is around the corner from the lace school. You can enjoy a superb dinner here, which might consist of *risotto di pesce* (the Italian version of the Valencian paella), followed by *fritto misto di pesce,* a mixed fish fry from the Adriatic, with savory bits of mullet, squid, and shrimp.

TORCELLO

Of all the islands of the lagoon, Torcello—the so-called Mother of Venice—offers the most charm. If Burano is behind the times, Torcello is positively antediluvian. You can follow in the footsteps of Hemingway and stroll across a grassy meadow, traverse an ancient stone bridge, and step back into that time when the Venetians first fled from invading barbarians to create a city of Neptune in the lagoon.

To reach Torcello, take vaporetto no. 12 from Fondamenta Nuova on Murano. The trip takes about 45 minutes.

Warning: If you go on your own, don't listen to the savvy gondoliers who hover at the ferry quay. They'll tell you that both the cathedral and the locanda are miles away. Actually, they're both reached after a leisurely 12- to 15-minute stroll along the canal.

EXPLORING THE ISLAND

Torcello has two major attractions: a church with Byzantine mosaics good enough to make the empress Theodora at Ravenna turn as purple with envy as her robe, and a locanda (inn) that converts day-trippers into inebriated angels of praise. First the spiritual nourishment, then the alcoholic sustenance.

Cattedrale di Torcello, also called the Church of Santa Maria Assunta Isola di Torcello (☎ 041/730-084), was founded in A.D. 639 and was subsequently rebuilt. It stands in a lonely, grassy meadow beside a campanile that dates from the 11th century. It's visited chiefly because of its Byzantine mosaics. Clutching her child, the weeping Madonna in the apse is a magnificent sight, whereas on the opposite wall is a powerful *Last Judgment.* Byzantine artisans, it seems, were at their best in portraying hell and damnation. In their Inferno, they have re-created a virtual human stew with the fires stirred by wicked demons. Reptiles slide in and out of the skulls of cannibalized sinners. Open April to October, daily from 10am to 12:30pm and 2:30 to 6:30pm; November to March, daily from 10am to 12:30pm and 2:30 to 5pm. Admission is 1,500L (90¢).

WHERE TO DINE

Locanda Cipriani. Piazza San Fosca 29. ☎ 041/730-150. Reservations recommended. Main courses 34,000L–43,000L ($20.40–$25.80). AE, DC, MC, V. Wed–Mon noon–3pm; Fri–Sat 7–10pm. Closed Jan 15–Feb 15. VENETIAN.

It's operated by the same folks who bring you some of the grandest, most paralyzingly expensive, and most society-conscious hangouts in Venice. They're the heirs of Harry Cipriani (i.e., Hotel Cipriani, Harry's Bar). But, in the case of this artfully simple locanda, the venue is low-key, deliberately rustic, and light-years removed from the family's grander venues closer to Venice's touristic core. You'll reach the place—a 19th-century villa—after a boat ride from other parts of the city, in a position across from the island's landmark church. Menu items are uncompromisingly classic, with roots that go deep into the collective unconscious of Venice and the Cipriani family. A good example is *filleto di San Pietro alla Carlina* (fillet of John Dory in the style of Carla, a late and much-revered matriarch, who concocted the dish for decades using tomatoes and capers). Also look for *carpaccio Cipriani; risotto alla Torcellano* (with fresh vegetables and herbs from the family's garden); fish soup; *tagliolini verdi gratinati;* and a traditional roster of veal, liver, fish, and beef dishes.

Tearing yourself away from Piazza San Marco in Venice is a task that requires an iron will. However, Venice doesn't have a regional monopoly on art or tourist treasures. Of the cities of interest easily reached from Venice, three tower above the rest: Verona, the home of the eternal lovers, Romeo and Juliet; Padua, the city of Mantegna, with frescoes by Giotto; and Vicenza, the city of Palladio, with streets of Renaissance palazzi and villa-studded hills. If time remains, you can also explore the Riviera del Brenta with its Venetian palazzi, and such historic old cities as Treviso and Bassano del Grappa. The miracle of all these cities is that, although Venice dominated them for centuries, the Serene Republic did not siphon off their creative drive completely.

1 Riviera del Brenta

The Brenta Canal, running from Fusina to Padua, functioned as a sort of mainland extension of Venice during the Renaissance, when the wealthy merchants of Venice began using the area as a retreat from the summer heat of the city—a trend that remained popular among the patrician class from the 16th through the 19th centuries. Dubbed the Riviera del Brenta, a 10^1/2-mile stretch along the banks of the canal from Malcontenta to Stra is renowned for the gracious villas to which Venetians escaped, 44 of which are still visible.

The primary architect of the region was **Andrea Palladio** (1508–80), who designed 19 of the villas. Inspired by his study of ancient Roman architecture, Palladio's singular design—square, perfectly proportioned, functionally elegant—became the standard by which villas were judged. Palladio's designs are familiar to Americans as the basis for most state capitals as well as Jefferson's Monticello, and to the British as the most common design for country estates. The importance of villa life to the Venetians was such that it gained immortality in *The Merchant of Venice,* in which Portia's home is set in a villa at Belmont along the Brenta.

ESSENTIALS

GETTING THERE   By Boat   Consider an all-day guided excursion by boat to the Brenta Canal that extends as far as Padua, including many of the most important Renaissance monuments en route. American Express (☎ 041/520-0844) will sell you tickets aboard the **Burchiello Excursion Boat.** Excursions depart from the piers at

Piazza San Marco every Tuesday, Thursday, and Saturday at 9am for an all-day boat ride that includes running bilingual commentary from an on-board host. The price of 114,000L ($68.40) per person, plus a supplement of 40,000L ($24) for an (optional) lunch in the historic town of Oriago, covers the cruise offering glimpses of the elegant villas that seem to cling to the shorelines, including guided visits through the evocative villas at Malcontenta and Oriago, plus a somewhat rushed tour through the most spectacular sights of Padua after the boat docks. At 6:10pm, you board a bus for rapid transit back to Venice.

By Bus   You can tour the Brenta Riviera by buses leaving from Venice headed for Padua. The buses, operated by the local ACTV line (☎ 041/528-7886), depart from the Venetian company's ticket office in the Piazzale Roma Monday through Saturday from 8am to 2:30pm. A one-way ticket to Villa Foscari costs 1,200L (70¢) per person, and a one-way fare to the Villa Pisano sells for 4,000L ($2.40).

By Car   All villas open to the public are on the north bank of the canal directly along Route S11 headed west out of Venice toward Padua. The road follows the canal, offering you a chance to glimpse the other villas, which are situated on both banks. At the APT in Venice, you can pick up the visitor's guide "Riviera del Brenta Venezia," which offers background information on the villas and a map of their locations between Malcontenta and Stra.

By Personal Guide   The most opulent way to tour the villas is by personal guide. Rates depend on where you want to go and how much you want to take in during a day. A list of guides along with their fixed fees is available from the principal APT tourist office at the Palazzetto Selva, right off Piazza San Marco in Venice (☎ 041/522-6356). You can also contact the Guides Association in Venice at Calle San Antonio 5448-A, Castello (☎ 041/523-9902).

VISITOR INFORMATION   For additional information, contact the APT tourist office of Riviera del Brenta, Via Don Minzoni 26, 30030 Mira Porte, Venezia (☎ 041/424-973).

TOURING THE VILLAS

The closest villa to Venice among those that you can currently tour, the **Villa Foscari (Villa La Malcontenta),** (☎ 041/520-3966), is about 2½ miles west of where the canal empties into the Venetian Lagoon, on Route S11. It was constructed by Palladio for the Foscari family in 1560. A Foscari wife was exiled here for some alleged misdeed to her husband, and the unhappiness surrounding the incident gave the name Malcontenta—unhappy one—to both the villa and its village. It is open only Tuesday and Saturday from 9am to noon, with an admission fee of 10,000L ($6), or you can call and make reservations to see the villa on other days, when admission will cost you 15,000L ($9).

In Stra, 20 miles west of Venice on S11, stands the **Villa Pisani,** also known as Villa Nazionale (☎ 049/502-074). Built in 1720 as a palatial retreat for Doge Alvise Pisani, it became the Italian home of Napoléon, and later served as the initial meeting site of Mussolini and Hitler. Given this historical context, it's no surprise that the villa is the largest and grandest of them all. A reflecting pool out front gives the structure added dimension and a small army of statues stand guard over the premises, dotting the facade, the edges of the pool, and scattered throughout the grounds. The highlights of the visit are the magnificent frescoes of Giambattista Tiepolo, painted on the ballroom ceiling to depict the *Glory of the Pisani Family,* in which family members are surrounded by a host of hovering angels and saints. The villa is open

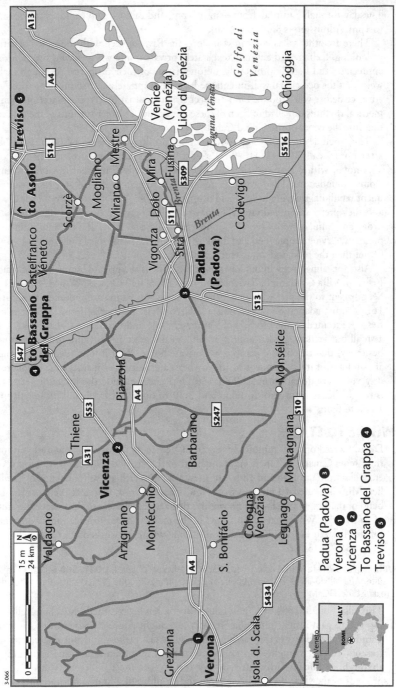

Padua (Padova) ❸
Verona ❶
Vicenza ❷
To Bassano del Grappa ❹
Treviso ❺

Tuesday through Saturday from 9am to 4pm, and Sunday and holidays from 9am to 1pm. Admission is 8,000L ($4.80).

There are other villas you can visit along the Riviera, each with the added benefit of looking, feeling, and acting like a stately private home whose owners recognize, appreciate, and fiercely protect the unique nature of their property. Although each welcomes the occasional well-intentioned and appropriately respectful visitor, call in advance before you drop in. Don't expect structures that follow the gracefully symmetrical rhythms of Palladio: Each of these is evocative of larger versions of the palazzi that line the edges of the Grand Canal in Venice.

They include the **Villa Sagredo,** Via Sagredo, in Vigonovo (☎ 049/503-174; after hours, call ☎ 041/412-967). Set a half mile northwest of the hamlet of Vigonovo, within a venerable, suitably gnarled garden, it was built on ancient Roman foundations. The form it has today dates from around 1700, the result of frequent rebuildings during its long and distinguished life. You must reserve in advance, and they prefer scheduled visits Tuesday to Friday between 6pm and 8pm, or Saturday and Sunday from 2pm to around 8pm. There's a bar and a restaurant on the premises, serving simple food and drink that might act as the focal point of your visit. Other than the food and wine, entrance is free.

Also appealing, but without any public facilities, is the private home of Dr. Bruno Bellemo, **Villa Gradenigo,** Riviera San Pietro 75, 30030 Oriago (☎ 041/429-631). Set adjacent to the pier where boats from Venice and Padua are moored, it's a pure 16th-century adaptation of a Venetian palazzo whose interior is noted for a series of frescoes executed by the brothers of Veronese, Paolo and Benedetto Caliari. Look for a small but verdant garden around it, and all the grace notes (and understandable hesitancy) that accompany its role as a private home. Well-intentioned visitors and art students, if it's convenient for the owners, are welcomed inside, usually for free or a voluntary donation of 10,000L ($6), but never outside the hours of Tuesday through Friday from 9am to noon and 2:30 to 6pm, Saturday and Sunday from 10am to 6pm.

WHERE TO STAY

Dolo, located only 15 minutes by car from Venice or Padua, is at the midpoint of the Brenta Canal, and functions as the heart of the district. As such, it contains several villas from the 17th and 18th centuries, most of which are still inhabited by families. **Mira** is located 10 minutes from Venice and 20 from Padua at the most scenic bend of the Brenta Canal—it's no wonder that several villas lie in the immediate area of this village. While here, drop a card in the mail at the post office, situated in the former Palazzo Foscarini, Lord Byron's home where he worked on *Childe Harold* from 1817 to 1819.

Villa Ducale. Riviera Martiri della Libertà 75, 30031 Dolo. ☎ and fax **041/560-8020.** 11 rms, 1 suite. A/C MINIBAR TV TEL. 220,000L ($132) double; 280,000L ($168) suite. Rates include breakfast. AE, DC, MC, V.

This villa, built in 1884 by Count Giulio Rocca, has been turned into a hotel, allowing you to gain insight into villa life as an overnight guest. Restored to its original grandeur, the villa is graced with Murano glass chandeliers and mirrors, elaborate frescoes, ornate wrought-iron railings, luxurious fabrics, and antique furnishings throughout. Beautifully furnished guest rooms look over the statue-filled grounds of the villa. Besides being large and comfortable, rooms are equipped with a safe-deposit box, trouser press, and hair dryer. The hotel restaurant, La Colonne, specializes in Venetian seafood dishes, and there's a private parking lot for lodgers.

Villa Margherita. Via Nazionale 416–417, 30030 Mira, Venezia. ☎ **041/426-5800.** Fax 041/426-5838. 19 rms. A/C MINIBAR TV TEL. 220,000L–250,000L ($132–$150) double. Rates include breakfast. AE, DC, MC, V.

Arriving through an avenue of limes interspersed with antiquated statuary, this 17th-century villa is situated on a particularly scenic bend of the Brenta River, and the beauty of its interiors justifies its setting. Features include marble columns and fireplaces, marble and terra-cotta floors, immaculate frescoes and stucco work, a sunny breakfast room, and guest rooms that blend individualized traditional elegance with modern comfort. An immense park opens up behind the villa, and a stroll of 100 yards brings you to the Ristorante Margherita. The restaurant prepares the freshest Venetian seafood specialties, available with a large selection of fine wines and champagnes.

WHERE TO DINE AT MIRA

Ristorante Nalin. Via Nuovissimo 29, Mira. ☎ **041/420-083.** Reservations recommended. Main courses 16,000L–20,000L ($9.60–$12). AE, DC, MC, V. Tues–Sun noon–2:30pm, Tues–Sat 7:30–10pm. Closed Aug and Dec 26–Jan 6. VENETIAN/SEAFOOD.

Most of the restaurants of the Riviera del Brenta focus on seafood dishes, and this one is no exception. Set within a century-old building originally designed as a private home, the restaurant has flourished within its solid walls as a family-run enterprise since the 1960s. It is adjacent to the canal, near the town center, and you'll probably gravitate to the outdoor terrace, where potted shrubs and flowers add touches of spring throughout the summer. Specialties vary with whatever happens to be in season, but are likely to include *tagliatelle con salsa di calamaretti* (with squid sauce), *spaghetti al nero* (with octopus ink), crabs culled from the nearby Venetian lagoon, and seasonal variations on polenta and risotto. Seafood dishes are always prepared with fresh fish and vary according to what's readily available.

2 Padova (Padua)

25 miles W of Venice, 50 miles E of Verona, 145 miles E of Milan

Padua no longer looks as it did when Burton tamed shrew Taylor in the Zeffirelli adaptation of *The Taming of the Shrew*. However, it remains a major art center of the Veneto. Shakespeare called Padua a "nursery of arts."

Padua is sometimes known as *La Città del Santo* (City of the Saint), a reference to St. Anthony of Padua, who is buried at a basilica that the city dedicated to him. *Il Santo* was an itinerant Franciscan monk—not to be confused with St. Anthony of Egypt, the hermit who could resist all the temptations of the Devil. Many visitors stay in the cheaper Padua and commute to Venice. Of course, it doesn't have Venice's beauty, and it has been defaced by high-rises and urban blight, but its inner core has a wealth of attractions. Its university, the second oldest in Italy, adds life and vibrancy to Padua, although visitors and professors like Dante and Galileo haven't been seen here in a while.

ESSENTIALS

GETTING THERE By Train   The train is best if you're coming from Venice, Milan, or Bologna. Trains depart for and arrive from Venice once every 30 minutes (trip time: 30 minutes), at a one-way cost of 3,400L ($2.05). Trains to and from Milan run every hour (trip time: 2½ hours), charging 19,000L ($11.40) one-way. For information and schedules call ☎ **049/875-1800.** The main rail terminus lies at Piazza Stazione, north of the historic core and outside the 16th-century walls. A bus will connect you to the center.

By Bus   Buses from Venice arrive every 30 minutes (trip time: 45 minutes); a one-way fare is 4,800L ($2.90). There are also connections from Vicenza every 30 minutes (trip time: 30 minutes), charging 5,000L ($3). The **bus station** is at Via Trieste 40 (☎ 049/820-6844), near Piazza Boschetti, 5 minutes from the rail station.

By Car   Take autostrada A4 west from Venice.

VISITOR INFORMATION   The **tourist information center** is at the train station (☎ 049/875-2077). It's open Monday to Saturday from 9:30am to 5:30pm and Sunday from 9am to noon. Tickets valid for admission to all museums in Padua cost 15,000L ($9) adults and 10,000L ($6) students and children at the tourist office or at any of the city's museums.

SEEING THE SIGHTS

A university that grew to fame throughout Europe was founded here as early as 1222 (poet Tasso attended). The physics department counts Galileo among past professors and Petrarch also lectured here, and the **University of Padua** has remained one of the great centers for learning in Italy. Today its buildings are scattered throughout the city. The historic main building of the university is called **Il Bo,** after an inn on the site that used an ox as its sign, the major font of learning in the heyday of the Venetian Republic. The chief entrance is on Via Otto Febbraio. Of particular interest is an anatomy theater, which dates from 1594 and was the first of its kind in Europe. You can join a guided tour of the university on Tuesday from 9 to 11am, Wednesday and Thursday from 9 to 11am and 3 to 5pm, and Friday from 3 to 5pm. Tours cost 5,000L ($3). For information contact the Associazione Guide di Padova (☎ 049/820-9711).

If you're on a tight schedule, concentrate on the Cappella degli Scrovegni (Giotto frescoes) and the Basilica di San Antonio.

✪ **Cappella degli Scrovegni (also Arena Chapel).** Piazza Ermitani, off Corso Garibaldi. ☎ **049/820-4550.** Admission (including admission to the Musei Civici di Padova) 10,000L ($6) adults, 7,000L ($4.20) children 6–17, free for children 5 and under. Feb–Oct, daily 9am–7pm; Nov–Jan, daily 9am–6pm.

This modest (on the outside) chapel is the best reason for visiting Padua. Sometime around 1305 and 1306 Giotto did a cycle of more than 35 remarkably well-preserved frescoes inside, which, along with those at Assisi, form the basis of his claim to fame. Like an illustrated storybook, the frescoes unfold biblical scenes. The third bottom panel (lower level on the right) depicts Judas kissing a most skeptical Christ and is the most reproduced and widely known panel in the cycle. On the entrance wall is Giotto's *Last Judgment,* in which hell wins out for sheer fascination. The master's representation of the *Vices and Virtues* is bizarre; it reveals the depth of his imagination in personifying nebulous evil and elusive good. One of the most dramatic panels depicts the raising of Lazarus from the dead. This is a masterfully balanced scene, rhythmically ingenious for its day. The swathed and cadaverous Lazarus, however, looks indecisive as to whether or not he'll rejoin the living.

Chiesa degli Eremitani. Piazza Eremitani 9. ☎ **049/875-6410.** Free admission (donations accepted). Apr–Sept Mon–Sat 8:15am–noon and 4–6:30pm. Sun and religious holdays 9:30am–noon and 4–6pm. Closes 30 min earlier the rest of the year.

One of Padua's tragedies was when this church was bombed on March 11, 1944, during World War II. Before that time it housed one of the greatest treasures in Italy, the Ovetari Chapel, with the first significant cycle of frescoes by Andrea Mantegna (1431–1506). The church was rebuilt, but, unfortunately, you can't resurrect 15th-century frescoes. Inside, to the right of the main altar, are the fragments left after the bombing, a glimpse of what we lost of Mantegna's work. The most interesting fresco saved is a panel depicting the dragging of St. Christopher's body through the streets. Note also the *Assumption of the Virgin*. Like da Vinci, the artist had a keen eye for architectural detail.

⚙ **Basilica di Sant'Antonio.** Piazza del Santo 11. ☎ **049/824-2811.** Free admission. Apr–Sept, daily 7:30am–7:45pm; Oct–Mar, daily 7:30am–7pm.

This building was constructed in the 13th century and dedicated to St. Anthony of Padua, who's interred within. The basilica is a synthesis of styles, with mainly Romanesque and Gothic features. Campaniles and minarets combine to give it an Eastern appearance. Inside it's richly frescoed and decorated, and filled with pilgrims devoutly touching the saint's marble tomb. One of the more unusual relics is in the treasury—the seven-centuries-old, still-uncorrupt tongue of St. Anthony.

The great art treasurers are the Donatello bronzes at the main altar, with a realistic *Crucifix* towering over the rest. Seek out, too, the Donatello relief depicting the removal of Christ from the cross (at the back of the high altar), a unified composition that expresses in simple lines and with an unromantic approach the tragedy of Christ and the sadness of the mourners.

Among his other innovations, Donatello restored the lost art of the equestrian statue with the well-known example in front of the basilica. Although the man it honors—called Gattamelata—is of little interest to art lovers, the 1453 statue is of prime importance. The large horse is realistic, as Donatello was a master of detail. He cleverly directs the eye to the forceful, commanding face of the Venetian military hero, nicknamed "Spotted Cat." Gattamelata was a dead ringer for the late Lord Laurence Olivier.

Musei Civici di Padova. Piazza Eremitani 8. ☎ **049/820-4550.** Admission included with admission to Cappella degli Scrovegni (see above). Apr–Oct, Tues–Sun 9am–7pm; Nov–Mar, Tues–Sun 9am–6pm. Bus: 3, 8, 12, or 18.

This picture gallery is filled with minor works by major Venetian artists, some of which date from the 14th century. Look for a wooden *Crucifix* by Giotto and two miniatures by Giorgione. Other works include Giovanni Bellini's *Portrait of a Young Man* and Jacopo Bellini's miniature *Descent into Limbo*, with its childlike devils. The 15th-century Arras tapestry is also on display. Other works are Veronese's *Martyrdom of St. Primo and St. Feliciano*, plus Tintoretto's *Supper in Simone's House* and his *Crucifixion*, probably the finest single painting in the gallery.

Palazzo della Ragione. Via VIII Febbraio, between Piazza delle Erbe and Piazza dell Frutta. ☎ **049/820-5006.** Admission 9,000L ($5.40) adults, 5,000L ($3) children under 18. Feb–Oct, Tues–Sun 9am–7pm; Nov–Jan, Tues–Sun 9am–6pm.

This "Palace of Law," which dates from the early 13th century, is among the most remarkable buildings of northern Italy. Ringed with loggias, and with a roof shaped like the hull of a sailing vessel, it sits in the marketplace of Padua. Climb the steps and enter the grandiose Salone, a 270-foot assembly hall containing a gigantic, 15th-century wooden horse. The walls are richly frescoed with symbolic paintings that replaced the frescoes by Giotto and his assistants destroyed by a fire in 1420.

SHOPPING

Padua is an elegant town with a rich university life, a solid industrial base, and an economy that's too diversified to rely exclusively on tourism. Therefore, you'll find a wide roster of upscale consumer goods and luxury items and less emphasis on tourist souvenirs and handcrafts. For insights into the good life *alla Padovese*, make a trek through the city's densest concentration of shops, the neighborhood around the landmark Piazza Insurrezione, especially the **Galleria Borghese,** a conglomeration of shops off the Via San Fermo.

Droves of shoppers head to the **Prato delle Valle** on the third Sunday of every month, when more than 200 antique and collectible vendors set up shop for the day. The square, one of the largest in all of Europe, also hosts a smaller weekly market on Saturday. Shoes from nearby Brenta factories are the prevalent product, but the range of goods offered remains eclectic.

WHERE TO STAY
MODERATE

Hotel Donatello. Piazza del Santo 102–104, 35123 Padova. ☎ **049/875-0634.** Fax 049/875-0829. 49 rms, 4 suites. A/C MINIBAR TV TEL. 238,000L ($142.80) double; from 385,000L ($231) suite. AE, DC, MC, V. Closed Dec 15–Jan 15. Parking 28,000L ($16.80).

The Donatello is a renovated hotel with an ideal location near the Basilica of St. Anthony—although the Plaza has more amenities and is better equipped. The Donatello's terraced restaurant is its most alluring feature. The hotel's buff-colored facade is pierced by an arched arcade, and the oversized chandeliers of its lobby combine with the checkerboard marble floor for a hospitable ambience. The rooms are well maintained and reasonably comfortable, although furnished in a standard and uninspired style.

Hotel Plaza. Corso Milano 40, 35139 Padova. ☎ **049/656-822.** Fax 049/661-117. 142 rms, 5 suites. A/C MINIBAR TV TEL. 270,000L ($162) double; from 370,000L ($222) suite. Rates include buffet breakfast. AE, DC, MC, V. Parking 20,000L ($12).

The Plaza is Padua's leading inn, a business hotel with brown ceramic tiles and concrete-trimmed square windows. Constructed in the 1970s, it was last renovated in 1992. The entrance is under a modern concrete arcade, which leads into a contemporary lobby. Its angular lines are softened with an unusual Oriental needlework tapestry, brown leather couches, and a pair of gilded baroque cherubs. The rooms are comfortable and well decorated. The bar, which you reach through a stairwell and an upper balcony dotted with modern paintings, is a relaxing place for a drink. The restaurant is open Monday through Friday for lunch and Monday through Saturday for dinner.

Majestic Hotel Toscanelli. Piazzetta dell'Arco 2, 35122 Padova. ☎ **049/663-244.** Fax 049/876-0025. 29 rms, 3 suites. A/C MINIBAR TV TEL. 180,000L–280,000L ($108–$168) double; from 280,000L ($168) suite. Rates include buffet breakfast. AE, DC, MC, V. Parking 25,000L ($15).

Wrought-iron balconies protect the stone-edged French windows on this pastel-pink building fronting a cobblestone square in the heart of town. There's a Renaissance well and dozens of potted shrubs in front. Inside, you'll find a breakfast room surrounded by a garden of green plants. The lobby has white marble floors, Oriental rugs, an upper balcony, and a mishmash of old and new furniture. The bedrooms were completely overhauled in 1992. Elegant cherrywood furniture crafted by Tuscan artisans was added, along with mahogany and white marble. Pastel colors predominate in the bedrooms, with traditional Louis XV or Louis XVI decorating styles. On-site is a budget pizzeria that makes some of the best pies in town and serves several savory and freshly made pastas as well.

INEXPENSIVE

✪ **Albergo Leon Bianco.** Piazzetta Pedrocchi 12, 35122 Padova. ☎ **049/657-225.** Fax 049/875-0814. 22 rms. A/C TV TEL. 151,000L–157,000L ($90.60–$94.20) double. AE, MC, V. Parking 25,000L ($15).

This is the most nostalgic hotel in Padua, permeated with a sense of bittersweet regret for grander, more ostentatious eras. It was built "sometime after 1850." At the time, this "White Lion" was much, much larger that it is today, but during the economic uncertainties and conflicts of the 20th century, the hotel was whittled away to only 22 rooms. In 1985, a major renovation added bright, sometimes jarring colors, a rather odd-looking modern entrance set into the massive archway of the front, and a cafe and breakfast area to the panoramic rooftop. (Throughout the warm-weather months, it blossoms with the largest and most exotic collection of geraniums in Padua.) Breakfast is the only meal served, and the staff is much more articulate and charming than at similar hotels in the region.

Europa-Zaramella. Largo Europa 9, 35137 Padova. ☎ **049/661-200.** Fax 049/661-508. 59 rms. A/C MINIBAR TV TEL. 195,000L ($117) double. Rates include breakfast. AE, DC, MC, V. Parking 25,000L ($15).

Europa-Zaramella, near the post office, was built in the 1960s and looks its age, but is a recommendable choice because of its fairly modest rates. The tasteful bedrooms are compact and serviceable and have pastel walls and simple built-in furnishings. The rooms open onto small balconies. The public rooms are enhanced by cubist murals, free-form ceramic plaques, and furniture placed in conversational groupings. The American bar is popular, as is the dining room. The Zaramella Restaurant features a good Paduan cuisine, with an emphasis on seafood dishes from the Adriatic.

Hotel al Fagiano. Via Locatelli 45, 35123 Padova. ☎ **049/875-0073.** Fax 049/875-3396. 32 rms. A/C TV TEL. 110,000L ($66) double. AE, MC, V.

In 1988, the owners of this 18th-century town house completed a radical restoration of their three-story premises, and opened their doors to a growing trade of business and pleasure travelers from throughout Italy and the world. Its location (less than 100 yards from the Bascilica of St. Anthony) is among its most appealing assets. But despite its age, don't expect too many of the baroque trappings of a grander era. Ceilings inside some of the bedrooms are higher than within a modern building, but other than that, the venue is modern, streamlined, contemporary, and strongly influenced by design as practiced in industrialized Milan. A replica of a Renaissance fresco in the reception area adds one of the few historic touches, and the staff, not all of whom speak English, is particularly helpful. Breakfast is the only meal served.

WHERE TO DINE

✪ **Antico Brolo.** Corso Milano 22. ☎ **049/664-455.** Reservations recommended. Main courses 23,000L–40,000L ($13.80–$24). AE, DC, MC, V. Tues–Sun 12:30–2:30pm and 7:30 to 10:30pm. ITALIAN.

Set across from the ornate facade of the Teatro de Padova (Civic Theater), this is acknowledged by every hotelier in town as the city's best restaurant. Even though the 16th-century dining room evokes the Renaissance, many diners prefer a candlelit table within the carefully cultivated terrace garden. Cuisine follows the tenets of most of Italy, with special emphasis on seasonal ingredients and the regional traditions of the Veneto and Emilia-Romagna. Especially delicious are the made-on-the-premises *garganelli* (similar to the tubular shape of penne) with garlic sauce; an appetite-inducing version of onion soup baked in a crust; chateaubriand steak with balsamic vinegar; and grilled fish. The perfect dessert is a *zuppa inglese,* a cream-enriched dessert similar to a zabaglione.

✪ **Belle Parti—Toulà.** Via Belle Parti 11. ☎ **049/875-1822.** Reservations required. Main courses 20,000L–28,000L ($12–$16.80). AE, DC, MC, V. Mon–Sat 12:30–2:30pm and 8–10:30pm. Closed 3 weeks in Aug. INTERNATIONAL/ITALIAN.

Cappuccino in the Elegance of 19th-Century Padua

The **Caffè Pedrocchi,** Piazzetta Pedrocchi 15 (☎ 049/663-944), located off Piazza Cavour, is a neoclassical landmark. Hailed as the most elegant coffeehouse in
Europe when it opened in 1831 under Antonio Pedrocchi, its green, white, and
red rooms reflect the national colors of Italy. On sunny days you might want to sit
out on one of the two stone porches, and in winter you'll have plenty to distract
you inside. The sprawling bathtub-shaped travertine bar has a brass top and brass
lion's feet. The velvet banquettes have maroon upholstery, red-veined marble tables,
and Egyptian Revival chairs. And if you tire of all this 19th-century outrageous-
ness, you can retreat to a more conservatively decorated English-style pub on the
premises, whose entrance is under a covered arcade a few steps away. Renovated in
1997, it's now as good as new. Coffee costs 1,300L (80¢) at the stand-up bar, 2,800L
($1.70) at a table. Drinks begin at 5,000L ($3) at the bar, 8,000L ($4.80) at a table.
Although drinks cost more than they would in a lesser cafe, you haven't heard the
heartbeat of Padua until you've been at the Pedrocchi. It's open Tuesday to Sunday from 9:30am to 12:30pm and 3:30 to 8pm.

Toulà was established in 1982 under ceiling beams that are at least 500 years old. The
age of the structure, however, didn't stop a team of designers from creating a sensual
decor that showcases Italian style at its best. The ground floor includes a slick black
bar, and the main dining area offers the excellent service this most sophisticated of
nationwide restaurant chains is eager to provide. The palate-pleasing menu changes
monthly, but might include crayfish salad with artichokes; scampi salad with fennel,
orange slices, and olives; a salad of radicchio with bacon; a savory salad composed of
bottargha fish, beans, and celery; or filet of beef with a sauce of rosemary and balsamic vinegar. The cookery isn't always as refined as that of its sibling in Rome, but
is first-rate nevertheless.

Ristorante Dotto. Via Squarcione 23. ☎ **049/625-469.** Main courses 16,000L–25,000L
($9.60–$15); fixed-price menu 50,000L ($30). AE, DC, MC, V. Tues–Sat 12:30–2pm and 7:30–
10pm, Sun 12:30–2pm. Closed Aug 8–20. PADUAN.

Ristorante Dotto takes its name from the *dottori* (doctors) of the university for which
Padua is famous. The discreet, elegant restaurant is in the heart of the city, suitable
not only for an academic or business meal but also for an intimate tête-à-tête dinner. Try the pasta e fagioli, grilled sole, risotto made with fresh asparagus, or the chef's
pâté. You could top all this off with a feathery dessert soufflé, the most elaborate of
which must be ordered at the beginning of a meal. The cookery is solid and reliable,
without ever rising to the sublime.

Taverna del Teatro. Corso Milano 22. ☎ **049/664-455.** Main courses 20,000L–30,000L
($12–$18). AE, DC, MC, V. Tues–Sun 7pm–1am. ITALIAN.

This is the simple and unpretentious conterpart to Antico Brolo (see above), with
which it shares the same management. Set in Antico Brolo's stone-sided cellar, it's
open only for dinner and combines many of the functions of beer tavern and wine
bar. No one will mind if you descend into its depths just for a beer, priced at around
5,000L ($3), or some of the local wine, priced from 18,000L ($10.80) a bottle. But
if you're hungry, there's a wide medley of pizzas, pastas, simple platters of food, and
ice creams awaiting your pleasure.

PADUA AFTER DARK

You can network with students in town at any of the crowded cafes along the Via Cavour, or walk over to the wine and beer dives around the Piazza delle Frutte to find out where most of the college crowd is being cool. But other than a quiet stroll through the town's historic core, there is little happening in the city. The most popular discos lie outside the city along the road between Padua and the spa town of Abano Terme, where the music is louder and the lights are dimmer than within comparable inner-city venues. Examples include **King's Club,** in Abano Terme (☎ **049/667-895**), 10 miles from Padua. En route, about 2 miles west of Padua, you'll find **Disco Extra Extra,** Via Ciamician 5 (☎ **049/620-044**), and its neighbor **Disco P1,** Viale Giusti (☎ **049/860-1633**). Looking for something within Padua itself? Try **Disco-Bar Limbo,** Via San Fermo 44 (☎ **049/656-882**), where electronic games alternate with recorded and (occasionally) live music.

3 Treviso

19 miles N of Venice

A city of sweets and art, Treviso is known to culinary fans for cherries and the creation of *tiramisù*—translated "pick me up"—a delicious blend of ladyfingers, mascarpone cheese, eggs, cocoa, liqueur, and espresso. Art aficionados know it for its many works by Tomaso da Modena.

ESSENTIALS

GETTING THERE   By Train   There are three trains per hour from Venice, a trip of 30 minutes costing 3,800L ($2.30), and hourly trains from Udine, a trip of 1 hour 40 minutes for 8,000L ($4.80). There are a half-dozen daily trains from Vicenza, a trip of 1 hour 10 minutes priced at 4,300L ($2.60). Treviso's station (☎ **0422/541-352**) is at Piazza Duca d'Aosta on the southern end of town.

By Bus   The station at Lungosile Mattei 29 receives buses on the La Marca bus line (☎ **0422/412-222**) from Bassano del Grappa nine times daily, a trip of 1 hour 15 minutes costing 5,700L ($3.40), and every 30 minutes from Padua, a 1-hour 10-minute excursion for 5,000L ($3). The ACT line (☎ **0422/541-821**) runs two buses an hour from Venice, a 30-minute trip priced at 3,800L ($2.30).

By Car   From Venice, take the autostrada A11 through Mestre, a distance of 6 miles; head northeast on A4 for 3 miles, then take Route S13 for 10 miles north to Treviso.

VISITOR INFORMATION   The **tourist office,** Via Toniolo 41 (☎ **0422/540-600**), is open Monday through Friday from 8:30am to 1:30pm and 2:30 to 6pm, Saturday 8:30am to noon.

SEEING THE SIGHTS

Tomaso da Modena painted 40 portraits in the **Capitolo dei Dominicani** of the Seminario Vescovile, Via San Nicolò (☎ **0422/412-010**). They capture the diverse personalities of a series of Dominican monks seated at their desks. There is no admission fee, and daily hours are from 9am to 12:30pm and 3 to 7:30pm; in winter, it closes at 5:30pm.

No longer a church, **Chiesa di Santa Caterina,** Piazzetta Mario Botter, houses the frescoes that comprise da Modena's depiction of the Christian legend of the *Ursula Cycle,* with its 11,000 virgins all accounted for. Call the **Museo Civico,** Borgo Cavour

24 (☎ 0422/658-442), for hours or an appointment. The museum itself houses the strange *Il Castragatti (The Cat Fixer)* by Sebastiano Florigero, a *Crucifixion* by Bassano, and the fresco *San Antonio Abate* by Pordenone. Hours are Tuesday through Saturday from 9am to 12:30pm and 2:30 to 5pm, and Sunday from 9am to noon. Admission is 3,000L ($1.80).

You can visit the **Duomo,** Piazza del Duomo at Via Canoniche 2 (☎ 0422/ 545-720), Monday through Saturday from 7:30 to 11:30am and 3:30 to 6:45pm. It contains more frescoes by Pordenone as well as an *Annunciation* by Titian. The crypt is open after 10:30am. A stroll through the **Piazza dei Signori** offers views of several interesting Romanesque buildings, including the municipal bell tower, the Trecento Palace, and the nearby Loggia dei Cavalieri on Via Martiri della Libertà.

SHOPPING   The city is known for its production of wrought iron and copper utensils, and the best places to find these goods are **Prior,** Via Palesto 12 (☎ 0422/ 545-886), **Fontebasso,** Via Calmaggiore 1 (☎ 0422/547-774), and **Morandin,** Via Palestro 50 (☎ 0422/543-651).

WHERE TO STAY

Al Fogher. Viale della Repubblica 10, 31100 Treviso. ☎ **800/528-1234** in the U.S., or 0422/ 432-950. Fax 0422/430-391. 55 rms, 1 suite. A/C TV TEL. 230,000L ($138) double; 280,000L ($168) suite. Rates include breakfast. AE, DC, MC, V.

Of the hotels in town, we recommend this business favorite of wine merchants. Set just north of the medieval fortifications of Treviso, this six-story Best Western affiliate was built in the 1960s and completely renovated in 1995. The decor contrasts antique statuary with modern art prints and marble with glass bricks. The brightly painted guest rooms are done in cool pastels and floral prints, and outfitted in an internationally modern style—solid and comfortable but not majestic or cutting edge in any way. The top floor has a panoramic terrace where guests congregate for views over the Veneto countryside, and the well-regarded basement restaurant serves seasonal Venetian dishes made from the market's freshest ingredients. It's a popular eatery, so reservations are suggested. Meals are highlighted with real silver service and a substantial wine list. The restaurant is closed in August and the second week of January.

Ca'del Galletto. Via Santa Bona Vecchia 30, 31100 Treviso. ☎ **0422/432-550.** Fax 0422/ 432-510. 62 rms. A/C MINIBAR TV TEL. 220,000L–270,000L ($132–$162) double. Rates include breakfast. AE, DC, MC, V. Parking 20,000L ($12).

This thoroughly modern hotel offers comfortable soundproof rooms with safe-deposit boxes, trouser presses, and hair dryers. Deluxe accommodations also include Jacuzzis. An enclosed garden allows you outdoor privacy in the city, and two tree-shaded clay tennis courts offer exercise. The lobby bar is open 24 hours for your convenience, and the Ristorante Albertini next door serves rich Venetian seafood dishes and other traditional specialties.

Hotel Continental. Via Roma 16, 31100 Treviso. ☎ **0422/411-216.** Fax 0422/55-054. 80 rms. A/C MINIBAR TV TEL. 220,000L ($132) double. Rates include breakfast. AE, DC, MC, V.

Located close to the sights within the old city walls, this four-star hotel has been in business since 1958 providing dependable service and comfortable accommodations. The building itself, though only about 40 years old, pays homage to Italian design through various eras, mixing and matching antique furnishings so that each room gains an individuality that is elegantly highlighted by beautiful fabrics and Oriental rugs. There is no restaurant or parking at the hotel, but a number of eateries and parking lots are close by.

Hotel Scala. Viale Felissent 5, 31100 Treviso. ☎ **0422/307-600.** Fax 0422/305-048. 21 rms. A/C MINIBAR TV TEL. 160,000L ($96) double. Rates include breakfast. AE, DC, MC, V.

This immense villa sitting privately in the midst of a tree-filled garden combines old country elegance with modern hospitality. Arched entryways, beamed ceilings, and eclectic antiques grace environs that include a bar, an acclaimed restaurant serving Venetian and international fare, and a private car park. Bedrooms are comfortably and traditionally furnished, and extremely well maintained.

A NEARBY PLACE TO STAY

✪ **Villa Condulmer.** Via Zermanese 1, 31021 Zerman di Mogliano Veneto. ☎ **041/457-100.** Fax 041/457-134. 22 rms, 12 junior suites, 8 apts. A/C MINIBAR TEL. 260,000L–360,000L ($156–$216) double; 290,000L ($174) junior suite; 380,000L ($228) apartment. Rates include breakfast. AE, DC, MC, V. Drive 7 miles south on S13 to Zerman, just outside Mogliano Veneto.

The finest place to stay is 7 miles outside Treviso. Giuseppe Verdi fled here in 1853 after the Venetian debut of *La Traviata* was met with catcalls. This illustrious house was built in 1743 by the Condulmer family, whose wealth and power can be traced to 14th-century ancestor Pope Eugene IV. The villa passed from the family's hands in the early 19th century, when frescoes by Moretti Laresi were added. The kind of luxury Ronald Reagan found here in 1987 includes elaborate stucco work, marble floors, crystal chandeliers, Oriental carpets, period furnishings, and large guest rooms located in the main house, as well as in two annexes with lofts. The back garden houses a private chapel, and beyond it stretches a park with a small lake, hillocks, ruins, a swimming pool, 27-hole golf course, tennis court, and riding grounds. There's also a piano bar and a restaurant, which grows its own produce to supplement the market's freshest fish and game.

WHERE TO DINE

Al Fogher, reviewed as a hotel above, houses a good restaurant.

Beccherie. Piazza Ancilotto 10. ☎ **0422/56-601.** Reservations recommended. Main courses 18,000L–30,000L ($10.80–$18). AE, DC, MC, V. Tues–Sun 12:30–2pm; Tues–Sat 7:30–10pm. Closed July 15–31. VENETIAN.

Despite the prevalence of the car park, this stone-sided building still evokes the era of its construction (1830) when it was built as a coaching inn for the care and feeding of humans and horses. Cuisine and the flavorings of the dishes vary with the seasons, and include such midwinter game dishes as *faraona in salsa peverada* (guinea hen in a peppery sauce), and a spring and summer favorite, *pasticcio di melanzane* (eggplant casserole). In between, look for such enduring traditions as fried crabs from the Venetian lagoon, served with herb-flavored polenta; fresh fried sardines; osso buco; fiery hot pastas; and roasted loin of pork.

El Toulà da Alfredo. Via Collalto 26. ☎ **0422/540-275.** Reservations required Sat–Sun. Main courses 25,000L–40,000L ($15–$24). AE, DC, MC, V. Tues–Sun noon–2:30pm and 7:30–11pm. Closed Aug 8–24. INTERNATIONAL/VENETIAN.

Founded in 1960, this is the elegant and upscale restaurant that launched what has become a nine-member chain known throughout Italy for its well-conceived food and elegant service. It offers Veneto-based dishes whose inspiration varies with the seasonality of the ingredients and the chef's intelligent permutations on local traditions. Within a pair of dining rooms built in 1790 and outfitted in an upscale Liberty art nouveau style, you can order succulent versions of risotto with baby peas, pappardelle pasta studded with baby asparagus tips and herbs, Venetian-style calves' liver, veal kidneys in mustard sauce, *risotto con funghi* (rice with mushrooms), and blinis with caviar. The lengthy dessert roster includes an array of light sweet sorbets, often concocted from local fruit. Service is impeccable.

THE WINE ROADS FROM TREVISO

Many travelers indelibly associate wine and the cultivation of grapes with the gently rolling foothills of the Dolomites around Treviso. For a view of the ancient vines that have produced thousands of gallons of the region's most drinkable wine, take a drive along the two local highways whose adjacent vineyards are the most respected in the region. Together, they're known as the **Strade dei Vini del Piave** in honor of the nearby Piave River, and both begin at the medieval town of Conegliano where the local tourist office is at Via Columbo 45 (☎ **0438/21-230**).

Confusingly, you won't find route numbers associated with either of these wine roads. But each is clearly signposted en route, beginning in central Conegliano, the originating point of them both. The less interesting is the **Strada del Vino Rosso** (Red Wine Road), which runs through 25 miles of humid flatlands that stretch southeast of Conegliano. Significant points en route include the scenic hamlets of Oderzo, Motta, and Ponte di Piave, a site on the outskirts of the province of Treviso.

Much more scenic, and evocative, is the **Strada del Vino Bianco** (or, more specifically, **Strada del Prosecco),** which meanders through the rolling foothills of the Dolomites for about 24 miles northwest of Conegliano, ending at the hamlet of Valdobbiadene. En route, it passes through particularly prestigious, DOC-designated regions famous for their sparkling Prosecco. This is a quality white wine, meant to be drunk young, with the characteristic taste and smell of ripe apples, wisteria, and acacia honey. The most charming of the many hamlets you'll encounter en route (blink an eye and you'll miss them) include San Pietro di Feletto, Follina, and Pieve di Soligno. Each of those medieval hamlets is awash with family-run cantinas, kiosks, and roadside stands, all selling the fermented fruits of the local harvest and offering platters of prosciutto, local cheese, and crusty bread to accompany your vintages.

Don't expect mega-agriculture here, as the low-slung stone buildings baking in the sun amid verdant vines look virtually unchanged since they were built, and curiously timeless. The Strada del Vino Bianco was the first wine road established by the Italian government. The year was 1966, and the designation immediately prompted equivalent regions throughout Italy to apply for official recognition.

The two best hotels for establishing a base in the region lie in Conegliano. The three-star **Canon d'Oro,** Via XX Settembre 129, 31015 Conegliano (☎ and fax **0438/34-246**), lies in a 15th-century building near the railway station and offers 135,000L ($81) for a double. The more upscale, four-star **Hotel Città de Conegliano** (☎ **0438/21-445;** fax 0438/410-950) is the best in town, an elegant landmark with unusual frescoes on the facade and doubles for 108,000L to 130,000L ($64.80 to $78).

FOOD & DRINK EN ROUTE

Rest assured that if you opt for an excursion along this wine route, you won't lack for options for food and drink.

IN CONEGLIANO　Among the many rustic, country-comfortable sites that dot the local landscapes, our personal favorite is **Tre Panoce,** Via Vecchia Trevigiano 50 (☎ **0438/60-071**). Set within a 16th-century (or perhaps older) stone building originally conceived as an annex to a local convent, it charges around 50,000L ($30) for full meals, without wine, that include a culinary celebration for whatever is in season at the moment. Your pasta might be flavored with radicchio, fresh mushrooms, wild herbs, or local cheese, depending on the whim of the chef, but will always be a suitable foil for whatever local wine might tempt you. It's set in the hills above Conegliano, a half-mile from the town center, within earshot of both the autostrada and flotillas of wild birds.

More formal (indeed, the most formal and upscale restaurant in town), is **Al Salisà,** Via XX Settembre 2 (☎ **0438/24-288**), which occupies a stone building with 12th-century foundations in the historic core of town. Excellent food, complemented by the authentically old-fashioned setting that includes one large dining room and an outdoor terrace, attracts the best-heeled visitors in town. Menu items include roasted veal prepared with wild herbs, sea bass with seasonal vegetables and a basil-flavored white wine sauce, and fettuccine with wild duck. It's closed Tuesday evening and all day Wednesday.

IN VALDOBBIADENE   You might not be too hungry by the time you reach this hamlet because of the many edible temptations you're likely to have sampled en route. But if you're in the mood for a meal, the two most appealing restaurants in town are **Al Pesce,** Via Erizza 287 (☎ **0423/980-296**), and **Valle Mariana,** Via Cal Vecchia del Col 8 (☎ **0423/972-616**). Both feature the region's seasonal produce, fresh fowl, fish, and meat, and a time-honored skill at blending food with the local wines.

4 Asolo

11 miles E of Marostica, 7 miles E of Bassano, 20 miles NW of Treviso

Known as the "Town of a Hundred Horizons" because of its panoramic views, this hamlet entered the mainstream of Renaissance politics in the late 1400s, when Caterina Cornari, daughter of a prominent Venetian family, became a pawn in a strategic treaty between Venice and the king of Cyprus. After the king's death, Queen Caterina struggled unsuccessfully, with Venetian help, to keep the Turks off Cyprus. When they conquered the island and ousted the Venetians, Caterina was given this hamlet as a consolation prize.

Between 1498 and her death in 1510, she shuttled between Venice and her country estate in Asolo, building up the local economy and supporting the arts, creating the village you see today. Partly because of her patronage of music, literature, and painting, the town's reputation as a centerpiece for the arts flourished through the turn of this century as home to both English poet Robert Browning and Italy's grande dame of the stage, Eleonora Duse, a figurehead of the Liberty art nouveau movement.

ESSENTIALS

GETTING THERE   By Bus   There is daily bus service from Bassano, Treviso, and Venice. For information, contact Sta. La Marca in Treviso (☎ **0422/412-222**).

By Car   From Treviso, take Route 348 for 16 miles northwest to Cornuda, then take Route 248 for 5¹/₂ miles west to Asolo. From Bassano, take Route 248 for 7 miles east to reach the town.

VISITOR INFORMATION   The APT tourist office is at Piazza Gabriele d'Annunzio 1 (☎ **0423/529-046**). It's open Monday to Saturday from 8:30am to 1pm and 2:30 to 6pm.

EXPLORING CATERINA'S TOWN

Most of the allure of Asolo derives from its well-preserved Renaissance architecture and timeless agrarian charm, but there are a handful of monuments worth visiting. You can visit Queen Caterina's rebuilt home, the **Castello Cornaro**, Via Regina Cornaro (☎ **0423/55-842**). Of its former grandeur, only the tower is original, and in the late 1800s, much of its interior was transformed into a municipal theater, the

Teatro Municipio Eleonora Duse (same phone). About 10 different venues of chamber music concerts and light, Italian-language comedies are presented every year, at ticket prices that begin at around 10,000L ($6).

Brooding over the eastern edge of town, less than a quarter-mile from the center, is **La Rocca.** Originally conceived as a medieval stronghold by the Venetians, and now only a weathered rampart with a panoramic view, it can be visited only on Saturday from 2 to 6pm and Sunday from 10am to sunset, for an entrance fee of 2,500L ($1.50).

Asolo's only museum, the **Museo Civico,** Piazza Garibaldi 207 (☎ 0423/952-313), has been closed for renovation but may tentatively be reopened during the lifetime of this edition. Call or ask anyone in town prior to your visit, and expect lots of memorabilia devoted to Caterina Cornaro, Robert Browning, Eleonora Duse, and her lover, romantic poet Gabriele d'Annunzio. Within the town's **Cimiterio di Sant'Anna** on Via Sant'Anna you can find the gravestones of Duse and also Robert Browning's son, Pen. The oft-renovated **Duomo** on Via Browning (☎ 0423/952-376) houses *Assumptions* by Bassano and Lorenzo Lotto.

Regardless of what you see and do in Asolo, you'll pass several times through the landmark **Piazza Maggiore,** lined with Renaissance palaces and workaday, turn-of-the-century cafes where Browning, Duse, and other greats inevitably gathered for refreshment, socializing, and/or gossip.

WHERE TO STAY

Hotel Duse. Via Browning 190, 31001 Asolo. ☎ **0432/55-241.** Fax 0432/950-404. 14 rms. A/C MINIBAR TV TEL. 200,000L–250,000L ($120–$150) double. Rates include breakfast. AE, MC, V.

Set opposite the Duomo on Asolo's main square, this four-story hotel occupies a stone building that's at the very least a century old and is named for the great stage actress Eleonora Duse. Staffed by a charming, partly English-speaking staff, it contains cozy bedrooms outfitted with Liberty art nouveau–style accessories and bright colors. No meals are served other than breakfast, but nearby are many restaurants—and many much more expensive hotels.

✪ **Hotel Villa Cipriani.** Via Canova 298, 31001 Asolo. ☎ **800/325-3535** or 0423/952-166. Fax 0423/952-095. 31 rms. A/C TV TEL. 360,000L ($216) deluxe double, 460,000L ($276) superior double. AE, DC, MC, V.

Once the home of Actress Eleonora Duse and poet Robert Browning, this 18th-century villa has been a hotel since 1962, and is now part of the ITT Sheraton chain. The individualized rooms are divided between the main house and a "garden house," and feature wood-beamed ceilings, period furnishings, Oriental carpets, and incredible views of the grounds, town, and surrounding hills. There is abundant plant life everywhere, from ivy creeping down an internal balcony or scaling the exterior walls, to the bright blossoms of window boxes, potted plants, and the garden, often riotous with the bloom of azaleas and roses. The two restaurants, Sala Contarini and Veranda, even grow the vegetables that are combined with fresh market fish and game in creative seasonal Venetian and international dishes. There is an American-style bar and a terrace for enjoying the weather while partaking of meals and drinks.

WHERE TO DINE

Ca'Derton. Piazza d'Annunzio 11. ☎ **0423/529-648.** Reservations recommended. Main courses 18,000L–25,000L ($10.80–$15). AE, MC, V. Tues–Sun noon–3pm and 7:30–10pm. Closed July 15–31 and Jan 7–17. VENETIAN.

It's hard to miss this well-managed, family-run restaurant, as it occupies one of Asolo's most visible palaces, a white-fronted stately edifice built in the early 1700s near the fountain in the center of town. Run by members of the Baggio family since 1978, it has room for only 45 diners, who admire the venerable paintings and antiques, and consume large quantities of such dishes as potato-based gnocchi, oven-roasted lamb with rosemary and herbs, and fettuccine with asparagus. Especially delicious are the various risotto dishes with peas, mushrooms, or whatever else happens to be seasonal at the time—when it's available, order the succulent version with local cheeses and braised radicchio. Also look for the roast duckling marinated in balsamic vinegar; and bigoli (a local pasta) flavored with tomatoes, herbs, and duck meat.

OFF THE BEATEN PATH: A PALLADIAN VILLA

Take SS248 for 4¹/₂ miles northeast of Asolo to the **Villa Barbaro,** Via Cornuda 2 (☎ 0423/923-004), in Maser. Built in 1559, it is Palladio's second-greatest Renaissance villa, after La Rotonda in Vicenza. It's still in private hands, and the owners will make you put scuffs over your shoes so you won't mark up their polished floors. Once inside, you can admire beautiful stuccos and frescoes by Paolo Veronese. In the back garden there's an ornate grotto by Alessandro Vittorio. The villa is open April through September, Tuesday, Saturday, and Sunday from 3 to 6pm, and October through March, Saturday and Sunday from 2:30 to 5pm. Admission is 8,000L ($4.80).

5 Bassano del Grappo

23 miles N of Venice

Situated at the foot of Mount Grappa in the Valsugana Valley, this hideaway along the Brenta River draws Italian vacationers because of its proximity to the mountains and its panoramic views. It's best known for its liquor, *grappa,* a brandy usually made from grape pomace left in a winepress, but it's also known for pottery, porcini mushrooms, white asparagus, and radicchio.

ESSENTIALS

GETTING THERE **By Train** There is direct train service from Trento 8 times a day, a 2-hour journey that costs 8,000L ($4.80). There are also trains requiring a change at Castelfranco from Padua and Venice. The former is a 1-hour trip arriving 12 times daily for 4,200L ($2.50); the latter, 16 trains daily taking 1 hour 20 minutes, costs 5,000L ($3). Contact the train station (☎ 0424/525-034) for information and schedules.

By Bus There are many more buses to Bassano than trains. The FTV bus line (☎ 0424/30-850) offers service from Asiago (trip time: 1 hour 30 minutes) 7 times daily for 5,600L ($3.35), hourly from Vicenza (trip time: 1 hour) for 4,800L ($2.90), and hourly from Marostica, 10 minutes away, for 2,000L ($1.20). ACTM buses run from Asolo (trip time: 30 minutes) 7 times daily for 2,800L ($1.70), Maser (trip time: 30 minutes) 10 times daily for 4,000L ($2.40), and Possagno (trip time: 40 minutes) 7 times daily for 3,800L ($2.30). Both lines arrive at Bar Trevisiani, Piazzale Trento 13 (☎ 0424/525-025), a ticket booth/bar/restaurant. La Marca buses (☎ 0422/412-222) from Treviso pull in at Osteria La Pergola, Piazzale Trento 7 (☎ 0424/27-154), 6 times daily. The trip takes 1 hour 20 minutes and costs 5,700L ($3.40).

By Car From Asolo, take Route 248 for 7 miles west.

VISITOR INFORMATION The **tourist office** is located at Largo Cordona d'Italia 35, off Via Jacopo del Ponte (☎ 0424/524-351). They hand out the *Bassano News,* a monthly information and accommodation guide with a town map. It's open

Monday through Friday from 9am to 12:30pm and 2 to 5pm, and Saturday from 9am to 12:30pm.

EXPLORING THE TOWN

The village is lovely and the liquor is strong, but there aren't a lot of specific sights here. Its best-known landmark is the **Ponte dei Alpini,** a covered wooden bridge over the Brenta, which has been replaced numerous times over the years because of flooding, but each version is faithful to the original 1209 design.

Housing numerous paintings by Bassano, the **Museo Civico,** in Piazza Garibaldi at Via Museo 12 (☎ 0424/522-235), also has works by Canova, Tiepolo, and others. It's open Tuesday through Saturday from 9am to 12:30pm, and Tuesday through Sunday from 3:30 to 6:30pm, with an admission fee of 5,000L ($3) adults or 2,500L ($1.50) children under 18 and seniors. That ticket will also admit you to the **Palazzo Sturm,** Via Schiavonetti (☎ 0424/522-235), home of the Ceramics Museum, featuring four centuries of finely crafted regional pottery. Summer hours are the same as the Civic Museum, and off-season hours are from 9am to noon on Friday, and 3:30 to 6:30pm on Saturday and Sunday.

SHOPPING If you don't get sick from overindulging on grappa, you may want to pick some up to take home. The best-known distillery is the 18th-century **Nardini,** Via Madonna Monte Berico 4 (☎ 0424/567-040), next to the Ponte degli Alpini, where juniper, pear, peach, and plum versions supplement the grape standard. Other grappa shops include **Poli,** Via Gamba (☎ 0424/524-426), and **Bassanina,** Via Angarano (☎ 0424/502-140). Because you're in the heart of grappa country, you can also find good smaller labels like Folco Portinari, Maschio, Jacopo de Poli, Rino Dal Tosco, Da Ponte, and Carpene Malvolti.

WHERE TO STAY

✪ **Al Castello.** Piazza Terraglio 19, 36061 Bassano del Grappa. ☎ or fax **0424/228-665.** 11 rms. A/C TV TEL. 100,000L ($60) double. AE, MC, V.

Opened by the Cattapan family 25 years ago, this is a small simple hotel outfitted to provide you with a comfortable stay at a bargain rate. Conveniently located in the heart of town near the medieval Civic Tower, this antique town house was renovated 5 years ago but retains a classical style. Each comfortably furnished, tasteful room has a shower. There is no restaurant, but at a cafe-bar with a sidewalk terrace you can relax over coffee or a drink.

Hotel Belvedere. Piazzale Generale Giardino 14, 36061 Bassano del Grappa. ☎ **0424/522-204.** Fax 0424/529-849. 91 rms. A/C MINIBAR TV TEL. 260,000L ($156) double. Rates include breakfast. AE, DC, MC, V. Parking 20,000L ($12).

The first inn in the village, the Belvedere was established in the 15th century as a place to rest and change horses before traveling to the Republic of Venice. The third-floor rooms attest to the hotel's age with rustic, exposed beams. Bedrooms incorporate classical, Venetian, and Bassanese styles in a blend of antiquity and comfort. Public rooms are luxuriously clad in Oriental rugs and tapestries, fresh-cut flowers, and curvaceous wooden furniture covered with richly colored and patterned fabrics. The lounge houses a baby grand piano, large fireplace, glass and beamed ceiling, and wooden balcony overhung with ivy. There's a bar, and the chandeliered restaurant, Del Buon Ricordo, specializes in *baccalà alla vicentina,* and you get to take your plate, illustrated with a drawing of the Bassano bridge, home as a souvenir. The restaurant is shared with the Hotel Palladio, 500 yards away, whose gym facilities are open to Belvedere guests.

Hotel Palladio Bassano. Via Gramsci 2, 36061 Bassano del Grappa. ☎ **0424/523-777.**
Fax 0424/524-050. 54 rms, 12 junior suites. A/C MINIBAR TV TEL. 220,000L ($132) double;
260,000L ($156) junior suite. Rates include breakfast. AE, DC, MC, V. Parking 20,000L ($12).

A sibling to the Hotel Belvedere—they sit 500 yards apart and share a restaurant,
gym, and parking facilities—you'd never guess they were related. Contrasting to the
Belvedere, this hotel's facade is modern with cut stone and stepped glass panels. The
interior is contemporary as well, as the lobby attests with a curved wood and brass
service counter and modern receded lighting. It does have common interior elements
though, mainly in the form of mottled marble floors and Oriental rugs. Furniture
runs the gamut, from curved wood with richly patterned fabrics, to overstuffed black
leather and tassled velveteen—sometimes all in one area. Bedrooms are modern,
streamlined, sunny, painted in pastels and off-whites, and very comfortable. On the
premises, there's a bar, gym, sauna, hydromassage bath, solarium, and beauty and
massage parlor. Step over to the Belvedere to partake in meals at Del Buon Ricordo.

Villa Palma. Via Chemin Palma 30, 36065 Mussolente. ☎ **0424/577-407.** Fax 0424/87-687.
12 rms, 8 junior suites, 1 suite. A/C MINIBAR TV TEL. 300,000L ($180) double; 420,000L ($252)
junior suite; 480,000L ($288) suite. Rates include breakfast. AE, DC, MC, V.

Located just 3 miles from Bassano del Grappa, this 18th-century villa was opened as
a hotel in 1991 after renovations that carefully preserved features such as its beamed
and vaulted brick ceilings. Guest rooms are spread across three floors and are individualized by mixing antiques, carpets, and tapestries to create a comfortable yet elegant atmosphere. Some bathrooms have sauna showers or Jacuzzis. The hotel
restaurant, La Loggia, is closed on Monday and for 2 weeks in August and 1 week
following New Year's, but at other times creates an environment and regional meals
as well appointed as the hotel itself.

WHERE TO DINE

Al Sole. Via Jacopo Vittorelli 41. ☎ **0424/523-206.** Main courses 15,000L–23,000L ($9–
$13.80). AE, DC, MC, V. Tues–Sun noon–3pm and 7:30–10pm. Closed July. VENETIAN.

Gian-Franco Chiurato's successful restaurant originally opened nearby in 1949, then
moved into this cavernous early 19th-century palazzo in 1961, where both dining
rooms are decorated with local ceramics. The cuisine is firmly rooted in the traditions
of the Veneto, and celebrates two annual crops that sweep at 6-month intervals across
the menus: In springtime, look for the region's distinctive white asparagus *(asperagi
de Bassano)* blended into pastas and risottos, as a garnish for main courses, and often featured as a refreshing course on its own. In autumn and winter, look for similar variations on mushrooms, especially porcini, which its fans claim is absolutely
addictive with game birds and venison. The rest of the year, expect polenta with codfish, warm versions of puff pastry layered with local cheeses and mushrooms, homemade bigoli pasta drenched with duck meat and mushrooms, and baked lamb served
with herbed polenta.

San Bassiano. Viale dei Martiri 36. ☎ **0424/521-453.** Reservations recommended. Main
courses 13,000L–22,000L ($7.80–$13.20); fixed-price menu 55,000L ($33), including wine. DC,
MC, V. Mon–Sat 12:30–3pm and 7:30–10pm. ITALIAN/SEAFOOD.

The Carotenuto family have done their best to retain the original wood paneling of
this grand restaurant in the finest condition possible to serve as an attractive backdrop for the Pan-Italian cuisine that emerges from the steaming kitchens. Established
in the early 1980s, it maintains a cozy bar adjacent to the dining rooms, and an emphasis on the bounty produced throughout the Italian peninsula. Examples include
potato-based gnocchi with eggplant; fettuccini with crayfish; risotto with radicchio

and herbs or, when they're available, with shrimp; *baccalà alla vincentina* (codfish braised in wine and milk with herbs, anchovies, and garlic); and succulent pappardelle noodles with porcini mushrooms. The single most opulent pasta served here is *imperiali,* prepared with a lavish array of fresh shellfish and served with appropriate theatricality.

OFF THE BEATEN PATH: A HUMAN CHESS GAME

Four-and-a-half miles west of Bassano del Grappa on Route 248, **Marostica** hosts **"The Game of Life,"** a reminder of just how far sexual relations have actually progressed over the years. On the second week of September in even-numbered years, the checkerboard town square in front of the Castello da Basso is used as a chessboard and costumed townspeople as its pieces in order to re-create the medieval practice of playing *scacchi* to claim the hand of the kingdom's most beautiful woman (the loser got a homelier maiden). For more information contact the Associazione Pro Marostica, Piazza Castello (☎ **0424/72-127;** fax 0424/72-800). While you're here, you might want to indulge in the succulent cherries, which are the town's other claim to fame.

6 Vicenza

126 miles E of Milan, 32 miles NE of Verona

In the 16th century Vicenza was transformed into a virtual laboratory for the architectural experiments of Andrea Palladio (1508–80) from Padua. One of the greatest architects of the High Renaissance, he was inspired by the classical art and architecture of ancient Greece and Rome. Palladio peppered the city with palazzi and basilicas, and the surrounding hills with villas for patrician families.

The architect was particularly important to England and America. In the 18th century Robert Adam was especially inspired by him, as reflected by many country homes in England today. Then, through the influence of Adam and others even earlier, the spirit of Palladio was imported across the waves to America (examples include Jefferson's Monticello and plantation homes in the antebellum South). Palladio even lent his name to this architectural style—"Palladianism"—identified by regularity of form, massive, often imposing size, and an adherence to lines established in ancient Greece and Rome. Visitors arrive in Vicenza today virtually for one reason only— to see the works left by Palladio, and it is for this reason that the city was designated as a UNESCO World Heritage Site in 1994.

Vicenza today isn't entirely living off its former glory. Dubbed the Venice of Terra Firma, Vicenza is ringed with light industry on its outskirts, its citizens earning one of the highest average incomes in the country. Federico Faggin, inventor of the silicon chip, was born here, and many local computer component industries are prospering. Gold manufacturing is another traditional and rich industry.

ESSENTIALS

GETTING THERE   By Train   Most visitors arrive from Venice (trip time: 50 minutes); a one-way ticket costs 5,700L ($3.40). Trains also arrive frequently from Padua (trip time: 25 minutes), charging 3,400L ($2.05) one-way. There are also frequent connections from Milan (trip time: 2¹/₂ hours), at 15,500L ($9.30) one-way. For information and schedules call ☎ **0444/325-045.** The rail station lies at Piazza Stazione, also known as Campo Marzio, at the southern edge of Viale Roma.

By Bus   It's best to arrive by train. Once at Vicenza, however, you'll find good bus connections for the province of Vicenza if you'd like to tour the environs. The service is operated by **FTV,** Viale Milano 138 (☎ **0444/223-111**), to the left as you exit from the rail station.

By Car   From Venice, take autostrada A4 west toward Verona, bypassing Padua.

VISITOR INFORMATION   The **tourist information center** is at Piazza Matteotti 12 (☎ **0444/320-854**). It's open Monday to Saturday from 9am to 1pm and 2:30 to 6pm and Sunday from 9am to 1pm.

EXPLORING THE WORLD OF PALLADIO

To introduce yourself to the world of Palladio, head for **Piazza dei Signori.** In this classical square stands the **Basilica Palladiana,** partially designed by Palladio. The loggias rise on two levels, the lower tier with Doric pillars, the upper with Ionic. In its heyday this building was much frequented by the Vicentino aristocrats, who lavishly spent their gold on villas in the neighboring hills. They met here in a kind of social fraternity, perhaps to talk about the excessive sums being spent on Palladio-designed or -inspired projects. The original basilica here was done in the Gothic style and served as the Palazzo della Ragione (hall of justice). The roof collapsed following a 1945 bombing, but has been subsequently rebuilt. To the side is the **Torre Bissara,** which dates from the 13th century and soars almost 270 feet. Across from the basilica is the **Loggia del Capitanio** (captain of the guard), designed by Palladio in his waning years.

✪ Teatro Olimpico (Olympic Theater). Piazza Matteotti. ☎ **0444/323-781.** Admission 5,000L ($3) adults, 3,000L ($1.80) students. Mon–Sat 9:30am–12:30pm and 2:15–5pm, Sun 9:30am–12:30pm.

The masterpiece and last work of Palladio—ideal for performances of classical plays—is one of the world's greatest theaters still in use. It was completed in 1585, 5 years after Palladio's death, by Vincenzo Scamozzi, and the curtain went up on the Vicenza premiere of Sophocles's *Oedipus Rex.* The arena seating area, in the shape of a half moon, is encircled by Corinthian columns and balustrades. The simple proscenium is abutted by the arena. What is ordinarily the curtain in a conventional theater is here a permanent facade, U-shaped, with a large central arch and a pair of smaller ones flanking it. The permanent stage setting represents the ancient streets of Thebes, combining architectural detail with trompe l'oeil. Above the arches (to the left and right) are rows of additional classic statuary on pedestals and in niches. Over the area is a dome, with trompe l'oeil clouds and sky, giving the illusion of an outdoor Roman amphitheater.

Museo Civico (City Museum). In Palazzo Chiericati, Piazza Matteotti 37–39. ☎ **0444/ 321-348.** Admission 5,000L ($3) adults, 3,000L ($1.80) children under 14 and seniors over 60. Tues–Sat 9am–12:30 and 2:15–5pm, Sun 9:30am–12:30pm.

This museum is housed in one of the most outstanding buildings by Palladio. Begun in the mid-16th century, it was not finished until the late 17th century, during the baroque period. Visitors today come chiefly to view its excellent collection of Venetian paintings on the second floor. Works by lesser-known artists—Paolo Veneziano, Bartolomeo Montagna, and Jacopo Bassano—hang alongside paintings by such giants as Tintoretto *(Miracle of St. Augustine),* Veronese *(The Cherub of the Balustrade),* and Tiepolo *(Time and Truth).*

Tempio di Santa Corona. Via Santa Corona. ☎ **0444/323-644.** Free admission. Daily 8:30am–noon and 2:30–6:30pm.

This much-altered Gothic church was founded in the mid-13th century. Visit it to see Giovanni Bellini's *Baptism of Christ* (fifth altar on the left). In the left transept,

---

La Città del Palladio

His name was Andrea di Pietro, but his friends called him "Palladio." In time he would become the most prominent architect of the Italian High Renaissance, living and working in his beloved Vicenza, which remains in spite of the destruction of 14 of his buildings during World War II air raids (luckily, lavishly photographed and documented before their demise), a living museum of his architectural achievements. In time Vicenza would become known as La Città del Palladio. Palladio was actually born in Padua in 1508, where he was apprenticed to a stone carver, but fled in 1523 to Vicenza where he would live for most of his life, dying there in 1580.

In his youth Palladio journeyed to Rome where he studied the architecture of the Roman Vitruvius, who was to have a profound influence on him. Returning to Vicenza, Palladio in time perfected the "Palladian style," with its use of pilasters and a composite structure on a gigantic scale. The "attic" in his design was often surmounted by statues. One critic of European architecture wrote, "The noble design, the perfect proportions, the rhythm, and the logically vertical order invites devotion." Palladio's treatise on architecture, published in four volumes, is required reading for aspiring architects.

By no means was Palladio a genius, in the way the Florentine Brunelleschi was. No daring innovator, Palladio was more like an academician who went by the rules. Although all his buildings are harmonious, there are no surprises in them.

One of his most acclaimed buildings is the Villa Rotonda in Vicenza, a cube with a center circular hall crowned by a dome. On each external side is a pillared, rectangular portico. The classic features, although dry and masquerading as a temple, captured the public's imagination. This same type of villa was to reappear all over England and America.

The main street of Vicenza, Corso Andrea Palladio, honors its most famous hometown boy, who spent much of his life building villas for the wealthy. The street is a textbook illustration of the great architect's work (or that of his pupils), and a walk along the Corso is one of the most memorable in Italy.

---

a short distance away, is another of Vicenza's well-known works of art—this one by Veronese—depicting the three Wise Men paying tribute to the Christ child. The high altar with its intricate marble work is also worth a look. A visit to Santa Corona is more rewarding than a trek to the Duomo, which is only of passing interest.

La Rotonda. Via della Rotonda 25. ☎ **0444/321-793.** Admission 10,000L ($6) to the interior; 5,000L ($3) to the grounds. Interior, Wed 10am–noon and 3–6pm; grounds, Tues–Thurs 10am–noon and 3–6pm. Closed Nov 5–Mar 14.

This is Palladio's most famous villa, featuring his trademark design inspired by the Roman temples. The interior lacks the grand decor of many lesser-known villas, but the exterior is the focus anyway, having inspired Christopher Wren's English country estates, Jefferson's Monticello, and the work of a slew of lesser-known architects designing U.S. state capitals and Southern antebellum homes. On the World Heritage List of UNESCO, it was begun by Palladio in 1567, although he did not live to see its completion. The final work was carried out by Scamozzi between Palladio's death in 1580 and 1592. If you are not here during the limited open hours, you can still view it clearly from the road.

Villa Valmarana dei Nani. Via San Bastiano 8. ☎ **0444/543-976,** or 0444/544-546 for winter appointments. Admission 8,000L ($4.80) adults, 5,000L ($3) students and children. May–Sept, Wed–Sat 10am–noon and 3–6pm; call for off-season hours, which vary.

The most magnificent thing about this 17th-century villa, built by Palladio disciple Mattoni, is the series of frescoes by Giambattista Tiepolo that, taken together, create an elaborate mythological world. In the garden, you will find miniature statues, which are the *nani,* or dwarves, referred to in its name. Winter tours, available by appointment, require a group of 10 or more and have an increased admission fee of 11,000L ($6.60) per person.

SHOPPING

Shopping and tourism-industry insiders note a lackluster number of shops within Vicenza devoted to retail sales of one of the region's biggest industries, goldsmithing. Likewise, most of Vicenza's shops, conscious of the city's role as an aesthetic style-setter since the days of the Renaissance, devote most of their energies to distributing high-fashion, upscale products whose layout might remind you in some ways of fashionable neighborhoods of Milan.

Your better bet in Vicenza involves pursuing the good life, Italian style, as defined by such high-style emporiums as **Max Mara,** Corso Palladio 141 (☎ **0444/543-058**), selling stylish upscale garments for women; and two other outfits with both men's and women's departments, **Duca d'Este,** Contrà Santa Barbara (☎ **0444/320-846**), and **EMO,** Contrà Cavour 22 (☎ **0444/545-939**).

WHERE TO STAY

Continental. Viale G. G. Trissino 89, 36100 Vicenza. ☎ **0444/505-478.** Fax 0444/513-319. 55 rms. MINIBAR TV TEL. 225,000L ($135) double. Rates include breakfast. AE, DC, MC, V.

The Continental is among the best choices for an overnight stopover in a town not known for its hotels. It has been renovated in a modern style and offers comfortably appointed bedrooms, about 70% of which are air-conditioned. The hotel has a good restaurant; however, there's no meal service on Saturday, Sunday, or in August or around Christmas. There's a solarium on the premises.

Hotel Campo Marzio. Viale Roma 21, 36100 Vicenza. ☎ **0444/545-700.** Fax 0444/320-495. 35 rms. A/C MINIBAR TV TEL. 280,000L ($168) double. Rates include breakfast. AE, DC, MC, V. Parking 15,000L ($9).

This contemporary hotel is ideally situated in a peaceful part of the historic center of Vicenza, adjacent to a park. The hotel's bedrooms have undergone complete renovation. The sunny lobby has a conservatively comfortable decor that extends into the bedrooms. A cozy restaurant offers regional dining Monday to Friday.

Hotel Cristina. Corso San Felice e Fortunato 32, 36100 Vicenza. ☎ **0444/323-751.** Fax 0444/543-656. 34 rms. A/C MINIBAR TV TEL. 190,000L ($114) double. Rates include buffet breakfast. AE, DC, MC, V. Parking 12,000L ($7.20).

The well-maintained, contemporary Hotel Cristina is a cozy place near the city center, with an inside courtyard where visitors can park. The recently refurbished decor consists of large amounts of marble and parquet flooring and lots of exposed paneling, coupled with comfortable furniture in the public rooms. The high-ceilinged bedrooms are also well furnished, although some are small. A breakfast buffet is the only meal served.

Jolly Hotel Europa. Viale San Lorenzo 11, 36100 Vicenza. ☎ **800/221-2626** in the U.S., or 0444/564-111 in Italy. Fax 0444/564-382. 120 rms. A/C MINIBAR TV TEL. 243,000L–340,000L ($145.80–$204) double. Rates include buffet breakfast. AE, DC, MC, V. Free parking.

Outside of town, the Jolly is the finest hotel in the area—although it doesn't face much competition. It's a somewhat sterile but well-run and well-maintained hotel flying the flags of many nations. It's geared to the business traveler, as it lies in the Exhibition Center with easy access to the autostrada; however, it can also serve the leisure visitor. The bedrooms are done in a jazzy Italian style, and are medium-sized, each with a small safe, a hair dryer, and a green color scheme. Some rooms are set aside for nonsmokers. Le Ville restaurant offers both international dishes and regional food of the Veneto.

WHERE TO DINE

Antica Trattoria Tre Visi. Corso Palladio 25. ☎ **0444/324-868.** Reservations required. Main courses 20,000L–30,000L ($12–$18). AE, DC, MC, V. Tues–Sat 12:30–2:30pm and 7:30–10:30pm, Sun 12:30–2:30pm. Closed July. VICENTINO/INTERNATIONAL.

This restaurant was established as a simple tavern in the early 1600s. After many variations, it was named "The Three Faces" more than a century ago after the rulers of Austria, Hungary, and Bavaria, whose political influence was very powerful in the Veneto. The decor is rustic, with a fireplace, ceramic wall decorations, baskets of fresh fruit, tavern chairs, and an open kitchen. Together with the good selection of regional wines you can enjoy a rich choice of international dishes. They might feature *baccalà* (salt codfish) *alla vicentina,* roast goat, *zuppa di fagioli* (bean soup), or spaghetti with duck sauce. Another specialty is *capretto alla gambalaro* (kid marinated for 4 days in wine, vinegar, and spices, then roasted). The best-known dessert is the traditional *pincha alla vicentina,* made with yellow flour, raisins, and figs.

✪ Cinzia e Valerio. Piazzetta Porta Padova 65–67. ☎ **0444/505-213.** Reservations required. Main courses 18,000L–35,000L ($10.80–$21); fixed-price menu 65,000L ($39). AE, DC, V. Tues–Sun noon–2:30pm; Tues–Sat 7:30–9:30pm. Closed Aug 4–25. SEAFOOD.

Cinzia is the chef, Valerio the maître d'hôtel, and this is the best and the most elegant restaurant in Vicenza. You'll be greeted by a polite staff and views of masses of seasonal flowers. The house fish specialties are time-tested recipes from the Adriatic coast. Your meal might begin with mollusks and shellfish arranged into an artfully elegant platter. Other dishes include risotto flavored with squid, a collection of crab and lobster that might surprise you by its size and weight, and an endless procession of fish cooked any way you prefer.

Ristorante Grandcaffè Garibaldi. Piazza dei Signori 5. ☎ **0444/542-455.** Main courses 9,000L–16,000L ($5.40–$9.60). AE, DC, MC, V. Restaurant: Thurs–Mon 12:30–3pm and 7:30–11pm, Tues 12:30–3pm. Cafe: Thurs–Tues 8am–midnight. VICENTINO/ITALIAN.

The most impressive cafe and restaurant in town has a design worthy of the city of Palladio. In the heartbeat center, it has a wide terrace and an ornate ceiling, marble tables, and a long glass case of sandwiches from which you can make a selection before you sit down (the waitress will bring them to your table). In the cafe, *panini* (sandwiches) cost 4,000L ($2.40), or a cappuccino, 3,000L ($1.80). Prices are slightly lower if you stand at the bar. There's also an upstairs restaurant with trays of antipasti and arrangements of fresh fruit set up on a central table. The menu's array of familiar Italian specialties is among the best in town.

VICENZA AFTER DARK

Faithful to its role as a staid town with a distinct bourgeois overcast, Vicenza places great emphasis on musical expressions within settings whose architectural splendor enhances (and sometimes dominates) the music. Two important series of concerts define the cultural context of the town. The more comprehensive of the two series revolves around the above-described **Teatro Olimpico,** where, thanks to its outdoor venue, cultural events are scheduled only between April and late September. Look for a changing program of classical Greek tragedy (*Oedipus Rex* is an enduring favorite), Shakespeare plays—sometimes translated into Italian—chamber music concerts, and dance recitals. You can pick up schedules and buy tickets either at the gate or from the series' administrative headquarters near Vicenza's basilica at Agenzia Viaggi Palladio, Contrà Cavour 16 (☎ 0444/546-111). Tickets cost from 20,000L to 40,000L ($12 to $24), although in rare instances some nosebleed seats go for as little as 12,000L ($7.20).

More esoteric, and with a shorter season, is a series of concerts scheduled in June, the **Concerti in Villa.** Every year, the venue changes to include performances of chamber music recitals performed in or near often privately owned villas in the city's outskirts. Look for orchestras set up on loggias or under formal pediments, and audiences sitting on chairs in gardens or inside. Note that these depend on the whims of both local musicians and owners of the villas. Contact the tourist information office (see above) for more information.

7 Verona

71 miles W of Venice, 312 miles NW of Rome, 50 miles W of Padua

The home of a pair of star-crossed lovers, Verona was the setting for the most famous love story in the English language, Shakespeare's *Romeo and Juliet.* A long-forgotten editor of an old volume of the Bard's plays once wrote: "Verona, so rich in the associations of real history, has even a greater charm for those who would live in the poetry of the past." It's not known if a Romeo or a Juliet ever existed, but the remains of Verona's recorded past are much in evidence today. Its Roman antiquities, for example, are unequaled north of Rome.

In the city's medieval golden age under the despotic, cruel Scaligeri princes, Verona reached the pinnacle of its influence and prestige, developing into a town that, even today, is among the great cities of Italy. The best-known member of the ruling Della Scala family, Cangrande I, was a patron of Dante. His sway over Verona has often been compared to that of Lorenzo the Magnificent over Florence.

Verona stands in contrast to Venice, even though both are tourist towns. At least in Verona you can put your feet on solid land—not on water. It overflows with visitors today, and, like Venice, it hustles and often lives off a glorious past. But most of the people walking the streets of Verona are actually residents and not visitors. For a city that hit its peak in the 1st century A.D., Verona is doing admirably well today. However, stick to the inner core and not the newer sections, which are blighted by industry and tacky urban development.

ESSENTIALS

GETTING THERE   By Train   A total of 37 trains a day make the 2-hour run between Venice and Verona, at 9,800L ($5.90) one-way. If you're in the west—say, at Milan—there are even more connections, some 40 trains a day, taking 2 hours to reach Verona at a cost of 11,700L ($7) one-way. Six daily trains arrive from Rome, a 6-hour trip, costing 40,500L ($24.30) one-way. Rail arrivals are at the Stazione Porta Nuova (☎ 045/590-688), which lies south of the centrally located Arena and Piazza Brà. At least 6 bus lines service the area, taking you frequently into the monumental core.

By Bus   APT buses arrive and depart from the bus station at Piazza XXV Aprile (☎ 045/800-4129), which lies across from the main rail station (see above). Buses serve the province and fan out to such cities as Brescia, Mantua, and Riva del Garda.

From mid-June to mid-September, you can go from Venice to Verona without changing buses (although it's still better to take the train).

By Car From Venice, take autostrada A4 west to the signposted cutoff for Verona—marked Verona Sud. If you're reaching Verona from the south or north, take the A22 autostrada and get off at the exit marked Verona Nord.

VISITOR INFORMATION The main **tourist information office** is adjacent to the Arena at Piazza Leoncini 61 (☎ **045/592-828**), and is open in summer Monday to Saturday from 8am to 8pm, Sunday from 9am to noon. Off-season hours are Monday to Saturday from 8am to 7pm and Sunday from 9am to noon. There's another information office at the centrally located Piazza delle Erbe (☎ **045/ 803-0086**), which is open in summer Monday to Saturday from 9am to 12:30pm and 2:30 to 7pm. Finally, there's another small office at the Porta Nuova rail station (☎ **045/800-0861**), open Monday to Saturday from 8am to 7:30pm and Sunday from 9am to noon.

EXPLORING THE CITY

Verona lies along the Adige River. It's most often visited on a quick half-day excursion, but Verona deserves more time. It's meant for wandering and for contemplation. If you're rushed, head first to the old city to begin your explorations. In addition to the sights listed below, there are other attractions that might merit a visit.

Opening onto Piazza dei Signori, the handsomest in Verona, is the **Palazzo del Governo,** where Cangrande extended the shelter of his hearth and home to that fleeing Florentine, Dante Alighieri. A marble statue of the "divine poet" stands in the center of the square, with an expression as cold as a Dolomite icicle, but unintimidated pigeons perch on his pious head. Facing Dante's back is the late 15th-century **Loggia del Consiglio,** frescoed and surmounted by five statues. Five different arches lead into **Piazza dei Signori,** the innermost chamber of the heart of Verona.

The **Arche Scaligere** are outdoor tombs surrounded by highly decorative wrought iron that form a kind of open-air pantheon of the Scaligeri princes. One tomb, that of Cangrande della Scala, rests directly over the door of the 12th-century Santa Maria Antica Church. The mausoleum contains many Romanesque features. It's crowned by a copy of an equestrian statue (the original is now at the Castelvecchio). The tomb nearest the door is that of Mastino II; the one behind it—and the most lavish of all— that of Cansignorio.

The ✪ **Piazza delle Erbe,** or "Square of the Herbs," is a lively, palace-flanked square that was formerly the Roman city's forum. Today it's the fruit and vegetable market milling with Veronese, both shoppers and vendors. In the center of the square is a fountain dating from the 14th century and a Roman statue dubbed *The Virgin of Verona.* The pillar at one end of the square, crowned by a chimera, symbolizes the many years that Verona was dominated by *La Serenissima,* Venice. Important buildings include the early 14th-century **House of Merchants;** the **Gardello Tower,** built by one of the Della Scala princes; the restored former city hall and the **Lamberti Tower,** soaring about 260 feet; the baroque **Maffei Palace;** and the **Casa Mazzanti.**

From the vegetable market, you can walk down **Via Mazzini,** the most fashionable street in Verona, to **Piazza Brà,** with its neoclassical town hall and the Renaissance palazzo, the Gran Guardia. If you want to visit the Duomo, San Zeno, and Sant'Anastasia, it is cheaper to purchase a joint ticket costing 9,000L ($5.40) from March through October, lowered to 6,000L ($3.60) off-season.

Arena di Verona. Piazza Brà. ☎ **045/800-3204.** Admission 6,000L ($3.60); free the first Sun of each month. Tues–Sun 8am–6:30pm (on performance days, 8am–1:30pm).

The elliptical amphitheater on Piazza Brà, resembling Rome's Colosseum, dates from the 1st century A.D. Four arches of the "outer circle" and a complete "inner ring" still stand. This is rather remarkable considering that in the 12th century an earthquake hit. From mid-July to mid-August it's the setting for an opera house, where more than 20,000 people are treated to Verdi and Mascagni. The acoustics are considered perfect, even after all these centuries, and performances are still able to be conducted without microphones. Attending an outdoor evening performance here (see "Verona After Dark") can be one of highlights of your visit to Italy. In one season alone, you might be able to hear and see *Macbeth* performed, as well as *Madama Butterfly, Aïda, Carmen, Rigoletto,* and Verdi's *Requiem Mass.*

✪ **Castelvecchio.** Corso Castelvecchio 2. ☎ **045/594-734.** Admission 5,000L ($3) adults, 1,500L (90¢) students; free the first Sun of each month. Tues–Sun 7:45am–6:30pm.

Built on the order of Cangrande II in the 14th century, the Old Castle stands alongside the Adige River (head out Via Roma) near the Ponte Scaligero, a bridge bombed by the Nazis in World War II and subsequently reconstructed. The former seat of the Della Scala family, the restored castle has been turned into an art museum, with important paintings from the Veronese school and other masters of northern Italy. Fourteenth- and fifteenth-century sculpture are displayed on the ground floor, and on the upper floor you'll see masterpieces of painting from the 15th to the 18th centuries.

In the Sala Monga is Jacopo Bellini's *St. Jerome,* in the desert with his lion and crucifix. Two sisterlike portraits of Saint Catherina and Veneranda by Vittore Carpaccio grace the Sala Rizzardi Allegri. The Bellini family is also represented by a lyrical *Madonna con Bambino* painted by Giovanni, a master of that subject.

Between the buildings is the most provocative equestrian statue we've ever seen, that of Cangrande I, grinning like a buffoon, with a dragon sticking out of his back. In the Sala Murari dalla Corte Brà is one of the most beguiling portraits in the castle—Giovanni Francesco Caroto's smiling red-haired boy. In the Sala di Canossa are paintings by Tintoretto, a *Madonna Nursing the Child* and a *Nativity,* and by Veronese, a *Deposition from the Cross* and the *Pala Bevilacqua Lazise.*

In the Sala Bolognese Trevenzuoli is a rare self-portrait of Bernardo Strozzi, and in the Sala Avena, among paintings by the most famous Venetian masters such as Gianbattista and Giandomenico Tiepolo and Guardi, hangs an almost satirical portrait of an 18th-century patrician family by Longhi.

Basilica San Zeno Maggiore. Piazza San Zeno. ☎ **045/800-6120.** Admission 4,000L ($2.40). Mar–Oct, Mon–Sat 9am–6pm, Sun 1–6pm; Nov–Feb, Mon–Sat 10am–4pm, Sun 1–4pm.

This near-perfect Romanesque church and campanile constructed between the 9th and 12th centuries is graced with a stunning entrance—two pillars supported by puce-colored marble lions and surmounted by a rose window called the *Ruota della Fortuna,* or "wheel of fortune." On either side of the portal are bas-reliefs depicting scenes from the Old and New Testaments, as well as a mythological story portraying Theodoric as a huntsman lured to hell (the king of the Goths defeated Odoacer in Verona). The panels on the bronze doors, nearly 50 in all, are a remarkable achievement of medieval art, sculpted perhaps in the 12th century. They reflect a naive handling of their subject matter—see John the Baptist's head resting on a platter. The artists express themselves with such candor that they achieve the power of a child's storybook. The interior, somber and severe, contains a major Renaissance work at the main altar, a triptych by Andrea Mantegna, an enthroned Madonna and Child with saints. Although not remarkable in its characterization, it reveals the artist's genius for perspective.

Basilica di Sant'Anastasia. Piazza Sant'Anastasia. ☎ **045/800-4325.** Admission 4,000L ($2.40). Mar–Oct, daily 9am–7pm; Nov–Mar, daily 10am–4pm.

The largest church in Verona was constructed between 1290 and 1481. Its facade isn't complete, yet nevertheless it's the finest representation of Gothic design in Verona. Many artists in the 15th and 16th centuries decorated the interior, but few of the works are worthy of being singled out. The exception is the Pellegrini Chapel, with terra-cotta reliefs by the Tuscan artist Michele, and the Giusti Chapel, with a fresco by Pisanello representing St. George preparing to face his inevitable dragon. The patterned floor is especially impressive. As you enter, look for two *gobbi,* or hunchbacks, supporting holy water fonts. The church also has a beautiful companile from the 1300s that is richly decorated with sculpture and frescoes.

Duomo. Piazza del Duomo. ☎ **045/595-627.** Admission 4,000L ($2.40). Mar–Oct, Mon–Sat 9am–6pm, Sun 1–6pm; off-season, Mon–Sat 10am–4pm, Sun 1:30–4pm.

The cathedral of Verona is less interesting than San Zeno Maggiore, but it still merits a visit. It was begun in the 12th century but not completed until the 17th century. A blend of the Romanesque and Gothic styles, its facade contains (lower level) 12th-century sculptured reliefs by Nicolaus that depict scenes of Roland and Oliver, two of the legendary dozen knights attending Charlemagne. In the left aisle (first chapel) is an *Assumption* by Titian, the stellar art work of the Duomo. The other major work of art is the rood screen in front of the presbytery, with Ionic pillars, designed by Samicheli.

Chiesa di San Fermo. Piazza San Fermo. ☎ **045/800-7287.** Admission 4,000L ($2.40). Apr–Oct, Mon–Fri 9am–6pm, Sat noon–6pm; Nov–Mar, Mon–Fri 10am–5pm, Sat noon–5pm.

This Romanesque church, which dates from the 11th century, forms the foundation of the 14th-century Gothic building that surmounts it. Through time it has been used by both the Benedictines and the Franciscans. The interior is unusual, with a single nave and a splendid roof constructed of wood and exquisitely paneled. The most important work inside is Pisanello's frescoed *Annunciation,* to the left of the main entrance (at the Brenzoni tomb). Delicate and graceful, the work reveals the artist's keen eye for architectural detail and his bizarre animals.

✪ **Teatro Romano (Roman Theater) and Archeological Museum.** Rigaste Redentore 2. ☎ **045/800-0360.** Admission 5,000L ($3) adults, 1,500L (90¢) students and children; free the first Sun of each month. Tues–Sun 8am–6:30pm. Closes 1:30pm in winter.

The **Teatro Romano,** built in the 1st century A.D., now stands in ruins at the foot of St. Peter's Hill. For nearly a quarter of a century a Shakespearean festival has been staged here in July and August, and, of course, a unique theater-going experience is to see *Romeo and Juliet* or *Two Gentlemen of Verona* in this setting. The theater is across the Adige River (take the Ponte di Pietra). After seeing the remains of the theater, you can take a rickety elevator to the 10th-century Santi Siro e Libera Church towering over it. In the cloister of St. Jerome is the **Roman Archeological Museum,** which has interesting mosaics and Etruscan bronzes.

Giardino Giusti. Via Giardino Giusti 2. ☎ **045/803-4029.** Admission 5,000L ($3) adults, 2,000L ($1.20) students and children. Summer, daily 9am–8pm; off-season, daily 9am–5pm.

One of the oldest and most famous gardens in Italy, the Giardino Giusti was created at the end of the 14th century. These well-manicured Italian gardens, studded with cypress trees, form one of the most relaxing and coolest spots in Verona for strolls. You can climb up to the "monster balcony" for an incomparable view of the city.

The layout you see today was given to the gardens by Agostino Giusti. All its 16th-century characteristics—the grottoes, the statues, the fountains, the mascarons, the box-enclosed flower garden, and the maze—have remained intact. In addition to the flower displays, you can admire the statues by Lorenzo Muttoni and Alessandro Vittoria, Roman remains, and the great cypress mentioned by Goethe. The gardens, with their adjacent 16th-century palazzo, form one of Italy's most interesting urban complexes. The maze, constructed with myrtle hedges, faithfully reproduces the 1786 plan of the architect Trezza. Its complicated pattern and small size make it one of the most unusual in Europe. The gardens lie near the Roman Theater, only a few minutes' walk from the heart of the city.

La Tomba di Giulietta. Via del Pontiere 5. ☎ **045/800-0361.** Admission 5,000L ($3) adults; 1,500L (90¢) students and children; free the first Sun of each month. Tues–Sun 7:45am–7pm.

The so-called Juliet's tomb is sheltered in a Franciscan monastery entered on Via Luigi da Porto, off Via del Pontiere. "A grave? O, no, a lantern. . . . For here lies Juliet, and her beauty makes this vault a feasting presence full of light." Don't you believe it! Still, the cloisters, near the Adige River, are graceful. Adjoining the tomb is a museum of frescoes, dedicated to G. B. Cavalcaselle.

Casa Giulietta. Via Cappello 23. ☎ **045/803-4303.** Admission 5,000L ($3) adults, 1,500L (90¢) students and children. Tues–Sun 7:45am–6:30pm.

"Juliet's house" is a small home with a balcony and a courtyard. Although there is no evidence that the Capulets lived here, it was acquired by the city of Verona in 1905 and turned into this contrived sight. So powerful is the legend of Juliet that millions flock to this house, not seeming to care whether Juliet lived here or not. To many of these visitors, Juliet was a real person, and this is where she lived. Tradition calls for visitors to rub the right breast of a bronze statue of Juliet. It is now brightly polished by millions of hands. With a little bit of imagination, it's not difficult to hear Romeo say: "But, soft! What light through yonder window breaks? It is the east, and Juliet is the sun!"

SHOPPING

The byword for shopping in Verona is elegance, and shops feature a diffusion of the fashion being touted in faraway Milan and Rome. Consequently, don't look for touristic products that involve country-cousin crudeness or rustic-looking crafts and souvenirs, but rather for more upscale versions of all-Italian fashion and accessories for men and women. A worthwhile shop for women is **New Galles,** Via Cantore 4 (☎ **049/803-1555**); a noteworthy shop for men is **Class Uomo,** Via San Rocchetto 13B (☎ **049/595-775**). Every Veronese knows the allure for both genders of **Armani,** Via Cappello 25 (☎ **049/594-727**).

If you yearn for a Veronan antique to haul back to your private world, look for a dense concentration of vendors selling antiques or old bric-a-brac in the streets around the Church of Sant'Anastasia, or head for the **Piazza delle Erbe** for a more or less constant roster of merchants in flimsy flea-market-style kiosks selling the dusty, and often junkier, collectibles of yesteryear, along with aromatic herbs, fruits, and vegetables.

WHERE TO STAY

Hotel rooms tend to be scarce during the County Fair in March and the opera and theater season in July and August.

VERY EXPENSIVE

✪ **Due Torri Hotel Baglioni.** Piazza Sant'Anastasia 4, 37121 Verona. ☎ **045/595-044.** Fax 045/800-4130. 81 rms, 10 suites. A/C MINIBAR TV TEL. 410,000L–630,000L ($246–$378) double; from 700,000L ($420) suite. Rates include breakfast. AE, DC, MC, V. Parking 40,000L ($24).

Owned by the national, upscale Cogeta Palace Hotels chain, this was originally the 1400s home of the Scaligeri dynasty. During the 18th and 19th centuries the palace hosted VIPs like Mozart, Goethe, and Tsar Alexander I. Set in the monumental heart of Verona, the palace is still the best address in town. In the 1950s, legendary hotelier Enrico Wallner transformed it into a hotel with a stunning collection of antiques. Despite the 1990 takeover by Cogeta, which richly renovated and restored the entire hotel over 4 years, many of these antiques remain in both the public areas and bedrooms—a splendid range of Directoire, Empire, Louis XVIII, and Biedermeier. There are also many old oil paintings, a large lobby sited in the palace's old courtyard, and a series of well-upholstered salons permeated with charm and serviced by a discreet staff.

Dining/Entertainment: The hotel's restaurant, All'Aquila, serves typical local and light cuisine. This is one of the most distinguished restaurants of Verona, and is open to nonguests as well. There's also an elegant bar.

Services: Room service (24 hours), baby-sitting, laundry, valet.

✪ **Hotel Gabbia d'Oro.** Corso Porta Borsari 4A, 37121 Verona. ☎ **045/800-3060.** Fax 045/590-293. 8 rms, 19 suites. A/C MINIBAR TV TEL. 350,000L–450,000L ($210–$270) double; 650,000L–800,000L ($390–$480) suite. Rates include breakfast except in July–Aug. AE, DC, MC, V. Parking 50,000L ($30) first day, 40,000L ($24) each additional day.

This upscale hotel in a historic 18th-century palazzo in Verona's historic center was inaugurated in 1990, the first hotel in years to give the Due Torri Baglioni serious competition. It has a more romantic Romeo-and-Juliet atmosphere than the more fabled hostelry. Small, discreet, and devoted to the privacy of its guests, it contains many of the building's original grandiose frescoes, its beamed ceiling, and (in the cozy bar area) much of the original carved paneling. Only hotel guests are allowed into the bar and restaurant, where advance reservations are strictly required. Even the hotel's name, "Golden Cage," seems to enhance its exclusivity. The interior courtyard contains potted plants, flowering shrubs, and tables devoted to drinking and dining facilities during clement weather. The bedrooms contain framed engravings, antique furniture, and—in some cases—narrow balconies with wrought-iron detailing overlooking either the street or the courtyard below.

EXPENSIVE

Hotel Accademia. Via Scala 12, 37121 Verona. ☎ and fax **045/596-222.** 92 rms, 5 suites. A/C MINIBAR TV TEL. 240,000L–380,000L ($144–$228) double; 335,000L–550,000L ($201–$330) suite. Rates include buffet breakfast. AE, DC, MC, V. Parking 25,000L ($15).

This is one of the few older hotels of Verona that was custom built as a hotel, rather than having been transformed from a monastery or palazzo. Dating from the late 1800s, when it welcomed a goodly percentage of English visitors on their grand tour of Italy, it contains Oriental carpets, a medieval tapestry, and a pair of grandiose marble columns flanking the polished stone stairwell leading to the three floors of bedrooms. The rooms are conservatively traditional and high-ceilinged. There's a paneled, modern bar at the lobby's far end and a restaurant (the Accademia) that operates under a separate management. Guests receive a 10% discount on meals.

MODERATE

Colomba d'Oro. Via C. Cattaneo 10, 37121 Verona. ☎ **045/595-300.** Fax 045/594-974. 49 rms, 2 suites. A/C MINIBAR TV TEL. 260,000L–310,000L ($156–$186) double; 300,000L–372,000L ($180–$223.20) suite. Rates include buffet breakfast. AE, DC, MC, V. Parking 25,000L ($15).

Venerable and historic, Colomba d'Oro was built as a private villa during the 1600s and was later transformed into a monastery. During the 18th and 19th centuries it served as an inn for travelers and employees of the postal service, and eventually grew into the large and much-renovated hotel it is today. The building is efficiently organized and has an atmosphere somewhere between semitraditional and contemporary. The bedrooms are nicely furnished with matching fabrics and comfortable furniture. Only breakfast is served, but there are many restaurants nearby.

INEXPENSIVE

Hotel Aurora. Piazza delle Erbe, 37121 Verona. ☎ 045/594-717. Fax 045/801-0860. 32 rms. A/C TV TEL. 145,000L–170,000L ($87–$102) double. AE, MC, V. Parking free on the street; 15,000L ($9) in a public parking lot (a 10-minute walk).

The foundations of this tall and narrow hotel were already at least 400 years old when the building itself was constructed in the 1500s. In 1994, its owners completed a radical renovation that improved all the hidden systems (structural beams, electricity, and plumbing) but retained hints of the building's antique origins. It's set behind a sienna-colored facade on a square that's transformed every morning, beginning around 7:30am, into Verona's busiest emporium of fruits and vegetables. Views from all but a few of the simply furnished bedrooms encompass a full or partial look at the activity within the square, a fact that considerably enhances the charm of the panorama over the town's historic core. You have to climb a flight of steps to reach the reception area, but after that there's a cramped but serviceable elevator. The hotel's bar is open 24 hours.

Hotel de'Capuleti. Via del Pontiere 26, 37122 Verona. ☎ 045/800-0154. Fax 045/803-2970. 42 rms. A/C MINIBAR TV TEL. 230,000L ($138) double. Rates include breakfast. AE, DC, MC, V. Closed Dec 22–Jan 10.

Hotel de'Capuleti is an attractively pristine little hotel, conveniently located a few steps from Juliet's (supposed) tomb and the chapel where she is said to have been married. The reception area has stone floors and leather couches, along with a tastefully renovated decor that's reflected upstairs in the comfortable bedrooms.

Hotel Giulietta e Romeo. Vicolo Tre Marchetti 3, 37121 Verona. ☎ 045/800-3554. Fax 045/801-0862. 32 rms. A/C MINIBAR TV TEL. 140,000L–260,000L ($84–$156) double. Rates include breakfast. Add 30% to these rates during trade fairs. AE, MC, V.

Permeated with a slightly saccharine replay of Shakespeare's great love affair between Verona's most literate lovers, and set within a few paces of the ancient Roman arena, most of the bedrooms in this once-stately palazzo look out over the ancient monument. In honor of the maiden Juliet, the hotel maintains at least one marble balcony that might be appropriate in a modern-day revival of the great play itself. Bedrooms are tastefully modernized, not overly large, and have marble-sheathed bathrooms, touches of burnished hardwoods that include cherry, comfortable furnishings, and lighting that you can actually read by.

Hotel Torcolo. Vicolo Listone 3, 37121 Verona. ☎ 045/800-4058. Fax 045/800-4058. 19 rms. A/C MINIBAR TV TEL. 134,000L–165,000L ($80.40–$99) double. MC, V. Parking 12,000L ($7.20) in a nearby public lot.

The setting is modest but, thanks to the devoted efforts of its trio of hardworking owners (Silvia Pomari and her colleagues, Marina and Diana), it's spotlessly clean. You'll find the Torcolo in the historic core of town, near both the Roman Arena and the Piazza Brà, in a building erected around 1825. The plain bedrooms' furnishings run the gamut from modern and banal to simple but antique. The staff speaks English, the hotel's three floors are accessible via elevator, and the hotel's name—if you ask—is dialect for winepress.

WHERE TO DINE
EXPENSIVE

✪ **Arche.** Via Arche Scaligere 6. ☎ **045/800-7415.** Reservations required. Main courses 32,000L–45,000L ($19.20–$27); fixed-price menu 100,000L ($60). AE, DC, MC, V. Mon 7:30–9:30pm, Tues–Sat 12:30–2:30pm and 7:30–9:30pm. Closed Jan. ITALIAN.

Classic and elegant, this restaurant is acclaimed by some critics as the finest in Verona. We'd give that honor to Il Desco (see below), but Arche is a close runner-up. Giancarlo and Paola Gioco, the owners, insist on market-fresh fish from nearby Chioggia. The restaurant was founded in 1879 by Giancarlo's great-grandfather, and the seafood dishes are based on traditional recipes passed down from generation to generation, including some discovered in ancient cookbooks. Sole, sea bass cooked with delectable porcini mushrooms, and scampi are among the eternal favorites here. Baked "sea scorpion" with black olives is one of the chef's finest specialties, as is his ravioli stuffed with sea bass and served with a clam sauce. The furnishings in this 1420 building are Liberty style, the setting enhanced by candlelight and fresh flowers.

✪ **Ristorante il Desco.** Via Dietro San Sebastiano 7. ☎ **045/595-358.** Reservations recommended. Main courses 37,000L–40,000L ($22.20–$24); *menu degustazione* 130,000L ($78). AE, DC, MC, V. Mon–Sat 12:30–2pm and 7:30–10pm. Closed Jan 1–7 and Dec 25–26. ITALIAN.

Ristorante il Desco is a handsome restaurant, the tops in Verona. It's located in the city's historic center, inside a tastefully renovated palazzo that's one of the civic prides of the city. The menu steers closer to the philosophy of cuisine moderne than anything else in town. Specialties make use of the freshest ingredients, including a purée of shrimp; potato pie with mushrooms and black truffles; calamari salad with shallots; tortellini with sea bass; risotto with radicchio and truffles; and tagliolini with fresh mint, lemon, and oranges. The wine cellar is superb, and your sommelier will help you if you're unfamiliar with regional vintages. The cheese selection is wide-ranging, featuring choices from France.

MODERATE

Nuovo Marconi. Via Fogge 4. ☎ **045/591-910.** Reservations required. Main courses 20,000L–35,000L ($12–$21)). AE, DC, MC, V. Mon–Sat 12:30–2:45pm and 8–11:30pm. ITALIAN.

Nuovo Marconi is one of the best and most glamorous restaurants in Verona, in an ocher-colored villa on a narrow street just around the corner from Piazza dei Signori. The doors are covered with an art nouveau wrought-iron grill, and the interior has stone columns, silk-shaded lamps, and lots of framed paintings. The menu reflects the best of traditional and regional dishes, and changes daily depending on the availability of ingredients at the market. The kitchen uses only fresh products, whether it be pasta, fish, or meat. In season, the chef likes to specialize in game dishes and the fish antipasti are reason enough to visit. The wine list is updated every 6 months, and the service is agreeable.

Ristorante 12 Apostoli. Vicolo Corticella San Marco 3. ☎ **045/596-999.** Reservations recommended. Main courses 28,000L ($16.80). AE, DC, MC, V. Tues–Sat 12:30–2:30pm and 7:30–10pm, Sun 12:30–2:30pm. Closed June 15–July 5. ITALIAN.

This is the oldest restaurant in Verona, in business for 250 years. It's a festive place, steeped in tradition, with frescoed walls and two dining rooms separated by brick arches. It's operated by the two Gioco brothers. Giorgio, the artist of the kitchen, changes his menu daily in the best tradition of great chefs, whereas Franco directs the dining room. Just consider some of these delicacies: salmon baked in a pastry shell (the fish is marinated the day before, seasoned with garlic, and stuffed with scallops), or chicken stuffed with shredded vegetables and cooked in four layers of paper. To begin, we recommend the tempting *antipasti alla Scaligera*. For dessert, try the home-made cake.

INEXPENSIVE

Ristorante Re Teodorico. Piazzale di Castel San Pietro 1. ☎ **045/834-9990.** Reservations required. Main courses 25,000L–30,000L ($15–$18). AE, DC, MC, V. Thurs–Tues noon–3pm and 7–10pm. Closed Jan. REGIONAL/INTERNATIONAL.

Ristorante Re Teodorico is perched high on a hill at the edge of town, with a panoramic view of Verona and the Adige River. From its entrance, you descend a cypress-lined road to the ledge-hanging restaurant suggestive of a lavish villa. Tables are set out on a wide flagstone terrace edged with a row of classical columns and an arbor of red, pink, and yellow vines. Specialties include homemade pasta, which is always delectable; swordfish with tomatoes, capers, and fresh basil; and chateaubriand with a béarnaise sauce. The dessert specialty is crêpes Suzette.

VeronAntica. Via Sottoriva 10. ☎ **045/800-4124.** Reservations recommended. Main courses 12,000L–23,000L ($7.20–$13.80). AE, DC, MC, V. Sept–June, Wed–Mon noon–2:30pm and 7–10:45pm; July–Aug, Wed–Mon 6–10:45pm. INTERNATIONAL.

VeronAntica is a distinguished local restaurant housed on the ground floor of a five-story town house a short block from the river, across from a cobblestone arcade similar to the ones used in the film *Romeo and Juliet.* This place attracts the locals—not just tourists. It's made even more romantic at night by a hanging lantern that dimly illuminates the street. The chef knows how to prepare all the classic Italian dishes as well as some innovative ones too. Try the *bretelline* (tagliatelle made with flower of rice) with rughetta salad and asparagus or the salmon in papillote with fresh mussels, seafood, and fresh tomatoes. From June to September you can dine on an open-air terrace.

VERONA AFTER DARK

Opera festivals on a scale more human and accessible than regular venues in cities like Milan are presented in Verona every summer between July and August. The setting is the ancient Arena di Verona, a site that's grand enough to include as many elephants as might be needed for a performance of *Aïda.* Schedules vary every year, so for more information and tickets contact the Ente Lirico Arena di Verona, Piazza Brà 28, 37121 Verona (☎ **045/590-109**). Prices of tickets vary widely with view lines and whatever is being staged, but usually range from 40,000L to 250,000L ($24 to $150) each.

For tickets and information on the opera or ballet in Verona, **Edwards & Edwards** has a New York office from which you can purchase tickets before you go at 1270 Ave. of the Americas, Suite 2414, New York, NY 10020 (☎ **800/223-6108** or 914/328-2150; fax 914/328-2752). A personal visit is not necessary and they can mail vouchers or fax a confirmation to allow you to pick up the tickets half an hour prior to curtain call.

Looking for a break from too much Verdi? Head for **Disco Berfis Club,** Via Lussemburgo (☎ **045/508-024**), or **Bar/Disco Tribu,** Via Calderara 17 (☎ **045/566-470**), where rhythms derivative from what's being broadcast in New York and Milan help local folk to get down and boogey. More closely linked to Verona's historic core is **Bar Campidoglio,** Piazza Tira Bosco (☎ **045/594-448**), where the venue is softer, more subdued, less frenzied and electronic, and more evocative of the Italy of long ago.

12 Trieste, the Dolomites & South Tyrol

The limestone Dolomites (Dolomiti), one of Europe's greatest natural attractions, are a peculiar mountain formation of the northeastern Italian Alps. Some of their peaks soar to a height of 10,500 feet. The Dolomiti are a year-round pleasure destination, with two high seasons: in midsummer, and then in winter when the skiers slide in.

At times the Dolomiti form fantastic shapes, combining to create a landscape that looks primordial, with chains of mountains that resemble a giant dragon's teeth. Clefts descend precipitously along jagged rocky walls, whereas at other points a vast flat tableland—spared by nature's fury—emerges.

The provinces of Trent and Bolzano (Bozen in German) form the Trentino–Alto Adige region. The area is rich in health resorts, attracting many German-speaking visitors to its alpine lakes and mountains. Many of its waters—some of which are radioactive—are said to have curative powers.

The Alto Adige province around Bolzano, surrounded by the Dolomite Alps, was until 1919 known as South Tyrol, and was part of Austria. And even though today it belongs to Italy, it's still very much Tyrolean in character, both in its language (German) and in its dress. Today, the entire Trentino–Alto Adige region functions with a great deal of autonomy from the national government.

Before we proceed to details, readers with an extra day or so to spare may first want to postpone their Dolomite or Tyrolean adventure for a detour to Trieste.

1 Trieste

72 miles NE of Venice, 414 miles NE of Rome, 253 miles E of Milan

The remote city of Trieste, a shimmering, bright city with many neoclassical buildings, is perched on the half-moon Gulf of Trieste, which opens into the Adriatic.

As an Adriatic seaport, Trieste has had a long history, with many changes of ownership. The Habsburg emperor Charles VI declared it a free port in 1719, but by the 20th century it was an ocean outlet for the Austro–Hungarian Empire. After the war and a secret deal among the Allies, Trieste was ceded to Italy in 1918. In the late summer of 1943 Trieste again fell to foreign troops—this time the Nazis, who were ousted by Tito's Yugoslav army in the spring of

1945. In 1954, after much hassle, the American and British troops withdrew as the Italians marched in, with the stipulation that the much-disputed Trieste would be maintained as a free port. Today that status continues. Politics, as always, dominates the agenda in modern Trieste. There is racial tension here, and many Italian Fascists are centered here, as are anti-Slav parties.

Trieste has known many glamorous literary associations, particularly in the pre–World War II years. As a stopover on the *Orient Express,* it became a famed destination. Dame Agatha Christie came this way, as did Graham Greene. James Joyce, eloping with Nora Barnacle, arrived in Trieste in 1904. Out of both work and money, Joyce got a job teaching at the Berlitz School. He was to live here for nearly 10 years. He wrote *A Portrait of the Artist as a Young Man* here and may have begun his masterpiece *Ulysses* here as well. The poet Rainer Maria Rilke also lived in the Trieste area. Author Richard Burton, known for his *Arabian Nights* translations, lived in Trieste from 1871 until he died, about 20 years later.

Today, Trieste, squashed between Slovenia and the Adriatic, has been more vulnerable to conditions following the collapse of Yugoslavia than any other city in Italy. Civil war and turmoil have halted the flow of thousands who used to cross the border to buy merchandise from the west—mainly blue jeans and household appliances. The port has also suffered from crisis in the shipbuilding and steel industries. Trieste remains Italy's insurance capital, and one-fourth of its population of 150,000 residents are retired (it has the highest per capita pensioner population in Italy).

ESSENTIALS

GETTING THERE   By Plane   Trieste is serviced by an airport at **Ronchi dei Legionari** (☎ **0481/7731** for airport information), 21½ miles northwest of the city. Daily flights on Alitalia connect the airport with Linate airport in Milan (trip time: 50 minutes), Franz Josef Strauss airport in Munich (1 hour 10 minutes), and Leonardo da Vinci in Rome (1 hour 10 minutes).

By Train   Trieste lies on a direct rail link from Venice. Trip time to Venice is 2½ hours and a one-way ticket costs 13,600L ($8.15). The station is on Piazza della Libertà (☎ **040/418-207**), northwest of the historic center.

By Bus   It's better to fly, drive, or take the train to Trieste. Once here, you'll find a network of **local buses** servicing the region from Corso Cavour (☎ **040/425-020** for schedules).

By Car   From Venice, continue northeast along autostrada A4 until you reach the end of the line at Trieste.

VISITOR INFORMATION   The **tourist information office** is at Via San Nicolò 20 (☎ **040/679-6111**). It's open Monday to Friday from 8:30am to 7pm and Saturday from 8:30am to 1pm. A second **tourist information center** is located in the train station (☎ **040/420-182**). It's open Monday to Saturday from 9am to 7pm and Sunday from 10am to 1pm and 4 to 7pm.

EXPLORING THE CITY

The heart of Trieste is the neoclassic ✪ **Piazza dell'Unità d'Italia,** the largest square in Italy that fronts the sea. Opening onto the square is the town hall with a clock tower, the Palace of the Government, and the main office of the Lloyd Triestino ship line. Flanking the square are numerous cafes and restaurants, popular at night with the denizens of Trieste who sip an aperitif, then later promenade along the seafront esplanade.

After visiting the main square, you may want to view Trieste from an even better vantage point. Head up the hill for another cluster of attractions—you can take an antiquated tram, leaving from Piazza Oberdan, and get off at Obelisco. Here, at the **belvedere,** the city of the Adriatic will spread out before you.

Cathedral of San Giusto. Piazza Cattedrale, Colle Capitolino. ☎ **040/302-874.** Free admission. Daily 8:30am–noon and 4–7pm.

Dedicated to the patron saint (St. Just) of Trieste, who was martyred in A.D. 303, the basilica atop Colle San Giusto was consecrated in 1330, incorporating a pair of churches that had been separate until then. The front is in the Romanesque style, enhanced by a rose window. Inside, the nave is flanked by two pairs of aisles. To the left of the main altar are the best of the Byzantine mosaics in Trieste (note especially the blue-robed Madonna and her Child). The main altar and the chapel to the right contain less interesting mosaics. To the left of the basilica entrance is a small campanile from the 14th century, which you can scale for a view of Trieste and its bay. At its base are preserved the remains of a Roman temple from the 1st century A.D. You may prefer to take a taxi up to the cathedral, then walk a leisurely 15 minutes back down. From the basilica you can also stroll to the nearby Castle of San Giusto.

Castle of San Giusto. Piazza Cattedrale 3. ☎ **040/309-362.** Castle, 2,000L ($1.20); museum, 3,000L ($1.80). Castle, daily 9am–sunset; museum, Tues–Sun 9am–1pm.

Constructed in the 15th century by the Venetians on the site of a Roman fort, this fortress maintained a sharp eye on the bay, watching for unfriendly visitors arriving by sea. From its bastions, panoramic views of Trieste unfold. Inside is a **museum** (☎ 040/313-636) with a collection of arms and armor. The castle's open-air theater hosts a film festival in July and August.

✪ **Castello di Miramare.** Viale Miramare, Grignano (4¹/₂ miles northwest of town). ☎ **040/ 224-143.** Castle, 8,000L ($4.80) adults, free for children 18 and under and seniors 60 and over; grounds, free. Castle, Apr–Sept, daily 9am–6pm; Oct–Mar, daily 9am–1pm. Grounds, Apr–Sept, daily 9am–7pm; Oct–Mar, daily 9am–5pm. Bus 36 from center.

Overlooking the Bay of Grignano, this castle was erected by Archduke Maximilian, the brother of Franz Joseph, the Habsburg emperor of Austria. Maximilian, who married Princess Charlotte of Belgium, was the commander of the Austrian navy in 1854. In an ill-conceived move, he and "Carlotta" sailed to Mexico in 1864, where he became the emperor in an unfortunate reign. He was shot in 1867 in Querétaro, Mexico. His wife lived until 1927 in a château outside Brussels, driven insane by the Mexican episode. (Late-night-movie TV staple *Juárez* about Maximilian and Carlotta stars Bette Davis and Paul Muni.) On the ground floor of the castle, you can visit the bedroom of Maximilian (built like a ship's cabin) and that of Charlotte, as well as an impressive receiving room and more parlors, including a chinoiserie salon.

Enveloping the castle are magnificently designed park grounds (Parco di Miramare), ideal for pleasant strolls. In summer a sound-and-light presentation in the park depicts Maximilian's tragedy in Mexico. Tickets to the presentation, staged in July and August, begin at 15,000L ($9).

TOURING THE GROTTA GIGANTE

In the heart of the limestone plateau called Carso that surrounds the city, you can visit the ✪ **Grotta Gigante** (☎ 040/327-312), an enormous cavern and one of the most interesting phenomena of speleology. First explored in 1840 via the top ceiling entrance, this huge room, some 380 feet deep, was opened to the public in 1908. It's the biggest single-room cave ever opened to visitors and one of the

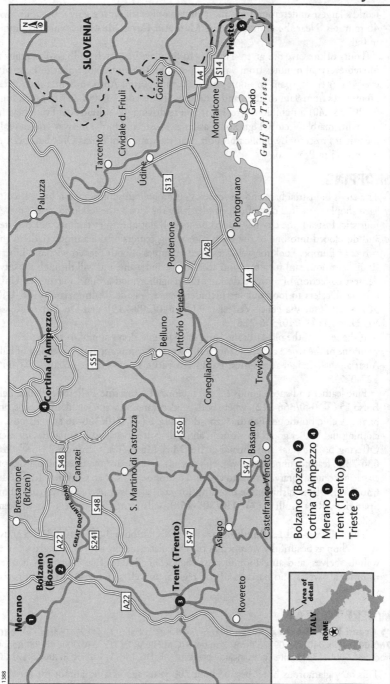

Bolzano (Bozen) ❷
Cortina d'Ampezzo ❹
Merano ❶
Trent (Trento) ❸
Trieste ❺

world's largest underground rooms. You can only visit with a guide; the tour takes 40 minutes. Near the entrance is the **Man and Caves Museum,** which is unique in Italy.

Tours of the cave are given Tuesday to Sunday; in March and October, they're offered every 30 minutes from 9am to noon and 2 to 5pm; November to February, every hour from 10am to noon and 2:30 to 4:30pm; April to September, every 30 minutes from 9am to noon and 2 to 7pm. Tours cost 13,000L ($7.80) for adults, 9,000L ($5.40) for children 6 to 12. If you're driving, take Strada del Friuli beyond the white marble Victory Lighthouse as far as Prosecco. On the freeway you can take the exit at Prosecco. By public transport, take the tram from Piazza Oberdan and then bus no. 45 to Prosecco.

SHOPPING

The city's industrial base and its sense of cosmopolitan sophistication have discouraged shopkeepers in Trieste from emphasizing the kitsch, the folkloric, or the merely touristic. Instead, the city has traded on its polyglot of former regimes and cultures, and developed into one of the most interesting centers of the antique trade in this corner of Europe. Look for well-preserved examples of both Biedermeier and Liberty (Italian art nouveau) furniture and accessories, and wander at will through the city's densest collection of antique dealers, the neighborhood around Piazza dell'Unità d'Italia. Dealers to look out for include: **Davia,** Via de l'Annunziata 6 (☎ 040/304-321); **Jésu,** Via Felice Venezian 9 (☎ 040/300-719); and **Dr. Fulvio Rosso,** Via Diaz 13 (☎ 040/306-226).

If the sense of the old-fashioned and deep patinas don't appeal to you, you might want one of the wood carvings from Trieste's most comprehensive collection of half-Austrian, half-Italian accessories, **Paolo Hrovatin,** Borgo Grotte Gigante (☎ 040/327-077).

Fine leather and suede goods fill the interior of **Christine Pellettrie,** Piazza della Borso 15 (☎ 040/366-212), where both genders can find well-crafted shoes, bags, and pants. A chic boutique, **Fendi,** Capo di Piazza 1 (☎ 040/366-464), sells upscale clothing and leather goods for women, and well-crafted belts, wallets, and ties for men. Offering both casual and formal attire, **Max Mara,** Via Carducci 23 (☎ 040/636-723), features impeccable women's designs, accessorized by shoes and bags. From classic to contemporary, formal to casual, **Le Monde,** Passo San Giovanni 1 (☎ 040/636-343), offers fashionable clothing for men and women. A waterfront shop, **Spangher,** Riva Gulli 8 (☎ 040/305-158), sells trendy sportswear for weekend sailors.

The 130-year-old **La Bomboniera,** Via XXX Ottobre 3 (☎ 040/632-752), is a sweets shop as beautifully wrapped as the chocolates it sells, with etched glass, carved walnut shelves, and an elaborate glass chandelier. Besides fine chocolates it offers traditional sweets and pastries of the region, as well as a few Austro-Hungarian specialties.

WHERE TO STAY

✪ **Grand Hotel Duchi d'Aosta.** Piazza dell'Unità d'Italia 2, 34121 Trieste. ☎ **040/760-0011.** Fax 040/366-092. 52 rms, 2 suites. A/C MINIBAR TV TEL. 330,000L ($198) double; from 585,000L ($351) suite. Rates include breakfast. AE, DC, MC, V. Parking 37,000L ($22.20).

This now-glamorous hotel began about 200 years ago as a restaurant for the dock workers who toiled nearby. Today many savvy business and pleasure travelers check in, preferring it over the Savoia Excelsior, which is not as well managed or maintained. In 1873, one of the most beautiful facades in Trieste—a white neo-classical shell with delicate carving, arched windows, and a stone crown of heroic sculptures—was erected over the existing building. The design is very much that of an 18th-century palace, an effect enhanced by views over the fountains and lamps of the square and the sea beyond it, while the Victorian-style public rooms inside give it a 19th-century ambience. The interior was practically rebuilt in the 1970s, and each accommodation has a well-stocked minibar, antiqued walls, and tasteful furniture. The restaurant, Ristorante Harry's Grill, is so good we reviewed it separately below under "Where to Dine."

Hotel al Teatro. Capo di Piazza G. Bartoli 1, 31131 Trieste. ☎ **040/366-220.** Fax 040/366-560. 46 rms, 36 with bath. TEL. 115,000L ($69) double without bath, 155,000L ($93) double with bath. Rates include breakfast. AE, MC, V.

The theatrical mask carved into the stone arch above the entrance is an appropriate symbol of this hotel, a favorite with many of Trieste's visiting opera stars. It's located a few steps from the seaside panorama of Piazza dell'Unità d'Italia and about a 10-minute walk from the station. The simply furnished and slightly old-fashioned rooms have parquet floors, lots of space, comfortable but minimal furniture, and a tub or shower in the rooms with bath. The hotel was built in 1830 as a private house and later served as headquarters of the British army in the aftermath of World War II.

Novo Hotel Impero. Via Sant'Anastasio 1, 34132 Trieste. ☎ **040/364-242.** Fax 040/365-023. 48 rms, 2 suites. TV TEL. 140,000L–198,000L ($84–$118.80) double; 288,000L ($172.80) suite. Rates include breakfast. AE, DC, MC, V.

Bargain hunters seek out this completely restored hotel in a neoclassic building just in front of the railway station. Next to the historical center and the business area, the hotel offers tastefully, albeit a bit sparsely, furnished bedrooms. A member of Fenice hotels, the property is well run and has completely modernized baths. The building, which has seen marching armies pass by over the decades, still retains much of the original glamor of its facade.

Savoia Excelsior Palace. Riva del Mandracchio 4, 34124 Trieste. ☎ **040/77-941.** Fax 040/638-260. 146 rms, 5 suites. A/C MINIBAR TV TEL. 320,000L–380,000L ($192–$228) double; 390,000L–460,000L ($234–$276) suite. Rates include breakfast. AE, DC, MC, V. Parking 40,000L ($24).

This leading choice stands next to the headquarters of the Lloyd Triestino shipping company, right off Piazza dell'Unità d'Italia. Fronting the water, the hotel has witnessed much of the pageantry of Trieste. It was originally built by the Austrians in 1912, and still retains many Habsburg-style frills in its ornate decor. The rooms in this first-class hotel are equipped with radios and other amenities, and many are furnished in bold modern designs. There's an American bar, plus an excellent restaurant.

WHERE TO DINE

Ai Due Triestini. Via Cadorna 10. ☎ **040/303-759.** Main courses 20,000L–30,000L ($12–$18). No credit cards. Mon–Sat noon–2:30pm. Closed Sept. AUSTRIAN/INTERNATIONAL/TRIESTINO.

For one of the best lunch bargains in Trieste, we suggest this tavern behind Piazza dell'Unità d'Italia. Run by a husband-and-wife team, this little trattoria covers its tablecloths with plastic and doesn't even bother to print a menu. Some of the cookery is heavily influenced by neighboring Austria. Try spezzatino, chunks of beef in a goulash ragoût, with fresh peas and potatoes. The Hungarian goulash is quite good, as is a rich strudel in the tradition of Budapest.

Al Bragozzo. Riva Nazario Sauro 22. ☎ **040/303-001.** Reservations required. Main courses 15,000L–40,000L ($9–$24); fixed-price all-you-can-eat menu 60,000L ($36). AE, DC, MC, V. Tues–Sat 11am–3pm and 7pm–midnight. Closed June 23–July 10 and 3 weeks in Dec. SEA-FOOD.

This is the best-known fish restaurant at the port, established in the late 1960s in a Jugenstil building originally constructed as a private house by the Austro-Hungarians a century ago. The outdoor tables, sheltered by a canopy, are popular in summer, although the paneled dining room is better during inclement weather. Specialties include *spaghetti al'Giorgio* (with tomatoes and herbs), ravioli stuffed with herbs, and many different preparations of salmon and shrimp. The cooks bring considerable experience and talent to turning out their time-tested recipes.

Al Granzo. Piazza Venezia 7. ☎ **040/306-788.** Reservations recommended. Main courses 20,000L–30,000L ($12–$18); fixed-price menu 38,000L ($22.80). AE, DC, MC, V. Mon–Tues and Thurs–Sat 12:30–3pm and 7:30–10pm, Sun 12:30–3pm. SEAFOOD.

This restaurant was established in 1923 by the ancestors of the three brothers who run it today. It began life as a simple fish house, serving seafood stews and grilled fish to the mariners who worked in the then-nearby dockyards. Today it's one of the leading seafood restaurants of Trieste, serving flavorful versions of that curious mixture of Italian, Austrian, and Yugoslav cuisines known as Triestino. Menu items include *brodetto*, a traditional bouillabaisse spiced with saffron and other herbs; vermicelli with black mussels; and risotto with seafood. Fresh fish are displayed on a bed of crushed ice in a wagon, and there's an impressive selection of fresh *contorni* (vegetables, sold individually) from nearby farms. A suitable wine might be a local Tocai Friulano, aromatic, harmonious, and somewhat tart, and lemon yellow to pale green in color. Dessert might be homemade strudel.

Antica Trattoria Suban. Via Comici 2, at San Giovanni. ☎ **040/54-368.** Reservations recommended. Main courses 18,000L–25,000L ($10.80–$15). AE, DC, MC, V. Mon 7:30–10pm, Wed–Sun 12:30–2:30pm and 7:30–10pm. Closed Aug 1–20. ITALIAN/AUSTRO-HUNGARIAN.

Established in 1865, this country tavern is 2 miles north of Trieste in the district of San Giovanni, on a spacious terrace opening onto a view of the hills. Today the surrounding landscape contains glimpses of the industrial age, but the brick and stone walls, the terrace, and the country feeling are still intact. The restaurant is run by descendants of the founding family. The cuisine is both hearty and delicate. In the true Triestino tradition, it draws its inspiration from northeastern Italian, Slavic, Hungarian, and Germanic recesses of what used to be the Austro-Hungarian Empire. The chefs concoct specialties from fresh ingredients gathered from surrounding farmlands. Dishes include a flavorful risotto with herbs, basil-flavored crêpes, beef with garlic sauce, a perfectly prepared chicken Kiev, and veal croquettes with Parmesan and egg yolks. The chef's handling of grilled meats is adept, and the rich pastries are worth the extra calories.

Ristorante Harry's Grill. In the Hotel Duchi d'Aosta, Piazza dell'Unità d'Italia 2. ☎ **040/365-646.** Reservations required. Main courses 30,000L–40,000L ($18–$24); Sun brunch 40,000L ($24). AE, DC, MC, V. Daily 12:15–3pm and 7:15–10:30pm. INTERNATIONAL.

Set in Trieste's most upscale hotel, this restaurant manages to be both elegant and relaxed, a place where you can have an American-style martini followed by either a simple plate of pasta or a complete, rather sumptuous meal. The big lace-covered curtains complement the paneling, the polished brass, and the blue Murano chandeliers. In summer, tables are set up in the traffic-free Piazza dell'Unità d'Italia. The outdoor terrace, which is sheltered by a canopy, has a separate area for bar clients. The Mediterranean-inspired cuisine is good, but not great, and includes fresh shrimp with oil and lemon, pasta and risotto dishes, boiled salmon in sauce, butter-fried calves' liver with onions, and an array of beef and fish dishes. The adjoining bar—not related to Italy's other famed Harry's Bars—is one of the most popular rendezvous spots in town, particularly for the business community.

TRIESTE AFTER DARK

For the greatest night out, head for **Teatro Verdi,** Corso Cavour (☎ 040/367-816), an opera house compared favorably to La Scala in Milan. That is, if it's open follow-ing a massive restoration—it was constructed in 1801 and needed a major overhaul. If the opera house hasn't opened at the time of your visit, check with the tourist office (see above) for its temporary venue, usually the **Sala Tripcovich,** Piazza Libertà (reached by the same phone).

You might begin an evening on the town at a cafe that seems descended directly from the world of the Hapsburgs, **Caffè Tommaseo,** Riva III Novembre 3 (☎ 040/366-765). After that, the neighborhood around the Piazza dell'Unità d'Italia offers the town's most interesting disco, **Mandracchio,** Passo di Piazza (☎ 040/366-292), which is rivaled by its most animated competitor, **Disco Machiavelli,** Viale Miramare 285 (☎ 040/44-104), a crowded see-and-be-seen dance hall whose only drawback is its location 4 miles north of the Piazza dell'Unità d'Italia. The city also has lots of pubs, some of which appeal to the young, rock-oriented crowd. Examples include **Juice,** on Via Madonnina (no phone), and **Round Midnight,** Via Gynnastica (no phone). Others, usually catering to a more mature clientele, try to capture the mellow and congenial ambience of the Habsburg age. An example is **Pub Jamin,** within the Il Giulia Trade Center, Via Giulia 75 (☎ 040/578-401).

2 Cortina d'Ampezzo

100 miles N of Venice, 82 miles E of Bolzano, 255 miles NE of Milan

This fashionable resort is your best center for exploring the snowy Dolomiti. Its repu-tation as a tourist mecca dates back to before World War I, but its recent growth has been phenomenal, spurred by the 1956 Olympics held here. Cortina d'Ampezzo draws throngs of nature lovers in summer and both Olympic-caliber and neophyte skiers in winter. It's a hotel owner's Shangrila, charging maximum prices in July and August as well as in the 3 months of winter.

A public relations *signora* once insisted, "Just say Cortina has everything." Such statements of propaganda, even when they come from charming Italian ladies, are suspect—but in this case she's nearly right. "Everything," in the Cortina context, means—first and foremost—people of every shape and hue; New York socialites rub elbows in late-night spots with frumpy Bremen hausfraus. Young Austrian men, clad in Loden jackets and stout leather shorts, walk down the streets with feathers in their caps and gleams in their eyes. French women in red ski pants sample Campari at cafe tables, whereas the tweedy English sit at rival establishments drinking "tea like mother made."

Then, too, "everything" means location. Cortina is in the middle of a valley ringed by enough Dolomite peaks to cause Hannibal's elephants to throw up their trunks and flee in horror. Regardless of which road you choose for a motor trip, you'll find the scenery rewarding. Third, "everything" means good food. Cortina sets an excellent table, inspired by the cuisine of both Venice and Tyrol. Fourth, "everything" means summer and winter sporting facilities—chiefly golf, horseback riding, curling, tennis, fishing, mountain climbing, skiing, skating, and swimming. The resort has an Olympic ice stadium, bobsled track, and ski jump. In addition, it has a skiing school, a large indoor swimming pool, an Olympic downhill track, and a cross-country track.

Finally, "everything" means top-notch hotels, *pensioni,* private homes, and even mountain huts for the rugged. The locations, facilities, types of service, price structures, and decor in these establishments vary considerably, but we've never inspected an accommodation here that wasn't clean. Most of the architecture of Cortina, incidentally, seems more appropriate to Zell am See, Austria, than to an Italian town.

ESSENTIALS

GETTING THERE   By Train   Frequent trains run between Venice and Calalzo di Cadore (trip time: 2 hours 20 minutes), 19 miles south of Cortina. You proceed the rest of the way by bus. For information about schedules call ☎ **01478/88-088** in Calalzo.

By Bus   About 14 to 16 buses a day connect Calalzo di Cadore with Cortina. Buses arrive at the **Cortina bus station** on Viale Marconi (☎ **0436/2741** for information about schedules).

By Car   Take autostrada A27 from Venice to Pian de Vedoia, continuing north along Route S51 all the way to Cortina d'Ampezzo.

VISITOR INFORMATION   The **tourist information office** is at Piazzetta San Francesco 8 (☎ **0436/3231**). The staff can assist you in arranging accommodations. Hours are Monday through Friday from 9am to 12:30pm and 4 to 7pm, Saturday 10am to 12:30pm and 4 to 7pm, and Sunday from 10am to 12:30pm.

CLIMBING TO THE STARS

One of the main attractions in Cortina is to take a cable car "halfway to the stars," as the expression goes. On one of them, at least, you'll be just a yodel away from the pearly gates. It's the **Freccia nel Cielo,** or "Arrow of the Sky." Beginning at 9am, from the base 200 yards west of town, cars depart every 20 minutes, July 12 to September 28 and December 16 to May 1 (call ☎ **0436/5052** for departure information the rest of the year). A round-trip costs 28,000L ($16.80). The first station is Col Druscie at 5,752 feet; the second station, Ra Valles, stands at 8,027 feet; and the top station, Tofana di Mezzo, is at 10,543 feet. At Tofana on a clear day, you can see as far as Venice.

SKIING & OTHER OUTDOOR ACTIVITIES

DOWNHILL SKIING   The Faloria-Cristallo area in the surroundings of Cortina is known for its 18¹/₂ miles of ski slopes and 10 miles of fresh-snow runs. At 1,224 meters (4,014 feet) above sea level, the altitude of Cortina is not particularly forbidding, at least compared to other European ski resorts, and although snowfall is usually abundant between late December and early March, a holiday in November or April might leave a serious skier stranded without an adequate amount of snow. Die-hard Cortina enthusiasts usually compensate for that, at least during the tail end of the winter season, by remaining only at the surrounding slopes' higher altitudes (there's lots of skiability at 9,000 feet in the surrounding peaks) and traversing lower-altitude snowfields by cable car.

As Italy's premier ski resort, and the focus of the holiday dreams of millions of residents of sultrier Italian climates, Cortina boasts more than 50 cable cars and lifts spread out across the valley of the Boite River. The surrounding mountains also contain about two dozen restaurants, 140km (approximately 87 miles) of clearly designated ski trails, and, at least in theory, a virtually unlimited number of off-piste trails for cross-country enthusiasts.

Frankly, Cortina is not the richest ski venue for supreme ski experts—who might be happiest spending 4 or 5 days in Cortina, then moving on to sojourns within the colder (and often more brutal) heights of more vertiginous resorts such as Zermatt (Switzerland), Courchevel (France), or Zürs (Austria).

Cortina's ample sunshine, the relative lack of crowding, and the lush array of slopes well suited to intermediate, advanced intermediate, and novice skiers can pay off handsomely. During the winter season, ski lifts are open throughout the day from 9am to between 4 and 5pm, depending on the time of sunset.

Cortina boasts a half-dozen distinctly different ski areas, each with its own challenges and charms. Regrettably, because they sprawl rather disjointedly across the surrounding terrain, they're not always easy to interconnect into a massively integrated whole. The most appealing of the area's six different ski areas include the Tofana-Promedes and the Faloria-Tondi complexes, both of which are usually judged as Cortina's most nerve-tingling and athletically diverse. The Pocol, Piera, Mietres, and Cinque Torri areas are specifically designated for novices, and the outlying Falzarego site is a long, dramatic, and sometimes terrifying downhill jaunt not recommended for anyone except a very competent skier.

Despite the easy availability of dozens of cable cars that originate outside the town center along the valley floor, Cortina's most dramatic cable cars are the **Freccia nel Cielo** ("arrow to the sky"), the region's longest and most panoramic (see above), and the **Funivia Faloria** (Faloria chairlift), 200 yards east of town. Both are patronized even by visitors who would never dream of actually trusting their eventual descent to a pair of skis. A single round-trip ticket on either costs 42,000L ($25.20)

Ski passes are issued in daily increments of 1 to 21 days. They can include access to either just the lifts around Cortina (about 50) or access to all the ski lifts within the Dolomiti (around 464). By far the better value is the latter, more comprehensive pass. This Dolomiti Super Ski Pass allows you unlimited access to a vast network—one of the largest in the world—of chairlifts and gondolas stretching over Cortina and the mountains flanking at least 10 other resorts nearby. The single-day pass sells for 58,000L ($34.80), but the daily cost goes down as you increase the days on the pass. For example, a 7-day pass costs 303,000L ($181.80), or 43,285L ($25.95) per day, and the 21-day pass goes for 691,000L ($414.60), which is 32,904L ($19.75) per day. Children born after January 1, 1984, receive about a 12% discount. The less comprehensive, and hence less desirable, Cortina-only pass sells for about 10% less, but few people opt for it.

Included in any pass is free transport on any of Cortina's bright yellow ski buses that run the length of the valley in season, connecting the many cable cars. Depending on snowfall, the two ski lifts mentioned above, as well as most of the other lifts in Cortina, are closed from around April 20 to July 15, and from September 15 to around December 1. For information, call ☎ **0436/5062.**

CROSS-COUNTRY SKIING   The trails start about 2 miles north of town. Some, but not all of them, run parallel to the region's roads and highways. For information about their location, instruction, and rental of equipment, contact Cortina's **Scuola Italiana Sci Fondo Cortina** in Fiames (☎ 0436/867-088).

CURLING   When weather is cold enough, the center for this sport is at the **Stadio Olimpico del Ghiaccio,** Via dello Stadio (☎ 0436/2661).

FISHING   The best stocked of the three lakes around Cortina is the Lago di Aial. You won't be charged for a permit until you actually catch something—lake access

Exploring the Peaks of the Dolomiti

The very existence of the high, snowy peaks of the Dolomiti comes as a surprise to foreigners who assume that Italy is an exclusively maritime country of rolling hills, steamy flatlands, and sun-flooded harbors. The Dolomiti add verticality and alpine charm to Italy, contributing a distinctive high-altitude wealth and Germanic overtones to the peninsula's diversity of cultures. Both the rock of which they're composed (dolomitic limestone) and the peaks themselves are named after an 18th-century French geologist, Déodat Guy Silvani Trancrède Gratet de Domolieu, who spent most of his life analyzing their mineral content.

Part of the eastern Alps, the Dolomiti stretch along the northwestern tier of Italy, following the line of the Austrian border between the valleys of the Adige and the Brenta rivers. Although the highest peak is the Marmolada (a few feet shy of 11,000 feet above sea level), the range contains an additional 17 peaks in Italian territory that rise above 10,000 feet. Escaping from the often intense heat of other parts of their country, Italians travel from more low-lying regions to breathe the Dolomiti's cool mountain air and to ski and play in such glittering resorts as Cortina.

The mountains' mixture of limestone and porphyry, combined with the angle of the rising and setting sun, contributes to the dramatic coloration of the mountain peaks. Most pronounced in the morning and at dusk, their colors range from soft pinks to brooding tones of russet. When the sun shines directly overhead, the hues fade to a homogenized and rather dull tone of gray. Fortunately for tourists, trekkers, and skiers, the climate isn't as bone-chillingly cold as it is in the alpine regions of western Italy and in the Alps of the Tyrol, farther to the north.

As you explore the Dolomiti, don't expect lush vegetation. When not camouflaged with snow, the slopes tend to be stony and relatively bare of groundcover. And don't rush out to gather hillside bouquets for your beloved, as many of the wildflowers (including the Austrian national flower, the edelweiss) are endangered species. Picking flowers or destroying vegetation is punishable by stiff fines.

The Dolomiti are redolent with natural beauty and trekking opportunities. Networks of hiking trails are clearly marked with painted signs, and any local tourist office (as well as most hotel reception staffs) are well versed in the length, duration, and degree of difficulty of most treks in their neighborhood. Maps of hiking trails are broadly distributed, and any local tourist office can refer you to the nearest branch of whatever Associazione Guide Alpine proliferates in the region.

If you decide to ramble across the Dolomiti for a day or two, stout shoes, warm clothing, and a waterproof jacket (storms erupt quickly at these altitudes) would be prudent. Chairlifts, cog railways, and alpine gondolas usually operate in both summer and winter, and offer an alternative means of enjoying sweeping views over ferociously beautiful mountain scenery. Networks of hiking trails usually radiate outward from the top and bottom of most mechanical lifts, and rustically charming *refugi* (mountain huts, sometimes with dining and overnight facilities) offer the opportunity for an overnight stay or just a rest.

roads leading from Cortina have checkpoints with the Italian equivalent of a park ranger, who charges you a small fee based on the size of your catch. For information on the best sites, contact the tourist office or the Municipio de Cortina (town hall) at Corso Italia 33 (☎ **0436/4291**).

ICE SKATING In winter, the town's main outlet for the sport is the **Stadio Olimpico del Ghiaccio,** Via dello Stadio (☎ **0436/2661**). In summer, after the ice has melted, participants change from ice blades to roller blades, and the action continues.

MOUNTAIN CLIMBING   No one should head into the Dolomiti for a spate of rock climbing or mountain climbing without consulting local authorities on climbing conditions, local bylaws, and well-intentioned advice about safety. The center for all this information, as well as a repository of local guides and teachers, is **Scuola di Roca Cortina,** Piazzetta San Francesco 6 (☎ 0436/4740).

WHERE TO STAY

The **tourist information office** in Cortina has a list of all the private homes in town that take in paying guests, lodging them family style for a moderate cost. It's a good opportunity to live with a Dolomite family in comfort and informality. The office, however, will not personally book you into a private home. Those arrangements you must make independently. Even though there are nearly 4,700 hotel beds available, it's best to reserve in advance, especially in August and December 20 to January 7.

VERY EXPENSIVE

✪ **Miramonti Majestic Grand Hotel.** Via Pezzie 103, 32043 Cortina d'Ampezzo. ☎ **0436/ 4201.** Fax 0436/867-019. 106 rms, 11 suites. MINIBAR TV TEL. 540,000L–740,000L ($324– $444) double; from 500,000L ($300) per person suite. Rates include half board. AE, DC, MC, V. Closed Apr–June and Sept–Dec 25. Parking 30,000L ($18) in garage, free outside. Hotel shuttle bus to/from the town center every 30 minutes.

Built in 1893, this hotel, one of the grandest in the Dolomiti, is a short distance from the center of town. It consists of two ocher-colored buildings with alpine hipped roofs and dignified facades. The rustic interior is filled with warm colors, lots of exposed timbers, and the most elegant clientele in Cortina. The well-furnished bedrooms look like those of a private home, complete with matching accessories, built-in closets, and all the modern amenities. A sports facility is on the premises, with an indoor swimming pool, exercise and massage equipment, a sauna, hydrotherapy, and physical therapy. Other sports facilities for winter and summer exercises are nearby, including golf and tennis.

MODERATE

✪ **Ancora.** Corso Italia 62, 32040 Cortina d'Ampezzo. ☎ **0436/3261.** Fax 0436/3265. 64 rms, 6 suites. TV TEL. 540,000L ($324) double; 470,000L ($282) per person suite. Rates include half board. AE, DC, MC, V. Closed after Easter to June and Sept 15–Dec 20.

This "Romantik Hotel," originally a private home back in 1826, is the domain of that hearty empress of the Dolomiti, Flavia Bertozzi, who believes in her guests having a good time. The hotel attracts sporting guests from all over the world and plays hostess to modern art exhibitions and classical concerts. The antique sculptures and objets d'art filling the place were gathered from Signora Flavia's trips to every province of Italy. Hers is a revamped hotel flanked on two sides by terraces with outdoor tables and umbrellas—the town center for sipping and gossiping. Garlanded wooden balconies encircle the five floors, and most bedrooms open directly onto these sunny porches. The bedrooms are all well furnished, comfortable, and especially pleasant— many with sitting areas. All is kept shiny clean, the service is polite and efficient, and the food is reason enough to check in.

Hotel Corona. Via Val di Sotto 12, 32040 Cortina d'Ampezzo. ☎ **0436/3251.** Fax 0436/ 867-339. 44 rms. TV TEL. 260,000L–360,000L ($156–$216) double. Rates include half board. MC, V. Closed Apr 2–July and Sept–Dec 20.

Dating from 1935, the Corona was one of the first hotels built at Cortina and its loyal clients will stay nowhere else. For anyone interested in modern Italian art, a stopover here is an event. The interior walls are hung with hundreds of carefully inventoried artworks. Many of the most important artists of Italy (and a few from France) from 1948 to 1963 are represented by paintings, sculptures, and ceramic bas-reliefs. These were acquired over the past quarter of a century by Luciano Rimoldi, the athletic manager who doesn't overlook sports either. Rimoldi is also a ski instructor—he once coached Princess Grace in her downhill technique—and was head of the Italian ice-hockey team during the 1988 Winter Olympics at Calgary. His hotel was chosen for the World Cup competition by a U.S. ski team just before they headed for the Sarajevo Olympics. The hotel prefers guests to take half board.

Menardi. Via Majon 110, 32043 Cortina d'Ampezzo. ☎ **0436/2400.** Fax 0436/86-2183. 51 rms. TEL. 230,000L–460,000L ($138–$276) double. Rates include half board. AE, MC, V. Closed Apr 10–June 20 and Sept 20–Dec 20. Parking 15,000L ($9).

This eye-catcher in the upper part of Cortina looks like a great country inn, with its wooden balconies and shutters. Its rear windows open onto a meadow of flowers and a view of the rough Dolomite crags. The inn is 100 years old and is run by the Menardi family, who still know how to speak the old Dolomite tongue, Ladino. Decorated in the Tyrolean fashion, each bedroom has its distinct personality. Considering what you get—the quality of the facilities, the reception, and the food—we'd rate this as one of the best values in Cortina. The living rooms and dining rooms have homelike furnishings: lots of knickknacks, pewter, antlers, spinning wheels.

INEXPENSIVE

Hotel Dolomiti. Via Roma 118, 32043 Cortina d'Ampezzo. ☎ **0436/861-400.** Fax 0436/862-140. 42 rms. TV TEL. 100,000L–200,000L ($60–$120) double. Rates include breakfast. AE, DC, MC, V. Parking 10,000L ($6).

This former Hotel Agip offers many amenities, although admittedly it's a sterile choice after the atmospheric places previously considered. But if you're watching your lire, this isn't a bad stopover. It's also a good bet if you arrive in Cortina in the off-season, when virtually everything else is closed. Its convenient location on the main road just outside the center of town—coupled with its clean, comfortable, contemporary, and no-nonsense format—has gained it increasing favor with visitors. The bedrooms are predictably furnished and fairly quiet, and the management is helpful. The restaurant serves good food, featuring regional specialties.

WHERE TO DINE

Da Beppe Sello. Via Ronco 68. ☎ **0436/3236.** Reservations recommended. Main courses 20,000L–35,000L ($12–$21). AE, DC, MC, V. High season, daily 12:30–2pm and 7:30–10pm; low season, Wed–Sun 12:30–2pm and 7:30–10pm. Closed Easter–May 15 and Sept 30–Oct 31. ALPINE/INTERNATIONAL/ITALIAN.

When you tire of the sometimes oppressive glamor of the more expensive restaurants in town, head for this simple but charming, Tyrolean-style restaurant in a hotel at the edge of the village. Named after the double nicknames of the hotel's founder, Joseph (Beppe) Menardi (Sello), and run today by his multilingual niece, Elisa, it's a bastion of superb regional cuisine and has been visited by some of the resort's most elegant clients. Food items include filet of venison from the Dolomiti served with pear, polenta, and *marmellata di mirtilli* (marmalade made from an alpine berry resembling a huckleberry or blueberry); diners get to keep the plate the dish was served on as a souvenir. Other dishes include pappardelle with rabbit sauce, tagliolini with porcini mushrooms, roast chicken with bay leaves, and filet steak flavored with bacon.

El Toulà. Località Ronco 123. ☎ **0436/3339.** Reservations required. Main courses 35,000L–40,000L ($21–$24). AE, DC, MC, V. Tues–Sun 12:30–2:30pm and 8–11pm. Closed Easter to late July and Sept–Christmas. ITALIAN/VENETIAN.

Located 2 miles east of Cortina toward Pocol, this was the first El Toulà—today a chain with 11 restaurants scattered throughout Italy and the world. Established in the early 1960s, under a name that in the dialect of Cortina translates as "The Hayloft," it's a wood-framed structure with picture windows and an outside terrace. You get excellently prepared dishes here, including squab grilled to perfection and served with an expertly seasoned sauce and veal braised with a white truffle sauce. Try the frittata of sea crabs in the "Saracen" style, *pasta e fagioli* (pasta and beans) in the style of the Veneto, a pasticcio of eggplant, or Venetian-style calves' liver. In the 1960s this place was terribly chic, an exclusive of Cortina's jet set crowd. In the 1990s, the rich and flavorful cuisine is appreciated by more down-to-earth clients.

✪ **Ristorante Tivoli.** Località Lacedel. ☎ **0436/866-400.** Reservations required. Main courses 20,000L–35,000L ($12–$21). AE, DC, MC, V. High season, daily 12:30–2:30pm and 7:30–10pm; off-season, Tues–Sun 12:30–2:30pm and 7:30–10pm. Closed May–June and Oct–Nov. ALPINE.

The best restaurant in Cortina, and one of the finest in the area, is this low-slung alpine chalet whose rear seems almost buried in the slope of the hillside. Standing high above the resort, about a mile from the center, it's beside the road leading to the hamlet of Pocol. Vastly popular with an athletic European clientele, it derives its excellence from the hardworking efforts of the gracious Calderoni family, who make this place the most fun and interesting at the resort. They use only the freshest of ingredients to create the savory dishes and aromas emerging from the kitchen. Try the stuffed rabbit in an onion sauce, wild duck with honey and orange, veal filet with basil and pine nuts, or salmon flavored with saffron. The pastas are made fresh daily. For dessert, you might sample an aspic of exotic fruit.

CORTINA AFTER DARK

In true European alpine resort style, the bar and disco scene of Cortina does a roaring business during winter, virtually closes down during spring and autumn, and reopens rather halfheartedly in midsummer. Most clubs lie off or along the pedestrian-only length of Cortina's Corso Italia, and by the time you read this, the nightlife landscape will probably feature two or three newcomers. Anyway, the popularity rating of any of them is about as fleeting as the mountain snow in June. Here are a few of the more enduring establishments.

Area, Via Ronco (☎ 0436/867-393), is modern and up-to-date with the latest nightlife trends of Rome, Milan, and London. You enter a bar on street level, but go downstairs to the basement to dance. A rocking competitor popular with a roster of mostly European club-goers is **Bilbo Club,** Galleria Nuovo Centro 7 (☎ 0436/5599), whose interior is dark, woodsy, and alpine-looking, and just battered enough so that no one minds if you happen to spill your beer on the floor. More dancing is available in the cellar of the **Hyppo Dance Hall,** Largo Poste (☎ 0436/2333), where you can preface your boogeying with a drink in the street-level bar. Better synchronized to a wider spectrum of ages is **Limbo,** Corso Italia 97 (☎ 0436/860-026), where a restaurant on the premises that's open later than virtually anything else in town (until 3am) assuages the hunger pangs of a dance-a-holic crowd.

A less frenetic setting that features an esoteric roster of wines from every wine-growing region of Italy is **Enoteca Cortina,** Via del Mercato 5 (☎ 0436/862-040). Its owners claim that it's the first wine bar in Italy, with a success story going back to 1964, and a carefully polished interior that might remind you of an English pub or a compartment aboard the Orient Express. Only 200 yards from the town's bell tower, locals happily mingle with skiers in winter and mountain climbers in summer. A roughly equivalent kind of calm is available at the **Piano Bar** in the lobby of the Splendid Hotel Venezia, Corso Italia 209 (☎ **0436/5527**), with soothing music during midwinter and midsummer from dusk until midnight.

EN ROUTE TO BOLZANO VIA THE GREAT DOLOMITE ROAD

From Cortina d'Ampezzo in the east to Bolzano in the west, the ✪ **Great Dolomite Road** follows a circuitous route of about 68 miles and ranks among the grandest scenic drives in all of Europe. The first panoramic pass you'll cross (Falzarego) is about 11 miles from Cortina and 6,900 feet above sea level. The next great pass is called Pordoi, at about 7,350 feet above sea level, the loftiest point along the highway (you can take a cable car to the top). Here you'll find restaurants, hotels, and cafes. In the spring, edelweiss grows in the surrounding fields. After crossing the pass, you'll descend to the little resort of Canazei, then much later pass by sea-blue Carezza Lake.

3 Bolzano

177 miles NE of Milan, 298 miles N of Rome, 95 miles N of Verona

The terminus of the Great Dolomite Road (or the gateway, depending on your approach), Bolzano is a town of mixed blood, reflecting the long rule that Austria enjoyed until 1919. Many names, including that of the town (Bozen), appear in German. As the recipient of considerable Brenner Pass traffic (55 miles north), the city is a melting pot of Italians and both visitors and residents from the Germanic lands. Bolzano lies in the center of the Alto Adige region and is traversed by two rivers, the Isarco and Talvera, one of which splits the town into two sections.

ESSENTIALS

GETTING THERE   By Train   Bolzano is a 1¼-hour train ride north of Verona; a one-way fare is 11,700L ($7). For information and schedules call ☎ **01478/ 88-088.** The Austrian city of Innsbruck, which is reached Via the Brenner Pass, lies about a 95-minute train ride north of Bolzano. Trains arrive at Piazza Stazione in the center of town—300 feet up Viale Stazione is the very heart of the city, Piazza Walther.

By Bus   Four buses a day make the 3½-hour trip from Cortina d'Ampezzo. A one-way ticket costs 14,500L ($8.70). For information about schedules call ☎ **0471/ 974-292.**

By Car   From Trent (see section 5 in this chapter), continue north to Bolzano on autostrada A22; or head west from Cortina d'Ampezzo along Route 48 until you reach the signposted junction with Route 241, which covers the final circuitous lap into Bolzano.

VISITOR INFORMATION   The **tourist information center** is at Piazza Walther 8 (☎ **0471/307-001**). It's open Monday to Friday from 9am to 6:30pm and Saturday from 9am to 12:30pm.

EXPORLING BOLZANO & DOLOMITE EXCURSIONS

Bolzano is a modern industrial town, yet a worthwhile sightseeing attraction in its own right. It has many esplanades for promenading along the river and a 15th-century Gothic **Duomo** with a colorful roof on Piazza Walther, the main square in town. The most interesting street is the colonnaded **Via dei Portici.** You can begin your stroll down this street of old buildings at either **Piazza Municipio** or **Piazza delle Erbe,** the latter a fruit market for the orchards of the province.

Bolzano makes a good headquarters for exploring the Dolomiti and the scenic surroundings, such as **Monte Renon** (Ritten in German) on the alpine plateau, with its cog train; the village of **San Genesio,** reached by cable north of Bolzano; and **Salten,** 4,355 feet up, an alpine tableland. If you have time for only one of these excursions, make it Monte Renon, connected to Bolzano by cable car daily from 7am to 8pm, a round-trip costing 7,500L ($4.50). You are taken to a lofty 3,000 feet up the slopes to the village of Soprabolzano. The terminus for the cable car lies about a 6-minute walk northwest from the rail station on Via Renon.

SHOPPING You'll get a whiff of what's being produced in the nearby mountains of western Austria after a quick perusal of the folkloric shops of Bolzano. One of the town's biggest and best-stocked is **Tschager,** Piazza Municipio (☎ 0471/973-675), where three floors of wood carvings include depictions of everything from a panoply of saints to rifle-toting huntsmen. Also look for ceramics, pottery, metalwork, and fabrics. A worthy competitor is **Artigiani Atesini,** Via Portici 39 (☎ 0471/978-590).

Looking for outdoor and/or flea markets? Check out the *frutta e verdura* (fruits and vegetables) sold every Monday to Saturday (8am to 1pm) in the Piazza delle Erbe; and the flea market (lots of used clothing, but only the occasional genuine heirloom) that takes place every Saturday morning (8am to around 2pm) in the Piazza della Vittoria. If you happen to visit in December, attend the Christkindlmarkt, held every year from November 28 to December 23, in the Piazza Walther, adjacent to the town's cathedral. Here, crafts and trinkets of every imaginable sort, with lots of emphasis on the Teutonic versions of Tannenbaum, will surround you from temporary kiosks laden with evergreen boughs and reminders of Christmas.

WHERE TO STAY

Hotel Alpi. Via Alto Adige 35, 39100 Bolzano. ☎ **0471/970-535.** Fax 0471/971-929. 110 rms. A/C MINIBAR TV TEL. 240,000L ($144) double. Rates include breakfast. AE, DC, MC, V. Parking 15,000L ($9).

The exterior of this tastefully contemporary hotel—the second-best choice in town—is dotted with recessed balconies, large aluminum-framed windows, and the flags of many nations. The spacious public rooms are richly covered with paneling, exposed stone, and ceramic wall sculptures, and contain comfortable upholstered seating areas. The hotel is located in the commercial center of town, and has a bar, a restaurant, a well-trained staff, and cozy rooms.

✪ **Park Hotel Laurin.** Via Laurin 4, 39100 Bolzano. ☎ **800/223-5652** in the U.S. or 0471/311-000 in Italy. Fax 0471/311-148. 96 rms, 10 suites. A/C MINIBAR TV TEL. 260,000L–375,000L ($156–$225) double; from 440,000L ($264) suite. Rates include breakfast. AE, MC, V. Parking 19,000L ($11.40).

The town's best address, the Park Laurin captures the glamor of the past. It was built in 1910 and is set on landscaped grounds. It's the only superior hotel in Bolzano, and its rooms and suites have been refurbished, with baths in Italian marble. In fact, the Park Hotel is among the top first-class hotels in the Dolomiti. The private garden is dominated by old shade trees and a flagstone-enclosed swimming pool. The garden terrace is ideal for lunches or dinners. The Laurin Bar offers piano entertainment daily, with jazz performances every Friday.

✪ **Scala Hotel Stiegl.** Via Brennero 11 (Brennerstrasse 11), 39100 Bolzano. ☎ **0471/976-222.** Fax 0471/981-141. 60 rms, 5 suites. MINIBAR TV TEL. 180,000L ($108) double;

350,000L ($210) suite. Rates include breakfast. AE, DC, MC, V. Closed Dec 27–Jan 12. Parking 15,000L ($9) in garage, free outside.

The Scala is the best of the middle-bracket hotels of Bolzano. Its trilingual staff speaks fluent English and keeps the interior spotless. The neobaroque yellow-and-white facade is well maintained, with plenty of ornamentation scattered symmetrically over its five-story expanse. On the premises is an outdoor pool, plus a summer-garden restaurant specializing in Tyrolean dishes. The hotel affords easy access to the train station and the historic center of town.

WHERE TO DINE

Da Abramo. Piazza Gries 16 (Grieserplatz 16). ☎ **0471/280-141.** Reservations recommended. Main courses 21,000L–29,000L ($12.60–$17.40); fixed-price menu 38,000L ($22.80). AE, DC, MC, V. Mon–Sat noon–2:15pm and 7–9:45pm. Closed Jan 6–13 and 3 weeks in Aug. MEDITERRANEAN/SEAFOOD.

In a century-old Liberty-style villa, the best and the most elegant restaurant in Bolzano took great pains to introduce a chic modern airiness to its physical decor. Across the river from the historic center of town, they offer a summer garden covered with vine arbors, plus a labyrinthine arrangement of rooms. Full meals cost upward of 50,000L ($30) and might include, depending on the mood of the chef, veal in a sauce of tuna and capers, roast quail with polenta, fish soup, warm seafood antipasti, codfish Venetian style, shellfish with seafood, tagliatelle with prosciutto, and beefsteak flambé with cognac. Flavors are robust, some thanks to the best of herbs and spices.

Zur Kaiserkron. Piazza della Mostra 1 (Mustergasse 1). ☎ **0471/970-770.** Reservations recommended. Main courses 20,000L–30,000L ($12–$18). AE, DC, MC, V. Mon–Fri noon–2:30pm and 7–9:30pm, Sat noon–2:30pm. SOUTH TYROLEAN/FRENCH/INTERNATIONAL.

The food is excellent, the decor appealing, and the multilingual management preserves the bicultural ambience for which Bolzano is known. The restaurant is housed a block from the cathedral in a yellow-and-white baroque building constructed in 1740 as the home of a wealthy Austrian merchant. For warm-weather dining, there's a canopy-covered wooden platform in front surrounded with greenery. Inside are tables under vaulted ceilings and wrought-iron chandeliers. Favorite dishes include an assortment of alpine-dried charcuterie; pâté of minced pheasant and duck liver; ravioli stuffed with spinach and minced beef; homemade tagliatelle with truffles; a traditional recipe of grüstl made from minced veal fried together with onions, eggs, and potatoes; home-smoked salmon; filet of venison with rosemary, pine nuts, and sweet-and-sour sauce; roast lamb or kid; and beef goulash with polenta.

BOLZANO AFTER DARK

The high altitudes and vestiges of alpine gemütlich from its days as an Austrian possession help contribute to good times and high energy after dark. Three discos (only one of which lies in the town center) are ready for you to get down and boogey. The cellar-level **Club Miro,** Piazza Dominicani 3B (☎ **0471/976-464**), is the smallest but most central and convivial of the three. It features a piano bar, a disco, lots of beer and wine from the German-speaking world, and the occasional live concert.

Within the city's less evocative industrial zone are the town's biggest and flashiest discos, **Disco Pathos,** Via Siemens 14 (☎ **0471/201-188**), a site that features dancing and drinking on two floors; and **Disco Big,** Via Galvani (☎ **0471/931-810**), the city's newest, biggest, most imaginative, and most widely publicized. Both emulate New York, Milan, and Los Angeles more aggressively than they do the evergreen folklore of the Italian Dolomiti.

4 Merano

18 miles NW of Bolzano, 202 miles NE of Milan

Once the capital of Tyrol before Innsbruck, Merano (Meran) was ceded to Italy at the end of World War I, but it retains much of its Austrian heritage today. In days gone by it was one of the most famous resorts in Europe, drawing kings and queens and a vast entourage from many countries, who were attracted to the alpine retreat by the grape cure. (Eating the luscious Merano grapes is supposed to have medicinal value.) After a slump, Merano now enjoys popularity, especially in autumn when the grapes are harvested. Before World War II Merano also became known for its radioactive waters, in which ailing bathers supposedly secured relief for everything from gout to rheumatism.

The Passirio River cuts through the town, banked by promenades that evoke the heyday of 19th-century resorts. Situated in the Valley of the Adige at the foot of Kuchelberg, Merano makes a good base for excursions in several directions, particularly to Avelengo. A bus from Sandplatz will deliver you to a funicular in which you can ascend 3,500 feet above sea level to Avelengo, with its splendid vista and mountain hotels and pensions. Merano is rich with tourist facilities and attractions, such as open-air swimming pools at its Lido, tennis courts, and a race track.

ESSENTIALS

GETTING THERE   By Train   Five trains per day make the short run from Bolzano. The trip takes 40 minutes and costs 3,600L ($2.15) one-way. For schedules and information call ☎ **0473/47-500.** Directly to the right of the station, Via Europa leads into the Piazza Mazzini, the center of town. It's a 15-minute walk or else you can take the frequent ACT bus no. 5, which will also take you to the center.

By Bus   From Bolzano, buses run frequently throughout the day northwest to Merano. The one-way fare is 4,000L ($2.40). Buses leave from Via Perathoner 4 (☎ **0471/450-111**) in Bolzano.

By Car   From Bolzano, head northwest along Route S38.

VISITOR INFORMATION   The **tourist information center** is at Corso della Libertà 35 (☎ **0473/235-223**). It's open Monday to Saturday from 9am to 6:30pm and Sunday from 9am to 12:30pm.

EXPLORING THE TOWN

On the Tappeinerweg promenade, the **Museo Agricolo Brunnenburg,** Ezra Pound Weg 6 (☎ **0473/923-533**), is housed in a castle owned by the daughter and grandson of Ezra Pound, who lived in Merano from 1958 to 1964. The museum has displays of Tyrolean country life, including a blacksmith's shop and grain mill. There are also ethnology exhibits, plus a room dedicated to Pound. It's open Wednesday to Monday from 9:30am to 5pm. Admission is 4,000L ($2.40) for adults, 1,500L (90¢) for children. You can reach the castle by taking bus no. 3 from Merano to Dorf Tirol, every hour on the hour, or by climbing the Tappeinerweg. The house is closed November to March.

The **Merano Thermal Spa Centre,** Via Piave 9 (☎ **0473/237-724**), is a well-laid-out spa complex in the heart of town, set in a landscaped park with flowering shrubs and shade trees. Here you'll find a small ornamental lake, along with an Olympic-sized heated outdoor pool, plus an indoor pool filled with spa water. This health center specializes in radon baths, mud-pack treatments, medicinal herb baths, and full massage treatments.

SPORTS & OUTDOOR ACTIVITIES   The **Maia Racehouse,** Via Palade
(☎ 0473/446-222), which opened in the 19th century, is one of the largest and most
attractive in Europe. It features steeple-chasing. Its major event is the Grand Premier
di Merano, the most important race of the season, run in connection with a national
lottery on the last Sunday in September. The racing season here lasts from May to
the end of October, with a break in July.

The **Merano Tennis Club,** Via Piave 46 (☎ 0473/230-313), offers nine open-
air hard-earth courts and four indoor hard-earth courts. In addition, the **Merano
Horse Riding Club,** Via E. Toti 1 (☎ 0473/232-246), gives riding lessons for
beginners and experts.

Merano is also the gateway to the ✪ **Parco Nazionale della Stelvio**—with
1.3 million acres, the largest national park in Italy. Offering countless possibilities
for hikes and hill climbing, the park has some 50 lakes and 100 glaciers (ensuring
year-round skiing). It also contains Europe's second highest pass, Passeo dello Stelvio,
open only between June and October. At Silandro, you can visit the park visitor
center at Via dei Cappuccini 2 (☎ 0473/70-443) to pick up a map outlining
hiking trails and the locations of mountain huts where campers can spend the night.
Several buses a day leave from the Merano station at Piazza Stazione heading for
Silandro, which lies 18 miles east along S38.

SHOPPING   Merano, thanks to its sometimes uncomfortable position midway
between the German- and Italian-speaking worlds, stresses Teutonic-style handcrafts
much more energetically than the *O Sole Mio* types of pottery you'd expect in Naples
or Genoa. Look for wood carvings, pewterware, alpine textiles and weavings,
commemorative spoons, and neobaroque plate racks at the town's largest gift shop,
Südtiroler Handwerk, Via Casa di Risparmio. (Surprisingly, it doesn't release its
phone number to the public.) If you're inspired by the local scenery to trek across
the hills and forests that surround Merano, and feel underaccessorized, you can
buy the appropriate clothing at **Runggaldier,** Via Portici (☎ 0471/237-454).
Also for sale are the kinds of loden and leather clothing you'd see across the border
in Austria.

WHERE TO STAY

Accommodations are also available at Kurhotel Castel Rundegg (see "Where to
Dine," below).

✪ **Castel Labers (Schloss Labers).** Via Labers 25, 39012 Merano. ☎ **0473/234-484.** Fax
0473/234-146. 30 rms, 1 suite. TEL. 180,000L–280,000L ($108–$168) double; 280,000L–
380,000L ($168–$228) suite. Rates include breakfast. Half board 115,000L–165,000L ($69–$99)
per person extra. AE, DC, MC, V. Closed Nov to 1 week before Easter.

The earliest documentation of this site dates from the 11th century, when the
feudal lords of the region, the von Labers, erected a modest fortress here. Since around
1890 the much enlarged and improved structure has functioned as a hotel, attracting visitors from around the Italian- and German-speaking world. The establishment
is one of the highest hotels in Merano, located on a hillside about 2 miles east of the
center of town. Owned and managed by the same family for more than a century,
the hotel maintains solid traditions and comfortably rustic bedrooms, usually with
panoramas and simple but solid accessories. There's an on-site tennis court, an outdoor swimming pool, and a flowered patio for outside drinking and dining.

Hotel Fragsburg. Via Fragsburg 3 (Fragsburgerstrasse 3) (Postfach 210), 39012 Merano–
Labers. ☎ 0473/244-071. Fax 0473/244-493. 20 rms, 4 suites. TV TEL. 240,000L–340,000L
($144–$204) double; 280,000L–380,000L ($168–$228) suite. Rates include half board. No credit
cards. Closed Nov–Apr 3.

This hotel is perched midway up the side of a sun-flooded mountain, high above Merano—the views from its verandas and decks are spectacular. Built around 1520 as a hunting lodge and hideaway for the count of Memmingen, it became a hotel in 1904 when an Austrian entrepreneur built a road leading here from the town center, and transformed the building into summertime lodgings for guests from throughout the Habsburg Empire. Since 1932 the hotel has been restored and improved, and it resembles an impeccably maintained historic chalet like you might find in the Austrian Tyrol. It's full of pinewood paneling, hunting trophies, art nouveau accessories, and elegantly rustic bedrooms, each with a safe and an outdoor balcony. There is a heated swimming pool, a cocktail lounge, access to nearby tennis courts, a dining room serving Italian-style meals, and one offering Tyrolean meals. The highest waterfall in Italy is a 20-minute trek from the hotel.

Hotel Minerva. Via Cavour 95, 39012 Merano. ☎ **0473/236-712.** Fax 0473/230-460. 45 rms. TV TEL. 150,000L–190,000L ($90–$114) double. Rates include breakfast. AE, DC, MC, V. Closed Jan 8–Mar and Nov 2–Mar 27.

Built in 1909 in the Teutonic style favored by the then-rulers of Merano, this hotel is large, comfortable, and just antique enough to give its clients a sense of tradition. Surrounded by a private garden, near several more expensive hotels, it's a 10-minute pedestrian trek eastward from the center of town. All but a few of the rooms have balconies with views over the town. There is an outdoor pool and an unpretentious dining room.

✪ **Hotel Palace.** Via Cavour 2–4 (Cavourstrasse 2), 39012 Merano. ☎ **0473/211-300.** Fax 0473/234-181. 120 rms, 7 suites. MINIBAR TV TEL. 300,000L–410,000L ($180–$246) double; 310,000L–1,050,000L ($186–$630) suite. Rates include breakfast. Special packages for health and diet available. AE, DC, MC, V.

The most deluxe hotel at the resort is a turn-of-the-century neobaroque palace set in the most beautiful formal gardens in town. The gilt- and cream-colored public rooms contain good copies of 18th-century furniture and massive crystal chandeliers. From the rear terrace there's a view of the large marble slabs that make a chessboard on the lawn. The gardens contain a free-form swimming pool whose waters flow below a tile annex to an indoor pool. Many of the bedrooms have their own stone or wrought-iron balconies overlooking the garden. Accommodations vary widely, but most have air-conditioned and other mdoern comforts; rates depend on the size, the season, and the view.

Dining/Entertainment: Guests gather in the piano bar before going into the Tiffany Grill restaurant, which features both regional and international cuisine.

Services: Room service, baby-sitting, laundry, valet, medical supervision for spa, health, and fitness programs.

Facilities: Fitness equipment, sauna, solarium, hot whirlpool, thermal treatments, and beauty farm.

WHERE TO DINE

Flora. Via Portici 75. ☎ **0473/231-484.** Reservations required. Main courses 16,000L–30,000L ($9.60–$18); fixed-price menus 40,000L–55,000L ($24–$33). AE, DC, MC, V. Mon–Sat noon–3pm and 7pm–midnight. Closed Dec 1–Feb 28. ITALIAN/TYROLEAN.

The Flora serves a refined, creative Tyrolean and Italian cuisine of consistently good quality in its conservative, elegant confines. Full meals are likely to include ravioli stuffed with chicken and exotic mushrooms, pasta blackened with squid ink, rack of lamb cooked in a shell of salt, and marinated trout with fines herbes. The menu changes seasonally, and this restaurant is the most solid and dependable choice in town.

Kurhotel Castel Rundegg. Via Scena 2, 39012 Merano. ☎ **0473/234-100.** Fax 0473/
237-200. Main courses 28,000L–45,000L ($16.80–$27). Daily noon–1:15pm and 7–8:30pm.
AE, DC, MC, V. ITALIAN/SOUTH TYROL.

This schloss and spa hotel offers the most creative food and refined atmosphere in
town. The setting has a kind of fairy-tale aura, a romantic building surrounded by
a beautiful park. The schloss dates from the 12th century, is devoted to health and
beauty care, and attracts the most demanding palates in Merano to its elegantly
appointed room under a vaulted ceiling. The chefs are internationally trained and
equally adept at both haute cuisine and delicate, low-calorie recipes. Begin with South
Tyrolean and Italian hors d'oeuvres such as farmer's speck (raw smoked pork) or
snails in herb butter, or try something more innovative like pumpkin dumplings with
cheese sauce. They offer nearly a dozen soups nightly, including fennel cream with
salmon strips or Terlano wine soup, a local specialty. Fish and meat dishes are
delectable, ranging from Tyrolean sirloin steak to grilled frogfish. Desserts are among
the finest in Merano, especially the apricot dumplings and "fruits of the forest"
cocktail. The hotel rents 28 luxuriously furnished bedrooms, all with minibar, TV,
and phone, costing 274,000L to 496,000L ($164.40 to $297.60) per person in a
double. Half board is 65,000L ($39) per person.

MERANO AFTER DARK

There are more discos here than you might have expected, partly because of a
population scattered in hamlets throughout the region, but despite that, know that
clubbing is likely to be fun and animated only on Friday and Saturday nights. Two
of Merano's most youth-oriented and techno-conscious discos lie within the town
center, easily accessible to local residents under 25 and foreign, dance-a-holic
travelers without cars. The more cutting edge of the two is **Manhattan Disco,** Corsa
Libertà (☎ **0471/449-655**), where the music includes garage, techno, and funk like
you might find in London. It's inner-city competitor for the youth crowd is the **Sugar
Shake,** Via Portici 242 (☎ **0471/233-333**), which has the added advantage of an
occasional live concert that's usually (but not always) scheduled for Tuesday, Friday,
or Saturday night.

More elegant, and geared toward a less frenetic, older, and perhaps more staid
clientele, is **Dancing Club Exclusif** (☎ **0471/561-711**). It's carefully signposted
within the alpine hamlet of Lana, 6 miles east of Merano, and sometimes plays 1980s
disco themes that any North American in his or her 40s probably remembers with
nostalgia.

5 Trento (Trent)

36 miles S of Bolzano, 144 miles NE of Milan, 63 miles N of Verona

A northern Italian city that basks in its former glory, this medieval town on the left
bank of the Adige is known throughout the world as the host of the Council of Trent
(1545–63). Beset with difficulties, such as the rising tide of "heretics," the Ecumenical
Council convened at Trent, a step that led to the Counter-Reformation. Trent lies
on the main rail line from the Brenner Pass, and many visitors like to stop off here
before journeying farther south into Italy.

Although it has an alpine aura, Trento is much more Italian in flavor than either
Murano or Bolzano. As capitals of provinces go, Trent is rather sleepy and provincial. Visitors often use it as a hub for trips into the surrounding mountains. The city
has not been overly commercialized, and it is still richly imbued with a lot of architectural charm, with a small array of attractions—none to get too excited about.

Nonetheless, it makes a good refueling stop for those exploring this history-rich part of Italy.

ESSENTIALS

GETTING THERE **By Train** Trent enjoys excellent rail connections. It lies on the Bologna–Verona–Brenner Pass–Munich rail line, and trains pass through day and night. The trip from Milan takes 2 hours 40 minutes; from Rome, 7 hours. Trains also connect Trent with Bolzano once every hour. Seven trains per day make the 3¹/₂-hour run from Venice. For rail information and schedules call ☎ 04478/ 88-088.

Both the train and bus stations lie between the Adige River and the public gardens of Trent. The heart of town is to the east of the Adige. From the station, turn on Via Pozzo, which becomes Via Orfane and Via Cavour before reaching the heartbeat Piazza del Duomo.

By Bus It's better to take the train to Trent and then rely on local buses once you get there. The **local bus station** is next to the train station (☎ 0461/821-000 for schedules), and has service to such places as Riva del Garda (see chapter 13) departing once an hour during the day.

By Car Trent lies on the autostrada A22, south of Bolzano and north of Verona.

VISITOR INFORMATION The **tourist information center** is on Via Alfieri 4 (☎ 0461/983-880). It's open in July and August, Monday to Saturday from 9am to noon and 3 to 6pm and Sunday from 10am to noon; the rest of the year, Monday to Friday from 9am to noon and 3 to 6pm and Saturday from 9am to noon.

EXPLORING THE TOWN

The city has much old charm. For a quick glimpse of the old town, head for **Piazza del Duomo,** dominated by the **Cathedral of Saint Vergilio.** Built in the Romanesque style and much restored over the years, it dates from the 12th century. A medieval crypt under the altar holds a certain fascination, and the ruins of a 6th-century Christian basilica were recently discovered underneath the church. You're admitted to these remains along with your admission to the **Museo Diocesano** (☎ 0461/234-419), with its religious artifacts on display relating to the Council of Trent, which met in the Duomo from 1545 to 1563. The museum is open Monday through Saturday from 9:30am to 12:30pm and 2:30 to 6pm, costing 5,000L ($3). The duomo is open daily from 8:30am to noon and 2:30 to 8pm. In the center of the square is a mid-18th-century Fountain of Neptune.

The ruling prince-bishops of Trent, who held sway until they were toppled by the French in the early 19th century, resided at the medieval **Castello del Buonconsiglio** (☎ 0461/233-770), reached from Via Bernardo Clesio 3. Now the old castle has been turned into a **Museo Provincale d'Arte,** with a collection of paintings and fine art, some quite ancient, including early medieval mosaics. Its most interesting art is a fresco cycle from the 1400s, *Cico dei Mesi,* or "cycle of the months." The **Museo del Risorgimento,** also at the castle, contains mementos related to the period of national unification between 1796 and 1948. The museums are open September to May, Tuesday to Sunday from 9am to noon and 2 to 5pm; June to August, Tuesday to Sunday from 9am to noon and 2 to 5:30pm. Admission is 7,000L ($4.20) adults, 3,000L ($1.80) for children under 18 and seniors 60 and over, free for children under 12.

Trent makes a good base for exploring **Monte Bondone,** a sports resort about 22 miles from the city center; **Paganella,** slightly more than 12 miles from Trent (the summit is nearly 7,000 feet high); and the **Brenta Dolomiti.** The latter excursion, which will require at least a day for a good look, will reward you with some of the finest mountain scenery in Italy. En route from Trent, you'll pass by **Lake Toblino,** then travel a winding, circuitous road past jagged boulders. A 10-minute detour from the main road at the turnoff to the Genova valley offers untamed scenery. Take the detour at least to the thunderous **Nardis waterfall.** A good stopover point is the fast-rising little resort of **Madonna di Campiglio.**

SHOPPING   Hoping to carry home some of the abundant agrarian bounty of the Trentino region as a souvenir of your visit? The most memorable food and wine shop in town is **Enoteca de Corso,** Corso 3 Novembre 54 (☎ **0471/916-424**), with wines from the region and everywhere else in Italy, as well as the salamis, olives, cheeses, and other salty tidbits that go well with them. If you're looking for handcrafts, head for the largest store of its type in town, **Artigianato Trentino,** Via Manchi 62 (☎ **0471/234-892**).

WHERE TO STAY

Albergo Accademia. Vicolo Colico 6, 38100 Trento. ☎ **0461/233-600.** Fax 0461/230-174. 41 rms, 2 suites. A/C MINIBAR TV TEL. 250,000L ($150) double; from 310,000L ($186) suite. Rates include breakfast. AE, DC, MC, V. Parking 20,000L ($12).

This alpine inn in the center of town behind the Renaissance church of Santa Maria Maggiore is made up of three buildings that have been joined to create a comfortable and attractive hostelry. One of the structures is believed to be of 11th- or 12th-century origin, based on a brick wall similar to the city walls found during renovation work. According to legend, the older part of the Accademia housed church leaders who attended the Council of Trent in the 16th century. The rooms are done in light natural wood. A suite at the top of the house has a terrace with a view of the town and the mountains. The alpine influence is carried over to the bar and the restaurant (closed on Monday).

Hotel America. Via Torre Verde 50, 38100 Trento. ☎ **0461/983-010.** Fax 0461/230-603. 50 rms. A/C MINIBAR TV TEL. 140,000L ($84) double. AE, DC, MC, V. Parking 20,000L ($12).

This simple, attractive hotel is located in the heart of the historic old town, a short walk from the rail station. Iron balconies look out to the Dolomite mountains and a vine-wreathed arbor shelters the main entrance. The newly redecorated rooms are clean and comfortable. The founder of the hotel worked in Wyoming from 1909 to 1923 and named the hotel after the country where he made the money to build it. There is also a restaurant.

Hotel Buonconsiglio. Via Romagnosi 16–18, 38100 Trento. ☎ **0461/272-888.** Fax 0461/ 272-889. 45 rms, 1 suite. A/C MINIBAR TV TEL. 180,000L–255,000L ($108–$153) double; 280,000L ($168) suite. AE, DC, MC, V. Rates include breakfast. Parking 10,000L ($6).

Built shortly after World War II as the Hotel Alessandro Vittorio, and renamed the Buonconsiglio in 1990 at the time of a massive renovation, this is an immaculate, well-administered hotel with pleasant bedrooms and an English-speaking staff. It's located on a busy street near the railway station. This place has a slight edge over the Accademia, but both hotels are virtually on a par. In the lobby is a collection of abstract modern paintings. Each bedroom contains a personal safe, satellite TV reception, and soundproofing against traffic noises from outside.

WHERE TO DINE

Orso Grigio. Via degli Orti 19. ☎ **0461/984-400.** Reservations recommended. Main courses 16,000L–22,000L ($9.60–$13.20). AE, DC, MC, V. Mon–Sat 12:30–2:30pm and 7:30–9:30pm. ITALIAN/TRENTINE.

This elegant and spacious restaurant lies about 30 yards from Piazza Fiera, in an old building whose origins may go back to the 1500s. When you see the immaculate table linen, the well-cared-for plants, and the subdued lighting, you know something is going right. Menus are seasonally adjusted to take in the finest fresh produce. The place enjoys local popularity—a good sign, since the Trentino is noted for a refined palate. Rufioli, a green tortellini, is a specialty. Another good regional dish is *squazzet con polenta,* Trentine-style fried tripe. Finish the feast with a chocolate mousse. Wines of the province are a special feature of the restaurant.

○ **Restaurant Chiesa.** Via San Marco 64. ☎ **0461/238-766.** Reservations recommended. Main courses 17,000L–25,000L ($10.20–$15); fixed-price "apple menu" 75,000L ($45). AE, DC, MC, V. Mon–Tues and Thurs–Sat 12:30–2:30pm and 7:30–9:30pm, Wed 12:30–2:30pm. TRENTINE.

Restaurant Chiesa offers the largest array of dishes we've ever seen made with apples. Owners Allesandro and Alberto recognized that Eve's favorite fruit, which grows more abundantly around Trent than practically anywhere else, was the base of dozens of traditional recipes. Specialties include risotto with apple, liver pâté with apple, fillet of perch with apple, and a range of other well-prepared specialties (a few of which, believe it or not, don't contain apples).

TRENTO AFTER DARK

Trento enjoys a reputation as an industrial workhorse, with an early-to-bed and early-to-rise philosophy that has never fostered large-scale emphasis on nighttime carousing. Your most appealing option might be an after-dark stroll around the Piazza Duomo, where three different bars offer the hope of conviviality and dialogue. Still in the town center, but farther afield, you might be attracted to **Bar Picaro,** Via San Giovanni 36 (☎ **0461/230-145**), where live, loud music attracts the under-30 crowd. A more soothing venue is the **Piano Bar Le Bollicine,** Via Ventuno 1 (☎ **0461/983-161**), where a live *artiste* executes highly drinkable music to a polyglot of locals and international travelers.

If discomania should happen to infect you during your time here (something the bishops who convened here during the Council of Trent would find highly irreverent), head for the hamlet of Pergine, 6 miles east of Trent, to the region's most popular disco, **Paradisi,** Via al Lago (☎ **0461/532-694**). Here, within easy access of at least two bars, one side is devoted to amusing versions of such old-fashioned dances as the waltz and jitterbug; the other to the more exuberant kinds of boogeying of conventional discos.

13 Milan, Lombardy & the Lake District

The vicissitudes of Italy's history are reflected in Lombardy as perhaps in no other region. Conquerors from barbarians to Napoléon have marched across its plain. Even Mussolini came to his end here. He and his mistress—both already dead—were strung up in a Milan square as war-weary residents vented their rage upon the two bodies.

Among the most progressive of all the Italians, the Lombards have charted an industrial empire unequaled in Italy. Often the dream of the underfed and jobless worker in the south is to go to Milano for the high wages and the good life, although thousands end up finding neither.

Lombardy isn't all manufacturing. Milan, as we'll soon see, is filled to the brim with important attractions, and nearby are old Lombard art cities—Bergamo, Cremona, and Mantova (Mantua). The Lake District, with its flower-bedecked promenades, lemon trees and villas, parks and gardens, and crystal-clear blue waters, may sound a bit dated, like a penny-farthing bicycle or an aspidistra in the bay window. But the lakes—notably Garda, Como, and Maggiore—continue to form one of the most enchanting splashes of scenery in northern Italy.

Like the lake district in northwestern England, the Italian lakes have attracted poets and writers—everybody from Goethe to Gabriele d'Annunzio. But after World War II the Italian lakes seemed to be largely the domain of matronly English and German types. In our more recent swings through the district, however, we've noticed an increasing *joie de vivre* and a rising influx of the 25-to-40 age group, particularly at such resorts as Limone on Lake Garda. Even if your time is limited, you'll want to have at least a look at Lake Garda.

1 Milan

355 miles NW of Rome, 87 miles NE of Turin, 88 miles N of Genoa

Italians in the south, perhaps resentful of the hard-earned prosperity of the north, sometimes declare that the Milanese are not unlike their nearby neighbors, the no-nonsense Swiss. With two million inhabitants, Milan doesn't evoke the languor and garrulousness of the rest of Italy, it doesn't muck about with excessive manners, and it doesn't snooze somnolently in the midday heat. It works, it moves,

Lombardy & the Lake District

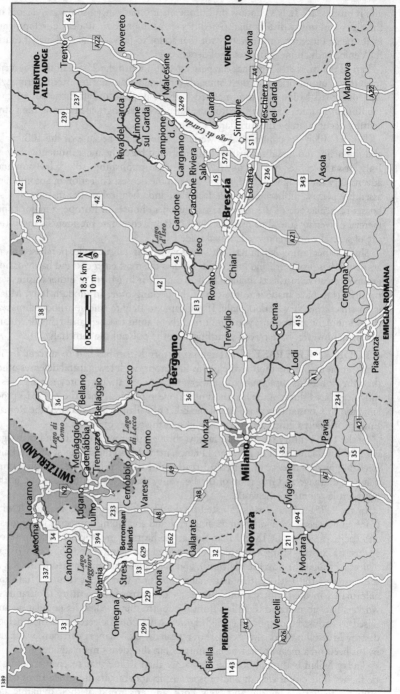

and it bustles. It's Italy's window on Europe, its most advanced showcase, devoid of the dusty and musty history that sometimes seems to paralyze modern developments in Rome or Florence, or the watery rot that seems to pervade the sublimely beautiful Venice with an inevitable sense of decay.

Part of the work ethic that has catapulted Milan toward the 21st century may stem from the Teutonic origins of the Lombards (originally from northwestern Germany), who occupied Milan and intermarried with its population after the collapse of the Roman Empire. Later the Teutonic influence was strengthened during the 18th-century occupation by the Austrians.

Today, Milan is a commercial powerhouse and, partly because of the 400 banks and the major industrial companies headquartered here, the most influential city in Italy. It's the center of the country's industries: publishing, silk, television and advertising, and design; and it lies very close to the densest collection of automobile-assembly plants, rubber and textile factories, and chemical plants in Italy. It also boasts La Scala, one of the most prestigious opera houses in Europe, a major commercial university (the alma mater of most of Italy's corporate presidents), and is the site of several world-renowned annual trade fairs.

Since its beginning Milan has, with unashamed capitalistic style, purchased more art than it has produced, and lured to its borders the most energetic and hardworking group of creative intellects in all of Italy. To make it in Milan, in either business or the arts, is to have made it to the top of the pecking order in modern Italy. Milan is, in effect, the New York of Italy. If you came to Italy to find sun-flooded piazzas and somnolent afternoons, you won't find them amid the fogs and rains of Milan. You will, however, have placed your finger on the pulse of modern Italy.

A LOOK AT THE PAST Throughout history Milan has had to succeed by its wits. Set on one of the most fertile plains in Europe, with few natural defenses other than the skill of its diplomats and traders, the city has always more or less successfully negotiated through the labyrinth of European politics. Since the A.D. 313 proclamation by Constantine the Great of the Edict of Milan (which declared the Roman Empire officially Christian), Milan has been at the center of events.

In the 14th century the Visconti family, through their wits, wealth, and marriages with the royal families of England and France, made Milan the strongest state in Italy. Realizing its dependence on agriculture early on, Milan initiated a continuing campaign of drainage and irrigation of the Po Valley that helped to make it one of the most fertile regions in the world.

In the 1700s Milan was dominated by the Habsburgs, a legacy that left it with scores of neoclassical buildings in its inner core and an abiding appreciation for music and (perhaps) work. In 1848 Milan was at the heart of the northern Italian revolt against its Austro–Hungarian rulers, encouraged the development of a Pan-Italian dialect (through the novelist Manzoni), and, along with neighbor Piedmont, was at the center of the 19th-century nationalistic passion that swept through Italy and culminated in the country's unification. By the turn of the century thousands of workers had immigrated to Milan from the south; they swelled its population and raised its industrial output to envied figures. Milan both elected and then helped destroy Mussolini, who, after being shot repeatedly by Milanese partisans, was hung by his heels on a meat hook, with his mistress, in the town's main square.

Today Milan is the only Italian city other than Rome that receives transatlantic flights. The city is elegant and prosperous; its inhabitants are tuned in to developments in Paris, London, and New York, and are proud of their dynamic and unusual city.

Milan

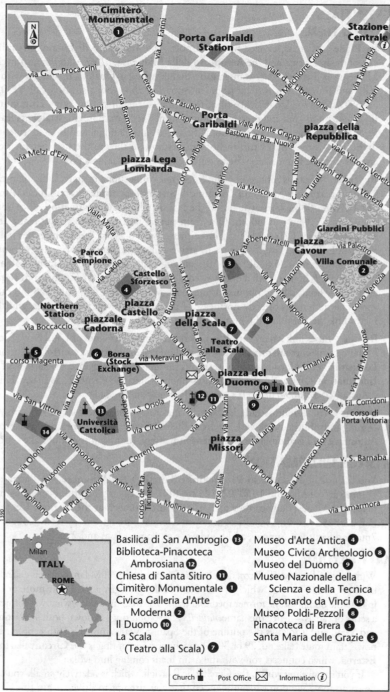

Basilica di San Ambrogio 🔟
Biblioteca-Pinacoteca
   Ambrosiana 🔟
Chiesa di Santa Sitiro 🔟
Cimitèro Monumentale ❶
Civica Galleria d'Arte
   Moderna ❷
Il Duomo 🔟
La Scala
   (Teatro alla Scala) ❼

Museo d'Arte Antica ❹
Museo Civico Archeologio ❽
Museo del Duomo ❾
Museo Nazionale della
   Scienza e della Tecnica
   Leonardo da Vinci 🔟
Museo Poldi-Pezzoli ❽
Pinacoteca di Brera ❸
Santa Maria delle Grazie ❺

Church ✝   Post Office ✉   Information ⓘ

ESSENTIALS
GETTING THERE

By Plane Milan is serviced by two airports, the **Aeroporto di Linate,** 4¹/₂ miles east of the inner city, and the **Aeroporto della Malpensa,** 31 miles to the northwest. Malpensa is used for most transatlantic flights, whereas Linate is for flights within Italy and Europe. For general flight information about both airports call ☎ 02/ 74-851. Buses for Linate leave from the Porta Garibaldi station every 20 minutes from 5:40am to 7pm and every 30 minutes from 7 to 9pm. Buses for Malpensa leave from the Stazione Centrale 2¹/₂ hours before all international and intercontinental flight departures. (Buses run in both directions, so they're the best bet for new arrivals to come into town.) This is much cheaper than taking a taxi.

By Train Milan is serviced by the finest rail connections in Italy. The main rail station for arrivals is Mussolini's mammoth **Stazione Centrale,** Piazza Duca d'Aosta (☎ 1478/88-088), where you'll find the National Railways information office open daily from 7:30am to 9:30pm. One train per hour arrives from both Genoa and Turin (trip time: 1¹/₂ to 2 hours from either city); a one-way fare from either point is 13,700L ($8.20). Twenty-five trains arrive daily from Venice (trip time: 3 hours), at a one-way fare of 20,800L ($12.50); and one train per hour arrives from Florence (trip time: 2¹/₂ hours), with a one-way cost of 26,200L ($15.70). Trains from Rome arrive every hour, taking 5 hours for the journey and costing 47,700L ($28.60) each way. The station lies directly northeast of the heart of town; trams, buses, and the metro link the station to the Piazza del Duomo in the very center.

By Bus Buses link Milan with Pavia, Bergamo, and other cities of Lombardy. Some of these companies are privately owned and others are under the control of Regione Lombardia. For information about various routings in the province, ask at the **ATM Information Office,** on the departures floor of Stazione Centrale, at Piazza Duca d'Aosta (☎ 02/669-7081). It's open daily from 8am to 8pm.

By Car The A4 autostrada is the principal east–west route for Milan, with A8 coming in from the northwest, A1 from the southeast, and A7 from the southwest. Autostrada A22 is another major north–south artery, running just east of Lake Garda.

VISITOR INFORMATION

You'll find the **Azienda di Promozione Turistica del Milanese,** on Piazza del Duomo at Via Marconi 1 (☎ 02/7252-4300), particularly helpful, dispensing free maps and whatever advice they can. There's also a branch at the Stazione Centrale (☎ 02/7252-4370). The offices are open Monday through Friday from 8:30am to 7pm and Saturday, Sunday, and holidays from 9am to 1pm and 2 to 5pm.

CITY LAYOUT

With its spired cathedral, Piazza del Duomo lies at the heart of Milan. Milan is encircled by three "rings," one of which is the **Cerchia dei Navigli,** a road that more or less follows the outline of the former medieval walls. The road runs along what was formerly a series of canals—hence the name *navigli*. The second ring is known both as **Bastioni** and **Viali,** and it follows the outline of the Spanish Walls from the 16th century. It's now a tram route (take no. 29 or 30). A much more recent ring is the **Circonvallazione Esterna,** which connects you with the main roads coming into Milan.

If you're traveling within the Cerchia dei Navigli, which is relatively small, you can do so on foot. We don't recommended that you attempt to drive within this circle unless you're heading for a garage. All the major attractions, including Leonardo's *Last Supper,* La Scala, and the Duomo, lie within this ring.

One of Milan's most important streets, **Via Manzoni,** begins near the Teatro alla Scala, and will take you to Piazza Cavour, a key point for the traffic arteries of Milan. The **Arch of Porta Nuova,** a remnant of the medieval walls, marks the entrance to Via Manzoni. To the northwest of Piazza Cavour lie the Giardini Pubblici, and to the northwest of these important gardens is **Piazza della Repubblica.** From this square, Via Vittorio Pisani leads into **Piazza Duca d'Aosta,** site of the cavernous Stazione Centrale.

Back at Piazza Cavour, you can head west along Via Fatebenefratelli into the **Brera district,** whose major attraction is the Accademia di Brera at Via Brera 28. This district in recent years has become a major center in Milan for offbeat shopping and after-dark diversions.

GETTING AROUND

The tourist office sells a special 5,000L ($3) 1-day or 9,000L ($5.40) 2-day **travel pass,** good for unlimited use on the city's tram, bus, and subway network. Those planning a longer stay can purchase a weekly pass, costing 20,000L ($12) and requiring a photo.

The city **bus** system covers most of Milano, and regular tickets costs 1,500L (90¢), as does the **subway** at the same fare. Take heed: Planned modification of Milan's bus lines may create a bit of pandemonium throughout 1998. Wise travelers may wish to find alternative modes of transportation. Some subway tickets are good for continuing trips on city buses at no extra charge, but they must be used within 75 minutes of purchase.

To phone a **taxi,** dial ☎ 02/6767, 02/5353, 02/8585, or 02/8388; fares start at 6,000L ($3.60), with a nighttime surcharge of 5,000L ($3).

FAST FACTS: Milan

American Express   There's an American Express office at Via Brera 3 (☎ 02/7200-3693 or 02/8646-0930), open Monday to Friday from 9am to 5pm.

Consulates   The Consulate of the **United States,** Via Prìncipe Amedeo 2/10 (☎ 02/290-351), is open Monday to Friday from 9am to noon and 2 to 4pm. The consulate of **Canada** is at Via Vittor Pisani 19 (☎ 02/67-581), open Monday to Friday from 9am to 5pm. Citizens of the **United Kingdom** will find their consulate at Via San Paolo 7 (☎ 02/723-001), open Monday to Friday from 9:15am to 12:15pm and 2:30 to 4:30pm. **Australia** has a consulate at Via Borgogna 2 (☎ 02/777-041), open Monday to Thursday from 9am to noon and 2 to 4pm and Friday from 9am to noon. Citizens of **New Zealand** should contact their consulate in Rome.

Emergencies   For the police, call ☎ 62261; for an ambulance, ☎ 118; for any emergency, ☎ 113.

Hospital   About a 5-minute ride from the Duomo, the **Ospedale Maggiore Policlinico,** Via Francesco Sforza 35 (☎ 02/55-031), has English-speaking doctors.

Newspapers   You'll find foreign newspapers at all major newsstands. If you read Italian (even just a little bit), you can pick up information about present attractions and coming events, such as cinema and theater schedules, by buying the daily *La Repubblica,* a useful newspaper. If you're seeking secondhand bargains, you can learn about sales in *Secondamano,* which comes out on Monday and Thursday.

Pharmacies   You can find an all-night pharmacy by phoning ☎ 192. The pharmacy (☎ 02/669-0735) at the Stazione Centrale never closes. For information on pharmacies open on Sunday and after-hours, call ☎ 0661-14471.

Post Offices   Most branches are open from 8:30am to 1:30pm Monday to Saturday. The Central Post Office is at Via Cordusio 4 (☎ 02/869-2069), and is open

Monday to Friday from 8:30am to 7:15pm and Saturday from 8:30am to 3:30pm. You can also call the Information Office at Piazza Cordusio (☎ 02/805-6812). **Telephone** The best place is the Central Post Office (see above), where telephone booths and operators maintain a 24-hour service.

THE TOP ATTRACTIONS

Despite its modern architecture and industry, Milan is still a city of great art. The serious sightseer will give the metropolis at least 2 days for exploration. If your schedule is frantic, see the Duomo, the Brera Picture Gallery, and one of the most important galleries of northern Italy, the Biblioteca-Pinacoteca Ambrosiana.

✪ Il Duomo. Piazza del Duomo. ☎ **02/8646-3456.** Cathedral, free; roof, 6,000L ($3.60) stairs, 8,000L ($4.80) elevator. Daily 9am–5:30pm. Metro: Duomo.

In the very center of Milan, opening onto the heart of the city's life, is Piazza del Duomo. Its impressive lacy Gothic cathedral ranks with St. Peter's in Rome and the cathedral at Seville, Spain, among the largest in the world. It's 479 feet long and 284 feet wide at the transepts. The cathedral, started in 1386, has seen numerous architects and builders. The conqueror of Milan, Napoléon, even added his own decorating ideas to the facade in the early years of the 19th century. The imposing structure of marble is the grandest and most flamboyant example of the Gothic style in Italy.

Built in the shape of a Latin cross, the cathedral is divided by soaring pillars into five naves. The overall effect is like a marble-floored Grand Central Terminal—that is, in space—with far greater dramatic intensity. In the crypt rests the tomb of San Carlo Borromeo, the cardinal of Milan. To experience the Duomo at its most majestic, you must ascend to the roof, from which you can walk through a forest of pinnacles, turrets, and marble statuary—like a promenade in an early Cocteau film. A gilded Madonna towers over the tallest spire.

Museo del Duomo. In the Palazzo Reale, Piazza del Duomo 14. ☎ **02/860-358.** Admission 8,000L ($4.80) adults, 4,000L ($2.40) children and seniors 60 and over. Tues–Sun 9:30am–12:30pm and 3–6pm. Metro: Duomo.

Museo del Duomo is housed in the Palazzo Reale (Royal Palace). It's like a picture storybook of the cathedral's six centuries of history. The museum has exhibits of statues and decorative sculptures, some of which date from the 14th century. There are also antique art objects, stained-glass windows (some from the 15th century), and ecclesiastical vestments, many as old as the 16th century. The museum also houses the **Museo d'Arte Contemporanea** upstairs, with a permanent exhibition of Italian futurist art, along with some Picasso works.

✪ Biblioteca-Pinacoteca Ambrosiana. Piazza Pio XI no. 2. ☎ **02/8645-1435.** Admission 8,000L ($4.80). Sun–Fri 9:30am–5pm. Metro: Duomo–Cordusio.

Near the Duomo, the Ambrosiana Picture Gallery and Library were founded in the early 17th century by Cardinal Federico Borromeo. On the second floor, the Pinacoteca contains a remarkable collection of art, mostly from the 15th through the 17th centuries. Among the notable works are a *Madonna and Angels* by Botticelli; works by Brueghel (which have impressive detail and are among the best art in the gallery); paintings by Lombard artists, including Bramantino's *Presepe,* in earthy, primitive colors; a curious miniature *St. Jerome with Crucifix* by Andrea Solario; and works by Bernardino Luini. The museum owns a large sketch by Raphael on which he labored before painting *The School of Athens* for the Vatican. The most celebrated treasures are the productions of Leonardo da Vinci's *Codice Atlantico.* (In Milan, the master had as a patron the powerful Ludovico Sforza, known as "The Moor.")

After seeing the sketches (in facsimile), you can only agree with Leonardo's evaluation of himself as a genius without peer. Attributed to him is a portrait of a musician, believed to have been Franchino Gaffurio. The Library contains many medieval manuscripts, which are shown for scientific examination only.

✪ Chiesa di Santa Maria delle Grazie (The Last Supper). Piazza Santa Maria delle Grazie (off Corso Magenta). ☎ **02/498-7588.** Church, free; *The Last Supper*, 12,000L ($7.20). Church, Mon–Sat 7:30am–noon and 3–7pm, Sun 3:30–6:30pm; *The Last Supper*, Tues–Sun 8am–1pm. Metro: Cadorna or Conciliazione.

This Gothic church was erected by the Dominicans in the mid-15th century. A number of its more outstanding features, such as the cupola, were designed by the great Bramante. But visitors from all over the world flock here to gaze upon a mural in the convent next door. In what was once a refectory, the incomparable Leonardo da Vinci adorned one wall with *The Last Supper.*

Commissioned by Ludovico the Moor, the painting was finished about 1497 and began to disintegrate almost immediately. The 28-by-15-foot mural was totally repainted—once in the 1700s and again in the 1800s. The gradual erosion of the painting makes for one of the most intriguing stories in art. It narrowly escaped being bombed in 1943. The bomb demolished the roof, and—astonishingly—the painting was exposed to the elements for 3 years before a new roof was built at the end of World War II. The current restoration has been controversial, drawing fire from some art critics, as did the Sistine Chapel restoration. The chief restorer of *The Last Supper,* Pinin Brambilla Barcilon, said the Sistine Chapel was a "simple window wash" compared to the da Vinci.

It has been suggested that all that's really left of *The Last Supper* created by da Vinci is a "few isolated streaks of fading color"—everything else is the application and color of artists and restorers who followed in his wake. What remains today, however, is Leonardo's "outline"—and even it is suffering badly. As one Italian newspaper writer put it: "If you want to see *Il Cenacolo,* don't walk—run!" A painting of grandeur, the composition portrays Christ at the moment he announces to his shocked apostles that one of them will betray him. Vasari called the portrait of Judas "a study in perfidy and wickedness."

Viewers are admitted 25 at a time, and are required to pass through antechambers designed to remove pollutants from their bodies. After they view the painting—for 10 minutes only—visitors must walk through two additional filtration chambers as they exit.

✪ Pinacoteca di Brera. Via Brera 28. ☎ **02/867-518.** Admission 8,000L ($4.80). Tues–Sat 9am–5pm, Sun 9am–12:15pm. Metro: Cairoli, Lanza, or Montenapoleone.

Pinacoteca di Brera, one of Italy's finest art galleries, contains an exceptionally good collection of works by both Lombard and Venetian masters. Like a Roman emperor, Canova's nude Napoléon—a toga draped over his shoulder—stands in the courtyard (fittingly, a similar statue ended up in the Duke of Wellington's house in London).

Among the notable artworks, the *Pietà* by Lorenzo Lotto is a work of great beauty, as is Gentile Bellini's *St. Mark Preaching in Alexandria* (it was finished by his brother, Giovanni). Seek out Andrea Mantegna's *Virgin and the Cherubs,* a great work from the Venetian school. Two of the most important prizes at the Brera are Mantegna's *Dead Christ* and Giovanni Bellini's *La Pietà,* as well as Carpaccio's *St. Stephen Debating.*

Other paintings include Titian's *St. Jerome,* as well as such Lombard art as Bernardino Luini's *Virgin of the Rose Bush* and Andrea Solario's *Portrait of a Gentleman.* One of the greatest panels is Piero della Francesca's *Virgin and Child Enthroned with Saints and Angels and the Kneeling Duke of Urbino in Armor.* Seek out, in addition, the *Christ* by Bramante. One wing, devoted to modern art, offers works by such artists as Boccioni, Carrà, and Morandi. One of our favorite paintings in the gallery is Raphael's *Wedding of the Madonna,* with a dancelike quality. *The Last Supper at Emmaus* is another moving work, this one by Caravaggio.

EXPLORING THE REST OF MILAN

✪ **Museo Poldi-Pezzoli.** Via Manzoni 12. ☎ **02/794-889.** Admission 10,000L ($6) adults, 5,000L ($3) children under 17 and seniors over 60. Tues–Fri 9:30am–12:30pm and 2:30–6pm, Sat 9:30am–12:30pm and 2:30–7:30pm, Sun 9:30am–12:30pm and 2:30–6pm (closed Sun afternoon Apr–Sept). Metro: Duomo or Montenapoleone.

This fabulous museum is done in great taste and is rich with antique furnishings, tapestries, frescoes, and Lombard wood carvings. It also displays a remarkable collection of paintings by many of the old masters of northern and central Italy, including Andrea Mantegna's *Madonna and Child,* Giovanni Bellini's *Cristo Morto,* and Filippo Lippi's *Madonna, Angels, and Saints* (superb composition). One portrait here that virtually enjoys the same fame in Milan that the *Mona Lisa* does world wide is Antonio Pollaiolo's *Portrait of a Lady,* one of the most reproduced paintings of all time and a work of haunting originality. One buyer from Paris's garment district says he comes here on every trip to Milan—regardless of how rushed—just to gaze in wonder at this stunning portrait. One room is devoted entirely to Flemish artists, and there's a collection of ceramics and also one of clocks and watches. The museum grew out of a private collection donated to the city in 1881.

Museo d'Arte Antica. In Castello Sforzesco, Piazza Castello. ☎ **02/7600-2378.** Free admission. Tues–Sun 9:30am–5:30pm. Metro: Cairoli.

Castle Sforzesco, the Castle of Milan, is an ancient fortress rebuilt by Francesco Sforza, who launched another governing dynasty. It's believed that both Bramante and Leonardo da Vinci contributed architectural ideas to the fortress. Following extensive World War II bombings, it was painstakingly restored and continued its activity as a Museum of Ancient Art. Displayed on the ground floor are sculpture from the 4th century A.D., medieval art mostly from Lombardy, and armor. The most outstanding exhibit, however, is Michelangelo's *Rondanini Pietà,* on which he was working the week he died. In the rooms upstairs, besides a good collection of ceramics, antiques, and bronzes, is the important picture gallery, rich in paintings from the 14th to the 18th centuries, including works by Lorenzo Veneziano, Mantegna, Lippi, Bellini, Crivelli, Foppa, Bergognone, Cesare da Sesto, Lotto, Tintoretto, Cerano, Procaccini, Morazzone, Guardi, and Tiepolo.

Museo Nazionale della Scienza e della Tecnica Leonardo da Vinci. Via San Vittore 21. ☎ **02/4801-0040.** Admission 10,000L ($6) adults, 6,000L ($3.60) children 18 and under and seniors 60 and over. Tues–Fri 9:30am–5pm, Sat–Sun 9:30am–6:30pm. Metro: S. Ambrogio.

If you're a fan of Leonardo da Vinci, as we are, you'll want to visit this vast museum complex where you could practically spend a week devouring the exhibits. For the average visitor the most interesting section is the Leonardo da Vinci Gallery, which displays copies and models from the Renaissance genius. There's a reconstructed pharmacy from a convent, along with a monastic cell, even a sewing-machine collection. You'll also see antique carriages plus exhibits relating to astronomy, telecommunications, watchmaking, goldsmithery, motion pictures, and the subjects of classic physics.

Civica Galleria d'Arte Moderna. Via Palestro 16. ☎ **02/7600-2819.** Free admission. Tues–Sun 9:30am–5:30pm. Metro: Palestro.

The Civica Galleria d'Arte Moderna (Civic Modern Art Gallery) used to be known as the royal villa before its name was changed to the Villa Comunale. Constructed between 1790 and 1793, it was designed by the architect Leopold Pollack. For a short time it was the residence of Napoléon and Eugène de Beauharnais. The gallery has a large collection of works from the Milanese neoclassical period, along with many paintings that show the development of Italian romanticism. It's predictably rich in the works of Lombard artists. Important collections that have been donated are those of Carlo Grassi and the Vismara art accumulation. Also significant is the Marino Marini Museum, which was opened in 1973. Marini, a famous Italian sculptor, has some 200 works displayed, including not only sculpture but paintings and graphics, all a gift of the artist himself. Many artists are on parade: Picasso, Matisse, Rouault, Renoir, Modigliani, Corot, Millet, Manet, Cézanne, Bonnard, and Gauguin.

Basilica di Sant'Eustorgio. Piazza Sant'Eustorgio 1. ☎ **02/5810-1583.** Basilica, free; chapel, 2,000L ($1.20). Daily 8:30am–noon and 3–6:30pm. Metro: Genova.

The bell tower of the 4th-century Basilica of Sant'Eustorgio dates from the 13th century; it was built in the romantic style by patrician Milanese families. It has the first tower clock in the world, made in 1305. Originally this was the tomb of the Three Kings (4th century A.D.). Inside, its greatest treasure is the Capella Portinari, designed by the Florentine Michelozzo in Renaissance style. The chapel is frescoed and contains a bas-relief of angels at the base of the cupola. In the center is an intricately carved tomb, supported by marble statuary of the 13th century by Balduccio of Pisa. Inside are the remains of St. Peter Martyr. The basement has a Roman crypt.

Basilica di San Ambrogio. Piazza San Ambrogio 15. ☎ **02/8645-0895.** Basilica, free; museum, 3,000L ($1.80). Basilica, Mon–Sat 9:30am–noon and 2:30–6:30pm; museum, Mon–Sat 10am–noon and 3–5pm, Sun 3–5pm. Closed Aug. Metro: San Ambrogio.

This church was originally erected by St. Ambrose in the later years of the 4th century A.D. The present structure was built in the 12th century in the Romanesque style. The remains of St. Ambrose rest in the crypt. The church, entered after passing through a quadrangle, is rather stark and severe, in the style of its day. The atrium is its most distinguishing architectural feature. In the apse are interesting mosaics from the 12th century. The Lombard tower at the side dates from 1128, and the facade, with its two tiers of arches, is impressive. In the church is the **Museo della Basilica di S. Ambrogio,** containing some frescoes, 15th-century wood paneling, silver and gold objects originally for the altar, paintings, and sculpture, including Flemish tapestries.

Cimitèro Monumentale. Piazzale Cimitero Monumentale 1. ☎ **02/659-9938.** Free admission. Tues–Fri 8:30am–4:15pm, Sat–Sun 8:30am–4:45pm. Metro: Garibaldi. Tram: 4, 8, 12, or 14.

Cimitèro Monumentale (Monumental Cemetery) has catered for more than 100 years to the whims of Milan's elite society. The only requirements for burial in the cemetery are, first, that you are dead, and second, that you can buy your way into a plot. Some families have paid up to 200,000,000L ($120,000) just for the privilege of burying their dead here. The graves are marked not only with brass plates or granite markers, but also with Greek temples, elaborate obelisks, or such original works as an abbreviated version of Trajan's Column.

This outdoor museum has become such an attraction that a superintendent has compiled an illustrated guidebook—a sort of "Who *Was* Who." Among the cemetery's outstanding sights is a sculpted version of *The Last Supper.* Several fine examples of art nouveau sculpture dot the hillside, and there's a tasteful example of Liberty-style architecture (Italy's version of art nouveau) in a tiny chapel designed to hold the remains of Arturo Toscanini's son, who died in 1906. Among the notables buried here are Toscanini himself and novelist Alessandro Manzoni. In the Memorial Chapel is the tomb of Salvatore Quasimodo, who won the 1959 Nobel prize in literature. Here also rest the ashes of Ermann Einstein, father of the scientist. In the Palanti Chapel is a monument commemorating the 800 Milanese citizens slain in Nazi concentration camps. (A model of this monument is displayed in the Museum of Modern Art in New York.) It's located a few blocks east of Stazione Porta Garibaldi.

WHERE TO STAY

In the city are some deluxe hostelries, as well as a superabundance of first- and second-class hotels, most of which are big on comfort but short on romance. In the third- and fourth-class bracket and on the *pensione* (boardinghouse) level there are dozens of choices—many of which rank at the bottom of the totem pole of comparably classed establishments in all of Italy's major cities, with the exception of Naples. Some places are outright dangerous, and others so rock-bottom and unappealing as to hold little interest for the average visitor. In several places, men sit around in the lobby in their bathrobes watching soccer games on TV.

Our recommendation is—if you can afford it—to stay in a better grade of hotel in Milan, and to leave your serious budgeting to such tourist meccas as Rome, Florence, and Venice, which have clean, comfortable, and often architecturally interesting third- and fourth-class hotels and *pensioni*. However, for the serious economizer we have included the best of the budget lot. We present them as safe and (hopefully) clean shelters, but with no particular enthusiasm.

VERY EXPENSIVE

Four Seasons Hotel Milano. Via Gesù 8, 20121 Milano. ☎ **02/77-088.** Fax 02/7708-5000. 70 rms, 28 suites. A/C MINIBAR TV TEL. 738,000L–1,028,000L ($442.80–$616.80) double; from 1,392,000L ($835.20) suite. AE, DC, MC, V. Metro: Montenapoleone or San Babila.

Milan's most exciting five-star hotel started in 1993 on a side street opening onto the most elegant concentration of upscale boutiques in Italy, Via Montenapoleone. Housed in what was a three-story monastery in the 14th century, its acquisition was a real-estate coup by Four Seasons. The building was the residence of the Habsburg-appointed governor of northern Italy in the 1850s, and later housed luxury apartments. The medieval facade, many of the frescoes and columns, and the original monastic details were incorporated into a modern edifice flooded with sunlight and accented with bronze, stone floors, glass, pearwood cabinetry, Murano chandeliers, and acres of Fortuny fabrics. The accommodations are cool, conservative, spacious, and discreetly outfitted in tones of beige and pale green, always with a sense of understated luxury.

Dining/Entertainment: The hotel lounge contains the architectural renderings for stage sets used at the nearby La Scala opera house. Nearby is Il Teatro, serving dinner daily from 8pm to midnight. Less formal, La Veranda serves meals daily and continuously from 11am to 11pm.

Services: Concierge, room service (24 hours), same-day valet and laundry.

Facilities: High-tech fitness center and spa, business center.

Palace Hotel. Piazza della Repubblica 20, 20124 Milano. ☎ **800/221-2340** in the U.S., 800/955-2442 in Canada, or 02/6336. Fax 02/654-485. 220 rms, 6 suites. A/C MINIBAR TV TEL. 528,000L–638,000L ($316.80–$382.80) double; from 913,000L ($547.80) suite. AE, DC, MC, V. Parking 45,000L–70,000L ($27–$42). Metro: Repubblica.

The Palace Hotel, blithely ignoring the noisy pell-mell commercial world around it, stands aloof on a hill near the railway station; it has a formal car entrance and a facade of 14 floors with tiers of balconies. Primarily a business hotel catering to some of Europe's most prominent figures, the Palace also welcomes tourists and occasional entertainers. The Prìncipe di Sovoia, its Ciga sibling across the street, is superior to the Palace in sheer old-world opulence—and the Four Seasons leaves both properties behind. The bedrooms are furnished with pastel upholstery and carpeting, and reproductions of Italian antiques. Modern conveniences include heated towel racks and minibars concealed behind mahogany chests.

Dining/Entertainment: The hotel bar attracts an international clientele, and the Grill Casanova is acclaimed as one of the finest in Milan, offering both regional and international dishes.

Services: Room service, baby-sitting, laundry, valet.

Facilities: Fitness center.

Principe di Savoia. Piazza della Repubblica 17, 20124 Milano. ☎ **800/325-3535** in the U.S. and Canada, or 02/6230. Fax 02/659-5838. 252 rms, 47 suites. A/C MINIBAR TV TEL. 594,000L–759,000L ($356.40–$455.40) double; from 1,000,000L ($600) suite. AE, DC, MC, V. Parking 60,000L ($36) and up. Metro: Repubblica.

The Prìncipe was built in 1927 to fill the need for a luxurious hotel near the Stazione Centrale and is still a regal address, although overtaken by the Four Seasons. It was completely restored in 1991. Substantial and luxurious, the six stories offer solid comfort amid crystal, detailed plasterwork, fine carpets, and polished marble. The rooms are spacious and modern, decorated in a 19th-century Lombard style. Many are paneled in hardwoods, and all contain leather chairs and other stylish furniture. The front rooms face the hysterical traffic of Piazza della Repubblica, whereas the ones in back are more tranquil, opening onto the Alps.

Dining/Entertainment: There's a spacious bar area off the main lobby. The hotel has a notable restaurant, Galleria, serving both regional and international dishes. It also offers the popular Doney cafe (see "Where to Dine," below).

Services: Room service, baby-sitting, laundry, valet.

Facilities: Sauna, health club, solarium, indoor pool, limited facilities for the disabled.

EXPENSIVE

Excelsior Gallia. Piazza Duca d'Aosta 9, 20124 Milano. ☎ **800/225-5843** in the U.S. and Canada, or 02/6785. Fax 02/6671-3239. 237 rms, 13 suites. A/C MINIBAR TV TEL. 400,000L–460,000L ($240–$276) double; from 700,000L ($420) suite. AE, DC, MC, V. Parking 20,000L–40,000L ($12–$24). Metro: Stazione Centrale. Tram: 33 or 59.

This Liberty-style (art nouveau) monument was built by the Gallia family in 1933. Set near the main railway station, the hotel is one of the most expensive and visible in Milan, and once one of the top hotels of Italy—but today is more of an upmarket rail station hotel. The 1994 renovations combined some of the smaller rooms into larger and more comfortable accommodations. The bedrooms fall into two categories: modern and comfortable in the newer wing and graciously old-fashioned and charming in the original core. All are soundproofed against the roar of traffic in the piazza outside. The noted restaurant, Gallia's, serves haute Lombard and international dishes. The Baboon Bar is stylish, and a piano player sometimes performs in the lobby. On the premises are baby-sitting, laundry, valet, and room service, along with a business center, a fitness club with a massage center, a gym, a whirlpool, and a sauna.

MODERATE

Casa Svizzera. Via San Raffaele 3, 20121 Milano. ☎ **02/869-2246.** Fax 02/7200-4690. 45 rms. A/C MINIBAR TV TEL. 270,000L ($162) double. Rates include breakfast. AE, DC, MC, V. Parking 30,000L ($18). Metro: Duomo.

Casa Svizzera, right off Piazza del Duomo, is one of the most serviceable hotels in the city, following a reconstruction in 1970. Two elevators service five floors of rooms. Features include paneled double windows and soundproofing to keep out the noise. The homelike bedrooms have air-conditioning that can be independently regulated and satellite TV.

Hotel Galles-Milano. Via Ozanam 1 (Corso Buenos Aires), Milano 20129. ☎ **800/528-1234** in the U.S. and Canada or 02/204-841. Fax 02/204-8422. 100 rms, 5 suites. A/C MINIBAR TV TEL. 300,000L–500,000L ($180–$300) double; from 500,000L ($300) suite. Rates include breakfast. AE, DC, MC, V. Parking 40,000L ($24). Metro: Lima.

This hotel was built in 1901 as one of the then-most-glamorous hotels in Milan. In 1990 a consortium of Italian investors poured millions of lire into an elegant rehabilitation, producing an aggressively marketed hotel that's much favored by businesspeople, conventioneers, and visitors looking for safe, comfortable, and unpretentious lodgings. The interior lacks the art nouveau glamor of many of its competitors, but this doesn't seem to bother the many clients who approve of the building's functional lines and conservatively modern bedrooms. The hotel contains a big-windowed rooftop restaurant (La Terrazza) with additional seating on a canopy-covered terrace, and a cocktail bar with a drink for virtually everyone's taste. In use in spring or summer is a roof garden with a solarium and Jacuzzi.

INEXPENSIVE

✪ **Antica Locanda dei Mercanti.** Via San Tomaso 6, 20123 Milano. ☎ **02/805-4080.** Fax 02/805-4090. 10 rms. TEL. 180,000L ($108) double; 220,000L–250,000L ($132–$150) triple. AE, DC, MC, V. Tram: 1, 14, or 24.

The antique building that contains this reasonably priced but sophisticated hotel was built in the late 1800s by a wealthy merchant who used it as a *pied-à-terre* during trips to Milan. In 1996, a former model for Milan Schön, the charming Paola Ora, gutted the building's second floor and installed a streamlined and well-conceived hotel, custom designing each bedroom and naming each after a successful Milanese mercantile family. Furnishings are upholstered in top-echelon Milanese fabrics with embroidered floral designs or pale monochromes, and bathrooms are sheathed in slabs of marble. Don't be startled by the building's severe-looking monumental entrance, or the businesslike appearance of three of the building's four floors, most of which are occupied by crafts studios for the jewelry industry and a ground-floor travel agency. Breakfast—in bed—is the only meal served. The neighborhood was intricately described in Alessandro Manzoni's 19th-century clasic *I Promessi Sposi (The Promised Spouse).*

✪ **Antica Locanda Solferino.** Via Castelfidardo 2, 20121 Milano. ☎ **02/657-0129.** Fax 02/657-1361. 11 rms. TV TEL. 180,000L ($108) double. Rates include breakfast. AE, DC, MC, V. Parking 25,000L–30,000L ($15–$18) nearby. Metro: Moscova or Repubblica.

When this country-style hotel opened in 1976, the neighborhood was a depressed backwater of downtown Milan. Today it's an avant-garde community of actors, writers, and poets, and this inn deserves some of the credit for the transformation. The hotel got off to a fortuitous start soon after it opened when editors from *Gentleman's Quarterly* stayed here while working on a fashion feature. Since then celebrities have become clients, either staying in one of the old-fashioned bedrooms or dining at the ground-floor restaurant (see "Where to Dine," below). Each bedroom is different, reflecting the 19th-century floor plan of the building; there are no singles. The furnishings include Daumier engravings and art nouveau or late 19th-century bourgeois pieces. But the baths are modern. Since the hotel is small and often fully booked, reserve as far in advance as possible.

Hotel Gran Duca di York. Via Moneta 1A (Piazza Cordusio), 20123 Milano. ☎ **02/874-863.** Fax 02/869-0344. 33 rms. TV TEL. 230,000L ($138) double; 280,000L ($168) triple. Rates include breakfast. AE, V. Closed Aug. Parking 35,000L ($22.40). Metro: Cordusio.

When it was built by the Catholic Church in the 1890s, this Liberty-style palace housed dozens of priests from the nearby Duomo. Among them was the cardinal of Milan, who later became Pope Pius XI. Today anyone can rent one of the pleasantly furnished and well-kept bedrooms, each with a private bath sheathed with patterned tiles. Behind the ocher-and-stone facade, you'll find a bar in an alcove of the severely elegant lobby, where a suit of armor and leather-covered armchairs contribute to the restrained tone.

Hotel Manzoni. Via Santo Spirito 20, 20121 Milano. ☎ **02/7600-5700.** Fax 02/784-212. 52 rms. TEL. 220,000L ($132) double. AE, DC, MC, V. Parking 22,000L–50,000L ($13.20–$30). Metro: Montenapoleone or San Babila.

Hotel Manzoni, built around 1910 and renovated frequently since then, charges reasonable prices considering its location near the most fashionable shopping streets of Milan. It lies behind a facade of stone slabs on a fairly quiet one-way street. Each of its bedrooms is outfitted with color-coordinated, comfortable functional furniture and carpeting. Many of the rooms have TVs. A brass-trimmed winding staircase leads from the lobby into a bar and TV lounge. The English-speaking staff is cooperative.

Hotel Star. 5 Via dei Bossi, 20121 Milano. ☎ **02/801-501.** Fax 02/861-787. 30 rms. A/C MINIBAR TV TEL. 230,000L ($138) double. Rates include buffet breakfast. AE, MC, V. Closed Aug and Christmas. Parking 35,000L–40,000L ($21–$24). Metro: Cordusio or Duomo.

The Ceretti family welcomes guests to their well-run little hotel on a narrow street a few blocks from La Scala and the Duomo. The lobby has been refurbished, making it brighter than before, and the bedrooms are comfortably furnished but a bit dour. Amenities such as hair dryers have been installed in the bathrooms. Double-glass windows cut down on the noise from the street. They serve a rich buffet breakfast, including jams, pâté, yogurts, cheese, eggs, ham, and fruit salad, along with cereal, croissants, and various teas, juices, and coffee.

Hotel Valgauna. Via Vare 32, 20158 Milano. ☎ **02/3931-0089.** Fax 02/3931-2566. 40 rms. A/C MINIBAR TV TEL. 100,000L–240,000L ($60–$144) double. Rates include buffet breakfast. AE, DC, MC, V. Bus: 82 or 92.

This newly renovated hotel is tasteful, modern, and centrally located to the local sites and motorways. It offers amenities such as satellite TV and piped music in each room, and each accommodation has been renovated and tastefully furnished. Some of the rooms, however, are a bit cramped. For the grand buffet, there is the breakfast lounge, and for later in the day a refined bar to welcome you. Laundry service is also available. For those who fancy sunbathing, there is a spacious terrace, and the reception staff is happy to assist you with transportation tickets to get to the nearby lakes of Como and Maggiore.

WHERE TO DINE

The wide economic levels of the population—from textile manufacturer to factory worker—are reflected in the prices in the restaurants, which range from haute cuisine to the pizza parlor.

EXPENSIVE

✪ **Giannino.** Via Amatore Sciesa 8. ☎ **02/5519-5582.** Reservations required. Main courses 40,000L–75,000L ($24–$45). AE, DC, MC, V. Mon–Sat 12:30–3pm and 7:30pm–midnight. Tram: 12 or 30. MILANESE/SEAFOOD/TUSCAN.

Giannino continues to enchant its loyal patrons and win new adherents every year. It's one of the top restaurants in all of Lombardy, and has been since 1899. The chef approaches every day as if he must make his reputation anew. Diners have a choice of several attractive rooms, and eyes rivet on the tempting underglass offerings of the *specialità gastronomiche milanesi*. The choice is excellent, including such characteristic Lombard dishes as tender, breaded veal cutlet and risotto simmered in broth and coated with Parmesan cheese. It's difficult to recommend any one dish, as everything we've ordered, or even seen going by, piqued our taste. However, we have special affection for *tagliolini con scampi al verde*, fresh homemade noodles with prawn tails in herb sauce. Also superb are the cold fish and seafood salad and the beautifully seasoned *orata al cartoccio* (fish baked in a paper bag with shrimp butter and fresh herbs).

Il Teatro. In the Four Seasons Hotel Milano, Via Gesù 8. ☎ **02/7708-1435.** Reservations recommended. Main courses 33,000L–40,000L ($19.80–$24). Fixed-price dinner 85,000L ($51). AE, DC, MC, V. Mon–Sat 7:30pm–midnight. Closed Aug. Metro: Montenapoleone or San Babila. MEDITERRANEAN.

This is the culinary showcase of the shopping district's newest and most glamorous hotel. Favored since its opening in 1993 by such luminaries as Versace, Calvin Klein, and members of the Agnelli family, the restaurant lies in a Milanese palazzo built in the 1400s as a cloister. The outdoor patio overlooks a garden, and the dining room is sheathed in burnished paneling and nut-colored leather under a tented ceiling of champagne-colored silk. Prices are lower than you might think. The menu changes at least four times a year, but might include a tantalizing involtini of eggplant with ricotta and mint, crispy crayfish with a purée of tomatoes, and a fillet of red mullet with essence of tomato and black truffles. Everything tastes as fresh as the day it was picked, harvested, or caught. Dessert might be a *mille-feuille croquante* layered with walnuts, chocolate mousse, and raspberries.

St. Andrews. Via Sant'Andrea 23. ☎ **02/798-236.** Reservations required. Main courses 35,000L–70,000L ($21–$42). AE, DC, MC, V. Mon–Sat 12:30–3:30pm and 8pm–1am. Closed Aug. Metro: Montenapoleone or San Babila. INTERNATIONAL.

This restaurant has given much pleasure to many people for many years. It offers one of the finest kitchens in Lombardy, preparing both international and regional food. The cuisine is superior. The menu includes an unusual appetizer of steak tartare mixed with caviar and seasonings, John Dory in a salt crust, and rack of lamb in the Provençal style. The dessert specialty is a tartatelli, composed of pastry with a honey-and-strawberry sauce. At lunch it has somewhat the atmosphere of a private club and is apt to be filled with businesspeople. The armchairs are covered in black leather, the paneling is dark wood, and the lighting is discreet from hooded lamps. Formally attired waiters give superb service to regular guests and to such celebrities as famous Italian fashion stylists, including Gianfranco Ferré, Armani, Versace, and Missoni.

✪ **Savini.** Galleria Vittorio Emanuele II. ☎ **02/7200-3433.** Reservations required. Main courses 25,000L–45,000L ($15–$27); fixed-price lunch (with wine) 70,000L ($42); fixed-price dinner (without wine) 80,000L ($48). AE, DC, MC, V. Mon–Fri noon–3pm and 7:30–11pm, Sat 7:30–11pm. Closed Dec 24–Jan 2 and Aug 10–25. Metro: Duomo. LOMBARD/INTERNATIONAL.

Savini provides a heavenly introduction to the aromatic cookery of Lombardy and has attracted everybody from Puccini to Pavarotti. Perched in the heart of the great glass-enclosed arcade opposite the Duomo, the *classico* restaurant, which dates from 1867, draws both the out-of-towner and the discriminating local. Guests sit on the terrace outside, or dine in the old-world room with its crystal chandeliers and glittering silverware. Waiters in black jackets hover over you to see that you enjoy every mouthful. Many of the most memorable dishes are unassuming, including the Lombardy specialty *costoletta alla milanese,* tender veal coated with egg batter and bread crumbs, then fried a rich brown. The *pièce de résistance* of Milan, most often ordered before the main course, is *risotto alla milanese*—rice simmered in a broth and dressed with whatever the artiste in the kitchen selects that night. Savini is excellently stocked with a wide range of wine (the staff will gladly assist you).

MODERATE

Al Chico di Uva. Via Sirtori 24, ☎ **02/2940-6883.** Reservations recommended. Main courses 18,000L–36,000L ($10.80–$21.60). AE, DC, MC, V. Mon–Sat noon–2:30pm and 7–10:30pm. Closed Aug 3–27. Metro: Porta Venezia. TUSCAN/ITALIAN.

Al Chico, a good neighborhood restaurant specializing in such fare as onion soup and fondue bourguignonne, was established in the 1970s in a much-renovated, century-old building. Tuscan specialties such as Florentine beefsteak are also featured, and portions are tasty and satisfying. The chef is rightly proud of his pappardelle with porcini mushrooms, branzini (sea bass) cooked in a salt crust, and spaghetti with mushrooms and spring onions. The place is usually crowded, but it's worth the wait for a table. The service is good, and the ingredients are fresh and well selected at the market. They stock good house wines from Tuscany, including the classic Chianti. In summer you can eat on the veranda.

Alfio-Cavour. Via Senato 31. ☎ **02/7600-0633.** Reservations recommended. Main courses 25,000L–45,000L ($15–$27). AE, DC, MC, V. Mon–Fri 12:30–3pm and 7:30–11pm, Sun 7:30–11pm. Closed Aug. Metro: Montenapoleone or San Babila. ITALIAN/INTERNATIONAL.

There's a luminous quality to the lavish displays of antipasti served with relish at this family-run restaurant. It stems partly from the Tahitian-style decor, where trees grow through the glass panels of a greenhouse-like roof and vines entwine themselves among bamboo lattices. The restaurant is best known for its serve-yourself display of antipasti, where the polite but sharp-eyed staff bills you for what you select. A pasta specialty is the flavorful *spaghetti pescatore,* with bits of seafood. You might follow with large grilled shrimp or a *gran misto* fish fry, or else one of the many excellent beef or veal dishes.

Al Porto. Piazzale Generale Cantore. ☎ **02/832-1481.** Reservations required. Main courses 25,000L–40,000L ($15–$24). AE, DC, MC, V. Mon 7:30–10:30pm, Tues–Sat 12:30–2:30pm and 7:30–10:30pm. Closed Dec 24–Jan 3 and Aug. Metro: Porta Genova or S. Agostino. SEAFOOD.

Established in 1907, this is among the most popular seafood restaurants in Milan. As you enter, you pass by tanks of "demons of the deep" (which might later end up on your plate). The glassed-in garden room is the most sought after by loyal habitués. It's especially popular among business patrons; you may need to reserve several days in advance. Menu items include *orata* (dorado) with pink peppercorns and *branzini* (sea bass) with white Lugurian wine and olives. Many come here just for *risotto ai frutti di mare,* the classic Lombard dish served with an assortment of sea creatures. One of the staff confided that the "best patrons" begin with a warm antipasto, then follow with a risotto, and then order the traditional *fritto misto*—almost anything that swims is likely to turn up on the plate—although some find this far too much food. Everything tastes better with a Friuli wine.

A Santa Lucia. Via San Pietro all'Orto 3. ☎ **02/7602-3155.** Reservations recommended. Main courses 25,000L–30,000L ($15–$18). V. Tues–Sun noon–2:30pm and 7:30pm–2:30am. Closed Aug. Metro: San Babila. MEDITERRANEAN/SEAFOOD.

A Santa Lucia pulls out hook, line, and sinker to lure you with some of the best fish dinners in Milan. A festive place, the restaurant is decked out with photographs of pleased celebs, who attest to the skill of its kitchen. You can order such specialties as a savory fish soup, which is a meal in itself; fried baby squid; or good-tasting sole. Spaghetti alla vongole evokes the tang of the sea with its succulent clam sauce. Pizza also reigns supreme. Try either the calzone of Naples or the *pizza alla napoletana*.

Bistrot di Gualtiero Marchesi. Via San Raffaele 2. ☎ **02/877-120.** Reservations required. Main courses 28,000L–32,000L ($16.80–$19.20); fixed-price menu 45,000L–55,000L ($27–$33). AE, DC, MC, V. Mon 7:30–10:30pm, Tues–Sat 12:30–2:30pm and 7:30–10:30pm. Closed 2 weeks in Aug. Metro: Duomo. LOMBARD/ITALIAN.

Near the Duomo, this bistro was created by Signor Gualtiero Marchesi, the patron saint of *cucina nuova* in Italy. Once hailed by *Time* magazine as among the 10 top chefs in the world, he operated a very expensive restaurant in another part of town that moved to Erbusco, near Brescia; but this bistro was left as a love token to Milan. It boasts one of the best views of the cathedral in the city, set on the top floor of the Rinascente Center, which rises seven stories across a narrow street from the cathedral, "almost within touching distance." The bistro has big walls of glass to better admire the view. The menu depends on the inspiration of the chef, but in the past we've enjoyed an unusual form of half-opened ravioli, or crayfish cooked very al dente with cucumbers. You're almost certain to find a perfect veal cutlet milanese.

Boeucc Antico Ristorante. Piazza Belgioioso 2. ☎ **02/7602-0224.** Reservations required. Main courses 25,000L–32,000L ($15–$19.20). AE. Mon–Fri 12:40–2:30pm and 7:40–10:40pm, Sun 7:40–10:40pm. Closed Aug, Easter, and Christmas. Metro: Duomo, Montenapoleone, or San Babila. INTERNATIONAL/MILANESE.

This restaurant, established in 1696, is a trio of rooms in a severely elegant old palace, within walking distance of the Duomo and the major shopping streets. Throughout you'll find soaring stone columns and modern art. In summer guests gravitate to a terrace for open-air dining. The hearty specialties come from regions of Italy. You might enjoy a spaghetti in clam sauce, a salad of shrimp with arugula and artichokes, or grilled liver, veal, or beef with aromatic herbs. In season sautéed zucchini flowers accompany some dishes.

Doney. In the Prìncipe di Savoia Hotel, Piazza della Repubblica 17. ☎ **02/6230.** Main courses 16,000L–29,000L ($9.60–$17.40); fixed-price menu 70,000L–110,000L ($42–$66); afternoon tea 23,000L ($13.80). AE, DC, MC, V. Daily noon–12:30am (afternoon tea 4–7pm). Metro: Repubblica. Tram: 1, 4, 11, 29, or 30. LIGHT INTERNATIONAL/AFTERNOON TEA/LOMBARD/ VEGETARIAN.

Its burnished paneling, plush upholstery, and soaring frescoed ceiling are some of the high points of one of Milan's most recent (and most expensive) hotel restorations. Doney borrowed its name from a historic cafe in Rome, and much of its decorative allure from the turn-of-the-century Liberty style of Italy's gilded age. Its menu features elegant but simple preparations of salads (lobster, artichokes, and pear), sandwiches (smoked salmon on brown bread), and steaks. During teatime you can select from nine kinds of tea, and pastries and finger sandwiches from a trolley. At any hour the place functions as a popular meeting point.

La Scaletta. Piazza Stazione Genova 3. ☎ **02/5810-0290.** Reservations required. Main courses 40,000L–42,000L ($24–$25.20). AE, MC, V. Mon 8–9:30pm, Tues–Sat noon–1:15pm and 8–9:30pm. Closed 1 week at Easter, Aug, and Dec 24–Jan 6. Metro: Stazione Genova. ITALIAN.

La Scaletta emerges near the top in the highly competitive world of Milanese restaurants, housed in a Liberty-style building from the turn of the century. The chefs practice modern Italian cuisine with a certain flair. Some have likened the elegant setting to a small and exclusive London club. Because this place is so popular with the Milan business community, reserve as far in advance as possible. The quality of the ingredients is superb—the chefs demand that every item be fresh. The veal dishes are heavenly. You might begin with a tripe terrine in gelatin or a scampi salad, before giving serious attention to your main course. Specialties include risotto made with green peas and wild mushrooms, a carpaccio with herbs, tagliatelle with clams and broccoli, and a pâté of snails. The signature dessert is freshly made gelato with rosemary and sage.

✪ Peck's Restaurant. Via Victor Hugo 4. ☎ **02/876-774.** Main courses 30,000L–40,000L ($18–$24); fixed-price menu 60,000L–80,000L ($36–$48). AE, DC, MC. V. Mon–Sat 12:15–2:30pm and 7:15–10:30pm. Closed 10 days in Jan and July 1–21. Metro: Duomo. MILANESE/ITALIAN.

Peck's is owned by the famous delicatessen of Milan, which gastronomes view as the Milanese equivalent of Fauchon's in Paris. It was established by Francesco Peck, who came to Milan from Prague in the 19th century. His small restaurant eventually became a food empire. In an environment filled with shimmering marble and modern Italian paintings, an alert staff will serve you an elegant cuisine. The fresh specialties include a classic version of risotto milanese, rack of lamb with fresh rosemary, *ravioli alla fonduata,* and *lombo di vitello* (veal) with artichokes, followed by chocolate meringue for dessert. Its cured meats are said to be the richest in Italy.

Taverna del Gran Sasso. Piazza Principessa Clotilde 10. ☎ **02/659-7578.** All-you-can-eat meal 60,000L ($36). MC, V. Mon–Sat 12:30–2pm and 7:30–10:30pm. Closed Jan 1 and Aug. Metro: Repubblica. ABRUZZI.

This tavern, dating from 1962, provides regional meals. Filled with lots of sentimental baubles, its walls are crowded ceiling to floor with copper molds, ears of corn, strings of pepper and garlic, and cart wheels. A tall, open hearth burns with a charcoal fire, and a Sicilian cart is laden with baskets of bread, dried figs, nuts, and kegs of wine. As you enter, you'll find a mellowed wooden keg of wine with a brass faucet (you're supposed to help yourself, using glass mugs). The cuisine features a number of specialties from the Abruzzi—regional dishes such as *maccheroni alla chitarra,* a distinctively shaped macaroni with a savory meat sauce. Meals are an all-you-can-eat feast.

✪ Trattoria Bagutta. Via Bagutta 14. ☎ **02/7600-2767.** Reservations required. Main courses 25,000L–50,000L ($15–$30). AE, DC, MC, V. Mon–Sat 12:30–2:30pm and 7:30–10:30pm. Closed Dec 24 and Jan 6. Metro: San Babila. INTERNATIONAL.

Patronized by artists, this restaurant is the most celebrated trattoria in Milan. A venerable-looking establishment from 1927, the Bagutta is known for the caricatures—framed and frescoed—that cover its walls. Of the many large and bustling dining rooms, the rear one with its picture windows is most enticing. The tempting food draws on the kitchens of Lombardy, Tuscany, and Bologna for inspiration. On offer are assorted antipasti, and main-dish specialties include fried squid and scampi, *lingua e puré* (tongue with mashed potatoes), linguine with shrimp in a tomato-cream sauce, and scaloppine alla Bagutta. The Bagutta enjoys a vogue among out-of-towners, who consider it chic to patronize the sophisticated little trattoria, as opposed to the more deluxe restaurants.

INEXPENSIVE

Al Tempio d'Oro. Via delle Leghe 23. ☎ **02/2614-5709.** Main courses 10,000L–20,000L ($6–$12). No credit cards. Mon–Sat 8pm–2am. Closed 2 weeks in mid-Aug. Metro: Pasteur. ITALIAN/INTERNATIONAL.

This restaurant, near the central railway station, offers inexpensive and well-prepared meals in an ambience similar to what you might have found if an ancient Greek temple had decided to serve beer on tap along with international food specialties. The chef is justifiably proud of his fish soup, Spanish paella, and North African couscous. The crowd scattered among the ceiling columns is relaxed, and they contribute to an atmosphere somewhat like that of a beer hall. No one will mind if you stop by just for a drink.

La Magolfa. Via Magolfa 15. ☎ **02/832-1696.** Reservations required. Main courses 18,000L ($10.80); fixed-price meal from 35,000L ($21). AE, DC, MC, V. Tues–Sun 8pm–1am. Closed Sat in July–Aug. Metro: Porta Genova. LOMBARD/INTERNATIONAL.

La Magolfa, one of the city's dining bargains, offers a gargantuan fixed-price meal. The building is a country farmhouse whose origins go back to the 1500s, although the restaurant opened only in 1960. It's likely to be crowded, as is every other restaurant in Milan that offers such value. If you don't mind its location away from the center of town, in Zona Ticinese in the southern part of the city, you'll be treated to some very good regional cookery that emerges fresh from battered pots and pans. A general air of conviviality reigns, and there's music of local origin nightly.

✪ **Peck.** Via Victor Hugo 4. ☎ **02/876-774.** Reservations required. Main courses 18,000L–22,000L ($10.80–$13.20). AE, DC, MC, V. Mon–Sat 7:30am–9pm. Closed 10 days in Jan and July 1–21. Metro: Duomo. MILANESE/LOMBARD.

Peck offers one of the best values in Milan—food served in a glamorous cafeteria associated with the most famous delicatessen in Italy (the higher-priced restaurant in the basement is listed under "Moderate," above). Only a short walk from the Duomo, Peck has a stand-up bar in front, and, in the rear, well-stocked display cases of specialties fresh from their treasure trove of produce. Armed with a plastic tray, you can sample such temptations as artichoke-and-Parmesan salad, marinated carpaccio, slabs of tender veal in an herb sauce, risotto marinara, and selections from a carving table laden with a juicy display of roast meats.

SHOPPING

London has Harrods, Paris has all the big-name boutiques you can think of, and Rome and Florence instill an acquisitional fever in the eyes of anyone who even window-gazes. Milan, however, is blessed with one of the most unusual concentrations of shopping possibilities in Europe. Most of the boutiques are infused with the style, humor, and sophistication that has made Milan the dynamo of the Italian fashion industry, a place where the sidewalks sizzle with the hard-driving entrepreneurial spirit that has been part of the northern Italian textile industry for centuries. The shops say it all—Dolce & Gabbana, Gianfranco Ferre, Moschino, Krizia, Prada, Giorgio Armani, and Gianni Versace have all catapulted to international stardom from design studios based here.

THE SHOPPING SCENE

THE GOLDEN TRIANGLE   One well-heeled shopper from Florida recently spent the better part of her vacation in Italy shopping for what she called "the most unbelievable variety of shoes, clothes, and accessories in the world." A walk on the fashion subculture's focal point, **Via Montenapoleone,** heart of the "Golden Triangle," will quickly confirm that impression. It's one of Italy's three great shopping streets, a mile-long strip that has become a showcase for famous (and high-priced) makers of clothes and shoes.

Note carefully that beauty does not come cheaply in the garment industry, and the attention you receive will often be based directly on the salesperson's impression of how much money you plan to spend. But as a handful of American models, along with design imitators from around the world, know, there are indeed riches to be discovered.

ORSO BUENOS AIRES   Bargain hunters leave the Golden Triangle and head for a 1-mile stretch called Corso Buenos Aires, where today's Evita on a budget shops for style at affordable prices. There is a dazzling array of some 400 shops along this strip. What to look for here? Virtually everything. Saturday is the worst time to go because of over-crowding. Most shopping tours begin here at the **Piazza Oberdan,** which is the square closest to the heart of Milan. Clothing abounds on this street, especially casual wear. But you'll find a vast array of merchandise, ranging from scuba-diving equipment to soft luggage. Some of the shops hawk rip-offs of designer merchandise, especially in clothing. You get the look, but not the craftsmanship.

THE BRERA AREA   The other street of bargains in Milan is the Brera area, the name given to a sprawling shopping district around the Brera Museum. This area is far more attractive than Corso Buenos Aires and has often been compared to New York's Greenwich Village because of its cafes, shops, antique stores, and art students. Skip the main street here, Via Brera, and concentrate on the side streets, especially **Via Solferino, Via Madonnina,** and **Via Fiori Chiari.** To reach the district, you can start by the La Scala opera house and continue to walk along Via Verdi, which becomes Via Brera. Running off from Via Brera to the left is the pedestrian-only street, **Via Fiori Chiari,** which is a good venue for bric-a-brac, and even some fine art deco and art nouveau pieces. Via Fiori Chiari will lead to another traffic-free street, **Via Madonnina,** which has some excellent buys in store after store in clothing. Some well-made leather goods are also hawked here. Via Madonnina eventually connects with Corso Garibaldi, a busy thoroughfare. This will take you to Via Solferino, the third-best shopping street of the district. In addition to traditional clothing and styling, a lot of eye-catching but eccentric modern clothing is sold here.

The best time to visit the Brera area is for the Mercantone dell'Antiquariato, which takes place on the third Saturday of each month (it's especially hectic at Christmastime) along Via Brera in the shadow of La Scala. Artists and designers, along with antique dealers and bric-a-brac peddlers, turn out in droves.

SHOPPING HOURS   Early-morning risers will be welcomed only by silent streets and closed gates. Most shops are closed all day Sunday and Monday (although some open on Monday afternoon). Some stores open at 9am unless they're very chic, and then they're not likely to open until 10:30am. They remain open, for the most part, until 1pm, reopening again between 3:30 and 7:30pm.

SALES   The best time for the savvy shopper to visit Milan is for the January sales, when *saldi* or "sale" signs are placed in the windows. Sales usually begin the middle of January and in some cases extend all the way through February. Prices in some emporiums are cut by as much as 50% (but don't count on it). Of course, items offered for sale are most often last season's merchandise, but nevertheless many good buys are possible. Items bought on sale cannot be returned.

BOOKS
American Bookstore. Via Camperio 16. ☎ **02/878-920.**

There are bigger and flashier bookstores in Rome, but this one will probably stock that paperback novel you're looking for, or the scholarly exegesis of Milanese artwork you should have reviewed before your trip and never did. They only stock English-language books and periodicals.

DEPARTMENT STORES
La Rinascente. Piazza del Duomo. ☎ **02/88-521.**

La Rinascente bills itself with accuracy as Italy's largest fashion department store. In addition to clothing, the basement carries a wide variety of giftware for the home, including handwork from all regions of Italy. There's an information desk on the ground floor, and on the seventh, a bank, a travel agency, Rolando hairdresser, Estée Lauder Skincare Center, a coffee bar, and the Brunch and Bistro restaurants.

Incidentally, the name of the store was suggested by the poet Gabriele d'Annunzio, for which he received a compensation of 5,000L ($3). The store was officially opened right before Christmas in the closing year of World War I, but it burned down on Christmas Eve. Rebuilt, it later met total destruction in an Allied bombing raid in 1943. But it has always rallied from disaster and now is better than ever.

FASHION

For Men

Darsena. Corso Buenos Aires 16. ☎ **02/2952-1535.**

This shop, which has far better prices than competitors in the Golden Triangle, carries very high-quality men's clothing that is both casual and elegant. Most items are the store brand, but they also sell items with such names as Armani, Valentino, and Trussardi.

Ermenegildo Zenga. Via Pietro Verri 3. ☎ **02/7600-6437.**

This shop, which opened in 1985, offers a complete range of menswear, beginning with the Sartorial line, the Zenga *haute couture* offering of suits, jackets, trousers, and accessories. The "soft line" is dedicated to a younger customer, and the sportswear collection and yachting line allow you to wander the globe with the right apparel. The shop also offers a "made-to-measure" service with a selection of 300 fabrics per season. They can make an outfit in about 4 weeks, then ship it to any destination.

✪ **Giorgio Armani.** Via San Andrea 9. ☎ **02/7600-3234.**

Giorgio Armani houses the style we've come to expect in a large showroom vaguely reminiscent of a very upscale aircraft hangar. Armani's trademark look incorporates loose-fitting, unstructured, and unpadded clothing draped loosely over firm bodies. Although there's a bit more structure to the clothes since Richard Gere made the look popular in *American Gigolo,* Armani still creates elegant upholstery for elegant people.

Mila Schön. Via Montenapoleone 2. ☎ **02/781-190.**

The sophisticated look is casually chic, hip, and expensive. If you're male, thin, and relatively muscular, you'll look terrific in Mila Schön. Mila's women's line is on the ground floor. Even the somewhat flippant accessories are stratospherically expensive.

For Women

✪ **Gianfranco Ferré.** Via della Spiga 11–13. ☎ **02/7600-0385.**

This is the only outlet in Milan for a famous designer whose women's fashions are worn by some of the world's most elegant dressers. The range is wide—perfect tailleurs and soft knitwear, organza shirts, or sensual evening dresses, along with refined leather accessories, bijoux, and foulards. Next door to the women's shop is an outlet for the designer's men's clothing. Closed in August.

✪ **Giuseppe Falzone.** Corso Cristoforo Colombo 5. ☎ **02/5810-3673.**

This shop offers stacks of designer clothing for women. Discounts are about 70% of regular boutique prices.

Micro Store. Corso Buenos Aires 23. ☎ **02/5832-0078.**

This store offers both casual and classical maternity clothes. They also sell terrific children's clothes. Prices here are most affordable, especially during the winter sales.

✪ Prada. Via della Spiga 1. ☎ **02/7600-2019.**

Prada has the best leather goods and other stylish accessories for women in Milan. *Travel & Leisure* called it "a fashion industry phenomenon." The black nylon backpack is the most popular item.

Spiga 31 di R. Bilancioni. Via della Spiga 31. ☎ **02/7602-3502.**

The inventory here includes an unusual look that the casually elegant night owl might like. Clothing ranges somewhere between sportswear and formal evening wear, without really fitting into either category. If you choose to show off a purchase from the sometimes flamboyant, sometimes discreet inventory at the country club, you won't need to worry that another woman will be wearing the same dress.

For Men & Women
Accademia. Via Solferino 11. ☎ **02/659-5961.**

In the Brera district, this is the store for men and women's outdoor clothing. They carry a variety of classical and casual styles. This is also the store to go to for men who need clothes in hard-to-find dimensions because you can order an item made-to-measure; however, it takes more than 1 month, and to have alterations, it takes 4 to 5 additional days.

Drogheria Solferino. Via Solferino, at the corner of Via Pontaccio. ☎ **02/878-740.**

In the Brera district, and quite affordable, this store stocks a wide range of clothing. Look especially for the line of knitwear and the cotton or silk blouses. You can find rather elegant men's and women's ready-to-wear clothing and shoes.

Gemelli. Corso Vercelli 16. ☎ **02/433-404.**

This store sells well-made clothes for men, women, babies, and teenagers, which, while stylish and serviceable, are neither as glamorous nor as chillingly expensive as some of the city's more famous clothiers. Everything here is off the rack; there's no custom-tailoring service.

Il Drug Store. Corso Buenos Aires 28. ☎ **02/2951-5592.**

Despite its name, this shop sells men's and women's clothing for the young and for the young at heart. It's one of the best places to shop along this bargain-flanked street. "It's cheap, but trendy," one young customer told us. There is an interesting selection of sweaters both embroidered and ornamented. Knits and dresses with that young look are always sold here but there's a fast turnover in merchandise.

Primavera. Via Torino 47. ☎ **02/874-565.**

When the high prices of Milano fashion are beyond your means, go here for stylish clothing (both men and women) at bargain-basement prices.

Urrah. Via Solferino 3. ☎ **02/864-385.**

This shop offers high-quality, casual clothing for men and women. The store in the Brera district is known for its "no name" but well-designed fashions. They carry rather modern styles, so traditional dressers beware.

GIFTS
G. Lorenzi. Via Montenapoleone 9. ☎ **02/7602-2848.**

In this tiny store, you'll find everything you were looking for in the way of small gifts—and a lot of stuff you've never seen before. Many are one-of-a-kind items.

JEWELRY

✪ Mario Buccellati. Via Montenapoleone 4. ☎ 02/7600-2153.

Mario Buccellati offers the best-known—and the most expensive—silver and jewels in Italy. The designs of the cast-silver bowls, tureens, and christening cups are nothing short of rhapsodic, and the quality is among the finest in the world.

✪ Meru. Via Solferino 3. ☎ 02/8646-0700.

Back in the Brera district, Meru sells consciously avant-garde jewelry, rumored to have been worn and privately publicized by young and beautiful European film stars. Many of the pieces are set into enameled backgrounds and often include unusual types of gemstones such as rose quartz, coral, and amber. Leather-and-gold combinations are also used. All pieces are made by Meru craftspeople. Closed July 30 to September 10.

LACE

✪ Jesurum. Via Verri 4. ☎ 02/7601-5045.

This is the Milanese outlet of a Venice-based lace company that has been famous since 1870. Set on a very short street where none of the buildings have an obvious street number, it sells all-lace or lace-edged tablecloths, doilies, and all the handmade textiles that a bride might like to add to her trousseau. It also sells lace blouses, even a swimming suit (which might be better suited to a photo session than to a game of water polo) and lace by the meter for trimming curtains or whatever.

LEATHER GOODS & SHOES

Alfonso Garlando. Via Madonnina 2. ☎ 02/8646-3733.

The prices on the merchandise here at the Brera area shop range up to the very expensive, but the shop's size and lack of concern for a stylish showroom almost guarantees a reasonable choice of merchandise at a reasonable price. They sell shoes for men and women, but not children.

✪ Beltrami. Via Montenapoleone 16. ☎ 02/7602-3422.

Prices are chillingly high here, but the leather goods for men and women are among the best you'll find in the world. The showroom is appropriately glamorous, the merchandise appropriately chic. Beltrami has another shop at Piazza San Babila 4A (☎ 02/7600-0546).

Calzaturificio di Parabiago. Corso Buenos Aires 52. ☎ 02/2940-6851.

This factory-outlet store carries classical and casual shoes for men and women. The price range varies from relatively inexpensive to expensive. But most of the merchandise is sold at discount prices along this "street of bargains." Parabiago is one of the major shoe-manufacturing areas of the country.

Gucci. Via Montenapoleone 5. ☎ 02/7601-3050.

Gucci is the Milanese headquarters for the most famous leather-goods distributor in Italy. Its shoes, luggage, and wallets for men and women, handbags, and leatherware accessories usually have the colors of the Italian flag (olive and crimson) stitched in the form of a more-or-less discreet ribbon across the front of most merchandise.

✪ Salvatore Ferragamo. Via Montenapoleone 3. ☎ 02/7600-6660.

The label is instantly recognizable and the quality high at this shop that has created and designed shoes since the 1930s for the fashion goddesses and gods of Europe and Hollywood. Rigidly controlled by a large and extended second generation of the original founders, it's still a leader in style and allure. The store contains inventories of shoes, luggage, and accessories for women and men. Also for sale are Ferragamo leather jackets, pants, and a small selection of clothing.

Sebastian. Via Borgospesso 18. ☎ **02/780-532.**

Sebastian sells excellent shoes for men and women from a ready-made stockpile of over 150 fashionable models, which Sebastian makes in its own factories. For almost the same price (if you don't mind waiting 2 months or more) you can order custom-made shoes, shipped anywhere. Custom-made shoes are usually available only in women's styles. This is a boon for clients with wide, narrow, large, or small feet, who consider Sebastian something of a sartorial and orthopedic blessing.

Tanino Crisci. Via Montenapoleone 3. ☎ **02/7602-1264.**

Its showroom of oiled paneling and conservative leather chairs evokes the interior of a private club in London. Its inventory includes elegantly conservative footwear for men and women, but its most famous products are the leather boots that will make you look like an ace equestrian, polo player, or stalker of big game—even if they haven't been your lifelong hobbies.

LINGERIE

B. Finzi. Galleria Vittorio Emanuele. ☎ **02/8646-0920.**

Styles of underwear have changed since this shop was established in 1859, but the Milanese demand for both practical and frivolous unmentionables has continued unabated. (The polite Italian word for these is *biancheria intima*.) Most of the stock here is for all kinds and types of women—look especially for the satin-trimmed silk camisoles—but there's also a selection of underwear for men (most of which seems to be bought by wives or companions).

MALLS

Caffè Moda Durini. Corso Venezio 8. ☎ **02/7602-0658.**

Despite the implications of its name, this is actually a shopping complex filled with the deliberately informal offshoots of some of the most renowned clothing designers in Italy. Its focal point is a ground-floor cafe and bar around which all the gossip of the neighborhood seems to ebb and flow. Radiating outward, and stretching over three different levels, are at least 20 different shops. These include jeans outlets of both Valentino and Gianfranco Ferré, and informal (but still expensive) outlets for Missoni, Valentino Uomo, and Krizia Poi. Each boutique maintains its own hours, but most of them are open nonstop Monday to Saturday from 10am to 7pm. A few of the smaller shops might close briefly for lunch. The complex is located about a block behind the Palazzo Reale.

✪ Galleria Vittorio Emanuele II. Corso Vittorio Emanuelle II.

One of the most famous landmarks in Milan, this huge three-story complex is reminiscent of a railway station and the architectural details may impress you as much—or more—than any shop located within it. Its features include vaulted glass ceilings merging in a huge central dome, decorative window and door casings, elaborate bas-reliefs, huge arched frescoes, wrought-iron globe lamps, and a decorative tile floor with increasingly intricate patterns in the main concourse. You can browse in shops that include a Prada boutique and a Rizzoli bookstore, or grab a caffè from one of the bistros and relax while people-watching. It's worth a stop even if shopping isn't your top priority.

Italian Design: From Retro to the Restless

Since the laissez-faire indulgences of *La Dolce Vita,* no one has denied the whimsy, the allure, and the sheer intelligence of Italian design. Many people born after the age of Sputnik know how Olivetti used to win awards for designs of everything from typewriters to office calculators, and there isn't a red-blooded movie star in Beverly Hills who doesn't experience a meltdown at the possibility of acquiring a Lamborghini whose organic-looking, air-streamed lines are more alluring in some circles than (dare we admit it) sex?

Why is Italian design so wonderful? Murry Moss, owner of Moss, a design store in New York's Soho that's made a living bringing the real Italian McCoy to the Anglo-Saxon world, says, "The Italians are good at taking something simple, like a plain white tile, and making a big deal out of it. The point is that everyone who looks at it, goes, 'Ah.'"

Consumers began to say "Ah!" to Italian objects during the *belle époque,* when Liberty style carried art nouveau to more serpentine limits. In 1918, Adele Fendi, matriarch of the worldwide empire, convinced thousands of chic Italians they'd be underdressed without a wardrobe of fur coats—hardly a necessity in steamy Italy, but commercially viable nonetheless. In 1920, Elsa Schiaparelli elevated a simple black sweater with a trompe l'oeil bow into high chic. Within a decade, her "pagoda sleeve" hats, inspired by the shape of a veal cutlet, and "Schiaparelli (i.e., hot) pink" entered the mainstream of chic. In 1925, an obscure Neapolitan shoemaker (Salvatore Ferragamo) emigrated to Hollywood, where Greta Garbo, Marion Davies, and Gloria Swanson quickly became visibly devoted to his products, and where the divine Ms. Crawford wore his wedge heels more glamorously than any other woman before or since. (Later clients, after the maestro's return to Italy, included Queen Elizabeth *Secondo*—who did not wear wedgies—and her more fashionable sister, Margaret.)

In 1948, Ottavio Missoni, later part-owner of the knitwear empire, installed zippers along the length of his track suits, revolutionizing the design of form-fitting ski suits ever since. (In 1978, the Whitney Museum exhibited his geometric designs as works of art in their own right.) In 1950, Emilio Pucci—a designer who elevated Italian temperament to heights not known since Emperor Nero—introduced what's now proclaimed as the precursor of psychedelic fashion. In 1951, the Fontana sisters raised their mother's small dressmaking shop to the level of haute couture, scoring their biggest success with their design for the wedding dress of Margaret (daughter of Harry) Truman. In 1957, Mariuccia Mandeli, an ex-elementary school teacher, elevated photo-printed fabric to worldwide notoriety. Her corporate logo (Krizia) was inspired from a line within an essay by Plato on the nature of women's vanity.

In 1968, Jacqueline Kennedy wore a Valentino dress during her much-photographed marriage to "the Greek." In a buying spree that had never before happened in the rarefield world of haute couture, the same dress was then ordered by 38 other women. Between 1970 and 1985, Giorgio Armani, Gianfranco Ferré (later the artistic director of Dior), Moschino, Versace, Domenico Dolce and Stefano Gabbana (founders of Dolce & Gabbana), and Trussari all burst upon the world's fashion scenes. In 1996, in honor of the 50th anniversary of the bikini, Italian designers "reinvented" the two-piece bathing suit.

In today's fashion, the look has fragmented into sideshows that reflect the varied cultural origins that combine to form big-city life. It's fashionable to revisit fashion history, often in ways that stress the tongue-in-cheek and the whimsical. At the Milan fashion shows of 1997, Alessandro Dell'Acqua offered an image lifted straight from the novels of Jack Kerouac, mixing high heels with cut-off T-shirts and a minimum of fabric. Gucci's collection mixed colors and leather-metallic accessories that might appeal to a rock-and-roll star with slinky silk and stretchy knits, often in very basic black. Milan's hot new designer, Lawrence Steele, combined blue velvet army boots with lace—a look somewhere between the bedroom and the battlefield—in a way that would never have been approved by Il Duce.

Romeo Gigli wowed Milan in 1997 with intricate needlepoint embroideries on softly contoured designs crafted from some of the most appealing velvet in decades. Even bad-boy Moschino, accused of resorting to cheap voyeuristic thrills and exhibitionism in the past, now offers a strong sense of the geometric, plus inspirations from avant-garde, post–Cold War Russia. The ever-appealing Versace entered a new period of sternness with tailored black suits, contrasting materials, and subtle references to 1980 fashion visionary Yves St-Laurent. The ever-so-stylish darling of Hollywood, Armani—lately the most visible designer at the Academy Awards— continues to produce artfully simple suits and jackets for men and women that seem to conform gracefully to the bodies of the young, the beautiful, the restless, and those rich enough to afford it.

What about utilitarian objects in the Italian style? In the recent past, Italian design has been identified by a coolly calculated minimalism and graceful references to American corporate culture. Furniture was well considered and elegant, patterned after the High Temple of the style as exemplified in Philip Johnson's Seagram Building in New York, reflecting overscale proportions, smoothly rectangular but not particularly dramatic forms, high gloss, and a sophisticated mixture of natural and synthetic materials. Adam Tihany, well-known decorator of the most recent version of Le Cirque in Manhattan, referred to Milan's recent design trends as "sophisticated American corporate retro."

But in 1997, during Milan's 36th International Furniture Fair—when anyone who was anyone in the rarefied world of cutting-edge design could be seen rummaging through the display areas of the artists who matter—there were lots of opportunities for spectators to say, "Ah!" The drama resulted from a new crop of upstarts whose sheer, unexpected whimsy was presented in ways that either irritated or delighted. Couches were upholstered in red vinyl, looking like daybeds large enough for four to sleep (or whatever) comfortably, accessorized by outrageously poofy pillows. Tables were composed of grandmother's lace tablecloth dipped in epoxy, floor tiles designed for bathrooms were covered with glass contours as a means of massaging the feet, and bathroom sinks were fashioned from a flexible, rubberlike plastic that can be bashed during arguments or bent to allow passage for bodies through cramped spaces.

Chairs identified by their designers as "swinging divans" might combine uncomfortable-looking metal spikes with a single piece of triple-thick felt, and be marketed directly to people relaxing during "downtime off the Internet." Lots of the new look in furniture is designed as cost-conscious furniture for nomadic apartment dwellers, and can be disassembled and rolled into an easy-to-transport bundle—presumably for setup near another Internet station.

How can you identify a cutting-edge piece of Italian design? In the words of one designer, "I hope that if someone digs up one of the season's best designs in someone's garden a century from now, it will be instantly recognized as coming from right now."

PAPER
I Giorni di Carta. Corso Garibaldi 81. ☎ **02/655-2514.**

In the Brera district, this is one of the city's most unusual outlets for writing paper and stationery, with dozens of different colors, textures, and weights. Much of the inventory is made from recycled paper. They do not always sell the same things. It depends on what they find. The establishment also sells briefcases to carry your letters, pens and ink, notebooks, lamps, dishes, dolls, and ornamental paperweights.

PERFUMES
Profumo. Via Brera 6. ☎ **02/7202-3334.**

Profumo in the Brera district sells some of Italy's most exotic perfumes for women, plus cologne and aftershave lotions for men. Some Italian scents are exclusively distributed here near the American Express office.

PORCELAIN & CRYSTAL
Richard-Ginori. Corso Buenos Aires 1. ☎ **02/2951-6611.**

Since 1735 this company has manufactured and sold porcelain to dukes, duchesses, and ordinary bourgeois consumers, who seek out the best deals along the street of affordable merchandise. A household word in Italy, Ginori sells ovenproof porcelain in both modern and traditional themes, as well as crystal and silverware that they either make themselves or inventory from other manufacturers such as Baccarat or Wedgwood.

PRINTS & ENGRAVINGS
Raimondi di Pettinaroli. Corso Venezia 6. ☎ **02/7600-2412.**

This is considered the finest shop in Milan for antique prints and engravings, plus reprints of old engravings made from the original copper plates. It was originally established in 1776. Of particular interest are the engravings of Italian cityscapes during the 19th century, and the many treasures worth framing after you return home.

SUNGLASSES
Salmoiraghi Vigano. Corso Matteotti 22. ☎ **02/7600-0100.**

This shop is known for having the best-looking sunglasses in Italy, attracting all trendoids. It's for those who want to look like Marcello Mastroianni in *La Dolce Vita*.

MILAN AFTER DARK

As in Rome, many of the top nightclubs in Milan shut down for the summer, when the cabaret talent and the bartenders pack their bags and head for the hills or the seashore. However, Milan is a big city, and there are always plenty of after-dark diversions. This sprawling metropolis is also one of the cultural centers of Europe.

THE PERFORMING ARTS

The most complete list of cultural events appears in the large Milan newspaper, the left-wing *La Repubblica*. Try for a Thursday edition, usually with the most complete listings.

✪ **Teatro alla Scala.** Piazza della Scala. ☎ **02/809-126,** or 02/861-772 or 02/861-781 for tickets Tues–Sun noon–3pm. Tickets 10,000L–270,000L ($6–$172.80). Metro: Duomo.

If you have only a night for Milan and are here between mid-December and September, try to attend a performance at the world-famous Teatro alla Scala. Built to the designs of Piermarini, the neoclassic opera house was restored after World War II bomb damage. The greatest opera stars appear here, and the Milanese first-night audience is the hardest to please in the world. Tickets are also extremely hard to come by and are sold out weeks in advance. However, you do stand a chance of getting gallery tickets—seats so far up they should be called celestial. The box office is open Tuesday to Sunday from noon to 7pm. You may also reserve by phone. Note that the opera house will be closing for restorations at the end of the spring 1998 season until sometime after the year 2000.

Opera lovers will also want to visit the **Museo Teatrale alla Scala (☎ 02/ 805-3418)** in the same building. Established in 1913, it contains a rich collection of historical mementos and records of the heady world of opera. Among them are busts and portraits of such artists as Beethoven, Chopin, Donizetti, Verdi, and Puccini. Two halls are devoted to Verdi alone, with objects including scores written in his own hand and the spinet on which he learned to play. Rossini's eyeglasses and his pianoforte tuning key are in a case, and there are many other such treasures, including a death-cast of Chopin's left hand. A small gallery honors Toscanini, with his batons, medals, and pince-nez on display. One of the greatest thrills for opera lovers who may not be in Milan at the time of a performance at La Scala—or may not be able to get tickets—will be the view from the third floor. From here, you can look down on the theater's ornate auditorium with its velvet draperies. Charging 5,000L ($3) for admission, the museum is open May to October, Monday to Saturday from 9am to 12:30pm and 2 to 5:30pm; November to April, Monday to Sunday from 9am to 12:30pm and 2 to 5:30pm.

Conservatorio. Via del Conservatorio 12. ☎ **02/762-1101.** Tickets 25,000L–60,000L ($15–$36). Metro: San Babila.

The Conservatorio, in the San Babila sector, features the finest in classical music. Year-round, a cultured Milanese audience enjoys high-quality programs of widely varied classical concerts.

Piccolo Teatro. Via Rovello 2 (near Via Dante). ☎ **02/7233-3222.** Tickets 50,000L ($30). Metro: Cordusio or Cairoli.

The Piccolo Teatro became a socialist theater in the years after World War II, but now the city of Milan is the landlord. Programs are varied today, and performances are in Italian. Its director, Giorgio Strehler, is acclaimed as one of the most avant garde and talented in the world. The theater lies between the Duomo and the Castle of the Sforzas. It's sometimes hard to obtain seats here. No shows are presented on Monday, and it's closed in August. For more information call ☎ 02/762-1101 Monday through Saturday from 10am to 7pm and Sunday from 10am to 6:30pm.

THE CLUB & MUSIC SCENE

Ca'Bianca Club. Via Lodovico il Moro 117. ☎ **02/8912-5777.** Cover 30,000L ($18) including show and the first drink, 90,000L–100,000L ($54–$60) with dinner.

Ca'Bianca has a changing offering of live music and dancing on Wednesday night, which ranges from folk music to cabaret to Dixieland jazz. Technically this is a private club, but no one at the door will prevent nonmembers from entering. The show—whatever it may be—begins at 11pm. The club is open daily from 8:30pm to 1am; closed in August.

Capolinea. Via Lodovico II Moro 119. ☎ **02/8912-2024.** No cover.

Since its establishment in the 1970s, this has been one of the most appealing jazz clubs in town, with an ongoing roster of jazz acts of every imaginable ilk. Doors open nightly at 8pm and music is performed from 10:30pm to 1 or 1:30am, depending on business and the night of the week.

Club Astoria. Piazza Santa Maria Beltrade 2. ☎ **02/8646-3710.** No cover.

This popular nightclub is one of the most frequented in town, especially by the expense-account-junket crowd. When there's a floor show, a drink might cost around 50,000L ($30), which takes the place of a cover charge. Otherwise, drinks begin at 30,000L ($18). Open Monday to Saturday from 10:30pm to 4am.

Coquetel. Via Vetere 14. ☎ **02/836-0688.** No cover.

It's loud, it's wild, and it celebrates the American-style party-colored cocktail with a whimsy that could only be all Italian. The action around here, coupled with babble from dozens of regular clients, ain't exactly sedate, and you might just get swept away by the energy of it all. It's open Monday to Saturday from 8pm to 2am.

Facsimile. Via Tallone 11. ☎ **02/738-0635.** No cover, but a one-drink minimum.

This bar and *birreria* is a popular rendezvous point where Milanese rockers can commune with their favorite video stars in living color. The decor is almost entirely gray and red, and there are outdoor tables for stargazing. Drinks range upward from 4,000L to 8,000L ($2.40 to $4.80). The bar is open Tuesday to Sunday from 9am to 1am.

Killer Plastic. Viale Umbria 120. ☎ **02/733-996.**

This is the most oft-changed disco in Milan, and also the most often cited as everybody's favorite. Your experience will depend largely on the night you happen to show up. Thursday is gay night, welcoming gay men—and to a lesser extent, lesbians—onto the high-tech dance floors, whereas Saturday is crammed with the crème of the city's *alta moda* nightlife crowd. Other nights, the site is animated, high-energy, and exhibitionistic in see-and-be-seen modes that seem completely appropriate to the glamor of Milano. Doors usually open Thursday to Sunday, from 10:30pm to around 3am or later, depending on the crowd.

Le Scimmie. Via Ascanio Sforza 49. ☎ **02/8940-2874.** No cover.

Established in 1981, this place echoes with applause and approval for the various types of live music that are the norm here. Depending on the venue, bands play everything from funk to blues to creative jazz to an appreciative audience that shows up every night except Tuesday. Doors open around 8pm, and music is presented between 10pm and around 12:30am.

Rock Hollywood. Corso Como 15. El. **02/659-8996.** Cover 25,000L–30,000L ($15–$18) includes the first drink.

It's small, intimate, and has a sound system that's so good you might get swept up in the animated fun of it all. Let your hair down, dress whimsically or in your best party-down costume, and dance, dance, dance. No matter how attractive you might think you are, be assured that there will be dozens of contenders here whose main business seems only to maintain themselves as beautifully as possible. It's open Tuesday to Sunday from 10:30pm to at least 3am.

Rolling Stone. Corso XXII Marzo 32. ☎ **02/733-172.** Cover Fri 20,000L ($12), Sat 25,000L ($15), other days 12,000L ($7.20).

This club was established for the Beat Generation of the 1950s, later attracting *la dolce vita* crowd in the 1960s. In 1984 it adopted its present rock-and-roll preoccupation, featuring heavy metal and an ocean of aggressively energetic groups in their 20s. Its open every night, usually from 10:30pm to 4am, but don't even consider showing up here until at least midnight (otherwise you'll have the place to yourself). For some concerts, the place doesn't open until 1am. Closed in July and August.

Gay Clubs

Nuova Idea International. Via de Castillia 30. ☎ **02/6900-7859.** Cover 15,000L ($9) Thurs–Fri and Sun, 25,000L ($15) Sat, includes the first drink.

This is the largest, oldest, most active, and most fun gay disco in Italy, very much tied in to the urban bustle of modern Milan. Its sense of freedom would be unthinkable in smaller towns in the provinces. It prides itself on mimicking the examples of the large, all-gay discos of northern Europe. It draws a patronage of young and not-so-young men, many of whom are film or theater actors. There's a large video screen and occasional live entertainment. It's open Thursday to Sunday from 9:30pm to 2:30am.

Zip. Corso Sempione 76 (at Via Salvioni). ☎ **02/331-4904.** Cover 30,000L–40,000L ($18–$24) includes the first drink.

One of the most deliberately raunchy gay clubs in southern Europe, Zip is a *club privato,* although non-Italian newcomers can enter upon presentation of a passport. This dive contains a labyrinth of inner rooms devoted to a disco with a clientele of gay males, a late-night cafeteria, a screen showing gay porno, and a dark room where the action is uninhibited. The disco opens Wednesday through Sunday night at 12:30am, but no one arrives before 2:30 or 3am. It shuts down for a much-needed rest at 6am (on Saturday, not until 8am). The establishment lies in back of Castello Sforzesco. If you attend, be alert to the neighborhood at this late hour, and exercise caution once you're inside.

THE BAR SCENE

Al Teatro. Corso Garibaldi 16. ☎ **02/864-222.**

Decorated a bit like a bohemian parlor of the last century, this is a popular bar across the street from the Teatro Fossati. It opens for morning coffee Tuesday to Sunday at 4pm, and closes (after several changes of ambience) at 3am. At night there's sometimes musical entertainment, but most of the time clients seem perfectly happy to drink, gossip, and flirt. In addition to coffee and drinks, the establishment serves toasts and tortes. In fine weather tables are set outside on Corso Garibaldi.

Bar Giamaica. Via Brera 32. ☎ **02/876-723.**

The place is loud and bustling, and seats its customers with a no-nonsense kind of gruff humor. That, however, is part of the allure of a bar that has attracted writers and artists for many years, and is one of the mainstays of the Milanese night scene. The personalities who work here haven't changed in years. If you want only a drink, you'll have lots of company among the office workers who jostle around the tiny tables, often standing because of the lack of room. It's open as a restaurant Monday to Saturday from noon to 2:30pm and 7:30 to 10pm. Meals range from 20,000L ($12) (for a salad and a beer) to as much as 45,000L ($27) (for a full Italian regalia). Reservations are not accepted, but you won't lack company while waiting at the bar for a table. The bar opens at 9am Monday to Saturday and remains open until around 12:30am or later. Closed 1 week in mid-August.

Grand Hotel Pub. Via Ascanio Sforza 75. ☎ **02/8951-1586.**

Despite its name, this establishment does not rent rooms, or even pretend to be grand. Instead, it's a large, animated restaurant and pub with frequent live music or cabaret. In summer the crowds can move quickly from the smoky interior into a sheltered garden. The evening's entertainment is live jazz and rock music. Most visitors come here only for a drink, but if you're hungry, the restaurant charges around 50,000L ($30) for a full meal. The place is open Tuesday to Sunday from 8pm to 2am. Entrance is usually free.

THE CAFE SCENE

Every city in Italy seems to have a cafe or two filled with 19th-century detailing and memories of Verdi or some such famous person. It usually offers a wide variety of pastries and a particular kind of clientele who gossip, sip espresso, munch snacks, and compare notes on shopping. All service at the tables is more expensive, as is the rule in Europe.

Berlin Café. Via Gian Giacomo Mora 9. ☎ **02/839-2605.**

As its name implies, the decor emulates a cafe in turn-of-the-century Berlin; the ambience is enhanced with etched glass and marble-topped tables. It's a great spot for coffee or a drink. A variety of simple snack food is available, primarily during the day. One drawback is the surly staff. It's open Tuesday to Sunday from 10am to 2am.

Café Cova. Via Montenapoleone 8. ☎ **02/7600-0578.**

Amid a chic assemblage of garment-district personnel and the shoppers who support them, this cafe follows a routine established in 1817. This involves concocting gallons of heady espresso and dispensing staggering amounts of pralines, chocolates, brioches, and sandwiches from behind a glass display case. The more elegant sandwiches contain smoked salmon and truffles. Clients drink their espresso from fragile gold-rimmed cups at one of the small tables in an elegant inner room or while standing at the prominent bar. Most of the action takes place at the bar, so you don't really need a table unless you're exhausted from too much shopping. Open Monday to Saturday from 8am to 8pm; closed in August.

Pasticceria Taveggia. Via Visconti di Modrone 2. ☎ **02/7602-1257.**

Established in 1910, this is one of the oldest and most historic cafes of Milan. Behind ornate glass doors set into the 19th-century facade, Taveggia makes the best cappuccino and espresso in town. To match this quality, a variety of brioches, pastries, candies, and tortes is offered. Freshly made on the premises, they can be enjoyed while standing at the bar or seated in the Victorian tearoom. Food items range from 8,000L to 25,000L ($4.80 to $15). Taveggia is open Tuesday to Sunday from 7:30am to 8:30pm; closed in August.

SIDE TRIPS FROM MILAN

The ✪ **Certosa** (Charter House) of Pavia, Via Monumento 4 (☎ **0382/925-613**), marks the pinnacle of the Renaissance statement in Lombardy. The Carthusian monastery is 5 miles north of the town of Pavia and 19 miles south of Milan. It was founded in 1396, but not completed until years afterward, and is one of the most harmonious structures in Italy. The facade, studded with medallions and adorned with colored marble and sculptural work, was designed in part by Amadeo, who worked on the building in the late 15th century. Inside, much of its rich decoration is achieved by frescoes reminiscent of an illustrated storybook. You'll find works by Perugino *(The Everlasting Father)* and Bernardino Luini *(Madonna and Child)*. Gian Galeazzo Visconti, the founder of the Certosa, is buried in the south transept.

Through an elegantly decorated portal you enter the cloister, noted for its exceptional terra-cotta decorations. In the cloister is a continuous chain of elaborate "cells," attached villas with their own private gardens and loggia. Admission is free, but donations are requested. It's open May to August, daily from 9 to 11:30am and 2:30 to 6pm; in March, April, September, and October, Tuesday to Sunday from 9 to 11:30am and 2:30 to 5pm; November to February, Tuesday to Sunday from 9 to 11:30am and 2:30 to 4:30pm.

Buses run between Milan and Pavia every hour from 5am to 10pm daily, taking 50 minutes and costing 4,500L ($2.70) one-way. Trains leave Milan bound for Pavia once every hour, at a one-way fare of 3,600L ($2.15). Motorists can take Route 35 south from Milan or take A7 to Binasco and continue on Route 35 to Pavia and its Certosa.

2 Bergamo

31 miles NE of Milan, 373 miles NW of Rome

Known for its defenses and wealth since the Middle Ages, Bergamo is one of the most characteristic Lombard hill towns. Many of the town's stone fortifications were built on Roman foundations by the medieval Venetians, who looked upon Bergamo as one of the gems of their trading network during several centuries of occupation. Set on a hilltop between the Seriana and the Brembana valleys, Bergamo lies in the alpine foothills, in a setting similar to what you might expect in the hills of Umbria or Tuscany.

The Old Town (Città Alta), set 900 feet above sea level, is buttressed by and terraced upon the original Venetian fortifications. About half a mile downhill is the New Town (usually identified by residents simply as "Bergamo"), with many 19th- and early 20th-century buildings. A settlement of wide streets and northern Italian bourgeois prosperity, this modern metropolis and industrial center contains the bus and railway stations, most hotels, and the town's commercial and administrative center. The two-in-one aspect of Bergamo, as well as its role in the mercantile history of Lombardy, was analyzed and praised by one of its strongest champions, the 19th-century French novelist Stendhal.

Bergamo has many famous native sons, including the *maestro of bel canto* in the composer, Gaetano Donizetti. The great Venetian painters, Palma Vecchio and Lorenzo Lotto, were actually from Bergamo, as was the master of the portrait, Gian Battista Moroni. Bergamo even gave the world the "Bergomask," the peasant dance at the end of *A Midsummer's Night Dream.*

ESSENTIALS

GETTING THERE   By Train   Trains arrive from Milan once every hour, depositing passengers in the center of the new town. The trip takes an hour, and a one-way ticket costs 5,100L ($3.05). For information about rail connections in Bergamo call ☎ **035/247-624.**

By Bus   The bus station in Bergamo is across from the train station. For information or schedules call ☎ **035/240-240.** Buses arrive from Milan once every 30 minutes; a one-way ticket costs 7,200L ($4.30).

By Car   From Milan, head east on autostrada A4.

VISITOR INFORMATION   The **tourist information office** is on Piazzale Marconi, Vicolo Aquila Nera 2 (☎ **035/242-226**). From April through September, hours are 9am to 12:30pm and 2:30 to 5:30pm.

EXPLORING THE UPPER TOWN

For the sightseer, the higher the climb the more rewarding the view. The ✪ **Città Alta** is replete with narrow circuitous streets, old squares, splendid monuments, and imposing and austere medieval architecture that prompted d'Annunzio to call it "a city of muteness." To reach the Upper Town, take bus no. 1 or 3, then a 10-minute walk up Viale Vittorio Emanuele.

The heart of the Upper Town is **Piazza Vecchia,** which has witnessed most of the town's upheavals and a parade of conquerors ranging from Attila to the Nazis. On the square is the Palazzo della Ragione (the town hall), an 18th-century fountain, and the Palazzo Nuovo of Scamozzi (the town library).

A vaulted arcade connects Piazza Vecchia with Piazza del Duomo. Opening onto the latter is the cathedral of Bergamo, which has a baroque overlay. D'Annunzio said of the **Basilica di Santa Maria Maggiore** that it seemed "to blossom in a rose-filtered light." Built in the Romanesque style, the church was founded in the 12th century. Much later it was baroqued on its interior and given a disturbingly busy ceiling. There are exquisite Flemish and Tuscan tapestries displayed that incorporate such themes as the Annunciation and the Crucifixion. The choir, designed by Lotto, dates from the 16th century. In front of the main altar is a series of inlaid panels depicting such themes as Noah's Ark and David and Goliath. The basilica is open Monday to Saturday from 8am to noon and 3 to 6pm and Sunday from 9am to 12:45pm and 3 to 6pm.

Also opening onto Piazza del Duomo is the ✪ **Colleoni Chapel,** which honors the already-inflated ego of the Venetian military hero. The Renaissance chapel, with an inlaid marble facade reminiscent of Florence, was designed by Giovanni Antonio Amadeo, who is chiefly known for his creation of the Certosa in Pavia. For the *condottiere,* Amadeo built an elaborate tomb, surmounted by a gilded equestrian statue (Colleoni was also the subject of one of the world's most famous equestrian statues, which now stands on a square in Venice). The tomb sculpted for the soldier's daughter, Medea, is much less elaborate. Giovanni Battista Tiepolo painted most of the frescoes on the ceiling. From March through October, it is open Tuesday through Sunday from 9am to noon and 2 to 6:30pm; off-season, Tuesday through Sunday from 9am to noon and 2:30 to 4:30pm. Admission is free.

Facing the cathedral is the baptistery, which dates from Giovanni da Campione's design in the mid-14th century but was rebuilt at the end of the 19th century.

EXPLORING THE NEW TOWN

✪ **Galleria dell'Accademia Carrara.** Piazza Giacomo Carrara 82A. ☎ **035/399-643.** Admission 5,000L ($3) adults, free for children 17 and under and seniors 60 and over. Wed–Mon 9:30am–12:15pm and 2:30–5:15pm.

Filled with a wide-ranging collection of the works of homegrown artists, as well as Venetian and Tuscan masters, the academy draws art lovers from all over the world. The most important works are on the top floor—head here first if your time is limited. The Botticelli portrait of Giuliano di Medici is well known, and another room contains three different versions of Giovanni Bellini's favorite subject, the *Madonna and Child.* It's interesting to compare his work with that of his brother-in-law, Andrea Mantegna, whose *Madonna and Child* is also displayed, as is Vittore Carpaccio's *Nativity of Maria,* which was seemingly inspired by Flemish painters.

Farther along you encounter a most original treatment of the old theme of the *Madonna and Child*—this one the work of Cosmé Tura of Ferrara. Also displayed are three tables of a predella by Lotto and his *Holy Family with St. Catherine* (wonderful composition), and Raphael's *St. Sebastian.* The entire wall space of another room is taken up with paintings by Moroni (1523–78), a local artist who seemingly did portraits of everybody who could afford it. In the salons to follow, foreign masters, such as Rubens, van der Meer, and Jan Brueghel, are represented, along with Guardi's architectural renderings of Venice and Longhi's continuing parade of Venetian high society.

WHERE TO STAY

Agnello d'Oro. Via Gombito 22, 24100 Bergamo. ☎ **035/249-883.** Fax 035/235-612. 20 rms. TV TEL. 125,000L ($75) double. AE, DC, V.

Agnello d'Oro is an intimate, old-style country inn right in the heart of Città Alta, facing a handkerchief square with a splashing fountain. It's an atmospheric background for good food or an adequate bedroom, all refurbished in 1995. When you enter the cozy reception lounge, ring an old bell to bring the owner away from the kitchen. You dine at wooden tables and sit on carved ladderback chairs. Among the à la carte offerings are three worthy regional specialties. Try *casoncelli alla bergamasca,* a succulent ravioli dish, or *quaglie farcite* (quail stuffed and accompanied by slices of polenta). The room becomes a tavern lounge between meals. The restaurant is closed Sunday night and Monday.

Hotel Cappello d'Oro. Viale Papa Giovanni XXIII 12, 24100 Bergamo. ☎ **035/232-503.** Fax 035/242-946. 124 rms. MINIBAR TV TEL. 221,000L ($132.60) double. Rates include breakfast. AE, DC, MC, V. Parking 30,000L ($18).

Hotel Cappello d'Oro is a renovated 150-year-old corner building on a busy street in the center of New Town, at Porta Nuova near the railway station. The 19th-century facade has been stuccoed, and the public rooms and the bedrooms are functional, high-ceilinged, and clean. The rooms are adequately but rather plainly furnished, and 80 of them are air-conditioned. If you need a parking space, reserve it along with your room.

Hotel Excelsior San Marco. Piazza della Repubblica 6, 24122 Bergamo. ☎ **035/366-111.** Fax 035/223-201. 163 rms, 3 suites. A/C MINIBAR TV TEL. 301,000L ($180.60) double; 430,000L ($258) suite. Rates include breakfast. AE, DC, MC, V. Parking 30,000L ($18) indoors, 20,000L ($12) outdoors.

This 35-year-old establishment at the edge of a city park is about midway between the old and new towns, both of which might be visible from the balcony of your room. The lobby contains a small bar, reddish stone accents, and low-slung leather chairs. The most prominent theme of the ceiling frescoes is the lion of St. Mark. The bedrooms are attractively furnished and comfortable.

WHERE TO DINE

✪ **Ristorante da Vittorio.** Viale Papa Giovanni XXIII 21. ☎ **035/218-060.** Reservations required. Main courses 25,000L–40,000L ($15–$24); fixed-priced menus 60,000L–130,000L ($36–$78). AE, DC, MC, V. Thurs–Tues noon–2:30pm and 7:30–9:30pm. Closed 3 weeks in Aug. INTERNATIONAL.

This restaurant on the main boulevard in New Town serves a cuisine almost better than anything found in Milan. Set on a corner, the establishment lights its entrance with lanterns. The menu offers more than a dozen risottos, more than 20 pastas, and around 30 meat dishes, as well as just about every kind of fish that swims in Italy's waters. Examples include grilled "fantasy of the sea" with fresh seasonal vegetables, a breast of goose with a tapenade of black olives, and a tartare of salmon with avocado. The service is efficient, all of it directed by members of the Cerea family, who by now are among the best-known citizens of Bergamo.

Taverna del Colleoni dell'Angelo. Piazza Vecchia 7. ☎ **035/232-596.** Reservations required. Main courses 25,000L–37,000L ($15–$22.20); fixed-price lunch 50,000L ($30); fixed-price dinner 95,000L ($57); fixed-price Sunday meal 75,000L ($45). AE, DC, MC, V. Tues–Sat noon–2:30pm and 7:45–10:30pm, Sun noon–2:30pm. Closed Aug 12–25. LOMBARDO/NORTH ITALIAN.

In the heart of the Città Alta, this restaurant is known to many a gourmet who journeys here to try regional dishes of exceptional merit. The building dates from the 14th century, and is the most historic restaurant in Bergamo. The sidewalk tables are popular in summer, and the view is part of the reward of dining here. Inside, the decor suggests medievalism, but with a fresh approach. The ceiling is vaulted, the chairs are leather, and there's a low-floor dining room with a wood-burning fireplace. Known for its creative interpretations of Lombard cuisines, the establishment features such dishes as a casserole of jumbo shrimp with polenta, homemade flat pasta with a delicate ragoût of wild duck, and Adriatic turbot on a bed of crispy potatoes.

BERGAMO AFTER DARK

Citizens are passionate about opera, the season lasting from September to November with a drama being staged from then until April at the **Donizetti Theater,** Piazza Cavour (☎ 035/249-631). A program of free events, *Viva La Tua Città,* is staged every summer. The tourist office (see above) will provide a pamphlet.

If visiting a *birreria* (beer hall) is what you want, head for Via Gombito in the upper city. It's lined with places to drink. One of the most popular joints is **Papageno Pub,** Via Colleoni (☎ 035/236-624), which makes the best sandwiches and *bruschetta* in town. In Città Bassa the young people's favorite is **Capolinea,** Via Giacomo Quarenghi 29 (☎ 035/320-981), with an active bar up front.

3 Cremona

59 miles SE of Milan, 61 miles S of Bergamo

This city of the violin is found on the Po River plain. Music lovers from all over the world flock to the birthplace of Monteverdi (the father of modern opera) and of Stradivari (latinized to Stradivarius), who made violin making an art. Born in Cremona in 1644, Antonio Stradivari became the most famous name in the world of violin crafting, far exceeding the skill of his teacher, Nicolò Amati. The third great family name associated with the craft, Giuseppe Guarneri (1687–1745), was also of Cremona. Today students still flock here to the International School for Violin Making. Graduates of the school have opened some 60 workshops all over town.

ESSENTIALS

GETTING THERE   By Train   At least nine trains per day run between Milan and Cremona (trip time: 1¹/₂ hours), at a one-way fare of 7,200L ($4.30). Call the **rail station** in Cremona, at Via Dante 68 (☎ 0372/28-757). Arrivals are in the north of town. Via Palestro leads south to the Piazza Cavour, which connects with the heartbeat Piazza del Comune and the adjoining Piazza del Duomo.

By Bus   One bus a day makes the run from Milan to Cremona, at a one-way fare of 9,300L ($5.60). The **bus station** is on Via Dante (☎ 0372/29-212 for schedules and information).

By Car   From Milan, take Route 415 southeast.

VISITOR INFORMATION   The **tourist information office** is at Piazza del Comune 5 (☎ 0372/23-233), open Monday to Saturday from 9:30am to 12:30pm and 3 to 6pm and Sunday from 9:45am to 12:15pm.

EXPLORING CREMONA

Most of the attractions of the city are centered on the harmonious **Piazza del Comune.** The Romanesque **cathedral** dates from 1107, although over the centuries, Gothic, Renaissance, even baroque elements were incorporated. In the typical

Lombard style, the pillars of the main portal rest on lions, an architectural detail matched in the nearby octagonal 13th-century baptistery. Surmounting the portal are some marble statues in the vestibule, with a Madonna and Bambino in the center. The rose window over it, from the 13th century, is inserted in the facade like a medallion.

Inside, the pillars are draped with Flemish tapestries. Five arches on each side of the nave are admirably frescoed by such artists as Boccaccio Boccaccino (see his *Annunciation* and other scenes from the life of the Madonna, painted in the early 16th century). Other artists who worked on the frescoes were Gian Francesco Bembo (*Adoration of the Wise Men* and *Presentation at the Temple*), Gerolamo Romanino (scenes from the life of Christ), and Altobello Melone (a *Last Supper*). It's open Monday to Saturday from 7am to noon and 3 to 7pm and Sunday from 7am to 1pm and 3:30 to 7pm. Admission is free.

Beside the cathedral is the **Torrazzo,** which dates from the late 13th century and enjoys a reputation as the tallest campanile (bell tower) in Italy, soaring to a height of 353 feet. It's open Monday to Saturday from 10:30am to noon and 3 to 6pm and Sunday from 10:30am to 12:30pm and 3 to 7pm; from November to Easter, however, it's open only Sunday and holidays. Admission is 5,000L ($3) for adults and 3,000L ($1.80) for children.

From the same period, and also opening onto the Piazza, are the **Loggia dei Militi** and the **Palazzo Comunale** in the typical Lombardy Gothic style. The Palazzo Comunale (☎ 0372/4071-31971), displays a collection of violins crafted by the Armatis, Guarneri, and, of course, Stradivari. It also displays antiques and paintings, some dating from the 17th century. Hours are Tuesday to Saturday from 8:30am to 6pm and Sunday from 9am to 12:15pm and 3 to 6pm. Admission is 6,000L ($3.60).

Museo Stradivariano. Via Palestro 17. ☎ **0372/461-886.** Admission 6,000L ($3.60) adults, 3,000L ($1.80) children. Tues–Sat 8:15am–6pm, Sun 9:15am–12:15pm and 3–6pm.

At this museum you can see a collection of models, designs, and shapes and tools of Stradivari (1644–1737). This Italian violin maker produced more than 1,000 strong instruments, many of which are among the best ever made.

SHOPPING

Cremona is famous for bars of **torrone,** a nougat made with honey, egg, and nuts. The best ones are sold at **Spelari,** 25 Via Solferino (☎ 0372/22-346), in business since 1836. The torrone made at **Pasticceria Duomo,** Via Boccaccino 6 (☎ 0372/22-273), are shaped like violins. This is a pastry shop from the past century, following recipes the owner calls "legendary."

WHERE TO STAY

Hotel Agip. Località San Felice, 26100 Cremona. ☎ **0372/450-490.** Fax 0372/451-097. 77 rms. A/C MINIBAR TV TEL. 180,000L ($108) double. Rates include breakfast. AE, DC, MC, V. Motorists exit autostrada A21 at Casello and drive 1¹/₂ miles.

This motel, part of a nationwide chain, is at the San Felice exit of the superhighway between Piacenza and Brescia. It's a modern establishment with comfortable bedrooms outfitted with hair dryers and soundproofed against the noise of the nearby highway. A good restaurant on the premises serves copious amounts of food, with a fixed-price menu as well as a self-service area.

Hotel Continental. Piazza della Libertà 26, 26100 Cremona. ☎ **0372/434-141.** Fax 0372/454-873. 57 rms, 7 suites. A/C MINIBAR TV TEL. 185,000L ($111) double; from 280,000L ($168) suite. Rates include breakfast. AE, DC, MC, V.

Roads from many parts of northern Italy converge on the busy piazza where the comfortable 1980s Hotel Continental stands. It's the best choice in the town, having more atmosphere and personality than the Agip. The staff show an obvious pride in the musical history of Cremona as they eagerly point out their collection of early 20th-century copies of violins by Amati and Stradivari housed in illuminated glass cases. There are also instruments made by master luthiers of Cremona, some of whom seem to be on a first-name basis with the management. A bronze bust of Claudio Monteverdi, the 17th-century composer, looks out over the lobby, and there's a restaurant that can seat 500 people. Each of the hotel's comfortably furnished bedrooms has sound-insulated windows.

WHERE TO DINE

✪ **Ceresole.** Via Ceresole 4. ☎ **0372/30-990.** Reservations required. Main courses 25,000L–30,000L ($15–$18). DC, MC, V. Tues–Sat noon–2:30pm and 8–10:30pm. Closed Jan 22–30 and Aug 6–28. ITALIAN.

Near the Duomo, Ceresole is an elegant and well-known culinary institution, lying in a century-old building in the historic heart of Cremona. It's the finest restaurant in the entire surrounding area, and is richly deserving of its star. Behind a masonry facade on a narrow street, it has windows covered with elaborate wrought-iron grills. Specialties include rice with rhubarb, a wide array of delicately seasoned fish (some of them served with fresh seasonal mushrooms and truffles), and the most delectable grilled baby piglet this side of Segovia, Spain. Some of the dishes are based on time-honored regional recipes, including *spaghetti alla marinara, straccotto di manzo* (a beef stew), and grilled fillets of eel.

CREMONA AFTER DARK

The prospect is a bit bleak unless you're here in May or June. At that time, classical music is performed at the **Teatro Ponchielli,** Corso Vittorio Emanuele (for tickets call the tourist office at ☎ 0372/23-233). Tickets range from 25,000L to 30,000L ($15 to $18). The opera season, also at Teatro Ponchielli, runs from mid-October to early December, with tickets beginning at 25,000L ($15). All that jazz is heard at **Cremona Jazz** in March and April, with tickets costing 15,000L ($9) and up. Call the tourist office for tickets to all these events.

If you'd like a bar that overflows with local life, patronize **Ristorante Centrale,** Via Pertusio 4, off Via Solferino (☎ 0372/28-701). If you get hungry, you can dine on Cremonese cuisine at its on-site restaurant. *Bollito misto,* a medley of boiled meats, is the specialty.

4 Mantova (Mantua)

25 miles S of Verona, 95 miles SE of Milan, 291 miles NW of Rome, 90 miles SW of Venice

Once a duchy, Mantova had a flowering of art and architecture under the Gonzaga dynasty that held sway over the town for nearly four centuries. Originally an Etruscan settlement, later a Roman colony, it has known many conquerors, including the French and Austrians in the 18th and 19th centuries. Virgil, the great Latin poet, has remained its most famous son (he was born outside the city in a place called Andes). Verdi set *Rigoletto* here, Romeo (Shakespeare's creation, that is) took refuge here, and writer Aldous Huxley called Mantova "the most romantic city in the world."

Mantova is an imposing, at times even austere city, despite its situation near three lakes, Superiore, di Mezzo, and Inferiore. It's very much a city of the past and is within easy reach of a number of cities in northern Italy. The historic center is traffic-free.

ESSENTIALS

GETTING THERE   By Train   Mantova has excellent rail connections, lying on direct lines to Milan, Cremona, Modena, and Verona. Nine trains a day arrive from Milan, taking 2¹/₄ hours; a one-way ticket costs 14,700L ($8.80). From Cremona, trains arrive every hour (trip time: 1 hour), a one-way ticket costing 6,000L ($3.60). The **train station** is on Piazza Don Leoni (☎ **0376/321-646**). Take bus no. 3 from outside the station to get to the center of town.

By Bus   Most visitors arrive by train, but Mantova has good bus connections with Brescia; 17 buses a day make a 1-hour 40-minute journey at a cost of 9,300L ($5.60) for a one-way ticket. The **bus station** is on Piazza Mondadori (☎ **0376/327-237**).

By Car   From Cremona, continue east along Route 10.

VISITOR INFORMATION   The **tourist information center** is at Piazza Andrea Mantegna 6 (☎ **0376/328-253**), open Monday to Saturday from 8:30am to 12:30pm and 3 to 6pm.

EXPLORING THE PALACES & THE BASILICA

✪ Museo di Palazzo Ducale. Piazza Sordello 40. ☎ **0376/320-283**. Admission 12,000L ($7.20) adults, free for children 17 and under and seniors 60 and over. Sun–Mon 9am–1pm, Tues–Sat 9am–1pm and 2:30–6pm.

The ducal apartments of the Gonzagas, with more than 500 rooms and 15 courtyards, are the most remarkable in Italy—certainly when judged from the standpoint of size. Like Rome, the compound wasn't built in a day, or even in a century. The earlier buildings, erected to the specifications of the Bonacolsi family, date from the 13th century. The later 14th and early 15th centuries saw the rise of the Castle of St. George, designed by Bartolino da Novara. The Gonzagas also added the Palatine Basilica of St. Barbara by Bertani.

Over the years the historic monument of Renaissance splendor has lost many of the art treasures collected by Isabella d'Este during the 15th and 16th centuries in her efforts to turn Mantova into "La Città dell'Arte." Her descendants, the Gonzagas, sold the most precious objects to Charles I of England in 1628, and 2 years later most of the remaining rich collection was looted during the sack of Mantova. Even Napoléon did his bit by carting off some of the objects still there.

What remains of the painting collection is still superb, including works by Tintoretto and Sustermans, and a "cut-up" Rubens. The display of classical statuary is impressive, gathered mostly from the various Gonzaga villas at the time of Maria Theresa of Austria. Among the more inspired sights are the Zodiac Room, the Hall of Mirrors (with a vaulted ceiling constructed at the beginning of the 17th century), the River Chamber, the Apartment of Paradise, the Apartment of Troia (with frescoes by Giulio Romano), and a scale reproduction of the Holy Staircase in Rome. The most interesting and best-known room in the castle is the Camera degli Sposi (bridal chamber), frescoed by Andrea Mantegna. Winged cherubs appear over a balcony at the top of the ceiling. Look for a curious dwarf and a mauve-hatted portrait of Christian I of Denmark. There are many paintings by Domenico Fetti, along with a splendid series of nine tapestries woven in Brussels and based on cartoons by Raphael. A cycle of frescoes on the age of chivalry by Pisanello has recently been discovered. A guardian takes visitors on a tour to point out the many highlights.

Basilica di Sant'Andrea. Piazza Mantegna. ☎ **0376/328-504**. Free admission. Mon–Sat 8am–noon and 3–6pm, Sun 3–6pm.

Built to the specifications of Leon Battista Alberti, this church opens onto Piazza Mantegna, just off Piazza delle Erbe, where you'll find fruit vendors. The actual work on the basilica was carried out by a pupil of Alberti's, Luca Fancelli. However, before Alberti died in 1472, it's said that, architecturally speaking, he knew he had "buried the Middle Ages." The church wasn't completed until 1782, when Juvara crowned it with a dome.

As you enter, the first chapel to your left contains the tomb of the great Mantegna (the paintings are by his son, except for the *Holy Family* by the old master himself). The sacristan will light it for you. In the crypt you'll encounter a representation of one of the more fanciful legends in the history of church relics: St. Andrew's claim to possess the blood of Christ, "the gift" of St. Longinus, the Roman soldier who is said to have pierced his side. Beside the basilica is a 1414 bell tower.

Palazzo Te. Viale Te 13. ☎ **0376/323-266.** Admission 12,000L ($7.20) adults, 10,000L ($6) seniors 60 and over, 5,000L ($3) children 12 to 18, free for children under 12. Tues–Sun 9am–6pm, Mon 1–6pm.

This Renaissance palace, built in the 16th century, is known for its frescoes by Giulio Romano and his pupils. Fun-loving Federigo II, one of the Gonzagas, had the villa built as a place where he could slip away to see his mistress, Isabella Boschetto, for amorous dallyings. The name, *Te*, is said to have been derived from the word *tejeto*, which in the local dialect means "a cut to let the waters flow out." This was once marshland drained by the Gonzagas for their horse farm.

The frescoes in the various rooms, dedicated to everything from horses to Psyche, rely on mythology for subject matter. The Room of the Giants, the best known, has a scene that depicts heaven venting its rage on the giants who had moved threateningly against it. Federico's motto was, "What the lizards lack is that which tortures me," an obscure reference to the reptile's cold blood as opposed to his hot blood. The banquet hall, Sala di Psiche, forever immortalizes the tempestuous love affair of these swingers. The hall is decorated with erotic frescoes on the theme of the marriage of Cupid and Psyche, two other "hot bloods."

SHOPPING

The best shopping is at the **open-air market** that operates only on Thursday morning at the Piazza delle Erbe and Piazza Sordello. Here you can find a little bit of everything—from cheap clothing (often designer rip-offs) to bric-a-brac. The place is like an outdoor traveling department store.

WHERE TO STAY

✪ **Albergo San Lorenzo.** Piazza Concordia 14, 46100 Mantova. ☎ **0376/220-500.** Fax 0376/327-194. 23 rms, 9 junior suites. A/C MINIBAR TV TEL. 290,000L ($174) double; 340,000L ($204) suite. Rates include breakfast. AE, DC, MC, V. Parking 30,000L ($18).

Your best bed in Mantova awaits at this four-star hotel in the historic center. The building is ancient, but after a careful restoration in 1996, San Lorenzo emerged as the finest hotel in town. Restorers paid great attention to the architectural details and the furnishings, most of which are antique, with marble floors, oil paintings, and Oriental carpets. The aim was to re-create the luxurious feel of the 19th century. The great service makes guests feel at home in a pleasant, intimate atmosphere. The hotel offers a panoramic terrace with a view of the historic city. The bedrooms, painted mostly in soft muted whites and blues, are furnished with dark woods (antique reproductions) and gilded mirrors. Baths are completely up-to-date and, as a godsend in steamy Mantova, there is adjustable air-conditioning. Breakfast is the only meal served.

Hotel Dante. Via Corrado 54, 46100 Mantova. ☎ **0376/326-425.** Fax 0376/221-141. 40 rms. TV TEL. 140,000L–145,000L ($84–$87) double. AE, DC, MC, V. Parking 20,000L ($12).

Built in 1968, this boxy, modern hotel has a recessed entrance area and a marble-accented interior, parts of which look out over a flagstone-covered courtyard. On a narrow street in the busy commercial center, some of the simply furnished but clean rooms have air-conditioning and a minibar. It's your best bet when funds are low.

Mantegna Hotel. Via Fabio Filzi 10B, 46100 Mantova. ☎ **0376/328-019.** Fax 0376/368-564. 34 rms, 3 suites. A/C TV TEL. 160,000L ($96) double; 230,000L ($138) suite. AE, DC, MC, V. Closed Dec 24–Jan 5.

Mantegna is in a commercial section of town, a few blocks from one of the entrances to the old city. This six-story hotel has bandbox lines and a facade of light-gray tiles. The lobby is accented with gray and red marble slabs, along with enlargements of details of paintings by (as you probably guessed) Mantegna. About half the units look out over a sunny rear courtyard, although the rooms facing the street are fairly quiet as well. The hotel is a good value for the rates charged.

Rechigi Hotel. Via P. F. Calvi 30, 46100 Mantova. ☎ **0376/320-781.** Fax 0376/220-291. 60 rms, 5 suites. A/C TV TEL. 230,000L ($138) double; 280,000L ($168) suite. AE, DC, MC, V. Parking 25,000L ($15).

Near the center of the old city stands the Rechigi, a comfortable modern hotel, rivaled only by the San Lorenzo. It's a comfortable, cozy nest, but short on style. Its lobby is warmly decorated with modern paintings, with an alcove bar. The owners maintain the property well, and they have decorated the attractively furnished rooms in good taste. Only breakfast is served.

WHERE TO DINE

The local specialty is donkey stew *(stracotto di asino)*. Local legend claims you'll never be a man until you've sampled it.

Il Cigno Trattoria dei Martini. Piazza Carlo d'Arco 1. ☎ **0376/327-101.** Reservations recommended. Main courses 25,000L–35,000L ($15–$21). DC, MC, V. Wed–Sun 12:30–1:45pm and 8–9:45pm. Closed Jan 7–14 and Aug 1–22. MANTOVANO.

This trattoria overlooks a cobblestone square in the old part of Mantova. The exterior is a faded ocher, with wrought-iron cross-hatched window bars within sight of the easy parking on the piazza outside. After passing through a large entrance hall studded with frescoes, you'll come upon the bustling dining rooms. They feature both freshwater and saltwater fish, and such dishes as *agnoli* (a form of pasta) in a light sauce or risotto. *Bollito misto* (a medley of boiled meats) is served with various sauces, including one made of mustard. One excellent pasta, *tortelli di zucca*, is stuffed with pumpkin.

✪ **L'Aquila Nigra (The Black Eagle).** Vicolo Bonacolsi 4. ☎ **0376/327-180.** Reservations recommended. Main courses 22,000L–25,000L ($13.20–$15). AE, DC, MC, V. June–Aug and Nov–Mar, Tues–Sat noon–2pm and 8–10pm; Apr–May, Tues–Sat noon–2pm and 8–10pm, Sun noon–2pm; Sept–Oct, Tues–Sat noon–2pm and 8–10pm, Sun noon–2pm. Closed Jan 1–15 and Aug. MANTOVANO/ITALIAN.

This restaurant is in a Renaissance mansion on a narrow passageway by the Bonacolsi Palace. The building's foundations were laid in the 1200s, but the restaurant dates from 1984. Among the excellent food served in the elegant rooms, you can choose from such dishes as pike from the Mincio River, called *luccio,* served with *salsa verde* (green sauce) and polenta, as well as other specialties of the region. You also might order a pasta, *gnocchi alle ortiche* (potato dumplings tinged with puréed nettles), eel marinated in vinegar (one of the most distinctive specialties of Mantova), or *tortelli di zucca* (with a pumpkin base).

Ristorante Pavesi. Piazza delle Erbe 13. ☎ **0376/323-627.** Reservations recommended. Main courses 13,000L–25,000L ($7.80–$15). AE, DC, MC, V. Fri–Wed 12:30–2:30pm and 7:30–9:30pm. Closed Jan 25–Feb 14. MANTOVANO.

Ristorante Pavesi has the advantage of being located under an ancient arcade on the most beautiful square in Mantova. The walls partially date from the 1200s, although the restaurant itself goes back before World War II. It's an intimate family-run establishment with hundreds of antique copper pots hanging randomly from the single-barrel vault of the plaster ceiling. There's an antipasti table near the door loaded with delicacies, and in summer, tables spill out into the square. Specialties include *agnolotti* (a form of tortellini) with meat, cheese, sage, and butter, as well as *risotto alla mantovana* (with pesto). Also try the roast filet of veal (deboned and rolled), and a well-made blend of *fagioli* (white beans) with onions.

MANTOVA AFTER DARK

The major cultural venue is **Teatro Sociale di Mantova,** Piazza Cavallotti (☎ **0376/ 323-860**), lying off Corso Vittorio Emanuele. They put on operas in October, followed by a season of Italian dramas lasting from November through May. Tickets cost from 20,000L ($12). In lieu of any other major entertainment, locals depend on festivals, beginning with a series of chamber music series in April and May, followed by the **Mantova (Mantua) Jazz Festival** at the end of July. The tourist office (see above) has details.

If you're just looking for a place to drink and meet some companions, head for **Leoncino Rosso,** Via Giustiziati 33 (☎ **0376/323-277**), behind Piazza Erbe. This osteria opened in 1750 and hasn't changed some of its recipes such as tortellini with nuts or pumpkin since then. It stays open until 10pm except Sunday and is the best place for drinking and general carousing. It's closed August and 2 weeks in January. The best selection of beer in town is at **Oblo,** Via Arrivabene 50 (☎ **0376/360-676**), which also has a good offering of reasonably priced wine, such as the red, fizzy Lambrusco.

5 Lake Garda

The easternmost of the northern Italian lakes, Garda is also the largest, 32 miles long and 11½ miles wide at its fattest point. Sheltered by mountains, its scenery, especially the part on the western shore that reaches from Limone to Salo, has been compared to that of the Mediterranean; you'll see olive, orange, and lemon trees, even palms. The almost-transparent lake is ringed with four art cities: Trent to the northeast, Brescia to the west, Mantova (Mantua) to the south, and Verona to the east.

The eastern side of the lake is more rugged, less trampled, but the resort-studded western strip is far more glamorous to the first-timer. On the western side, a circuitous road skirts the lake through one molelike tunnel after another. You can park your car at several secluded belvederes for a panoramic lakeside view. In spring the scenery is splashed with color, everything from wild poppy beds to oleander. Garda is well served by buses, or you can traverse the lake on steamers or motorboats. The lake, once a mandatory stopover on the Grand Tour, has attracted everyone from the Romans to Mussolini.

ESSENTIALS

GETTING THERE   By Bus & Train   Eight buses a day make the 1-hour trip from Trent to Riva del Garde. A one-way fare is 5,200L ($3.10). For information and schedules call the **Autostazione** on Viale Trento in Riva (☎ **0365/552-323**). The nearest train station is at Roverto, a 20-minute ride from Riva. Frequent buses make the 20-minute trip from the train station to Riva; the one-way bus fare is 3,200L ($1.90). For getting around Lake Garda, you'll need a car.

By Car   From Milan or Brescia, autostrada A4 east runs to the southwestern corner of the lake. From Montova, take A22 north to A4 west. From Verona and points east, take A4 west.

GETTING AROUND   By Car   Most visitors take the road along the western shore, Route S572, north to Riva di Garda. For a less-touristed jaunt, try heading back down the lake along its eastern shore on the Gardesana Orientale (S249). Route S11 runs along the south shore.

Warning to motorists: The twisting roads that follow the shores of Lake Garda would be enough to rattle even the most experienced driver. Couple the frightening turns, dimly lit tunnels, and emotional local drivers with convoys of tour buses and trucks that rarely stay in their lane, and you have one of the more frightening drives in Italy. Use your horn around blind curves, and be warned that Sunday is especially risky, since everyone on the lake and from the nearby cities seems to take to the roads after a long lunch with lots of heady wine.

By Boat & Hydrofoil   Both boats and hydrofoils operate on the lake from Easter through September. For schedules and information contact **Navigazione Lago di Garda** (☎ **030/914-1321**). Boats connect Riva's Porto San Nicolò with all the major lakeside towns, including Gardone (trip time: 2¹/₂ hours), costing 9,000L ($5.40) one-way; Sirmione (trip time: 4 hours), costing 12,600L ($7.55) one-way; and Desenzano (trip time: 4 hours 20 minutes), costing 15,000L ($9) one-way. These boats are the best and most affordable way to see the lake. If you opt to board one of the hydrofoils (instead of a boat) at Riva's port, you'll pay a one-way supplement ranging from 1,500L to 5,200L (90¢ to $3.10) per person. These hydrofoils are a lot faster if you're in a rush, but you won't enjoy the lakeside scenery with such leisure as you would aboard a slow-moving boat.

RIVA DEL GARDA

Some 195 feet above sea level, Riva is the oldest and most traditional resort along the lake. It consists of both an expanding new district and an old town, the latter centered at Piazza III Novembre. On the harbor are the Tower of Apponale, dating from the 13th century, and La Rocca, built in 1124 and once owned by the ruling Scaligeri princes of Verona. **La Rocca** has been turned into a museum (☎ **0464/ 573-869**), which you might visit on a rainy day, as it exhibits mainly local artworks. Admission is 4,000L ($2.40), and it's open Tuesday to Sunday from 9am to 12:30pm and 2 to 6pm (in July and August, afternoon hours are 4:30 to 8:30pm).

On the northern banks of the lake, between the Benacense plains and towering mountains, Riva offers the advantages of the Riviera and the Dolomites. Its climate is classically Mediterranean—mild in winter and moderate in summer. Vast areas of rich vegetation combine with the deep blue of the lake. Many people come for health cures; others for business conferences, meetings, and fairs. Riva is popular with tour groups from the Germanic lands and from England.

Riva del Garda is linked to the Brenner–Modena motorway (Rovereto Sud/Garda Nord exit) and to the railway (Rovereto station), and is near Verona's Airport.

VISITOR INFORMATION   Tourist information is available at the **Palazzo dei Congressi,** Giardini di Porta Orientale 8 (☎ **0464/554-444**), open mid-September to Easter, Monday to Friday from 9am to noon and 2 to 7pm; Easter to mid-September, Monday to Saturday from 9am to noon and 2 to 7pm; mid-June to mid-September, also open Sunday from 10am to noon and 4 to 6:30pm.

OUTDOOR ACTIVITIES Riva is the windsurfing capital of Italy. Windsurfing schools offer lessons and also rent equipment. The best one is **Nautic Club Riva,** Viale Rovereto 132 (☎ 0464/552-453), which is closed November to Easter. It has full rentals, including life jackets, wet suits, and boards, for 22,000L ($13.20) per hour. You might also try **Paolo Fazi** at Sabbioni beach (☎ 0337/459-785), where charges are 10,000L ($6) per hour. If you'd like to explore the lake by bike, go to **Girelli Mountain Bike,** Viale Damiano Chiesa, 15–17 (☎ 0464/554-719), where rentals are 18,000L ($10.80) per day.

SHOPPING Retailers mainly peddle souvenirs of only passing interest; however, a large **open-air market,** the best on Lake Garda, comes to town on the second and fourth Wednesday of every month. It mainly sprawls along three streets: Viale Dante, Via Prati, and Via Pilati. You can buy virtually anything here, from alpine handcrafts to busts of Mussolini. While shopping, drop in to **Pasticceria Copat di Fabio Marzari,** Viale Dante 27 (☎ 0464/551-885). It sells the most delectable pastries in Riva.

WHERE TO STAY

✪ **Hotel du Lac et du Parc.** Viale Rovereto 44, 38066 Riva del Garda. ☎ 0464/551-500. Fax 0464/555-200. 172 rms, 6 suites. MINIBAR TV TEL. 190,000L–430,000L ($114–$258) double; from 480,000L ($288) suite. Rates include breakfast. AE, DC, MC, V. Closed Oct 20–Mar 20. Parking 25,000L ($15).

This deluxe Spanish-style hotel, the best in town, is set back from the busy road behind a shrub-filled parking lot dotted with stone cherubs. The interior of the main building is freshly decorated, with arched windows and lots of spacious comfort; an enclosed and manicured lawn is visible from the lobby. There's a huge dining room, two additional restaurants, an attractive bar, unusual accessories, and a comfortably sprawling format, each corner of which gives the impression of being part of a large private home. The well-trained staff speaks a variety of languages and seems genuinely concerned with the well-being of their guests. A garden stretches behind the hotel, containing two pools, a lakeside beach, and two tennis courts. Other amenities include a sauna, fitness room, and beauty salon. The bedrooms are well furnished, and 54 are air-conditioned.

Hotel Sole. Piazza III Novembre 35, 38066 Riva del Garda. ☎ 0464/552-686. Fax 0464/552-811. 52 rms, 3 suites. MINIBAR TV TEL. 230,000L–270,000L ($138–$162) double; from 350,000L ($210) suite. Rates include breakfast. AE, DC, MC, V. Closed Jan 8–Mar and Nov–Dec 25. Parking 10,000L ($6).

The medium-priced Hotel Sole had far-sighted founders who snared the best position on the waterfront. The hotel has amenities worthy of a first-class rating, even though it charges second-class prices. It's an overgrown villa with arched windows and colonnades, and the interior has time-clinging traditional rooms. The lounge has a beamed ceiling and centers around a hooded fireplace; clusters of antique chairs sit on islands of Oriental carpets. The character and quality of the bedrooms vary considerably according to their position (most have lake views). Some are almost suites, with living-room areas; the smaller ones are less desirable. Nevertheless, all rooms are comfortable and spotless. You can dine in the formal interior room or on the flagstone lakeside terrace. There is a sauna and a solarium.

Hotel Venezia. Viale Rovereto 62, 38066 Riva del Garda. ☎ 0464/552-216. Fax 0464/556-031. 24 rms. TV TEL. 138,000L–175,000L ($82.80–$105) double. Rates include breakfast. AE, V. Closed Nov–Easter.

The is one of the most attractive budget hotels in town. The main section of the Venezia's angular modern building is raised on stilts above a private parking lot set back from the lakefront promenade. The hotel was designed as a villa in 1968, but in the early 1990s it was renovated to become a small, personalized, and unpretentious hotel. The complex is surrounded by trees on a quiet street bordered with flowers and private homes. The reception area is at the top of a flight of red marble steps. There's a private pool surrounded by palmettos, and a clean and sunny dining room with Victorian reproduction chairs. The rooms are pleasantly furnished.

WHERE TO DINE

Ristorante San Marco. Viale Roma 20. ☎ **0464/554-477.** Reservations recommended. Main courses 18,000L–30,000L ($10.80–$18). AE, DC, MC, V. Tues–Sun noon–2:30pm and 7–10pm. Closed Feb. ITALIAN/SEAFOOD.

Set back from the lake on one of the main shopping streets of the resort, the San Marco was built in the 19th century as a hotel and converted into a restaurant in 1979. If you arrive early for your reserved table, you can enjoy an aperitif at the bar. The superb food is classically Italian and the service is excellent. You might begin with pasta, such as spaghetti with clams or tortellini with prosciutto. They serve many good fish dishes, including sole and grilled scampi. Among the meat selections, try the tournedos opera or the veal cutlet bolognese. During the summer you may dine in the open-air garden.

RIVA AFTER DARK

Begin your evening with a drink at **Pub al Gallo,** Via San Rocca 11 (☎ **0464/ 551-177**), which stays open until 3am. The best disco is **Discoteca Tiffany,** Giardini di Porta Orientale (☎ **0464/552-512**), open only Thursday through Sunday. You can also shake it at **Après Club,** Via Monte d'Oro 14 (☎ **0464/552-187**) most of the year Wednesday to Sunday from 9pm to 2:30am (although the owners will often cut hours to just Friday and Saturday in the slow periods of spring and autumn).

LIMONE SUL GARDA

Limone sul Garda lies 6 miles south of Riva on the western shore of Lake Garda. Taking its name from the fruit of the abundant local lemon tree, Limone is one of the liveliest resorts on the lake, once praised by Goethe and D. H. Lawrence.

Snuggling close to the water at the bottom of a narrow, steep road, Limone's shopkeepers, faced with no building room on their narrow strip of land, dug right into the rock. There are 2¹/₂ miles of beach from which you can bathe, sail, or surf. The only way to get about is on foot, but at Limone you can enjoy tennis, soccer, and other sports, as well as discos.

If you're bypassing Limone, you may still want to make a detour south of the village to the turnoff to Tignale, in the hills. You can climb a modern highway to the town for a sweeping vista of Garda, one of the most scenic spots on the entire lake.

VISITOR INFORMATION   From April to September, a **tourist information center** is operated at Via Comboni 15 (☎ **0365/954-070**). It's open Monday to Friday from 8:30am to noon and 2:30 to 6pm.

WHERE TO STAY & DINE

Hotel Capo Reamol. Via IV Novembre 92, 25010 Limone sul Garda. ☎ **0365/954-040.** Fax 0365/954-262. 60 rms. MINIBAR TV TEL. 316,000L–360,000L ($189.60–$216) double. Rates include half board. MC, V. Closed Nov–Mar.

You won't even get a glimpse of this 1960s hotel from the main highway because it nestles on a series of terraces stretching down to the edge of the lake, well below road level. Pull into a roadside area indicated 1¹/₄ miles north of Limone, and then follow the driveway down a steep and narrow hill. Bedrooms are well furnished and freshly decorated. The bar, restaurant, and sports facilities are on the lowest level, sheltered from the lakeside breezes by windbreaks. Many of the public rooms are painted in pastels. Clients can swim in the lake or in the pool and rent Windsurfers on the graveled beach. The restaurant serves an Italian cuisine and many fine Italian wines. Live music is offered on weekends. A tavern profits, like everything else in the hotel, from views of the water.

Hotel Le Palme. Via Porto 36, 25010 Limone sul Garda. ☎ **0365/954-681.** Fax 0365/954-120. 28 rms. TEL. 140,000L–200,000L ($84–$120) double. Rates include breakfast. AE, MC, V. Closed Nov–Mar 15.

Completely renovated, this well-known antique Venetian-style villa with period furniture stands in the shade of two-centuries-old palm trees in the historic center of Limone, opening directly onto the shores of Lake Garda. Although extensively remodeled, this four-star hotel retains many of its original architectural features. The hotel offers well-furnished bedrooms, each individually decorated, containing a radio. The second floor has a comfortable reading room with a TV, and the third floor has a wide terrace. The ground floor contains a large dining room with decorative sculpture, opening onto a wide terrace where in fair weather you can order meals and drinks. The cuisine, backed up by a good wine list, is excellent. Because of the popularity of the hotel, it's best to make reservations.

GARDONE RIVIERA

On Garda's western shore 60 miles east of Milan, Gardone Riviera is well equipped with a number of good hotels and sporting facilities. Its lakeside promenade attracts a wide range of predominantly European tourists for most of the year. When it used to be chic for patrician Italian families to spend their holidays by the lake, many of the more prosperous built elaborate villas not only in Gardone Riviera, but in neighboring Fasano (some have been converted to receive guests). The town also has the major attraction along the lake, d'Annunzio's Villa Vittoriale, which you may want to visit even if you're not lodging for the night.

GETTING THERE   The resort lies 26 miles south of Riva on the west coast. Three buses per day arrive from Riva. The trip takes 1¹/4 hours, and a one-way ticket costs 5,000L ($3). Two buses make the 3-hour trip from Milan; a one-way ticket is 15,100L ($9.05). For schedule information call ☎ **0365/21-061.**

VISITOR INFORMATION   The tourist information office is at Corso della Repubblica 35 (☎ **0365/20-347**). It's open April to October, Monday to Saturday from 9am to 12:30pm and 4 to 7pm; November to March, Monday to Friday from 9am to 12:30pm and 3 to 6pm and Saturday from 9am to 12:30pm.

VISITING D'ANNUNZIO'S VILLA

✪ **Vittoriale,** Via Vittoriale 12 (☎ **0365/20-130**), was once the private home of Gabriele d'Annunzio (1863–1938), the poet and military adventurer, another Italian who believed in *la dolce vita*, even when he couldn't afford it. Most of the celebrated events in d'Annunzio's life occurred before 1925, including his love affair with Eleonora Duse and his bravura takeover as a self-styled commander of a territory being ceded to Yugoslavia. In the later years of his life, until he died in the winter before World War II, the national hero lived the grand life at his private estate on Garda.

North of the town, Vittoriale is open year-round; in the winter, Tuesday to Sunday from 9am to 12:30pm and 2 to 6pm (until 5pm in spring and autumn); in summer, Tuesday to Sunday from 8:30am to 8pm. Admission to the grounds is only 8,000L ($4.80), or 16,000L ($9.60) to the house and grounds. The furnishings and decor passed for avant garde in their day, but now evoke the Radio City Music Hall of the 1930s. D'Annunzio's death mask is of morbid interest, and his bed with a "Big Brother" eye adds a curious touch of Orwell's *1984* (over the poet's bed is a faun casting a nasty sneer). The marble bust of Duse—"the veiled witness" of his work—seems sadly out of place, but the manuscripts and old uniforms perpetuate the legend. In July and August, d'Annunzio plays are presented at the amphitheater on the premises. Vittoriale is a bizarre monument to a hero of yesteryear. To reach it, head out Via Roma, connecting with Via Colli.

WHERE TO STAY

Bellevue Hotel. Via Zanardelli 81, 25083 Gardone Riviera. ☎ and fax **0365/290-088.** 33 rms. TEL. 135,000L ($81). Rates include breakfast. V. Closed Oct 10–Mar 27.

This villa perched up from the main road has many terraces surrounded by trees and flowers—and an unforgettable view. You can stay here even on a budget, enjoying the advantages of lakeside villa life complete with swimming pool. The lounges are comfortable, and the dining room affords a view through the arched windows and excellent meals (no skimpy helpings here). In fair weather you can dine in a large garden.

✪ **Grand Hotel.** Via Zanardelli 74, 25083 Gardone Riviera. ☎ **0365/20-261.** Fax 0365/22-695. 180 rms, 14 junior suites. MINIBAR TV TEL. 280,000L–320,000L ($168–$192) double; 350,000L–400,000L ($210–$240) junior suite. Rates include breakfast. Half board 35,000L ($21) per person extra. AE, DC, MC, V. Closed Oct 18–Mar 26. Parking 20,000L ($12).

When it was built in 1881, this was the most fashionable hotel on the lake and one of the biggest resorts of its kind in Europe. Its massive tower is visible for miles around. The hotel's reputation drew Churchill for an extended stay in 1948, during which he fished and recovered from World War II and his rejection by British voters. Other famous guests have included Gabrielle d'Annunzio and W. Somerset Maugham. It's only a rumor that Vladimir Nabokov was inspired to write *Lolita* after spotting a young girl here. The establishment still boasts a distinguished clientele of regulars. The main salon's sculpted ceilings, parquet floors, and elegantly comfortable chairs make it an ideal spot for reading or watching the lake. The dining room offers good food and old-time splendor. All rooms face the lake, and a series of garden terraces, a private beach, and a swimming pool are scattered throughout the extensive gardens.

A NEARBY PLACE TO STAY

Fasano del Garda is a satellite resort of Gardone Riviera, 1¼ miles to the north. Many prefer it to Gardone.

✪ **Hotel Villa del Sogno.** Via Zanardelli 107, Fasano del Garda, 25080 Gardone Riviera. ☎ 0365/290-181. Fax 0365/290-230. 33 rms, 5 suites. TV TEL. 330,000L–480,000L ($198–$288) double; 490,000L–640,000L ($294–$384) suite. Rates include breakfast. AE, DC, MC, V. Closed Oct 20–Apr 1.

This 1920s re-creation of a Renaissance villa offers sweeping views of the lake and spaciously comfortable, old-fashioned bedrooms. This "Villa of the Dream" resort is far superior to anything in the area, having long ago surpassed the Grand (above). Set a few hundred yards above the water, with easy access to a private beach, the hotel also has a pool and is ringed with terraces filled with cafe tables and pots of petunias and geraniums, which combine with bougainvillea and jasmine to brighten the surroundings. The baronial stairway of the interior, as well as many of the ceilings and architectural details, were crafted from wood. The bedrooms are well furnished, each with private bath (tub or shower). Nine rooms are air-conditioned.

WHERE TO DINE

Most visitors to this resort take their meals at their hotels. However, there are some good independent dining selections.

Ristorante La Stalla. Strade per Il Vittoriale. ☎ **0365/21-038.** Reservations recommended. Main courses 15,000L–30,000L ($9–$18); fixed-price menu 25,000L ($15). AE, DC, MC, V. Wed–Mon 12:30–2:30pm and 7:30–9:30pm. Closed Jan 8–20. INTERNATIONAL.

This charming restaurant is frequented by local families for miles around. In a handcrafted stone building with a brick-columned porch, outdoor tables, and an indoor ambience loaded with rustic artifacts and crowded tables, the restaurant is set in a garden ringed with cypresses on a hill above the lake. To get here, follow the signs toward Il Vittoriale (the building was commissioned by d'Annunzio as a horse stable) to a quiet street with singing birds and residential houses. Depending on the shopping that day, the specialties might include a selection of freshly prepared antipasti, risotto with cuttlefish, or crêpes fondue. Polenta is served with Gorgonzola and walnuts, or you may prefer filet of beef in a beer sauce. Sunday afternoon can be crowded.

✪ **Villa Fiordaliso.** Via Zanardelli 132. ☎ **0365/20-158.** Reservations required. Main courses 24,000L–55,000L ($14.40–$33); fixed-price menu 85,000L ($51) for five courses, 120,000L ($72) for seven courses. AE, DC, MC, V. Tues–Sun 12:30–2pm and Wed–Sun 7:30–10:30pm. Closed Jan–Feb. ITALIAN.

This deluxe establishment is a Liberty-style (art nouveau) villa from 1924 with gardens stretching down to the edge of the lake. The restaurant is not only the most scenic and beautiful on Lake Garda, it also serves the finest cuisine. This is personalized by the chef and likely to include a terrine of eel and salmon in an herb-and-onion sauce, a timbale of rice and shellfish with curry, and several succulent fish and meats grilled over a fire. Other specialties include ravioli with Bergoss (a salty regional cheese), sardines from a nearby lake baked in an herb crust, and scampi in a sauce of tomatoes and wild onions. This little bastion of fine food has impeccable service to match.

GARDONE AFTER DARK

Although we agree with Goethe that, "It is not possible to express in words the enchantment of this luxuriant riviera," there is time when even scenery is tiring. If so, make your way to **Winnie's Bar** in the previously recommended Grand Hotel, Via Zanardelli 74 (☎ 0365/20-261), named after its most famous guest, Sir Winston Churchill, who preferred a bottle of cognac a day. Here you can drink and dance, following in the footsteps of Maugham, who preferred the drink (Soave), not the dance. Sabin, Nabokov, even Mussolini, are long gone from here, but some of the glory and grandeur of the *belle époque* still live on.

SIRMIONE

Perched at the tip of a narrowing strip on the southern end of the Lake, Sirmione juts out 2¹/₂ miles into Lake Garda. Noted for its thermal baths (used to treat deafness), the town is a major resort, just north of the autostrada connecting Milan and Verona, that blooms in spring and wilts in late autumn.

The resort was a favorite of Giosuè Carducci, the Italian poet who won the Nobel prize for literature in 1906. In Roman days it was frequented by still another poet, the hedonistic Catullus, who died in 54 B.C. Today the **Grotte di Catullo,** on Via Catullo (☎ 030/916-157), is the chief sight, an unbeatable combination of Roman ruins and a panoramic view of the lake. You can wander at leisure through the remains of this once-great villa from April to September, Tuesday to Sunday from 9am to 6pm; October to March, Tuesday to Sunday from 9am to 4pm. Admission is 8,000L ($4.80) for adults, free for children 17 and under and seniors 60 and over.

At the entrance to the town stands the moated 13th-century **Castello Scaligera,** Piazza Castello (☎ 030/916-468), which once belonged to the powerful Scaligeri princes of Verona. You can climb to the top and walk the ramparts April to September, daily from 9am to 6pm; October to March, Tuesday to Sunday from 9am to 1pm. Admission is 8,000L ($4.80).

GETTING THERE   Sirmione lies 3¹/₂ miles from the A4 autostrada exit and 5 miles from the town of Desanzano. Buses run from Brescia and from Verona to Sirmione every hour (trip time from either, depending on traffic: 1 hour). A one-way ticket from Brescia costs 5,400L ($3.25), and a one-way ticket from Verona is 4,600L ($2.75). There is no rail service. The nearest train terminal is at Desenzano, which is on the Venice–Milan rail line. From here, there is frequent bus service to Sirmione; the bus trip takes 30 minutes and a one-way fare is 2,100L ($1.25).

VISITOR INFORMATION   The **tourist information center** is at Viale Marconi 2 (☎ 030/916-245). It's open April to October, daily from 9am to 12:30pm and 3 to 6pm; November to March, Monday to Friday from 9am to 12:30pm and 3 to 6pm and Saturday from 9am to 12:30pm.

OUTDOOR ACTIVITIES   Known for its beaches, which are invariably overcrowded in summer, Sirmione is Garda's major lakeside resort. The best beach is **Lido delle Bione,** which you reach by taking Via Dante near the castle. Here vendors will rent you a chaise longue with an umbrella for 10,000L ($6). If you're feeling more athletic, other vendors will hook you up with a pedal boat for 12,000L ($7.20) per hour or a kayak costing 8,000L ($4.80) for an hour. If you'd like to go biking in the area, head for **Garda Noleggia,** Via Verona 47 (☎ 030/990-5973), where rentals cost 5,000L ($3) per hour.

SHOPPING   The resort is filled with souvenir shops, many hawking cheaply made trinkets aimed at the day-tripper. However, the best buys are on Friday from 8am to 1pm when an **outdoor market** blossoms in Piazza Montebaldo. Vendors bring their wares here (likely to be anything) not only from nearby lake villages but from towns and villages to the south.

WHERE TO STAY

During the peak summer season motorists need a hotel reservation to take their vehicles into the crowded confines of the town. However, there's a large parking area at the entrance to the town. Accommodations are plentiful. The only way to visit Sirmione is on foot. All the hotels below are in the center of town.

Flaminia Hotel. Piazza Flaminia 8, 25019 Sirmione. ☎ **030/916-078.** Fax 030/916-193. 45 rms. A/C TV TEL. 165,000L–210,000L ($99–$126) double. Rates include breakfast. AE, DC, MC, V.

This is one of the best little hotels in Sirmione, recently renovated with a number of facilities and amenities. One of Sirmione's more modern inns, it lies near the town center right on the lakefront, with a terrace extending into the water. The bedrooms are made attractive by French doors opening onto private balconies. The lounges are furnished in a functional modern style. Breakfast is the only meal served.

Grand Hotel Terme. Viale Marconi 1, 25019 Sirmione. ☎ **030/916-261.** Fax 030/916-568. 58 rms, 15 junior suites, 1 suite. A/C MINIBAR TV TEL. 400,000L ($240) double; 450,000L ($270) junior suite; 800,000L ($480) suite. Rates include breakfast. AE, DC, MC, V. Closed Oct 27–Mar 21.

This rambling, three-story hotel at the entrance of the old town is on the lake next to the Scaligeri Castle. After Villa Cortine (see below), it's the second-best choice in the town center, known especially for its lake-bordering garden. The wide marble halls and stairs lead to well-furnished, balconied bedrooms. Constructed in 1948, the hotel has contemporary furnishings, plus a number of spa and physical-therapy facilities and a swimming pool. The food served in the indoor-outdoor dining room is excellent, with such offerings as prosciutto and melon, risotto with snails, fettuccine with fresh porcini, and a wide choice of salads and fruits.

Olivi. Via San Pietro 5, 25019 Sirmione. ☎ **030/990-5365.** Fax 030/916-472. 60 rms. A/C TV TEL. 180,000L–240,000L ($108–$144) double. Rates include breakfast. AE, DC, MC, V. Closed Dec–Jan.

A creation of the sun-loving owner Cerini Franco, this hotel has an excellent location, on the rise of a hill in a grove of olive trees at the edge of town. The all-glass walls of the major rooms never let you forget you're in a garden spot of Italy. Even the compact and streamlined bedrooms have walls of glass leading onto open balconies. The hotel serves typically Italian meals. Sometimes live music is featured— even country music when the hotel stages a barbecue. The hotel offers an outdoor swimming pool, a solarium, and laundry and room service.

✪ **Villa Cortine Palace.** Via Grotte 12, 25019 Sirmione. ☎ **030/990-5890.** Fax 030/916-390. 43 rms, 6 suites. A/C TV TEL. 460,000L–590,000L ($276–$354) double; 770,000L– 1,050,000L ($462–$630) suite. Rates include breakfast. AE, DC, MC, V. Closed end of Oct–Easter.

This first-class choice is luxuriously set apart from the town center, surrounded by imposing, sumptuous gardens. For serenity, atmosphere, professional service, and even good food, there's nothing to equal it in Sirmione. The hotel was built in 1905, although in 1957 a new wing greatly increased its amenities and capacities. Today all but a handful of its bedrooms are in this new wing, with the bar and reception area in the original building. The century-old landscaping in the hotel's park contains a formal entrance through a colonnade, and winding lanes lined with cypress trees, wide-spreading magnolias, and flower-bordered marble fountains with classic sculpture. Some rooms offer a minibar. The interior has one formal drawing room, with much gilt and marble—it's positively palatial.

WHERE TO DINE

La Rucola. Vicolo Strentelle 5. ☎ **030/916-326.** Reservations recommended. Main courses 25,000L–30,000L ($15–$18); fixed-price menu 80,000L ($48). AE, MC, V. Fri–Wed 12:30– 2:30pm and 7:30–10:30pm. Closed Jan–Feb 9. ITALIAN.

In the heart of town, this restaurant lies on a small alley a few steps from the main gate leading into Sirmione. The building looks like a vine-laden, sienna-colored country house and was originally a stable 150 years ago. Full meals, served in a mod-ernized interior, could include fresh salmon, langoustines, mixed grilled fish, and a more limited meat selection. Meats are most often grilled or flambéed, including Florentine beefsteak. Newer items on the menu include *gnocchetti di riso* with baby squid and squid ink, and fillet of turbot with potatoes and a zabaglione of spinach. Good pasta dishes include spaghetti with clams and several local specialties. Many of the desserts are made for two, including crêpes Suzette and banana flambé.

Ristorante Grifone da Luciano. Via delle Bisse 5. ☎ **030/916-097.** Main courses 10,000L– 20,000L ($6–$12). AE, DC, MC, V. Thurs–Tues noon–2:30pm and 7–10:30pm. Closed Nov–Easter. INTERNATIONAL.

One of the most attractive restaurants in town is separated from the castle by a row of shrubbery, a low stone wall, and a moat. From your seat on the flagstone terrace, you'll have a view of the crashing waves and the plants that ring the dining area. The main building is an old stone house surrounded with olive trees, but many diners gravitate toward the low glass-and-metal extension stretching toward the lake. The place doesn't necessarily rate a rave, but traditionalists like it. They have a charming and fun staff, and the chef is talented, keeping the quality high and the prices moderate. The food includes many varieties of fish and many standard Italian dishes such as *gnocchetti dragoncella* (with tomatoes and aromatic herbs), risotto with shellfish, Venetian-style calves' liver with onions, filet of beef flambéed with whisky, tournedos of beef, and beef cutlets *(costello di Manzo)*.

6 Lake Como

Everything noble, everything evoking love—that was how Stendhal characterized fork-tongued Lake Como. Others have called it "the looking glass of Venus," and Virgil pronounced it "our greatest lake." More than 30 miles north of Milan, it's a shimmering deep blue spanning $2^1/2$ miles at its widest point. With its flower-studded gardens, villas built for the wealthy of the 17th and 18th centuries, and mild climate, Larius (as it was known to the Romans) is among the most scenic spots in all of Italy.

ESSENTIALS

GETTING THERE   By Train   Trains arrive daily at Como from Milan every hour. The trip takes 40 minutes, and a one-way fare is 7,700L ($4.60). The main station, **Stazione San Giovanni,** Piazzale San Gottardo (☎ **031/261-494**), lies at the end of Viale Gallio, a 15-minute walk from the center (Piazza Cavour).

By Car   The city of Como is 25 miles north of Milan and is reached via the autostrada A9. Once at the Como, a small road (S583) leads to the popular resort of Bellagio.

GETTING AROUND   By Bus   SPT, Piazza Matteotti (☎ **031/247-247**), offers bus service to the most important centers on the lake. A one-way fare to the most popular resort at Bellagio costs 4,100L ($2.45). Travel time depends on the traffic.

By Boat & Hydrofoil   From Como, there are seven boat trips daily exploring the lake, each lasting 2 hours. There are also seven 45-minute hydrofoil trips offered daily. Boats and hydrofoils dock at Lungo Lario in front of Piazza Cavour in Como. For information or schedules call ☎ **031/304-060,** or stop at the dockside ticket office. If you want information on boating and hydrofoils in the nearby area, call in Cernobbio: **BCS Centro Nautico Barche Legno,** c/o Villa Pizzo, 48 (☎ **031/511-262**); in Menaggio: **Centro Nautico "Riva Boat Service,"** Via Cipressi (☎ **0344/310-033**); or in Ossuccio: **Idro Sciatori Isola,** Via Provinciale 80 (☎ **0344/55-142**). Either at the dock in Como or at the tourist office, you can pick up a copy of a booklet, *Orari e Traffie,* listing prices and departures of public lake transport. Depending on where you are heading, fares range from 2,000L to 12,500L ($1.20 to $7.50).

COMO

At the southern tip of the lake, 25 miles north of Milan, Como is known for its silk industry. Most visitors will pass through here to take a boat ride on the lake. The lakeside Piazza Cavour is the center of local life.

Because Como is also an industrial city, we have generally shunned it for overnighting, preferring to anchor into one of the more attractive resorts along the lake, like Bellagio. However, train passengers who don't plan to rent a car may prefer Como (the city, that is) for convenience.

For centuries the destiny of the town has been linked to that of Milan. Como is still called the world capital of silk, the silk makers of the city joining communal hands with the fashion designers of Milan. Como has been making silk since Marco Polo first returned with silkworms from China (since the end of World War II Como has left the cultivating of silk to the Chinese and just imported the thread to weave into fabrics). Designers such as Giorgio Armani and Bill Blass come here to discuss the patterns they want with silk manufacturers.

VISITOR INFORMATION   The **tourist information center** is at Piazza Cavour 17 (☎ 031/269-712), open Monday to Saturday from 9am to 12:30pm and 2:30 to 6pm.

EXPLORING THE TOWN

Before rushing off on a boat for a tour of the lake, you may want to look at the **Cattedrale di Como,** Piazza del Duomo (☎ 031/265-244). Construction began in the 14th century in the Lombard Gothic style, and labored on through the Renaissance until the 1700s. The exterior, frankly, is more interesting than the interior. Dating from 1487, it's lavishly decorated with statues, including those of Pliny the Elder (A.D. 23–79) and the Younger (A.D. 62–113), who one writer once called "the beautiful people of ancient Rome." Inside, look for the 16th-century tapestries depicting scenes from the Bible. The cathedral is open Monday through Saturday from 7am to noon and 3 to 6:30pm.

On the other side of the Duomo lie the colorfully striped **Brolette** (town hall), and adjoining it, the **Torre del Comune.** Both are from the 13th century.

If time remains, head down the main street, Via Vittorio Emanuele, where, just two blocks south of the cathedral, rises the five-sided **San Fedele,** a church from the 12th century standing on Piazza San Fedele. It is known for its unusual pentagonal apse and a doorway carved with "fatted" figures from the Middle Ages. Further along, you come to the **Museo Civico del Risorgimento Garibaldi,** Piazza Medaglie d'Oro Comasche (☎ 031/271-343), the virtual "attic" of Como, displaying artifacts collected by the city from prehistoric times through World War II. It's open Tuesday through Saturday from 9:30am to 12:30pm and 2 to 5pm; Sunday from 9:30am to 12:30pm. Admission is 4,000L ($2.40).

The art museum of Como is of passing interest: The small **Pinacoteca Palazzo Volpi** at Via Diaz 84 (☎ 031/269-869) has several old and quite wonderful paintings from the Middle Ages, most of which were taken here from the monastery of Santa Margherita del Broletto. Two of the museum's best paintings are anonymous— that of St. Sebastian riddled with arrows (though appearing quite resigned to the whole thing) and a moving *Youth & Death.* The museum is open Monday through Saturday from 9:30am to 12:30pm and 2 to 5pm and Sunday from 10am to 1pm. Admission is 4,000L ($2.40) adults, 2,500L ($1.50) students and children.

After the museum, continue down Via Giovio until you come to the gate, **Porta Vittoria,** dating from 1192 with five tiers of arches. A short walk away, passing through a dreary commercial area, leads you to Como's most interesting church, the 11th-century **Sant-Abbondio,** a Romanesque gem. From Porta Vittoria, take Viale Cattaneo to Viale Roosevelt, turning left onto Via Sant'Abbondio on which the church stands. Because of its age, it was massively restored in the 19th century. Heavily frescoed, the church has five aisles.

The heartbeat of life in Como is **Piazza Cavour** with its hotels, cafes, and steamers departing for lakeside resorts. Immediately to the west, the **Giardini Pubblici** make for a pleasant stroll, especially if you're heading for the **Tempio Voltiano,** Viale

Marconi (☎ 031/574-705), honoring native son Alessandro Volta, the physicist and pioneer of electricity. The temple contains memorabilia of his life and experiments. It is open April to September, Tuesday to Sunday from 10am to noon and 3 to 6pm; October to March, Tuesday to Sunday from 10am to noon and 2 to 4pm. Admission is 5,000L ($3).

To bid adieu to Como, take the funicular at Lungolario Trieste (near the main beach at Villa Genio) to the top of **Brunante,** a hill overlooking Como. Here is the most panoramic view possible on Lake Como. Departures are every 30 minutes during the day, a round-trip costing 6,800L ($4.10).

OUTDOOR ACTIVITIES   The best swimming is at a pool, **Lido Villa Olmo,** Via Cantoni (☎ 031/570-968), which adjoins a sandy stretch of beach for sunbathing. Admission is 7,500L ($4.50), and it's open daily 10am to 6pm.

SHOPPING   This lakeside city has been known throughout Europe as a focal point of the silk industry since the era of Marco Polo. Consequently, slinky fashion accessories, especially scarves, blouses, pillows, and neckties, are literally bursting the seams of many merchants throughout the town. Before you buy, you might be interested in viewing a museum devoted exclusively to the history and techniques of the silk industry, the **Museo Didactico delle Sete,** Via Vallegio 3 (☎ 031/303-180). Maintained by a local trade school, it displays antique weaving machines and memorabilia going back to the Renaissance concerning the world's most elegant fabric. Entrance, priced at 15,000L ($9) per person, is relatively expensive. It's open Tuesday to Saturday from 9am to noon and 3 to 6pm.

Not all of the silk factories will sell retail to individuals, but the best of those that do include the following: One of the largest outlets in the region is **Ratti,** Via per Chernobbio 17 (☎ 031/233-111). On the premises of an antique villa, accessible via a formal-looking gate on the periphery of town (follow the signs to Chernobbio), you'll find a duet of rooms stuffed with retail goods of a local producer. Look for yard goods and ties that look very similar to the high-fashion accessories of some of the world's most prestigious names, at extremely reasonable prices. Within Como, two somewhat smaller but eminently tasteful outlets with the same style of merchandise are **Binda,** Viale Geno (☎ 031/303-440); and **Martinetti,** Via Torriani 41 (☎ 031/269-053).

WHERE TO STAY

Hotel Barchetta Excelsior. Piazza Cavour 1, 22100 Como. ☎ **031/261-817.** Fax 031/302-622. 80 rms, 4 suites. A/C MINIBAR TV TEL. 230,000L–270,000L ($138–$162) double; 340,000L ($204) suite. Rates include breakfast. AE, DC, MC, V. Parking 28,000L ($16.80).

This first-class hotel is set at the edge of the main square in the commercial section of town. Major additions have been made to the original 1957 structure, including the alteration of its restaurant and an upgrading of the bedrooms, which are comfortably furnished, often with a balcony overlooking this heartbeat square and the lake. All accommodations have radios, among other amenities, and most have lake views. There's a parking lot behind the hotel, plus a covered garage just over 50 yards away.

Metropole & Suisse. Piazza Cavour 19, 22100 Como. ☎ **031/269-444.** Fax 031/300-808. 71 rms, 3 suites. A/C MINIBAR TV TEL. 270,000L ($162) double; 290,000L–320,000L ($174–$192) suite. AE, DC, MC, V. Closed Dec 18–Jan 7. Parking 20,000L ($12).

This hotel offers good value in clean, convenient accommodations. Near the cathedral and the major lake-fronting square, it's composed of three lower floors dating from around 1700, with upper floors added about 60 years ago. The hotel began life as a waterfront store (the square itself is an 1850 landfill). A photograph of the Swiss creator of the hotel with his staff in 1892 hangs behind the reception desk. Each of the bedrooms is different, rich with character for the most part. Many repeat clients have staked out their favorite rooms. A parking garage and the city marina are nearby. A popular restaurant, Imbarcadero, under separate management (below), fills most of the ground floor of the hotel.

WHERE TO DINE

Ristorante Imbarcadero. In the Hotel Metropole & Suisse, Piazza Cavour 20. ☎ **031/ 270-166.** Reservations recommended. Main courses 24,000L–32,000L ($14.40–$19.20); fixed-price menu 40,000L ($24). AE, DC, MC, V. Daily 12:30–2:30pm and 7:30–10pm. Closed Jan 1–8. INTERNATIONAL/LOMBARD.

Established more than a decade ago in a 300-year-old building near the edge of the lake, this restaurant is filled with a pleasing blend of carved Victorian chairs, panoramic windows with marina views, and potted palms. The summer outdoor terrace set up on the square is ringed with shrubbery and illuminated with evening candlelight. The restaurant attracts clients with demanding tastes who take pleasure in the first-class ingredients deftly handled by the kitchen. The chef makes his own tagliatelle, or you may want to order spaghetti with garlic, oil, and red pepper. The fish dishes are excellent, especially slices of sea bass with braised leek and aromatic vinegar or else sage-flavored Como lake whitefish. Try the breaded veal cutlet Milanese style or else breast of pheasant flavored with port and shallots. Desserts might include a parfait of almonds, hazelnuts, and apple sorbet flavored with Calvados.

COMO AFTER DARK

The most fun is in July when **Jazz & Co.** stages five concerts at Piazza San Federale. The tourist office (see above) will supply details.

CERNOBBIO

Cernobbio, 3 miles northwest of Como and 33 miles north of Milan, is a small, fashionable resort frequented by the wealthy of Europe for its deluxe hotel, the 16th-century Villa d'Este. But its idyllic anchor on the lake has also attracted a less affluent tourist, who'll find a number of third- and fourth-class accommodations as well.

VISITOR INFORMATION   The **tourist information center** is at Via Regina 33B (☎ **031/510-198**) and is open Monday to Saturday from 9:30am to 12:30pm and 2:30 to 5:30pm; closed January.

WHERE TO STAY

✪ **Grand Hotel Villa d'Este.** 22010 Cernobbio. ☎ **031/3481.** Fax 031/348-844. 108 rms, 54 suites. A/C MINIBAR TV TEL. 700,000L–900,000L ($420–$540) double; from 1,100,000L ($660) suite. Rates include breakfast. AE, DC, MC, V. Closed Nov 15–Mar 1.

One of Italy's most legendary hotels, the Villa d'Este was built in 1568 as a lakeside home and pleasure pavilion for Cardinal Tolomeo Gallio. One of the most famous Renaissance-era hotels in the world, designed in the neoclassical style by Pellegrino Pellegrini di Valsolda, it passed from owner to illustrious owner for 300 years until it was transformed into a hotel in 1873.

The hotel remains a kingdom unto itself, a splendid palace surrounded by 10 acres of some of the finest hotel gardens in Italy. The interior lives up to the enthralling beauty of the grounds. The silken wall coverings of the Salon Napoleone were embroidered especially for the emperor's visit; the Canova room is centered around a statue of Venus by the room's namesake; and a Grand Ballroom is suitable for some of the most festive banquets in Europe. Throughout, frescoed ceilings, impeccable antiques, and attentive service create one of the world's most envied hotels. Each bedroom has an individual decor, and a roster of famous former occupants. Some 34 of the hotel's 156 accommodations are in the Queen's Pavilion, an elegant annex built in 1856.

Dining/Entertainment: The hotel contains two restaurants, both of culinary merit serving formal à la carte dinners. The cookery is sublime. Lunches are less expensive, especially in summer when light buffets are set on long tables within view of the gardens. Throughout the year there's always at least a live pianist on most nights, and in midsummer a small orchestra plays dance music three evenings a week.

Services: Concierge, room service, baby-sitting, laundry, valet, hairdresser, massage.

Facilities: Swimming pool floating atop Lake Como; access to the world-class golf course at nearby Montofano; red-clay tennis courts; gym, sauna, Turkish bath; squash court; waterskiing and other sports.

Hotel Asnigo. Via Noseda 2, 22012 Cernobbio. ☎ **031/510-062.** Fax 031/510-249. 30 rms, 3 suites. MINIBAR TV TEL. 190,000L–257,000L ($114–$154.20) double; 260,000L–320,000L ($156–$192) suite for three. Rates include buffet breakfast. AE, DC, MC, V.

The Asnigo, 1 mile northeast of Cernobbio, calls itself *un piccolo grand hotel.* Commanding a view of Como from its hillside perch, this is a good little first-class hotel set in its own garden. Its special and subtle charms have been known to a lake-loving set of British visitors since 1914.

An Englishwoman writes: "Last summer . . . I went on a trip to Italy with my nephew and his wife from America, who quite frankly patronize a higher type of establishment than I do. Naturally, they were lured to the Villa d'Este on Como. I, fortunately, was able to find a splendid little hotel in the hills, the Asnigo. The proprietor was most helpful, the meals flawless and beautifully served, the room spotlessly clean and comfortable. After being a dinner guest one night at the Villa d'Este, I returned the hospitality the following evening by inviting my relatives for a most enjoyable meal at my hotel. At least they learned that good food and comfort are not the sole domain of a deluxe hotel." We echo her sentiments.

BELLAGIO

Sitting on a promontory at the point where Lake Como forks, 48 miles north of Milan and 18 miles northeast of Como, Bellagio is with much justification labeled "The Pearl of Larius." It has also been called "the prettiest town in Europe." A sleepy veil hangs over the arcaded streets and little shops. Bellagio is rich in memories, having attracted fashionable, even royal visitors such as Leopold I of Belgium, who used to own the 18th-century Villa Giulia. Still going strong, although no longer the aristocratic address today that it was, Bellagio is a 45-minute drive north of Como.

VISITOR INFORMATION The **tourist information center** is at Piazza della Chiesa 14 (☎ 031/950-204). It's open May to September, daily from 9am to noon and 3 to 6pm; October to April, Monday and Wednesday to Saturday from 8:30am to 12:15pm and 2:30 to 6pm.

EXPLORING LAKESIDE GARDENS

To reach many of the places in Bellagio, you must climb streets that are really stair-ways. Its lakeside promenade blossoms with flowering shrubbery. From the town, you can take tours of Lake Como and enjoy sports such as rowing and tennis, or just lounge at Bellagio Lido (the beach).

The most important attraction of Bellagio is the garden of the **Villa Melzi** museum and chapel, on Lungolario Marconi (☎ **031/950-318**). The villa was built in 1808 for Duke Francesco Melzi d'Eril, vice-president of the Italian republic founded by Napoléon. Franz Liszt and Stendhal are among the illustrious guests who have stayed here. The park has many well-known sculptures, and if you're here in the spring you can enjoy the azaleas. Today it's the property of Count Gallarti Scotti, who opens it from March 22 to the end of October, daily from 9am to 6pm. Admission is 5,000L ($3).

If time allows, try to explore the gardens of the **Villa Serbelloni,** Piazza della Chiesa (☎ **031/950-204**), the Bellagio Study and Conference Center of the Rockefeller Foundation (not to be confused with the Grand Hotel Villa Serbelloni by the waterside in the village). The landlord here used to be Pliny the Younger. The villa is not open to the public, but you can visit the park on 1¹/₂-hour guided tours starting at 11am and 4pm. Tours are conducted mid-April to mid-October, Tuesday to Sunday, at a cost of 6,000L ($3.60) per person; the proceeds go to local charities.

A NEARBY VILLA

From Como, car ferries sail back and forth across the lake to Cadenabbia on the western shore, another lakeside resort, with hotels and villas. Directly south of Cadenabbia on the run to Tremezzo, the **Villa Carlotta** (☎ **0344/40-405**) is the most-visited attraction of Lake Como—and with good reason. In a serene setting, the villa is graced with gardens of exotic flowers and blossoming shrubbery, especially rhododendrons and azaleas. Its beauty is tame, cultivated, much like a fairy tale that recaptures the halcyon life available only to the very rich of the 19th century. Dating from 1847, the estate was named after a Prussian princess, Carlotta, who married the duke of Sachsen-Meiningen. Inside the villa are a number of art treasures, including Canova's *Cupid and Psyche,* and neoclassical statues by Bertel Thorvaldsen, a Danish sculptor who died in 1844. There are also neoclassical paintings, furniture, and a stone-and-bronze table ornament that belonged to Viceroy Eugene Beauharnais on display. From March 15 to 31 and in October, it's open daily from 9am to 11:30am and 2 to 4:30pm; April to September, daily from 9am to 6pm. Admission is 8,000L ($4.80) for adults, 6,000L ($3.60) for seniors 65 and over, and 5,000L ($3) for children 7 to 14.

WHERE TO STAY & DINE

✪ **Grand Hotel Villa Serbelloni.** Via Roma 1, 22021 Bellagio. ☎ **800/223-6620** in the U.S., or 031/950-216. Fax 031/951-529. 95 rms, 5 suites. MINIBAR TV TEL. 440,000L–651,000L ($264–$390.60) double; 840,000L–1,045,000L ($504–$627) suite. Rates include breakfast. AE, DC, MC, V. Closed Nov 1–Mar 27.

This lavish old hotel is for those born to the grand style of life. On the lake, its surpassed only by the Villa d'Este. It stands proud and serene at the edge of town against a backdrop of hills, surrounded by beautiful gardens of flowers and semi-tropical plants. It's perched on the lakefront, and guests sunbathe on the waterside terrace or doze under a willow tree. Inside, the public rooms rekindle the spirit of the baroque: the grand drawing room with painted ceiling, marble columns, a glittering chandelier, and ornate gilt furnishings and the mirrored neoclassical dining room. The bedrooms are wide-ranging, from elaborate suites with a recessed tile bath, baroque furnishings, and lake-view balconies to more chaste quarters. The most desirable rooms open onto the lake; 13 are air-conditioned. In 1993 it opened a fitness and beauty center.

Hotel du Lac. Piazza Mazzini 32, 22021 Bellagio. ☎ **031/950-320.** Fax 031/951-624. 48 rms. A/C MINIBAR TV TEL. 195,000L–210,000L ($117–$126) double. Rates include breakfast. MC, V. Closed Nov–Mar 25. Parking 12,000L ($7.20).

Hotel du Lac was built 150 years ago, when the waters of the lake came directly up to the front door of the ocher facade. Landfill has since created Piazza Mazzini, and today there's a generous terraced expanse of flagstones in front with cafe tables and an arched arcade. The bedrooms are comfortably furnished, containing such amenities as satellite TV and hair dryers. On the second floor is a glassed-in terrace restaurant, and guests can also bask in the sun or relax in the shade on the rooftop garden, opening onto panoramic views of the lake.

Hotel Florence. Piazza Mazzini 45, 22021 Bellagio. ☎ **031/950-342.** Fax 031/951-722. 36 rms. TV TEL. 205,000L–220,000L ($123–$132) double; 308,000L ($184.80) suite. Rates include breakfast. AE, MC, V. Closed Oct 25–Apr 1.

The entrance to this green-shuttered villa, one of the most charming middle-bracket choices in the resort, is under a vaulted arcade near the ferryboat landing. Wisteria climbs over the iron balustrades of the lake-view terraces. The entrance hall's vaulted ceilings are supported by massive timbers and granite Doric columns; there's even a Tuscan fireplace. The main section of the hotel was built around 1720, although most of what you see today was added around 1880. For 150 years the hotel has been run by the Ketzlar family. You'll probably be welcomed by the charming Roberta Ketzlar, her brother Ronald, and their mother, Friedl. The bedrooms are scattered amid spacious sitting and dining areas, and often have high ceilings, antiques, and lake views. In the 1990s the hotel was vastly improved, with the addition of a gourmet restaurant and an America Bar, which becomes a kind of jazz club on Sunday evening.

TREMEZZO

Reached by frequent ferries from Bellagio, Tremezzo, 48 miles north of Milan and 18 miles north of Como, is another popular west-shore resort that opens onto a panoramic view of Lake Como. Around the town is a district known as Tremezzina, with luxuriant vegetation that includes citrus trees, palms, cypresses, and magnolias. Tremezzo is the starting point for many excursions. Its accommodations are much more limited than those in Bellagio.

VISITOR INFORMATION   There's a **tourist information center** at Via Regina 3 (☎ **0344/40-493**). It's open May to October, Monday to Wednesday and Friday to Saturday from 9am to noon and 3:30 to 6:30pm.

WHERE TO STAY

Grand Hotel Tremezzo Palace. Via Regina 8, 22019 Tremezzo. ☎ **0344/40-446.** Fax 0344/40-201. 98 rms, 2 suites. MINIBAR TV TEL. 300,000L–320,000L ($180–$192) double; from 350,000L ($210) suite. Rates include breakfast. AE, DC, MC, V. Closed Nov–Mar 1.

Built in 1910 on a terrace several feet above the traffic of the lakeside road, this hotel is one of the region's best examples of the Italian Liberty style, and the unquestioned leading choice at this resort. In 1990 most of the pale-yellow hotel was discreetly modernized, and the bedrooms on two of the hotel's four floors were garnished with air-conditioning. (Many guests still reject the air-conditioning in favor of open-windowed access to lakefront breezes.) The bedrooms are comfortable, traditionally furnished, high-ceilinged, and priced according to views of either the lake (most expensive, often with blaconies) or the park and garden extending from the back of the hotel.

   Dining/Entertainment: There are three restaurants and an outdoor dining terrace (closed during inclement weather). All serve regional and international cuisines.

On a platform beside the lake is the Club l'Escale, a bar popular with residents of surrounding communities.

Services: Room service, baby-sitting, laundry, valet.

Facilities: Very large park, two pools, tennis court, lido beside the lake, jogging track, billiard room, heliport, and conference facilities.

Hotel Bazzoni & du Lac. Via Regina 26, 22019 Tremezzo. ☎ **0344/40-403.** Fax 0344/41-651. 123 rms. TEL. 160,000L–170,000L ($96–$102) double. Rates include breakfast. AE, DC, MC, V. Closed Oct 10–Apr 24. Ferry from Ballagio or hydrofoil from Como.

There was an older hotel on this spot during Napoléon's era, bombed by the British 5 days after the official end of World War II. Today the reconstructed hotel is a collection of glass-and-concrete walls, with prominent balconies at the edge of the lake. It's one of the best choices in a resort town filled with hotels of grander format but much less desirable accommodations. The main restaurant on the ground floor has a baronial but unused fireplace, contemporary frescoes of the boats on the lake, and scattered carvings. The pleasantly furnished sitting rooms include antique architectural elements from older buildings. A summer restaurant near the hotel's entrance is constructed like a small island of glass walls.

A NEARBY PLACE TO STAY

✪ **Grand Hotel Victoria.** Via Lungolago Castelli 7–11, 22017 Menaggio. ☎ **0344/32-003.** Fax 0344/32-992. 49 rms, 4 junior suites. A/C MINIBAR TV TEL. 320,000L–370,000L ($192–$222) double; from 450,000L ($270) junior suite. Rates include breakfast. Half board 55,000L ($33) per person extra. AE, DC, MC, V.

This is one of the best hotels on the lake, built in 1806 along a lakeside road bordered with chestnut trees. It was luxuriously renovated in 1983, with attention paid to the preservation of the ornate plasterwork of the ceiling vaults. There is a lavish use of marble, big windows, and carving on the white facade that resembles the heads of water sprites. The modern furniture and amenities in the bedrooms include bathroom tiles designed by Valentino. The beach in front of the hotel is one of the best spots on Lake Como for windsurfing, especially between 3 and 7pm.

Dining/Entertainment: Guests enjoy drinks on the outdoor terrace near the stone columns of the tree-shaded portico, or in the antique-filled public rooms. The restaurant has well-prepared food, art nouveau chandeliers, and an embellished ceiling showing the fruits of an Italian harvest and mythical beasts.

Services: Room service, baby-sitting, laundry, valet.

Facilities: Pool, beach, tennis court, private boats.

WHERE TO DINE

Al Veluu. Via Rogaro 11, Rogaro di Tremezzo. ☎ **0344/40-510.** Reservations recommended. Main courses 18,000L–35,000L ($10.80–$21). AE, MC, V. Wed–Mon noon–2pm and 7:30–9:30pm. Closed Nov–Mar 1. LOMBARD/INTERNATIONAL.

Al Veluu, 1 mile north of the resort in the hills, is an excellent regional restaurant with plenty of relaxed charm and lots of personalized attention from owner Carlo Antonini and his son, Luca. The terrace tables offer a panoramic sweep of the lake, and the rustic dining room with its fireplace and big windows is a welcome refuge in inclement weather. Most of the produce comes freshly picked from the garden; even the butter is homemade, and the best cheeses come from a local farmer. The menu is based on the fresh, light, and flavorful cuisine of northern Italy. Examples include *missoltini* (dried fish from the lake, marinated, and grilled with olive oil and vinegar), *penne al Veluu* (made with spicy tomato sauce), *risotto al Veluu* (made with champagne sauce and fresh green peppers), and an unusual lamb pâté.

7 Lake Maggiore

The waters of this lake wash up on the banks of Piedmont and Lombardy in Italy, but its more austere northern basin (Locarno, for example) lies in the mountainous region of Switzerland. It stretches more than 40 miles and is 6 1/2 miles at its widest point. A wealth of natural beauty awaits you: mellowed lakeside villas, dozens of lush gardens, sparkling waters, panoramic views. A veil of mist seems to hover at times, especially in early spring and late autumn. Such men as Hemingway, Flaubert, Goethe, and Wagner have cited its charms.

Maggiore is a most rewarding lake to visit from Milan, especially because of the Borromean Islands in its center (most easily reached from Stresa). If you have time, drive around the entire basin; on a more limited schedule, you may find the western, resort-studded shore the most scenic.

ESSENTIALS

GETTING THERE   By Train   The major resort of the lake, Stresa, is just 1 hour by train from Milan on the Milan–Domodossola line. Service is every hour, and a one-way ticket costs from 7,200L to 15,000L ($4.30 to $9), depending on the train. There is no bus service to the lake. For information and schedules call ☎ **0323/30-472.**

By Car   From Milan, a 51-mile drive northwest along autostrada A8 (staying on E62 out of Gallarate until it joins Route SS33 up the western shore of the lake) will take you to Stresa, the major resort.

GETTING AROUND   By Car   Route S33 goes up the west side of the lake to Verbania, where it becomes S34 on its way to the Swiss town of Locarno, a distance of about 25 miles. If you want to encircle the lake you'll have to clear Swiss Customs before passing through such famed tourist resorts as Ascona and eventually Locarno. From Locarno you can head south again along the eastern, less touristy shore, which becomes Route SS493 on the Italy side. At Luino, you can cut off on SS233, then A8 to return to Milan, or continue along the lake shore (the road becomes SS629) to the southern point again where you can get E62 back toward Milan.

By Boat   Cruising Lake Maggiore with modern boats and fast hydrofoils is a very developed activity. There is a frequent ferry service for cars and passengers between Intra (Verbania) and Laveno. Boats leave from the Piazza Marconi along Corso Umberto I in Stresa. For boat schedules, contact **Navigazione Sul Lago Maggiore,** Viale F. Baracca 1 (☎ **0322/46-651**), in the lakeside town of Arona.

STRESA

On the western shore, 407 miles northwest of Rome and 51 miles northwest of Milan, Stresa has skyrocketed from a simple village of fisherfolk to a first-class international resort. Its vantage on the lake is almost unparalleled, and its level of hotel accommodations is superior to that of other Maggiore resorts in Italy. Scene of sporting activities and an international **Festival of Musical Weeks** (beginning in late August), it swings into action in April, then dwindles in popularity at the end of October.

VISITOR INFORMATION   The **tourist information center** is at Via Prìncipe Tomaso 70–72 (☎ **0323/30-150**). It's open May to September, Monday to Saturday from 8:30am to 12:30pm and 3 to 6:15pm and Sunday from 9am to noon; October to April, Monday to Friday from 8:30am to 12:30pm and 3 to 6:15pm and Saturday from 8:30am to 12:30pm.

WHERE TO STAY

Albergo Ariston. Corso Italia 60, 28049 Stresa. ☎ **0323/31-195.** Fax 0323/31-195. 11 rms. 140,000L ($84) double. Rates include breakfast. Half board 95,000L ($57) per person extra. AE, DC, MC, V. Closed Dec–Apr 1. Free parking.

Here is a good bargain. The hotel is listed as third class, but its comfort is superior. The rooms are well kept and attractively furnished. Nonresidents can stop in for a meal, ordering a lunch or dinner on the terrace, which has a panoramic view of the lake and gardens. Your hosts are the Balconi family.

✪ Grand Hotel des Iles Borromées. Corso Umberto I 67, 28049 Stresa. ☎ **0323/30-431.** Fax 0323/938-938. 173 rms, 13 suites. A/C MINIBAR TV TEL. 528,000L–595,000L ($316.80–$357) double; from 759,000L ($455.40) suite. AE, DC, MC, V.

Set on the edge of the lake in a flowering garden, this is by far Stresa's leading resort hotel. You can see the Borromean Islands from many rooms, furnished in an Italian/French Empire style, including rich ormolu, burnished hardwoods, plush carpets, and pastel colors. The baths look as if every quarry in Italy was scoured for matched marble. The hotel opened its doors in 1863, attracting titled notables and guests like J. P. Morgan. Hemingway had the hero of *A Farewell to Arms* stay here to escape World War I. The elegant public rooms, with two-tone ornate plasterwork and crystal chandeliers, once hosted a top-level meeting among the heads of state of Italy, Great Britain, and France in an attempt to stave off World War II. The hotel also operates a 27-room Residenza in a building separate from the main hotel. Prices are 20% lower, and each room is decorated in a modern style, with air-conditioning, TV, and minibar.

Dining/Entertainment: The restaurant serves specialties of Lombardy and the Piedmont. Special dishes include fillet of perch with sage and tenderloin cooked on a black stone.

Services: Room service, laundry, baby-sitting.

Facilities: Medically supervised health and exercise program, two outdoor pools, tennis court, sauna.

Hotel Astoria. Corso Umberto I 31, 28049 Stresa. ☎ **0323/32-566.** Fax 0323/933-785. 95 rms, 4 suites. MINIBAR TV TEL. 180,000L–290,000L ($108–$174) double; 350,000L ($210) suite. Rates include breakfast. AE, DC, MC, V. Closed late Oct–Mar 27.

A 5-minute walk from either the railway station or the center of Stresa, this hotel fronting the lake was partially rebuilt in 1993, giving an even more modern gloss to an already contemporary hotel. A medium-priced establishment, it's expressly for sunseekers who want a heated swimming pool, Turkish bath, small gym, roof garden, and Jacuzzi. It features triangular balconies—one to each bedroom—jutting out for the view. The bedrooms are streamlined and spacious. The public lounges have walls of glass opening toward the lake view and the garden. The portion of the dining room favored by most guests is the wide-paved, open-air front terrace, where under shelter you dine on good Italian and international cuisine while enjoying a view of Maggiore.

Hotel Moderno. Via Cavour 33, 28049 Stresa. ☎ **0323/933-733.** Fax 0323/933-775. 53 rms. MINIBAR TV TEL. 200,000L ($120) double. Rates include breakfast. AE, DC, MC, V. Closed Nov–Mar. Parking 15,000L ($9).

A block from the lake and boat-landing stage, the Moderno lies in the center of Stresa. The hotel dates from the turn of the century, but subsequent modernization, most recently in 1989, has rendered the building's original lines unrecognizable. The bedrooms each have a personalized decor and good beds. The Moderno has three restaurants, unusual for such a small hotel.

Regina Palace. Corso Umberto I 33, 28049 Stresa. ☎ **0323/933-777.** Fax 0323/933-776. 167 rms, 7 suites. MINIBAR TV TEL. 380,000L ($228) double; from 700,000L ($420) suite. Rates include breakfast. AE, DC, MC, V. Closed Oct–Easter. Parking 15,000L ($9) in garage, free outside.

Regina Palace was built in 1908 in a boomerang shape whose central curve faces the lakefront. The art deco illuminated-glass columns inside are capped with gilded Corinthian capitals, and a wide marble stairwell is flanked with carved oak lions. There's a swimming pool in the rear, and a guest roster that has included George Bernard Shaw, Ernest Hemingway, Umberto I of Italy, and Princess Margaret. Lately, about half the guests are American, many of them with the tour groups that stream through Stresa. The bedrooms are equipped with all the modern comforts, and many have views of the Borromean Islands. Facilities include tennis and squash courts, a Jacuzzi, saunas, a health club, and a Turkish bath. The hotel also has two dining rooms, one reserved only for residents. The other dining choice is the Charleston, an à la carte restaurant.

WHERE TO DINE

Ristorante Emiliano. Corso Italia 50. ☎ **0323/31-396.** Reservations required. Main courses 20,000L–38,000L ($12–$22.80); fixed-price menu 55,000L ($33). AE, DC, MC, V. Wed–Mon 12:30–2:30pm and 7:30–10pm. Closed Jan–Feb. EMILIANA.

As its name suggests, the cuisine comes from the Emilia-Romagna region of Italy, and the decor makes it the most elegant nonhotel restaurant in Stresa. The entrance is sheltered by a wrought-iron and glass canopy, which extends partially over the outdoor tables with their view of the lake. Changing menu specialties might include slices of fresh goose liver served with a fondant of onions, pink cannelloni stuffed with a purée of fish, braised Piedmont pigeon in wine and herb sauce, or roulades of fillet of lakefish prepared with saffron. Desserts include several kinds of crêpes and cassatas.

Taverna del Pappagallo. Via Principessa Margherita 46. ☎ **0323/30-411.** Reservations recommended. Main courses 15,000L–20,000L ($9–$12); pizzas 8,000L–16,000L ($4.80–$9.60). No credit cards. Thurs–Mon 11:30am–2:30pm and 6:30–10:30pm. ITALIAN/PIZZA.

This formal little garden restaurant and tavern is operated by the Ghiringhelli brothers, who turn out some of the least expensive meals in Stresa. Specialties include gnocchi, many types of scaloppine, *scalamino allo spiedoe fagioli* (grilled sausage with beans), and *saltimbocca alla romana* (a veal-and-prociutto dish). At night pizza is king (try the pizza Regina). The service has a personal touch.

THE BORROMEAN ISLANDS

The heart of Lake Maggiore is occupied by this chain of tiny islands, which were turned into sites of lavish villas and gardens by the Borromeo clan. Boats leave from Stresa about every 30 minutes in summer, and the trip takes 3 hours. The **navigation offices** at Stresa's center port (☎ **0323/30-393**) are open daily from 7am to 7pm. The best deal is to purchase an excursion ticket for 13,000L ($7.80) entitling you to go back and forth to all three islands during the day.

EXPLORING THE ISLANDS

The major stopover is on the **Isola Bella** (Beautiful Island). Dominating the island is the 17th-century **Borromeo Palazzo** (☎ **0323/30-556**). From the front the figurines in the garden evoke the appearance of a wedding cake. On conducted tours, you are shown through the light and airy palace, from which the views are remarkable. Napóleon slept here. A special feature is the six grotto rooms, built piece by piece like a mosaic. In addition, there's a collection of quite good tapestries, with gory, cannibalistic animal scenes. Outside, the white peacocks in the garden enchant year after year. The palace and its grounds are open March 27 to October 24, daily from 9am to noon and 1:30 to 5:30pm. Admission is 13,000L ($7.80) for adults and 6,000L ($3.60) for children 6 to 15.

The largest of the chain, **Isola Madre** (Mother Island) is visited chiefly for its *Orto Botanico,* or botanical garden. You wander through a setting ripe with pomegranates, camellias, wisteria, rhododendrons, bougainvillea, hibiscus, hydrangea, magnolias, even a cypress tree from the Himalayas. You can also visit the 17th-century **palace** (☎ 0323/31-261), which contains a rich collection of 17th- and 18th-century furnishings. Of particular interest is a collection of 19th-century French and German dolls belonging to Countess Borromeo and the livery of the House of Borromeo. The unique 18th-century marionette theater, complete with scripts, stage scenery, and devices for sound, light, and other special effects, is on display. Peacocks, pheasants, and other birds live and roam freely on the grounds. Visits are March 27 to October 24, daily from 9am to noon and 1:30 to 5:30pm. Admission to both the palace and grounds is 13,000L ($7.80) for adults, 6,000L ($3.60) for children 6 to 15.

Isola del Pescatori (Fisher's Island) is without major sights or lavish villas, but in many ways it's the most colorful. Less a stage setting than its two neighbors, it's inhabited by fisherfolk who live in cottages that haven't been converted to souvenir shops. Good walks are possible in many directions.

VILLA TARANTO

Back on the mainland near the resort of Pallanza, north of Stresa, the **Giardini Botanici** at Villa Taranto, Via Vittorio Veneto 111, Verbania–Pallanza (☎ 0323/556-667), are spread over more than 50 acres of the Castagnola Promontory jutting out into Lake Maggiore. In this dramatic setting between the mountains and the lake, more than 20,000 species of plants from all over the world thrive in a well-tended and cultivated institution, begun in 1931 by a Scotsman, Capt. Neil McEacharn. Plants range from rhododendrons and azaleas to specimens from such faraway places as Louisiana. Seasonal exhibits include fields of Dutch tulips (80,000 of them), Japanese magnolias, giant water lilies, cotton plants, and rare varieties of hydrangeas. The formal gardens are carefully laid out with ornamental fountains, statues, and reflection pools. Among the more ambitious creations is the elaborate irrigation system that pumps water from the lake to all parts of the gardens, and the Terrace Gardens, complete with waterfalls and swimming pool.

The gardens are open March 28 to October 31, daily from 8:30am to 6:30pm. To arrange an hour-long **guided tour** (for groups only), contact the Palazzo dei Congressi di Stresa (☎ 0323/30-389). You may also take a round-trip boat ride from Stresa, which docks at the Villa Taranto pier adjoining the entrance to the gardens. You pay an admission of 10,000L ($6) for adults, 9,000L ($5.40) for children 6 to 14.

Piedmont & Valle d'Aosta

Towering, snowcapped alpine peaks; oleander, poplar, and birch trees; sky-blue lakes; river valleys and flower-studded meadows; the chamois and the wild boar; medieval castles; Roman ruins and folklore; the taste of vermouth on home ground; Fiats and fashion—northwestern Italy is a fascinating area to explore.

Piedmont (Piemonte) is largely agricultural, although its capital, Torino (Turin), is one of Italy's front-ranking industrial cities (with more mechanics per square foot than any other location in Europe). The influence of France is strongly felt, both in the dialect and in the kitchen.

Valle d'Aosta (really a series of valleys) has traditionally been associated with Piedmont, but in 1948 it was given wide-ranging autonomy. Most of the residents in this least-populated district in Italy speak French. Closing in Valle d'Aosta to the north on the French and Swiss frontiers are the tallest mountains in Europe, including Mont Blanc (15,780 ft.), the Matterhorn (14,690 ft.), and Monte Rosa (15,200 ft.). The road tunnels of Great St. Bernard and Mont Blanc (opened in 1965) connect France and Italy.

1 Torino (Turin)

140 miles SW of Milan, 108 miles NW of Genoa, 414 miles NW of Rome

In Turin, the capital of Piedmont, the Italian *Risorgimento* (unification movement) was born. During the years when the United States was fighting its Civil War, Turin became the first capital of a unified Italy, a position it later lost to Florence. Turin was once the capital of Sardinia. Much of the city's history is associated with the House of Savoy, a dynasty that reigned for 9 centuries, even presiding over the kingdom of Italy when Victor Emmanuel II was proclaimed king in 1861. The family ruled, at times in name only, until the monarchy was abolished in 1946.

In spite of extensive bombings, Turin found renewed prosperity after World War II, largely because of the Fiat manufacturers based here. The city has been called the Detroit of Italy. Many buildings were destroyed, but much of its 17th- and 18th-century look remains. Located on the Po River, Turin is well laid out, with wide streets, historic squares, churches, and parks. For years it has had a reputation as the least-visited and least-known of Italy's major cities.

Torino's biggest draw, the Cathedral of San Giovanni, home to the Shroud of Turin, was damaged by fire in 1997. The Chapel of the Holy Shroud, where the silver reliquary that protects the controversial Christian symbol is usually on display, and the west wing of the neighboring Royal Palace sustained most of the damage. Luckily, the Shroud had been moved into the cathedral itself because the dome of its chapel was being renovated. As this book went to press, the Vatican had moved the Shroud to an undisclosed location while deciding which local venue will temporarily display the cloth.

Turin is one of Italy's richest cities, with some one million Turinese, many of whom are immigrants who came here to get a piece of the pie. "Car Capital of Italy," Turin is surrounded by some hideous suburbs that are ever growing, but its Crocietta district is home to some of the most aristocratic residences in Italy and its inner core is one of grace and harmony. One of Italy's most feared and powerful men, Gianni Agnelli, lives here. It was once the home of Antonio Gramsci who staged "occupations" of the Fiat factory and later helped found the Italian Communist Party before dying in a Fascist prison. On a cultural note, Turin is the center of modern Italian writing; it was here that such major authors as Primo Levi, Cesare Pavese, and Italo Calvino were first published.

ESSENTIALS

GETTING THERE   By Plane   Alitalia flies into the **Caselle International Airport** (☎ 011/567-6111), about 9 miles north of Turin. It receives direct scheduled flights from 22 cities (7 domestic and 15 from major European centers); it's used by 13 scheduled carriers that operate regular flights. In 1993, it inaugurated the New Air Passenger Terminal, one of the most technologically advanced structures in Europe, covering a total area of more than 43,000 square yards. The New Air Terminal handles up to three million passengers a year.

By Train   Turin is a major rail terminus, with arrivals at **Stazione di Porta Nuova** (☎ 011/561-3333) or **Stazione Centrale,** Corso Vittorio Emanuele II (for information call ☎ 01478/88-088), in the heart of the city. It takes 1¼ hours to reach Turin by train from Milan, but anywhere from 9 to 11 hours to reach Turin from Rome, depending on the connection. The one-way fare from Milan is 15,600L ($9.35); from Rome, 70,400L ($42.25).

By Bus   It's possible to catch a bus in Chamonix (France) and go to Turin. Three buses a day run through the Mont Blanc Tunnel. The trip takes 3½ hours; a one-way ticket is 37,000L ($22.20). There are also 15 buses a day arriving from Milan. This trip is 2 hours and costs 15,700L ($9.40) one-way. For **bus information** call SATEM (☎ 011/311-1616).

By Car   If you're coming from France Via the Mont Blanc Tunnel, you can pick up the autostrada at Aosta. You can also reach Turin by autostrada from both the French and Italian Rivieras, and there's an easy link from Milan.

VISITOR INFORMATION   For tourist information, go to the office of **APT,** Via Roma 226 (☎ 011/535-901), open Monday to Saturday from 9am to 7pm. There's another office at the train station, Porta Nuova (☎ 011/531-327), which is open the same hours.

CITY LAYOUT   The Stazione di Porta Nuova is in the very center of town. The **Po River,** which runs through Turin, lies to the east of the station. One of the main arteries running through Turin is **Corso Vittorio Emanuele II,** directly north of the station. Turin is also a city of fashion, and you may want to walk along the major

Piedmont & Valle d'Aosta

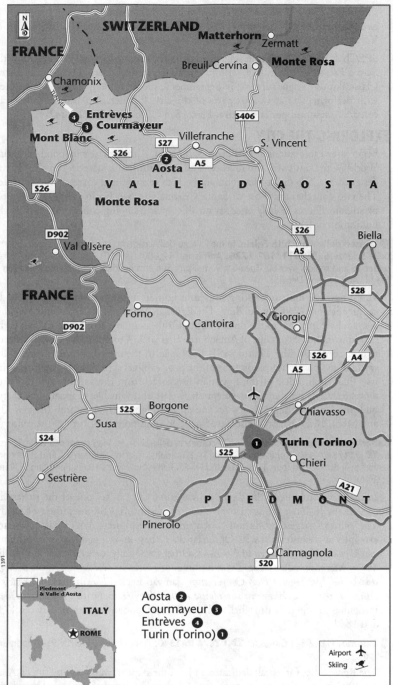

SWITZERLAND

FRANCE

Matterhorn
Zermatt
Breuil-Cervína
Monte Rosa

Chamonix

TUNNEL

Entrèves
④ ③ Courmayeur
Mont Blanc
Villefranche
S406
S. Vincent
S27
S26
② A5
Aosta

S26
V A L L E   D'   A O S T A

Monte Rosa

S26
A5
Biella

D902
Val d'Isère

S28

FRANCE

Forno
Cantoira
S. Giorgio

S26
A4

D902
A5

Borgone
Chiavasso

S25
① Turin (Torino)
Susa
S24
S25
Chieri

Sestrière
A21

P I E D M O N T

Pinerolo

Carmagnola
S20

Piedmont
& Valle d'Aosta

ITALY

★ ROME

Aosta ②
Courmayeur ③
Entrèves ④
Turin (Torino) ①

Airport ✈
Skiing 🎿

569

shopping street, **Via Roma,** which begins north of the station, leading eventually to two squares that join each other, Piazza Castello and Piazza Reale. In the middle of Via Roma is **Piazza San Carlo,** which is the heartbeat of Turin.

SPECIAL EVENTS Turin stages two major cultural *feste* every year, including the **Sere d'Estate** festival in July, with programs devoted to dance, music, and theater. Classical music reigns supreme in September at the monthlong **Settembre Musica,** with performances at various parts of the city. For details about these festivals contact **Assesorato per la Cultura,** Piazza San Carlo 161 (☎ 011/442-4715).

EXPLORING THE CITY

Begin your explorations at ✪ **Piazza San Carlo.** Although heavily bombed during World War II, it's still the loveliest and most unified square in the city. It was designed by Carlo di Castellamonte in the 17th century, and covers about 3¹/₂ acres. The two churches are those of Santa Cristina and San Carlo. Some of the most prestigious figures in Italy once sat on this square, sipping coffee and plotting the unification of Italy.

✪ **Museo delle Antichità Egizie.** In the Palazzo dell'Accademia delle Scienze, Via Accademia delle Scienze 6. ☎ **011/561-7776.** Admission 12,000L ($7.20) adults, free for children under 18 and seniors over 60. Tues–Sat 9am–7pm, Sun and holidays 9am–2pm. Closed Jan 1, May 1, Aug 15, and Dec 25.

You'll find the most interesting museums housed in the Guarini-designed, 17th-century Science Academy Building. The Egyptian Museum's collection is so vast that it's rated second only to the one at Cairo. Of the statuary, that of Ramses II, is the best known, but there's one of Amenhotep II as well. A room nearby contains a rock temple consecrated by Thutmose III in Nubia. In the crowded wings upstairs, the world of the pharaohs lives on (one of the prize exhibits is the "Royal Papyrus," with its valuable chronicle of the Egyptian monarchs from the 1st through the 17th dynasties). The funerary art is exceptionally rare and valuable, especially the chapel built for Maia and his young wife, and an entirely reassembled tomb (that of Kha and Merit, 18th Dynasty), discovered in good condition at the turn of the century.

Galleria Sabauda. In the Palazzo dell'Accademia delle Scienze, Via Accademia delle Scienze 6. ☎ **011/547-440.** Admission 8,000L ($4.80) adults, free for children 17 and under and seniors over 60. Guided tours Tues–Wed and Fri–Sat 9am–2pm, Thurs 10am–7pm, Sun 9:30am–1:30pm.

In the same building as the Egyptian Museum, you can see one of the richest art collections in Italy, acquired over a period of centuries by the House of Savoy. The gallery's largest exhibition is of Piedmontese masters, but it has many fine examples of Flemish art as well. Of the latter, the best-known painting is Sir Anthony van Dyck's *Three Children of Charles I.* Other important works include Botticelli's *Venus,* Memling's *Passion of Christ,* Rembrandt's *Sleeping Old Man,* Duccio's *Virgin and Child,* Mantegna's *Holy Conversation,* Jan van Eyck's *The Stigmata of Francis of Assisi,* Veronese's *Dinner in the House of the Pharisee,* Bellotto's *Views of Turin,* intriguing paintings by Brueghel, and a section of the royal collections between 1730 and 1832.

✪ **Duomo.** Piazza San Giovanni. ☎ **011/436-1540.** Free admission. Daily 9am–noon and 3–5pm.

The Renaissance cathedral, dedicated to John the Baptist, was swept by fire on April 12, 1997, with major damage sustained by Guarini's Chapel of the Holy Shroud, the usual resting place of the contested Christian relic. The Shroud, purported to be the one that Joseph of Arimathea wrapped around the body of Christ after it was removed from the Cross, was undamaged and has been removed to an undisclosed location until the Vatican decides where to display it temporarily. At press time, local and church officials were rushing to re-restore the cathedral—unfortunately, already near the end of a long and expensive restoration when the fire hit—in time for Jubilee Year 2000. Since visits will be curtailed through much of 1998, you must check with local authorities to find out when you can get into the cathedral.

The authorities supervising the administration of the Shroud maintain a small, rather dusty library and research center near the cathedral, which is open to ecclesiastics and qualified scholars only upon special request. It's the **Museo della Sindone** (Holy Shroud Museum), Via San Domenico 28 (☎ 011/436-5832).

Palazzo Reale (Royal Palace). Piazza Castello. ☎ **011/436-1455.** Admission 8,000L ($4.80) adults, free for children 17 and under and seniors 60 and over. Tues–Sun 9am–5pm.

The palace that the Savoys called home was begun in 1645. The halls, the columned ballroom by Palagi, the tea salon, and the "Queen's Chapel" are richly baroque in style. The original architect was Amedeo de Castellamonte, but numerous builders supplied ideas and effort before the palazzo was completed. As in nearly all ducal residences of that period, the most bizarre room is the one bedecked with flowering chinoiserie.

The Throne Room is of interest, as is the tapestry-draped Banqueting Hall. Le Nôtre, the famous Frenchman, mapped out the gardens, which may also be visited along with the Royal Armory (Armeria Reale), with its large collection of arms and armor and many military mementos. Guided tours are offered every 20 minutes.

The west wing of the palace was damaged when fire spread through the chapel of the neighboring cathedral on April 12, 1997. Check with the toruist office to find out how and when renovations will affect your visit.

SHOPPING

The most adventurous shopping is at the **Gran Balôn,** an old-fashioned flea market set up every second Sunday in Piazza della Repubblica. Some of the merchandise peddled here is from the home of various immigrants.

The antiques market at **Galleria Principe Eugenio,** Via Cavour 17 (☎ 011/562-4209), offers an eclectic mix of Italian styles. Sharp eyes can occasionally find a real deal.

Some of the best-known drinks in the world are manufactured in Torino. For the best sampling, head for **Paissa,** Piazza San Carlo 196 (☎ 011/562-8364), where among the wine and food items available, you'll find the best deals on Cinzano and Martini & Rossi vermouths.

WHERE TO STAY

Like Milan, Turin is an industrial city first and a tourist center second. Most of its hotels were built after 1945 with an eye toward modern comfort but not necessarily style. The hotels generally lack distinction, except those in the expensive range.

EXPENSIVE

✪ **Jolly Hotel Prìncipi di Piemonte.** Via Gobetti 15, 10123 Torino. ☎ **212/685-3700** in the U.S. or 011/562-9693. Fax 011/562-0270. 107 rms, 8 suites. A/C MINIBAR TV TEL. 420,000L ($252) double; from 690,000L ($414) suite. Rates include breakfast. AE, DC, MC, V. Parking 30,000L ($18).

A favorite choice of Fiat executives, this 10-story hotel is in the center of the city, near the railway station. Today it's the finest address in town, having surpassed the Turin Palace. The building itself is from 1939. Owned by Italy's Jolly chain, it employed some of Italy's finest architects and designers in its wholesale revamping. The public rooms are grand in style and furnishings, with bas-relief ceilings, gold wall panels, silk draperies, Louis XVI–style chairs, and baroque marble sideboards. There are both formal and informal dining rooms serving Piedmontese food, as well as a fashionable drinking lounge.

✪ **Villa Sassi.** Via Traforo del Pino 47, 10132 Torino. ☎ **011/898-0556.** Fax 011/898-0095. 15 rms, 2 suites. MINIBAR TV TEL. 400,000L ($240) double; 500,000L ($300) suite. AE, DC, MC, V.

This classic 17th-century-style estate lies 4 miles east of the town center and is surrounded by park grounds and approached by a winding driveway. If you want tranquility, head here. It was converted long ago into a top-grade hotel and restaurant. The impressive original architectural details are still intact, including the wooden staircase in the entrance hall. The drawing room features an overscale mural and life-sized sculpted baroque figures holding bronze torchiers. Each bedroom has been individually decorated with a combination of antiques and reproductions. The manager sees that the hotel is run in a personal way, with "custom-made" service. The intimate drinking salon features draped red-velvet walls, a bronze chandelier, black dado, and low seat cushions. See "Where to Dine," below, for a recommendation of the hotel restaurant.

MODERATE

Hotel Due Mondi. Via Saluzzo 3, 10125 Torino. ☎ **011/650-5084.** Fax 011/669-9383. 36 rms. A/C TV TEL. Mon–Fri 145,000L–210,000L ($87–$126) double; weekends 120,000L ($72) double. Rates include buffet breakfast. AE, MC, V. Closed Aug 10–20.

Located off the Corso Vittorio Emanuele, within walking distance of the Stazione di Porta Nuova, this little hotel surfaces near the top for those seeking old-fashioned style and grace at an affordable price. In a sea of characterless hotels, it has a real Italian aura—not deluxe or first class by any means, but with traditional furnishings. Everything is smartly outfitted, often in dark patterns and woods. This three-star address has been totally refurbished and now is one of the most worthy choices in its price range. Only breakfast is served, but there are many restaurants nearby.

INEXPENSIVE

Hotel Genio. Corso Vittorio Emanuele II 47, 10125 Torino. ☎ **011/650-5771.** Fax 011/650-8264. 90 rms. A/C MINIBAR TV TEL. Mon–Thurs 200,000L ($120) double; Fri–Sun 150,000L ($90) double. Rates include breakfast. AE, DC, MC, V. Parking 20,000L ($12).

Built at the end of the 19th century, this four-story hotel in the center of town was renovated into a streamlined, modern format in 1990. Set close to the railway station, its accommodations contain a comfortable blend of contemporary and early 20th-century furniture, and have double-paned windows for soundproofing.

Hotel Piemontese. Via Berthollet 21, 10125 Torino. ☎ **011/669-8101.** Fax 011/669-0571. 35 rms, 5 suites. A/C MINIBAR TV TEL. Mon–Thurs 220,000L ($132) double; 280,000L ($168) suite. Fri–Sun 150,000L ($90) double; 180,000L ($108) suite. Rates include breakfast. AE, DC, MC, V. Parking 15,000L ($9).

Hotel Piemontese is in a 19th-century building near the historic center and the Stazione Centrale. The facade is covered with iron balconies and ornate stone trim. The restructured interior is well maintained, and the comfortable bedrooms and public places have undergone a complete restoration. Breakfast, taken in an airy, sunny room, is the only meal served, but nearby restaurants are willing to offer ample fixed-price menus to guests of the Piemontese. Laundry and 24-hour room service are available. Guests can patronize a nearby sports center with a swimming pool.

WHERE TO DINE
EXPENSIVE
Del Cambio. Piazza Carignano 2. ☎ **011/546-690.** Reservations required. Main courses 31,000L–37,000L ($18.60–$22.20); fixed-price menu 95,000L ($57). AE, DC, MC, V. Mon–Sat noon–2:30pm and 7:45–10:30pm. PIEDMONTESE/MEDITERRANEAN.

Del Cambio is a classic restaurant of old Turin, where you dine amid a grand old-world setting of white-and-gilt walls, crystal chandeliers, and gilt mirrors. Founded in 1757, it's the oldest restaurant in Turin—possibly in all of Italy. The statesman Camillo Cavour was a loyal patron, and his much-frequented corner is immortalized with a bronze medallion. The chef has received many culinary honors and the white truffle is featured in many specialties. The assorted fresh antipasti are excellent; the best pasta dish is the regional *agnolotti piemontesi.* Among the main dishes, the fondue with truffles from Alba and the beef braised in Barolo wine deserve special praise. Some trademark specialties derive from very old recipes of the southwestern Alps: artichokes stewed with bone marrow and truffles; *girello aromatizzato alla piemontese* (flank steak marinated in sugar, salt, and aromatic herbs, sliced paper thin, and served with Parmesan and vegetables); and *tonno di coniglio à la manière antica* (rabbit).

✪ **Due Lampioni da Carlo.** Via Carlo Alberto 45. ☎ **011/817-9380.** Reservations required. Jacket and tie required for men. Main courses 18,000L–30,000L ($10.80–$18); fixed-price menu 45,000L ($27). AE, V. Mon–Sat 12:30–3pm and 7:30–11pm. Closed Aug. Bus: 61. PIEDMONTESE.

Giovanni Agnelli, the head of Fiat, has a gift for finding the best restaurants in Turin, and he's been known to patronize this elegant 17th-century palace in the heart of the city, run by chef Carlo Bagatin. Specialties are founded in Piedmont traditions, and only the finest of ingredients go into the tasty dishes. The antipasto selection is among the best in Turin, and you can follow with agnolotti, stuffed with duck and cooked with local white truffles, or perhaps tournedos with olive purée. Other favorite dishes include tripe soup, ravioli stuffed with ricotta and pesto, brains fried in an herb liqueur, a mosaic of fish served as a beautiful antipasto, and a *bollito misto* (medley of boiled meats) in the "style of the stockbrokers." An informal brasserie is open for lunch on the ground floor and serves an international cuisine for dinner with a fixed-price menu of 40,000L ($24).

✪ **El Toulà—Villa Sassi.** In the Villa Sassi, Via Traforo del Pino 47. ☎ **011/898-0556.** Reservations required. Main courses 30,000L–42,000L ($18–$25.20); fixed-price menu 80,000L ($48). AE, DC, MC, V. Mon–Sat noon–2pm and 8–10:30pm. Closed Aug, Dec 24, and Jan 6. PIEDMONTESE/INTERNATIONAL.

This spacious 17th-century villa is on the rise of a hill 4 miles east of the town center on the road to Chieri. The stylish, antique-decorated establishment has seen the addition of a modern dining room, with glass walls extending toward the gardens (most of the tables have an excellent view). Some of the basic foodstuff is brought in from the villa's own farm—not only the vegetables, fruit, and butter, but the beef as well. For an appetizer, try the frogs' legs cooked with broth-simmered rice, or fonduta, a Piedmont fondue, made with Fontina cheese and local white truffles. If it's featured, you may want to sample the prized specialty of the house: *camoscio in salmì*—that is, chamois (a goatlike antelope) prepared in a sauce of olive oil, anchovies, and garlic, laced with wine and served with polenta.

✪ **Vecchia Lanterna.** Corso Re Umberto 21. ☎ **011/537-047.** Reservations required. Main courses 30,000L–45,000L ($18–$27)); fixed-price menu 80,000L–110,000L ($48–$66). DC, MC, V. Mon–Fri noon–3pm and 8pm–midnight, Sat 8pm–midnight. Closed Aug 10–20. PIEDMONTESE/INTERNATIONAL.

This is one of Turin's most popular upper-bracket restaurants, and it usually proves to be a rewarding gastronomic experience. It's housed in a building dating from 1740. The bar area near the entrance has *belle époque* lighting fixtures, heavy gilt mirrors, ornate 19th-century furniture, and Oriental rugs over carpeting. The dining room evokes old Venice. The antipasti selection is a treat—king crab Venetian style, asparagus flan, pâté de foie gras, grilled snails on a skewer, and marinated trout. This could be followed by ravioli stuffed with duck and served with a truffle sauce, your choice of risotto, or snail soup. Main courses change seasonally, but often include goose-liver piccata on a bed of fresh mushrooms, sea bass Venetian style, or garnished frogs' legs. The seafood grill is especially delectable; each element is prepared individually and then assembled.

MODERATE

✪ Ristorante C'Era una Volta. Corso Vittorio Emanuele II 41. ☎ **011/655-498.** Reservations required. Fixed-price menus 35,000L–45,000L ($21–$27). AE, DC, MC, V. Mon–Sat 8:30pm–midnight. Closed Aug. PIEDMONTESE.

Located near the Porta Nuova train station, this restaurant is entered from the busy street through carved doors; you take an elevator one floor above ground level. Because the restaurant adheres to the classic dishes of the Piedmontese cuisine, it's a good introduction to the food of the Italian alpine regions. Many clients are faithful fans. The decor is in the typical Piedmontese style, with hanging copper pots and thick walls of stippled plaster. Fixed-price meals feature an aperitif, a choice of seven or eight antipasti, and two first and two main courses, with vegetables, dessert, and coffee. Typical regional fare includes polenta, crêpes, rabbit, and guinea fowl. The restaurant's name means "Once upon a time."

INEXPENSIVE

Caffè Torino. Piazza San Carlo 204. ☎ **011/545-118.** Main courses 18,000L–25,000L ($10.80–$15). AE, DC, MC, V. Daily 7am–1am. ITALIAN.

Established in 1903, this famous coffeehouse is the best re-creation in Turin of the days of Vittorio Emanuele. It's decorated with faded frescoes, brass and marble inlays, and a somewhat battered 19th-century formality. Set on one of the most elegant squares in northern Italy, it has a staff that adheres to a confusing series of rules about where and when clients can and should be seated. There's a stand-up bar near the entrance, a rather formal dining room off to the side, display cases filled with snack food, and a cafe area with tiny tables and unhurried service.

Da Mauro. Via Maria Vittoria 21. ☎ **011/817-0604.** Reservations not accepted. Main courses 9,000L–15,000L ($5.40–$9). No credit cards. Tues–Sun noon–2:30pm and 7:30–10pm. Closed July. ITALIAN/TUSCAN.

Located within walking distance of Piazza San Carlo, this place, the best of the town's low-cost trattorie, is generally packed (everybody loves a bargain). The food is conventional, but it does have character; the chef borrows freely from most of the gastronomic centers of Italy, although the cuisine is mainly Tuscan. An excellent pasta specialty is the cannelloni. Most main dishes consist of well-prepared fish, veal, and poultry. The desserts are consistently enjoyable.

TURIN AFTER DARK

This city of Fiat is also the cultural center of northwestern Italy. Turin is a major stopover for concert artists performing between Genoa and Milan. The daily newspaper of Piedmont, *La Stampa,* lists complete details of current cultural events.

Classical music concerts are presented at the **Auditorium della RAI,** Via Rossini 15 (☎ **011/8800**), throughout the year, although mainly in the winter months. Tickets range from 20,000L to 200,000L ($12 to $120), depending on the production. Turin is also home to one of the country's leading opera houses, **Teatro Regio,** Piazza Castello 215 (☎ **011/88-151**). Concerts and leading ballets are also presented here. The box office (☎ **011/881-5241** or 011/881-5242) is open Tuesday to Sunday from 1 to 6:30pm; closed in August. Tickets cost 20,000L to 250,000L ($12 to $150).

Opera and other classical productions are presented in summer outside the gardens of the **Palazzo Reale.** The last remaining government-subsidized (RAI) orchestra performs at Via Nizza 262. The **orchestra hall** (☎ **011/664-4111**) is part of the extensive Lingotto exhibition and conference center that grew out of Fiat's first large-scale automobile assembly plant. Ticket prices vary for each performance.

The city's other nightlife is like a smaller version of urbanized Milan, with one of the most diverse collections of electronic options in northern Italy. Look for establishments that combine bar hopping with highly amplified music, and in many cases, dancing. Worthy examples include **Alcatraz,** Manzani Po (☎ **011/838-900**), a hypermodern patchwork of avant-garde design and late-breaking music from virtually everywhere. An important competitor is **Discoteca Atlantide,** Via Monginevro 10 (☎ **011/936-7783**), and a somewhat corny contender, **Il Scoppiato,** Via Villarbasse 26 (☎ **011/338-567**), where karaoke contests from local wannabes might intrigue or repel you, depending on your tastes and whoever happens to grab the microphone. Another karaoke club worth a mention is **Luca's,** Via Fredour 26 (☎ **011/776-4604**), where sports talk and karaoke contests bring out the exhibitionism of cinematic hopefuls. **Ziegfild Follies,** Via Pomba 7 (☎ **011/812-5368**), offers disco music, restaurant service, and a bar where you might strike up a dialogue. On a hill looking down over Torino is **Disco Masko,** Calle della Maddalena 170 (☎ **011/862-0342**), which is somewhat less cutting-edge than the more punkish **Exit,** Via Barge 4C (☎ **011/434-8233**), which describes itself as a pub devoted to "trend music." Some (but not all) music here is performed by a roster of north Italian punkers, techno artists, and rockers.

2 Aosta

114 miles NW of Milan, 78 miles N of Turin, 463 miles NW of Rome

Founded by the Emperor Augustus who called it Augusta Praetoria, the capital of the Valle d'Aosta has lost much of its quaintness today, but makes a good stopover for touring in the area. It's called the "Rome of the Alps," but that is just tourist propaganda. Aostanas today number about 40,000 and live in the shadow of the peaks of Mont Blanc and San Bernardo. The economy is increasingly dependent on tourism.

Lying as it does on a major artery, Aosta makes for an important stopover point, either for overnighting or as a base for exploring Valle d'Aosta or taking the cable car to the Conca di Pila, the mountain that towers over the town.

ESSENTIALS

GETTING THERE **By Train** Thirteen trains per day run directly from Turin to Aosta (trip time: 2 hours); a one-way ticket costs 11,700L ($7). From Milan, the trip takes 4¹/₂ hours and costs 17,200L ($10.30) one-way; you must change trains at Chivasso. For information and schedules call ☎ **0165/562-057.** The train station is at Piazza Manzetti in the center of town, only a 5-minute stroll over to the Piazza Chanoux, the very core of Aosta.

By Bus Ten buses a day travel between Turin and Aosta (trip time: 2½ hours); a one-way ticket costs 10,300L ($6.20). There are seven buses a day arriving from Milan (4 hours); a one-way ticket costs 20,500L ($12.30). For schedules and information call ☎ **0165/262-027.**

By Car From Turin, continue north along autostrada A5, which comes to an end just east of Aosta.

VISITOR INFORMATION The **tourist information center** is at Piazza Chanoux 8 (☎ **0165/236-627**). It's open Monday to Saturday from 9am to 1pm and 3 to 8pm and Sunday from 9am to 1pm.

EXPLORING AOSTA

The town's **Roman ruins** include the Arch of Augustus, built in 24 B.C., the date of the Roman founding of the town. Via Sant'Anselmo, part of the old city from the Middle Ages, leads to the arch. Even more impressive are the ruins of a Roman theater, reached by the Porta Pretoria, a major gateway built of huge blocks that dates from the 1st century B.C. A Roman forum is today a small park with a crypt, lying off Piazza San Giovanni near the cathedral. The ruins of the theater are open year-round Monday to Friday from 9am to 6:30pm and Saturday and Sunday from 9am to noon and 2 to 5pm. Entrance is free.

The town is also enriched by its medieval relics. The Gothic **Collegiata dei Santi Pietro e Orso,** founded in the 12th century, is characterized by its landmark steeple designed in the Romanesque style. You can explore the crypt, but the cloisters, with capitals of some three dozen pillars depicting biblical scenes, are more interesting. The church lies directly off Via Sant'Anselmo and is open April to September, Tuesday to Sunday from 9am to 7pm. Off-season hours are Tuesday to Sunday from 9:30am to noon and 2:30 to 5:30pm.

A SIDE TRIP TO A GREAT NATIONAL PARK

Aosta is a good base for exploring the ✪ **Parco Nazionale di Gran Paradiso,** five lake-filled valleys which in 1865 were a royal hunting ground of Vittorio Emanuele II. Even back then, long before the term *endangered species* was common, he awarded that destination to the ibex, a nearly extinct species of mountain goat. In 1919, Vittorio Emanuele III gave the property to the Italian state, which established a national park in 1922. The park encompasses some 1,400 square miles of forest, pastureland, and alpine meadows, filled not only with ibex but the chamois and other animals who roam wild here.

The main gateway to the park is Cogne, a popular resort. The best time to visit the park is in June, when the wildflowers are at their most spectacular. You can get a sampling of this rare alpine fauna by visiting **Giardino Alpino Paradiso,** near the village of Valnontey, a mile south of Cogne. It is open June 10 to September 10, daily from 9:30am to 12:30pm and 2:30 to 6:30pm, charging an admission of 3,000L ($1.80) (free for children under 10). For information about the park, visit the park headquarters at Via Losanna 5 in Aosta (☎ **0165/44-126**). Cogne lies about 18 miles south of Aosta, reached along S35 and S507.

SHOPPING

The Valle d'Aosta is known for its wood carvings and its wrought-iron work. For a sampling, head for the **permanent craft exhibitions** in the arcades of Piazza Chanoux, the center of Aosta. You're not expected to pay the first price quoted, so test your bargaining power here. The big explosion of handcrafts, however, takes place the last 2 days in January, when alpine dwellers appear en masse to sell their handcrafts, mostly carved wood and stonework. Count yourself lucky if you pick up some handmade lace from neighboring Cogne. It's highly valued for its workmanship.

Valdostan handcrafts can be found at **IVAT**, Via Xavier de Maistre 1 (☎ **0165/41-462**), where sculpture, bas-relief, and wrought iron are offered for sale. The shop owners can also provide you with a list of local furniture makers. Antique furniture and paintings are the domain of **Bessone**, Via Edouard Aubert 53 (☎ **0165/40-853**), whereas **New Gallery**, Via Sant'Anselmo 115 (☎ **0165/40-929**), features a more diverse selection of antiquated goods.

WHERE TO STAY

Hotel Roma. Via Torino 7, 11100 Aosta. ☎ **0165/41-000.** Fax 0165/32-404. 33 rms. TEL. 115,000L–140,000L ($69–$84) double. Rates include breakfast. AE, DC, MC, V. Parking 10,000L ($6).

Silvio Lepri and Graziella Nicoli are the owners of this hotel, which is on a peaceful alleyway in a cubist-style white stucco building; it's surrounded by the balconies and windows of what appear to be private apartments. Rooms are well maintained, modern, and simple, with touches of varnished pine and modern tiled bathrooms. The entrance is at the top of an exterior concrete stairwell. The public rooms include a warmly paneled bar area, big windows, and a homelike decor filled with bright colors and rustic accessories. There's a garage on the premises, plus public parking nearby.

Hotel Valle d'Aosta. Corso Ivrea 146, 11100 Aosta. ☎ **0165/41-845.** Fax 0165/236-660. 104 rms. MINIBAR TV TEL. 170,000L–230,000L ($102–$138) double. Rates include breakfast. AE, DC, MC, V. Closed Dec 1–27.

This modern hotel with its zigzag concrete facade is one of the leading choices in Aosta. Located on a busy road leading from the old town to the entrance of the autostrada, it's a prominent stopover for motorists using the Great Saint Bernard and Mont Blanc tunnels into Italy. The sunny lobby has beige stone floors, paneled walls, deep leather chairs, and an oversized bar. All bedrooms have double windows and views angled toward the mountains. The Ristorante Le Foyer on the premises, under a different management, is reviewed under "Dining," below. The hotel also offers room service, baby-sitting, laundry, and a garage (free parking).

Le Pageot. Via Giorgio Carrel 31, 11100 Aosta. ☎ **0165/32-433.** Fax 0165/33-217. 18 rms. TV TEL. 110,000L–120,000L ($66–$72) double. AE, DC, MC, V. Parking 10,000L ($6).

Built in 1985, this is one of the best-value hotels in town. It has a modern, angular facade of brown brick with big windows and floors crafted from carefully polished slabs of mountain granite. The bedrooms are clean and functional, and the well-lit public areas include a breakfast room and a TV room. The hotel's name is antiquated local dialect for "bed." There's no restaurant.

WHERE TO DINE

Ristorante Le Foyer. Corso Ivrea 146. ☎ **0165/32-136.** Reservations recommended. Main courses 17,000L–30,000L ($10.20–$18); fixed-price menu 37,000L ($22.20). AE, DC, MC, V. Mon 12:15–1:50pm, Wed–Sun 12:15–1:50pm and 7:30–9:30pm. Closed Jan 8–25 and July 5–20. VALDOSTAN/INTERNATIONAL.

This restaurant sits beside a traffic artery on the outskirts of town. The full Valdostan meals you get here are both flavorful and cost-conscious. In a wood-paneled dining room that's illuminated by a wall of oversized windows, you can dine on specialties such as salmon trout, beef tagliata with balsamic vinegar, vegetable flan with fondue, or fresh noodles with smoked salmon and asparagus. There's also a good selection of French and Italian wines.

Ristorante Piemonte. Via Porta Pretoria 13. ☎ **0165/40-111.** Main courses 12,000L–25,000L ($7.20–$15); fixed-price menu 27,000L ($16.20). MC, V. Sat–Thurs noon–3pm and 7–10pm. Closed Jan 6–Jan 31. VALDOSTAN/INTERNATIONAL.

On a relatively traffic-free street lined with shops, this family-run place is one of the best of the low-cost trattorie inside the walls of the old town. Established in 1910, it has been popular and unpretentious ever since. In a setting of vaulted ceilings and tile floors, you can savor *bagna cauda,* cannelloni of the chef, risotto with roast pork, sautéed octopus with ginger, and an array of refreshing desserts, which could include fresh strawberries with lemon.

Vecchia Aosta. Piazza Porta Pretoria 4. ☎ **0165/361-186.** Reservations recommended. Main courses 16,000L–27,000L ($9.60–$16.20); fixed-price menus 28,000L–35,000L ($16.80–$21). AE, DC, MC, V. Thurs–Tues noon–3pm and 7:30–10pm. Closed Feb 15–30 and Nov 15–30. VALDOSTAN/INTERNATIONAL.

The most unusual restaurant in Aosta lies in the narrow niche between the inner and outer Roman walls of the Porta Pretoria. It's in an old structure which, although modernized, still bears evidence of the superb building techniques of the Romans, whose chiseled stones are sometimes visible between patches of modern wood and plaster. Full meals are served on at least two different levels in a labyrinth of nooks and isolated crannies, and might include homemade ravioli, filet of beef with mushrooms, pepperoni flan, eggs with cheese fondue and truffles, and a cheese-laden version of Valdostan fondue.

AOSTA AFTER DARK

You won't lack for diversions within this alpine capital. The town's newest disco is **La Compagnia dei Motori,** Piazza Arco d'Augusto (☎ **0165/363-484**), where a glossy, partially metallic interior includes a network of dance floors, bars, and a deserved self-image as the trendiest and most happening disco-of-the-minute in Aosta. Competitors include the **Duit Club,** Piazza Wuillermin 12 (☎ **0165/238-868**), which seems to be more closely geared to student life than business generated by the over-30 crowd. A site whose decor and ambience was inspired purely by Olde England and the pub traditions there is the **Old Distillery Pub,** Via Prés Fossés 7 (☎ **0165/230-511**), where taps dispense foaming mugs full of lager and stout within a paneled ambience that might remind you of an alpine, much-updated version of something out of Charles Dickens.

3 Courmayeur & Entrèves

COURMAYEUR

Courmayeur, a 22-mile drive northwest of Aosta, is Italy's best all-around ski resort, with two "high seasons," attracting the alpine excursionist in summer, the ski enthusiast in winter. Its popularity was given a considerable boost with the opening of the Mont Blanc road tunnel, feeding traffic from France into Italy (estimated trip time: 20 minutes). The cost for an average car is 43,000L ($25.80) one-way.

With Europe's highest mountain in the background, Courmayeur sits snugly in a valley. Directly to the north of the resort is the alpine village of Entrèves, sprinkled with a number of chalets (some of which take in paying guests).

In the vicinity, you can take a cable-car lift—one of the most unusual in Europe and a spectacular achievement in engineering—across Mont Blanc all the way to

Chamonix, France. It's a ride across glaciers that's altogether frightening and thrilling—for steel-nerved adventure seekers only. Departures on the Funivie Monte Bianco are from La Palud, near Entrèves. The three-stage cable car heads for the intermediate stations, Pavillon and Rifugio Torino, before reaching its peak at Punta Helbronner at 11,254 feet. At the latter, you'll be on the doorstep of the glacier and the celebrated 11¹/₂-mile Vallée Blanche ski run to Chamonix, France, which is usually opened at the beginning of February every year. The round-trip price for the cable ride is 40,000L ($24) per person. Departures are every 20 minutes, and service is daily from 8am to 1pm and 2 to 5pm. At the top is a terrace for sunbathing, a bar, and a snack bar. Bookings are possible at **Esercizio Funivie,** Frazione La Palud 22 (☎ **0165/89-925**).

ESSENTIALS

GETTING THERE   Proceed to Aosta by rail. In Aosta, you can take any of 11 buses leaving daily for Courmayeur from the bus terminal, Piazza Narbonne (☎ **0165/841-305**), adjacent to the train station. Trip time is 1 hour, and a one-way ticket costs 3,600L ($2.15). Motorists should continue west from Aosta on Route 26 heading toward Monte Bianco.

VISITOR INFORMATION   The **tourist information center** for Courmayeur is on Piazzale Monte Bianco (☎ **0165/842-060**). It's open Monday to Friday from 9am to 12:30pm and 3 to 6:30pm and Saturday to Sunday from 9am to 7:30pm.

GETTING AROUND   You can easily get around Courmayeur itself on foot. However, if you're going somewhere in the environs, such as Entrèves or La Palud (to catch the cable car for Mont Blanc), you'll need to take a local bus. Each bus is labeled by destination. The tourist office has a complete schedule, and buses depart from just outside the office.

WHERE TO STAY

Courmayeur has a number of attractive hotels, many of which are open seasonally. Always reserve ahead in high season, either summer or winter.

Expensive

Grand Hotel Royal e Golf. Via Roma 87, 11013 Courmayeur. ☎ **0165/846-787.** Fax 0165/842-093. 87 rms, 4 suites. A/C MINIBAR TV TEL. 380,000L–600,000L ($228–$360) double; 500,000L–1,000,000L ($300–$600) suite. Rates include breakfast. AE, DC, MC, V. Closed Apr 27–June 20 and Sept 20–Nov. Parking 18,000L ($10.80) inside, free outside.

Built in 1950, this hotel is in a dramatic location above the heart of the resort between the most fashionable pedestrian walkway and a heated outdoor pool. As a hotel, it's tops except for the more tranquil and elegant Pavillon (see below). Much of its angular facade is covered with rocks, so it fits in neatly with the surrounding mountainous landscape. The rooms are generally large, with built-in furnishings and streamlined bathrooms.

   Dining/Entertainment: A large and comfortable lounge is flanked by a bar and a dais with a pianist nightly in season. The deluxe dining room, La Grill dell'Hotel Royal e Golf, is reviewed in "Where to Dine," below. There's also a regular dining room open daily.

   Services: Room service, baby-sitting, laundry, valet, hydromassage.

   Facilities: Pool, sauna, Jacuzzi, solarium, Turkish bath.

Hotel Pavillon. Strada Regionale 60, 110113 Courmayeur. ☎ **0165/846-120.** Fax 0165/846-122. 50 rms, 10 suites. MINIBAR TV TEL. 200,000L–310,000L ($120–$186) per person double; 260,000L–410,000L ($156–$246) per person suite. Rates include half board. AE, DC, MC, V. Closed May–June 15 and Oct 2–Dec 2. Parking 12,000L ($7.20).

This is easily the swankiest and most important hotel at the resort, in spite of its small size. Many of the clients warming themselves around the stone fireplace are from England, Germany, and France, which adds a continental allure. Built in 1965, renovated in 1990, and designed like a chalet, the hotel is located a 4-minute walk south of Courmayeur's inner-city pedestrian zone. The bedrooms, entered through leather-covered doors, feature built-in furniture and a comfortable conservative decor; all but two have private balconies. The hotel is only a short walk from the funicular that goes to Plan Checrouit. Room service, baby-sitting, laundry, and valet are available. In the basement is a full array of hydrotherapy facilities; there's also a solarium and a covered pool.

Moderate

✪ **Palace Bron.** Località Plan Gorret 41, 11013 Courmayeur. ☎ **0165/846-742.** Fax 0165/844-015. 26 rms, 1 suite. TV TEL. 250,000L–530,000L ($150–$318) double; 550,000L–690,000L ($330–$414) suite. AE, DC, MC, V. Closed Easter–July 1 and mid-Sept to Dec 8.

Located about 1¼ miles from the heart of the resort, this tranquil oasis is one of the plushest addresses in town. The white-walled chalet is the most noteworthy building on the pine-studded hill, and it has a commanding view over Courmayeur and the mountains beyond. Guests are made to feel like members of a baronial private household. The bedrooms are handsomely furnished and well maintained. Winter visitors appreciate its proximity to the many ski lifts in the area. Walking from the chalet to the center of town is a good way to exercise after formal dining on the kitchen's filling international cuisine. The hotel's piano bar is especially lively in winter, hosting skiers from all over Europe and America. Other hotel services include room service, baby-sitting, laundry, and valet.

Inexpensive

Bouton d'Or. Strada Traforo del Monte Bianco 10 (off Piazzale Monte Bianco), 11013 Courmayeur. ☎ **0165/846-729.** Fax 0165/842-152. 35 rms. TV TEL. 150,000L–180,000L ($90–$108) double. AE, DC, MC, V. Rates include breakfast. Closed June and Nov.

Named after the buttercups that cover the surrounding hills in summer, this hotel is owned by the Casale family, who built it in 1970 and renovated it in 1990. It features an exterior painted yellow and gray, stone trim, and a flagstone roof. French windows lead from the clean, comfortable bedrooms onto small balconies. The hotel is about 100 yards (toward the Mont Blanc Tunnel) from the most popular restaurant in Courmayeur, Le Vieux Pommier, which is owned by the same family. The hotel also has a garage, sauna, solarium, and garden.

Hotel Courmayeur. Via Roma 158, 11013 Courmayeur. ☎ **0165/846-732.** Fax 0165/845-125. 26 rms. TV TEL. 90,000L–170,000L ($54–$102) per person double. Rates include half board. AE, DC, V. Closed Apr 6–June 21 and Oct–Nov.

Hotel Courmayeur, located right in the center of the resort, was constructed so that most of its rooms would have unobstructed views of the nearby mountains. It is a small, unpretentious hotel with clean rooms and low prices. A number of the bedrooms, furnished in the mountain chalet style, also have wooden balconies. Even nonresidents can dine on regional food in the hotel restaurant.

Hotel del Viale. Viale Monte Bianco 74, 11013 Courmayeur. ☎ **0165/846-712.** Fax 0165/844-513. 23 rms. MINIBAR TV TEL. 120,000L ($72) per person double. Rates include half board. AE, DC, MC, V. Closed May and Nov. Parking 10,000L ($6) inside, free outside.

This old-style mountain chalet at the edge of town is a good place to enjoy the indoor-outdoor life. There's a front terrace with tables set under trees in fair weather, and the rooms inside are cozy and pleasant in the chillier months. In the winter, guests can gather in the taproom to enjoy *après-ski* life, drinking at pine tables and warming their feet before the open fire. The clean and comfortable bedrooms, with natural wood, have a rustic air about them.

WHERE TO DINE

Expensive

✪ **La Grill dell'Hotel Royal e Golf.** In the Grand Hotel Royal e Golf, Via Roma 87. ☎ **0165/846-787.** Reservations required in winter. Fixed-price menu 70,000L–80,000L ($42–$48). AE, DC, MC, V. Tues–Sun 7:30–10pm. Closed Apr 27–June 20 and Sept 20–Dec 1. VALDOSTAN.

On the lobby level of this previously recommended hotel is the most fashionable—and certainly the most expensive—restaurant in town. It has only 30 places for diners interested in the cultivated cuisine inspired by the legacy of Harry Cipriani, of Harry's Bar fame. It's sparsely decorated, with a carved Gothic screen from an English church standing against one wall. The relatively simple but fresh and well-prepared dishes include *pasta e fagioli,* carpaccio, risotto with radicchio, and rosettes of veal Cipriani style. The hotel's foie gras—served on a brioche—is rumored to be the best anywhere. The menu changes daily.

Inexpensive

✪ **Cadran Solaire.** Via Roma 122. ☎ **0165/844-609.** Reservations required. Main courses 20,000L–30,000L ($12–$18). AE, DC, MC, V. Wed–Sun 12:30–3pm and 7:30–11pm. Closed May and Oct. VALDOSTAN.

In the center of town is the most interesting restaurant in Courmayeur. It's named after the sundial *(cadran solaire)* that embellishes the upper floor of its chalet facade, and is owned by Leo Garin, whose La Maison de Filippo (see under Entrèves, below) is the most popular restaurant in the Valle d'Aosta. Try to come for a before-dinner drink in the vaulted bar; its massive stones were crafted into almost alarmingly long spans in the 16th century using construction techniques that the Romans perfected. A few steps away, the rustically elegant dining room has its own stone fireplace, a beamed ceiling, and wide plank floors. Specialties change with the season but are likely to include warm goat cheese blended with a salad, noodles with seasonal vegetables, a baked cheese and spinach casserole, and duck breast with plums. The desserts are sumptuous.

Leone Rosso. Via Roma 73. ☎ **0165/846-726.** Reservations recommended. Main courses 18,000L–35,000L ($10.80–$21); fixed-price menus 35,000L–60,000L ($21–$36). AE, MC, V. Dec–Mar, daily noon–2:30pm and 7–10pm; Apr and July–Sept, Fri–Sun and Tues–Wed noon–2:30pm and 7–10pm; Nov, Fri–Sun noon–2:30pm and 7–10pm; May–June and Oct, Sat noon–2:30pm and 7–10pm, Sun noon–2:30pm. VALDOSTAN.

Leone Rosso is in a stone- and timber-fronted house in a slightly isolated courtyard, a few paces from the busy pedestrian traffic of Via Roma. It serves well-prepared and seasoned Valdostan specialties, including fondues, a thick and steaming regional version of minestrone, tagliatelle with mushrooms and en papillote, and a selection of rich, creamy desserts. Some meats you grill yourself at your table. This place is not to be confused with the Red Lion pub.

Le Vieux Pommier. Piazzale Monte Bianco 25. ☎ **0165/842-281.** Reservations recommended. Main courses 23,000L–28,000L ($13.80–$16.80); fixed-price menu 28,000L ($16.80). AE, DC, MC, V. Daily noon–2pm and 7–9:30pm. Closed Oct and 10–15 days in May. VALDOSTAN/INTERNATIONAL.

The hacked-up trunk of the "old apple tree" that was cut down to build this place was re-erected inside and now serves as the sculptural focal point of the restaurant, located on the main square of town. Filmmaker Ingmar Bergman, like everyone else, has appreciated the exposed stone, the copper-covered bar, and the thick pine tables arranged in an octagon. Today Alessandro Casale, the son of the founder, directs the kitchen assisted by his wife, Lydia. They have toured Europe teaching the technique of their regional cuisine. Your meal might consist of three kinds of dried alpine beef, followed by noodles in a ham-studded cream sauce, and an arrangement of three pastas or four fondues, including a regional variety with Fontina, milk, and egg yolks. Then it's on to chicken suprême en papillote (parchment) or four or five unusual meat dishes that are cooked mountain style, right at your table.

COURMAYEUR AFTER DARK

American Bar. Via Roma 43. ☎ **0165/846-707.**

Not to be confused with a less desirable bar of the same name at the end of the same street, this is one of the most popular bars on the *après-ski* circuit. It's rowdy and sometimes outrageous, but most often a lot of fun. Most guests end up in one of the two rooms, beside either an open fireplace or a long, crowded bar. The place is open in winter daily from 9am to 1am; it's sometimes closed on Tuesday, but never in ski season.

Café della Posta. Via Roma 51. ☎ **0165/842-272.**

Café della Posta, the oldest, most venerable café in Courmayeur, is as sedate as its neighbor, the American Bar, is unruly. Many guests prefer to remain in the warmly decorated bar area, never venturing into the large and comfortable salon with a glowing fireplace in an adjacent room. The place changes its stripes throughout the day, opening as a morning cafe at 8:30am.

Le Clochard. Route de Frazione Dolonne. ☎ **0165/89-950.** Cover 20,000L ($12) includes the first drink.

"The Drunkard" is one of the most popular clubs in town, catering to an over-25 crowd of skiers, hikers, and sports enthusiasts. It lies at the edge of the resort. Near the busy bar and a blazing wintertime fireplace, you'll find a warm and comfortable spot to watch the international goings-on. It's open every evening in winter from 9:30pm to 1:30am. In summer its schedule varies with business at the resort.

ENTRÈVES

Even older than Courmayeur, Entrèves is an ancient community that's small and compact, really a mountain village of wood houses. Many discriminating clients prefer its alpine charm to the more bustling resort of Courmayeur. It's reached by a steep and narrow road. Many gourmets book in here just to enjoy the regional fare, for which the village is known.

Just outside Entrèves on the main highway lies the **Val Veny cable car,** which skiers take in winter to reach the Courmayeur lift system.

Entrèves is located 2 miles north of Courmayeur (signposted off Route 26). Buses from the center of Courmayeur run daily to Entrèves. For more information contact Courmayeur's tourist office.

WHERE TO STAY & DINE

La Brenva. Frazione Entrèves di Courmayeur, 11013 Courmayeur–Entrèves. ☎ **0165/ 869-780.** Fax 0165/869-726. Reservations required. Main courses 20,000L–30,000L ($12–$18); fixed-price menus 30,000L–45,000L ($18–$27). AE, MC, V. Tues–Sun 12:30–1:30pm and 7:30–10:30pm. Closed May and Oct. VALDOSTAN/FRENCH.

Many skiers make a special trek to Entrèves just for a drink at the old-fashioned bar of this hotel and restaurant. The copper espresso machine topped by a brass eagle and many of the other decorative accessories are at least a century old. The core of the building was constructed in 1884 as a hunting lodge for Victor Emmanuel. In 1897 it became a hotel, and in 1980 the owners enlarged its stone foundations with the addition of extra bedrooms and a larger eating area. The restaurant consists of exposed stone walls, wide flooring planks, hunting trophies, copper pots, and straw-bottomed chairs. Fires burn in winter, and many diners prefer an aperitif in the unusual salon, within view of the well-chosen paintings. On any given day the menu could include prosciutto, fonduta for two, carbonada with polenta, scaloppine with fresh mushrooms, Valle d'Aostan beefsteak, and zabaglione for dessert.

Each of the 12 simple and comfortable bedrooms has a private bath, TV, phone, and lots of peace and quiet. Many of them have covered loggias. With breakfast included, they rent for 110,000L to 180,000L ($66 to $108) per person daily. The inn takes a vacation in either May or June.

✪ **La Grange.** 11013 Courmayeur–Entrèves. ☎ **0165/869-733.** Fax 0165/869-744. 21 rms, 2 suites. MINIBAR TV TEL. 200,000L ($120) double; from 400,000L ($240) suite. Rates include breakfast. AE, DC, MC, V. Closed May–June and Oct–Nov.

This will be one of the first buildings you'll see as you enter this rustic alpine village. A few foundation stones date from the 1300s, when the building was a barn. What you'll see today is a stone building whose balconies and gables are outlined against the steep hillside into which it's built. The Berthod family transformed a dilapidated property into a rustic and comfortable hotel in 1979, surrounding the establishment with summer flower beds. It's enthusiastically managed by Bruna Berthod Perri and her nephew, Stefano Pellin. The unusual decor includes a collection of antique tools and a series of thick timbers, stucco, and exposed stone walls. There is a piano in the bar, and an exercise room and sauna. A rich breakfast is the only meal served, but several restaurants are nearby.

La Maison de Filippo. Frazione Entrèves di Courmayeur. ☎ **0165/869-797.** Reservations required. Fixed-price menu 45,000L–55,000L ($27–$33). MC, V. Wed–Mon 12:30–2:30pm and 7:30–10:30pm. Closed June–July 10 and Nov–Dec 20. VALDOSTAN.

This colorful tavern, the creation of Leo Garin, is for those who enjoy a festive atmosphere and bountiful regional food. The three-story open hallway seems like a rustic barn, with an open worn wooden staircase leading to the various dining nooks. You pass casks of nuts, baskets of fresh fruits, bowls of salad, fruit tarts, and loaves of freshly baked bread. It's one of the most charming inns of the valley. The outdoor summer beer garden has a full view of Mont Blanc. Mr. Garin features local specialties on an all-you-can-eat basis, earning the place the nickname "Chalet of Gluttony." A typical meal might begin with a selection of antipasti, followed by a 2-foot-long platter of about 60 varieties of sausage. Next comes a parade of pasta dishes. For a main course, you can pick everything from fondue to camoscio (chamois meat) to trout with an almond-and-butter sauce. Huge hunks of coarse country bread are served from a wicker basket the size of a laundry bin.

15 Genova & the Italian Riviera

For years the retreat of the wintering wealthy, the Italian Riviera now enjoys a broad base of tourism. Even in winter (the average temperature in January hovers around the 50° Fahrenheit mark) the Riviera is popular, although not for swimming. The protection provided by the Ligurian Apennines that loom in the background makes the balmy weather possible.

The winding coastline of the Rivieras, particularly the one that stretches from the French border to San Remo, is especially familiar to moviegoers as the background for countless flicks about sportscar racing, jewel thieves, and spies. Over the years the northwestern coast of Italy has seen the famous and the infamous, especially literary figures: the poet Shelley (who drowned off the shore), d'Annunzio, Byron, Katherine Mansfield, George Sand, and D. H. Lawrence.

The Mediterranean vegetation is characterized by pines, olives, citrus trees, and cypresses. The Western Riviera—the Riviera di Ponente, from the border to Genova—is sometimes known as the Riviera of Flowers because of its profusion of blossoms. Starting at the French border, Ventimiglia is the gateway city to Italy. Along the way you'll encounter the first big resort, Bardighera, followed by San Remo, the major center of Riviera tourism.

Genova (Genoa), which divides the Riviera into two parts, is the capital of Liguria. It's a big, bustling port city that has charm for those willing to take the time to seek out its treasures.

On the Riviera di Levante (eastern) are three small, dramatically situated resorts—Rapallo, Santa Margherita, and Portofino (the favorite of the yachting set).

The Ligurians are famous for ceramics, lace, silver and gold filigree, marble, velvet, olive wood, and macramé, and all of the towns and villages of the region hold outdoor markets either in the main square or on the waterfront. Haggling is a way of life here, so good deals do exist, but English speakers be warned that prices may not fall as low as they would if you were negotiating in the local dialect.

1 San Remo

10 miles E of the French border, 85 miles SW of Genova, 397 miles NW of Rome

San Remo's reputation has grown ever since Emperor Frederick William wintered in a villa here. In time, the Empress Maria

Alexandrova, wife of Czar Alexander II, showed up, trailed by a Russian colony that included Tchaikovsky, who composed the *Fourth Symphony* here during a stay in 1878. Alfred Nobel, the father of dynamite and the founder of the famous prizes in Stockholm, died here in 1896. The flower-filled resort today has been considerably updated, and its casino, race track, 18-hole golf course, and deluxe Royal Hotel still attract the fashionable on occasion. But mostly it's called a "mini-Vegas by the sea." Its climate is the mildest on the entire western Riviera, and the town offers miles upon miles of cultivated beaches.

ESSENTIALS

GETTING THERE   By Train   Since San Remo lies on the coast between Ventimiglia and Imperia—6 miles from each—it's a major stop for many trains. A train leaves Genova heading for the French border once per hour, stopping in San Remo. Rome is 8 hours by train from San Remo. For train information and schedules call ☎ **01478/88-088.**

By Bus   If you've arrived in Italy from France in the gateway town of Ventimiglia, you'll find a bus leaving for San Remo about every 15 minutes. The trip takes 30 minutes, and a one-way ticket costs 3,000L ($1.80). On Saturday a bus departs Milan for San Remo at 8am, arriving at 1:45pm. For information call ☎ **0184/ 502-030.**

By Car   Autostrada A10, which runs east–west along the Riviera, is the fastest way for motorists to reach San Remo from either the French border or Genova.

VISITOR INFORMATION   The **tourist information center** is on Corso Nuvoloni (☎ **0184/571-571**). It's open Monday to Saturday from 8am to 7pm and Sunday from 9am to 1pm.

THE TOP ATTRACTIONS

Even if you're just passing through, you might want to stop off and visit **La Città Vecchia** (also known as La Pigna), the Old City on the top of the hill. Far removed in spirit from the burgeoning, sterile-looking town near the water, old San Remo blithely ignores the present, and its tiny houses on narrow, steep lanes seem to capture the past. In the new town, the palm-flanked **Passeggiata dell'Imperatrice** attracts promenaders. For a scenic view, drive to the top of **San Romolo** and **Monte Bignone** (4,265 feet).

From October to June you can visit the most famous flower market in Italy, the **Mercato di Fiori,** open daily from 6 to 8am. It's held in the market hall between Corso Garibaldi and Piazza Colombo. In this market you'll see some 20,000 tons of roses, mimosa, and carnations, which are grown in the balmy climate of the Riviera in winter before shipment to all parts of Europe.

As an offbeat excursion you can visit **Bussana Vecchia,** which lies 5 miles west of San Remo (signposted). Too well inhabited to really be considered a ghost town, Bussana Vecchia is, however, a rather unofficial town. A substantial earthquake of February 23, 1887, killed thousands of its residents, destroying many buildings in the process. The survivors, too frightened to stay, started a new Bussana 1 1/4 miles closer to the sea. The original town, with several buildings still standing, has gradually been taken over by artist-squatters who have revamped interior spaces—but not exteriors, no reason to draw that much attention to themselves— and hooked up water, electricity, and telephones. They live off their art, so haggling can get you a good deal on a painting. As a bit of trivia, one survivor of the 1887 earthquake, Giovanno Torre detto Merlo, would go on to invent the ice-cream cone in 1902.

SHOPPING   Frankly, San Remo is too sophisticated a resort to assume that its sun-loving and sybaritic clients will be particularly interested in acquiring a suitcase filled with folkloric artifacts. More prevalent are the stylish boutiques that line the town's busiest thoroughfare, Via Matteotti. Most are devoted to high-style Milan-inspired beachwear and slinky cocktail dresses. Wander up and down the street, making it a point to stop at **Annamoda,** Via Matteotti 141 (☎ **0184/505-550**), or **Moro Gabrielle,** Via Matteotti 126 (☎ **0184/531-614**), both of which sell sporty-looking as well as relatively formal garments for men and women. If you absolutely can't live without another piece of local craft, there's one noteworthy shop selling wood carvings and ceramics, **Pon Pon,** Via Matteotti 140 (☎ **0184/509-069**).

WHERE TO STAY
EXPENSIVE

✪ **Royal Hotel.** Corso dell'Imperatrice 80, 18038 San Remo. ☎ **0184/5391.** Fax 0184/661-445. 132 rms, 14 suites. A/C MINIBAR TV TEL. 310,000L–505,000L ($186–$303) double; 545,000L–990,000L ($327–$594) suite. Rates include breakfast. AE, DC, MC, V. Closed Oct 6–Dec 21. Parking 16,000L–25,000L ($9.60–$15).

Although long past its heyday, this resort is still a formidable challenger because of its sheer size and facilities. It's complete with terraces and gardens, a heated free-form saltwater pool, a forest of palms, bright flowers, and hideaway nooks for shade. Activity centers around the garden terrace—little emphasis is put on the public lounges decked out in the grand old dowager style. Bedrooms vary considerably—some are tennis-court size with private balconies, many have sea views, and others face the hills. The furnishings range from traditional to modern. The luxurious fifth-floor rooms—all doubles—have the best views and are more expensive.

Dining/Entertainment: There's an American bar with piano music nightly. Lunch is served in fair weather on the veranda. The more formal restaurant features regional and international cuisine.

Services: Room service, baby-sitting, laundry, valet.

Facilities: Heated pool, sauna, solarium, minigolf, gym, tennis court, facilities for children, hairdresser, covered and open-air parking areas, garage (with a mechanic, a car wash, and a gas pump), 18-hole golf course and horseback riding nearby.

MODERATE

✪ **Grand Hotel Londra.** Corso Matuzia 2, 18038 San Remo. ☎ **0184/668-000.** Fax 0184/668-073. 149 rms, 7 suites. MINIBAR TV TEL. 250,000L–265,000L ($150–$159) double; 500,000L–565,000L ($300–$339) suite. Rates include breakfast. AE, DC, MC, V. Closed Sept 30–Dec 18.

Built around 1900 as a two-story hotel, this place was later expanded into the imposing structure you see today. Located within a 10-minute walk of the commercial district, it's set in a park with a view of the sea. Like the Royal it continues to coast on its past glory. The well-furnished interior is filled with framed engravings, porcelain in illuminated cases, gilt mirrors, and brass detailing. Many of the bedrooms have wrought-iron balconies, and some rooms are air-conditioned. There's also a bar and an outdoor swimming pool.

Hotel Méditerranée. Corso Cavallotti 76, 18038 San Remo. ☎ **0184/571-000.** Fax 0184/541-106. 62 rms, 3 suites. A/C MINIBAR TV TEL. 250,000L–300,000L ($150–$180) double; 350,000L–400,000L ($210–$240) suite. Rates include breakfast. Children staying in parents' room receive a 30% discount. AE, DC, MC, V. Parking 35,000L ($21) in garage, free outside.

The traffic in front of this steel-and-glass structure can be profuse, especially in peak season, but once you're inside, or in the rear garden with its Olympic-sized pool, you'll scarcely be aware of it. Built about a century ago, the hotel received its present

Italian Riviera

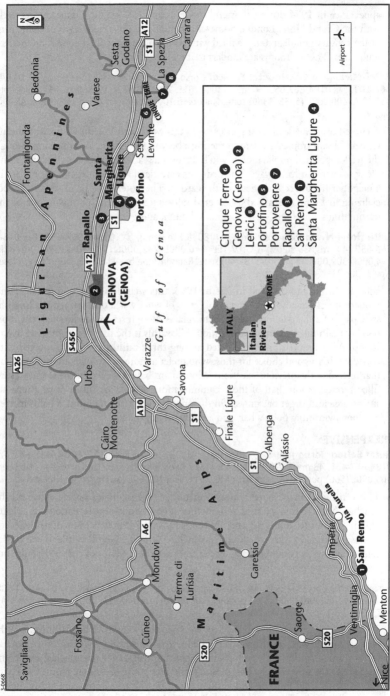

Cinque Terre **6**
Genova (Genoa) **2**
Lerici **8**
Portofino **5**
Portovenere **7**
Rapallo **3**
San Remo **1**
Santa Margherita Ligure **4**

appearance in 1974 during a tasteful modernization. Today it competes effectively with the Grand Hotel Londra. Some of the public rooms retain signs of their turn-of-the-century grandeur and are filled with potted plants, polished floors, and modern sculptures. The bedrooms are modernized and well furnished.

Hotel Miramare Continental Palace. Corso Matuzia 9, 18038 San Remo. ☎ **0184/667-601.** Fax 0184/667-655. 60 rms, 6 suites. TEL. 270,000L–330,000L ($162–$198) double; 430,000L–600,000L ($258–$360) suite. Full board 100,000L ($60) per person extra. AE, DC, MC, V.

A curved driveway leads past palmettos to this well-maintained traditional building set behind semitropical gardens bordering a busy thoroughfare. After passing through the well-appointed public rooms, you'll discover a seaside garden with sculptures and plenty of verdant hideaways. The bedrooms are clean and comfortable; some are in a neighboring annex with views of the garden. The hotel has a good restaurant specializing in Ligurian seafood. A covered saltwater swimming pool is in one of the outbuildings, and there's also a sauna, solarium, and gym.

Suite Hotel Nyala. Strada Solaro 134, 18038 San Remo. ☎ **0184/667-668.** Fax 0184/666-059. 44 rms, 36 suites. A/C TV TEL. 146,000L–232,000L ($87.60–$139.20) double; 194,000L–309,000L ($116.40–$185.40) suite. Rates include breakfast. AE, DC, MC, V. Closed Nov 3–Dec 23.

Built in 1984, and doubled in size in 1993, this well-designed, comfortable, and modern hotel lies among the venerable trees of what was a century ago the English-style park of a since-demolished private villa. Although set in a residential neighborhood containing some impressive antique villas, this is the most modern hotel in San Remo. Accommodations are divided among three buildings interconnected with corridors. It's a good choice for those who prefer a more up-to-date atmosphere than that offered at the previous selections. Most rooms have a view over the sea and a sun-filled terrace. About half of the accommodations are junior suites, with a separate sitting area and larger balconies. On the premises are a dining room, a palm-fringed outdoor swimming pool, a bar, and a hardworking staff.

INEXPENSIVE

Hotel Belsoggiorno Juana. Corso Matuzia 41, 18038 San Remo. ☎ **0184/667-631.** Fax 0184/667-471. 43 rms. TV TEL. 136,000L ($81.60) double. Rates include breakfast. Half board 100,000L ($60) per person extra. DC, MC, V. Parking 10,000L ($6) in garage, free outside.

This centrally located hotel is near Imperatrice, the main sea promenade, and the beaches. Attractively furnished and inviting, it contains a large reception area, plenty of living rooms for lounging, and TV rooms. Manager Luciana Maurizi de Benedetti has also provided a pleasant garden in which to sit and enjoy the sun and plants. Because the food is good, you may prefer to order the fixed-price menu if you're not staying here on half board.

Hotel Eletto. Corso Matteotti 44, 18038 San Remo. ☎ **0184/531-548.** Fax 0184/531-506. 29 rms. TV TEL. 140,000L ($84) double. Half board 120,000L ($72) per person extra. AE, MC, V.

This hotel is on the main artery of town, near more expensive hotels. It has a 19th-century facade with cast-iron balconies and ornate detailing. The rear of the hotel is set in a small garden with perhaps the biggest tree in San Remo casting a welcome shade over the flower beds. This pleasant stopover point has public rooms filled with carved panels, old mirrors, and antique furniture. The bedrooms are old-fashioned and comfortable. The sunny and well-maintained dining room serves inexpensive meals, and the hotel also provides a cabana on the beach.

Hotel Mariluce. Corso Matuzia 3, 16038 San Remo. ☎ **0184/667-805.** Fax 0184/667-655.
23 rms, 19 with bath (tub or shower). 70,000L–100,000L ($42–$60) double without bath,
80,000L–120,000L ($48–$72) double with bath. V. Closed Nov–Dec 20.

As you're walking along the flowered promenade away from the commercial center
of town, you'll notice a flowering garden enclosed on one side by the neighboring
walls of a Polish church; one of the walls is emblazoned with a gilded coat-of-arms.
Behind the garden is the building that until 1945 was a refugee center that Poles
throughout Europe used as a base for finding friends and relatives. Today it's one of
the most reasonably priced hotels in the resort, a bargain for San Remo, offering simply furnished but comfortable bedrooms and sunny public rooms. A passage under
the street leads from the garden to the beach.

WHERE TO DINE

✪ Da Giannino. Lungomare Trento e Trieste 23. ☎ **0184/504-014.** Reservations recommended. Main courses 30,000L–45,000L ($18–$27); fixed-price menus 65,000L–100,000L
($39–$60). AE, DC, MC, V. Tues–Sat 12:30–2:30pm and 7:30–10pm, Sun 12:30–2:30pm.
LIGURIAN/SEAFOOD.

This is still acclaimed as the finest restaurant in San Remo, although Paolo e Barbara
is closing in fast. In a conservatively comfortable and elegant setting, you can enjoy
such specialties as a warm seafood antipasti, a flavorful risotto laced with cheese and
a pungently aromatic green sauce, and a selection of main courses that changes with
the availability of ingredients. Some of the more exotic selections are likely to include
marinated cuttlefish gratinée. The wine list features many of the better vintages of
both France and Italy.

Il Bagatto. Via Matteotti 145. ☎ **0184/531-925.** Reservations required. Main courses
25,000L–38,000L ($15–$22.80); fixed-price menu 45,000L–65,000L ($27–$39). MC, V. Mon–
Sat noon–3pm and 7:30–10pm. Closed July. LIGURIAN/SEAFOOD.

Il Bagatto provides good meals in the 16th-century home of an Italian duke, with
dark beams, provincial chairs, and oversized pepper grinders brought to the tables.
It's located in the shopping district of the town, about two blocks from the sea. Our
most recent dinner began with a choice of creamy lasagne and savory hors d'oeuvres.
The scaloppine with artichokes and asparagus was especially pleasing, as was (on another occasion) a mixed grill of Mediterranean fish. All orders were accompanied by
potatoes and a choice of vegetables, then followed by crème caramel for dessert. They
serve many kinds of Ligurian fish, including fillet of sea bass in a sauce made with
fresh peppers, and a gallinella, the quintessential white-flesh Ligurian fish, roasted
with potatoes and olives.

La Lanterna. Via Molo di Ponente al Porto 16. ☎ **0184/506-855.** Reservations
required Sat–Sun. Main courses 20,000L–35,000L ($12–$21); fixed-price menu
46,000L ($27.60). AE, DC, MC, V. Fri–Wed 12:30–2:30pm and 7:30–10pm. Closed Dec–Jan.
SEAFOOD.

Many local residents recommend this place, a nautically decorated enclave of good
seafood in a building near the harbor. Established around 1917, it's one of the few
restaurants that has survived in San Remo from the heady days of its Edwardian grandeur. The clientele can get very fashionable here, especially in summer, when outdoor tables are set within view of the harbor. Meals might include an excellent fish
soup *(brodetto di pesce con crostini)*, a Ligurian fish fry, or a meat dish such as scaloppine in marsala wine sauce. Sea bass and red snapper are both readily available and
might be grilled; fried with olive oil, herbs, and lemon; or baked with artichokes,
olives, and white-wine sauce.

✪ **Paolo e Barbara.** Via Roma 47. ☎ **0184/531-653.** Reservations recommended. Main courses 32,000L–77,000L ($19.20–$46.20); fixed-price lunch (with wine) 75,000L ($45); *menu degustazione* (without wine) 100,000L ($60). AE, DC, MC, V. Fri–Tues 12:30–2pm and Thurs–Tues 8–10pm. LIGURIAN/ITALIAN.

Named after the husband-and-wife team who owns it (the Masieri family), this restaurant near the casino has caught the imagination of San Remo since it was established in 1987. It specializes in traditional regional recipes, as well as a handful of innovative dishes created by its staff. Meals here tend to be drawn-out affairs, so allow adequate time. Depending on the season, the menu might feature a tartare of raw marinated mackerel served with a garlic mousse and a potato-tomato and basil-flavored garnish, trenette (a regional pasta) with freshly pulverized pesto, or grilled crayfish served on a bed of onion purée with fresh herbs, olive oil, and pine nuts.

SAN REMO AFTER DARK

The high life holds forth at the **San Remo Casino,** Corso Inglesi 18 (☎ **0184/ 5951**), located in the very center of town. For decades fashionable visitors have dined in high style in the elegant restaurant, reserved tables at the roof garden's cabaret, or tested their luck at the gaming tables. Like a white-walled palace, the pristine-looking casino stands at the top of a steep flight of stone steps above the main artery of town.

Visitors today can attend a variety of shows, fashion parades, concerts, and theatrical presentations staged throughout the year. The entrance fee is 15,000L ($9) for the French and American gaming rooms, which are open Sunday to Friday from 2:30pm to 3am and Saturday from 2:30pm to 4am. Presentation of a passport is required, and a jacket and tie are requested as proper attire for men. For the slot machines section, entrance is free and there's no particular dress code; it's open Sunday to Friday from 10am to 2am and Saturday from 2:30pm to 3am. The casino's restaurant is open nightly from 8:30pm to 1:30am, charging 60,000L to 100,000L ($36 to $60) per person for dinner. The restaurant has an orchestra playing everything from waltzes to rock music. The roof-garden cabaret is open only June to September on Friday and Saturday nights, with shows beginning at 10pm. If you visit for drinks only (not dinner), the cost is 35,000L ($21) per drink.

At least part of your nocturnal adventures will transpire within the lobby of either your hotel or one of the grand palaces (especially the Royal, recommended above) whose bars are always open to well-behaved nonresidents. You can always strike out for the cafes along the town's main artery, the Via Matteotti, which serve drinks until late at night, then drop into the resort's most elegant and whimsical disco, a favorite for everyone except the most hard-core crowd, **Discoteca Nifa Igaria,** Via Matteotti 178 (☎ **0184/509-009**). Don't even think of showing up before 10pm.

2 Genova (Genoa)

88 miles SW of Milan, 311 miles NW of Rome, 120 miles NE of Nice

It was altogether fitting that "Genova the Proud" (Repubblica Superba) gave birth to Christopher Columbus. Its link with the sea dates back to ancient times. However, Columbus did his hometown a disservice. By blazing the trail to the New World, he dealt a devastating blow to Mediterranean ports in general, as the balance of trade shifted to newly developing centers on the Atlantic.

Even so, Genova today is Italy's premier port, and ranks with Marseilles in European importance. In its heyday (the 13th century), its empire, extending from colonies on the Barbary Coast to citadels on the Euphrates, rivaled that of Venice. Apart from Columbus, its most famous son was Andrea Doria (the ill-fated oceanliner was named after him), who wrested his city from the yoke of French domination in the early 16th century.

With a population of some 820,000, Genova is the capital of Liguria. It's one of the richest cities in Italy. Although shipping remains its major business, other industries have been increasingly highly developed in recent years, including insurance, communications, banking, and electronics.

Like a half moon, the port encircles the Gulf of Genova. Its hills slope right down to the water, so walking is likely to be an up- and downhill affair. Because of the terrain, the Christopher Columbus Airport opened quite late in Genova's development.

The center of the city's maritime life, the **harbor of Genova** makes for an interesting stroll, particularly in the part of the old town bordering the water. Sailors from many lands search for adventure and women in the little bars and cabarets that occupy the back alleyways. Often the streets are merely medieval lanes, with foreboding buildings closing in.

Word of warning: The harbor, particularly after dark, is not for the squeamish. It can be dangerous. If you go wandering, don't go alone and don't carry valuables. Genova is rougher than Barcelona, more comparable to Marseilles. Not only in the harbor area, but on any side street that runs downhill, a woman is likely to lose her purse.

The present harbor is the result of extensive rebuilding, following massive World War II bombardments that crippled its seaside installations. The best way to view the overall skyline is from a **harbor cruise.** Tours depart from the Stazione Marittima daily every half hour and cost 10,000L ($6) for adults and 7,000L ($4.20) for children 9 and under and seniors 60 and over.

ESSENTIALS

GETTING THERE   By Plane   Alitalia and other carriers fly into the **Aeroporto Internazionale de Genova Cristoforo Colombo,** 4 miles west of the city center in Sestri Ponente (☎ **010/2411** for flight information).

By Train   Genova has good rail connections with the rest of Italy; it lies only 1$^{1}/_{2}$ hours from Milan, 3 hours from Florence, and 1$^{1}/_{2}$ hours from the French border. Genova has two major rail stations, the **Stazione Prìncipe** and the **Stazione Brignole.** Chances are you'll arrive at the Prìncipe, Piazza Acquaverde, which is nearest to the harbor and the old part of the city. Brignole, on Piazza Verde, lies in the heart of the modern city. Both trains and municipally operated buses run between the two stations. You can phone for **train information** (☎ **0147/88-088**).

By Car   Genova is right along the main autostrada (A10) that begins at the French border and continues along the Ligurian coastline.

By Ferry   There's a 22-hour service to Genova originating in Palermo (Sicily); a one-way ticket costs 98,000L ($58.80) per person. Ferries also leave Porto Torres (Sardinia) for Genova; the one-way fare is 90,000L ($54). The number to call in Genova for information is the **Stazione Marittima** (☎ **010/261-466**).

VISITOR INFORMATION   The **Azienda di Promozione Turistica** is on Via Roma (☎ **010/576-791**). It's open daily from 8:30am to 6:30pm. You'll also find information booths dispensing tourist literature at the rail stations and the airport. The rail station office at Prìncipe (☎ **010/246-2633**) is open Monday to Saturday from 8am to 8pm and Sunday from 9am to noon; the airport office (☎ **010/ 601-5247**), is open Monday to Saturday from 8am to 8pm.

CITY LAYOUT   Genova opens onto the Porto di Genova, and most of the section of interest to visitors lies between the two main rail stations, **Stazione Prìncipe,** on the western fringe of the town, near the port, and **Stazione Brignole,** to the north-east, which opens onto Piazza Verdi. A major artery is **Via XX Settembre,** which runs between Piazza Ferrari in the west and Piazza della Vittoria in the east. **Via Balbi** is another major artery, beginning its run east of the Stazione Prìncipe, off Piazza Acquaverde. Via Balbi ends at Piazza Nunziata. From here, a short walk along Via Cairola leads to the most important tourist street in Genova, the palazzo-flanked **Via Garibaldi** (but more about that later).

FAST FACTS: GENOVA

Currency Exchange   You can exchange money at **Delfino,** Via Balbi 161R. Both the Brignole and Prìncipe railway stations have exchange offices open daily from 7am to 10pm.

Drugstores   Genova has no 24-hour pharmacies, but for a supplement of 5,000L ($3) after midnight, Pescetto, Via Balbi 185R (☎ 010/246-2696), will fill your order. For the names of other pharmacies operating at night call ☎ 192.

Emergencies   Dial ☎ 113 for assistance in a general emergency. If it's automobile trouble, call ACI, Soccorso Stradale (☎ 116). For an ambulance, call ☎ 010/570-5951.

Gas Station   If you don't mind self-service, there's an Agip station open at night on Viale Brigate Partigiane. You must have the right change.

Medical Care   If you're in need of a doctor, try Ospedale San Martino, Viale Benedetto XV 10 (☎ 010/5551).

Police   Dial ☎ 113.

Post Office   The post office, at Via Dante and Piazza de Ferrari (☎ 010/593-811), has a telex and fax. It's open Monday to Saturday from 8:15am to 7:20pm (telex until 10pm).

Taxi   To call a radio taxi, dial ☎ 5966.

Telephone   If you need to make a long-distance call, it's cheapest to go to the office at Via XX Settembre 139, which is open 24 hours a day (your hotel is likely to impose heavy surcharges). You can also place calls at both the Brignole and Prìncipe railroad stations until 9pm.

SEEING THE SIGHTS

In the heart of the city, you can stroll down ✪ **Via Garibaldi,** the street of patricians, on which noble Genovese families erected splendid palazzi in late Renaissance times. The guiding hand behind the general appearance and most of the architecture was Alessi, who grew to fame in the 16th century (he studied under Michelangelo).

Civica Galleria di Palazzo Rosso. Via Garibaldi 18. ☎ 010/247-6368. Admission 6,000L ($3.60), free for children 17 and under and seniors 60 and over. Tues and Thurs–Fri 9am–1pm; Wed and Sat 9am–7pm; Sun 10am–6pm.

This 17th-century palace was once the home of the Brignole-Sale, a local aristocratic family who founded a Genovese dynasty. It was restored after having been bombed in World War II, and now contains a good collection of paintings, with such exceptional works as *Giuditta* by Veronese, *St. Sebastian* by Guido Reni, and *Cleopatra* by Guercino. Perhaps the best-known exhibit is Sir Anthony van Dyck's portrait of Pauline and Anton Giulio Brignole-Sale from the original collection, and the magnificent frescoes by Gregorio de Ferrari *(Spring* and *Summer)* and Domenico Piola *(Autumn* and *Winter).* There are also collections of ceramics and sculpture and a display of gilded baroque statuary. Across from this red palace is the white palace, the Palazzo Bianco Gallery.

Genoa

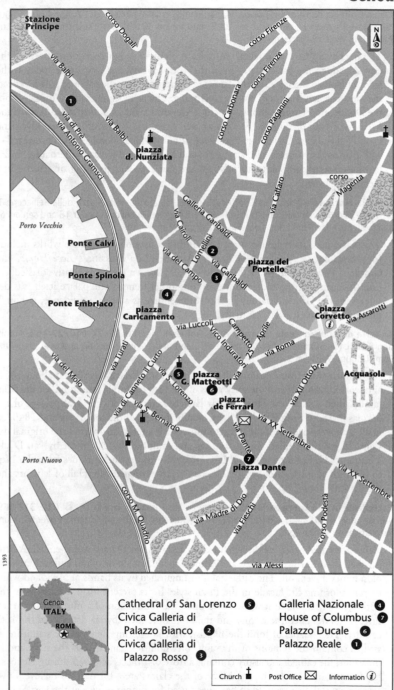

Cathedral of San Lorenzo ⑤
Civica Galleria di
Palazzo Bianco ②
Civica Galleria di
Palazzo Rosso ③

Galleria Nazionale ④
House of Columbus ⑦
Palazzo Ducale ⑥
Palazzo Reale ①

Church ☗   Post Office ✉   Information ⓘ

Civica Galleria di Palazzo Bianco. Via Garibaldi 11. ☎ **010/247-6377.** Admission 6,000L ($3.60) adults, free for children 17 and under and seniors 60 and over. Tues, Thurs–Fri, and Sun 9am–1pm; Wed and Sat 9am–7pm.

The duchess of Gallier donated this palace, along with her collection of art, to the city. Although the palace dates from the 16th century, its appearance today is the work of later architects. Gravely damaged during the war, the restored palace reflects the most recent advances in museum planning. The most significant paintings—from the Dutch and Flemish schools—include Gerard David's *Polittico della Cervara* and Memling's *Jesus Blessing the Faithful,* as well as works by Sir Anthony van Dyck and Peter Paul Rubens. A wide-ranging survey of European and local artists is presented— with paintings by Caravaggio, Zurbarán, and Murillo, and works by Bernardo Strozzi (a whole room) and Alessandro Magnasco (an excellent painting of a scene in a Genovese garden).

Galleria Nazionale (National Gallery). In the Palazzo Spinola, Piazza della Pellicceria 1. ☎ **010/294-661.** Admission 8,000L ($4.80) adults, free for children under 18 and seniors 60 and over. Monday 9am–1pm, Tues–Sat 9am–7pm, Sun 2–7pm.

The National Gallery houses a major painting collection. Its notable works include Joos van Cleve's *Madonna in Prayer,* Antonello da Messina's *Ecce Homo,* and Giovanni Pisano's *Guistizia.* The gallery is also known for its decorative arts collection (furniture, silver, and ceramics, among other items). The palace itself was designed for the Grimaldi family in the 16th century as a private residence, although the Spinolas took it over eventually.

Galleria di Palazzo Reale (Royal Palace Gallery). Via Balbi 10. ☎ **010/27-101.** Admission 8,000L ($4.80) adults, free for children 18 and under and seniors 60 and over. Sun–Tues 9am–1:30pm, Wed–Sat 9am–7pm.

A 5-minute walk from Stazione Prìncipe, the Royal Palace was started about 1650, and work continued until the early years of the 18th century. It was built for the Balbi family, then sold to the Durazzos. It later became one of the royal palaces of the Savoias in 1824. King Charles Albert modified many of the rooms around 1840. As in all Genovese palazzi, some of these subsequent alterations marred the original designs. Its gallery is filled with paintings and sculpture, works of art by van Dyck, Tintoretto, G. F. Romanelli, and L. Giordano. Frescoes and antiques from the 17th to the 19th centuries are displayed. Seek out, in particular, the Hall of Mirrors and the Throne Room.

Cattedrale of San Lorenzo. Piazza San Lorenzo, Via Tommaso Reggio 17. ☎ **010/311-269.** Admission 9,000L ($5.40) adults, 7,000L ($4.20) students, children, and seniors over 60. Mon– Sat 9am–noon and 3–6pm.

Genova is noted for its medieval churches, and this one towers over them all. A British shell fired during World War II almost spelled its doom—miraculously the explosion never went off. The cathedral is distinguished by its bands of black-and-white marble adorning the facade in the Pisan style. In its present form it dates from the 13th century, although it was erected upon the foundation of a much earlier structure. Alessi designed the dome, and the campanile (bell tower) dates from the 16th century. The Chapel of John the Baptist, with interesting Renaissance sculpture, is said to contain the remains of the saint for whom it's named. Off the nave and in the vaults, the cathedral treasury contains a trove of artifacts acquired during Genova's heyday as a mercantile empire. Some of the claims are a bit hard to believe, however—a crystal dish reputed to have been used for dinner service at the Last Supper and a blue chalcedony platter on which the head of John the Baptist was rested for its delivery to Salome. Other treasures include an 11th-century arm reliquary of St. Anne and a jewel-studded Byzantine Zaccaria Cross.

SHOPPING

Shopping in Genova includes a good selection of apparel, all things antiquated, jewelry, and foodstuff. Classic but contemporary, **Berti,** Via XII Ottobre 94R (☎ 010/540-026), carries a line of Burberry items, as well as British-inspired designs by designers such as Valentino and Pedroni. Assuming there's a sailor in all of us, **Lucarda,** Via Sottoripa 61 (☎ 010/297-963), offers nautically inspired clothing for men and women. They do not, however, carry beachwear. **Le Mimose,** Via XXV Aprile 58R (☎ 010/292-615), is a small room filled with women's lingerie of impeccable quality and design. An elegant shop, **Pescetto,** Via Scurreria 8 Rosso (☎ 010/247-3433), offers men's and women's designer outfits and fragrances, coupled with accessories that include leather bags and wallets. Located in a street overrun with goldsmiths, the reputable **Codevilla,** Via Orefici 53 (☎ 010/247-2567), fashions jewelry and small objects out of gold, silver, and a wide variety of precious and semiprecious stones.

Appropriately situated in the historical center of the town, **Dallai Libreria Antiquaria,** Piazza de Marini 11R (☎ 010/247-2338), handles first editions and rare books and prints from the 18th and 19th centuries. Displaying their wares in a 16th-century chapel featuring elaborate frescoes, the proprietors of **Galleria Imperiale,** Piazza Campetto 8 (☎ 010/299-290), are estate liquidators, specializing in 19th- and early 20th-century household goods, including objets d'art, all types of furniture, and paintings.

With bakers working around the clock, **Il Fornaio di Sattanino,** Via Fiasella 18r (☎ 010/580-972), turns out versions of the region's famous *focaccia* filled with almost any ingredient available at the market. They also offer other types of bread and various pastries. A death-by-chocolate lover's dream, **Pietro Romanengo fu Stefano,** Via Soziglia 74 Rosso (☎ 010/297-869), allows you to indulge your sweet tooth on handmade confections coated, sprinkled, glazed, or composed of the dark sugary concoction. When your hunger turns to thirst, the retail-only **Vinoteca Sola,** Piazza Colombo 13 (☎ 010/561-329), offers a huge selection of wines from all over the world.

Combining Old World beliefs with New Age enthusiasm, **Antica Erboristeria San Giorgio,** Via Luccoli 47R (☎ 010/206-888), prepares and sells herbs, teas, and natural personal-care products. **Pecchiolo,** Via Pisa 13 (☎ 010/362-5082), sells upscale dinner- and cookware of ceramic, crystal, and silver; and if you'd rather just have a one-stop shopping excursion, **La Rinascente,** Via Vernazza 1 (☎ 010/586-995), and **Coin,** Via XII Ottobre 4 (☎ 010/570-5821), are the two biggest department stores in town.

WHERE TO STAY

Generally, hotels in Genova are second rate, but some good finds await those who search diligently.

Warning: Some of the cheap hotels and pensions in and around the waterfront are to be avoided. Our recommendations, however, are suitable even for women traveling alone.

EXPENSIVE

Bristol-Palace. Via XX Settembre 35, 16121 Genova. ☎ **010/592-541.** Fax 010/561-756. 128 rms, 5 suites. A/C MINIBAR TV TEL. 380,000L ($228) double; 490,000L ($294) suite. Rates include breakfast. AE, DC, MC, V. Parking 40,000L ($24).

Bristol-Palace, dating from the late 19th century, has a number of features that will make your stay in Genova special, even though it's in the grimy heart of old town. Its obscure entrance behind colonnades on a commercial street is misleading; the salons and drawing rooms inside are furnished nicely with traditional pieces, although both fabrics and furnishings are beginning to show their age. The larger of the bedrooms have an old-fashioned elegance, are spacious and comfortable, and are tastefully furnished, often with chandeliers, Queen Anne desks, and padded headboards. The hotel's stairway is one of the most stunning in Genova. The English bar is a favorite rendezvous point, and a small but elegant restaurant, Il Caffè de Bristol, offers daily lunches and dinners.

City Hotel. Via San Sebastiano 6, 16123 Genova. ☎ **010/5545.** Fax 010/586-301. 66 rms, 3 suites. A/C MINIBAR TV TEL. 360,000L ($216) double; 600,000L ($360) suite. Rates include breakfast. AE, DC, MC, V. Parking 40,000L ($24).

One of the best hotels in its category, last renovated in 1990, is located in a starkly angular stucco and travertine postwar building, surrounded by a crumbling series of town houses. The convenient location, near Piazza Corvetto and Via Garibaldi, is one of the hotel's best features. Other pluses include a welcoming staff, a comfortable wood-and-granite lobby, and modernized rooms. The bedrooms have parquet floors, specially designed furniture, and up-to-date amenities. The hotel also has a cocktail bar serving snacks and a first-class restaurant that offers many regional specialties. A short list of cold and hot foods are served room service–style throughout the day and early evening.

Hotel Savoia Majestic. Via Arsenale di Terra 5, 16126 Genova. ☎ **010/261-641.** Fax 010/261-883. 123 rms, 5 suites. MINIBAR TV TEL. 290,000L–340,000L ($174–$204) double; from 410,000L ($246) suite. Rates include breakfast. AE, DC, MC, V. Parking 25,000L ($15).

Located across from Piazza Prìncipe, the 1887 Hotel Savoia Majestic still contains some of its original accessories, although its heyday when it entertained dukes and their duchesses has long since past. These days clients tend to be European business travelers. The decor of the high-ceilinged bedrooms ranges from modern to conservatively old-fashioned. Try for a room on the sixth floor for the best views of the harbor. All but 20 of the rooms are air-conditioned. Some of the bathrooms are unusually large with pink marble surfaces, whereas others are extremely cramped. Because the rooms vary so widely from good to bad, your experience will depend entirely on where you're stashed for the night. The lobby and reception area is shared with another establishment, the Hotel Londra & Continentale. The restaurant here is so routine you'll want to seek better fare at one of the nearby trattorie.

Jolly Hotel Plaza. Via Martin Piaggio 11, 16122 Genova. ☎ **800/221-2626** in the U.S., 800/237-0319 in Canada, or 010/839-3641. Fax 010/839-1850. 146 rms, 1 suite. A/C MINIBAR TV TEL. 320,000L–400,000L ($192–$240) double; 900,000L ($540) suite. Rates include breakfast. AE, DC, MC, V. Parking 30,000L ($18).

A four-star member of the Jolly chain, this hotel is newer than its modified classic facade would suggest. Centrally located near Piazza Corvetto, it was built in 1950 to replace an older hotel destroyed during an air raid in World War II. In 1992 the hotel was renovated, upgraded, and enlarged. The Jolly links two former hotels, the Baglioni Eliseo and the Plaza. The rooms in the old Eliseo are generally more spacious than those in the former Plaza. Elegant touches include mother-of-pearl inlay in the doors and marble baths. The rooms in the old Plaza are more cramped and decorated with a dull brown decor. On the premises are an American-style bar and a grill room, La Villetta di Negro. When business is slow, the management sometimes opts not to open the restaurant on weekends.

MODERATE

Columbus Sea Hotel. Via Milano 63, 16126 Genova. ☎ **010/265-051.** Fax 010/255-226. 80 rms, 7 junior suites. A/C MINIBAR TV TEL. 200,000L–250,000L ($120–$150) double; 280,000L–350,000L ($168–$210) junior suite. AE, DC, MC, V.

One of the best moderate hotels in town, Columbus Sea looks out at the new cruise ship terminal and stands close to Genova's World Trade Center. The city center and old town lie only a mile away. It's warmer and more inviting inside than its cold boxy exterior suggests. Bedrooms are roomy for the most part, furnished in muted colors with Oriental carpeting. The public rooms are more gracious, outfitted with a certain taste and flair. A popular rendezvous point in Genova is Il Mandraccio, the hotel's American bar. La Lanterna restaurant serves excellent Ligurian specialties and also treats diners to a panoramic view of the harbor and city.

INEXPENSIVE

○ **Albergo Viale Sauli.** Viale Sauli 5, 16121 Genova. ☎ **010/561-397.** Fax 010/590-092. 56 rms. A/C MINIBAR TV TEL. 160,000L ($96) double. Rates include breakfast. AE, DC, MC, V.

This hotel is located on the second floor of a modern concrete office building, just off a busy shopping street in the center of town. It's scattered over three floors, each of them reachable by elevator from the building's lobby. The high-ceilinged public rooms include a bar, a breakfast room, and a reception area, all with big windows and lots of comfort. Enore Sceresini is the opera-loving owner, and his clients usually include businesspeople who appreciate cleanliness and comfort. Each of the units has marble floors and a spacious bath.

Hotel Agnello d'Oro. Vico delle Monachette 6, 16126 Genova. ☎ **010/246-2084.** Fax 010/ 246-2327. 38 rms. TV TEL. 140,000L ($84) double. AE, MC, V.

When the Doria family owned this structure and everything around it in the 1600s, they carved their family crest on the walls of the building near the top of the alley so that all of Genova would know the point at which their property began. The symbol was a golden lamb, and you can still see one at the point where the narrow street joins the busy boulevard leading to the Stazione Prìncipe. The hotel, which was named after the animal on the crest, is a 17th-century building that includes vaulted ceilings and paneling in the lobby. About half the units are in a newer wing, but if you want the oldest accommodations, ask for Room 6, 7, or 8. Today the hotel is maintained by a family who has installed a small bar and restaurant off the lobby.

Hotel Astoria. Piazza Brignole 4, 16122 Genova. ☎ **010/873-316.** Fax 010/831-7326. 73 rms. TV TEL. 190,000L ($114) double. AE, DC, MC, V. Parking 20,000L ($12).

Built in the 1920s but opened as a hotel only in 1978, this establishment has lots of polished paneling, wrought-iron accents, beige marble floors, and a baronial carved fireplace in one of the public rooms. The rooms are comfortably furnished and well maintained. The hotel sits on an uninspiring square that contains a filling station, and its view encompasses a traffic hub and many square blocks of apartment buildings. There's a bar on the premises, but no restaurant. There's no garage—street parking only.

Hotel Vittoria Orlandi. Via Balbi 33–45, 16126 Genova. ☎ **010/261-923.** Fax 010/ 246-2656. 56 rms. A/C TV TEL. 100,000L–140,000L ($60–$84) double. AE, DC, MC, V. Parking 20,000L ($12).

Since this hotel is constructed on one of the hillsides for which Genova is famous, its entrance is under a tunnel that opens at a point about a block from the Stazione Prìncipe. An elevator will take you up to the reception area. The establishment, built in 1926, welcomes a wide variety of guests to its simple but clean rooms. Many of the rooms have balconies, and about half are air-conditioned and contain a minibar. Best of all, the hotel is quiet because of the way it's sheltered from the busy boulevards by other buildings.

WHERE TO DINE

Genova, which has been praised for its cuisine, has lots of restaurants and trattorie, many of which are strung along the harbor. The following recommendations will give you several opportunities to judge it for yourself.

✪ **Da Giacomo.** Corso Italia 1R. ☎ **010/362-9647.** Reservations required. Main courses 25,000L–45,000L ($15–$27); fixed-price menu 80,000L ($48). AE, DC, MC, V. Mon–Sat 12:30–2:30pm and 7:30–10pm. Closed 1 week in Aug. LIGURIAN.

Many food critics regard Da Giacomo, established in 1965, as the premier restaurant of Genova. The service is deluxe, as is the ambience, decorated in an elegant modern style and graced with plants. Ligurian cooking is dominated by the sea and so is the menu here, beginning with superb seafood antipasti, some of which is raw but cut and carved with the exquisite care you find in Tokyo. Meat, fish, and poultry dishes are prepared with unusual flair. Pesto sauce accompanies many dishes, especially the pasta. (During the Crusades it was reported that the Genovese contingent could always be identified by the aroma of pesto surrounding them.) They offer some of the finest regional wines in Italy, and desserts are made fresh daily on the premises. There is also a piano bar where you can dance.

✪ **Gran Gotto.** Viale Brigate Bisagno 69R. ☎ **010/564-344.** Reservations recommended. Main courses 30,000L–40,000L ($18–$24); fixed-price menu 85,000L ($51). AE, MC, V. Mon–Fri 12:30–2:30pm and 7:30–10pm, Sat 7:30–10pm. Closed Aug 17–31. SEAFOOD.

Although it was established in 1937, and has been in the same family ever since, this restaurant moved to new quarters in 1995. Amid a setting of modern art and vaguely Austrian accessories, we consider it the top restaurant in Genova. Its name translates from Genovese dialect as "large glass." The emphasis is on seafood, but the meat and pasta dishes aren't neglected. In fact, the most typical offering, *trenette al pesto,* is quite famous, a pasta of paper-thin noodles served with the characteristic pesto. The delicately simmered risotto is also tempting. The main dishes are reasonably priced and of high standard, including the mixed fish fry and the French baby squid. The *zuppa di pesce* (fish soup) has made many a luncheon for many a gourmet. The *rognone al cognac* is another superb choice—tender calves' kidneys that have been cooked and delicately flavored in cognac.

Ristorante Saint Cyr. Piazza Marsala 4. ☎ **010/886-897.** Reservations required. Main courses 30,000L ($18). AE, DC, MC, V. Mon–Fri noon–2:30pm and 7:30–10pm, Sat 7:30–10pm. Closed Dec 23–Jan 7 and 1 week in Aug. LIGURIAN/PIEDMONTESE.

Our favorite time to come to this restaurant is at night, when some of the most discriminating palates in Genova might be seen enjoying dishes generously adapted from regional recipes. The restaurant was established in 1971 near Piazza Corvetto in a 1900 printing factory. Menu items change daily, although recent offerings featured rice with truffles and cheese, a timbale of fresh spinach, a charlotte of fish, and a variety of braised meats, each delicately seasoned and perfectly prepared. Specialties include *scamone* (a certain cut of beef) cooked in Barolo wine and *ravioli al sugo di carne* (ravioli with sauce made from meat juices). The restaurant is also open for lunch, when the clientele are likely to be conservatively dressed businesspeople discussing shipping contracts.

Ristorante Zeffirino. Via XX Settembre 20. ☎ **010/591-990.** Reservations recommended. Main courses 30,000L–60,000L ($18–$36); fixed-price menu 60,000L ($36). AE, DC, MC, V. Thurs–Tues noon–3pm and 7pm–midnight. LIGURIAN.

Located in a cul-de-sac just off one of the busiest boulevards of Genova, this place has hosted everyone from Frank Sinatra to Luciano Pavarotti, and Pope John Paul II to Liza Minnelli. Established in the 1930s, it moved to its present location in the 1950s. At least 14 members of the Zeffirino family prepare the best pasta in the city, from recipes collected from all over Italy. These include lesser-known varieties such as quadrucci, pettinati, and cappelletti, as well as the more familiar tagliatelle and lasagne. Next, you can select from a vast array of meat and fish, along with 1,000 kinds of wine. Ligurian specialties, including risotto alla pescatore and beef stew with artichokes, are featured. Try a wide array of shellfish—either baked or steamed—and served with seasonal vegetables.

GENOVA AFTER DARK

The port has understood the allure of nocturnal pleasures since the city's heyday as a magnet for mariners and merchants from around north Europe and the Mediterranean. But be alert to the unsavory aspects of nightlife in Genova, especially within the labyrinthine alleyways of the town's medieval core. Equally unadvisable are the dubious neighborhoods around the bus station and the Piazza Matteotti, where drug sales and commercial sex are only two of the preoccupations of many of the night owls there.

You'll find enough *discoteche* to keep you fully occupied every night of your stay. The best of them include **Caffè Nessundorma,** Via Porta d'Arci 74 (☎ 010/561-773), where bouts of live music, beginning at 11pm, usually segue into recorded disco, often with retro music from the disco-crazed 70s and 80s, for a crowd milling in a setting that combines aspects of both a singles bar and a very hip cafe. Somewhat more elegant is **Mako,** Corso Italia 28 (☎ 010/367-652), which has a piano bar, a disco, and a restaurant. Two other centrally located contenders for the bar and disco trade include **Vanilla,** Via Brigata Salerno (☎ 010/399-0872), and **Eccentrica,** Via Ceccardi 24 (☎ 010/570-2809), which are neither as vanilla nor as eccentric as their names make them appear. (Eccentrica is not particularly geared to punk-rockers, as its name implies, as at least some of its clients come here with neckties.) **M&M,** Piazza Fontana Marose, Salita Santa Caterina (☎ 010/586-787), offers a small-scale environment that's either intimate or cramped, depending on who happens to be here at the time. It features recorded music, and, after the evening brings rock and roll, some live jazz and blues as well.

Looking for a simple pint of beer, some pub grub, and access to a dose of English humor? Head for the **Brittania Pub,** Vico Calzana, near the Piazza de Ferrari (no phone), where groups of friends fill a woodsy-looking setting that evokes Winston Churchill with an Italian accent.

3 Rapallo

296 miles NW of Rome, 17 miles SE of Genova, 100 miles S of Milan

A top seaside resort—known for years to the chic and wealthy crowd who live in the villas studding the hillside—Rapallo occupies a remarkable site overlooking the Gulf of Tigullio. In summer the crowded heart of Rapallo takes on a carnival air, as hordes of bathers occupy the rocky sands along the beach. In the area is an 18-hole golf course, as well as an indoor swimming pool, a riding club, and a modern harbor. You can also take a cable car to the **Sanctuary di Montallegro,** then walk to **Monte Rosa** for one of the finest views of the Ligurian coast. There are many opportunities for summer **boat trips,** not only to Portofino but to the Cinque Terre.

Rapallo's long history is often likened to Genova's. It became part of the Repubblica Superba in 1229, but Rapallo had existed long before that. Its **cathedral** dates from the 6th century when it was founded by the bishops of Milan. Walls once enclosed the medieval town, but now only the **Saline Gate** remains. Rapallo has also been the scene of many an international meeting, the most notable of which was the 1917 conference of wartime allies.

Today Rapallo is a bit past its heyday, although it was once known as one of Europe's most fashionable resorts, numbering among its residents Ezra Pound and D. H. Lawrence. Other artists, poets, and writers have been drawn to its natural beauty, which has been marred in part by an uncontrolled building boom brought on by tourism. At the innermost corner of the Gulf of Tiguillio, Rapallo is still the most famous resort on the Riviera di Levante, a position it owes to its year-round mild climate.

ESSENTIALS

GETTING THERE　By Train　Three trains from Genova stop off here each hour from 4:30am to midnight. A one-way fare is 2,700L ($1.60). A train also links Rapallo with Santa Margherita every 30 minutes, costing 1,500L (90¢) for a one-way fare.

By Bus　From Santa Margherita, a bus operated by Tigullio runs every 30 minutes to Rapallo, costing 1,400L (85¢) for a one-way fare and taking half an hour. The bus information office is at Piazza Vittorio Veneto in Santa Margherita (☎ **0185/ 288-834**).

By Car　From Genova, continue southeast along the A12 autostrada.

VISITOR INFORMATION　The **tourist information center** is at Via Diaz 9 (☎ **0185/230-346**). It's open Monday to Saturday from 9am to 12:30pm and 2:30 to 5:30pm, Sunday from 9am to 12:30pm.

WHERE TO STAY
EXPENSIVE

Eurotel. Via Aurelia di Ponente 22, 16035 Rapallo. ☎ **0185/60-981.** Fax 0185/50-635. 65 rms. A/C MINIBAR TV TEL. 190,000L–230,000L ($114–$138) double. Rates include buffet breakfast. AE, MC, V. Parking 20,000L ($12) in the garage, free outdoors.

With seven floors and three elevators, this vivid sienna-colored structure is one of the tallest hotels in town, set above the port at the top of a winding road where you'll have to negotiate the oncoming traffic with care. (Many of the units, though, are privately owned condominiums.) The lobby has marble floors and a helpful staff. All rooms contain built-in cabinets, arched loggias with views over the gulf of Rapallo, and beds that fold, Murphy style, into the walls. A bar and a second-floor panoramic restaurant, Antica Aurelia, are on the premises, as is a small rectangular swimming pool set in a verdant garden.

✪ **Grand Hotel Bristol.** Via Aurelia Orientale 369, 16035 Rapallo. ☎ **0185/273-313.** Fax 0185/55-800. 85 rms, 6 suites. A/C MINIBAR TV TEL. 280,000L–380,000L ($168–$228) double; from 800,000L ($480) suite. Rates include breakfast. AE, MC, V. Parking 20,000L ($12) in the garage, free outdoors.

This hotel, one of the Riviera's grand old buildings and Rapallo's finest resort with a polite staff, is still a viable choice in spite of falling standards. Built in 1908, it was reopened in 1984, and the turn-of-the-century pink-and-white facade, with surrounding shrubbery and iron gates, was spruced up but basically unchanged during the 5-year rebuilding program. The interior, however, was gutted. Some bedrooms have private terraces, and all contain electronic window blinds, lots of mirrors, and oversized beds. The inviting waters of a pool are visible from many, and the kitchens are about the most modern anywhere.

Dining/Entertainment: The hotel has several restaurants, including a rooftop restaurant that's often closed when it's too hot. If the house count is low, only one restaurant might be open.

Services: Room service, baby-sitting, laundry, valet, hairdresser, beautician, massage salon.

Facilities: Free-form pool (one of the biggest in the region), conference rooms.

Hotel Giulio Cesare. Corso Cristoforo Colombo 52, 16035 Rapallo. ☎ **0185/50-685.** Fax 0185/60-896. 33 rms. TV TEL. 140,000L ($84) double; 95,000L ($57) per person double with half board. AE, DC, MC, V. Closed Nov 6–Dec 20. Free parking in low season, 10,000L–20,000L ($6–$12) in high season.

This modernized, four-story villa is a bargain for the Italian Riviera. When the genial owner skillfully renovated the establishment, he kept expenses down to keep room rates lower. The hotel, which lies on the coast road about 90 feet from the sea, offers bedrooms with a homelike atmosphere, which feature good views of the Gulf of Tigullio and are furnished with tasteful reproductions (most of the rooms have sunny balconies). Ask for the rooms on the top floor if you want a better view and quieter surroundings. The meals are prepared with fine ingredients (the fresh fish dishes are superb).

Hotel Miramare. Lungomare Vittorio Veneto 27, 16035 Rapallo. ☎ **0185/230-261.** Fax 0185/273-570. 22 rms, 6 suites. MINIBAR TV TEL. 140,000L–160,000L ($84–$96) double; 150,000L–180,000L ($90–$108) suite. Half board 110,000L–140,000L ($66–$84) per person. AE, DC, MC, V. Closed Nov. Parking 20,000L ($12).

Located on the water near a stone gazebo is this jazz-age (1929) re-creation of a Renaissance villa, with exterior frescoes that have faded in the salt air. The gardens in front have been replaced by a glass extension that contains a contemporary restaurant (see "Where to Dine," below). The accommodations inside are clean and simple, comfortable, and high-ceilinged. Many on them have iron balconies that stretch toward the harbor.

WHERE TO DINE

Ristorante da Monique. Lungomare Vittorio Veneto 6. ☎ **0185/50-541.** Reservations required. Main courses 20,000L–30,000L ($12–$18). AE, DC, MC, V. Wed–Mon 12:30–2:30pm and 7:30–10pm. Closed Jan 7–Feb 15. SEAFOOD.

This is one of the most popular seafood restaurants along the harbor since the 1930s, especially in summer when the tavern chairs are almost filled. It features nautical decor and big windows that overlook the boats in the marina. As you'd expect, fish is the specialty, including seafood salad, fish soup, risotto with shrimp, spaghetti with clams or mussels, grilled fish, and both tagliatelle and scampi "Monique." Some of these dishes may not always hit the mark, but you'll rarely go wrong ordering the grilled fish.

Ristorante Elite. Via Milite Ignoto 19. ☎ **0185/50-551.** Main courses 14,000L–28,000L ($8.40–$16.80); fixed-price menu 35,000L ($21). AE, MC, V. Fri–Wed noon–2:30pm and 7:30–10pm. Closed several days in Nov. SEAFOOD.

This restaurant is set back from the water on a busy commercial street in the center of town. It was established in the 1960s in a building from the 1930s. Mainly fish is served; the offering depends on the catch of the day. Your dinner might consist of mussels marinara, minestrone Genovese style, *risotto marinara, trenette al pesto,* scampi, *zuppa di pesce,* sole meunière, turbot, or a mixed fish fry from the Ligurian coast. A limited selection of the standard meat dishes is available, too. At the peak of the midsummer tourist invasion, the restaurant is likely to remain open every day.

Ristorante Miramare. In the Hotel Miramare, Lungomare Vittorio Veneto 27. ☎ **0185/230-261.** Reservations recommended. Main courses 16,000L–35,000L ($9.60–$21); fixed-price menu 45,000L ($27). AE, DC, MC, V. Daily 12:30–2pm and 7:30–9:30pm. SEAFOOD/LIGURIAN.

Set in a previously recommended hotel, a building originally conceived as a private villa, this restaurant serves well-prepared and unpretentious food in a modern dining room overlooking the sea. Your dinner might include fried calamari, spaghetti with clams, sea bass or turbot baked with potatoes and artichokes, veal in marsala sauce, or flavorful versions of fish soup.

4 Santa Margherita Ligure

19 miles E of Genova, 3 miles S of Portofino, 296 miles NW of Rome

A resort rival to Rapallo, Santa Margherita Ligure also occupies a beautiful position on the Gulf of Tigullio. Its attractive harbor is usually thronged with fun seekers, and the resort offers the widest range of accommodations in all price levels on the eastern Riviera. It has a festive appearance, with a promenade, flower beds, and palm trees swaying in the wind. As is typical of the Riviera, its beach combines rock and sand. Santa Margherita Ligure is linked to Portofino by a narrow road. The climate of Santa Margherita Ligure is mild, even in the winter months, when many elderly clients visit the resort.

The town dates back to A.D. 262. The official name of Santa Margherita Ligure was given to the town by Victor Emmanuel II in 1863. Before that it had many other names, including Porto Napoleone, an 1812 designation from Napoléon.

You can visit the richly embellished **Sanctuary of Santa Maria della Rosa,** Piazza Caprera, with its Italian and Flemish paintings, along with relics of the saint for whom the town was named.

ESSENTIALS

GETTING THERE By Train Three trains per hour arrive from Genova daily from 4:30am to midnight. The one-way fare is 2,700L ($1.60). The **train station** is at Piazza Federico Raoul Nobili.

By Bus Buses run frequently between Portofino and Santa Margherita Ligure daily. A one-way ticket costs 1,700L ($1). You can also catch a bus in Rapallo to Santa Margherita; during the day one leaves Rapallo every 30 minutes. For information call ☎ 010/231-108.

By Car Take Route 227 southeast from Genova.

VISITOR INFORMATION The **tourist information center** is at Via 25 Aprile 2B (☎ 0185/287-485). It's open Monday to Saturday from 9am to 12:30pm and 2:30 to 5:30pm, Sunday from 9am to 12:30pm.

WHERE TO STAY
VERY EXPENSIVE

Imperiale Palace Hotel. Via Pagana 19, 16038 Santa Margherita Ligure. ☎ **0185/288-991.** Fax 0185/284-223. 89 rms, 13 junior suites. A/C MINIBAR TV TEL. 380,000L–540,000L ($228–$324) double; from 700,000L ($420) suite. Rates include breakfast. AE, DC, MC, V. Closed Dec–Mar.

The Imperial looks like an ornate gilded palace, and many guests, attracted to its faded grandeur, choose to spend their "season on the Riviera" here. Although still regal, it's fading a bit, and the Grand Hotel Miramare (below) has overtaken it. It's built against a hillside at the edge of the resort, surrounded by semitropical gardens. The time-worn public rooms live up to the hotel's name—old courtly splendor dominates, with vaulted ceilings, satin-covered antiques, ornate mirrors, and inlaid marble floors. The bedrooms vary widely, from royal suites to simple singles away from the sea. Many have elaborate ceilings, balconies, brass beds, chandeliers, and white antique furniture, but others are rather bare.

Dining/Entertainment: The formal dining room serves Ligurian and international meals. There's also a two-decker open-air restaurant. There's a music room, with a grand piano and satin chairs, for teatime. In summer, live music is presented on the terrace.

Service: Room service, baby-sitting, laundry, valet.

Facilities: A festive recreation center along the water's edge, with an oval flagstone swimming pool, an extended stone wharf, and cabanas.

EXPENSIVE

✪ **Grand Hotel Miramare.** Via Milite Ignoto 30, 16038 Santa Margherita Ligure. ☎ **800/ 223-6800** in the U.S., or 0185/287-013. Fax 0185/284-651. 75 rms, 9 suites. A/C MINIBAR TV TEL. 370,000L–450,000L ($222–$270) double; 650,000L–800,000L ($390–$480) suite. Rates include breakfast. Reduced rates available for children under 12 in parents' room. AE, DC, MC, V. Parking 30,000L–35,000L ($18–$21).

Now the prestige address of the resort, this old-world choice, a palatial 1929 building, has kept more up with the times than has the Imperial. It was on the terrace of this hotel in 1933 that Marconi succeeded in transmitting for the first time telegraph and telephone signals a distance of more than 90 miles. Separated from a stony beach by a busy boulevard, it's a 3-minute walk from the center of town. The hotel building has a festive confectionery look, surrounded by meticulously maintained gardens. To one side is a curved outdoor pool with heated seawater. This adjoins a raised sun terrace dotted with parasols and iron tables. The bedrooms are classically furnished, and many of the baths are spacious and packed with amenities from hair dryers to makeup mirrors. Even some of the standard rooms have large terraces with sea views.

Dining/Entertainment: The hotel restaurant has many Victorian touches, including fragile chairs and blue-and-white porcelain set into the plaster walls.

Services: Room service, baby-sitting, laundry, valet.

Facilities: Heated saltwater outdoor pool, private beach, Miramare Skywater School.

MODERATE

Hotel Continental. Via Pagana 8, 16038 Santa Margherita Ligure. ☎ **0185/286-512.** Fax 0185/284-463. 76 rms. A/C MINIBAR TV TEL. 235,000L–295,000L ($141–$177) double, including breakfast; 160,000L–205,000L ($96–$123) per person double with half board. AE, DC, MC, V. Parking 15,000L–25,000L ($9–$15).

You'll see this hotel's grandiose facade from the winding road into town. The high-ceilinged, airy public rooms give a glimpse of terraced gardens that stretch down to a private beach. The Continental is the only hotel directly on the water. In fair weather, it operates a snack bar there, where guests enjoy views of Santa Margherita bay. The bedrooms are filled with comfortable, conservative, if somewhat fading furnishings, and often have tall French windows that open onto wrought-iron balconies. Try for a room on the top floor; the annex contains very lackluster lodgings. The view from the restaurant encompasses the curved harbor in the center of town, a few miles away. Since the turn of the century the Ciana family has managed this property, along with the Regina Elena and Metropole and Laurin. With such a command of rooms, they can almost always accommodate you in any season.

Hotel Regina Elena. Lungomare Milite Ignoto 44, 16038 Santa Margherita Ligure. ☎ 0185/
287-003. Fax 0185/284-473. 103 rms. A/C MINIBAR TV TEL. 232,000L–280,000L ($139.20–
$168) double, including breakfast; 298,000L–366,000L ($178.80–$219.60) double with half
board. AE, DC, MC, V.

This pastel-painted hotel is situated by the sea, along the scenic thoroughfare leading to Portofino. The well-maintained bedrooms are furnished with modern styling,
and most of them open onto a balcony with a sea view. An annex in the garden contains additional rooms. The hotel was built in 1908 and many turn-of-the-century
details remain, including a marble staircase. The hotel is operated by the Ciana family,
which has been receiving guests for almsot a hundred years. They also operate the
Continental (above) and the Metropole and Laurin. The dining room is the most
interesting part of the hotel, a 12-sided glass-walled structure serving excellent cuisine. The hotel offers room service, baby-sitting, laundry, and valet. There's also a
conference center and a roof garden pool with a Jacuzzi.

Park Hotel Suisse. Via Favale 31, 16038 Santa Margherita Ligure. ☎ 0185/289-571. Fax
0185/281-469. 85 rms. TV TEL. 130,000L–360,000L ($78–$216) double. Rates include continental breakfast. No credit cards.

Set in a garden above the town center, the Park Hotel Suisse features a panoramic
view of the sea and harbor. It has seven floors, all modern in design, with deep
private balconies that are like alfresco living rooms for some of the bedrooms. On the
lower terrace is a large, free-form, saltwater swimming pool surrounded by semitropical vegetation. A modernistic water chute, diving boards, and a cafe with para-
sol tables for refreshments all give one the advantages of seaside life and then some.
The comfortable bedrooms that open onto the rear gardens, without sea view, cost
slightly less. The hotel, although built in 1957, has been renovated many times since
then, and lies 800 yards from the rail station above a small harbor about 100 yards
from the sea. You have to cross a small street to reach the water.

INEXPENSIVE

Albergo Conte Verde. Via Zara 1, 16038 Santa Margherita Ligure. ☎ 0185/287-139. Fax
0185/284-211. 35 rms, 30 with shower. 70,000L–100,000L ($42–$60) double without shower,
80,000L–150,000L ($48–$90) double with shower. Rates include breakfast. AE, DC, MC, V.
Closed Mar 1–15 and Dec 1–25. Parking 15,000L ($9).

This place offers one of the warmest welcomes in town to the budget traveler.
Located only two blocks from the sea, this third-class hotel has been revamped, and
its rooms are simple but adequate. The front terrace has swing gliders, and the lounge
has period furnishings, including rockers. All is consistent with the villa exterior of
shuttered windows, flower boxes, and a small front garden and lawn where tables are
set out for refreshments. Open year-round, the hotel also has a good and inexpensive restaurant.

Albergo Fasce. Via Bozzo 3, 16038 Santa Margherita Ligure. ☎ 0185/286-435. Fax 0185/
283-580. 16 rms. MINIBAR TV TEL. 145,000L ($87) double. Rates include breakfast. AE, DC,
MC, V. Parking 20,000L ($12).

A family-run hotel, the Fasce is functional yet welcoming. Each of its streamlined
modern rooms has a safe-deposit box. On the roof is a panoramic solarium.
English-born Jane McGuffie Fasce runs the hotel along with her husband, Aristide;
everything functions in a homelike way. Extra amenities include 4-hour laundry service. The hotel also provides free bicycles and a 3-day bus pass for touring the area.

Hotel Jolanda. Via Luisito Costa 6, 16038 Santa Margherita Ligure. ☎ 0185/287-513. Fax
0185/284-763. 40 rms. TV TEL. 130,000L–160,000L ($78–$96) double, including breakfast;
80,000L–120,000L ($48–$72) per person double with half board. AE, MC, V. Parking 10,000L
($6) in garage, free outdoors.

Since the 1940s the Pastine family has been welcoming visitors to their little hotel, a short walk from the sea. A patio serves as a kind of open-air living room. The pensione lies on a peaceful little street, away from traffic noise. The rooms are comfortably furnished. Guests often gather in the bar before proceeding to the restaurant, where an excellent Ligurian cuisine is served. A meal costs about 35,000L ($21).

WHERE TO DINE

Ristorante La Ghiaia. In the Lido Palace Hotel, Via Andrea Doria 5. ☎ **0185/283-708.** Reservations recommended. Main courses 10,000L–25,000L ($6–$15); fixed-price menu 45,000L ($27). AE, DC, MC, V. Thurs–Tues 12:30–2pm and 8–10pm. Closed Nov. SEAFOOD.

This establishment's name in translation means "sea rocks," and that's precisely what you'll see from the windows that overlook the water. It's set on the ground floor of one of the town's most centrally located hotels, and the modern decor includes paintings throughout the sunny dining rooms. Outdoor tables are shielded from the pedestrian traffic by rows of shrubbery. Your meal might begin with *antipasti di mare, tagliolini al pesto, zuppa di pesce* (fish soup), *risotto di mare* (rice with seafood), or spaghetti with lobster sauce. Fresh fish, including turbot, scampi, gamberini, and sea bass, is priced by the gram. This restaurant, although not particularly distinguished, is still one of the best in town.

Trattoria Cesarina. Via Mameli 2C. ☎ **0185/286-059.** Reservations recommended, especially in midsummer. Main courses 15,000L–35,000L ($9–$21). AE, DC, MC, V. Wed–Mon 12:30–2:30pm and 7:30–10pm. Closed Dec. SEAFOOD.

This is the best of the trattorie in town. It lies beneath the arcade of a short but monumental street that runs into Piazza Fratelli Bandiere. In an atmosphere of bentwood chairs and discreet lighting, you can enjoy a variety of Ligurian dishes. Specialties include meat, vegetables, and seafood antipasti, along with such classic Italian dishes as taglierini with seafood and pappardelle in a fragrant sausage sauce, plus seasonal fish such as red snapper or dorado, best when grilled, that has been caught off the nearby coast.

SANTA MARGHERITA LIGURE AFTER DARK

Nightlife here seems geared to sipping wine or parti-colored cocktails on terraces with sea views, flirting with sunburned strangers, and flip-flopping through the town's sand-strewn beachfront promenades looking for dialogues or whatever. But if a day in the sun has activated your dancing shoes, head for either of the town's most appealing discos, **Covo di Nortest,** Via Rossetti 1 (☎ **0195/286-558**), or **Disco Carillon,** Localitá Paragi (☎ **0185/286-721**). Both cater to dance and music lovers aged 20 to 40, and you might get the sense that most clients are temporary visitors, residing in other parts of Europe and in town on holiday, and looking for a laugh and perhaps a romp.

Looking for something completely pretentious where you can show your skill as a pool jockey? Head for the **Old Inn Bar,** Piazza Mazzini 40 (☎ **0185/286-041**), where you can play pool for 8,000L ($4.80) per person per hour, drink bottled beers, and generally hang out with a crowd of locals, many of them under 20.

5 Portofino

22 miles SE of Genova, 106 miles S of Milan, 301 miles NW of Rome

Portofino is located about 4 miles south of Santa Margherita Ligure, along one of the most beautiful coastal roads in all of Italy. Favored by the yachting set, the resort is in an idyllic location on a harbor, where the water reflects all the pastel-washed little houses that run along it. In the 1930s it enjoyed a reputation with artists; later, a chic crowd moved in—and they're still here, occupying villas in the hills and refusing to surrender completely to the tourists who pour in by the busloads during the day.

The thing to do in Portofino: **take a walk,** preferably before sunset, that leads toward the tip of the peninsula. You'll pass the entrance to an old castle (where a German baron once lived), old private villas, towering trees, and much vegetation, before you reach the lighthouse. Allow an hour at least. When you return to the main piazza, proceed to one of the two little drinking bars on the left side of the harbor that rise and fall in popularity.

Before beginning that walk to the lighthouse, however, you can climb the steps from the port leading to the little parish **Church of St. George.** From here you'll get a panoramic view of the port and bay. In summer you can also take **boat rides** around the coast to such points as San Fruttuoso.

ESSENTIALS

GETTING THERE   By Train   Go first to Santa Margherita Ligure, then continue the rest of the way by bus.

By Bus   Tigullio buses leave Santa Margherita Ligure once every 30 minutes bound for Portofino. The one-way ticket is 1,700L ($1), and you can purchase tickets aboard the bus. Call ☎ **0185/288-8334** for information and schedules.

By Car   From Santa Margherita Ligure, continue south along the only road, which hugs the promontory, until you reach Portofino. In summer, traffic is likely to be heavy.

VISITOR INFORMATION   The **tourist information center** is at Via Roma 35 (☎ **0185/269-024**). It's open in summer, daily from 9:30am to 1pm and 1:30 to 6:30pm; off-season, daily from 9:30am to 12:30pm and 2:30 to 5:30pm.

WHERE TO STAY

Portofino is severely limited in hotels. In July and August you may be forced to book a room in nearby Santa Margherita Ligure or Rapallo.

Albergo Nazionale. 16034 Portofino. ☎ **0185/269-575.** Fax 0185/269-578. 12 rms, 4 suites. MINIBAR TV TEL. 280,000L–450,000L ($168–$270) double; 450,000L–480,000L ($270–$288) suite. MC, V. Closed Nov 20–Mar 20.

At stage center, right on the harbor, this old villa is modest, yet well laid out. It was restored and renovated in the mid-1980s. The suites are tastefully decorated, and the little lounge has a brick fireplace, coved ceiling, antique furnishings, and good reproductions. Most of the bedrooms, furnished in a mixture of styles (hand-painted Venetian in some of the rooms), have a view of the harbor.

✪ **Albergo Splendido.** Viale Baratta 13, 16034 Portofino. ☎ **800/237-1236** in the U.S., or 0185/269-551. Fax 0185/269-614. 42 rms, 25 suites. A/C MINIBAR TV TEL. 1,120,000L–1,380,000L ($672–$828) double; 1,790,000L–2,300,000L ($1,074–$1,380) suite for two. Rates include half board. AE, DC, MC, V. Closed Jan 3–Mar 20. Parking 35,000L ($21).

This Relais & Châteaux property is reached by a steep and winding road from the port. It provides a luxury base for those who moor their yacht in the harbor or have closed down their Palm Beach residences for the summer and can afford its outrageous prices. The four-story structure was built as a monastery during the Middle Ages, but pirates attacked so frequently that the monks abandoned it. Later it became a family summer home. The building opened as a hotel in 1901, set on 4 acres of semitropical gardens, and has attracted the likes of Winston Churchill. The rambling villa offers several levels of public rooms, terraces, and "oh, that view" bedrooms. Each room is furnished in a personal way—no two alike.

Dining/Entertainment: The dining room is divided by arches and furnished with Biedermeier chairs, flower bouquets, and a fine old tapestry. The restaurant terrace enjoys a fine view and serves traditional Ligurian and international specialties.

Services: Room service, baby-sitting, laundry, valet, massage.

Facilities: Hotel speedboat, heated saltwater swimming pool, beauty center, solarium, sauna.

Hotel Eden. Vico Dritto 18, 16034 Portofino. ☎ **0185/269-091.** Fax 0185/269-047. 9 rms. MINIBAR TV TEL. 250,000L–300,000L ($150–$180) double. Rates include breakfast. AE, DC, MC, V. Closed Dec 1–20. Public parking 30,000L ($18).

Located just 150 feet away from the harbor in the heart of the village, this little albergo is a budget holdout in an otherwise high-fashion resort. Set in a garden (hence its name), it's a good choice in this pricey town. Although the inn doesn't have a view of the harbor, there's a winning vista from the front veranda, where breakfast is served. The hotel is run by Mr. Ferruccio, and life here is decidedly casual.

WHERE TO DINE

Da U'Batti. Vico Nuovo 17. ☎ **0185/269-379.** Reservations recommended. Main courses 40,000L–45,000L ($24–$27); fixed-price menu 75,000L ($45). AE, DC, MC, V. Tues–Sun noon–3pm and 8–11pm. Closed Dec–Jan. SEAFOOD.

Informal, chic, and colorful, this place is on a narrow cobblestone-covered piazza a few steps above the port. Founded in 1963, it still perpetuates some of the *la dolce vita* aura of that heady time. A pair of barnacle-encrusted anchors hanging above the arched entrance hint at the seafaring specialties that have become this establishment's trademark. Owner and sommelier Giancarlo Foppiano serves delectable dishes, which might include a soup of "hen clams," rice with shrimp or crayfish, or fish *alla Battista*. It has a good selection of grappa, as well as French and Italian wines.

Delfino. Piazza Martiri delli Olivetta 40. ☎ **0185/269-081.** Reservations recommended Sat. Main courses 30,000L–45,000L ($18–$27); fixed-price fish menu 150,000L ($90). AE, DC, MC, V. Apr–Oct, daily noon–3pm and 7–11pm; Nov–Mar, Tues–Sun noon–3pm and 7–11pm. SEAFOOD.

Delfino is located right on the village square that fronts the harbor. This is Portofino's most fashionable dining spot (along with Il Pitosforo, below). It's both nautically rustic and informally chic. Less expensive than Il Pitosforo, it offers virtually the same type of food, such as *lasagne al pesto*. Again, the fish dishes are the best bets: *zuppa di pesce* (a soup made of freshly caught fish with a secret spice blend) and risotto with shrimp, sole, squid, and other sea creatures. If you can't stand fish, the chef also prides himself on his sage-seasoned *vitello all'uccelletto*, roast veal with a gamey taste. Try to get a table near the front so you can enjoy (or at least be amused by) the parade of visitors and villagers.

Il Pitosforo. Molo Umberto I 9. ☎ **0185/269-020.** Reservations required. Jackets required for men. Main courses 40,000L–60,000L ($24–$36). AE, DC, MC, V. Wed–Mon noon–2:30pm and 7:30–11pm. Closed from the end of Nov to Feb and for lunch Apr–Oct. LIGURIAN/ITALIAN.

You have to climb some steps to reach this place, which draws raves when the meal is served and, most likely, wails when the tab is presented. While not blessed with an especially distinguished decor, its position right on the harbor gives it all the native chic it needs, and has ever since Bogey and Bacall and Taylor and Burton came this way long ago. *Zuppa di pesce* is a delectable Ligurian fish soup, or you may prefer the bouillabaisse, which is always reliable here. The pastas are especially tasty, and include *lasagne al pesto*, wide noodles prepared in the typical Genovese sauce. Fish dishes feature mussels alla marinara and *paella valenciana* for two, saffron-flavored rice studded with seafood and chicken. Some meat and fish dishes are grilled over hot stones, others over charcoal.

Ristorante da Puny. Piazza Martiri delli Olivetta. ☎ **0185/269-037.** Reservations required. Main courses 28,000L–38,000L ($16.80–$22.80). No credit cards. Fri–Wed noon–3pm and 7–11pm. Closed Dec 15–Feb 20. SEAFOOD.

Da Puny is set up on the stone square that opens onto the harbor. Because of its location, it's practically in the living room of Portofino, within sight of the evening activities of the oh-so-chic and oh-so-tan yachting set. Green-painted tables are set under trees at night on a slate-covered outdoor terrace. The menu includes pappardelle Portofino, antipasto of the house, spaghetti with clams, baked fish with potatoes and olives, fried zucchini flowers, and an array of freshly caught fish.

PORTOFINO AFTER DARK

La Gritta American Bar. Calata Marconi 20. ☎ **0185/269-126.** Drinks 13,500L–19,000L ($8.10–$11.40). Fri–Wed 8:30pm–3am.

La Gritta vies for business with its rival a few storefronts away. Between the two of them, they attract the biggest names, from Onassis to Frank Sinatra to John Wayne. It's said that Rex Harrison, while drinking here with the duke of Windsor, excused himself to go and purchase a package of cigarettes. He never came back—on the way for the cigarettes, he ran into actress Kay Kendal and the two eloped. These celebrities have intermingled with dozens of tourists and a collection of U.S. Navy personnel in the small, well-appointed restaurant. As James Jones, author of *From Here to Eternity,* noted: "This is the nicest waterfront bar this side of Hong Kong." That's true, but it's always wise to check your bar tab carefully before you stagger out looking for a new adventure.

Scafandro American Bar. Calata Marconi 10. ☎ **0185/269-105.** Drinks 13,500L–19,000L ($8.10–$11.40). Wed–Mon 10:30am–3am.

This is one of the village's chic rendezvous points, a place that has attracted a slew of yachting guests. The three-quarter-round banquettes inside contribute to the general feeling of well-being. If some international celebrity doesn't happen to come in while you're here, you can always study one of the series of unusual nautical engravings adorning the walls.

6 Cinque Terre

Monterosso: 56 miles E of Genova, 6 miles W of La Spezia

Set among olive and chestnut groves on steep, rocky terrain overlooking the gulf of Genova, the communities of Corniglia, Manarola, Riomaggiore, and Vernazza offer a glimpse into another time. These rural villages, inaccessible by car, are an agricultural belt where garden and vineyard exist side-by-side. Together with their "city cousin" Monterosso, they are known as the Cinque Terre, or "five lands." The northernmost town of the five lands, Monterosso, is the tourist hub of the region, with traffic, crowds, and the only notable glimpse of contemporary urban life here.

The area is best known for its culinary delights, culled from forest, field, and sea. Here the land yields an incredible variety of edible mushrooms, and oregano, borage, rosemary, and sage grow abundantly in the wild. The pine nuts essential to pesto are easily collected from the forests, as are chestnuts for making flour, and olives for the oil at the base of all dishes. Garlic and leeks flavor sautéed dishes, whereas beets turn up unexpectedly in ravioli and other dishes. Fishing boats add their rich hauls of anchovies, mussels, squid, octopus, and shellfish, and to wash it all down, vineyards produce Sciacchetra, a DOC wine, rarer than many other Italian varieties because of the low 25% yield characteristic of the Vermentino, Bosco, and Albarola grapes from which it is derived.

Most visitors explore the villages by excursion boat. To avoid these crowds and really get to know the region, you may want to stroll along its renowned walking paths that meander scenically for miles across the hills and through the forests.

ESSENTIALS

GETTING THERE   By Train   Hourly trains run from Genova to La Spezia, a trip of 1½ hours, where you must backtrack by rail to any of the five towns you wish to visit. Once in the Cinque Terre, local trains, which run frequently between the five stops, offer daily unlimited travel at a cost of 4,500L ($2.70).

By Car   From Genova, take autostrada A12, and exit at Monterosso—the only town of the five you can actually approach by car. A gigantic parking lot accommodates visitors, who then travel between the towns by rail, boat, or foot.

By Boat   Navagazione Golfo dei Porto (☎ 0185/967-676) plies the waters between Monterosso and Manarola or Riomaggiore five times daily, whereas Motobarca Vernazza runs hourly to Vernazza.

VISITOR INFORMATION   The **APT** office for the five villages is located in Monterosso, Via Fegina 38 (☎ 0185/817-506), open April to October, Monday to Saturday from 10am to noon and 5 to 7:30pm, and Sunday from 10am to noon.

EXPLORING THE COAST

There are 14 walking trails laid out for exploring the wilds of the area, as well as functioning as a viable way of going from town to town. The APT office listed above offers a brochure, "Footpaths Along the Cinque Terre and the Eastern Riviera," which defines and maps out routes ranging as far north as Deiva Marina and as far south as Portovenere, but suggests several that stay within the boundaries of the Cinque Terre as well. Each hike takes from 1 to 5 hours. Some turn inland, emphasizing the hills and forests of the region. The longest and most scenic, highlighting both coast and forest, is the Sentieri Azzurri, or "azure path along the coast," which runs from Monterosso, starting near the town hall, to Riomaggiore, ending along the Via dell'Amore. In the process you pass through Vernazza, Corniglia, and Manarola.

Good walking shoes, long pants, and a rain jacket are suggested gear for even the least strenuous of the routes, along with a water bottle and snacks. Many routes are steep and some include hazards such as frequent landslides. A walking companion is recommended, and in case of accident the local emergency telephone number is ☎ 115.

WHERE TO STAY
IN MONTEROSSO

Baia. Via Fegina 72, 19016 Monterosso. ☎ **0187/817-512.** Fax 0187/818-322. 29 rms. TV TEL. 170,000L ($102) double. Rates include breakfast. MC, V. Closed Nov–Feb.

Opened in 1911, this hotel features a private beach and comfortable rooms where the whitewashed furniture lends an illusion of size and space. The on-premises restaurant serves regional seafood specialties and patio dining is available overlooking the beach. What it doesn't offer is air-conditioning, which management says is in the works, or shuttle service—but the train station is only 110 yards away.

Jolie. Via Gioberti 1, 19016 Monterosso. ☎ **0187/817-539.** Fax 0187/817-273. 31 rms. TV TEL. 180,000L–312,000L ($108–$187.20) double. Rates include breakfast. MC, V. Closed Jan 10–Feb 7.

A pleasant inn located in the middle of town, it's still only 160 yards to the beach. The hotel features well-furnished and soundproofed rooms, a solarium, a garden, and a restaurant serving local and national cuisine prepared by the owner himself. Don't expect a lot of excitement if you stay here, but you can be moved by scenes on local life: a rainbow of laundry flapping in the wind, grandmothers sitting in ancient door-ways watching life drift by, and kids playing soccer on the breakwater.

Palme. Via IV Novembre 18, 19016 Monterosso. ☎ **0187/829-013.** Fax 0187/829-081. 49 rms. A/C MINIBAR TEL. 190,000L–230,000L ($114–$138) double. Rates include breakfast. AE, DC, MC, V. Closed Nov–Mar.

Located one street away from the beach, this 30-year-old hotel was renovated 14 years ago. The decor leaves something to be desired: bright abstract fabrics looking gaudy in contrast to dark wood furniture, and the fluorescent lighting in the dining room is unflattering. Nevertheless, it is comfortable, with a staff providing customer service that avoids the glaring inconsistencies of the hotel's interior. Actually, the guest rooms are more inviting than the public areas, relying more on muted blues and whites to create a relaxed atmosphere. There's a game room, bar, and shaded garden. Although the hotel doesn't have its own restaurant, the staff recommends one adjacent to it.

Pasquale. Via Fegina 4, 19016 Monterosso. % 0187/817-477. Fax 0187/817-056. 15 rms. A/C TV TEL. 170,000L ($102) double. Rates include breakfast. MC, V.

This small hotel sits right by the beach, offering both intimacy and privacy since its small number of guest rooms are spread out across four floors. It was built and opened as a hotel 35 years ago and was updated in 1994. It's modern and has been decorated in the manner of a private Genovan home. The bar-restaurant is reminiscent of an Italian coffee shop, with gleaming marble floors, shiny glass cases, and dark wood wainscoting, window frames, and service counter accented with a brass rail and foot guard.

Porto Roca. Via Corone 1, 19016 Monterosso. ☎ **0187/817-502.** Fax 1087/817-692. 43 rms. A/C MINIBAR TV TEL. 250,000L–320,000L ($150–$192) double. Rates include breakfast. AE, MC, V. Closed Nov–Mar.

You give up direct beach access to stay here, but it's a small price to pay for accommodations as gracious as these. Set on a cliff offering panoramic views of the village and harbor below, every corner of this hotel is filled with eclectic antiques, knick-knacks, and art, mixing Oriental rugs with wooden furniture ranging from the simple to the ornate. The terrace, hemmed in by a curvaceous wrought-iron railing and lit by matching globe lamps, is alive with lush greenery and brightly flowered plants that complement the blue of the bay it overlooks. The restaurant serves local seafood and its large dining room offers privacy through the placement of columns and Liberty-style glass screens throughout the room. The bar also allows privacy, clustering furniture together to create cozy pockets in which to relax and converse. Its fanciful fireplace adds warmth on cool off-season days.

IN MANAROLA

Ca'd'Andrean. Via Lo Scalo 101, 19010 Manarola. ☎ **0187/920-040.** Fax 0187/920-652. 10 rms. TEL. 100,000L ($60) double. No credit cards. Closed Nov.

A small garden is the nicest feature of this barebones three-story hotel, which opened in a former private home in 1988. The building that contains it was owned a century ago by the grandparents of the present owners. Bedrooms, each with a simple, white-walled decor, are clean, uncomplicated, and straightforward. There is a bar, but no restaurant, on the premises.

Marina Piccola. Via Discovolo 38, 19010 Manarola. ☎ **0187/920-103.** Fax 0187/920-966. 10 rms. TEL. 110,000L ($66) double. AE, DC, MC, V. Closed Jan.

With 10 rooms spread across 5 floors, this former home is a hotel as vertical as the town that houses it. Opened in 1981, there's a rustic charm to the small bedrooms, which feature wrought-iron beds. There's no bar, but the on-premises restaurant, as simply decorated as the hotel, offers a great view of the harbor. The cuisine is typical of the region (see "Where to Dine," below).

IN VERNAZZA

Locanda Barbara. Piazza Marconi 21, 19018 Vernazza. ☎ and fax **0187/812-201.** 10 rms without bath. 70,000L ($42) double. MC, V. Closed Dec–Jan.

Offering small, simple rooms with no amenities or private bathrooms, this is the economical way to sample the simplicity of life in this undeveloped region. Your room will lie on the street level of the circa 1965 modern building that also, under separate management, contains the town's most appealing restaurant, the *Taverna del Capitano* (see "Where to Dine", below).

IN RIOMAGGIORE

Villa Argentina. Via de Gaspari 187, 19017 Riomaggiore. ☎ **0187/920-213.** 15 rms. TV. 95,000L ($57) double. AE, DC, MC, V. Closed Nov.

This 20-year-old hotel has a maritime theme throughout, and its greatest asset is its quiet country setting just outside of town. If you don't feel like walking, an efficient shuttle service will transport you into the village. There's no air-conditioning, but each room has a ceiling fan—somewhat more effective than it would be in the heart of the village. There is a small restaurant and a bar on the premises. Although it's a simple choice, its prices evoke Italy of the late 60s.

WHERE TO DINE
IN MONTEROSSO

Il Gigante. Via IV Novembre 9. ☎ **0187/817-401.** Reservations recommended on holidays. Main courses 16,000L–22,000L ($9.60–$13.20). AE, DC, MC, V. Daily noon–3pm and 7–10pm. Closed some Tues. LIGURIAN.

This traditional trattoria is one of the best places to introduce yourself to the flavorful cuisine of Liguria, and there is no better introduction than the *zuppa di pesce.* Actually the fish soup is enough for a main course, but locals are rarely satisfied with just soup. Another pleasing first course—and one most typical of the area—is *minestrone alla genovese,* a bean-and-vegetable soup flavored with the inevitable pesto. Waiters cite the daily specials, none more delectable than a risotto made with freshly plucked shellfish. To go truly Ligurian, you'll opt for the spaghetti with octopus sauce. The mixed grill is another savory offering. Although the restaurant in theory is open daily, watch for those erratic and unannounced closings on Tuesday.

IN MANAROLA

Aristide. Via Lo Scalo 138. ☎ **0187/920-000.** Reservations recommended. Main courses 18,000L–25,000L ($10.80–$15). Fixed-price menu Mon–Fri 30,000L–40,000L ($18–$24); Sat–Sun 50,000L–60,000L ($30–$36). No credit cards. Tues–Sun and holidays noon–2:30pm and 7–10pm. LIGURIAN.

This old, comfortable trattoria showcases the simplicity of the region's cuisine, combining a few key ingredients in tasty combinations. The weekday fixed-price menu includes wine with the meal, and the weekend version also features antipasto and coffee. House specialties include *lasagne al pesto, penne all'aragosta,* and *zuppa di pesce,* one of the most savory kettles of fish in the "five lands." Traditional recipes have never been forgotten and are always part of the menu.

Marina Piccola. Via Discovolo 38. % 0187/920-103. Reservations recommended. Main courses 15,000L–25,000L ($9–$15). AE, DC, MC, V. Fri–Wed noon–3pm and 7–9:30pm. LIGURIAN.

Located next door to the hotel of the same name, this restaurant is as old and simple as the inn (see above). For a Ligurian palate tantalizer, try cozze ripiene, mussels cooked in white wine and served with a butter sauce. Squid in its own ink tastes best when combined with homemade spaghetti. Fresh sardines are a local crowd pleaser, and another homemade pasta, trenette, comes flavored with some of the best-tasting pesto along the coast. Grilled fish is the invariable favorite for a main dish. It's always fresh and perfectly prepared, though seasoned simply, as is the Ligurian style.

In Vernazza

Gianni Franzi. Via Visconti 2. ☎ **0187/812-228.** Reservations recommended. Main courses 15,000L–18,000L ($9–$10.80). AE, DC, MC, V. Closed Wed from Jan 10–Mar 8. LIGURIAN.

With a view of the sea and a savory and perfectly flavored fish platter before you, it's easy to understand why this is a local favorite. Of course, day-trippers and hill hik-ers descend on the place too, enjoying "a good tuck in," as an English visitor recently confided to us. That tuck in, for many diners, invariably begins with penne con scampi, a quill-shaped pasta with shrimp recently plucked from the sea. The antipasto mare or hors d'oeuvres from the sea is one of the finest along the coast. The mixed grill of fresh fish is a sure-fire palate pleaser, as are the white sardines of the area that might appear in a salad or else baked with savory seasonings.

Il Gambero Rosso. Piazza Marconi 7. ☎ **0187/812-265.** Reservations recommended Sat–Sun. Main courses 20,000L–30,000L ($12–$18); fixed-price menu 55,000L ($33). AE, DC, MC, V. Tues–Sun 12:30–3pm and 7:30–10:30pm. Closed Feb. LIGURIAN.

Situated high up on a rocky cliff overlooking the sea, ask for a table on the terrace to make the most of this restaurant's setting. Here, too, the food is typically Ligurian, and house specialties include ravioli stuffed with fresh fish. The wonderful porcini mushrooms that are harvested in the area figure into some dishes. Many of the reci-pes served here were passed by word of mouth from mother to daughter. A lot of the flavoring is based on the use of herbs and other ingredients that grow in the hills. The pesto sauce is made with the best olive oil and mixed with basil, grated cheese, pine nuts, and fresh marjoram.

Taverna del Capitano. Piazza Marconi 21, in the Locanda Barbara. ☎ **0187/ 812-224.** Reservations recommended. Main courses 15,000L–25,000L ($9–$15). MC, V. Thurs–Tues 12:30–3pm and 7:30–9:30pm. Closed Jan. LIGURIAN.

This tavern is set on the top floor of a two-story hotel whose street level contains an also-recommended hotel (Locanda Barbara) under separate management. It is one of the best eateries in all of Cinque Terre. It seats 60 in three informal and nautically rustic dining rooms. Among it's most popular dishes are grilled prawns, grilled filet of beef, potato-based gnocchi, pasta with pesto sauce, and linguine flavored with crabmeat.

Naples, Pompeii & Ischia

Campania is in many ways the most eerie, memorable, and beautiful region of Italy, sociologically different from anything else in Europe—haunting, confusing, and satisfying, all at the same time. Campania forms a fertile crescent around the bays of Naples and Sorrento, and stretches inland into a landscape of limestone rocks dotted with patches of fertile soil. It was off the shores of Campania that Ulysses ordered his crew to tie him, ears unstopped, to the mast of his ship, so that he alone would hear the songs of the sirens without throwing himself overboard to sample their pleasures. Today the siren song of Campania still lures, with a chemistry that some visitors insist is an aphrodisiac.

The geological oddities of Campania include a smoldering and dangerous volcano (already famous for having destroyed Pompeii and Herculaneum), sulfurous springs that belch steam and smelly gases, and lakes that ancient myths refer to as the gateway to Hades. Its seaside highway is the most beautiful, and probably the most treacherous, in the world, combining danger at every hairpin turn with some of Italy's most reckless drivers (this "Amalfi Drive" is covered in chapter 17). Despite such dark images, Campania is one of the most captivating regions of Italy, sought out by native Italians and visitors alike for its combination of earth, sea, and sky. Coupled with this are what might well be the densest collection of ancient ruins in Europe, each celebrated by classical scholars as among the very best of its kind.

The ancient Romans dubbed the land Campania Felix, which may reflect their satisfaction with the district that inspired the construction of hundreds of private villas. In some ways the beauty of Campania contributed to the decay of the Roman Empire, as Caesars, their senators, and their courtiers spent more and more time pursuing its pleasures and abandoning the cares of Rome's administrative problems.

Even today seafront land in Campania is so desirable that hoteliers have poured their life savings into foundations of buildings that are sometimes bizarrely cantilevered above rock-studded cliffs. Despite their numbers, these hotels tend to be profitably overbooked in summer.

Although residents of Campania sometimes stridently extol the virtues of its cuisine, it's not the most renowned in Italy. Its produce, however, is superb, its wine heady, and its pizzas highly memorable.

Today Campania typifies the conditions that northern Italians label "the problem of the south." Although the inequities are the most pronounced in Naples, the entire region, outside the resorts along the coast, has a lower standard of living and education, and higher crime rates, plus less developed standards of health care, than the more affluent north.

Television has contributed to leveling regional differences. Nevertheless, Campania is still rife with superstitious myths, vendettas, and restrictive problems. It's also home to a people who can sometimes overwhelm you with kindnesses and spontaneity. Despite, or perhaps because of, these tendencies, it's worth investing your vacation time in Campania. In some ways, it captures the soul and soulfulness of southern Italy.

1 Naples

136 miles SE of Rome, 162 miles W of Bari

In spite of some honest officials, its city government remains corrupt; many of its businesses are dominated by the Camorra, the Neapolitan Mafia; it indisputedly has the worst air pollution and traffic in Italy; and its hordes of street children make it the juvenile delinquency capital of Europe. Naples is Italy's most controversial city: You'll either love it or hate it. Is it *paradiso* or the *inferno?* It's louder, more intense, more unnerving, but perhaps ultimately more satisfying for the traveler than almost anywhere else in Italy.

Naples has changed a lot since the cholera outbreak of 1973, when the world discovered that the city had no sewers and was basking on the edge of a picturesque but poisoned bay. New civic centers have been planned, and some of the city's baroque palaces have been restored. But to the foreigner unfamiliar with the complexities of the multifarious "Italys" and their regional types, the Neapolitan is still the quintessence of the country—easy to caricature ("O Sole Mio," "Mamma Mia," bel canto). If Sophia Loren (a native who moved elsewhere) evokes the Italian woman for you, you'll find more of her look-alikes here than in any other city. In addition to Ms. Loren, Naples also gave the world Enrico Caruso.

Perhaps more visible are the city's children. In one of the most memorable novels to come out of World War II, *The Gallery* by John Horne Burns, there is this passage: "But I remember best of all the children of Naples, the *scugnizzi.* Naples is the greatest baby plant in the world. Once they come off the assembly line, they lose no time in getting onto the streets. They learn to walk and talk in the gutters. Many of them seem to live there." If Burns were writing this novel today, he might also have warned you that these scugnizzi specialize in *lo scippo* (local dialect for petty thievery). Of course, if it's your purse or wallet that has been stolen, it may be no petty crime to you. Guard your person and your valuables carefully as you explore the tangled, often dangerous streets of Naples.

In spite of all its many problems, Naples remains one of our most favorite Italian cities. Life is lived here with such vivacity that you can fall under its spell. There have even been some improvements in recent years, such as the closing off of certain streets to traffic, allowing visitors the chance to explore more without fear of being run down by a car. "The comedy is broad," Herbert Kubly noted in his *American in Italy.* "The tragedy violent. The curtain never rings down." We agree. Naples remains a raw theater of life, with the Neapolitans themselves being the number one attraction.

A LOOK AT THE PAST   Neapolitan legends claim that the city was founded after the body of Parthenope (a nymph who committed suicide after being spurned by

Ulysses) washed ashore in the nearby bay. Archeological evidence suggests that it was founded by Greek colonists late in the 5th century B.C.

During the height of the Roman Empire, Naples was only one of dozens of important cities that surrounded the famous bay. Roman emperors, especially Nero, perhaps in order to show that they appreciated the finer (Greek-inspired) things in life, treated Naples as a resort, away from the pressure of Imperial Rome. They also used it as a departure point for their nearby villas on Capri. It was visited by poets (Virgil wrote the *Georgics* here) and sybarites alike. Under the Byzantine administration of the remnants of the Roman Empire, Naples actually grew and prospered—unlike many of its Italian neighbors. This was in part because of its excellent harbor and in part because many of its competitors (Pompeii and Herculaneum, for example) were destroyed by economic stagnation or by cascades of molten lava and ash.

Over the centuries Naples has known many conquerors, and lived in constant fear of the potential for a volcanic eruption that might annihilate the city. These facts might help to explain its "live for today" philosophy. Among its conquerors and leaders have been everyone from the Normans in 1139, to Charles of Anjou in 1266, to the Aragonese of Spain under Alfonso V in 1435, to Archduke Charles of Austria in 1707, to the French Bourbons in 1734, to the Pan-Italian nationalist armies of Garibaldi in 1861, to the Americans, after the fiasco of Mussolini's brand of Fascism during World War II.

During the 18th and 19th centuries, French, English, and German tourists visited the Bay of Naples as an essential part (perhaps the highlight) of their grand European tour. They flooded the northern European consciousness with legends and images of Naples as the most beautiful and carefree city in the world. "See Naples and die," the popular wisdom claimed. Some historians write that the unabashed sexual permissiveness of 18th- and 19th-century Naples was more of a lure to northern Europeans than the region's archeology.

AND ON TO THE PRESENT   Today the only "dying" you're likely to experience is being run over by a car. Each of the city's 2.2 million inhabitants seems to have a beat-up Fiat, battalions of which speed erratically and incessantly over hopelessly narrow roads laid out more than 2,000 years ago. To add to the confusion, hordes of Neapolitan children will blithely throw lit firecrackers into moving traffic, stop traffic to beg or smear your windshield with a soiled towel, or (sometimes more or less endearingly) try to pick your pocket.

Surely, the Neapolitans are the most spontaneous people on earth, wearing their emotions on the surface of their skin. No Neapolitan housewife gets overheated running up and down steps to convey a message to someone on the street—she handles the situation by screaming out the window.

The Neapolitan dialect is one of the most distinctive and difficult in all of Italy, with an almost alarming number and diversity of words (a source of pride) for describing intimate body parts and functions. Naples even bears the dubious honor of having introduced syphilis to the world in 1495, the outbreak of which was immediately blamed on a group of French soldiers quartered there at the time.

Naples is a city to be savored in bits and pieces. It comes at you like a runaway car, with tour-ticket sellers, car thieves, hotel hawkers, and pimps and hustlers, and a series of human encounters that seesaw between extraordinary warmth and kindness and a kind of surrealistic nightmare.

With its almost total absence of parks, its lack of space (it has the highest population density of any city in Europe), and the constant and unrelieved perception that it will disintegrate into total anarchy at any moment, it's not a destination for queasy palates and weak hearts. Add to this the 35% unemployment rate, the unending prevalence of both major and minor larceny, the highest infant mortality rate in Italy, the heat, and the pollution, and you have a destination many visitors rush through quickly on their way to somewhere else.

Still, the tattered splendor of baroque palaces (whose charm is enhanced by shrubs and bushes growing from cracks in their cornices), the sense of history, and the un-alloyed spectacle of humanity struggling, with humor and perseverance, to survive, make Naples one of the most memorable places you'll visit in Italy. Only one thing, *don't show up on Monday*—most attractions will be closed.

Naples is a fantastic adventure. It's also a bubbling, infectious stew. The best ap-proach, from its bay, is idyllic—a port set against the backdrop of a crystal-blue sky and volcanic mountains. The rich attractions inside the city and in the environs (Pompeii, Ischia, Capri, Ischia, Vesuvius, the Phlaegrean Fields, Herculaneum) make Naples one of the five top tourist meccas of Italy. The inexperienced may have dif-ficulty coping with it. The seasoned explorer will find it worthy ground, and might even try venturing down side streets, some of which teem with prostitutes and a major source of their upkeep: the ubiquitous sailor.

ESSENTIALS

GETTING THERE   By Plane   Domestic flights from Rome and other major Ital-ian cities put you into **Aeroporto Capodichino,** Via Umberto Maddalena (☎ 081/789-6259), 4 miles north of the city. A city ATAN bus (no. 14) makes the 15-minute run between the airport and Naples's Piazza Garibaldi in front of the main rail ter-minus. The bus fare is 1,200L (70¢); a taxi will run about 40,000L to 50,000L ($24 to $30). Domestic flights are available on Alitalia, Alisarda, and Ati. Flying time from Milan is 1 hour 20 minutes; from Palermo, 1 hour 15 minutes; from Rome, 50 min-utes; and from Venice, 1 hour 15 minutes.

By Train   Frequent trains connect Naples with the rest of Italy. One or two trains per hour arrive from Rome, taking 2¹/₂ hours and costing 17,200L ($10.30) for a one-way passage. It's also possible to reach Naples from Milan in about 7 hours, cost-ing 83,700L ($50.20) for a one-way ticket.

The city has two main centrally located rail terminals: **Stazione Centrale,** at Piazza Garibaldi, and **Stazione Mergellina,** at Piazza Amadeo. For general rail information call ☎ 01478/88-088.

Alitalia, in collaboration with FS, the Italian State Railways, links Naples with Rome's Leonardo da Vinci International Airport without intermediate stops. Twice a day, 7 days a week, the "Alitalia Airport Train by FS" departs from Stazione Margellina, heading north to Rome and the airport. To travel on the airport train, you must have an Alitalia airline ticket.

By Car   In the old days the custom was to sail into the Bay of Naples, but today's traveler is more likely to drive here, heading down the autostrada from Rome. The Rome–Naples autostrada (A2) passes Caserta 18 miles north of Naples and the Naples–Reggio di Calabria autostrada (A3) runs by Salerno, 33 miles north of Naples.

By Ferry   From Sicily, you can go on a ferry to Naples from Palermo on **Tirrenia Lines,** Molo Angionio, Stazione Marritima (☎ 081/720-1111), in the port area of Palermo. A one-way ticket costs 60,000L ($36) armchair and 90,000L ($54) first-class cabin per person for the 10¹/₂-hour boat trip to Naples.

ORIENTATION

VISITOR INFORMATION   The **Ente Provinciale per il Turismo,** at the Stazione Centrale (☎ 081/268-779), is open daily from 8:30am to 8:30pm. There's another office at Piazza del Gesù Nuovo 7 (☎ **081/552-3328**). They're open Monday to Saturday from 9am to 2:30pm and 3:30 to 7:30pm and Sunday from 9am to 2pm.

CITY LAYOUT   If you arrive by train at the Stazione Centrale, in front of Piazza Garibaldi, you'll want to escape from that horror by taking one of the major arteries of Naples, **Corso Umberto,** in the direction of the Santa Lucia district. Along the water, many boats, such as those heading for Capri and Ischia, leave from **Porto Beverello.**

Many visitors to Naples confine their visit to the bayside **Santa Lucia** area, and perhaps venture into another section to see an important museum. Most of the major hotels lie along **Via Partenope,** which looks out not only to the Gulf of Naples but to the Castel dell'Ovo. To the west is the **Mergellina** district, site of many restaurants and dozens of apartment houses. The far western section of the city is known as **Posillipo.**

One of the most important squares of Naples is **Piazza del Plebiscito,** north of Santa Lucia. The Palazzo Reale opens onto this square. On a satellite square, you can visit **Piazza Trento y Trieste,** with its Teatro San Carlo and entrance to the famed Galleria Umberto I. To the east is the third most important square, **Piazza Municipio.** From Piazza Trento y Trieste, you encounter the main shopping street of Naples, **Via Toledo/Via Roma,** on which you can walk as far as Piazza Dante. From that square, take Via Enrico Pessina to the most important museum in Naples, located on Piazza Museo Nazionale.

GETTING AROUND   By Metro   The Metropolitana line will deliver you from the Stazione Centrale in the west all the way to the Stazione Mergellina. Get off at Piazza Amadeo if you wish to take the funicular to Vómero. The Metro uses the same tickets as buses and trams.

By Bus or Tram   It's dangerous to ride buses at rush hours. Never have we seen such pushing, shoving, and jockeying for position. On one recent trip we saw a middle-aged woman fall from a too-crowded bus, injuring her leg. We were later told that this was a routine occurrence. If you're a linebacker, take your chances. Many people prefer to leave the buses to the battle-hardened Neapolitans and take the subway or tram no. 1 or 4, which run from the Stazione Centrale to the Mergellina station. (It will also let you off at the quayside points where the boats depart for Ischia and Capri.) For a **ticket** valid for 90 minutes with unlimited transfers during that time slot, the cost is 1,200L (70¢). However, for a full day of unlimited travel, you can purchase a ticket for 4,000L ($2.40).

By Taxi   If you survive the reckless driving (someone once wrote that all Neapolitans drive like the anarchists they are), you'll only have to do battle over the bill. You will inevitably be overcharged. Many cab drivers claim that the meter is broken, and proceed to assess the cost of the ride, always to your disadvantage. Some legitimate surcharges are imposed, including night drives and extra luggage. However, many taxi drivers deliberately take you "the long way there" to run up costs. In repeated visits to Naples, we've never yet been quoted an honest fare. We no longer bother with the meter; instead, we estimate what the fare would be worth, negotiate with the driver, and take off into the night. If you want to take a chance, you can call a radio taxi at ☎ **081/556-4444,** 081/556-0202, or 081/570-7070.

By Car   Getting around Naples is a nightmare! Motorists should pay particular attention, as Neapolitans are fond of driving the wrong way on one-way streets and speeding hysterically along lanes reserved for public transportation, sometimes cutting into your lane without warning. Red lights, if they're turned on at all, seem to hold no terror for a Neapolitan driver. You may want simply to park your car and walk, but there are two dangers in that. One is that your car can be stolen, as ours once was, even though apparently "guarded" by an attendant in front of a deluxe hotel. The other danger is that you're likely to get mugged (nearly a third of the city is unemployed, and people have to live somehow).

By Funicular　Funiculars take passengers up and down the steep hills of Naples. The **Funicolare Centrale** (☎ 081/714-5583), for example, connects the lower part of the city to Vómero. Departures are from Piazzetta Duca d'Aosta, just off Via Roma. The cable cars run daily from 7am to 10pm. Watch that you don't get stranded by missing the last car back. The same tickets valid for buses and the Metro are good for funicular travel.

FAST FACTS: NAPLES

Consulates　You'll find the consulate of the **United States** on Piazza della Repubblica (☎ 081/583-8111), where the staff has long since grown weary of hearing about another stolen passport. Its consular services are open Monday to Friday from 8am to noon. The consulate of the **United Kingdom** is at Via Francesco Crispi 122 (☎ 081/663-511), open Monday to Friday from 9am to 12:30pm and 2 to 4:30pm. Citizens of Canada, Australia, and New Zealand will need to go to the embassies or consulates in Rome (see "Fast Facts: Rome," in chapter 4).

Drugstores　Try Farmacia Helvethia, Piazza Garibaldi 11, near Stazione Centrale (☎ 081/554-8894).

Emergencies　If you have an emergency, dial ☎ **113.** To reach the police or carabinieri, call ☎ **112.** For an ambulance, call ☎ **113** or **752-0696.**

Medical Care　Try the Guarda Medica Permanente, located in each area of town, or call ☎ **113** or ask for directions to the nearest Guarda Medica Permanente at your hotel.

Post Office　The main post office is on Piazza G. Matteotti (☎ 081/551-1456). Look for the POSTA TELEGRAFO sign. It's open Monday to Friday from 8:15am to 7:30pm and Saturday from 8:15am to noon.

Telephone　If you need to make a long-distance call, you can do so at the Stazione Centrale, where an office is open 24 hours; if you make calls from your hotel, you'll likely be hit with an excessive surcharge.

SEEING THE SIGHTS

Before striking out for Pompeii (see section 3 in this chapter) or Capri (see chapter 17), you should try to see some of the sights inside Naples. If you're hard-pressed for time, then settle for the first three museums of renown.

THE TOP MUSEUMS

Reconfirm any museum hours before going there. A book issued annually can't keep up with the changes—they've been known to change from month to month, depending on how little money is in the city treasury. Even the posted opening hours seem more ornamental than reliable.

✪ **Museo Archeologico Nazionale.** Piazza Museo 18–19. ☎ **081/440-166.** Admission 12,000L ($7.20) adults, free for children 18 and under and seniors 60 and over. Wed–Mon 9am–2pm. Metro: Piazza Cavour.

With its Roman and Greek sculpture, this museum contains one of the most valuable archeological collections in Europe—the select Farnese acquisitions are notable in particular, as are the mosaics and sculpture excavated at Pompeii and

Naples

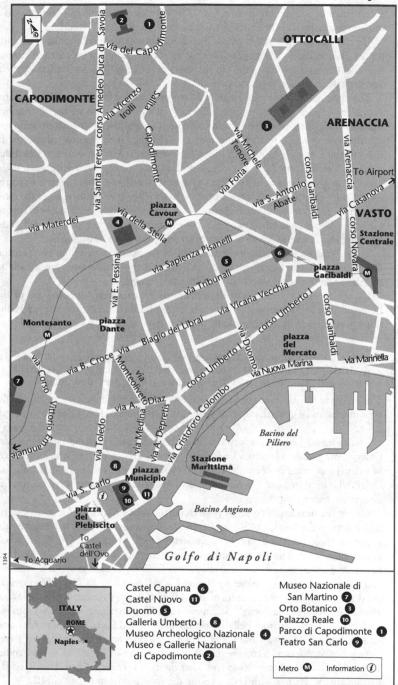

Castel Capuana **6**
Castel Nuovo **11**
Duomo **5**
Galleria Umberto I **8**
Museo Archeologico Nazionale **4**
Museo e Gallerie Nazionali
di Capodimonte **2**

Museo Nazionale di
San Martino **7**
Orto Botanico **3**
Palazzo Reale **10**
Parco di Capodimonte **1**
Teatro San Carlo **9**

ITALY

ROME

Naples

Metro **M**   Information **i**

Herculaneum. The building dates from the 16th century, and was turned into a museum some two centuries later by Charles and Ferdinand IV Bourbon.

On the ground floor is one of the treasures of the Farnese collections: The nude statues of Armodio and Aristogitone are the most outstanding in the room. A famous bas-relief (from an original of the 5th century B.C.) in a nearby salon depicts Orpheus and his wife, Eurydice, with Mercury.

The nude statue of the spear-bearing *Doryphorus,* copied from a work by Polyclitus the Elder and excavated at Pompeii, enlivens another room. Also see the gigantic but weary *Hercules,* a statue of remarkable boldness; it's a copy of an original by Lysippus, the 4th-century B.C. Greek sculptor for Alexander the Great, and was discovered in the Baths of Caracalla in Rome. On a more delicate pedestal is the decapitated but exquisite *Venus* (Aphrodite). The *Psyche of Capua* shows why Aphrodite was jealous. The *Group of the Farnese Bull* presents a pageant of violence from the days of antiquity. A copy of either a 2nd- or 3rd-century B.C. Hellenistic statue—one of the most frequently reproduced of all sculptures—it, too, was discovered at the Baths of Caracalla. The marble group depicts a scene in the legend of Amphion and Zethus, who tied Dirce, wife of Lycus of Thebes, to the horns of a rampaging bull.

The galleries on the mezzanine are devoted to mosaics excavated from Pompeii and Herculaneum. These include scenes of cock fights, dragon-tailed satyrs, an aquarium, and the finest one of all, *Alexander Fighting the Persians.*

On the top floor are some of the celebrated bronzes that were dug out of the Pompeii and Herculaneum lava and volcanic mud. Of particular interest is a Hellenistic portrait of Berenice, a comically drunken satyr, a statue of a *Sleeping Satyr,* and *Mercury on a Rock.*

✪ **Museo e Gallerie Nazionali di Capodimonte.** Parco di Capodimonte (off Amedeo di Savoia), Via Milano 1. ☎ **081/744-1307.** Admission 8,000L ($4.80) adults, free for children 18 and under and seniors 60 and over. Tues–Sat 10am–7:30pm, Sun 10am–2pm.

The gallery and museum are in the 18th-century Palace of Capodimonte (built in the time of Charles III), which stands in a park. It houses one of Italy's finest picture galleries.

Seven Flemish tapestries, which were made according to the designs of Bernart van Orley, show grand-scale scenes from the Battle of Pavia (1525), in which the forces of Francis I of France—more than 25,000 strong—lost to those of Charles V. Van Orley, who lived in a pre-*Guernica* day, obviously didn't consider war a horror, but a romantic ballet.

One of the pinacoteca's greatest possessions is Simone Martini's *Coronation* scene, which depicts the brother of Robert of Anjou being crowned king of Naples by the bishop of Toulouse. You'll want to linger over the great Masaccio's *Crucifixion,* a bold expression of grief. The most important room is literally filled with the works of Renaissance masters, notably an *Adoration of the Child* by Luca Signorelli, a *Madonna and Child* by Perugino, a panel by Raphael, a *Madonna and Child with Angels* by Botticelli, and—the most beautiful of all—Fillipino Lippi's *Annunciation and Saints.*

Look for Andrea Mantegna's *St. Eufemia* and his portrait of Francesco Gonzaga, his brother-in-law Giovanni Bellini's *Transfiguration,* and Lotto's *Portrait of Bernardo de Rossi* and his *Madonna and Child with St. Peter.* In one room is Raphael's *Holy Family and St. John* and a copy of his celebrated portrait of Pope Leo X. Two choice sketches include Raphael's *Moses* and Michelangelo's *Three Soldiers.* Displayed farther on are the Titians, with Danae taking the spotlight from Pope Paul III.

Another room is devoted to Flemish art: Pieter Brueghel's *Blind Men* is an outstanding work, and his *Misanthope* is devilishly powerful. Other foreign works include

Impressions

The museum is full, as you know, of lovely Greek bronzes. The only bother is that they all walk about the town at night.

—Oscar Wilde, letter to Ernest Dowson, October 11, 1897

Joos van Cleve's *Adoration of the Magi.* You can climb the stairs for a panoramic view of Naples and the bay, a finer landscape than any you'll see inside.

The State Apartments downstairs deserve inspection. Room after room is devoted to gilded mermaids, Venetian sedan chairs, ivory carvings, a porcelain chinoiserie salon (the best of all), tapestries, the Farnese armory, and a large glass and china collection.

Museo Nazionale di San Martino. Largo San Martino 5 (in the Vómero district). ☎ 081/578-1769. Admission 8,000L ($4.80) adults, free for children 17 and under and seniors 60 and over. Tues–Sun 9am–2pm. Funicular: Centrale from Via Toledo.

Magnificently situated on the grounds of the Castel Sant'Elmo, this museum was founded in the 14th century as a Carthusian monastery, but fell into decay until the 17th century, when it was reconstructed by architects in the Neapolitan baroque style. Now a museum for the city of Naples, it displays stately carriages, historic documents, ship replicas, china and porcelain, silver, Campagna paintings of the 19th century, military costumes and armor, and the lavishly adorned crib by Cuciniello. A balcony opens onto a panoramic view of Naples and the bay, as well as Vesuvius and Capri. Many people come to the museum just to drink in the view. The colonnaded cloisters have curious skull sculptures on the inner balustrade.

MORE ATTRACTIONS

Royal Palace (Palazzo Reale). Piazza del Plebiscito 1. ☎ 081/580-8216. Admission 8,000L ($4.80) adults, free for children 17 and under and seniors 60 and over. Tues–Sun 9am–2pm. Bus: 106 or 150.

This palace was designed by Domenico Fontana in the 17th century. The eight statues on the facade are of Neapolitan kings. Located in the heart of the city, the square is one of the most architecturally interesting in Naples, with a long colonnade and a church, San Francesco di Paolo, that evokes the style of the Pantheon in Rome. Inside the Palazzo Reale you can visit the royal apartments, lavishly and ornately adorned in the baroque style with colored marble floors, paintings, tapestries, frescoes, antiques, and porcelain. Charles de Bourbon, son of Philip IV of Spain, became king of Naples in 1734. A great patron of the arts, he installed a library in the Royal Palace, one of the greatest of the south, with more than 1,250,000 volumes.

New Castle (Castel Nuovo). Piazza del Municipo. ☎ 81/795-2003. Admission 10,000L ($6), free for children under 12 and seniors over 65. Mon–Sat 9am–7pm. Tram: 1 or 4.

The New Castle, which houses municipal offices, was built in the late 13th century on orders from Charles I, king of Naples, as a royal residence for the House of Anjou. It was badly ruined and virtually rebuilt in the mid-15th century by the House of Aragón. The castle is distinguished by a trio of three round imposing battle towers at its front. Between two of the towers, and guarding the entrance, is an arch of triumph designed by Francesco Laurana to commemorate the expulsion of the Angevins by the forces of Alphonso I in 1442. It has been described by art historians as a masterpiece of the Renaissance. The Palatine Chapel in the center dates from the 14th century, and the city commission of Naples meets in the Barons' Hall, designed by

Segreta of Catalonia. You'll find some frescoes and sculptures (of minor interest) from the 14th and 15th centuries inside the castle.

Santa Chiara. Via Santa Chiara 49. ☎ **081/552-6209.** Free admission. Mon–Sat 8:30am–12:30pm and 3:30–6pm, Sun 8:30am–12:30pm. Metro: Montesanto.

On a palazzo-flanked street, this church was built on orders from Robert the Wise, king of Naples, in the early 14th century. It became the church for the House of Anjou. Although World War II bombers heavily blasted it, it has been restored somewhat to its original look, a Gothic style as practiced by Provençal architects. The altarpiece by Simone Martini is displayed at the Capodimonte Galleries (see above), which leave the Angevin royal sarcophagi as the principal art treasures, especially the tomb of King Robert in back of the main altar. The Cloister of the Order of the Clares was restored by Vaccaro in the 18th century and is marked by ornate adornment, particularly in the tiles.

Il Duomo. Via del Duomo 147. ☎ **081/449-097.** Free admission. Mon–Sat 8am–12:30pm and 5–7:30pm, Sun 9am–noon. Metro: Piazza Cavour.

The Duomo of Naples may not be as impressive as some in other Italian cities, but it merits a visit nevertheless. Consecrated in 1315, it was Gothic in style, but the centuries have witnessed many changes. The facade, for example, is from the 1800s. A curiosity of the Duomo is that it has access to the Basilica of St. Restituta, which was the earliest Christian basilica erected in Naples and goes back to the 4th century. But an even greater treasure is the chapel dedicated to St. Januarius (San Gennaro), which you enter from the south aisle. The altar is said to contain the blood of St. Gennaro, patron saint of Naples. St. Gennaro may have been a Christian assimilation of Janus, the Roman god. The church contains two vials of the saint's blood, which is said to liquify and boil three times annually—the first Sunday in May, September 19, and December 16.

Castle of the Egg (Castel dell'Ovo). Puerto Santa Lucia (follow Via Console along the seafront from Piazza del Plebiscito to port Santa Lucia; Castel dell'Ovo is at the end of the promontory). ☎ **081/764-5688.** Free admission. Mon–Sat 9am–3pm. Tram: 1 or 4.

This 2,000-year-old fortress overlooks the Gulf of Naples. The site of the castle was important centuries before the birth of Christ, and was fortified by early settlers. In time a major stronghold to guard the bay was erected and duly celebrated by Virgil. It is said that Virgil built it on an enchanted egg of mystical powers submerged on the floor of the ocean. Legend has it that if the egg breaks, the city of Naples will collapse. Actually, most of it was constructed by Frederick II and later expanded by the Angevins. Although there's little to see here today, Egg Castle is one of the most historic spots in Naples, perhaps the site of the original Greek settlement of Parthenope. In time it became the villa of Lucullus, the Roman general and philosopher. By the 5th century, the villa had become the home in exile for the last of the western Roman emperors, Romulus Augustulus. The Goths found him too young and stupid to be much of a threat to their ambitions and pensioned him off here. In the castle's dungeons, columns of Lucullus's villa can still be viewed. In one epoch of its long history it served as a state prison. The view from here is panoramic. It's not open to the public except for special exhibits.

Acquario. Villa Comunale 1, Via Caracciolo. ☎ **081/583-3111.** Admission 6,000L ($3.60) adults, 3,000L ($1.80) children. Tues–Sat 9am–5pm, Sun 9am–2pm. Tram: 1 or 4.

The Aquarium is in a municipal park, Villa Comunale, between Via Caracciolo and the Riviera di Chiaia. Established by a German naturalist in the 1800s, its the oldest aquarium in Europe. It displays about 200 species of marine plants and fish, all found in the Bay of Naples (they must be a hardy lot).

Catacombe di San Gennaro (St. Januarius). In the Chiesa del Buon Consiglio, Via di Capodimonte 16. ☎ **081/741-1071.** Admission 5,000L ($3), free for children. Tours Mon–Fri between 9:30am and 12:30pm. Tram: 1 or 4.

A guide will show visitors through this two-story underground cemetery, which dates back to the 2nd century and has many interesting frescoes and mosaics. You enter the catacombs on Via di Capodimonte (head down an alley going alongside the Madre del Buon Consiglio Church).

ESPECIALLY FOR KIDS

Children can enjoy the **Aquarium** (see above) and the **Giardino Zoologico** (☎ 081/ **239-5943**), which is in the Mostra d'Oltremare at the entrance to Viale Kennedy. The zoo, established by a German naturalist in 1873, is open daily from 9am to 7pm (until 4pm from November to February). Admission is 5,000L ($3) for adults and 3,000L ($1.80) for children 4 to 9, free for children 3 and under. And to cap it off, take them to the **Edenlandia Amusement Park** (☎ 081/239-1182), also in the area of Mostra d'Oltremare (entrance on Viale Kennedy). It's open all year. In the Naples area, children often delight in wandering through the ruins of **Pompeii** as much as their parents do.

WHERE TO STAY

With some exceptions, the accommodations in Naples are a sad lot. Most of the large hotels are in the popular (also dangerous) district of Santa Lucia. Many of the so-called first-class establishments line Via Partenope along the water. In and around the central railway station are other clusters, many built in the late 1950s (and some that seemingly haven't been changed since).

Regardless of the price range in which you travel, there's a bed waiting for you in Naples. Regrettably, that bed often isn't clean or comfortable. We'll present a selection of what are generally conceded to be the "best" hotels in Naples, but know that with an exception or two, none of the other candidates leave us with much enthusiasm. Many of the innkeepers we've encountered seem an indifferent lot.

EXPENSIVE

Grande Albergo Vesuvio. Via Partenope 45, 80121 Napoli. ☎ **800/223-6800** in the U.S. or 081/764-0044. Fax 081/764-0044. 167 rms, 16 suites. A/C MINIBAR TV TEL. 450,000L ($270) double; from 700,000L ($420) suite. Rates include breakfast. AE, DC, MC, V. Parking 35,000L–40,000L ($21–$24).

Built in 1882, the Vesuvio was restored about 50 years later and features a marble-and stucco-sheathed facade evocative of art deco with curved balconies extending toward the Castel dell'Ovo. It was—and, with the decline of the Excelsior, again is—the first and foremost hotel along the fabled bay; many aristocratic English flocked here, to be followed later by Bogie and Errol Flynn. The 1930s-style rooms have lofty ceilings, rich cove moldings, parquet floors, renovated tiled bathrooms with lots of

---

Impressions

Whoever it was who said (I believe it was Nelson), "See Naples and die," perpetrated one of the greatest hoaxes in history. Or perhaps I am unlucky when I go there.
                                          —Geoffrey Harmsworth, *Abyssinian Adventure*, 1935

space, and large closets. Only the bedrooms at the Grand Hotel Parker's are as good. Traditionalists should request rooms on the second floor, decorated in a 1700s style. You'll also find a scattering of antiques throughout the echoing hallways. The hotel also has a first-class restaurant, Caruso; a roof garden; and a comfortable bar that evokes the most stylish decor of the 1950s.

Hotel Excelsior. Via Partenope 48, 80121 Napoli. ☎ **800/325-3535** in the U.S. or 081/764-0111. Fax 081/764-9743. 135 rms, 12 suites. A/C MINIBAR TV TEL. 440,000L–470,000L ($264–$282) double; 650,000L–1,050,000L ($390–$630) suite. Rates include breakfast. AE, DC, MC, V. Parking 35,000L ($21).

The Excelsior is situated in a most dramatic position right on the waterfront, with views of Santa Lucia and Vesuvius. Standards are slipping here and it has lost its number one position to the Vesuvio. Nevertheless, there are many elegant details, such as Venetian chandeliers, Doric columns, wall-sized murals, and bronze torchiers. Most of the accommodations are, in reality, bed/sitting rooms, furnished in a heavy Empire style. Others are much less grand.

Dining/Entertainment: Both Neapolitan and international cuisine are served in a windowless room. Breakfast can be ordered on a covered roof terrace.

Services: Room service, baby-sitting, laundry, valet.

MODERATE

Grand Hotel Parker's. Corso Vittorio Emanuele 135, 80121 Napoli. ☎ **081/761-2474.** Fax 081/663-527. 73 rms, 10 suites. A/C TV TEL. 310,000L–350,000L ($186–$210) double; from 750,000L ($450) suite. Rates include breakfast. AE, DC, MC, V. Parking 20,000L ($12). Metro: Piazza Amedeo.

This 1870 hotel sits up and away from the harbor commotion on one of the better hillside avenues of Naples, and many guests check in just to enjoy the view of Naples. It has been fully restored and has reclaimed its position as one of the finest hotels in Naples. It's topped only by the Vesuvio and is much better managed than the Excelsior. It was created when architects cared about the beauty of their work— neoclassic walls, fluted pilasters, and ornate ceilings. The bedrooms are traditionally furnished, some quite formal. Each room is in a different style, including Louis XVI, Directoire, Empire, and Charles X. Naturally, all guests try for a "room with a view." The roof garden restaurant offers a fine view along with an international Mediterranean cuisine. The hotel provides laundry, valet, baby-sitting, and room service, and operates a currency exchange and business center.

Hotel Majestic. Largo Vasto a Chiaia 68, 80121 Napoli. ☎ and fax **081/416-500.** 129 rms, 6 junior suites. MINIBAR TV TEL. 260,000L ($156) double; 350,000L–400,000L ($210–$240) suite. Rates include breakfast. AE, DC, MC, V. Parking 25,000L–35,000L ($15–$21). Metro: Piazza Amedeo.

This four-star hotel was built in 1959 on 10 floors. It's now one of the most up-to-date hostelries in a city too often filled with decaying mansions. A favorite with the conference crowd, it lies in the antique district of Naples—at your doorstep will be dozens of fashionable boutiques. Reservations are important, as this hotel is often fully booked. There's a cozy American bar and a restaurant, the Magic Grill, which serves Neapolitan dishes and international specialties Monday to Saturday. The garage is small, so reserve parking space with your room.

Hotel Miramare. Via Nazario Saura 24, 80132 Napoli. ☎ **081/764-7589.** Fax 081/764-0775. 31 rms. A/C MINIBAR TV TEL. Mon–Thurs, 290,000L–350,000L ($174–$210) double; Fri–Sun, 250,000L–290,000L ($150–$174) double. Rates include breakfast. AE, DC, MC, V. Parking: 25,000L–35,000L ($15–$21).

In a superb location, seemingly thrust out toward the harbor on a dockside boulevard, the Miramare is central and sunny. Originally the hotel was an aristocratic villa, but in 1944 it was transformed into a hotel after serving for a short period as the American consulate. Its lobby evokes a little Caribbean hotel with a semitropical look. The bedrooms have been renovated and now are pleasantly furnished and decently maintained. They have soundproof windows to protect against the traffic noise outside. An American bar and a roof garden are on the premises.

Hotel Paradiso. Via Catullo 11, 80122 Napoli. ☎ **800/528-1234** in the U.S. or 081/761-4161. Fax 081/761-3449. 71 rms, 2 suites. A/C MINIBAR TV TEL. 280,000L ($168) double; from 450,000L ($270) suite. Rates include breakfast. AE, DC, MC, V. Parking 24,000L ($14.40). Funicular: C21.

This hotel might be paradise, but only after you reach it. It's only 3½ miles from the central station, but one irate driver claimed that it also takes about 3½ hours to get here. Once you arrive, however, your nerves are soothed by the view, one of the most panoramic of any hotel in Italy. The Bay of Naples unfolds before you, and in the distance Mount Vesuvius looms menacingly. The hotel is one of the best in Naples, with well-furnished and comfortably equipped bedrooms. When you take your breakfast, you may want to linger here before facing the traffic of Naples again. Should you elect not to go out at night, you can patronize the fine hotel restaurant, which serves both Neapolitan and Italian specialties.

Hotel Royal. Via Partenope 38, 80121 Napoli. ☎ **081/764-4800.** Fax 081/764-5707. 273 rms, 14 suites. A/C MINIBAR TV TEL. 230,000L–340,000L ($138–$204) double; 560,000L ($336) suite. Rates include breakfast. AE, DC, MC, V. Parking 26,000L ($15.60). Tram: 1.

The 10-story Hotel Royal, built in 1955, is in a desirable location on this busy but dangerous street beside the bay in Santa Lucia. A very commercial aura prevails, and the hotel is often filled with groups. You enter a greenery-filled vestibule, where the stairs that lead to the modern lobby are flanked by a pair of stone lions. Each of the bedrooms has a balcony and aging modern furniture. Some, but not all, offer a water view. A seawater pool with an adjacent flower-dotted sun terrace is on the hotel's roof—swimming here is vastly preferred over the polluted bay. The hotel's restaurant has panoramic views but only mediocre food.

Hotel Santa Lucia. Via Partenope 46, 80121 Napoli. ☎ **081/764-0666.** Fax 081/764-8580. 95 rms, 12 suites. A/C MINIBAR TV TEL. 370,000L–400,000L ($222–$240) double; from 600,000L ($360) suite. Rates include breakfast. AE, DC, MC, V. Parking 25,000L–30,000L ($15–$18).

Santa Lucia's imposing neoclassical facade overlooks a sheltered marina on the bay. It competes effectively with the nearby Royal and is better maintained. From the windows of about half the bedrooms you can watch motorboats and yachts bobbing at anchor, fishermen repairing nets, and all the waterside life that Naples is famous for. But beware of muggers if you do go wandering around the area at night. The interior has undergone extensive renovations, and is decorated in a family-conscious Neapolitan style, with terrazzo floors and lots of upholstered chairs scattered throughout the lobby. The bedrooms are large and high-ceilinged, with French doors that open onto tiny verandas. The noisier rooms overlook the traffic of Via Santa Lucia. There's an American-inspired bar on the premises, plus the Restaurant Jardin, serving a superb Mediterranean cuisine.

INEXPENSIVE

Albergo San Germano. Via Beccadelli 41, 80125 Napoli. ☎ **800/528-1234** in the U.S. or 081/570-5422. Fax 081/570-1546. 104 rms. A/C MINIBAR TV TEL. 250,000L ($150) double. Rates include breakfast. AE, DC, MC, V.

Designed like an Italian version of a Chinese pagoda, this brick-and-concrete hotel is ideal for late-arriving motorists who are reluctant to negotiate the traffic of Naples. A terraced swimming pool and garden are welcome respites after a day in Naples. The hotel's bedrooms are clean but simple, and each has a tile bath. There's a lobby bar, along with a modern restaurant. From the autostrada, follow the signs to Tangenziale Napoli; exit 8 miles later at Agnano Terme. The hotel is on your right less than a mile from the toll booth. You can take bus no. C52 the 4 miles into the center of Naples.

Hotel Rex. Via Palepoli 12, 80132 Napoli. ☎ **081/764-9389.** Fax 081/764-9227. 40 rms. A/C TV TEL. 170,000L ($102) double. Rates include breakfast. AE, DC, MC, V. Parking 30,000L ($18). Bus: 104.

The most famous budget hotel in Santa Lucia, Hotel Rex has played host to lira-watchers around the world since its opening in 1938. Some like it and others don't, but proof of its popularity is that its bedrooms are often fully booked when other hotels have vacancies. The building itself is lavishly ornate architecturally, but the bedrooms are simple and some are very cramped. Breakfast is the only meal served.

Hotel Serius. Viale Augusto 74, 80125 Napoli. ☎ **081/239-4844.** Fax 081/239-9251. 69 rms. A/C MINIBAR TV TEL. 175,000L ($105) double. Rates include breakfast. AE, MC, V. Metro: Piazza Leopardi. Tram: 1 or 4.

Built in 1974 to provide well-organized comfort, this hotel is on a palm-lined street of a relatively calm neighborhood known as Fuorigrotto, a short bus ride north of the center. The paneled split-level lobby contains an intimate bar and several metal sculptures of horses and birds. The bedrooms are simply furnished with boldly patterned fabrics and painted furniture. In addition to the bar, there's a pleasant, contemporary dining room.

WHERE TO DINE

Naples is the home of pizza and spaghetti. If you're mad for either of those items, then you'll delight in sampling the authentic versions. However, if you like subtle cooking and have an aversion to olive oil or garlic, you won't fare as well.

One of the major problems is overcharging. It's not uncommon for four foreign visitors to have a meal in a Naples restaurant, particularly those once-famous ones in Santa Lucia, and be billed for five dinners. Service in many restaurants tends to be poor. As with the hotels, we'll attempt to pick out the best of the lot.

EXPENSIVE

✪ **Giuseppone a Mare.** Via Ferdinando Russo 13. ☎ **081/575-6002.** Reservations required. Main courses 15,000L–36,000L ($9–$21.60). AE, DC, MC, V. Tues–Sun 12:30–3:30pm and 8pm–midnight. Closed Aug 16–31. SEAFOOD.

Here you can dine in Neapolitan sunshine on an open-air terrace with a view of the bay. The only better restaurant in Naples is La Cantinella (see above). The restaurant at Capo Posillipo is known for serving the best and the freshest seafood in Campania. Diners make their selections from a trolley likely to include everything from crabs to eels. You might precede your fish dinner with some fritters (a batter whipped up with seaweed and fresh squash blossoms). Naturally, they serve linguine with clams—the chef here adds squid and mussels. Much of the day's catch is deep-fried a golden brown. The *pièce de résistance* is an octopus casserole. If the oven's going, you can also order a pizza. They stock some fine southern Italian wines, too, especially from Ischia and Vesuvio.

Il Gallo Nero. Via Torquato Tasso 466. ☎ **081/643-012.** Reservations recommended. Main courses 45,000L–55,000L ($27–$33); fixed-price menu 65,000L ($39) meat, 75,000L ($45) fish.

AE, DC, MC, V. Tues–Sat 7pm–midnight, Sun 12:30–3pm. Closed Aug. Metro: Mergellina. PASTA/NEAPOLITAN.

Dinner here is almost like a throwback to the mid-19th century. Gian Paolo Quagliata, with a capable staff, maintains this hillside villa with its period furniture and accessories. In summer the enthusiastic clientele is served on an elegant outdoor terrace. Many of the dishes are based on 100-year-old recipes from the classical Neapolitan repertoire, although a few are more recent inventions of the chef. You might enjoy the Neapolitan linguine with pesto, rigatoni with fresh vegetables, tagliatelle primavera, or macaroni with peas and artichokes. The fish dishes are usually well prepared, whether grilled, broiled, or sautéed. The meat dishes include slightly more exotic creations, such as prosciutto with orange slices, veal cutlets with artichokes, and a savory array of beef dishes.

✪ **La Cantinella.** Via Cuma 42. ☎ **081/764-8684.** Reservations required. Main courses 20,000L–30,000L ($12–$18). AE, DC, MC, V. Mon–Sat 12:30–3pm and 7:30pm–midnight. Closed 1 week in mid-Aug. Tram: 1 or 4. SEAFOOD.

You get the impression of 1920s Chicago as you approach this place, where speakeasy-style doors open after you ring. The restaurant is on a busy street that skirts the bay in Santa Lucia, with a terrace overlooking the sea. Inside, you'll find a well-stocked antipasto table and—get this—a phone on each table. We consistently find the highest-quality meals in Naples served here. The chefs have a deft way of handling the region's fresh produce and they turn out both Neapolitan classics and more imaginative dishes. The menu includes four different preparations of risotto (including one with champagne), many kinds of pasta (including penne with vodka, and linguine with scampi and seafood), and most of the classic beef and veal dishes of Italy. Best known for its fish, Cantinella serves grilled seafood at its finest.

MODERATE

Don Salvatore. Strada Mergellina 4A. ☎ **081/681-817.** Reservations recommended. Main courses 10,000L–28,000L ($6–$16.80); fixed-price menu 65,000L ($39). AE, DC, MC, V. Thurs–Tues 1–4pm and 8pm–1am. Metro: Mergellina. SEAFOOD.

Don Salvatore is the creative statement of a serious restaurateur, who directs his waterfront establishment with passion and dedication. Antonio Aversano takes his wine as seriously as his food. The latter is likely to include linguine with shrimp or with squid, an array of fish, and a marvelous assortment of fresh Neapolitan vegetables grown in the surrounding countryside. The fish, priced according to weight, comes right out of the Bay of Naples, which may, but possibly may not, be a plus. Rice comes flavored in a delicate fish broth, and you can get a reasonably priced bottle from the wine cellar, said to be the finest in Campania. The restaurant is on the seafront near the departure point of hydrofoils for Capri.

La Sacrestia. Via Orazio 116. ☎ **081/761-1051.** Reservations required. Main courses 12,000L–30,000L ($7.20–$18); fixed-price menu 80,000L ($48). AE, DC, MC, V. Daily 12:30–4:30pm and 7:40–11:30pm. Closed 2 weeks in mid-Aug. Funicular: From Mergellina. PASTA/SEAFOOD.

The trompe-l'oeil frescoes on the two-story interior and the name La Sacrestia vaguely suggest the ecclesiastical, but that's not the case here. One of the best restaurants in Naples, this bustling place is sometimes called "the greatest show in town." It's perched near the top of a seemingly endless labyrinth of streets winding up from the port (take a taxi). In summer an outdoor terrace with its flowering arbor provides a view over the lights of the harbor. Meals emphasize well-prepared dishes with strong doses of Neapolitan drama. You might, for example, try what's said to be the most luxurious macaroni dish in Italy ("Prince of Naples"), concocted with truffles and mild cheeses. The *fettuccine alla Gran Caruso* is made from fresh peas, mushrooms, prosciutto, and tongue. Less ornate selections include a full array of pastas and dishes composed of octopus, squid, and shellfish.

Rosolino. Via Nazario Sauro 5–7. ☎ **081/764-0547.** Reservations required. Main courses 12,000L–25,000L ($7.20–$15); fixed-price menu 50,000L ($30). AE, DC, MC, V. Mon–Sun 12:30–3:30pm; Mon–Sat 8pm–midnight. Tram: 1 or 4. INTERNATIONAL/ITALIAN/SEAFOOD.

This stylish place is not defined as a nightclub by its owners, but rather as a restaurant with dancing. Set on the waterfront, it's divided into two distinct areas; there's a piano bar near the entrance, where you might have a drink before passing into a much larger dining room. Here, in interiors ringed with stained glass set into striking patterns, you can dine within sight of a bandstand reminiscent of the Big Band Era. Live music is only on Saturday night. The food is traditional—not very imaginative—but well prepared with fresh vegetables. Dishes include rigatoni with zucchini and meat sauce, an impressive array of fresh shellfish, and such beef dishes as tournedos and veal scaloppine. Most fresh fish is priced according to weight. There are three different wine lists, including one for French wines and champagne.

INEXPENSIVE

Dante e Beatrice. Piazza Dante 44–45. ☎ **081/549-9438.** Reservations recommended. Main courses 10,000L–22,000L ($6–$13.20); fixed-price menu 28,000L ($16.80). No credit cards. Tues–Sun 12:30–3:30pm and 7:30–11pm. Closed Aug 15–30. Tram: 1 or 4. NEAPOLITAN.

Gregarious and unpretentious, and named after the players in one of the great romantic tragedies of the Middle Ages, Dante e Beatrice was established in 1956 and remains one of the best restaurants in its neighborhood. Specializing in all the staples of the Neapolitan cuisine, it serves simple, flavorful, and filling portions of lasagne, minestrone, spaghetti with clams, tagliatelle, pasta e fagiole, and grilled fish to the many workday clients who seek this place out.

Ristorante La Fazenda. Via Marechiaro 58A. ☎ **081/575-7420.** Reservations required. Main courses 15,000L–25,000L ($9–$15); fixed-price menu 40,000L ($24). AE, MC, V. Tues–Sat 1–4pm and 7:30pm–12:30am. Closed 1 week in mid-Aug. SEAFOOD.

It would be hard to find a more typically Neapolitan restaurant than this one, offering a panoramic view that on a clear day can include the island of Capri. The decor is rustic, loaded with agrarian touches and filled with an assortment of Neapolitan families, lovers, and visitors who have made it one of their preferred dining locales since it opened in 1973. In summer the overflow from the dining room spills onto the terrace. Menu specialties include linguine with scampi, an array of fresh grilled fish, sautéed clams, a mixed Italian grill, several savory stews, and many chicken dishes, along with lobster with fresh grilled tomatoes.

Umberto. Via Alabardieri 30. ☎ **081/418-555.** Reservations required. Main courses 9,000L–22,000L ($5.40–$13.20). AE, DC, MC, V. Thurs–Tues 12:30–3:30pm and 7:30–10:30pm. Closed Aug. NEAPOLITAN.

Located off Piazza dei Martiri, Umberto is one of the most atmospheric places to dine in all of Naples. The tasteful dining room has been directed for many a year by the same interconnected family. There's likely to be an evening dance band playing. The excellent Italian specialties served here include pizzas, gnocchi with potatoes, and grilled meats and fishes, as well as savory stews and a host of pasta dishes. The bel canto era lives on here.

Vini e Cucina. Corso Vittorio Emanuele 761. ☎ **081/660-302.** Reservations not accepted. Main courses 6,000L–12,000L ($3.60–$7.20). No credit cards. Mon–Sat noon–4:30pm and 7pm–midnight. Closed Aug 10–26. Metro: Mergellina. NEAPOLITAN.

The best ragù sauce in all of Naples is said to be made at this trattoria, which has only 10 tables and is known for its home cookery. You can get a really satisfying meal here, but we must warn you—it's almost impossible to get in. Dedicated diners might do as we do: Arrive early and wait for a table. The cooking is the best home-style version of Neapolitan cuisine we've been able to find in this tricky city. The spaghetti, along with that fabulous sauce, is served al dente. The restaurant is in front of the Mergellina station.

A HISTORIC PIZZERIA

Brandi. Via Miano 27–29. ☎ **081/741-0455.** Reservations required. Main courses 9,000L–20,000L ($5.40–$12). No credit cards. Tues–Sun noon–3pm and 6:30pm–midnight. NEAPOLITAN/PIZZA.

The most historic pizzeria in Italy, Brandi was established by Pietro Colicchio in the 19th century. His successor, Raffaele Esposito, who enjoyed the reputation that his hard work had earned, was requested one day to prepare a banquet for Margherita di Savoia, the queen of Italy. So successful was the reception of the pizza made with tomato, basil, olive oil, and mozzarella (the colors of the newly united Italy's flag) that the queen accepted the honor of having it named after her. Thus was pizza Margherita born from the kitchens of Naples's Restaurant Brandi. Today you can order the pizza that pleased a queen, as well as such other specialties as linguine with scampi, fettuccine "Regina d'Italia," and a full array of seafood dishes.

SHOPPING

Naples is hardly the shopper's paradise that Milan, Venice, Florence, and Rome are. Nevertheless, there are some good buys here for those willing to seek them out. The finest shopping area lies around **Piazza dei Martiri** and along such streets as Via dei Mille, Via Calabritto, and Via Chiaia. There's more commercial shopping between Piazza Trieste e Trento and Piazza Dante along Via Toledo/Via Roma.

Coral is much sought after by collectors. Much of the coral is now sent to Naples from Thailand, but it's still shaped into amazing jewelry at one of the workrooms at Torre del Greco, on the outskirts of Naples, off the Naples–Pompeii highway. Cameos are also made there.

ANTIQUES

Arte Antica. Via Domenico Morelli 6. ☎ **081/764-3704.**

One of the finest antique stores in Naples, Arte Antica has been at this address since 1900. The Falanga family, the owners, specialize in Italian antiques. Their specialty is the kind of florid and exquisitely detailed porcelain that has always been prized in Naples.

Salvatore Iermano. Via Domenico Morelli 30. ☎ **081/764-3913.**

The specialties here are antique versions of an art form practiced in southern Italy for hundreds of years, the *crèche.* Usually sold as a set of wood or terra-cotta figures that represent all the important characters at the birth of Jesus, they are sought after as antiques.

BOOKS

De Perro. Via dei Mille 17. ☎ **081/418-687.**

Most of the books here are in Italian, although there are some English titles. Many deal with the art and architecture of southern Italy, with photographs that are souvenirs in their own right. As one young Italian said, "Here we read all the time, because we're very intelligent and have little else to do."

DEPARTMENT STORES

Coin. Via Alessandro Scarlatti 100. ☎ 081/578-0111.

Coin sells everything from housewares to clothing.

La Rinascente. Via Toledo 343. ☎ 081/411-511.

This is the Neapolitan branch of Italy's most interesting department-store chain. Some of the best items to buy here include cameos, coral, jewelry, and leather goods. There's also a good assortment of shoes, handbags, and fashionable clothing.

FABRIC & LINENS

D'Andrea. Via Santa Brigida 34. ☎ 081/551-0621.

D'Andrea is a well-stocked outlet for tablecloths, napkins, and towels, a few of which are hand-embroidered, although most are machine-made. The establishment also sells undergarments for men, women, and children.

La Tienda. Via dei Mille 63. ☎ 081/415-249.

La Tienda is one of the best-known fabric shops in Naples. If you've ever been tempted to take up sewing, you'll find all the tools you'll need right here. Some of the fabrics are the same as those used by Italy's well-known designers.

FASHION

Eddy Monetti. Piazza Santa Catarina 7. ☎ 081/403-229.

This is the women's branch of a fine clothing empire still owned by Signor Eddy Monetti. The men's branch, at Via dei Mille 45 (☎ 081/407-064), sells elegant men's clothing, well tailored and well selected.

Salvatore Balbi. Via Chiaia 258. ☎ 081/418-551.

Here you can get underwear, nightshirts, socks, and shirts for men, in a shop filled with colorfully artistic underwear displays, and crowds of women making their selections. Many of their garments, especially the bathrobes, are very elegant.

Stefanel. Via Chiaia 195. ☎ 081/407-562.

Stefanel sells fun and informal sports clothes and casual clothes in bright colors for women and men.

FOOD

Codrington & Co. Via Chiaia 94. ☎ 081/418-257.

Codrington & Co. was founded about a century ago by a British family, and has a reputation in Naples as a purveyor of mostly English foodstuffs, sold and displayed from a briskly English-inspired shop near the Ponte di Chiaia. There are food and spices from throughout the world, as well as Devonshire marmalade, Stilton cheese, and old-fashioned chutney, but along with these edibles you'll find an array of small household objects, kitchen utensils, soap, and those gadgets that—once you discover them—you might not want to do without.

JEWELRY & GIFTS

Bottega della Carta. Via Cavallerizza a Chiaia 22–23. ☎ 081/421-903.

The specialty here is party supplies, carnival masks, and writing supplies, plus unusual gifts to take back home.

Theo Brinkmann. Piazza Municipio 21. ☎ 081/552-0555.

Theo Brinkmann is one of the leading jewelers of Naples, a strictly local, Naples-based establishment with a long history and no other branches. The store carries one of the best and most varied collections of cameos in the city.

LEATHER & SHOES

D'Aria. Via dei Mille 71. ☎ **081/415-309.**

This is a large and well-stocked shoe outlet that sells Italian and other shoes for both men and women.

Salvatore Spatarella. Via Calabritto 1. ☎ **081/764-3794.**

Here you can inspect a full array of well-made leather goods such as purses, luggage, shoes, handbags, and wallets. It's run by the Spatarella family, who also have a carefully selected array of women's clothing.

NAPLES AFTER DARK

A sunset **walk through Santa Lucia** and along the waterfront never seems to dim in pleasure, even if you've lived in Naples for 40 years. Visitors are also fond of riding around town in one of the **carrozzelle** (horse-drawn wagons).

Or you can stroll by the glass-enclosed **Galleria Umberto,** off Via Roma in the vicinity of the Teatro San Carlo. The 19th-century gallery, which evokes many a memory for aging former GIs, is still standing today, although a little the worse for wear. It's a kind of social center for Naples. John Horne Burns used it for the title of his novel *The Gallery,* in which he wrote: "In August 1944, everyone in Naples sooner or later found his way into this place and became like a picture on the wall of the museum."

On its nightclub and cabaret circuit, Naples offers more sucker joints than any other port along the Mediterranean. If you're starved for action, you'll find plenty of it—and you're likely to end up paying for it dearly.

Teatro San Carlo, Via San Carlo (across from the Galleria Umberto) (☎ **081/797-2331**), is one of the largest opera houses in Italy, with some of the best acoustics. Built in only 6 months' time for King Charles's birthday in November 1737, it was restored in a gilded neoclassical style. Grand-scale productions are presented here on the main stage. The box office is open December to June, Tuesday to Sunday from 10am to 1pm and 4:30 to 6:30pm. Tickets cost from 110,000L to 250,000L ($66 to $150).

Young Neapolitans hang out at discos such as **Accadémia,** Via Porta Posillippo 43 (☎ **081/769-2500**), which has the advantage of being sited on one of the most romantic-looking streets of Naples. A high-energy competitor is **Chez Moi,** Parco Margherita 17 (☎ **081/407-526**), where music is likely to derive from London, Los Angeles, or Milan and may be experimental. Two other establishments, unassociated but both named in homage to the song by everybody's favorite Italian American, Frank Sinatra, include **Discoteca My Way,** Via Cappella Vecchia 30 (☎ **081/764-4735**), and a beer pub **Bar My Way,** Piazza San Pasquale 30 (☎ **081/764-2615**). Looking for a dress-up and show-off kind of venue where clothes and high fashion are about as upscale as Naples is likely to provide? Head for **La Mela** (also known as "Big Apple"), Via de Mille 40 (☎ **081/413-881**). Carefully monitored by an understated cadre of bouncers and doormen, it does everything it can to maintain a sense of order amid the frenzy otherwise known as nocturnal Naples.

Chez Moi, Via dei Parco Margherita 13 (☎ **081/407-526**), is one of the city's best-managed nightclubs, strictly refusing entrance to anyone who looks like a troublemaker. This is appreciated by the designers, government ministers, and visiting

A Sweet Shop & a Grand Cafe

Giovanni Scaturchio, at Piazza San Domenico Maggiore 19 (☎ **081/551-6944**), offers the most caloric collection of pastries in Naples, and is famous for both satisfying and fattening local residents since around 1900. Representative pastries include the entire selection of Neapolitan sweets, cakes, and candies, including brioches soaked in liqueur, cassate (pound cake) filled with layered ricotta, Moor's heads, and cheesy ricotta pastries known as *sfogliatelle,* dear to the heart of most Neapolitans since childhood. Another specialty is *ministeriale,* a chocolate cake filled with liqueur and chocolate cream. Pastries start at 1,800L ($1.10) if consumed standing up, or at 3,000L ($1.80) if enjoyed at a table. It's open Wednesday to Monday from 7:20am to 8:40pm; closed 2 weeks in August.

The decor of the **Gran Caffè Gambrinus,** Via Chiaia 1, near the Galleria Umberto (☎ **081/417-582**), the oldest cafe in Naples, dating from 1860, would fit easily into a grand Bourbon palace. Along the vaulted ceiling of an inner room, Empire-style caryatids spread their togas in high relief above frescoes of mythological playmates. The cafe is known for its espresso and cappuccino, as well as pastries and cakes whose variety dazzles the eye. These pastries are the most famous in Naples. You can also order potato and rice croquettes and fried pizzas for a light lunch. Tea costs 3,500L ($2.10); cappuccino goes for 4,000L ($2.40) at a table. The cafe is open daily from 8am to midnight; closed 2 weeks in August.

socialites who enjoy the place. Clients tend to be over 25, and have included the mayor of Naples. You'll be ushered to a table amid a decor of soft blues and greens, where you'll order your first drink. The place is open Friday and Saturday from 10:30pm to 4 or 5am. Occasionally there is a cabaret act or a live pianist at the bar, but more frequently the music is highly danceable disco. The cover is 25,000L ($15).

Madison Street, Via Sgambati 47 (☎ **081/546-6566**), is huge—the largest disco in Naples. The youngish crowd, usually between 18 and 25, mingles and dances and generally has an uninhibited good time. If you tire of the human melee going on at the several bars or on the dance floor, you can watch video movies or videotaped rock concerts on one of several different screens. There's a restaurant and piano bar on the premises, called the Harem Café, set up in a separate (and quieter) room. The place is open only on Tuesday and Thursday through Saturday from 10pm to 3am and Sunday from 8pm to 2am. The Friday-night crowd tends to be older and slightly more sedate. Reservations are required for the Harem Café because of the limited space; call ☎ 081/770-1310. Cover charges range from 15,000L to 20,000L ($9 to $12).

Looking for gay action? Head for **Tongue,** Via Mazonik 207 (☎ **081/769-0800**), which has a mixed clientele, a large part of whom are gay, dancing to techno music. It is open only on weekends from 9pm to 3am, charging a cover of 10,000L to 15,000L ($6 to $9). There are no all-exclusive lesbian or gay clubs in Naples, but **ARCI-Gay/Lesbica** (☎ **081/551-8293**), offers information about gay-friendly night spots and local clubs that sponsor gay and lesbian nights.

2　The Environs of Naples

PHLAEGREAN FIELDS

One of the bizarre attractions of southern Italy, the Phlaegrean Fields (Campi Flegrei) form a backdrop for a day's adventure of exploring west of Naples and along its bay.

An explosive land of myth and legend, the fiery fields contain a dormant volcano (Solfatara), the cave of the Cumaean Sibyl, Virgil's gateway to the "Infernal Regions," the ruins of thermal baths and amphitheaters built by the Romans, deserted colonies left by the Greeks, and lots more.

If you're depending on public transportation, the best center for exploring the area is **Pozzuoli,** which is reached by Metropolitana (subway) from the Stazione Centrale in Naples. The fare is 1,500L (90¢). Once in Pozzuoli, you can take one of the SEPSA buses at any bus stop, which will take you to places such as Baia in 20 minutes. You can also go to Cumae on one of these buses, or to Solfatara or Lago d'Averno.

✪ **SOLFATARA**   About 7¹/₂ miles west of Naples, near Pozzuoli, is the ancient **Vulcano Solfatara,** Via Solfatara 161 (☎ **081/526-7413**). It hasn't erupted since the final year of the 12th century, but it has been threatening ever since. It gives off sulfurous gases and releases scalding vapors through cracks in the earth's surface. In fact, the activity—or inactivity—of Solfatara has been observed for such a long time that the crater's name is used by *Webster's* dictionary to define any "dormant volcano" emitting vapors.

The crater may be visited daily from 8:30am to 1 hour before sunset, at a cost of 7,000L ($4.20) for adults, 4,000L ($2.40) for children. Take bus no. 152 from Naples or the Metropolitana line from the Stazione Centrale to Solfatara. Once you get off at the train station, you can board one of the city buses that go up the hill, or you can walk to the crater in about 20 minutes.

POZZUOLI   Just 1¹/₂ miles away from Solfatara, the seaport of Pozzuoli opens onto a gulf screened from the Bay of Naples by a promontory. The ruins of the **Anfiteatro Flavio,** Via Nicola Terracciano (☎ **081/526-6007**), built in the last part of the 1st century A.D., testify to past greatness. One of the finest surviving examples of the arenas of antiquity, it's particularly distinguished by its "wings"—which, considering their age, are in good condition. You can see the remains where exotic beasts from Africa were caged before being turned loose in the ring to test their jungle skill against a gladiator. The amphitheater, which may be visited September to March, daily from 9am to 4pm; April and May, daily from 9am to 5pm; and June to August, daily from 9am to 6pm, is said to have entertained 40,000 spectators at the height of its glory. Admission is 4,000L ($2.40).

In another part of town, the **Tempio di Serapide** was really the "Macellum," or market square, and some of its ruined pillars still project upward today. It was erected during the reign of the Flavian emperors. You can reach Pozzuoli by subway from the Stazione Centrale in Naples.

BAIA   In the days of Imperial Rome, the emperors—everybody from Julius Caesar to Hadrian—came here to frolic in the sun while enjoying the comforts of their luxurious villas and Roman baths. Nero is said to have murdered his mother, Agrippina, at nearby Bacoli, with its Pool of Mirabilis. (The ancient "Baiae" was named for Baios, helmsman for Ulysses.) Parts of its illustrious past have been dug out, including both the **Temple of Baiae** and the **Thermal Baths,** said to have been among the greatest erected in Italy.

You can explore this archeological district (☎ **081/868-7592**) daily from 9am to 2 hours before sunset. Admission is 6,000L ($3.60). The town is 15 minutes by rail from Naples. Ferrovia Cumana trains depart from Stazione Centrale at Piazza Garibaldi in the center of Naples.

LAGO D'AVERNO   About 10 miles west of Naples, a bit to the north of Baia, is a lake occupying an extinct volcanic crater. Known to the ancients as the Gateway

Treading Lightly on Mount Vesuvius

*Stand at the bottom of the great market-place of Pompeii, and look up at the silent
streets . . . over the broken houses with their inmost sanctuaries open to the day, away
to Mount Vesuvius, bright and snowy in the peaceful distance; and lose all count of
time, and heed of other things, in the strange and melancholy sensation of seeing the
Destroyed and the Destroyer making this quiet picture in the sun.*

—Charles Dickens, *Pictures from Italy*

A volcano that has struck terror in Campania, the towering, pitch-black Vesuvius
looms menacingly over the Bay of Naples. August 24, A.D. 79, is the infamous date
when Vesuvius burst forth and buried Pompeii, Herculaneum, and Stabiae under
its mass of lava and volcanic mud. What many fail to realize is that Vesuvius has
erupted periodically ever since (thousands were killed in 1631): The last major
spouting of lava occurred in this century (it blew off the ring of its crater in 1906).
The last spectacular eruption was on March 31, 1944. The approach to Vesuvius is
dramatic, with the terrain growing forlorn and foreboding as you near the top. Along
the way you'll see villas rising on its slopes and vineyards (the grapes produce an
amber-colored wine known as lacrimae Christi; the citizens of Pompeii enjoyed wine
from this mountainside, as excavations revealed). Closer to the summit the soil
becomes colored puce and an occasional wildflower appears.

Although it may sound like a dubious invitation to some (Vesuvius, after all, is
an active volcano), it's possible to visit the rim—or lips, so to speak—of the crater's
mouth. As you look down into its smoldering core, you may recall that Spartacus,
in a century before the eruption that buried Pompeii, hid in the hollow of the crater, which was then covered with vines.

To reach Vesuvius from Naples, you can take the Circumvesuviana Railway, or
(in summer only) a motorcoach service from Piazza Vittoria, which hooks up with
bus connections at Pugliano. You get off the train at the Ercolano station, the 10th
stop. Six SITA buses per day go from Herculaneum to the crater of Vesuvius, costing 4,000L ($2.40) round-trip. Once at the top you must be accompanied by a
guide, which costs another 5,000L ($3).

to Hades, it was for centuries shrouded in superstition. Its vapors were said to produce illness and even death, and Averno could well have been the source of the expression, "Still waters run deep." Facing the lake are the ruins of what has been
known as the **Temple of Apollo** from the 1st century A.D., and what was once
thought to be the Cave of the Cumaean Sibyl (see Cuma, below). According to legend, the Sibyl is said to have ferried Aeneas, son of Aphrodite, across the lake, where
he traced a mysterious spring to its source, the River Styx. In the 1st century B.C.,
Agrippa turned it into a harbor for Roman ships by digging out a canal. Take the
Napoli–Torre Gaveta bus from Baia to reach the site.

CUMA   Ancient Cuma was one of the first outposts of Greek colonization in what
is now Italy. Located 12 miles west of Naples, it's of interest chiefly because it's said
to have contained the cave of the legendary Cumaean Sibyl. The **cave of the oracle,**
really a gallery, was dug by the Greeks in the 5th century B.C. and was a sacred spot
to them. Beloved by Apollo, the Sibyl is said to have written the *Sibylline Oracles,* a
group of books of prophecy purchased, according to tradition, by Tarquin the Proud.
You may visit not only the caves, but also the ruins of temples dedicated to Jupiter
and Apollo (later converted into Christian churches), daily from 9am to 1 hour

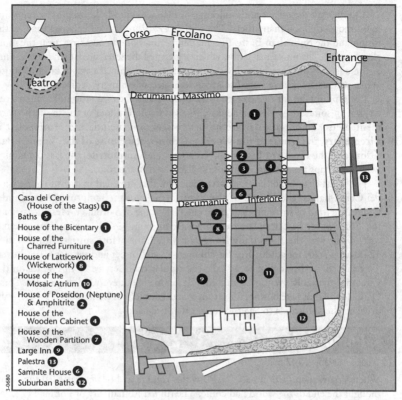

Casa dei Cervi
(House of the Stags) **11**
Baths **5**
House of the Bicentary **1**
House of the
  Charred Furniture **3**
House of Latticework
  (Wickerwork) **8**
House of the
  Mosaic Atrium **10**
House of Poseidon (Neptune)
  & Amphitrite **2**
House of the
  Wooden Cabinet **4**
House of the
  Wooden Partition **7**
Large Inn **9**
Palestra **13**
Samnite House **6**
Suburban Baths **12**

before sunset, for 8,000L ($4.80), free for children under 18 and seniors over 60. On Via Domitiana, to the east of Cuma, you'll pass the **Arco Felice,** an arch about 64 feet high, built by the emperor Domitian in the 1st century A.D. Ferrovia Cumana trains run here. They depart from Stazione Centrale at Piazza Garibaldi in the center of Naples.

✪ HERCULANEUM

The builders of Herculaneum (Ercolano in Italian) were still working to repair the damage caused by an A.D. 62 earthquake when Vesuvius erupted on that fateful August day in A.D. 79. Herculaneum, a much smaller town (about one-fourth the size of Pompeii), didn't start to come to light again until 1709, when Prince Elbeuf launched the unfortunate fashion of tunneling through it for treasures, more intent on profiting from the sale of objets d'art than in uncovering a dead Roman town.

Subsequent excavations at the site, **Ufficio Scavi di Ercolano,** Corso Resina, Ercolano (☎ **081/739-0963**), have been slow and sporadic. In fact, Herculaneum, named after Hercules, is not completely dug out today. One of the obstacles has been that the town was buried under lava, which was much heavier than the ash and pumice stone that piled onto Pompeii. Of course, this formed a greater protection for the buildings buried underneath—many of which were more elaborately constructed than those at Pompeii, as Herculaneum was a seaside resort for patrician families. The complication of having the slum of Resina resting over the yet-to-be-excavated district has further impeded progress and urban renewal.

Although all the streets and buildings of Herculaneum hold interest, some ruins merit more attention than others. The **baths** *(terme)* are divided between those at the forum and the **Suburban Baths** (Terme Suburbane) on the outskirts, near the more elegant villas. The municipal baths, which segregated the sexes, are larger, but the ones at the edge of town are more lavishly adorned. The **Palestra** was a kind of sports arena, where games were staged to satisfy the spectacle-hungry denizens.

The typical plan for the average town house was to erect it around an uncovered atrium. In some areas, Herculaneum possessed the forerunner of the modern apartment house. Important private homes to seek out include the **House of the Bicentenary,** the **House of the Wooden Cabinet,** the **House of the Wooden Partition,** and the **House of Poseidon** (Neptune) and **Amphitrite,** the last containing what is perhaps the best-known mosaic discovered in the ruins.

The finest example of how the aristocracy lived is provided by a visit to the Casa dei Cervi, named the **House of the Stags** because of the sculpture found inside. Guides are fond of showing their male clients a statue of a drunken Hercules urinating. Some of the best of the houses are locked and can be seen only by permission.

You can visit the ruins daily from 9am to 1 hour before sunset. Admission is 12,000L ($7.20) for adults, free for children 17 and under and seniors 60 and over. To reach the archeological zone, take the regular train service from Naples on the Circumvesuviana Railway, a 20-minute ride leaving about every half hour from Corso Garibaldi 387; or take bus no. 255 from Piazza Municipio. Otherwise, it's a 4½-mile drive on the autostrada to Salerno (turn off at Ercolano).

3 Pompeii

15 miles S of Naples, 147 miles SE of Rome

When Vesuvius erupted in A.D. 79, Pliny the Younger, who later recorded the event, thought the end of the world had come. The ruined Roman city of Pompeii (*Pompei* in Italian), now dug out from the inundation of volcanic ash and pumice stone rained on it by Vesuvius, vividly brings to light the life of 19 centuries ago, and has sparked the imagination of the world.

Numerous myths have surrounded Pompeii, one of which is that a completely intact city was rediscovered. Actually the Pompeiians—that is, those who escaped—returned to their city when the ashes had cooled and removed some of the most precious treasures from the thriving resort. But they left plenty behind to be uncovered at a later date and carted off to museums throughout Europe and America.

After a long medieval sleep, Pompeii was again brought to life in the late 16th century, quite by accident, by the architect Domenico Fontana. However, it was in the mid-18th century that large-scale excavations were launched. Somebody once remarked that Pompeii's second tragedy was its rediscovery, that it really should have been left to slumber for another century or two, when it might have been better excavated and maintained.

ESSENTIALS

GETTING THERE   By Train   The Circumvesuviana Railway departs Naples every half hour from Piazza Garibaldi. A round-trip fare is 2,700L ($1.60); trip time is 45 minutes each way. There's an entrance about 50 yards from the railway station at Villa Misteri.

By Bus   At the railway station in Pompeii, bus connections take you to the entrance to the excavations.

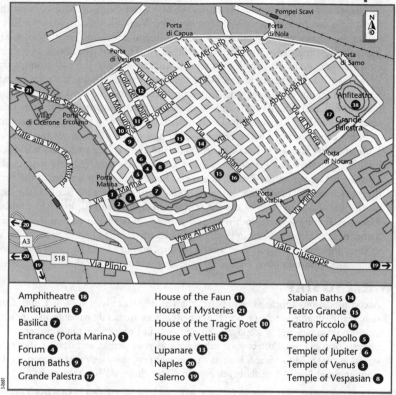

Amphitheatre **18**	House of the Faun **11**	Stabian Baths **14**
Antiquarium **2**	House of Mysteries **21**	Teatro Grande **15**
Basilica **7**	House of the Tragic Poet **10**	Teatro Piccolo **16**
Entrance (Porta Marina) **1**	House of Vettii **12**	Temple of Apollo **5**
Forum **4**	Lupanare **13**	Temple of Jupiter **6**
Forum Baths **9**	Naples **20**	Temple of Venus **3**
Grande Palestra **17**	Salerno **19**	Temple of Vespasian **8**

By Car   To reach Pompeii from Naples, take the 13½-mile drive on the autostrada to Salerno.

VISITOR INFORMATION   The **tourist information center** is at Via Sacra 1 (☎ 081/850-7255), open October to March, Monday to Friday from 8am to 3:40pm and Saturday from 8am to 2pm; April to September, Monday to Friday from 8am to 7pm and Saturday from 8am to 2pm.

✪ EXPLORING THE RUINS

The best preserved 2,000-year-old ruins in Europe, most of the curious visit the **Ufficio Scavi di Pompei,** Piazza Esedra (☎ 081/861-0744), on a day trip from Naples (allow at least 4 hours for even a superficial look at the archeological site). The ruins are open daily from 9am to 1 hour before sunset. Admission is 12,000L ($7.20) for adults, free for children under 18 and seniors over 60. The most elegant of the patrician villas, the **House of Vettii** has a courtyard, statuary (such as a two-faced Janus), paintings, and a black-and-red Pompeiian dining room frescoed with cupids. The house was occupied by two brothers named Vettii, both of whom were wealthy merchants. As you enter the vestibule, you'll see a painting of Priapus resting his gargantuan phallus on a pair of scales. The guard will reveal other erotic fertility drawings and statuary, although most such material has been removed from Pompeii to the Archaeological Museum in Naples. This house is the best example of a villa and garden that's been restored, and is also known for its frescoes of delicate miniature cupids.

The second important villa, the **House of Mysteries** (Villa dei Misteri), near the Porto Ercolano, lies outside the walls (go out along Viale alla Villa dei Misteri). What makes the villa exceptional, aside from its architectural features, are its remarkable frescoes, depicting scenes associated with the sect of Dionysus (Bacchus), one of the cults that was flourishing in Roman times. Note in some of the backgrounds the Pompeiian red. The largest house, called the **House of the Faun** (Casa del Fauno) because of a bronze statue of a dancing faun found here, takes up a city block and has four different dining rooms and two spacious peristyle gardens. It sheltered the celebrated Battle of Alexander the Great mosaic, which is now in a Naples museum.

In the center of town is the **Forum**—although rather small, it was the heart of Pompeiian life, known to bakers, merchants, and the wealthy aristocrats who lived luxuriously in the villas. Parts of the Forum were severely damaged in an earthquake 16 years before the eruption of Vesuvius and had not been repaired when the final destruction came. Three buildings that surround the Forum are the **basilica** (the largest single structure in the city) and the **temples of Apollo and Jupiter.** The **Stabian Thermae** (baths)—where both men and women lounged and relaxed in between games of knucklebones—are in good condition, among the finest to come down to us from antiquity. Here you'll see some skeletons, and in a building called Lupanare, some erotic paintings (these frescoes are the source of the fattest tips to the guides).

WHERE TO STAY

Accommodations appear to be for earnest archeologists only. The Villa Laura is the only really suitable hotel in town; the other choices are barely passable and are suggested only as emergency stopovers. Some hotels in Pompeii are not considered safe because of robberies. Protect your valuables and your person and don't wander the streets at night. Most visitors look at the excavations, then seek better accommodations at either Naples (see above) or Sorrento (see chapter 17) for the night.

Hotel del Santuario. Piazza Bartolo Longo 2–6, 80045 Pompei. ☎ 081/850-6165. Fax 081/850-2822. 52 rms. TEL. 100,000L–120,000L ($60–$72) double. Rates include breakfast. AE, MC, V. Free parking.

This hotel is in the very center of Pompeii, and opens onto the major square across from the basilica. It rents simply furnished bedrooms, very basic, and also offers a ristorante, pizzeria, gelateria, and tearoom. The restaurant serves reasonably priced meals. You can enjoy such dishes as beefsteak pizzaiola or a mixed fry of shrimp and squid. There's limited parking.

Hotel Villa dei Misteri. Via Villa dei Misteri 11, 80045 Pompei–Scavi. ☎ 081/861-3593. Fax 081/862-2983. 41 rms. 80,000L ($48) double. DC, MC, V. From the Pompeii rail station, take the Sorrento train and get off at the Villa dei Misteri stop.

Located 250 yards from the Scavi Station, this 1930s hotel is suitable for motorists. About 1 1/2 miles south of the center of town, it features a swimming pool, a little garden, and a place to park your car. The family-style welcome may compensate for a certain lack of facilities and amenities. The place could stand a face-lift, but many readers have expressed their fondness for it. The only rooms are barebone doubles.

Villa Laura. Via della Salle 13, 80045 Pompei. ☎ 081/863-1024. Fax 081/850-4893. 24 rms. A/C TV TEL. 120,000L ($72) double. AE, DC, MC, V. Parking 9,000L ($5.40).

Villa Laura is the best hotel in town, which isn't saying a lot. Located on a somewhat hidden street, it escapes a lot of the street noise that plagues many Pompeii hotels. The hotel is mercifully air-conditioned, and the bedrooms are comfortably but not spectacularly furnished. Try for a room with a balcony. There's a breakfast room with a bar in the basement. The breakfasts are a bit dull, but for lunch and dinner you can escape to many trattorie nearby—or better yet, patronize one of the restaurants recommended below. The hotel also has a garden.

WHERE TO DINE

✪ **Il Prìncipe.** Piazza Bartolo Longo 8. ☎ **081/850-5566.** Reservations required. Main courses 25,000L–35,000L ($15–$21); fixed-price menu 50,000L ($30). AE, DC, MC,V. Summer, daily 12:30–3pm and 7:30–11:30pm; off-season, Tues–Sun 12:30–3pm and 7:30–11:30pm. CAMPANIAN/MEDITERRANEAN.

The leading restaurant of Pompeii, Il Prìncipe is also acclaimed as one of the best restaurants in Campania. The decor incorporates the best decorative features of ancient Pompeii, including a scattering of brightly colored frescoes and mosaics. Guests can dine in its beautiful interior or select a sidewalk table at the corner of the most important square in Pompeii, with views of the basilica. For your first course, you might start with carpaccio or a salad of porcini mushrooms; then follow with one of the pasta dishes, perhaps *spaghetti vongole* (with baby clams). You can also order superb fish dishes, such as sea bass and turbot, *saltimbocca* (sage-flavored veal with ham), or steak Diane.

Zi Caterina. Via Roma 20. ☎ **081/850-7447.** Reservations recommended. Main courses 15,000L–20,000L ($9–$12). AE, DC, MC, V. Wed–Mon noon–11pm. SEAFOOD/NEAPOLITAN.

This good choice is conveniently located in the center of town near the basilica, with two spacious dining rooms. The antipasto table might tempt you with its seafood, but don't rule out the *pasta e fagiole* (pasta and beans) with mussels. The chef's special rigatoni, with tomatoes and prosciutto, is tempting, as is the array of fish or one of the live lobsters fresh from the tank.

POMPEII AFTER DARK

The hot spot in town used to be the Lupanare, or bordello, but Vesuvius ended those nocturnal adventures long ago. Today you must settle for the **Panatenee Pompeiane,** a festival of the performing arts, a series of classical plays in July and August. For more information contact the tourist offices in Pompeii or Naples.

4 Ischia

21 miles W of Naples

Dramatically situated in the Gulf of Gaeta, the island of Ischia is of volcanic origin. Some of its beaches are radioactive, and its thermal spas claim cures for most anything that ails you—be it "gout, retarded sexual development, or chronic rheumatism." Called the Green Island or Emerald Island, Ischia is bathed in brilliant light and surrounded by sparkling waters that wash up on many sandy beaches (a popular one: Sant'Angelo). The island is studded with pine groves. In Greek mythology, this volcanic island was the home of Typhoeus, or Typhon, who created volcanoes and fathered the three-headed canine Cerberus, guardian of the gateway to Hades, and the incongruous Chimera and Sphinx. Covering just over 18 square miles, its prominent feature is Monte Epomeo, near the center of the island, a volcano that was a powerful force and source of worry for the Greek colonists who settled here in the 8th century B.C.

Today, the 2,590-foot peak is considered dead, having last erupted in the 14th century, but it's still responsible for warming the island's thermal springs. Ischia slumbered for centuries after its early turbulence, although many discerning visitors knew of its charms. Ibsen, for example, lived in a villa near Casamicciola to find the solitude necessary to complete *Peer Gynt.* However, by the 1950s, Ischia was suddenly discovered—this time by wealthy Italians who built a slew of first-class hotels in the process of trying to avoid the overrun resorts of Capri.

The island is known for its sandy beaches, health spas (which utilize the hot springs for hydromassage and mud baths), pine groves, and vineyards that produce a red and white Monte Epomeo, a red and white Ischia, and the white Biancolella. The largest community is at Ischia Porto on the eastern coast, a circular town seated in the crater of an extinct volcano that functions as the island's main port of call. The most lively settlement is at Forio on the western coast, with its many bars along tree-lined streets. The island's other major communities are Lacco Ameno and Casamicciola Terme, on the north shore, and Serrara Fontana and Barano d'Ischia, inland and to the south.

ESSENTIALS

GETTING THERE   The easiest and most frequent route of access is from Naples, from which both hydrofoils (passengers only) and conventional ferryboats (passengers with their cars) make frequent runs throughout the year. A hydrofoil is the most convenient and most rapid option, charging fares of 17,000L ($10.20) per person, each way, and departures between three and seven times a day, depending on the season. Transit by hydrofoil takes about 40 minutes each way; transit by ferryboat requires around 1 hour 20 minutes each way, but costs only 9,000L ($5.40) each way for foot passengers. Ferries also transport cars; a medium-sized vehicle, with as many passengers as will fit inside, costs around 70,000L ($42) each way. Both hydrofoils and conventional ferryboats depart from Naples's Mergellina Pier, near the Hotel Vesuvio, whereas conventional ferryboats leave from Molo Beverello, near Piazza Municipio. Two companies maintain both hydrofoils and ferryboats: They include **Caremar** (☎ **081/551-3882** in Naples or 081/991-953 in Ischia) and **Linee Lauro** (☎ **081/552-2838** in Naples or 081/991-888 in Ischia). Caremar is somewhat more upscale, with better-maintained ships and a more cooperative staff.

VISITOR INFORMATION   In Porto d'Ischia, the **Azienda di Turismo** has two offices, one located right by the docks on Via Iasolino (☎ **081/991-146**). It's open throughout the year, Monday to Saturday from 9am to noon and 1:30 to 5pm. There's another, primarily administrative office, at Corso Vittoria Colonna 116 (☎ **081/991-464**).

ISCHIA PORTO

This harbor actually emerged from the crater of a long-dead volcano. Most of the population and the largest number of hotels are centered here. **Castello Aragonese** (☎ **081/992-834**) once guarded the harbor from raids. At the castle lived Vittoria Colonna, the poetess and confidante of Michelango, to whom he wrote the celebrated letters.

References to a fortress on this isolated rock date from as early as 474 B.C. Today it's the symbol of Ischia, jutting like a Mediterranean version of France's Mont-St-Michel from the sea surrounding it. It's connected to the oldest part of town by the Ponte d'Ischia, a narrow bridge barely wide enough for a car. If you're driving, park on the "mainland" side of the bridge and cross on foot. The fortress is privately owned, and you pay 8,000L ($4.80) to get inside. The castle is closed between January and March, but open daily otherwise from 9am to sunset.

WHERE TO STAY

Continental Terme. Via M. Mazzella 74, 80077 Ischia Porto. ☎ **081/991-588.** Fax 081/982-929. A/C MINIBAR TV TEL. 310,000L–350,000L ($186–$210) double; from 470,000L ($282) suite. Rates include half board. AE, DC, MC, V. Closed Nov–Mar.

The thermal springs at this sprawling complex are among the largest and most fully equipped on the island. There are five thermal water swimming pools, three covered, surrounded by the exotic greenery of 32,700 square yards of gardens. Public spaces feature polished marble and terra-cotta floors, padded contemporary Italian seating, and wicker and glass tables, accented by cut flowers and plant life. In sleek, contemporary styling, bedrooms are well decorated and rather luxuriously furnished, set in a diverse collection of town-house villas scattered throughout the grounds. There's a bar lounge, a poolside bar, and a piano bar that provides evening entertainment. If you want to shop, there are boutiques dedicated to fashion and art. The spa facilities contain a gymnasium, the thermal pools, advanced physiotherapy equipment, and a full-service beauty salon offering thermal mud treatments. Meals, which can be taken in the dining room or on the terrace, feature the island's bountiful local seafood offered with a lengthy list of wines.

✪ **Grand Hotel Excelsior.** Via Emanuele Gianturco 19, 80077 Ischia Porto. ☎ **081/991-020.** Fax 081/984-100. 72 rms, 2 suites. A/C MINIBAR TV TEL. 460,000L–640,000L ($276–$384) double; from 700,000L ($420) suite. Rates include half board. AE, DC, MC, V. Closed Nov 3–Apr 23.

The superior accommodation in Ischia, this palatial hotel, the private retreat of English nobleman James Nihn at the end of the 19th century, was opened by the counts of Micangeli early in this century. The rich, textural decor is a bit ostentatious, but never lets you forget that you are relaxing in the lap of luxury. The public spaces contain huge multitiered chandeliers, terra-cotta tile floors, the occasional Oriental carpet, and thickly padded furniture, the wooden frames of which are curved, carved, or scrolled elaborately. In the guest rooms, curvaceous wrought-iron headboards rise above loudly colorful bedspreads matched to the lampshades, curtains, and sheers. Each room has a private patio beyond French doors. There are covered and outdoor swimming pools—the latter surrounded by a small but lush garden—a fitness room, and minigolf course. There's a small but fastidious bar, and dining indoors or on a covered terrace, where rich specialty dishes of seafood are served with local and international wines.

Grand Hotel Punta Molino Terme. Lungomare Cristoforo Colombo 23, 80070 Ischia Porto. ☎ 081/991-544. Fax 081/991-562. 82 rms, 2 suites. A/C MINIBAR TV TEL. 450,000L–560,000L ($270–$336) double; from 760,000L ($456) suite. Rates include half board. AE, DC, MC, V. Closed Nov–Apr 14.

Standing in the midst of cliffs of olive groves, this large, modern hotel combines comfort with excellent service and a full-service health spa. Public areas feature a mixture of contemporary with 17th- and 18th-century furnishings, with reproductions in the guest rooms, and are floored with stone, marble, or terra-cotta—some tiles of which are painted. Fresh cut flowers and living plants add life and color, unifying the interior with the lush greenery of the surrounding grounds. Thermal springs fill an indoor and an outdoor swimming pool, and there's also a freshwater outdoor pool. There are both a poolside bar and an interior piano bar. The health facilities offer a wide range of beauty treatments and fitness training. Candlelit dining in the restaurant offers a wide selection of Italian dishes including succulent seafood specialties. Meals taken on the terrace feature regional barbecued specialties. Both offer views of the sea and a lengthy wine list.

Il Moresco. Via Emanuele Gianturo 16, 80077 Ischia Porto. ☎ 081/981-355. Fax 081/992-338. 72 rms. 240,000L–340,000L ($144–$204) per person. Rates include half board. AE, DC, MC, V. Closed Nov–Feb.

This hotel's spa facilities and health and beauty center are so complete that some guests check in for the entire duration of their vacation. It sits in a sun-dappled park whose pines and palmettos grow close to the arched loggias of its thick concrete walls. From some angles, the Moorish-inspired exterior looks almost like a cubist fantasy. Inside, the straightforward design re-creates a modern oasis in the southern part of Spain—matador-red tiles couple with stark-white walls and Iberian furniture. Each of the well-furnished accommodations has a terrace or balcony. The hotel offers a landscaped cluster of thermal swimming pools, tennis courts, access to a nearby beach, and several bars and dining areas both in- and out-of-doors. Wide solarium terraces face the sea.

✪ **La Villarosa.** Via Giacinto Gigante 5, 80077 Ischia Porto. ☎ **081/991-316.** Fax 081/992-425. 37 rms. TV TEL. 220,000L ($132) double or 105,000L–125,000L ($63–$75) per person half board. AE, DC, MC, V. Closed Nov–Mar.

This is the finest pensione in Ischia. Set in a garden of gardenias, banana, eucalyptus, and fig trees, it is like a private villa, charmingly furnished with antiques. The dining room is in the informal country style, with terra-cotta tiles, lots of French windows, and antique chairs. The meals are a delight, served with a variety of offerings, including the local specialties. And what looks like a carriage house in the garden has been converted into an informal tavern with more antiques—relaxing, and attractive. The staff is selected to maintain the personal atmosphere. The bright and airy bedrooms are well kept, conveying a homelike flavor.

WHERE TO DINE

Ristorante Damiano. Via Nuova Circumvallazione/Highway SS-270. ☎ **081/983-032.** Reservations recommended. Main courses 25,000L–55,000L ($15–$33). MC, V. Daily 8pm–midnight. Apr–June and Sept, Sun 1–3pm. Closed Oct–Mar. ISCHIAN.

Set in a circa 1980 building that was angled for maximum exposure to the Ischian coastline, this charming restaurant lies about a mile southwest of the ferryboat terminal at Ischia Porto. Its guiding spirit is culinary entrepreneur Damiano Caputo, who infuses his seafood with zest and very fresh ingredients. Within the consciously rustic setting that includes long communal tables and fresh flowers, you can select from an array of succulent antipasti arranged on a sturdy buffet; linguine that might be studded with lobster, shrimp, or clams; steamy bowls of minestrone; at least four different kinds of seafood salad, including a version that focuses on mussels; and grilled fresh fish or lobster. Desserts include tiramisù and a soothing assortment of *gelati*.

LACCO AMENO

Jutting up from the water, a rock named **Il Fungo** (The Mushroom) is the landmark natural sight of Lacco Ameno. The spa is the center of the good life (and contains some of the best and most expensive hotels on the island). People come from all over the world either to relax on the beach and be served top-level food or to take the cure. The radioactive waters at Lacco Ameno have led to the development of a modern spa with extensive facilities for thermal cures, everything from underwater jet massages to mud baths.

WHERE TO STAY

La Reginella. Piazza Santa Restituta 1, 80076 Lacco Ameno d'Ischia. ☎ **081/994-300.** Fax 081/980-481. 78 rms. A/C MINIBAR TV TEL. 320,000L–500,000L ($192–$300) double. Rates include half board. AE, DC, MC, V. Closed Nov 3–Mar 26.

Set in a lush garden typical of the island's accommodations, this hotel's Mediterranean decor combines printed tile floors with light woods and pastel or floral fabrics to create a relaxed atmosphere in which to enjoy its solarium, gymnasium, and tennis courts. Its spa features Finnish saunas, an outdoor thermal pool, and an indoor version with an underwater jet massage and against-current swimming. Residents can also use the private beach at the nearby Regina Isabella complex. Indoor and outdoor meal service is provided by the O'Pignatiello restaurant, where fresh seafood dishes and a selection of wines will revitalize you from the activities of the day.

Regina Isabella e Royal Sporting. 80076 Lacco Ameno d'Ischia. ☎ **081/994-322.** Fax 081/900-190. 117 rms, 17 suites. A/C MINIBAR TV TEL. 340,000L–900,000L ($204–$540) double; from 540,000L ($324) suite. Rates include half board. AE, DC, MC, V.

Requiring a minimum stay of 3 days, this resort, dating from 1950, offers the finest accommodations and service available in Lacco Ameno, in a refined setting that successfully contrasts contemporary furnishings with rococo and less ornate antique styles. In bedrooms, serene blues and greens prevalent in upholstery, draperies, and some printed tile floors are offset by earthy brown tiles and woodwork, whereas elaborate chandeliers illuminate public spaces. There is an outdoor freshwater swimming pool, an indoor thermal pool, and a private beach offering windsurfing and motorboat rental. Spa offerings include regimented stretching and walking programs, various types of massages and mud baths, and "cures" for almost anything. You can take a break in the piano bar. The hotel restaurant features dining room and terrace service of seafood specialties and eclectic wines with a view over the gardens to the sea beyond.

Terme di Augusto. Viale Campo 128, 80076 Lacco Ameno d'Ischia. ☎ **081/994-944.** Fax 081/980-244. 118 rms. A/C MINIBAR TV TEL. 220,000L–320,000L ($132–$192) double. Rates include half board. AE, DC, MC, V. Closed Dec 1–27.

This hotel, located some 50 yards from the shore, provides comfortable accommodations and excellent service in a setting that's less ostentatious than many competing resorts. It combines prominent arched ceilings, patterned tile floors, and floral drapery and upholstery to create the light, airy spaces typical of Mediterranean style. Fitness activities are provided by a freshwater outdoor pool, fully equipped gymnasium, and tennis courts, whereas thermal treatments are represented by an indoor swimming pool with a temperature range up to 96.8°F and a thermal beauty center offering mud packs, massage, and "cures" for symptoms ranging from dandruff to vaginal infections. The dining room and terrace restaurants offer local, national, and international cuisine and wines, served with great attention to detail.

✪ Terme San Montano. Via Monte Vico, 80076 Lacco Ameno d'Ischia. ☎ **081/994-033.** Fax 081/980-242. 65 rms. A/C MINIBAR TV TEL. 440,000L–620,000L ($264–$372) double. Rates include half board. AE, DC, MC, V. Closed Nov–Apr 26.

This facility was built in 1972, and Man Ray was once a faithful guest, as were opera stars Mario del Monaco and Giuseppi di Stefano. The grounds spread out around the hotel in a luxuriant garden. A nautical decor features recurring elements of outdated sailing ships in public and guest rooms. Aged woods, leather, and brass are combined in furnishings, and marine lamps shed light on almost every room. Headboards resemble a ship's helm, windows are translated as portholes, and miniature ships and antiquated diving gear are decoratively scattered about. Facilities include a full gymnasium, solarium, natural sauna, thermal and freshwater swimming pools, spa and beauty center, and private beach. Services range from boat and car rental to babysitting. Tennis, squash, or water-skiing lessons, massage, mud baths, and a full range of health-related treatments are also available.

FORIO

A short drive from Lacco Ameno, Forio stands on the west coast of Ischia opening onto the sea near the Bay of Citara. Long a favorite with artists—filmmaker Lucchino Visconti maintains a villa here—it is now developing a broader base of tourism. Locals produce some of the finest wines on the island. On the way from Lacco Ameno, stop at the beach of San Francesco, with its sanctuary. At sunset many visitors head for a rocky spur upon which sits the Church of Santa Maria del Soccorso. The lucky ones get to witness the famous "green flash" over the Gulf of Gaeta. It appears on occasion immediately after the sun sets.

WHERE TO STAY

✪ **Grande Albergo Mezzatorre.** Via Mezzatorre, 80075 Forio d'Ischia. ☎ **081/986-111.** Fax 081/986-015. 50 rms, 5 suites. A/C MINIBAR TV TEL. 420,000L–540,000L ($252–$324) double; 520,000L–640,000L ($312–$384) suite. Rates include half board. AE, DC, MC, V. Closed Nov–Apr.

The best accommodation in Forio, this complex is built around a 16th-century villa whose stone tower once guarded against invaders; now it houses the least expensive of the double rooms. The inn's five postmodern buildings, erected in 1989, run a few hundred feet downhill to a waterfront bluff. The setting is placid and romantic, with matching rough stone sea walls and paths under tall twisted evergreens. A casual airiness prevails in public spaces that contrast soft lighting with terra-cotta floors. Recurring elements include woven straw mats, vaulted ceilings, and round and lancet arched doorways and nooks. The decor is bright and contemporary, with wooden furniture and brightly upholstered seating, mimicked in the fabrics of bedspreads and drapery. The hotel features tennis courts, a chapel, a seaside outdoor pool, stairway access to the rocky coastline, a chapel, a private dock, and thermal baths. The restaurant offers a bounty of fresh seafood.

WHERE TO DINE

La Romantica. Via Marina 46. ☎ **081/997-345.** Reservations recommended. Main courses 15,000L–35,000L ($9–$21). AE, DC, MC, V. Daily noon–3pm and 7pm–midnight. Closed Wed from Oct–Mar. NEAPOLITAN/ISCHIAN.

Set near the drydocked fishing vessels of Forio's old port, this is the most appealing nonhotel restaurant in town. Established in 1966, it occupies a Neapolitan-style building whose facade has been enlarged with the addition of a jutting wooden extension that has welcomed everyone from Josephine Baker to heart surgeon Christian Barnard. Your meal might incude linguine with clams or scampi, or a house specialty, "penne 97," garnished with artichoke hearts and shrimp. Swordfish, grilled and served either with lemon sauce or an herb-flavored green sauce, is delicious, as are the baked spigola and several different risotto and veal dishes. You might prefer, weather permitting, a seat on the outdoor terrace.

SANT'ANGELO

The most charming settlement on Ischia, Sant'Angelo juts out on the southernmost tip. The village of fishers is joined to the "mainland" of Ischia by a 300-foot-long lava-and-sand isthmus. Driving into the town is virtually impossible. In summer, you may have to park a long way away and walk. Its beach is among the best on the island.

WHERE TO STAY

Park Hotel Miramare. 80070 Sant'Angelo d'Ischia. ☎ **081/999-219.** Fax 081/999-325. 50 rms. MINIBAR TV TEL. 306,000L ($183.60) double. Rates include breakfast. DC, V. Closed Nov–Feb.

Located right on the sea, this hotel has no beach to speak of, but there is a concrete terrace with chairs and umbrellas and a stairway that clears the rocky shore, leading directly into the water. Within the hotel, boldly patterned floor tiles and contemporary furnishings favor hues of blue. Curved wrought-iron balconies, white wickerwork, and canopied iron bed frames are recurring decorative elements. The hotel's health spa is not on the premises, but it's only a short walk away, down a flower-lined path. Among its offerings are 12 thermal pools, mud treatments, massage, sauna, and designated nudist areas. The hotel's dining room features the seafood the island is known for, and a snack bar offers a quick, informal, and inexpensive option to restaurant service.

17 The Amalfi Coast & Capri

When the English say "see Naples and die," they mean the city and the bay, with majestic Mt. Vesuvius in the background. When the Germans use the expression, they mean the Amalfi Drive. And, indeed, several motorists do die each year on the dangerous coastal road, too narrow to accommodate the heavy stream of summer traffic, especially the large tour buses that almost sideswipe each other as they try to pass. Moreover, in driving along the coast you sometimes find it difficult to concentrate on the road because of the view. The drive, remarked André Gide, "is so beautiful that nothing more beautiful can be seen on this earth."

Capri and Sorrento have long been known to international travelers. But the popularity of the resort-studded Amalfi Drive is a more recent phenomenon. It was discovered by German officers in World War II, then later by American and English servicemen (Positano was a British rest camp in the last months of the war). Later, when the war was over, many returned, often bringing their families. The little fishing villages in time became major tourism centers, with hotels and restaurants in all categories.

Sorrento and Amalfi are in the vanguard, with the widest range of facilities; Positano has more snob appeal and remains popular with artists; Ravello is still the choice of the discriminating few, such as Gore Vidal, who desire relative seclusion. To cap off an Amalfi Coast adventure, you can take a boat from Sorrento to Capri, which needs no advance billing. Three sightseeing attractions in this chapter—in addition to the towns and villages—are worthy of a special pilgrimage: The Emerald Grotto between Amalfi and Positano, the Blue Grotto of Capri, and the Greek temples of the ancient Sybarite-founded city of Paestum, south of Salerno.

1 Sorrento

31 miles S of Naples, 159 miles SE of Rome, 31 miles W of Salerno

Borrowing from Greek mythology, the Romans placed the legendary abode of the Sirens—those wicked mermaids who lured seamen to their deaths with their sweet songs—at Surrentum (Sorrento). Ulysses resisted their call by stuffing the ears of his crew with wax and having himself bound to the mast of his ship. Perched on high cliffs, overlooking the bays of Naples and Salerno, Sorrento has been sending out its siren call for centuries—luring everybody from

Homer to Lord and Lady Astor. It's the birthplace of Torquato Tasso, author of *Jerusalem Delivered.* Some aging locals still get wet-eyed hearing Vic Damone sing "Come Back to Sorrento."

The streets in summer tend to be as noisy as a carnival. The hotels on the "racing strip," Corso Italia, need to pass out earplug kits when they tuck you in for the night. Perhaps you'll have a hotel on a cliffside in Sorrento with a view of the "sea of the sirens." If you want to swim in that sea, you'll find both paths and private elevators that take guests down.

To enjoy the beauty of the Amalfi Drive, whose perils are noted above, don't drive it yourself. Take a blue SITA bus which runs between Sorrento and Salerno or Amalfi. In Sorrento, bus stations with timetables are outside the railway station and in the central piazza.

ESSENTIALS

GETTING THERE   By Train   Sorrento is served by frequent express trains from Naples (trip time: 1 hour). The high-speed train, called Ferrovia Circumvesuviana, leaves from one floor underground at the Stazione Centrale.

By Car   From Naples, head south on Route 18, cutting west at the junction with Route S145.

VISITOR INFORMATION   The **tourist information office** is at Via de Maio 35 (☎ 081/807-4033), which winds down to the port where ships to Capri and Naples anchor. It's open April to September, Monday to Saturday 8:30am to 2:30pm and 4 to 7pm (to 6pm October to March).

EXPLORING THE TOWN

For such a famous beach resort, the actual beaches are very limited—most of them being just bathing piers extending into the water. Chaise longues and umbrellas line these decks along the rock-strewn coastline. The best beach is **Punta del Capo,** reached by going along Corso Italia to Via del Capo. If you'd like to go hiking, you can explore the green hills above Sorrento. Many of the trails are marked, and the tourist office will advise.

Although few visitors come to Sorrento to look at churches and monuments, there are some worth exploring. **Chiesa di San Francesco,** Via San Francesco (☎ 081/878-1269), dates from the 14th century. This cloister is a pocket of beauty in overcrowded Sorrento, with delicate archways and a garden studded with flowering vines. The convent here is also an art school offering exhibits, and in July and August jazz and classical music is performed almost nightly in the outdoor atrium. Show time is 9pm, with an admission of 25,000L ($15) for adults or 15,000L ($9) under 26. The cloister is otherwise open daily 9am to noon and 3 to 6pm.

If time remains, visit **Museo Correale di Terranova,** Via Correale (☎ 081/878-1846), north of Piazza Tasso. A former palace, it has displays of ancient statues, antiques, and Italian art. Here is a chance to introduce yourself to intarsia, a technique of making objects with paper-thin pieces of patterned wood. Neapolitan bric-a-brac and other curiosities finish off the exhibits. Hours are daily 9am to 12:30pm and 3 to 5pm. Admission is 5,000L ($3).

SHOPPING   A Gargiulo & Jannuzzi, Piazza Tasso (☎ 081/878-1041) is the best-known maker of marquetry furniture in the region. They demonstrate the centuries-old technique in the basement, where an employee will combine multihued pieces of wood veneer to create patterns of arabesques and flowers. The sprawling showrooms, right in the heart of town, feature an array of card tables, clocks, and partners' desks, each inlaid with patterns of elmwood, rosewood, bird's-eye maple, and mahogany. Upstairs is a collection of embroidered napery and table linen, and the outlet also has its own ceramic factory. The pottery can be packed and shipped anywhere in the world. Embroidery and lace are two of the best shopping bargains here, and **Luigia Gargiulo,** Corso Italia 48 (☎ **081/878-1081**), comes recommended for embroidered sheets and tablecloths but also offers children's clothing.

WHERE TO STAY

In its first- and second-class hostelries, Sorrento is superior to almost any resort in the south, and offers accommodations in all price ranges.

EXPENSIVE

✪ **Grand Hotel Excelsior Vittoria.** Piazza Tasso 34, 80067 Sorrento. ☎ **081/807-1044.** Fax 081/877-1206. 106 rms, 12 suites. MINIBAR TV TEL. 415,000L–536,000L ($249–$321.60) double; from 683,000L ($409.80) suite. Rates include breakfast. AE, DC, MC, V.

This luxury bastion, built between 1834 and 1882 on the edge of a cliff and surrounded by semitropical gardens with lemon and orange trees, combines 19th-century glamor with modern amenities. Overlooking the Bay of Naples, it towers over the competition. The terrace theme predominates, especially on the water side where you can enjoy the cold drinks served at sunset while gazing at Vesuvius across the bay. Three elevators take bathers down to the harbor. Inside, the atmosphere is old worldish, especially in the mellow dining room. In 1921, Enrico Caruso stayed in the suite now named for him. The huge bedrooms have their own drama, some with balconies that open onto the perilous cliffside drop. The rooms have a wide mixture of furnishings, with many antique pieces.

Dining/Entertainment: The dining room is festive and formal, with ornate, hand-painted ceilings and a panoramic view. You'll sit in ivory and cane provincial chairs while enjoying topnotch Sorrento cuisine. In summer you can dine in the open air. Live entertainment is presented twice a week.

Services: Room service, baby-sitting, laundry, valet.

Facilities: Large swimming pool.

MODERATE

Hotel Bristol. Via del Capo 22, 80067 Sorrento. ☎ **081/878-4522.** Fax 081/807-1910. 137 rms, 5 suites. A/C TV TEL. 210,000L–330,000L ($126–$198) double; 300,000L–430,000L ($180–$258) suite. Rates include breakfast. AE, DC, MC, V.

The Bristol was built pueblo style in 1958 on a hillside at the edge of town, and every room has a view of Vesuvius and the Bay of Naples. The hotel lures with its contemporary decor and spaciousness, and with well-appointed public and private rooms. The bedrooms are warm and inviting, with bright covers and built-in niceties. Most have balconies that overlook the sea, and some contain minibars. The hotel also has a restaurant, swimming pool, minigolf, solarium, and a Finnish sauna. In the summer you can dine outside on the terrace.

Grand Hotel Ambasciatori. Via Califano 18, 80067 Sorrento. ☎ **081/878-2025.** Fax 081/807-1021. 103 rms, 6 suites. A/C TV TEL. 220,000L–330,000L ($132–$198) double; 320,000L–430,000L ($192–$258) suite. Rates include breakfast. AE, MC, V.

The heavily buttressed foundation that prevents this cliffside hotel from plunging into the sea looks like something from a medieval monastery. Built in a style reminiscent of a private villa, it was landscaped to include several rambling gardens along the precipice. A set of steps and a private elevator lead to the wooden deck of a bathing wharf. Inside, a substantial collection of Oriental carpets, marble floors, and

The Bay of Naples & the Amalfi Coast

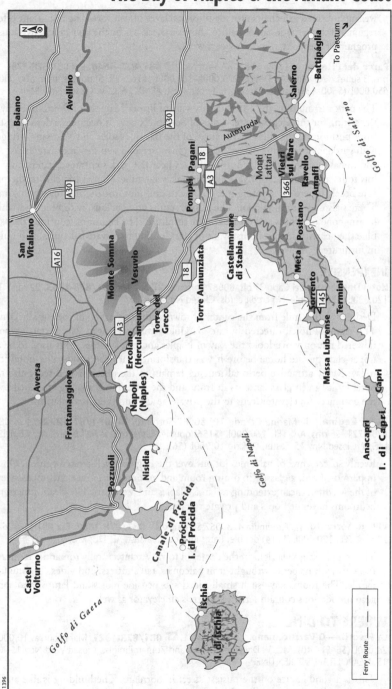

Ferry Route

well-upholstered armchairs provide plush enclaves of comfort. The restaurant offers regional and international specialties, there's a snack bar by the pool, and a live-music program of Neapolitan songs twice a week.

Parco dei Prìncipi. Via Rota 1, 80067 Sorrento. ☎ **081/878-4644.** Fax 081/878-3786. 93 rms, 3 suites. A/C MINIBAR TV TEL. 270,000L–360,000L ($162–$216) double; from 500,000L– 650,000L ($300–$390) suite. Rates include breakfast. AE, DC, MC, V. Closed Nov–Mar.

The park surrounding the 18th-century villa of Prince Leopold of Bourbon Sicily is the setting for this elegant hotel—one of Sorrento's best. It occupies a desirable sea-front position on the cliffs—with views of the Bay of Naples and Vesuvius—ringed with gardens of towering palms, acacias, olives, scented lemons, and magnolias. An additional building, set inland from the sea near the park's entrance, caters only to bus tours and groups. A private elevator takes swimmers down the cliff to the private beach. There's a mooring pier for yachts and motorboats, and for waterskiing. There's also a swimming pool. The public rooms are spacious, with blue-and-white herringbone tile floors and cerulean-blue furniture. The bedrooms continue the sky-blue theme, with striped floors, walls of glass leading to private balconies, and built-in furniture.

INEXPENSIVE

Hotel Désirée. Via del Capo 31 bis, 80067 Sorrento. ☎ and fax **081/878-1563.** 22 rms. TEL. 120,000L ($72) double. No credit cards. Closed Nov–Mar 10.

Désirée is half a mile from the center of town at the beginning of the Amalfi Drive. This tranquil hotel, directed by the Gargiulo family, is ringed with terraces whose flowered masonry overlooks the Bay of Naples and nearby trees. This used to be an upper-class private home before it was transformed into the good-value hotel it is today. Many attractive personal touches remain in the decor. You'll recognize the hotel by its green glass lanterns in front and the welcoming awning stretched over the entrance. An elevator leads to the private beach, and there is a solarium.

Hotel Regina. Via Marina Grande 10, 80067 Sorrento. ☎ **081/878-2722.** Fax 081/ 878-2721. 36 rms. A/C TEL. 260,000L ($156) double. Rates include half board. AE, CB, DISC, MC, V. Closed Nov 15–Easter. Parking 10,000L ($6).

Evenly spaced rows of balconies jut out over the Regina's well-tended garden. On its uppermost floor, a glassed-in dining room and an outdoor terrace encompass views of the Mediterranean extending as far as Naples and Vesuvius. The clean, functional bedrooms have tile floors and private terraces.

Villa di Sorrento. Via Fuorimura 4, 80067 Sorrento. ☎ **081/878-1068.** Fax 081/807-2679. 20 rms. TEL. 190,000L ($114) double. Rates include breakfast. AE, DC, MC, V.

This is a pleasant villa right in the center of town. Architecturally romantic, it attracts travelers with its petite wrought-iron balconies, tall shutters, and vines climbing the facade. The rooms have such small niceties as bedside tables and lamps, and some accommodations contain terraces. There's an elevator as well.

WHERE TO DINE

La Favorita—O'Parrucchiano. Corso Italia 71. ☎ **081/878-1321.** Main courses 10,000L– 24,000L ($6–$14.40). MC, V. Daily noon–4pm and 7pm–midnight. Closed Wed Nov 15–Mar 15. NEAPOLITAN/SORRENTINE.

This is a good choice on the busiest street in Sorrento. The building is like an old tavern, with an arched ceiling in the main dining room. On the terrace in the rear you can dine in a garden of trees, rubber plants, and statuary. Among the à la carte dishes, classic Italian fare is offered, including ravioli Caprese (filled with fresh cheese and covered with a tomato sauce), cannelloni, a mixed fish fry from the Bay of Naples, and a veal cutlet Milanese. The chef will also prepare a pizza for you.

L'Antica Trattoria. Via P. R. Giuliani 33. ☎ **081/807-1082.** Reservations recommended. Main courses 10,000L–25,000L ($6–$15); fixed-price menu 30,000L ($18). AE, MC, V. Tues– Sun noon–12:30am and 7pm–midnight. Closed Jan 10–Feb 10. CAMPANESE/INTERNATIONAL.

Set inside the weather-beaten walls of what was built 300 years ago as a stable, this 200-year-old restaurant is warm, charming, polite, and one of the best recommended in Sorrento. Although all of its food is well prepared, its real virtue lies in its anti- pasti. Each is homemade and features several varieties of fish cooked in a salt crust, which transforms the dish into a sweetly scented, firm but flaky delicacy, and a daunt- ing array of pastas from lasagne to ravioli, which in its best version is stuffed with sea- food. The house special pasta, *spaghetti alla ferrolese,* is made with fish roe, shrimp, red cabbage, and cream. A particularly delicious specialty is seafood pezzogna, made with pulverized cherry tomatoes, olive oil, garlic, parsley, crushed red pepper, and shellfish. The assortment of ice creams is especially tempting, some of the best in town.

SORRENTO AFTER DARK

At **Taverna dell' 800,** Via dell'Accademia 29 (☎ **081/878-5970**), owner "Tony" dispenses flavorful house-style maccheroni (pink-tinged, it combines tomatoes with ham, cream, and bacon) and good cheer. From 9pm to midnight, the music of a gui- tar and a piano duet enlivens a cozy, small-scale bar with flickering candles and a cross-cultural polyglot of languages. There's no cover charge, and main courses cost from 12,000 to 20,000L ($7.20 to $12). The joint is open Tuesday to Sunday 8am to 2am, and does lots of business throughout the day as a cafe and pub.

For a dose of Neapolitan-style folklore, head for **Circolo de Forestière,** Via Luigi de Maio 35 (☎ **081/877-3012**). The venue is that of a bar/cafe whose views extend out over a flowering terrace and the wide blue bay. Music from the live pianist is in- terrupted only for episodes of folkloric dancing and cheerful music from a troupe of players who might actually help you begin to like the song *O Sole Mio* again. The town's central square, Piazza Tasso, is the site of two worthwhile nightclubs. The one that's more closely geared to folkloric music is **Fauno** (☎ **081/878-1153**), where you can slug down a beer or two during the sporadic performances of *tarantella.* Brief but colorful, they interrupt a program that's otherwise devoted to recorded dance— usually disco—music. Less nostalgic is **The Club,** Piazza Tasso (☎ **081/878-4052**), where music derived from popular discos in London and Los Angeles blares out to a youngish crowd from throughout Europe and North America who love to dance.

2 Positano

35 miles SE of Naples, 10 miles E of Sorrento, 165 miles SE of Rome

A hillside, Moorish-style village on the southern strip of the Amalfi Drive, Positano opens onto the Tyrrhenian Sea with its legendary Sirenuse Islands, Homer's siren is- lands in the *Odyssey,* which form the mini-archipelago of Li Galli. Still privately owned, these islands were once purchased by Leonid Massine, the Russian-born cho- reographer. It's said that the town was "discovered" after World War II when Gen. Mark Clark stationed troops in nearby Salerno. It has jackrabbited along the classic postwar route of many a European resort: a sleeping fishing village that was visited by painters and writers (Paul Klee, Tennessee Williams), and then was taken over by bohemia-sampling visitors.

Once Positano was part of the powerful Republic of the Amalfis, a rival of Venice as a sea power in the 10th century. Today smart boutiques dot the village, and bikinis add vibrant colors to the mud-gray beach where you're likely to get pebbles in your sand castle. Prices have been rising sharply over the past few years. The 500-lire-a-night rooms popular with sunset-painting artists have gone the way of your baby teeth.

The topography of the village, you'll soon discover, is impossibly steep. But, as John Steinbeck once wrote, "Positano bites deep. It is a dream place that isn't quite real when you are there and becomes beckoningly real after you have gone."

ESSENTIALS

GETTING THERE **By Bus** SITA buses leave from Sorrento frequently throughout the day, more often in summer than in winter, for the rather thrilling ride to Positano; a one-way fare is 4,300L ($2.60). For information, call SITA at ☎ 089/871-016.

By Car Positano lies along the Amalfi Drive (Route 145, which becomes Route 163 at the approach to the resort).

VISITOR INFORMATION The **tourist information center** is at Via del Saracino 4 (☎ 089/875-067), open Monday to Friday 8:30am to 2pm, and Saturdays June to September 8:30am to noon.

SHOPPING

In a town known for beach and casual wear, **La Brezza,** Via del Brigantino 1 (☎ 089/875-811), located on the shore, has the perfect location for selling its bathing suits, beach towels, and summer clothes. Bright regional pottery can be found at **Umberto Carro,** Via Pasitea 90 (☎ 089/811-596), where dishes, cookware, and surface tiles are emphasized.

WHERE TO STAY

VERY EXPENSIVE

✪ **Il San Pietro.** Via Laurito 2, 84017 Positano. ☎ **089/875-455.** Fax 089/811-449. 43 rms, 16 suites. A/C MINIBAR TV TEL. 620,000L–700,000L ($372–$420) double; 800,000L–1,100,000L ($480–$660) suite. Rates include breakfast. AE, DC, MC, V. Closed Nov 3–Easter.

A mile from Positano toward Amalfi, San Pietro is signaled only by a miniature 17th-century chapel projecting out on a high cliff. The hotel was established in 1970 and has been renovated virtually every winter since. An elevator takes you down to the cliff ledges of the choicest resort along the Amalfi Coast and one of the grandest resort hotels in Europe. The suitelike bedrooms are super-glamorous, and many have a picture window beside the bathtub (there's even a huge sunken Roman bath in one suite). Bougainvillea from the terraces reaches into the ceilings of many living rooms filled with antiques and reproductions. Privacy of guests is zealously guarded. Some of the more distinguished have included Lord Laurence Olivier, Rudolf Nureyev, and Gregory Peck.

Dining/Entertainment: Guests gather at sunset in the piano bar. A dining room cut into the cliff features picture windows and a refined international cuisine.

Services: Room service, baby-sitting, laundry, valet.

Facilities: Swimming pool, private beach, tennis court.

✪ **Le Sirenuse.** Via Christoforo Colombo 30, 84017 Positano. ☎ **089/875-066.** Fax 089/811-798. 58 rms, 2 suites. A/C MINIBAR TV TEL. 400,000L–700,000L ($240–$420) double; from 710,000L ($426) suite. Rates include breakfast. AE, DC, MC, V.

A feel of the 50s still lingers around this candy box of a hotel, and Jean Cocteau could have (but didn't) designed some of the decor. The sophisticated clientele includes numerous artists and writers. The hotel, an old villa only a few minutes' walk up from the bay, is owned by the Marchesi Sersale family and was their private residence until 1951. The marchesa personally selects all furnishings, which include fine carved chests, 19th-century paintings and old prints, a spinet piano, upholstered pieces in bold colors, and a Victorian cabinet from an old jewelry shop. The bedrooms, many with Jacuzzi, are varied, and all have terraces that overlook the village. Your room may have an iron bed, high and ornate and painted red, as well as a carved chest and refectory tables.

Dining/Entertainment: Meals are well served on one of the three terraces, and the chef caters to the international palate with a regional cuisine. It's one of the best dining rooms along the coast.

Services: Room service, baby-sitting, laundry, valet.

Facilities: Narrow swimming pool, sauna, gym.

EXPENSIVE

✪ **Hotel Poseidon.** Via Pasitea 148, 84017 Positano. ☎ **089/811-111.** Fax 089/875-833. 48 rms, 2 suites. A/C MINIBAR TV TEL. 280,000L–380,000L ($168–$228) double; 450,000L–580,000L ($270–$348) suite. Rates include breakfast. AE, DC, MC, V. Closed Nov 4–Mar 29. Parking 30,000L ($18).

This hotel, among the very finest in Positano, was built in 1950 by the Aonzo family as their summer residence. In 1955 it was enlarged and transformed into a hotel, still owned and managed by the hospitable Aonzos. Centrally located, it's charming, discreet, and elegant, with tastefully selected antique furniture and objects. The bedrooms are traditionally furnished and beautifully maintained. Along with its terraces and garden, the hotel offers both indoor and outdoor dining; its chefs feature both a regional and continental cuisine, in summer served on the panoramic terrace, covered with a portico of bougainvillea and ivy. There's a freshwater swimming pool and health club (the first and only one in Positano), with a sauna, hydromassage spa, and gym with a professional trainer.

MODERATE

Albergo L'Ancora. Via Colombo 36, 84017 Positano. ☎ **089/875-318.** Fax 089/811-784. 18 rms. MINIBAR TV TEL. 210,000L–250,000L ($126–$150) double. AE, DC, MC, V. Closed Nov–Apr 1.

This is a stand-out choice, a hillside villa turned hotel with the atmosphere of a private club. It's fresh and sunny here—each room, 11 of them air-conditioned, is like a bird's nest on a cliff. Designed to accommodate the maximum of sun terraces and sheltered loggias for shade, the hotel is a 5-minute climb from the beach. Its main lounge has clusters of club chairs, tile floors, and teardrop chandeliers. But the bedrooms—which cater to couples only—are the stars, with their individualized treatments. Well-chosen antiques, such as fine inlaid desks, are intermixed with more contemporary pieces. Each room opens onto a private terrace. Only guests can dine on the informal outdoor terrace under a vine-covered sun shelter.

Albergo Miramare. Via Trara Genoino 31, 84017 Positano. ☎ **089/875-002.** Fax 089/875-219. 18 rms, 4 suites. A/C TEL. 220,000L–330,000L ($132–$198) double; 270,000L–380,000L ($162–$228) triple; 290,000L ($174) suite. Rates include breakfast. AE, MC, V. Closed Nov 15–Mar 15.

This is one of the most charming accommodations in Positano, for those who like the personalized touch only a small inn can provide. On a cliff in the heart of town, the hotel attracts a discriminating clientele who appreciate the terraces where one can sip Campari and soda and contemplate the sea. Guests stay in one of two tastefully furnished buildings in a setting of citrus trees and flamboyant bougainvillea. Your bed will most likely rest under a vaulted ceiling, and the white walls will be thick. Even the bathrooms are romantic. The conversation piece of the hotel is a glass bathtub on a flowery terrace. What might seem like questionable taste in Los Angeles—a pink porcelain clamshell serving as a wash basin—becomes charming at the Miramare, even when the water rushes from a sea-green ceramic fish with coral-pink gills. The beach is a 3-minute walk away on a series of stairs.

Albergo Ristorante Covo dei Saraceni. 84017 Positano. ☎ **089/875-400.** Fax 089/ 875-878. 48 rms, 10 junior suites. A/C MINIBAR TV TEL. 230,000L–340,000L ($138–$204) double; 350,000L–450,000L ($210–$270) junior suite. Rates include buffet breakfast. AE, DC, MC, V. Closed Nov–Mar. Parking 25,000L–30,000L ($15–$18).

You'll find this rambling yellow-ochre building a few steps above the port. It's a desirable choice for those who want to be in the swim of the summer action. The side closest to the water culminates in a rounded tower of rough-hewn stone, inside of which is an appealing restaurant open to the breezes and a firsthand view of the crashing waves. The bedrooms are comfortably furnished.

Buca di Bacco. Via Rampa Teglia 8, 84017 Positano. ☎ **089/875-699.** Fax 089/875-731. 54 rms. A/C MINIBAR TV TEL. 230,000L–280,000L ($138–$168) double. Rates include breakfast. AE, DC, MC, V. Closed Oct 31–Mar. Parking 30,000L–35,000L ($18–$21).

This is one of the best moderately priced hotels at the resort, with one of the best restaurants in the area (see "Dining," below). The main beach of Positano often draws guests who patronize only its bar, one of the best-known rendezvous points along the Amalfi Drive. A large terrace opens onto the beach, and you can enjoy a Campari and soda while still in your bathing suit. The oldest and most expensive part, the Buca Residence, was an old seaside mansion at the dawn of the 19th century. The rooms are well-furnished, with many facilities, including balconies that face the sea.

INEXPENSIVE

Casa Albertina. Via Tavolozza 4, 84017 Positano. ☎ **089/875-143.** Fax 089/811-540. 20 rms. A/C MINIBAR TV TEL. 180,000L–220,000L ($108–$132) double with breakfast; 300,000L– 320,000L ($180–$192) double with half board. Half board compulsory Apr–Oct. AE, DC, MC, V. Parking 30,000L ($18).

This villa guesthouse, up a steep and winding road, offers a view of the coastline from its hillside perch. Each bedroom is a gem, color coordinated in either mauve or blue. The rooms are furnished with well-selected pieces, such as gilt mirrors, fruitwood end tables, and bronze bed lamps. Each accommodation has wide French doors that lead out to a private balcony, and a few have Jacuzzis. You can have breakfast on the terra-cotta–tile terrace. The hotel also has a good restaurant that specializes in fresh grilled fish. Laundry service and a baby-sitter are available on request, and the hotel has both a bar and a solarium.

✪ **Palazzo Murat.** Via dei Mulini 23, 84017 Positano. ☎ **089/875-177.** Fax 089/811-419. 28 rms. MINIBAR TV TEL. 245,000L–320,000L ($147–$192) double. Rates include breakfast. AE, DC, MC, V. Closed Jan 1–one week before Easter. Parking 30,000L–35,000L ($18–$21).

For nostalgic atmosphere and Baroque style, this place has no equal in all of Positano. The jasmine and bougainvillea are so profuse in its garden that they spill over their enclosing wall onto the arbors of the narrow street outside. Once this was the sumptuous retreat of Napoléon I's brother-in-law, the king of Naples. Shell designs cap the villa windows, which look out over a cluster of orange trees and the wrought-iron tendrils of the gate that leads into the garden. To enlarge the property, a previous owner erected a comfortable annex in a style compatible with the original villa. Only breakfast is served. Nineteen rooms are air-conditioned.

WHERE TO DINE

Buca di Bacco. Via Rampa Teglia 8. ☎ **089/875-699.** Reservations required. Main courses 18,000L–40,000L ($10.80–$24). AE, DC, MC, V. Daily 12:30–3:30pm and 8–11pm. Closed Oct 31–Mar. CAMPANIA/ITALIAN.

Right on the beach you'll find one of Positano's top restaurants. Guests often stop for a drink in the bar before heading up to the dining room on a big covered terrace that faces the sea. On display are fresh fish, special salads, and fruit, including luscious black figs and freshly peeled oranges soaked in caramel. An exciting opener is a salad made with fruits of the sea, or you may prefer the *zuppa di cozze* (mussels), prepared with flair in a tangy sauce. The pasta dishes are homemade, and the meats are well prepared with fresh ingredients. Finish off with the chic after-dinner drink, *limoncello,* the lemon liqueur celebrated along the Amalfi Drive.

Chez Black. Via del Brigantino. ☎ **089/875-036.** Reservations required in summer. Main courses 10,000L–40,000L ($6–$24). AE, DC, MC, V. Apr–Oct, daily 12:30–3pm and 7:30–11pm; Nov–Mar, daily 12:30–3pm. Closed Jan 10–Feb 10. SEAFOOD.

The owner is Salvatore Russo, but for his restaurant he uses the suntan-inspired name that his friends gave him in college. Founded after World War II, the restaurant occupies a desirable position near the beach. In summer it's in the "eye of the hurricane" of action. The interior emulates an expensive yacht with varnished ribbing, a glowing sheath of softwood and brass, and semaphore symbols, which make it one of the most beautiful restaurants in town. A stone-edged aquarium holds fresh lobsters, and rack upon rack of local wines give diners a choice. Seafood is the specialty, as well as a wide selection of pizzas. The best-known dish is the spaghetti with crayfish, but you might also be tempted by linguine with fresh pesto, grilled swordfish, sole, or shrimp, along with an array of veal, liver, chicken, and beef dishes.

POSITANO AFTER DARK

Virtually anyone in town will agree that Positano and the nearby coast contain only two nightclubs that appeal to visitors' sense of style and whimsy. More convenient to Positano is **Music on the Rocks,** Spiaggia Grande (☎ **089/875-874**), designed on two levels, one of which contains a contemplative piano bar. Similar in its choice of music, clientele, and setting is **L'Africana,** Vettica Maggiore (☎ **089/874-042**), in the satellite resort of Praiano, about two miles from Positano. Local fishers come in during the most frenzied peak of the dancing, and dredge a sinkhole in the edge of the dance floor with nets, pulling up a bountiful catch of seafood for consumption in local restaurants. The contrast of new-age music with old-world folklore is as riveting as it is bizarre. Many chic guests from Positano often arrive here by boat. Both clubs are open nightly from June to August, but only Friday and Saturday in May and September, and they're closed the rest of the year—both occupy rough-edged grottos set close to sea level, and in winter storms they risk flooding.

3 Amalfi

38 miles SE of Naples, 11 miles E of Positano, 21 miles W of Salerno, 169 miles SE of Rome

From the 9th to the 11th century the seafaring Republic of Amalfi rivaled those great maritime powers, Genoa and Venice. Its maritime code, the Tavole Amalfitane, was used in the Mediterranean for centuries. But raids by Saracens and a flood in the 14th century devastated the city. Its power and influence weakened, until it rose again in modern times as the major resort on the Amalfi Drive.

From its position at the slope of the steep Lattari hills, it overlooks the Bay of Salerno. The approach to Amalfi is very dramatic, whether you come from Positano or from Salerno. Today Amalfi depends on tourist traffic, and the hotels and pensioni in dead center are right in the milling throng of holiday makers. The finest and most highly rated accommodations are on the outskirts.

ESSENTIALS

GETTING THERE   By Bus   SITA buses run every 2 hours during the day from Sorrento, for a one-way fare of 4,000L ($2.40). There are also SITA bus connections from Positano, a one-way ticket costing 2,000L ($1.20). Information about schedules is available in Amalfi by calling the **bus terminal** at the waterfront on Piazza Flavio Gioia (☎ **089/871-016**).

By Car   From Positano continue east along the Amalfi Drive (S163) with its narrow, hairpin turns.

VISITOR INFORMATION   The **tourist information center** is at Corso delle Repubbliche Marinare 19–21 (☎ **089/871-107**), open Monday to Friday 8am to 2pm and Saturday 8am to noon.

EXPLORING THE CATHEDRAL & THE EMERALD GROTTO

The ✪ **Duomo,** Piazza del Duomo (☎ **089/871-059**)—named in honor of St. Andrew (Sant'Andrea), whose remains are said to be buried inside the crypt—evokes Amalfi's rich past. Reached by climbing steep steps, the cathedral is characterized by its black-and-white facade and its mosaics. Inside, the one nave and two aisles are all richly baroqued. The cathedral dates back to the 11th century, although the present structure has been rebuilt. Its bronze doors were made in Constantinople and its campanile (bell tower) is from the 13th century, erected partially in the Romanesque style. The Duomo is open daily 7:30am to 8pm.

You can also visit the **"Cloister of Paradise" (Chiostro del Paradiso),** to the left of the Duomo, originally a necropolis for members of the Amalfitan "establishment." This graveyard dates from the 1200s and contains the broken columns and statues, as well as sarcophagi, of a long-gone civilization. The aura here is definitely Moorish, with a whitewashed quadrangle of interlaced arches. One of the treasures here is fragments of Cosmatesque work—brightly colored geometric mosaics. Once they formed parts of columns and altars, a specialty of this region of Italy. The arches here created an evocative setting for concerts, both piano and vocal, held here on Friday nights from July through September, with tickets costing 5,000L ($3). The cloister is open daily 9am to 7pm and charges 5,000L ($3) for admission. The crypt is reached from the cloister. Here lie the remains of St. Andrew—that is, everything, except his face. The Pope donated his face to St. Andrew's in Patras, Greece, but the back half of his head remained here.

A minor attraction, good for that rainy day, is the **Museo Civico,** Piazza Municipio (☎ **089/871-001**), which displays original manuscripts of the *Tavoliere Amalfitane.* This was the maritime code that governed the entire Mediterranean until 1570. Some exhibits relate to Flavio Gioia, Amalfi's most famous merchant adventurer. Amalfitani claim he invented the compass in the 12th century. "The sun, the moon, the stars and—Amalfi," locals used to say. What's left from the "attic" of their once great power is preserved here. The museum is free and open Monday to Saturday 9am to 1pm.

For your most scenic walk in Amalfi, start at Piazza del Duomo and head up Via Genova. The classic stroll will take you to the **Valle dei Mulini** (the Valley of the Mills), so called because of the paper mills along its rocky reaches (the seafaring republic is said to have acquainted Italy with the use of paper). You'll pass by fragrant gardens and scented citrus groves. If the subject interests you, you can learn more details about the industry at the **Museo della Carta,** Via Valle dei Mulini (☎ 089/ 872-615). It's filled with antique presses and yellowing manuscripts from yesterday. It's open Tuesday to Thursday and Saturday and Sunday 9am to 1pm. Admission is 2,000L ($1.20).

For the biggest attraction of all, head west to the ✪ **Emerald Grotto (Grotta di Smeraldo).** This ancient cavern, known for its light effects, is a millennia-old chamber of stalagmites and stalactites. Three miles west of Amalfi, the grotto is reached from the coastal road via a descent by elevator, which costs 5,000L ($3), including the boat ride. Then you board a boat that traverses the eerie world of the grotto. The stalagmites are unique in that some are underwater. You can visit daily 10am to 4pm. Take the SITA bus in Amalfi going toward Sorrento. The best way to go is by boat from Amalfi, leaving from the docks and costing 10,000L ($6) round trip, plus the 5,000L ($3) entry fee.

HITTING THE BEACH

Amalfi makes some pretension at being a beach resort, and tiny public beaches do flank both sides of the harbor. Many of the first-class and deluxe hotels have their own private beaches. However, better beaches are found at either Maiori or Minori, further along the coast and reached by buses leaving from Amalfi's Piazza Flavio Gioia (☎ 089/871-009). For fun, you can rent a boat at **Raffaele Florio** (☎ 089/ 872-147) on the beach close to the port area. Small boats cost 25,000L ($15) per hour. A little farther down, **Lido delle Sirene,** Piazza dei Protontini (☎ 089/ 871-489), also rents small boats, costing 60,000L ($36) for 2 hours. Lido della Sirene also offers waterskiing, costing 60,000L ($36) for 15 minutes.

SHOPPING

The coast has long been known for its ceramics, and the area at Piazza Duomo is filled with hawkers peddling "regional" ware. However, that region today often means Asia, especially Taiwan. But the real thing is still made at nearby **Vietri sul Mare,** west of Amalfi for 8 miles. The pottery made in Vietri is distinguished by its florid colors and sunny motifs. The best outlet in Vietri sul Mare is **Ceramica Solimene,** Via Madonna degli Angeli 7 (☎ 089/210-243), which has been producing quality terracotta ceramics for centuries. It's fabled for its production of lead-free surface tiles, dinner and cookware, umbrella holders, and stylish lamps. Although Solimene is the best, you might also check out **La Taverna Paradiso,** Via Diego Taiani (☎ 089/ 212-509); **La Sosta,** Via Costiera 6 (☎ 089/211-790), and **Pinto,** Corso Umberto I, 27 (☎ 089/210-271).

In Amalfi itself, the town's two most famous products involve drinking and writing, a combination that lots of professional journalists might find appealing. Limoncello, a sweet lemon-derived liqueur that tastes best chilled, is manufactured most visibly in town by the **Aceto** factories. You can drop by their headquarters on Via Chiarito to buy a bottle of the stuff (call ☎ 089/873-288 or 089/873-211 for information). The Aceto Group's product is marketed under the *Limoncello Cata* label, and is sold at many outlets throughout the town.

Looking for fancy paper whose design and high-rag content has been perfected in and around Amalfi for longer than virtually anyone can remember? You can visit the showroom at the **Amatruda** group, one of the town's larger and much-respected manufacturers, on Via Fiume, near the corner of the Valle dei Mulini (☎ 089/971-315). A worthy competitor, who manufactures the luxury items on a smaller scale, is **Antonio Cavaliere,** Via Fiume (☎ 089/871-954). Both outfits sell traditional, cream-colored, high-fiber versions that seem appropriate for invitations to a royal wedding, as well as versions that amalgamate dried flowers, faintly visible through the surface, into the manufacturing process.

If items other than paper appeal to you, head for one of Amalfi's most deeply entrenched retail outlets, **Criscuolo,** Largo Scario 2 (☎ 089/871-089). Established by the ancestors of the present owners in 1935 as a site selling only cigarettes and newspapers, it expanded over the decades into an outlet that specializes in jewelry, including a charming collection of cameos, locally crafted ceramics, and general memorabilia commemorating your visit to Amalfi.

WHERE TO STAY
VERY EXPENSIVE

✪ **Santa Caterina.** Strada Amalfitana, 84011 Amalfi. ☎ **089/871-012.** Fax 089/871-351. 70 rms, 11 suites. A/C MINIBAR TV TEL. 450,000L–540,000L ($270–$324) double; from 780,000L ($468) suite. Rates include breakfast. Half board 75,000L ($45) per person extra. AE, DC, MC, V. Parking 25,000L ($15) in the garage, free outside.

Perched on top of a cliff, the six-story Santa Caterina has an elevator that will take you down to a private beach. This "saint" is one of the most scenic accommodations around, dating from 1902, although the look today is more from the 30s. You're housed in the main structure or one of the small "villas" in the citrus groves along the slopes of the hill. The rooms are furnished in good taste, with an eye toward comfort. Most have private balconies that face the sea. The furniture respects the tradition of the house, and in every room there's an antique piece. The bathrooms are spacious, with luxurious fittings, and each has a hair dryer.

Dining/Entertainment: The food here is among the best at Amalfi. Many of the vegetables are grown in the hotel's garden, and the fish tastes so fresh that we suspect the chef has an agreement with local fishers to bring in the "catch of the day." Once or twice a week there's a special evening buffet accompanied by music.

Services: Room service, baby-sitting, laundry, valet.

Facilities: Saltwater pool.

EXPENSIVE

Hotel Luna Convento. Via Pantaleone Comite 33, 84011 Amalfi. ☎ **089/871-002.** Fax 089/871-333. 45 rms. TV TEL. 250,000L–300,000L ($150–$180) double including breakfast; half board (compulsory in summer) 350,000L–420,000L ($210–$252) per person. AE, DC, MC, V. Parking 20,000L ($12).

This hotel—the best in Amalfi except for the Santa Caterina—boasts a 13th-century cloister said to have been founded by St. Francis of Assisi. Most of the building, however, was rebuilt in 1975. The long corridors, where monks of old used to tread, and in time Wagner and Ibsen, are lined with sitting areas used by the most unmonastic guests seeking a tan. The bedrooms have sea views, terraces, and modern furnishings, although many are uninspired in decor. The rather formal dining room has a coved ceiling, high-backed chairs, arched windows that open toward the water, and good food (Italian and international). The hotel has a nightclub that projects toward the sea, and in summer dancing is offered in the piano bar. A free-form swimming pool is nestled on the rocks, near the sound of the surf and sea gulls.

MODERATE

Excelsior Grand Hotel. Via Pogerola, 84011 Amalfi. ☎ **089/830-015.** Fax 089/830-255. 97 rms. TEL. 120,000L–185,000L ($72–$111) per person. Rates include full board. AE, DC, MC, V.

Two miles north of Amalfi at Pogerola, the Excelsior is a modern first-class hotel on a high mountain perch. All its rooms are angled toward the view so you get the first glimmer of sunrise and the last rays of sunlight. The social center is the terrazzo-edged swimming pool filled with filtered mountain spring water. The hotel structure is unconventional—a high octagonal glass tower that rises above the central lobby, with exposed mezzanine lounges and an open staircase. The bedrooms are individually designed, with plenty of room, with many good reproductions, some antiques, king-size beds, and tile floors. The private balconies, complete with garden furniture, are the most important feature. The dignified dining room serves Italian cuisine with Gallic overtones. At the Bar del Night, musicians play for dancing on weekends. Transportation to and from the private beach is provided by boat and bus for 15,000L ($9).

INEXPENSIVE

Hotel Belvedere. Via Smeraldo, Conca dei Marini, 84011 Amalfi. ☎ **089/831-282.** Fax 089/831-439. 36 rms. TEL. 145,000L–170,000L ($87–$102) per person, per day, double occupancy, depending on the season. Rates include half board. AE, DC, MC, V. Closed Oct 15–Apr 15.

Lodged below the coastal road outside Amalfi on the drive to Positano, the aptly named Belvedere has one of the best pools in the area. The house originated as a private villa in the 1860s and was transformed by its present owners into a hotel in 1962. It's in a prime location, just two miles from the center of Amalfi, hidden from the view and noise of the heavily traveled road, and thrust out toward the sea. The rooms have terraces that overlook the water, and some offer air conditioning. Signor Lucibello, who owns the hotel, sees to it that guests are content, and there's a shuttle bus into Amalfi. You can dine on well-prepared Italian meals either inside (where walls of windows allow for views of the coast) or on the front terrace. There's also a cocktail bar.

Hotel Lidomare. Largo Duchi Piccolomini 9, 84011 Amalfi. ☎ **089/871-332.** Fax 089/871-394. 15 rms. MINIBAR TV TEL. 90,000L–100,000L ($54–$60) double. Rates include breakfast. AE, DC, MC, V. Parking 15,000L ($9).

This pleasant, small hotel is just a few steps from the sea, and its building dates from the 13th century. The high-ceilinged bedrooms are airy and clean, and contain a scattering of modern furniture mixed with Victorian-era antiques. The Camera family extends a warm welcome to their never-ending stream of foreign visitors. Most of the bedrooms have air-conditioning, and they promise to add it to all by the end of 1998. Breakfast is the only meal served, but you can order it until 11:30am. This hotel is one of the best bargains in Amalfi.

Hotel Miramalfi. Via Quasimodo 3, 84011 Amalfi. ☎ **089/871-588.** Fax 089/871-287. 43 rms, 4 suites. A/C MINIBAR TV TEL. 180,000L–230,000L ($108–$138) double; 280,000L–330,000L ($168–$198) suite. Rates include breakfast. Half board 125,000L–170,000L ($75–$102) per person extra. AE, DC, MC, V. Parking 15,000L ($9).

On the western edge of Amalfi, the Miramalfi lies below the coastal road and beneath a rocky ledge on its own beach. The rooms are wrapped around the curving contour of the coastline and have unobstructed views of the sea. The stone swimming pier—used for sunbathing, diving, and boarding motor launches for waterskiing—is down a winding cliffside path, past terraces of grapevines. The dining room has glass windows and some semitropical plants; the food is good and served in abundant portions. Breakfast is served on one of the main terraces or on your own balcony. Each bedroom is well equipped, with built-in headboards, fine beds, cool tile floors, and efficient maintenance. There's a swimming pool and an elevator to the private beach.

Marina Riviera. Via Comite 9, 84011 Amalfi. ☎ **089/872-394.** Fax 089/871-024. 20 rms. A/C MINIBAR TV TEL. 180,000L–200,000L ($108–$120) double. Rates include breakfast. AE, MC, V. Closed Oct 31–Mar. Parking 15,000L ($9).

Just 50 yards from the beach, this hotel offers rooms with terraces that overlook the sea. Directly on the coastal road, it rises against the foot of the hills, with side verandas and balconies. Two adjoining public lounges are traditionally furnished, and a small bar provides drinks whenever you want them. The newly refurbished rooms are comfortable, with a balcony and such amenities as a hair dryer. There's a gracious dining room with high-backed provincial chairs, but we suggest that you dine alfresco. A restaurant called Eolo opened in the spring of 1995 right below the hotel and is under the same management.

WHERE TO DINE

Da Gemma. Via Frà Gerardo Sassi 9. ☎ **089/871-345.** Reservations required. Main courses 18,000L–50,000L ($10.80–$30). AE, DC, MC, V. Feb–July and Sept–Dec, Thurs–Tues 12:30–3pm and 8pm–midnight, Aug, Thurs–Tues 8pm–midnight. SEAFOOD/MEDITERRANEAN.

One of the best restaurants in town, Da Gemma takes inspired liberties with the regional cuisine and gives diners a strong sense of the family unity that makes this place popular. The kitchen sends out plateful after plateful of savory spaghetti, sautéed mixed shellfish, fish casserole, and a full range of other sea creature dishes. In summer the intimate dining room more than doubles with the addition of an outdoor terrace.

La Caravella-Amalfi. Via Matteo Camera 12. ☎ **089/871-029.** Reservations required. Main courses 15,000L–45,000L ($9–$27). AE, DC, MC, V. Daily 12:30–2:30pm and 7:30–11pm. Closed Nov and Tues Sept 1–July 31. CAMPANIA.

La Caravella is a leading restaurant and, happily, it's inexpensive. A grottolike, air-conditioned place, it's off the main street next to the road tunnel, only a minute from the beach. You get well-cooked, authentic Italian specialties, such as spaghetti Caravella with a seafood sauce, or fresh fish with lemon. *Scaloppine alla Caravella* is served with a tangy clam sauce, and a healthy portion of *zuppa di pesce* (fish soup) is also ladled out. You can have a platter of the mixed fish fry, with crisp, tasty bits of shrimp and squid, followed by an order of fresh fruit served at your table in big bowls.

4 Ravello

171 miles SE of Rome, 41 miles SE of Naples, 18 miles W of Salerno

Known to long-ago personages ranging from Richard Wagner to Greta Garbo—even D. H. Lawrence, who wrote *Lady Chatterley's Lover* here—Ravello is the choice spot along the Amalfi Drive. It's where "poets go to die," or so it is said. Its reigning celebrity at the moment is Gore Vidal, who purchased a villa as a writing retreat. Other writers have also been inspired by the spot, including André Gide. William Stryon set his novel, *Set This House on Fire*, here. Boccaccio dedicated part of the *Decameron* to Ravello, and John Huston used it as a location for his film, *Beat the Devil*, with Bogie. The village seems to hang 1,100 feet up, between the Tyrrhenian Sea and some celestial orbit. You approach this sleepy (except for summer tour buses) village from Amalfi, 4 miles to the southwest, by a wickedly curving road that cuts through the villa- and vine-draped hills that hem in the Valley of the Dragone. Celebrated in poetry, song, and literature are Ravello's major attractions, two villas.

ESSENTIALS

GETTING THERE   By Bus   Buses from Amalfi leave for Ravello from the terminal at the waterfront at Piazza Flavio Gioia (☎ **089/871-016** for schedules and information) every hour from 7am to 10pm. The one-way fare to Ravello is 1,500L (90¢).

By Car   From Amalfi, take a circuitous mountain road north of the town (the road is signposted to Ravello).

VISITOR INFORMATION   The **tourist information center** is at Piazza del Duomo 10 (☎ **089/857-096**). It's open May to September, Monday to Saturday 8am to 8pm (to 7pm October to April).

FABULOUS VILLAS & THE DUOMO

Villa Cimbrone. Via Santa Chiara 26. ☎ **089/857-459**. Admission 8,000L ($4.80) adults, 5,000L ($3) children. Daily 9am–sunset.

A long walk past grape arbors and private villas takes you to the Villa Cimbrone. After ringing the bell for admission, you'll be shown into the vaulted cloisters (on the left as you enter); note the grotesque bas-relief. Later you can stroll (everybody "strolls" in Ravello) through the gardens, past a bronze copy of Donatello's *David*. Along the rose-arbored walkway is a tiny, roofless chapel. At the far end of the garden is a cliffside view of the Bay of Salerno, a scene that the devout might claim was the spot where Satan took Christ to tempt him with the world. Gore Vidal called the view "the most beautiful in the world." Look for the Temple of Bacchus, where Lord Grimthorpe is buried. This eccentric Englishman who created the villa died in London in 1917 but wished to be buried here with his enigmatic inscription: "Lost to a world in which I crave no part, I sit alone and commune with my heart, pleased with my little corner of earth. Glad that I came not sorry to depart."

Villa Rufolo. Piazza Vescovado. ☎ **089/857-657**. Admission 5,000L ($3) adults, 3,000L ($1.80) children. Oct–Apr, daily 9am–6pm; May–Sept, daily 9am–8pm.

Villa Rufolo was named for the patrician family who founded it in the 11th century. Once the residence of kings and popes, such as Hadrian IV, it's now remembered chiefly for its connection with Richard Wagner. He composed an act of *Parsifal* here in a setting he dubbed the "Garden of Klingsor." Boccaccio was so moved by the spot that he included it as background in one of his tales. The Moorish-influenced architecture evokes the Alhambra at Granada. The large tower was built in what is known as the "Norman-Sicilian" style. You can walk through the flower gardens that lead to lookout points over the memorable coastline.

Duomo. Piazza Vescovado. Admission: Duomo, free; museum, 2,000L ($1.20). Duomo, daily 9am–1pm and 3–7pm. Museum, May–Sept, daily 9am–7:30pm; Oct, daily 9am–5pm.

It's unusual for such a small place to have a cathedral, but Ravello boasts one because it was once a major bishopric. The building itself dates from the 11th century, although its bronze doors are the work of Barisano da Trani, crafted in 1179. Its campanile or bell tower was erected in the 13th century. One of its major treasures is the family pulpit of the Rufolo family, decorated with intricate mosaics and supported by spiral columns resting on the backs of a half dozen white marble lions. This is the work of Nicolò di Bartolomeo da Foggia in 1272. Another less intricate pulpit from 1130 features two large mosaics of Jonah being eaten and regurgitated by a dragon-like green whale. Left of the altar is the Chapel of San Pantaleone, the patron saint of Ravello to whom the cathedral is dedicated. His "unleakable" blood is preserved here in a cracked vessel. The saint was beheaded at Nicomedia on July 27, 290 A.D. When Ravello holds a festival on that day every year the saint's blood is said to liquefy. A minor museum of religious artifacts is also on site.

WHERE TO STAY

The choice of accommodations at Ravello is limited in number, but large on charm. Ristorante Garden (see "Dining," below) also rents rooms.

VERY EXPENSIVE

✪ Hotel Palumbo/Palumbo Residence. Via San Giovanni del Toro 28, 84010 Ravello. ☎ **089/857-244.** Fax 089/858-133. 27 rms, 3 suites. A/C MINIBAR TV TEL. Hotel, 400,000L–600,000L ($240–$360) double; from 650,000L ($390) suite. Residence, 260,000L–320,000L ($156–$192) double. Rates include breakfast. AE, DC, MC, V. Parking 25,000L ($15).

This elite retreat on the Amalfi Coast, a 12th-century palace, has been favored by the famous ever since composer Richard Wagner persuaded the Swiss owners, the Vuilleumier family, to take in paying guests. If you stay here you'll understand why Humphrey Bogart, Henry Wadsworth Longfellow, Ingrid Bergman, Zsa Zsa Gabor, Tennessee Williams, Richard Chamberlain, and a young John and Jacqueline Kennedy found it ideal. D. H. Lawrence even wrote part of *Lady Chatterley's Lover* while staying here.

The hotel offers gracious living in its drawing rooms, furnished with English and Italian antiques. Most of the snug but elegantly decorated bedrooms have their own terrace. The original Hotel Palumbo contains by far the more glamorous and better-accessoried accommodations; seven functional rooms are in the modern annex (1950s vintage) in the garden, but a few have sea views.

Dining/Entertainment: Meals are served in a 17th-century dining room with Baroque accents and a panoramic dining terrace. The cuisine, the finest in Ravello, shows the influence of the Swiss-Italian ownership. It's worth visiting just for the lemon and chocolate soufflés. The Palumbo also produces its own Episcopio wine, stored in 50,000L–liter casks in a vaulted cellar.

Services: Room service, baby-sitting, laundry, valet.

Facilities: Solarium overlooking the Gulf of Salerno.

✪ Hotel Villa Cimbrone. Via Santa Chiara 26, 84010 Ravello. ☎ **089/857-459.** Fax 089/857-777. 17 rms, 2 suites. MINIBAR TEL. 330,000L–400,000L ($198–$240) double; 500,000L ($300) suite. Rates include breakfast. AE, V. Closed mid-Nov–Easter.

Enchantment itself, this villa rises at the south side of Ravello on its most panoramic point. Set in lush gardens, a 10-minute walk from the center, it stands on a site of a patrician palace from the 12th century, which was probably constructed on the ruins of a Roman villa. In the 20th century, eccentric English nobleman Lord Grimthorpe built a villa here, which has hosted the likes of D. H. Lawrence, E. M. Forster, Virginia Woolf, Churchill, and even those "illicit" lovers, Greta Garbo running off with Leopold Stokowsky. Recently renewed, the hotel rooms offer living on a grand style as you sleep in the same bedrooms once enjoyed by the Duke and Duchess of Kent. Period furniture and frescoed ceilings along with all the grace, charm, and style of the early part of this century reacquaint visitors with a way of life virtually faded. Breakfast is the only meal served.

EXPENSIVE

Hotel Caruso Belvedere. Via San Giovanni del Toro, 84010 Ravello. ☎ **089/857-111.** Fax 089/857-372. 26 rms. TEL. Nov–Mar 180,000L–280,000L ($108–$168) double; Apr–Oct and Christmas 147,000L–197,000L ($88.20–$118.20) per person with compulsory half board. AE, DC, MC, V. Parking 10,000L ($6) in the garage, free outside.

This spacious clifftop hotel, built into the remains of an 11th-century palace, is operated by the Caruso family, descended from the great Enrico himself. Some of the most famous people of the 20th century, including Greta Garbo, have stayed here. This property has semitropical gardens and a belvedere that looks over terraced rows of grapes, used to make their "Grand Caruso" wine, to the Bay of Salerno. Although antiques appear here and there, many bedrooms are rather plain, about on the same level as some of the town's economy-minded inns. The best rooms have sunrooms for breakfast and open onto "oh, that view" terraces.

Dining/Entertainment: The indoor dining room has the original coved ceiling, plus tile floors. It opens onto a wide terrace where meals are also served under a canopy. Naturally, the locally produced wines are touted.

Services: Room service, baby-sitting, laundry, valet.

MODERATE

Hotel Giordano e Villa Maria. Piazza del Duomo, Via S. Chiara 2, 84010 Ravello. ☎ **089/857-255.** Fax 089/857-071. 46 rms, 2 suites. A/C TV TEL. Hotel Giordano: 160,000L–180,000L ($96–$108) double; Villa Maria: 210,000L–240,000L ($126–$144) double; 320,000L–460,000L ($192–$276) suite. Rates include breakfast. AE, DC, MC, V.

The older, but more obviously modernized, of these two hotels is the Giordano, built in the late 1700s as a private manor house of the family who runs it today. In the 1970s the owners bought the neighboring 19th-century Villa Maria. The two operate as quasi-independent hotels with shared facilities. Accommodations in the Villa Maria are more glamorous than those in the Hotel Giordano, and usually contain high ceilings, a scattering of antiques, and sea views. The rooms in the Hotel Giordano have garden views and conservative reproductions of traditional furniture. You'll find a large heated pool near the Giordano, at least two bars, and a pair of restaurants. (Unlike its twin, the Villa Maria restaurant remains open throughout the winter and has a panoramic view of the sea.) The beach is a 15-minute walk along ancient pathways (you can also take a public bus from Ravello's central square every hour).

Hotel Parsifal. Via G. D'Anna 5, 84010 Ravello. ☎ **089/857-144.** Fax 089/857-972. 19 rms. TV TEL. 105,000L–115,000L ($63–$69) per person double. Rates include half board. AE, DC, MC, V. Closed Oct 15–Easter.

This little hotel incorporates portions of a convent founded in 1288 by Augustinian monks, who had an uncanny instinct for picking spots with inspiring views on which to build their retreats. The cloister, with stone arches and a tile walk, has a multitude of potted flowers and vines, and the garden spots, especially the one with a circular reflection pool, are the favorites of all. There are chairs placed for watching the setting sun that illuminates the twisting shoreline in fiery lights. Dining is on the trellis-covered terrace where bougainvillea and wisteria scents mix with that of lemon blossoms. The living rooms have bright and comfortable furnishings, set against pure white walls. The bedrooms, although small, are tastefully arranged, and a few have terraces.

Hotel Rufolo. Via San Francesco 3, 84010 Ravello. ☎ **089/857-133.** Fax 089/857-935. 26 rms, 6 suites. A/C MINIBAR TV TEL. 270,000L–300,000L ($162–$180) double; 380,000L–410,000L ($228–$246) suite. Rates include breakfast. AE, DC, MC, V.

This little gem housed D. H. Lawrence for a long while in 1926. The view from the sun decks is superb, and chairs are placed on a wide terrace and around the pool. The bedrooms are cozy and immaculate, some with air-conditioning, and the suites have Jacuzzis. Recently enlarged and modernized, the hotel lies in the center between cloisters of pine trees of the Villa Rufolo, from which the hotel takes its name, and the road that leads to the Villa Cimbrone. Mr. Schiavo and his family take good care of their guests. The restaurant is quite good, and the service is efficient.

INEXPENSIVE

Albergo Toro. Viale Wagner 3, 84010 Ravello. ☎ and fax **089/857211.** 9 rms. TEL. 95,000L–105,000L ($57–$63) double. Rates include breakfast, 140,000L–180,000L ($84–$108) double including half-board. AE, MC, V. Closed Nov 6–Mar.

This place is a real bargain. It's a small, charming villa that has been converted to receive paying guests. The Toro—entered through a garden—lies just off the village square with its cathedral. It has semimonastic architecture, with deeply set arches, long colonnades, and a tranquil character. The rooms are decent, and the owner is especially proud of the meals he serves.

WHERE TO DINE

Most guests take meals at their hotels. But try to escape the board requirement at least once to sample the goods at the following establishments.

Cumpa'Cosimo. Via Roma. ☎ **089/857-156.** Reservations recommended. Main courses 12,000L–35,000L ($7.20–$21); fixed-price menus 18,000L–25,000L ($10.80–$15). AE, DC, V. Daily 12:30–3pm and 7:30–10pm. Closed Mon Nov 10–Dec 9 and Jan 11–Mar 10. CAMPANIA.

You're likely to find here everyone from the electrician down the street to a well-known movie star searching for the best home-cooking in town. It was established as an offshoot to a nearby butcher shop in 1929 by a town patriarch known affectionately as Cumpa' (godfather) Cosimo and his wife, Cumma' (godmother) Chiara. Today their daughter, the kindly Netta Bottone, runs the place, turning out well-flavored regional food in generous portions. Menu items include homemade versions of seven different pastas, served with your choice of seven different sauces. Any of these might be followed by a mixed grill of fish, giant prawns, or roasted lamb well seasoned with herbs. The seasonal availability of vegetables is respected, as the restaurant offers artichokes, asparagus, or mushrooms. Certain fish dishes are priced according to weight based on daily market quotations.

Ristorante Garden. Via Boccacio 4. ☎ **089/857-226.** Main courses 13,000L–25,000L ($7.80–$15). AE, DC, MC, V. Apr–Sept, daily noon–2:30pm and 7:30–10pm; Nov–Mar, Wed–Mon noon–2:30pm and 7:30–10pm. CAMPANIA.

This pleasant restaurant's greatest claim to fame occurred in 1962 when Jacqueline Onassis, then the wife of President Kennedy, came from a villa where she was staying to dine here with the owner of Fiat. Today some of that old glamor is still visible on the verdant terrace, which was designed to cantilever over the cliff below. The Mansi family offers well-prepared meals, which might include one of four kinds of spaghetti, cheese crêpes, and an array of soups, a well-presented antipasto table, brochettes of grilled shrimp, a mixed fish fry, and sole prepared in several ways. One of the local wines will be recommended. They also rent 10 well-scrubbed double rooms, each with its own bath and terrace, for 100,000 to 120,000L ($60 to $72), including breakfast.

RAVELLO AFTER DARK

The hilltop town is known for its summer classical music festivals. Sometimes internationally famed artists appear here. The venues range from the Duomo to the gardens of Villa Rufolo. Tickets, which can be purchased at the tourist office, start at 30,000L ($18).

5 Paestum

25 miles S of Salerno, 62 miles SE of Naples, 189 miles SE of Rome

The ancient city of Paestum (Poseidonia) dates back to 600 B.C., founded by colonists from the Greek city of Sybaris, which was located in today's Calabria (the "toe" of Italy's boot). It was abandoned for centuries and fell to ruins. But the remnants of its past, excavated in the mid-18th century, are glorious—the finest heritage left from the Greek colonies that settled in Italy. The roses of Paestum, praised by the ancients, bloom two times yearly, splashing the landscape of the city with a scarlet red, a good foil for the salmon-colored temples that still stand in the archeological garden.

ESSENTIALS

GETTING THERE   By Train   Paestum is within easy reach of Salerno, an hour away. Both buses and trains service the route. You can catch a southbound train, which departs Salerno with a stop at Paestum about every 2 hours. For schedules, call ☎ 089/252-200 in Salerno. A one-way fare is 4,200L ($2.50), and the journey takes an hour.

By Bus   The bus from Salerno leaves from Piazza Concordia (near the rail station) about every 30 minutes. Call ☎ 089/255-899 for information. A one-way fare is 4,300L ($2.60).

By Car   From Salerno, take S18 south.

VISITOR INFORMATION   The **tourist information center** is at Via Magna Grecia 151—156 (☎ 0828/811-016), in the archeological zone. It's open Monday to Saturday 8am to 2pm.

EXPLORING THE TEMPLES

The ✪ **basilica** is a Doric temple that dates from the 6th century B.C., the oldest temple from the ruins of the Hellenic world in Italy. The basilica is characterized by 9 columns in front and 18 on the sides. The Doric pillars are approximately five feet in diameter. The walls and ceiling, however, long ago gave way to decay. Animals were sacrificed to the gods on the altar.

The **Temple of Neptune** is the most impressive of the Greek ruins at Paestum. It and the Temple of Haphaistos ("Theseum") in Athens remain the best-preserved Greek temples in the world, both dating from around 450 to 420 B.C. Six columns in front are crowned by an entablature, and there are 14 columns on each side. The **Temple of Ceres,** from the 6th century B.C., has 34 columns still standing and a large altar for sacrifices to the gods.

The temple zone may be visited daily 9am to sunset for 8,000L ($4.80) adults; children under 18 and seniors over 60 are admitted free. Using the same ticket, you can visit the **Museo Archeologico Nazionale di Paestum,** Via Magna Grecia 169 (☎ 0828/811-023), across the road from the Ceres Temple. It displays the metopes removed from the treasury of the Temple of Hera (Juno) and some of southern Italy's finest tomb paintings from the 4th century B.C. *The Diver's Tomb* is an extraordinary example of painting from the first half of the 5th century B.C. The museum is open 9am to 7pm daily (closed the first and third Monday of every month).

New discoveries have revealed hundreds of Greek tombs, which have yielded many Greek paintings. Archeologists have called the finds astonishing. In addition, other excavated tombs were found to contain clay figures in a strongly impressionistic vein.

WHERE TO STAY & DINE

Strand Hotel Schuhmann. Via Laura Mare, 84063 Paestum. ☎ **0828/851-151.** Fax 0828/851-183. 36 rms. A/C MINIBAR TV TEL. 180,000L–310,000L ($108–$186) double. Rates include half board. AE, DC, MC, V.

If you'd like to combine serious looks at Italy's archeological past with the first-class amenities of a beachside resort, try the Strand Hotel Schuhmann, a delightful choice for a holiday. Set in a pine grove removed from traffic noises, the hotel has a large terrace with a view of the sea and a subtropical garden that overlooks the Gulf of Salerno and the Amalfi Coast to Capri. Its bedrooms are well furnished and maintained, and each has a balcony or terrace. Guests get use of the beach facilities and deck chairs. The hotel also has a restaurant.

Nettuno Ristorante. Zona Archeologica. ☎ **0828/811-028.** Main courses 20,000L–30,000L ($12–$18). AE, MC, V. July–Aug, daily 7:30–10pm; May–June and Sept–Oct, daily 12:30–3pm; Nov–Feb, Tues–Sun 12:30–3pm. CAMPANESE.

If you're looking for lunch, try this special place standing in a meadow just at the edge of the ruins, like a country inn or villa. The interior dining room has vines growing over its arched windows, and from the tables there's a good view of the ruins. The ceilings are beamed, the room divided by three Roman stone arches. Outside is a dining terrace that faces the temples—like a stage for a Greek drama. Under pine trees, hedged in by pink oleander, you can order such a typical selection as beefsteak or roast chicken, a vegetable or salad, plus dessert. Menu suggestions include spaghetti with filets in tomato sauce, veal cutlet, and crème caramel.

6 Capri

3 miles off the tip of the Sorrentine peninsula

The broiling dog-day July and August sun that beats down on Capri illuminates a circus of humanity. The parade of visitors would give Ripley's "Believe It or Not" material for months. In the upper town, a vast snakelike chain of gaudily attired tourists promenades through the narrow quarters (many of the lanes evoke the casbahs of North Africa).

The Greeks called Capri (pronounced *Cap*-ry, not Ca-*pree*) "the island of the wild boars." Before the big season rush, which lasts from Easter to the end of October, Capri is an island of lush Mediterranean vegetation (olives, vineyards, flowers) encircled by emerald waters, an oasis in the sun even before the emperor Tiberius moved the seat of the empire here. Writers such as D. H. Lawrence have in previous decades found Capri a haven. Some have written of it, including Axel Munthe (*The Story of San Michele*) and Norman Douglas (*Siren Land*). The latter title is a reference to Capri's reputation as the "island of the sirens" that tempted Ulysses. Other distinguished visitors have included Mendelssohn, Dumas, and Hans Christian Andersen.

Don't visit Capri, incidentally, for great beaches. The mountainous landscape doesn't make for long sandy beaches. There are some spots for bathing, but many of these have been turned into clubs called *stabilimenti balneari*, which you must pay to visit.

Capri

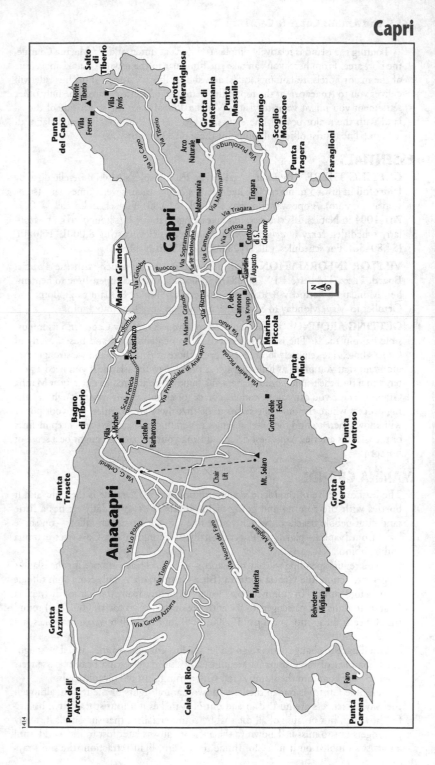

Touring the island is relatively simple. You dock at unremarkable **Marina Grande,** the port area. From here, you can take the funicular to the town of **Capri** above, site of the major hotels, restaurants, cafés, and shops. From Capri, a short bus ride will deliver you to **Anacapri,** at the top of the island near Monte Solaro. The only other settlement you might want to visit is **Marina Piccola,** on the south side of the island with the major beach. There are also beaches at Punta Carnea and Bagni di Tiberio. The tourist office will pinpoint these on a map for you.

ESSENTIALS

GETTING THERE   By Boat   You can go from Naples's Molo Beverello dock by **hydrofoil** in just 45 minutes. The hydrofoil (*aliscafo*) leaves several times daily (some stop at Sorrento). A one-way trip costs 18,000L ($10.80). For schedules, call ☎ **081/ 761-1004** in Naples. It's cheaper, but takes longer (about 1¹/₂ hours), to go by regularly scheduled **ferry** (*traghetto*), with a one-way ticket costing 8,000L–10,000L ($4.80–$6). For schedules, call ☎ **081/551-3882** in Naples.

VISITOR INFORMATION   For information, get in touch with the **Tourist Board,** Piazza Umberto I 19 (☎ **081/837-0686**), at Capri, open June to September, Monday to Saturday 8:30am to 8:30pm and Sunday 8:30am to 2:30pm; and October to May, Monday to Saturday 9am to 1pm and 3:30 to 6:45pm.

GETTING AROUND   There's no need to have a car in tiny Capri with its impossible hairpin roads. The island is serviced by funiculars, taxis, and buses. Many of Capri's hotels are remotely located, especially those at Anacapri, and we strongly recommend that you bring as little luggage as possible to the island. If you need a porter, you'll find their union headquarters in a building connected to the jetty at Marina Grande. There you can cajole, coddle, coerce, or connive your way through the hiring process where the only rule seems to be that there are no rules. But your porter will know where to find the hotel among the winding passageways and steep inclines of the island's arteries. Your best defense during your pilgrimage might be a sense of humor.

MARINA GRANDE

The least attractive of the island's communities, Marina Grande is the port, and it bustles with the coming and going of hundreds of visitors daily. It has a little sand-cum-pebble beach, on which you're likely to see American sailors—on shore leave from Naples—playing ball, occasionally upsetting a Coca-Cola over mamma and bambino.

If you're just spending the day on Capri, you should leave at once for the island's biggest attraction, the **Grotta Azzurra (Blue Grotto),** open daily from 9am till one hour before sunset. In summer boats leave frequently from the harbor at Marina Grande to transport passengers to the entrance of the grotto for 10,000L ($6) round trip. Once at the grotto, you'll pay 15,000L ($9) for the small rowboat that takes you inside.

You'll have to change boats to go under the low entrance to the cave. The toughened boatmen of the Campania are unusually skilled at getting heavier passengers from the big boat into the skimpy craft with a minimum of volcanic spills.

The Blue Grotto is one of the best-known natural sights of the region, although the way passengers are hustled in and out of it makes it a tourist trap. It *is* beautiful, however, but because of all the shabby commercialism that surrounds it, many passengers opt to miss it. Known to the ancients, it was later lost to the world until an artist stumbled on it in 1826. Inside the cavern, light refraction (the sun's rays entering from an opening under the water) achieves the dramatic Mediterranean cerulean color. The effect is stunning, as thousands testify yearly.

If you wish, you can take a **trip around the entire island,** passing not only the Blue Grotto, but the Baths of Tiberius, the "Palazzo al Mare" built in the days of the empire, the Green Grotto (less known), and the much-photographed rocks called the Faraglioni. Motorboats circle the island in about 1¹/₂ hours at a cost of 25,000L ($15) per person.

Connecting Marina Grande with Capri (the town) is a frequently running **funicular** that charges 1,500L (90¢) one-way. However, the funicular, really a cog railway, doesn't operate off-season. Instead, you take a bus from Marina Grande to Capri (same price).

SOME GOOD PLACES TO GO SWIMMING

In lieu of great beaches, the **Bagni Nettuno,** Via Grotta Azzurra 46 (☎ 081/837-1362), is often a magnet in summer. This swimming pool is found above the Blue Grotto in Anacapri, and it's surrounded by scenic cliffsides, the most dramatic place to swim on the island. From the cove here, you can actually swim into the Blue Grotto. The entrance to the grotto, however, is small and rocky, and boats during the day will prevent swimming. Admission to the pool is 15,000L ($9), and hours are daily 9am to 7pm but only from mid-March to mid-November.

Another preferred spot is **Bagni di Tiberio,** a bathing beach amid the ruins of an imperial villa. To reach it, take a boat for 8,000L ($4.80) from Marina Grande to the site. Or else you can walk it, descending north between vineyards to Piazza Umberto. Another place to swim is **Marina Piccola,** where you can swim among lava rocks. At Marina Piccola from a beach kiosk you can rent a motor boat for 30,000L ($18) per hour or else a kayak for 8,000L ($4.80) per hour. Call **Bagni le Sirene** at ☎ 081/837-7688 for rental information. Also at Marina Grande you can contact **Sercomar,** largo Fontana 64 (☎ 081/837-8781) about snorkeling or scuba diving. They'll also rent you an inflatable motorboat from 60,000L ($36) per hour.

CAPRI—A PARK, A PLEASURE PALACE & A MONASTERY

The main town is the center of most of the hotels, restaurants, and elegant shops—and the milling throngs. The heart of the resort, Piazza Umberto I, is like a grand living room.

One of the most popular walks from the main square is down Via Vittorio Emanuele, past the deluxe Quisisana, to the **Giardini di Augusto.** The park is the choice spot on Capri for views and relaxation. From this perch, you can see the legendary I Faraglioni, the rocks, once inhabited by the "blue lizard." At the top of the park is a belvedere that overlooks emerald waters and Marina Piccola. Nearby you can visit the **Certosa,** a Carthusian monastery erected in the 14th century in honor of St. James. The monastery is open Tuesday to Sunday 9am to 2pm and charges no admission.

Back at Piazza Umberto I, head up Via Longano, then Via Tiberio, all the way to Monte Tiberio. Here is the **Villa Jovis,** the splendid ruin of the estate from which Tiberius ruled the empire from A.D. 27 to 37. Actually, the Jovis was one of a dozen villas that the depraved emperor erected on the island. Apparently Tiberius couldn't sleep, so he wandered from bed to bed, exploring his "nooks of lechery," a young girl one hour, a young boy the next. From the ruins there's a view of both the Bay of Salerno and the Bay of Naples, as well as of the island. The ruins of the imperial palace may be visited daily 9am to one hour before sunset for 4,000L ($2.40) admission. For information, call the tourist board (☎ 081/837-0686).

SHOPPING   A little shop on Capri's luxury shopping street, **Carthusia-Profumi di Capri** Via Camerelle 10 (☎ 081/837-0368) specializes in perfume made on the island from local herbs and flowers. Since 1948 this shop has attracted such clients as Elizabeth Taylor—before she started touting her own perfume. The scents are unique, and many women consider Carthusia perfumes collector's items.

Carthusia also has a **perfume laboratory,** at Via Matteotti 2 (☎ **081/837-0368**), which you can visit daily 9am to 7pm. There's another Carthusia shop in Anacapri, at Via Capodimonte 26 (☎ 081/837-3668), next to the Villa Axel Munthe. The shops close January to March and on Sunday in March, October, November, and December.

Limoncello, Via Capodimonte 27 (☎ 081/837-2927), is the home of *Limoncello,* the most famous liqueur in the world. The liqueur contains alcohol, is made from lemons, and is often mixed with wines and liquors such as champagne and vodka. Some people even use it as an aid to digestion following meals. The liqueur is packaged in a variety of ways, usually with a lemon motif, and make ideal gifts.

Shoppers here also look for deals on sandals, cashmere, and jewelry, the town's big bargains. The cobblers at **Canfora,** Via Camerelle 3 (☎ 081/837-0487), make all the sandals found in their shop. If you don't find what you need, you can order custom-made footwear. They also sell shoes, but they don't make those themselves. You can find a good selection of men's cashmere pullover sweaters at **Russo Uomo,** Piazzetta Quisisina (☎ **081/838-8208**). But for pullovers for the whole family, go to **Russo Donna,** Via Vittorio Emanuele 55 (☎ 081/838-8207). The eight talented jewelers at **La Perla,** Piazza Umberto 10-21 (☎ 081/837-0641), work exclusively with gold and gems, and they can design and create anything you want.

WHERE TO STAY

Finding your own bed for the night can be a real problem if you arrive in July or August without a reservation when the demand far exceeds the supply. Capri is also an exclusive enclave of the wealthy, and even the lesser accommodations are able to charge high prices. Many serious economizers find that they have to return to the mainland for the night.

Very Expensive

✪ **Grand Hotel Quisisana Capri.** Via Camerelle 2, 80073 Capri. ☎ 081/837-0788. Fax 081/837-6080. 150 rms, 15 suites. A/C MINIBAR TV TEL. 380,000L–750,000L ($228–$450) double; from 900,000L ($540) suite. Rates include breakfast. AE, DC, MC, V. Closed Nov 1 to mid-March.

The deluxe choice on the island, this is the favorite nesting place for a regular international clientele. Established as a sanitorium in 1845, it became a resort in 1880, and functioned as an R&R site for American GIs in the final months of WWII. More spacious than its central location would indicate, its private garden is shut off from the passing tourists. The sprawling premises are painted a distinctive yellow and accented with vines and landscaping. It has bedrooms ranging from cozy singles to spacious suites—all of which open onto wide arcades with a view of the seacoast. They vary greatly in decor, with both traditional and conservatively modern furnishings. Capri's social center, the terrace of the hotel, is where everybody who is anybody goes for cocktails before dinner.

Dining/Entertainment: The hotel has two restaurants, both under the famed chef Gualtiero Marchesi. Colombaia, which serves lunch only, is proud of its fresh-tasting and attractively displayed fish dishes, as well as its lush fruits and vegetables. The Quisi Restaurant, which serves dinner only, is alluring with candlelight, serving a creative Mediterranean and local cuisine. The American bar overlooks the swimming pool on the lower terrace.

Services: Room service, baby-sitting, laundry, valet.

Facilities: Sauna, Turkish bath and massage facilities, indoor and outdoor swimming pools, beauty shop, gymnasium, tennis courts. The hotel's two golf courses are covered with artificial grass. Facilities are not as complete as at Europa Palace (below).

La Scalinatella (Little Steps). Via Tragara 8, 80073 Capri. ☎ **081/837-0633.** Fax 081/837-8291. 30 junior suites. A/C MINIBAR TV TEL. 550,000L–670,000L ($330–$402) suite. Rates include breakfast. AE, MC, V. Closed Nov–Easter.

One of the most delightful hotels in Capri is constructed like a private villa above terraces that offer a panoramic view of the water and a nearby monastery. Many former Quisisana guests have deserted to this more intimate and exclusive pair of 200-year-old houses, with a vaguely Moorish design, run by the Morgano family. The ambience is one of unadulterated luxury; the suites include a phone beside the bathtub, beds set into alcoves, elaborate wrought-iron accents that ring both the inner stairwell and the ornate balconies, and a sweeping view over the gardens and pool. The hotel contains a restaurant, open only at lunchtime, where simple but flavorful dishes are served on a terrace beside the pool.

Expensive

Hotel Flora. Via Federico Serena 26, 80073 Capri. ☎ **081/837-0211.** Fax 081/837-8949. 24 rms. A/C MINIBAR TV TEL. 330,000L–400,000L ($198–$240) double. Rates include breakfast. AE, DC, MC, V. Closed Jan 9–Mar 1 and Oct–Dec 15.

The terraces—edged with oleander, bougainvillea, and geraniums—overlook the monastery of St. James and the sea. There are several tile courtyards with garden furniture, pots of tropical flowers, and spots where you can either sunbathe or be cooled by the sea breezes. The public and private rooms are a wise blend of the old and new. The bedrooms are well furnished. There's a less desirable but comfortable annex across the street. The first-class, reasonably priced restaurant, La Certosa di San Giacomo, offers an impressive cuisine and many excellent regional wines.

Hotel Luna. Viale Matteotti 3, 80073 Capri. ☎ **081/837-0433.** Fax 081/837-7459. 54 rms. A/C TV TEL. 240,000L–460,000L ($144–$276) double. Rates include breakfast. AE, DC, MC, V. Closed Oct 1–Easter.

This first-class hotel, built in the mid-1960s, stands on a cliff overlooking the sea and the rocks of Faraglioni. Even more tranquil and inviting than the Flora, it's set almost between the Gardens of Augustus and the Carthusian monastery of St. James. The building is nondescript, the furnishings reproductions of antiques. The bedrooms, a mixture of contemporary Italian pieces and Victorian decor, incorporate wood and padded headboards and gilt mirrors over the desk, all in good style. Some of the bedrooms have arched, recessed private terraces that overlook the garden of flowers and semitropical plants. There's a clubby drinking lounge, and the dining room lures with good cuisine.

Hotel Punta Tragara. Via Tragara 57, 80073 Capri. ☎ **081/837-0844.** Fax 081/837-7790. 17 rms, 30 suites. A/C MINIBAR TV TEL. 380,000L–520,000L ($228–$312) double; 530,000L–630,000L ($318–$378) suite. Rates include breakfast. AE, DC, MC, V. Closed Nov–Easter.

This former private villa—designed by Le Corbusier—stands above rocky cliffs at the tip of the most desirable panorama on Capri. Its sienna-colored walls and Andalusian-style accents are designed so that each of the apartment accommodations is subtly different. It ranks just under the Quisisana and Scalinatella, but far grander than either the Luna or the Flora. Outfitted with mottled carpeting, big windows, substantial furniture, and all the modern comforts, each unit opens onto a private terrace or a balcony studded with flowers and vines, plus a sweeping view. The premises include two pools (one heated), quiet retreats near a baronial fireplace, and a grotto disco. An often-debated point on Capri involves this hotel's isolation from the other activities of the island, although many clients consider this a virtue, especially in high season when other sections of the island can be very crowded.

La Palma. Via Vittorio Emanuele 39, 80073 Capri. ☎ **081/837-0133.** Fax 081/837-6966. 70 rms. A/C MINIBAR TV TEL. 210,000L–430,000L ($126–$258) double. Rates include breakfast. AE, DC, MC, V.

On par with the Flora, this hotel was established a century ago as one of the first symbols of modern tourism on the island. Right in the center of Capri town, it caters to guests who seek first-class amenities and comforts—and who are willing to pay the piper for the privilege. Restored and renovated in an appealing style that blends modern and traditional styles, the hotel has a white-walled exterior, and a forecourt with palms and potted shrubs, which is hardly the equal of the Flora's flowery terrace and sea views. Each bedroom is handsomely furnished. Its restaurant, Relais la Palma, is one of the finest on Capri (but it operates only from Easter to late September).

Moderate

La Vega. Via Occhio Marino 10, 80073 Capri. ☎ **081/837-0481.** Fax 081/837-0342. 24 rms. A/C MINIBAR TV TEL. 280,000L–350,000L ($168–$210) double. Rates include breakfast. AE, DC, MC, V. Closed Nov–Easter.

This hotel originated in the 1930s as the private home of the family that continues to run it today. Renovated in 1993, it has a clear view of the sea and is nestled amid trees against a sunny hillside. Each of the oversize rooms has a private balcony that overlooks the water. Below the rooms is a garden of flowering bushes, and on the lower edge is a free-form swimming pool with a grassy border for sunbathing and a little bar for refreshments. The rooms have decoratively tiled floors and some of the beds have wrought-iron headboards while all units have a Jacuzzi. Breakfast is served on a terrace surrounded by trees and large potted flowers or on your balcony.

Regina Cristina. Via Serena 20, 80073 Capri. ☎ **081/837-0744.** Fax 081/837-0550. 50 rms, 5 suites. A/C MINIBAR TV TEL. 200,000L–350,000L ($120–$210) double; from 380,000L ($228) suite. Rates include breakfast. Midwinter discounts up to 45%. AE, DC, MC, V.

The white facade of the Regina Cristina rises four stories above one of the most imaginatively landscaped gardens on Capri. It was built in 1959 and renovated in 1993 in a sun-flooded design of open spaces, sunken lounges, cool tiles, and *la dolce vita* armchairs. Each accommodation has its own balcony and is very restful. Most of the rooms have Jacuzzi bathtubs. In general, for what you get this hotel appears overpriced. But on Capri in July and August you're sometimes lucky to find a room at any price.

Villa Brunella. Via Tragara 24, 80073 Capri. ☎ **081/837-0122.** Fax 081/837-0430. 9 rms, 11 suites. A/C MINIBAR TV TEL. 360,000L ($216) double; 470,000L ($282) suite. Rates include breakfast. AE, DC, MC, V. Closed Nov 6–Mar 20.

Located a 10-minute walk from many of Capri's largest hotels, this hotel was built in the late 1940s as a private villa. In 1963 it was transformed into a well-appointed and comfortable hotel by its present owner, Vincenzo Ruggiero, who named it after his hard-working wife, Brunella. The hotel has been completely renovated. Although lacking the ambience of the Flora, it competes with that hotel in its sea views and its flowery terrace. All the doubles have balconies or terraces and views of the sea. There's also a carefully landscaped pool, a bar, and a cozy restaurant.

Inexpensive

Villa Krupp. Via Matteotti 12, 80073 Capri. ☎ **081/837-0362.** Fax 081/837-6489. 15 rms. TEL. 180,000L–230,000L ($108–$138) double. Rates include breakfast. MC, V. Closed Nov 4– Mar 15.

During the early years of the 20th century the Russian revolutionaries Gorky and Lenin called this villa home. Surrounded by shady trees, it offers panoramic views of the sea and the Gardens of Augustus from its lofty terraces. At this intimate, family-run place, the front parlor is all glass with views of the seaside and semitropical plants set near Hong Kong chairs, all intermixed with painted Venetian-style pieces. Your bedroom may be large, with a fairly good bathroom. Many of the rooms have a terrace. Breakfast is the only meal offered.

Villa Sarah. Via Tiberio 3A, 80073 Capri. ☎ **081/837-7817.** Fax 081/837-7215. 20 rms. MINIBAR TV TEL. 220,000L–280,000L ($132–$168) double. Rates include breakfast. AE, MC, V. Closed late Oct–Mar 19.

The modern Villa Sarah, although far removed from the day-trippers from Naples, is still very central. A steep walk from the main square, it seems part of another world with its Capri garden and good views. All it lacks is a pool. One of the bargains of the island, it's often fully booked, so reserve ahead in summer. The sea is visible only from the upper floors. Some bedrooms have terraces. Breakfast, the only meal, is sometimes served on the terrace.

WHERE TO DINE

Moderate

'Ai Faraglioni. Via Camerelle 75. ☎ **081/837-0320.** Reservations required. Main courses 22,000L–36,000L ($13.20–$21.60). AE, DC, V. Mar–Oct, daily 12:30–3pm and 7:30pm– midnight; Apr–June and Oct, Tues–Sun 12:30–3pm and 7:30pm–midnight. Closed Nov–Feb. SEAFOOD/CONTINENTAL.

Some locals say that the food is only a secondary consideration to the social ferment of this popular restaurant. In any event, the kitchen turns out a well-prepared collection of European specialties, usually based on seafood from the surrounding waters. Examples might include linguine with lobster, seafood crêpes, rice Créole, fisherman's risotto, grilled or baked fish of many different varieties, and a wide assortment of meat dishes such as pappardelle with rabbit. For dessert, try one of the regional pastries mixed with fresh fruit.

La Capannina. Via Le Botteghe 14. ☎ **081/837-0732.** Reservations required for dinner. Main courses 18,000L–38,000L ($10.80–$22.80). AE, DC, MC, V. May–Oct, daily noon–3pm and 7:30–10:30pm; Mar–Apr, Nov, and Dec 29–Jan 6, Thurs–Tues noon–3pm and 7:30–10:30pm. Closed Dec 1–Dec 28 and Jan 7–Feb 28. CAMPANA/ITALIAN.

This restaurant is not pretentious, although it's patronized by a host of famous people from actresses to dress designers to royalty. It's your best bet for non-hotel dining on the island. A trio of inside rooms is decorated in a tavern manner, although the main draw in summer is the inner courtyard, with its ferns and hanging vines. At a table covered with a colored cloth, you can select from baby shrimp au gratin, pollo (chicken) alla Capannina, or scaloppine Capannina. If featured, a fine opener is Sicilian macheroni. The most savory skillet of goodies is the *zuppa di pesce,* a soup made with fish from the bay. Some of the dishes were obviously inspired by the nouvelle cuisine school. Wine is from vineyards owned by the restaurant.

La Pigna. Via Roma 30. ☎ **081/837-0280.** Reservations recommended. Main courses 18,000L–35,000L ($10.80–$21). AE, DC, MC, V. Aug, daily noon–3pm and 8pm–2am; July and Sept, Tues 8pm–2am, Wed–Mon noon–3pm and 8pm–2am; Apr–June and Oct, Wed–Mon noon–3pm and 8pm–2am; Nov–Mar, daily noon–3pm. NEAPOLITAN.

La Pigna serves the finest meals for the money on the island. Dining here is like attending a garden party, and this has been true since 1875. This restaurant isn't as chic as it once was, but the food is as good as ever. The owner loves flowers almost as much as good food, and the greenhouse ambience includes purple petunias, red geraniums, bougainvillea, and lemon trees. Much of the produce comes from the restaurant's gardens in Anacapri. Try in particular the penne tossed in an eggplant sauce, and the specialty chicken suprême with mushrooms. Another recommended dish is the herb-stuffed rabbit. The dessert specialty is an almond-and-chocolate torte. Another feature of the restaurant is homemade liquors, one of which is distilled from local lemons. The waiters are courteous and efficient, and the atmosphere is nostalgic, as guitarists stroll by singing sentimental Neapolitan ballads.

Inexpensive

Casanova. Via Le Botteghe 46. ☎ **081/837-7642.** Reservations required at dinner in summer. Main courses 12,000L–40,000L ($7.20–$24). AE, DC, MC, V. Mar–Nov, daily noon–3pm and 7–11pm. Closed Dec–Easter. NEAPOLITAN/CAPRESE/SEAFOOD.

Run by the D'Alessio family, and only a short walk from Piazza Umberto I, this is one of the finest dining rooms on Capri. Its cellar offers a big choice of Italian wines, with most of the favorites of Campania, and its cooks turn out a savory blend of Neapolitan and Italian specialties. You might begin with a cheese-filled ravioli, then go on to veal Sorrento or even red snapper "crazy waters" (with baby tomatoes). The seafood is always fresh and well prepared. A large and tempting buffet of antipasti is at hand. In a small wine cellar you can enjoy a good selection of Italian and foreign wines with a variety of cheeses. Most meals are inexpensive, but some exotic dishes and specialties that appear infrequently can cause your check to soar.

Da Gemma. Via Madre Serafina 6. ☎ **081/837-7113.** Reservations required. Main courses 22,000L–30,000L ($13.20–$18); fixed-price menus 35,000L–50,000L ($21–$30). AE, DC, MC, V. Tues–Sun 12:30–3pm and 7:30pm–midnight. CAPRESE/SEAFOOD.

You'll find this place, long a favorite with painters and writers, by going up an arch-covered walkway, reminiscent of Tangier, from Piazza Umberto I. Some tables are arranged for the view. Everything's cozy and atmospheric. The cuisine is provincial, with a reliance on fish dishes. The best beginning is the mussel soup, and the finest main dish is the boiled fish of the day with creamy butter, priced according to weight. You can get pizza in the evening, and the desserts are mouth-watering. It has an annex across the street that has a covered terrace offering sea views.

La Cantinella di Capri. In the Giardini Augusto, Viale Matteotti 8. ☎ **081/837-0606.** Reservations recommended. Main courses 18,000L–30,000L ($10.80–$18). AE, DC, MC, V. Tues–Sun 12:30–3pm and 7:30–12:30pm. Closed: Nov–Mar. NEAPOLITAN/FRENCH.

One of the most scenically located restaurants on Capri, this restaurant occupies a circa 1750 villa set within a verdant park (The Gardens of Augustus) a short but soothing distance from the congestion of the town center. It was acquired in 1996 by the owners of a popular restaurant in Naples, who shuttle between Naples and Capri, thereby catering to as broad-based a clientele as possible. Menu items include lots of pungent sauces and fresh seafood that's sometimes combined into pastas such as linguine Sant Lucia (with octopus, squid, whitefish, and tomato sauce). Try the veal scallopine prepared with lemon and white wine, or with cheese, parmigiana-style. *Pasta fagiole* (beans and pasta) is succulent and hearty, and such desserts as tiramisu are invariably velvety smooth.

La Cisterna. Via Madre Serafina 5. ☎ **081/837-5620.** Reservations required. Main courses 13,000L–25,000L ($7.80–$15). AE, DC, MC, V. Fri–Wed noon–3:30pm and 7pm–midnight. Closed mid-Nov to mid-Mar. SEAFOOD.

This excellent small restaurant is run by two brothers, Francesco and Salvatore Trama, who extend to guests a warm welcome. Ask what the evening specials are. They might be mamma's green lasagne, or whatever fish was freshest at the dock that afternoon, marinated in wine, garlic, and ginger and broiled. You could also try the lightly breaded and deep-fried baby squid and octopus, a mouth-watering *saltimbocca*, spaghetti with clams, and a filling *zuppa di pesce* (fish soup). Pizza begins at 8,000L ($4.80). La Cisterna lies only a short walk from Piazza Umberto I via a labyrinth of covered "tunnels."

Ristorante al Grottino. Via Longano 27. ☎ **081/837-0584.** Reservations required for dinner. Main courses 15,000L–28,000L ($9–$16.80). AE, MC, V. Daily noon–3pm and 7pm–midnight. Closed Nov 3–Mar 30. SEAFOOD/NEAPOLITAN.

Founded in 1937, this was the retreat of the rich and famous during its *la dolce vita* 1950s heyday. Ted Kennedy, Ginger Rogers, the Gabor sisters, and Princess Soraya of Iran once dined here, and the place remains popular among ordinary folk. To reach it you must walk down a narrow alleyway that branches off from Piazza Umberto I. The chef knows how to rattle his pots and pans. Bowing to the influence of the nearby Neapolitan cuisine, he offers four different dishes of fried mozzarella cheese, any one highly recommended. Try a big plate of the mixed fish fry from the seas of the Campania. The *zuppa di cozze* (mussel soup) is a savory opener, as is the *ravioli alla caprese*. The linguine with scampi is truly succulent.

CAPRI AFTER DARK

You'll find an amusing roster of nightclubs on the island. Foremost among them is **Number Two,** Via Camerelle 1 (☎ 081/837-7078), rivaled closely by **Disco New Pentothal,** Via Vittorio Emmanuele 45 (☎ 081/837-6793). Both cater to clients of all ages, and all nationalities, of holidaymakers who either like to dance or enjoy watching people who do, but only between May and September. The presence of these electronicized hideaways doesn't detract from the allure of dozens of cafes, bars, and taverns scattered through the narrow streets of Capri's historic center. Among the most appealing of these is **Taverna Guarracino,** Via Castello 7 (☎ 081/837-0514), where bouts of convivial beer-and-wine-drinking might be interrupted by quasi-spontaneous performances of Neapolitan songs. More consciously stylish and aloof is **The Blue Bar,** Via Camerelle 85 (☎ 081/837-6650), where music from a live pianist amuses and distracts crowds from window-shopping and people-watching along the town's main street.

One of the major pastimes in Capri is to occupy an outdoor table at one of the cafés on Piazza Umberto I. Even some permanent residents (and this is a good sign) patronize **Bar Tiberio,** Piazza Umberto I (☎ 081/837-0268), open daily 7am to 2am (sometimes until 4am). Larger and a little more comfortable than some of its competitors, this cafe has tables both inside and outside that overlook the busy life of the square.

ANACAPRI

Capri is the upper town of Marina Grande. To see the upper town of Capri, you have to get lost in the clouds of Anacapri—more remote, secluded, and idyllic than the main resort, and reached by a daring 3,000L ($1.80) round-trip bus ride more thrilling than any roller coaster. One visitor once remarked that all bus drivers to Anacapri "were either good or dead." At one point in island history, Anacapri and Capri were connected only by the Scala Fenicia, the Phoenician Stairs.

When you disembark at Piazza della Victoria, you'll find a Caprian Shangri-la, a village of charming dimensions.

To continue your ascent to the top, you then hop aboard a chair lift (Segiovia) to **Monte Solaro,** the loftiest citadel on the island at 1,950 feet. The ride takes about 12 minutes, operates winter, spring, and fall from 9:30am to sunset, and charges 7,500L ($4.50) for a round-trip ticket. At the top, the panorama of the Bay of Naples is spread before you.

You can head out on Viale Axel Munthe from Piazza Monumento for a 5-minute walk to **Villa San Michele,** Capodimonte 34 (☎ 081/837-1401). This was the home of Axel Munthe, the Swedish author (*The Story of San Michele*), physician, and friend of Gustav V, King of Sweden, who visited him several times on the island. The villa is as Munthe (who died in 1949) furnished it, in a harmonious and tasteful way. From the rubble and ruins of an imperial villa built underneath by Tiberius, Munthe purchased several marbles, which are displayed inside. You can walk through the gardens for another in a series of endless panoramas of the island. Tiberius used to sleep out here alfresco on hot nights. You can visit the villa daily 9am to 6pm May to September, 9:30am to 5pm in April and October, from 9:30am to 4:30pm in March, and from 10:30am to 3:30pm November to February. Admission is 6,000L ($3.60) for adults, free for children 12 and under.

WHERE TO STAY

Expensive

Europa Palace. Via Capodimonte 2, 80071 Anacapri. ☎ 081/837-3800. Fax 081/837-3191. 92 rms, 20 junior suites, 4 suites. A/C MINIBAR TV TEL. 350,000L–500,000L ($210–$300) double; from 900,000L ($540) suite. Rates include breakfast. AE, DC, MC, V. Closed Nov 15–Easter.

On the slopes of Monte Solaro, the first-class Europa sparkles with *moderne* and turns its back on the past to embrace the semiluxury of today. Its bold designer obviously loved wide open spaces, heroic proportions, and vivid colors. The landscaped gardens with palm trees and plenty of bougainvillea have a large swimming pool, which most guests use as their outdoor living room. Although lacking the intimate charms of Scalinatella, it is alluring because of its setting and its Capri Beauty Farm, offering spa treatments. Each of the bedrooms is attractively and comfortably furnished, and from some on a clear day you can see smoking Vesuvius. Each of the four special suites has a private pool.

Dining/Entertainment: The hotel restaurant is known for its fine cuisine with Neapolitan and other Mediterranean specialties, even with some nouvelle cuisine. A snack bar with light lunches is in the pool area.

Services: Room service, baby-sitting, laundry, valet.

Facilities: Swimming pool, beauty spa.

Hotel San Michele di Anacapri. Via Orlandi 1-3, 80071 Anacapri. ☎ **081/837-1427.** Fax 081/837-1420. 56 rms. TV TEL. 190,000L–230,000L ($114–$138) double. Rates include breakfast. AE, DC, MC, V. Closed Nov 5–Dec 27 and Jan 5–Mar 31.

This well-appointed contemporary hotel has spacious cliffside gardens and unmarred views as well as enough shady or sunny nooks to please everybody. It also has the largest swimming pool on Capri. Guests linger long and peacefully in its private and well-manicured gardens, where the green trees are softened by splashes of color from hydrangea and geraniums. The view for diners includes the Bay of Naples and Vesuvius. The bedrooms carry out the same theme, with a respect for the past, but also with sufficient examples of today's amenities, such as a tile bath in most rooms, good beds, and plenty of space.

Moderate

Bella Vista. Via Orlandi 10, 80071 Anacapri. ☎ **081/837-1821.** Fax 081/837-0957. 15 rms. TEL. 140,000L–170,000L ($84–$102) double. Rates include breakfast. Half board 100,000L–125,000L ($60–$75) per person extra. AE, MC, V. Closed Nov 30–Easter.

Only a 2-minute walk from the main piazza, this is a modern holiday retreat with a panoramic view. Lodged into a mountainside, the hotel is decorated with primary colors and has large living and dining rooms, and terraces with a view of the sea. The breakfast and lunch terrace has garden furniture and a rattan-roofed sun shelter, and the cozy lounge features an elaborate tile floor and a hooded fireplace, ideal for nippy nights. The bedrooms are pleasingly contemporary (a few have a bed mezzanine, a sitting area on the lower level, and a private entrance). The restaurant is closed Monday.

Inexpensive

Hotel Loreley. Via Orlandi 12, 80071 Anacapri. ☎ **081/837-1440.** Fax 081/837-1399. 18 rms. TEL. 100,000L–160,000L ($60–$96) double. Rates include breakfast. AE, MC, V. Closed Oct 15–Mar 30.

Loreley has more to offer than economy: It's a cozy, immaculately kept accommodation, with a genial homelike atmosphere. Opened in 1963, it features an open-air veranda with a bamboo canopy, rattan chairs, and of course, a good view. The rooms overlook lemon-bearing trees that have (depending on the season) either scented blossoms or fruit. The bedrooms are quite large, with unified colors and enough furniture to make for a sitting room. Each room has a balcony. You approach the hotel through a white iron gate, past a stone wall. It lies off the road toward the sea, and is surrounded by fig trees and geraniums.

MARINA PICCOLA

You can reach the little south-shore fishing village and beach of Marina Piccola by bus (later you can take a bus back up the steep hill to Capri). The village opens onto emerald-and-cerulean waters, with the Faraglioni rocks of the sirens jutting out at the far end of the bay. Treat yourself to lunch at **La Canzone del Mare,** Marina Piccola (☎ **081/837-0104**), daily noon to 4pm, closed Wednesdays from October to Easter. Seafood and Neapolitan cuisines are served.

18 Apulia (Puglia)

Known to the Italians as *La Puglia,* the district of Apulia encompasses the southeasternmost section of Italy, the heel of the geographic boot. It is the country's gateway to the Orient, but more specifically, for most North Americans, the gateway to Greece from the port of Brindisi. Through it marched the Crusaders, and even earlier, the Romans, on their way to the possessions in the East.

For most foreigners, it is a little-known but fascinating region of Italy, embracing some of its most poverty-stricken areas and some of its most interesting sections (see the Trulli District, below). Many signs of improved living conditions are in the air, however.

The land is rich in archeological discoveries and some of its cities were shining sapphires in the crown of Magna Graecia (Greater Greece). The Ionian and Adriatic Seas wash up upon its shores, which have seen the arrival of cross-currents of civilizations and of the armies of tribes and countries seeking to conquer this access route to Rome. The Goths, Germanic hordes, Byzantines, Spanish, and French sought to possess it. Saracen pirates and Turks came to see what riches they might find.

Apulia offers the beauty of marine grottoes and caverns as well as turquoise seas and sandy beaches. Forests, wind-twisted pines, huge old carob trees, junipers, sage and rosemary grow near the sea, whereas orchards, vineyards, fields of grain, and vegetable gardens grow inland. Flocks of sheep and goats dot the landscape.

1 Foggia

60 miles W of Bari, 108 miles NE of Naples, 225 miles SE of Rome

Foggia, the capital city of Capitanata, is Apulia's northernmost province. A history of tragedy, including a serious earthquake in 1731 and extensive bombing of the city during World War II, has left Foggia with little in the way of attractions, although it is a good base for exploring nearby attractions such as Lucera and Troia. It is also used by many motorists as a base for a day's motor tour of the Gargano Peninsula. A 12th-century cathedral remains; the rest of the city is pleasant, but thoroughly modern. Foggia is clean and has parks and wide boulevards lined with a decent selection of hotels and restaurants. This is a good place to take care of business—rent a car, exchange money, mail postcards, or whatever, because it's relatively safe, easy to get around in, and in a central location.

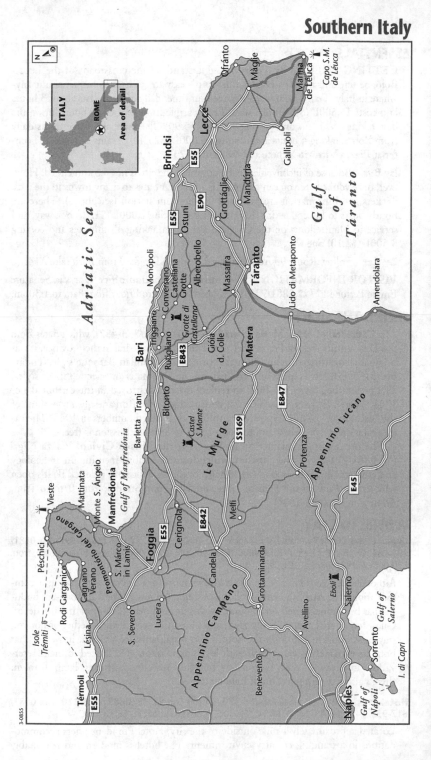

Southern Italy

ITALY
ROME
Area of detail

Adriatic Sea

Ofranto
Ófranto
Màglie
Marina de Léuca
Capo S.M. de Léuca
Lecce
Brindsi
E55
Gallipoli
Mandúria
Grottáglie
E90
E55
Ostuni
Monópoli
Conversano
Castellana
Grotte
Alberobello
Massafra
Táranto
Gulf of Táranto
Lido di Metaponto
Triggiano
Grotte di Castellana
Rutigliano
E843
Gióia d. Colle
Matera
Amendolara
Bari
Bitonto
Le Murge
SS169
Trani
Castel S.Monte
E847
Barletta
Appennino Lucano
Manfrédonia
Gulf of Manfredonia
Monte S. Ángelo
Mattinata
Vieste
Potenza
E45
Melfi
Cerignola
E842
Promontório del Gargano
S. Márco in Lamis
Foggia
E55
Candela
Grottaminarda
Eboli
Péschici
Cagnano
Verano
Appennino Campano
Gulf of Salerno
Rodi Garganico
Lucera
Salerno
Lésina
S. Severo
Avellino
Sorrento
Isole Trémiti
Benevento
Gulf of Nápoli
I. di Capri
Térmoli
E55
Naples
Sorrento
I. di Capri

3-0855

679

ESSENTIALS

GETTING THERE **By Train** Foggia stands at the crossroads of the Lecce-Bologne line and the Bari-Naples run, so it's easy to get here from just about anywhere in Italy. Trains from Naples arrive four times daily; the trip lasts about 3 hours and costs 15,500L ($9.30) one way. Trains arrive from Bari every hour during the day, taking 1¹/₂ hours and costing 9,800L ($5.90). There are also three trains daily from Rome, taking 4 hours and costing 39,000L ($23.40). Trains arrive in the center at **Piazza Vittorio Veneto** (☎ **0881/608-234**).

By Bus Because of inconvenience, bus travel to the city is not recommended. However, once you're here you can ride **ATAF** and **SITA** buses to many towns in the area. Tickets and information are provided by the train station (see above). There are hourly buses to Lucera, taking 30 minutes and costing 2,000L ($1.20) one way, and service to Manfredonia on the Gargano Peninsula, taking 45 minutes and costing 3,500L ($2.10) one way.

By Car Follow Route 90 from Naples directly to Foggia. From Bari, take A14.

VISITOR INFORMATION The **tourist information office** is at Via Senatore Emilio Perrone 17 (☎ **0881/723-141**), open Monday to Friday from 8am to 1:30pm.

SEEING THE SIGHTS

The **Cathedral of Santa Maria Icona Vetere** (☎ **0881/773-482**), which dates from the 12th century, lies off Piazza del Lago. The largest cathedral in the province, it was originally constructed in an unusual Norman and Apulian Baroque style. Today, because of extensive repairs and expansions, the Duomo is an eclectic mix of styles. The present bell tower was built to replace the one destroyed in the earthquake of 1731. There's also a crypt, which was constructed in the Romanesque style; some of the "excavation" of this crypt was compliments of Allied bombers in 1943. The cathedral is open daily from 9am to noon and 5 to 8pm. Admission is free.

The other notable attraction in Foggia is the **Museo Civico,** Piazza Nigri (☎ **0881/771-823**). The museum, which features exhibits focusing on archeology and ethnography, is housed in the remains of the residence of Frederick II. It's open Monday to Friday from 9am to 1pm and 5 to 7pm, Sunday from 9am to 1pm. Admission is 1,000L (60¢).

WHERE TO STAY

Grand Hotel Cicolella. Viale XXIV Maggio 60, 71100 Foggia. ☎ **0881/688-890.** Fax 0881/778-984. 98 rms, 8 suites. A/C MINIBAR TV. 250,000L–290,000L ($150–$174) double; from 320,000L ($192) suite. AE, DC, V.

Although the 1920s Hotel Cicolella is known more for its restaurants than its accommodations, the establishment is still the best hotel in town. The Victorian-era building has been modernized throughout, with glass and marble dominating the decor. Guest rooms are large, well equipped, and pleasantly decorated. Whether or not you stay here, you can patronize the hotel's two restaurants. Be warned, however, that both are extremely popular with both locals and visitors; you'll need to make reservations in advance. Many patrons say that they serve the best roast lamb in town; there's also a superb selection of Italian cheeses.

Hotel President. Viale degli Aviatori 130, 71100 Foggia. ☎ **0881/618-010.** Fax 0881/617-930. 140 rms. A/C MINIBAR TV TEL. 115,000L ($69) double. AE, DC, MC, V.

Located approximately 1 mile outside of the city, Hotel President offers accommodations in a tranquil, country environment. The hotel is modern and reasonably comfortable. Rooms are a bit barren, but provide all the necessary amenities. The hotel also operates a large restaurant that offers regional and international cuisine.

White House Hotel. Via Sabotino 24, 71100 Foggia. ☎ **0881/721-644.** Fax 0881/721-646. 40 rms. A/C MINIBAR TV TEL. 288,000L ($172.80) double. AE, DC, MC, V.

This first-class hotel is located in the heart of Foggia, just a few steps from the train station. It's a good choice for convenience and comfort. Although there is no restaurant, room service is provided upon request. There is a bar on the premises and a comfortable lounge area.

WHERE TO DINE

✪ **Il Ventaglio.** Via Gaetano Postiglione 6. ☎ **0881/661-500.** Reservations not required. Main courses 25,000L ($15). AE DC MC, V. Tues–Sat 1–2:45pm and 8:30–10:30pm, Sun 8:30–10:30pm. ITALIAN.

This elegant restaurant is known for its inventive cuisine, among the finest in southern Italy. The proprietor, who likes to add a personal touch to each dish she creates, says that she "never makes the same dish twice." Some of her specialties include *fagottino di pesce* (fish), and *agnolotti ripieni,* her pasta specialty studded with fish. The orecchiette come in a clam sauce and with the freshest vegetables of the season. The area is known for its migratory birds and swamp game, which appear in many dishes with a great variety of sauces. Here is also a chance to sample some of the finest cheese in the area, including pecorino, scamorza, and manteca. Service is discreet and with a certain charm.

A SIDE TRIP TO LUCERA & TROIA

From Foggia, you can take an hourly bus, a 30-minute trip that costs 2,000L ($1.20), or drive 12 miles northwest to the small medieval town of **Lucera.** Its hilltop site opens onto the Tavoliere, the largest tract of flat country in Italy. Its large castello dominates the terrain for miles around.

Once it was a city of Saracens who carried out a thriving trade here, after their banishment from Sicily. Frederick II resettled about 20,000 of these Arabs here in the early 13th century on the site of a long-abandoned Roman town.

A bus from Foggia will deposit you at Piazza del Popolo, and from here you can walk up Via Gramsci to the **Duomo,** at Piazza del Duomo (☎ **0881/941-705**), the heart of the old walled town of the Middle Ages. Today's building was constructed over the site of a mosque that the Angevins destroyed when they massacred the Arab residents of Lucera in the early 1300s. One of the major architectural treasures of southern Italy, the Byzantine-Gothic cathedral, was constructed by Charles III of Anjou in 1305. The Arabic layout of Lucera is said to still exist, although the Islamic buildings have long turned to dust. Hours are daily from 7am to noon and 4:30 to 8pm.

Near the Duomo, you can visit the **Museo Civico G. Fiorelli** (☎ **0881/547-041**), by heading down Via de Nicastri to No. 36. The building housing the museum was the ancestral home of Baroness de Nicastri. Some of her antiques are still here. Otherwise, exhibits relate to the archeological finds in the area. Look for the old Arab teapots and some mosaics from even earlier Roman times. It is open May through August, Tuesday to Friday from 9am to 1pm and 3 to 6pm. Off-season hours are Tuesday to Friday from 9am to 1pm and 5 to 7pm. Admission is 1,500L (90¢) for adults, 1,000L (60¢) for children and seniors.

Northwest of town are the ruins of a **Roman amphitheater,** Viale Augusto (☎ **0881/549-214**), constructed in 27 B.C. It was dedicated to the Emperor

Augustus, and the site is open Tuesday to Sunday from 8am to 1:30pm and 2:30 to 8pm.

From the amphitheater, you can walk to the **castle** (no phone), the largest in Apulia, topped with two dozen towers. This fortress was built for Frederick II in 1230, and it measures more than a kilometer in circumference. It's open Tuesday to Sunday, 9am to 1pm, charging no admission. From Piazza del Duomo, head out Via Bovio and Via Frederico II to Piazza Matteotti. Follow the signs to "castello."

If time remains, you can also make an offbeat excursion to the small town of **Troia**, 12 miles due south of Lucera. If you're driving, take Route 160. Frequent buses make the run from both Foggia and Lucera. No one seems to know the origins of the town's name. *Troia* in Italian means "bitch." That bizarre twist sets the stage for one of the strangest towns in Apulia, a village that time forgot. Once the Roman town of Aecae, Troia was refounded in 1017.

It is now a dusty place visited by those wishing to see its **duomo,** an 11th-century medley of many architectural styles, from Romanesque to Byzantine, even Saracen, but with a distinctive Apulian flavor and a Baroque interior. Look for the bronze doors decorated with biblical characters and animals such as apes and elephants which are surmounted by a rose window.

DINING IN LUCERA

Ristorante Alhambra. Via De Nicastri 10-14. ☎ **0881/547-066.** Reservations recommended. Main courses 15,000L–25,000L ($9–$15). No credit cards. Daily noon–3pm and Mon–Sat 7:30–11pm. Closed Aug 25–Sept 10. APULIAN.

It's the most historic, and best-recommended, restaurant in town, within a stone's throw of the town's duomo. The well-prepared Apulian and classic Italian cuisine is served in a setting that was originally the private palace of an Arab patriarch. Menu items include a sprawling selection of seafood antipasti; a savory version of clam soup, or another version that combines a medley of shellfish; pasta flavored either with mushrooms or fresh clams; grilled lamb; and a wide selection of fish (including *spigola* and *brodetto*) served either as grilled filets or baked, with herbs and vegetables, in an oven.

2 The Gargano Peninsula

Called the Gargano, this mountainous wooded promontory is the "Spur of Italy." It's best seen in the autumn when you can enjoy the colors of the Umbra Forest, featuring such trees as maple, ash, cedar, and chestnut. The world here has a timeless quality. Unspoiled salt-lake areas are found at Lesina and Varano, and bathing and water sports are prevalent because of the mild climate and calm seas. The coast is a series of cliffs, rocks, caves, islets, and beaches, whereas vegetable gardens grow inland on a landscape dotted with flocks of sheep and goats. In addition to nature's wild and varied landscape, the promontory is rich in historic interest, showing off monuments that are Byzantine, Romanesque, Norman, and medieval.

It will take a leisurely seven hours to drive all around the Gargano (perhaps longer depending on your stopovers), staying on Route 89. We consider this sometimes difficult route among the most scenically rewarding in Italy. In ancient times the peninsula was an island, until the sediment from a river eventually formed a "bridge" linking it to the mainland of Italy.

Train service into the peninsula is limited to a private spur running along the northwestern coast of the peninsula, so for travelers who wish to fully explore the area by bus or car, the gateway will be Manfredonia.

ESSENTIALS

GETTING THERE   By Train   From Foggia, make a connection to San Severo, 24 miles to the north, an hourly trip of 25 minutes costing 3,500L ($2.10), and transfer to the Ferrovia del Gargano (☎ **0884/707-495**), Gargano's private railway, which travels the northwestern edge of the peninsula to Rodi Garganico and Peschici six times daily. You can also take an hourly train to Manfredonia, 27 miles northeast of Foggia, for 3,500L ($2.10), where buses depart to explore the peninsula.

By Bus   Bus services are provided by the **ATAF** and **SITA** lines, which overlap, with hourly buses running from Foggia to Manfredonia, a 45-minute trip costing 3,500L ($2.10), where you can make connections 7 times daily to Vieste, a 2-hour trip costing 5,000L ($3), 16 times daily to Mattinata, a 30-minute trip costing 1,500L (90¢), and 17 times daily to Monte Sant'Angelo, a 45-minute trip costing 3,000L ($1.80). Buses also leave from the parking lot of Camping Sports, Via Montesanto 34-40 (☎ **0884/964-015**) in Peschici, following the coastal route 89 to Vieste, a 40-minute trip that costs 3,000L ($1.80).

From Vieste, contact **Gargano Viaggi,** Piazza Roma 7 (☎ **0884/708-501**), to take a rather rushed 4-hour bus tour of the peninsula that costs 20,000L ($12).

By Car   Three roads dissect the peninsula and connect its major sights. Route 89 runs an 81-mile circuit around the coast; Route 528 cuts through the heart of the peninsula, starting 5 miles west of Peschici on the northern coast and running south through the Umbra Forest before ending at Route 272 just west of Monte Sant'Angelo; Route 272 slices east to west through the southern part of the region, from San Marco in Lamis, in the west, through San Giovanni Rotondo, and over to Monte Sant'Angelo, ending on the coast near Punta Rossa.

VISITOR INFORMATION   The tourist information center in **Manfredonia,** Corso Manfredi 26 (☎ **0884/581-998**), is open Monday to Saturday from 8:30am to 1:30pm. Here you can pick up a map and get data about touring the Gargano district, including bus and train schedules—especially since in most towns there are no actual bus stations. In **Vieste,** the tourist information center, Piazza Kennedy (☎ **0884/708-806**), will give you information about the many excursion possibilities in the area, especially the excellent beaches along the southern Gargano shoreline. From June 20 to September 20, hours are Monday to Saturday from 8:30am to 1:30pm and 4 to 9pm, and Sunday from 8:30am to 1pm. In the off-season, hours are Monday to Saturday from 8:30am to 1:30pm and 3 to 8pm. Operating only June to September, the tourist information center in **Peschici,** Corso Garibaldi 57 (☎ **0884/962-796**), is open Monday to Saturday from 10am to 12:30pm and 6 to 10:30pm.

MANFREDONIA

27 miles NE of Foggia, 74 miles NW of Bari, 135 miles NE of Naples

If you approach Gargano from the south, your first stop, perhaps at lunchtime, will be at Manfredonia, a small port known for its castle. It was named for Manfred, illegitimate son of Frederick II. In the heyday of the Crusades, this was a bustling port town, with knights and pilgrims leaving for the Levant. Much later in history, the town is noted in World War I documents as the place where the first blow of the conflict was launched—the Austrians bombed the railroad station in 1915. Manfredonia lies on a rail route from Foggia.

After arriving in town, turn right and go along Viale Aldo Moro to Piazza Marconi. Across the square, Corso Manfredi leads to the **Manfredonia Castello,** built for

Manfred and later enlarged by the Angevins. Other bastions were constructed in 1607 by the Spanish fearing an invasion from Turkey. Regrettably, it didn't do the job, as the Turks arrived in 1620 and destroyed a lot of Manfredonia, leaving some of its former walls standing. Today the castle is home to the **Museo Nazionale di Manfredonia** (☎ 0884/587-838), open Tuesday to Sunday from 8:30am to 1:30pm and 3:30 to 6:30pm, charging no admission. Archeological remnants and finds include a collection of Stone Age objects from villages of the area, most striking of which are the Daunian stelae, stone slabs decorated like human torsos and topped with stone heads, the legacy of the Daunian civilization that settled in the region around the 9th century B.C.

Two miles outside town is **Santa Maria di Siponto,** a church in a setting of pine woods that once was the site of the ancient city of Siponte, abandoned after being ravaged by an earthquake and a plague. The church, dating from the 11th century, is in the Romanesque style, showing both Tuscan and Arabic influences.

WHERE TO STAY & DINE

Hotel Gargano. Viale Beccarini 2, 71043 Manfredonia. ☎ and fax **0884/586-021.** 46 rms. A/C TV TEL. 150,000L–160,000L ($90–$96) double. MC, V. Closed Jan.

This is the largest and most appealing hotel in Manfredonia, a four-star medium-sized hotel that, while comfortable, is not horrendously expensive. Built by the sea in 1959 and expanded in 1970, the hotel's bedrooms are outfitted in simple, summery furnishings, with monochromatic color schemes of blue or white. Each faces the sea from a private terrace or veranda. There's a swimming pool filled with sea water close to a dance bar whose recorded music floats over chairs and tables angled for the best panorama of sea and shore. There's no room service, but the hotel bar remains open 24 hours a day.

Trattoria Il Barrocchio. Corso Roma 38. ☎ **0884/583-874.** Reservations recommended. Main courses 11,000L–18,000L ($6.60–$10.80). AE, DC, MC, V. Fri–Wed 12:30–2:30pm and 7:30–10:30pm. APULIAN/SEAFOOD.

Set in a turn-of-the-century building very close to Piazza Municipio, this is the most appealing restaurant in town. It attracts civic and business leaders at lunch, and groups of friends for dinners accompanied with a succulent roster of (mostly seafood and vegetarian) antipasti. Pasta dishes include spaghetti, or more typically *orecchiette,* prepared in simple versions of tomatoes, pesto, and local cheese; with garlic, olive oil, and fresh broccoli; or more elaborately garnished with seafood, especially octopus. Look for succulent portions of grilled baby lamb, as savory and aromatic as the nearby hills on which the animals were raised.

MONTE SANT'ANGELO

37 miles NE of Foggia, 84 NW of Bari, 145 miles NE of Naples

Motorists will find the principal town in the interior, Monte Sant'Angelo, 10 miles to the north of Manfredonia, in the great Umbra Forest, to be a good starting point for a tour. From here you can venture into a landscape of limes, laurels, towering yews, along with such animal life as foxes and gazelles. Narrow passageways, streets that are virtually stairways, and little houses washed a gleaming white characterize the town.

The site of Monte Sant'Angelo, standing on a spur, commands panoramic views of the surrounding terrain. Before leaving town, you may want to visit the **Sanctuary of San Michele,** built in the Romanesque-Gothic style. The campanile is octagonal, dating from the last years of the 13th century. The sanctuary commemorates the legend of St. Michael, who is said to have left his red cloak after he appeared to some shepherds in a grotto in A.D. 490. You can also visit the grotto in which the saint is alleged to have appeared. To enter from the church, go through some bronze doors, made in Constantinople in the 11th century. Crusaders stopped here to worship before going to the Holy Land. The sanctuary (no phone) is on Via Reale Basilica, and is open daily from 7:30am to 12:30pm and 2:30 to 6:30pm, charging no admission.

Opposite the campanile, or bell tower, you can also visit the **Tomba di Rotari** (Tomb of Rotharis). The tomb is said to hold the bones of the king of the Lombards, Rotharis, although it is in fact a baptistery dating from as early as the 12th century.

Past the sanctuary leads to the semirestored ruins of the **Norman Swabian Aragonese Castle** (☎ 0884/565-444), which is open daily from 9am to 5pm, charging 3,000L ($1.80) admission. Its Torre dei Giganti was constructed in 837, although most of the castle dates from the Middle Ages. From its ramparts is one of the most sweeping views in the Gargano. You can also visit **Museo Tancredi,** Piazza San Francesco d'Assisi (☎ 0884/562-098), which exhibits artifacts that local farmers and vintners used in their trade. It is open from May to September, Monday from 8:30am to 2pm, Tuesday to Saturday from 8:30am to 2pm and 2:30 to 8pm, and Sunday from 10am to 12:30pm and 3:30 to 7pm. Off-season hours are Monday to Saturday from 8am to 2pm. Admission is 3,000L ($1.80).

SHOPPING   As you wander about, look for local shops that sell wrought-iron goods, which are among the finest in Italy. It's been a long tradition here with sons following in their father's footsteps. The locals also make wooden furniture and utensils.

WHERE TO STAY & DINE

Hotel Rotary. Via per Pulsano km 1, 71037 Monte Sant'Angelo. ☎ **0884/562-146.** Fax 0884/562-146. 24 rms. TV TEL. 100,000L–110,000L ($60–$66) double. Rates include breakfast. AE, MC, V. Closed Nov.

You'll find this 1981 hotel a half-mile west of town, amid sloping terrain dotted with ancient olive groves and almond trees. Many visitors appreciate it for the panoramas of the Adriatic, about six miles to the southeast, that sweep across the landscape from many of the windows. There aren't many amenities on site, no swimming pool, and none of the simple bedrooms has air conditioning, but because of its location within relative high altitudes, ocean breezes usually keep temperatures comfortable. The in-house restaurant serves cuisine based on local culinary traditions, usually with competency and generosity.

Ristorante Medioevo. Via Castello 21. ☎ **0884/565-356.** Reservations recommended. Main courses 10,000L–23,500L ($6–$14.10). AE, MC, V. Tues–Sun noon–2:30pm and 7:30pm–11pm. CONTADINA.

Set in the heart of this medieval town, the Medioevo's single dining room takes its name from the weather-beaten but historic neighborhood that surrounds it, and as such is almost guaranteed a busy trade from midsummer passersby. Despite the fact that it has served countless numbers of diners from other parts of Europe, there remain vague hints of suspicion toward newcomers. Cuisine is firmly entrenched in recipes rehearsed by countless generations of *contadine* (peasant women). Examples include *zuppe di panne cotte,* a savory soup made of chicory and fava beans, homemade pasta, especially orecchiette, accessorized with a wide roster of meat or fish, and roasted lamb from rocky nearby meadows.

ISOLE TREMITI
7 miles NW of Gargano

While in the area, consider visiting the jewel-like cluster of the **Isole Tremiti** or Tremiti Islands, lying northwest of the Promontorio del Gargano in the Adriatic Sea. These small limestone islands have lovely reefs, gin-clear waters, and towering peaks.

GETTING TO THE ISLANDS   Between June and September, boats and hydro-foils travel from Vieste, Manfredonia, and Peschici to the Tremiti Islands, and you should make advance reservations in the peak weeks of summer, when the vessels get crowded. In Vieste, contact **Motonave Vieste,** Corso Fazzini 33 on the dock (☎ 0884/707-489), about boat service, a 1 hour and 45 minute trip costing 18,000L ($10.80), or **Adriatica,** Piazza Roma 7 at the Gargano Viaggi office (☎ 0884/ 708-501), which provides 1-hour hydrofoil service from Vieste for 20,000L ($12), as well as a 2-hour trip from Manfredonia for 30,900L ($18.55), leaving from the dock a three-minute walk south along Piazza Marconi toward Siponto. In Peschici, **Onda Azzurra,** Corso Umberto I, 16 (☎ 0884/964-234), makes daily boat runs to the islands, a trip of just over an hour that costs 17,500L ($10.50). Departures from all ports leave at 9:05am daily, with a return at 6pm.

EXPLORING THE TREMITI

By boat or hydrofoil, you'll arrive at the docks of **San Nicola,** the smaller of the two inhabited islands, where you can explore the castle from the 15th century (it's not much of a sight, but the view is spectacular). You might also want to visit the **Santa Maria a Mare,** the Church of Santa Maria, which grew out of a 9th-century abbey, one of many monasteries which once stood in the Tremiti. It has been largely rebuilt over the years, retaining only an intricate mosaic floor and early Byzantine cross from its early history. All of its treasures were plundered by pirates in 1321.

Between the islands of San Nicola and **San Domino,** the other inhabited island, you can take a shuttle boat, which runs every 15 minutes at a cost of 2,000L ($1.20). This is the largest island of the group, with a rock-strewn shoreline, which is best known for its grottoes—Grotta del Bue Marino, Grotta di Sale, and Grotta delle Viole. The only beaches of the Tremiti are found here, and the **Cala delle Arene,** located near the dock, is generally crowded with visitors, but you can also make your way to the west and south sides of the island where the only other approachable beaches (most are located at the foot of treacherous cliffs) offer stretches of solitude. As a historical footnote, Charlemagne's quarrelsome Italian father-in-law and Augustus's daughter were both exiled on the island, and Julia, granddaughter of Augustus, died here.

WHERE TO STAY

Hotel Gabbiano. Isola San Domino, 71040 San Nicola di Tremiti. ☎ **0882/463-410.** Fax 0882/663-428. 40 rms. A/C MINIBAR TV TEL. 160,000L–258,000L ($96–$154.80) per person, with half board included. AE, MC, V.

Built in 1973, and radically renovated from top to bottom in 1992, this is the best-managed and most appealing hotel on the island. It lies about a half-mile from the port, on San Domino's most beautiful stretch of coastline, in a palm garden that, after the sun-baked terrain around it, seems like a lush oasis. Most of the ground floor is devoted to a bar, a restaurant that's open to nonresidents, a solarium, and the reception area. Bedrooms are airy, summery, and painted in pastel shades that go well with the relentless sunshine streaming through the big windows.

Hotel San Domino. Isola San Domino, 71040 San Nicola di Tremiti. ☎ **0882/463-404.** Fax 0882/663-221. 24 rms. TV TEL. 140,000L–250,000L ($84–$150) double. Rates include half board. AE, DC, MC, V.

Less elegant than the preferred choice, Gabbiano (above), this is a simple three-star hotel that was built in 1975 in a position about a mile from the port. It's within a 5-minute walk from the nearest beach, and contains serviceable but simple white-walled bedrooms designed for escapist holidays near the beach. There's a restaurant on the premises, and a bar, but few other amenities.

VIESTE

57 miles NE of Foggia, 111 miles NW of Bari, 170 miles NE of Naples

At Vieste, on the far eastern shore of the Gargano, a legendary monolith stands firmly rooted in the sea. The rock is linked to the woeful tale of Vesta, a beautiful girl supposedly held prisoner on the stone by jealous sirens.

In recent years the town has blossomed as a summer resort, as it offers some of the beast beaches in the south. If you're just passing through, take time out to walk through the charming medieval quarter, with its whitewashed houses built on terraces overlooking the sea. Vieste is also a good center from which to explore the other excellent sandy beaches along the southern shoreline.

WHERE TO STAY

✪ Pizzomunno Vieste Palace Hotel. Lungomare Enrico Mattei, 71019 Vieste. ☎ **0884/ 708-741.** Fax 0884/707-325. 170 rms, 10 junior suites. 460,000L–640,000L ($276–$384) double; 660,000L–840,000L ($396–$504) junior suites. Rates include half board. AE, DC, MC, V. Closed late Oct to mid-Mar.

This five-star hotel is much better than any other contender in Gargano, and proud of its 80% Italian clientele. Its Mediterranean architecture, with five stories growing smaller as they rise, allows lots of private terraces on the fourth and fifth floors. Bed-rooms are airy and relatively spacious with big windows. There's an outdoor pool, a spa-style "beauty farm," an in-house movie theater, a piano bar, a high-energy disco, direct access to a beach, and facilities for water sports such as sailing. Ristorante Trabucco is the best hotel dining room in the region, with main courses that include roasted lamb with potatoes, baked or grilled fish such as sea wolf, lobster, and shrimp, salads, and pastas. Within 30 yards of the hotel is this establishment's companion hotel, (La Pineta), with which it shares the same management and the same prices. Even the staff is charming, a grace note that adds a lot to the allure of this well-conceived hotel.

Hotel Seggio. Piazza del Seggio/Via Vieste 7, 71019 Vieste. ☎ **0884/708-123.** Fax 0884/ 708-727. 28 rms. A/C TV TEL. 132,000L–262,000L ($79.20–$157.20) double. Rates include half board. AE, DC, MC, V.

This is the best cost-conscious hotel in town, with a historic pedigree more impres-sive than any of the town's grander palaces, and a simple three-star format. It occu-pies a three-story civic monument that functioned between its construction in the 1600s and around 1910 as the town's city hall. In 1983, it was renovated to become a hotel, with comfortable but basic bedrooms. One edge of it abuts the seafront, the other, one of the town's keynote squares. There's a smallish swimming pool on an outdoor terrace, and a restaurant, open to nonresidents, charging from 12,000L to 17,000L ($7.20 to $10.20) for main courses.

WHERE TO DINE

Al Dragone. Via Duomo 8. ☎ **0884/701-212.** Reservations recommended. Main courses 9,000L–30,000L ($5.40–$18). MC, V. Daily noon–3pm and 7–11:30pm. Closed mid-Oct to mid-Mar. APULIAN.

Its name derives from the dragon you'd expect to emerge from the primeval cave that houses it. Set near the cathedral, in the heart of town, it's usually the first restaurant that anyone mentions when honeymooners are looking for a secluded, romantic, candlelit hideaway that's memorable as much for its rock walls and reminders of the region's tortured topography. Decor includes flickering candles and raffia-sheathed Chianti bottles, and cuisine is based on the folkloric traditions of old Apulia. Look for seafood pastas, antipasti buffets, lamb roasted with herbs and potatoes in the oven, and flavors lush with garlic, rosemary, and pesto.

Box 19. Via Santa Maria di Merino 13. ☎ **0884/705-229.** Reservations recommended. Main courses 8,500–26,000L ($5.10–$15.60). MC, V. Daily noon–3pm and 7pm–midnight. Closed Mon Oct–Mar. APULIAN.

Box 19 makes less of an attempt to capitalize on local folklore than some other competitors, and as such offers a more culturally neutral and relatively sophisticated dining experience that appeals to the many northern Italian visitors. Despite that, cuisine is characteristically Apulian, with lots of emphasis on fresh fish, tomato-based pastas, roasted lamb with potatoes, and antipasti offerings that might wow you with their emphasis on pungent fresh fish (especially anchovies and sardines) and fresh marinated vegetables. It was established in the early 1980s in a former car repair shop—its post office box was no. 19. Despite that, accessories are antique (or antique-looking) and much older than the premises that contain them.

3 Bari

162 miles SE of Naples, 281 miles SE of Rome

The teeming seaport of Bari, often called the "doorway to the Orient," has been an important port since ancient times. Because of the central location of the city, almost every one of the major European powers has made use of the port. The crusaders passed through here on their way to the Holy Land. In more recent times, planes and ships departed from Bari during World War II to stage attacks on Yugoslavia and Greece.

The capital city of Apulia, Bari is divided into two parts. The modern section dates from the 19th century. Here, wide streets lined with palms follow a strict grid pattern. The area is home to the best restaurants of Bari, along with the more upscale hotels and shops.

In contrast, a twisting maze of narrow lanes characterizes the other section, called Città Vecchia (old city). Buildings here date from Byzantine times, although the present look is medieval. This area is definitely worth a visit—the streets are filled with shops, old women in black hanging laundry out to dry, and hordes of children, many of whom bathe in the public fountains. Unfortunately, the old town is also peopled with petty thieves and pickpockets who target tourists. Don't let fear keep you from enjoying the area though—just guard your belongings closely and be very aware of your surroundings.

To reach the old city from the Stazione Centrale, head north to Piazza Umberto I and continue along one of several streets, perhaps Via Andrea da Bari, until you come to it. In the southwestern corner of Città Vecchia is Piazza Garibaldi, a heartbeat center of the area. From here you can head west along Corso Vittorio Emanuele to Porto Vecchia or the "old port." A pedestrians-only thoroughfare, Via Sparano is the major shopping street of Bari. Finally, you may want to either drive or walk along one of the most scenic streets of Bari, Lungomare Nazario Sauro, running along the Porto Vecchia, which provides distant views of the Adriatic.

ESSENTIALS

GETTING THERE By Plane Air France (☎ 080/538-2370), **Alitalia** (☎ 080/521-6511), **British Airways** (☎ 080/558-4944), and **Lufthansa** (☎ 080/

466-014) all provide service to Bari from the major airports of Europe. Flights land at the **Bari Palese Airport** (☎ 080/538-2370), situated less than 15 miles west of the city. A shuttle bus will take you to the bus station in Bari for 6,000L ($3.60).

By Train The main FS train network has six trains per day that leave Rome for the 8-hour trip to Bari, arriving at the **city station** in Piazza Aldo Moro (☎ 080/ 521-6801) in the center. The one-way fare is 37,000L ($22.20). More frequent trips between Bari and some of the larger towns in the region are also provided by FS. The 2-hour ride from Brindisi or Taranto will cost you 9,800L ($5.90); a 2½-hour trip from Lecce goes for 11,700L ($7). Several private lines also use the station.

By Bus Several companies serve the Bari area. Of these, the most convenient service is **AMET** (☎ 080/579-3819), whose buses arrive just outside the train station. **FSE** (☎ 080/556-2111), just south of the train station, is an equally good choice.

By Car The Autostrada A14, coming down Italy's Adriatic coast and passing by Foggia, leads to Bari. The A16 from Naples meets up with the A14 about 72 miles west of Bari.

VISITOR INFORMATION The **tourist information center** is located at Piazza Aldo Moro 32 (☎ 080/524-2244). It's open Monday to Friday from 8:30am to 1pm. During the summer, the center also opens Monday to Friday from 3 to 7pm and Saturday from 8:30am to 1pm.

EXPLORING BARI

Bari's most famous attraction is the **Basilica of San Nicola,** Via Palazzo di Città (☎ 080/521-1205), which was built during the 11th and 12th centuries to house the bones of the city's patron saint, known to many as Santa Claus. The saint was known for his kindness for children; in fact, he is said to have raised three children from the dead after a butcher sliced them up and preserved their bodies in brine. A painting depicting the resurrection of the children fills the back wall of the church. The bones of the saint, which legend says in 1087 were brought home from Mira in Asia Minor (now part of Turkey) by Barese sailors, are housed in an underground crypt. The church's other chief treasure is the white-marble bishop's throne in the upper part of the basilica. The basilica itself was built in the Apulian-Romanesque style and incorporates parts of a palace once occupied by Byzantine rulers. The church is open daily from 7am to noon and 4:30 to 7pm.

The narrow Strada di Carmine in back of the basilica leads to the **Cattedrale di Bari,** Piazza dell'Odegitria (no phone), which is built in much the same style. It is primarily from the 12th century, but has been rebuilt and restored many times. A big rose window "protected" by monsters and grotesques, along with a squat bell tower, dominate the exterior. The interior is rather austere. The cathedral is open daily from 7am to noon and 4:30 to 7pm.

Looming behind the cathedral, the **Castello Svevo** (Swabian Castle), Piazza Federico di Svevia (☎ 080/521-4361), was built on a Roman fort but was later redesigned by Frederick II. During the 16th century, Queen Isabella of Spain held court here. Although the castle is often closed to allow archeologists to excavate mementos from Roman and Byzantine times, you can sometimes pass under the Gothic portal into the harmonious courtyard. Normal hours for touring the castle are Monday to Saturday from 8:30am to 1pm and 3:30 to 7pm, Sunday from 8:30am to 1pm. Admission is 4,000L ($2.40).

The most complete collection of Apulian archeological material in Italy is shown at the **Museo Archeologico,** Palazzo dell'Anteneo at Piazza Umberto I (☎ 080/521-1559). Greek and Roman artifacts found in excavations in Bari province, including a rich collection of ancient vases and a remarkable array of bronzes, are displayed. The museum has been closed for renovations but should reopen sometime in 1999.

On the seaside promenade of Lungomare Nazario Sauro, the **Pinacoteca Provinciale,** Via Spalato 19 (☎ **080/541-2461**), presents a collection of Italian art. The rather boring collection covers late medieval to present times and features several paintings by well-known artists. Among these, paintings by Bellini, Veronese, and Tintoretto are the major attractions. The museum is open Tuesday to Saturday from 9:30am to 1pm and 4 to 7pm and Sunday from 9am to 1pm. There is no admission charge.

A CASTLE NEAR BARI

Situated atop a hill 35 miles from Bari is the **Castel del Monte,** an impressive structure built by Frederick II between 1240 and 1250. The somewhat mysterious castle is arranged in a perfect octagon, with eight corner towers and eight trapezoidal rooms on each floor. Theories abound as to why the castle was erected. Scholars have ruled out its use as a military defense, and rumors of its construction as a prison have gone unproved. It is known that the castle was used as a hunting lodge at some point and may have also served as an observatory. Although fully restored, many of the sculptures and decoration that characterized the interior were lost before the 18th century. Today the castle is mostly visited for its unique architecture and the views the upper levels provide of the Tavoliere and the surrounding countryside. The Castel del Monte is open April through September, Monday to Saturday from 3:30am to 7pm, Sunday from 9am to 1pm. The rest of the year, it opens Monday to Saturday from 8:30am to 1pm and 2pm to sunset, Sunday from 9am to 1pm. Admission is 4,000L ($2.40). To get here from Bari, take the Bari-Nord train to Andria and then a bus toward Spinazzola. The round-trip ticket costs 10,000L ($6). To drive from Bari, take route 96 toward Modugno. After 6 miles, transfer to autostrada 98 west for 17 miles, passing Bitonto and Terlizzi. Just past Ruvo di Puglia, get on route 170 west and go 12 miles to reach Castel del Monte.

WHERE TO STAY

The **Stop-Over Bari program** (☎ 080/521-4538), a cooperative effort between the city government and grassroots organizations to make Bari more attractive to backpackers headed for Greece, offers tourists under 30 a free campsite and other invaluable assistance. If you're older, or just not willing to rough it, but still on a budget, Bari is probably not the place for you. Medium-priced or first-class lodgings are your best bet when you visit this fascinating but often difficult city.

Grand Hotel Ambasciatori. Via Omodeo 51, 70125 Bari. ☎ **080/501-0077.** Fax 080/502-1678. 177 rms, 14 suites. A/C MINIBAR TV TEL. 220,000L–290,000L ($132–$174) double; 500,000L ($300) suite. Rates include breakfast. AE, DC, MC, V. Parking 20,000L ($12).

This is a comfortable first-class facility on the outskirts of the city. Equipped with its own rooftop heliport, the hotel also has a heated swimming pool and panoramic elevators that provide sweeping views of the surrounding gardens and cityscape. Rooms are soundproof, attractively furnished, and well kept. A garage ensures that guests do not have to leave their cars unguarded on the streets at night. The hotel also operates a well-appointed restaurant, La Mongolfiera, which serves both classic Italian dishes and occasional specialties of Puglia.

Jolly Hotel. Via Giulio Petroni 15, 70124 Bari. ☎ **080/556-4366.** Fax 080/556-5219. 164 rms. A/C MINIBAR TV TEL. 270,000L ($162) double. AE, DC, MC, V.

Part of one of Italy's foremost 4-star hotel groups, the Jolly Hotel is an up-to-date and well-equipped establishment. Located approximately 1¹/₂ miles from the harbor, the hotel is convenient to most of Bari's important attractions. The rooms are spacious and well furnished and provide a comfortable respite from touring hot, sticky Bari. The hotel also has a restaurant that serves a variety of local fish main courses along with international cuisine.

Hotel Boston. Via Piccinni 155, 70122 Bari. ☎ **800/528-1234** in the U.S. or 080/521-6633 in Italy. Fax 080/524-6802. 70 rms. A/C TV TEL. 150,000L–210,000L ($90–$126) double. AE, DC, MC, V.

Hotel Boston is a modern hotel near the center of town, the port, and the railway station. The hotel lies on a major street, just off of Piazza Garibaldi, and is just a short walk from the Bari's major attractions. A member of the Best Western chain, it is one of the best middle-bracket hotels in Bari, with comfortable, well-maintained, but uninspired bedrooms.

Palace Hotel. Via Lombardi 13, 70122 Bari. ☎ **080/521-6551.** Fax 080/521-1499. 200 rms, 7 suites. A/C MINIBAR TV TEL. 230,000L–300,000L ($138–$180) double; from 390,000L ($234) suite. AE, DC, MC, V.

This first-class hotel offers the best accommodations in Bari. The severe exterior lines belie the comfortable luxury of the hotel's interior. Antique furniture and reproductions of classic Italian art characterize the decor, and each floor is furnished in a different decorative style, from Louis XVI to Liberty of London. The Murat restaurant, an exclusive rooftop dining establishment, is well known for its sophisticated cuisine and view over the city. Also popular is the hotel's piano bar.

Villa Romanazzi Carducci. Via Giuseppe Capruzzi 326, 70124 Bari. ☎ **080/542-7400.** Fax 080/556-0297. 89 rms. A/C MINIBAR TV TEL. 250,000L–360,000L ($150–$216) double. Rates include breakfast. AE, DC, MC, V. Parking 20,000L ($12).

Old meets new in this hotel as structures of metal and glass rise from century-old Italian gardens complete with fountains and exotic plants. Although the rooms here are a bit spartan, the Villa Romanazzi-Carducci provides comfortable accommodations, and it's more intimate than the Palace, attracting a chic clientele. An inviting dining room serves Italian and international cuisine. The hotel also has a swimming pool and garage.

WHERE TO DINE

Even if you're here only for a short time, try to visit one of the restaurants in the old town, who serve authentic Apulian cuisine at reasonable prices. However, these places often do not provide menus or itemized checks, so be careful—you may end up with something you can't eat that costs more than you had bargained for. Most of the modern restaurants of Bari are located in the commercial center of town. Here, you'll find menus catering to a more international clientele.

Ai Due Ghiottoni. Via Putignani 11. ☎ **080/523-2240.** Reservations recommended. Main courses 18,000L–25,000L ($10.80–$15). AE, DC, MC, V. Mon–Sat 12:30–3:30pm and 7:30pm–midnight. Closed Sun and Aug. ITALIAN/INTERNATIONAL.

This is a well-decorated restaurant located in the commercial center of the city, a short distance from the burnt out Petruzzelli Theater. The cuisine includes both international and northern-Italian specialties as well as those from Puglia. *Risotto ai frutti di mare*, pasta with a variety of seafood, is a favorite. Also deservedly popular are the grilled lamb and the *pappardelle* (wide noodles) *ai Due Ghiottoni*. You might also try a local favorite, fava bean purée with chicory leaves. Various Adriatic fish are available, and the chef will prepare it as you like it. Translated, the name of the restaurant means "two gluttons."

✪ **La Nuova Vecchia Bari.** Via Dante Alighieri 47. ☎ **080/521-6496.** Reservations recommended. Main courses 14,000L–30,000L ($8.40–$18); menu degustazione 50,000L–60,000L ($30–$36). AE, DC, MC, V. Sat–Thurs noon–3:30pm and 7:30–11pm. Closed Aug. ITALIAN/APULIAN.

This restaurant, operated by the members of the Lagrasta family, serves the best food in Bari. Concentrating on regional cuisine, menu items include spicy meats, fish, pastas, and seasonal vegetables. The restaurant is most known for its antipasti trolley, which features a wide selection, including local mortadella and sausages, and focaccia with anchovy, ricotta, onion, and olives. Desserts often use almonds as a base. The decor is strictly regional, and a meal here is a bit Rabelaisian. Locals really know how to tuck it in.

La Pignata. Via Melo 9. ☎ **080/523-2481.** Reservations recommended. Main courses 16,000L–25,000L ($9.60–$15); fixed-price menu 50,000L ($30). AE, DC, MC, V. Tues–Sun noon–3:30pm and 7:30pm–12:30am. Closed Aug. ITALIAN/APULIAN.

The proprietors of this restaurant welcome their guests with a warm greeting and good food. Some consider La Pignata one of the finest restaurants in southern Italy. The modern setting and traditional food combine to create a pleasant dining experience. The many varieties of homemade pasta are favorites of diners, especially when accompanied by fresh local seafood. Other specialties include the *Tiella alla barese* (a kind of Italian paella) and a purée of fava beans and chicory leaves. The owners toil in the kitchens and dining room, offering old-world service and a style of cookery adhering to the ancient concepts of the Pugliese cuisine.

BARI AFTER DARK

Teatro Petruzzelli (☎ **080/524-1761**), which featured performances of drama, opera, and ballet, was almost completely destroyed in a fire in 1991. It's closed indefinitely as workers try to rebuild it, but it never hurts to call to see if it will be up and running by the time you visit. If it's not, call the **Teatro Piccinni** (☎ **080/521-3717**), which still offers concerts during the spring.

Most of the young people in Bari gather on the streets between Piazza Armando Diaz and Largo Eroi del Mare. You may want to stop in for a drink in this area at **Baraonda,** Largo G. Bruno (no phone), or **Reiff,** Largo Adua 1 (no phone), which has live music and American food. To keep the American atmosphere, try a drink at the **Yankee Pub,** Corso Vittorio Emanuele 98 (no phone). If you're looking for a more authentic Italian good time, catch a bus to the nearby town of Bisceglie. Here you'll find **Divanae Follie,** Via Ponte Lama 3 (☎ **080/958-0033**), a dance club packed with sweaty patrons moving to the music. The cover here is 25,000L ($15). Closer, but not as popular, is **Arena,** Via Tridente 15/21 (no phone). The mix of Italian, American, and English music keeps dancers grooving into the night.

During the summer, festivals keep the air in Bari filled with music. The **Fest della Musica** brings an eclectic mix of locals and visitors into the streets to enjoy free concerts that last all day and part of the night. The **Bari Rock Contest** at the Pineta San Francesco is held every year in August.

The largest fair in southern Italy, the **Levante Fair** attracts vendors from all over the world. Held adjacent to the municipal stadium, the event runs for 10 days in mid-September. The **Festival of San Nicola,** held from mid-April to early June, celebrates the city's patron saint. The tourist office will supply information and details about all these festivals.

4 The Trulli District

45 miles NW of Brindisi, 37 miles SE of Bari, 28 miles N of Taranto

The center of a triangle made up by Bari, Brindisi, and Taranto, the Valley of Itria has long been known for olive cultivation and for the beehive-shaped houses that dot its landscape. The curious structures, called *trulli*, were built at least as early as the 13th century, possibly even before. Their whitewashed limestone walls and conical fieldstone roofs utilize the materials available in the area in such a way that mortar is not used to keep the pieces together. Several theories abound as to why the trulli aren't built with mortar—the most popular being that the buildings, which were considered substandard peasant dwelling, had to be easily dismantled in case of a royal visit. See the box, "The Mystery of the Trulli," below for more speculation.

The center of the district, and home to the greatest concentration of trulli, is **Alberobello.** Here, the streets are lined with some 1,000 of the buildings. You may feel as if you've entered into some page of a child's storybook as you walk through the maze of cobbled streets that curve through Italy's most fantastic village. The crowds of visitors will quickly relieve you of any such thoughts, however. Many of the trulli have been converted into souvenir shops where you can buy everything from postcards to miniature models of the dwellings. Be careful though; if you enter you're expected to buy something—and the shop owners will let you know it.

ESSENTIALS

GETTING THERE   By Train   FSE trains leave Bari every hour (every two hours on Sunday) heading to Alberobello. The trip takes approximately an hour and 40 minutes and costs 5,700L ($3.40). To find the trulli, follow Via Mazzini, which turns into Via Garibaldi, until you reach Piazza del Popolo. Turn left on Largo Martellotta, which will take you directly to the edge of the popular tourist area.

By Car   Head south of Bari on S100, then east (signposted) on S172.

VISITOR INFORMATION   The **tourist information office** in Alberobello is just off of the central square, Piazza del Popolo, at Piazza Ferdinando IV (☎ **080/932-5161**). It's open daily from 9am to noon and 4 to 8pm.

SEEING THE SIGHTS

The most well-known of the trulli is the *trullo sovrano,* or sovereign trullo in Alberobello. The 50-foot structure, the only true two-story trullo, was built during the 19th century to serve as headquarters for a religious confraternity and carbonari sect. To find it, head down Corso Vittorio Emanuele until you get to the church, then take a right. The trullo sovrano is open daily from 10am to 1pm and 3 to 7pm, charging no admission.

On the outskirts of Alberobello, you can also visit **Castellana,** a small town that is home to a series of caverns that have been carved out over the centuries by water streaming through the rocky soil. A wide stairway leads visitors down through a tunnel into a cavern called the Grave. From here, a series of paths winds through other underground rooms that are filled with the strange shapes of stalagmites and stalactites. The culmination of the journey into the earth ends with the majestic Grotta Bianca. Here, alabaster concretions are the result of centuries of Mother Nature's work. Grotte di Castellana can only be visited on guided tours, usually one per hour until early afternoon. The tours cost from 15,000L to 30,000L ($9 to $18); call ☎ 080/496-5511 for a schedule of tours. Be sure to bring a sweater—the average underground temperature is 59°F, even on hot summer days.

The Mystery of the Trulli

The architectural mystery of Southern Italy, the igloo-shaped trulli are the most idiosyncratic habitations of Italy. They are constructed of local limestone without mortar. A hole in the top allows smoke to escape.

Southwest of Bari, in an area roughly hemmed in by Gioia del Colle to the west, Ostuni to the south, and the Adriatic coastline to the east, these strange whitewashed limestone buildings are roofed with tall spiraling cones of a stone prevalent in the region. Trulli are found nowhere else in the entire country.

The structures look somewhat primitive, giving them an air of being ancient, though most of the existing buildings are less than two centuries old. Many are new constructions, since the people of the area are quite attached to their unique architectural form, using it to house businesses as well as homes. The trulli are of a uniformly small size. If more space is needed, local custom dictates the construction of several connected trulli rather than a single larger one. In fact, the one trullo in the entire area that dared expand into a two-story structure is of such renown that the residents of Alberobello will point it out to you or tell you where to find it (in the Piazza Sacramento).

Some locals call trulli signalmen's houses, and others refer to them as monuments and point out obscure symbols that adorn the most traditional of the structures. These symbols were copied over the centuries from the emblems that embellish the few remaining ancient structures. One of the most puzzling things is that, despite great attachment to the buildings, no one in the region can tell you why the form came into favor in the first place, what the traditional emblems symbolize, or even why they're called by any of the names associated with them.

SHOPPING   Most popular among visitors to the Trulli District are the hand-painted clay figurines that abound in every souvenir shop. You can also find a good assortment of fabrics and rugs at reasonable prices. If you'd like to take a trullo home with you, visit the shop of **Giuseppe Maffei,** 741 Via Duca d'Aosta (☎ 080/721-9325), which has the best selection.

WHERE TO STAY & DINE IN ALBEROBELLO

Most visitors choose to visit the area for a one-day excursion; therefore, hotels in Alberobello are limited. You may be able to find individual renovated trulli that are rented to two to eight people for a relatively cheap rate. Call the tourist office for information. Otherwise, the accommodations here are usually more expensive than those in Bari and other nearby towns.

Colle del Sole. Via Indipendenza 63, 70011 Alberobello. ☎ **080/721-814.** Fax 080/721-370. 24 rms. TV TEL. 80,000L ($48) double. AE, DC, MC, V.

On the edge of town, a few minutes walk from the trulli zone, this hotel is a modern two-story structure. The bedrooms are basic, yet comfortable, and have small balconies. A friendly staff is eager to make your stay a pleasant one. The hotel also has a restaurant that serves both local and international dishes.

Dei Trulli. Via Cadore 32, 70011 Alberobello. ☎ **080/932-3555.** Fax 080/932-3560. 19 suites. MINIBAR TV TEL. Half board 170,000L–180,000L ($102–$108) per person. AE, DC, MC, V.

The people of Alberobello don't seem to care where the trulli came from. Only a few scholars have tackled the problem, in the end making half-hearted suggestions that perhaps they are of Saracenic or Greek origin—theories that have neither been proven nor dispelled. One line of logic points out that limestone, a calcareous rock that is found in abundant stratiform throughout the region, is easily separated into thin layers which can readily be shaped into crude bricks that don't require mortar when relayered. The dome design also allows heat to rise, perhaps slightly cooling the living space, a significant factor in the brutal summer heat of the region. Given that the area has long been impoverished, perhaps the design is nothing but good old ingenuity, a means of cheaply constructing homes and businesses with the materials at hand—but that still doesn't explain the hieroglyphics.

One suggestion is that the origin of the trulli had to do with outwitting the Spanish ruler, Ferdinand I of Aragón. This king ordered that Apulians could not build permanent dwellings. That way, he could move the labor force around as he chose. Apulians constructed these houses so that they could be dismantled when they spotted the king's agents. Another theory suggests that also during Spanish rule a tax was levied on individual homes, except for unfurnished homes for which the trulli qualified when their roofs were removed.

Other theories link them with similar structures in Mycenae and suggest their origins may be as old as 3000 B.C. Apulia was part of Magna Graecia and could have come under the influence. Similarities have been noted between the trulli of Apulia and the "sugarloaf" houses of Syria. It's been suggested this idea, traveling west, influenced builders in southern Italy who initially used the trulli as tombs. It's also been noted that soldiers returning from the Crusades may have brought the architectural curiosity to Alberobello.

In what is almost a village unto itself, Dei Trulli, offers visitors the experience of living in one of the unique beehive-shaped houses for which this area is famous. Each of the mini-apartments may have one, two, or even three cones—circular buildings wedged together in the Siamese fashion. Most have a bedroom with bath, a small sitting room with a fireplace, and a patio. The complex also has a swimming pool, attractively landscaped grounds, and a restaurant. The cuisine served here is predominantly regional and is presented in individual ceramic pots. The pignata—a veal stew—accompanied by a glass of red Primotivo wine from Turi makes a good meal.

✪ **Il Poeta Cantadino.** Via Indipendenza 21. ☎ **080/721-917.** Reservations recommended. Main courses 30,000L–35,000L ($18–$21). AE, DC, MC, V. Daily noon–3pm and 7–11pm. Closed Mon during off-season and two weeks in Jan. ITALIAN.

This restaurant is understated but elegant, with linen tablecloths set with silver and crystal enclosed by stone walls. Candlelight casts a romantic glow. The antique furniture and Persian rugs that characterize the place are a perfect setting for the well-prepared and succulent regional cuisine that Chef Marco Leonardo presents. The restaurant specializes in fish and seafood dishes. Favorites include *agnello* (lamb) *con cicoriella* and a mixture of beans, wheat, and rice served with octopus and a medley of other seafood. There is also a large antipasti selection.

Trullo d'Oro. Via Cavallotti 27. ☎ **080/932-3909.** Reservations required Sat–Sun. Main courses 15,000L–20,000L ($9–$12). AE, DC, MC, V. Tues–Sun noon–3pm and 8–11pm. Closed Jan.

With a rustic decor within several linked trulli, this restaurant is one of the town's best. The cuisine consists mainly of well-prepared local and regional dishes. Specialties of the restaurant include purée of fava beans and chicory leaves, roast lamb with lampasciuni (a wild onion that grows in the region), and the chef's special pasta, orecchiette served with bitter greens or else with tomatoes, olive oil, garlic, and arugula. Southern desserts, such as ricotta cooked with marmalade, are also served.

5 Brindisi

563 miles SE of Rome, 45 miles E of Taranto

Known to the Romans as Brundisium, this was the terminus of the Appian Way. Many famous Romans passed through here: Augustus, Marc Anthony, Cicero, and Virgil to name a few. An important seaport throughout its history, Brindisi figured in many historical movements in Europe, including the Crusades. More recently, the town was a strategic Adriatic port in both world wars.

Although the Italian word *brindisi* has come into the language of the world as a toast, at first you may not want to raise your glass to this town. It is today, as it has been throughout history, an embarkation point for those crossing the Adriatic to Greece. This means that the place is filled with sweaty backpackers and loads of students waiting to catch a boat across. Get away from the main streets, though, and you'll find a pleasant, if not overly exciting city. *A warning:* Because of the constant flow of people through the town, Brindisi has more than its share of petty thieves; guard your money and passport closely. If you're not heading straight to Greece, it's probably best to store your bags—lone backpackers are considered easy targets.

ESSENTIALS

GETTING THERE   By Train   The **FS** line (☎ **01831/521-975**) has service to the main station in Piazza Crispi, about 1½ miles from the ferry port. Four trains per day leave Rome for the 7-hour trip; towns closer to Brindisi, such as Taranto and Lecce, have more frequent service. During the summer, two trains daily go all the way to the Brindisi Marittima station at the port.

By Bus   Miccolis, Corso Garibaldi 109 (☎ **0831/560-678**), has three buses a day running between Naples and Brindisi. The trip takes five hours and costs 40,000L ($24) for a one-way ticket.

By Car   From Naples, it is a 233-miles drive to Brindisi. Take the Autostrada A3 for 30 miles to autostrada E45/A3, driving toward Salerno where you get the E847/SS407 east. Drive east past Potenza and continue another 62 miles to the E90/route 106. Head north on this road for 30 miles, curving around the Gulf of Taranto. At Taranto, veer northwest on the E90/route 7 to drive into Brindisi.

VISITOR INFORMATION   The **tourist information office** is located at Via Cristoforo Colombo 88 (☎ **0831/562-126**), open Monday to Friday from 8am to 2pm; on Tuesday it's also open from 4 to 7pm.

SEEING THE SIGHTS

While waiting for your ferry to Greece, you may want to explore some of Brindisi. Most of the sights of interest are close to the port, so you won't have to go far and risk missing the boat. Start your tour by heading toward the cathedral or **Duomo,** at Piazza Duomo; you'll be able to find it by the steeple that pokes out from the surrounding cityscape. A mosaic floor that dates from the 12th-century is worth seeing, although the rest of the structure was rebuilt in the 18th century and is unremarkable.

Gateway to Greece

Ferry companies are abundant in Brindisi and most offer very comparable rates. **Adriatica,** Corso Garibaldi 85 (☎ **01831/523-825**), offers free deck seats to passengers who have valid Eurail or InterRail passes on a space-available basis; fares for those wanting to sit inside begin at 29,000L ($17.40). **Fragline,** Corso Garibaldi 88 (☎ **01813/590-334**) and **Minoan Lines,** Corso Garibaldi 65 (☎ **01813/562-200**), are two of the least expensive ferry companies. Depending on the season and where you prefer to sit, one-way fares range from 30,000 to 66,000L ($18 to $39.60). Also note that posted fares do not include a port tax of 10,000L ($6). Instead of taking the time to find one of these agencies, you may want to check with a few of the maritime agents that are scattered throughout the crowds, especially along the commercial promenade Corso Garibladi that leads to the main port. These agents usually represent many of the same ferry companies and offer a much broader range of options for the same price.

To the left of the duomo, near steep stairs leading to the water, is a **Roman column** crowned with carvings of several deities. Neptune, Jove, Mars, and eight tritons tower on the marble cylinder that marks the end of the ancient Appian way. Nearby, a small **Museo Archeologico,** Piazza Duomo 8 (☎ **0831/221-401**), presents numerous finds from excavations along with pottery and sculpture. It's open Monday, Wednesday, and Friday from 9am to 1pm; Tuesday from 9am to 1pm and 3:30 to 6:30pm. Admission is free.

Also in the area is the **Castello Svevo,** a defense fortification built by Frederick II in the 13th century. Although it is not open to the public, from the harborfront side you can look back at the oldest part of Brindisi and the Roman column.

If you just want a break from Roman ruins and artifacts, you may want to take a good book and head to the **Cloister of San Benedetto.** A short walk down Via Tarantini takes you to the cloister where a peaceful courtyard awaits travelers looking for place to relax before boarding their ferries to Greece.

To see Brindisi's greatest attraction, you'll have to leave the harbor area. The **Church of Santa Maria del Casale** lies just north of the city, on the way to the airport (follow Via Provinciale S. Vito around the harbor; it becomes Via E. Ciciriello, then Via Benedetto Brin, then Via U. Maddalena before heading toward the airport; the church is near a sports complex). Started in the 1320s, the structure cannot be confined to one particular period style or cultural influence. The two-toned sandstone facade consists of delicate patterns that contrast with the vertical lines and severe arches of the structure. Inside, Byzantine-inspired frescoes adorn the walls. Most notable is the brightly colored portrayal of the Last Judgment. Painted by Rinaldo, an artist from Taranto, the work graphically depicts saints and sinners as they are judged and meet their fate. Sadly, many of the other frescoes are faded and in disrepair, although they are still of interest to those who take time to examine them. It's officially open daily from 9am to 4pm, but is often closed for no apparent reason.

For a different kind of experience, you may want to visit the **open-air market** off Corso Umberto on Via Battisti. Here you can join the Brindisi locals as they search for the best ingredients for their meals. You may come here to wander through just for fun, but the massive quantities of fresh fruit overflowing from the stalls and scent of fresh pizza and focaccia drifting through the air will probably tempt you to buy at least a small snack.

WHERE TO STAY

Most travelers only spend a few hours in Brindisi; few choose to stay overnight. Because of this, hotel owners are reluctant to invest in their hotels—most are dull and uninspired.

Hotel Majestic. Corso Umberto I, 151, 72100 Brindisi. ☎ **0831/222-941.** Fax 0831/524-071. 65 rms, 3 suites. A/C MINIBAR TV TEL. 210,000L ($126) double; 280,000L ($168) suite. Rates include buffet breakfast. AE, DC, MC, V.

Although it's one of Brindisi's first-class hotels, Hotel Majestic is so modern that it tends to be a bit sterile. The popular chain hotel is located directly on the station plaza and provides a comfortable place to spend the night before or after a boat ride across the Adriatic. If you don't want to venture into the crowd-filled streets to search for a place to dine, the hotel also has a restaurant and grill.

Hotel Mediterraneo. Via Aldo Moro 70, 72100 Brindisi. ☎ **0831/582-811.** Fax 0831/587-858. 66 rms. A/C TV TEL. 178,000L ($106.80) double. Rates include continental breakfast. AE, DC, MC, V.

This modern and fairly comfortable hotel just outside the city center is considered second best in Brindisi. The rooms are rather blandly furnished, but many have balconies and look over the city toward the sea. The hotel's restaurant serves an international menu that centers around well-prepared seafood. Service is prompt and friendly. An added bonus at this hotel is the private minibus, which offers service throughout the city on request.

WHERE TO DINE

Tourist menus are served by most restaurants along the main street. These are best avoided—although they're low in price, the portions are so small you'll need to eat twice to get your fill. Depending on the strength of your stomach, there are also some Brindisi dishes you may want to stay away from. These include *gnummarieddi* (spit-cooked goat entrails) and *stacchiodde* (pig ears in tomato sauce).

La Lanterna. Via Tarantini 14. ☎ **0831/564-026.** Reservations recommended. Main courses 15,000L–22,000L ($9–$13.20); fixed-price menu 45,000L ($27). AE, DC, MC, V. Mon–Sat 12:30–2:30pm and 8–11:30pm. Closed Aug 10–30. ITALIAN.

Set near the Piazza Vittoria near the center of town, this restaurant is elegant and refined. It's located in a building constructed as an inn during the 1400s and has its own garden where diners can enjoy their meals during the summer. Along with a well-chosen collection of wines, La Lanterna specializes in seafood. The pasta is all homemade with whole wheat and is served in rich sauces. The *ravioli ripieni di pesce* made with fresh seafood is savory and filling. Also good is the *maccheroncini alla contadina,* the old-fashioned "housewife" style of cooking macaroni.

BRINDISI AFTER DARK

A citywide celebration, the **City of Brindisi Festival** is held throughout the summer months. Folklore, art, and music can be enjoyed most nights. The tourist office has complete details.

6 Lecce

25 miles SE of Brindisi, 54 miles E of Taranto, 562 miles SE of Rome

Often called "the Florence of the South," Lecce lies in the heart of the Salento Peninsula—the "heel" of the Italian boot. Although the town was founded before the time of the ancient Greeks, it is most known for the architecture, *barocco leccese* (Lecce

Baroque), that defines many of its buildings. Dating from Lecce's heyday in the 16th, 17th, and 18th centuries, these structures are made mostly of fine-grained yellow limestone. Masons delighted in working with the golden material; their efforts turned the city into what one architectural critic called a "gigantic bowl of overripe fruit." Unfortunately, recent restorations have taken away much of the color as workers have whitewashed the buildings.

For centuries Lecce has been neglected by tourists. Perhaps it's for this reason that many of the Baroque-style buildings have remained intact—progress has not over-run the city with modern development. The charm of the city lies in these displays of the lighter Baroque (although many buildings are now in dire need of repair).

ESSENTIALS

GETTING THERE   By Train   Lecce is connected to Brindisi by hourly train ser-vice on the state-run **FS** line. For service from points east and south of the city, you'll have to take the **FSE** line—which isn't known for its speed. Several trains coming from Otranto and Gallipoli enter Lecce each day. The train station is about a 1 1/2 miles from Piazza Sant'Oronzo, in the center of the old quarter.

By Bus   STP buses provide service to Lecce from areas not serviced by train. The tourist information office has schedules.

By Car   Route 613 leads here from Brindisi.

VISITOR INFORMATION   The **tourist information center** (☎ 0832/317-766) is located at Piazza Sant'Oronzo 25. It's open Monday to Saturday from 9am to 1pm and Monday to Friday from 5 to 7pm.

SEEING THE SIGHTS

Piazza Sant'Oronzo is a good place to begin a stroll through Lecce. The 2nd century A.D. **Roman column,** or Colonna Romana, erected here once stood near its mate in Brindisi and together served to mark the end of the Appian Way. Lightning toppled this column in 1528, and the Brindisians left it lying on the ground until 1661, at which time Lecce purchased it and set the pillar up in their home town instead. Saint Oronzo, for whom the square is named, now stands atop it guarding the area. At the southern side of the piazza, you can see the remains of a **Roman amphitheater.** Dat-ing from the 1st century B.C., it accommodated 20,000 fans who came to watch bloody fights between gladiators and wild beasts.

North of the piazza, Via Umberto I leads to the **Basilica di Santa Croce** (☎ 0832/261-957). This ornate display of Leccese Baroque architecture took almost 1 1/2 centuries to complete. Architect Gabriele Riccardo began work in the mid-15th century; the final touches were not added until 1680. The facade bears some similarity to the Spanish Plateresque style and is peopled by guardian angels, gro-tesque demons, and a variety of flora and fauna. St. Benedict and St. Peter are also depicted. The top part of the facade—the flamboyant part—is the work of Antonio Zimbalo, who was called "Zingarello" or gypsy. The interior is laid out in a Latin cross plan and is in a simple Renaissance style. The basilica is open daily from 7am to 12:30pm and 4 to 7pm.

Down Via Vittorio Emanuele, the **Duomo** (cathedral) of Lecce, Piazza Duomo (☎ 0832/308-557), stands in a closed square. The building, which has two facades, was reconstructed between 1659 and 1670 by "the gypsy." To the left of the duomo, the campanile towers 210 feet above the piazza. The cathedral is open daily from 7:30am to 12:30pm and 4 to 7pm. On the opposite side of the cathedral is the **Palazzo Vescovile (Bishop's Place).** Lecce's archbishop still lives here today. Also in the courtyard is a seminary, which was built between 1694 and 1709 by Giuseppe Cino, who was a student of Zimbalo. Its decorations have been compared to those of a wedding cake. A baroque well, extraordinarily detailed with garlands and clusters of flowers and fruit, stands in the seminary's courtyard.

The collection of bronze statuettes, Roman coins, and other artifacts at the **Museo Provinciale,** Viale Gallipoli (☎ **0832/307-415**), will keep your interest for a while. It's worth the time to stop by to have a look at the ornately decorated 13th-century gospel cover. Inlaid with enamel of blue, white, and gold, it's a rare treasure. There is also a small picture gallery in the museum. It's open Monday to Friday from 9am to 1:30pm and 2:30 to 7:30pm. Admission is free.

SHOPPING   To see artisans practicing the centuries-old craft of *cartapesta* (*papier-mâché*), head to **Mario di Donfrancesco's** workshop, Via d'Amelio (☎ **0832/ 312-593**). The workers fashion a variety of objects that you can purchase through the shop, but also make and repair religious reliquaries. The best store for wrought-iron goods in Lecce is **Salvatore Mancarella,** Via Fanteria 95 (☎ **0832/634-544**). For a wide selection of local crafts, including cartapesta, ceramics, and terra-cotta, visit **Mostra dell'Artigianato,** Via Rubichi 21 (☎ **0832/246-758**). **Enoteca**, Via Cesare Battisti 23 (☎ **0832/302-832**), sells red, white, and rosé wines from Salento and other regions of Italy. You may be able to try a glass before deciding to buy a bottle.

WHERE TO STAY

The baroque architecture that Lecce is famous for is lacking in the hotels of the city. Most are modern structures built to accommodate large numbers of visitors who care more about seeing the town and surrounding area than spending time in their rooms.

Albergo Delle Palme. Via di Leuca 90, 73100 Lecce. ☎ and fax **0832/347-171.** 96 rms. A/C TV TEL. 150,000L–180,000L ($90–$108) double. Rates include breakfast. AE, DC, MC, V.

This is the best hotel of the middle-bracket choices in Lecce. In the center of town, it's within easy walking distance of the major Baroque monuments. The common rooms, with their overstuffed leather furniture and paneled walls, are warm and inviting. The guest rooms are comfortably decorated with painted iron beds and small sitting areas. The hotel also operates a good restaurant, serving both regional and national cuisine.

Hotel Cristal. Via Marinosci 16, 73100 Lecce. ☎ **0832/372-314.** Fax 0832/315-109. 63 rms. A/C TV TEL. 160,000L ($96) double. AE, DC, MC, V. Parking 16,000L ($9.60).

This high-rise, metal and glass hotel is a good choice for comfort at a reasonable price. The glossy marble lobby and lounge area is severe, but not sterile, and offers a pleasant place to sit down and enjoy a drink. The rooms vary in size and are decorated monochromatically in purples, pinks, or blues. A small refrigerator and a safe are standard in the accommodations. The hotel also has tennis courts and a large garage.

Hotel President. Via Salandra 6, 73100 Lecce. ☎ **0832/311-881.** Fax 0832/372-283. 154 rms. A/C MINIBAR TV TEL. 250,000L ($150) double; from 300,000L ($180) suite. Rates include buffet breakfast. AE, DC, MC, V.

Although this hotel lies near the historical baroque center of the city, it is a severely modern structure, and Lecce's finest address. The rooms are decorated in the browns and oranges that were the rage during the 1970s, but are large and comfortable. Luckily, the service here makes up for the not-so-appealing decor. Fresh pastries and breads are the highlights of the breakfast buffet. The restaurant serves good regional and international dishes at lunch and dinner.

WHERE TO DINE

During your stay, be sure to sample some of the specialties of the Salento region. These include a tasty combination of mozzarella and tomato wrapped in a light pastry shell.

I Tre Moschettieri. Via Paisiello, 73100 Lecce. ☎ **0832/308-484.** Main courses 8,000L–18,000L ($4.80–$10.80). DC, MC, V. Mon–Sat noon–3pm and 7pm–midnight. Closed Aug. ITALIAN/PIZZA.

Although this restaurant has two rooms in which to seat diners, most visitors choose to have their meal outside on the alfresco patio. The tables throughout the restaurant are widely spaced and allow for undisturbed conversation. Offerings from the *cucina rustica* here include a variety of fresh seafood dishes along with a vast selection of made-to-order pizzas. Local politicians often frequent this place where formal service at moderate prices is the rule. The cuisine is respectful of old traditions, yet aware of new developments in the field of gastronomy.

LECCE AFTER DARK

Because of the large student population at the University of Lecce, there's usually something to keep night owls entertained here. Nightfall usually sees the emergence of young people who flock to the main piazza to join friends for a drink. Piazzetta del Duca d'Atena is an especially popular hangout. For a more active night, you may want to head to **Corto Maltese,** located at Via Giusti 23 (no phone). Wednesday to Monday from 9pm to 2am, crowds gather to dance the night away.

July and August are good times to come to Lecce if you're interested in enjoying authentic Italian night life. During these months the **Estate Musicale Leccese** has nightly festivals of music and dance. Tamer tourists may want to visit the public gardens of the city during July when plays (and sometimes operas) are performed for the public. In September, the churches of Lecce are venues for a festival of Baroque music. The tourist information office (see above) will provide complete details about these diversions.

A SIDE TRIP TO GALLIPOLI

Southwest of Lecce for 23 miles, on the Gulf of Taranto side of the Salento Peninsula, lies Gallipoli. This is not the Gallipoli that is infamous in history books as the sight of one of the bloodiest battles ever fought; that World War I landmark is part of Turkey. The Italian town has a much quieter, and less tragic, past. Originally named Kallipolis, or beautiful city, by the Greeks, the present-day town still has a distinct Greek look. The medieval quarter, once a small island, is especially inviting to explore, with its twisting lanes and plain whitewashed houses.

SEEING THE SIGHTS

Many tourists who come to Gallipoli head straight for the beaches. **Baia Verde,** which is located just south of the town, is especially popular. However, if you take the time to drive down from Lecce, you might as well see what the town has to offer.

One of the most interesting places to visit is the **Museo Civico,** on Via De Pace. There's a little of everything here; it's almost as if the townspeople cleaned out their closets and made what they found into a museum. The collection covers several centuries and many different aspects of life—there's everything from unexploded sea mines to clothing from the 18th century. The museum is open daily, excluding Wednesday and Saturday, from 8:30am to 1pm and 4 to 6pm.

The Greek **nymphaion,** a fountain elaborately decorated with mythological scenes, can be found in the new town near the bridge. It's the only fountain of this type left in Italy, although there are a few still left in Greece.

The town also has a **cathedral** dating from the 1400s and a **castle** that juts out into the Ionian sea. The circular fortress has protected the city for centuries; locals fought off Charles of Anjou's men for seven months here and troops from England attacked the castle in 1809.

If you drive to Gallipoli, you can continue on to discover the tip of the Salento Peninsula, often called **Finibus Terrae,** or Land's End. The Temple of Minerva that was once used by ancient sailors to trace their course has been replaced with the Church of Santa Maria di Leuca, although stones and dolmens that stand in the area are reminders of the long-ago civilization.

Also nearby is **Casarano,** the birthplace of Boniface IX, who was pope from 1339 to 1404. The small Church of Casaranello is here; early Christian mosaics adorn the walls.

It's best to rent a car for this trip; train service to Gallipoli from Lecce is extremely slow and public transportation in the area is limited. It's a quick 25-minute drive down to the town from Lecce, perfect for a day trip to the beach.

WHERE TO STAY & DINE

Grand Hotel Costa Brada. Strada Litoranea, 73014 Gallipoli. ☎ **0833/202-551.** Fax 0833/ 202-555. 78 rms. A/C TV TEL. 230,000L ($138) double. AE, DC, MC, V.

With a swimming pool, tennis courts, a private beach, and its own nightclub, the Costa Brada is more of a resort than a hotel. The hotel is outside of Gallipoli, about four miles down a scenic seaside road. This is the best place to stay in the area, with attractively furnished and well-maintained bedrooms. Its cuisine relies heavily on fresh fish and is served only to residents of the hotel.

Lungomare Marconi. ☎ **0833/266-143.** Reservations recommended. Main courses 15,000L–20,000L ($9–$12); fixed-price menu 30,000L ($18); menu degustazione 55,000L ($33). AE, DC, MC, V. Daily noon–4pm and 7pm–midnight. Closed Tues in winter. GALLIPOLI.

This restaurant, located on a small island connected to the mainland by a bridge, is a popular favorite of the locals. The proprietor, Antonio Giungato, serves authentic Gallipoli cuisine and attracts diners from all along the coast. Using the freshest ingredients available, he adds special spices and a skillful touch to create mouthwatering dishes. Fish dishes are, of course, staples of the restaurant. Specialties include *zuppa di pesce* (fish soup), *risotto alla pescatora* (rice flavored with seafood), and a variety of *dolci della casa* (handmade sweets).

7 Taranto

44 miles W of Brindisi, 62 miles SE of Bari, 331 SE of Rome

Taranto, known to the ancient Greeks as Taras, is said to have been named for a son of Poseidon who rode into the harbor on a dolphin's back. A less fantastic theory, trumpeted by historians, is that a group of Spartans was sent here in 708 B.C. to found a colony. Taranto was once a major center of Magna Graecia and continued as an important port on the Ionian coast throughout the 4th century. A long period of rule under Archytas, a Pythagorean mathematician and philosopher, was the high point in the city's history. According to some, Plato himself came to Taranto during this time to muddle through the mysteries of life with the wise and virtuous ruler.

Ten years of war with the Romans in the 3rd century ended in defeat for Taranto. Although the city lost much of the power and prestige it had once been known for, it did survive through the dark ages and became an important port once more during the time of the Crusades.

Taranto did lend its name to the tarantula, but don't be alarmed; the only spiders here are rather small, harmless brown ones. The dance known today as the *tarantella* also takes its name from this city. Members of various dancing cults believed that individuals who had been bitten by spiders should dance wildly to rid their bodies of the poison; the inflicted person would sometimes dance for days. In modern times the dance is characterized by hopping and foot tapping and is one of the most popular folk dances of southern Italy.

Taranto is a modern, industrial city that many visitors pass by. The once prosperous old city has begun to crumble and the economy of the town has hit a slump, in part because of the scaling back of naval forces stationed in Taranto. However, the new city, with its wide promenades and expensive shops, still draws crowds. Come here if only to taste some of Italy's best seafood. Taranto's location on a peninsula between two seas, the Mare Piccolo and the Mare Grande, is perfect for cultivation of oysters, mussels, and other shellfish.

ESSENTIALS

GETTING THERE   By Train   Regular service from both Bari and Brindisi is provided by the **FS** and **FSE** train lines. Trains leave Bari approximately once an hour for Taranto; the trip takes 1¹/₂ to 2 hours and costs 8,500L ($5.10). For 5,700L ($3.40), you can take the hour ride from Brindisi; trains leave every two hours. Arrivals are on the western outskirts of town, from which you can proceed into the center by bus or taxi.

By Bus   Three bus companies, **FSE, SITA, and CTP,** provide service to Taranto. From Bari, take the FSE bus, which departs every two hours. The trip takes from one to two hours and costs 8,500L ($5.10). The tourist information office has schedules.

By Car   The Autostrada A14 leads here from Bari; the E90 comes in from Brindisi; and Route 7ter makes the trek west from Lecce.

VISITOR INFORMATION   The **tourist information center** is located at Corso Umberto I, 113 near Piazza Garibaldi (☎ 099/453-2392). Hours are Monday to Friday from 9am to 1pm and 4:30 to 6:30pm, Saturday from 9am to noon.

SEEING THE SIGHTS

For the best view of the city, walk along the waterfront promenade, Lungomare Vittorio Emanuele. The heart of the old town, **Città Vecchia,** lies on an island, separating the Mare Piccolo from the Mare Grande. The modern city, or Città Moderna, lies to the north of Lungomare Vittorio Emanuele.

Evidence of Taranto's former glory as an important city in Magna Graecia can be found at the ✪ **Museo Nazionale di Taranto,** Corso Umberto 41 (☎ 099/453-2112). Here, an assortment of artifacts that document Pugliese civilization from the Stone Age to modern times is displayed. Most of the items are the results of archeological digs in the area, especially the excavated necropolis. The museum boasts the largest collection of terra-cotta figures in the world along with a glittering array of Magna Grecian art such as vases, goldware, marble and bronze sculpture, and mosaics. The designs of many of these works would be considered sophisticated even by today's standards. The museum is open daily from 9am to 1:30pm; admission is 8,000L ($4.80).

SHOPPING   If the ornate vases at the National Museum enchanted you, you may want to visit **Grottaglie,** a small town near Taranto that is the ceramics capital of southeast Italy. Hordes of visitors take the 15-minute train ride east of Taranto to buy pottery in a town that boasts a tradition of ceramics work dating from the Middle Ages. Modern styles are crafted here, but most shoppers prefer to purchase traditional pieces, such as the giant vases that originally held laundry or the glazed wine bottles that mimic those of the ancient Greeks. Here, you can buy pieces for a standard 50% discount over what you'd pay anywhere else for Grottaglie pottery, which is sold all over Italy. The whole village looks like one great china shop. Plates and vases are stacked on the pavements and even on the rooftops. Just walk along looking to see what interests you—and bargain, bargain, bargain.

WHERE TO STAY

Choices here are limited. Inexpensive accommodations, in fact, may be impossible to find. Many third- or fourth-class hotels, especially the ones around the waterfront, are unsafe. Proceed with caution. Make reservations in advance—the good hotels, though expensive, fill up fast. It's dangerous to walk around at night; muggings are frequent.

Grand Hotel Delfino. Viale Virgilio 66, 74100 Taranto. ☎ **099/732-3232.** Fax 099/730-4654. 198 rms, 6 suites. A/C MINIBAR TV TEL. 180,000L ($108) double; 300,000L ($180) suite. Rates include breakfast. AE, DC, MC, V.

The Delfino stands on the waterfront, much like a beach club, and is the best place to stay in Taranto. A swimming pool and garden overlooking the sea and a tile sundeck with garden furniture and potted semitropical plants attract many guests. There's also a cozy country-style drinking lounge and bar with ladderback chairs and wood paneling. The rooms are modern and beachy, with tile floors, wooden furniture, and small balconies. The hotel's restaurant serves regional cuisine, including excellent fish dishes. The seaview dining room is a perfect setting in which to try such specialties as Taranto oysters.

Hotel Palace. Biale Virilio 10, 74100 Taranto. ☎ **099/459-4771.** Fax 099/459-4771. 73 rms. A/C MINIBAR TV TEL. 243,000L ($145.80) double. Rates includes breakfast. AE, MC, V. Parking 12,000L ($7.20).

Hotel Palace is the nearest rival to Delfino, but is often preferred by visitors. A first-class hotel, it lies at the eastern end of Lungomare Vittorio Emanuele III, opening onto the Mare Grande. The modern building offers good rooms, each well maintained, all with balconies. A restaurant, bar, and cafe are operated on the premises. Garage parking is available; the peace of mind it provides is worth the extra charge.

Hotel Plaza. Via d'Aqhino 46, 74100 Taranto. ☎ **099/459-0775.** Fax 099/459-0675. 112 rms, 7 suites. A/C TV TEL. 140,000L ($84) double; 240,000L ($144) suite. Rates include breakfast. AE, DC, MC, V.

This is the choice hotel for those who want style along with comfort. The modern hotel opens onto a main square; each well-furnished guest room of the hotel has a balcony overlooking it. Inside, glossy marble and classic furnishings give the place a dignified and contemporary feeling. The hotel is well maintained and a good choice.

WHERE TO DINE

Taranto is blessed with a bountiful supply of seafood; it's fresh from the water, delicious, and best of all, inexpensive. However, avoid anything raw; although the locals like some fish dishes this way, you don't want to risk spending your vacation in the hospital.

Al Gambero. Vico del Ponte 4. ☎ **099/471-1190.** Reservations not necessary. Main courses 8,000L–15,000L ($4.80–$9); fixed-price menu 35,000L ($21). AE, DC, MC, V. Tues–Sun noon–3pm and 8–11pm. Closed Nov. ITALIAN/SEAFOOD.

This restaurant is devoted to the fish dishes that Taranto is known for, including oysters and black mussels. Diners have a choice of enjoying their meal either alfresco or in one of the rooms overlooking the harbor and the old city fish market. The view is supplemented by a collection of colorful contemporary paintings. To start your meal, try the *antipasti frutti di mare*—an assortment of seafood hors d'oeuvres. Main courses include *spaghetti al Gambero* and a filling *orecchiette alla Pugliese,* the most known pasta dish of Apulia.

L'Assassino. Lungomare Vittorio Emanuele II, 29. ☎ **099/459-3477.** Reservations recommended. Main courses 14,000L–20,000L ($8.40–$12); fixed-price menu 32,000L ($19.20). AE, DC, MC, V. Sat–Thurs noon–4pm and 9pm–midnight. Closed Christmas and Aug. ITALIAN/INTERNATIONAL.

Described by its owners as "normal but nice," this restaurant is exactly that—nothing too fancy, but a pleasant place for a good and affordable meal. The dining area offers a panoramic view of the water and a wide range of well-prepared Italian dishes. Of course, L'Assassino has a variety of fresh fish dishes, including *risotto al frutti di mare* (rice with the "fruits of the sea"). Other specialties include orecchiette and *spaghetti marinara.* The proprietors, who have run the place for more than 30 years, are friendly and provide good service.

OFF-THE-BEATEN-TRACK

For years, movie buffs have visited the little town of Castellaneta, birthplace of Rudolph Valentino, the silent screen actor known for starring roles in such films as *The Sheik* (1921), *Blood and Sand* (1922), and *Four Horsemen of the Apocalypse* (1921). Valentino was born in 1895 at Via Roma 114; for decades, the young men of the town modeled themselves, heavily oiled hair and all, after the star. The town still sells mementos of the matinee idol and souvenir photographs. In the town piazza a statue of Valentino stands in the full costume of the character Sheik of Araby. Castellaneta is also known for its "cave churches" and views of the Gulf of Taranto and the Basilicata mountains. Set high in a ravine, the village is not easily accessible except by car. From Taranto, take S7 to the turnoff for Castellaneta.

19 Sicily

Sicily is an ancient land of myth and legend. It is also, according to many Italians, a land unto itself, different from the rest of Italy in customs and traditions—and proudly so. On the map, the toe of the Italian boot seems poised to kick Sicily away from the mainland, as if it did not belong to the rest of Italy. The largest of the Mediterranean islands, it's located some 80 miles from the coast of Africa and is swept by winds that dry its fertile fields every summer, crisping the harvest into a sun-blasted palette of browns. Like its landscape, Sicily is a hypnotic place of dramatic turbulence, as absurdly emotional and intense as a play by native son Luigi Pirandello.

For centuries Sicily's beauty and charm have attracted the greedy eye of foreigners: Greeks (before the island was conquered by Rome), Vandals, Arabs, Normans, Swabians, the fanatically religious House of Aragon, and the French Bourbons.

Homer, in the *Odyssey*, recorded ancient myths about cannibalistic tribes (the Laestrygones) living near the site of modern Catania. Centuries later legends grew about Sicily's patron saint, Agatha, martyred by having her breasts cut off. The island still teems with all kinds of tales shrouded in primeval lore and legend, as well as with stories, many fervently believed, about the curative powers of water from certain caves and the harmful powers of the evil eye. That the Sicilians should have created and held on to such phantasmagoric tales and legends is not surprising, in view of their island's history of natural and political disasters.

Through the centuries, a series of plagues, ferocious family vendettas, volcanic eruptions, earthquakes, and economic hardships have threatened many times to destroy the interwoven cultures of Sicily. Always, the island has persevered. Its archeology and richly complex architecture are endlessly fascinating, and the masses of almond and cherry trees in bloom in February make it one of the most beautiful places in Italy.

Too long neglected by travelers wooed by the art cities of the north, Sicily is today attracting greater numbers of foreign visitors. This land of volcanic islands is full of sensual sights and experiences: a sirocco whirling out of the nearby Libyan deserts, horses with plumes and bells pulling gaily painted carts, vineyards and fragrant citrus groves, Greek temples and classical dramas performed in ancient theaters, and the aromatic fragrance of a glass of marsala.

Sicily

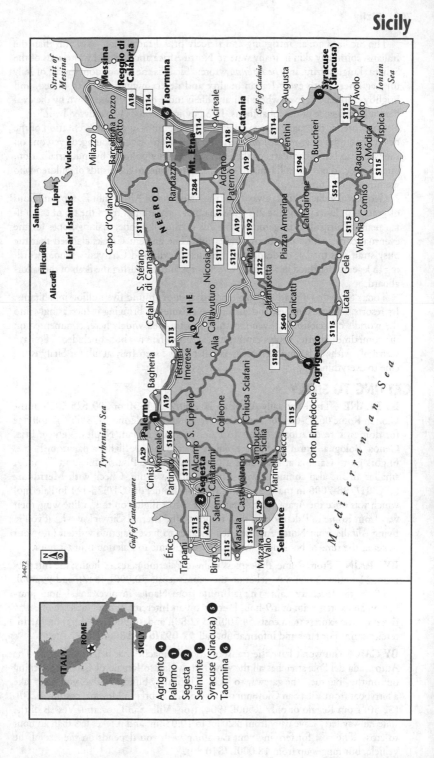

Strait of Messina

Tyrrhenian Sea

Gulf of Castellammare

Lipari Islands

Alicudi
Filicudi
Salina
Lipari
Vulcano

Milazzo
Reggio di Calabria
Messina
Barcellona Pozzo di Gotto
Taormina
Capo d'Orlando
S. Stéfano di Camastra
Cefalù
Términi Imerese
Bagheria
Palermo
Monreale
Cinisi
Partinico
S. Cipirello
Alcamo
Segesta
Calatafimi
Castelvetrano
Salemi
Marsala
Birgi
Mazara d.o Vallo
Marinella
Sciacca
Sambuca di Sicilia
Chiusa Sclafani
Corleone
Alia
Caltavuturo
Nicosia
Randazzo
Adrano
Paternò
Bronte
Biancavilla
Catánia
Acireale
Leníini
Buccheri
Avola
Noto
Óspica
Módica
Ragusa
Cómiso
Vittória
Gela
Licata
Canicattì
Caltanissetta
Enna
Piazza Armerina
Caltagirone
Calascibetta
Mt. Etna

NEBROD
MADONIE

Érice
Trápani

Gulf of Catánia

Ionian Sea

Mediterranean Sea

A29
A19
A18
A19
S186
S113
S113
S115
S115
S115
S115
S113
S117
S117
S121
S121
S120
S114
S114
S114
S284
S192
S122
S194
S514
S640
S189
S113

N

ITALY
SICILY
ROME

Agrigento 4
Palermo 1
Segesta 2
Selinunte 3
Syracuse (Siracusa) 5
Taormina 6

1 Palermo
2 Segesta
3 Selinunte
4 Agrigento
5 Syracuse (Siracusa)
6 Taormina

3-0672

707

The Sicilians are an intriguing and fiercely proud racial mix, less Latin than the Italians, spiritually akin in many ways to North Africa and the wild wastelands of the Sahara. Luigi Barzini, in *The Italians,* wrote: "Sicily is the schoolroom model of Italy for beginners, with every Italian quality and defect magnified, exasperated, and brightly colored. . . . Everywhere in Italy, life is more or less slowed down by the exuberant intelligence of the inhabitants: In Sicily it is practically paralyzed by it."

There are far too many cars in Palermo, a sometimes-unpleasant reflection of the new (sometimes drug-related) prosperity that seems to have encouraged everyone on the island to buy a car. Parts of the island are heavily polluted by industrialization, but the age-old poverty still remains in the streets, home to thousands of children who seemingly grow up there.

Geologically, Sicily broke away from the mainland of Africa (not Europe) millions of years ago. Even today, the 2¹/₂-mile channel separating it from the tip of the Italian peninsula is still a dangerously unstable earthquake zone, making hopes for the eventual construction of a bridge unfeasible. The ancient Greeks claimed that the busy strait was the lair of deadly sea monsters, Scylla and Charybdis, who, according to legend, delighted in wrecking Greek ships and devouring the flesh of the sailors aboard.

Today Sicily has a relatively stable population of around five million inhabitants. Its resorts, ancient temples, and distinctive cuisine are bringing it increasingly into the world's consciousness. Even Goethe, who traveled widely here, commented on the sometimes bizarre, always captivating, symbols he saw, but concluded, "To have seen Italy without having seen Sicily is not to have seen Italy at all, for Sicily is the clue to everything."

GETTING TO SICILY

BY PLANE   There are daily **Alitalia** (☎ **800/223-5730** or 800/625-4825 in the U.S.; in Rome 06/65-641 for domestic reservations; in Palermo 1478/65-641 toll free for domestic reservations) flights to Palermo from Milan, Naples, Venice, Pisa, Genoa, Bologna, Turin, and Rome. There are around six flights a day from Rome. Flights go to Catania at least once a day from Milan, Pisa, Rome, and Turin. A smaller airline also competes with Alitalia on this route. Check with **Meridiana** (☎ **201/798-7000** in the U.S.; 06/478-041 in Rome; or 091/323-141 in Palermo) which was once the Aga Khan's Alisarda line. Most flights on this airline wing their way from Rome to Palermo and then return to the Eternal City. However, if you're flying Alitalia from North America, it's cheaper to have Palermo written into your ticket at the time of booking. Flying time from Rome to Palermo is just 1 hour.

BY TRAIN   From Rome, the express train to Palermo takes 13 hours; the Intercity train, 11 hours. A one-way ticket on the express costs 70,000L ($42), and 95,000L ($57) on the Intercity train. The rail route from Naples involves an 11-hour journey on an express train or a 9-hour journey on an Intercity. From Naples, a one-way ticket on the express train costs 54,700L ($32.80), and 74,900L ($44.95) on the Intercity train. For fares and information, call ☎ **091/616-1806.**

BY CAR   You won't have the transportation headache that plagued Goethe. The Autostrada del Sole stretches all the way from Milan to Reggio di Calabria, sticking out on the "big toe," the gateway to Sicily. Until they build a bridge, you must take a ferryboat from Villa San Giovanni or Reggio di Calabria to Messina, costing 4,200L ($2.50) from Reggio or only 1,500L (90¢) from Villa San Giovanni. Vessels of the state railway ferry leave daily from 3:20am to 10:05pm, and it takes less than an hour to cross. The cost for ferrying your car along with you depends on the size of the vehicle, but ranges up from 18,000L ($10.80).

BY HYDROFOIL (NO CAR)   Much quicker, shaving at least 22 minutes off the crossing time, is an *aliscafo* (hydrofoil) leaving from Reggio di Calabria. You'll pay 4,200L ($2.50) one-way, and the higher price usually means fewer passengers—hence, less crowding. You cannot take your vehicle on a hydrofoil. Call ☎ 0965/29-568 for various connections.

Near Reggio di Calabria, incidentally, is a much smaller community, Scilla, famous in Homeric legend. Mariners of old, including Ulysses, crossed the Strait of Messina from here, and faced the double menace of the two monsters, Charybdis and Scylla.

FROM NAPLES TO SICILY BY SEA   The night ferry from Naples leaves at 8pm, arriving in Palermo the next morning at 7am. On Friday there's another departure at 10pm. The service is run by **Tirrenia S.A.** For information, call the company's office in Naples (☎ 081/720-1111). If you're already in Palermo and want to take the ferry to Naples, dial ☎ 091/333-300; unfortunately, you won't always find someone who speaks English. Sleeping compartments are often booked days in advance, and there may be space available only on deck. The cost for a ferry is 93,600L to 117,000L ($56.15 to $70.20) depending on the car length. First-class passage costs 81,000L ($48.60) per person for a one-way ticket, 71,000L ($42.60) in second class.

1 Taormina

33 miles N of Catania, 33 miles S of Messina, 155 miles E of Palermo

Runaway bougainvillea, silvery olive branches, a cerulean sky, cactuses adorning the hills like modern sculpture, pastel-plastered walls, garden terraces of geraniums, trees laden with oranges and lemons, ancient ruins—all that and more is Taormina, Sicily's most desirable oasis.

Dating from the 4th century B.C., Taormina hugs the edge of a cliff overlooking the Ionian Sea. Writers for English Sunday supplements rave of its unspoiled charms and enchantment. The sea, even the railroad track, lie down below, connected by bus routes. Looming in the background is Mount Etna, the active volcano. Noted for its mild climate, the town enjoys a year-round season.

A lot of people contributed to putting Taormina on the tourist map. Since it was first inhabited by a tribe known as the Siculi, it has known many conquerors, including Greeks, Carthaginians, Romans, Saracens, French, and Spanish. Its first tourist was said to have been Goethe, who arrived in 1787. He recorded his impressions in his *Journey to Italy*. Other Germans were to follow over the centuries, including a red-haired Prussian, Otto Geleng. Arriving at the age of 20 in Taormina, he recorded its beauties in his painted landscapes. These were exhibited in Paris and caused much excitement—people had to go themselves to find out if Taormina was all that beautiful.

Another German, Wilhelm von Gloeden, arrived to photograph not only the town, but also nude boys crowned with laurel wreaths. These pictures sent European high society flocking to Taormina. Von Gloeden's photographs, some of which are even printed in official tourist literature to this day, form one of the most enduring legends of Taormina. Souvenir shops still sell his pictures, which, although considered scandalous in their day, would be tame, even innocent, by today's X-rated standards.

Following in the footsteps of von Gloeden came a host of long-faded international celebrities hoping to see what all the excitement was about: Truman Capote, Tennessee Williams, Marlene Dietrich, Joan Crawford, Rita Hayworth, and Greta Garbo. Always in disguise, sometimes as Harriet Brown, Ms. Garbo used Taormina as a vacation retreat from 1950 until her last mysterious arrival in 1979. Many of these stars, including Garbo, stayed at a villa on the road to Castel Mola owned by Gayelord

Hauser, the celebrated dietitian to Hollywood stars back in the golden age. In time another wave of stars were to arrive: Taylor and Burton, Cary Grant, and the woman who turned him down, Sophia Loren.

The rich and famous still come here, along with a lot of middle-class visitors as well. Taormina remains chic.

ESSENTIALS

GETTING THERE   By Train   You can make rail connections on the Messina line from Syracuse. Telephone ☎ **0942/51-026** in Taormina for schedules. There are 29 trains a day each from Messina and Catania, both taking 45 to 50 minutes and costing 4,200L ($2.50) for a one-way ticket. The train station at Taormina is a mile from the heart of the resort; buses will take you up a hill every 15 to 45 minutes (schedules vary throughout the year), daily 9am to 9pm; a one-way ticket costs 2,500L ($1.60).

By Bus   Most visitors arrive in Messina, the gateway to Sicily. There you can board a Taormina-bound bus; 13 leave per day, taking 1¹/₂ hours. More details are available in Messina by calling **SAIS,** the bus company (☎ **090/771-914**).

By Car   From Messina, head south along autostrada A18. From Catania, continue north along A18.

VISITOR INFORMATION   A **tourist information center** is in the Palazzo Corvaja, Largo Santa Caterina (☎ **0942/23-243**). It's open Monday to Saturday from 8am to 2pm and 4 to 7pm.

SEEING THE SIGHTS

The ✪ **Teatro Greco,** Via Teatro Greco (☎ **0942/23-220**), is the most visited monument, offering a view of rare beauty of Mount Etna and the seacoast. At an unrecorded time the Greeks hewed the theater out of rock on the slope of Mount Tauro, but the Romans remodeled and modified it greatly for their amusement. The conquering Arabs, who seemed intent on devastating the town in the 10th century, slashed away at it. On the premises is an antiquarium, containing not only artifacts from the classical period but early Christian ones as well. The theater is open Tuesday to Sunday from 9am to two hours before sunset. Admission is 2,000L ($1.20) for adults; children 17 and under and seniors 60 and over are admitted free.

Behind the tourist office, on the other side of Piazza Vittorio Emanuele is the **Roman Odeon,** a small theater partly covered by the Church of Santa Caterina next door. This theater was constructed by the Romans when Taormina was under their rule around A.D. 21. Much smaller than the Greek theater, it was discovered in 1892 by a blacksmith digging in the area. Its architecture is very similar to that of the larger theater. A peristyle (colonnade) was discovered here, perhaps all that was left of a Greek temple dedicated to Aphrodite.

Next door you can visit the **Church of Santa Caterina,** whose exact consecration date is unknown. Opposite the Palazzo Corvaja, the church, consecrated to St. Catherine of Alexandria, lies in the center of town. It may have been built in the mid-17th century, and the sacristy may have been constructed even earlier. The facade of the sacristy is decorated with two small windows decorated with sea shells, the same decor used on the architrave of its doors. The opening hours of this church are erratic.

Further along the main drag, **Corso Umberto I,** you arrive at the Piazza del Duomo and the **Duomo** or cathedral of Taormina. Built around 1400 on the ruins of a church from the Middle Ages, this is a fortress cathedral with a Latin cross plan and a trio of aisles. The nave is held up by half a dozen monolithic columns—three on each side in pink marble. Their capitals are graced with a fish-scale decoration. The ceiling of the nave is an attraction, with its wooden beams held up by carved corbels decorated with Arabian scenes. Other features include a main portal reconstructed in 1636 with a large Renaissance-inspired rosette sculpted on it. The cathedral is often open in the early morning or early evening, but is likely to be closed during the day. The monsignor here opens it apparently when he feels in the mood.

The other thing to do in Taormina is to walk through the **Giardino Pubblico,** Via Bagnoli Croce, a flower-filled garden overlooking the sea, a choice spot for views as well as a place to relax. At a bar in the park you can order drinks.

OTHER ACTIVITIES   Many visitors to Taormina come for the beach, although the sands aren't exactly at the resort. For the best and most popular beach, **Lido Mazzarò,** you have to go below the town. From Taormina, you can reach the beach by cable car leaving from Via Pirandello. Departures are every 15 minutes, a one-way ticket costing 2,000L ($1.20). After 8:15pm, the fare is raised to 2,500L ($1.50).

The most popular excursion, other than to Mount Etna, is to the **Gole Alcantara,** a series of beautiful gorges, complete with rapids and waterfalls. Unlike the rest of Sicily, waters here are extremely cold but how refreshing in August. To reach the Alcantara, take one of the SAIS buses which run from Taormina to here three times a day, with departures at 9:15am, 12:15pm, and again at 2pm. There's only one bus back, leaving at 2:20pm. The cost of a round-trip fare is 7,300L ($4.40). For more information, contact the Gole Alcantara office at ☎ 0942/985-810.

SHOPPING   Shopping is easy in Taormina—just get on Corso Umberto I and go. The trendy shops along this street sell everything upscale, from lacy linens and fashionable clothing to antique furniture and jewelry.

Hand-embroidered lace is the draw at **Galeano (Concetta),** Corso Umberto I, 233 (☎ 0942/625-144), where bedspreads and tablecloths are meticulously crafted from fine cotton and linen. If it's old, wearable, and gold, it's at **Gioielleria Giuseppe Stroscio,** Corso Umberto I, 169 (☎ 0942/24-865), where the collection of antique gold jewelry dates from 1500 to the turn of this century. Favoring aesthetic over utility, the jewelers at **Estro,** Corso Umberto I, 205 (☎ 0942/24-991), sell contemporary adornments including rings, necklaces, and bracelets.

Featuring refined fashions for men and women, **Giovanni Vadala,** Corso Umberto I, 189-191 (☎ 0942/625-163), emphasizes casual clothing accessorized by belts and bags. Formerly a Fendi fur store, now **Maru,** Corso Umberto I, 83 (☎ 0942/24-218), offers only shirts and jumpers. Elegant styles for women over 40 can be found at **Mira Boutique,** Corso Umberto I, 48 (☎ 0942/24-960), where you'll find outfits, by the likes of Castigliani and Domino, but not accessories. Feminine fashions are emphasized at **Mazzullo,** Corso Umberto I, 35 (☎ 0942/23-152), which does, however, offer upscale clothing and accessories for both sexes.

Mixing the new and the old, **Carlo Panarello,** Corso Umberto I, 122 (☎ 0942/23-910), offers Sicilian ceramics varying from pots to tables, and also deals in eclectic antique furnishings, paintings, and engravings. A small shop filled with a bounty of national treasures, **Casa d'Arte M. Forin,** Corso Umberto I, 148 (☎ 0942/23-060), sells Italian antiques, ranging from furniture to prints, silver, and bronze, with an emphasis on Sicilian and Venetian pieces. From curios to furniture, **Giovanni Panarello,** Corso Umberto I, 110 (☎ 0942/23-823), offers a wide range of antiques, one of the best selections in town.

WHERE TO STAY

The hotels in Taormina are the best in Sicily—in fact, the finest in Italy south of Amalfi. All price levels and accommodations are available, from sumptuous suites to army cots.

VERY EXPENSIVE

✪ **Palazzo San Domenico.** Piazza San Domenico 5, 98039 Taormina. ☎ **0942/23-701.** Fax 0942/625-506. 101 rms, 9 suites. A/C MINIBAR TV TEL. 550,000L–685,000L ($330–$411) double; 1,050,000L–1,185,000L ($630–$711) suite. AE, DC, MC, V. Parking 30,000L ($18).

This is one of the great old hotels of Europe, converted from a 14th-century Dominican monastery. In 1996, it was used for meetings of top NATO officials. Past clients have included François Miterrand, Winston Churchill, and the aristocrats of old Europe. In 1997, it was discreetly renovated. For sheer luxury there's no other equal in Sicily. Its position is legend to discriminating travelers—high up from the sea coast, on different levels surrounded by terraced gardens of almond, orange, and lemon trees. In the 19th century it blossomed as a hotel, with no expense spared, and was a favorite of the elite.

The large medieval courtyard is planted with semitropical trees and flowers. The encircling enclosed loggia—the old cloister—is decorated with potted palms and ecclesiastical furnishings (high-backed carved choir stalls, wooden angels and cherubs, oil paintings). Off the loggia are great refectory halls turned into sumptuously furnished lounges. Although antiques are everywhere, the atmosphere is not museumlike but gracious. Ornate ceilings climb high and arched windows look out onto the view. The bedrooms, opening off the cloister, would impress a cardinal, filled with one-of-a-kind furniture including elaborate carved beds, gilt, Chinese red, provincial pieces, Turkish rugs, and Venetian chairs and dressers.

Dining/Entertainment: The cuisine, supervised by a masterful chef and the most refined in Taormina, is a combination of Sicilian and Italian dishes. Dining in the main hall is an event. Meals are served around the pool in summer.

Services: Room service, baby-sitting, laundry, valet.

Facilities: Flower-edged swimming pool.

MODERATE

Bristol Park Hotel. Via Bagnoli Croce 92, 98039 Taormina. ☎ **0942/23-006.** Fax 0942/24-519. 50 rms, 2 suites. A/C MINIBAR TV TEL. 250,000L–600,000L ($150–$360) double; 360,000L ($216) suite. Rates include breakfast. Half-board 110,000L–170,000L ($66–$102) per person extra. AE, DC, MC, V. Closed mid-Nov to Feb. Parking 15,000L ($9) in garage.

This four-star hotel, built in the 1950s with improvements and upgrades made virtually every year since, is one of the all-out comfort hotels. Constructed high on the cliffside at the edge of Taormina, close to the public gardens of Duca di Cesaro, it offers a panoramic view of the coastline and Mount Etna from most of its private sun balconies. The interior decor is amusing with tufted satin, plush and ornate. In contrast, the bedrooms are traditional. The dining room, with arched windows framing the view, offers international meals with an occasional Sicilian dish. There's a private beach with free deck chairs and parasols, plus bus service to the beach (June to September). The hotel has a pool.

Excelsior Palace. Via Toselli 8, 98039 Taormina. ☎ **0942/23-975.** Fax 0942/23-978. 89 rms. A/C TV TEL. 260,000L ($156) double with breakfast; 190,000L ($114) per person double with half-board. AE, DC, MC, V.

Designed a century ago in a fanciful late Victorian style reminiscent of a Moorish palace, this hotel lies in the rocky foothills at the edge of town. It's the number two hotel in town, topped only by the San Domenico Palace. It was massively renovated in the early 1990s, and is as foreboding as a fortress on two sides, but the severity dissolved into style and comfort inside. The verdant gardens have terraces of scented semitropical flowers, date palms, yucca, and geraniums and a pool. The view of Etna and the seacoast below is of a rare enchantment. Superior facilities and service await all guests. The bedrooms have plenty of space and are decorated in a traditional manner. The hotel minivan makes a half-dozen trips daily (June to October only) to the beach at Lido Caparena. Here, residents get free use of deck chairs, chaise longues, showers, and changing facilities.

Hotel Monte Tauro. Via Madonna delle Grazie 3, 98039 Taormina. ☎ **0942/24-402.** Fax 0942/24-403. 30 rms, 40 junior suites. A/C MINIBAR TV TEL. 270,000L ($162) double; from 300,000L ($180) junior suite. Rates include breakfast. AE, DC, MC, V. Closed Jan 15–Mar.

Engineering skills and tons of poured concrete went into this dramatic, early 1970s hotel built into the side of a scrub-covered hill rising high above the sea, within view of the coastline. Although not as good as the hotels previously recommended, it does compete successfully against the Hotel Villa Diodoro. Renovated in the early 1990s, each bedroom has a circular balcony with a sea view, often festooned with flowers, and a private bath or shower. The social center is the many-angled swimming pool, whose cantilevered platform is ringed with a poolside bar and dozens of plants. The velvet-covered chairs of the modern, tile-floored interior are upholstered in the same blues, grays, and violets of the sunny bedrooms where Mondrian-style rectangles and stripes decorate the bedspreads and accessories.

Hotel Villa Diodoro. Via Bagnoli Croce 75, 98039 Taormina. ☎ **0942/23-312.** Fax 0942/23-391. 102 rms. A/C MINIBAR TV TEL. 280,000L–320,000L ($168–$192) double with breakfast; 200,000L–260,000L ($120–$156) per person double with half-board. AE, DC, MC, V.

The Diodoro is one of the most luxurious of the first-class hotels. The design of everything—the public lounges, the bedrooms—is well coordinated, on a high taste level. The dining room, with tall windows on three sides, is projected toward the sea and Mount Etna. The outdoor swimming pool is a sun trap; you can sunbathe, swim, and enjoy the view of mountains, trees, and flowers. The bedrooms are tasteful and comfortable, with well-designed furniture and the latest gadgets. Each has a private bath or shower, and many of the rooms are angled toward the sea, with wide-open windows.

INEXPENSIVE

Ariston. Via Bagnoli Croce 128, 98039 Taormina. ☎ **0942/23-838.** Fax 0942/21-137. 176 rms. A/C MINIBAR TEL. 70,000L–140,000L ($42–$84) per person. Rates include half-board. AE, MC, V.

Substantial and cost-conscious, and favored by families from Italy and the rest of Europe, this modern hotel was built in 1975 with four stories rising above a verdant park about 400 yards from the center of Taormina. The well-maintained bedrooms are airy, streamlined, and comfortable, in shades of off-white. About 36 of its rooms are in a low-rise garden annex nearby. Although the hotel is located inland, a short walk from the sea, there's a pool on the premises, a piano bar, and a restaurant with efficient service and both Sicilian and international specialties.

La Campanella. Via Circonvallazione 3, 98039 Taormina. ☎ **0942/23-381.** Fax 0942/625-248. 12 rms. TEL. 120,000L ($72) double. Rates include breakfast. No credit cards.

This hotel is rich in the aesthetics of gardening, painting, and hospitality. It sits at the top of a seemingly endless flight of stairs, which begin at a sharp curve of the main road leading into town. You climb past terra-cotta pots and dangling tendrils of a terraced garden, eventually arriving at the house. The owners maintain clean and uncluttered bedrooms.

Pensione Svizzera. Via Pirandello 26, 98039 Taormina. ☎ **0942/23-790.** Fax 0942/625-906. 26 rms. TEL. 90,000L ($54) double; 105,000L ($63) triple; 120,000L ($72) quad. Rates include breakfast. AE, DC, MC, V. Closed Jan.

This is a pleasant place to stay, about an eighth of a mile from the center of town. Constructed in 1926, the hotel has been run by the same family for three generations, currently Antonino Vinciguerra and his German-born wife, both of whom speak English. Try to get a room that overlooks the sea and Isola Bella. All bedrooms have hair dryers, and 12 open onto sea views. There's also a garden with shady palm trees where breakfast is served in summer. The funicular going down to the beach at Mazzarò is a little over 100 yards from the pensione, as is the bus terminal.

Villa Belvedere. Via Bagnoli Croci 79, 98039 Taormina. ☎ **0942/23-791.** Fax 0942/ 625-830. 30 rms. TEL. 150,000L–239,500L ($90–$143.70) double. Rates include breakfast. MC, V. Closed Nov 15–Dec 15 and Jan 15–Mar 15. Parking 8,000L ($4.80).

This five-story building was conceived as a private villa in 1904, and soon thereafter transformed into the charming hotel you see today. This gracious old villa is bathed in Roman gold near the Giardino Pubblico. In its garden is a heated swimming pool. From the cliffside terrace in the rear—a social center for guests—is that view: the clear blue sky, the gentle Ionian Sea, the cypress-studded hillside, and menacing Mount Etna. It's the same view enjoyed by clients at the more expensive first-class hotels nearby. The formal entrance is enhanced by potted plants and wall-covering vines, and the interior is captivating. The bedrooms have been restored, and 30 of them are air-conditioned. Breakfast is served, and there are two bars. Lunch is at a snack bar by the pool.

✪ **Villa Fiorita.** Via Pirandello 39, 98039 Taormina. ☎ **0942/24-122.** Fax 0942/625-967. 24 rms, 2 suites. A/C MINIBAR TV TEL. 175,000L ($105) double; from 200,000L ($120) suite. Rates include breakfast. AE, MC, V. Parking 15,000L ($9).

One of the most charming hotels in its category, Villa Fiorita stretches toward the town's Greek theater from its position beside the road leading up to the top of this cliff-hugging town. Designed in 1976, its imaginative decor includes a handful of ceramic stoves, which the owner delights in collecting. A well-maintained flowering garden with a swimming pool is bordered by an empty but ancient Greek tomb whose stone walls have been classified as a national treasure. The bedrooms are arranged in a step-like labyrinth of corridors and stairwells, some of which bend to correspond to the rocky slope on which the hotel was built. Each unit contains some kind of antique, and usually a flowery private terrace as well.

Villa Nettuno. Via Pirandello 33, 98039 Taormina. ☎ **0942/23-797.** Fax 0942/626-035. 13 rms. 80,000L–100,000L ($48–$60) double. MC, V. Closed Jan 15–Mar 15 and Nov 15–Dec 15. Parking 8,000L ($4.80).

A favorite budget accommodation in town is this geranium-colored villa with Renaissance-style stone trim. It lies near the city center, opposite a cableway that transports passengers down to the sea. You must climb several flights of steps after leaving the traffic of the main street, passing beneath an archway whose keystone is carved with a grotesque stone face. The villa built in 1860, was acquired by the Sciglio family in 1887 and converted into a well-managed hotel in 1955 by the warm-hearted but highly discerning Maria Sciglio, assisted by her hardworking son, Antonio. Guests enjoy breakfast in a garden with hibiscus and night-blooming jasmine. The dining room is like the rococo living quarters of an elegant Sicilian family. Each of the attractive, well-scrubbed bedrooms contains either a panoramic terrace or balcony, in most cases with views out to sea.

Villa Paradiso. Via Roma 2, 98039 Taormina. ☎ **0942/23-922.** Fax 0942/625-800. 35 rms. A/C TV TEL. 220,000L–280,000L ($132–$168) double. Rates include breakfast. AE, DC, MC, V. Parking 20,000L ($12).

This charming hotel is at one end of the main street of town, near the Greek theater and overlooking the public gardens and tennis courts. The creation of Signore Salvatore Martorana, it's a reasonably priced choice for those who want to live well. He loves his establishment, and that attitude is reflected in the personal manner in which the living room is furnished, with antiques and reproductions. Each bedroom is individually decorated, containing a balcony. Guests spend many sunny hours in the rooftop solarium, the TV room, or the informal drinking bar and lounge. Between June and October, the hotel's management offers free access to the Paradise Beach Club in the seaside district of Letojanni. There's a free minivan to the beach, plus use of sun umbrellas, deck chairs, and showers, plus changing cabins, swimming pool, hydromassage, and garden. Guests can also play 45 minutes of tennis free per day.

Villa Schuler. Piazzetta Bastione, Via Roma, 98039 Taormina. ☎ **0942/23-481.** Fax 0942/23-522. 27 rms. TEL. 145,000L ($87) double. Rates include breakfast. AE, MC, V. Parking 12,000L ($7.20) in the garage, free outside.

Family-owned and run, this hotel was converted from a Sicilian villa in 1905. High above the Ionian Sea, it offers views of snow-capped Mount Etna and the Bay of Naxos. The hotel lies only a 2-minute stroll from the central Corso Umberto I, and about a 15-minute walk from the cable car to the beach below. It's also near the ancient theater of Taormina. Surrounded by its own gardens and filled with the fragrance of bougainvillea and jasmine, the hotel is an ideal retreat. The bedrooms are comfortably furnished and many have a small balcony or terrace opening onto a view of the sea. Breakfast can be served in your room or taken on a panoramic palm terrace overlooking the coastline. Facilities and services include a roof terrace solarium, small library, 24-hour bar and room service, and laundry.

PLACES TO STAY IN NEARBY MAZZARÒ

If you arrive in Taormina in summer, you may prefer to stay at Mazzarò, about 3 miles from the more famous resort. This is the major beach of Taormina, and has some fine hotels. A bus for Mazzarò leaves from the center of Taormina every 30 minutes daily from 8am to 9pm, charging 1,500L (90¢).

Grande Albergo Capotaormina. Via Nazionale 105, 98039 Taormina. ☎ **0942/24-000.** Fax 0942/625-467. 200 rms, 3 suites. A/C MINIBAR TV TEL. 320,000L ($192) double; from 380,000L ($228) suite. Rates include buffet breakfast. AE, DC, MC. V. Closed Oct 30–Feb 28. Parking 15,000L ($9).

Grande Albergo is a world unto itself, nestled atop a rugged cape projecting into the Ionian Sea. It was designed by one of Italy's most famous architects, Minoletti. There are five floors on five wide sun terraces, plus a saltwater swimming pool at the edge of the cape. Elevators take you through 150 feet of solid rock to the beach below. The bedrooms are handsomely furnished and well proportioned, with wide glass doors opening onto private sun terraces. There are two bars—one intimate, the other more expansive with an orchestra for dancing. The lobby blends the cultures of Rome, Carthage, and Greece, and an open atrium reaches skyward through the center. The food is lavishly presented, and is effectively enhanced by Sicilian wines.

Mazzarò Sea Palace. Via Nazionale 147, 98030 Mazzarò. ☎ **0942/24-004.** Fax 0942/ 626-237. 76 rms, 8 suites. A/C MINIBAR TV TEL. 250,000L–520,000L ($150–$312) double; 680,000L ($408) suite for two. Rates include half-board. AE, DC, MC, V. Parking 20,000L ($12).

The Sea Palace is a leading four-star hotel in this little satellite resort of Taormina. It opens onto the most beautiful bay in Sicily. Its modern design was completed in 1962 and renovated frequently since then, most recently in the mid-1990s. It's graced with big windows to let in cascades of light and offer views of the coastline. The food in the restaurant terrace is served on fine china and crystal, and guests are pampered by the staff. The piano bar is a popular nighttime spot. There's also a private beach for guests. The rooms are well furnished, most opening onto panoramic views. It's customary to stay here on the half-board plan.

Villa Sant'Andrea. Via Nazionale 137, 98030 Mazzarò. ☎ **0942/23-125.** Fax 0942/24-838. 67 rms. A/C MINIBAR TV TEL. 310,000L–530,000L ($186–$318) double. Rates include breakfast. AE, DC, MC, V. Parking 22,000L ($13.20).

Converted from a villa, this first-class hotel stands at the base of the mountain, directly on the sea with a private beach. You'll feel like part of a house party. The rooms are informal, with a homelike prettiness, and there's a winning dining terrace where you can enjoy good food. Even if you're not a guest, you might want to try the hotel restaurant, Oliviero, which is one of the finest on the island, having won many awards. A cable car, just outside the front gates of the hotel, will whisk you to the heart of Taormina.

WHERE TO DINE
MODERATE

Giova Rosy di Turi Salsa. Corso Umberto 38. ☎ **0942/24-411.** Reservations recommended. Main courses 18,000L–36,000L ($10.80–$21.60). AE, DC, V. Fri–Wed noon–3pm and 7–midnight. Closed Jan–Feb. SICILIAN.

This rustically old-fashioned place serves a variety of local specialties, including an array of linguine, risotto dishes, and a spiedini with shrimp and lobster dosed with a generous shot of cognac, tagliolini with seafood, and swordfish cooked *in cartoccio* (in a paper bag). You might also enjoy Sicilian antipasti or eggplant with ricotta. You'll have a view of the ancient theater.

Ristorante da Lorenzo. Via Roma, near Via Michele Amari. ☎ **0942/23-480.** Reservations required. Main courses 16,000L–40,000L ($9.60–$24). AE, DC, MC, V. Thurs–Tues noon–3pm and 6:30–11pm. Closed Nov 15–Dec 15. SICILIAN/ITALIAN.

This is a clean and bright restaurant on a quiet street near the landmark San Domenico Hotel, in front of the town hall. The restaurant has a terrace shaded by an 850-year-old tree—the botanical pride of the town—and oil paintings decorating its white walls. You can enjoy meals that might include a fresh selection of antipasti, spaghetti with sea urchins, scaloppine mozzarella, grilled swordfish, and filet of beef with Gorgonzola.

INEXPENSIVE

Il Ciclope. Corso Umberto. ☎ **0942/23-263.** Reservations not accepted. Main courses 16,000L–28,000L ($9.60–$16.80). AE, MC, V. Thurs–Tues 12:30–3pm and 7:30–10pm. Closed Jan 10–31. SICILIAN/ITALIAN.

This is one of the best of the low-priced trattorie of Taormina. Set back from the main street, it opens onto the pint-sized Piazzetta Salvatore Leone. In summer, try for an outside table if you'd like both your food and yourself inspected by the passing parade. Meals are fairly simple but the ingredients are fresh and the dishes well prepared. Try the fish soup or Sicilian squid. If those don't interest you, then go for the entrecôte Ciclope, or the grilled shrimp. Most diners begin their meal with a selection from the *antipasti di mare,* a savory collection of seafood hors d'oeuvres.

Ristorante La Griglia. Corso Umberto 54. ☎ **0942/23-980.** Reservations recommended. Main courses 16,000L–28,000L ($9.60–$16.80). AE, DC, MC, V. Wed–Mon 12:30–2:30pm and 7:30–11:30pm. Closed Nov 20–Dec 20. SICILIAN/INTERNATIONAL.

Opened in 1974, this restaurant is still one of the best in town. The vestibule that funnels visitors from the main street of the old city into the interior contains a bubbling aquarium and a menagerie of carved stone lions. The masses of plants inside almost conceal the terra-cotta floors and big-windowed views over the feathery trees of a garden. Your meal might include a selection from the antipasto display, a fresh fish carpaccio, and an involtino of spaghetti and eggplant.

Ristorante Luraleo. Via Bagnoli Croce 27. ☎ **0942/24-279.** Reservations recommended. Main courses 15,000L–60,000L ($9–$36). DC, MC, V. Summer, daily noon–3pm and 7–11pm. Closed Wed off-season. SICILIAN/INTERNATIONAL.

Acclaimed by a handful of city residents as the best place in town, Ristorante Luraleo is eager to offer excellent value for an attractive price. Many diners prefer the flowering terrace, where pastel tablecloths are shaded by a vine-covered arbor. If you prefer to dine indoors, there's a country-rustic dining room with tile accents, flowers, evening candlelight, racks of wine bottles, and a richly laden antipasto table. The grilled fish is good here, as are the pastas, such as house-made maccheroni with tomato, eggplant, and basil, regional dishes, and herb-flavored steak. Risotto with salmon and pistachio nuts is a specialty, as are the house tortellini and *involtini siciliana.*

Ristorante U'Bossu. Via Bagnoli Croce 50. ☎ **0942/23-311.** Reservations required. Main courses 12,000L–18,000L ($7.20–$10.80); fixed-price menu 20,000L ($12). MC, V. Tues–Sun 12:30–3pm and 7:30–10pm. Closed Jan 14–Feb 20. SICILIAN/MEDITERRANEAN.

Vines entwine around the facade of this small and crowded restaurant in a quiet part of town. Amid a pleasing decor of fresh flowers, wagon-wheel chandeliers, prominently displayed wine bottles, and burnished wooden panels, you can enjoy a meal pungent with all the aromas of a herb garden. Meals begin with complimentary bruschetta, grilled bread with oil and garlic or tomato. Specialties include *pasta con la sarde* (pasta with fish), and *involtini di pesce spada* (a swordfish stew), and a groaning antipasti table. The restaurant is decorated with a folkloric scene from *Cavalleria Rusticana,* and the chef pays homage to the famed opera by naming his best pasta dish *maccheroni alla Turidda* after the principal character. For dessert, nothing else can top the zabaglione with fresh strawberries.

A RESTAURANT IN NEARBY MAZZARÒ

Ristorante Angelo a Mare—Il Delfino. Via Nazionale, Mazzarò. ☎ **0942/23-004.** Main courses 16,000L–28,000L ($9.60–$16.80). AE, DC, MC, V. Daily noon–3pm and 7pm–midnight. Closed Nov–Mar. MEDITERRANEAN/ITALIAN.

Located in Mazzarò, about 3 miles from Taormina, this restaurant offers a flowering terrace with a view over the bay. Both the decor and the menu items are inspired by the sea, and carefully supervised by the chef and owner. Mussels are a specialty, as well as a house-style steak, along with involtini of fish, cannelloni, and *risotto marinara* (fisher's rice).

TAORMINA AFTER DARK

Begin your evening at the **Caffè Wunderbar**, Piazza IX Aprile 7, Corso Umberto I (☎ **0942/625-302**), a popular spot that was once a favorite watering hole of

Tennessee Williams and his longtime companion, Frank Merlo. It's on the most delightful square in town. Beneath a vine-covered arbor, the outdoor section is perched as close as is safely possible to the edge of the cliff. We prefer one of the Victorian armchairs in the elegant interior, where an impressionistic pair of sculpted figures fill wall niches beneath chandeliers. There's a well-stocked bar, as well as a piano bar. An espresso costs 4,200L ($2.50), and a cappuccino, 5,200L ($3.10) if you sit. It's open daily from 8:30am to 2:30am; closed Tuesday in December and January.

The entire town is geared to holidaymaking, and thus—scattered among Taormina's medieval masonry—a healthy roster of nightclubs. The best of the lot include **Bella Blu,** Guardiola Vecchia (☎ 0942/24-239), which caters to the high-energy, dance-a-holic jinx of patrons from throughout Europe. There's also the **Club Septimo,** Via San Pancrazio 50 (☎ 0942/625-522), where a sweeping view of the town and sea is framed with reproductions of ancient Roman columns, and an interior has all the strobe lights and ultraviolet you might want. More elegant than either of these is **La Jarra,** Via La Floresta 1, off Corso Umberto (☎ 0942/23-370), the only one of the three that's open year-round, thanks to the on-site premises of an upscale restaurant. A bar with recorded music and occasional bouts of dancing is **Le Perroquet,** on Piazza San Domenico de Guzman, corner of Via Roma (☎ 0942/24-462), a site more closely geared to gay life than any of the others reviewed here.

Taormina also has a cultural side, with its Greek and Roman theater (see above) offering regular theatrical performances July to September. In addition, churches and other venues in summer are the settings for a summer festival of classical music, staged from May to September. Each July the resort sponsors an international film festival in its Roman Greek amphitheater. For more information on all these cultural events, contact the tourist office or call ☎ 0942/23-220.

A SIDE TRIP TO MOUNT ETNA

Looming menacingly over the coast of eastern Sicily, **Mount Etna** is the highest and largest active volcano in Europe—and we do mean active! The peak changes in size over the years, but is currently somewhere in the neighborhood of 10,800 feet. Etna has been active in modern times (in 1928 the little village of Mascali was buried under its lava), and eruptions in 1971 and 1992 have rekindled the fears of Sicilians.

Etna has figured in history and in Greek mythology. Empedocles, the 5th-century B.C. Greek philosopher, is said to have jumped into its crater as a sign that he was being delivered directly to Mount Olympus to take his seat among the gods. It was under Etna that Zeus crushed the multiheaded, viper-riddled dragon Typhoeus, thereby securing domination over Olympus. Hephaestus, the god of fire and blacksmiths, was believed to have made his headquarters in Etna, aided by the single-eyed Cyclops.

The Greeks warned that whenever Typhoeus tried to break out of his prison, lava erupted and earthquakes cracked the land. Granted that, the monster must have nearly escaped on March 11, 1669, the date of one of the most violent eruptions ever recorded—it destroyed Catania, about 17 miles away.

Always get the latest report from local tourist offices before contemplating a trip to Mount Etna, as adventurers have been killed by a surprise "belch" (volcanic explosion).

For a good view of the ferocious, lava-spewing mountain, take one of the trains operated by **Ferrovia Circumetnea** that circumnavigate the base of the mighty volcano. Board at the Stazione Borgo, Via Caronda 350 (☎ 095/531-402), in Catania, off Viale Leonardo da Vinci. A 5-hour circular tour from Catania costs 15,000L ($9).

If you'd prefer not to attempt this rather cumbersome do-it-yourself means of seeing Etna, consider a package tour offered from Taormina. Contact **CIT,** Corso Umberto I, 101 (☎ 0942/23-301), to see if any tours are being offered. Generally CIT organizes tours to Etna about two times a week in summer, costing around 70,000L ($42) per person. There are no plans yet to offer tours in winter, but this may change if demand is sufficient.

2 Siracusa (Syracuse)

35 miles SE of Catania

Of all the Greek cities of antiquity that flourished on the coast of Sicily, Siracusa was the most important, a formidable competitor of Athens in the West. In the heyday of its power, it dared take on Carthage, even Rome. At one time its wealth and size were unmatched by any other city in Europe.

On a site on the Ionian Sea, colonizers from Corinth founded the city in about 735 B.C. Much of its history was linked to despots, beginning in 485 B.C. with Gelon, the "tyrant" of Gela who subdued the Carthaginians at Himera. Siracusa came under attack from Athens in 415 B.C., but the main Athenian fleet was destroyed and the soldiers on the mainland captured. They were herded into the Latoma di Cappuccini at Piazza Cappuccini, a stone quarry. The "jail," from which there was no escape, was particularly horrid, as the defeated soldiers weren't given food and were packed together like cattle and allowed to die slowly.

Dionysius I was one of the greatest despots, reigning over the city during its particular glory in the 4th century B.C., when it extended its influence as a sea power. But in 212 B.C. the city fell to the Romans who, under Marcellus, sacked its riches and art. Incidentally, in this rape Siracusa lost its most famous son, the Greek physicist and mathematician Archimedes, who was slain in his study by a Roman soldier.

Before you go, you might want to read Mary Renault's novel *The Mask of Apollo,* set in Syracuse of the 5th century B.C. As one critic put it, "It brings the stones to life."

Today the city's harborfront is lined with a distinguished collection of 18th- and 19th-century town houses, each brightly painted in a spectrum of colors, whose ensemble provides one of the most charming vistas in Sicily.

Siracusa is a caldron in summer. You can do as the locals do and head for the sea. The finest beach, regrettably, is about 12 miles away at **Fontane Bianche,** but it's reached by bus 21 or 22, leaving from the post office in Siracusa at Piazza delle Poste 15. The same bus will also take you to another beach, Lido Arenella, only 5 miles away, but it's not as good.

ESSENTIALS

GETTING THERE   By Train   From other major cities in Sicily, you'll find Siracusa best reached by train: 1 1/2 hours from Catania, 2 hours from Taormina, and 5 hours from Palermo. Most trains transfer in Catania (for rail information on connections into Siracusa, call ☎ 095/531-625). Trains arrive in Siracusa at the station at Via Francesco Crispi, centrally located midway between the archeological park and Oritigia.

By Bus   From Siracusa, 15 SAIS buses daily make the 1 1/2 hour trip to Catania for a one-way fare of 2,500L ($1.50). From Catania, you can continue south by SAIS bus to Syracuse. Eight buses make the 1 1/2-hour trip per day, costing 6,100L ($3.65) one-way. Phone **SAIS** (☎ 0931/66-710 in Syracuse) for information and schedules, or else call ☎ 095/536-168 in Catania.

By Car　From Taormina, continue south along Route 114, past Catania.

VISITOR INFORMATION　The **tourist information center** is at Via della Maestranza 33 (☎ **0931/464-255**), facing the Church of San Giovanni, with a branch office at the entrance to the archeological park, on Largo Paradiso (☎ 0931/ 60-510). It's open Monday to Saturday from 8:30am to 2pm and 4:30 to 7:30pm.

ANCIENT SIGHTS

✪ **Zona Archeologica.** Via Augusto (off intersection of Corso Gelone and Viale Teocrito). ☎ **0931/66-206.** Admission 2,000L ($1.20). Apr–Oct daily 9am–6pm, Nov–Mar daily 9am–3pm.

Siracusa's archeological park contains the town's most important attractions: the Greek theater (Teatro Greco), the Roman Amphitheater (Anfiteatro Romano), as well as the Latomia del Paradiso.

On the Temenite Hill, the ✪ **Teatro Greco** was one of the great theaters of the classical period. Hewn from rocks during the reign of Hieron I in the 5th century B.C., the ancient seats have been largely eaten away by time. You can, however, still stand on the remnants of the stone stage that once hosted plays by Euripedes. The theater was much restored in the time of Hieron II in the 3rd century B.C. In the spring of even-numbered years the Italian Institute of Ancient Drama presents classical plays by Euripedes, Aeschylus, and Sophocles. In other words, the show hasn't changed much in 2,000 years!

Outside the entrance to the Greek theater is the most famous of the ancient quarries, the **Latomia del Paradiso,** one of four or five latomies from which stones were hauled to erect the great monuments of Siracusa in its glory days. On seeing the cave in the wall, Caravaggio is reputed to have dubbed it "The Ear of Dionysius," because of its unusual shape. But what an ear! It's nearly 200 feet long. You can enter the inner chamber of the grotto where the tearing of paper sounds like a gunshot. Although dismissed by some scholars as fanciful, the story goes that the despot Dionysius used to force prisoners into the "ear" at night, where he was able to hear every word they said. Nearby is the **Grotta dei Cordari,** where ropemakers plied their ancient craft.

The ✪ **Anfiteatro Romano** was created at the time of Augustus. It ranks among the top five amphitheaters left by the Romans in Italy. Like the Greek theater, part of it was carved from rock. Unlike the Greek theater and its classical plays, the Roman amphitheater tended toward more gutsy fare. Gladiators—prisoners of war and "exotic" blacks from Africa—faced each other with tridents and daggers, or naked slaves would be whipped into the center of a to-the-death battle between wild beasts. Either way the victim lost. If his combatant, man or beast, didn't do him in, the crowd would often scream for the ringmaster to slit his throat. The amphitheater is near the entrance to the park, but you can also view it in its entirety from a belvedere on the panoramic road.

✪ **Museo Archeologico Regionale Paolo Orsi.** Viale Teocrito 66. ☎ **0931/464-022.** Admission 2,000L ($1.20) adults, free for children 17 and under and for seniors 60 and over. Tues–Sun 9am–1pm.

One of the most important archeological museums in southern Italy, it's modern quarters survey the Greek, Roman, and early Christian epochs in sculpture and fragments of archeological remains. The museum also has a rich coin collection. Of the statues here (and there are several excellent ones), the best known is the headless *Venus Anadyomene* (rising from the sea), dating from the Hellenistic period in the 2nd century B.C. One of the earliest-known works is of an earth mother suckling two babes, from the 6th century B.C. The pre-Greek vases have great style and elegance. The museum stands in the gardens of the Villa Landolina in Akradina.

Impressions

I have heard it said that Sicilians can't use the telephone because they need both hands to talk with.

—Anonymous

✪ **Catacombe di San Giovanni (St. John).** Piazza San Giovanni, at the end of Viale San Giovanni. ☎ **0931/67-955.** Admission 3,000L ($1.80) adults, 1,000L (60¢) for children 10 and under. Mar 15–Nov 14, daily 10am–noon and 3–6pm; Nov 15–Mar 14, Thurs–Tues 10am–noon.

These honeycombed tunnels of empty coffins evoke the catacombs along the Appian Way in Rome. You enter the world down below from the Chiesa di San Giovanni, from the 3rd century A.D.; the present building is of a much later date. Included in the early Christian burial grounds is the crypt of St. Marcianus, which lies under what was reportedly the first cathedral erected in Sicily. *Warning:* Make sure you exit in plenty of time before closing. Two women readers who entered the catacombs after 5pm were accidentally locked in for the night, and managed to escape only after a harrowing and dangerous ordeal of wandering around in the dark.

EXPLORING ORTYGIA ISLAND

Ortygia, inhabited for many thousands of years, is also named Città Vecchia, and contains the town's Duomo, many rows of houses spanning 500 years of building styles, most of the city's medieval and Baroque monuments, and some of the most charming vistas in Sicily. Its beauties praised by Pindar, the island, reached by crossing the Ponte Nuova, was the heart of Siracusa, having been founded by the Greek colonists from Corinth. In Greek mythology, it's said to have been ruled by Calypso, daughter of Atlas, the sea nymph who detained Ulysses (Odysseus) for 7 years on the island. The island is about a mile long and half again as wide.

Heading out the Foro Italico, you'll come to the **Fonte Arethusa,** also famous in mythology. Alpheius, the river god, son of Oceanus, is said to have fallen in love with the sea nymph Arethusa. The nymph turned into this spring or fountain, but Alpheius became a river and "mingled" with his love. According to legend, the spring ran red when bulls were sacrificed at Olympus.

At Piazza del Duomo, the **Duomo** of Syracuse, with a Baroque facade, was built over the ruins of the Temple of Minerva, and employs the same Doric columns, 26 of the original still in place. The temple was erected after Gelon the Tyrant defeated the Carthaginians at Himera in the 5th century B.C. The Christians converted it into a basilica in the 7th century A.D. Visits are possible daily from 8am to noon and 4 to 7pm.

Palazzo Bellomo, at Via Capodieci 14, off Foro Vittorio Emanuele II, dates from the 13th century, with many alterations, and is today the home of the Galleria Regionale, (☎ **0931/69-617**). Not only is the palace fascinating, with its many arches, doors, and stairs, but it also has a fine collection of paintings. The most notable is an *Annunciation* by Antennal da Messina from 1474. There's also a noteworthy collection of antiques and porcelain. It's open Monday to Saturday from 9am to 1:30pm and on Sunday from 9am to 12:30pm, charging an admission of 2,000L ($1.20).

WHERE TO STAY

Hotel Bellavista. Via Diodoro Siculo 4, 96100 Siracusa. ☎ **0931/411-355.** Fax 0931/37-927. 49 rms, 37 with bath. TV TEL. 90,000L ($54) double without bath, 148,000L ($88.80) double with bath. Rates include breakfast. AE, MC, V.

Family owned and run, this four-story hotel was built in 1960, then renovated several times. It lies in the commercial center, close to the archeological zone. There's an annex in the garden for overflow guests. The main lounge has a sense of space, with leather chairs and semitropical plants. The bedrooms are informal and comfortable, often furnished with traditional pieces. Most rooms feature a sea-view balcony. There is a restaurant serving Sicilian cuisine for hotel guests and groups only.

Hotel Forte Agip. Viale Teracati 30-32, 96100 Siracusa. ☎ **0931/463-232.** Fax 0931/67-115. 87 rms. A/C MINIBAR TV TEL. 199,000L–214,000L ($119.40–$128.40) double. Rates include breakfast. AE, DC, MC, V.

Located a short drive inland from the medieval Città Vecchia, near the ancient Greek theater and most of the city's classical monuments, this member of a national hotel chain is designed for ease of access and convenience to motorists. Each of the monochromatic bedrooms is simple and streamlined. The in-house restaurant is often visited by residents of Syracuse who consider the generous portions, unpretentious service, and flavorful specialties worth the trip. Menu items include pastas, stuffed veal, American-style tournedos, salads, and a changing array of fresh fish.

Jolly. Corso Gelone 45, 96100 Siracusa. ☎ **800/221-2626** in the U.S., 800/237-0319 in Canada, or 0931/461-1111 in Italy. Fax 0931/461126. 100 rms. A/C MINIBAR TV TEL. 240,000L ($144) double. Rates include breakfast. AE, DC, MC, V.

A major group stop, the six-story Jolly is part of the chain that's the Holiday Inn of Italy. You get no surprises here—just clean, modern, tropical-style rooms, short on soul but good on comfort, though a bit worn. The hotel restaurant—better than the hotel itself—offers a standard lunch or dinner of Sicilian or International cuisine. At least the view of Mount Etna and the sea is panoramic.

Panorama. Via Necropoli Grotticelle 33, 98100 Siracusa. ☎ and fax **0931/412-188.** 51 rms. TV TEL. 100,000L ($60) double. AE, MC, V.

Near the entrance to the city, on a rise of Temenite Hill, is this bandbox-modern hotel, built on a busy street about five minutes from the Greek theater and Roman amphitheater. It's not a motel, but it does provide parking space. Inside, a contemporary accommodation awaits you. The bedrooms are pleasant and up-to-date, with comfortable but utilitarian pieces. There's a dining room serving only a continental breakfast (not included in the room prices).

WHERE TO DINE

Arlecchino. Via dei Tolomei 5. ☎ **0931/66-386.** Reservations recommended. Main courses 16,000L–20,000L ($9.60–$12). AE, DC, MC, V. Daily 12:30–3:30pm and 7:30pm–midnight. Closed Sun Apr–Sept. SEAFOOD/PIZZA.

This restaurant occupies the street level of a 250-year-old palace in the heart of the Città Vecchia, a short walk from the cathedral. Despite its understated decor, Arlecchino is the best restaurant in town. Many specialties emerge from the fragrant kitchen. These include a wide array of homemade pastas, a cheese-laden crespelline of the house, pasta with sardines, spiedini with shrimp, and a selection of pungent beef, fish, and veal dishes. There is also a pizzeria on site.

Darsena da Ianuzo. Riva Garibaldi 6. ☎ **0931/66-104.** Reservations required. Main courses 12,000L–26,000L ($7.20–$15.60). AE, MC, V. Thurs–Tues 12:30–3pm and 7:30–10:30pm. Closed Nov. SEAFOOD.

This might not differ all that much from dozens of other seafood restaurants in the Città Vecchia, except that the food seems to be exceptionally good, the welcome warm, and there is a veranda overlooking the sea. Specialties include fresh shellfish, spaghetti with clams, a wide collection of fresh grilled and baked fish, and the ever-present fish soup. Locals devour the sea urchins, a specialty of the chef, although many visitors wonder what the excitement is all about after downing a few. Mercifully, the place is air conditioned in summer.

Gambero Rosso. Via Eritrea 2. ☎ **0931/68-546.** Reservations recommended. Main courses 12,000–26,000L ($7.20–$15.60). AE, MC, V. Fri–Wed 12:30–3pm and 8–10pm. SICILIAN/ MEDITERRANEAN/SEAFOOD.

Ideal for those who want to dine at an old tavern, this restaurant is near the entrance to the bridge leading to the Città Vecchia. It's a mellow building, close to the fishing boats, with a certain charm, and a cuisine dedicated to the best of Sicilian dishes. A reliable dish is the *zuppa di pesce* (fish soup). An alternative choice is the *zuppa di cozze,* a plate brimming with fresh mussels in a savory marinade. Among the asciutte, the Sicilian cannelloni are good. The meat dishes feature a number of choices from the kitchens of Lazio, Tuscany, and Emilia-Romagna.

Ristorante Jonico-a Rutta e Ciauli. Riviera Dionisio il Grande 194. ☎ **0931/65-540.** Reservations recommended. Main courses 18,000–26,000L ($10.80–$15.60). AE, MC, V. Wed– Mon 12:30–3pm and 8–10pm. SICILIAN.

This is one of the best restaurants on the island serving the typical cuisine and local wines of Sicily. The restaurant offers a veranda and garden setting right on the sea, with a panoramic view about 100 yards from the Piazzale dei Cappuccini. The decoration is typically Sicilian. The antipasti array alone is dazzling, and the homemade pasta dishes are superb (ask one of the English-speaking waiters to explain the many variations or settle for spaghetti with caviar). One of the most interesting fish dishes we recently sampled was *spada a pizzaiola* (swordfish in a savory, garlic-flavored sauce). Meat specialties include *polpettone* (rolled meat) *alla siracusana,* and a delectable stew made of various fish. The dessert specialty is a *cassatine siciliana.* There is also a roof garden with pizzeria which serves typical Sicilian pizza for 15,000L ($9).

Ristorante Rossini. Via Savoia 6. ☎ **0931/24-317.** Reservations recommended. Main courses 18,000L–25,000L ($10.80–$15). AE, DC, MC, V. Wed–Mon 12:30–3:30pm and 8– 10pm. Closed Dec 25. MEDITERRANEAN.

Ristorante Rossini is a homelike and comfortable enclave of regional gastronomy, offering meals to 50 fortunate diners a night. You might begin with an assortment from the amply stocked buffet table of antipasti, then select one of many main dishes, including a mousse of fish with fresh shrimp, perhaps a shellfish risotto with roast peppers and tomato purée. Twice-roasted swordfish is also a specialty.

SIRACUSA AFTER DARK

After you tire of the spectacular vista beside the ancient harbor, you might want to stray farther afield for an evening of dancing. The region's most appealing disco is **Fontana Bianci,** Via Dei Lidi (☎ **0931/753-633**), 12 miles southwest of the town center. It contains a walled garden, verdant shrubbery, a swimming pool that at night seems mostly ornamental, and a clientele that's older and better established from what you'll find within the student hangouts at nightclubs closer to the town center. Another option is the **Discotecca Malibu,** Via Elorina (☎ **0931/721-888**), about 3½ miles southwest of town on the SS115, where a younger crowd seems full of the energy it takes to dance all night at a seaside pavilion that evokes something like its California namesake.

Malibu's most visible competitor is **La Nottola,** Via Gargallo 61 (☎ **0931/ 60-009**). Set on a small street near the larger Via Maestanza, and permeated with a sense of restrained style and at times, even glamor, it mingles aspects of a jazz club, piano bar, and disco for a crowd that's usually better dressed than the norm. If you should happen to arrive in midsummer, head for the **Sporting Cub Terrauzza** (☎ 0931/714-505), centerpiece of the hamlet of Terrauzza, about 6 miles southwest of Siracusa, where whomever happens to be making holidays on the local beaches shows up to mingle with 20-somethings from the region.

Count yourself lucky if you arrive in Siracusa during even numbered years. From May through August, the Istituto Nazionale del Dramma Antico presents **classic plays** by Aeschylus and Euripides, among others, in the ancient Teatro Greco of the Parco Archeologico. Tickets range from 20,000L to 60,000L ($12 to $36). For more information and tickets, get in touch with **INDA** at C.G. Matteotti 29 (☎ 0931/ 67-415).

3 Agrigento

80 miles S of Palermo, 109 miles SE of Trápani, 135 miles W of Siracusa

Greek colonists from Gela (Caltanissetta) named it Akragas when they established a beachhead here in the 6th century B.C. In time their settlement grew to become one of the most prosperous cities in Magna Graecia. A great deal of that growth is attributed to the despot Phalaris, who ruled from 571 to 555 B.C. and is said to have roasted his victims inside a brazen bull, eventually meeting the same fate himself.

Empedocles, the Greek philosopher and politician (also credited by some as the founder of medicine in Italy), was the most famous son of Akragas, born around 490 B.C. He formulated the four-elements theory (earth, fire, water, and air), modified by the agents love and strife. In modern times the town produced Luigi Pirandello, the playwright (*Six Characters in Search of an Author*) who won the Nobel Prize in literature in 1934.

Like nearby Selinunte, the city was attacked by war-waging Carthaginians, the first assault in 406 B.C. In the 3rd century B.C. the Carthaginians and Romans played Russian roulette with the city until it finally succumbed to Roman domination by 210 B.C. The city was then known as Agrigentium.

The modern part of town (in 1927 the name was changed from Girgenti to Agrigento) occupies a hill site. The narrow streets—casbahlike—date back to the influence of the conquering Saracens. Heavy Allied bombing in World War II necessitated much rebuilding, which for the most part was full and uninspired, and it's not helped by all the cement factories in the area.

Below the town stretch the long reaches of La Valle dei Templi, containing some of the greatest Greek ruins in the world.

You obviously visit Agrigento for its past—one of the most impressive classical sites in all of Italy—and not for the present modern city. It's been a long time since Pindar lauded Agrigento as "Man's Finest City." However, once here and once you've been awed by the ruined temples, you can visit the **centro storico** with its tourist boutiques hawking postcards and T-shirts, and enjoy people-watching at a cafe along the Via Atenea. When it gets too hot (as it so often does here), flee to one of the nearby beaches at San Leone.

ESSENTIALS

GETTING THERE   By Train   There are 10 daily trains arriving from Palermo (trip time: 2 hours), costing 11,700L ($7) for a one-way ticket. The **main rail station,** Stazione Centrale, Piazza Marconi (☎ 0922/29-007), is just downhill from Piazzale Aldo Moro, a public park, and Piazza Vittorio Emanuele, both landmark squares in the center of town. From Siracusa by rail, you must first take one of nine daily trains to Ragusa, a 2¹/₂ hour trip costing 9,800L ($5.90) one way, where you transfer to one of three daily trains to Agrigento, costing 15,500L ($9.30) for a one-way ticket (trip time: 3¹/₂ hours).

By Bus You can get one of six daily **AST** buses (☎ **0932/621-249**) in Siracusa that will take you to Ragusa, taking two hours and costing 7,500L ($4.50) one way. Once at Ragusa, the connection is somewhat awkward and unreliable. The changing schedules are posted where the buses depart on Piazza Gramsci, and you can buy tickets on board the bus. For information in **Agrigento** call ☎ **0922/20-414.**

By Car From Siracusa, take the SS115 through Gela. From Palermo, cut southeast along Route S121, which becomes S188 and S189 before it finally reaches Agrigento and the Mediterranean.

VISITOR INFORMATION The **tourist information center** is at Via Cesare Battisti, 15 (☎ **0922/20-454**). There's another office at Via Empedocle 73 (☎ 0922/20-391). Both are open Monday to Saturday from 8:30am to 1:45pm and 4 to 7pm.

WANDERING AMONG THE RUINS

Many writers are fond of suggesting that Greek ruins in the **Valle dei Templi** be viewed at either dawn or sunset. Indeed, their mysterious aura is heightened then. But for details you can search them out under the bright cobalt-blue Sicilian sky. The backdrop for the temples is idyllic, especially in spring when the striking almond trees blossom into pink.

Riding out the Strada Panoramica, you'll first approach (on your left), the ✪ **Tempio di Giunone (Juno).** With many of its Doric columns now restored, this temple was erected sometime in the mid-5th century B.C., at the peak of a construction boom that skipped across the celestial globe honoring the deities. As you climb the blocks, note the remains of a cistern as well as a sacrificial altar in front. There are good views of the entire valley from the perch here.

The ✪ **Tempio della Concordia,** next, ranks along with the Temple of Hephaestos (the "Theseum") in Athens as the best-preserved Greek temple in the world. Flanked by 13 columns on its side, along with 6 in front and 6 in back, the temple was built in the peripteral hexastyle. You'll see the clearest example in Sicily of what an inner temple was like. In the late 6th century A.D. the pagan structure was transformed into a Christian church, which may have saved it for posterity, although today it has been stripped down to its classical purity.

The **Tempio di Ercole (Hercules)** is the most ancient, dating from the 6th century B.C. Badly ruined (only eight pillars are standing), it once ranked in size with the Temple of Zeus. At one time the temple sheltered a celebrated statue of Hercules. The infamous Gaius Verres, the Roman magistrate who became an especially bad governor of Sicily, attempted to steal the image as part of his temple-looting tear on the island. Astonishingly you can still see signs of black searing from fires set by the long-ago Carthaginian invaders.

The ✪ **Tempio di Giove (Jove or Zeus)** was the largest in the valley, similar in some respects to the Temple of Apollo at Selinunte, until it was ruined by an earthquake. It even impressed Goethe. In front of the structure was a large altar. The giant on the ground was one of several telamones (atlases) used to support the edifice. Carthaginian slave labor was used to build what was then the largest Greek temple in the world and one of the most remarkable.

The so-called **Tempio di Dioscuri,** with four Doric columns intact, is a *pasticcio*— that is, it's composed of fragments from different buildings. At various times it has been designated as a temple honoring Castor and Pollux, the twin sons of Leda, and deities of seafarers; or Demeter (Ceres), the goddess of marriage and of the fertile earth; or Persephone, the daughter of Zeus who became the symbol of spring. Note that on some maps this temple is called Tempio di Castore e Polluce.

The temples can usually be visited daily from 9am until one hour before sunset. City bus nos. 8, 9, 10, and 11 leave from the train station in Agrigento, taking you to the site of the temples.

OTHER ATTRACTIONS

The **Museo Regionale Archeologico** (☎ 0922/49-726) stands near the Church of Saint Nicholas (Chiesa di San Nicola), on Contrada San Nicola at the outskirts of town on the way to the Valle dei Templi, and is open daily from 8am to 12:30pm, admission is free. Its single most important exhibit is a head of the god Telamon from the Tempio di Giove. The collection of Greek vases is also impressive. Many of the artifacts on display were dug up when Agrigento was excavated. Take buses numbered 8, 9, 10, or 11 here.

Casa di Pirandello, Contrada Caos, Frazione Kaos (☎ 0922/48326), is the former abode of the 1934 Nobel Prize winner who is known worldwide for his plays *Six Characters in Search of an Author* and *Enrico IV*. He died two years after winning the prize and its subsequent world acclaim. Although Agrigentans back then might not have liked his portrayal of Italy, all is forgiven now and Pirandello is the local boy who made good. In fact, they named a theater after him, the Teatro Luigi Pirandello at Piazza Minicipio. The "Casa Natale" of Pirandello is now a museum devoted to memorabilia pertaining to the playwright's life, including his study and murals he painted. The playwright's tomb lies under his favorite pine tree ("One night in June I dropped down like a firefly beneath a huge pine tree in the garden.") The tomb lies a few hundred yards from the house and the admission-free grounds which are open Monday to Saturday from 8:30am to one hour before sunset. The birthplace lies outside of town in the village of Kaos (catch bus no. 11 from Piazza Marconi) just west of the temple zone.

The Settimana Pirandelliana is a weeklong festival of plays, operas, and ballets staged in Piazza Kaos at the end of July and August. The tourist office will supply details; tickets range from 10,000L to 20,000L ($6 to $12).

WHERE TO STAY & DINE

Hotel Tre Torri. Strada Statale 115, Viale Canatello, Viallagio Mosè, 92100 Agrigento. ☎ 0922/606-733. Fax 0922/607-839. 118 rms. A/C TV TEL. 160,000L ($96) double. Rates include breakfast. AE, MC, V.

Some 4¹/₂ miles south of Agrigento in the village of Villaggio Mosè, this selection lies near an unattractive commercial district, yet it's among the best hotels in the area. Sheltered behind a mock-medieval facade of white stucco, chiseled stone blocks, false crenellations, and crisscrossed iron balconies, the hotel, which opened in 1982, is a favorite with Italian business travelers. A swimming pool in the small, terraced garden is visible from a restaurant. There's also an indoor swimming pool, sauna, and fitness center. For entertainment, the hotel contains a bar, sometimes with live piano music, and a disco. The bedrooms are comfortable, with modern furnishings.

Hotel Villa Athena. Via dei Templi 33, 92100 Agrigento. ☎ 0922/596-288. Fax 0922/402-180. 40 rms. A/C TV TEL. 250,000–300,000L ($150–$180) double. Rates include breakfast. AE, DC, MC, V. Free parking outdoors.

This 18th-century former private villa rises from the Sicilian landscape in the Valley of the Temples, less than 2 miles from town. It's the best place to stay in the area.

Its grounds have been planted with fruit trees that bloom in January. During the day guests sit in the paved courtyard, enjoying a drink and the fresh breezes. At night you have a view of the floodlit temples, a string of Doric ruins, from one of the windows. There's a pool in a setting of gardenia bushes and flowers. The dining room is in a separate building, serving both regional specialties and international dishes. In summer, make a reservation about two weeks in advance. The rooms are modern, with Italian styling. Room 205 frames a perfect view of the Temple of Concord.

Le Caprice. Strada Panoramica dei Templi 51. ☎ **0922/26-469.** Reservations required. Main courses 20,000L–32,000L ($12–$19.20). AE, DC, MC. V. Sat–Thurs 12:30–3pm and 7:30–11pm. Closed July 1–15. SEAFOOD/SICILIAN.

A loyal clientele return to this well-directed restaurant for special celebrations as well as for everyday fun. Le Caprice is the only restaurant of any consequence in Agrigento; the rest are simple trattorie. Specialties of the house include an antipasti buffet and a mixed fish fry from the gulf, along with rolled pieces of veal in a savory sauce. The chef takes justifiable pride in his local specialty, stuffed swordfish. One German visitor came here seven nights in a row, ordering the dish each time.

Trattoria del Vigneto. Via Cavalleri Magazzeni 11. ☎ **0922/414-319.** Main courses 12,000L–18,000L ($7.20–$10.80); fixed-price menu 30,000L ($18). V. Wed–Mon noon–2:30pm and 7pm–midnight. Closed Nov. SICILIAN.

This is a simple place to go for a Sicilian meal after a visit to the Valley of the Temples, just a short distance away. Menu items include homemade pasta flavored with sardines, pine nuts, and balsamic vinegar; pasta alla Norma, with eggplant, ricotta, tomatoes, and fresh basil; and a *bistecca vignolo,* where steaks are garnished with proscuitto, mozzarella, and tomatoes. The welcome is sincere, and the food is perfectly acceptable and often quite flavorful.

4 Selinunte

76 miles SW of Palermo, 70 miles W of Agrigento, 55 miles SE of Trápani

One of the lost cities of ancient Sicily, Selinunte traces its history to the 7th century B.C. when immigrants from Megara Hyblaea (Syracuse) set out to build a new colony. They succeeded, erecting a city of power and prestige adorned with many temples. But that was like calling attention to a good thing. Much of Selinunte's fate was tied up with seemingly endless conflicts with the Elymi people of Segesta (see section 5, below). Siding with Selinunte's rival, Hannibal virtually leveled the city in 409 B.C. The city never recovered its former glory, and ultimately fell into decay.

ESSENTIALS

GETTING THERE   By Train   From Palermo, Trápani, or Marsala, you can make rail connections to Castelvetrano. Once at Castelvetrano, you must board a bus for Selinunte. Most passengers reach Selinunte from Palermo (call ☎ **091/616-1806** in Palermo for rail information).

By Bus   From Agrigento, take one of four daily buses to Castelvetrano, a ¼-hour trip, costing 9,600L ($5.75) one way. Buses (about five per day) depart from in front of the rail terminal at Castelvetrano. A one-way fare is 2,000L ($1.20). For information, call ☎ **091/617-5411.**

By Car   Selinunte is on the southern coast of Sicily and is best explored by car, as public transportation is awkward. From Agrigento, take Route 115 northwest into Castelvetrano. From here, follow the signposted secondary road marked SELINUNTE which leads south to the sea.

VISITOR INFORMATION   There are no tourist offices in the area; it is a very informal site.

AN ARCHEOLOGICAL GARDEN

Today Selinunte's temples lie in scattered ruins, the mellowed stone, the color of honey, littering the ground as if an earthquake had struck (as one did in ancient times). From 9am to dusk daily you can walk through the monument zone, exploring such relics as the remains of the Acropolis, the heart of old Selinunte. Parts of it have been partially excavated and reconstructed, as much as is possible with the bits and fragments remaining. Admission is 2,000L ($1.20).

The temples, in varying states of preservation, are designated by letters. They are dedicated to such mythological figures as Apollo and Hera (Juno), and most date from the 6th and 5th centuries B.C. The Doric **Temple E** contains fragments of an inner temple. Standing on its ruins before the sun goes down, you can look across the water that washes up on the shores of Africa, from which the Carthaginian fleet emerged to destroy the city. **Temple G,** in scattered ruins, was one of the largest erected in Sicily, and was also built in the Doric style.

WHERE TO STAY & DINE IN NEARBY MARINELLA

The site of the ruins of Selinunte contains virtually no hotels, restaurants, or watering holes of note. Most visitors stop at the temple for a daylight visit, heading on to other locales at night. There are a handful of overnight accommodations, however, in the little seafront village of Marinella, which lies about a mile east of Selinunte. To reach Marinella, you'll travel along a narrow country road.

Hotel Alceste. Via Alceste 23, 91020 Marinella di Selinunte. ☎ **0924/46-184.** Fax 0924/ 46-143. 26 rms. A/C TV TEL. 110,000L ($66) double. AE, DC, MC, V.

After they erected the concrete walls of this hotel, the builders painted it a shade of sienna and filled its three-sided courtyard with dining tables and plants. This hotel, which is most busy in the summer season (and occasionally closed for periods in winter) is about a 15-minute walk from the ruins. The recently renovated bedrooms each have new furniture. Most visitors, however, stop only for a meal, enjoying a regional Sicilian dinner for 35,000L ($21) and up. In summer, there is musical entertainment, dancing, cabaret, and theater in the garden in front of the hotel.

5 Segesta

41 miles SW of Palermo, 91 miles NW of Agrigento

Segesta was the ancient city of the Elymi, a people of mysterious origin, although they've been linked by some to the Trojans. As the major city in western Sicily, it was brought into a series of conflicts with the rival power nearby, Selinus (Selinunte). From the 6th through the 5th century BC there were near-constant hostilities. The Athenians came from the east to aid the Segestans in 415 B.C., but the expedition ended in disaster, forcing the city to turn eventually for help to Hannibal of Carthage.

Twice in the 4th century B.C. it was besieged and conquered, once by Dionysius and again by Agathocles, the latter a particularly brutal victor who tortured, mutilated, or made slaves of most of the citizenry. Recovering eventually, Segesta in time turned on its old (but dubious) ally, Carthage. Like all Greek cities of Sicily, it ultimately fell to the Romans.

ESSENTIALS

GETTING THERE   By Train   Trains leave Palermo, bound for Segesta, at 6:50am. They make the return trip at 1pm.

By Bus   If you're going to see one of the classical plays (see below), you can take a bus from Piazza Politeama in Palermo approximately 2 hours before the show is presented. For information, call ☎ **091/616-7919.** Buses to the site are run by **Autoservizi Tarantola** (☎ **091/31-020** or 091/32-598) in Palermo. Six buses per day go here Monday to Saturday, two on Sunday. A round-trip ticket costs 6,700L ($4).

By Car   Drive west from Palermo along autostrada A29, branching onto the A29dir past Álcamo. From Segesta, head to Castelvetrano to connect to the A29 headed north, branching onto the A29dir.

VISITOR INFORMATION   Consult the tourist information office in Palermo (see section 6 of this chapter, below).

EXPLORING ANCIENT RUINS & ATTENDING CLASSICAL PLAYS

Visit Segesta for its remarkable ✪ **Doric temple,** dating from the 5th century B.C. Although never completed, it's in an excellent state of preservation (the entablature still remains). The temple was far enough away from the ancient town to have escaped leveling during the "scorched earth" days of the Vandals and Arabs.

From its position on a lonely hill, the Doric temple commands a majestic setting. Although you can scale the hill on foot, you're likely to encounter Sicilian boys trying to hustle you for a donkey ride. From mid-July until the first of August, **classical plays** are performed at the temple. Ask at the tourist information office in Palermo for details. Local travel agents in Palermo sell tickets for 15,000L to 25,000L ($9 to $15).

In another spot on Mount Barbaro, a theater, built in the Greek style into the rise of the hill, has been excavated. It was erected in the 3rd century B.C.

There's a cafe in the parking area leading to the temple; otherwise, Segesta is bereft of dining or accommodation selections.

6 Palermo

145 miles W of Messina, 448 miles S of Naples, 580 miles S of Rome

As the ferryboat docks in the Bay of Palermo, and you start spotting blond, blue-eyed *bambini* all over the place, don't be surprised. If fair-haired children don't fit your conception of what a Sicilian should look like, remember that the Normans landed here in 1060, six years before William the Conqueror put in at Hastings, and launched a campaign to wrest control of the island from the Arabs. Both elements were to cross cultures, a manifestation still seen today in Palermo's architecture—a unique style, Norman-Arabic.

The city is the largest port of Sicily, its capital, and the meeting place of a regional parliament granted numerous autonomous powers in postwar Italy. Against a backdrop of the citrus-studded Conca d'Oro plain and Monte Pellegrino, it's a city of wide boulevards, old quarters in the legendary Sicilian style (laundry lapping against the wind, smudge-faced kids playing in the street), town houses, architecturally harmonious squares, Baroque palaces, and modern buildings (many erected as a result of Allied bombings in 1943). It also has the worst traffic jams in Sicily.

Palermo was founded by the Phoenicians, but it has known many conquerors, some of whom established courts of great splendor (Frederick II), others of whom brought decay (the Angevins).

Today the city of 900,000 is *la brutta* and *la bella,* the ugly and the beautiful. Overcrowded, decaying in parts, and with unemployment and poverty rampant, it is nevertheless a showcase of artistic treasures and historical significance. It has the dubious reputation of being the home turf of the Mafia, sheltering some of the world's most powerful dons (none of whom look like Marlon Brando). As you make your way through the city occasionally seeing an armor-plated Alfa Romeo pass by, just avoid Vespa-riding bag snatchers and some of the most brilliant pickpockets in all the world, and you should have a fine time.

ESSENTIALS

GETTING THERE   By Plane   If you fly from Rome or Naples, you'll land at **Cinisi-Punta Raisi** (☎ 091/591691 for domestic, 091/591295 for international), 19 miles west of Palermo. It's best to catch a local airport bus from the airport to Piazza Castelnuovo; the fare is 4,500L ($2.70). For the same trip a taxi is likely to charge at least 60,000L ($36)—more if the driver thinks he can get away with it.

By Train   See "Getting to Sicily," above. After a 3½-hour ride from Messina across the north coast of Italy, you arrive at Palermo's station at **Piazza Giulio Césare** (☎ 091/616-1806), which lies on the eastern side of town and is linked to the center by buses and taxis.

By Bus   Palermo has bus connections with other major cities in Italy, operated by **SAIS** (☎ 091/616-6028). Some 16 buses a day make the 2½-hour trip from Catania, at a one-way cost of 18,000L ($10.80). One bus a day (except Sunday) arrives from Siracusa; the trip lasts 4 hours and costs 20,000L ($12) one-way. The bus terminal is near the rail station at Via Balsamo 16.

By Car   After your arrival from mainland Italy at Messina, head west on autostrada A20, which becomes Route 113, then A20 again, and finally A19 before its final approach to Palermo.

VISITOR INFORMATION   There are tourist information offices at strategic points, including the Palermo airport (☎ 091/591-698). The principal office, however, is the **Azienda Autonoma Turismo**, Piazza Castelnuovo 35 (☎ 091/583-847), open Monday to Friday from 8am to 8pm and Saturday 8am to 2pm.

GETTING AROUND   Municipally operated buses in Palermo charge 1,500L (90¢) for a ticket, or else you can purchase a full-day ticket for 4,000L ($2.40). For information and schedules, call **AMAT** at ☎ 091/222-398. Most passengers purchase their tickets at tobacco shops (*tabacchi)* before getting on. Otherwise, you'll need some 100-lira coins handy.

FAST FACTS: PALERMO

American Express   The agent for American Express is Giovanni Ruggieri e Figli, Via Emerico Amari 40 (☎ 091/587-144), which is open Monday to Friday from 9am to 1pm and 4 to 7pm and Saturday from 9am to 1pm.

Consulate   You'll find the **U.S. Consular Agency** at Via Re Federico 18 bis, 90141 Palermo (☎ 091/611-0020), open Monday to Friday from 9am to noon.

Crime   Be especially alert. Some citizens here are the most skilled pickpockets on the continent. Keep your gems locked away (in other words, don't flaunt any sign of wealth). Women who carry handbags are especially vulnerable to purse-snatchers on Vespas (wear the strap over one shoulder and across your chest with the purse hanging on the wall side of the sidewalk). Don't leave valuables in your car. In fact, we almost want to say don't leave your car alone, even knowing how impossible that is unless you put it in a garage (highly recommendable). Police squads operate mobile centers through the town to help combat street crime.

Emergencies   To call police, report a fire, or summon an ambulance, dial ☎ 113.

Post Office   The major post office is at Via Roma 322 (☎ **091/589-737**) and is open Monday to Saturday from 8:10am to 6:30pm.

SEEING THE SIGHTS

"The four corners" of the city, **Quattro Canti di Città,** is in the heart of the old town, at the junction of Corso Vittorio Emanuele and Via Maqueda. The ruling Spanish of the 17th century influenced the design of this grandiose Baroque square, replete with fountains and statues. From here you can walk to **Piazza Bellini,** the most attractive square of the old city. In an atmosphere reminiscent of the setting for an operetta, you're likely to hear strolling singers with guitars entertaining pizza eaters. Opening onto it is the **chiesa di Santa Maria dell'Ammiraglio** (also known as "La Martorana"), Piazza Bellini 3 (☎ **091/616-1692**), erected in 1143 with a Byzantine cupola by an admiral to Roger II. Its decaying but magnificent bell tower was built from 1146 to 1185. It's open Monday to Saturday from 9:30am to 1pm and 3:30 to 7pm and Sunday from 8:30am to 1pm. Admission is free.

Also fronting the square is the **chiesa di San Cataldo,** erected in 1160 in the Arab-Byzantine style with a trio of faded pink cupolas. In a 12th-century building constructed in a cubic form, it belonged to the order of the Knights of the Holy Sepulchre. Also opening onto the Piazza Bellini is the **chiesa di Santa Caterina,** attached to a vast Dominican monastery constructed in 1310. The church is late 16th century, containing interesting 18th-century multicolored marble ornamentation.

Adjoining the square is **Piazza Pretoria,** dominated by a fountain designed in Florence in 1554 for a villa, but acquired by Palermo about 20 years later. A short walk will take you to the cathedral of Palermo.

Il Duomo. Piazza di Cattedrale. Corso Vittorio Emanuele. ☎ **091/334-376.** Free admission (donation appreciated). Apr–Oct, daily 7am–7pm; Nov–Mar, daily 7am–noon and 4–7pm.

This cathedral is a curious spectacle where East meets West. It was built in the 12th century on the foundation of an earlier basilica that had been converted by the Arabs into a mosque. The cathedral—much altered over the centuries—was founded by an English archbishop known as Walter of the Mill. The impressive "porch" was built in the 15th century on the southern front in the Gothic style. But the cupola, added in the late 18th century, detracts from the overall appearance, and the interior was revamped unsuccessfully at the same time, resulting in a glaring incongruity in styles. The "pantheon" of royal tombs includes that of the emperor Frederick II, in red porphyry under a canopy of marble.

San Giovanni degli Eremiti. Via dei Benedettini Bianchi 3. ☎ **091/651-5019.** Free admission. Mon–Sat 9am–1pm, Mon and Thurs 3–6pm, Sun 9am–12:30pm.

The other church (now deconsecrated) worthy of note is Saint John of the Hermits. Perhaps in an atmosphere appropriate for the recluse it honors, this little church with its twin-columned cloister is one of the most idyllic spots in all of Palermo. A medieval veil hangs heavy in the gardens, with their citrus blossoms and flowers, especially on a hot summer day as you wander around in its cloister. Ordered built by Roger II in 1132, the church adheres to its Arabic influence, surmounted by pinkish cupolas, while showing the Norman style as well.

Palazzo di Normanni. Piazza del Parlamento. ☎ **091/656-1737.** Free admission. Tours of the palace given by advance reservation only. Chapel, Mon–Fri 9am–noon and 3–5pm, Sat 9am–noon, Sun 9–10am and noon–1pm.

This Palace of the Normans contains one of the greatest art treasures in Sicily, the Cappella Palatina (Palatine Chapel). Erected at the request of Roger II in the 1130s,

Exploring La Kalsa

Although it's a bit dangerous, especially at night, the crumbling Kalsa is the most interesting district of Palermo. In the southwestern sector of the old city, it was built by the Arabs as a walled seaside residence for their chief ministers. It is bounded by the port and Via Garibaldi and Via Paternostro to the east and west and by Corso Vittorio Emanuele and Via Lincoln to the north and south. Later, much of the fine work of the Arabs was destroyed when the Spanish viceroys took over, adding their own architectural interpretations.

Kalsa has been called one of the least restored neighborhoods in Europe. To reach the sector, begin at the Quattro Canti di Città (see above) and head east down the Corso, crossing the bustling Via Roma. Turn right down Via Paternostro until you reach the **chiesa di San Francesco d'Assisi,** a church from the 13th century on Piazza San Francesco d'Assisi (☎ **091/616-2819**). Visit the church if for no other reason than to see its magnificent Cappella Mastrotonio carved in 1468. Don't always count on the church being open, however.

From Piazza San Francesco d'Assisi, go along Via Merlo to the **Palazzo Mirto,** 2 Via Merlo (☎ **091/616-4751**) to see how the nobility used to live back in the days when this was an upmarket neighborhood. The palace is a splendid example of a princely residence of the early 20th century, still maintaining its original 18th- and 19th-century furnishings. It is open Monday, Wednesday, and Friday from 9am to 1pm, charging 2,000L ($1.20) admission.

Via Merlo leads into the landmark **Piazza Marina,** one of the most evocative parts of Palermo. Once the port of La Cala was here but it silted up the 1100s. Like something out of the U.S.'s Deep South, a garden is found at the Villa Garibaldi in the center of the square. The square is dominated by the Palazzo Chiaramonte on the southeast corner, dating from the early 14th century. A trio of Renaissance churches occupy the other corners of this historic square.

it's the finest example of the Arabic-Norman style of design and building. The effect of the mosaics inside is awe-inspiring. Almond-eyed biblical characters from the Byzantine art world in lush colors create a panorama of epic pageantry, illustrating such Gospel scenes as the Nativity. The overall picture is further enhanced by inlaid marble and mosaics and pillars made of granite shipped from the East. For a look at still more mosaics, this time in a more secular vein depicting scenes of the hunt, you can visit the Hall of Roger II upstairs, the seat of the Sicilian Parliament, where security is likely to be tight. Visitors are taken through on guided tours.

Galleria Regionale della Sicilia. Via Alloro 4. ☎ **091/616-4317.** Admission 2,000L ($1.20) adults, free for children 17 and under and for seniors 60 and over. Mon, Wed, Fri, and Sat 9am–1:30pm; Tues and Thurs 9am–1:30pm and 3–5:30pm; Sun 9am–12:30pm.

The Palazzo Abatellis was built in the Gothic and Renaissance styles. Today it houses the Regional Gallery, which shows the evolution of art in Sicily from the 13th to the 18th century. On the ground floor is a most famous work, a 15th-century fresco *Triumph of Death,* in all its gory magnificence. A horseback-riding skeleton, representing death, tramples his victims under hoof. Worthy of mention are three majolica plates, valuable specimens of Loza dorada manufactured in the workshops of Manises, and the Giara produced in the workshops of Málaga at the end of the 13th century.

Francesco Laurana's slanty-eyed *Eleonora d'Aragona* is worth seeking out, as are seven grotesque D'Roleries painted on wood. Of the paintings on the second floor,

L'Annunziata by Antonello da Messina, a portrait of the Madonna with depth and originality, is one of the most celebrated paintings in Italy. The 13th room contains a very good series of Flemish paintings from the 15th and 16th centuries, among which the best is the *Trittico Malvagna* by Jean Gossaert, called Mabuse.

Museo Archeologico Regionale. Piazza Olivella 4. ☎ **091/611-6805.** Admission 2,000L ($1.20). Mon, Wed–Thurs, and Sat 9am–1:30pm; Tues and Fri 9am–1:30pm and 3–5:30pm; Sun 9am–1pm.

Located in a former convent for Philippine friars, this is one of the greatest archeological collections in southern Italy, where the competition's stiff. Many works displayed here were excavated at Selinunte, once one of the major towns in Magna Graecia (Greater Greece). See, in particular, the Sala di Selinunte, displaying the celebrated metopes that adorned the classical temples, as well as slabs of bas-relief. The gallery also owns important sculpture from the Temple of Himera. The collection of bronzes is exceptional, including the athlete and the stag discovered in the ruins of Pompeii (a Roman copy of a Greek original) and a bronze ram that came from Syracuse, dating from the 3rd century B.C. Among the Greek sculpture is *The Pouring Satyr*, excavated at Pompeii (a Roman copy of a Greek original by Praxiteles).

Catacombe dei Cappuccini. Piazza Cappuccini 1. ☎ **091/212-117.** Free admission (donations accepted). Tours, Mon–Sat 9am–noon and 3–5pm, Sun and holidays 9am–noon and 3–5pm.

The final attraction, on the outskirts of the city, is the most bizarre of all. The fresco you might have seen in the Galleria Regionale della Sicilia, *Triumph of Death,* dims by comparison to the real thing. The catacombs, it was discovered, contained a preservative that helped to mummify dead people. Sicilians, everyone from nobles to maids, were buried here in the 19th century, and it was the custom on Sunday to go and visit Uncle Luigi to see how he was holding together. If he fell apart, he was wired together again or wrapped in burlap sacking. The last person buried in the catacombs was placed to rest in 1920—a little girl almost lifelike in death. But many Sicilians of the 19th century are in fine shape, considering—with eyes, hair, and even clothing fairly intact (the convent could easily be turned into a museum of costume). Some of the expressions on the faces of the skeletons take the fun out of Halloween—a grotesque ballet. The catacombs may be visited on guided tours.

SHOPPING

The most colorful place to shop even if you don't buy anything is **Vucciria,** lying off Via Roma in the rear of the Church of San Domenico. This is one of the great casbahlike markets of Europe. Here are the mountains of food, from fish to meat and vegetables, that the denizens of Palermo consume daily. The array of wild fennel, long-stemmed artichokes, and blood oranges, as well as giant octopus and squid, calls for a painter at least. In Sicilian dialect, the name "vucciria" means hubbub, and that's an apt name for this market. As an offbeat adventure, try dining at **Shangai,** Vicolo Mezzani 34 (☎ **091/589-702**), which cooks virtually anything that is sold in the market. You can sample several fish specialties, including eel, by ordering the mixed fish fry. The market is open Monday through Saturday but Shangai stays open until 11pm. You don't have to eat at a restaurant but can also sample the wares offered at various food stalls, including chickpea flour fritters or deep-fried meat- or cheese-filled pockets of dough (calzoni). To go really local, ask for guasteddi. This is a fresh bun stuffed with narrow strips of calf's spleen and ricotta, dished up with a fiery hot sauce. Everything shuts down on Sunday. After all, this is Sicily.

Actually two shops in one, **Battaglia,** Via Ruggero Settimo 74/M (☎ **091/ 580-224**), sells women's wear and within it, **Hermès** offers men's and women's wear, all of an upscale nature that includes prêt-à-porter and alta moda collections. There's also a limited selection of casual and sports shoes as well as leather accessories, but this shop is really about clothing. Offering well-made men's wear, **Giovanni Alongi,** Via Ruggero Settimo 46/A (☎ 091/582-927), also has shoes and accessories. Carrying everything from women's knitwear to sequined evening gowns, **Napoléon,** Via della Libertà 1 (☎ 091/587-173) has just enough men's accessories to keep males preoccupied while women do the real shopping.

If it comes in linen, **Frette,** with locations at Via Ruggero Settimo 12 (☎ 091/585-166), Via G. Sciutti 85 (☎ 091/343-288), and Via della Libertà 36/B (☎ 091/625-0075) sells it. The shop offers sheets, tablecloths, towels, bedspreads, pajamas, night gowns, curtains, and tapestries. Call for an appointment at **Miroslava Tasic,** Largo di Malta (☎ 091/588-126), if you're interested in purchasing handmade sheets, towels, tablecloths, or upholstery fabrics in fine cottons, silks, and linens, adorned with embroidery or lace trim.

Offering jewelry in silver or gold, plain or inlay with the gems of your choice, **Ma Gi,** Via Ruggero Settimo 45 (☎ 091/585-446), also markets dishes and cutlery in silver. If you can afford it, they can make it. Selling sterling and Sheffield silver pieces from various eras, **Fecarotta,** Via Principe di Belmonte 103/B (☎ 091/331-518) is a market leader. They also sell antique furniture and paintings.

Featuring traditional fruit-filled tarts as well as *cassata siciliana,* tarts with ricotta-based filling, **Fratelli Magri,** Via Isidoro Carini 42 (☎ 091/584-788), also makes other types of sweets, and in the summer offers *gelato* as well. A meat-eaters fantasy shop, **Mangia Charcuterie,** Via Principe di Belmonte 116 (☎ 091/587-651) presents a smorgasbord of meats and meat dishes, including imported French pâtés and German sausages. You can carry out or have items mailed directly to your favorite carnivore. A celebration of local and national confections, **I Peccatucci di Mamma Andrea,** Via Principe di Scordia 67 (☎ 091/334-835) temps with such delectables as pralines, *torrone, panettoni,* jams, fruits in honey, *ghirlande di croccantini,* marzipan, and even liqueurs. If it's sweet and Italian, it's here.

If you don't read Italian, your book selections are limited at **Libreria Flaccovio,** Via Ruggero Settimo 37 (☎ 091/589-442), but they do offer English versions of guide books about Sicily and Palermo, as well as a lovely volume featuring the art of Palermo. They emphasize handcrafted tortoise-shell picture frames at **Meli,** Via Dante 294 (☎ 091/682-4213), but you can also find a selection of prints, etchings, and engravings from the 16th through 19th centuries. The two pottery shops of **De Simone,** at Largo San Severino 24, in Piazza Leoni (☎ 091/363-190), and Via Gaetano Daita 13B (☎ 091/584-876), carry only majolica. They sell interior and exterior tiles as well as dinnerware, lamps, and assorted other pieces. It may seem like an odd marriage of merchandise, but **Verde Italiano,** Via delle Croci 33 (☎ 091/326-002), sells its own line of ceramics and a selection of liqueurs. You can visit their pottery studio at Via Principe di Villafranca 42 (☎ 091/320-282) without an appointment.

WHERE TO STAY

Generally you'll find a poor lot of hostelries, aided by only a few fine choices. Hunt and pick carefully.

EXPENSIVE

Villa Igiea Grand Hotel. Salita Belmonte 43, 90142 Palermo. ☎ **091/543-744.** Fax 091/547-654. 117 rms, 6 suites. A/C MINIBAR TV TEL. 377,000L ($226.20) double; from 630,000L ($378) suite. Rates include breakfast. AE, DC, MC, V.

This deluxe hotel was built at the turn of the century as one of Sicily's great aristocratic estates, and today it's one of the top two luxury hotels on the island (it lags behind the San Domenico in Taormina). The exterior resembles a medieval Sicilian fortress whose carefully chiseled walls include crenellated battlements and forbidding watchtowers. It was constructed of the same buff-colored stone that Greek colonists used during the Punic Wars when they erected a circular temple which, although heavily buttressed with modern scaffolding, still stands in the garden. Nearby, nestled amid a grove of pines and palms, is an Art Nouveau statue of Igiea, goddess of flowers. Everywhere are clusters of antiques. The accommodations vary from sumptuous suites with private terraces to rooms of lesser size and glamor. The hotel, reached by passing through an industrial portside north of Palermo, sits on a cliff with a view of the open sea.

Dining/Entertainment: The hotel's bar is baronial, with a soaring stone vault. You dine on Sicilian and classic Italian meals in a grand and glittering room against a backdrop of paneled walls, ornate ceilings, and chandeliers.

Services: Room service, baby-sitting, laundry, valet.

Facilities: Terrace overlooking the water, swimming pool, tennis court.

MODERATE

Centrale Palace Hotel. Corso Vittorio Emanuele 327, near the corner of Via Maqueda, 91039 Palermo. ☎ **091/588-409.** Fax 091/334-881. 57 rms, 6 junior suites. A/C TV TEL. 280,000L ($168) double, 370,000L ($222) junior suite. Rates include breakfast. Parking 15,000L ($9). AE, MC, V.

One of the most appealing hotels in Palermo occupies the four-story premises of what was built in the 1600s as an opulent private home in the historic core of Palermo. About a century ago, it was transformed into a hotel, and in the early 1990s was thoroughly renovated into a plush and comfortable favorite of traveling business executives. You'll find flowers in the public rooms, a congenial, well-informed staff, and enough comforts (including air conditioning whenever it matters) to make you appreciate the amenities of the modern age. Look for an enlargement and improvement of the in-house dining facilities, perhaps during the lifetime of this edition. At presstime, there was a simple restaurant, along with a bar, but plans are in effect to transform it into something larger and much more dramatic.

Grande Albergo Sole. Corso Vittorio Emanuele 291, 90133 Palermo. ☎ **091/581-811.** Fax 091/611-0182. 150 rms. A/C MINIBAR TV TEL. 210,000L ($126) double. Rates include breakfast. AE, DC, MC, V. Parking 10,500L ($6.30).

This pleasant, second-class hotel lies in the busy historic center of Palermo. A 1960s remake of a century-old building, it houses a helpful staff and simple and uncomplicated bedrooms, each with radio and modern furniture, often reproductions of Sicilian 19th-century pieces. There's a residents' lounge, a bar, a restaurant, and a roof garden terrace for sunbathing.

Jolly Hotel del Foro Italico. Via Foro Italico 22, 90133 Palermo. ☎ **800/221-2626** in the U.S., 800/247-1277 in Canada, or 091/616-5090 in Italy. Fax 091/616-1441. 268 rms, 5 suites. A/C MINIBAR TV. 200,000L ($120) double; 220,000L ($132) suite. Rates include breakfast. Half board 53,000L ($31.80) per person extra. AE, DC, MC, V.

Off a busy boulevard facing the Gulf of Palermo, this aging 1960s chain hotel invites with shafts of pale blue supporting triangular balconies. Try for the quieter bedrooms on the upper floors or at the rear. One of the best hotels in town (popular for Sicilian wedding receptions), it offers a contemporary atmosphere and good accommodations. The public rooms have bright colors and serviceable furnishings. The well-organized bedrooms have lots of built-in pieces and comfortable beds. The bedrooms on the top floors provide you with at least a glimpse of the Mediterranean. The Jolly also has a garden, a pool, a restaurant, and an American bar. The food is both Sicilian and Italian.

President Hotel. Via Francesco Crispi 230, 90139 Palermo. ☎ **091/580-733.** Fax 091/ 611-1588. 129 rms. A/C TV TEL. 200,000L ($120) double. Rates include breakfast. AE, DC, MC, V. Parking 7,000L ($4.20).

Its eight-story concrete-and-glass facade rising above the harborfront quays, this is one of the better and more up-to-date of the middle-bracket hotels in town, superior to the Grande Albergo Sole. Built in 1978, it was renovated in the early 1990s. You'll pass beneath the facade's soaring arcade before entering the informal stone-trimmed lobby. One of the most appealing coffee shop/bars in town lies at the top of a short flight of stairs next to the reception area. There's a panoramic restaurant on the uppermost floor, plus a guarded parking garage in the basement. The bedrooms are comfortably furnished, although short on style.

INEXPENSIVE

Albergo Cavour. Via Alessandro Manzoni 11, 90133 Palermo. ☎ **091/616-2759.** 9 rms, 4 with bath (tub or shower). 45,000L ($27) double without bath, 55,000L ($33) double with bath. No credit cards. Parking 10,000L ($6).

Albergo Cavour is on the fifth floor of a 1920s building conveniently located in front of the central station. The rooms are functional, suitable for overnight stopovers, and the manager sees to it that they're well kept and decently furnished, with comfortable mattresses on the beds. No meals are served, but many cafes are nearby.

Hotel Sausele. Via Vincenzo Errante 12, 90127 Palermo. ☎ **091/616-1308.** Fax 091/ 616-7525. 36 rms. TEL. 135,000L ($81) double. Rates include breakfast. AE, DC, MC, V. Parking 14,000L ($8.40).

This hotel near the railway station is the best in a run-down area. It's owned and managed efficiently by Swiss-born Signora Sausele, who has created a clean establishment. It's a modest but quite pleasant albergo, with bedrooms just adequate for a good night's rest. The hotel has an elevator, garage, bar, and TV room. The lounges are air-conditioned.

WHERE TO DINE
MODERATE

L'Approdo da Renato. Via Messina Marine 224. ☎ **091/630-2881.** Reservations required Fri–Sat. Main courses 18,000L–25,000L ($10.80–$15). AE, MC, V. Tues–Sun 12:30–3pm and 8–11pm. Closed Aug 10–25. SICILIAN.

This restaurant lies in an elegant villa built in 1880. From its dining room, or from its flowering outdoor terrace, you'll have a view over the Gulf of Palermo. Run by a husband-and-wife team, it's infused with gaiety. Some visitors are invited to explore the wine cellar, whose contents are said to rival the best in all of Italy. The kitchen adheres to time-tested Sicilian recipes, and the menu depends on the season and the finest of available ingredients. Nearly all diners begin with a selection of Sicilian antipasti, both vegetarian and seafood, with tuna factored in somehow. You never know what dishes will be offered, but memorable past meals have included fresh fish marinated in refined olive oil and flavored with herbs, crêpes filled with seafood, swordfish in a mandarin orange sauce, and roast goat flavored with Sicilian herbs.

Charleston. Piazzale Ungheria 30. ☎ **091/321-366.** Reservations required. Jacket and tie required. Main courses 28,000L–35,000L ($16.80–$21). AE, DC, MC, V. Mon–Sat 1–3pm and 8–11pm. Closed June 16–Sept 25. SICILIAN/INTERNATIONAL.

For years Charleston was regarded as the finest restaurant in Sicily, although today there's competition for that title. Nevertheless, it remains a national culinary monument of Sicilian hospitality and old-fashioned virtues, an appealing choice in Palermo. The owners create a refined and perfect milieu for their presentation of Sicilian dishes, which naturally concentrate on fresh fish, especially roast swordfish. The kitchen prepares a number of international dishes as well, but we prefer to stick to their regional fare, especially if it's the chef's special *spaghetti all'aragosta* with a delectable lobster sauce. Begin with *caponata* (one of Sicily's best eggplant dishes), and finish off with a torta Charleston, a sweet, and oh-so-rich cake.

Gourmand's. Via della Libertà. ☎ **091/323-431.** Reservations recommended. Main courses 15,000L–22,000L ($9–$13.20). AE, DC, MC, V. Mon–Sat 1–3pm and 8–11pm. Closed Aug 5–25. SICILIAN.

Gourmand's is among the best restaurants in Palermo for an introduction to the rich, aromatic cookery of Sicily. The cuisine is on par with that of Charleston, although the atmosphere is less elegant. A corner restaurant in the commercial district of town, it's a light and airy room filled with original paintings and Chinese-red ceiling lattices. You'll admire the richly laden antipasti table before you're ushered to your table. For a first course, try spaghetti Gourmand's or an involtino of eggplant. Fresh fish is always available—try it grilled. The chef does many Italian dishes well, including veal escalope in the Valdostan style and pepper steak or, if available, roast quail. Risotto with salmon is often featured on the menu, as is rigatoni Henry IV made with mushrooms and ham in white sauce and tomato sauce.

La Scuderia. Viale del Fante 9. ☎ **091/520-323.** Reservations recommended. Main courses 18,000L–40,000L ($10.80–$24). AE, DC, MC, V. Mon–Sat 12:30–3pm and 8:30pm–midnight. Closed 2 weeks in Aug. INTERNATIONAL/ITALIAN.

Dedicated professionals direct this appealing restaurant surrounded by trees at the foot of Monte Pellegrino, north of the city center and directly south of Parco della Favorita. It's the only restaurant in Palermo to equal the cuisine of Gourmand's and Charleston. The inside is augmented in summer with one of the prettiest flowering terraces in town, sought after by everyone from erstwhile lovers to extended families to glamour queens on vacation. The sound of falling water, followed by the tunes of a piano player, greet you as you enter. The imaginative cuisine includes a mixed grill of fresh vegetables with a healthy dose of a Sicilian cheese called caciocavallo, along with stuffed turkey cutlet, a wide array of beef and veal dishes, involtini of eggplant, risotto with seafood, veal spiedino, and many tempting desserts, including one known as *pernice all'erotica*.

INEXPENSIVE

Al Vicolo. Cortile Scimecaz (off Piazza San Francesco Saverio). ☎ **091/651-2464.** Reservations recommended. Main courses 10,000L–14,000L ($6–$8.40); fixed-price menu 24,000L ($14.40). No credit cards. Mon–Sat 12:30–3pm and 7–11:30pm. Closed Aug 10–25. SICILIAN.

This is one of the most characteristic trattorie of the city, and deserves more acclaim than it receives. The dining rooms were converted from a produce warehouse. For antipasti, try *panelle* (chickpea or garbanzo fritters) and *arancini* (rice croquettes) or potato croquettes, or the sardines *à beccafico* (stuffed and flavored with laurel). They serve many of the most typical dishes of Sicily, including pasta mixed with sardines and wild fennel—for some, an acquired taste, for the devotee of Sicilian cuisine, reason enough to visit the restaurant. Any pasta labeled "alla Norma" comes with vine-ripened tomatoes and eggplant. The local fish is fresh and abundant, and local meats including lamb and kid are always offered. You can wash down the meal—Sicilians say "irrigate"—with a selection of regional wines.

Friend's Bar. Via Filipo Brunelleschi 138, Borgo Nuovo. ☎ **091/201-401.** Reservations required. Main courses 22,500L–24,500L ($13.50–$14.70). AE, DC, MC, V. Tues–Sun 1–3:30pm and 8–11:30pm. Closed Aug 10–31. SICILIAN.

This is one of the finest restaurants in Palermo, located in a suburb called Borgo Nuovo. A meal here is an event to many Sicilians. Friend's Bar has become one of the sought-after places on the island, and a reservation for one of the garden seats is almost essential to get past the bar. First, you might enjoy a few of the delicacies from the antipasti table, followed by one of the many regional specialties such as subtly flavored pastas, and an array of steamed or grilled fish dishes or one of the meat dishes that have made this place so well known locally. The house red wine is a good accompaniment for most any meal.

PALERMO AFTER DARK

We always like to begin our evening by heading to the century-old **Caffè Mazzara,** Via Generale Magliocco 15 (☎ 091/321-443), where you can sample Sicilian ice cream—among the best in the world—and order the richest coffee in all the country. Or perhaps you'll prefer to sit quietly, sipping the heady Sicilian wines in the corner where Giuseppe di Lampedusa in the late 1950s wrote a great many chapters of his novel *The Leopard*. Besides an espresso bar and pastry shop on the first floor, there's a so-called American grill on the second floor as well as the prestigious Restaurant Charleston. If you can't find a place to eat in Palermo on a Sunday, when virtually everything is shut, the Mazzara is a good bet. It's open daily from 7:30am to 10pm.

All three of Palermo's most popular dance clubs lie in the modern, commercial center of the city, and all feature late-breaking music and loudspeaker systems that encourage patrons to dance. They include **Gazebo Club,** Viale Piemonte 6 (☎ 091/348-917); **Il Cherchio,** Viale Strasbourg 312 (☎ 091/688-5421); and **Grant's Club,** Via Principe de Paterno 8 (☎ 091/346-772). This trio is animated and crowded, especially after 10:30pm, sometimes oppressively so thanks to the city's notorious heat.

Calmer, more contemplative evenings can be enjoyed at a stylish piano bar, **Villa Jiuditta,** Via San Lorenzo Colli 17 (☎ 091/688-6257), whose well-groomed premises lie about a half-mile west of the town center. Here, evenings in a cool and carefully decorated bar sometimes segue into dinners at the establishment's restaurant. If you're looking for relief from Palermo's oppressive heat, consider short trek north of the city to Mondello, where an attractive piano bar in the **Mondello Palace Hotel** beckons from Via Principe de Scalea 12 (☎ 091/450-001).

Palermo is also a cultural center of some note, its opera and ballet season lasting from January through June. The principal venue for these presentations is the **Teatro Politeama Garibaldi,** Piazza Ruggero Séttimo (☎ 091/605-3315), where tickets cost from 35,000L ($21). The box office is open Tuesday to Saturday 10am to 1pm and 5 to 7pm. The city is known also for its puppet performances, the best of which are staged by **Compagnia Bradamante di Anna Cuticchio,** Via Lombardia 25 (☎ 091/625-9223). Tickets range from 10,000L to 30,000L ($6 to $18), and the box office opens one hour before show time.

The tourist office will advise about times and dates of performances for the major summer event, a festival taking place at an open-air seaside theater, **Teatro di Verdura Villa Castelnuovo.** The festival usually begins the first week of July, lasting an entire month, with classical music, jazz, and ballet performances. For more information or to purchase tickets, contact **Teatro Politeama Garibaldi,** Piazza Ruggero Séttimo (☎ **091/605-3315**), across from the tourist office, Tuesday to Saturday from 10am to 1pm and 5 to 7pm.

SIDE TRIPS FROM PALERMO
MONREALE

The town of Monreale is 6 miles from Palermo, up Monte Caputo and on the edge of the Conca d'Oro plain. If you don't have a car, you can reach it by taking bus no. 389 from Piazza Indipendenza in Palermo. The Normans under William II founded a Benedictine monastery at Monreale some time in the 1170s. Near the ruins of that monastery a great cathedral was erected.

As with the Alhambra in Granada, Spain, the ✪ **Chiostro del Duomo di Monreale,** Piazza Guglielmo il Buono (☎ **091/640-4403**), has a relatively drab facade, giving little indication of the riches inside. The interior is virtually covered throughout with shimmering mosaics, illustrating scenes from the Bible, such as the story of Adam and Eve and Noah and the Ark. The artwork provides a distinctly original interpretation of the old, rigid Byzantine form of decoration. The mosaics make for an Eastern look despite the Western-style robed Christ reigning over his kingdom. The ceiling is ornate, even gaudy. On the north and west facade of the church are two bronze doors in relief depicting biblical stories. The cloisters are also of interest. Built in 1166, they consist of twin mosaic columns, every other pair an original design (the lava inlay was hauled from the active volcano, Mount Etna). Admission to the cathedral is free, although if you visit the cloisters, there is a charge of 2,000L ($1.20). The cathedral is open daily 8am to noon and 3:30 to 6pm. From July to September, the cloister is open Monday, Wednesday, and Friday from 9am to 1pm and 3 to 6pm; Tuesday, Thursday and Saturday from 9am to 1pm; and Sunday from 9am to 12:30pm. In off-season, ask at the cathedral, as hours vary.

You can also visit the treasury and the terraces, each charging another 2,000L ($1.20) for admission. They're open from 8:30am to 12:30pm and 3 to 6:30pm. The terraces are actually the rooftop of the church, from which you'll be rewarded with a view of the cloisters.

Where to Stay & Dine

Park Hotel Carrubella. Corso Umberto 1, 90046 Monreale. ☎ **091/640-2188.** Fax 091/ 640-2189. 30 rms. A/C TEL. 120,000L ($72) double. AE, DC, MC, V.

The aging Park Hotel is one of the tallest buildings in town, its terraces providing a sweeping view over the famous church, the surrounding valleys, and the azure coastline of faraway Palermo. To reach it, follow a one-lane road from the piazza near the church along a serpentine series of terraces; the hotel is 800 yards from the cathedral. The spacious but tattered interior is filled with luxurious mirrors and deep and comfortable armchairs, along with scattered pieces of sculpture. In the public rooms, as well as in the bedrooms, the floors are covered with rows of Sicilian tiles hand-painted into flowery designs. The hotel offers comfortably furnished accommodations, each with its own balcony. Well-prepared meals are served in the conservatively elegant dining room.

La Botte. Contrada Lenzitti 20 (SS186). ☎ **091/414-051.** Reservations required. Main courses 16,000L–22,000L ($9.60–$13.20). AE, DC, MC, V. Fri–Sun 1–2:45pm and 8–10:45pm. Closed June 20–Sept 20. SICILIAN/ITALIAN.

Most of the dishes are derived from ancient recipes of Palermo, whose origins have long been forgotten. Perhaps you'll begin with an aromatic antipasto of such local ingredients as artichokes, tuna, or shrimp. Pasta specialties are always smooth choices, followed by creative Sicilian meat dishes. This is the best restaurant in the area.

MONDELLO LIDO

When the summer sun burns hot, old men on the square seek a place in the shade, *bambini* tire of their toys, it's beach weather. For the denizen of Palermo, that means Mondello, 7¹/₂ miles to the east. Originally, before this beachfront started attracting the wealthy class of Palermo, it was a fishing village (it still is), and you can see rainbow-colored fishing boats bobbing up in the harbor. A sandy beach, a good one, stretches for about a mile and a half, and it's filled to capacity on a July or August day. You might call it a Palermitan seaside experience. Some women traveling alone have found Mondello more inviting and less intimidating than the center of Palermo. In summer an express bus (no. 6, "Beallo") leaves for Mondello from the central train station in Palermo.

Where to Stay

✪ **Mondello Palace Hotel.** Viale Prìncipe di Scalea 2, 90151 Mondello. ☎ **091/450-001.** Fax 091/450-657. 83 rms, 10 suites. A/C MINIBAR TV TEL. 250,000L ($150) double; from 360,000L ($216) suite. Rates include breakfast. AE, DC, MC, V.

Set in a garden of palms and semitropical shrubs across the coastal road from the beach, this is the most visible, the best, and most famous hotel in Mondello. Built in 1950 and renovated several times since, it offers four stories of airy and comfortable bedrooms outfitted in tones of blue, red, and white. All doubles have balconies and sea views. Clients of yesteryear have included Sophia Loren and Luchino Visconti; today the place might house families vacationing en masse from the hinterlands of Sicily or northern Europe. There's a large swimming pool set into the garden, a bar, and a sea-view indoor/outdoor restaurant serving full meals.

Splendid Hotel la Torre. Via Piano di Gallo 11, 90151 Mondello. ☎ **091/450-222.** Fax 091/ 450-033. 170 rms. A/C MINIBAR TV TEL. 198,000L ($118.80) double; 255,000L ($153) triple. Rates include breakfast. AE, DC, MC, V.

Built in 1962 and renovated in 1984, this beach-side hotel lies half a mile north of Mondello's center. From your comfortable bed you can get up and walk out onto a private terrace overlooking the sea. Some of the well-furnished chambers are quite spacious. All are well maintained. During the day there are many sports and recreational activities to occupy your time, including swimming pools, a tennis court, a garden, and plenty of games for children. La Torre is very much a family resort, not a romantic retreat. It is crowded during the peak summer months, so reservations are important. It attracts some heavy drinkers as well—the bar opens at 9am, staying open until 1am. The place is not a gourmet haven, but we've enjoyed our meals here, especially the pasta and fish dishes. The cookery is quite good, the choice is ample, and the staff takes good care of you.

Where to Dine

✪ **Charleston le Terrazze.** Viale Regina Elena. ☎ **091/450-171.** Reservations required. Main courses 29,000L–35,000L ($17.40–$21). AE, DC, MC, V. Daily 1–3pm and 8–11pm. Closed Oct–May. SICILIAN/INTERNATIONAL.

The best food in Mondello is served at this buff-colored seaside fantasy of art nouveau, with spires and gingerbread detailing. The Sicilian staff add to the sense of luxury and refinement—but bring lots of money. The chef specializes in many dishes, including such favorites as *melanzana Charleston* (in our modest opinion, Sicilians do the best eggplant dishes in the world). Try also the *pesce spada* (swordfish) al gratin and scaloppe Conca d'Oro. For dessert, you can have a smooth finish by ordering a parfait di caffè. For a wine, we recommend a Corvo, which comes both bianco and rosso. Of course, with a name like Le Terrazze it's got to deliver the mandatory terrace with a view.

CEFALÙ

For another day's excursion, we recommend a trek east from Palermo for 50 miles to this fishing village, which is known all over Europe for its Romanesque cathedral, an outstanding achievement of the Arab-Norman architectural style.

GETTING THERE   From Palermo, it's relatively easy, as 14 trains per weekday make the one-hour trip, costing 5,700L ($3.40) for a one-way ticket. For information and schedules, call ☎ 0921/21-169. In addition, SPISA, Via Umberto I, 28 (☎ 0921/24-301), runs buses between Palermo and Cefalù, costing 7,600L ($4.55) one way. Motorists can follow Route 113 east from Palermo to Cefalù.

VISITOR INFORMATION   You'll find visitor information at Corso Ruggero 77 (☎ 0921/21-050), open Monday to Friday from 8am to 2pm and 4 to 7pm and Saturday from 8am to 2pm.

Seeing the Sights

Il Duomo. Piazza di Duomo, off Corso Ruggero. ☎ 0921/922-021. Free admission. Daily 8am–noon and 3:30–7pm.

Resembling a military fortress, the Duomo was built by Roger II to fulfill a vow he made when faced with a possible shipwreck. Construction began in 1131, and in time two square towers dotted the landscape of Cefalù, curiously placed between the sea and a rocky promontory. The architectural line of the cathedral has a severe elegance, and inside are some outstanding Byzantine-inspired mosaics. Seek out especially Christ the Pantocrator in the dome of the apse.

Museo Mandralisca. Via Mandralisca 13. ☎ 0921/421-547. Admission 5,000L ($3). Daily 9:30am–12:30pm and 3:30–6:30pm.

Before leaving town, try to visit this museum opposite the cathedral, with its outstanding collection of art, none more notable than the 1470 portrait of an unknown by Antonello da Messina. Some art critics have journeyed all the way down from Rome just to stare at this handsome work. This face is often featured on most Sicilian tourist brochures.

Where to Dine

Al Gabbiano da Saro. Viale Lungomare 17. ☎ 0921/421-495. Reservations recommended Sat–Sun. Main courses 10,000L–30,000L ($6–$18). AE, DC, MC, V. Thurs–Tues noon–3pm and 7pm–midnight. Closed mid-Dec to mid-Jan. SEAFOOD/SICILIAN.

In a century-old building, this rustic seaside trattoria is typical of the area, attracting both locals and visitors in almost equal measure. Fresh fish is the item to order, making your way through a list of unpronounceable sea creatures. You might begin with *zuppa di cozze*, a savory mussel soup. The vegetables and pastas are good, too, especially *pennette alla Norma* (with eggplant). Involtini of swordfish is another specialty. The cookery is consistent, as is the service. If you speak a little Italian, it helps.

Da Nino al Lungomare. Viale Lungomare 11. ☎ **0921/422-582.** Reservations required. Main courses 14,000L–22,000L ($8.40–$13.20); fixed-price menu 22,000L ($13.20). AE, MC, V. June–Sept, daily noon–3pm and 7–11pm; Oct and Dec–May, Wed–Mon noon–3pm and 7–11pm. Closed Nov. SOUTHERN ITALIAN/SICILIAN/PIZZA.

In a century-old salt warehouse, this is a reasonably good choice for southern Italian and Sicilian cuisine served al fresco in a seaside setting. That means that the kitchen is in no way influenced by trends or food fads. Time-tested recipes are served here, including a delectable *risotto marinara* (fisher's rice) and involtini of meat. Fresh fish, however, is the featured item. You can also order some delectable pizzas fresh from the oven.

7 Journeys off the Beaten Path

If you want to spend more time in Sicily, the northwest corner offers scenic, historic towns and villages shaped by mythology and the multicultural influences of nearby Africa and the numerous civilizations that have dominated the territory over the centuries. From here, it's a short ferry ride to the remote Egadi Islands.

ÉRICE   Located 60 miles southwest of Palermo, Érice sits 2,300 feet above the sea on Mount Érice. A well-preserved medieval town composed of steep cobblestone streets and narrow twisted alleys, it has a long history as a mystical, mythic place. It is laid out in a triangle composed of two outer walls built in the 11th century by the Normans over pre-existing walls that dated to at least the 4th century B.C. It was home of a long-standing temple dedicated to the reigning goddess of love, with cult worship evolving from the Phoenician Astarte, to the Greek Aphrodite, and finally to the Roman Venus.

At the western corner of the town, the **Temple of Venus,** Viale Conte Pepoli, is represented only by its base and the **Well of Venus,** down which young girls were thrown in sacrifice after being deflowered. The Normans, outraged by such behavior, destroyed the pagan structure that was also associated with orgies, prostitution, and self-castration rituals. Still standing at its side is the **Norman castle** they built to replace it, surrounded by the lush **Balio Gardens** that make for a pleasant stroll. The grounds including the temple, castle, and gardens are open daily 8am to sunset, with no admission fee. Housing artifacts that trace the town's long and varied history, **Museo Communale Cordici,** Piazza Umberto I (☎ **0923/866-9258**), also contains a collection of works by the Gaginis, Sicily's leading family of sculptors. It's open Monday to Saturday from 8:30am until 1:30pm, with admission costing 2,000L ($1.20).

The best accommodations in town can be found at **Hotel Elimo,** Via Vittorio Emanuele 75, 91016 Érice, Trápani (☎ **0923/869-388,** fax 0923/869252), a restored villa featuring original limestone masonry, beamed ceilings, and a decoratively tiled fireplace, where a double room with half board costs 250,000L ($150). Serving regional Trápani cuisine in its romantic shaded courtyard, **Cortile di Venere,** Via Sales 31 (☎ **0923/869-362**), offers meals priced between 25,000L and 55,000L ($15 to $33). Additional information about sights and accommodations is available from the **tourist information office,** Viale Conte Pepoli 11 (☎ **0923/869-388**).

TRÁPANI   Located on the western coast of Sicily 64 miles southwest of Palermo and about 8 miles west of Érice, Trápani is blasted by the hot winds of nearby northern Africa. African cultural influence is evident in the local cuisine, which includes a seafood condiment made of cucumbers, celery, capers, and olives, as well as the staple coucous flavored with fish. Trápani's inland growth has been as a bland modern town, but a charming historical district lies on its narrow western peninsula. On the northern perimeter, Via Torrearsa is home to the local fish markets, whereas Viale Regina Elene to the south is the port to the Egadi and other nearby islands. The main street of the peninsula is Corso Vittorio Emanuele, which is blocked off at its mainland end by the Baroque **Palazzo Cavaretta,** from the balcony of which the patriotic hero Garibaldi made a cry of "Rome or death!" in 1860, a reference to his exhausting efforts to unify the then-splintered nation.

Of the many churches in the town, the most important in this area is the **Church of Santa Maria del Gesu,** behind the palace off Corso Italia, with a marble canopy constructed by Antonello Gagini in 1521 to shelter Andrea della Robbia's enameled terra-cotta *Madonna of the Angels.* The small Baroque **Santuario dell'Purgatorio,** Via Gen. Giglio, houses 21 wooden statues, dating mainly from the 18th century, that represent scenes from the Passion. On Good Friday, the statues are carried through the streets in an Easter procession, but the rest of the year they can be viewed on Monday, Wednesday, and Friday from 9am to 1pm.

Moving into the mainland along Via Fardella, you can view the most important church in the town, the 14th-century **Church of the Annunciation,** which includes a Renaissance arch by the Gaginis and a statue of the *Madonna of Trápani* attributed to Nino Pisano. Nearby, set in a 16th-century palace, the **Pepoli National Museum** features art by Titian and Roberto di Oderisio, as well as archeological remnants gathered from around the area. It's open Tuesday, Thursday, and Friday from 9am to 1pm and 3 to 6pm, Wednesday and Saturday from 9am to 1pm, and Sunday from 9am to 12:30pm. Admission is 2,000L ($1.20) except on Sunday, when it's free.

The best local accommodation is the newly constructed **Crystal,** Via San Giovanni Bosco 17, 91100 Trápani (☎ **0923/20-000**), which substitutes creature comforts for atmosphere. A double here runs 205,000L ($123) a night. Specializing in seafood, **Da Peppe,** Via Spalti 54 (☎ **0923/28-246**), offers dining inside or outdoors under their gazebo. Further information can be obtained at the **tourist information center,** Villa Aula, Via Sorba 15 (☎ **0923/27-077**).

ÍSOLE ÉGADI (THE EGADI ISLANDS)   Lévanzo, Favignana, and Maréttimo, known for their solitude, caves, and calm clear waters, are the three islands that make up this chain, which sits just a few miles off Sicily's west coast. To get to the islands, call **Siremar** (☎ **0923/540-515**) in Trápani, which runs ferries to all three islands several times a day from the docks at Viale Regina Elena. The trip to nearby Lévanzo takes 20 minutes and costs 9,200L ($5.50) each way, from which you can continue by ferry to the other two islands. Additional information on the Egadi can be obtained at the tourist information center in Trápani, listed above.

The closest island to the mainland, **Lévanzo** lies 10 miles west of Trápani, with the only real community being the small port town of the same name. It is the smallest of the islands, with an area of just over 2 square miles, and its main attraction is the **Grotta del Genovese,** which holds skillfully rendered Paleolithic drawings of animals and humans (there are 33 figures total) believed to be at least 10,000 years old. There are additional Neolithic drawings, added 5,000 years later, but they aren't as impressive. The cave is privately owned by Giuseppe Castiglione, Via Calvario 11 (☎ **0923/921-704**), who will take you from the dock to the cave for a fee of 15,000L ($9) per person—or less if you have a large enough party to get a group rate.

Sitting $3^1/_2$ miles south of Lévanzo, the larger, more populous **Favignana** occupies $7^1/_2$ square miles of land mass. The port village shares the island's name, and hosts a well-developed tuna industry and a maximum-security prison housed in the **Forte S. Giacomo,** which dates from 1120. The oldest section of town, the **Rione Sant'Anna,** is worthy of a stroll just to look at the homes made entirely out of tufa, but here, too, the main attraction is caves, which are found west of town on the Punta

San Nicolà. **Grotta del Pazzo** is inscribed with Punic and early Christian messages, whereas **Grotta degli Archi** houses 4th- and 5th-century Christian tombs. The most developed of the islands, Favignana offers the chain's only accommodations, and the best of these is **Aegusa,** Via Garibaldi 11/17, Favignana, Egadi, Trápani (☎ **0923/922-430,** fax 0923/922-440), an 11-room inn open from April 10 to October 15, which charges 180,000L ($108) for a double room with half board. Other meals can be taken at **Egadi,** Via Cristoforo Colombo 12 (☎ **0923/921-232**), where the cost of a seafood-based meal ranges from 40,000L to 55,000L ($24 to $33).

Located 13 miles west of Favignana, **Maréttimo** is the most remote of the islands in population, activity, and distance from the mainland. A small community of fishers live in the village named after the island, and **beaches** extend north and south of the town. Follow the hiking trail that leads west into the island's interior and you'll come to the **Case Romane,** ruins of a late Roman fort. Head north out of the village instead, and you'll skirt the base of the island's highest peak, the 2,243-foot **Monte Falcone,** on your way to the **Castello di Punta Troia,** which sits on a precipice 379 feet above the sea at the northeastern corner of the island.

8 Isole Eolie o Lipari (Aeolian Islands)

Lipari: 18^1/$_2$ miles N of Milazzo; Strómboli: 50 miles N of Milazzo; Vulcano: 12^1/$_2$ miles N of Milazzo

The Aeolian Islands have been inhabited for more than 3,000 years in spite of volcanic activity that even now issues forth sulfuric belches, streams of molten lava, and hissing clouds of steam. These seven windswept islands were believed by ancient Greek sailors to be the home of Aeolus, god of the winds, who supposedly lived in a cave on Vulcano, keeping the winds of the world in a bag to be opened only with great caution and for limited use. Today, visitors only seeks out the limited accommodations at Lipari (14 square miles), the largest and most developed island, Strómboli (5 square miles), the most distant and volcanically active, and Vulcano (8 square miles), the closest island to the Sicilian mainland with its brooding, potentially volatile cone and therapeutic mud baths. The other islands, including Salina, Filicudi, Alicudi, and Panarea, offer only barebone facilities and are visited mainly by day trippers.

In spite of the volcanos, the area attracts tourists—mainly Germans and Italians—inspired by crystalline waters that foster active snorkeling, scuba, and spear fishing industries, and photogenic beaches composed of hot black sand and rocky outcroppings jutting into the Tyrrhenian Sea. The volcanos themselves offer hikers the thrill of peering into a bubbling crater.

ESSENTIALS

GETTING THERE   By Boat   Ferry and hydrofoil service to Lipari, Strómboli, and Vulcano is available in Milazzo, on the northeastern coast of Sicily 20 miles west of Messina, from **Societa Siremar,** Via Dei Mille (☎ **090/928-3242**), and hydrofoil service is offered by **Societa SNAV,** Via L. Rizzo 17 (☎ **090/928-4509**).

Siremar has two ferry routes, which are cheaper but also slower than the hydrofoils, the Milazzo-Vulcano-Lipari-Salina line leaves Milazzo 4 to 6 times daily, between 7am and 6:30pm. It takes 1^1/$_2$ hours to reach Vulcano, with a one-way ticket costing 10,800L ($6.50), and 2 hours to reach Lipari, at a cost of 11,600L ($6.95) one way. To reach Strómboli, take the Milazzo-Panarea-Strómboli line, which departs from Milazzo at 7am Friday to Wednesday, and at 2:30pm on Thursday. The Strómboli trip takes 5 hours and costs 18,500L ($11.10) for a one-way ticket.

There are also two hydrofoil lines, each run by both companies. The Milazzo-Vulcano-Lipari-Salina line reaches Vulcano in 40 minutes, with a one-way ticket costing 18,400L ($11.05), and it takes 55 minutes to reach Lipari, at a cost of 19,700L ($11.80) one way. Siremar makes the trip 6 to 12 times daily between 7:05am and 7pm, whereas SNAV makes six runs daily between 7:30am and 7:30pm. To arrive at Strómboli, travel on the Milazzo-Panarea-Strómboli line, which takes 2¹/₂ hours at a cost of 28,700L ($17.20) one way. Siremar leaves 4 times daily between 6:15am and 3pm; SNAV makes runs daily at 6:40am, 7:25am, and 2:20pm.

VISITOR INFORMATION   The tourist information center in **Lipari** is at Via Vittorio Emanuele (☎ 090/988-0095). Hours are July to August, Monday to Saturday from 8am to 2pm and 4:30 to 10pm, Sunday from 8am to 2pm; September to June, Monday to Saturday from 8am to 2pm and 4:30 to 7:30pm. There are also information centers in **Strómboli** (☎ 090/986-023) and **Vulcano,** Via Porto do Levante (☎ 090/985-2028). They keep the same hours as the Lipari office but are open only from June through September.

LIPARI

Homer called it, "A floating island, a wall of bronze and splendid smooth sheer cliffs." The offspring of seven volcanic eruptions, Lipari is the largest of the Aeolians. Lipari is also the name of the only real town on the island. It's the administrative headquarters of the Aeolian Islands (except for autonomous Salina). The town of Lipari is seated on a plateau of red volcanic rock on the southeastern shore. It's framed by two beaches, Marina Lunga, which functions as the harbor, and Marina Corta.

It's dominant feature is a 16th-century Spanish castle, within the walls of which lie a **17th-century cathedral** featuring a 16th-century *Madonna* and an 18th-century silver statue of San Bartolomeo, as well as an **archeological park** that has uncovered stratified clues about continuous civilizations dating back to 1700 B.C.

Excellent artifacts from the Stone and Bronze ages, as well as relics from Greek and Roman acropoli that once stood here, are housed next door in the former bishop's palace, now the **Museo Archeologico Eoliano** (☎ 090/988-0174), one of Sicily's major archeological museums. It houses one of the world's finest Neolithic collections, the oldest discoveries dating from 4200 B.C. From the last Neolithic period, lustrous red ceramics—known as "the Diana style"—date from 3000 to 2500 B.C. Other exhibits include reconstructed necropolises from the Middle Bronze Age, and a 6th-century depiction of Greek warships. Some 1,200 pieces of 4th and 3rd century B.C. painted terra-cotta, including stone theatrical masks, are also on exhibit. The museum also houses the only Late Bronze Age (8th century B.C.) necropolis ever found in Sicily. It is open from 9am to 2pm Monday to Saturday, and from 9am to 1pm on Sunday. Admission is free.

The most popular beaches are at **Canneto,** lying about a 20-minute walk north of Lipari on the eastern coast, and just north of it, **Spiaggia Bianca,** named for the white sand that is an oddity among the predominant black sands of the region. At the latter nudists gather in spite of the hot sun and sharp rocks. To reach the beach from Canneto, take the waterfront road, climb the stairs of Via Marina Garibaldi, and then veer right down a narrow cobbled path for about 325 yards.

Acquacalda, or "hot water," is the island's northernmost city but nobody likes to go on its beaches. The town is also named for its obsidian and pumice quarries. West of Acquacalda at **Quattropani,** you can make a steep climb to the **Duomo de Chiesa Barca,** where the point of interest is not the cathedral, but the panoramic view from the church grounds. On the west coast, 2¹/₂ miles from Lipari, the island's other great view is available by making another steep climb up to the **Quattrocchi Belvedere.**

Eighteen miles of road circle the island, connecting all of its villages and attractions. Buses run by Lipari's **Autobus Urso Guglielmo,** Via Cappuccini (☎ 090/981-1262), make 10 circuits of the island per day, with passage to Quattropani and Acquacalda on the north coast costing 2,000L ($1.20), and closer destinations, 1,500L (90¢).

Agriculturally, Lipari yields fields of capers, prevalent in the local cuisine, and Malvasia grapes, producing a malmsy-like wine too acidic to compare favorably with many other Italian wines. Figs, ginger, rosemary, and wild fennel also manage to grow in the sulfuric soil.

WHERE TO STAY

Carasco. A Porto delle Genti, 98005 Lipari. ☎ **090/981-1606.** Fax 090/981-1828. 86 rms, 2 suites. TEL. 200,000L–350,000L ($120–$210) double including breakfast; 240,000L–390,000L ($144–$234) double including half board. AE, DC, MC, V. Closed Oct 19–Mar 31.

This large hotel is actually two buildings connected by an addition, sitting on a bluff by the sea with a staircase leading down to the rocky coastline. The interior contrasts the bright heat of the outdoors with brown terra-cotta floors, and dark wood furniture upholstered with fabrics striped in shades of brown. Wall-mounted lights and potted trees complete the decor, and each well-furnished guest room features a ceiling fan. Just above the sea, a terrace of umbrella tables surrounds a large sea-water swimming pool. The hotel offers its own limited nightlife in the form of a full bar and a piano bar, and the hotel restaurant serves Aeolian seafood typical of the islands.

Gattopardo Park Hotel. Via Diana, 98055 Lipari. ☎ **090/981-1035.** Fax 090/988-0207. 60 rms. 170,000L–360,000L ($102–$216) double. Rates include half board. DC, V. Closed Nov 1–Feb 28.

Situated in an 18th-century villa, this hotel is entered through wide white wrought-iron doors. You come into a lobby featuring a rough log-beamed ceiling, white stucco walls, and a patterned tile floor of subdued gray and black. There are also numerous flat-roofed bungalows that allow for some added privacy. All rooms are equipped with a ceiling fan. Public rooms feature wooden framed furniture with canvas seats, and the dining area includes a covered terrace with ceiling fans to help fight the heat while you dine on the regional seafood dishes. A flagstone terrace is decorated with wrought-iron tables and chairs around a small fountain, and geraniums, palm trees, and other greenery create a lush oasis in the midst of the largely barren island. At night, ornate wrought-iron globe lamps illuminate this patio for evening relaxation.

Giardino sul Mare. Via Maddalena 65, 98055 Lipari. ☎ **090/981-1004.** Fax 090/988-0150. 30 rms. A/C TEL. 130,000L–180,000L ($78–$108) double, including breakfast; 180,000L–310,000L ($108–$186) double, including half board. AE, DC, MC, V. Closed Nov 16–Mar 14.

A short walk from the port at Marina Corta, this hotel stands on a rock outcropping overlooking the bay and the distant Sicilian coastline. It is a typical Mediterranean structure of white stucco with a red tile roof. The hotel pool stands mimicking the bright blue waters of the sea just beyond it. Throughout the hotel there are bright tile floors, and public rooms feature padded white wicker furniture. Guest rooms opt for simple, comfortable dark hardwood furnishings. The restaurant terrace is protected from the brutal heat by a canopy of trees, allowing you to endure the outdoors so that you can enjoy the sea view while dining on the fresh seafood prepared here.

Hotel Oriente. Via Guglielmo Marconi 35, 98055 Lipari. ☎ **090/981-1493.** Fax 090/988-0198. 25 rms. A/C TEL. 80,000–200,000L ($48–$120) double including continental breakfast; 140,000L–320,000L ($84–$192) double including half board. AE, DC, MC, V.

The lobby of this hotel is cluttered with contemporary and antique bric-a-brac, but when you get into the guest rooms, the decor is much simpler, featuring natural woods and bright solid fabrics. The main terrace here is somewhat protected from the heat by shade trees and lush greenery, and the covered breakfast terrace is simply furnished with lawn furniture, looking out at a misleading jungle of greenery on a barren island. There is a fully stocked piano bar, a game room, snack shop, solarium, and large-screen satellite television room. Although the hotel does not have a restaurant, half-board rates are available in conjunction with an eatery serving Aeolian seafood just 100 yards away. The hotel is situated inland, three blocks from the coast.

Meligunis. Via Marte 7, 98005 Lipari. ☎ **090/981-2426.** Fax 090/988-0149. 32 rms. A/C MINIBAR TV TEL. 180,000L–300,000L ($108–$180) double; 250,000L–390,000L ($150–$234) double with half board. AE, DC, MC, V.

Set fewer than 50 yards from the ferryboat docks, this is a four-star, appealingly contemporary hotel that arose from the core of what was built in the 17th century as a cluster of fisher's cottages at Marina Corta. Bedrooms are rustic but uncluttered, larger than you might have expected, usually with views out over the harbor, and summery furniture. Its name, incidentally, derives from the ancient name that Greek colonists originally gave to Lipari, Meligunia.

WHERE TO DINE

Filippino. Piazza Municipio. ☎ **090/981-1002.** Reservations recommended. Main courses 15,000L–22,000L ($9–$13.20). AE, DC, MC, V. Daily noon–2:30pm and 7:30–10:30pm. Closed Mon Oct–Mar. SICILIAN.

This restaurant has thrived from a position in the heart of town, near Town Hall, since 1910, when it was established by the ancestors of the family that runs it today. You'll dine in one of two large airy rooms, or on an outdoor terrace that's ringed with flowering shrubs and potted flowers and flanked with a view over the town and the sea. Menu items are based on old-fashioned Sicilian recipes, and prepared with flair and gusto. Examples include *ravioloni* (a local form of ravioli) stuffed with pulverized pork and served with *salsa paysana* that's made from tomatoes, capers, and herbs. Homemade maccheroni enriched with mozzarella, prosciutto, and ricotta is baked in the oven. Veal scallopine here is especially tempting when cooked in Malvasina wine, and the array of fresh fish is very broad.

E Pulera. Via Diana 51. ☎ **090/981-1158.** Reservations recommended. Main courses 14,500L–26,000L ($8.70–$15.60). AE, DC, MC, V. Daily 7:30pm–2am. Closed June–mid-Oct. SICILIAN/AEOLIAN.

More than its counterpart, Filippino, which is owned by the same family, this restaurant stresses its Aeolian Island origins through such means as maps of the islands fashioned from ceramic tiles, and folkloric artifacts that are scattered throughout the premises. Some tables occupy a terrace whose views extend over a flowering lawn accented with an ornate pergola where you'll probably want to linger. Specialties include a delightful version of *zuppe di pesce alla pescatora* (fisher's stew), *bocconcini di pesce spada* (swordfish ragoût), risotto with either crayfish or squid in its own ink; a rich assortment of seafood antipasti that's usually laden with basil and garlic; an involtini of eggplant, and herb-laden versions of roasted lamb. Desserts are tied to local traditions, and feature a Sicilian *cassata* and *tiramisù*.

STRÓMBOLI

The most distant island in the archipelago, Strómboli achieved notoriety and became a household word in America in 1950 with the release of the Rossellini cinéma vérité film starring Ingrid Bergman. The American public was far more interested in the "illicit" affair between Bergman and Rossellini than in the film. Although the affair seems tame by today's standards, it temporarily ended Bergman's American career, and she was denounced from the Senate floor. Movie fans today are more likely to remember Strómboli from the Jules Verne film, *Voyage to the Center of the Earth.* The volcanic island was used as the exit of the heroes.

The entire surface of Strómboli is the cone of a sluggish but active volcano. Puffs of smoke can be seen during the day. Almost as smoldering is a night view of the **Sciara del Fuoco** (Slope of Fire), where lava glows red-hot on its way down to meet the sea with a loud hiss and a cloud of steam—a memorable vision that may leave you feeling a little too vulnerable while you're actually here.

In fact, the island can serve as a fantasyland for those who've been bitten by Hollywood's volcano-mania of 1997. The main attraction is a steep, difficult climb to the lip of the 3,000-foot **Gran Cratere,** where a view of bubbling pools of ooze (glowing with heat if you're here at night) is accompanied by rising clouds of steam and a sulfuric stench. The journey is a 3-hour hike best taken in early morning or late afternoon to avoid the worst of the brutal sunshine—and even then requiring plenty of sunscreen and water and a good pair of shoes. You'll be following in the footsteps of Malcolm Lowry's sad characters who sloshed their way to trouble in *Under the Volcano.* A 1990 ordinance has made it illegal to climb the slope without a guide, although many daring visitors defy this ban. The island's authorized guide company is Guide Alpine Autorizzate (☎ **090/986-211**), which leads groups up the mountain at 6am, returning six hours later (the return trip is an hour quicker than the climb, which leaves you an hour at the rim), for a charge of 20,000L ($12).

In spite of the volcano and its sloped terrain, two settlements do actually exist here: **Ginostra** on the southwestern shore, little more than a cluster of summer homes where there are only 15 year-round residents, and **Strómboli** on the northeastern shore, a conglomeration of the villages of **Ficogrande, San Vincenzo,** and **Piscità,** where the only in-town attraction is the black sand beaches.

WHERE TO STAY & DINE

La Sirenetta-Park Hotel. Via Marina 33, 98050 Ficogrande, Strómboli. ☎ **090/986-025.** Fax 090/986-124. 43 rms. 163,200L–252,000L ($97.90–$151.20) double including breakfast; 259,200L–412,000L ($155.50–$247.20) double including half board. AE, DC, MC, V. Closed Nov 1–Mar 22.

This is a clean, uncluttered hotel, with white-tiled floors and walls offset in guest rooms by contemporary dark wood furniture and trim. The public rooms are graced by natural wicker furnishings upholstered with blue floral prints. A large swimming pool is on the terrace overlooking the sea. There's also an Italian fashion boutique, plus a full bar and a restaurant featuring Aeolian and Sicilian seafood dishes.

La Sciara Residence. Via Soldato Cincotta, 98050 Piscita, Strómboli. ☎ **090/986-004.** Fax 090/986-284. 60 rms. TEL. 200,000L–430,000L ($120–$258) double. Rates include half board. AE, DC, MC, V. Closed Oct 11–Apr 30.

The volcano looms imminently behind this hotel where each room is individually furnished in an eclectic combination of Sicilian, Neapolitan, and Florentine antiques. Fifteen rooms are in the main hotel and the rest are split among six villas enveloping the 10,900 square-yard central garden terrace, which is made of flagstones surrounded by lush greenery. The interior bar and seafood restaurant are bright and busy, combining a blue bar decorated with contrasting navy rectangles and red diamonds, colorful floral fabrics and tablecloths, ladderback chairs with red seat cushions, rococo picture frames, and more of the above-mentioned mix of antiques.

Even the dinnerware features a lively yellow design. A covered terrace allows you the option of dining outside, with a view of the volcano in one direction and the sea in the other. There is a swimming pool with a poolside bar as well as a tennis court.

VULCANO

The island closest to the mainland, the ancient Thermessa figured heavily in the mythologies of the region, as the still-active **Vulcano della Fossa** was thought to be not only the home of Vulcan, but also the gateway to Hades. Thucydides, Siculus, and Aristotle each recorded eruptions. Three dormant craters also exist on the island, but it is a climb to the rim of active **Gran Cratere** that most draws attention. It hasn't erupted since 1890, but one look inside the sulfur-belching hole is more than enough to understand how it could have activated the imaginings that led to the hellish legend surrounding it. The 1,372-foot peak is an easier climb than the one on Stròmboli, taking just about an hour—though it's just as hot, and the same precautions of avoiding midday, and loading up with sunscreen, plenty of water, and good hiking shoes still prevail.

Here the risks of mounting a volcano are not addressed with any sort of legislation, so you can make the climb without a guide, but breathing the sulfuric air at the summit has its risks, since the steam is tainted with numerous toxins. To get to the peak from Porto Levante, the main port, follow Via Piano away from the sea for about 220 yards until you see the first of the CRATERE signs, then just go along the marked trail.

Laghetto di Fanghi, famous mud baths that claim to cure every known ailment, are located along Via Provinciale a short way from the port. Be warned that the mud will discolor anything from cloth to jewelry, which is one explanation for the prevalent nudity here. Within sight, the **acquacalda** features hot-water jets that act as a natural Jacuzzi. Either can scald you if you step or sit on the vents that release the heat, so take care if you decide to enter.

The island offers one of the few smooth beaches of the entire chain, **Spiaggia Sabbie Nere,** or "Black Sands Beach," featuring dark sand that is so hot in the midday sun that thongs or wading shoes are suggested if you plan to while away your day along the shore. You can find the beach by following signs posted along Via Ponente.

In reality, a knowledge of street names is worthless, since there are no signs. Not to worry, the locals who gather at the dock are friendly and experienced at giving directions to tongue-tied foreign visitors, especially since all they ever really have to point out are the paths to the crater, the mud baths, and the beach, the island's only attractions.

WHERE TO STAY & DINE

Hotel Conti. À Porto Ponente, 98050 Vulcano. ☎ **090/981-1004.** Fax 090/988-0150. 67 rms. TEL. 162,000L–240,000L ($97.20–$144) double. Rates includes half board. V. Closed Oct 19–May 9.

The rooms in this inn feature latticed wooden furniture and brightly patterned tile floors and bedspreads. A sunny terrace leads down onto the black sand beach. The covered dining terrace features cane chairs and tables, all with matching green linens and seat cushions, separated by columns. The restaurant serves local seafood, and a summertime alternative is the on-premises pizzeria (open June 25 to September 15). There is also a full bar.

Eolian. Localita Porto Ponente, 98050 Vulcano. ☎ **090/985-2151.** Fax 090/985-2153. 88 rms. 184,000L–270,000L ($110.40–$162) double including breakfast; 224,000L–330,000L ($134.40–$198) double including half board. AE, DC, MC, V. Closed Oct 1–Apr 24.

Spread through a series of typical white stucco buildings and bungalows surrounded by palms and evergreens, the hotel rooms feature contemporary wooden furniture components painted white with offsetting bright solid fabrics. Additional features are a television room, solarium, and full bar. A stairway leads down from a two-tone brown checkerboard terrace to the black sand beach adjacent to the hotel. Evening dining on a covered terrace features column-mounted globe lamps and a wrought-iron railing offers a panoramic sea view. The restaurant, naturally, serves Aeolian and Sicilian seafood.

Restaurant Vincencino. Vulcano Porto. ☎ **090/985-2016.** Main courses 10,000L–25,000L ($6–$15). AE, DC, MC, V. Daily 12:30–3pm and 7:30–9:30pm. Closed Oct–Mar. SICILIAN.

Set fewer than 30 yards from the waterfront, this is the most appealing of the limited number of restaurants that are convenient to the port that receives the ferryboats. Within a modernized but rustic setting that has thrived here since the early 1960s, you can order filling portions that are redolent with the bounty of Sicily, which provides many of the raw ingredients that go into such dishes as house-style maccheroni, *spaghetti Vincencino* (with crayfish, capers, and tomato sauce); grilled steaks, and all sorts of fish. Between October and March, the menu is limited to a simple array of platters served from the bar, which otherwise remains open throughout the winter.

Index

Accademia (Venice), 421–23
Accommodations
    best hotels, 9–10
    tips on, 70–71
    youth hostels, 59
Acquario (Naples), 622–23
Aeolian Islands, 744–50
Agrigento, 724–27
Airlines, 59
    from North America, 59–61
    from the United Kingdom, 62–63
Alba, 55
Alberobello, 19, 693–95
Alberti, Leon Battista, 34, 255, 543, 544
Alexander VI, Pope, 140, 142, 252,
    358–59
Altar of Peace (Rome), 154
Alto Adige, 16
Amalfi, 655–60
Amalfi Coast, 19, 646
American Cemetery and Memorial,
    Florence, 258
American Express, 51
Amphitheaters, Roman, 2, 6, 54, 200,
    283, 475, 633, 681–82, 699, 720
Anacapri, 675–77
Andrea Doria, 150, 590
Anfiteatro Flavio (Pozzuoli), 633
Anfiteatro Romano (Lucca), 283
Anfiteatro Romano (Siracusa), 720
Antelami, Benedetto, 39, 373
Antiques
    Ferrara, 361
    Florence, 260
    Naples, 629
    Padua, 456
    Rome, 176–77
    Taormina, 711
    Trieste, 486
    Venice, 435–36
Antonello da Messina, 423, 594, 733, 741
Aosta, 53, 575–78
Aosta Valley (Valle d'Aosta), 18, 567, 575
    cuisine, 43
Apartments, renting, 70
Apollo of Belvedere, 139
Appian Way (Rome), 84, 127, 159–60
Apulia (Puglia), 19, 45, 678–705

Arch of Constantine (Rome), 144
Arch of Septimius Severus (Rome), 164
Arch of Titus (Rome), 167–68
Archeological museums and exhibits. *See
    also* Archeological sites and ruins
    Agrigento, 726
    Bari, 689–90
    Bologna, 349
    Brindisi, 697
    Ferrara, 360–61
    Fiesole, 271
    Florence, 255
    Foggia, 680
    Lipari, 745
    Lucera, 681
    Manfredonia, 684
    Naples, 4–5, 618, 620
    Orvieto, 340
    Paestum, 665–66
    Palermo, 733
    Palestrina, 201
    Ravenna, 366
    Rome, 4, 38, 147, 156
    Siracusa, 720
    Taranto, 703
    Tarquinia, 203
    Vatican, 139
    Verona, 476
Archeological sites and ruins, 31–32. *See
    also and specific sites and ruins;* Archeo-
    logical museums and exhibits; Etruscans;
    Greeks, ancient; Romans, ancient
    Agrigento, 725–26
    Aosta, 576
    Baia, 633
    best, 5–6
    Capri, 669
    Cuma, 634–35
    Herculaneum (Ercolano), 635–36
    Lake Averno, 634
    Lecce, 699
    Lévanzo, 743
    Lipari, 745
    Lucera, 681–82
    Monte Sant'Angelo, 685
    Ostia Antica, 2
    Paestum, 2, 665
    Perugia, 322

Archeological sites and ruins, *cont.*
   Pompeii, 2, 636–38
   Pozzuoli, 633
   Ravenna, 366
   Segesta, 729
   Selinunte, 728
   Siracusa, 720
   Sirmione, 552–53
   Taormina, 710
   Todi, 338
Architecture, 31–37. *See also and specific
   architects;* Castles and palaces; Churches
   and cathedrals; Villa(s)
Arena Chapel (Padua), 454
Arena di Verona, 474–75
Arezzo, 315–17
Armani stores, 179, 477, 526
Arnolfo di Cambio, 135, 249, 251, 256,
   322
Art, 1, 38–42. *See also* Art museums;
   Churches and cathedrals; Egyptian art;
   Etruscans; Greeks, ancient, art and
   architecture; Prints and engravings
   shopping for
      Bologna, 350
      Florence, 260
Art museums
   Asolo, 464
   Bari, 690
   Bassano del Grappa, 466
   Bergamo, 538
   Bologna, 348, 349–50
   Cefalù, 741
   Como, 556
   Érice, 742
   Ferrara, 360–61
   Florence
      Casa Buonarroti, 256–57
      Galleria degli Uffizi, 4, 243, 246
      Galleria dell'Accademia, 208,
         246–47
      Loggia della Signoria, 252
      Museo Archeologico, 255
      Museo dell'Opera del Duomo, 251
      Museo di San Marco, 248–49
      Museo Nazionale del Bargello, 4,
         248
      Palazzo Pitti, 4, 247
      Palazzo Vecchio, 252–53
   Genova, 592, 594
   Mantova, 543, 544
   Milan, 512–15
      Museo Poldi-Pezzoli, 4
      Pinacoteca di Brera, 4

   Modena, 370
   Naples
      Museo Archeologico Nazionale,
         4–5, 618, 620
      Museo e Gallerie Nazionali di
         Capodimonte, 620–21
   Orvieto, 341
   Padua, 455
   Palermo, 732–33
   Parma, 374
   Perugia, 4, 322–23
   Ravenna, 365
   Rome
      Galleria Borghese, 154–55
      Galleria Doria Pamphilj, 150
      Galleria Nazionale d'Arte Antica,
         157–58
      Galleria Nazionale d'Arte
         Moderna, 155
      Museo Capitolino and Palazzo dei
         Conservatori, 147
      Museo Nazionale del Palazzo di
         Venezia, 148
      Museo Nazionale di Villa Giulia,
         4, 156
      National Roman Museum, 158
   Siena, 298, 300–301
   Sorrento, 647
   Torino, 570
   Trent, 503
   Vatican City, 3, 138–42
   Venice, 421–25
      Ca'd'Oro, 424
      Collezione Peggy Guggenheim,
         379, 424–25
      Gallerie dell'Accademia, 4, 421–23
      Museo Civico Correr, 423
      Palazzo Ducale, 418–19
   Vicenza, 469
Asolo, 463–65
Assisi, 327–34
   accommodations, 331–33
   attractions, 328, 330–31
   restaurants, 333–34
   sights, 5
ATM networks, 50
Augustus, 3, 24, 25, 140, 148, 154, 156,
   169–71, 575, 576
Augustus Mausoleum (Rome), 156
Averno, Lago d', 633–34

Baia, 633
Bargello, Museo Nazionale del (Florence),
   4, 248

Bari, 688–92

Baroque art, 41

Bartolomeo, Fra, 247–49

Basilica Aemilia (Rome), 164

Basilica di St. Domenico (Bologna), 348

Basilica di San Ambrogio (Milan), 515

Basilica di San Clemente (Rome), 146

Basilica di San Francesco (Arezzo), 316

Basilica di San Francesco (Assisi), 5, 330–31

Basilica di San Giorgio Maggiore (Venice), 427

Basilica di San Giovanni in Laterano (Rome), 146–47

Basilica di San Lorenzo (Florence), 254

Basilica di San Marco (Venice), 415, 418–19

Basilica di San Paolo Fuori le Mura (Rome), 162

Basilica di San Petronio (Bologna), 347

Basilica di San Pietro (Vatican City). See St. Peter's Basilica

Basilica di Santa Croce (Florence), 256

Basilica di Santa Croce (Lecce), 699

Basilica di Santa Maria Assunta (San Gimignano), 292–93

Basilica di Santa Maria Gloriosa dei Frari (Venice), 426

Basilica di Santa Maria Maggiore (Bergamo), 538

Basilica di Santa Maria Maggiore (Rome), 158

Basilica di Santa Maria Novella (Florence), 255–56

Basilica di Sant'Anastasia (Verona), 476

Basilica di Sant'Andrea (Mantova), 543–44

Basilica di Sant'Antonio (Padua), 455

Basilica di Sant'Eustorgio (Milan), 515

Basilica Julia (Rome), 166

Basilica of Constantine (Rome), 167

Basilica of St. Apollinare in Classe (Ravenna), 366

Basilica of San Nicola (Bari), 689

Basilica of Santa Chiara (Assisi), 328, 330

Basilica San Zeno Maggiore (Verona), 475

Bassano, Jacopo, 427, 460, 464, 469

Bassano del Grappo, 465–68

Baths of Caracalla (Rome), 147

Baths of Diocletian, 84, 158, 159

Battistero (Parma), 373

Battistero (Pisa), 288–89

Battistero (Siena), 300

Battistero San Giovanni (Florence), 250–51

Beers, 47

Bellagio, 559–61

Bellini, Gentile, 423, 513

Bellini, Giovanni, 41, 138, 246, 422, 426–28, 446, 455, 469, 513, 514, 538, 620, 690

Bellini, Jacopo, 41, 455, 475

Bergamo, 12, 537–40

Bernini, Giovanni, 36, 41, 133, 135, 149, 152, 155, 157, 158, 163, 183, 196, 199, 370

Bernini, Pietro, 153

Biblioteca-Pinacoteca Ambrosiana (Milan), 512

Blue Grotto (Capri), 668–69

Boboli Gardens (Florence), 257

Boccaccio, 204, 274, 660, 661

Bologna, 15, 344–58

   accommodations, 352–54

   attractions, 347–50

   nightlife, 358

   restaurants, 354–58

   shopping, 350–52

   transportation to and within, 346–47

Bolzano, 496–98

Bonaparte, Elisa, 283

Bookstores

   Florence, 261

   Milan, 525

   Naples, 629

   Rome, 178

Borghese, Scipione, 155, 157

Borgia, Lucrezia, 119, 142, 334, 361

Borgia Apartments (Vatican City), 140

Borromean Islands, 565–66

Bossi, Umberto, 20–21

Botticelli, Sandro, 4, 141, 204, 246, 247, 255, 512, 538, 570, 620

Bramante, 35, 36, 119, 135, 140, 152, 513, 514

Brenta Riviera, 449–53

Brindisi, 696–98

   ferries to Greece, 697

Browning, Elizabeth Barrett, 258

Browning, Robert, 258, 360, 421, 424, 463

Brunante, 557

Brunelleschi, Filippo, 5, 34, 204, 208, 247, 249–51, 254–56

Bucket shops (consolidators), 60

Burano, 384, 447

Business hours, 72

Bus travel

   from the United Kingdom, 63

   within Italy, 67

Bussana Vecchia, 585

Cacciari, Massimo, 20
Ca'd'Oro (Venice), 424
Calendar of events, 53–55. *See also specific cities and towns*
Campania, 19, 613–14
   wines and vineyards, 45
Campanile (Giotto's Bell Tower) (Florence), 250
Campanile di San Marco (Venice), 419
Campi Flegrei, 632–33
Camposanto (Pisa), 289
Canneto, 745
Canova, Antonio, 42, 135, 155, 426, 466, 513, 559, 560
Capitoline Hill (Campidoglio) (Rome), 146, 185
Capitoline Museum (Rome), 147
Cappella degli Scrovegni (Padua), 454
Cappelle Medici (Florence), 253–54
Capri, 3, 19, 666–77
   accommodations, 10, 670–73
   nightlife, 675
   restaurants, 673–75
   swimming, 669
   traveling to and in, 668
Car travel
   breakdowns/assistance, 69
   driving rules, 69
   to Italy, 65–66
   rentals, 68
   road maps, 69
   within Italy, 67–69
Caravaggio, Michelangelo da, 41, 139, 147, 150, 155, 158, 246, 514, 594, 720
Ca'Rezzonico (Venice), 424
Carnevale (Venice), 53
Carpaccio, Vittore, 421–24, 426, 475, 513, 538
Carracci, 41, 370
Casa Buonarroti (Florence), 256–57
Casa di Dante (Florence), 257–58
Casa di Pirandello (Agrigento), 726
Casa Giulietta (Verona), 477
Casa Guidi (Florence), 258
Casarano, 702
Casa Romei (Ferrara), 361
Casinos
   San Remo, 590
   Venice, 445
Castel dell'Ovo (Naples), 622
Castel del Monte (near Bari), 690
Castel Nuovo (Naples), 621–22
Castel Sant'Angelo (Rome), 28, 142–43
Castelgandolfo, 198–99

Castellana, 693
Castellaneta, 705
Castellina in Chianti, 312–14
Castelli Romani, 198–99
Castello di Miramare (Trieste), 484
Castello di Querceto (near Greve), 310
Castello di Uzzano (near Greve), 308
Castello di Verrazzano (near Greve), 308
Castello Estense (Ferrara), 360
Castello Gardens (Venice), 379
Castello Scaligera (Sirmione), 553
Castello Svevo (Bari), 689
Castelvecchio (Verona), 475
Castle of San Giusto (Trieste), 484
Castle of the Egg (Naples), 622
Catacombe dei Cappuccini (Palermo), 733
Catacombe di San Callisto (Callixtus) (Rome), 159–60
Catacombe di San Gennaro (Naples), 623
Catacombe di San Giovanni (Siracusa), 721
Catacombe di San Sebastiano (Rome), 159
Caterina, Queen (Caterina Cornari), 463, 464
Cathedral of San Giovanni (Torino), 568, 570–71
Cathedral of San Giusto (Trieste), 484
Cathedral of Santa Maria del Fiore (Duomo) (Florence), 5, 34, 207–8, 249–50
Cathedral of Santa Maria Icona Vetere (Foggia), 680
Cattedrale di Bari, 689
Cattedrale di Como, 556
Cattedrale di San Rufino (Assisi), 328
Cattedrale of San Lorenzo (Genova), 594
Caverns
   Emerald Grotto (Amalfi), 657
   Grotta Azzurra (Capri), 668–89
   Grotta del Genovese (Lévanzo), 743
   Grotta Gigante (Trieste), 484, 486
   Grotte di Castellana, 693
Cefalù, 741–42
Cellini, Benvenuto, 143, 204, 208, 252
Ceramics, 12
   museums
      Ceramics Museum (Bassano del Grappa), 466
      Museo della Ceramica Umbra (Deruta), 324
      Museo Internazionale delle Ceramiche (Faenza), 351
   shopping for, 12, 302, 318, 342, 375
      Amalfi, 657
      Deruta, 323–24

Ferrara, 361
Grottaglie, 703–4
Lucca, 283
Milan, 532
Palermo, 734
Perugina, 323
Positano, 652
Sorrento, 648
Taormina, 711
Cernobbio, 10, 558–59
Certosa (Charter House) of Pavia, 536–37
Cerveteri (Caere), 4, 23, 156, 202
Charles of Bourbon, 6
Charter House of Pavia, 536–37
Chianti district (La Chiantigiana),
306–11
Chiaramonti Museum (Vatican City), 140
Chiesa degli Eremitani (Padua), 454
Chiesa del Gesù (Rome), 150
Chiesa di San Agostino (Rome), 150
Chiesa di San Fermo (Verona), 476
Chiesa di San Francesco (Sorrento), 647
Chiesa di San Giacomo Maggiore
(Bologna), 349
Chiesa di San Luigi dei Francesi (Rome),
150
Chiesa di Santa Cecilia in Trastevere
(Rome), 162
Chiesa di Santa Maria d'Aracoeli (Rome),
148–49
Chiesa di Santa Maria degli Angeli
(Rome), 158–59
Chiesa di Santa Maria della Pace (Rome),
152
Chiesa di Santa Maria delle Grazie
(Milan), 513
Chiesa di Santa Maria in Cosmedin
(Rome), 148
Chiesa di Santa Maria in Trastevere
(Rome), 162
Chiesa di Santa Maria Sopra Minerva
(Rome), 152
Chiesa di San Zaccaria (Venice), 427
Chiesa Madonna dell'Orto (Venice), 427
Chiesa San Frediano (Lucca), 282
China. See Ceramics
Chiostro del Duomo di Monreale, 739
Chocolates
Perugina, 323
Churches and cathedrals
architecture, 31–37
Arezzo, 316
Assisi, 328, 330–31
Bari, 689

Bergamo, 538
best, 5
Bologna, 347–49
Como, 556
Cremona, 540–41
Ferrara, 360
Fiesole, 271
Florence, 34
Basilica di San Lorenzo, 254
Basilica di Santa Croce, 256
Basilica di Santa Maria Novella,
255–56
Il Duomo (Cathedral of Santa
Maria del Fiore), 5, 34, 207–8,
249–50
Santa Maria del Carmine, 257
Foggia, 680
Genova, 594
Gubbio, 318
Lecce, 699
Lucca, 282
Mantova, 543–44
Milan, 512, 513
Modena, 369–70
Murano, 446
Orvieto, 339–40
Padua, 454–55
Palermo, 731, 732
Parma, 373, 374
Perugia, 322
Pisa, 288
Ravenna, 365, 366
Rome
Basilica di San Clemente, 146
Basilica di San Giovanni in
Laterano, 146–47
Basilica di Santa Maria Maggiore,
158
Chiesa del Gesù, 150
Chiesa di San Agostino, 150
Chiesa di San Luigi dei Francesi,
150
Chiesa di Santa Cecilia in
Trastevere, 162
Chiesa di Santa Maria d'Aracoeli,
148–49
Chiesa di Santa Maria degli Angeli,
158–59
Chiesa di Santa Maria della Pace,
152
Chiesa di Santa Maria in
Cosmedin, 148
Chiesa di Santa Maria in
Trastevere, 162

Churches and cathedrals, *cont.*
    Chiesa di Santa Maria Sopra
      Minerva, 152
    St. Paul Outside the Walls (Basilica
      di San Paolo Fuori le Mura), 162
    St. Peter's Basilica, 2, 5, 36, 135,
      138
    Saint Peter in Chains (Chiesa di
      San Pietro in Vincoli), 147–48
    San Nicola, 686
    Siena, 299–300
    Spoleto, 334
    Todi, 338
    Torcello, 448
    Torino, 570–71
    Trent, 503
    Treviso, 459–60
    Trieste, 484
    Venice
      Basilica di San Giorgio Maggiore,
        427
      Basilica di San Marco, 418–19
      Basilica di Santa Maria Gloriosa
        dei Frari, 426
      Chiesa di San Zaccaria, 427
      Chiesa Madonna dell'Orto, 427
      Santa Maria della Salute, 427–28
      Santi Giovanni e Paolo Basilica,
        428
    Verona, 475–76
    Vicenza, 469
Church of Santa Maria del Casale
    (Brindisi), 697
Cimabue, 39, 243, 300, 330
Cimitèro Monumentale (Milan), 515–16
Cimitero Monumentale dei Padri
    Cappucini (Rome), 157
Cinque Terre, 608–12
Circus Maximus (Rome), 172
Civica Galleria d'Arte Moderna (Milan),
    514–15
Civica Galleria di Palazzo Bianco
    (Genova), 594
Civica Galleria di Palazzo Rosso (Genova),
    592
Clement VII, Pope, 5, 28, 340
Clement VIII, Pope, 163, 359
Climate, 51–52
Cloister of Paradise (Amalfi), 656
Cogne, 576
Collegio del Cambio (Perugia), 323
Colleoni Chapel (Bergamo), 538

Collezione Peggy Guggenheim (Venice),
    379, 424–25
Colli, 228–29
Colosseum (Rome), 6, 31, 144–45, 169
Column of Phocas (Rome), 166
Como, 555–58
Como, Lake, 555–62
Conegliano, 462–63
Constantine, 5, 25, 135, 144, 146, 147
    Basilica of (Rome), 167
Corniglia, 608
Correggio, 246, 370, 372–74
Cortina d'Ampezzo, 9, 11, 489–96
Courmayeur, 578–82
Credit cards, 49
Cremona, 540
Crystal. *See* Glass
Cuisine, 1, 42–44. *See also under specific*
    regions
Cuma, 634
Curia (Rome), 164
Currency, 48–49
Currency exchange, 49
Customs regulations, 72

D'Annunzio, Gabriele, 288, 421, 526,
    537, 538, 552
    Vittoriale (Gardone Riviera), 550–51
Dante Alighieri, 39, 188, 204, 256, 293,
    327, 348, 474
    Casa di Dante (Florence), 257–58
    Tomba di Dante (Ravenna), 366
David (Donatello), 40, 248, 254, 661
David (Michelangelo), 40, 208, 246–48,
    252, 257, 348
Da Vinci, Leonardo, 40, 138, 140, 204,
    246, 252, 307, 310, 374, 512–14
    Museo Nazionale della Scienza e della
      Tecnica Leonardo da Vinci (Milan),
      514
Della Robbia, Andrea, 255, 743
Della Robbia, Luca, 250, 251, 255, 256,
    262, 271
Department stores
    Milan, 525–26
    Naples, 630
Deruta, 323–24
Design, Italian, 530–31
Diocletian, 25
    Baths of, 84, 158, 159
Disabled travelers, 56–57
Dolo, 452

Dolomites, the (Dolomiti), 16, 482
  exploring, 492, 497
Domus Augustana (Rome), 168
Domus Aurea (Rome), 144
Donatello, 40, 148, 204, 208, 248,
  250–52, 254–56, 300, 426, 455, 661
Doric temple (Segesta), 729
Drinks, 47. *See also* Wines and vineyards
Duccio di Buoninsegna, 300, 322
Duomo (Amalfi), 656
Duomo (Cefalù), 741
Duomo (Ferrara), 360
Duomo (Florence), 5, 34, 207–8,
  249–50
Duomo (Foggia), 681
Duomo (Milan), 5, 512
Duomo (Modena), 369–70
Duomo (Naples), 622
Duomo (Orvieto), 5, 339–40
Duomo (Palermo), 731
Duomo (Parma), 373
Duomo (Pisa), 288
Duomo (Ravello), 661–62
Duomo (Siena), 299–300
Duomo (Siracusa), 721
Duomo (Taormina), 710–11
Duomo (Torino), 570–71
Duomo (Verona), 476
Duomo Collegiata (San Gimignano),
  292–93
Duse, Eleonora, 421, 463, 464, 550, 551

Economy, 21
Egadi Islands, 743
Egyptian art, 135, 156, 191, 289, 375
  Egyptian-Gregorian Museum (Vatican
    City), 139
  Museo Archeologico (Florence), 255
  Museo Civico Archeologico (Bologna),
    349–50
  Museo delle Antichità Egizie (Turin),
    570
El Greco, 158, 370
Electricity, 73
Embassies/consulates, 73
Emergencies, 73
Emilia-Romagna, 15–16, 20
  cuisine, 44
  wines and vineyards, 8, 45
Emilio Greco Museum (Orvieto), 341
Enoteca Italica Permanente (Siena), 301
Entrèves, 582–83

Entry requirements, 48
Ercolano (Herculaneum), 5, 6, 620,
  635–36
Eremo delle Carceri (Assisi), 331
Érice, 742
Estate Musicale Leccese, 701
Estruscan-Gregorian Museum (Vatican
  City), 139
Etna, Mount, 718–19
Etruscan Necropolis (Tarquinia), 203
Etruscans, 4, 22–23, 42, 44, 139, 209,
  274, 289, 339, 340, 343, 350, 375, 476
  art and architecture, 31, 38
  Cerveteri (Caere), 23, 202
  Estruscan-Gregorian Museum
    (Vatican City), 139
  Museo Archeologico (Florence), 255
  Museo Nazionale di Villa Giulia
    (Rome), 156
  Tarquinia, 23, 202–3
Eurailpass, 64–65
Europass, 65

Fabrics
  Florence, 261
  Naples, 630
Faenza, 12, 351
Faloria-Cristallo ski area, 490
Farmhouse accommodations, 70
Farnese family, 5, 153, 344, 374
Farnese Gardens (Rome), 6, 169
Fasano del Garda, 551
Fashion, shopping for, 12, 323
  Bologna, 351–52
  Florence, 261–62
  Genova, 595
  Milan, 524, 526–27
  Naples, 630
  Palermo, 733–34
  Rome, 179–81
  Taormina, 711
  Trieste, 486
  Venice, 437
  Verona, 477
  Vicenza, 471
Favignana, 743–44
Ferrara, 358–63
Ferries, 69
  to Greece, 697
  to Sicily, from Naples, 709
Festival dei Due Mondi/Festival di
  Spoleto, 54, 334, 335

Festivals, 53–55. *See also specific cities and towns*
Fiesole, 9, 207, 209, 271–73
Finibus Terrae, 702
Flavian Palace (Rome), 168
Florence, 15, 20, 40, 204–73
  accommodations, 213–29
  across the Arno (Oltrarno), 206, 209
    accommodations, 227–28
    attractions, 257
    restaurants, 240–42
  arriving in, 205–6
  business hours, 211
  Centro, 207
    accommodations, 216–17
    restaurants, 229, 232
  for children
    accommodations, 222
    restaurants, 237
  churches and cathedrals
    Basilica di San Lorenzo, 254
    Basilica di Santa Croce, 256
    Basilica di Santa Maria Novella, 255–56
      Il Duomo (Cathedral of Santa Maria del Fiore), 5, 34, 207–8, 249–50
    Santa Maria del Carmine, 257
  consulates, 211
  currency exchange, 211
  doctors and dentists, 211
  emergencies, 211, 212
  gelato, 242
  layout of, 206–7
  museums, 4, 243, 246–49, 251, 255, 256–57
  neighborhoods, 207–9
  nightlife, 267–70
    gay nightlife, 270
  Piazza del Duomo, 207–8
    accommodations, 217–18
    restaurants, 232–33
  Piazza della Santissima Annunziata, 254–55
  Piazza della Signoria, 208
    attractions, 251–53
    restaurants, 233
  Piazza Massimo d'Azeglio
    accommodations, 227
  Piazza San Lorenzo, 253–54
  Piazza San Marco, 208
    accommodations, 222–24
    restaurants, 238
  Piazza Santa Croce, 209
    accommodations, 225
    restaurants, 238–40
  Piazza Santa Maria Novella & Termini, 208
    accommodations, 213, 218–22
    restaurants, 234–38
  Ponte Vecchio, 206–7, 209, 253
    accommodations, 225–27
    restaurants, 240
  post office, 212
  restaurants, 229–42
  safety, 213
  shopping, 13, 259–67
  side trip to Fiesole, 271
  sights, 242–58
  special events, 53
    Maggio Musicale Fiorentino, 54, 267
  sports and outdoor activities, 258–59
  transportation, 209–11
  visitor information, 206
Foggia, 678, 680–82
Fontana dei Trevi (Rome), 154
Fontana del Nettuno (Bologna), 348
Fonte Arethusa (Ortygia), 721
Food. *See* Cuisine
Forio, 644
Foro Romano (Rome), 6, 143–44, 163
Forum of Augustus (Rome), 170
Forum of Julius Caesar (Rome), 171
Forum of Nerva (Rome), 170
Forum of Trajan (Rome), 171
Fra Angelico, 138, 140, 152, 208, 243, 248, 249, 322, 331, 340
Francia, Francesco, 158, 349, 350
Francis of Assisi, Saint, 39, 148, 188, 256, 275, 327, 328
  Basilica di San Francesco (Arezzo), 316
  Basilica di San Francesco (Assisi), 5, 330–31
Frascati, 199–200
Fregene, 201–2
Friuli-Venezia Giulia, 16
  wines and vineyards, 8, 45–46

Gaiole in Chianti, 311, 312
Galleria Borghese (Rome), 154–55
Galleria degli Uffizi (Florence), 4, 243, 246
Galleria dell'Accademia (Florence), 246–47
Galleria dell'Accademia Carrara (Bergamo), 538

Galleria di Palazzo Reale (Genova), 594
Galleria Doria Pamphilj (Rome), 150
Galleria Estense (Modena), 370
Galleria Nazionale (Genova), 594
Galleria Nazionale (Parma), 374–75
Galleria Nazionale d'Arte Antica (Rome),
    157–58
Galleria Nazionale d'Arte Moderna
    (Rome), 155
Galleria Nazionale dell'Umbria (Perugia),
    4, 322–23
Galleria Regionale della Sicilia (Palermo),
    732–33
Galleria Sabauda (Torino), 570
Gallerie dell'Accademia (Venice), 4
Gallipoli, 701–2
Galluzzo, 229
Garda, Lake, 546–55
Gardens
    Bellagio, 560
    Farnese Gardens (Rome), 6, 169
    Giardini di Boboli (Florence), 257
    Giardino Alpino Paradiso (near Aosta),
        576
    Giardino Giusti (Verona), 476–77
    Isola Madre, 566
    Vatican City, 142
    Villa Taranto, 566
Gardone Riviera, 550–52
Gargano Peninsula, 682–88
Garibaldi, Giuseppe, 28, 29, 162, 743
Gasoline, 69
Gay & lesbian travelers, 57–58
Genova (Genoa), 19, 584, 590–99
    accommodations, 595–97
    attractions, 592, 594
    essential information, 591–92
    harbor, 591
    nightlife, 599
    restaurants, 12, 598–99
    shopping, 595
Ghiberti, Lorenzo, 40, 204, 250, 251, 300
Ghirlandaio, Domenico, 141, 208, 249,
    255, 256, 289, 293
Giambologna, 248, 252, 257, 348
Giardini di Boboli (Florence), 257
Giardino Giusti (Verona), 476–77
Giordano, Luca, 254, 283, 594
Giorgione, 41, 246, 247, 422, 455
Giotto, 15, 34, 39–40, 138, 146, 204, 207,
    243, 250, 256, 271, 330, 350, 454, 455
Giotto's Bell Tower (Campanile)
    (Florence), 250

Glass
    factory tours (Murano), 445
    shopping for, 12
        Florence, 262
        Milan, 532
        Murano, 445
        Rome, 178
        Venice, 434, 437–38
Golden House of Nero (Rome), 144, 161
Gole Alcantara (near Taormina), 711
Golf, 174, 258
Gothic period, 33, 39
Gozzoli, Benozzo, 4, 249, 254, 293, 322
Grand Canal (Venice), 381, 421
    boat rides, 2, 385
Grappa, 47, 465, 466
Great Dolomite Road, 496
Greco, Emilio, 340, 341
Greece
    ferries to, 697
Greeks, ancient, 615, 639
    Agrigento, 724, 725–26
    art and architecture, 33, 34, 37, 38, 198,
        246, 300, 340, 349, 375, 618, 620
        Rome, 147, 158, 167, 171
        Taormina, 710
        Vatican museums, 139, 140
    Bari, 689–90
    Cuma, 634
    Gallipoli, 701, 702
    Mount Etna, 718
    Paestum, 6, 665, 666
    Segesta, 7
    Selinunte, 7
    Sicily, 708
    Siracusa, 719, 720
Greve in Chianti, 308, 312, 313
Grotta Azzurra (Capri), 668–69
Grotta del Genovese (Lévanzo), 743
Grotta Gigante (Trieste), 484, 486
Grottaglie, 703–4
Grotte di Catullo (Sirmione), 552–53
Grotte, 317–20
Gubbio, 317–20
Gucci stores, 182, 263–64, 528
Guggenheim, Peggy, 425

Hadrian, Emperor, 80, 142
    Pantheon (Rome), 31, 149
    Villa Adriana (near Tivoli), 6, 196–97
Harry's Bar
    Florence, 234
    Rome, 191
    Venice, 11, 383, 403, 442

Health concerns, 55–56
Hemingway, Ernest, 11, 389, 403, 442, 564
Herculaneum (Ercolano), 5, 620, 635–36
Hippodrome (Rome), 168
Historical and cultural museums. *See also*
   Archeological museums and exhibits
      Amalfi, 656
      Como, 556
      Fiesole, 271
      Merano, 499
      Monte Sant'Angelo, 685
      Museo di Criminologia Medioevale
         (San Gimignano), 293
      Trento, 503
      Venice
         Museo Comunità Ebraica, 428–29
         Museo Storico Navale, 425
History of Italy, 22–31
Holidays, 52
Homer, 45, 651, 706, 745
Horseback riding, 311, 343
      Merano, 500
      Rome, 174–75
House of Livia (Rome), 169

Il Duomo. *See* Duomo
Imperial Forums (Rome), 169–71
Information sources, 48
Insurance, 56
Ischia, 2, 639–45
Ischia Porto, 640–42
Isola Bella, 565–66
Isola del Pescatori, 566
Isola Madre, 566
Isole Égadi, 743
Isole Eolie o Lipari, 744–50
Isole Tremiti, 686–87
Italian design, 530–31
Italian Riviera, 18–19, 584

Jacopo della Quercia, 40, 250, 282, 298,
      300, 347, 349, 360
Jewelry, 302
      Bologna, 352
      Florence, 263
      Milan, 528
      Naples, 630–31
      Rome, 181–82
      Taormina, 711
      Venice, 439
Jewish Ghetto
      Rome. *See* Rome, Campo de' Fiori/
         Jewish Ghetto district
      Venice, 383, 428–29

John XXIII, Pope, 135, 159, 340
Julius Caesar, 23, 24, 46, 81, 117, 166
Julius II, Pope, 40

Kalsa (Palermo), 732
Keats, John, 84, 161, 193
      Keats-Shelley Memorial (Rome),
         155–56
Keats-Shelley Memorial (Rome), 155

Lacco Ameno, 642–43
Lace, 13
      Burano, 447
      Milan, 528
      Orvieto, 342
      Taormina, 711
      Venice, 435, 439
La Chiantigiana (Chianti district),
      306–11
Lago d'Averno, 633–34
Lapis Niger (Rome), 164
La Rotonda (Vicenza), 470
La Scala (Milan), 2, 532–33
Last Judgment (Michelangelo), 141
Last Supper, The (da Vinci), 40, 513
Latium, 15
      wines and vineyards, 8–9, 45
Latomia del Paradiso (Siracusa), 720
Leaning Tower (Pisa), 288
Leather goods, 13. *See also* Shoes
      Florence, 256, 263–64
      Milan, 528–29
      Naples, 631
      Rome, 182
      Venice, 439–40
Lecce, 698–701
Lévanzo, 743
Libreria Piccolomini (Siena), 300
Liguria, 18
      cuisine, 44
      wines and vineyards, 46
Limoncello, 47, 670
Limone sul Garda, 549–50
Lingerie
      Florence, 264
      Milan, 529
      Rome, 183
Lipari, 745
Lippi, Filippino, 152, 257, 293, 620
Lippi, Filippo, 150, 158, 246, 282, 334,
      514
Liqueurs, 47
Liquor laws, 73–74
Lira, 49

Livia, 25, 154, 169
Lombardy, 18, 27, 28, 506
  art and architecture, 32, 39
  cuisine, 43
  wines and vineyards, 7, 46
Longhi, Pietro, 424, 475, 538
Lorenzetti, Ambrogio, 298, 301
Lorenzetti, Pietro, 301, 316, 330
Lorenzo the Magnificent, 252–54
Lotto, Lorenzo, 464, 513, 514, 537, 538, 620
Lucca, 280–86
Lucera, 681

Machiavelli, Niccolò, 252, 256, 284
Maderno, Carlo, 135, 157, 200
Mafia, 19–21, 246, 730
Maggio Musicale Fiorentino (Florence), 54
Maggiore, Lake, 563–66
Mail, 74
Man and Caves Museum (Trieste), 486
Manarola, 608, 610, 611–12
Manfredonia, 683–84
Mannerism, 41
Mantegna, Andrea, 246, 422, 424, 454, 455, 475, 513, 514, 538, 543, 544, 570, 620
Mantova (Mantua), 12, 20, 542–46
Marches, the
  wine, 45
Maréttimo, 744
Marina Grande (Capri), 668–89
Marina Piccola (Capri), 677
Marinella, 728
Marini, Marino, 155, 515
Marostica, 468
Martini, Simone, 243, 289, 298, 301, 330, 620, 622
Masaccio, 242–43, 255, 257, 274, 289, 620
Matisse, Henri, 351, 515
Mausoleum of Galla Placidia (Ravenna), 365–66
Mazzarò, 715–17
Medici family, 4, 28, 40, 243, 247, 253, 255, 274
  Biblioteca Medicea Laurenziana, 254
  Cappelle Medici, 253
  Palazzo Medici-Riccardi, 254
  tombs, 253
Menotti, Gian Carlo, 54, 334
Merano, 499–502
Mestre, 379

Michelangelo, 35, 36, 40, 110, 133, 135, 138, 146, 147, 348
  in Florence, 209, 242–43, 248–51, 256
    Biblioteca Medicea Laurenziana, 254
    burial place, 256
    Casa Buonarroti, 256–57
    David, 40, 208, 246–48, 252, 257, 348
    Medici tombs, 253–54
  Sistine Chapel (Vatican City), 138, 140, 141, 243, 513
Michelozzo, 248, 249, 254, 515
Middle Ages, 26–27
Milan, 18, 32, 506–37
  accommodations, 516–19
  attractions, 512–16
  churches and cathedrals, 5
  cuisine, 43
  history of, 508
  layout of, 510–11
  museums, 4
  nightlife, 532–36
  restaurants, 12, 519–24
  shopping, 2, 12, 524–32
  side trips from, 536–37
  Teatro alla Scala, 2, 532–33
Mira, 452, 453
Modena, 368–72
Modigliani, Amedeo, 42, 155, 515
Mona Lisa (da Vinci), 40, 150, 310
Mondello, 740–41
Money, 48–51
Monreale, 739–40
Montecatini Alto, 275
Montecatini Terme, 2, 275–80
Monteriggioni, 296
Monterosso, 608–11
Monte Sant'Angelo, 684–85
Monteverdi, Claudio, 540, 542
Morandi, Giorgio, 42, 155, 348, 350, 514
Mosaics, 33, 38, 146, 158, 159, 162, 197, 251, 384, 415, 448, 484, 503, 515, 618, 620, 623, 656, 661, 662, 732, 739, 741
  Monreale, 739
  Nile Mosaic (Colonna-Barberini Palace), 201
  in Ravenna, 364–66
  shopping for, 183, 262, 265, 366
Moses (Michelangelo), 148
Mount Etna, 718–19
Murano, 384, 445–46
Musei Civici di Padova, 455

Musei Vaticani (Vatican City), 3
Museo Agricolo Brunnenburg (Merano), 499
Museo Archeologico (Bari), 689–90
Museo Archeologico (Florence), 255
Museo Archeologico Eoliano (Lipari), 745
Museo Archeologico Nazionale (Naples), 4–5, 618, 620
Museo Archeologico Nazionale di Paestum, 665–66
Museo Archeologico Regionale (Palermo), 733
Museo Archeologico Regionale Paolo Orsi (Siracusa), 720
Museo Capitolino and Palazzo dei Conservatori (Rome), 147
Museo Civico (Amalfi), 656
Museo Civico (Foggia), 680
Museo Civico (Gallipoli), 701
Museo Civico (San Gimignano), 293
Museo Civico (Vicenza), 469
Museo Civico Archeologico (Bologna), 349
Museo Civico Correr (Venice), 423
Museo Civico G. Fiorelli (Foggia), 681
Museo Communale Cordici (Érice), 742
Museo d'Arte Antica (Milan), 514
Museo del Duomo (Milan), 512
Museo delle Antichità Egizie (Turin), 570
Museo dell'Opera (Pisa), 289
Museo dell'Opera del Duomo (Florence), 251
Museo dell'Opera Metropolitana (Siena), 300
Museo del Risorgimento (Trento), 503
Museo di Criminologia Medioevale (San Gimignano), 293
Museo Diocesano (Trento), 503
Museo di Palazzo Ducale (Mantova), 543
Museo di San Marco (Florence), 248–49
Museo e Gallerie Nazionali di Capodimonte (Naples), 620–21
Museo Mandralisca (Cefalù), 741
Museo Missionario Francescano Fiesole, 271
Museo Nazionale del Bargello (Florence), 4, 248
Museo Nazionale del Palazzo di Venezia (Rome), 148
Museo Nazionale della Scienza e della Tecnica Leonardo da Vinci (Milan), 514
Museo Nazionale di Manfredonia, 684
Museo Nazionale di San Martino (Naples), 621

Museo Nazionale di San Matteo (Pisa), 289
Museo Nazionale di Taranto, 703
Museo Nazionale di Villa Giulia (Rome), 4, 23, 156
Museo Poldi-Pezzoli (Milan), 4, 514
Museo Regionale Archeologico (Agrigento), 726
Museo Storico Navale (Venice), 425
Museo Stradivariano (Cremona), 541
Museo Tancredi (Monte Sant'Angelo), 685
Mussolini, Benito, 15, 29–30, 37, 77, 80, 133, 148, 156, 169, 170, 174, 198, 199, 450, 506

Naples, 19, 614–32
    accommodations, 623–26
    attractions, 618, 620–23
    for children, 623
    consulates, 618
    cuisine, 44
    ferry to Sicily, 709
    history of, 614–15
    layout of, 617
    museums, 4–5
    nightlife, 631–32
    restaurants, 626–29, 632
    shopping, 629–31
    transportation, 617–18
    traveling to, 616
    visitor information, 616–17
    wines and vineyards, 45
Napoléon Bonaparte, 28, 283, 294, 415, 418, 450, 512, 513, 515, 543, 565
National Roman Museum (Rome), 158
Nero, 25, 84, 144, 191, 349, 615, 633
New Castle (Naples), 621–22
Nile Mosaic (Colonna-Barberini Palace), 201
Northern League, 20–21

Opera, 2
Ortygia (Città Vecchia), 721
Orvieto, 5, 339–43
Ospedale degli Innocenti (Florence), 254–55
Ostia, 197–98
Ostia Antica, 6, 198

Package tours, 61–64
Padova (Padua), 453–59
Paestum, 2, 6, 665

Palatine Hill (Il Palatino, Rome), 6, 167–68
Palazzo Bellomo (Ortygia), 721
Palazzo Comunale (Bologna), 348
Palazzo dei Conservatori (Rome), 147
Palazzo dei Diamanti (Ferrara), 361
Palazzo del Quirinale (Rome), 156
Palazzo della Ragione (Padua), 455
Palazzo di Normanni (Palermo), 731–32
Palazzo Ducale (Venice), 418–19
Palazzo Faina (Orvieto), 340
Palazzo Farnese (Rome), 153
Palazzo Mansi (Lucca), 282–83
Palazzo Medici-Riccardi (Florence), 254
Palazzo Mirto (Palermo), 732
Palazzo Pitti (Florence), 4, 247
Palazzo Pubblico (Siena), 298
Palazzo Reale (Naples), 621
Palazzo Reale (Torino), 571
Palazzo Schifanoia (Ferrara), 360–61
Palazzo Spada (Rome), 153
Palazzo Te (Mantova), 544
Palazzo Vecchio (Florence), 252–53
Palermo, 729–42
    accommodations, 734–36
    attractions, 731–33
    crime, 730
    nightlife, 738–39
    restaurants, 736–38
    shopping, 733–34
    side trips from, 739–42
    traveling to, 730
Palestrina, 201
Palio delle Contrade (Siena), 54, 296, 298, 299
Palladio (Andrea di Pietro), 35, 374, 382, 427, 449, 450, 452, 465, 468, 469–71
    in Vicenza, 470–71
Pantheon (Rome), 84, 149
Panzano, 310, 314
Papacy (popes), 26–28, 55, 142. *See also* Vatican City; *and individual popes*
    Castelgandolfo (summer retreat), 198–99
    Christmas Blessing of the Pope, 55
    papal audiences, 142
Paper products, 302
    Amalfi, 657–58
    Florence, 265, 266
    Milan, 532
    Venice, 440
Parco Nazionale della Stelvio (near Merano), 500
Parco Nazionale di Gran Paradiso, 576

Parma, 372–77
Parmigianino, Il, 41, 246, 372, 374
Paul VI, Pope, 140, 141
Peggy Guggenheim Collection (Venice), 379, 424–25
Perugia, 4, 320–27
Perugino, 4, 141, 246, 247, 275, 322–23, 325, 327, 536, 620
Petrarch, 274, 315, 316, 454
Pets, 74
Phlaegrean Fields, 632–33
Piazza Barberini (Rome), 157
Piazza Colonna (Rome), 152
Piazza delle Erbe (Verona), 474
Piazza dell'Unità d'Italia (Trieste), 483–84
Piazza IV Novembre (Perugia), 320, 321–22
Piazza Marina (Palermo), 732
Picasso, Pablo, 351, 425, 512, 515
Piedmont (Piemonte), 18, 567
    cuisine, 43
    wines and vineyards, 7, 46
Piero della Francesca, 274, 316, 322, 513
Pietà (Michelangelo), 40, 135
Pinacoteca di Brera (Milan), 4, 513–14
Pinacoteca Nazionale (Siena), 300–301
Pinacoteca Nazionale di Bologna, 350
Pinacoteca Nazionale e Museo di Palazzo Mansi (Lucca), 282–83
Pinacoteca Palazzo Volpi (Como), 556
Pinturicchio, 140, 141, 148, 293, 300, 323
Pio Clementino Museum (Vatican City), 139
Pirandello, Luigi, 724, 726
Pisa, 33, 54, 286–91
Pisano, Andrea, 250, 251, 340
Pisano, Giovanni, 288, 289, 299, 300, 321, 594
Pisano, Nicola (Niccolò), 39, 288, 289, 300, 321, 348
Pisano, Nino, 271, 289, 743
Pitti Palace (Florence), 4, 247
Pius II, Pope, 300
Pius XI, Pope, 15, 138, 519
Pius XII, Pope, 135, 198, 301, 328
Politics, 20–21
Pompeii, 2, 5, 6, 620, 636–39
Ponte Sant'Angelo (Rome), 163
Popes. *See* Papacy; *and individual popes*
Porcelain. *See* Ceramics
Portofino, 3, 10, 605–8
Positano, 10, 651
Pottery. *See* Ceramics

Pozzo di San Patrizio (Orvieto), 340
Pozzuoli, 633
Prints and engravings, 13
    Florence, 265–66
    Milan, 532
    Rome, 177–78
    Venice, 438–39
Prodi, Romano, 20, 31
Protestant Cemetery (Rome), 161
Puccini, Giacomo, 280, 284, 533
Pyramid of Caius Cestius (Rome), 162

Radda in Chianti, 310, 312–14
Rainfall, monthly, 52
Rapallo, 599–602
Raphael, 3, 35, 40, 119, 135, 138, 149,
    150, 152, 155, 158, 187, 204, 246–48,
    274, 300, 322–24, 350, 512, 514, 538,
    543, 620
    Stanze of Raphael (Vatican City), 140
Ravello, 3, 660–65
Ravenna, 364–68
Religious institutions, accommodations in,
    71
Religious objects and vestments, 13
Renaissance, 27–28, 31, 39–41, 54, 55.
    See also specific persons and buildings
    art and architecture, 34–36
Reni, Guido, 350, 370, 592
Rest rooms, 74
Restaurants
    best, 11–12
    tipping in, 76
    tips on, 71
Riomaggiore, 608, 611
Riva del Garda, 547–49
Riviera, Italian. See Italian Riviera
Riviera del Brenta, 449–53
Rocca Maggiore (Assisi), 331
Rococo style, 36–37, 41–42
Roman Empire, 24–26. See also Romans,
    ancient
Romanesque art, 39
Romanesque art and architecture, 31–33
Roman Forum (Rome), 6, 143–44, 163
Roman Holiday (film), 148
Roman Odeon (Taormina), 710
Roman republic, 23
Romans, ancient, 2. See also Archeological
    museums and exhibits; Archeological
    sites and ruins
    amphitheaters, 2, 6, 54, 200, 283,
        475, 633, 681–82, 699, 720
    architecture, 31

art, 38, 158, 201, 255, 289, 349
    history of, 22–26
    Ostia Antica, 6, 198
    Pompeii, 6
Roman Theater and Archeological
    Museum (Verona), 476
Rome, 15, 77–203. See also Vatican City
    accommodations, 91–114
    American Express, 88–89
    ancient (historic distric), 81. See also
        Romans, ancient
        accommodations, 94
        attractions, 143–49
        restaurants, 114–16
        walking tour, 163–72
    Appian Way (Via Appia Antica), 84,
        127
        attractions, 159–60
    arriving in, 78
    business hours, 89
    Campo de' Fiori/Jewish Ghetto
        district, 81
        accommodations, 95
        attractions, 152–53
        restaurants, 116–18
    for children
        accommodations, 98
        attractions, 173
        fashion, 180–81
        restaurants, 119
    churches and cathedrals
        Basilica di San Clemente, 146
        Basilica di San Giovanni in
            Laterano, 146–47
        Basilica di Santa Maria Maggiore,
            158
        Chiesa del Gesù, 150
        Chiesa di San Agostino, 150
        Chiesa di San Luigi dei Francesi,
            150
        Chiesa di Santa Cecilia in
            Trastevere, 162
        Chiesa di Santa Maria d'Aracoeli,
            148–49
        Chiesa di Santa Maria degli Angeli,
            158–59
        Chiesa di Santa Maria della Pace,
            152
        Chiesa di Santa Maria in
            Cosmedin, 148
        Chiesa di Santa Maria in
            Trastevere, 162
        Chiesa di Santa Maria Sopra
            Minerva, 152

St. Paul Outside the Walls (Basilica
    di San Paolo Fuori le Mura), 162
St. Peter's Basilica, 2, 5, 36, 135, 138
Saint Peter in Chains (Chiesa di
    San Pietro in Vincoli), 147–48
cuisine, 43
currency exchange, 89
doctors and dentists, 89
drinking water, 91
drugstores, 89
emergencies, 89
finding an address in, 80
history of, 22–29
Jewish Ghetto, 81
layout of, 80–81
Monte Mario, 85
    accommodations, 113–14
museums, 4, 147, 148, 150, 154–58
neighborhoods, 81–85
nightlife, 185–94
    ballet & dance, 186
    bar & cafe scene, 191–94
    cinemas, 194
    classical music, 185
    gay clubs, 190–91
    Irish pubs, 194
    jazz, soul & funk, 189–90
    nightclubs, 187–89
    opera, 186
    restaurants with entertainment,
        186–87
Parioli, 85
    accommodations, 112–13
    restaurants, 131–32
Piazza del Popolo
    cafes, 191–92
    restaurants, 120
Piazza di Spagna (Spanish Steps), 84
    accommodations, 97–98, 100–103
    cafes, 193
    restaurants, 120–23
Piazza Navona/Pantheon district, 81, 84
    accommodations, 95, 97
    cafes, 192, 193–94
    restaurants, 118–20
post office, 90
Prati, 85
restaurants, 11
    Rome ancient, 114–32
restoration projects, 134
safety, 90
shopping, 13, 175–84
side trips from, 194–203
    Castelli Romani, 198–99

Etruscan historical sights, 202–3
    Frascati, 199–200
    Fregene, 201–2
    Nemi, 199
    Ostia, 197–98
    Palestrina, 201
    Tivoli, 194, 196–97
special events, 53–55
sports and outdoor activities, 174–75
street maps, 80–81
Termini, 84
    accommodations, 106–10
    attractions, 158–59
    restaurants, 125–27
Testaccio, 84–85
    attractions, 161–62
    restaurants, 127–28
tours
    organized, 173–74
    underground, 161
    walking, 163–72
traffic, 81
transportation, 85–88
    information, 91
Trastevere, 85
    attractions, 162
    cafes, 192
    restaurants, 128–30
underground, 160–61
Via Veneto, 84
    accommodations, 103–4
    attractions, 157–58
    bar & cafe scene, 191
    restaurants, 123–25
visitor information, 79–80
walking in, 88
Romeo and Juliet, 476, 477, 542
Rosso, Medardo, 42
Rostra (Rome), 164
Royal Palace (Naples), 621
Ruins. *See* Archeological sites and ruins

Safety concerns, 74
St. Catherine's Sanctuary (Siena), 301
St. Francis Basilica (Assisi), 5, 330–31
St. Mark's Basilica (Venice), 415, 418–19
St. Paul Outside the Walls (Basilica di San
    Paolo Fuori le Mura) (Rome), 162
St. Peter's Basilica (The Vatican, Rome),
    2, 5, 36, 135, 138
Saint Peter in Chains (Chiesa di San
    Pietro in Vincoli) (Rome), 147–48
Sanctuary of San Michele (Monte
    Sant'Angelo), 684–85

San Domino, 686
San Genesio, 497
San Gimignano, 291
San Giovanni degli Eremiti (Palermo), 731
San Michele in Foro (Lucca), 282
San Nicola, 686
San Polo, 307
San Remo, 53, 584–86, 588–90
Sangallo, Antonio da, 153, 322, 340
Santa Chiara (Naples), 622
Santa Margherita Ligure, 602–5
Santa Maria del Carmine (Florence), 257
Santa Maria del Fiore (Il Duomo,
    Florence), 5, 34, 207–8, 249–50
Santa Maria della Salute (Venice),
    427–28
Santa Maria di Siponto (Manfredonia),
    684
Sant'Angelo, 644–45
Santi Giovanni e Paolo Basilica (Venice),
    428
Santo Stefano (Bologna), 349
Santuario e Casa di Santa Caterina
    (Siena), 301
Savonarola, 208, 249, 252, 253
Scuola di San Giorgio degli Schiavoni
    (Venice), 426
Scuola di San Rocco (Venice), 426
Segesta, 728–29
Segesta (Sicily), 7
Selinunte, 7, 727–28
Senior travelers, 58
Shakespeare, William, 453
    in Verona, 473, 476
Shelley, Percy Bysshe, 155, 161
Shoes, 351
    Florence, 266
    Milan, 528–29
    Naples, 631
    Rome, 184
Shopping. *See also* Antiques; Bookstores;
    Ceramics, shopping for; Fashion,
    shopping for; Glass; Lace; Prints and
    engravings; *and under specific cities*
    best buys, 12–13
Shroud of Turin, 568, 570–71
Sicily, 19, 27–29, 32, 33, 706–50
    cuisine, 44
    traveling to, 708–9
    wines and vineyards, 9, 46
Siena, 296–306
    accommodations, 302–5
    attractions, 298–301
    Il Palio, 54, 296–97

    nightlife, 306
    Palio delle Contrade, 54, 296, 298, 299
    restaurants, 305–6
    shopping, 301–2
    traveling to, 298
Signorelli, Luca, 141, 274, 322, 331, 340,
    620
Silver
    Florence, 266–67
Sinagoga di Firenze, 258
Siracusa (Syracuse), 719–24
Siremar, 743
Sirmione, 552–55
Sistine Chapel (Vatican City), 138, 140,
    141, 243, 513
Skiing
    Cortina, 490–91
    Courmayeur, 578
Soccer
    Florence, 259
    Rome, 174
Solfatara, 633
Sorpasso, il, 21
Sorrento, 646–51
South Tyrol (Trentino-Alto Adige), 16
Spanish Steps (Piazza di Spagna) (Rome),
    153
Spas, 2–3
    Ischia, 639–43
    Merano Thermal Spa Centre, 499
    Montecatini Terme, 275, 278–80
Special events, 53–55. *See also specific cities
    and towns*
Spoleto, 3, 334–39
    Festival dei Due Mondi/Festival di
        Spoleto, 54, 334, 335
Stadium of Domitian (Rome), 168
Stanze of Raphael (Vatican City), 140
Strada, 307
Stradivari, Antonio (Stradivarius), 540–42
Stresa, 12, 563–65
Strómboli, 747–49
Student travelers, 59
Syracuse. *See* Siracusa

Taormina, 3, 10, 709–19
    accommodations, 712–16
    attractions, 710–11
    nightlife, 717–18
    restaurants, 716–17
    shopping, 711
    traveling to, 710
Taranto, 702–5
Tarquinia, 23, 202–3

Tasso, Torquato, 359, 454, 647
Taxes, 75
Teatro alla Scala (Milan), 2, 532–33
Teatro di Marcello (Rome), 171–72
Teatro Greco (Siracusa), 720
Teatro Greco (Taormina), 710
Teatro Olimpico (Vicenza), 469, 472–73
Teatro Romano (Verona), 476
Telephone, 75–76
Television, 74, 76
Temperatures, average monthly, 52
Tempio della Concordia (Agrigento), 725
Tempio di Dioscuri (Agrigento), 725–26
Tempio di Ercole (Hercules) (Agrigento), 725
Tempio di Giove (Jove or Zeus) (Agrigento), 725
Tempio di Giunone (Agrigento), 725
Tempio di Santa Corona (Vicenza), 469
Tempio di Serapide (Pozzuoli), 633
Temple of Antoninus and Faustina (Rome), 166
Temple of Apollo (Lake Averno), 634
Temple of Fortuna Virile (Rome), 172
Temple of Julius Caesar (Rome), 166
Temple of Neptune (Paestum), 665
Temple of Romulus (Rome), 166–67
Temple of the Castors (Rome), 166
Temple of Vesta (Rome), 166
Terme di Caracalla (Rome), 147
Tiberius, 3, 25, 154, 167, 169, 669, 676
Tiepolo, Giambattista (Giovanni Battista), 424, 450, 466, 471, 475, 514, 538
Tintoretto, 41, 158, 246, 283, 370, 383, 418, 423, 425–28, 446, 455, 469, 475, 514, 543, 594, 690
Tipping, 76
Titian, 138, 147, 150, 155, 158, 246, 247, 423, 424, 426–28, 434, 460, 476, 513, 620, 743
Tivoli, 194, 196–97
Todi, 338
Tomba di Giulietta (Verona), 477
Tomb of St. Sebastian (Rome), 159
Torcello, 384, 448
Torino (Turin), 567–75
Torrazzo (Cremona), 541
Torre degli Asinelli (Bologna), 348–49
Torre dell'Orologio (Venice), 419–20
Toscanini, Arturo, 374, 515, 516, 533
Tourist information, 48
Tours
    grand tour of Italy, 3
    package, 61–64

Tower of the Milizie (Rome), 171
Train travel
    from the United Kingdom, 63
    within Italy, 66–67
Trajan's Column (Rome), 171
Trajan's Market (Rome), 170
Trápani, 742
Traveler's checks, 50
Traveling
    to Italy, 59–64
        from North America, 59–62
        from the United Kingdom, 62–64
        from within Europe, 64–66
    within Italy, 66–69
Tremezzo, 561–62
Tremiti Islands, 686–87
Trentino-Alto Adige area, 16
    cuisine, 43
    wines and vineyards, 7–8, 46
Trento (Trent), 502–5
Trevi Fountain (Rome), 154
Treviso, 459–63
Trieste, 16, 18, 482–84, 486–89
Troia, 682
Trulli district, 693–96
Tura, Cosmé, 360, 361, 370, 422, 423, 538
Turin
    restaurants, 12
    special events, 570
Tuscany, 15, 274
    art and architecture, 33
    tours, 279
    wines and vineyards, 8, 45

Uffizi, Galleria degli (Florence), 4, 243, 246
Umbria, 15, 274–75
    wines and vineyards, 8
University of Padua, 454
Urbino, 55

Valdobbiadene, 463
Valle d'Aosta, 18, 567, 575
Valle dei Templi (Sicily), 7
Vasari, Giorgio, 141, 148, 209, 243, 249, 250, 252, 255, 256, 300, 315, 316, 374, 513
Vatican City, 14–15, 29, 85
    accommodations, 110–12
    attractions, 135–43
        Castel Sant'Angelo, 142–43
        gardens, 142
        museums, 3, 138–42

Vatican City, *cont.*
  papal audiences, 142
  restaurants, 130–31
  Sistine Chapel, 138, 140, 141, 243, 513
Venetia, 28, 29
  wines and vineyards, 45
Venetian glass, 12, 435
  shopping for, 12
Veneto, 16, 35, 449–81
  wines and vineyards, 7
Veneziano, Lorenzo, 422, 514
Veneziano, Paolo, 422, 469
Venice, 16, 378–448
  accommodations, 388–402
  American Express, 386
  arriving in, 379–80
  art and architecture, 33, 41
  Cannaregio, 383
    accommodations, 397
    restaurants, 410–11
  Carnevale, 53
  Castello, 383
  for children
    attractions, 433
    hotels, 398
    restaurants, 408
  churches and cathedrals, 418–19,
    425–28
  cuisine, 43
  currency exchange, 387
  Dorsoduro, 381, 384
    accommodations, 398–99
    restaurants, 411–12
  finding an address in, 382
  Grand Canal, 381, 421
    boat rides, 2, 385
  guild houses, 425, 426
  International Film Festival, 55
  Isola della Giudecca, 430
    accommodations, 400
    restaurants, 412–13
  Jewish Ghetto, 383, 428–29
  layout of, 381–82
  the Lido, 384, 420–21
    accommodations, 400–402
    restaurants, 413
  museums & galleries, 4, 418–19,
    421–25
  neighborhoods, 383–84
  nightlife, 440–45
    bars, 441–43
    cafes, 444
    casinos, 445

    ice cream & pastries, 444–45
    performing arts, 440–41
  Piazza San Marco, 383
    accommodations, 389, 392–94
    attractions, 414–15, 418–20
    restaurants, 402–7
  Piazzetta San Marco, 420
  Ponte di Rialto, 383
    accommodations, 396–97
    restaurants, 408–10
  restaurants, 11, 402–13
  Riva degli Schiavoni, 383
    accommodations, 394–96
    restaurants, 407–8
  safety, 388
  San Marco district, 383
  San Polo, 383–84
    accommodations, 397–98
    restaurant, 411
  Santa Croce, 384
    accommodations, 398
    restaurant, 411
  shopping, 12, 13, 434–40
  side trips from, 445–48
  special events, 54, 55
  street maps, 382
  tours, organized, 433–34
  transportation, 385–86
  visitor information, 380–81
  walking in, 2, 386
  walking tour, 429–33
Verdi, Giuseppi, 275, 372, 373, 461, 475,
  533, 542
Vernazza, 608, 611, 612
Verona, 54, 473–81
  accommodations, 477–79
  nightlife, 481
  restaurants, 11, 480–81
  shopping, 477
  sights, 474–77
  traveling to, 473–74
  visitor information, 474
Veronese, Paolo, 41, 246, 283, 370, 418,
  423, 427, 428, 446, 455, 465, 469, 470,
  475, 570, 592, 690
Verrazzano, 308
Verrocchio, Andrea del, 246, 248, 252
Versace, Gianni, 531
Vesuvius, Mount, 634
Via dei Fori Imperiali (Rome), 169–70
Vicenza, 468–73
Victor Emmanuel II (Vittorio Emanuele
  II), 29, 148, 149, 576, 583, 602

Vieste, 687–88
Villa(s)
    Adriana (near Tivoli), 6, 196–97
    Barbaro (near Asolo), 465
    Borghese (Rome), 157
    Carlotta (on Lake Como), 560
    d'Este (Tivoli), 196
    Gregoriana (Tivoli), 196
    Jovis (Capri), 669
    La Rotonda (Vicenza), 470
    Melzi (Bellagio), 560
    Palladian, 465, 470–71
    in Ravello, 661
    renting, 70
    in Riviera del Brenta, 450, 452
    San Michele (Anacapri), 676
    Serbelloni (Bellagio), 560
    Taranto, 566
    Vittoriale (Gardone Riviera), 550–51
Vineyards. See Wines and vineyards
Virgil, 348, 542, 555, 615, 622, 633
Visitor information, 48
Vittoriale (Gardone Riviera), 550–51
Vittorio Emanuele II (Victor Emmanuel
    II), 29, 148, 149, 576, 583, 602

Vittorio Emanuele Monument (Rome),
    80, 171
Vulcano, 749–50
Vulcano Solfatara, 633

Water, drinking, 76
Wines and vineyards, 44–46. See also
    specific regions
    best, 7–8
    buying wines
        Florence, 267
        Orvieto, 341–42
        Rome, 184
        San Gimignano, 295
        Siena, 302
    Enoteca Italica Permanente (Siena), 301
    La Chiantigiana (Chianti region),
        306–11
    around Treviso, 462
World War II, 29–30, 201, 258, 278,
    315, 365, 374, 454, 614, 646, 688

Youth hostels, 59

Zona Archeologica (Siracusa), 720

WHEREVER
YOU TRAVEL,
*H*ELP IS NEVER
FAR AWAY.

**From planning your trip to providing travel assistance
along the way, American Express® Travel Service Offices
are always there to help.**

Italy

Bigtours Travel Service (R)
Via Indipendenza 12
Bologna
51/224-923

American Express Travel Service
Via Brera 3
Milan
2/720-03-693

American Express Company S.P.A.
Via Guicciardini 49/R
Florence
55/288-751

American Express Travel Service
Piazza Di Spagna 38
Rome
6/676-41

American Express Travel Service
Via Dante Alighieri 22R
Florence
55/509-81

American Express Travel Service
1471 San Marco, San Moise
Venice
41/520-0844

Viatur SRL (R)
Piazza Fontane Marose 3
Genoa
10/561-241

Fabretto Viaggi E Turismo (R)
Corso Porta Nuova 11
Verona
45/800-9040

Travel

http://www.americanexpress.com/travel

**American Express Travel Service Offices are
found in central locations throughout Italy.**